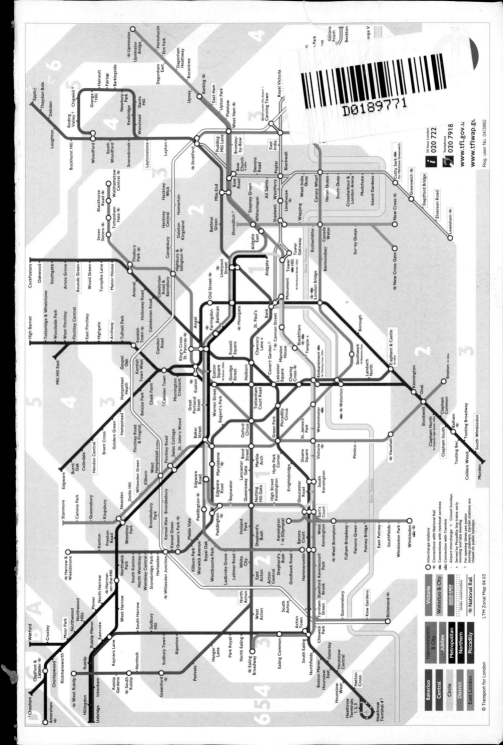

© Transport for London

www.tfl.gov.u
www.tflwap.g

Reg. user No. 0473982

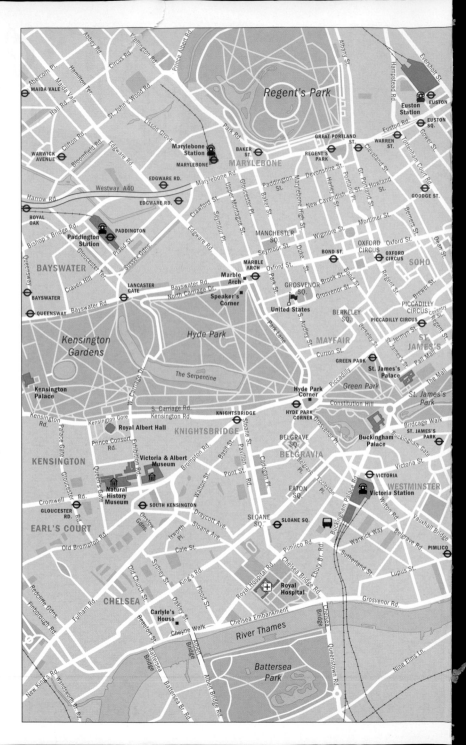

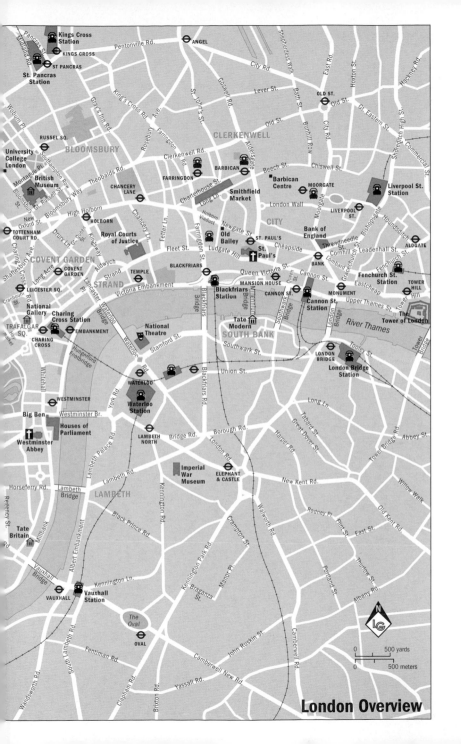

London Overview

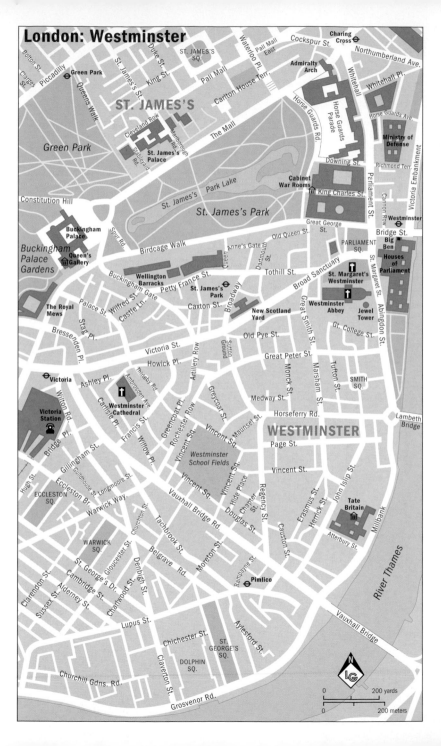

London: Westminster

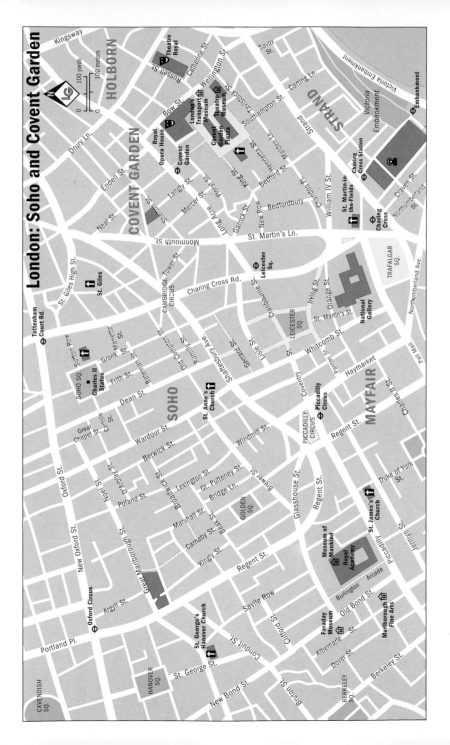

London: Soho and Covent Garden

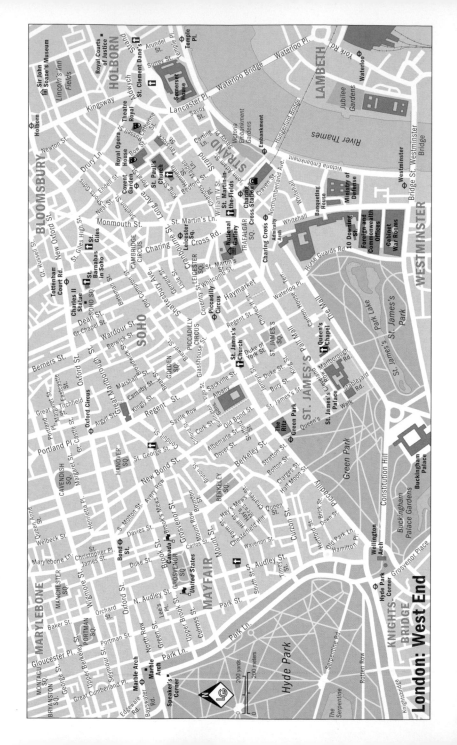

London: West End

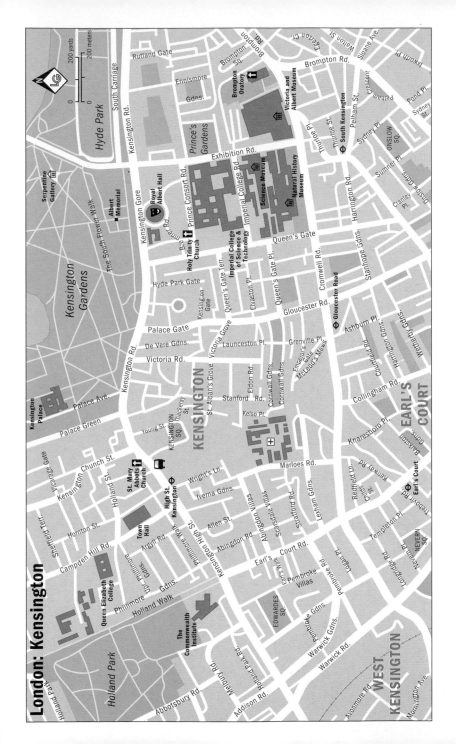

London: Kensington

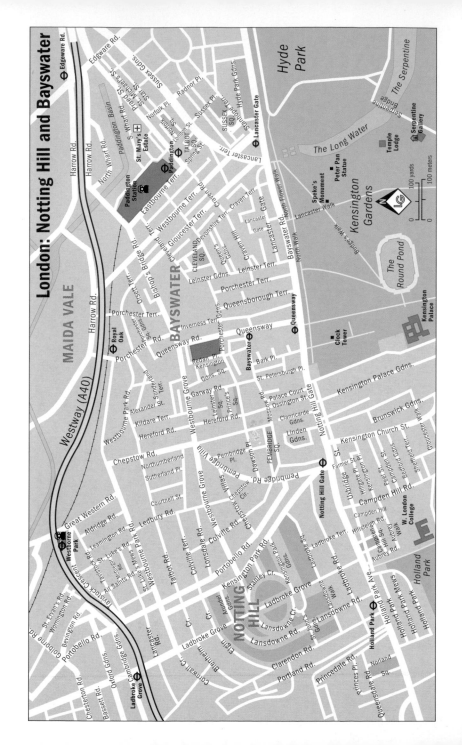

London: Notting Hill and Bayswater

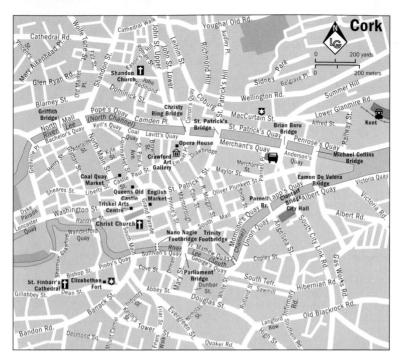

Cork

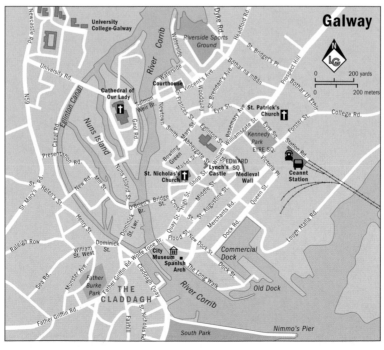

Galway

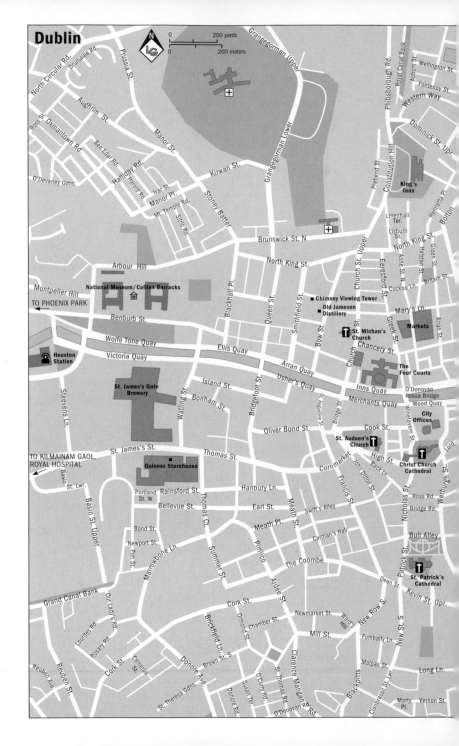

Dublin

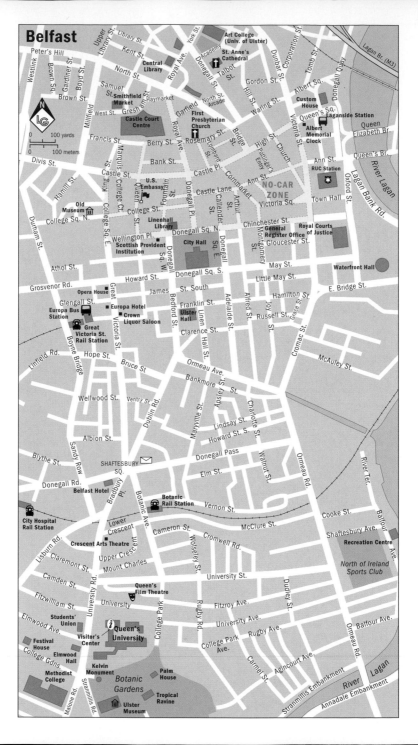

Belfast

LET'S GO

■ THE RESOURCE FOR THE INDEPENDENT TRAVELER

"The guides are aimed not only at young budget travelers but at the indepedent traveler; a sort of streetwise cookbook for traveling alone."

—*The New York Times*

"Unbeatable; good sight-seeing advice; up-to-date info on restaurants, hotels, and inns; a commitment to money-saving travel; and a wry style that brightens nearly every page."

—*The Washington Post*

"Lighthearted and sophisticated, informative and fun to read. [Let's Go] helps the novice traveler navigate like a knowledgeable old hand."

—*Atlanta Journal-Constitution*

"A world-wise traveling companion—always ready with friendly advice and helpful hints, all sprinkled with a bit of wit."

—*The Philadelphia Inquirer*

■ THE BEST TRAVEL BARGAINS IN YOUR PRICE RANGE

"All the dirt, dirt cheap."

—*People*

"Anything you need to know about budget traveling is detailed in this book."

—*The Chicago Sun-Times*

"Let's Go follows the creed that you don't have to toss your life's savings to the wind to travel—unless you want to."

—*The Salt Lake Tribune*

■ REAL ADVICE FOR REAL EXPERIENCES

"The writers seem to have experienced every rooster-packed bus and lunar-surfaced mattress about which they write."

—*The New York Times*

"Value-packed, unbeatable, accurate, and comprehensive."

—*The Los Angeles Times*

"[Let's Go's] devoted updaters really walk the walk (and thumb the ride, and trek the trail). Learn how to fish, haggle, find work—anywhere."

—*Food & Wine*

LET'S GO PUBLICATIONS

TRAVEL GUIDES
Australia 8th edition
Austria & Switzerland 12th edition
Brazil 1st edition
Britain & Ireland 2005
California 10th edition
Central America 9th edition
Chile 2nd edition
China 5th edition
Costa Rica 2nd edition
Eastern Europe 2005
Ecuador 1st edition **NEW TITLE**
Egypt 2nd edition
Europe 2005
France 2005
Germany 12th edition
Greece 2005
Hawaii 3rd edition
India & Nepal 8th edition
Ireland 2005
Israel 4th edition
Italy 2005
Japan 1st edition
Mexico 20th edition
Middle East 4th edition
Peru 1st edition **NEW TITLE**
Puerto Rico 1st edition
South Africa 5th edition
Southeast Asia 9th edition
Spain & Portugal 2005
Thailand 2nd edition
Turkey 5th edition
USA 2005
Vietnam 1st edition **NEW TITLE**
Western Europe 2005

ROADTRIP GUIDE
Roadtripping USA **NEW TITLE**

ADVENTURE GUIDES
Alaska 1st edition
New Zealand **NEW TITLE**
Pacific Northwest **NEW TITLE**
Southwest USA 3rd edition

CITY GUIDES
Amsterdam 3rd edition
Barcelona 3rd edition
Boston 4th edition
London 2005
New York City 15th edition
Paris 13th edition
Rome 12th edition
San Francisco 4th edition
Washington, D.C. 13th edition

POCKET CITY GUIDES
Amsterdam
Berlin
Boston
Chicago
London
New York City
Paris
San Francisco
Venice
Washington, D.C.

LET'S GO

BRITAIN & IRELAND 2005

LAURA KRUG EDITOR
ADRIÁN MALDONADO ASSOCIATE EDITOR

RESEARCHER-WRITERS
KRISTEN KEATING
ALEX LEMANN
PATRICK MCKEE
MATTHEW NAUNHEIM
LILY STOCKMAN

JOHN P. KIERNAN MAP EDITOR
JEREMY TODD MANAGING EDITOR

ST. MARTIN'S PRESS ❧ NEW YORK

HELPING LET'S GO. If you want to share your discoveries, suggestions, or corrections, please drop us a line. We read every piece of correspondence, whether a postcard, a 10-page email, or a coconut. **Address mail to:**

Let's Go: Britain & Ireland
67 Mount Auburn Street
Cambridge, MA 02138
USA

Visit Let's Go at **http://www.letsgo.com,** or send email to:

feedback@letsgo.com
Subject: "Let's Go: Britain & Ireland"

In addition to the invaluable travel advice our readers share with us, many are kind enough to offer their services as researchers or editors. Unfortunately, our charter enables us to employ only currently enrolled Harvard students.

Maps by David Lindroth copyright © 2005 by St. Martin's Press.

Distributed outside the USA and Canada by Macmillan.

Let's Go: Britain & Ireland Copyright © 2005 by Let's Go, Inc. All rights reserved. Printed in the United States of America. No part of this book may be used or reproduced in any manner whatsoever without written permission except in the case of brief quotations embodied in critical articles or reviews. Let's Go is available for purchase in bulk by institutions and authorized resellers. For information, address St. Martin's Press, 175 Fifth Avenue, New York, NY 10010, USA.

ISBN: 0-312-33543-1
EAN: 978-312-33543-4
First edition
10 9 8 7 6 5 4 3 2 1

Let's Go: Britain & Ireland is written by Let's Go Publications, 67 Mount Auburn Street, Cambridge, MA 02138, USA.

Let's Go® and the LG logo are trademarks of Let's Go, Inc.
Printed in the USA.

CONTENTS

V

VII

PRICE RANGES>>UNITED KINGDOM

Our researchers list establishments in order of value from best to worst; our favorites are denoted by the Let's Go thumbs-up (📖). Since the best value is not always the cheapest price, however, we have also incorporated a system of price ranges, based on a rough expectation of what you will spend. For **accommodations,** we base our range on the cheapest price for which a single traveler can stay for one night. For **restaurants** and other dining establishments, we estimate the average amount a traveler will spend. The table below tells you what you will *typically* find in the United Kingdom at the corresponding price range; keep in mind that a particularly expensive ice cream shop may still be marked with a ②, depending on what you are likely to spend there.

ACCOMMODATIONS	RANGE	WHAT YOU'RE *LIKELY* TO FIND
❶	under £11	Dorm-style rooms. Expect bunk beds and a communal bath; you may have to bring or rent towels and sheets.
❷	£11-19	Upper-end hostels or small hotels. You may have a private bathroom (ensuite), or there may be a sink in your room and communal shower in the hall.
❸	£20-29	Most B&Bs or a small room with a private bath. Should have decent amenities, such as phone and TV. Breakfast may be included in the price of the room.
❹	£30-59	Similar to 3, but may have more amenities or be in a more touristed area.
❺	£60 and up	Large hotels, upscale chains, or even castles. If it's a 5 and it doesn't have the perks you want, you've paid too much.
FOOD	**RANGE**	**WHAT YOU'RE *LIKELY* TO FIND**
❶	under £5	Mostly street-corner stands, pizza places, or sandwich and tea shops. Rarely ever a sit-down meal.
❷	£5-9	Some take-out options, but also quite a few ethnic restaurants or options outside of London.
❸	£10-14	Entrees are more expensive, but chances are you're paying for decor and ambience.
❹	£15-20	As in 3, the higher prices are probably related to better service, but in these restaurants, the food will tend to be a little fancier.
❺	£21 and up	These better be the best—or at least the best looking—bangers n' mash you've ever had.

ABOUT LET'S GO

GUIDES FOR THE INDEPENDENT TRAVELER

At Let's Go, we see every trip as the chance of a lifetime. If your dream is to grab a machete and forge through the jungles of Brazil, we can take you there. If you'd rather bask in the Riviera sun at a beachside cafe, we'll set you a table. We write for readers who know that there's more to travel than sharing double deckers with tourists and who believe that travel can change both themselves and the world—whether they plan to spend six days in London or six months in Latin America. We'll show you just how far your money can go, and prove that the greatest limitation on your adventures is not your wallet, but your imagination. After all, traveling close to the ground lets you interact more directly with the places and people you've gone to see, making for the most authentic experience.

BEYOND THE TOURIST EXPERIENCE

To help you gain a deeper connection with the places you travel, our researchers give you the heads-up on both world-renowned and off-the-beaten-track attractions, sights, and destinations. They engage with the local culture, writing features on regional cuisine, local festivals, and hot political issues. We've also opened our pages to respected writers and scholars to hear their takes on the countries and regions we cover, and asked travelers who have worked, studied, or volunteered abroad to contribute first-person accounts of their experiences. We've also increased our coverage of responsible travel and expanded each guide's Alternatives to Tourism chapter to share more ideas about how to give back to local communities and learn about the places you travel.

FORTY-FIVE YEARS OF WISDOM

Let's Go got its start in 1960, when a group of creative and well-traveled students compiled their experience and advice into a 20-page mimeographed pamphlet, which they gave to travelers on charter flights to Europe. Four and a half decades later, we've expanded to cover six continents and all kinds of travel—while retaining our founders' adventurous attitude toward the world. Our guides are still researched and written entirely by students on shoestring budgets, experienced travelers who know that train strikes, stolen luggage, food poisoning, and marriage proposals are all part of a day's work. This year, we're expanding our coverage of South America and Southeast Asia, with brand-new *Let's Go: Ecuador*, *Let's Go: Peru*, and *Let's Go: Vietnam*. Our adventure guide series is growing, too, with the addition of *Let's Go: Pacific Northwest Adventure* and *Let's Go: New Zealand Adventure*. And we're immensely excited about our new *Let's Go: Roadtripping USA*—two years, eight routes, and sixteen researchers and editors have put together a travel guide like none other.

THE LET'S GO COMMUNITY

More than just a travel guide company, Let's Go is a community. Our small staff comes together because of our shared passion for travel and our desire to help other travelers see the world. We love it when our readers become part of the Let's Go community as well—when you travel, drop us a postcard (67 Mt. Auburn St., Cambridge, MA 02138, USA) or send us an e-mail (feedback@letsgo.com) to tell us about your adventures and discoveries.

For more information, visit us online: www.letsgo.com.

IX

RESEARCHER-WRITERS

Kristen Keating   *Midlands, Heart of, Southwest, and Northern England*

Kristen threw herself into it all, thumping Northwest nightlife and quiet Southwest towns alike. Backpack-snatchers and connections from hell were no match for her quiet toughness as she zigzagged from one coast of the UK to the other within days, putting in hard work, enthusiasm, and respect for the places she saw. This champ also thoroughly trounced her itinerary—in an excellent way.

Alex Lemann   *Northern England, Edinburgh, Southern and Central Scotland*

Straight outta upstate NY, this classical archaeology buff can boast a route that took him island-hopping and ruin-climbing. From big city Edinburgh to uninhabited Staffa, Alex soared through the country with a love of learning and a thirst for single malts, stopping to expound on the merits of castles vs. stately homes while quoting rap lyrics. It was our pleasure working with such a well-rounded scholar.

Patrick McKee   *South and Heart of England, Midlands, East Anglia, Yorkshire*

Faulty parallelism beware: this stalwart lover of cathedrals, the *Anglo-Saxon Chronicle*, and real ales took as much care with his write-ups as with his research. Patrick studied the aesthetics of the pint and took in the academia of Cambridge's colleges even as he struggled with a dying computer and a mysteriously-missing passport, and always had a new and interesting historic tidbit at the ready.

Matthew Naunheim   *Wales, Isle of Man, Midlands, Northwest England*

Charming literary magnates and sidestepping sheep, Matt cruised through the coasts and hills of Wales, the Isle of Man, and Northwest England with resourcefulness, cheer, and an eye for every detail. Whether he was receiving instant canonization, relaxing on Tenby's beaches, or figuring out what makes Swansea tick, Matt's brio made every phone call a joy and his polished copy made our jobs fun.

Lily Stockman   *Glasgow, Central Scotland, Highlands and Islands*

Like a bat out of hell, or at least New Jersey, Lily jumped into her tiny European car and fell head-over-heels for tiny Orkney outposts, sipping a tiny bit of whisky every now and then. Her time in the mountains of Montana prepared her for the Highlands, and she joyfully met every backpacker, crofter, and hairy coo on her route. We have no doubt she'll have an amazing time studying art history in Mongolia.

X

CONTRIBUTING WRITERS

John Blickstead *Western Ireland*

John braved mononucleosis, torrential rains, clingy vagrants, and aggressive Quebecoise grad students to deliver brilliantly funny copy. Irrepressibly energetic and outgoing, John made friends wherever he went.

Feargus Denman *Northwest Ireland, Northern Ireland*

Hailing from Maynooth in Co. Kildare, Feargus eased his way through the Donegal wilds and sectarian murals of Derry and Belfast as only a native could.

Brian Fairley *Cork, Dublin, Eastern Ireland, Southeast Ireland*

Brian came to the Isle with a nose for culture and quirky shopping, and soon developed a nose for Irish whiskey as well. He became an expert on distilling and tasting, and spilled the fruits of his labor throughout the book.

Ariel Fox *Dublin, Eastern Ireland*

A three-year *Let's Go* veteran, Ariel came to Dublin with a background in British literature and a love of those authors who had fled Ireland. She was won over by St. Stephen's Green, and covered Dublin with gumption and a gentle, dark wit.

David Huyssen *Southwest Ireland*

A *Let's Go* veteran and soon-to-be Yalie, David accepted the call to Southwest Ireland with unbridled zest. He charmed his way through seaside villages and scenic peninsulas with an eye for detail and a seasoned touch.

Aviva Gilbert *London*

Aviva brought the heat of Berkeley, California to her coverage of London. Tearing up accommodations listings during the day and the dance floor at night, Aviva's exhaustive copy often made it seem like she was in twenty places at once.

Robert Hodgson *London*

Professional, candid and prone to slapstick misfortunes, Bobby traveled from New England to England where, from the confusion of London's transport system to its mélange of cuisines, he could find his way through all.

Andrew Noble Sodroski *Editor, Let's Go: Ireland 2005*

Jakub Jan Kabala *Associate Editor, Let's Go: Ireland 2005*

Rabia Mir *Editor, Let's Go: London 2005*

Simon Schama is an author and a professor at Columbia University. He writes for *The New Yorker* and was recently the writer and host of the BBC's *History of Britain*.
Lily Brown graduated from Harvard University in 2004 with a degree in Women, Gender, and Sexuality Studies.
Brenna Powell works with the Stanford Center on Conflict and Negotiation.
Brian Algra, a former researcher for *Let's Go: California*, is currently pursuing a doctoral degree in English Literature at the University of Edinburgh.
Sarah Kerman graduated from Harvard University with a degree in literature. She has worked as a writing tutor at the Johns Hopkins Center for Talented Youth.

ACKNOWLEDGMENTS

LET'S GO

TEAM B&I THANKS: To our ▨Xtreme RWs for your love, wit, and ridiculous adventures. To Jeremy, for tirelessly keeping us on track. Andrew, Kuba, and Rabia for crunch. John, for our sexy maps. Teresa, for your baby. Jenny, for support and typing. Proofers, Prod, Thom Yorke, Skee-lo, Kendal mint cake, and sheep.

LAURA THANKS: Adrián, thank you for your tirelessness, jokes, knowledge, and pure excitement—this project could not have happened without you. Best of luck amid your castles in Scotland next year. BAM! Jeremy, for learning to stop worrying and love the sheep. Andrew and Kuba, for cider and for endowing me with mystique and funk, Ireland-style. The whole basement crew. Pegglet, for donuts and love. My sixth RW, for advice and answers. My wonderful roommates KJT and LEM. Mom, Dad, and Sammi—for understanding my deadlines and for crossword puzzles. Bridget, for *français* and France. Everyone for procrastination and love. The Druid, the 80s, and B&I, for the best kind of inspiration.

ADRIÁN THANKS: Much love to all my people in the ▨Basement, especially my fellow medievalists in team ▨ÉIRE; Kuba and The Dros, you kept the *craic* on tap all summer. Gigantor thanks to ▨Laura, who hired me even after she read a sample of my writing. ▨Jeremy, whose music and high-pitched rodent shrieks fueled everything that is creative in our writing. All sorts of good love to ▨▨Katie, for trying so hard to coax me out of the office. This book's for us! ▨Mom for the groceries, ▨LG for funding my Thai and Indian addiction; curry wrote this book. And ▨Scotland, you got me this gig; I'm coming back, baby. HOT!

JOHN THANKS: Laura and Adrián, for tireless map edits. Jeremy, for midnight snack goodness. Elizabeth, for map-making magic. His family, for everything.

Editor
Laura Krug
Associate Editor
Adrián Maldonado
Managing Editor
Jeremy Todd
Map Editor
John P. Kiernan
Typesetter
Ariel Fox

Publishing Director
Emma Nothmann
Editor-in-Chief
Teresa Elsey
Production Manager
Adam R. Perlman
Cartography Manager
Elizabeth Halbert Peterson
Design Manager
Amelia Aos Showalter
Editorial Managers
Briana Cummings, Charlotte Douglas,
Ella M. Steim, Joel August Steinhaus,
Lauren Truesdell, Christina Zaroulis
Financial Manager
R. Kirkie Maswoswe
Marketing and Publicity Managers
Stef Levner, Leigh Pascavage
Personnel Manager
Jeremy Todd
Low-Season Manager
Clay H. Kaminsky
Production Associate
Victoria Esquivel-Korsiak
IT Director
Matthew DePetro
Web Manager
Rob Dubbin
Associate Web Manager
Patrick Swieskowski
Web Content Manager
Tor Krever
Research and Development Consultant
Jennifer O'Brien
Office Coordinators
Stephanie Brown, Elizabeth Peterson

Director of Advertising Sales
Elizabeth S. Sabin
Senior Advertising Associates
Jesse R. Loffler, Francisco A. Robles, Zoe M. Savitsky
Advertising Graphic Designer
Christa Lee-Chuvala

President
Ryan M. Geraghty
General Manager
Robert B. Rombauer
Assistant General Manager
Anne E. Chisholm

XII

HOW TO USE THIS BOOK

COVERAGE LAYOUT. *Let's Go: Britain & Ireland* launches out of **London,** and follows with a whirling tour through **England.** From the idyllic **South,** venture down into the **Southwest,** through the storybook **Heart of England,** to **East Anglia** and the misunderstood **Midlands,** then across the cities and lakes of the **Northwest** (with a quick hop out to the **Isle of Man**) and finally the moors of the **Northeast.** Your travels begin anew in **Wales,** sweeping from Cardiff up through **South Wales** into mountainous **North Wales.** From Edinburgh, wheel around **Southern Scotland** to Glasgow, then trek north to the castles of **Central Scotland** and embark on a tour of the rugged and remote **Highlands and Islands.** Next, it's across the sea to the Emerald Isle. Beginning in Belfast, tour the people and places of **Northern Ireland,** then, bidding farewell to the UK, career through Dublin and the **Republic of Ireland.**

TRANSPORTATION INFO. For making connections between destinations, information is generally listed under both the arrival and departure cities. Parentheticals usually provide the trip duration followed by the frequency, then the price. For more general information on travel, consult the **Essentials** (p. 11) section.

COVERING THE BASICS. The first chapter, **Discover Britain & Ireland** (p. 1), contains highlights of the British Isles, complete with **Suggested Itineraries.** The **Essentials** (p. 11) section contains practical information on planning a budget, making reservations, and other useful tips for traveling in Britain and Ireland. Take some time to peruse the **Life and Times** sections, which introduce each separate country (England, p. 71; Wales, p. 445; Scotland, p. 533; Northern Ireland, p. 695; Republic of Ireland, p. 722) and briefly sum up the history, culture, and customs of each destination. The **Appendix** (p. 813) has climate information, a list of bank holidays, measurement conversions, and a glossary. For study abroad, volunteer, and work options in Britain and Ireland, **Alternatives to Tourism** (p. 58) is all you need.

SCHOLARLY ARTICLES. Five contributors with unique regional insight wrote articles for *Let's Go: Britain and Ireland.* Columbia University professor and famous British historian **Simon Schama** discusses his favorite ruins (p. 10), expert **Brenna Powell** describes Belfast's walls (p. 721), former *Let's Go* researcher **Brian Algra** chronicles the Glasgow football rivalry (p. 585), Harvard graduate **Sarah Kerman** weighs current immigration issues (p. 184), and Harvard graduate **Lily Brown** reflects on her experience studying at Oxford (p. 65).

PRICE DIVERSITY. Our researchers list establishments in order of value from best to worst, with absolute favorites denoted by the *Let's Go* thumbs-up (🖎). Since the cheapest price does not always mean the best value, we have incorporated a system of price ranges for food and accommodations; see p. viii.

PHONE CODES AND TELEPHONE NUMBERS. Area codes for each region appear opposite the name of the region and are denoted by the ☎ icon. Phone numbers in text are also preceded by the ☎ icon.

A NOTE TO OUR READERS. The information for this book was gathered by *Let's Go* researchers from May through August of 2004. Each listing is based on one researcher's opinion, formed during his or her visit at a particular time. Those traveling at other times may have different experiences since prices, dates, hours, and conditions are always subject to change. You are urged to check the facts presented in this book beforehand to avoid inconvenience and surprises.

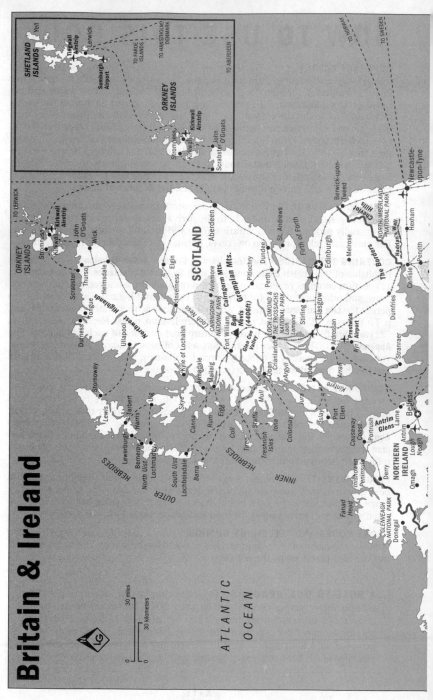

Britain & Ireland

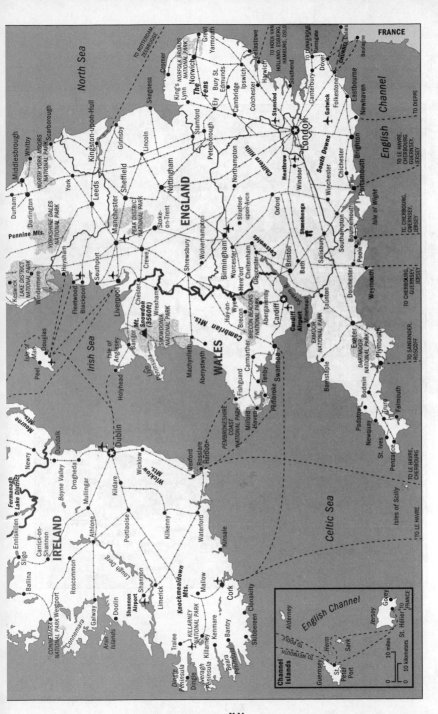

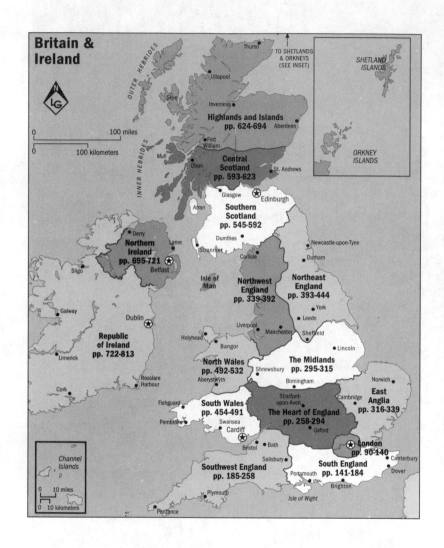

Britain & Ireland

TO SHETLANDS & ORKNEYS (SEE INSET)

SHETLAND ISLANDS

ORKNEY ISLANDS

OUTER HEBRIDES

INNER HEBRIDES

Thurso

Ullapool

Skye

Inverness

Highlands and Islands pp. 624-694

Aberdeen

Fort William

Mull

Oban

Central Scotland pp. 593-623

St. Andrews

Glasgow

Arran

Edinburgh

Southern Scotland pp. 545-592

Derry

Larne

Northern Ireland pp. 695-721

Belfast

Sligo

Galway

Dublin

Republic of Ireland pp. 722-813

Limerick

Cork

Dumfries

Stranraer

Carlisle

Newcastle-upon-Tyne

Durham

Isle of Man

Northwest England pp. 339-392

Northeast England pp. 393-444

York

Leeds

Liverpool

Manchester

Sheffield

Lincoln

Holyhead

Bangor

North Wales pp. 492-532

Shrewsbury

The Midlands pp. 295-315

Norwich

Aberystwyth

Birmingham

East Anglia pp. 316-339

Fishguard

Stratford-upon-Avon

Cambridge

Pembroke

South Wales pp. 454-491

Swansea

Cardiff

The Heart of England pp. 258-294

Oxford

London pp. 90-140

Canterbury

Bristol

Bath

Salisbury

Dover

Southwest England pp. 185-258

Portsmouth

South England pp. 141-184

Brighton

Plymouth

Isle of Wight

Penzance

Rosslare Harbour

Channel Islands

0   10 miles
0   10 kilometers

0   100 miles
0   100 kilometers

DISCOVER BRITAIN AND IRELAND

Welcome to Britain. You've arrived on an island half the size of Spain with a population almost twice that of California, whose people have managed to colonize two-fifths of the globe and win just about every war they've gotten into. If they seem to keep more to themselves these days, it's because they feel safe in the knowledge that the world is coming to them—in the form of an endless spate of visitors. Though small, Britain somehow has enough variety of terrain and regional flavor to keep you occupied for your entire stay and then some. The rolling farms of the south and the rugged peaks of the north are only hours apart by train, and even on a two-week trip, you'll come across peoples as diverse as London clubbers, Welsh students, and Scottish crofters. Prepare to experience a multiplicity of cultures living in remarkably close quarters, a quirk that has resulted in a bloody past whose defiant fortresses, subterranean dungeons, and ensuing ruins account for much of the island's appeal. But even if the disparate regions of Britain are perpetually at odds, they all embrace the fruits of the cultures they've come across in their globetrotting days: Brits eat kebab and curry as often as they do scones and lemon curd, and watch American TV shows as much as the BBC. Despite the survival of a bucolic "Merry Olde England," in today's Great Britain, the hum of the big city draws as much attention as the picturesque views of a country inn.

Make sure to set aside plenty of time for Ireland as well; between the dramatic mist-cloaked mountain peaks and the dazzling green of the landscape, you'll find that the "Emerald Isle" is no mere marketing slogan. But perhaps nothing will stay with you more than the vibrant Irish culture, where traditional music and pub life survive in village and city alike. Wherever in the British Isles you choose to swing through, one thing is decidedly clear: you've chosen the right place to travel.

WHEN TO GO

Britain and Ireland's popularity as tourist destinations makes it wise to plan around high season (June-Aug.). Spring or autumn (Apr.-May and Sept.-Oct.) are more appealing times to visit; the weather is still reasonable and flights are cheaper. If you intend to visit the cities and linger indoors, the low season (Nov.-Mar.), is most economical. Keep in mind, however, that sights and accommodations often run reduced hours or close completely, especially in rural areas.

"Rain, Rain, Go Away" is less a hopeful plea than an exercise in futility. Regardless of when you go, **it will rain.** Have warm, waterproof clothing on hand at all times. Relatively speaking, April is the driest month. The mild weather has few extremes; excluding Highland altitudes, temperatures average around 15-20°C (the mid-60°s F) in summer and 5-7°C (the low 40°s F) in winter. Another factor to consider is daylight—the Isles are more northerly than you may think. In Scotland, the midsummer sun lasts almost all day, and in winter sets as early as 3:45pm.

DISCOVER

THINGS TO DO

With Manchester's clubs only an hour from the Lake District fells, Britain and Ireland provide unparalleled opportunities in an amazingly compact space. For more specific regional attractions, see the **Highlights** box at the start of each chapter.

AU NATURAL

Forget the madding crowds: the diversity of Britain and Ireland's natural landscapes is worthy of a small continent. Discover your inner romantic (or Romantic) among the gnarled crags and crystalline waters of the peaceful **Lake District** (p. 372). The **South Downs Way** (p. 154) ambles through the gentle hills of Southern England. With sea-sprayed bravura, Wales meets the Atlantic Ocean at **Pembrokeshire Coast National Park** (p. 484), where sandy beaches are fringed with lofty cliffs and idyllic harbors. **Loch Lomond and The Trossachs** (p. 611) recently became Scotland's first national park—a trip on the **West Highland Railway** slices through the Highlands north from Glasgow, steps away from those bonnie, bonnie banks, and passes imposing **Ben Nevis** (p. 672). Farther north, the misty peaks of the **Isle of Skye** (p. 654) and the **Northwest Highlands** (p. 672) lend themselves to postcard snapshots from just about any angle. Find endless expanses of grass in the isolated **Orkneys** (p. 680), where the winds are so strong that trees can't survive. In Northern Ireland, the honeycomb columns of the **Giant's Causeway** (p. 716) are a geological anomaly among Antrim's rocky outcrops and pristine white beaches. Southwest in the Republic, the **Ring of Kerry** (p. 779) encircles a peninsula rippled with mountains and waterfalls. The **Cliffs of Moher** (p. 812) supply dramatic seascapes, with sheer 700 ft. drops.

HISTORY, PRE-1066

Britain and Ireland were some of Europe's most popular residences long before the arrival of William the Conqueror and the Normans. Walk through a perfectly preserved Neolithic village at **Skara Brae** (p. 684) in the Orkneys. **Stonehenge** (p. 192) is the best-known marker of Bronze Age inhabitants, though nearby **Avebury** (p. 192) is a bigger, less touristed site. In Ireland's Co. Meath, the underground passages and 5000-year-old designs of the **Boyne Valley** (p. 760) stump engineers. On Scotland's Isle of Lewis, the **Callanish Stones** (p. 664) reveal ancient knowledge of astronomy and math, while the burial tomb of Wales's **Bryn Celli Ddu** (p. 519) pokes up from the middle of a modern farm. Fabulous mosaics and a theater have been excavated at **St. Albans** (p. 258), once the raging capital of Roman Britannia, while **Bath** (p. 193) provided a regenerative retreat for Roman colonists. On the then-border with Scotland, **Hadrian's Wall** (p. 436) marks an emperor's frustration with rebellious tribes to the north. Finding the light in the Dark Ages, early Christianity got its start in Canterbury, where the **Church of St. Martin** (p. 146) is Britain's oldest house of worship. But a new era of British history was soon to be inaugurated in that fateful year when William trounced the Saxons at **Hastings** (p. 154).

CHURCH AND STATE

Wherever a castle or cathedral could be imposingly built (or defiantly razed) in Britain and Ireland, it was. Edward I of England had a rough time containing the Welsh; his massive fortresses—like **Caernarfon** (p. 508), the Robocop of Welsh castles, or the begging-to-be-explored **Caerphilly** (p. 461)—are lined like spectacular soldiers along the northwestern coast of Wales. Two castles, equally grand, top

FACTS AND FIGURES

POPULATIONS England: 49.1 million, Wales: 2.9 million, Scotland: 5.1 million, Northern Ireland: 1.7 million, Republic of Ireland: 3.9 million.

PATRON SAINTS George (England), David (Wales), Andrew (Scotland), Patrick (Ireland).

MONARCHS Kings: 35. Queens: 7. Longest reign: 64 years (Victoria). Shortest reign: 9 days (Lady Jane Grey).

SUN STATS Average hours of sunshine per day in South England: 4.65, in Wales: 4, in Ireland: 3.5, in the Scottish Highlands: 3. Hours of total darkness, midsummer, Shetland Islands: 0.

MOST COMMON NAMES Jack (it's a boy!), Emily (it's a girl!), The Red Lion (it's a pub!).

BEVERAGES Tea (per person per year): 860 cups. Beer: 228 pints.

extinct volcanoes in Scotland, one ringed with gargoyles, in **Stirling** (p. 607), the other perched high above **Edinburgh** (p. 546). You'll notice there isn't a scratch on **Dover Castle** (p. 151); this fortress of power has reigned supreme over the coast since England ruled half of France. Join the camera-toters if you must at **Eilean Donan Castle** (p. 673), but you can't leave Scotland without visiting **Dunnottar Castle** (p. 630); it's even more mind-exploding on a stormy day. On your way south, stop by the ruined **St. Andrews Castle** (p. 597) and scurry through Britain's only surviving countermine tunnel. In the Heart of England, get the full medieval experience at **Warwick Castle** (p. 296), complete with banquets, jousts, and all the wax figures you can handle. You can also play the lord or lady at hilltop **Durham Castle** (p. 427), which lets out its rooms to travelers, as does 15th-century **St. Briavel's Castle** (p. 465), now a hostel near Tintern. The sumptuous **Castle Howard** (p. 415), not strictly a castle at all, and the magnificent **Alnwick Castle** (p. 442) both afford a heady taste of how the other 0.001% still lives. Finally, cross the Irish Sea to discover the hidden gem **Ross Castle** (p. 780) deep inside Killarney National Park.

In northeast England, **York Minster** (p. 412), the country's largest Gothic house of worship, jockeys with **Durham Cathedral** (p. 426) to inspire the most awe in its visitors, while **Canterbury Cathedral** (p. 144) has attracted pilgrims even before the time of Geoffrey Chaucer. **Salisbury Cathedral** (p. 190) sets a record of its own with England's tallest spire. In London, thousands flock to **Westminster Abbey** (p. 110) and **St. Paul's Cathedral** (p. 111), where Poets' Corner and the Whispering Gallery take their breath away. Up in Scotland, the ruined **Border Abbeys—Jedburgh** (p. 569), **Melrose**, (p. 567), **Kelso** (p. 570), and **Dryburgh** (p. 568)—draw fewer visitors, but way more introspection. Across the Irish Sea, the quiet interior of Dublin's **Christ Church Cathedral** (p. 747) belies its contested history. Ruins of another medieval cathedral crown the magnificent **Rock of Cashel** (p. 765).

LITERARY LANDMARKS

Even if you've never been to Britain or Ireland, their landscapes may appear familiar from the pages of your English Lit notes. **Jane Austen** grew up in Winchester (p. 179), wrote in **Bath** (p. 193), and took the odd trip to **Lyme Regis** (p. 215). Farther north, the **Brontës**—Charlotte, Emily, and Anne—lived in the parsonage in **Haworth** (p. 399), and captured the wildness of the **Yorkshire moors** (p. 415) in their novels. **Thomas Hardy** was a **Dorchester** (p. 212) man, whose fictional county of Wessex mirrored Southwest England perfectly. **Sir Arthur Conan Doyle** set Sherlock Holmes's house on 221b Baker St. in London (p. 118), but sent the sleuth to **Dartmoor** (p. 223) to find the Hound of the Baskervilles. **Virginia Woolf** drew inspiration for her novel *To the Lighthouse* from **St. Ives** (p. 250) and the **Isle of Skye** (p. 654). Long after shuffling off his mortal coil, **Wil-**

THE QUEST FOR THE HOLY GRAIL

1. Get psyched for your journey at Henry III's Round Table in the **Winchester Great Hall** (p. 182).

2. Reenact Arthur's final battle with his son Mordred at **Slaughter Bridge** (p. 237), using plastic swords bought from the nearby **Arthurian Centre** gift shop.

3. Go back to where it all began at **Tintagel Castle** (p. 238), Arthur's legendary birthplace, or poke around **Merlin's Cave** on the water just below.

4. Sleuth carefully at **Glastonbury Tor** (p. 209), the real Isle of Avalon and Grail-hunter hotspot.

5. Hike up the **Brecon Beacons** (p. 471) looking for bits of Camelot sticking up through the grass (or just relive the movie *King Arthur,* partially filmed here).

6. Get your legends straight in the caverns of **King Arthur's Labyrinth** in Machynlleth (p. 497).

7. Be wary for the Grail (or ghosts) at the forlorn ruins of **Castell Dinas Brân** (p. 531).

8. Explore the **Eildon Hills** (p. 567), keeping an eye out for any underground caverns where Arthur and his knights sleep until Britain needs them once more.

9. Follow *Da Vinci Code* enthusiasts to **Rosslyn Chapel** (p. 565) and practice your knowledge of Templar symbology among the thousands of stone carvings.

10. Paddle out to the end of your Quest with Monty Python fans at **Castle Aaargh** (p. 616). Just don't let any rude French knights break your resolve!

liam **Shakespeare** lives on in **Stratford-upon-Avon** (p. 275). **William Wordsworth** grew up in the **Lake District** (p. 372), and his friend **Samuel Taylor Coleridge** envied him deeply for it—much of their poetry was inspired by walks near its waters and mountain ridges. **J.R.R. Tolkien** and **C.S. Lewis** chatted fantasy over pints at The Eagle and Child in **Oxford** (p. 263). Welshman **Dylan Thomas** was born in **Swansea** (p. 476), moved to **Laugharne** (p. 483), and today enjoys a fanatical following in both locations. Scotland's national poet is **Robert Burns,** and every town in **Dumfries and Galloway** (p. 571) pays tribute to him, while **Edinburgh** (p. 546) cherishes its favorite **Scott, Sir Walter.** Irishman **W.B. Yeats** scattered his poetic settings throughout the island, but chose **Co. Sligo** (p. 803) for his gravesite; and **James Joyce** is the most famous of the dear, dirty **Dubliners** (p. 750).

A SPORTS FAN'S PARADISE

Football (soccer, if you must) fanaticism is unavoidable: the Queen Mum was an Arsenal fan, and the police run a National Hooligan Hotline. At the **football grounds** of London, become a gunner for a day at Highbury, chant for the Spurs at White Hart Lane, or don the Chelsea blue. Then head up to **Old Trafford** (p. 358), Manchester United's hallowed turf on Sir Matt Busby Way, or move west to the stadia of bitter rivals **Everton** and **Liverpool** (p. 345). **Rugby** scrums are held in gaping **Millennium Stadium,** Cardiff (p. 460). Discouraged by the terrace yobs and the mud? Throwers of tree-trunks and other wearers of kilts reach their own rowdy heights annually at the festival-like Highland Games in **Braemar** (p. 631) and other towns throughout Scotland. **Cricket** is more refined; watch the men in white at London's **Lords** grounds. **Tennis,** too, demands genteel conduct to balance sport with strawberries and cream at **Wimbledon.** The **Royal Ascot** horse races and the **Henley** regatta draw Britain's blue-bloods, but the revered coastal golf courses of **St. Andrews** (p. 593) attract enthusiasts from all over. Surfers catch a wave along the Atlantic coast at alternative **Newquay** (p. 239), artsy **St. Ives** (p. 250), and hardcore **Lewis** (p. 662). Go canyoning or whitewater rafting at **Fort William** (p. 646), or try the more tranquil punting at **Oxford** (p. 263) or **Cambridge** (p. 316). **Snowdonia National Park** (p. 510) and the **Cairngorm Mountains** (p. 632) challenge hikers, while every park has cycling trails. Any town will offer spontaneous kickabouts: go forth and seek your game.

FEELING FESTIVE?

It is difficult to travel in Britain without bumping into some kind of festival. The **Edinburgh International Festival** and its **Fringe** (p. 564) take over Scotland's capital with a head-spinning program of performances. The whole of Scotland hits the streets to welcome the New Year for **Hogmanay**, while torch-lit Viking revelry ignites the Shetlands during **Up Helly Aa** (p. 694). Back in London, things turn fiery during the **Chinese New Year.** In Manchester's Gay Village, **Mardi Gras** (p. 354) is the wildest of street parties, while the summer **Notting Hill Carnival** blasts the streets of London with Caribbean color. The three-day **Glastonbury Festival** (p. 208) is Britain's biggest homage to rock, drawing the biggest names (and crowds) year after year. The **International Musical Eisteddfod** is Wales's version of the mega-fest, annually swelling modest Llangollen (p. 530) to nearly 30 times its normal size. For a celebration of all things Welsh, check out the **National Eisteddfod** (p. 453).

In warmer months, virtually all of Ireland's villages find reason to tune their fiddles and gather their sheep (or goats, or bachelors) for show. Joycean scholars join an 18hr. ramble through Dublin's streets on June 16, **Bloomsday** (p. 753). Around August, every set in Ireland tunes in to the nationally televised **Rose of Tralee Festival and Pageant** (p. 785), a personality contest of epic proportions.

ADDITIONAL RESOURCES

NON-FICTION

A History of Britain, by Simon Schama
A History of the English-Speaking Peoples, by Winston Churchill
A History of Wales, by John Davies
How the Scots Invented the Modern World, by Arthur Herman
The Troubles: Ireland's Ordeal and the Search for Peace, by Tim Pat Coogan
How the Irish Saved Civilization, by Thomas Cahill

FICTION AND POETRY

The Adventures of Sherlock Holmes, by Sir Arthur Conan Doyle
Alice in Wonderland, by Lewis Carroll
Danny, Champion of the World, by Roald Dahl
England, England, by Julian Barnes
Sarum, by Edward Rutherfurd
How Green Was My Valley, by Richard Llewellyn
Trainspotting, by Irvine Welsh
Poems, Chiefly in the Scottish Dialect, by Robert Burns
Dubliners, by James Joyce

TRAVEL BOOKS

Let's Go: Ireland
Let's Go: London
In Search of England, by H.V. Morton.
The Kingdom by the Sea, by Paul Theroux
A Writer's House in Wales, by Jan Morris
Journal of a Tour to the Hebrides, by James Boswell
Round Ireland with a Fridge, by Tony Hawks
The Hitchhiker's Guide to the Galaxy, by Douglas Adams

DISCOVER

DISCOVER

LET'S GO PICKS

BEST PLACE FOR A PINT In Penzance, **Admiral Benbow** (p. 249) adorns its walls with shipwreck relics. Students prowl **"The Turf"** (p. 268) in Oxford. Tradition mandates a pub crawl in **Edinburgh** (p. 561). If the blonde in the black skirt is your drink of choice, the pubs of **Dublin's** Grafton St. (p. 741) serve up copious pints of Guinness. Unruly trad sessions liven **The Crane** (p. 798) in Galway.

BEST QUIRKY MUSEUMS A collection of antiquities and architectural marvels, **Sir John Soane's Museum** (p. 129) is worth a look. In Boscastle, the **Museum of Witchcraft** (p. 238) confirms the hocus pocus with biographies of living witches. The **Dog Collar Museum** in Leeds Castle (p. 148) displays medieval pooch attire. Near Shrewsbury, **The Land of Lost Content** (p. 306) salvages souvenirs of popular culture from trash cans.

BEST PLACE TO CATCH A WAVE Hang ten at **Newquay** (p. 239) on the dazzling Cornwall coast, or brave the 20 ft. rollers at **Lewis** (p. 662). Unspoiled sands stretch near **Aberdaron** (p. 507) and on the colorful **Isle of Wight** (p. 175). The stunning seascapes in **St. Ives** (p. 250) have long inspired artists.

BEST INDULGENCES It is easy to overload on clotted cream and cucumber sandwiches as you sip **high tea** in London (p. 102). Sate chocolate cravings and Willy Wonka fantasies at **Cadbury World,** in Birmingham (p. 301). Eager volunteers can sample the best of **Old Jameson Distillery's** liquid gold (p. 748) or a pint straight from the source at the **Guinness Storehouse** (p. 747).

BEST WAY TO TEMPT FATE Tourists bend over backwards to kiss a stone at **Blarney Castle** (p. 776). Legend holds that nappers on Snowdonia's **Cader Idris** (p. 501) will awake either poets or madmen. In Snowdonia, mountaineers celebrate the summit of **Tryfan** (p. 515) by jumping between its two peaks.

BEST SUNSETS The walled Welsh city of **Caernarfon** (p. 508) sits on the water, facing the western horizon full on. In Ireland, Yeats still can't get enough of the views from **Drumcliff** (p. 806) toward Benbulben. The extreme northern location of **Shetland** (p. 688) makes for breathtaking skies, while **Arthur's Seat** (p. 559) grants 360° views of the shimmering Edinburgh skyline.

BEST LIVESTOCK Don't pet Northumberland's psychotic **Wild Cattle,** inbred for seven centuries (p. 442). The Highlands have the harrowing **Bealach-na-ba ("Cattle") Pass** (p. 674), featuring plunging cliffs, hairpin turns, and daredevil cows. Famous **seaweed-eating sheep** sustain themselves on North Ronaldsay's beaches (p. 688). The fine goats on Ireland's **Cape Clear Island** (p. 777) produce fine goat's-milk ice cream.

BEST NIGHTLIFE The Beatles' hometown, **Liverpool** (p. 345), comes together every night. **Brighton** (p. 159) does native son Fatboy Slim proud. Students command most of **Newcastle** (p. 429), while funkier folks try Oldham St. in **Manchester** (p. 354) or Broad St. in **Birmingham** (p. 297). Oh, and **London** (p. 90) is rumored to have the odd club, here and there.

BEST OF THE MACABRE The morbid can sample the gallows at Nottingham's **Galleries of Justice** (p. 309). The plague struck down most of the residents of Eyam (p. 371), where visitors can examine 17th-century **Plague Cottages** and purchase plastic rats. Some 250,000 bodies supposedly slumber around Edinburgh's **Greyfriars Tolbooth and Highland Kirk** (p. 557), while corpses are put to more interesting use at **Moyses' Hall Museum** (p. 336) in Bury St. Edmunds. Don't miss the reenactments of torture and killing at the **London Dungeon** (p. 119), and a walk through the somber ruins of **Kilmainham Gaol** (p. 747) will leave you chilled to the bone.

SUGGESTED ITINERARIES

THE BEST OF BRITAIN AND IRELAND

THE BEST OF BRITAIN AND IRELAND (6 WEEKS)

Start in hip **London** (4 days; p. 90) to take in the world's best museums, shopping, theater, and nightlife. Head down to **Salisbury** (1 day; p. 186) for a visit to **Stonehenge** (p. 192), the giants on the plain. Zoom through Cornwall to **Penzance** (1 day; p. 246) and the breathtaking inlets of the **Lizard Peninsula** (p. 245). Explore **Exmoor National Park** (1 day; p. 219), then plunge into spa town **Bath** (1 day; p. 193) to take the waters and picture-perfect vistas.

In **Oxford** (2 days; p. 263), stroll the university quads, then head to **Stratford-upon-Avon** (1 day; p. 275), for a little Shakespeare. Cross into Wales through the quaint villages of the **Cotswolds** (1 day; p. 287), then head west for a stopover in **St. David's** (1 day; p. 489) or a trek into **Pembrokeshire Coast National Park** (p. 484). Head north past fantastic coastal fortresses like **Harlech** (1 day; p. 501). Take on steadfast **Caernarfon** (1 day; p. 508), with its world-famous castle and proximity to towering **Mt. Snowdon** (1 day; p. 515).

From Holyhead (p. 520), ferry over to **Dublin** (2 days; p. 732), home to Joyce, Guinness, and the *Book of Kells.* Run along the coast to trendy **Cork** (1 day; p. 770), and inland to **Killarney** (1 day; p. 779), where you can follow the tourists around the gorgeous **Ring of Kerry** (p. 779), then relax on the stunning **Dingle**

Peninsula (1 day; p. 783). Next, hit **Galway** (2 days; p. 793), an Irish cultural capital, and brave the plunging **Cliffs of Moher** (p. 812). Slip into the traditional *gaeltacht* culture in County **Donegal** (1 day; p. 806), and head for politically-divided **Belfast** (2 days; p. 700), with a daytrip to see the **Antrim Coast** (p. 713). Cross the Irish Sea to Stranraer (p. 575), where a train leads to hip **Glasgow** (2 days; p. 581) and verdant **Loch Lomond** (p. 611). Take the West Highland Railway through **Fort William** (p. 646) to **Mallaig** (1 day; p. 652), where you can catch a boat to the **Isle of Skye** for a taste of the glorious **Hebrides** (2 days; p. 626). Search for Nessie as you pass through **Inverness** (p. 638) on your way to Aberdeen and the clifftop **Dunnottar Castle** (1 day; p. 630). Swing through medieval **St. Andrews** (p. 593) on the way to exuberant **Edinburgh** (3 days; p. 546), where castles and *ceilidhs* meet cosmopolitan life. Cross back into England for the picturesque **Lake District** (2 days; p. 372), and on to historic **York** (1 day; p. 409). Rock out in **Liverpool** (1 days; p. 345), where the Beatles still top the charts, and let loose in happening **Manchester** (1 day; p. 354), the capital of urban nightlife. Swing southward to **Cambridge** (1 day; p. 316) for culture and a punt on the Cam, then wash it all away in debauched **Brighton** (1 day; p. 159). Finish your trip with a hike along part of the **South Downs Way,** ambling through the gentle Sussex landscape (1 day; p. 154).

THE BEST OF ENGLAND (1 MONTH)

All-encompassing England offers highlights from pastoral plains to cutting-edge clubs. Start in **London** (5 days; p. 90), the cosmopolitan center of everything English. Then head southeast for a panorama of the Continent from the white cliffs of **Dover** (1 day; p. 148). For a classic, infamous "dirty weekend," trace the coast to **Brighton** (2 days; p. 159). Catch a piece of the idyllic **South Downs Way** (1 day; p. 154), stopping to admire the fairy-tale castle at **Arundel** (p. 166). Use **Salisbury** (2 days; p. 186), as a base to explore the stone circles at **Stonehenge** (p. 192) and **Avebury** (p. 192), as well as its own cathedral—with the tallest spire in Britain. Then swing southwest around the tip of the striking Cornish coast, to **Penzance** (p. 246) and **St. Ives** (2 days; p. 250), and up to **Newquay** (1 day; p. 239) for an incongruous slice of surfer culture. Devon's **Exmoor National Park** is perfect for a day of

THE BEST OF ENGLAND

rambling (1 day; p. 219). After stunning **Bath** (1 day; p. 193), Georgian England's most fashionable watering hole, you can unwind by hiking between rustic **Cotswold villages** (2 days; p. 287). Next, snatch a pint and a punt in the medieval university city of **Oxford** (2 days; p. 263) and catch a play in **Stratford-upon-Avon** (1 day; p. 275), Shakespeare's hometown. Live it up in the northwestern cities—the post-industrial clubbing mecca of **Manchester** (1 day; p. 354), Beatles-mad **Liverpool** (1 day; p. 345), and terrifically gaudy **Blackpool** (1 day; p. 360). Partied too hard? Wander north to the peaceful, Wordsworthian **Lake District** (2 days; p. 372). Scuttle along **Hadrian's Wall** (p. 436) to **Newcastle,** home of the famous brown ale and great nightlife (1 day; p. 429), then make your way south to age-old **York** (1 day; p. 400). Finish your trip in elegant **Cambridge** (1 day; p. 316), topped off with a quick train back to London.

THE BEST OF WALES (2 WEEKS)

With vast expanses of untouristed country punctuated by ancient and dramatic towns, Wales may be Britain's last undiscovered realm. **Cardiff** (2 days; p. 454), the resurgent

nation's young, international capital, boasts a newly developed waterfront and a flourishing arts scene. From picturesque **Chepstow** (1 day; p. 462), it's just a quick jaunt to haunting **Tintern Abbey** (p. 463), which inspires Wordsworthians to this day. Make your way north into the hills and dales of the **Wye Valley** (2 days; p. 461), with a stop in bookish **Hay-on-Wye** (p. 465), then to **Brecon** (p. 469) in the rugged **Brecon Beacons** (1 day; p. 471). Head west to soak up some rays at **Tenby,** a beach resort town with flair (1 day; p. 481). Magical, mystical **St. David's** (1 day; p. 489) is crowned with a majestic cathedral; and **Pembrokeshire Coast National Park** (p. 484) beckons with scenic coastal hikes.

Then it's up to wild, mountainous North Wales, starting with a dip into **Snowdonia** and stops in **Machynlleth** (1 day; p. 497) and tiny **Dolgellau** (1 day; p. 499). Coastal **Harlech** (1 day; p. 501) boasts sea, sand, and summits—not to mention Wales's most dramatic fortress. A Byzantine castle and Roman ruins draw visitors to ancient, walled **Caernarfon** (1 day; p. 508). From idyllic **Llanberis** (1 day; p. 513), ascend lofty **Mt. Snowdon** (p. 515) then head to eclectic **Conwy** (1 day; p. 522), where curious attractions flank a turquoise harbor. From here, let your wanderlust be your guide, whether east to **Liverpool** (p. 345), in England, or west to **Holyhead** (p. 520), to hop a ferry to Dublin.

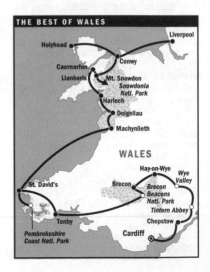

THE BEST OF WALES

THE BEST OF SCOTLAND (2 WEEKS)

Home to more than just men in kilts, Scotland balances remote, unspoiled islands with lively cities. Start off in **Glasgow** (2 days; p. 581), a city of art, culture, and nightlife, and base for a daytrip to the bonnie banks of **Loch Lomond** (p. 611). The scenery only gets better as you trek to **Fort William** and scale Scotland's highest peak, **Ben Nevis** (1 day; p. 646). From Mallaig (p. 652), make the quick crossing to the **Isle of Skye** (2 days; p. 626) for enviable hiking and dramatic views of the **Cuillin Mountains.**

Cross back to the mainland at Kyle of Lochalsh (p. 655), and into the beautiful Highlands. Pass through scenic **Durness** (p. 678) on your way to **John O'Groats,** ferryport for timeless **Orkney** (2 days; p. 680). Head back south to **Inverness** (1 day; p. 638)—more transport hub than destination, but a good base for seeing **Loch Ness** (p. 644) and perhaps its infamous resident. Hit up **Aberdeen** (1 day; p. 626) for city life and a trip to clifftop **Dunnottar Castle** (p. 630), then drop by medieval and musical **Dunkeld** and **Birnam** (1 day; p. 602). Hit the homestretch with a stop in golf-mad **St. Andrews** (p. 593) and **Stirling** (1 day; p. 607), home of Scottish heroes and a stunning castle. Finish your tour in **Edinburgh** (4 days; p. 546), fantastic during festival time in

THE BEST OF IRELAND

August, but sparkling year-round with the historic Royal Mile and unbeatable pubs.

THE BEST OF IRELAND (3½ WEEKS).

Spend a few days in **Dublin** (p. 732) exploring its pubs. Drink a pint of the dark stuff at the Guinness Brewery and catch a football match at Croke Park before moving on to **Belfast** (p. 700). The complex history of this capital is illustrated in the murals decorating its sectarian neighborhoods. Catch the bus to the **Giant's Causeway** (p. 714), a formation of octagonal rocks referred to as the earth's eighth natural wonder. Ride back to the Republic and on to **Donegal Town** (p. 806). Get a good night's rest at one of Ireland's best hostels—tomorrow it's on to **Slieve League** (p. 809) to hike up Europe's tallest sea cliffs. For after-dark action, dip down to **Sligo** (p. 803), once Yeats' beloved home. **Galway** (p. 793), a raging student center, draws Ireland's best musicians. Jump on a ferry to the desolate **Aran Islands** (p. 790) and chill for a few days. Return via **Doolin,** which rests near the **Cliffs of Moher** (p. 789). Take a bus or bike around the **Ring of Kerry** (p. 779), a peninsula captured on postcards worldwide. Return to civilization in **Cork** (p. 770), where you can daytrip out to the **Blarney Stone** (p. 776). Take a detour to medieval **Kilkenny** (p. 761), where a former monastery is now Ireland's oldest brewery.

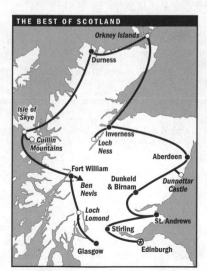

THE BEST OF SCOTLAND

DISCOVER

THE PLEASURE OF RUINS

The inexpressible delight in ruin, shared by all classes and passed from generation to generation, is one of those cultural tics which make the British truly singular among the nations. This instinct to commune with melancholy, to wax wistful about the ambitions of ages past chastened and brought low by history's pratfalls, is as British as milky tea and cow parsley in the country lanes.

It's possible to enter this great British romance of ruins in many of the most celebrated piles of stones such as **Tintern Abbey,** near the River Avon where Wordsworth made intimations of mortality a national obligation. But the danger of sampling the poetry of dereliction amidst the Top Sites is, of course, the buzzing business of the present; so many tourist coaches, so much bad ice cream, so many postcards. Better by far to head to the lesser known and commune in the company of bumblebees and the occasional wandering fellow-pilgrim.

Go, for instance, to Northamptonshire to see what's left of **Lyveden New Bield,** the late 16th-century oratory of the Anglo-Catholic Thomas Tresham and a ruin almost as soon as it was constructed. An exquisite echo of French Renaissance limestone architecture, the oratory was supposed to be a place where the Elizabethan gentleman, who tried to be loyal to both his Queen and his Church, could practice his devotions safe from the prying eyes of authorities. Lyveden displays a delicate, haunting frieze of the stations of the cross on its exterior walls; and from above, the entire structure takes the form of a cross, the sign which Tresham dared not make. A great rotunda was to crown the structure, but Tresham ran out of money and time and was jailed for failing to pay the "recusancy" fines imposed for not subscribing to the official church. The entire building was left open to the elements where it stands in knee-high meadowland.

Most of the ruins in Britain are the work of sudden disaster rather than the slow crumblings of time. **Corfe Castle** (a major destination in Dorset but still worth the trip) looks the charred and blackened pile because it held out against Oliver Cromwell's besieging army to the bitter end during the Second Civil War of 1647-1648. And some of the imposing, pitted "brochs" of Iron Age **Orkney** (like Gurness) and

Shetland look as brutal as they do, not through long centuries of decay but because, at some point they failed in their mission of holding back the oncoming wave of invaders and local rivals. Stunning, sandstone-red **Lindisfarne,** occupying its heart-stopping site on the Northumbrian shore, was twice ravaged, first by Vikings who, despite their recent cultural makeover as seaborn traders, still sacked the place and slaughtered the monks. Then again, predictably emptied it of its community and treasures in the Reformation. Equally sudden was the end of the spectacularly beautiful **Binham Priory** in southern Norfolk, also succumbing to the enforcers of the Protestant Reformation under Henry VIII and Edward VI, who turned what had obviously been one of the most palatial and gorgeously decorated Benedictine foundations into a strangely truncated and spare parish church (where you can still hear choral concerts in the evenings). Miraculously, the Reformation's erasures of the richly painted rood screen (the screen separating the nave from the choir) have themselves become ruins, peeling away to reveal beneath some of the most astonishing church painting of saints and apostles that survived from the world of Roman Catholic England.

Some of the most powerfully evocative ruins, though, can be modern. A little way from the center of Dublin stands one of the great monuments to imperial obtuseness: Kilmainham Gaol. Now a stunning historical museum, the urge to create an Irish national martyrology has been resisted for the sake of genuine historical intelligence. The exterior is just standard issue, banal, mock-castellated prison. But the interior is a cathedral of incarceration; simultaneously shocking, almost operatically grand, with its multi-story iron staircase and rat-hole cells where ancient pallets and fragments of anonymous rags gather grime—morally as well as architecturally squalid. If it all gets too much, head for the tea room and munch on Irish cakes, drink in the giggly chatter of schoolchildren scripted by James Joyce, and reflect that this is how ruins are supposed to get you, not a cheap rush of sentiment, much less a pang of nostalgia, but the tender inspection of ancient scars which linger obstinately to remind us of the redeeming vulnerability of the human condition.

Simon Schama is University Professor of Art History at Columbia University. He writes for The New Yorker and was recently the writer and host of the BBC's History of Britain. His most recent book is A History of Britain, Volume III: The Fate of Empire.

ESSENTIALS

PLANNING YOUR TRIP

ENTRANCE REQUIREMENTS

Passport (p. 13). Required for all foreign nationals, though they may not be checked for citizens of the EU.

Visa (p. 14). Not required for citizens of Australia, Canada, New Zealand, the US, and many other Western countries. If you are unsure, call your local embassy or complete an inquiry at www.ukvisas.gov.uk. Students planning to study in the UK or Ireland for six months or more must obtain a student visa.

Work Permit (p. 14). Required of all foreign nationals planning to work in the UK or Ireland.

EMBASSIES AND CONSULATES

UK CONSULAR SERVICES ABROAD

For addresses of British embassies in countries not listed here, consult the **Foreign and Commonwealth Office** (☎ 020 7008 1500; www.fco.gov.uk). Some cities have a local British consulate that can handle most of the same functions as an embassy.

Australia: British High Commission, Commonwealth Ave., Yarralumla, ACT 2600 (☎ 02 6270 6666; www.britaus.com). Visa and British Consulate-General, The Gateway, Level UK (16), 1 Macquarie Place, Sydney, NSW 2000. Consulates-General in Brisbane, Melbourne, and Perth; Consulate in Adelaide.

Canada: British High Commission, 80 Elgin St., Ottawa, ON K1P 5K7 (☎ 613-237-1530; www.britain-in-canada.org). British Consulate-General, 777 Bay St., Ste. 2800, Toronto, ON M5G 2G2 (☎ 416-593-1290). Consulates-General also in Montreal, Toronto, and Vancouver; Honorary consuls in St. John's, Quebec City, Dartmouth, and Winnipeg.

Ireland: British Embassy, 29 Merrion Rd., Ballsbridge, Dublin 4 (☎ 01 205 3700; www.britishembassy.ie).

New Zealand: British High Commission, 44 Hill St., Thorndon, Wellington 1 (☎ 04 924 2888; www.britain.org.nz); mail to P.O. Box 1812, Wellington. Consulate-General, Level 17, IAG House, 151 Queen St., Auckland (☎ 09 303 2973); or Private Bag 92014, Auckland.

US: British Embassy, 3100 Massachusetts Ave. NW, Washington, D.C. 20008 (☎ 202-588-6500; www.britainusa.com). Consulate-General, 845 Third Ave., New York, NY 10022 (☎ 212-745-0200). Other Consulates-General in Atlanta, Boston, Chicago, Houston, Los Angeles, San Francisco. Consulates in Denver, Miami, Seattle.

IRISH CONSULAR SERVICES ABROAD

Australia: Irish Embassy, 20 Arkana St., Yarralumla, Canberra ACT 2600 (☎ 062 73 3022).

Canada: Irish Embassy, Ste. 1105, 130 Albert St., Ottawa, K1P 5G4, Ontario (☎ 613-233-6281; embassyofireland@rogers.com).

New Zealand: Honorary Consul General, 18 Shortland St. 1001, 6th Fl., Auckland 1 (☎09 997 2252, www.ireland.co.nz).

UK: Irish Embassy, 17 Grosvenor Pl., London SW1X 7HR (☎020 7235 2171). Consulates: 16 Randolph Crescent, Edinburgh EH3 7TT (☎0131 226 7711); Brunel House, 2 Fitzalan Rd., Cardiff CF24 0EB (☎029 7225 7700).

US: Irish Embassy, 2234 Massachusetts Ave. NW, Washington, D.C. 20008 (☎202-462-3939). Consulates: 345 Park Ave., 17th Fl., New York, NY 10154-0037 (☎212-319-2555); 400 N. Michigan Ave., Chicago, IL 60611 (☎312-337-1868); 100 Pine St., 33rd Fl., San Francisco, CA 94111 (☎415-392-4214); 535 Boylston St., Boston, MA 02116 (☎617-267-9330).

CONSULAR SERVICES IN THE UK

Australia: Australian High Commission, Australia House, The Strand, London WC2B 4LA (☎020 7379 4334; www.australia.org.uk).

Canada: Canadian High Commission, 38 Grosvenor Sq., London W1K 4AA (☎020 7258 6600; www.canada.org.uk).

Ireland: See **Irish Consular Services Abroad,** above.

New Zealand: New Zealand High Commission (consular section), New Zealand House, 80 The Haymarket, London SW1Y 4TQ (☎020 7930 8422; www.nzembassy.com).

US: American Embassy, 24 Grosvenor Sq., London W1A 1AE (☎020 7499 9000; www.usembassy.org.uk). Consulate in Scotland at 3 Regent Terr., Edinburgh EH7 5BW (☎0131 556 8315).

TOURIST OFFICES

VISIT BRITAIN. Formerly known as the **British Tourist Authority (BTA),** Visit Britain administrates UK tourist boards. Thames Tower, Blacks Road, London, W6 9EL (☎020 8563 3000; www.visitbritain.com).

Australia: Level 2, 15 Blue St., North Sydney NSW 2060 (☎02 9377 4400; www.visitbritain.com/au).

Canada: 5915 Airport Rd., Ste. 120, Mississauga, Ontario L4V 1T1 (☎905-405-1720; www.visitbritain.com/ca).

Ireland: 18/19 College Green, Dublin 2 (☎01 670 8000; www.visitbritain.com/ie).

New Zealand: Richwhite Building, 17th Fl., 151 Queen St., Auckland 1 (☎09 309 1899; www.visitbritain.com/nz).

US: 551 Fifth Ave., 7th Fl., New York, NY 10176 (☎800-462-2748 or 212-986-2266; www.travelbritain/us).

WITHIN THE UK AND IRELAND.

English Tourist Board, Britain Visitor Centre, 1 Lower Regent St., Piccadilly Circus, London SW1Y 4XT (☎020 8462 2748, www.visitbritain.com). Open M 9:30am-6:30pm, Tu-F 9am-6:30pm, Sa-Su 10am-4pm; June-Oct. extended hours Sa 9am-5pm.

Irish Tourist Board (Bord Fáilte): Baggot St. Bridge, Dublin 2 (☎01 602 4000; www.ireland.travel.ie).

Northern Ireland Tourist Board, 59 North St., Belfast BT1 1NB (☎028 9023 1221; www.discovernorthernireland.com).

Scottish Tourist Board, 23 Ravelston Terr., Edinburgh EH4 3TP (☎0131 332 2433; www.visitscotland.com).

Welsh Tourist Board, Brunel House, 2 Fitzalan Rd., Cardiff CF24 0UY (☎029 2049 9909 or 0870 121 1251; www.visitwales.com).

DOCUMENTS AND FORMALITIES

PASSPORTS

REQUIREMENTS

Citizens of all countries need valid passports to enter Britain and Ireland and to re-enter their home countries. EU citizens should carry their passports, though they may not be checked. Britain does not allow entrance if the holder's passport expires in under six months. Returning home with an expired passport is illegal.

NEW PASSPORTS

Citizens of Australia, Canada, Ireland, New Zealand, the United Kingdom, and the United States can apply for a passport at any passport office and many post offices and courts of law. New passport or renewal applications must be filed in advance of departure, although most passport offices offer rush services for a steep fee.

ONE EUROPE. European unity has come a long way since 1958, when the European Economic Community (EEC) was created to promote European solidarity and cooperation. Since then, the EEC has become the European Union (EU), a mighty political, legal, and economic institution. On May 1, 2004, 10 Southern, Central, and Eastern European countries—Cyprus, the Czech Republic, Estonia, Hungary, Latvia, Lithuania, Malta, Poland, Slovakia, and Slovenia—were admitted to the EU, joining 15 other member states: Austria, Belgium, Denmark, Finland, France, Germany, Greece, Ireland, Italy, Luxembourg, the Netherlands, Portugal, Spain, Sweden, and the UK.

What does this have to do with the average non-EU tourist? The EU's policy of **freedom of movement** means that border controls between the first 15 member states (minus Ireland and the UK, but plus Norway and Iceland) have been abolished, and visa policies harmonized. While you're still required to carry a passport (or government-issued ID card for EU citizens) when crossing an internal border, once you've been admitted into one country, you're free to travel to other participating states. Britain and Ireland have also formed a **common travel area,** abolishing passport controls between the UK and the Republic of Ireland. For more consequences of the EU for travelers, see **Customs in the EU** (p. 16).

PASSPORT MAINTENANCE

Be sure to photocopy the page of your passport with your photo, as well as visas, traveler's check serial numbers, and any other important documents. Carry one set of copies in a safe place, apart from the originals, and leave another at home. Consulates also recommend that you carry an expired passport or an official copy of your birth certificate in a part of your baggage separate from other documents.

If you lose your passport, immediately notify the local police and the nearest embassy or consulate of your home government. To expedite its replacement, you will need to know all information previously recorded and show ID and proof of citizenship. In some cases, a replacement may take weeks to process, and it may be valid only for a limited time. Any visas stamped in your old passport will be irretrievably lost. In an emergency, ask for immediate temporary traveling papers that will permit you to re-enter your home country.

ESSENTIALS

VISAS, INVITATIONS, AND WORK PERMITS

VISAS

EU citizens do not need a visa to enter Britain. As of August 2003, citizens of Australia, Canada, New Zealand, South Africa, and the US do not need a visa for visits shorter than six months; neither do citizens of Iceland, Israel, Japan, Malaysia, Mexico, Norway, Singapore, Switzerland, and some Eastern European, Caribbean, and Pacific countries. Citizens of most other countries must have a visa to enter Britain; citizens of certain countries will need a visa merely to pass through Britain. If you are uncertain, contact your embassy or complete an online inquiry at www.ukvisas.gov.uk. US citizens can consult www.state.travel.gov/foreigntryreqs. Tourist visas cost about US$66 for a one-time pass and allow you to spend up to six months in the UK. Visas can be purchased from your nearest British consulate (listed under **Embassies & Consulates,** p. 11). US citizens can take advantage of the **Center for International Business and Travel (CIBT;** ☎ 800-925-2428), which secures visas for travel for a variable service charge. If you need a **visa extension** while in the UK, contact the **Home Office, Immigration and Nationality Directorate** (☎ 0870 606 7766; www.ind.homeoffice.gov.uk).

WORK AND STUDY PERMITS

Admission as a visitor does not include the right to work, which is authorized only by a work permit. Entering Britain and Ireland to **study** requires a special visa if you are planning to do so for over six months; see **Alternatives to Tourism** (p. 58).

IDENTIFICATION

When you travel, always carry at least two forms of identification on your person, including a photo ID; a passport and a driver's license or birth certificate is usually adequate. Never carry all of your IDs together; split them up in case of theft or loss, and keep photocopies of all of them in your luggage and at home.

STUDENT, TEACHER, AND YOUTH IDENTIFICATION

The **International Student Identity Card (ISIC),** the most widely accepted form of student ID, provides discounts on sights, accommodations, food, and transport; access to a toll-free 24hr. emergency helpline for medical, legal, and financial emergencies overseas, and some insurance benefits for US cardholders. Applicants must be full-time secondary or post-secondary school students at least 12 years old. Because of the proliferation of fake ISICs, some services (particularly airlines) require additional proof of student identity.

The **International Teacher Identity Card (ITIC)** offers teachers the same insurance coverage as the ISIC and similar but limited discounts. For travelers who are 25 or under but are not students, the **International Youth Travel Card (IYTC)** also offers many of the same benefits as the ISIC, but with significantly fewer discounts.

ISIC and **ITIC** provide basic insurance benefits to US cardholders, including US$100 per day of in-hospital sickness for up to 60 days and US$5000 of accident-related medical reimbursement (see www.isicus.com). Each of these costs US$22 or equivalent. ISIC and ITIC cards are valid for roughly 1½ academic years; IYTC cards are valid for 1yr. from the date of issue. Many travel agencies (see p. 26) issue them; for a list of issuing agencies, see the **ISTC** website (www.istc.org).

The **International Student Exchange Card (ISE)** is a similar identification card available to students, faculty, and youth (12 to 26). The card provides discounts, medical benefits, access to a 24hr. emergency helpline, and the ability to purchase student airfares. However, it is not as widely recognized as the ISIC. The ISE costs US$25; call US ☎ 800-255-8000 for more info, or visit www.isecard.com.

INSTITUTE FOR STUDY ABROAD BUTLER UNIVERSITY

UNDERGRADUATE
STUDY ABROAD

Argentina • Australia • Chile • Costa Rica • Cuba • England • Mexico
New Zealand • Northern Ireland • Republic of Ireland • Scotland • Spain
WWW.IFSA-BUTLER.ORG • 800-858-0229

Institute
for Study
Abroad
BUTLER UNIVERSITY

CUSTOMS

Upon entering Britain or Ireland, you must declare certain items from abroad and pay a duty on the value of those articles if they exceed the allowance established by Britain's customs service. Note that goods and gifts purchased at **duty-free** shops abroad are not exempt from duty or sales tax; "duty-free" merely means that you need not pay a tax in the country of purchase. Upon returning home, you must likewise declare all articles acquired abroad and pay a duty on the value of articles in excess of your home country's allowance. In order to expedite your return, make a list of any valuables brought from home and register them with customs before traveling abroad, and be sure to keep receipts for all goods acquired abroad. If you're leaving for a non-EU country, you can claim back any **Value Added Tax** paid (see **Taxes,** p. 19). To expedite your return, make a list of any valuables brought from home and register them with customs before traveling abroad. Be sure to keep receipts for all goods acquired abroad.

The **Pet Travel Scheme (PETS)** allows dogs and cats from Western European nations, the US, and Canada to avoid a six month quarantine. Your dog or cat must be fitted with a microchip, treated for ticks and tapeworm, vaccinated for rabies, and tested for vaccine effectiveness six months prior to arrival. If your pet does not meet the provisions of the scheme or you are traveling from a country outside Western Europe, the US, or Canada, your pet will be quarantined. For a complete description of the stringent requirements, contact the **UK Department for Environment, Food, and Rural Affairs** (www.defra.gov.uk/animalh/quarantine/index.htm) or call the **PETS helpline** (☎ 0870 241 1710).

 CUSTOMS IN THE EU. As well as freedom of movement of people within the EU (see p. 13), travelers in the 15 original EU member countries (Austria, Belgium, Denmark, Finland, France, Germany, Greece, Ireland, Italy, Luxembourg, the Netherlands, Portugal, Spain, Sweden, and the UK) can also take advantage of the freedom of movement of goods. This means that there are no customs controls at internal EU borders (i.e., you can take the blue customs channel at the airport), and travelers are free to transport whatever legal substances they like as long as it is for their own personal (non-commercial) use—up to 800 cigarettes, 10L of spirits, 90L of wine (60L of sparkling wine), and 110L of beer. You should also be aware that duty-free allowances were abolished on June 30, 1999 for travel between EU member states; however, travelers between the EU and the rest of the world still get a duty-free allowance when passing through customs.

MONEY

CURRENCY AND EXCHANGE

The **pound sterling** is the main unit of currency in the **United Kingdom,** including Northern Ireland. Northern Ireland and Scotland have their own bank notes (including Scottish £1 and £100 notes), which can be used interchangeably with English currency, though they may not be accepted outside Northern Ireland and Scotland. The **Republic of Ireland** switched from the Irish pound to the **euro** in 2002.

The currency chart below is based on August 2005 exchange rates between local currency and Australian dollars (AUS$), Canadian dollars (CDN$), European Union euros (EUR€), New Zealand dollars (NZ$), British pounds (UK£), and US dollars (US$). Check the currency converter on websites like www.xe.com or www.bloomberg.com or a large newspaper for the latest exchange rates.

CURRENCY (£)		
AUS$1 = £0.40		£1 = AUS$2.52
CDN$1 = £0.42		£1 = CDN$2.36
EUR€1 = £0.68		£1 = EUR€1.48
NZ$1 = £0.37		£1 = NZ$2.70
UK£1 = £1		£1 = UK£1
US$1 = £0.55		£1 = US$1.82

As a general rule, it's cheaper to convert money in Britain or Ireland than at home. While currency exchange will probably be available in your arrival airport, it's wise to bring enough foreign cash to last for the first 24 to 72 hours of your trip.

When changing money abroad, try to go only to banks or bureaux de change that have at most a 5% margin between their buy and sell prices. Since you lose money with every transaction, **convert large sums** (unless the currency is depreciating rapidly), **but no more than you'll need.**

If you use traveler's checks or bills, carry some in small denominations (the equivalent of US$50 or less) for times when you are forced to exchange money at disadvantageous rates, but bring a range of denominations since charges may be levied per check cashed. Store your money in a variety of forms; ideally, at any given time you will be carrying some cash, some traveler's checks, and an ATM and/or credit card. All travelers should also consider carrying some US dollars (about US$50 worth), which are often preferred by local tellers.

TRAVELER'S CHECKS

Traveler's checks are one of the safest means of carrying funds. American Express and Visa are the most recognized brands. Many banks and agencies sell them for a small commission. Checks are readily accepted in heavily touristed areas, but often not in smaller towns and shops. Check issuers provide refunds if the checks are lost or stolen, and many provide additional services, such as toll-free refund hotlines abroad, emergency message services, and stolen credit card assistance. Always carry emergency cash. Visa and American Express also offer **prepaid travel cards** as a more convenient alternative to traveler's checks; call or visit their respective websites (below) for more information.

American Express: Checks available with commission at select banks, at all AmEx offices, and online (www.americanexpress.com; US residents only). American Express cardholders can also purchase checks by phone (☎800-721-9768).

Visa: Checks available (generally with commission) at banks worldwide. For issuing locations, call UK ☎0800 51 58 84; US 800-227-6811. **AAA** (see p. 37) offers commission-free checks to its members. Dual-signature checks also offered.

Travelex/Thomas Cook: For the nearest office, call Travelex service centers: In the US and Canada call ☎800-287-7362; www.travelex.com. In the UK ☎0800 62 21 01.

CREDIT, DEBIT, AND ATM CARDS

Credit cards are accepted by many businesses in Britain and Ireland. Some small establishments—including many B&Bs—either do not take them or add a surcharge. Where they are accepted, credit cards often offer superior exchange rates—up to 5% better than the retail rate used by banks and other currency exchange establishments. Credit cards may also offer services such as insurance or emergency help, and are sometimes required to reserve hotel rooms or rental cars. **Mastercard** (a.k.a. **Access** in Britain) and **Visa** (a.k.a. **Barclaycard**) are the most welcomed; **American Express** cards work at some ATMs and at major airports.

ESSENTIALS

ATM cards (a.k.a. **cash cards**) are widespread in Britain and Ireland and most banks have ATMs. Depending on the system that your home bank uses, you can most likely access your personal bank account from abroad. ATMs get the same wholesale exchange rate as credit cards, but there is often a limit on the amount of money you can withdraw per day (usually around US$500). There is typically also a surcharge of US$2-5 per withdrawal. The two major international money networks are **Cirrus** (to locate ATMs US ☎800-424-7787 or www.mastercard.com) and **Visa/ PLUS** (to locate ATMs US ☎800-843-7587 or www.visa.com). The ATMs of major British and Irish banks (including Barclays, HSBC, Lloyds TSB, National Westminster, Royal Bank of Scotland, Bank of Scotland, Allied Ireland Bank, and Ulster Bank) usually accept both networks.

Debit cards are a form of purchasing power as convenient as credit cards but with a more immediate impact on your funds. A debit card can be used wherever its associated credit card company (usually Mastercard or Visa) is accepted, yet the money is withdrawn directly from the holder's **checking account.** Debit cards often also function as ATM cards and can be used to withdraw cash from associated banks and ATMs throughout Britain and Ireland, and as such just might be the only form of payment you need to bring. Ask your bank about obtaining one.

PIN NUMBERS AND ATMS. To use a cash or credit card to withdraw money from a cash machine (ATM) in Europe, you must have a four-digit **Personal Identification Number (PIN).** If your PIN is longer than four digits, ask your bank whether you can just use the first four, or whether you'll need a new one. **Credit cards** don't usually come with PINs, so if you intend to hit up ATMs in Europe with a credit card to get cash advances, call your credit card company before leaving to request one.

Travelers with alphabetic, rather than numerical, PINs may also be thrown off by the lack of letters on European cash machines. The following are the corresponding numbers to use: 1=QZ; 2=ABC; 3=DEF; 4=GHI; 5=JKL; 6=MNO; 7=PRS; 8=TUV; and 9=WXY. Note that if you mistakenly punch the wrong code into the machine three times, it will swallow your card for good.

GETTING MONEY FROM HOME

If you run out of money while traveling, the easiest and cheapest solution is to have someone back home make a deposit to your credit card or ATM card. Failing that, consider one of the following options. The **International Money Transfer Consumer Guide** (http://international-money-transfer-consumer-guide.info) may help.

WIRING MONEY

It is possible to arrange a **bank money transfer,** which means asking your bank to wire money to a bank in Britain. This is the cheapest way to transfer cash, but also the slowest, generally taking 1-3 days or more. Banks may release your funds in local currency, potentially using a poor exchange rate. Transfer services like **Western Union** are faster and more convenient—but much pricier. To find one the nearest location, visit www.westernunion.com, or call US and Canada ☎800-325-6000, UK 0800 83 38 33, Australia 800 501 500, or New Zealand 800 27 0000. Money transfer services available at **American Express** and **Thomas Cook** offices.

US STATE DEPARTMENT (US CITIZENS ONLY)

In dire emergencies, the US State Department will forward money within hours to the nearest consular office, which will then disburse it according to instructions for a US$30 fee. If you wish to use this service, you must contact the Overseas Citizens Service division of the US State Department (☎317-472-2328; nights, Sundays, and holidays 202-647-4000).

COSTS

The cost of your trip will vary considerably, depending on where you go, how you travel, and where you stay. The most significant expenses will probably be your round-trip airfare to Britain and Ireland (see **Getting to Britain and Ireland: By Plane,** p. 26) and a **railpass** or **bus pass** (p. 31). Before you go, spend some time calculating a reasonable daily **budget.**

STAYING ON A BUDGET

To give you a general idea, a bare-bones day in Britain and Ireland (camping or sleeping in hostels/guesthouses, buying food at supermarkets) would cost about US$40 (£22/€33); a slightly more comfortable day (sleeping in hostels/guesthouses and the occasional budget hotel, eating one meal per day at a restaurant, going out at night) would cost US$91 (£50/€66); and for a luxurious day, the sky's the limit. Don't forget to factor in emergency reserve funds (at least US$200) when planning how much money you'll need.

TIPS FOR SAVING MONEY

Some simpler ways include searching out opportunities for free entertainment, splitting accommodation and food costs with trustworthy fellow travelers, and buying food in supermarkets rather than eating out. Bring a **sleepsack** (see p. 20) to save on linen fees in hostels, and do your **laundry** in the sink (unless you're explicitly prohibited from doing so). That said, don't go overboard. Staying within your budget is important, but don't do so at the expense of your health or a great trip.

TIPPING AND BARGAINING

Tips in restaurants are often included in the bill (sometimes as a "service charge"); if gratuity is not included, you should tip your server about 15%. Taxi drivers should receive a 10-15% tip, and bellhops and chambermaids usually expect between £1-3. To the great relief of budget travelers from the US, tipping is not required at pubs in Britain and Ireland. Bargaining is unheard of in UK shops.

TAXES

Both Britain and Ireland have a 17.5% **Value Added Tax (VAT),** a sales tax applied to everything but food, books, medicine, and children's clothing. The tax is **included** in the amount indicated on the price tag. The prices stated in *Let's Go* include VAT. Upon exiting Britain, non-EU citizens can reclaim VAT (minus an administrative fee) through the **Retail Export Scheme,** though the complex procedure is probably only worthwhile for large purchases. You can obtain refunds only for goods you take out of the country (i.e., not accommodations or meals). Participating shops display a "Tax Free Shopping" sign and may have a purchase minimum of £50-100 before they offer refunds. To claim a refund, fill out the form you are given in the shop and present it with the goods and receipts at customs upon departure (look for the Tax Free Refund desk at the airport). At peak times, this process can take up to an hour. You must leave the country within three months of your purchase in order to claim a refund, and you must apply before leaving the UK.

2 0 ■ PLANNING YOUR TRIP

PACKING

Pack lightly: Lay out only what you absolutely need, then take half the clothes and twice the money. The **Travelite FAQ** (www.travelite.org) is a good resource for tips on traveling light. If you plan to hike in the UK, see **Camping and the Outdoors**, p. 51.

Luggage: If you plan to cover most of your itinerary by foot, a sturdy **frame backpack** is unbeatable. (For the basics on buying a pack, see p. 52.) Toting a suitcase or trunk is fine if you plan to live in one or two cities and explore from there, but not if you plan to move around frequently. In addition to your main piece of luggage, a daypack (a small backpack or better, a courier bag) is useful.

Clothing: No matter when you're traveling, it's a good idea to bring a warm jacket or wool sweater, a rain jacket to protect against ever-present British rain (Gore-Tex® is both waterproof and breathable), sturdy shoes or hiking boots, and wool socks. Flip-flops or waterproof sandals are must-haves for grubby hostel showers. You will want a classy outfit for going out at night, as well as a nicer pair of shoes.

Sleepsack: Some travelers chose to bring a sleepsack while camping, or to certain accommodations; hostels may have grungy bedding, or worse, charge extra for linens. To save yourself a few quid, make a sleepsack: fold a full-size sheet in half the long way, then sew it closed along the long side and one of the short sides.

Converters and Adapters: In Britain and Ireland, electricity is 220 volts AC, enough to fry any 120V North American appliance. 220/240V electrical appliances don't like 120V current, either. Americans and Canadians should buy an adapter (which changes the shape of the plug; US$5) and a converter (which changes the voltage; US$20-30). Don't make the mistake of using only an adapter (unless appliance instructions explicitly state otherwise, like many laptops). New Zealanders and Australians (who use 230V at home) won't need converters, but will need adapters to use anything electrical. For more on all things adaptable, check out http://kropla.com/electric.htm.

Toiletries: The basics, from toothpaste to tampons to condoms, are often available, but bring extras to save money. **Contact lenses** are likely to be expensive and difficult to find, so bring enough extra pairs and solution for your entire trip. Also bring your glasses and a copy of your prescription in case you need emergency replacements.

First-Aid Kit: For a basic first-aid kit, pack bandages, pain reliever, antibiotic cream, a thermometer, a Swiss Army knife with tweezers, moleskine, decongestant, motion-sickness remedy, diarrhea or upset-stomach medication, an antihistamine like Benadryl for allergy emergencies, sunscreen, insect repellent, and burn ointment.

Film: Film and developing are expensive, so bring enough film for your entire trip and develop it at home. Despite disclaimers, airport security X-rays can fog film, so ask security to hand-inspect it. Always pack film in your carry-on luggage, since higher-intensity X-rays are used on checked luggage.

Other Useful Items: For safety purposes, you should bring a **money belt** and small **padlock**. Basic **outdoors equipment** (plastic water bottle, compass, waterproof matches, pocketknife, sunglasses, sunscreen, hat) may also prove useful. If you want to do laundry by hand, bring detergent, and string for a makeshift clothes line. **Other things** you're liable to forget are an **umbrella;** sealable **plastic bags** (for damp clothes, soap, food, shampoo, and other spillables); a **travel alarm clock;** safety pins; a flashlight; earplugs; and a small **calculator**. A **cell phone** can be a lifesaver (literally) on the road; see p. 44 for information on acquiring one that will work for your budget.

Important Documents: Don't forget your passport, traveler's checks, ATM and/or credit cards, ID, and photocopies of all of these in case they get lost or stolen (see p. 14). Also, if these apply: a hosteling membership card (see p. 47); driver's license (see p. 14); travel insurance forms; ISIC (p. 14), and rail or bus pass (see p. 31).

SAFETY AND HEALTH

GENERAL ADVICE

In any type of crisis situation, the most important thing to do is **stay calm.** Your country's embassy abroad (p. 12) is usually your best resource when things go wrong; **registering** with that embassy upon arrival in the country is always the right idea for peace of mind and to facilitate aid.

DRUGS AND ALCOHOL

Remember that you are subject to the laws of the country in which you travel. It's your responsibility to know these laws before you go. If you carry insulin, syringes, or other **prescription drugs** while you travel, it is vital to have a copy of the prescriptions themselves and a note from your doctor. The Brits and the Irish love their drink, and the vibrant pub scene is unavoidable. If you're trying to keep up with the locals, keep in mind the **Imperial pint is 20 oz.,** as opposed to the wussy 16 oz. of a US pint. The drinking age in Britain and Ireland is 18.

Needless to say, **illegal drugs** are best avoided altogether; the average sentence for possession in the United Kingdom is around two years. Carrying drugs across an international border can result in prison time and a "Drug Trafficker" stamp on your passport for the rest of your life. If arrested, call your country's consulate. Don't carry anyone's excess luggage onto a plane.

SPECIFIC CONCERNS

DEMONSTRATIONS AND POLITICAL GATHERINGS

Although sectarian violence in Ireland is dramatically less common than in the height of the Troubles, some neighborhoods and towns still experience unrest during sensitive political times. It's best to remain alert and cautious while traveling in Northern Ireland, especially during **Marching Season,** which reaches its height July 4-12. The 12th of August, when the **Apprentice Boys** march in Derry/Londonderry, is also a testy period when urban areas should be traversed with much circumspection. The most common form of violence is property damage, and tourists are unlikely targets (beware of leaving a car unsupervised, however, if it bears a Republic of Ireland license plate). In general, if traveling in Northern Ireland during marching season, prepare for transport delays and for some shops and services to be closed. Vacation areas like the Glens and the Causeway Coast are less affected. In general, use common sense in conversation and, as ever when traveling, be respectful of your hosts' religious and political perspectives.

TERRORISM

The Anti-Terrorism Crime and Security Act 2001, passed in the aftermath of the September 11, 2001 attacks, strengthens the 2000 Terrorism Act which outlaws certain terrorist groups and gives police extended powers to investigate terrorism. Having faced the threat of Irish Republican terrorism for several years, Britain is committed to an extensive program of prevention and prosecution. More information is available from the Foreign and Commonwealth Office (see box below) and the Home Office (☎0870 000 1585; www.homeoffice.gov.uk/terrorism). The US State Department Website (www.state.gov) provides information on the current situation. To have advisories and warnings emailed to you while abroad, just register with your home embassy or consulate when you arrive in Britain. If you see a suspicious unattended package or bag at an airport or other crowded public place, report it immediately at ☎999, or the free **Anti-Terrorism Hotline** (☎0800 789 321).

ESSENTIALS

PERSONAL SAFETY

EXPLORING AND TRAVELING

EXPLORING. To avoid unwanted attention, try to blend in as much as possible. Familiarize yourself with your surroundings before setting out, and carry yourself with confidence. Check maps in shops and restaurants rather than on the street. If you are traveling alone, be sure someone at home knows your itinerary, and never admit that you're by yourself. When walking at night, stick to busy, well-lit streets and avoid dark alleyways. If you feel uncomfortable, leave quickly and directly.

SELF DEFENSE. There is no sure-fire way to avoid all the threatening situations you might encounter while traveling, but a good **self-defense course** will give you concrete ways to react to unwanted advances. **Impact, Prepare, and Model Mugging** can refer you to local self-defense courses in the US (☎800-345-5425). Visit the website at www.impactsafety.org for a list of nearby chapters. Workshops (2-3hr.) start at US$50; full courses (20hr.) run US$350-500.

POSSESSIONS AND VALUABLES

Never leave your belongings unattended; crime occurs in even the most demure-looking hostel or hotel. Be particularly careful on **buses** and **trains;** horror stories abound about determined thieves who wait for travelers to fall asleep. Always keep your backpack in sight. When traveling with others, sleep in alternate shifts. When alone, use good judgment in selecting a train compartment: never stay in an empty one, and use a lock to secure your pack to the luggage rack. Try to sleep on top bunks with your luggage stored above you (if not in bed with you, but mind you do not sleep on or knock over your laptop).

There are a few steps you can take to minimize the financial risk associated with traveling. First, **bring as little with you as possible.** Second, buy a few combination **padlocks** to secure your belongings either in your pack or in a hostel or train station locker. Third, **carry as little cash as possible.** Keep your traveler's checks and ATM/credit cards in a **money belt**—not a "fanny pack"—along with your passport and ID cards. Fourth, **keep a small cash reserve separate from your primary stash.** This should be about US$50 (US$ or GB£ are best) sewn into or stored in the depths of your pack, along with your traveler's check numbers and important photocopies.

The best way to avoid getting **pickpocketed** is to use your common sense; never flash your cash on the street, **never wear your wallet in your back pocket.** In large cities **con artists** often work in groups and may involve children. **Never let your passport and your bags out of your sight.** Beware of **pickpockets** on public transportation.

If you will be traveling with electronic devices, such as a laptop or a PDA, check whether your insurance covers loss, theft, or damage when you travel. If not, you might consider a low-cost policy. **Safeware** (☎US 800-800-1492; www.safeware.com) specializes in covering computers and charges US$90 for 90-day comprehensive international travel coverage up to US$4000. If you stay in any hostels on your trip, ask to store electronic valuables in a safe—most keep one in reception.

PRE-DEPARTURE HEALTH

In your **passport,** write the names of any people you wish to be contacted in case of a medical emergency, and list any allergies or medical conditions. Matching a prescription to a foreign equivalent is not always easy, safe, or possible, so if you take prescription drugs, consider carrying up-to-date, legible prescriptions or a letter from your doctor stating the medication's trade name, manufacturer, chemical name, and dosage. Be sure to keep all medication with you in your carry-on luggage. For tips on packing a basic **first-aid kit** and other health essentials, see p. 20.

While no injections are specifically required for entry into the UK, travelers over two years old should make sure the following vaccines are up to date: MMR (for measles, mumps, and rubella); DTaP or Td (for diptheria, tetanus, and pertussis); OPV (for polio); HbCV (for haemophilus influenza B); and HBV (for Hepatitis B). Protection against Hepatitis A, Hepatitis B, and tetanus is highly recommended. For recommendations on immunizations and prophylaxis, consult the CDC (see below) in the US or the equivalent in your home country, and check with a doctor.

INSURANCE

Travel insurance covers four basic areas: medical/health problems, property loss, trip cancellation/interruption, and emergency evacuation. Though regular insurance policies may well extend to travel-related accidents, you may consider purchasing separate travel insurance if the cost of potential trip cancellation, interruption, or emergency medical evacuation is greater than you can absorb. Prices for travel insurance purchased separately generally run about US$50 per week for full coverage, while trip cancellation/interruption may be purchased separately at a rate of US$3-5 per day depending on length of stay.

Medical insurance (especially university policies) often covers costs incurred abroad; check with your provider. **US Medicare** does not cover foreign travel. **Canadian** provincial health insurance plans increasingly do not cover foreign travel; check with the provincial Ministry of Health or Health Plan Headquarters for details. **Australians** traveling in Ireland, New Zealand, the UK, the Netherlands, Sweden, Finland, Italy, or Malta are entitled to many of the services that they would receive at home as part of the Reciprocal Health Care Agreement. **Homeowners' insurance** (or your family's coverage) often covers theft during travel and loss of travel documents (passport, plane ticket, railpass, etc.) up to US$500.

INSURANCE PROVIDERS

STA (see p. 26) offers a range of plans that can supplement your basic coverage. Other private insurance providers in the US and Canada include: Access America (☎800-284-8300; www.accessamerica.com); Berkely Group (☎800-323-3149; www.berkely.com); Globalcare Travel Insurance (☎800-821-2488; www.globalcare-cocco.com); Travel Assistance International (☎800-821-2828; www.europassistance.com); and Travel Guard (☎800-826-4919; www.travelguard.com). Columbus Direct (☎020 7375 0011; www.columbusdirect.co.uk) operates in the UK and AFTA (☎02 9264 3299; www.afta.com.au) operates in Australia.

USEFUL ORGANIZATIONS AND PUBLICATIONS

The US **Centers for Disease Control and Prevention** (**CDC;** ☎877-FYI-TRIP/394-8747; www.cdc.gov/travel) maintains an international travelers' hotline and an informative website. The CDC's comprehensive booklet *Health Information for International Travel* (The Yellow Book), an annual rundown of disease, immunization, and general health advice, is free online or US$29-40 via the Public Health Foundation (☎877-252-1200; http://bookstore.phf.org). For quick information on health and other travel warnings call the **Overseas Citizens Services** (M-F 8am-8pm ☎888-407-4747; after-hours ☎202-647-4000; ☎317-472-2328 from overseas), or contact a passport agency, embassy, or consulate abroad. For information on medical evacuation services and travel insurance firms, see the US

ESSENTIALS

government's website at http://travel.state.gov/medical.html or the **British Foreign and Commonwealth Office** (www.fco.gov.uk). For general health info, contact the **American Red Cross** (☎800-564-1234; www.redcross.org).

STAYING HEALTHY

Common sense is the simplest prescription for good health while you travel. Drink lots of fluids to prevent dehydration and constipation, and wear sturdy, broken-in shoes and clean socks. Temperatures in Britain and Ireland rarely stray from about 40°F in winter and about 60°F in summer except in the Scottish highlands and mountains, where temperatures can reach greater extremes. When in areas of high altitude, be sure to dress in layers that can be peeled off as needed. Allow your body a couple of days to adjust to less oxygen before exerting yourself. Note that alcohol is more potent and UV rays are stronger at high elevations.

ONCE IN BRITAIN AND IRELAND

INSECT-BORNE DISEASES
Many diseases are transmitted by insects—mainly mosquitoes, fleas, ticks, and lice. Be aware of insects in wet or forested areas, especially while hiking and camping; wear long pants and long sleeves, tuck your pants into your socks, and use a mosquito net. Use insect repellents and soak or spray your gear with permethrin (licensed in the US only for use on clothing). **Ticks**—responsible for Lyme and other diseases—can be particularly dangerous in rural and forested regions.

FOOD- AND WATER-BORNE DISEASES
Tap water throughout Britain and Ireland is safe. When camping, purify your own water by boiling or treating it with **iodine tablets;** note that some parasites such as *giardia* have exteriors that resist iodine treatment, so boiling is more reliable.

Two recent diseases originating in British livestock have made international headlines. **Bovine spongiform encephalopathy (BSE),** better known as **mad cow disease,** is a chronic degenerative disease affecting the central nervous system of cattle. The human variety is called new variant Cruetzfeldt-Jakob disease (nvCJD), and both forms involve invariably fatal brain damage. Information on nvCJD is not conclusive, but the disease is thought to be caused by consuming infected beef. The risk is extremely small (around 1 case per 10 billion meat servings); regardless, travelers might consider avoiding beef and beef products while in the UK. Milk and milk products are not believed to pose a risk.

The UK and Western Europe experienced a serious outbreak of **Foot and Mouth Disease (FMD)** in 2001. FMD is easily transmissible between cloven-hoofed animals (cows, pigs, sheep, goats, and deer), but does not pose a threat to humans, causing mild symptoms, if any. In January 2002, the UK regained **international FMD free status.** Nearly all restrictions on rural travel have been removed. Further information on these diseases is available through the CDC (www.cdc.gov/travel) and the British Department for Environment, Food & Rural Affairs (www.defra.gov.uk).

INFECTIOUS DISEASES

AIDS and HIV: For detailed information on Acquired Immune Deficiency Syndrome (AIDS) in the UK, call the US Centers for Disease Control's 24hr. hotline at ☎800-342-2437, or contact the Joint United Nations Programme on HIV/AIDS (UNAIDS), 20, ave. Appia, CH-1211 Geneva 27, Switzerland (☎41 22 791 3666; fax 22 791 4187).

Sexually transmitted diseases (STDs): Gonorrhea, chlamydia, genital warts, syphilis, herpes, and other STDs are more common than HIV and can cause serious complications. **Hepatitis** B and C can also be transmitted sexually. Though condoms may protect you from some STDs, oral or even tactile contact can lead to transmission. If you think you may have contracted an STD, see a doctor immediately.

OTHER HEALTH CONCERNS

MEDICAL CARE ON THE ROAD

In both Britain and Ireland, medical aid is readily available and of the quality you would expect in major Western countries. For minor ailments, **chemists** (pharmacies) are plentiful. The ubiquitous **Boots** chain has a blue logo. **Late night pharmacies** are rare, even in big cities. If you need serious attention, most major hospitals have a **24hr. emergency room** (called a "casualty department" or "A&E," short for Accident and Emergency). Call the numbers listed below for assistance.

In Britain, the state-run **National Health Service (NHS)** encompasses the majority of healthcare centers (☎ 020 7210 4850; www.doh.gov.uk/nhs.htm). Cities may have private hospitals, but these cater to the wealthy and are not often equipped with full surgical staff or complete casualty units. Access to free care is based on residence, not British nationality or payment of taxes; those working legally or undertaking long-term study in the UK may also be eligible. **Health insurance** is a must for all other visitors. For more information, see **Insurance, p. 23.**

If you are concerned about obtaining medical assistance while traveling, you may wish to employ special support services. The *MedPass* from **GlobalCare, Inc.,** 6875 Shiloh Rd. East, Alpharetta, GA 30005, USA (☎ 800-860-1111; www.globalems.com), provides 24hr. international medical assistance, support, and medical evacuation resources. The **International Association for Medical Assistance to Travelers** (**IAMAT;** US ☎ 716-754-4883, Canada 519-836-0102; www.cybermall.co.nz/NZ/IAMAT) has free membership, lists doctors worldwide, and offers detailed info on immunization requirements and sanitation. If your regular **insurance** policy does not cover travel abroad, you may wish to purchase additional coverage (p. 23).

Those with medical conditions (such as diabetes, allergies to antibiotics, epilepsy, heart conditions) may want to obtain a **Medic Alert** membership (first year US$35, annually thereafter US$20), which includes a stainless steel ID tag, among other benefits, like a 24hr. collect-call number. Contact the Medic Alert Foundation, 2323 Colorado Ave., Turlock, CA 95382, USA (☎ 888-633-4298, outside US 209-668-3333; www.medicalert.org).

WOMEN'S HEALTH

Women traveling in unsanitary conditions are vulnerable to **urinary tract** and **bladder infections,** common and uncomfortable bacterial conditions that cause a burning sensation and painful (sometimes frequent) urination. Vaginal yeast infection is known in Britain and Ireland as **thrush** and can be treated with over-the-counter medicines like Diflucan One or Vagisil. Remember to pack **tampons, pads,** and **contraceptives** when camping, since pharmacies may be few and far between. Women who need an **abortion** or **emergency contraception** while in the UK should call the **FPA** (formerly the Family Planning Association) helpline (☎ 0845 310 1334; M-F 9am-6pm), visit the website (www.fpa.org.uk).

ESSENTIALS

GETTING TO BRITAIN AND IRELAND

BY PLANE

When it comes to airfare, a little effort can save you a bundle. If your plans are very flexible (read: you have no plans), courier fares are the cheapest. Standby seating is also a good deal, but last-minute specials, airfare wars, and charter flights often beat these fares. The key is to hunt around, be flexible, and ask about discounts. Students, seniors, and those under 26 should never pay full price for a ticket.

AIRFARES

Airfares to Britain and Ireland peak between June and September; holidays are also expensive. Midweek (M-Th morning) round-trip flights run US$40-50 cheaper than weekend flights, but they are generally more crowded and less likely to permit frequent-flier upgrades. Not fixing a return date ("open return") or arriving in and departing from different cities ("open-jaw") can be pricier than round-trip flights. Patching one-way flights together is the most expensive way to travel. Flights between London, Belfast, and Dublin or regional hubs tend to be cheaper.

If Britain or Ireland is only 1 stop on a more extensive globe-hop, consider a round-the-world (RTW) ticket. Tickets usually include at least 5 stops and are valid for about a year; prices range US$1200-5000. Try **Northwest Airlines/KLM** (US ☎800-447-4747; www.nwa.com) or **Star Alliance,** a consortium of 22 airlines including United Airlines (US ☎800-241-6522; www.staralliance.com). **Fares** for round-trip flights to London from the US or Canadian east coast cost US$400-600, US$300-500 in the low season (October-June); from the US or Canadian west coast US$800-1000/US$600-800 low season; from Australia AUS$3500 and up; from New Zealand NZ$3000 and up.

BUDGET AND STUDENT TRAVEL AGENCIES

While travel agents can make your life easy and help you save, they may not spend the time to find you the lowest possible fare—they get paid on commission. Travelers holding **ISIC** and **IYTC cards** (see p. 14) qualify for discounts from student travel agencies. Most flights are on major airlines, but may include charter flights.

CTS Travel, 30 Rathbone Pl., London W1T 1GQ, UK (☎0207 209 0630; www.ctstravel.co.uk). A British student travel agent with offices in 39 countries including the US, Empire State Building, 350 Fifth Ave., Suite 7813, New York, NY 10118 (☎877-287-6665; www.ctstravelusa.com).

STA Travel, 5900 Wilshire Blvd., Ste. 900, Los Angeles, CA 90036, USA (24hr. reservations and info ☎800-781-4040; www.sta-travel.com). A student and youth travel organization with over 150 offices worldwide (check their website for a listing), including offices in Boston, Chicago, Los Angeles, New York, San Francisco, Seattle, and D.C. Booking, insurance, railpasses, and more. Offices are located throughout Australia (☎03 9349 4344), New Zealand (☎09 309 9723), and the UK (☎0870 1 600 599).

Travel CUTS (Canadian Universities Travel Services Limited), 187 College St., Toronto, ON M5T 1P7 (☎416-979-2406; www.travelcuts.com). Offices across Canada and the US including Los Angeles, New York, Seattle, and San Francisco.

usit, 19-21 Aston Quay, Dublin 2 (☎01 602 1777; www.usitnow.ie), Ireland's leading student/budget travel agency has 22 offices throughout Northern Ireland and the Republic of Ireland.

ESSENTIALS

FLIGHT PLANNING ON THE INTERNET. The Internet may be the budget traveler's dream when it comes to finding and booking bargain fares, but the array of options can be overwhelming. Many airline sites offer special last-minute deals on the Web. Try BMI (www.flybmi.com), Virgin Atlantic (www.virginatlantic.com), or British Airways (www.ba.com). Others compile the deals for you. Try these: **STA** (www.sta-travel.com) and **StudentUniverse** (www.studentuniverse.com) provide quotes on student tickets, while **Orbitz** (www.orbitz.com), **Expedia** (www.expedia.com), and **Travelocity** (www.travelocity.com) offer full travel services. **Priceline** (www.priceline.com) lets you specify a price, and obligates you to buy any ticket that meets or beats it; **Hotwire** (www.hotwire.com) offers bargain fares, but won't reveal the airline or flight times until you buy. Other sites that compile deals for you include www.bestfares.com, www.flights.com, www.lowestfare.com, www.onetravel.com, and www.travelzoo.com. An indispensable resource on the Internet is the **Air Traveler's Handbook** (www.faqs.org/faqs/travel/air/handbook), a comprehensive listing of links to everything you need to know before you board a plane.

ESSENTIALS

COMMERCIAL AIRLINES

The commercial airlines' lowest regular offer is the **APEX** (Advance Purchase Excursion) fare, which provides confirmed reservations and allows "open-jaw" tickets. Generally, reservations must be made seven to 21 days ahead of departure, with 7- to 14-day minimum-stay and up to 90-day maximum-stay restrictions. Book high-season APEX fares early. Use **Expedia** (www.expedia.com) or **Travelocity** (www.travelocity.com) to get an idea of the lowest published fares, then use the resources outlined here to try and beat those fares. Low-season fares should be appreciably cheaper than the high-season (June to September) ones listed here.

Standard commercial carriers like American (☎800-433-7300; www.aa.com) and United (☎800-241-6522; www.united.com) will probably offer the most convenient flights, but they may not be the cheapest, unless you manage to grab a special promotion. The following "discount" airlines offer lower fares, but more connections.

Icelandair: (☎800-223-5500; www.icelandair.com.) Stopovers in Iceland for no extra cost on most transatlantic flights. US$500-730; Oct.-May US$390-$450.

Finnair: (☎800-950-5000; www.us.finnair.com.) Cheap round-trips from San Francisco, New York, and Toronto to Helsinki; connections throughout Europe.

Aer Lingus: (☎0818 365000; www.aerlingus.com.) Cheap round-trips from Boston, Chicago, Los Angeles, New York and Washington, D.C. to Birmingham, Bristol, London, Manchester, Glasgow, Dublin, and Shannon.

TRAVELING FROM AUSTRALIA AND NEW ZEALAND

Air New Zealand: (New Zealand ☎0800 73 70 00; www.airnz.co.nz.) Flights from Auckland to London.

Qantas Air: (Australia ☎13 13 13, New Zealand 0800 808 767; www.qantas.com.au.) Flights from Australia and New Zealand to London for around AUS$2400.

Singapore Air: (Australia ☎13 10 11, New Zealand 0800 808 909; www.singaporeair.com.) Flies from Auckland, Sydney, Melbourne, and Perth to London.

Thai Airways: (Australia ☎1300 65 19 60, New Zealand 09 377 02 68; www.thai-air.com.) Auckland, Sydney, and Melbourne to London.

AIR COURIER FLIGHTS

Those who travel light should consider courier flights. Couriers help transport cargo on international flights by using their checked luggage space for freight. Generally, couriers must travel with carry-ons only and deal with complex flight restrictions. Most flights are round-trip only, with short fixed-length stays (usually one week) and a limit of a one ticket per issue. Most of these flights also operate only out of major gateway cities, mostly in North America. Most flights leave from Los Angeles, Miami, New York, or San Francisco in the US; and from Montreal, Toronto, or Vancouver in Canada. Generally, you must be over 21. Super-discounted fares are common for "last-minute" flights (three to 14 days ahead).

FROM NORTH AMERICA

Round-trip courier fares from the US to London run about US$200-500. Most flights leave from New York, Los Angeles, San Francisco, or Miami in the US; from Montreal, Toronto, or Vancouver in Canada. Prices quoted below are round-trip.

Air Courier Association, 1767 A Denver West Blvd., Golden, CO 80401 (☎800-280-5973; www.aircourier.org). 10 departure cities in the US and Canada to London, and throughout western Europe (high-season US$130-640). 1yr. membership US$25.

International Association of Air Travel Couriers (IAATC), PO Box 847, Scottsbluff, NE 69363 (☎308-632-3273; www.courier.org). From 9 North American cities to London. 1yr. membership US$45.

Global Courier Travel, PO Box 3051, Nederland, CO 80466 (www.globalcourier-travel.com). Searchable online database. 6 departure points in the US and Canada to London. 1yr. membership US$50, 2 people US$65.

FROM THE UK

The minimum age for couriers from the **UK** is usually 18. **Brave New World Enterprises,** P.O. Box 22212, London SE5 8WB (info@courierflights.com; www.courierflights.com) publishes a directory of all the companies offering courier flights in the UK (£10, in electronic form £8). **The International Association of Air Travel Couriers** (www.courier.org; see above) often offers courier flights from London to Budapest. **British Airways Travel Shop** (☎0845 6060 747; www.batravelshops.com) arranges some flights from London to destinations in continental Europe (specials may be as low as £60; no registration fee). **Global Courier Travel** (see above) also offers flights from London and Dublin to continental Europe.

STANDBY FLIGHTS

Traveling standby requires considerable flexibility. Companies dealing in standby flights sell vouchers rather than tickets, along with the promise to get you to your destination (or near your destination) within a certain window of time (typically 1-5 days). You call in before your specific window of time to hear your flight options and the probability that you will be able to board each flight. You can then decide which flights you want to try to make, show up at the appropriate airport at the appropriate time, present your voucher, and board if space is available. Vouchers can usually be bought for both one-way and round-trip travel. You may receive a monetary refund only if every available flight within your date range is full; if you opt not to take an available (but perhaps less convenient) flight, you can only get credit toward future travel. Carefully read agreements with any company offering standby flights as tricky fine print can leave you in the lurch. To check on a company's service record in the US, call the **Better Business Bureau** (☎ 703-276-0100; www.bbb.org). It is difficult to receive refunds, and clients' vouchers will not be honored when an airline fails to receive payment in time.

BY CHUNNEL FROM THE UK

Traversing 27 mi. under the sea, the **Chunnel** is undoubtedly the fastest, most convenient, and least scenic route from England to France.

BY TRAIN. Eurostar, Eurostar House, Waterloo Station, London SE1 8SE (UK ☎ 08705 186 186; Belgium 02 528 28 28; France 08 92 35 35 39; www.eurostar.com) runs frequent trains between London and the continent. 10-28 trains per day run to 100 destinations including Paris (4hr., 2nd class US$75-300), Disneyland Paris, Brussels, Lille, and Calais. Book at major rail stations in the UK.

BY BUS. Eurolines and **Eurobus,** both run by National Express (UK ☎ 08706 808 080), provide bus-ferry combinations.

BY CAR. Eurotunnel, Customer Relations, P.O. Box 2000, Folkestone, Kent CT18 8XY (UK ☎ 08705 35 35 35; www.eurotunnel.co.uk) shuttles cars and passengers between Kent and Nord-Pas-de-Calais. Round-trip fares for vehicle and all passengers £283-317 with car. Same-day round-trip costs £19-34, five-day round-trip for either a car or a camper van £163-197. Book online or via phone. Travelers with cars can also look into sea crossings by ferry (see below).

BY FERRY

A directory of UK ferries can be found at www.seaview.co.uk/ferries.html.

Brittany Ferries: UK ☎ 08703 665 333; France ☎ 08 25 82 88 28; www.brittany-ferries.com. **Plymouth** to **Roscoff, France** and **Santander, Spain; Portsmouth** to **St.-Malo** and **Caen, France; Poole** to **Cherbourg;** and **Cork** to **Roscoff, France.**

DFDS Seaways: UK ☎ 08705 333 000; www.dfdsseaways.co.uk. **Harwich** to **Hamburg** and **Esbjerg, Denmark; Newcastle** to **Amsterdam, Kristiansand, Norway,** and **Gothenburg, Sweden.**

Fjord Line: UK ☎ 0191 296 1313; www.fjordline.no. **Newcastle** to **Stavanger** and **Bergen, Norway.**

Hoverspeed: UK ☎ 0870 240 8070, France 008 00 1211 1211; www.hoverspeed.co.uk. **Dover** to **Calais;** and **Newhaven** to **Dieppe, France.**

Irish Ferries: France ☎ 01 44 88 54 50, Ireland 1890 31 31 31, UK 08705 17 17 17; www.irishferries.ie. **Rosslare** to **Cherbourg** and **Roscoff, France,** and **Pembroke, UK;** and **Holyhead, UK** to **Dublin.**

P&O Ferries: UK ☎ 08705 202 020, from Europe 44 13 0486 4003; www.poferries.com. Daily ferries from **Hull** to **Rotterdam, Netherlands; Zeebrugge, Belgium;** and **Dover** to **Calais.**

Stena Line: (UK ☎ 08705 70 70 70; www.stenaline.co.uk.) **Harwich** to **Hook of Holland; Fishguard** to **Rosslare** and **Dún Laoghaire, Ireland; Stranraer** to **Belfast;** and car ferry only **Holyhead** to **Dublin.**

ESSENTIALS

GETTING AROUND BRITAIN AND IRELAND

Fares on all modes of transportation are referred to as **single** (one-way) or round-trip. "Period round-trips" or "open round-trips" require you to return within a specific number of days; "day round-trip" means you return on the same day. Unless stated otherwise, *Let's Go* always lists standard single fares.

BY PLANE

The recent emergence of no-frills airlines has made hopscotching around Europe (and even within the UK) by air increasingly affordable and convenient. Though these flights often feature inconvenient hours or serve less-popular regional airports, with one-way flights averaging about US$50, it's never been faster or easier to jet across the Continent.

The Irish and British national carriers, **Aer Lingus** (Ireland ☎0818 365 000, UK ☎0845 084 4444; www.aerlingus.ie) and **British Midland Airways** (UK ☎0870 607 0555; www.flybmi.com), fly regularly between London and Dublin (Aer Lingus 1¼hr., 15 flights per day; BA 1½hr., about 12 flights per day) and other major cities. The cheapest Aer Lingus round-trip fares to Dublin can be as low as US$67.

If you can book in advance and/or travel at odd hours, the discount airlines listed below are a great option. A good source of offers are the travel supplements of newspapers or the classifieds in *Time Out;* many airlines also advertise fares on their own websites. Because of the many carriers flying within the British Isles, we only include those with cheap specials here. The **Air Travel Advisory Bureau** in London (☎0785 737 0026; www.atab.co.uk) provides referrals to travel agencies and consolidators that offer discounted airfares out of the UK.

Aer Lingus: Ireland ☎0818 365 000, UK ☎0845 084 4444; www.aerlingus.ie. Services between Cork, Dublin, Galway, Kerry, Shannon, and many cities in Europe. Departures from Birmingham, Edinburgh, Glasgow, London, and Manchester in the UK.

British Midland Airways: UK ☎0870 607 0555; www.flybmi.com. Services between Aberdeen, Belfast, Dublin, Edinburgh, Glasgow, Inverness, and London. London to Brussels, Madrid, Paris, and Frankfurt.

easyJet: UK ☎0870 600 0000; www.easyjet.com. Departures from Aberdeen, Belfast, Bristol, Edinburgh, East Midlands, Glasgow, Inverness, Liverpool, London, Newcastle. Flights to many European cities. Frequent specials; online tickets.

EUJet: UK ☎0870 414 1414; www.eujet.com. From Kent (p. 141) to Edinburgh, Glasgow, Dublin, Manchester, Jersey, and many destinations on the continent. Online tickets.

KLM: UK ☎0870 507 4074; www.klmuk.com. Round-trip tickets from London and other cities in the UK to Amsterdam, Brussels, Frankfurt, Düsseldorf, Milan, Paris, and Rome.

Ryanair: Ireland ☎0818 303 030, UK 0870 156 9569; www.ryanair.ie. From Dublin, London, and Glasgow to destinations in France, Ireland, Italy, Scandinavia, and elsewhere. As low as £5 on limited weekend specials, but book in advance.

The **Star Alliance European Airpass** offers economy class fares as low as US$65 for travel within Europe to more than 200 destinations in 43 countries. The pass is available to transatlantic passengers on Star Alliance carriers, including Air Canada, Austrian Airlines, BMI British Midland, Lufthansa, Mexicana, Scandinavian Airlines, THAI, United Airlines, US Airways, and Varig, as well as on certain partner airlines. See www.staralliance.com for more information.

BY TRAIN

Britain's train network criss-crosses the length and breadth of the island. In cities with more than one train station, the city name is given first, followed by the station name (for example, "Manchester Piccadilly" and "Manchester Victoria" are Manchester's two major stations). In general, traveling by train costs more than by bus. Railpasses covering specific regions are sometimes available from local train stations and may include bus and ferry travel. Prices and schedules often change; find up-to-date information from **National Rail Inquiries** (☎08457 484 950) or online at **Railtrack** (www.railtrack.co.uk, schedules only).

TICKET TYPES. The array of available tickets on British trains is bewildering, and prices aren't always set logically—buying an unlimited day pass to the region may cost less than buying a one-way ticket. Prices rise on weekends and may be higher before 9:30am. Purchase tickets before boarding, except at unstaffed train stations, where tickets are bought on the train. There are several types of **discount tickets. APEX** (Advance Purchase Excursion) tickets must be bought at least 7 days in advance; **SuperAdvance** tickets must be purchased before 6pm the day before you travel. **Saver** tickets are valid any time, but may be restricted to certain trains at peak times; **SuperSaver** tickets are similar, but are only valid at off-peak times (usually Su-Th). It may seem daunting, but the general rule of thumb is simple: planning a week or more in advance can make a £30-60 difference.

BRITRAIL PASSES. If you plan to travel a great deal on trains within Britain, the **BritRail Pass** can be a good buy. Eurail passes are *not* valid in Britain, but there is often a discount on BritRail passes if you purchase the two simultaneously. BritRail passes are only available outside Britain; **you must buy them before traveling to Britain.** They allow unlimited train travel in England, Wales, and Scotland, regardless of which company is operating the trains, but they do not work in Northern Ireland or on Eurostar. **Youth** passes are for travelers under 26, while **senior** passes are for travelers over 60. Children 5-15 can travel free with each adult pass, as long as you ask for the **Family Pass** (free). All children under 5 travel free. The **Party Pass** gets the third and fourth travelers in a party a 50% discount on their railpasses. Check with BritRail (US ☎877-677-1066; www.britrail.net) or one of the distributors for details on other passes. Prices listed do not include shipping costs (usually US$15 for delivery in 2-3 days, US$30 for overnight delivery).

Classic: Consecutive days travel: 4 days (1st-class US$279, standard-class US$189), 8 days (US$405/$269), 15 days (US$599/$399), 22 days (US$765/$509), 1 month (US$909/$605).

Youth Classic: Standard-class only; consecutive days travel: 4 days US$142, 8 days US$202, 15 days US$299, 22 days US$382, 1 month US$454.

Senior Classic: 1st-class only; consecutive days travel: 4 days US$237, 8 days US$344, 15 days US$509, 22 days US$650, 1 month US$773.

Flexipass: Travel within a 2-month period: any 4 days (1st-class US$349, standard-class US$239), any 8 days (US$515/$345), any 15 days (US$775/$519).

Youth Flexipasses: Standard-class only; travel within a 2-month period: 4 days US$179, 8 days US$259, 15 days US$389.

Senior Flexipasses: 1st-class only; travel within a 2-month period: 4 days US$297, 8 days US$438, 15 days US$659.

BritRail Pass Plus Ireland: Travel within 1 month on British and Irish (both Northern Ireland and the Republic of Ireland) trains, plus a round-trip crossing on Stena Ferries: any 5 days (1st-class US$515, standard-class US$369), any 10 days (US$849/$595).

Freedom of Scotland Travelpass: Standard-class travel on all trains within Scotland, the Glasgow Underground, and selected ferry routes to the islands: 4 out of 8 days (US$145), 8 out of 15 days (US$189).

BRITRAIL DISTRIBUTORS. The distributors listed below will either sell you passes directly or tell you where to buy passes; also ask at travel agents (p. 26).

Australia: Rail Plus, Level 3, 459 Little Collins St., Melbourne, Victoria 3000 (☎09 9642 8644; www.railplus.com.au). **Concorde International Travel** (Rail Tickets), Level 9, 310 King St., Melbourne, Victoria 3000 (☎03 9920 3833; www.concorde.com.au).

Canada and US: Rail Europe, 226 Westchester Ave., White Plains, NY 10604 (Canada ☎800-361-7245, US 877-257-2887; www.raileurope.com), is the North American distributor for BritRail. Or try **Rail Pass Express** (☎800-722-7151; www.railpass.com).

Ireland: usit NOW, 19-21 Aston Quay, O'Connell Bridge, Dublin 2 (☎01 602 1600).

New Zealand: Holiday Shoppe, Gullivers Holiday Rep: Holiday Shoppe, 5th fl. 66 Wyndham St., Auckland (☎0800 80 84 80; www.holidayshoppe.co.nz).

RAIL DISCOUNT CARDS. Unlike BritRail passes, these can be purchased in the UK. Passes are valid for one year and generally offer one-third off standard fares. They are available for young people (£20; must be 16-25 or full-time student), seniors (£20; must be over 60), families (£20), and people with disabilities (£14). Visit the **Railcards** website (www.railcard.co.uk) for details.

TRAINS IN IRELAND

Iarnród Éireann (Irish Rail) is useful only for travel between urban areas. For schedule information, pick up an *InterCity Rail Travelers Guide* (€1.20), available at most train stations. A **Faircard** (€10-15) gets anyone age 16-26 up to 50% off any InterCity trip. Those over 26 can get the **Weekender** card (€8; up to a third off; valid Su-Tu and F-Sa only). Both are valid through the end of the year. The **Rambler** ticket allows unlimited train travel on 5 days within a 15-day period (€122). Information is available from the Irish Rail information office, 35 Lower Abbey St., Dublin (☎01 836 3333; www.irishrail.ie). Train tickets sometimes allow travelers to break a journey into stages while paying the price of a single-phase trip. Bikes can be carried on most trains for a small fee; check at the station for restrictions.

While the **Eurailpass** is not accepted in Northern Ireland, it *is* accepted on trains in the Republic. The BritRail pass does not cover travel in Northern Ireland, but the month-long **BritRail+Ireland** works in both the North and the Republic with rail options and round-trip ferry service between Britain and Ireland (see above). It's easiest to buy a Eurailpass before you arrive in Europe; contact a travel agent (p. 26). **Rail Europe** (p. 32) also sells point-to-point tickets.

Northern Ireland Railways (☎028 9066 6630; www.nirailways.co.uk) is not extensive but covers the northeastern coast. The major line connects Dublin to Belfast, then splits with one branch ending at Bangor and one at Larne. There is also service from Belfast and Lisburn west to Derry and Portrush, stopping at three towns between Antrim and the coast. BritRail passes are not valid here, but Northern Ireland Railways offers its own discounts. A valid **Translink Student Discount Card** (£6) will get you up to 33% off all trains and 15% discounts on bus fares over £1.45 within Northern Ireland. The **Freedom of Northern Ireland** ticket allows unlimited travel by train and Ulsterbus; 7 consecutive days £47, 3 out of 8 days £32, 1 day £13.

BY BUS AND COACH

The British and the Irish distinguish between **buses** (short local routes) and **coaches** (long distances). *Let's Go* generally uses the term "buses" for both. Regional **passes** offer unlimited travel within a given area for a certain number of days; these are often called **Rovers, Ramblers,** or **Explorers.**

BUSES IN BRITAIN

Long-distance coach travel is more extensive in Britain than most of Europe, and is the cheapest option. **National Express** (☎08705 808 080; www.nationalexpress.com) is the principal operator of long-distance coach services in Britain, although **Scottish Citylink** (☎08705 505 050; www.citylink.co.uk) has the most extensive coverage in Scotland. **Discount Coachcards** are available for seniors (over 50), students, and young persons (16-25) for £10 (valid for 1yr.) and reduced fares on National Express by up to 30%; other discount cards are available for families and repeated travel. The **Brit Xplorer passes** offer unlimited travel for a set number of days (7 days, £70; 14 days, £120; 28 days, £190; www.nationalexpress.com). For those who plan far ahead, the best option is National Express's **Fun Fares,** available only online, which offer a limited amount of seats on buses out of London from, amazingly, £1; another similar option is **Megabus** (☎01738 639095; www.megabus.com), which also offers the one-quid price but has fewer buses. Tourist Information Centres carry timetables for regional buses and will help befuddled travelers decipher them.

BUSES IN IRELAND

Buses in the Republic reach more destinations and are less expensive than trains. The national bus company, **Bus Éireann** (☎01 836 6111; www.buseireann.ie), operates both long-distance Expressway buses, which link larger cities, and local buses, which serve the countryside and smaller towns. The invaluable bus timetable book (€2) is difficult to obtain, though you may find one at Busáras Central Bus Station in Dublin as well as in the occasional tourist office. **Private bus services** can be faster and cheaper than Bus Éireann; *Let's Go* lists these private companies in areas they cover. In Donegal, private bus providers take the place of Bus Éireann's nearly non-existent local service. Bus Éireann's **Rambler** ticket offers unlimited bus travel within Ireland for 3 of 8 consecutive days (€53, under 16 €32), 8 of 15 consecutive days (€116/€74), or 15 of 30 consecutive days (€168/€105), but individual tickets may be more cost-effective. A combined **Irish Explorer Rail/Bus** ticket allows unlimited travel on trains and buses for 8 of 15 consecutive days (€176, under 16 €88).

    Ulsterbus (☎028 9066 6630; www.ulsterbus.co.uk), the North's version of Bus Éireann, runs extensive and reliable routes throughout Northern Ireland. Pick up a free regional timetable at any station. The **Irish Rover** pass covers Bus Éireann and Ulsterbus services. Unless you're planning to spend lots of time on the bus, its value is debatable (unlimited travel for 3 of 8 days €68, child €38; 8 of 15 days €152/84; 15 of 30 €226/124. The **Emerald Card** offers unlimited travel on: Ulsterbus; Northern Ireland Railways; Bus Éireann Expressway, Local, and city services in Cork, Galway, Limerick, and Waterford; and Intercity, DART, and Suburban Rail Iarnród Éireann services. The card works for 8 of 15 consecutive days (€198, under 16 €99) or 15 of 30 consecutive days (€341/170.50).

BUS TOURS

Staffed by young, energetic guides, these tours cater to backpackers and stop right at the doors of hostels. They are a good way to meet other independent travelers and get to places that public transport doesn't reach; most ensure a stay at certain hostels. "Hop-on, hop-off" tours allow you to stay as long as you like at each stop.

▣ **HAGGiS,** 60 High St., Edinburgh EH1 1TB (☎0131 557 9393; www.haggisadventures.com). Specialize in 3, 6, and 8-day prearranged tours of Scotland with small groups and witty, super-knowledgeable guides (from £85). Hop-on, hop-off flexitours also available (from £69). Sister tours **HAGGiS Britain** (same contact) and **The Shamrocker Ireland** (☎01 672 7651) run 3-7 days through England, Wales, and Ireland.

▣ **MacBackpackers,** 105 High St., Edinburgh EH1 1SG (☎0131 558 9900; www.macbackpackers.com). Hop-on, hop-off flexitour (£65) of Scotland and 1- to 7-day tours.

Celtic Connection, 7/6 Cadiz St., Edinburgh EH6 7BJ (☎0131 225 3330; www.thecelticconnection.co.uk). 5-12-day tours combining Scotland and Ireland (£109-265).

Karibuni (☎0118 961 8577; www.karibuni.co.uk) runs adventure tours in England and Wales from London, with activities like biking, kayaking, surfing, horseback riding, and camping (£120-150). Longer tours available for groups of 8 or more.

BY CAR

Cars offer speed, freedom, access to the countryside, and an escape from the town-to-town mentality of trains; but they introduce the hassle of driving, parking, and the high cost of petrol (gasoline). If you can't decide between train and car travel, you may benefit from a combination of the two; BritRail pass distributors (p. 26) sell combination rail-and-drive packages.

RENTING

Renters in Britain must be over 21; those under 23 (or even 25) may have to pay hefty additional fees. In Ireland, those under 23 generally cannot rent. Since the public transportation system in Britain and Ireland is so extensive and punctual, travelers should consider using it instead and saving loads of cash. However, for longer trips, journeys into many small, obscure destinations, or into the farthest reaches of Highlands and Islands of the north and west, the convenience of a car can mean the difference between an amazing trip and a tiresome trek.

RENTAL AGENCIES. You can rent a car from a US-based firm with European offices, from a Europe-based company with local representatives, or from a tour operator that arranges rentals from a European company at its own rates. Multinationals offer greater flexibility, but tour operators often strike better deals. At most agencies, all you need to rent a car is a driver's license; some will ask for an additional ID. The following agencies rent cars in Britain and Ireland:

Auto Europe: US and Canada ☎888-223-5555; www.autoeurope.com.

Avis: US ☎800-230-4898, Canada 800-272-5871, UK 0870 606 0100, Australia 136 333, New Zealand 0800 65 51 11; www.avis.com.

Budget: US and Canada ☎800-527-0700, Quebec ☎800-268-8900, UK 01442 276266; www.budgetrentacar.com.

Europe by Car: US ☎800-223-1516 or 212-581-3040; www.europebycar.com.

Europcar International: US ☎877-940-6900, UK 0870 607 5000; www.europcar.com.

ESSENTIALS

Hertz: US ☎800-654-3001, Canada ☎800-263-0600, UK 08705 996 699, Australia 9698 2555; www.hertz.com.

Kemwel: US ☎877-820-0668; www.kemwel.com.

COSTS. Rental prices vary by company, season, and pickup point; expect to pay at least £120 per week for a small car. Expect to pay more for 4WD and automatic transmission, though it is virtually impossible to find an automatic 4WD. If possible, reserve and pay well in advance; it's less expensive to reserve a car from the US than from Europe. Rental packages can offer unlimited kilometers, while others offer km per day with a surcharge per additional km. National chains often allow one-way rentals, picking up in one city and dropping off in another. There is usually a minimum hire period and sometimes an extra drop-off charge.

LEASING. For trips longer than a few weeks, leasing can be cheaper and often the only option for those aged 18-21. The cheapest leases are agreements to buy the car and then sell it back to the manufacturer at a prearranged price. Leases generally include insurance and are not taxed. Depending on car size, a 60-day lease starts around US$1300. **Auto Europe, Europe by Car,** and **Kemwel** (above) handle leases, as does **Renault Eurodrive** (US ☎800-221-1052; www.renaultusa.com) leases.

INSURANCE. Most credit cards cover standard **insurance.** However, cars rented on an American Express or Visa/Mastercard Gold or Platinum credit cards in Britain and Ireland might *not* carry automatic insurance; check with your credit card company. Be sure to ask whether the price includes insurance against theft and collision. If you rent, lease, or borrow a car, you will need a **Green Card,** or **International Insurance Certificate,** to certify that you have liability insurance that applies abroad. Green Cards can be obtained at rental agencies, car dealers, some travel agents, and some border crossings. Insurance plans almost always come with an **excess** (or deductible) averaging US$900 in the UK and US$600 in Ireland but can reach US$3000 for certain vehicles. The excess quote applies to collisions with other vehicles; collisions with non-vehicles, such as trees, ("single-vehicle collisions") costs more. The excess can often be reduced or waived entirely if you pay an additional charge, from US$5-25 per day. If you are driving a rented vehicle on an **unpaved road,** you are almost never covered.

ON THE ROAD

You must be 17 to drive in Britain. Be sure you can handle **driving on the left** side of the road, or driving **manual transmission** ("stick-shift" is far more common than automatic). Be particularly cautious at **roundabouts** (rotary interchanges), and remember to give way to traffic from the right. The **Association for Safe International Road Travel (ASIRT),** 11769 Gainsborough Rd., Potomac, MD 20854, USA (☎301-983-5252; www.asirt.org), sends travelers country-specific Road Travel Reports. Road atlases for the UK are available in travel bookshops and from many Tourist Information Centres. **Petrol** (gasoline) is sold by the liter; there are about four liters to the gallon. Prices vary, but average about 80p per liter. The country is covered by a high-speed system of **motorways** ("M-roads") that connect London with major cities around the country. These are supplemented by a tight web of "A-roads" and "B-roads" that connect towns: A-roads are the main routes, while B-roads are narrower but often more scenic. **Distances** on road signs are in miles (1 mi.= 1.6 km). **Speed limits** are 70mph (113km/hr.) on motorways (highways) and dual carriageways (divided highways), 60mph (97km/hr.) on single carriageways (non-divided highways), and usually 30mph (48km/hr.) in urban areas. Speed limits are marked at the beginning of town areas; upon leaving, you'll see a circular sign with a slash through it, signaling the end of the restriction. Drivers and all passengers are required to wear **seat belts**. Driving in central **London** is restricted during weekday working hours. Parking in London can be similarly nightmarish. The **Highway Code**, which details Britain's driving regulations, is accessible online (www.highwaycode.gov.uk) or can be purchased at most large bookstores or newsagents.

 DRIVING PRECAUTIONS. When traveling in the summer, bring substantial amounts of water (a suggested 5 liters of **water** per person per day) for drinking and for the radiator. For long drives to unpopulated areas, register with police before beginning the trek, and again upon arrival at the destination. Check with the local automobile club for details. When traveling for long distances, make sure tires are in good repair and have enough air, and get good maps. A **compass** and a **car manual** can also be very useful. You should always carry a **spare tire** and **jack, jumper cables, extra oil, flares, a flashlight (torch),** and **heavy blankets** (in case your car breaks down at night or in the winter). If you don't know how to **change a tire**, learn before heading out, especially if you are planning on traveling in deserted areas. Blowouts on dirt roads are exceedingly common. If you do have a breakdown, **stay with your car;** if you wander off, there's less likelihood trackers will find you.

DANGERS. Learn local driving signals and wear a seatbelt. Carseats for infants are available at most rental agencies. Study route maps before you hit the road, and consider bringing spare parts. If your car breaks down, wait for the police to assist you. For long drives in desolate areas, invest in a cellular phone and a roadside assistance program (p. 37). Driving in rural areas often requires extra caution on single-lane roads. These roads feature occasional "passing places," which cars use to make way for passing vehicles. Cars **flash their lights** to signal that they will pull aside; the other car should take the right of way. Also be wary of roaming **livestock** along these more remote roads. Be sure to park your vehicle in a garage or well traveled area, and use a steering wheel locking device in larger cities. **Sleeping in your car** is one of the most dangerous (and often illegal) ways to get your rest.

CAR ASSISTANCE. In the event of a breakdown in Britain, try contacting the **Automobile Association (AA;** ☎0800 028 9018) or the **Royal Automobile Club** (☎0800 828 282). Call ☎**999** in an emergency.

DRIVING PERMITS AND CAR INSURANCE

INTERNATIONAL DRIVING PERMIT (IDP)

If you plan to drive in Britain or Ireland, you must have a **valid foreign driver's license.** An **International Driving Permit (IDP)** is also advisable. Your IDP, valid for one year, must be issued in your own country before you depart. You must be 18. EU license-holders do not need an IDP to drive in Britain or Ireland. Purchase an IDP through one of the automobile associations listed below—those sold by irreputable online dealers may be overpriced, invalid, or illegal.

Australia: Royal Automobile Club (☎08 9421 4400; www.rac.com.au/travel) or National Royal Motorist Association (☎77 000 010 506; www.nrma.com.au). AUS$20.

Canada: Canadian Automobile Association, 1145 Hunt Club Rd., Ste. 200, Ottawa, Ontario K1V 0Y3 (☎613-820-1890; www.caa.ca). CDN$15.

New Zealand: New Zealand Automobile Association, 99 Albert St., Auckland City (☎09 377 4660; www.nzaa.co.nz). NZ$15.

US: American Automobile Association (AAA; ☎800-222-7448; www.aaa.com). US$10.

CAR INSURANCE
Most credit cards cover standard insurance. If you rent, lease, or borrow a car, you will need a **green card**, or **International Insurance Certificate**, to certify that you have liability insurance and that it applies abroad (p. 23). Green cards can be obtained at rental agencies, car dealers (for those leasing cars), and some travel agents.

BY FERRY

Prices vary widely depending on route, season, and length of stay.

Caledonian MacBrayne, The Ferry Terminal, Gourock PA19 1QP (☎01475 650 100; www.calmac.co.uk). The mac-daddy of Scottish ferries, with routes in the **Hebrides** and along the west coast of Scotland.

Irish Ferries, 2-4 Merrion Row, Dublin 2 (Republic of Ireland ☎1890 31 31 31, UK 08705 17 17 17; www.irishferries.ie), and Corn Exchange Building, Brunswick St., Liverpool L2 7TP (☎08705 171 717). **Rosslare** to **Pembroke** and **Holyhead** to **Dublin.**

Isle of Man Steam Packet Company serves the Isle of Man; see p. 386 for details.

P&O Irish Sea, Terminal 3, Dublin Port, Dublin 1 (☎01 800 409 049) and Larne Harbour, Larne, BT40 1AW (☎0870 242 4777; www.poirishsea.com). Vehicle ferries from **Dublin** to **Liverpool; Larne** to **Cairnryan** and **Troon** in Scotland.

Northlink Ferries, Stromness, Orkney, KW16 3BH (☎01856 851 144, reservations 0845 600 0449; www.northlinkferries.co.uk). Sails between **Aberdeen, Lerwick, Kirkwall, Stromness,** and **Scrabster.**

SeaCat, SeaCat Terminal, Donegal Quay, Belfast BT1 3AL (Belfast ☎08705 523 523; Dublin 01 836 4019; www.seacat.co.uk). **Belfast** to **Troon, Scotland; Dublin** to **Liverpool.** Several routes via **Isle of Man: Belfast, Dublin, Liverpool** and **Heysham.**

Stena Line: (UK ☎08705 70 70 70; www.stenaline.co.uk.) **Fishguard** to **Rosslare** and **Dún Laoghaire. Stranraer** to **Belfast.** Car ferry only **Holyhead** to **Dublin.**

Swansea-Cork Ferries: (UK ☎01792 456 116, Ireland ☎021 427 1166); www.swansea-cork.ie. **Swansea** and **Pembroke** to **Ringaskiddy, Co. Cork.**

BY BICYCLE

Much of the British and Irish countryside is well-suited for cycling as many roads are not heavily traveled. Consult tourist offices for local touring routes, and always bring along the appropriate **Ordnance Survey maps.** Keep safety in mind—even well-traveled routes often cover highly uneven terrain.

GETTING OR TRANSPORTING A BIKE. Many airlines will count a bike as part of your luggage, although a few charge an extra US$60-110 each way. If you plan to explore several widely separated regions, you can combine cycling with train travel; bikes often ride free on ferries. A better option for some is to buy a bike in Britain and Ireland and sell it before leaving. A bike bought new overseas is subject to customs duties if brought home. **Renting** ("hiring") a bike is preferable to bringing your own. *Let's Go* lists bike rental stores in many towns.

BICYCLE EQUIPMENT. Riding a bike with a frame pack strapped to it or your back is extremely unsafe; **panniers** are essential. You'll also need a suitable **bike helmet** (from US$30) and a U-shaped **Citadel** or **Kryptonite lock** (from US$25). British law requires a white light at the front, a red light and red reflector at the back.

INFORMATION AND ORGANIZATIONS. The **National Cycle Network** encompasses 7000 mi. of biking and walking trails in the UK and will be extended to 10,000 by 2005. Information and maps are available through **Sustrans** (☎0845 113 0065;

www.sustrans.org.uk). The **Cyclists Touring Club,** 69 Meadrow, Godalming, Surrey GU7 3HS (US ☎ 0870 873 0060; www.ctc.org.uk), provides maps and books. Membership costs £30.50 (under 26 £11, over 65 £18.75) and includes a bimonthly magazine. To purchase *England by Bike* or *Ireland by Bike* (each US$15), try **The Mountaineers Books** (US ☎ 800-553-4453; www.mountaineersbooks.org).

TOURS. Commercial tours are an alternative to cycling alone. **CBT Tours** (☎ 800-736-2453; www.cbttours.com) offers 7- to 14-day biking and hiking trips through Europe, including Britain and Ireland. **Bicycle Beano** (UK ☎ 01982 560 471; www.bicycle-beano.co.uk) offers vegetarian tours in Wales; **Cycle Scotland** (☎ 0131 556 5560; www.cyclescotland.co.uk) operates "Scottish Cycle Safaris"; and **Irish Cycle Tours** (☎ 028 9064 2222; www.irishcycletours.com) runs through Ireland.

BY FOOT

BRITAIN. An extensive system of well-marked and well-maintained long-distance paths cover Britain, ranging from the rolling paths of the **South Downs Way** (p. 154) to the rugged mountain trails of the **Pennine Way** (p. 396). Ordnance Survey 1:25,000 maps mark almost every house, barn, standing stone, graveyard, and pub; less ambitious hikers will want the 1:50,000 scale maps. The **Ramblers' Association,** Camelford House, 2nd Fl., 87-90 Albert Embankment, London SE1 7TW (☎ 020 7339 8500; www.ramblers.org.uk), publishes a *Yearbook* on walking and places to stay, as well as free newsletters and magazines. Their website abounds with information. (Membership £20, concessions £11.) The **National Cycle Network** (see **By Bicycle: Information and Organizations**) includes walking trails.

IRELAND. The **Wicklow Way,** a popular trail through mountainous Co. Wicklow, features hostels within a day's walk of each other. The best hillwalking maps are the *Ordnance Survey Discovery Series* (€7). Other trails include the **Kerry Way** and the **Burren Way.** Consult Bord Fáilte (p. 12) for more information. The 560 mi. Ulster Way of Northern Ireland has been split into regional **Waymarked ways.** Contact tourist offices in Northern Ireland for more information. **Guided tours,** though expensive (upwards of €80 per day), often include an expert guide, a bus for luggage, accommodations, and meals. Less expensive, more independent, **self-guided tours** include luggage transport and accommodations, but are often self-catering. For a list of tours, see www.walking.travel.ie. **Tír na nóg Tours,** 57 Lower Gardiner St., Dublin 1 (☎ 01 836 4684; www.tirnanogtours.com), is an acclaimed choice. **Contours Walking Holidays** (www.contours.co.uk) provides both guided and self-guided walking holidays in England, Scotland, Wales, and Ireland.

BY THUMB

Let's Go never recommends hitchhiking as a safe means of transportation, and none of the information presented here is intended to do so.

Let's Go strongly urges you to consider the risks before you choose to hitchhike. Hitching means entrusting your life to a random person, risking theft, assault, sexual harassment, and unsafe driving. Nonetheless, hitching can get you where you're going, especially in rural parts of Scotland, Wales, and Ireland (England is tougher for prospective hitchers), where public transportation is sketchy. Women traveling alone should never hitch. A man and a woman are safer; two men will have a hard time, and three will go nowhere. Experienced hitchers pick a spot outside built-up areas, where drivers can stop, return to the road without causing an accident, and have time to look over potential passengers as they approach. Hitching or even standing on motorways (any road labeled "M") is illegal.

Safety precautions are always necessary, even for those not hitching alone. Safety-minded hitchers will not get into a car that they can't get out of again in a hurry (especially the back seat of a two-door car) and never let go of their backpacks. If they feel threatened, they insist on being let off, regardless of location. Acting as if they are going to open the car door or vomit usually gets a driver to stop. Hitching at night can be particularly dangerous; experienced hitchers stand in well-lit places and expect drivers to be leery.

KEEPING IN TOUCH

BY MAIL

SENDING MAIL FROM BRITAIN AND IRELAND

Airmail is the best way to send mail home from Britain and Ireland. Just write "Par Avion—By Airmail" on the top left corner of your envelope, or swing by any post office and get a free Airmail label. **Aerogrammes,** printed sheets that fold into envelopes and travel via airmail, are also available at post offices. For priority shipping, ask for **Airsure**; it costs £4 on top of the actual postage, but your letter will get on the next available flight. If Airsure is not available to the country you wish to ship to, ask for **International Signed For** instead; for £3.30 your package will be signed for on delivery. **Surface mail** is the cheapest and slowest way to send mail taking one to three months to cross the Atlantic and two to four to cross the Pacific.

Royal Mail has taken great care to standardize their rates around the world. To check how much your shipment will cost, surf to the Royal Mail Postal Calculator at www.royalmail.com. From Britain, postcards cost 21p domestically, 40p to send within Europe and 43p to the rest of the world; airmail letters (up to 20g) are 21p domestically, 40p within Europe and 68p elsewhere. These are 2nd class mail rates, and take 2-3 business days to arrive. Next day delivery is also available.

International 2nd class rates are as follows: packages up to 500g cost £5.02 and take 5 business days to arrive; packages up to 2kg cost £18.52 and take 5 days around the world including Australia, Canada, New Zealand, and the US. Mail to Ireland has a separate rate. Letters and postcards (up to 20g) cost 40p; packages of up to 500g are £2.98 and take 3 business days; packages of up to 2kg cost £9.25 and take 3-5 business days.

SENDING MAIL TO BRITAIN AND IRELAND

To ensure timely delivery, mark envelopes "Par Avion—By Airmail." In addition to the standard postage system (rates are listed below), **Federal Express** (Canada and US 800-463-3339, Australia 13 26 10, Ireland 1800 535 800, New Zealand 0800 733 339, UK 0800 123 800; www.fedex.com) handles express mail services to Britain and Ireland; they can get a letter from New York to London in two days for US$30. Sending postcards or letters within the UK (up to 60g, or roughly 2oz) costs 28p for 1st class (usually 1-2 business days) or 21p for 2nd class (2-3 business days).

Australia: (www.auspost.com.au/pac). Allow 4-5 business days for regular airmail to Britain and Ireland. Postcards and letters up to 20g cost AUS$1; packages up to 0.5kg AUS$14, up to 2kg AUS$50. EMS can get a letter to Britain and Ireland in 3-4 work days for AUS$35.

Canada: (www.canadapost.ca). Allow 7-14 business days for regular airmail to Britain and Ireland. Postcards and letters up to 20g cost CDN$1.25; packages up to 0.5kg CDN$10.65, up to 2kg CDN$35.50.

New Zealand: (www.nzpost.co.nz/nzpost/inrates). Allow 4-8 business days for regular airmail to Britain and Ireland. Postcards NZ$1.50. Letters up to 20g cost NZ$2-7; small parcels up to 0.5kg NZ$17, up to 2kg NZ$55.

US: (http://ircalc.usps.gov). Allow 4-7 business days for regular airmail to Britain and Ireland. Postcards/aerogrammes cost US$0.70; letters under 1 oz. US$0.80. Packages under 1 lb. cost US$8.70; larger packages cost a variable amount (around US$15). US Express Mail takes 2-3 days and costs US$17. US Global Priority Mail delivers small/large flat-rate envelopes to Britain and Ireland in 4-6 business days for US$5/9.

RECEIVING MAIL IN BRITAIN AND IRELAND

There are several ways to arrange pick-up of letters sent to you by friends and relatives while you are abroad. Mail can be sent via **Poste Restante** (General Delivery) to almost any city or town in Britain and Ireland with a post office. Address *Poste Restante* letters like so:

William SHAKESPEARE
Poste Restante
2/3 Henley St.
Stratford-upon-Avon CV37 6PU
UK

The mail will go to a special desk in the central post office, unless you specify a post office by street address or postal code. It's best to use the largest post office. Bring your passport (or other photo ID) for pick-up. Have clerks check under your first name as well as your last. *Let's Go* lists post offices in the **Practical Information** section for every city and most towns.

American Express's travel offices throughout the world offer a free **Client Letter Service** (mail held up to 30 days and forwarded upon request) for cardholders who contact them in advance. Address the letter as shown above. Some offices offer these services to non-cardholders (especially AmEx Travelers Cheque holders), but call ahead to make sure. *Let's Go* lists AmEx office locations for most large cities in **Practical Information** sections; for a complete, free list, call ☎ 800-528-4800.

BY TELEPHONE

CALLING HOME FROM BRITAIN AND IRELAND

Using a **calling card** is often the cheapest option for travelers. You can frequently call collect without a calling card by calling a company's access number. **To obtain a calling card** from your national telecommunications service before leaving home, contact the appropriate company listed below. To **call home with a calling card,** contact the operator for your service provider in Britain or Ireland by dialing their toll-free access number. Many newsagents in the UK sell **prepaid international phonecards,** such as those offered by Swiftcall. These cards are usually the cheapest way to make long international phone calls, but sometimes carry a minimum charge per call. Stores such as **Call Shop** offer cheap international calls from their booths, and can be found in cities with large numbers of tourists or immigrants.

ESSENTIALS

To **call home with a calling card,** contact the operator for your service provider in Britain and Ireland by dialing the appropriate toll-free access number (listed below in the second column).

COMPANY	TO OBTAIN A CARD, DIAL:	TO CALL ABROAD, DIAL:
AT&T (US)	800-364-9292	0800 89 0011 or 0500 89 0011
Canada Direct	800-561-8868	0800 559 3141 or 0800 096 0634
Ireland Direct	800 40 00 00	0800 89 0353
MCI (US)	800 777 5000	0800 279 5088
New Zealand Direct	0800 000 000	0800 890 064
Australia AAPT	9377 7000	800 028 0890

You can make direct international calls from **payphones,** but if you aren't using a calling card you may need to drop coins as quickly as your words. Occasionally major credit cards can also be used for direct international calls. In-room **hotel calls** invariably include an arbitrary, sky-high surcharge (as much as £6); the rare B&B that has in-room phones tends to be less expensive, but still more costly than using calling cards. See the box (below) for directions on how to place a direct international call. Placing a **collect call** through an international operator is even more expensive. The number for the **international operator** in Britain is ☎ 155.

Let's Go has recently partnered with ekit.com to provide a calling card that offers a number of services, including email and voice messaging. Before settling on a calling card plan, be sure to research your options in order to pick the one that best fits both your needs and your destination.

For more information, visit www.letsgo.ekit.com.

PLACING INTERNATIONAL CALLS. To call Britain and Ireland from home or to call home from Britain and Ireland, dial:

1. The **international dialing prefix.** To dial *out of* Australia, dial 0011; Canada or the US, 011; the Republic of Ireland, New Zealand, or the UK, 00; South Africa, 09.

2. The **country code** of the country you want to call. To *place a call to* Australia, dial 61; Canada or the US, 1; the Republic of Ireland, 353; New Zealand, 64; South Africa, 27; the UK, 44.

3. The **city/area code.** *Let's Go* lists the city/area codes for cities and towns in Britain and Ireland opposite the city or town name, next to a ☎. If the first digit is a zero (e.g., 020 for London), omit the zero when calling from abroad (e.g., dial 20 from Canada to reach London).

4. The **local number.**

5. **Examples:** To call the US embassy in London from New York, dial ☎ 011 44 20 7499 9000. To call the British embassy in Washington from London, dial 00 1 202 588 6500.

CALLING WITHIN BRITAIN AND IRELAND

The simplest way to call within the country is to use a coin-operated phone, but **prepaid phone cards** (available at newspaper kiosks and tobacco stores), which carry a certain amount of phone time depending on the card's denomination, usually save time and money in the long run. The computerized phone will tell you how much time, in units, you have left on your card. Another kind of prepaid telephone card comes with a **Personal Identification Number** (PIN) and a toll-free access number. Instead of inserting the card into the phone, you call the access number and follow the directions on the card. These cards can be used to make international as well as domestic calls. Phone rates typically tend to be highest in the morning, lower in the evening, and lowest on Sunday and late at night.

To make a call within a city or town, just dial the number; from outside the region, dial the phone code and the number. For **directory inquiries,** call ☎118 500 in the UK (it'll run you a 40p connection charge and cost 15p/min. for the duration of the call) or 1190 in Ireland (for the price of a local call). *Let's Go* lists phone codes opposite the city or town name next to the ☎ symbol; all phone numbers in that town use that phone code unless specified otherwise. To call Britain from the Republic of Ireland, or vice versa, you will have to make an international call. Northern Ireland is part of the UK phone network.

PHONE CODES
Recent changes to British phone codes have produced a system in which the first three numbers of the phone code identify the type of number being called. **Premium rate calls,** costing about 50p per minute, can be identified by the 090 phone code. **Freephone** (toll-free) numbers have a 080 code. Numbers that begin with an 084 code incur the **local call rate,** while the 087 code incurs the **national call rate** (the two aren't significantly different for short calls). Calling a **mobile phone** (cell phone) is more expensive than a regular phone call. Mobile phone numbers carry 077, 078, or 079 codes, and pager numbers begin with 076.

PUBLIC PHONES IN BRITAIN
Public payphones in Britain are mostly run by **British Telecom (BT),** recognizable by the ubiquitous piper logo, although upstart competitors such as Mercury operate in larger cities. Public phones charge a minimum of 10p for calls and don't accept 1p, 2p, or 5p coins. The dial tone is a continuous purring sound; a repeated double-tone means the line is ringing. A series of harsh beeps will warn you to insert more money when your time is up. For the rest of the call, the digital display ticks off your credit. You may use any remaining credit on a second call by pressing the "follow on call" button (often marked "FC"). Otherwise, once you hang up, your remaining phonecard credit is rounded down to the nearest 10p, or unused coins are returned. Pay phones do *not* give change, so use 10p and 20p coins.

PUBLIC PHONES IN IRELAND
Using Irish pay phones can be tricky. Public coin phones will give you back unused coins, but not fractions of coins, so don't insert a €1 coin for a 20 cent call. Private pay phones (called "one-armed bandits") in hostels and restaurants do not return unused coins. Do not insert money into any pay phone until asked to or until the call goes through. Local calls cost 40 cents; "one-armed bandits" charge more. Local calls are not unlimited—one unit pays for four minutes.

The smart option for non-local calls is buying a **prepaid phone card,** which carries a certain amount of phone time depending on the card's denomination. The time is measured in minutes usually has a toll-free access telephone number and a PIN. Newsagents sell phone cards in denominations of €2, €5, €10, or €20. Card phones have a digital display that ticks off your units. When the unit number starts flashing, push the eject button on the card phone and replace the empty card with a fresh one. Don't wait until it gets to zero; eject your card early and use the remaining unit or two for a local call.

CELLULAR PHONES

Cell phones are ubiquitous in Britain and Ireland, though high rates for placing calls have created a text-messaging culture—almost everyone you see with a cell phone will be typing into, rather than talking into it.

The international standard for cell phones is **GSM,** a system that began in Europe and has spread to much of the rest of the world. Many high-end cell phones on sale today are already **GSM-compatible,** though they may not work in the UK (see box below); check your manual or contact a retailer. If you already have or plan to purchase a GSM-compatible phone, this is the best idea for travelers on a budget. You'll also need a **SIM (subscriber identity module) card,** a country-specific, thumbnail-sized chip that gives you a local phone number and plugs you into the local network. Most SIM cards are **prepaid,** meaning that they come with calling time included and you don't need to sign up for a monthly service plan. Incoming calls are usually free. When you use up the pre-paid time, you can buy additional cards or vouchers (usually available at convenience stores) to get more. For more information on rates, prices, and plans, check out the companies listed below.

TIP GSM PHONES. Just having a GSM phone doesn't mean you're necessarily good to go when you travel abroad. The majority of GSM phones sold in the United States operate on a different **frequency** (1900) than international phones (900/1800) and will not work abroad. Tri-band phones work on all three frequencies (900/1800/1900) and will operate through most of the world. As well, some GSM phones are **SIM-locked** and will only accept SIM cards from a single carrier. You'll need a **SIM-unlocked** phone to use a SIM card from a local carrier when you travel.

For longer visits (more than a month), a **pay-as-you-go plan** is the most flexible alternative. Once you arrive, pick up an eligible mobile (from £40) and you can recharge, or **top-up,** at most grocery stores or by phone. The best part is that **incoming calls and text messages are always free.** Call rates listed here are by the minute.

Orange (☎07973 100 150; www.orange.co.uk). Phones from £40. Calls to the US from 20p; to other Orange mobiles, 25p for the first 3 minutes, then 5p thereafter; to other UK networks, 40p; text messaging 12p.

O^2 (www.o2.co.uk). Phones from £60. Calls to the US from 35p, 10p weekends; calls to other O^2 mobiles and fixed lines, 25p for the first 3 minutes, then 2-5p for the rest of the day; to other UK networks, 40p; text messaging 10p.

T-Mobile (☎0845 412 5000; www.t-mobile.co.uk). Phones from £50; calls to US 90p flat rate; calls to any other phones from 10p if you use more than £20 of airtime per month; text messaging 10p.

TIME DIFFERENCES

Britain and Ireland are on **Greenwich Mean Time (GMT),** five hours ahead of New York, eight hours ahead of Vancouver and San Francisco, two hours behind Johannesburg, 10hr. behind Sydney, and 12hr. behind Auckland. Actual time differences depend on local time observances, such as daylight savings time. Both Britain and Ireland observe **daylight savings time** between the last Sunday of March and the last Sunday of October.

visit bonnie

SCOTLAND

Europe's prettiest country

and jump aboard
the amazing

HOSTEL
BUS SERVICE

for daily door to door,
hassle-free travel through the
beautiful Scottish Highlands

RUNNING YEAR ROUND

just £69

inc. Skye Tour £87

for more info check our website:

including full informal commentary from our
all-Scottish guides

MacBACKPACKERS.com

connecting

SCOTLAND'S TOP HOSTELS

- Edinburgh
  Castle Rock & High St. Hostels
- Pitlochry Backpackers Hotel
- Inverness Student Hotel
- Skye Backpackers
- Fort William Backpackers
- Oban Backpackers
- Glasgow Backpackers
- Edinburgh

or phone
+44 (0)131 558 9900
for tours, travel and accommodation

We also operate a fantastic range of set tours:

7 DAY Grand Tour of Scotland - £159

5 DAY Skye and Loch Ness Tour - £119

3 DAY Isle of Skye Tour - £75

3 DAY Highland Romp - £69

Wild Rover Round Britain Pass - £210

ESSENTIALS

BY EMAIL AND INTERNET

Cyber cafes or public terminals can be found almost everywhere in Britain and Ireland. (*Let's Go* lists them under **Internet Access** in the **Practical Information** section.) They tend to cost £4-6 per hour, but often you pay only for time used. Cyber cafes can also be found in the larger cities of Ireland and cost €4-6 per hour. Many hostels offer Internet access, charging about the same rates. **Libraries** usually have free Internet access, but you might have to wait or make an advance reservation. Two online guides to cyber cafes—updated daily—are **Cybercafes.com** (www.cybercafes.com) and **The Cybercafe Search Engine** (www.cybercaptive.com).

Increasingly, travelers find that taking their **laptops** on the road with them can be a convenient option for staying connected. Laptop users can find Internet cafes or wireless "hotspots" that allow wireless-enabled computers to get online for free or for a small fee. Computers can detect these hotspots automatically, or websites like www.jiwire.com, www.wi-fihotspotlist.com, and www.locfinder.net can help you find them. For information on insuring your laptop while traveling, see p. 22.

ACCOMMODATIONS

HOSTELS

If you want to save money, you will be staying in a hostel. In Britain and Ireland, hostels are generally clean and friendly places to spend the night, and in the larger cities students even choose to live in them for extended periods of time. They are usually laid out dorm-style, with large single-sex rooms and the inevitable bunk beds, although some offer private rooms. There are hostels with kitchens and utensils, bike or moped rentals, storage areas, transportation to airports, breakfast, and laundry facilities, but don't expect all of these in any one. Expect some to close during certain daytime "lockout" hours, enforce a curfew, or impose a maximum stay. In Britain, a hostel bed will cost about £10 in rural areas, £12-16 in larger cities, and £15-25 in London; in Ireland, €12.

A HOSTELER'S BILL OF RIGHTS. There are certain standard features that we do not include in our hostel listings. Unless we state otherwise, you can expect that every hostel has no lockout, no curfew, a kitchen, free hot showers, some system of secure luggage storage, and no key deposit.

HOSTELLING INTERNATIONAL

Joining the youth hostel association in your own country (listed below) automatically grants you membership privileges in **Hostelling International (HI)**, a federation of national hosteling associations. Non-HI members may be allowed to stay in some hostels, but will have to pay extra to do so. HI hostels are prevalent throughout the UK and Ireland. They are run by the **Youth Hostels Association** (England and Wales), the **Scottish Youth Hostels Association, Hostelling International Northern Ireland (HINI)**, and **An Óige (an-OYJ)** in the Republic of Ireland. HI's umbrella organization's web page (www.hihostels.com), which lists links and phone numbers of all national associations, can be a great place to begin researching hostels. Other comprehensive hostelling websites include www.hostels.com and www.hostelplanet.com.

Most HI hostels also honor **guest memberships**—you'll get a blank card with space for six validation stamps. Each night you'll pay a nonmember supplement (about one-sixth the membership fee) and earn one guest stamp; get six stamps, and you're a member. Most student travel agencies (see p. 26) sell HI cards, as do all of the national organizations listed below. All prices listed below are for **one-year memberships** unless otherwise noted.

Youth Hostels Association (YHA), Trevelyan House, Dimple Rd., Matlock, Derbyshire DE4 3YH, UK (☎0870 770 8868; www.yha.org.uk). £14.00, under 18 £7.00.

Scottish Youth Hostels Association (SYHA), 7 Glebe Cres., Stirling FK8 2JA (☎01786 89 14 00; www.syha.org.uk). £6, under 17 £2.50.

Hostelling International Northern Ireland (HINI), 22 Donegall Rd., Belfast BT12 5JN (☎02890 32 47 33; www.hini.org.uk). £13, under 18 £6.

An Óige (Irish Youth Hostel Association), 61 Mountjoy St., Dublin 7 (☎830 4555; www.irelandyha.org). €20, under 18 €10.

Australian Youth Hostels Association (AYHA), 422 Kent St., Sydney, NSW 200 (☎02 9261 1111; www.yha.com.au). AUS$52, under 18 AUS$19.

Hostelling International-Canada (HI-C), 205 Catherine St. #400, Ottawa, ON K2P 1C3 (☎613-237-7884; www.hihostels.ca). CDN$35, under 18 free.

Youth Hostels Association of New Zealand (YHANZ), Level 1, Moorhouse City, 166 Moorhouse Ave., P.O. Box 436, Christchurch (☎0800 278 299 (NZ only) or 03 379 9970; www.yha.org.nz). NZ$40, under 18 free.

Hostelling International-USA, 8401 Colesville Rd., Ste. 600, Silver Spring, MD 20910 (☎301-495-1240; www.hiayh.org). US$28, under 18 free.

BOOKING HOSTELS ONLINE. The easiest way to ensure you've got a bed for the night is by reserving online. Surf to the **Hostelworld** booking engine through **www.letsgo.com,** and you'll have access to bargain accommodations from Argentina to Zimbabwe with no added commission.

Independent hostels tend to attract younger crowds, be located closer to city centers, and have a more relaxed attitude about lockouts or curfews than YHA or An Óige counterparts. A number of Irish hostels belong to the IHH (Independent Holiday Hostels) organization. IHH hostels require no membership, and usually have no lockout or curfew; all are Bord Fáilte-approved. For a free booklet with complete descriptions of IHH hostels, contact the IHH office at 57 Lower Gardiner St., Dublin 1 (☎01 836 4700; www.hostels-ireland.com). A useful website for hostel listings throughout the UK is Backpackers UK (www.backpackers.co.uk).

BED & BREAKFASTS (B&BS)

For a cozy alternative to impersonal hotel rooms, B&Bs (private homes with rooms available to travelers) range from the acceptable to the sublime. B&B owners sometimes go out of their way to be accommodating, giving personalized tours or offering home-cooked meals. Some B&Bs, however, do not provide private bathrooms (rooms with private baths are referred to as **ensuite**) and most do not provide phones. A **double** room has one large bed for two people; a **twin** has two separate beds. *Let's Go* lists B&B prices by room type unless otherwise stated. You can book B&Bs by calling directly or by asking the local **Tourist Information Centre** (TIC) to help you find accommodations; most can also book B&Bs in other towns. TICs usually charge a 10% deposit on

REGENCY
HOUSE HOTEL
———— JVM HOTELS ————

A GEORGIAN TOWN HOUSE IN
THE HEART OF LONDON'S HISTORIC BLOOMSBURY
A SHORT STROLL AWAY FROM
THE BRITISH MUSEUM, WEST END THEATRES
AND OXFORD STREET SHOPS.

All rooms with en suite facilities.
All rooms have colour T.V, direct dial telephones,
tea and coffee making facilities.
Room rates are inclusive of all taxes and English breakfast.

71 GOWER STREET LONDON WC1 E6HJ
TEL: 020 7637 1804   FAX: 020 7323 5077
www.regencyhouse-hotel.com

the first night's or the entire stay's price, deductible from the amount you pay the B&B proprietor. Often a flat fee of £1-3 is added. To find B&Bs online, try www.innfinder.com, www.innsite.com, or www.bedandbreakfast.com.

The British tourist boards operate a B&B **rating system,** using a scale of one to five diamonds (in England) or stars (in Scotland and Wales). Rated accommodations are part of the tourist board's booking system, but it costs money to be rated and some perfectly good B&Bs choose not to participate. Approval by the Tourist Board is legally required of all Northern Ireland accommodations. Approved accommodations in the Republic are marked with a green shamrock.

OTHER TYPES OF ACCOMMODATIONS

YMCAS
Young Men's Christian Association (YMCA) lodgings are usually cheaper than a hotel but more expensive than a hostel. Not all YMCA locations offer lodging; those that do are often located in urban downtowns. Many YMCAs accept women and families; some will not lodge those under 18 without parental permission. The **World Alliance of YMCAs**, 12 Clos Belmont, 1208 Geneva, Switzerland (☎41 22 849 5100, fax 41 22 849 5110; www.ymca.int), has listings of YMCAs worldwide.

HOTELS AND GUESTHOUSES
Basic hotel singles in Britain cost about £70 per night, doubles £95. Some hotels offer "full pension" (all meals) and "half pension" (no lunch). Smaller guesthouses are often cheaper than hotels. If you make reservations in writing, indicate your night of arrival and the number of nights you plan to stay. The hotel will send you a confirmation and may request payment for the first night. Not all hotels take reservations, and few accept checks in foreign currency.

ESSENTIALS

UNIVERSITY DORMS

Many **colleges and universities** open their residence halls to travelers when school is not in session; some do so even during term-time. Getting a room may take a couple of phone calls and require advanced planning, but rates tend to be low, and many offer free local calls and Internet access.

HOME EXCHANGES AND HOSPITALITY CLUBS

Home exchange offers the traveler various types of homes (houses, apartments, condominiums, villas, even castles in some cases), plus the opportunity to live like a native and to cut down on accommodation fees. For more information, contact **HomeExchange.Com,** P.O. Box 787, Hermosa Beach, CA 90254 USA (☎800-877-8723; www.homeexchange.com), or **Intervac International Home Exchange** (UK ☎1249 461101, Ireland 041 983 0930; www.intervac.com).

   Hospitality clubs link their members with individuals or families abroad who are willing to host travelers for free or for a small fee to promote cultural exchange and general good karma. In exchange, members usually must be willing to host travelers in their own homes; a small membership fee may also be required. **Global-Freeloaders.com** (www.globalfreeloaders.com) and **The Hospitality Club** (www.hospitalityclub.org) are good places to start. **Servas** (www.servas.org) is an established, more formal, peace-based organization, and requires a fee and an interview to join. An Internet search will find many similar organizations, some of which cater to special interests (e.g., women, gay and lesbian travelers, or members of certain professions.) As always, use common sense when planning to stay with or host someone you do not know.

LONG-TERM ACCOMMODATIONS

Travelers planning to stay in Britain or Ireland for extended periods of time may find it most cost-effective to rent an **apartment,** though these can be expensive too. Besides the rent itself, prospective tenants usually are also required to front a security deposit (frequently one month's rent) and sometimes also the last month's rent. One place to look is **UK Flatshare** (www.flatshare-flatmate.co.uk), an extensive listing of available apartments and rooms for sublet.

CAMPING AND THE OUTDOORS

Britain and Ireland have quite a number of campsites that tend to be a hike away from many of the popular sights and cities. Campsites are often privately owned, with basic sites costing £3 per person, and posh ones costing up to £10 per person. Since much of the land in national parks is privately owned, never pitch your tent in a park without permission. The **Great Outdoor Recreation Pages** (www.gorp.com) provides excellent general information for travelers planning on camping or spending time in the outdoors.

LEAVE NO TRACE. *Let's Go* encourages travelers to embrace the "Leave No Trace" ethic, minimizing their impact on natural environments and protecting them for future generations. Trekkers and wilderness enthusiasts should set up camp on durable surfaces, use cookstoves instead of campfires, bury human waste away from water supplies, bag trash and carry it out with them, and respect wildlife and natural objects. For more detailed information, contact the **Leave No Trace Center for Outdoor Ethics,** P.O. Box 997, Boulder, CO 80306, USA (☎ 800-332-4100 or 303-442-8222; www.lnt.org).

USEFUL PUBLICATIONS AND RESOURCES

Campers heading to Europe should consider buying an International Camping Carnet. Similar to a hostel membership, it's required at some campgrounds and provides discounts. It is available in North America from the Family Campers and RVers Association and in the UK from The Caravan Club (see below).

Automobile Association, Contact Centre, Carr Ellison House, William Armstrong Drive, Newcastle-upon-Tyne NE4 7YA, UK (☎ 0870 600 0371; www.theAA.com). Publishes Caravan and Camping Europe and Britain (both £8) as well as Big Road Atlases for Europe, Britain, France, Germany, Italy, and Spain.

The Caravan Club, East Grinstead House, East Grinstead, West Sussex, RH19 1UA, UK (☎ 44 01342 326 944; www.caravanclub.co.uk). For £30, members receive travel equipment discounts, maps, and a monthly magazine.

Sierra Club Books, 85 Second St., 2nd fl., San Francisco, CA 94105, USA (☎ 415-977-5500; www.sierraclub.org). Publishes general resource books on hiking and camping.

The Mountaineers Books, 1001 SW Klickitat Way, Ste. 201, Seattle, WA 98134, USA (☎ 206-223-6303; www.mountaineersbooks.org). Boasts over 600 titles on hiking, biking, mountaineering, natural history, and conservation.

Ordnance Survey (☎ 08456 050 505, helpline 023 8079 2912; www.ordsvy.gov.uk). Britain's national mapping agency (also known as OS) publishes topographical maps, available at TICs and National Park Information Centres (NPICs) and many bookstores. Their excellent *Explorer* (£7) map series covers the whole of Britain in detailed 1:25,000 scale.

NATIONAL PARKS

Seeing the national parks of Britain is well worth the journey from London. The parks are in large part privately owned, but generally provide expansive areas for public use. There are 12 national parks in England and Wales. The Trossachs, Loch Lomond, and the Cairngorms were named Scotland's first national parks in 2002. Each park is administrated by its own National Park Authority.

WILDERNESS SAFETY

THE GREAT OUTDOORS

Staying **warm, dry,** and **well-hydrated** is key to a happy and safe wilderness experience. For any hike, prepare yourself for an emergency by packing a first-aid kit, a reflector, a whistle, high energy food, extra water, raingear, a hat, and mittens. For warmth, wear wool or insulating synthetic materials designed for the outdoors. Cotton is a bad choice since it dries painfully slowly.

Check **weather forecasts** often and pay attention to the skies when hiking, as weather patterns can change suddenly. Always let someone, either a friend, your hostel, a park ranger, or a local hiking organization, know when and where you are going hiking. See **Safety and Health,** p. 21, for information on outdoor ailments and medical concerns. If you are in trouble and can reach a phone, **call ☎999.** If not, six blasts on a **whistle** are standard to summon help (three are the reply); a constant long blast also indicates distress. For more information, see *How to Stay Alive in the Woods,* by Bradford Angier (Black Dog & Leventhal Books, $20).

CAMPING AND HIKING EQUIPMENT

WHAT TO BUY

Sleeping Bags: Most sleeping bags are rated by season; "summer" means 30-40°F (around 0°C) at night; "four-season" or "winter" often means below 0°F (-17°C). Bags are made of **down** (warm and light, but expensive, and miserable when wet) or of **synthetic** material (heavy, durable, and warm when wet). Prices range US$50-250 for a summer synthetic to US$200-300 for a good down winter bag. **Sleeping bag pads** include foam pads (US$10-30), air mattresses (US$15-50), and self-inflating mats (US$30-120). Bring a **stuff sack** to store your bag and keep it dry.

Tents: The best tents are free-standing (with their own frames and suspension systems), set up quickly, and only require staking in high winds. Low-profile dome tents are the best all-around. Worthy 2-person tents start at US$100, 4-person at US$160. Make sure your tent has a rain fly and seal its seams with waterproofer. Other useful accessories include a **battery-operated lantern,** a plastic **groundcloth,** and a nylon **tarp.**

Backpacks: Internal-frame packs mold well to your back, keep a lower center of gravity, and flex adequately to allow you to hike difficult trails, while **external-frame packs** are more comfortable for long hikes over even terrain, as they carry weight higher and distribute it more evenly. Make sure your pack has a strong, padded hip-belt to transfer weight to your legs. There are models designed specifically for women. Any serious backpacking requires a pack of at least 4000 in^3 (16,000cc), plus 500 in^3 for sleeping bags in internal-frame packs. Sturdy backpacks cost anywhere from US$125 to US$420, but remember that your pack (or your back) is an area where it doesn't pay to economize. Don't be afraid to strap on a few packs right in the store to find the best fit for you. Some packs include a **rain cover;** if not, pick one up (US$10-20).

Boots: Be sure to wear hiking boots with good **ankle support.** They should fit snugly and comfortably over 1-2 pairs of **wool socks** and a pair of thin **liner socks.** Break in boots over several weeks before you go to spare yourself blisters.

Other Necessities: Synthetic layers, like those made of polypropylene or polyester, and a pile jacket will keep you warm even when wet. A **space blanket** (US$5-15) will help you to retain body heat and doubles as a groundcloth. Plastic **water bottles** are vital; look for shatter- and leak-resistant models. Carry **water-purification tablets** for when you can't boil water. For those places (including virtually every organized campground) that forbid fires or the gathering of firewood, you'll need a **camp stove** (the classic Coleman starts at US$50) and a propane-filled **fuel bottle** to operate it. Also bring a **first-aid kit, pocketknife, insect repellent,** and **waterproof matches** or a **lighter.**

WHERE TO BUY IT

Campmor, 28 Parkway, P.O. Box 700, Upper Saddle River, NJ 07458, USA (US ☎800-525-4784; www.campmor.com).

Discount Camping, 880 Main North Rd., Pooraka, South Australia 5095, Australia (☎08 8262 3399; www.discountcamping.com.au).

Eastern Mountain Sports (EMS), 1 Vose Farm Rd., Peterborough, NH 03458, USA (☎888-463-6367; www.ems.com).

Karrimor International, Ltd., Petre Road, Clayton-le-Moors, Accrington, Lancashire BB5 5JZ, Australia (☎01254 893000; www.karrimor.co.uk). Many UK outlets.

L.L. Bean, Freeport, ME 04033, USA (US and Canada ☎800-441-5713; UK ☎0800 891 297; www.llbean.com).

Recreational Equipment, Inc. (REI), Sumner, WA 98352, USA (US and Canada ☎800-426-4840, elsewhere 253-891-2500; www.rei.com).

YHA Adventure Shop, 19 High St., Staines, Middlesex, TW18 4QY, UK (☎1784 458625). One of Britain's largest outdoor equipment suppliers.

CAMPERS AND RVS

Renting a camper van (RV in the US) will always be more expensive than camping or hosteling, but it's cheaper than staying in hotels and renting a car (see **Rental Cars,** p. 35). The convenience of bringing along your own bedroom, bathroom, and kitchen makes it an attractive option, especially for older travelers and families with children. Try **Vivanti Motorhomes** (☎08707 522225; www.vivanti.co.uk) or Just Go (☎0870 240 1918; www.justgo.co.uk).

ORGANIZED ADVENTURE TRIPS

Specialty Travel Index, 305 San Anselmo Ave., #313, San Anselmo, CA 94960 (US ☎800-442-4922, elsewhere 415-459-4900; www.specialtytravel.com).

TrekAmerica, PO Box 189, Rockaway, NJ 07866 (US ☎800-221-0596 or 973-983 1144, elsewhere 01295 256 777; www.trekamerica.com).

SPECIFIC CONCERNS

SUSTAINABLE TRAVEL

Ecotourism, a rising trend in **sustainable travel,** focuses on the conservation of natural habitats and using them to build up the economy without exploitation or over-development. Travelers can make a difference by doing advance research and by supporting organizations and establishments that pay attention to their impact on their natural surroundings and strive to be environmentally-friendly. For UK-specific trips, visit www.earthfoot.org/uk.htm.

ESSENTIALS

ECOTOURISM RESOURCES. For more information on environmentally responsible tourism, contact one of the organizations below:
The Centre for Environmentally Responsible Tourism (www.c-e-r-t.org).
Earthwatch, 3 Clock Tower Place, Ste. 100, Box 75, Maynard, MA 01754, USA (☎ 800-776-0188 or 978-461-0081; www.earthwatch.org).
International Ecotourism Society, 733 15th St. NW, Washington, D.C. 20005, USA (☎ 202-347-9203; www.ecotourism.org).

RESPONSIBLE TRAVEL

The impact of tourist dollars on the destinations you visit should not be underestimated. The choices you make during your trip can have potent effects on local communities—for better or for worse.

Community-based tourism aims to channel tourist money into the local economy by emphasizing tours and cultural programs that are run by members of the host community and that often benefit disadvantaged groups. An excellent resource on community-based travel is *The Good Alternative Travel Guide* (£10), a project of **Tourism Concern** (☎ 020 7133 3330; www.tourismconcern.org.uk).

The UK is filled with open-air historical sites such as ruinous cathedrals, bronze age settlements, and other ancient monuments. It is a rare privilege that such testaments to the multicultural heritage of the British Isles survive today, and an even greater privilege to be able to walk up, in, and among them. It is up to the tourists themselves to be responsible for not taking anything or leaving anything behind, however strong the temptation to maul/be part of history may be.

WOMEN TRAVELERS

Though Britain and Ireland are among the world's safest destinations, women on their own inevitably face some additional safety concerns, particularly in larger cities such as London, Cardiff, Glasgow, Belfast, and Dublin. The following suggestions shouldn't discourage women from traveling alone—it's easy to enjoy yourself without taking undue risks. Avoid solitary late-night treks or metro/Tube rides. Check that your hostel offers safe communal showers. Carry extra money for a phone call, bus, or taxi. If catching a bus at night, wait at a well-populated stop. Choose train or Tube compartments occupied by other women or couples. Look as if you know where you're going and approach older women or couples for directions if you're lost or uncomfortable.

Your best answer to verbal harassment is no answer at all; feigning deafness, sitting motionless, and staring straight ahead at nothing in particular will do a world of good that reactions usually don't achieve. The extremely persistent can sometimes be dissuaded by a firm, loud, and very public "Go away!" Wearing a conspicuous **wedding band** may help prevent unwanted overtures. Memorize emergency numbers and consider carrying a whistle or rape alarm on your keychain. Mace and pepper sprays are illegal in Britain.

The national **emergency** number is ☎ 999. **Rape Crisis UK and Ireland** (a full list of helplines can be found at www.rapecrisis.org.uk) provides referrals to local rape crisis and sexual abuse counseling services throughout the UK; the **Dublin Rape Crisis Centre** helpline is ☎ 1800 778 888 (www.drcc.ie). A self-defense course will prepare you for a potential attack and raise your level of awareness (see **Self Defense,** p. 22). For health concerns that women face when traveling, see p. 25.

GLBT TRAVELERS

Large cities, notably London, Dublin, Edinburgh, Manchester, and Brighton, are more open to GLBT culture than rural Britain, though evidence of bigotry and violence remains. The magazine *Time Out* (p. 57) has a Gay Listings section, and numerous periodicals make it easy to learn about the current concerns of Britain's gay community. Visit Britain publishes the essential guide *Britain: Inside and Out* (www.gaybritain.org). The *Pink Paper* (free) is available from newsagents in larger cities. **Out and About** (www.planetout.com) offers a bi-weekly newsletter.

 FURTHER READING: BISEXUAL, GAY, AND LESBIAN.
Spartacus International Gay Guide 2001-2002. Bruno Gmunder Verlag (US$33).
Damron Men's Guide, Damron's Accommodations, and *The Women's Traveller.* Damron Travel Guides (US$14-19). For more info, call ☎800-462-6654 or visit www.damron.com.
Ferrari Guides' Gay Travel A to Z, Ferrari Guides' Men's Travel in Your Pocket, and *Ferrari Guides' Inn Places.* Ferrari Publications (US$16-20). Purchase the guides online at www.ferrariguides.com.
The Gay Vacation Guide: The Best Trips and How to Plan Them. Mark Chesnut. Citadel Press (US$15).

Gay's the Word, 66 Marchmont St., London WC1N 1AB, UK (☎44 20 7278 7654; www.gaystheword.co.uk). UK's largest GLBT bookshop. Mail-order service available.

International Lesbian and Gay Association (ILGA), 81 rue Marché-au-Charbon, B-1000 Brussels, Belgium (☎32 2 502 2471; www.ilga.org). Provides political information such as homosexuality laws of individual countries.

Ireland's Pink Pages (www.pink-pages.org). Ireland's web-based bisexual, gay, and lesbian directory. Extensive urban and regional info for both the Republic and the North.

London Lesbian and Gay Switchboard (☎020 7837 7324; www.llgs.org.uk). Confidential advice, information, and referrals. Open 24hr.

TRAVELERS WITH DISABILITIES

With advance planning, Britain and Ireland can be accessible to travelers with disabilities. Those with disabilities should inform airlines and hotels of their disabilities when making reservations; time may be needed to prepare special accommodations. Call ahead to restaurants, museums, and other facilities to find out if they are handicapped-accessible. **Rail** may be the most convenient form of travel: many stations have ramps, and some trains have wheelchair lifts, special seating areas, and specially equipped toilets; call ahead to check. The National Rail website (www.nationalrail.co.uk) provides general information for travelers with disabilities and assistance phone numbers; it also describes the Disabled Persons Railcard ($14), which allows one-third off most fares for one year. Most **bus** companies will provide assistance if notified ahead of time. All National Express coaches entering service after 2005 must be equipped with a wheelchair lift or ramp; call the **Additional Needs Help Line** (☎0121 423 8479) for information. The London **Underground** is slowly improving accessibility; **Transport for London Access & Mobility** (☎020 7222 1234) can provide information on public transportation within the city. Some major **car rental** agencies (Hertz, Avis, and National), as well as local agencies can provide and deliver hand-controlled cars.

The British Tourist Boards have begun rating accommodations and attractions using the **National Accessible Scheme (NAS),** which designates three categories of accessibility. Look for the NAS symbols in Tourist Board guidebooks, or ask a site directly for their ranking. Many **theaters** and performance venues have space for wheelchairs; some larger theatrical performances include special facilities for the hearing-impaired. Guide dogs fall under the PETS regulations (p. 16).

USEFUL ORGANIZATIONS

Access Abroad, www.umabroad.umn.edu/access. A website devoted to making study abroad available to students with disabilities. The site is maintained by Disability Services Research and Training, University of Minnesota, University Gateway, Ste. 180, 200 Oak St. SE, Minneapolis, MN 55455, USA (☎612-624-6884).

Accessible Journeys, 35 West Sellers Ave., Ridley Park, PA 19078, USA (☎800-846-4537; www.disabilitytravel.com). Designs tours for wheelchair users and slow walkers. The site has tips and forums for all travelers.

Flying Wheels, 143 W. Bridge St., P.O. Box 382, Owatonna, MN 55060, USA (☎507-451-5005; www.flyingheelstravel.com). Specializes in escorted trips to Europe for people with physical disabilities; plans custom accessible trips worldwide.

The Guided Tour Inc., 7900 Old York Rd., #114B, Elkins Park, PA 19027, USA (☎800-783-5841; www.guidedtour.com). Organizes travel programs for persons with developmental and physical challenges in the US, Ireland, Iceland, Cancun, London, and Paris.

Mobility International USA (MIUSA), PO Box 10767, Eugene, OR 97440, USA (☎541-343-1284; www.miusa.org). Provides a variety of books and other publications containing information for travelers with disabilities.

Society for Accessible Travel & Hospitality (SATH), 347 Fifth Ave., #610, New York, NY 10016, USA (☎212-447-7284; www.sath.org). An advocacy group that publishes free online travel information and the travel magazine *OPEN WORLD* (annual subscription US$13, free for members). Annual membership US$45, students and seniors US$30.

MINORITY TRAVELERS

Minorities make up about 10% of Britain's population, the majority of which live in London and other cities. Ireland is only beginning to experience racial diversity, while rural Scotland and Wales remain predominantly white. Minority travelers should expect reduced anonymity in the latter regions, but onlookers are usually motivated by curiosity rather than in ill will and should not cause you to alter your travel plans. Contact the **Commission for Racial Equality (CRE),** St. Dunstan's House, 201-211 Borough High St., London SE1 1GZ (☎020 7939 0000; www.cre.gov.uk).

DIETARY CONCERNS

Vegetarians should be able to find meals in Britain and Ireland. Virtually all restaurants have vegetarian selections and many cater specifically to vegetarians. *Let's Go* notes restaurants with good vegetarian selections. Good resources include: www.veggieheaven.com, for a comprehensive listing of restaurants; www.vrg.org/travel, for links geared toward vegetarian and vegan travel; or contact **The Vegetarian Society of the UK** (☎0161 925 2000; www.vegsoc.org).

Travelers who keep **kosher** should contact synagogues in larger cities for information on kosher restaurants. Orthodox communities in North London (in neighborhoods such as **Golders Green** or **Stamford Hill**), Leeds, and Manchester provide a market for kosher restaurants and grocers. Kosher options decrease in rural areas, but most restaurants and B&Bs will try to accommodate your dietary restrictions. A good resource is the *Jewish Travel Guide*, edited by Michael Zaidner (Vallentine Mitchell; US$17).

OTHER RESOURCES

Time Out, Universal House, 251 Tottenham Court Road, London, W1T 7AB, (☎020 7813 3000; www.timeout.com), is the absolute best weekly guide to what's going on in London, Edinburgh, and Dublin. The magazine is sold at every newsstand in those cities, and the website is a virtual hub for the latest on dining, entertainment, and discounts.

Rand McNally, P.O. Box 7600, Chicago, IL 60680, USA (☎847-329-8100; www.randmcnally.com), publishes road atlases.

Adventurous Traveler Bookstore, P.O. Box 2221, Williston, VT 05495, USA (☎800-282-3963; www.adventuroustraveler.com) has a wide variety of adventure travel guides.

WORLD WIDE WEB

Almost every aspect of budget travel is accessible via the web. In 10min. at the keyboard, you can book a hostel bed, get advice from other travelers, or find out how much a train from London to Scarborough costs. Because website turnover is high, use search engines (such as www.google.com) to strike out on your own.

WWW.LETSGO.COM Our freshly redesigned website features extensive content from our guides; community forums where travelers can connect with each other and ask questions or advice—as well as share stories and tips; and expanded resources to help you plan your trip. Visit us soon to browse by destination, find information about ordering our titles, and sign up for our e-newsletter!

How to See the World: www.artoftravel.com. A compendium of great travel tips, from cheap flights to self defense to interacting with local culture.

Backpacker's Ultimate Guide: www.bugeurope.com. Tips on packing, transportation, and where to go. Also tons of country-specific travel information.

World Hum: www.worldhum.com. "Travel dispatches from a shrinking planet."

BootsnAll.com: www.bootsnall.com. Numerous resources for independent travelers, from planning your trip to reporting on it when you get back.

INFORMATION ON BRITAIN AND IRELAND

CIA World Factbook: www.odci.gov/cia/publications/factbook/index.html. Tons of vital statistics on (your country's) geography, government, economy, and people.

Geographia: www.geographia.com. Highlights, culture, and people of [your country].

Atevo Travel: www.atevo.com/guides/destinations. Detailed introductions, travel tips, and suggested itineraries.

PlanetRider: www.planetrider.com. A subjective list of links to the "best" websites covering the culture and tourist attractions of the UK.

Multimap: www.multimap.com. The Mapquest of the UK. Find any address, get directions, and often even aerial photos.

ESSENTIALS

ALTERNATIVES TO TOURISM

A PHILOSOPHY FOR TRAVELERS

Let's Go believes that the connection between travelers and their destinations is an important one. We've watched the growth of the 'ignorant tourist' stereotype with dismay, knowing that many travelers care passionately about the communities and environments they explore—but also knowing that even conscientious travelers can inadvertently damage natural wonders and harm cultural environments. With this "Alternatives to Tourism" chapter, *Let's Go* hopes to promote a better understanding of Britain and Ireland and enhance your experience there.

As a **volunteer** in Britain or Ireland, you can participate in projects from archaeological digs at Norman castles to working with political groups for peace in Northern Ireland. Later in this section, we recommend organizations that can help you find the opportunities that best suit your interests, whether you're looking to pitch in for a day or a year.

Studying in Britain and Ireland is another option. You can study medieval history for at the medieval institutions of Cambridge, Oxford, or St. Andrews. If economics is your passion, you can spend a summer or a year engaging in finance, accounting, management, and more at the London School of Economics.

Many travelers also structure their trips by the **work** that they can do along the way—either odd jobs as they go, or full-time stints in cities where they plan to stay for some time. Whether you'd like to take an internship in Parliament or teach, you can do so through a variety of organizations.

 Start your search at ▨ **www.beyondtourism.com,** *Let's Go's* brand-new searchable database of Alternatives to Tourism, where you can find exciting feature articles and helpful program listings divided by country, continent, and type.

VOLUNTEERING

Volunteering can be one of the most fulfilling experiences you have in life, especially if you combine it with the thrill of traveling in a new place. Though Britain and Ireland are considered wealthy in worldwide terms, there is no shortage of aid organizations to benefit the very real issues the region faces. Civil strife continues to challenge Northern Ireland, Britain's stunning landscapes and wildlife face threats of industrialization and ill-maintenance, and larger urban communities throughout the region suffer difficulties such as housing shortages.

Most people who volunteer in Britain and Ireland do so on a short-term basis, at organizations that make use of drop-in or once-a-week volunteers. These can be found in virtually every city and are referenced both in this section and in our town and city write-ups themselves. The best way to find opportunities that match your interests and schedule may be to check with local or national volunteer centers that list several options. **CharitiesDirect.com** offers extensive listings and profiles on hundreds of charities in the UK, and can serve as an excellent tool in researching volunteer options. The **Council on International Educational Exchange** (☎207-553-7600; www.ciee.org) offers a searchable online database listing volunteer opportunities according to region and project type. Northern Ireland's **Volunteer Development Agency** (☎028 9023 6100; www.volunteeringni.org) responds to enquiries concerning volunteer opportunities and hopes an annual Volunteer Week in early June. Their Freephone (☎0800 052 2212) connects callers to local volunteer bureaus listing services sites.

More intensive volunteer services may charge you a fee to participate. These costs can be surprisingly hefty (although they frequently cover airfare and most living expenses). Many people choose to go through a parent organization that takes care of logistical details and often provides a group environment and support system. There are two main types of organizations—religious and non-sectarian—although there are rarely restrictions on participation for either.

PEACE PROCESS

The conflict in Northern Ireland has plagued Britain and Ireland for centuries. It has resulted in violence from both sides and all over the UK. Demanding international attention, the peace process has been in the works for over 30 years. Volunteering for these organizations is a particularly good opportunity for foreigners whose primary objective is peace, not the furthering of one side over the other.

Corrymeela Community, Corrymeela Centre, 5 Drumaroan Rd., Ballycastle BT54 6QU (☎028 2076 2626; www.corrymeela.org). A residential community committed to bringing Protestants and Catholics together to work for peace. Volunteer openings from 1 wk. to 1 yr. Ages 18-30 preferred for long-term positions.

Northern Ireland Volunteer Development Agency, Annsgate House, 70-74 Anne St., Belfast, BT1 4EH (☎0232 236 100; info.nivda.@cinni.org), helps arrange individual and group volunteer efforts in Northern Ireland. IAVE membership fees for individuals US$30 per year; groups US$100.

Volunteers for Peace, 1034 Tiffany Rd., Belmont, VT 05730, USA (☎802-259-2759; www.vfp.org), arranges 2- to 3-week placements in work camps. Membership required for registration. Programs average US$200-500.

Kilcranny House, 21 Cranagh Rd., Coleraine BT51 3NN (☎028 7032 1816; www.kilcrannyhouse.org). A residential, educational, and resource center that provides a safe space for Protestants and Catholics to explore issues of non-violence, prejudice awareness, and conflict resolution. Volunteering opportunities from 6 mo. to 2 yr. Food and accommodation provided. £20 per wk. Drivers (23+) preferred.

Northern Ireland Volunteer Development Agency, Annsgate House, 70-74 Ann St., Belfast, BT1 4EH (☎028 9023 6100; www.ni.co.uk), arranges individual and group volunteer efforts in Northern Ireland. Individual fee US$30 per year; groups US$100.

Volunteers for Peace, 1034 Tiffany Rd., Belmont, VT 05730, USA (☎802-259-2759; www.vfp.org), arranges 2- to 3-week placements in work camps. Membership required for registration. Programs average US$200-400.

Volunteering Ireland, Coleraine House, Coleraine St., Dublin 7, Ireland (☎01 872 2622; www.volunteeringireland.com), offers opportunities for individuals or groups in various volunteering and advocacy settings.

Ulster Quaker Service Committee, 541 Lisburn Rd., Belfast BT9 7GQ (☎028 9020 1444; www.ulsterquakerservice.com), runs programs for Protestant and Catholic children from inner-city Belfast. 6-8 wk. summer posts and 1-2 yr. posts available. Short-term volunteers 18+, long-term volunteers 21+.

ALTERNATIVES TO TOURISM

CONSERVATION AND ARCHAEOLOGY

Britain's national parks and scenic natural landscapes provide idyllic venues for community service opportunities, from trail maintenance to archaeological expeditions. The largest organization in Britain for environmental conservation is the **British Trust for Conservation Volunteers (BTCV)**, 36 St. Mary's St., Wallingford, Oxfordshire OX10 0EU (☎01302 572 244; www.btcv.org). Their counterpart in Northern Ireland is **Conservation Volunteers Northern Ireland,** Beech House, 159 Ravenhill Rd., Belfast BT6 0BP (☎028 9064 5169; www.cvni.org). Many national parks have volunteer programs—the **Association of National Park Authorities** can contact individual park offices (see **National Parks,** p. 52). **i-to-i,** 190 East 9th Ave., Ste. 320, Denver, CO 80203, USA (☎800-985-4864; i-to-i.com), also lists opportunities for historical conservation in Ireland.

Archaeological Institute of America, Boston University, 656 Beacon St., Boston, MA 02215-2006, USA (☎617-353-9361; www.archaeological.org). The *Archaeological Fieldwork Opportunities Bulletin,* available on the website, lists fieldwork volunteer opportunities throughout Britain and Ireland with a wide range of costs and durations.

Earthwatch, 3 Clock Tower Pl., Ste. 100, Box 75, Maynard, MA 01754, USA (☎800-776-0188 or 978-461-0081; www.earthwatch.org) or **Earthwatch Europe,** 267 Banbury Rd., Oxford OX2 7HT (☎0186 531 8838, www.earthwatch.org/europe). Arranges 1- to 3-wk. programs to promote conservation of natural resources, awareness of endangered animal populations (such as the Eagles of Mull), and the study of archaeological remnants (like dinosaur footprints in Yorkshire). Fees vary based on location and duration, ranging from US$700 to US$4000 plus airfare.

Hessilhead Wildlife Rescue Trust, Gateside, Beith, KA15 1HT (☎01505 502 415; www.hessilhead.org.uk). Volunteers monitor and tend wild birds and mammals in Scotland. Accommodation provided. 2 wk. min. 16+.

The National Trust, Volunteering and Community Involvement Office, Rowan, Kembrey Park, Swindon, Wiltshire SN2 8YL (☎0870 609 5383; www.nationaltrust.org.uk/volunteering). Arranges numerous volunteer opportunities, including working holidays.

Orkney Seal Rescue, Dyke End, St. Margaret's Hope, Orkney KW17 2TJ (☎01856 831 463; selkiesave@aol.com), cares for orphaned seal pups in preparation for their return to the wild. Accommodation provided. 4 wk. min. £30 per wk. 18+.

Royal Society for the Protection of Birds (RSPB), UK Headquarters, The Lodge, Sandy, Bedfordshire SG19 2DL (☎01767 680 551; www.rspb.org.uk). Volunteer opportunities range from a day constructing nestboxes in East Anglia to several months monitoring invertebrates in the Highlands. Work for all levels of experience and for any duration.

The Wildlife Trusts, The Kiln, Waterside, Mather Rd., Newark, Nottinghamshire NG24 1WT (☎0870 036 7711; www.wildlifetrusts.org). Includes volunteer openings in conjunction with their 47 local Wildlife Trusts. Durations vary greatly.

WWF, Panda House, Weyside Park, Godalming, Surrey GU7 1XR (☎01483 426444; www.wwf.org.uk). Extensive conservation organization that lists volunteer opportunities from publicity to panda-keeping.

YOUTH AND THE COMMUNITY

There are countless social service opportunities offered in Britain and Ireland, including mentoring youths, working in homeless shelters, promoting mental health, andy any number of more specific concerns. The following represents a sampling of options; many more can be discovered upon further research.

Big Brothers Big Sisters of the United Kingdom, 1d Yukon Rd., London SW12 9PZ (☎020 8673 3030; www.mentors.org.uk). A mentoring program for youths in need of guidance on a longer term basis. Local agencies in Bristol, Birmingham, London, Edinburgh and Glasgow. **Big Brothers Big Sisters of Galway,** The Health Advice Cafe, 14 Francis St., Galway, Ireland (☎091 535 375), is the branch in the Republic of Ireland.

Christian Aid: Great Britain: 35 Lower Marsh, Waterloo, London SE1 7RL (☎020 7620 4444; www.christian-aid.org.uk). **The Republic:** 17 Clanwilliam Terr., Grand Canal Dock, Dublin 2 (☎01 6110 801). **Northern Ireland:** 30 Wellington Park, Belfast BT9 6DL (☎028 9038 1204). Individuals or groups of volunteers work in various fundraising and administrative roles, occasionally for a small stipend.

Citizens Advice Bureau, 39 High St., Stamford, Lincolnshire PE9 2BB (☎08701 22 44 22, M 10am-1pm, Tu 10am-3:30pm, W 5 pm-7 pm, F 10am-1pm; www.citizensadvice.org.uk). Addresses issues from employment to finance to personal relationships.

Community Service Volunteers, 237 Pentonville Rd., London, N1 9NJ (☎020 7278 6601; www.csv.org.uk). Part- and full-time volunteer opportunities with the homeless, the disabled, and underprivileged youth.

Habitat for Humanity Great Britain, 11 Parsons St., Banbury OX16 5LW (☎01295 264 240; www.habitatforhumanity.org.uk). Volunteers build houses in and around London. The website contains a list of work sites. Short-term programs US$1500-2000. **Habitat for Humanity Ireland,** Quadrant House, Chapelizod, Dublin 20, Ireland (☎086 384 2775; www.habitatireland.ie), offers the same services in the Republic of Ireland.

Mental Health Ireland, Mensana House, 6 Adelaide St., Dún Laoghaire, Co. Dublin, Ireland (☎01 284 1186; www.mentalhealthireland.ie). Fundraising, housing, and promoting mental health. Opportunities listed in newsletter, *Mensana News,* available online.

Simon Community of Ireland, 28-30 Exchequer St., Dublin 2, Ireland (☎01 671 1606; www.simoncommunity.com). Work and live in homeless shelters. 6 mo. min. 18+.

Service Civil International (SCI), SCI USA, 5474 Walnut Level Rd., Crozet, VA 22932, USA (☎434-823-9003; www.sciint.org), arranges placement in work camps. 18+.

DISABILITIES

The Disability Rights Commission recently launched an Educating for Equality campaign in Britain, designed to ensure the equal rights of individuals with disabilities in the education system. Despite this progressive measure and an increasing attitude of acceptance and tolerance, those possessing physical and mental handicaps continue to face discrimination in Britain and Ireland. Volunteer opportunities in this category include venues concerned with aiding the special needs of these individuals as well as boosting an attitude of acceptance and mutual respect.

Association of Camphill Communities, 56 Welham Rd., Malton, North Yorkshire YO17 9DP (☎01653 694197; www.camphill.org.uk). Private communities advocate Christian values and cater to both children and adults with special needs. Volunteers work from 3 mo. to 2 yr. Food, accommodation, and stipend provided. 18+.

International Volunteer Program (IVP), 678 13th St., Ste. 100, Oakland, CA 94612, USA (☎510-433-0414; www.ivpsf.org). Lists 6-wk. volunteer programs working with the disabled, the elderly, and underprivileged youth. US$1500, includes food, travel and accommodations. 18+.

The Share Centre, Smith's Strand, Lisnaskea, Co. Fermanagh, Northern Ireland BT92 0EQ (☎028 677 22122; www.sharevillage.org). Volunteer openings include outdoors and arts activities leaders. Opportunities range from 1 wk. to 1 yr. Food and accommodation provided. 16+.

ALTERNATIVES TO TOURISM

Winged Fellowship Trust, Angel House, 20-32 Pentonville Rd., London N1 9XD (☎020 7833 2594; www.wft.org.uk). Volunteers care for disabled people for 1-2 wk. working holidays. Food and accommodation provided. 16+.

Worcestershire Lifestyles, Woodside Lodge, Lark Hill Rd., Worcester WR5 2EF (☎01905 350 686; worcestershire-lifestyles.org.uk). Working one-on-one with disabled adults. Accommodation and weekly stipend provided. 18+.

STUDYING

VISA INFORMATION
As of November 2003, citizens of Australia, Canada, New Zealand, and the US require a visa if they plan to study in Britain or Ireland for longer than six months. Consult www.ukvisas.gov.uk to determine if you require a visa. Immigration officials will request a letter of acceptance from your UK university and proof of funding for your first year of study, as well as a valid passport from all people wishing to study in the UK. Student visas cost about US$66 and application forms can be obtained through the website listed above.

Study abroad programs range from basic language and culture courses to college-level classes. In order to choose a program that best fits your needs, research cost, duration, and type of accommodation as well as what kind of students participate in the program before making your decision. The **British Council** is an invaluable source of information. (10 Spring Gardens, London SW1A 2BN. ☎0207 930 8466; www.britishcouncil.org.) Devoted to educational mobility, the **Council for International Education** is another valuable resource. (9-17 St. Albans Pl., London N1 ONX. ☎0207 288 4330; www.ukcosa.org.uk.)

For accommodations, dorm life provides a better opportunity to mingle with fellow students, but there is less of a chance to experience the local scene. If you live with a family, there is a potential to build lifelong friendships with locals and to experience day-to-day life, but conditions can vary greatly from family to family.

UNIVERSITIES

Tens of thousands of international students study abroad in Britain and Ireland every year, drawn by the prestige of some of the world's oldest and most renowned universities. Apply early, as larger institutions fill up fast.

AMERICAN PROGRAMS

Studying abroad through an American program makes your life significantly easier in terms of arranging for course credit, planning your trip, orientation once you arrive, and support during your stay. The following is a list of organizations that can help place students abroad; you can search for more at **www.studyabroad.com**.

American Institute for Foreign Study, College Division, River Plaza, 9 West Broad St., Stamford, CT 06902, USA (☎800-727-2437, ext. 5163; www.aifsabroad.com), organizes programs for high school and college study in universities in Britain and Ireland.

Arcadia University for Education Abroad, 450 S. Easton Rd., Glenside, PA 19038, USA (☎866-927-2234; www.arcadia.edu/cea), operates programs at many universities throughout Britain. Costs range from US$3,450 (summer) to US$36,390 (1 yr.).

Butler University Institute for Study Abroad, 1100 W. 42nd St., Ste. 305, Indianapolis, IN 46208, USA (☎317-940-9336 or 800-858-0229; www.ifsa-butler.org), organizes both term-time and summer study at British and Irish universities, including orientation and daytrips. Prices vary greatly by location; US$3375 (summer) to US$30,000 (1 yr.).

Central College Abroad, Office of International Education, 812 University, Pella, IA, 50219, USA (☎800-831-3629 or 641-628-5284; www.central.edu/abroad), offers internships, as well as semester (US$10,000-14,000) and year-long (US$25,000-27,000) programs in Britain. US$30 application fee.

Council on International Educational Exchange (CIEE), 7 Custom House St., 3rd Floor, Portland, ME 01401, USA (☎800-407-8839; www.ciee.org/study), sponsors work, volunteer, academic, and internship programs in Britain and Ireland.

Institute for the International Education of Students (IES), 33 N. LaSalle St., 15th fl., Chicago, IL 60602, USA (☎800-995-2300; www.IESabroad.org), offers year-long (US$21,700-23,000), semester (US$12,000), and summer programs in London and Dublin. Internship opportunities. US$50 application fee. Scholarships available.

International Association for the Exchange of Students for Technical Experience (IAESTE), 10400 Little Patuxent Pkwy. Ste. 250, Columbia, MD 21044, USA (☎410-997-2200; www.aipt.org), offers 8- to 12-week programs in the UK for college students who have completed 2 years of technical study. US$50 application fee.

International Partnership for Service-Learning, 815 2nd Ave., Ste. 315, New York, NY 10017, USA (☎212-986-0989; www.ipsl.org), seeks to unite service and study at the University of Surrey Roehampton in London. Courses relating to volunteer work can be combined in semester (US$10,100) or full yr. (US$19,900) programs.

School for International Training, College Semester Abroad, Admissions, Kipling Rd., P.O. Box 676, Brattleboro, VT 05302, USA (☎800-257-7751 or 802-257-7751; www.sit.edu). Semester- and year-long programs in Britain and Ireland run US$10,600-13,700. Also runs the **Experiment in International Living** (☎800-345-2929; www.usexperiment.org), 3- to 5-week summer programs that offer high-school students cross-cultural homestays, community service, ecological adventure, and language training in Britain and Ireland and cost US$1900-5200.

BRITISH PROGRAMS

Many universities accommodate international students for summer, single-term, or full-year study. The most direct means to gather more information is to contact the university that interests you. Those listed below are only a few that open their gates to foreign students; the British Council (see p. 62) provides information on additional universities. Prices listed provide approximate estimate of university fees for non-EU citizens; in most cases room and board are not included. Also note that medical and other laboratory-based programs are more expensive.

University of Cambridge, Cambridge Admissions Office (CAO), 8/9 Jesus Ln., Cambridge CB5 8BA (☎01223 337733; www.cam.ac.uk). Open to overseas applicants for summer (£595-845) or year-long study (£8088-10,596).

University of Edinburgh, The International Office, University of Edinburgh, 57 George Sq., Edinburgh EH8 9JU (☎0131 650 4301; www.ed.ac.uk) offers summer programs (£1500) and year-long courses for international students (£12,400).

University of Glasgow, Student Recruitment and Admissions Service, University of Glasgow, 1 The Square, Glasgow G12 8QQ (☎0141 330 6150; www.gla.ac.uk), offers year-long courses (£7700-9700).

University of Leeds, Study Abroad Office, Leeds, West Yorkshire LS2 9JT (☎0133 343 4046; www.leeds.ac.uk/students/study-abroad). One of largest universities in England, the University offers semester (£3800) and full yr. (£7250) study abroad programs.

ALTERNATIVES TO TOURISM

University College London, Gower St., London WC1E 6BT (☎020 7679 2000; www.ucl.ac.uk). In the center of London. Various year-long programs (£9730-12,650).

London School of Economics, The Admissions Officer, London School of Economics, P.O. Box 13401, Houghton St., London WC2A 2AS (☎020 7955 7124; www.lse.ac.uk). Year- long courses for international students (about £10,000).

University of Oxford, College Admissions Office, Wellington Sq., Oxford OX1 2JD (☎0186 527 0105; www.admin.ox.ac.uk/io). Large range of summer programs (£400-4000) as well as semester- and year-long courses (£8900-£10,500).

University of St. Andrews, Application Centre, Old Union Building, North St., St. Andrews, Fife KY16 9AJ (☎01334 462150; www.st-andrews.ac.uk/services/admissions/intstud), welcomes students for term-time study. Also houses **Scottish Studies Summer Program,** Room C1, Old Union Building (☎01334 462238; www.st-andrews.ac.uk/admissions/summskool.htm). Courses in history, art history, literature, and music of the region for high-school students (£2500 all inclusive).

University of Westminster, International Education Office, 16 Little Tichfield St., London W1W 7UW (☎020 7911 5769; www.wmin.ac.uk/international), offers a range of semester (£3300) and full-year (£6600) programs of study in Schools of Biosciences, Integrated Health, Computer Science, Digital Technology and Design.

IRISH PROGRAMS

Most American undergraduates enroll in programs sponsored by US universities. Local universities in Ireland can be much cheaper, though it may be more difficult to receive academic credit. Some schools that offer study abroad programs to international students are listed below.

Irish Studies Summer School, USIT NOW, 19-21 Aston Quay, Dublin 2, Ireland (☎01 602 1777; www.usitnow.ie). 7-week-long program (€6150) offering courses in Irish history and contemporary culture. USIT also administrates the summer program **Ireland in Europe,** a 2-wk. course focusing on Irish civilization (€1550-1865).

National University of Ireland, Galway, University Rd., Galway, Ireland (☎091 524 411; www.nuigalway.ie), offers half- or full-year opportunities (€4660-12,200) for junior-year students who meet the college's entry requirements. Summer school courses include Irish Studies, Gaelic Language, and Creative Writing. Fees vary by field.

Queen's University Belfast, International Office, Belfast BT7 1NN, Northern Ireland (☎028 9097 5088; www.qub.ac.uk/ilo). Study in Belfast for a semester (UK£3305) or a full year (UK£6610).

Trinity College Dublin, Office of International Student Affairs, East Theatre, Trinity College, Dublin 2, Ireland (☎01 608 3150; www.tcd.ie/isa), offers semester or year programs of undergraduate courses for visiting students. Fees €4574-21,300.

University College Cork, International Education Office, West Wing, University College, Cork, Ireland (☎021-490-2543; www.ucc.ie/international). Students can choose from a wide array of subjects and classes. Semester €5605, full year €22,365.

University College Dublin, International Summer School, Newman House, 86 St. Stephen's Green, Dublin 2, Ireland (☎01 475 2004; www.ucd.ie/summerschool). A 2½ week international summer course on Irish culture. Fees €695, students €635.

University of Ulster, Shore Rd., Newtownabbey, Co. Antrim BT37 0QB, Northern Ireland (☎08 700 400 700; www.ulst.ac.uk/international), offers semester- or year-long programs for visiting international students. Fees UK£2650-7315.

A LEARNING EXPERIENCE
An education on the other side of the Atlantic.

When I started to think about my year off between high school and college, the furthest possibility from my mind was participating in any program that was remotely academic. I was interested in going abroad, however, and my desire to travel soon overwhelmed my aversion to academics. In the fall of 1999, then, freshly graduated from high school and with a year of freedom ahead of me, I moved to Oxford, England to spend a semester at Oxford Tutorial College.

I participated in a program for students taking a "gap year"—European for "year off"—and while I did meet other Americans, I also met students from Russia, England, Ireland and Switzerland.

I took three classes at Oxford: English literature, creative writing, and sociology. My literature and writing groups were both small, with just seven or eight students per class, and sociology became a one-on-one tutorial after the other students in the class switched into other courses early in the semester.

One benefit of going to Oxford Tutorial was that many of the teachers were young men and women either putting themselves through graduate school or teaching at a few different schools in the area. By mid-semester, many students I knew were playing sports with their teachers on the weekends, or meeting up for a beer after class. In some cases, teachers became mentors and trusted friends as well as instructors.

Now that I can reflect on my experience in England as it relates to my four years of college in America, I see major differences between the educational systems in which I have studied. First, at Oxford, all students were encouraged to work one or two days a week at an internship organized through the school. I spent one day a week working at a school for autistic children. My experience at this school was one that prepared me well for college. I was given no formal training in working with mentally handicapped children, but I was taught instead to learn from example and to do outside research on autism to supplement what I learned in the classroom and from interacting with the children. This experience prepared me well for the world of Harvard where students, rather than being spoon-fed, must learn to be aggressive about getting the most out of one's education.

Another difference between the systems at Oxford Tutorial College and at my American university was the very existence and protocol of the tutorial itself at Oxford. In my English literature class, each student was expected to meet with the teacher once a week to discuss readings and papers. When we wrote papers, we read them out loud to our teachers in tutorial. I will never forget the shock of finding out that I had to read a five-page paper out loud to a virtual stranger. My literature teacher, Royce, was young and very hip, and as I got to know him better, I felt more and more comfortable in our meetings—but at first I was terrified. This fear was, of course, the point. As I see it now, reading a paper aloud is a way of owning one's work in a way that I had never before experienced. This challenge dealt me by Oxford, to really experience what I had written, was a valuable one.

Reflecting on my experience now, I am struck by how great a part of my international experience took place in bars. This may sound ridiculous, but it's true. While a social life was similarly important in my four years of American college, in England, four years were compressed into four months. My roommate and I would go home after school every day to do our schoolwork, but most nights found us leaving again at ten or eleven to meet up with friends from school. Though I did take my schoolwork in England seriously, the very nature of going abroad for a semester begs one to experience all aspects of life in a new place. For this reason, my most enduring memories are of moments outside the classroom, of exploring Oxford alongside people from many different places and cultures.

Lily Brown graduated from Harvard University in 2004 with a degree in Women, Gender, and Sexuality Studies.

WORKING

WORK PERMIT AND VISA INFORMATION. European Economic Area (EEA) nationals (member countries include EU member states and Iceland, Liechtenstein, and Norway) do not need a work permit to work in the UK. If you live in a Commonwealth country (including Australia, Canada, and New Zealand) and if your parents or grandparents were born in the UK, you can apply for **UK Ancestry-Employment** and work without a permit. Commonwealth citizens ages 17-27 can work permit-free under a **working holiday visa.** Foreigners studying at an institution in the UK are able to work within restrictions without a work permit. American citizens who are full-time students and are over 18 can apply for a special permit from the **British Universities North America Club (BUNAC),** which allows them to work for up to six months in the UK and up to four months in Ireland. Contact BUNAC at: P.O. Box 430, Southbury, CT 06488, USA (☎203-264-0901) or 16 Bowling Green Lane, London EC1R 0QH (☎020 7251 3472; www.bunac.org.uk). Others will require a work permit to work in the UK. Applications must be made by the employer and can be obtained through the **Home Office,** Level 5, Moorfoot, Sheffield S1 4PQ (☎0114 259 4074; www.workpermits.gov.uk). Those wishing to work in the Republic of Ireland should contact the **Department of Enterprise, Trade & Employment,** Kildare St., Dublin 2 (☎01 631 2121; www.entemp.ie). As in Britain, the application for a work permit must be made by the employer. Applications for working visas must be made through your local consulate. See **Facts for the Traveler: Embassies and Consulates** (p. 11).

LONG-TERM WORK

If you plan to spend a substantial amount of time working in Britain or Ireland, search for a job well in advance. International placement agencies are often the easiest way to find employment abroad, especially for teaching English. **Internships,** usually for college students, are a good way to segue into working abroad, although they are often unpaid or poorly paid. Be wary of advertisements or companies that offer to get you a job abroad for a fee—often the same listings are available online or in newspapers. Some reputable organizations include:

Anders Glaser Wills, 1 Houndwell Pl., Southampton, SO14 1HU (☎0238 022 3511; www.andersglaserwills.com). Large job placement agency with 11 offices in Britain.

Hansard Scholar Programme, 9 Kingsway, 2nd Fl., London WC2B 6XF (☎020 7395 4000; www.hansard-society.org.uk), combines classes at the London School of Economics with internships in British government.

IAESTE–US, 10400 Little Patuxent Pkwy., Ste. 250, Columbia, MD 21044, USA (☎410-997-3069; www.aipt.org/iaeste.html), arranges paid internships from 8 wks. to 12 mo.

Working Ireland, 26 Eustace St., Templebar, Dublin 2, Ireland (☎01 677 0300; www.workingireland.ie), arranges job placement and accommodations throughout the country and provides general advice primarily for young people.

International Cooperative Education, 15 Spiros Way, Menlo Park, CA, 94025, USA (☎650-323-4944; www.icemenlo.com), finds summer jobs for students in England. Costs include a $200 application fee and a $600 fee for placement.

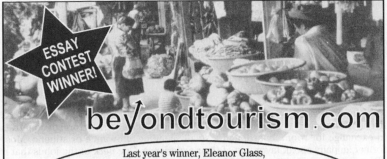

ESSAY CONTEST WINNER!

beyondtourism.com

Last year's winner, Eleanor Glass, spent a summer volunteering with children on an island off the Yucatan Peninsula. Read the rest of her story and find your own once-in-a-lifetime experience at www.beyondtourism.com!

"... I was discovering elements of life in Mexico that I had never even dreamt of. I regularly had meals at my students' houses, as their fisherman fathers would instruct them to invite the nice gringa to lunch after a lucky day's catch. Downtown, tourists wandered the streets and spent too much on cheap necklaces, while I played with a friend's baby niece, or took my new kitten to the local vet for her shots, or picked up tortillas at the tortilleria, or vegetables in the mercado. ... I was lucky that I found a great place to volunteer and a community to adopt me. ... Just being there, listening to stories, hearing the young men talk of cousins who had crossed the border, I know I went beyond tourism." - Eleanor Glass, 2004

LET'S GO

ALTERNATIVES TO TOURISM

TEACHING ENGLISH

The British school system is comprised of **state** (public, government-funded), **public** (independent, privately funded), and **international** (often for children of expatriates) schools, as well as **universities.** The academic year is divided into **autumn** (September to Christmas), **spring** (early January to Easter) and **summer** (Easter to late July) terms. Applications to teach at state schools must be made through the local government; independent and international schools must be applied to individually. University positions are typically only available through fellowship or exchange programs.

A graduate teaching degree is usually sufficient for casual or "supply" teaching positions that are paid by the day. To obtain a permanent position, you must have **Qualified Teacher Status (QTS).** The government-run **Teacher Training Agency** (☎0845 600 0991; www.canteach.gov.uk.) manages teacher qualification and provides general guidelines for those wishing to teach in the UK. European Union-qualified teachers can work in the UK. The **British Council** (p. 62) has extensive information for people wishing to teach abroad. A good website for information on student teaching in Ireland is **Americans in Ireland** (www.geocities.com/teachingirish). Placement agencies are useful in finding teaching jobs, although vacancies are also listed in major newspapers. The following organizations may be of help.

Council for International Exchange of Scholars, 3007 Tilden St. NW, Ste. 5L, Washington DC 20008, USA (☎202-686-4000; www.cies.org), administers the Fulbright program for faculty and professionals.

Eteach, Academy House, 403 London Rd., Camberley, Surrey GU15 3HL (☎0845 226 1904; www.eteach.com). Online recruitment service for teachers.

European Council of International Schools, 21B Lavant St., Petersfield, Hampshire GU32 3EL (☎01730 268244; www.ecis.org), runs recruitments services for several international schools in the UK and Ireland.

International Schools Services (ISS), 15 Roszel Rd., Box 5910, Princeton, NJ 08543-5910, USA (☎609-452-0990; fax 609-452-2690; www.iss.edu), hires teachers for more than 200 overseas schools, including some in England; candidates should have experience teaching or with international affairs, 2-year commitment expected.

The Teacher Recruitment Company, P.O. Box 6517, Burton Latimer, Kettering, Northamptonshire NN15 5XW (☎0870 922 0316; www.teachers.eu.com). International recruitment agency lists positions and provides information on jobs in the UK.

AU PAIR WORK

Au pairs are typically women (although sometimes men), aged 18-27, who work as live-in nannies, caring for children and doing light housework in foreign countries in exchange for room, board, and a small spending allowance or stipend. Most former au pairs speak favorably of their experience. One perk of the job is that it allows you to really get to know the country without the high expenses of traveling. Drawbacks, however, often include long hours of constantly being on duty and somewhat mediocre pay. Much of the au pair experience really does depend on the family with whom you're placed. The agencies below are a good starting point for looking for employment as an au pair in Britain or Ireland.

Au Pair Homestay, World Learning, Inc., 1015 15th St. NW, Suite 750, Washington, DC 20005, USA (☎800-287-2477; fax 202-408-5397).

Au Pair in Europe, P.O. Box 68056, Blakely Postal Outlet, Hamilton, Ontario, Canada L8M 3M7 (☎905-545-6305; fax 905-544-4121; www.princeent.com).

Childcare International, Ltd., Trafalgar House, Grenville Pl., London NW7 3SA (☎+44 020 8906-3116; fax 8906-3461; www.childint.co.uk).

Douglas Au Pair Agency Ltd., 28 Frankfield, Douglas, Cork, Ireland (☎/fax 01 489 1489; www.aupairhere.com), accepts applications for au pair positions in Ireland.

Dublin Childcare Recruitment Agency, Newcourt House, Strandville Ave., Clontarf, Dublin 3, Ireland (☎01 833 2281; www.childcare-recruitment.com).

InterExchange, 161 Sixth Ave., New York, NY 10013, USA (☎212-924-0446; fax 924-0575; www.interexchange.org).

Shamrock Au Pair Agency, Magheree, Kilmorony, Athy, Co. Kildare, Ireland (☎01 507 25533; www.aupairireland.com).

SHORT-TERM WORK

Traveling for long periods of time can get expensive; therefore, many travelers try their hand at odd jobs for a few weeks at a time to help finance another month or two of touring around. Though Britain typically does not issue work permits for short-term manual or domestic labor, a popular option is to work several hours at a hostel in exchange for free or discounted room and/or board. Pub work is widely available and may not require a permit, depending on the attitude of your employer. Most often, these short-term jobs are found by word of mouth, or simply by talking to the owner of a hostel or restaurant. Due to the high turnover in the tourism industry, many places are eager for help, even if it is only temporary. *Let's Go* tries to list temporary jobs like these whenever possible; look in the Practical Information sections of larger cities. **Vacation Work Publications,** 9 Park End St., Oxford, OX1 1HJ (☎01865 241 978; www.vacationwork.co.uk) publishes books on working overseas and maintains an up-to-date database of seasonal jobs in many countries including the UK. **BUNAC** (p. 66) has listings for establishments that have employed short-term workers in the past.

ENGLAND. Most English cities and larger towns have job spaces to fill, especially during the **high season,** and mainly in pubs or restaurants. **Brighton** (p. 159) is especially friendly to younger people looking for temporary work. Job hunting may be harder in the northern cities, where unemployment is higher. TICs can often be a good place to start your search (many post listings on their bulletin boards), though you will also be advised simply to check newspapers or individual establishments. **Job placement organizations** arrange temporary jobs in service or office industries. They can be found in most cities, including the Manpower office in **Manchester** (p. 355), Blue Arrow in **Cambridge** (p. 318) and throughout the southwest, and JobCentres throughout England. **Bournemouth** (p. 210), **Bristol** (p. 201), **Exeter** (p. 216), **Newquay** (p. 239) and **Torquay** (p. 228) are all good places to look for temporary work. The YHA website (www.yha.org.uk) lists openings for "general assistants"; you can also inquire personally at independent **hostels.**

WALES. Many areas of Wales are economically depressed and suffer unemployment rates higher than the British average. Picking up short-term work as a traveler may be more of a challenge here than in England. **Cardiff** (p. 454), a large, well-touristed city, is perhaps the most feasible option, especially during rugby season; smaller towns may have listings posted at TICs or outside markets. Opportunities for YHA hostel work extend to Wales as well as England (see above).

SCOTLAND. **Edinburgh** (p. 546) is an excellent place to look for short-term work, especially during Festival in August. The backpacker culture fosters plenty of opportunities, and most of the larger hostels post their own lists of job openings. **Glasgow** (p. 581) experiences a similar boom during the summer. In both cities, low-paying domestic and food service jobs are easy to procure; computer skills may net you higher-paying office work. **Inverness** has a JobCentre (p. 640) that can help you find temp placements. Archaeological digs are commonplace in both **Orkney** and **Shetland,** but the application is competitive. The fish-processing industry in Shetland (p. 688) provides hard work but good pay and excellent scenery. The SYHA hostel network has openings listed on its website (www.syha.org.uk); independent hostels also hire short-term workers from a pool of globetrotters.

IRELAND. Some of the most common forms of short-term employment in Ireland include **food service, domestic,** and **farm work.** As with all capital cities, **Dublin** and **Belfast** are good places to look for work: Dublin's Community and Youth Information Centre posts job listings (see p. 737), while **Belfast** has several placement agencies. **Galway** is another excellent city for short-term work; try FAS or the People's Resource Centre for guidance and advice (p. 793). Tourist towns in the Southwest—like **Kenmare** (p. 782), **Killarney** (p. 779), and **Dingle** (p. 784)—usually have openings during high season.

FOR FURTHER READING ON ALTERNATIVES TO TOURISM

How to Get a Job in Europe, by Sanborn and Matherly. Surrey Books, 1999 (US$22).

How to Live Your Dream of Volunteering Overseas, by Collins, DeZerega, and Heckscher. Penguin Books, 2002 (US$17).

International Directory of Voluntary Work, by Whetter and Pybus. Peterson's Guides and Vacation Work, 2000 (US$16).

International Jobs, by Kocher and Segal. Perseus Books, 1999 (US$18).

Work Abroad: The Complete Guide to Finding a Job Overseas, by Hubbs, Griffith, and Nolting. Transitions Abroad Publishing, 2000 (US$16).

Work Your Way Around the World, by Susan Griffith. Worldview Publishing Services, 2001 (US$18).

Invest Yourself: The Catalogue of Volunteer Opportunities, published by the Commission on Voluntary Service and Action (☎ 718-638-8487).

FARMING IN BRITAIN AND IRELAND

Working on a farm offers a chance to get away from the urban sprawl of London and the big cities and to wander for a time among sheep rather than tourist hordes. Run by the Home Office, the **Season Agricultural Workers Scheme** is a youth-oriented program that facilitates the placement of overseas nationals, especially students age 18-25, in seasonal positions in the agricultural industry. For more information, contact the Managed Migration division of the Home Office (☎0114 259 4074; www.workpermits.gov.uk). Below are a few organizations that can help set up short-term work and exchange programs in the farming industry:

Fruitful Ltd., Unit 3 Ind. Est., Honeybourne, Evesham, Worcester, WR11 7QF (☎0870 727 0050; www.fruitfuljobs.com), sets up farm work for backpackers and students all over the UK; online application available.

Irish Organic Farmers & Growers Association, Harbour Building, Harbour Rd., Kilbeggan, Westmeath (☎01 0506 32563; www.irishorganic.ie), maintains a list of organic farms across Ireland that offer work experience to students and other individuals interested in organic farming.

World Wide Opportunities on Organic Farms (WWOOF), P.O. Box 2675, Lewes, East Sussex BN7 1RB (www.wwoof.org), offers a list of organic farms across Britain and Ireland that welcome volunteer workers.

ENGLAND

This blessed plot, this earth, this realm, this England...
 —William Shakespeare, *Richard II*

While the terms "Great Britain" and "England" may seem interchangeable, England is in fact only one part, along with Scotland and Wales, of the island of Great Britain, the largest of the British Isles, which together with Northern Ireland forms Her Majesty's United Kingdom of Great Britain and Northern Ireland (more concisely known as the **UK**). United itself by the end of the first millennium AD, England had conquered Wales and Ireland by the 17th century, and Scotland in 1707. The Republic of Ireland won its independence in 1921, and while Wales and Scotland have long been a part of a nation administrated primarily from London, they are, like Ireland, separate and distinct lands with their own languages, culture, and customs. This chapter focuses on the history, literature, and culture of England; **Wales** (p. 445) and **Scotland** (p. 533) are treated separately, as are **Northern Ireland** (p. 695) and the **Republic of Ireland** (p. 722).

LIFE AND TIMES

ENGLAND OF OLDE

THE SCEPTERED ISLE. Once part of the continental landmass, Britain's first residents migrated from Europe. Only when the land bridge was severed (c. 6000-5000 BC) did the island colony physically and culturally develop its insular character. While little is known about the island's prehistoric residents, the megalithic, astronomically precise, and mysterious stone circles left behind at **Stonehenge** (p. 192) and **Avebury** (p. 192) testify to their technological prowess. Seeking shelter on Britain's isolated shores, **Celts** and **Druids** emigrated from the continent in the first millennium BC, only to be subdued by the carnage-loving armies of Emperor Claudius in AD 43. Despite agitation by Celtic warrior-queen **Boudicca,** by the end of the first century the **Romans** held all of "Britannia" (England and Wales) as their northernmost colony, having established cities at **Londinium** (London) and **Verulamium** (**St. Albans**, p. 258), as well as a resort spa (**Bath**, p. 193). Expansion north was to prove more difficult. To guard the northwest frontier from barbarian invaders, the Romans constructed **Hadrian's Wall** (p. 436) in the second century AD. The fourth century saw the decline of the Roman Empire in the face of increased raids. The Angles and Saxons—tribes from Denmark and northern Germany—were particularly successful invaders, establishing their own settlements and kingdoms in the south. The name "England" derives from "Anglaland," land of the Angles.

THE CONQUERORS. Christianity caught on in AD 597 when missionary **Augustine** converted King Æthelbert of the House of Wessex and founded England's first papal church at **Canterbury** (p. 141). From the 8th to the 10th century, Norsemen sacked Scotland, Ireland, and the north, while Danish Vikings raided England's east coast. In AD 878, legendary **Alfred the Great** defeated the Danes, curtailing their rapidly expanding influence. In the 11th century, **Edward the Confessor** allegedly brought about the end of the Anglo-Saxon dynasty by promising the throne to an up-and-coming Norman named William. Better known as **The Conqueror,** William I invaded the island in 1066, won the pivotal **Battle of Hastings** (p. 154), slaughtered his rival Harold II (and for good measure, his two brothers), and promptly set about cataloguing his new English acquisitions—down to each peasant, cow, and bale of hay—in the epic **Domesday Book** (p. 154). Able administrator as well as tyrant, William introduced **feudalism** to Britain during the "Norman yoke," doling out vast tracts of land to the king's cronies and subjugating English tenants to French lords. English was marginalized as Norman French became the language of the educated elite and Latin remained the language of the church; Henry IV (crowned 1399) was the next king whose mother tongue was English.

BLOOD AND DEMOCRACY. The Middle Ages were a time of bloody conquest and infighting. Henry Plantagenet ascended to the throne as Henry II in 1154, armed with an healthy inheritance and a dowry from his wife Eleanor of Aquitaine (King Louis VII of France's ex) that made him lord of most of France. During his reign he quelled interior uprisings and spread his influence north to Cumbria, Northumberland, and west to Ireland, proclaiming himself overlord in 1171. His notorious squabbles with the insubordinate Archbishop of Canterbury Thomas Becket resulted in Becket's murder (and immediate popular canonization) at **Canterbury Cathedral** (p. 144). Henry's son **Richard the Lionheart** was more interested in the Crusades than domestic insurgents and spent only six months of his 10-year reign on the island. Tired of such royal pains, noblemen forced his hapless brother and successor, King John, to sign the **Magna Carta** in 1215. Though the immediate impact was limited, the document is often seen as the precursor to modern English democracy; the first **Parliament** convened 50 years later. Defying this move toward egalitarian rule, **Edward I** absorbed Wales under the English crown in 1284 and waged war against the Scots, raising some of Britain's greatest castles along the way (see **Caernarfon,** p. 508). But while English kings expanded the nation's boundaries, the **Black Death** ravaged its population, killing over one-third of all Britons between 1348 and 1361. Many more fell in the **Hundred Years' War** (or the 116 Years' War, to be precise), a costly squabble over the French throne.

In 1399, Henry Bolingbroke invaded England and usurped the throne from his cousin Richard II (on holiday in Ireland), designating his own **House of Lancaster** in control. Bolingbroke's son **Henry V** defeated the French in the **Battle of Agincourt** (1415), a legendary victory for the British underdogs that rendered the young prince heir to the French throne. But his successor's failure to stave off revived French resistance under Joan of Arc resulted in the loss of almost all their land in France. The **Wars of the Roses** (1455-85)—a lengthy crisis of royal succession between the houses of Lancaster and York (whose respective emblems were a red and a white rose)—culminated when Richard of York put his nephew, boy-king Edward V, in the Tower of London for safe-keeping. When Edward disappeared, Richard was there, conveniently, to be crowned **Richard III.**

REFORMATION, RENAISSANCE, AND REVOLUTION. The last of the Lancasters, Henry VII won the throne in 1485 after defeating Richard III at the Battle of Bosworth Field, inaugurating the rule of the **House of Tudor.** Successor **Henry VIII** reinforced England's control over the Irish while he struggled with the more intimate, domestic concern of producing a male heir. Henry's equally infamous battle with the Pope over divorce resulted in his rejection of Catholicism and the establishment of the **Anglican Church.** Protestantism's fate was initially uncertain, however, as Henry's first successor, nine-year-old Edward VI, was quickly overshadowed by the fiery personality of his half-sister, staunch Catholic **Bloody Mary,** who earned her gory nickname after ordering mass burnings of Protestants. Though held under house arrest for much of her young life, **Elizabeth I** inherited control after Mary's death, reversed the religious convictions imposed by her sister, and cemented the success of the **Reformation.** Under her extraordinary reign, Britain became the leading Protestant power in Europe, the English defeated the **Spanish Armada** in 1588, and **Sir Francis Drake** circumnavigated the globe. Henry VII's great-granddaughter, Catholic **Mary, Queen of Scots,** briefly threatened the stability of the throne in this age of unparalleled splendor. Her implication in a plot against the Queen's life led to her 20-year imprisonment and execution.

The first union of England, Wales, and Scotland effectively took place in 1603, when philosopher prince **James VI** of Scotland ascended to the throne as **James I** of England. But James and his less able successor, **Charles I,** aroused suspicion within the largely Puritan parliament with their Catholic sympathies, extravagant spending, and insistence upon the "divine right" of kings. Charles ruled without Parliament for 11 years, after which the **English Civil Wars** (1642-51) erupted. The monarchy came to a violent end with the execution of Charles I and the founding of the first British Commonwealth in 1649.

REPUBLICANISM AND RESTORATION. Oliver Cromwell emerged as the charismatic but despotic leader of the new Commonwealth. His conquest of Ireland led to the death of nearly half its population, while his oppressive measures at home (swearing and the theater were outlawed) betrayed a deep religious fanaticism. To the relief of many, the Republic collapsed under the lackluster leadership of Cromwell's son Richard. According to **Thomas Hobbes** in his 1651 treatise **Leviathan,** life was "poor, nasty, brutish, and short" in the absence of an absolute sovereign, but even the **Restoration** of **Charles II** to the throne in 1660 did not cure England's troubles. Debate raged over the exclusion of Charles's Catholic brother **James II** from the succession. Side-taking spawned England's first political parties: the **Whigs,** who insisted on exclusion, and the **Tories,** who supported hereditary succession.

LAWS AND LOGIC. James II took the throne in 1685 but lost it three years later to his son-in-law, Dutch champion of Protestantism **William of Orange,** in the bloodless and **Glorious Revolution of 1688.** After James fled to France, William and his wife Mary ensured the Protestantism of future kings with their **Bill of Rights.** Supporters of James II (called **Jacobites**) remained a threat until 1745, when James II's grandson Charles (commonly known as **Bonnie Prince Charlie**) failed in his attempt to invade and recapture the throne (p. 538). The ascension of William and Mary marked the end of a century of upheaval and the debut of a more liberal age in which Britain rose to economic and political superstardom. By the end of the **Seven Years' War** (1756-1763), Britain controlled Canada and 13 unruly colonies to the south, as well as much of the Caribbean. Meanwhile, **Sir Isaac Newton** theorized the laws of gravity and invented calculus on the side, while **John Locke** cleared the philosophical slate by developing the theory of **empiricism.** Increased secularism was countered mid-century by a wave of religious fervor, with Bible-thumping **Methodists** preaching to outdoor crowds. Parliament prospered thanks to the ineffectual leadership of the Hanoverian kings, **George I, II,** and **III.** The Prime Minister eclipsed the monarchy as the seat of power, held by master negotiator **Robert Walpole,** fiery orator **William Pitt the Elder,** and first income-taxer **Pitt the Younger.**

EMPIRE AND INDUSTRY. At the start of the 18th century, British society ranged, in the words of **Daniel Defoe,** from "the great who lived profusely" to the "the miserable that really pinch and want." Attaining rule over more than one quarter of the world's population and two-fifths of its land during the 18th and 19th century, the British empire was even more diverse. This domination initially stemmed from private companies working in overseas trade—control of the Cape of Good Hope secured shipping routes to the Far East, while plantations in the New World produced lucrative staples like sugar and rum. The **Napoleonic Wars** (1800-15) marked the renewal of the Anglo-French rivalry and further colonization. By 1858, India, jewel of the imperial crown, was headlining a list that included Ceylon (Sri Lanka), South Africa, Hong Kong, the Falkland Islands, Australia, New Zealand, and the Western Pacific islands. In addition to the economic imperative, Britons consid-

ENGLAND

ered it their moral duty to "civilize" the non-Christians of their imperial domain. Despite losing the American colonies in 1776, the proud claim that "the sun never set on the British Empire" soon bore real meaning—although, as postcolonialists would remind us, perhaps it was that the sun never rose. The **Industrial Revolution** provided Britain with the economic fuel required for this frenzied colonizing. With the perfection of the steam engine by **James Watt** in 1765 and the mechanization of the textile industry, England soared ahead in machine-driven production. Massive portions of the rural populace, pushed off the land and lured by rapidly growing opportunities in industrial employment, migrated to towns like **Manchester** (p. 354) and **Leeds** (p. 400). The age-old gulf between landowners and farmers was replaced by a wider gap between factory owners and laborers. The **gold standard,** which Britain adopted in 1821, ensured the pound's value with gold and became an international financial system, securing Britain's economic supremacy.

VICTORIA AND COMPANY. The long and stable rule of **Queen Victoria** (1837-1901) dominated the 19th century in foreign and domestic politics as well as social mores. A series of **Factory** and **Reform Acts** throughout the century limited child labor, capped the average workday, and made sweeping changes in (male) voting rights. Prime Minister **Robert Peel** restored order by establishing the London police force in 1829. Prince Albert's 1851 **Great Exhibition** denoted the high point of the imperial era; over 10,000 consumer goods from Britain's far-flung realms were assembled in London's **Crystal Palace,** an immense glass construction erected in Hyde Park. Yet while commercial self-interest defined middle-class conservatism, not everyone approved. In *Utilitarianism* (1863), John Stuart Mill argued that citizens must do the greatest good for the greatest number of people. Similar crowd-pleasing jingles were taken up by the socialist **Fabian Society** in 1884, which benefited from the literary weight of **George Bernard Shaw** and **H.G. Wells.**

By the end of the century, trade unionism strengthened and found a political voice in the **Labour Party** in 1906. Yet pressures to improve the positions of other marginalized groups proved ineffectual, as the rich and bohemian embraced *fin de siecle* decadence. Increasing troubles with Ireland plagued the nation for half a century, and Prime Minister **William Gladstone's** attempts in 1886 and 1893 to introduce a **Home Rule Bill**—which would have seen the appointment of an Irish parliament to oversee the country's affairs—splintered the Liberal Party and ended in defeat (p. 727). Meanwhile, the **Suffragettes,** led by **Emmeline Pankhurst,** fought for voting rights by disrupting Parliament and staging hunger strikes. Women, however, would have to wait for the vote until after **World War I.**

A LOST GENERATION. The **Great War** (1914-1918), as WWI was known until 1939, brought British military action to the European stage, scarred the British spirit with the myth of a "lost generation," and dashed Victorian dreams of peaceful, progressive society. The technological explosion of the 19th century was manifested in horrific new weaponry coupled with outdated war strategies, resulting in unprecedented casualties on all sides. By the end of four years of fighting, almost a million British men were dead; twice as many were wounded.

The 1930s brought **depression** and mass unemployment; in a 1936 publication, social economist **John Maynard Keynes** argued that German war reparations would come to no good. That same year, King Edward VIII shocked the world and shamed the Windsor family with the announcement of his **abdication** for the sake of twice-divorced Baltimore socialite Wallis Simpson. Meanwhile, tensions in Europe escalated with the German reoccupation of the Rhineland. Prime Minister **Neville Chamberlain** pushed through a controversial (and notoriously disastrous) appeasement agreement with Hitler in Munich, naively promising "peace in our time." But following Hitler's subsequent invasion of Poland, Britain declared war on September 3, 1939, and for the second time in 25 years Europe went up in flames. Even the horror of the Great War failed to prepare the British Isles for the utter devastation of **World War II.** German air raids commenced the prolonged **Battle of Britain** in the summer of 1940. London, Coventry, and other English cities suffered extensive damage from thunderous **"blitzkriegs,"** which left scores of Britons orphaned or homeless. The near-immediate fall of France in 1940 precipitated the creation of a war cabinet, led by the determined and eloquent **Winston Churchill.** Britain first launched its offensive maneuvers in Europe with the 1944 **D-Day Invasion** of Normandy, augmented by American forces; the move swung the tide of the war and eventually produced peace in Europe in May 1945.

ENGLAND'S EVOLUTION. With increasing immigration to Britain from former colonies and a growing rift between the rich and poor, post-war Britain faced economic and cultural problems that still rankle today. In the immediate aftermath of WWII, left-wing politicians established the **National Health Service** in 1946, which guaranteed free medical care to all Brits. In keeping with the spirit of the 60s, the Labour government relaxed divorce and homosexuality laws and abolished capital punishment. Britain joined the **European Economic Community (EEC)** in 1971, a move that received a rocky welcome from many Britons and continues to inflame passions today. The nation's new economic liberalism, however, was unable to counter losses incurred by the decline of its colonial empire, which began in earnest after the infamous **Suez Crisis** of 1957. Unemployment and economic unrest culminated in a series of public service strikes during 1979's **"Winter of Discontent."**

It was against this backdrop that Britain grasped for change, electing "Iron Lady" **Margaret Thatcher** as Prime Minister, who advocated nationalism and Victorian values. Thatcher reversed the growing unpopularity that characterized her first term with the 1982 **Falkland Islands War.** The war heightened the rhetoric of British nationalism, while the political and social character of the nation changed dramatically. Thatcher denationalized nearly every industry the Labour government had brought under public control and dismantled vast segments of the welfare state with quips like "there is no such thing as society." Her policies brought dramatic prosperity to many but sharpened the divide between the haves and have-nots. Aggravated by her support of the unpopular **poll tax** and resistance to the EEC, the Conservative Party conducted a vote of no confidence that led to Thatcher's 1990 resignation and the election of **John Major.** In 1993, the Major government suffered its first embarrassment when the British pound toppled out of the EC's monetary regulation system. In August of the same year, Britain ratified (barely) the Maastricht Treaty on a tighter **European Union (EU).** Major remained unpopular, and by 1995 his ratings were so low that he resigned as Party leader to force a leadership election. He won the election, but the Conservatives lost parliamentary seats and continued to languish in the polls.

Under the leadership of charismatic **Tony Blair,** the Labour Party refashioned itself into the alternative for discontented voters. "New Labour" won a clear victory under Blair in 1997, with the biggest Labour majority to date, and garnered a second landslide victory in June 2001. Blair spent 1998 nurturing relations with the EU and maintaining a moderate economic and social position. Britain's stance on the **Kosovo** crisis gained Blair the title of "little Clinton" for what critics called his blind conformity to American foreign policy, a loyalty demonstrated again in the wake of the September 11, 2001 attacks.

Blair's Labour government has also tackled various constitutional reforms, beginning with domestic **devolution** in Scotland and Wales. The Scots voted in a 1997 referendum to have their own Parliament, which opened in 1999 (p. 539); the Welsh opened the first session of their National Assembly in 1999 (p. 450). Further expansion of local government occurred in May 1998 when London voters approved the plan for a city government, extinct since Thatcher's abolition of the Greater London Council in 1986. Progress has been more halting in attempts at

ENGLAND

Northern Irish autonomy. Though the Northern Ireland Assembly gained limited legislative and executive power at the end of 1999, the British government suspended Belfast's **Stormont Assembly** in 2000, hoping to instigate the decommissioning of arms by the IRA and their Unionist counterparts. A lack of progress led to a year of violence extending into 2002. The **Good Friday Agreement** continues a precarious existence between cease-fires, elections, and disarmament promises (p. 699).

TODAY

HOW BRITANNIA IS RULED. Britain managed to become one of the world's most stable constitutional monarchies without the aid of a written constitution. A combination of parliamentary legislation, common law, and convention creates the flexible system of British government. Since the 1700s the monarch has had a purely symbolic role; real political power resides with **Parliament,** consisting of the **House of Commons,** with its elected Members of Parliament (MPs), and the **House of Lords.** Power has shifted from the Lords to the Commons over the course of the centuries. Reforms in 1999 removed the majority of hereditary peers, replacing them with Life Peers—appointed by prime ministers to serve for life. Parliament holds supreme legislative power and may change and even directly contradict its previous laws. All members of the executive branch, which includes the **Prime Minister** and the **Cabinet,** are also MPs; this fusing of legislative and executive functions, called the "efficient secret" of the British government, ensures the quick passage of the majority party's programs into bills. Ruling from an elegant roost on **10 Downing Street** (or, in the case of Tony Blair and his large brood, No. 11; p. 122), the Prime Minister is generally the head of the majority party and chooses the members of the Cabinet, who serve as heads of the government's departments. British politics is a group effort; the Cabinet may bicker over policy in private, but their sense of collective responsibility ensures that they present a cohesive platform to the public. Political parties also keep their MPs in line on most votes in Parliament and provide a pool of talent and support for the smooth functioning of the executive. The two main parties in UK politics are **Labour** and the **Conservatives,** representing roughly the left and the right respectively; a smaller third party, the **Liberal Democrats,** tries its best to be the fulcrum on which power balances shift.

CURRENT EVENTS. Things are not looking good for Tony Blair these days. Even after an unpopular war in Iraq and its subsequent hardships, Britain remains the United States' staunchest ally in the **war on terrorism** and the **Road Map to Peace** in the Middle East, though rifts occasionally form over the latter. Blair's continued support of US foreign policy and his political alliance with President George Bush has incited increased resistance in Britain. February 2003 witnessed the largest demonstration in London's history, as an estimated 1,000,000 people gathered to oppose military intervention in Iraq. The rocky aftermath of the war in Iraq has been the most recent in a string of foreign policy troubles on Blair's plate.

Blair's detractors also point to the Prime Minister's position on the **euro.** Throughout 2002 the British government prepared to switch currencies, evaluating the economy to determine Britain's compatibility with the euro. In June 2003 Blair and chancellor Gordon Brown declared that joining the currency was not right for Britain. Setting an indeterminate time frame for a referendum, Blair and Brown delayed resolution of the issue, a move some argue was more political than economic. The fate of the pound remains a heated issue, but British opinion remains, as ever, distrustful of integration with the rest of Europe.

A ROYAL MESS? The royal family has had its share of trauma in recent years. In 1992, over a hundred rooms in Windsor Castle burned on Queen Elizabeth II's wedding anniversary, and in 1993 she started paying (gasp!) income tax. The spec-

ENGLAND

tacle of royal life took a tragic turn in 1997, when **Princess Diana** and **Dodi Al-Fayed** died in a car crash in a Paris tunnel. The outpouring of grief has since diminished, but tourists still mourn at the Diana memorial at Althorp, Northamptonshire. The fate of the royals now depends on whether the monarchy will embrace the populism Diana's legacy represents or retreat with traditional aloofness to the private realm. **Prince Charles** and his long-time paramour **Camilla Parker-Bowles** are making tentative steps toward public acceptance, if not a fully legitimized union—royal-watchers gaped at Camilla's seat in the Queen's box during the opening ceremonies for 2002's **Golden Jubilee** (a year-long bash celebrating the monarch's 50 years on the throne) and continue to titter at her increasingly frequent appearances at royal events. Royal-watchers also have their eyes on Charles's brother **Edward** and wife **Sophie Rhys-Jones,** who could surpass the divorce record of the other royal siblings (3-for-3 so far). A quick stop at a drug rehab clinic in 2002 heralded the onset of adult celebrity (and tabloid notoriety) for **Harry,** the younger of Charles and Diana's sons. Harry's increasing fame still cannot detract from the rapt attention devoted to future heir to the throne **Prince William.** After a rocky first two years at university in St. Andrews, whether "His Royal Sighness" will gracefully survive his trip to adulthood under the paparazzi's unforgiving lens remains to be seen.

ENGLISH CULTURE
FOOD AND DRINK

English cooking, like the English climate, is a training for life's unavoidable hardships.
—Historian R.P. Lister

England is not known for its food. Actually, perhaps it is best to say England is known for its lack of good food. Those with a stomach for meaty, milky, or otherwise heavy fare have come to the right place. But not to fear, hungry travelers! Ethnic cuisine has rapidly spread from the cities to the smallest of towns, so that most any village with a pub (and you'd be hard-pressed to find one without) will have an Indian takeaway to feed stumbling patrons after closing hours. Another surprising development is the extent to which **vegetarianism** has taken its hold on British culture, with even the most traditional pubs, and certainly the trendy cafe-bars, offering at least one meatless option. While England has yet to transform into a diner's paradise, enough progress has been made to challenge the national reputation for culinary blandness and close-mindedness.

Many Britons start their day off heartily with the famous, cholesterol-filled, meat-anchored **English breakfast,** which generally includes fried egg, bacon, sauteed mushrooms, grilled tomato, and black pudding (sausage made of grains and pork blood), and is served in most B&Bs across the country. Still, toast smothered in jam or Marmite (the most acquired of tastes—a salty, brown spread made from yeast) is perhaps the most common breakfast staple. The best dishes for lunch or dinner are **roasts**—beef, lamb, and Wiltshire hams—and **Yorkshire pudding,** a type of bread made with meat juices. **Bangers and mash** and **bubble and squeak,** despite their intriguing names, are basically left-overs (of sausages and potatoes, and cabbage and potatoes, respectively). Vegetables, often boiled into a flavorless, textureless mush, are typically the weakest part of the meal. Beware the British salad—often a plate of lettuce mixed with sweetened mayonnaise called "salad cream." The British like their **desserts** (or "afters") exceedingly sweet and gloopy. Sponges, trifles, tarts, the celebrated **spotted dick** (spongy currant cake), and puddings of endless variety will satiate even the severest of sweet teeth.

Pub grub is fast, filling, and a fine option for budget travelers. Hot meals could be meat pies like **Cornish pasties** (PASS-tees), meat pies like **shepherd's pie,** or meat pies like **steak and kidney pie.** For those really on the cheap, the **ploughman's lunch,** a staple in country pubs, is simply bread, cheese, and pickles. More cut-rate culinary options abound at the perennial "chippy" or chip shop—deep fried **fish and chips** are served in a cone of paper, dripping with grease, salt, and vinegar. A great low-cost lunch is the perennial sandwich and **crisps. Outdoor markets** and **supermarkets** provide the bread and the dairy—try Stilton cheese with digestive biscuits and find a suitably picturesque view. **Boots, Marks & Spencer,** and **Prêt à Manger** all sell an impressive array of ready-made sandwiches. Crisps, or potato chips, also come in astonishing variety, with flavors ranging from prawn cocktail to cheese 'n' onion. Most attractively for hungry travelers, there is an abundance of **ethnic restaurants** throughout the country. Try Chinese, Turkish, and especially Indian cuisines—Britain offers some of the best **tandoori** and **curry** outside of India. Finally, for the less adventurous, there are the ubiquitous American fast food chains (McDonald's, Burger King, Pizza Hut, and Subway), but travelers should look elsewhere; they'll still be there when you get home.

British **"tea"** refers both to a drink and a social ceremony. The ritual refreshment, accompanying almost every meal, is served strong and with milk. The standard tea, colloquially known as a nice **cuppa,** is mass produced by PG Tips or Tetleys; more refined cups specify particular blends such as **Earl Grey, Darjeeling,** or **Lapsang Souchong.** The oft-stereotyped ritual of afternoon **high tea** includes cooked meats, salad, sandwiches, and pastries. **Cream tea,** a specialty of Cornwall and Devon, includes toast, shortbread, crumpets, scones, and jam, accompanied by **clotted cream** (a cross between whipped cream and butter). The summer teatime potion **Pimms** is a sangria-esque punch of fruit juices and gin (the recipe is a well-guarded secret). And don't forget super-sweet fizzy drinks **Lilt** and **Tango.**

PUBS AND BEER

O Beer! O Hodgson, Guinness, Allsopp, Bass! Names that should be on every infant's tongue!
—C.S. Calverley in a poem entitled "Beer," 1861

Sir William Harcourt believed that English history was made in the pubs as much as in the Houses of Parliament. The spirit of the region certainly permeates the wood-panelled walls of the local tavern. The routine inspired by the pub is considerable; to stop in at lunchtime and after work is not uncommon. Brits rapidly develop affinities for neighborhood establishments, becoming loyal to their **locals,** and pubs in turn tend to cater to their regulars and develop a particular character. Pubs are ubiquitous; even the smallest village can support a decent **pub crawl.** The drinking age is a weakly-enforced 18, and you need only be 14 to enter a pub.

Bitter, named for its sharp, hoppy aftertaste, is the standard pub drink and should be hand-pumped or pulled from the tap at cellar temperature into government-stamped **pint** glasses (20oz.) or the more modest, rightfully scorned **halfpints. Real ale** retains a die-hard cult of connoisseurs in the shadow of giant corporate breweries; go to www.camra.org.uk to find out more about the movement for traditional brews and smaller breweries. **Brown, pale,** and **India pale ales**—less common varieties—all have a relatively heavy flavor with noticeable hop. **Stout,** the distinctive subspecies of ale, is rich, dark, and creamy; try the Irish **Guinness** (p. 731) with its silky foam head, rumored to be a recipe stolen from the older Beamish. Most draught ales and stouts are served at room temperature; if you can't stand the heat, try a **lager,** the tasty precursor of American beer that is typically served cold. **Cider,** like **Strongbow,** is fermented apple juice served sweet or dry, and is a potent, cold, and tasty alternative to beer. Variations on the standard pint include **black velvet,** or stout and champagne; **black and tan,** layers of stout and ale; and **snakebite,** a murky mix of lager and cider with a dash of blackcurrant Ribena. **Alcopops,** or designer drinks like **Bacardi Breezers** and hard lemonade, are also widespread, but you'd be hard-pressed to find a British male drinking one.

In almost all places in Britain government-imposed **closing times** restrict pub hours. Traditionally in England and Wales, drinks are served 11am-11pm Monday to Saturday, and noon-3pm and 7-10:30pm Sunday. A bell ten or so minutes before closing time signifies "last orders." In June 2003, the House of Commons voted to localize control of closing time, moving a step closer to allowing pubs to stay open as long as they want. Many establishments, particularly in larger towns and cities, find ways around closing times anyway such as serving food or having an entertainment license. Around pub-closing time people pack into clubs.

CULTURE AND CUSTOMS

Great Britain, roughly the size of the state of Oregon, is home to 60 million Britons. Such close quarters make the people around you as important to your trip as the castle ruins next on your itinerary. The English culture and character is as impossible to summarize as any on earth—Jane Austen, Sid Vicious, and Winston Churchill are each quintessentially "English," yet share almost nothing in common. Stiff upper lips sit next to football hooligans on the Tube, and the local who stares at you skeptically because you tried to strike up conversation at a bus stop would likely talk your ear off over a pint "down the local."

In a country full of such idiosyncrasies, there is very little a traveler can do that will inadvertently cause offense. That said, the English do place weight on proper decorum, including **politeness** ("thanks" comes in many varieties, including "ta" and "cheers," and you should use it), **queueing** (that is, lining up—never, ever line jump or otherwise disrupt the queue), and keeping a certain **respectful distance.** You'll find, however, that the British **sense of humor**—fantastically wry, explicit, even raunchy—is somewhat at odds with any notion of coldness and reserve.

THE ARTS

LANGUAGE AND LITERATURE

Eclipsed only by Mandarin Chinese in sheer number of speakers, the English language reflects in its history the diversity of the hundreds of millions who use it today. Once a minor Germanic dialect, English was enriched by words and phrases from Danish, French, and Latin, giving even its earliest wordsmiths a vast vocabulary rivaled by few world languages. Over centuries of British colonialism, the language has borrowed endlessly from other tongues and supplied a literary and popular voice for people far removed from the British Isles. A well-chosen novel or collection of poems will illuminate any sojourn in Britain, and the following survey hopes to give an idea of the range of choices. Welsh (p. 450), Scottish (p. 540), and Irish (p. 729) languages and literatures are treated separately.

BARDS AND BIBLES. One of Britain's biggest claims to fame is its undeniable position as the birthplace of much of the world's best literature. A strong oral tradition informed most of the earliest poetry in English, little of which survives. The finest piece of Anglo-Saxon (Old English) poetry is *Beowulf,* the 7th-century account of an egoistic prince, his heroic deeds, and his undoing in a battle with a dragon. The unknown author of *Sir Gawain and the Green Knight* (c. 1375) tells a romance of Arthurian chivalry in which the bedroom becomes a battlefield and a young knight seeks a mysterious destiny. **Geoffrey Chaucer** tapped into the more spirited side of Middle English; his *Canterbury Tales* (c. 1387) remain some

ENGLAND

of the sauciest, most incisive stories in the English canon and poke fun at all stations of English life. **John Wycliffe** made the Bible accessible to the masses by translating it from Latin to English in the 1380s. **William Tyndale** followed suit in 1525, translating from the original Greek and Hebrew, and his work became the model for the **King James** version (completed in 1611 under James I).

THE ENGLISH RENAISSANCE. English literature flourished under the reign of Elizabeth I. **Sir Philip Sidney's** sonnet sequences and **Edmund Spenser's** moral allegories (like *The Faerie Queene*) earned both of them favor at court, while **John Donne** wrote metaphysical poetry, as well as plenty of erotic verse. The era's greatest contributions were dramatic. Playwright **Christopher Marlowe** lost his life in a pub brawl, but not before he produced plays of temptation and damnation, such as *Dr. Faustus* (c. 1588). Meanwhile, **Ben Jonson,** when he wasn't languishing in jail, redefined satiric comedy in works like *Volpone* (1606). We shouldn't neglect to mention a certain son of a glove-maker from Stratford-upon-Avon (p. 275). A giant of the Elizabethan era, **William Shakespeare** continues to loom over all of English literature as the inventor of any number of words (try "scuffle," "whizzing," and "arouse") and the most successful playwright-poet of all time.

HOW NOVEL! Britain's Puritan turn in the late 16th and early 17th centuries influenced the huge volume of obsessive and beautiful literature of the time, like **John Milton's** epic *Paradise Lost* (1667) and **John Bunyan's** allegory-laden *Pilgrim's Progress* (1678). The 18th century saw the poetry of **John Dryden's** neoclassical revival, **Alexander Pope's** satires, and **Dr. Samuel Johnson's** lovably idiosyncratic dictionary, the first in the English language. In 1719, **Daniel Defoe** inaugurated the era of the English **novel** with his popular island-bound *Robinson Crusoe*. Authors like **Samuel Richardson** (*Clarissa*, 1749) and **Fanny Burney** (*Evelina*, 1778) cultivated the novel along more traditional lines, while **Henry Fielding's** wacky *Tom Jones* (1749) and **Laurence Sterne's** experimental *Tristram Shandy* (1759-67) invigorated the art form. **Jane Austen's** intricate narratives portrayed the modes and manners of the early 19th century. In the Victorian period, poverty and social change spawned the sentimental novels of **Charles Dickens;** *Oliver Twist* (1838) and *David Copperfield* (1849) draw on the bleakness of his childhood in Portsmouth (p. 170) and portray the harsh living conditions of working class Londoners. Secluded in the wild Yorkshire moors (see Haworth, p. 399), the **Brontë sisters** staved off tuberculosis to conjure the tumultuous landscapes and romances of *Wuthering Heights* (Emily; 1847) and *Jane Eyre* (Charlotte; also 1847). *Middlemarch* (1871) is **George Eliot's** (Mary Ann Evans's) intricately detailed "Study of Provincial Life," set in a fictional Midlands town. **Thomas Hardy** brought the Victorian age to a somber end in the fate-ridden Wessex (that is, southwest England) of *Tess of the d'Urbervilles* (1891) and *Jude the Obscure* (1895).

ROMANTICISM AND RESPONSE. Partly in reaction to the rationalism of the preceding century, the **Romantic** movement of the early 1800s found its greatest expression in turbulent verse. Painter-poet **William Blake's** *Songs of Innocence and Experience* (1794) was a precursor to the movement, but the watershed publication was the 1798 *Lyrical Ballads* by **William Wordsworth** and **Samuel Taylor Coleridge**, which included "Lines Composed a Few Miles above Tintern Abbey" (p. 463) and "The Rime of the Ancient Mariner." Romantic poets celebrated the transcendent beauty of nature, the power of the imagination, and the profound influence of childhood experiences. Wordsworth's poetry reflects on a long, full life—he drew inspiration from the Lakes (p. 372) and Snowdonia (p. 510), Cambridge, and London—but many of his colleagues died tragically young. **John Keats** succumbed to tuberculosis at 26, with just time enough to have penned the maxim "beauty is truth, truth beauty" in one of his astonishingly evocative odes. The poet

ENGLAND

Percy Bysshe Shelley drowned off the Tuscan coast at 29, and **Lord Byron's** *Don Juan* (1819-24) defined the heroic archetype and established the poet as the heartthrob of the age before he was killed in the Greek War of Independence at 36. The poetry of the Victorian age struggled with the impact of societal changes and religious skepticism. **Alfred, Lord Tennyson** spun verse about faith and doubt for over a half-century and inspired a medievalist revival with Arthurian idylls like "The Lady of Shalott" (1842). Celebrating the grotesque, **Robert Browning** composed piercing dramatic monologues, and his wife **Elizabeth Barrett** counted the ways she loved him in *Sonnets from the Portuguese* (1850). Meanwhile, fellow female poet **Christina Rossetti** envisioned the fantastical world of "Goblin Market" (1862). **Matthew Arnold** abandoned poetry in 1867 to become the greatest cultural critic of the day. Jesuit priest **Gerard Manley Hopkins** penned tortuous verse with a unique "sprung rhythm" that make him the chief forerunner of poetic modernism.

THE MODERN AGE. "On or about December 1910," wrote **Virginia Woolf,** "human nature changed." Woolf, a key member of London's bohemian intellectual **Bloomsbury Group,** tried to capture the spirit of the time and the real life of the mind in her novels; she and Irish expatriate **James Joyce** (p. 730) were among the most groundbreaking practitioners of **Modernism** (1910-1930). One of Modernism's poetic champions was **T.S. Eliot,** who grew up a Missouri boy but became the "Pope of Russell Square" (p. 103). *The Waste Land* (1922), among the last century's most important works, portrays London as a fragmented and barren desert awaiting redemption. **D.H. Lawrence** explored tensions in the British working-class family and broke sexual convention in *Sons and Lovers* (1913). Although he spoke only a few words of English when he arrived in the country at 21, **Joseph Conrad** demonstrated his mastery of the language in *Heart of Darkness* (1902). A similar disillusionment with imperialism surfaces in **E.M. Forster's** half-Modernist, half-Romantic novels, particularly *A Passage to India* (1924). Authors in the 1930s captured the tumult and depression of the decade: **Evelyn Waugh** turned a ruthlessly satirical eye on society, while **Graham Greene** studied moral ambiguity. The witty and often sardonic poet **W.H. Auden,** deeply disturbed by the gathering violence he saw in the world, left the world with this condition: "We must love one another or die."

LATER TWENTIETH-CENTURY. Fascism and the horrors of WWII motivated musings on the nature of evil, while the ravenous totalitarian state of **George Orwell's** *1984* (1949) strove to strip the world of memory and words of meaning. **Anthony Burgess's** *A Clockwork Orange* (1962), imagines the violence and anarchy of a not-so-distant future. The end of Empire, rising affluence, and the growing gap between classes splintered British literature. Nostalgia pervades the poems of **Philip Larkin** and **John Betjeman,** an angry working class found mouthpieces in **Allan Sillitoe** and **Kingsley Amis,** and postcolonial voices like **Salman Rushdie** and 2002 Nobel laureate **V.S. Naipaul** have become an important literary force. Though Britain no longer claims exclusive command of the English language, the home island still produces acclaimed works from writers like **A.S. Byatt, Martin Amis,** and **Ian McEwan.** British playwrights continue to innovate: **Harold Pinter** infused living rooms with horrifying silences, **Tom Stoppard** challenged theatrical convention in plays like *Rosencrantz and Guildenstern are Dead* (1967), and Carol Churchill provides blistering commentary on "the state of Britain," as well as its checkered past in *Cloud Nine* (1988) and other plays.

OUTSIDE THE CLASSROOM. English literature holds its own away from the ivory tower as well. The elegant mysteries of **Dorothy L. Sayers** and **Agatha Christie** are known the world over. The espionage novels of **John le Carré** and Fleming, **Ian Fleming,** provide thrills of another sort. **P.G. Wodehouse,** creator of Jeeves, the consummate butler, hilariously satirizes the idle aristocrat. **James Herriot** (Alf Wight), beloved

ENGLAND

author of *All Creatures Great and Small* (1972), chronicled his work as a young veterinarian. **Douglas Adams** parodied sci-fi in his hilarious series *Hitchhiker's Guide to the Galaxy*, and **Helen Fielding's** hapless *Bridget Jones* speaks for singletons everywhere. Britain has also produced volumes of children's literature. **Lewis Carroll's** *Alice's Adventures in Wonderland* (1865) and **C.S. Lewis's** *Chronicles of Narnia* (1950-56) continue to enchant generations. A linguist named **J.R.R. Tolkien,** Lewis's companion in letters and Oxford pub-readings (p. 263), wrote tales of elves, wizards, short folk, and rings (*The Hobbit*, 1934; *Lord of the Rings*, 1954-56). **Nick Hornby's** cool, witty novels tend to make good screenplays; you may have seen *High Fidelity* or *About a Boy*. More recently, **J.K. Rowling** has swept the world with her tale of juvenile wizardry in the blockbuster *Harry Potter* series, earning herself a fortune greater than that of the Queen.

ART AND ARCHITECTURE

 LEARN A NEW LANGUAGE. Church- and castle-spotting is more fun and rewarding when you know the lingo. Here's a brief introduction to the language of medieval architecture that will make you sound like an expert to all the tourists around you. A castle's **keep** is the main tower and residence hall. Some early keeps sit atop a steep mound called a **motte.** Laugh if you will, but **buttresses** are the slender external wall supports that hold up the tallest castles and the loftiest cathedrals. A **vault** is a stone ceiling; a ribbed vault is held up by spidery stone arcs or **ribs;** and the **webs** are the spaces in between ribs. Most churches are **cruciform,** or shaped like a cross. The head of the cross is the **choir,** the arms are the **transepts,** and the rest of it is the **nave,** usually flanked by **aisles.** Medieval churches usually have a three-tiered nave: the ground level is the **arcade,** the middle level (where monks used to walk and ponder scripture) is the **triforium,** and the highest level (where the light comes in) is the **clerestory.** Stained glass is awesome, but usually isn't original; old or new, the **tracery** is the lacy stonework that holds it in place.

HOUSES OF GODS AND MEN. Early English architecture has often been considered nothing more than a distillation of influences from the continent, but even those without a trained eye can spot a distinct British style. The Normans introduced **Romanesque** architecture (round arches and thick walls) in the eleventh century, but the British made it their own with Durham cathedral (p. 427). The **Gothic** style, originating in France (12th-15th century), ushered in a new world of intricate, elegant, and deceptively delicate buildings like the cathedrals of Wells (p. 205) and Salisbury (p. 186). By the 14th century, the English had developed the unique **perpendicular style** of window tracery, apparent at King's College Chapel in Cambridge (p. 316). Sadly, the **Suppression of Monasteries** in 1536 under Henry VIII spurred the wanton smashing of stained glass and even of entire churches, leaving picturesque **ruins** scattered along the countryside (like **Rievaulx,** p. 420; or **Glastonbury,** p. 209). After the **Renaissance,** architects utilized new engineering capabilities—attested to by **Christopher Wren's** fantastic dome on **St. Paul's Cathedral** (p. 122), built after the Great Fire of London in 1666.

Early domestic architecture in Britain progressed from the **stone dwellings** of pre-Christian folk (see **Skara Brae,** p. 684) to the Romans' **forts and villas** (see **Hadrian's Wall,** p. 436), and thence to the famed medieval castles. The earliest of these, the hilltop **motte-and-bailey** forts, arrived with William the Conqueror in 1066 (see the Round Tower of Windsor, p. 262, or Carisbrooke, p. 178), and progressed to towering, square **Norman keeps** like the **Tower of London** (p. 112). Warmongering Edward I constructed a string of astonishing **concentric castles** along the Welsh coast (Harlech, p. 501; Caernarfon, p. 508; Beaumaris, p. 520; Caerphilly, p. 461). By the 14th century, the advent of cannon had made castles obsolete as defensive structures, yet they lived on as **palaces** for the wealthy. A gorgeous example of these late castles, more aesthetic than bellicose, is in **Warwick** (p. 296). The Renaissance was ushered in with sumptuous **Tudor homes** like Henry VIII's Hampton Court (p. 126), which transitioned into an 18th-century competition between the heady **baroque** style of Castle Howard (p. 415) and the severe **Palladian** symmetry of Houghton Hall (p. 330). **Stately homes** like Howard and Houghton (all the rage until well into the 20th century) were furnished with **Chippendale** furniture and surrounded by equally stately **gardens** (see **Blenheim Palace**, p. 274). During the Victorian period, the English grew wistful for their heritage, spurring the **neo-Gothic revival** (**Houses of Parliament**, p. 109) and the **neo-Classical** British Museum (p. 127). Today, hotshot, high-profile types **Richard Rogers** and **Norman Foster** vie for bragging rights as England's most influential architect, littering London with wonderful, wacky new additions like the Lloyd's Building (p. 116), City Hall, and a host of Millennium constructions (including the **Millennium Bridge**, p. 119).

ON THE CANVAS. Britain's early religious art, including **illuminated manuscripts**, gave way to secular patronage and the institution of court painters; Renaissance art in England was largely dominated by foreign portraitists commissioned by the monarchy such as **Hans Holbein the Younger** (1497-1543) and Flemish masters **Peter Paul Reubens** (1577-1640) and **Anthony Van Dyck** (1599-1641). **Nicholas Hilliard** (1547-1619) was the first English-born success of the period. Vanity, and thus portraiture, continued to flourish into the 18th century, with the satirical London scenes of **William Hogarth** (1697-1764), classically-inspired poses of **Joshua Reynolds** (1723-1792), and provincial backdrops of **Thomas Gainsborough** (1727-1788). Encouraged by a nation-wide interest in gardening, **landscape painting** peaked during the 19th century. Beyond the literary realm, Romanticism inspired the vibrant rustic scenes of **John Constable** and the violent sense of the sublime inherent in **J.M.W. Turner's** stunning seascapes. The Victorian fascination for reviving old art forms sparked movements like the Italian-inspired, damsel-laden Pre-Raphaelite school, propagated by **John Everett Millais** (1829-1896) and **Dante Gabriel Rossetti** (1828-82). Victorians also dabbled in new art forms like photography and took advantage of early mass media with engravings and cartoons. Modernist trends from the Continent such as Cubism and Expressionism were picked up by **Wyndham Lewis** (1882-1957) and sculptor **Henry Moore** (1898-1986). WWII broke art wide open (as it did most things), yielding experimental, edgy works by **Francis Bacon** (1909-1992) and **Lucian Freud** (b. 1922; whose highly controversial portrait of the Queen was unveiled in 2002). **David Hockney** (b. 1937) gave American pop art a dose of British wit. Precocious **Young British Artists (YBAs)** of the 1990s include sculptor **Rachel Whitbread** and multimedia artist **Damien Hirst** (b. 1965). The factory-like Tate Modern (p. 128) is the place for contemporary art, while galleries in London (Tate Britain, p. 128; the British Museum, p. 127; the National Gallery p. 127) continue to hold their reputation among the world's greatest collections.

FASHION. Inspired by the hip street energy of London in the 1960s along with movements like Op and Pop Art, England's fashion designers have achieved international fame. A revolution was sparked when **Mary Quant** (b. 1934) invented the miniskirt. **Vivienne Westwood** (b. 1941) is credited with originating punk fashion in the early 1970s, and her label is still known for its references to costume history. Young British designers have made their marks at prestigious fashion houses, such as **John Galliano** (b. 1960) at Dior. Recent years, however, have seen the establishment of independent labels by both former Givenchy star **Alexander McQueen** (b. 1970) and Sir Paul's daughter, ex-Chloé designer **Stella McCartney** (b. 1972).

MUSIC

CLASSICAL. In the middle ages, traveling **minstrels** sang narrative folk **ballads** and **Arthurian romances** in the courts of the rich. During the Renaissance, English ears were tuned to cathedral anthems, psalms, and madrigals, along with the odd lute perfor-

ENGLAND

mance. **Henry Purcell** (1659-1695) rang in the baroque with instrumental music for Shakespeare's plays and England's first great opera, *Dido and Aeneas*. The 18th century, regarded as England's musical Dark Age, welcomed visits of foreign geniuses Mozart, Haydn, and **George Frideric Handel,** a German composer who wrote operas in the Italian style but spent most of his life in Britain. Thanks to Handel's influence, England experienced a wave of **operamania** in the early 1700s. Enthusiasm waned when listeners realized they couldn't understand what the performers were saying. The turning point occurred when **John Gay** satirized the opera house in *The Beggar's Opera* (1727), a low-brow comedy in which Italianate arias were set to English folk tunes. Today's audiences are familiar with the operettas of **W.S. Gilbert** (1836-1911) and **Arthur Sullivan** (1842-1900); the pair were rumored to hate each other, but produced gems such as *The Mikado* and *The Pirates of Penzance*. A second renaissance of more serious music began under **Edward Elgar** (1857-1934), whose *Pomp and Circumstance* is most often appreciated at graduation ceremonies. In contrast to his suites for military bands, **Gustav Holst** (1874-1934) adapted Neoclassical and folk methods to Romantic moods in *The Planets*.

Also borrowing elements from folk melodies, **Ralph Vaughan Williams** (1872-1958) and **John Ireland** (1879-1962) brought musical modernism to the island. The world wars provided adequate fodder for this continued musical resurgence, provoking **Benjamin Britten's** (1913-76) heartbreaking *War Requiem* and **Michael Tippett's** (1905-98) humanitarian oratorio, *A Child of Our Time*. Although the popular **Proms** at Royal Albert Hall (p. 139) afford a rousing evening surrounded by Brits waving flags, blowing whistles, and singing along to their favorite national songs, later 20th-century trends (like **Oliver Knussen's** one-act opera of Maurice Sendak's *Where the Wild Things Are* and **Andrew Lloyd Webber's** blend of opera, popular music, and falling chandeliers) demonstrate the commercially lucrative shift of British musical influence.

THE BRITISH ARE COMING. England's tag as "a land without music" (coined for the island's lack of an original classical composer since the Renaissance) can be disproved by a glance at any Billboard chart from the past 40 years. Invaded by American blues and rock 'n' roll following WWII, Britain staged an offensive unprecedented anywhere in history; the **British Invasion** groups of the 60s infiltrated the colonies with a more daring, controversial sound. Native Liverpudlians **The Beatles** were the ultimate trendsetters, still influential more than three decades after their break-up. The edgier lyrics and grittier sound of the **Rolling Stones** shifted teens' thoughts from "I Wanna Hold Your Hand" to "Let's Spend the Night Together." Over the next 20 years, England exported the hard-driving **Kinks,** the Urban "mod" sound of **The Who,** the psychedelia-meets-Motown **Yardbirds,** and guitar gurus Eric Clapton of **Cream** and Jimmy Page of **Led Zeppelin.**

ANARCHY IN THE UK. Despite (or perhaps because of) England's conservative national character, homosexuality became central to the flamboyant scene of the mid-70s. British rock schismed as the theatrical excesses of **glam rock** performers like **Queen, Elton John,** and **David Bowie** contrasted with the conceptual, album-oriented **art rock** emanating from **Pink Floyd** and **Yes.** With high unemployment and an energy crisis going on, dissonant **punk rock** bands like **Stiff Little Fingers** and **The Clash** emerged from Britain's industrial centers. Meanwhile, **The Sex Pistols** stormed the scene with profane and wildly successful antics—their angry 1977 single "God Save the Queen" topped the charts despite being banned in the UK. Sharing punk's anti-establishment impulses, the metal of **Ozzy Osbourne** and **Iron Maiden** was much less acclaimed but still attracts a cult following. Sheffield's **Def Leppard** carried the hard-rock-big-hair ethic through the 80s, while punk offshoots like **The Cure** and **goth** bands rebelled in the era of conservative Thatcherism.

I WANT MY MTV. Buoyed by a booming economy, British bands achieved popular success on both sides of the Atlantic thanks to the 1980s advent of America's Music Television. **Dire Straits** introduced the first computer-animated music video, while

GET YER ROCKS OFF If you're looking for road tunes, you could do worse than to pick something from this selection of albums.

British Invasion: The Beatles, *Rubber Soul;* The Rolling Stones, *Exile on Main St.;* and The Kinks, *Something Else by the Kinks.*

Punk/post-punk: The Clash, *London Calling;* The Sex Pistols, *Never Mind the Bollocks, Here's the Sex Pistols; and* Joy Division, *Permanent.*

Synth-pop: Duran Duran, *Decade;* Pet Shop Boys, *Discography;* and The Police, *Every Breath You Take: The Singles.*

Brit-pop: The Smiths, *The Queen is Dead;* Blur, *Parklife;* Oasis, *What's the Story (Morning Glory);* Pulp, *Different Class;* Radiohead, *OK Computer;* and Coldplay, *Parachutes.*

Dance: Fatboy Slim, *You've Come a Long Way, Baby;* Chemical Brothers, *Dig Your Own Hole;* Prodigy, *Fat of the Land.*

UK Garage: So Solid Crew, *They Don't Know;* The Streets, *Original Pirate Material;* Dizzee Rascal, *Boy in da Corner.*

Duran Duran, the **Eurythmics, Boy George, Tears for Fears,** and the **Police** enjoyed top-10 hits. England is also responsible for some of the giants of the lipstick-and-synthesizer age, including **George Michael** and **Bananarama.** At the end of the decade, a crop of bands from Manchester galvanized the post-punk era, spearheaded by **Joy Division,** and the early **rave** movement. Any clubber worth her tube-top can tell you about England's influence on dance music, from the **Chemical Brothers** and Brighton-bred **Fatboy Slim** to the house, trip-hop, and ska sounds of **Basement Jaxx, Massive Attack,** and **Jamiroquai.** The 90's saw the return of worldwide rock powerhouses during the Britpop era; **Blur** and **Oasis** embodied a dramatically indulgent breed of rock 'n' roll stardom, leaving trashed hotel rooms and screaming fans in their wake. The tremendous popularity of American **grunge rock** inspired a host of poseurs in the UK, including then-wannabes ▪️**Radiohead,** who have since become arguably the most influential British rock band since the Beatles. The UK is also a pop mecca, ruled for years by **Robbie Williams** (survivor of the bubblegummy **Take That**), who continues to be a stadium-filling force; sadly, the **Spice Girls** did not enjoy the same longevity, but they managed to do something Robbie hasn't: crack the US market. These days, **Coldplay** is still the UK's best-selling rock export. And after a significant dry spell, the British have finally created a true new genre: **UK Garage,** a blend of skittering beats, heavy bass, and unapologetically urban British-accented rapping, is now the official sound of every club. **The Streets** is the first to bring the sound to the US, but **Dizzee Rascal's** hardcore, nearly unintelligible flow is also winning fans abroad.

FILM

British film has endured an uneven history, characterized by cycles of relative independence from Hollywood influence followed by increasing emigration of talent to America. **Charlie Chaplin** and Archibald Alec Leach (a.k.a. **Cary Grant**) were both Briton-born but made their names in US films. The **Royal Shakespeare Company** has seen heavyweight alumni like **Dame Judi Dench, Sir Ian McKellen,** and **Jeremy Irons** make the transition to celluloid. Earlier Shakespeare impresario **Laurence Olivier** worked both ends of the camera in *Henry V* (the 1944 brainchild of government-sponsored WWII propaganda), and his *Hamlet* (1948) is still the hallmark Dane. Master of suspense **Alfred Hitchcock** snared audiences with films produced on both sides of the Atlantic, terrifying shower-takers everywhere. The 60s phenomenon of "swingin' London" created new momentum for the film industry and jump-started international interest in British culture. American Richard Lester made **The Beatles'** *A Hard Day's Night* in 1963, and a year later Scot **Sean Connery** downed the first of many martinis as **James Bond** in *Dr. No.*

ENGLAND

THE LOCAL STORY

COUNTRY LIFE

One of the most interesting things about a visit to Britain is experiencing the delightful stuffiness of the local aristocracy. Despite the changes of the last century, Britain is still a land of Dukes, Earls, and Lords, many of whom still live in stately homes set on thousands of acres of land. Of course, it's possible to get a feel for aristocratic life by visiting these palaces, out of course, paying the admission price and gawking at the antiques is for the common rabble.

To get a real taste of what it's like to be in Britain's landed aristocracy, simply pick up an issue of the weekly Country Life magazine, a notoriously snooty publication read religiously by anyone who's anyone. After the long section of mouth-watering real estate listings in the front, every issue announces a young lady into society with a tasteful picture and brief description. There are articles on all the important subjects in life—motoring, bridge, equestrian matters, and fox hunting—as well as longer inquiries into really pressing issues "which is Britain's oldest landed family?" There's always an update on important transactions made at Sotheby's, and even the comic strip at the back is geared towards the rich ("the maid gave my wine cellar a spring cleaning!"). At £4.80, it's not a bad way to break into the world's most exclusive society. Available at posher newsstands across Britain.

Elaborate costume drama and offbeat independent films characterized British film in the 80's and 90's. The sagas *Chariots of Fire* (1981) and *Gandhi* (1982) swept the Oscars in successive years. Director-producer team **Merchant-Ivory** led the way in adaptations of British novels like Forster's *A Room with a View* (1986). **Kenneth Branagh** focused his talents on adapting Shakespeare for the screen, with glossy, well-received works such as *Hamlet* (1996) and his less-acclaimed musical version of *Love's Labour's Lost* (2000). **Nick Park** took claymation and British quirk to a new level with the *Wallace and Gromit* shorts and the blockbuster feature film *Chicken Run* (2000). The dashing **Guy** "Mr. Madonna" **Ritchie** tapped into Tarantino-esque conventions with his dizzying *Lock, Stock and Two Smoking Barrels* (1998), followed by the trans-Atlantic smash *Snatch* (2000), though the film's success may or may not have had something to do with American stud Brad Pitt.

Recent British films have garnered a fair number of international awards; the working-class feel-goods *The Full Monty* (1997) and *Billy Elliot* (2000); **Mike Leigh's** affecting *Secrets and Lies* (1996) and costume extravaganza *Topsy-Turvy* (1999); and the endearing comedies *Bend it Like Beckham* (2002) and *Love, Actually* (2003) have all taken home awards from sources like the Academy, Cannes, and the Golden Globes. Then of course, there is the *Harry Potter* franchise (filmed at gorgeous Alnwick Castle (p. 442) and the Scottish Highlands), which kicked off in 2001 and continues to break box office records.

MEDIA

ALL THAT'S FIT TO PRINT. In a culture with a rich print-media history, the influence of newspapers remains enormous. The UK's plethora of national newspapers yields a range of political viewpoints. *The Times*, long a model of thoughtful discretion, has turned Tory under the ownership of Rupert Murdoch. *The Daily Telegraph*, dubbed "Torygraph," is fairly conservative and old-fashioned. *The Guardian* leans left, while *The Independent* answers for its name. Of the infamous tabloids, *The Sun*, Murdoch-owned and better known for its page-three topless pin-up than for its reporting, is the most influential. Among the others, *The Daily Mail*, *The Daily Express*, and *The London Evening Standard* (the only evening paper) make serious attempts at popular journalism, although the first two tend to position themselves as the conservative voice of Middle England. *The Daily Mirror, The News of the World*, and *The Star* are as shrill and lewd as *The Sun*. *The Financial Times*, on pleasing pink paper, distributes the news of the City of London as *The Wall Street Journal* does for Wall Street. Although closely associated with their sister dailies, Sunday newspapers are actually separate entities. *The Sunday Times, The Sunday Telegraph, The Independent on Sunday,* and the highly polished *Observer,* the world's oldest paper and sister to *The Guardian,* offer detailed arts, sports, and news coverage, together with more "soft bits" than the dailies.

A quick glance around any High St. newsagent will prove Britain has no shortage of magazines. World affairs are covered with refreshing candor and wit by *The Economist. The New Statesman* on the left and *The Spectator* on the right cover politics and the arts with verve. The satirical *Private Eye* is subversive, hilarious, and overtly political. Some of the best music mags in the world—*New Musical Express (NME), Q,* and *Gramophone*—are UK-based. Movie and other entertainment news comes in the over-sized *Empire.* The indispensable London journal *Time Out* is the most comprehensive listings guide to the city and features fascinating pieces on British culture; its website (www.timeout.com) also keeps tabs on events in Dublin, and Edinburgh. Recent years have seen the explosion of "lad's magazines" such as *FHM* and *Loaded,* which feature scantily-clad women and articles on beer, "shagging," and "pulling," while London-born *Maxim* offers similar content for a slightly older crowd. The insatiable appetites of royal-watchers and celebrity-gossipers are fed by *Hello* and *OK* magazines.

ON THE AIRWAVES. The **BBC** (British Broadcasting Corporation, affectionately known as the Beeb) established its reputation for cleverly styled fairness with its radio services. The World Service provides countries around the world with a glimpse into British life. Within the UK, the BBC has **Radios 1-7,** covering news (4), sports (5), and the whole spectrum of music from pop (1) to classical and jazz (3) to catch-all (2 and 6), and recently, for kids (7). Each region has a variety of local commercial broadcasting services. British radio is responsible for the introduction of the **soap opera** (*The Archers* is still broadcast weekdays on Radio 4), a form now dominated by the televised *Eastenders* and *Coronation Street.*

Aside from the daytime suds, British television has brought to the world such mighty comic wonders as *Monty Python's Flying Circus, Mr. Bean,* and most recently, the across-the-pond hit *The Office.* The BBC has made some stellar literary adaptations into **miniseries**—1996's *Pride and Prejudice* sparked an international "Darcy-fever" for **Colin Firth,** and is widely considered one of the best film versions of Austen's work. At the other end of the spectrum is Britain's current obsession with do-it-yourself home-improvement shows, cooking programs, and voyeur TV (remember, they invented *Big Brother* and *Pop* (aka *American) Idol).* A commercial-free repository of wit and innovation, the BBC broadcasts on two national channels. **BBC1** carries news as well as various Britcoms, while **BBC2** telecasts cultural programs and fledgling sitcoms (*Absolutely Fabulous* and *Blackadder* both started here). **ITV,** Britain's first and most established commercial network, carries drama, comedy, and news. **Channel 4** has morning shows, highly respected arts programming, and imported American shows. **Channel 5** features late-night sports shows and action movies. Rupert Murdoch's satellite **Sky TV** shows football, fútbol, soccer, and other incarnations of the global game on its Sky Sports channel, while its Sky One channel broadcasts mostly American shows.

SPORTS

There is a great noise in the city caused by hustling over large balls, from which many evils arise which God forbid.
   —King Edward II, banning football in 1314

FOOTBALL. The game of **football** (soccer), whose rules were formalized by the English Football Association (FA; www.thefa.com) in 1863, remains the island's—and the world's—most popular sport. In the highest echelon are the 20 **clubs** (teams) of the

ENGLAND

Premier League, which are populated with world-class players from Britain and abroad. Below the Premiership lie the three divisions of the Nationwide League. At the end of the season, the three clubs with the worst records in the Premiership face relegation to the First Division, whose top three clubs are promoted. The **F.A. Cup,** held every May, has been temporarily displaced from its hallowed home in **Wembley** as players and fans await the completion of a new **National Stadium,** due to open in 2006. The cup is the top knockout competition, and the ultimate achievement for an English football club is to "do the Double"—win the Premier League and the F.A. Cup in one season.

The English Premier League is dominated by teams like London Arsenal, Liverpool, Leeds, and Chelsea, but **Manchester United** (p. 354) is the red victory machine that every Brit loves to hate. "Man U" fans and paparazzi alike mourned the team's loss of celebrity star **David Beckham** to Real Madrid in 2003 in an unexpected £25 million trade. Unfortunately, the four British international teams (England, Scotland, Wales, and Northern Ireland compete as separate countries) have not performed well in **World Cups** and **European Championships**—England's 1966 World Cup victory being the glorious exception. The next round of mania is slated for Germany in 2006.

Over half a million fans attend professional matches in Britain every weekend from mid-August to May, and they spend the few barren weeks of summer waiting for the publication of the coming season's **fixtures** (match schedules). If you can get tickets, a match is well worth attending for a glimpse of British **football culture.** Worship at postmodern cathedrals—grand, storied stadiums full of painted faces and team colors, resounding with a rowdy chorus of uncannily synchronized (usually rude) songs and chants. Intracity rivalries (London's Arsenal-Tottenham or Glasgow's "Auld Firm," see p. 50) have been known to divide families. Violence and vandalism used to dog the game, causing tension between fans and the police who tried to control huge crowds in old stadiums. The atmosphere in stadiums has become safer (albeit pricier) now that clubs offer seating-only tickets, rather than standing spaces in the infamous terraces. **Hooligans** are usually on their worst behavior when the England national team plays abroad; things are tamer at home.

OTHER GAMES. According to legend, **rugby** was born one glorious day in 1823 when William Webb Ellis, an inspired (or perhaps slightly confused) Rugby School student, picked up a soccer ball and ran it into the goal. Since then, rugby has evolved into a complex, subtle, and thoroughly lunatic game. The amateur **Rugby Union** and professional **Rugby League,** both 19th-century creations, have slightly different rules and different numbers of players (15 and 13); in Britain, the former is associated with Scotland, Wales, and the Midlands, and the latter with northwest England. With little stoppage of play, no non-injury substitutions, and scanty protective gear, rugby is a *melée* of blood, mud, and drinking songs. An oval-shaped ball is carried or passed backward until the team is able to touch the ball down past the goal line (a "try" and worth five points) or kick it through the uprights (three points). Club season runs from September to May; the culmination of international rugby is the **Rugby World Cup,** to be hosted by France in October of 2007.

Though fanatically followed in the Commonwealth, **cricket** remains a phenomenally confusing spectacle to the uninitiated. The game is played by two 11-player teams on a 22-yard green, marked at each end by two **wickets** (made of three stumps and two bails; www.cricket.org has explanations and diagrams of these mysterious contraptions). In an inning, one team acts as **batsmen** and the other as **fielders.** The batting team sends up two batsmen, and a **bowler** from the fielding side throws the ball so that it bounces toward the wickets. The goal of the fielders is to try to get the batsmen out by **taking** the wickets (hitting the wickets so that the bails fall) or by catching the ball. The batsmen's goal is to make as many runs as possible while protecting their wickets, scoring every time they switch places. The teams switch positions once ten batsmen are out; usually both sides bat twice. Matches last one to five days. International games are known as **Test** matches; the **Ashes,** named for the remains of a cricket bail, are the prize in England's Test series with Australia. Cricket has its own **World Cup,** set for February and March of 2007. London's **Lords** cricket grounds is regarded as the spiritual home of the game.

Tennis, a sport with a long history, was becoming the game of the upper class at the end of the 15th century, when Henry VII played in slimming black velvet. As the game developed, cooler white became the traditional color, while today almost any high-tech garb goes. For two weeks in late June and early July, tennis buffs all over the world focus their attention on **Wimbledon,** a bastion of strawberries-and-cream lovers and home to the only Grand Slam event played on grass.

HORSES AND COURSES. The Brits have a special affinity for their horses, demonstrated in the tallyhooing of fox-killing excursions and Princess Anne's competition in **equestrian** during the 1976 Olympics. In late June, **polo** devotees flock to the **Royal Windsor Cup.** Horse-racing also pretends to noble status. An important society event, the Royal Gold Cup Meeting at **Ascot** has occurred in the second half of June for every summer since 1711, though some see it as an excuse for Brits of all strata to indulge in drinking and gambling while wearing over-the-top hats. Top hats also distinguish the famed **Derby** (DAR-bee), now the Vodafone Derby which has been run since 1780 on Epsom Racecourse, Surrey, on the first Saturday of June.

Britain remains a force in rowing, and the annual **Henley Royal Regatta,** on the Thames in Oxfordshire, is the most famous series of rowing races in the world. The five-day regatta ends on the first Sunday in July; Saturday is the most popular day, but some of the best races are the Sunday finals. The **Boat Race** (also on the Thames, but in London), between Oxford and Cambridge, enacts the traditional rivalry between the schools. Britain is the center of Formula One racecar design, and the **British Grand Prix** is held every July at Silverstone racecourse in Northamptonshire. Meanwhile, the **T.T. Races** bring hordes of screeching motorcycles to the Isle of Man during the first two weeks of June (p. 389).

HOLIDAYS AND FESTIVALS

It's difficult to travel anywhere in the British Isles without bumping into some kind of festival. Below is a not-at-all-comprehensive list of festivals in England; the local Tourist Information Centre for any town can point you toward the nearest scene of revelry and merry-making, and *Let's Go* tries to list individual events in the appropriate towns. The chart below also includes the UK-wide **public holidays;** see the corresponding sections of Scotland (p. 543), Wales (p. 453), and Ireland (p. 722) for more country-specific festivals. **Bank holidays** are listed in the Appendix.

DATE IN 2005	NAME AND LOCATION	DESCRIPTION
February 1	Chinese New Year, London	Fireworks! Lots of fireworks!
April 23	St. George's Day	Honoring England's dragon-slaying patron saint
May	Brighton Festival	Largest mixed-arts festival in England
May 13-15	Chelsea Flower Show	The world's premier garden event
May 28-June 10	T.T. Races, Isle of Man	The big event in the Road Racing Capital of the World
June	The Derby, Surrey	Horses and hats!
June	Glastonbury Festival	Britain's gigantic three-day homage to rock
June 14-18	Royal Ascot, York	Hats and horses!
June 20-July 3	Wimbledon	A lot of racquets and a BIG silver dish
June 29-July 3	Henley Royal Regatta	The world's premier boat race
August 20-30	Manchester Pride	A wild street party in Manchester's Gay Village
August 26-27	Notting Hill Carnival	Mad London street party

ENGLAND

LONDON

When a man is tired of London, he is tired of life; for there is in London all that life
can afford.
—Samuel Johnson

London offers the visitor a bewildering array of choices: Leonardo at the National
or Hirst at Tate Modern; tea at The Ritz or chilling in the Fridge; Rossini at the
Royal Opera or *Les Mis* at the Queen's; Bond Street couture or Camden cutting-
edge—you could spend your entire stay just deciding what to do and what to leave
out. London is often described as more a conglomeration of villages than a unified
city. While this understates the civic pride Londoners take in their city as a whole,
it is true that locals are strongly attached to their neighborhoods. Each area's traditions are still alive and evolving, from the City's 2000-year-old association with
trade to Notting Hill's West Indian Carnival. Thanks to the feisty independence
and diversity of each area, the London "buzz" is continually on the move—every
few years a previously disregarded neighborhood explodes into cultural prominence. In the 60s Soho and Chelsea swung the world; the late 80s saw grunge rule
the roost from Camden; and in the 90s the East End sprung Damien Hirst and the
Britpack artists on the world. More recently, South London has come to prominence with the cultural rebirth of the South Bank and the thumping nightlife of a
recharged Brixton. If you're spending a significant amount of time in London,
you'll find more extensive coverage in ⬛*Let's Go: London 2005.*

✈ INTERCITY TRANSPORTATION

BY PLANE

HEATHROW

Heathrow (☎ 0870 000 0123; www.baa.co.uk/main/airports/heathrow) is colossal,
crowded, and chaotic—what you'd expect from one of the world's busiest airports.

Underground: ☎ 7222 1234. Heathrow's two Tube stations form a loop on the end of
the **Piccadilly Line**—trains stop first at Heathrow Terminal 4 and then at Heathrow Terminals 1, 2, 3 (both Zone 6) before swinging back towards central London. Note that
stairs are an integral part of most Tube stations. (50-70min. from central London, every
4-5min. £3.80, under 16 £1.50.)

Heathrow Express: ☎ 0845 600 1515. Provides a speedy but expensive connection
from Heathrow to Paddington station. Buy tickets at Heathrow Express counters, on
board, or at self-service machines; railpasses and Travelcards not valid. (15min.,
every 15min. 5:10am-11:40pm. £13, round-trip £25; children £6/£11.50; £2 extra if
bought on board.)

Bus: National Express (☎ 08705 808 080) sends **Airbus A2** crawls from Heathrow to Russel
Square, stopping off at various points on the way. (1¼-1¾hr.; every 30-45min. 6am-8pm
Heathrow-King's Cross. £10; ages 5-15 £5.) **National Express** also runs coaches between
Heathrow and **Victoria Coach Station.** (40min-80min., approx. 3 per hr. Operates daily
5:35am-9:35pm Heathrow-Victoria, 7:30am-11:30pm Victoria-Heathrow.)

Taxis: Licensed (black) cabs cost at least £50 and take 1-1¾hr.

HIGHLIGHTS OF LONDON

ROYAL LONDON. Start at stately **Westminster Abbey** (p. 110), gaze up at **St. Paul's Cathedral** (p. 111), and watch your head at the imposing **Tower of London** (p. 112). To cover the highlights of the South Bank, follow our **Walking Tour** (p. 5).

IN THE GALLERIES. London's museums are some of the finest in the world—from the enormous **British Museum** (p. 127) and **National Gallery** (p. 127) to quirky **Sir John Soane's Museum** (p. 129) and the sleek new **Tate Modern** (p. 128).

ON THE STAGE. The **West End theater** boasts the very best of new drama—and for the best of old drama, check out **Shakespeare's Globe Theatre** (p. 119). Jostle with the other "groundlings" or cram onto hard wooden benches to see the Bard's best works.

GATWICK

Thirty miles south of the city, Gatwick (☎0870 000 2468; www.baa.co.uk/main/airports/gatwick) may look distant, but three train services to London make transport a breeze. The **train station** is in the **South Terminal.** The **Gatwick Express** (☎0845 850 1530; www.gatwickexpress.co.uk) service to **Victoria Station** would like you to think it's the only train to London (30min.; every 15min. 5am-midnight; £12). In fact, cheaper **Connex** (☎0845 5748 4950) trains run the same route almost as frequently and take only 7min. longer (£9.80). Additionally, **Thameslink** (☎0845 748 4950; www.thameslink.co.uk) trains head regularly to **King's Cross Station,** stopping at **London Bridge** and **Blackfriars** (50min.; 2 per hr.; £9.80). Gatwick's distance from London makes **road services** slow and unpredictable. National Express's **Airbus A5** travels to **Victoria Coach Station** (1½hr; every hr. 4:15am-9:15pm; £9.80). Never take a **licensed taxi** from Gatwick to London; the trip will take over an hour and cost at least £90. If you have heavy bags, take the train to Victoria and get a taxi from there.

STANSTED AND LUTON

Many discount airlines (see **By Plane,** p. 30) operate from London's secondary airports. **Stansted** (☎0870 000 0303; www.baa.co.uk/main/airports/stansted) is 30 mi. north of London. **Stansted Express** (☎0845 748 4950) trains run to **Liverpool St. Station** (45min.; every 2-4 per hr.; £13.80). National Express's **Airbus A6/A7** runs to **Victoria Station;** A6 via the West End, A7 via the City (1¼-1¾hr.; about 2 per hr. 5:30am-9:45pm; £10). From **Luton Airport** (☎0845 748 4950; www.londonluton.co.uk) **Thameslink** trains head to **King's Cross, Blackfriars,** and **London Bridge** (30-50min.; 2-4 per hr.; M-Sa 3:20am-1am, Su less frequently 6am-11:15pm), while **Green Line 757** (☎0870 608 7261; www.greenline.co.uk) buses serve the **West End** and **Victoria Station** (1-1¾hr.; 3 per hr.; 8am-6pm, 2 per hr. 6-11pm, every hr. 11pm-8am; £9, ages 5-15 £5.50).

BY TRAIN

London's array of mainline stations dates from the Victorian era, when each railway company had its own city terminus; see the box below for service information. All London termini are well served by bus and Tube; major stations sell various **Railcards,** which offer regular discounts on train travel (see **By Train,** p. 31).

BY BUS

Most long-distance buses trundle into **Victoria Coach Station** (⊖Victoria), Buckingham Palace Rd. **National Express** is the largest operator of intercity services. (☎08705 808 080; www.nationalexpress.com.) International services are domi-

LONDON

Central London

● SIGHTS

Albert Memorial, 59	B4
Apsley House, 61	C4
The Barbican, 17	E3
British Library, 2	D2
British Museum, 13	D3
Buckingham Palace, 63	C4
Cabinet War Rooms, 68	D4
Chelsea Physic Garden, 83	C5
Chinatown, 40	D4

Courtaud Institute Galleries, 45	D4
Design Museum, 55	F4
The Gilbert Collection, 46	D4
Guildhall, 21	E3
Hayward Gallery, 70	D4
The Houses of Parliament, 74	D4
ICA, 66	D4
Imperial War Museum, 87	E5
Kensington Palace, 57	B4
London Eye, 71	D4
London Planetarium, 7	C3
London Transport Museum, 32	D3

Madame Tussaud's, 8	C3
Marble Arch, 28	C3
Millennium Bridge, 47	E4
Monument, 52	F4
Museum of London, 18	E3
National Gallery, 42	D4
Natural History Museum, 79	B5
National Portrait Gallery, 41	D4
Royal Academy, 39	D4
Royal Albert Hall, 60	B4
Royal Courts of Justice, 33	E3
The Royal Hospital, 84	C5

LONDON

The Royal Mews, 64	C4	St. Paul's Church, 31	D3	Theatre Royal, Dury Lane, 30	D3
Royal Opera House, 29	D3	Savile Row, 38	D3	Tower Bridge, 54	F4
St. Bartholomew the Great, 16	E3	Science Museum, 80	B5	The Tower of London, 53	F4
St. Bride's, 35	E3	Shakespeare's Globe		Trafalgar Square, 43	D4
St. Etheldreda's, 14	E3	Theatre, 49	E4	University College London, 10	D3
St. James's Palace, 65	D4	Sir John Soane's Museum, 20	E3	Victoria and Albert Museum, 81	B5
St. John's Square, 11	E3	Smithfield Market, 15	E3	The Wallace Collection, 19	C3
St. Margaret's Westminster, 73	D4	South Bank Centre, 69	D4	The Wellington Arch, 62	C4
St. Martin-in-the-Fields, 44	D4	Southwark Cathedral, 51	E4	Westminster Abbey, 75	D4
St. Mary-le-Bow, 37	E3	Tate Britain, 86	D5	Westminster Cathedral, 85	D5
St. Pancras Station, 1	D2	Tate Modern, 48	E4	Whitehall, 67	D4
St. Paul's Cathedral, 36	E3	The Temple, 34	E3		

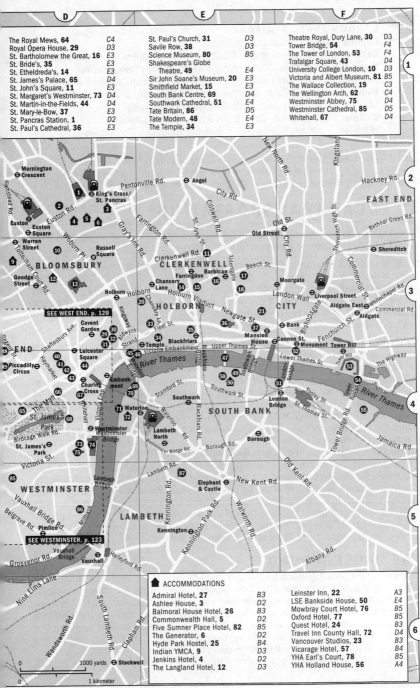

LONDON

ACCOMMODATIONS

Admiral Hotel, 27	B3	Leinster Inn, 22	A3
Ashlee House, 3	D2	LSE Bankside House, 50	E4
Balmoral House Hotel, 26	B3	Mowbray Court Hotel, 76	B5
Commonwealth Hall, 5	D2	Oxford Hotel, 77	B5
Five Sumner Place Hotel, 82	B5	Quest Hotel, 24	B3
The Generator, 6	D2	Travel Inn County Hall, 72	D4
Hyde Park Hostel, 25	B4	Vancouver Studios, 23	B3
Indian YMCA, 9	D3	Vicarage Hotel, 57	B4
Jenkins Hotel, 4	D2	YHA Earl's Court, 78	B5
The Langland Hotel, 12	D3	YHA Holland House, 56	A4

LONDON TRAIN STATIONS
Charing Cross: Kent (Canterbury, Dover)
Euston: Northwest (Birmingham, Glasgow, Holyhead, Liverpool, Manchester)
King's Cross: Northeast (Cambridge, Edinburgh, Leeds, Newcastle, York)
Liverpool St.: East Anglia (Cambridge, Colchester, Ipswich, Norwich), Stansted
Paddington: West (Oxford), Southwest (Bristol, Cornwall), South Wales (Cardiff)
St. Pancras: Midlands (Nottingham), Northwest (Sheffield)
Victoria: South (Brighton, Canterbury, Dover, Hastings), Gatwick
Waterloo: South and Southwest (Portsmouth, Salisbury), Paris, Brussels

nated by **Eurolines** (☎0870 514 3219; www.eurolines.co.uk). The area around London is served by **Green Line** coaches, which leave from the Eccleston Bridge mall behind Victoria station (☎0870 608 7261; www.greenline.co.uk. ⊖Victoria).

⎚ LOCAL TRANSPORTATION

Local gripes aside, London's public transport system is remarkably efficient. (☎7222 1234, 24 hr.; www.transportforlondon.gov.uk.)

ZONES. Public transport is divided into a series of **concentric zones;** ticket prices depend on the zones passed through during your journey. To confuse matters, the zoning system depends on type of transport. The Tube, DLR, and rail operate on a system of six zones, with **Zone 1** the most central. Buses reduce this to four zones, though Zones 1, 2, and 3 are the same as for the Tube. Almost everything of interest to visitors is found in Zones 1 and 2.

PASSES. You'll save money by investing in a travel pass. Passes work on the zone system, and can be purchased at Tube, DLR, and rail stations, and at newsagents. Beware **ticket touts** hawking secondhand passes—there's no guarantee the ticket will work, and it's illegal (penalties are stiff). Note that **all passes expire** at 4:30am the morning after the printed expiry date. Passes include **One Day Travelcards,** valid for bus, Tube, DLR, and commuter rail services after 9:30am weekdays and all day weekends; **LT Cards,** which differ only in being valid before 9:30am; **Family Travelcards,** for 1-2 adults and 1-4 children traveling together; **Weekend** and **Weekly Travelcards,** valid two consecutive days on weekends and public holidays or seven consecutive days, respectively; and **Bus Passes,** valid only on buses.

All children below the age of 5 can travel for free. Children from ages of 5-10 can travel for free on buses and pay half price on the train and tube. To qualify for child fares, teens aged 14-15 must display a **child-rate Photocard** when purchasing tickets and traveling on public transport. These can be obtained free of charge from any Tube station on presentation of proof of age and a passport-sized photo. Teens aged 16-17 are eligible for 30% discounts on period Travelcard and bus passes; you'll need a **16-17 Photocard,** available at Tube stations.

THE UNDERGROUND

Known as **"the Tube,"** London's Underground provides a fast and convenient way of getting around the capital. The Tube is best suited to longer journeys; within Zone 1, adjacent stations are so close that you might as well walk, and buses are cheaper and often get you closer to your destination. The **Docklands Light Railway (DLR)** is a driverless, overland version of the Tube running in East London; the ticketing structure is the same. If you'll be traveling by Tube a lot, you'll save money with a **Travelcard.** Regular ticket prices depend on two factors: how many zones traveled, and whether you traveled through Zone 1. Tickets must be bought at the **start of your journey** and are valid only for the day of purchase (including round-trips). **Keep your ticket** for the entire journey; it will be checked on the way out. A **carnet** is a pack of 10 tickets for travel in Zone 1, valid one year from purchase (£15); otherwise a single trip in Zone 1 costs £2.

The Tube runs daily approximately **6am-midnight,** giving clubbers that extra incentive to party till dawn. The exact time of the first and last train from each station is posted in the ticket hall: check if you plan on taking the Tube any time after 11:30pm. Trains run less frequently early mornings, late nights, and Sundays.

BUSES

Excellent signposting makes the bus system easy to use even for those with no local knowledge; most stops display a map of local routes and nearby stops, together with a key to help you find the bus and stop you need. Officially, bus stops are either **regular** or **request:** buses are supposed to stop at regular stops (red logo on white background), but only pull up at request stops (white on red) if someone on board rings the bell or someone at the stop indicates with an outstretched arm. In reality, it's safest to ring/indicate for all stops. On the older open-platform "Routemaster" buses, you're free to hop on or off as you like. Normal buses run approximately 5:30am-midnight; a reduced network of **Night Buses** fills in the gap. Double-deckers generally run every 10-15min., while single-decker hoppers should come every 5-8min. (These are averages—it's not uncommon to wait 30min. only for three buses to show up in a row.)

On newer buses, show your pass or buy a ticket from the driver as you board: state your destination or just say the price. Older buses still use conductors, who make the rounds between stops to collect fares. Despite the "exact change" warnings posted on buses, drivers and conductors will give change, though a £5 note will elicit grumbles and anything larger risks refusal. **Keep your ticket** until you get off the bus. Trips including Zone 1 cost £1; journeys wholly outside Zone 1 cost 70p, children aged 5-15 pay 40p regardless of zones traveled.

NIGHT BUSES. When honest folk are in bed, London's Night Buses come out to ferry party-goers home. Night Bus route numbers are prefixed with an **"N";** they typically operate on more or less the same routes as their daytime equivalents and cost the same. Many start from **Trafalgar Square.** Most Night Buses run 1-2 per hr. midnight-5:30am, then revert to pumpkins.

DOUBLE-DECKER DEMISE

Double-decker buses are a fixture in this city of high-profile public transportation. However, these distinctive buses are being quietly removed from the streets of London. This process began in late 2003, and now the London transportation authorities have announced that nearly all will be gone by early 2005. Replacement—single-decker "bendy buses" and bigger, boxier doubles—will lack the convenient open rear exit of their predecessors and will no longer employ the informative conductors, but they will be in compliance with European Union requirements of wheelchair accessibility and a lower floor that facilitates easy entrance/exit for people with disabilities.

Critics assert that the old buses offered a convenience and uniqueness that made the distinctly unsexy world of bus travel appealing to tourists and locals alike. In 2000, London mayor Ken Livingston was promising to add to the city's fleet, and as of 2002 the Transport Authority had "no intention" of withdrawing them. As it turns out, the sometimes-40 year old machines were just too dated to remain in circulation, and plans now call for a token few to remain in circulation on the heavily touristed "Heritage Routes." A grand era is London travel is coming to a close. Enjoy its last days.

THE MILLENIUM MILE: THE SOUTH BANK

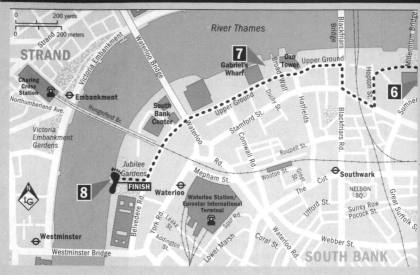

The timeless, understated grace of the Thames, best viewed from the spaceship-like pods of the London Eye, proves that both the area's rich past and its dynamic future fuel its current appeal. Once a rather seedy neighborhood, the South Bank is now home to London's densest concentration of cultural centers, varying from the cutting-edge design of the Tate Modern, which showcases the best of British contemporary

Distance: 2.5 mi. (4km)

When To Go: Start early morning

Start: Tower Hill Underground

Finish: Westminster Underground

Call Ahead: 5, 6, and 7

art, to the storied grandeur of Shakespeare's Globe Theatre, which celebrates British artistic traditions of a more mature vintage. Meanwhile, the Jubilee Line Extension, with its acclaimed underground architecture (including a revamped interior at London Bridge) makes transportation to the area enjoyable and easy.

1 TOWER OF LONDON. Begin your trek to the Tower early to avoid the crowds. Tours given by the Yeomen Warders meet every 90min. near the entrance. Listen as they expertly recount tales of royal conspiracy, treason, and murder. See the **White Tower,** once both fortress and residence of kings. Shiver at the executioner's stone on the tower green, and pay your respects at the Chapel of St. Peter ad Vinculum, holding the remains of 3 queens. Get the dirt on the gemstones at **Martin Tower,** before waiting in line to see the **Crown Jewels.** The jewels include such glittering lovelies as the First Star of Africa, the largest cut diamond in the world (p. 113).

2 TOWER BRIDGE. An engineering wonder that puts its plainer sibling, the London Bridge, to shame. Marvel at its beauty, but skip the **Tower Bridge Experience.** Or better yet, call ahead to inquire what times the Tower drawbridge is lifted (p. 115).

3 DESIGN MUSEUM. On Butler's Wharf, let the Design Museum introduce you to the latest innovations in contemporary design, from marketing to movements in haute couture. See what's to come in the forward-looking Review Gallery or home in on individual designers and products in the Temporary Gallery. From the Design Museum, walk along the **Queen's Walk,** where you will find the **HMS Belfast,** launched upon Normandy, France, on D-Day, 1938.

WALKING TOUR

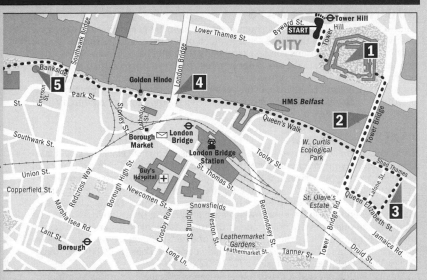

4 LONDON BRIDGE. See the fifth incarnation of a London classic, hopefully more sturdy than its predecessors. The 1832 Old London Bridge is now relocated in Lake Havasu City, Arizona. The **Golden Hinde** is docked on the other side of London Bridge, a full-size and functional replica of Sir Francis Drake's 16th-century war ship.

5 SHAKESPEARE'S GLOBE THEATRE. "I hope to see London once ere I die," says Shakespeare's Davy in *Henry IV, Part II*. In time, he may see it from the beautiful re-creation of Will's most famous theater. Excellent exhibits reveal the secrets of stage effects, explain how Shakespearean actors dressed, and tell of the painstaking process of rebuilding the theater almost 400 years after the original burned down. You might be able to catch a matinee performance if you time your visit right. Call ahead for tour and show times (p. 137).

6 TATE MODERN. It's hard to imagine anything casting a shadow over Shakespeare's Globe Theatre, but the massive former Bankside Power Station does just that. One of the world's premeir modern art museums, the Tate's arrangements promise a new conceptual spin on well-known favorites and works by emerging British artists. Be sure to catch one of the informative docent tours, and don't forget to ogle the rotating installation in the Turbine Room. Having fulfilled your theatrical and artistic appetites, sate your stomach at **Cafe 7** and the **East Room,** which offer meals and snacks, respectively, not to mention fabulous views of the City (p. 119).

7 GABRIEL'S WHARF. fCheaper alternatives to pricey Tate eateries can be found in the wharf's colorful cafés, bars and boutiques further west. If you missed the top floor of the Tate Modern, go to the public viewing gallery on the 8th floor of the OXO Tower. Pass by the South Bank Centre on your way to the London Eye. Established as a primary cultural center in 1951, it now exhibits a range of music from Philharmonic extravaganzas to low-key jazz. You may even catch one of the free lunchtime or afternoon events. Call ahead for dates and times.

8 LONDON EYE. Once known as the Millennium Wheel; given its siblings—the misbehaving "Bridge" and bloated ego of "Dome"—it's no surprise that it shed its Millennium maiden name at the first possible chance (p. 119). The London Eye has now firmly established itself as one of London's top attractions, popular with locals and tourists alike. It offers amazing 360° views from its glass capsules. If you time it right, you can see all of London lit up in the sunset. Book in advance to avoid the long queues.

WALKING TOUR

SUBURBAN RAILWAYS

Almost nonexistent in the city center, London's suburban **commuter rail network** is nearly as extensive as the Tube—and in much of South and East London, it's the only option. Though trains run less frequently than the Tube (generally every 20-30min.), they can dramatically reduce transit time thanks to direct cross-town links, and service often continues later into the night. For journeys combining rail travel with Tube and DLR, you can buy a single ticket valid for the entire trip. Travelcards are also valid on most suburban rail services, though not on intercity lines that happen to make a few local stops.

TAXIS

Taxis in London come in two forms: licensed taxis, known as **black cabs,** and **minicabs,** essentially private cars that offer pre-arranged pickups. Driving a black cab is skilled work: your driver has studied for years to pass a rigorous exam called "The Knowledge" to prove he or she knows the name of every street in central London and how to get there by the shortest possible route. These cabs are specially designed for London's narrow streets and can turn on a sixpence—don't be afraid to hail one from the other side of the road. Available cabs are indicated by the blue "for hire" light by the driver and the orange "taxi" sign on the roof. **Pickups** attach a minimum £2 fee; dispatchers include **Computer Cabs** (☎ 7286 0286), **Dial-a-Cab** (☎ 7253 5000), and **Radio Taxis** (☎ 7272 0272).

Anyone with a car and a driver's license can set themselves up as a "minicab" company; while only licensed cabs can ply the streets for hire, there are no regulations concerning pre-arranged pickups. As a result, competition is fierce and prices are lower than licensed cabs. Unless you know a reliable company, ordering a minicab is something of a crapshoot, though there's rarely any danger involved. Be especially careful with the dodgy drivers who turn up outside clubs at closing—jot down a phone number and call from the club, or arrange a pickup in advance. Always agree on a price with the driver before getting in; some firms have standardized price lists. One good choice is **London Radio Cars** (☎ 8905 0000).

🛈 PRACTICAL INFORMATION

 London's phone code is **020.**

TOURIST INFORMATION CENTRES AND LOCAL SERVICES

Britain Visitor Centre, 1 Regent St. (www.visitbritain.com). ⊖Oxford Circus. Open M 9:30am-6:30pm, Tu-F 9am-6:30pm, Sa-Su 10am-4pm.

London Information Centre, 1 Leicester Pl. (☎ 7930 6769; www.londoninformation.org). ⊖Leicester Sq. Open M 9:30am-6:30pm, Tu-F 9am-6:30pm, Sa-Su 10am-4pm.

Gay and Lesbian Resources: London Lesbian & Gay Switchboard (☎ 7837 7324; www.queery.org.uk). 24hr. helpline and information. **GAY to Z** (www.gaytoz.co.uk). Online and printed directory of gay resources and gay-friendly businesses in Britain.

EMERGENCY AND MEDICAL CARE

Emergency: ☎ 999.

Hospitals: Charing Cross, Fulham Palace Rd. (☎ 8846 1234), entrance on St. Dunstan's Rd., ⊖Hammersmith. **Royal Free,** Pond St. (☎ 7794 0500), ⊖Belsize Park. **St. Thomas's,** Lambeth Palace Rd. (☎ 7188 7982), ⊖Waterloo. **University College Hospital,** Grafton Way (☎ 7387 9300), ⊖Warren St.

LONDON

Pharmacies: Most chemists keep standard hours (usually M-Sa 9:30am-5:30pm); a "duty" chemist in each neighborhood opens Su, though hours may be limited. Late-night and 24hr. chemists are rare; one 24hr. option is **Zafash Pharmacy,** 233 Old Brompton Rd. (☎7373 2798). ⊖Earl's Ct.

Police: London is covered by 2 police forces: the **City of London Police** (☎7601 2222) for the City and the **Metropolitan Police** (☎7230 1212) for the rest. At least 1 station in each of the 32 boroughs is open 24hr. Call ☎7230 1212 to find the nearest station.

COMMUNICATIONS

Internet Access: If you're paying more than £2 per hr., you're paying too much. Try the ubiquitous **easyEverything** (☎7241 9000; www.easyeverything.com). Locations include 9-16 Tottenham Court Rd. (⊖Tottenham Court Rd.); 456/459 The Strand (⊖Charing Cross); 358 Oxford St. (⊖Bond St.); 9-13 Wilson Rd. (⊖Victoria); 160-166 Kensington High St. (⊖High St. Kensington). All open 24hr.

Post Office: Post offices are on almost every major road. When sending mail to London, be sure to include the full post code. The largest office is the **Trafalgar Square Post Office,** 24-28 William IV St. (☎7484 9304). ⊖Charing Cross. All mail sent *Poste Restante* or general delivery to unspecified post offices ends up here. Open M-Th and Sa 8am-8pm, F 8:30am-8pm. **Post Code:** WC2N 4DL.

⚓ ACCOMMODATIONS

Accommodations in London cost a good deal more than anywhere else in the UK. The area near Victoria station (Westminster) is convenient for major sights and transportation. **Bloomsbury,** near the British Museum, has affordable lodgings. In West London, posh **Kensington** and less-so **Bayswater** offer reasonably priced B&Bs. Book well in advance, especially in summer. Book YHAs online at www.yha.org.

WESTMINSTER

▦ **Melbourne House,** 79 Belgrave Rd. (☎7828 3516; www.melbournehousehotel.co.uk). ⊖Pimlico. A clean, well-kept, and recently refurbished establishment with a superbly friendly staff. All rooms with TV, phone, coffee-maker, and kettle; the pride and joy is the luxurious basement double, with a triangular bathtub for 2. No smoking. Continental breakfast included. Reserve 2 weeks ahead; 48hr. cancellation policy. Singles £38, ensuite £60; ensuite doubles £85; ensuite triples £95; ensuite quads £100. MC/V. ❸

Alexander Hotel, 13 Belgrave Rd. (☎7834 9738; www.alexanderhotel.co.uk). ⊖Victoria. Rooms are eclectically furnished with quality fittings, oak dressers, comfy beds, and satellite TV. Breakfast is served 7:30-9am (included). Prices vary according to demand. Singles £45; doubles £65; triples from £75; quads and quints £110. MC/V. ❸

Luna Simone Hotel, 47/49 Belgrave Rd. (☎7834 5897; www.lunasimonehotel.com). ⊖Victoria or Pimlico. Stuccoed Victorian facade conceals pleasant yellow rooms with TV, phone, safety deposit box, and hair dryer. Internet access. English breakfast included. Reserve 2 weeks ahead; 48hr. cancellation policy. Singles £40, ensuite £55; doubles £75; triples £100. Discounts for 1-week stays. AmEx/MC/V. ❸

Georgian House Hotel, 35 George's Dr. (☎7834 1438; www.georgianhousehotel.co.uk). ⊖Victoria. Rooms with TV, phone, hair dryer and kettle. Top-floor "student rooms" are smaller with fewer amenities. Professional staff and elegant decor. English breakfast included. Internet access. Reserve 1 month ahead for Sa-Su and student rooms. Singles £59; doubles £72; triples £90; quads £100. MC/V. ❸

BLOOMSBURY

■ **The Generator,** Compton Pl., off 37 Tavistock Pl. (☎ 7388 7655; www.generatorhostels.com). ⊖Russell Sq. or King's Cross. The ultimate party hostel. Under 18 not allowed unless part of a family group. All rooms have mirrors and washbasins; private doubles have tables and chairs. 4- to 8-bed dorms; some single-sex. Luggage storage, lockers (free—bring your own lock), linens, and laundry. Internet access. Continental breakfast included. Reserve 1 week ahead. Dorms £12.50-17. Mar.-Oct. singles £42; doubles £53; triples £67.50; quads £90; quints £112.50. Discounts for long stays, booking online, student IDs, or VIP Backpacker cards. MC/V. ❶

■ **Ashlee House,** 261-265 Gray's Inn Rd. (☎ 7833 9400; www.ashleehouse.co.uk). ⊖King's Cross St. Pancras. All about quiet, laid-back mellowness. Mixed-sex (all-female available) dorms are airy and bright, while private rooms include table, sink, kettle, luggage room, safe, laundry, and kitchen. Brand new bathrooms and TV room. Continental breakfast included. Towels £1. All rooms lock; no lockers. Internet access £1 per hr. 2-week max stay. 24hr. reception. May-Sept. 16-bed dorms £15; 8- to10-bed £17; 4- to 6-bed £19. Singles £36; doubles £48. Oct.-Apr. £2 less. MC/V. ❶

Jenkins Hotel, 45 Cartwright Gdns. (☎ 7387 2067; www.jenkinshotel.demon.co.uk), entry on Barton Pl. ⊖Euston or King's Cross St. Pancras. Rooms are airy and pleasant. Guests can use the tennis courts in Cartwright Gardens at a reduced rate (£5). Rooms have TV, kettle, phone, fridge, hair dryer, and safe. English breakfast included. No smoking. Reserve 1-2 months ahead in summer. 24hr. cancellation policy. Singles £52, ensuite £72; ensuite doubles (some with tub) £85; ensuite triples £105. MC/V. ❹

The Langland Hotel, 29-31 Gower St. (☎ 7636 5801; www.langlandhotel.com). ⊖Goodge St. The friendly staff keep their large rooms spotless; guests have access to a lounge with satellite TV. Recently refurbished rooms have TV, kettle, and fan. English breakfast included. 48hr. cancellation policy. Singles £45, ensuite £65; doubles £55/£80; triples £75/£95; quads £85/£105. Discounts available for longer stays, students, advance booking, and in winter. AmEx/MC/V. ❸

Indian YMCA, 41 Fitzroy Sq. (☎ 7387 0411; www.indianymca.org). ⊖Warren St. or Great Portland St. Standard student-dorm affair, an institutional (and somewhat musty) feel, but price includes both continental breakfast and an Indian (or Western) dinner. New laundry, lounge, and game room. Deluxe rooms are substantially larger and feature TV, fridge, desk, and kettle. Reserve ahead in summer. £1 membership fee. 1-night deposit required with reservations. £10 cancellation fee. Dorms £20; singles £34, ensuite £52; doubles £49/£55-72. AmEx/MC/V. ❷

Commonwealth Hall, 1-11 Cartwright Gdns. (☎ 7685 3500; www.lon.ac.uk/services/students/halls1/halls2/vacrates.asp). ⊖Russell Sq. Post-war block housing: 425 recently refurbished student singles with telephones; English breakfast included and garden tennis/squash courts. Pantry on each fl., bar, and cafeteria. Open mid-Mar. to late Apr. and mid-June to mid-Sept. Generally reserve at least 3 months ahead for July-Aug. No walkins. Singles £24, half-board £28; UK students half-board £20. MC/V. ❷

KENSINGTON AND EARL'S COURT

■ **Oxford Hotel,** 24 Penywern Rd. (☎ 7370 1161; www.the-oxford-hotel.com). Midsized, bright rooms, all with at least a shower. Comfortable beds, TV, kettle, safe, chair, and clothes rail. Continental breakfast included. Rooms in the annex down the road are less splendid, but still good. 24hr reception. Reserve 2-3 weeks ahead for June. Singles with shower only £37.50, ensuite £53; doubles £59/£69; triples £72/£81; quads £90/£96; quints £110/£120. Discount on stays over 1 week. AmEx/MC/V. ❸

■ **Vicarage Hotel,** 10 Vicarage Gate, (☎ 7229 4030; www.londonvicaragehotel.com). ⊖High St. Kensington. Beautifully kept Victorian house with ornate hallways, TV lounge, and charming bedrooms with kettle and hair dryer (ensuite rooms also have

TV). English breakfast included. Reserve several months ahead with 1 night's deposit; US$ personal checks accepted for deposit with at least 2 months' notice. Singles £46, ensuite £75; doubles £78/£102; triples £95/£130; quads £102/£140. ❸

YHA Holland House, Holland Walk, (☎ 7937 0748). ⊖High St. Kensington or Holland Park. In the middle of Holland Park, with half the rooms in a gorgeous 17th-century mansion. 12- to 20-bed single-sex dorms are less alluring (some bunks are 3-tiered), but a cleaner facility is hard to find. Internet access (7p per min.), TV room, luggage storage, lockers, laundry, and kitchen. Breakfast included; dinners £5-6. Book 2-3 weeks ahead in summer. 24hr reception. Dorms £21.60, under 18 £19.30. Singles £30; doubles £50; triples £70; quads £90. £3 discount w/student ID. MC/V. ❶

Five Sumner Place Hotel, 5 Sumner Pl. (☎ 7584 7586; www.sumnerplace.com). ⊖South Kensington. The amenities of a luxury hotel with the charm of a Victorian house. Spacious, elegant rooms have large windows; all ensuite, TV, fridge, phone, and hair dryer. English breakfast included. 14-day cancellation policy; book 1 month ahead in summer. Singles £85; doubles £130, extra bed £22. AmEx/MC/V. ❺

YHA Earl's Court, 38 Bolton Gdns. (☎ 7373 7083). Victorian townhouse that's considerably better-equipped than most YHAs. The bright single-sex dorms (4-8 people) have lockers (bring your own lock) and sink. Kitchen, 2 spacious TV lounges and luggage storage. Linen and laundry included. Internet access (at an ungodly 7p per min.). Breakfast included for private rooms; otherwise £3.50. 2-week max stay. 24hr. cancellation policy; £5 cancellation fee. Dorms £19.50; under 18 £17.20. Private rooms (book online only; at least 48hr. in advance): doubles £52; quads £76. MC/V. ❶

Mowbray Court Hotel, 28-32 Penywern Rd. (☎ 7373 8285; www.mowbraycourthotel.co.uk). Large 80 room B&B, TV lounge, and bar. Facilities include TV, trouser press, hair dryer, safe, and phone. Continental breakfast included. Reserve a week ahead; 24hr. cancellation policy. 24hr reception. Singles £45, ensuite £52; doubles £56/£67; triples £69/£80; quads £84/£95; quints £100/£110; sextuples £115/£125. Discounts for 1 week stays. AmEx/MC/V. ❸

BAYSWATER

🔲 **Vancouver Studios,** 30 Prince's Sq. (☎ 7243 1270; www.vancouverstudios.co.uk). ⊖Bayswater. Boasting the "convenience of a hotel, with the privacy of an apartment," it offers fully-serviced studios. Uniquely decorated rooms vary in size but all have kitchenette, TV, hair dryer, bath, phone, laundry, and maid service. The "Balcony Studio" for two (£95) is to die for. Single £65; doubles £85-95; triples £120. AmEx/MC/V. ❹

Quest Hostel, 45 Queensborough Terr. (☎ 7229 7782; www.astorhostels.com). ⊖Bayswater or Queensway. Many long-term visitors. Spacious dorms are mostly co-ed (2 female-only rooms available), and nearly all are ensuite. Otherwise, facilities on every other floor. Laundry, luggage storage, Internet access (50p per 15min.) and kitchen. Continental breakfast, linen, and lockers included. 4- to 8-bed dorms £14-17; doubles £42. MC/V. ❶

Admiral Hotel, 143 Sussex Gdns. (☎ 7723 7309; www.admiral-hotel.com). ⊖Paddington. Beautifully kept family-run B&B; all rooms ensuite, with hairdryer, TV, and kettle. Non-smoking. English breakfast included. Call 10-14 days ahead in summer; 4-day cancellation policy. Singles £40-50; doubles £58-75; triples £75-90; quads £88-110; quints £100-130. Ask about winter and long-stay discounts. MC/V. ❸

Hyde Park Hostel, 2-6 Inverness Terr. (☎ 7229 5101; www.astorhostels.com). ⊖Queensway or Bayswater. There's nothing fancy about the tightly-bunked dorms, but 260 beds and a veritable theme park of diversions set it apart. The recently renovated, jungle-themed basement bar and dancefloor hosts DJs and parties (open W-Sa 8pm-3am). Continental breakfast and linen included. Kitchen, laundry, TV lounge, and luggage room. Ages 16-35 only. Reserve 2 weeks ahead in summer; 24hr. cancellation policy.

Internet access 50p per 7min. Book online with 10% non-refundable deposit. 24hr. reception. 10- to 12-bed dorms £11-14; 8-beds £14.50-16; doubles £43-50. 10% ISIC discount. Weekly discounts available. MC/V. ❶

Balmoral House Hotel, 156-157 Sussex Gdns. (☎7723 7445; www.balmoralhousehotel.co.uk). ❺Paddington. Spacious, ensuite rooms with satellite TV, kettle, and hair dryer. English breakfast included. Singles £40; doubles £65; triples £80; quads £100, quints £120. MC/V (5% surcharge). ❸

Leinster Inn, 7-12 Leinster Sq. (☎7729 9641; www.astorhostels.com). ❺Bayswater. Small bar open W-Sa until 3am. Linen and Continental breakfast included. Safes, kitchen, Internet access, luggage room, TV/pool room, and laundry. £10 key deposit. 24hr. reception. 10-bed ensuite £12; 4- to 8-bed dorms £13-16, ensuite £16.50-18.50; singles £27.50-35/£33-40; doubles £44-50/£55-58; triples £54/£57-63. 10% ISIC discount. Weekly discounts available. MC/V. ❶

OTHER NEIGHBORHOODS

🎌 **YHA Oxford Street,** 14 Noel St. (☎0870 770 5984). ❺Oxford Circus. Small, clean, sunny rooms with limited facilities but an unbeatable location for Soho nightlife. Doubles have bunks, sink, mirror, and wardrobe; some triple-decker bunks. Comfy TV lounge. Internet access and well-equipped kitchen. Linen included. Towels £3.50. Pre-packed continental breakfast £3.60. Reserve at least 1 month ahead. 3- to 4-bed dorms £22.60, under-18s £18.20; 2-bed dorms £49.20. ❶

Travel Inn County Hall, Belvedere Rd. (☎0870 238 3300; www.travelinn.co.uk). ❺Westminster or Waterloo. Seconds from the South Bank and Westminster. All rooms are clean, ensuite, and modern with and color TV. Restaurant and bar. Reserve 1 month ahead; cancel by 4pm on day of arrival. English Breakfast £7. Singles/doubles and family rooms, M-Th £85, F-Su £80. AmEx/MC/V. ❹

High Holborn Residence, 178 High Holborn (☎7379 5589; www.lse.ac.uk/collections/vacations). ❺Holborn or Tottenham Crt. Rd. University dorm that converts into a hostel after summer school ends. Perfect location for Covent Garden and the West End. Rooms organized into clusters of 4-5 singles (some doubles), each with phone and shared kitchen and bath. Ensuite rooms are much larger. Bar, laundry, TV and game room. Continental breakfast included. Open Aug.-Sept. 2005. Singles £30; doubles £48, ensuite £58; ensuite triples £68. Some rooms wheelchair-accessible. MC/V. ❷

LSE Bankside House, 24 Sumner St. (☎7107 5750; www.lse.ac.uk/vacations). ❺Southwark or London Bridge. A residence of the London School of Economics, facing the back of the Tate Modern. 800 rooms, all with phone. Laundry, TV lounge, games room, restaurant, and bar. Open July-Sept. English breakfast included. Singles £30, ensuite £42; ensuite doubles £60; ensuite triples £78; ensuite quads £93. MC/V. ❸

🔲 FOOD

Forget stale stereotypes about British food: London's restaurants offer a gastronomic experience as diverse, stylish, and satisfying as you'll find anywhere. Any restaurant charging under £10 for a main course is relatively cheap; add drinks and service and you're nudging £15. That said, it *is* possible to eat cheaply—and well—in London. Lunchtime and early-evening **special offers** save cash. Many of the best budget meals are found in the amazing variety of **ethnic restaurants.** For the best and cheapest ethnic food, head to the source: **Whitechapel** for Bengali *balti*, **Islington** for Turkish *meze*, **Marylebone** for Lebanese *shwarma.* The cheapest places to get the ingredients for your own meal are local **street markets.** For all your food under one roof, the largest supermarket chains are **Tesco, Safeway,** and **Sainsbury's. Asda, Kwik-Save,** and **Somerfield** are "budget" supermarkets, while **Waitrose** and **Marks & Spencer** are more upmarket and a good source of fancier ingredients.

ASIAN		MODERN BRITISH	
busaba eathai	West End ❷	Bleeding Heart Tavern	Holborn ❸
Jenny Lo's Teahouse	Knightsbridge ❷	Books for Cooks	Notting Hill ❶
Mandalay	Marylebone ❶	Bug	South London ❸
Golden Dragon	West End ❷		
Mr. Kong	West End ❷	SANDWICHES & SNACKS	
		La Crêperie de Hampstead	North London ❶
BREAKFAST		Futures	City of London ❶
Chelsea Kitchen	Chelsea ❶		
		SEAFOOD	
CARIBBEAN		George's Portabello Fish Bar	Notting hill ❶
Mango Room	North London ❷	North Sea Fish Restaurant	Bloomsbury ❸
Mr. Jerk	Bayswater ❷		
		SPANISH/LATIN AMERICAN	
FRENCH		Anexo	Clerkenwell ❷
Gordon Ramsay	Chelsea ❺	Goya	Westminster ❸
Raison d'Être	Kensington ❶	Mö	West End ❸
INDIAN			
Aladin	East London ❷	VEGETARIAN	
Café Spice Namaste	City of London ❸	Chelsea Bun	Chelsea ❶
Masala Zone	West End ❷	The Gate	West London ❸
Zaika	Kensington ❺		
		WINE BARS	
ITALIAN		Gordon's Wine Bar	West End ❷
Cantina del Ponte	South Bank ❸	Vats	Bloomsbury ❸
ICCo	Bloomsbury ❷		
		WORLD	
LATE NIGHT		Giraffe	Marylebone ❷
Carmelli Bakery	North London ❶		
MIDDLE EASTERN			
Gallipoli	North London ❷		
Levantine	Bayswater ❷		
Tas	South Bank ❷		

Afternoon tea is a ritual as much as a meal. It involves a long afternoon of sandwiches, scones, pastries, and restrained conversation. The main attraction of afternoon tea is the chance to lounge in sumptuous surroundings and mingle with the upper crust. Most **major hotels** and hoity-toity **department stores** serve tea, but for the ultimate in old-fashioned luxury, take tea at **Ritz,** Piccadilly. Ritz serves tea (£32) M-F at noon, 1:30, 3:30 and 5pm. (☎ 7493 5181. ⊖Green Park. Dress smart.)

BAYSWATER

▨ **Mr. Jerk,** 19 Westbourne Grove (☎ 7221 4678). ⊖Bayswater or Royal Oak. **Branch** at 189 Wardour St. in the West End (☎ 7287 2878). Try their house specialty, jerk chicken (£6.50), or feast on Trinidadian *roti* (£5) or *ackee* (a savory Caribbean fruit) and saltfish (£6). Sip a Guinness Punch or go fully local with Soursap (both £2.50). Open M-Sa 10am-11pm, Su noon-8pm. AmEx/MC/V. ❷

▨ **Levantine,** 26 London St. (☎ 7262 1111). ⊖Paddington. Enter this elegant Lebanese restaurant to the faint aroma of incense and rose petals. Famous *meze* menu (lunches £8.50-15, dinners £19.50-28). A la carte from £3.25. Belly-dancing and *shisha* (water pipe). £1 cover. Open daily noon-1am (food served until midnight). MC/V. ❹

BLOOMSBURY

▨ **ICCo (Italiano Coffee Company),** 46 Goodge St. (☎ 7580 9688). ⊖Goodge St. ICCo serves delicious 11" pizzas (£3). Pre-packaged sandwiches and fresh-baked baguettes from £1.50 (rolls 50p). Buy any hot drink before noon and get a free croissant. Sandwiches ½ price after 4pm. Open M-F 7am-11pm, Sa-Su 9am-11pm. MC/V. ❶

TEA AT BROWN'S

Afternoon tea at Brown's is essential to any visit to London, however short. Here are some hints to make it less daunting:

1. Whenever possible, let your waiter pour your tea for you.

2. If you pour yourself a cup, do not forget to use the strainer provided. It is not optional. This fearless writer found herself with a cup full of silt, and hopes that you will learn from her error.

3. There is no way to drop sugar cubes in your tea without making a loud "plopping" noise, unless you were born an Englishman. I now limit myself to milk.

4. If you manage to finish any one of your three tiers of food, your waiter will bring you another one momentarily—they will feed you until you tell them to stop.

5. Make sure to stop by the bathroom, if only to sit in the armchairs and gawk at the full-length gilded mirrors.

6. People-watching is expected, but be subtle. Remember—if you appear aloof, you may be mistaken for a minor celebrity.

7. Dress appropriately—no jeans, no trainers. Do not, however, show up in full evening dress.

8. Finally, you did not "have" tea at Brown's. You "took" tea at Brown's. Good for you.

—Nicole Cliffe

North Sea Fish Restaurant, 7-8 Leigh St. (☎7387 5892). ⊖Russell Sq. or King's Cross St. Pancras. Fish and chips done right. Offers a boatload of fresh seafood in a warm setting. The takeaway shop sells heaping portions at unbeatable prices (£3.50-5). Entrees £8-17. Open M-Sa noon-2:30pm, 5:30-10:30pm; takeaway M-Sa noon-2:30pm, 5-11pm. AmEx/MC/V. ❸

Vats, 51 Lambs Conduit St. (☎7242 8963). ⊖Russell Square. Walk straight to the bar where the friendly staff is happy to let you taste before you commit (by-the-glass wines only). Monster wine list doesn't cover their entire cellar; don't be afraid to ask for something specific. "Good ordinary claret" £3.50 per glass, £14.50 per bottle. Lunch served noon-2:30pm, dinner (£10-16) 6-9:30pm. Open M-F noon-11pm. AmEx/MC/V. ❸

CHELSEA

Chelsea Bun, 9a Limerston St. (☎7352 3635). Tons of vegetarian and vegan options including faux-sausages in a full English breakfast. Early-bird specials 7am-noon (£2-3). Breakfasts (from £4) served until 6pm. Pasta, burgers, and omelettes £6-8. Min. £3.50 lunch, £5.50 dinner. Open M-Sa 7am-11:30pm, Su 9am-7pm. MC/V. ❶

Chelsea Kitchen, 98 King's Rd. (☎7589 1330). Unpretentious diner fare makes for one of the cheapest sit-down meals in town; entrees with chips and salad £3.30-5. Soup, salads, and sandwiches £2-4, wine £1.40 per glass and £6.80 per bottle. Min. £3 per person. Breakfast served until 11:30am. Open daily 7am-midnight. MC/V. ❶

Gordon Ramsay, 68 Royal Hospital Rd. (☎7352 4441; www.gordanramsay.com). Gordon Ramsay—eccentric artist, former footballer, and celebrity chef. Ramsay's light, innovative French concoctions have been awarded 3 Michelin stars (only 2 other UK restaurants can match that). Set lunch menu is £35, and multi-course dinners £65-80. Reserve 2 weeks ahead for lunch and 1 month for dinner. Open M-F noon-2:50pm and 6:30-11pm. AmEx/MC/V. ❺

THE CITY OF LONDON

Futures, 8 Botolph Alley (☎7623 4529), between Botolph Ln. and Lovat Ln. ⊖Monument. Suits and their lackeys besiege this tiny takeaway for lunch; come before noon. Rotating variety of vegetarian soups (£2-3), salads (£1.50-3), ready-made smoothies (£1.40), and hot dishes (£4). For breakfast there's a variety of pastries (80p), porridge, and hot cereal (£1). Wheelchair accessible. Open M-F 7:30-10am and 11:30am-3pm. Cash only. ❶

■ **Café Spice Namaste,** 16 Prescot St. (☎ 7488 9242). ⊖Tower Hill or DLR: Tower Gateway. While hard to find, Café Spice is worth a bit of a trek. The extensive menu of Goan and Parsee specialities helpfully explains each dish. Meat dishes are on the pricey side (£11-13), but vegetarian meals (£7-9) are affordable. Open M-F noon-3pm, 6:15-10:30pm, Sa 6:30-10:30pm. AmEx/MC/V. ❸

HOLBORN AND CLERKENWELL

■ **Anexo,** 61 Turnmill St. (☎ 7250 3401). ⊖Farringdon. This restaurant-bar serves tasty Iberian creations. Authentic paella (£7.50-9), fajitas (£8.50-10), and tapas (£3.25-5). 2- and 3-course lunch specials £7.50-9.50, 4-course tapas menu £15. M 2-for-1 tapas. Happy hour M-Sa 5-7pm. Takeaway available. Wheelchair accessible. Open M-F 10am-10pm, Sa 6-11pm, Su 4:30-10pm. Bar open until 2am. AmEx/MC/V. ❷

■ **Bleeding Heart Tavern,** corner of Greville St. and Bleeding Heart Yard (☎ 7404 0333). ⊖Farringdon. This "tavern" is in fact quite a good restaurant, split between a slightly posh upstairs pub and a luxurious restaurant below. Highlights include roast suckling pig with delicately spiced shards of apple (£11). Entrees £8-12. Open M-F 7-10:30am, noon-2:30pm and 6-10:30pm. Pub open M-F 11:30am-11pm. AmEx/MC/V. ❸

KENSINGTON AND EARL'S COURT

■ **Zaika,** 1 Kensington High St. (☎ 7795 6533; www.zaika-restaurant.co.uk). ⊖High St. Kensington. One of London's best Indian restaurants. Try the coconut poached prawns (£12). Excellent wine list. Starters £3-12, entrees £12-20 (2-course minimum dinner). Lunch menu £15 for 2 courses, £18 for 3. 5-course dinner menu £38, with wine £57. Reservations recommended. Dress smart. Open M-F noon-2:45pm and 6:30-10:45pm, Sa 6:30-10:45pm, Su noon-2:45pm and 6:30-9:45pm. AmEx/MC/V. ❹

Raison d'Être, 18 Bute St. (☎ 7584 5008). ⊖South Kensington. Catering to the local French community, this quiet eatery offers a bewildering range of filled baguettes and foccacia (£2.50-5). *Salades composées* (£3.20-5.20) and light dishes (like yogurt with fruit, £2.50) made to order. Open M-F 8am-6pm, Sa 9:30am-4pm. Cash only. ❶

KNIGHTSBRIDGE AND BELGRAVIA

■ **Jenny Lo's Teahouse,** 14 Eccleston St. (☎ 7259 0399). ⊖Victoria. The small interior bustles on weekdays, but delicious *cha shao* (pork noodle soup; £5.75) and the broad selection of pan-Asian noodles (£5.75-7.50) are worth the wait. Vegetarian options abound. Delivery and takeaway. Open M-F 11:30am-3pm, 6-10pm. Cash only. ❷

MARYLEBONE AND REGENT'S PARK

■ **Mandalay,** 444 Edgware Rd. (☎ 7258 3696). ⊖Edgware Rd. 5min. walk north from the Tube. Lunch specials are a great value (curry and rice £3.90; 4 courses, including a banana fritter, £6). Be sure to ask for the full menu, which includes an explanation of Burmese cuisine. Entrees £3-7.50. No smoking. Reservations recommended at peak hours. Open M-Sa noon-2:30pm and 6-10:30pm. AmEx/MC/V. ❶

Giraffe, 6-8 Blandford St. (☎ 7935 2333; www.giraffe.net). ⊖Bond St. or Baker St. Decor is eclectic-modern (lots of bamboo and greenery), food is eclectic-tasty (from noodles to Mexican burgers, £7-9). Early bird specials 5-7pm: 2 course dinner £7. Communal tables reduce privacy, but keep the atmosphere cheerful. Wheelchair accessible. Open M-F 8am-4pm and 5-10:45pm, Sa-Su 9am-4pm and 5-10:45pm. AmEx/MC/V. ❷

NOTTING HILL

■ **George's Portobello Fish Bar,** 329 Portobello Rd. (☎ 8969 7895). ⊖Ladbroke Grove. George opened up here in 1961, and the place has lived through various incarnations. It's currently disguised as a 50s-style diner, but the fish and chips are as good as ever (£4-5). Open M-F 11am-midnight, Sa 11am-9pm, Su noon-9:30pm. ❶

LONDON

THE BIG SPLURGE

TWO VIEWS FOR TWO

Forget the fancy restaurant dinners and walks on the beach. For a different kind of romantic evening, reserve a "Cupid's Capsule" just for two on the **London Eye,** and whisk your significant other nearly 450 ft. into the air. What could be more charming than cuddling up in your private glass pod as you slowly ascend to the top of the Eye and revel in the spectacular 360-degree bird's-eye views?

After returning to the ground, follow up the evening of sightseeing with a leisurely **champagne cruise** on the *Silver Bonito*, which departs from the pier at the Eye. St. Paul's, the Houses of Parliament, the Tower of London, the Globe Theatre, and the Tate Modern are all visible from the boat, which also offers live commentary, sun-deck seating, and covers in case of rain. On a clear night, the sunset on the river is beautiful.

(The Champagne Cruise Package, £45. Package guarantees fast-track entry (no long lines!) to the London Eye, followed by a 45-minute champagne cruise, souvenir guidebook, and single-use flash camera. The Cupid's Capsule, £300, is a "flight" on the Eye for two, including champagne served by your host, a guidebook, and a box of chocolates. Book on www.ba-londoneye.com, ☎ 870 443 9185, or in person in County Hall ticket office.)

Books for Cooks, 4 Blenheim Crescent (☎ 7221 1992). ⊖Ladbroke Grove. At lunchtime, owner Eric and his crew of chefs "test" recipes from new titles. There's no telling what will be served, but you can rely on the excellent cakes (£2). Daily workshops (£25; by reservation). Bookstore open Tu-Sa 10am-6pm. Food Tu-Sa 10am-2:30pm or so. ❶

THE SOUTH BANK

Cantina del Ponte, 36c Shad Thames, Butler's Wharf (☎ 7403 5403). ⊖Tower Hill or London Bridge. Given the quality of the Italian food (especially the desserts), the fixed menu is a bargain at £11 for 2 courses, £13.50 for 3 (M-F noon-3pm and 6-7:30pm). Pizzas £6-8. Entrees £10-15. Wheelchair accessible. Open M-Sa noon-3pm and 6-10:45pm, Su noon-3pm and 6-9:45pm. AmEx/MC/V. ❸

Tas, 33 The Cut (☎ 7928 2111). ⊖Southwark. Also 72 Borough High St. (☎ 7928 3300). **Tas Cafe,** 76 Borough High (☎ 7403 8559). **Tas Pide,** 20-22 New Globe Walk (☎ 7928 3300; www.tasrestaurant.com). ⊖London Bridge. A group of stylish Turkish spots. Entrees £6-9; 2-course menu £7.45 and *meze* menu £7-10. *Pide,* Anatolian pizza, has myriad options (£6-7). Live music daily 7:30pm. Reservations recommended. Wheelchair accessible. Open M-Sa noon-11:30pm, Su noon-10:30pm. AmEx/MC/V. ❷

THE WEST END

Mô, 23 Heddon St. (☎ 7434 3999). ⊖Piccadilly or Oxford Circus. Restaurant, tea room, and bazaar, Mô is an aesthetic slice of Marrakesh. Mix and match from their tapas-style dishes (£6-£7.50), and wash it down with some mint tea (£2.50). *Shisha* available (£9-20). Open M-W 11am-11pm, Th-Sa noon-midnight. AmEx/MC/V. ❸

Masala Zone, 9 Marshall St. (☎ 7287 9966; www.realindianfood.com). Also in Islington at 80 Upper St.; (☎ 7359 3399). ⊖Oxford Circus. Menu has typical favorites (£5-6), "street food," which comes in small bowls (£3-5), and the large *Thali* platter, which allows you to sample a variety of dishes (£8-11). Open M-F noon-2:45pm, 5:30-11pm, Sa 12:30-3pm, 5-11pm, Su 12:30-3:30pm, 6-10:30pm. MC/V. ❷

busaba eathai, 106-110 Wardour St. (☎ 7255 8686). Locals and students queue for marvelous Thai cuisine (£5-8) served at communal tables in a sea of polished wood. Open M-Th noon-11pm, F-Sa noon-11:30pm, Su noon-10pm. AmEx/MC/V. ❷

Golden Dragon, 28-29 Gerrard St. (☎ 7734 2763). The ritziest and best-known dim sum joint in Chinatown. From veggie staples to minced prawn and sugarcane treats (each dish £2-3). Regular dinner items £5.50-9. Set dim sum meal £12.50-22.50. Open M-Th noon-11:30pm, F-Sa noon-midnight, Su 11am-11pm. AmEx/MC/V. ❷

Mr. Kong, 21 Lisle St. (☎ 7437 7341). If you're up for some duck's web with fish lips (£12) or spicy pig's knuckles with jellyfish (£8.80), this is the place to go. Less-adventurous eats from £6. The menu is huge, and vegetarian options abound (try the mock crispy duck for £7. £7 minimum dinner. Open daily noon-3am. AmEx/MC/V. ❷

Gordon's Wine Bar, 47 Villiers St. (☎ 7930 1408; www.gordonswinebar.com). ⊖Embankment or Charing Cross. A wine bar has been on the site since 1890. Choose an entree, then pile on as much as you like from the salad bar (£6-10). Sherry and port from wood casks £3.50 per glass, vast wine list (£3.60 per glass, £14 per bottle). Open M-Sa 11am-11pm, Su noon-10pm. AmEx/MC/V. ❷

WESTMINSTER

Goya, 34 Lupus St. (☎ 7976 5309). ⊖Pimlico. One of two corner Goya tapas bars. Plentiful vegetarian options. Generous tapas mostly £3-5; 3 is more than enough. Special sangria £3. Wheelchair accessible. Open daily noon-11:30pm. AmEx/MC/V.

GREATER LONDON

NORTH LONDON

▨ **Gallipoli,** 102 Upper St. (☎ 7359 0630), **Gallipoli Again,** 120 Upper St. (☎ 7359 1578), **Gallipoli Bazaar,** 107 Upper St. Patterned tiles and hanging lamps provide the setting for Turkish delights like *Iskender Kebap* (grilled lamb with yogurt and marinated pita bread, £6). Reservations recommended F-Sa. Wheelchair accessible. Open M-Th 10:30am-11pm, F-Sa 10:30am-midnight, Su 10:30am-11pm. MC/V. ❷

▨ **Mango Room,** 10-12 Kentish Town Rd. (☎ 7482 5065). The small Caribbean menu favors fish, complemented with plenty of mango, avocado, and coconut sauces (entrees £9-12). Points for presentation. Potent tropical drinks served from the tiny bar at night. Reservations recommended for weekends. Wheelchair accessible. Open M 6pm-midnight, Tu-Sa noon-3pm and 6pm-midnight, Su noon-11pm. MC/V. ❷

Le Crêperie de Hampstead, 77 Hampstead High St. (metal stand on the side of the King William IV). Don't let the slow-moving line deter you; these phenomenal crepes are worth any wait. Try the mushroom with ham and tarragon cheese (£3.50), or the "Banana Butterscotch Cream Dream" (£2.60). 40p extra gets you gooey Belgian chocolate (plain, milk, or white). Open M-Th 11:45am-11pm, F-Su 11:45am-11:30pm. ❶

Carmelli Bakery, 128 Golders Green Rd. (☎ 8455 2074). Carmelli's golden, egg-glazed challah (£1.25-2) is considered the best in London. With the bagels and sinfully good pastries (£1.50), it's hard to go wrong here. Packed F afternoons, as every Jewish mother in London scrambles to get bread for the Sabbath. Wheelchair accessible. Hours vary, but generally open daily 6am-1am; Th and Sa 24hr. Cash only. ❶

SOUTH, EAST, AND WEST LONDON

▨ **Bug** (☎ 7738 3366; www.bugbar.co.uk), in the crypt of St. Matthew's Church, Brixton Hill. ⊖Brixton. Eerie lighting and decor give this small dining room and lounge a gothic atmosphere—then again, what else do you expect when dining in a crypt? North African lamb and Cajun chicken £7.50-13. Su "Bug Roast" gets you 2 courses (£11.50). Reservations essential. Open Tu-Th 5-11pm, F-Sa 5-11:30pm, Su 1-9pm. MC/V. ❸

LONDON

THE LOCAL STORY

QUEEN'S GUARD

Let's Go got the scoop on a London icon, interviewing Corporal of Horse Simon Knowles, an 18-year veteran of The Queen's Guard.

LG: What sort of training did you undergo?

SK: In addition to a year of basic military camp, which involves mainly training on tanks and armored cars, I was also trained as a gunner and radio operator. Then I joined the service regiment at 18 years of age.

LG: So it's not all glamour?

SK: Not at all, that's a common misconception. After armored training, we go through mounted training on horseback in Windsor for 6 months where we learn the tools of horseback riding, beginning with bareback training. The final month is spent in London training in full state uniform.

LG: Do the horses ever act up?

SK: Yes, but it's natural. During the Queen's Jubilee Parade, with 3 million people lining the Mall, to expect any animal to be fully relaxed is absurd. The horses rely on the rider to give them confidence. If the guard is riding the horses confidently and strongly, the horse will settle down.

LG: Your uniforms look pretty heavy. Are they comfortable?

🍴 **Aladin,** 132 Brick Ln. (☎ 7247 8210). Food that's a cut above the rest makes Aladin one of Brick Ln.'s more popular *balti* joints. Entrees £3-8.50, 3-course lunch £5.90. Open M-Th, Su noon-11:30pm, F-Sa noon-midnight. Cash only. ❷

The Gate, 51 Queen Caroline St. (☎ 8748 6932). ⊖Hammersmith. It feels like a hidden find: go through the garden gate and up the external stairs on the right. One of London's top vegetarian restaurants with plenty of vegan options. Entrees £8-13.50. Deservedly popular at all times; reserve a table for dinner. Wheelchair accessible. Open M-F noon-3pm and 6-11pm, Sa 6-11pm. AmEx/MC/V. ❸

🔎 SIGHTS

ORGANIZED TOURS. The classic London tour is on an open-top **double-decker bus**—and in fine weather, it's undoubtedly the best way to get a good overview of the city. **The Big Bus Company,** 48 Buckingham Palace Rd., runs hop-on, hop-off tours every 15min., 1hr. walking tours, and a mini Thames cruise. (☎ 7233 9533; www.bigbus.co.uk) ⊖Victoria. £18, children £9.) **London Duck Tours,** County Hall, operates a fleet of amphibious vehicles that follow a 60-70min. road tour with a 30min. splash into the Thames. (☎ 7928 3132; www.frogtours.com. ⊖Waterloo or Westminster. £17.50, concessions £14, children £12, families £50.) **Original London Walks** is the city's oldest and biggest walking-tour company, running 12-16 walks per day, from "The Beatles Magical Mystery Tour" to nighttime "Jack the Ripper's Haunts," and tours of museums. (☎ 7624 3978; www.walks.com. Most walks 2hr. £6, concessions £4, children free.) Departing from the LBTC store, Gabriel's Wharf, the **London Bicycle Tour Company** runs leisurely tours designed to keep contact with traffic to a minimum; prices include bike, helmet, and comprehensive insurance. (☎ 7928 6838; www.londonbicycle.com. ⊖Waterloo or Southwark. East Tour Sa 2pm, Royal West Su 2pm; both 9 mi., 3½hr. Middle London M-F 2pm; 6mi., 3hr. Book ahead. £16.) From Waterloo Pier and Embankment Pier, year-round **Catamaran Cruises** operates a nonstop Thames cruise with recorded commentary. (☎ 7925 1185; www.bateauxlondon.com. £7.50, concessions £5.80.)

MAJOR ATTRACTIONS

BUCKINGHAM PALACE

At the end of the Mall, between Westminster, Belgravia, and Mayfair. ⊖St. James's Park, Victoria, Green Park, or Hyde Park Corner. ☎ 7839 1377; www.royal.gov.uk.

THE STATE ROOMS. The Palace opens to visitors for two months every summer while the royals are off sunning themselves. Don't look for any insights into the Queen's personal life—the **State Rooms** are used only for formal occasions; as such, they are also the most sumptuous in all of Britain. The **Galleries** display many of the finest pieces in the outstanding Royal Collection, including Rembrandts and Vermeers. Since 2001, Elizabeth II has also allowed commoners into the gardens—keep off the grass! *(Entrance on Buckingham Palace Rd. Tickets available at ☎ 7766 7300 or the Ticket Office, Green Park. Book ahead. Open daily Aug.-late Sept. 9:30am-4:15pm. £12.95, concessions £11, under 17 £6.50, under 5 free, families £30.)*

CHANGING OF THE GUARD. The Palace is protected by a detachment of **Foot Guards** in full dress uniform, bearskin hats and all. Accompanied by a band, the "New Guard" starts marching down Birdcage Walk from Wellington Barracks around 10:30am, while the "Old Guard" leaves St. James's Palace around 11:10am. When they meet at the central gates of the palace, the officers of the regiments touch hands, symbolically exchanging keys, *et voilà*, the guard is officially changed. Show up well before 11:30am and stand directly in front of the palace, or watch from the steps of the Victoria Memorial. *(Daily Apr.-Oct., every other day Nov.-Mar., provided the Queen is in residence, it's not raining hard, and there are not pressing state functions. Call ☎ 7766 7300 to hear about any interruptions. Free.)*

THE HOUSES OF PARLIAMENT

Parliament Sq., in Westminster. Enter at St. Stephen's Gate, between Old and New Palace Yards. ⊖Westminster. Contact: Commons Info Office ☎ 7219 4272; www.parliament.uk. Lords Info Office ☎ 7219 3107; www.lords.uk. Debates: Both houses are open to all while Parliament is in session (Oct.-July M-W); afternoon waits can be over 2hr. M-Th after 6pm and F are least busy, but there may be an early adjournment. Tickets required for Prime Minister's Question Time (W noon). For tickets, write to your MP; non-residents contact your embassy. Commons usually in session M-W 2:30-9:30pm, Th 11:30am-7:30pm, F 9:30am-3pm. Lords usually sit M-W from 2:30pm, Th 3pm, occasionally F 11:30am; closing times vary. Tours: British residents: Tours held year-round M-W 9:30am-noon, F 2:30-5:30pm; contact your MP to book. Overseas visitors: Oct.-July, tours F 3:30-5:30pm. Non-residents must apply in writing at least 4 weeks ahead to: Parliamentary Education Unit, Norman Shaw Building, SW1A 2TT (☎ 7219 2105; edunit@parliament.uk). Summer tours: Open to all Aug.-Sept. M-Sa 9:15am-4:30pm. Reserve through Firstcall (☎ 0870 906 3773). £7, concessions £5, under 5 free.

SK: They're not comfortable at all. They were designed way back in Queen Victoria's time, and the leather trousers and boots are very solid. The uniform weighs about 3 stone [about 45 lb.].

LG: How do you overcome the itches, sneezes, and bees?

SK: Discipline is instilled in every British soldier during training. We know not to move a muscle while on parade no matter what the provocation or distraction—unless, of course, it is a security matter. But our helmets are akin to wearing a boiling kettle on your head; to relieve the pressure, sometimes we use the back of our sword blade to ease the back of the helmet forward.

LG: How do you make the time pass while on duty?

SK: The days are long. At Whitehall the shift system is derived upon inspection in Barracks. Smarter men work on horseback in the boxes in shifts from 10am-4pm; less smart men work on foot from 7am-8pm. Some guys count the number of buses that drive past. Unofficially, there are lots of pretty girls around here, and we *are* allowed to move our eyeballs.

LG: What has been your funniest distraction attempt?

SK: One day a taxi pulled up, and out hopped 4 Playboy bunnies, who then posed for a photo shoot right in front of us. You could call that a distraction if you like.

The **Palace of Westminster,** the building in which Parliament sits, has been at the heart of English government since the 11th century, when Edward the Confessor established court here. Westminster Hall aside, what little remained of the Norman palace was entirely destroyed in the massive fire of 1834; the rebuilding started a year later under the command of Charles Barry and Augustus Pugin. Access has been restricted since a bomb killed an MP in 1979. If you can't get on a tour, worry not: debates are open to all while the Houses are in session (Oct.-July).

OUTSIDE THE HOUSES. Facing the statue of Cromwell at about the midpoint of the complex, **Old Palace Yard** is the triangular area to the right. On the site of past executions (including those of Walter Raleigh and Guy Fawkes), a statuesque Richard I lords over parked cars. On the left, **New Palace Yard** is a good place to spy your favorite MPs entering the complex through the Members' entrance. Behind Cromwell squats **Westminster Hall,** sole survivor of the 1834 fire. Unremarkable from the outside, its chief feature is a 14th-century hammerbeam roof, considered the finest timber roof ever made. Famous defendants during its centuries as a law court include Saint Thomas More and Charles I. These days, it's used for public ceremonies and occasional exhibitions. The **Clock Tower** is universally, and wrongly, known as **Big Ben;** that name actually refers only to the bell within, cast in 1858 under the supervision of rotund Commissioner of Works Benjamin Hall.

DEBATING CHAMBERS. Visitors to the debating chambers must first pass through **St. Stephen's Hall,** which stands on the site of St. Stephen's Chapel. Formerly the king's private chapel, in 1550 St. Stephen's became the meeting place of the House of Commons. The Commons have since moved on, but four brass markers point out where the Speaker's Chair used to stand. At the end of the hall, the **Central Lobby** marks the separation of the two houses, with the Lords to the south and the Commons to the north. The ostentatious **House of Lords** is dominated by the sovereign's Throne of State under a gilt canopy. The Lord Chancellor presides over the Peers from the **Woolsack,** a red cushion the size of a VW Beetle. Next to him rests the man-sized **Mace,** brought in to open the House each morning. In contrast is the restrained **House of Commons,** with simple green-backed benches under a plain wooden roof. This is not entirely due to the difference in class—the Commons was destroyed by bombs in 1941, and rebuilding took place during an era of post-war austerity. The Speaker sits at the center-rear of the chamber, with government MPs to his right and the opposition to his left. The front benches are reserved for government ministers and their opposition "shadows"; the Prime Minister and the Leader of the Opposition face off across their dispatch boxes. With room for only 437 out of 635 MPs, things can get hectic when all are present.

WESTMINSTER ABBEY

Parliament Sq., in Westminster. Access Old Monastery, Cloister, and Garden from Dean's Yard, behind the Abbey. ↻Westminster. Abbey ☎7654 4900; Chapter House 7222 5152; www.westminster-abbey.org. Partially wheelchair accessible. Abbey open M-Tu and Th-F 9:30am-3:45pm, W 9:30am-3:45pm and 6-7pm, Sa 9:30am-1:45pm, Su open for services only. Museum open daily 10am-4pm. Chapter House daily 10am-4pm. Cloisters daily 8am-6pm. Garden Apr.-Sept. Tu-Th 10am-6pm; daily Oct.-Mar. 10am-4pm. Audioguides: Available M-F 9:30am-3pm, Sa 9:30am-1pm. £2. Tours: 90min. M-F 10, 11am, 2, 3pm; Sa 10, 11am; Apr.-Oct. also M-F 10:30am and 2:30pm. £3, includes Old Monastery. Abbey and Museum £6, concessions and ages 11-15 £4, under 11 free, families £12. Services free. Cloisters and Garden free. No photography.

On December 28, 1065, Edward the Confessor, last Saxon King of England, was buried in his still-unfinished abbey of the West Monastery; a year later, the abbey saw the coronation of William the Conqueror. Thus, even before it was completed, the abbey's twin traditions as figurative birthplace and literal resting place of royalty had been established. Later monarchs continued to add to it, but the biggest change was constitutional rather than physical: in 1540 Henry VIII dissolved the monasteries, expelling or slaughtering the monks and stripping churches of their wealth. Fortunately, the king's respect for his royal forebears outweighed his vindictiveness against the Pope, and Westminster escaped desecration.

INSIDE THE ABBEY. Visitors enter through the **Great North Door** into **Statesman's Aisle,** littered with monuments to 18th- and 19th-century politicians. From here, the ambulatory leads past a few chapels to the left and the **Shrine of St. Edward** to the right. Around the Confessor's shrine, the **House of Kings** displays the tombs of monarchs from Henry III (d. 1272) to Henry V (d. 1422). At the far end of the Shrine stands the **Coronation Chair,** built for Edward I. The shelf below the seat was made to house the Scottish Stone of Scone (see **Stone of Destiny,** p. 45), which Edward stole in 1296. Stairs lead from there to the **Lady Chapel,** now a Tudor mausoleum; side aisles hold **Elizabeth I,** in the north, and **Mary, Queen of Scots,** in the south. Returning to the center of the Lady Chapel, the nave is dominated by the carved stalls of the **Order of the Bath;** at its end, **Henry VII** lies within a wrought-iron screen.

The south transept holds the abbey's most famous and popular attraction: **Poets Corner.** Its founding member was buried here for reasons nothing to do with literary repute—**Chaucer** had a job in the abbey administration. Plaques at his feet commemorate both poets and prose writers. At the very center of the abbey, a short flight of steps leads up to the **Sanctuary,** where coronations take place. Admire the 13th-century mosaic floor from behind the rope. After a detour through the cloisters or optional visits to the Old Monastery and gardens, visitors return to the nave. At the west end is the **Tomb of the Unknown Warrior,** bearing the remains of an unidentified WWI soldier, with an oration poured from molten bullets. Just beyond is a memorial to **Winston Churchill.** Stretching east, the North Aisle starts with memorials to 20th-century prime ministers before becoming **Scientists Corner. Isaac Newton's** massive monument, set into the left choir screen, presides over a number of physicists; in the aisle floor, watch you don't step on **Charles Darwin.**

OLD MONASTERY, CLOISTERS, AND GARDENS. The abbey complex stretches far beyond the church itself. All these sights are accessible through Dean's Yard without going through the abbey. The **Great Cloisters** hold yet more tombs and commemorative plaques; a passage running off the southeastern corner leads to the idyllic **Little Cloister** and 900-year-old **College Gardens.** A door off the east cloister leads to the octagonal **Chapter House,** the original meeting place of the House of Commons, whose 13th-century tiled floor is the best-preserved in Europe. The windowless **Pyx Chamber** is one of the few surviving parts of the original 11th-century monastic complex. Originally a chapel, it was converted into a treasury in the 13th century. Next door, the **Abbey Museum** is housed in the Norman undercroft. The highlight of the collection is the array of **funeral effigies,** from wooden models of the 14th century to fully-dressed 17th-century wax versions.

ST. PAUL'S CATHEDRAL

St. Paul's Churchyard, the City. ⊖St. Paul's or Mansion House. ☎7246 8348; www.stpauls.co.uk. Open M-Sa 8:30am-4:30pm; last admission 4pm. Open for worship daily 7:15am-6pm. Dome and galleries open M-Sa 9:30am-4pm. Evensong M-Sa 5pm; arrive at 4:50pm for choir seats. Audioguides available 10am-3:30pm. 90min. tours M-F 11, 11:30am, 1:30, and 2pm. Cathedral £7, concessions £6, children £3; worshipers free. Audioguide £3.50, concessions £3. Tours £2.50, concessions £2, children £1.

Sir Christopher Wren's masterpiece is the fifth cathedral to occupy this site; the original was built in AD 604. **"Old St. Paul's"** was begun in 1087 and topped by a steeple one-third higher than the current 364 ft. dome. By 1666, when the Great Fire swept it away, Old St. Paul's was due for replacement. Even so, only in 1668 did authorities invite Wren to design a new cathedral. When the bishops rejected his third design, Wren simply ignored them and started building. Sneakily, he persuaded the king to let him make "necessary alterations" as work progressed, and the building that emerged from the scaffolding in 1708 bore a close resemblance to Wren's second "Great Model" design.

INTERIOR. The entrance leads to the north aisle of the **nave,** the largest space in the cathedral, with seats for 2500 worshipers. Unlike Westminster Abbey, no one is actually buried in the cathedral floor—the graves are all downstairs in the crypt. The second-tallest freestanding **dome** in Europe (after St. Peter's in the Vatican) seems larger from inside, exaggerated by the false perspective of the paintings on the inner surface. Stalls in the **choir** were spared during an air raid, but the altar was not. It was replaced with the current marble **High Altar,** above which looms the mosaic of *Christ Seated in Majesty.* The north choir aisle holds Henry Moore's magnificent *Mother and Child.* Soon after the sculpture's arrival, guides insisted a plaque be affixed because no one knew what it was. The **statue of John Donne** in the south choir aisle is one of the few monuments to survive from Old St. Paul's.

SCALING THE HEIGHTS. The dome is built in three parts: an inner brick dome, visible from the inside of the cathedral; an outer timber structure; and, between the two, a brick cone that carries the weight of the lantern on top. The narrow **Whispering Gallery,** reached by 259 shallow steps or (for those in need only) a small, non-wheelchair-accessible elevator. Encircling the base of the inner dome, the gallery is a perfect resounding chamber: whisper into the wall, and your friends on the other side should be able to hear you. From here, climb another 119 steep and winding steps to the **Stone Gallery,** outside the cathedral at the base of the outer dome. The heavy stone balustrade, not to mention taller modern buildings, results in an underwhelming view, so take a deep breath and persevere up the final 152 steps to the **Golden Gallery** at the base of the lantern.

PLUMBING THE DEPTHS. St. Paul's crypt is riddled with tombs of great Britons. **Admiral Nelson** commands pride of place, amid radiating galleries adorned with monuments to other heroes, including **Florence Nightingale** and Epstein's bust of **T.E. Lawrence** (of Arabia). The neighboring chamber holds the **Duke of Wellington's** massive tomb. The rear of the crypt bears the graves of artists, including **William Blake, J.M.W. Turner,** and **Henry Moore,** crowded around the black slab concealing **Wren** himself. Inscribed on the wall above is his epitaph: *Lector, si monumentum requiris circumspice* ("Reader, if you seek his monument, look around").

THE TOWER OF LONDON

Tower Hill, next to Tower Bridge, in the City, within easy reach of the South Bank and the East End. ⊖Tower Hill. ☎0870 756 6060; www.hrp.org.uk. Open Mar.-Oct. M 10am-6pm, Tu-Sa 9am-6pm, Su 10am-6pm; buildings close at 5:45pm, last ticket sold 5pm, last admission 5:30pm. Nov.-Feb. all closing times 1hr. earlier. Tickets also sold at Tube stations; buy ahead as queues can be horrendous. £13.50, concessions £10.50, children £9, under 5 free, families £37.50. Audioguide £3.

The Tower of London, palace and prison of English monarchs for over 900 years, is steeped in blood and history. Conceived by William the Conqueror more to provide protection from than for his new subjects, the wooden palisade of 1067 was replaced in 1078 by a stone structure that grew into the White Tower. **Yeomen Warders,** or "Beefeaters" (a reference to their daily allowance of meat in former times), still guard the fortress, dressed in their blue everyday or red ceremonial uniforms. Beware that the Tower is often swamped with visitors; arrive early in the morning or you'll have to wait for ages to get in, let alone to see the crown jewels. A 1hr. **Yeoman Warders' Tour** will fill you in on the Tower's history and legends. *(Meet near the entrance. Every 90min. M 10am-3:30pm, Tu-Sa 9:30am-3:30pm, Su 10am-3:30pm.)*

WESTERN ENTRANCE AND WATERLANE. From **Middle Tower,** where today tickets are collected and bags searched, you pass over the moat (now a garden) and enter the **Outer Ward** though **Byward Tower.** Just beyond Byward is the massive **Bell Tower,** dating from 1190; the nightly curfew bell has been rung for over 500 years. The stretch of the Outer Ward along the Thames is **Water Lane,** which until the 16th century was adjacent to the river. **Traitor's Gate** was built by Edward I for his personal use, but is now associated with the prisoners who passed through it.

MEDIEVAL PALACE. In this sequence of rooms, archaeologists have attempted to recreate the look and feel of the Tower during the reign of Edward I (1275-1279). The tour starts at **St. Thomas's Tower,** a half-timbered set of rooms above Traitor's Gate. The tour also includes **Wakefield Tower,** presented as a throne room. Tower lore claims that Henry VI was murdered while imprisoned here in 1471 by Edward IV, though recent evidence suggests he was kept in the adjacent **Lanthorn Tower.**

WALL WALK. A walk traces the eastern wall constructed by Henry III in the 13th century. The wall is entered via **Salt Tower,** long used as a prison and said to be haunted—dogs refuse to enter it. At the end of the walk is **Martin Tower,** home to a fascinating collection of retired crowns, *sans* gemstones, along with paste models of some of the more famous jewels, including the **Cullinan diamond,** the largest ever found. The stone was mailed third class from the Transvaal in an unmarked parcel, a scheme Scotland Yard believed was the safest way of getting it to London.

CROWN JEWELS. The queue at the **Jewel House** is a miracle of crowd management. After passing through room after room of videos of the jewels in action, the crowd is finally ushered into the vault and onto moving walkways that whisk them past the crowns. Most items come from Coronation regalia. The **Imperial State Crown** is home to the Stuart Sapphire and 16 other sapphires, 2876 diamonds, 273 pearls, 11 emeralds, and five rubies. Don't miss the **Sceptre with the Cross,** topped with First Star of Africa, the largest cut diamond in the world. The **Queen Mother's Crown** is set with the Koh-I-Noor diamond, which legend says will bring luck only to women.

WHITE TOWER. The Conqueror's original castle has served as royal residence, wardrobe, storehouse, records office, mint, armory, and prison. Visitors are given the option of long or short routes. The long version starts with the stunning ⬛**Chapel of St. John the Evangelist.** The spacious hall next door was most likely the royal **bedchamber,** adjacent to the larger **Great Hall.** Today it houses a collection of armor and weapons. The tour then passes through more weaponry displays before meeting up with the start of the short route. This trails through a set of historic misrepresentations, starting with the **Spanish Armory**—torture instruments displayed in the 17th century as being captured from the Spanish Armada (1588), but actually from the Tower's own repertoire of weapons.

TOWER GREEN. The grassy western side of the Inner Ward marks the site of the Tower's most famous executions, surrounded by residential buildings. The Tudor **Queen's House** (which will become the King's House when Charles ascends the throne) is occupied by the Governor of the Tower. Nearby, the **Beauchamp Tower** was usually reserved for high-class "guests," many of whom carved intricate inscriptions into the walls during their detention. On the north of Tower Green is the **Chapel Royal of St. Peter ad Vinculum.** Three queens— Anne Boleyn, Catherine Howard, and Lady Jane Grey—are buried here, along

LONDON

with Catholic martyrs Saint Thomas More and John Fisher. *(Open only by Yeoman tours or after 4:30pm.)* Across the green, **Bloody Tower** is named for the probability that here Richard III imprisoned and murdered his nephews, the rightful heir Edward V (aged 12) and his brother, before usurping the throne in 1483. In 1674, the bones of two children were unearthed nearby and subsequently reinterred in Westminster Abbey.

CENTRAL LONDON

BLOOMSBURY

ACADEMIA. The strip of land along Gower St. and immediately to its west is London's academic heartland. The stunning ■**British Library** (p. 129) is on Euston Rd. Established in 1828 to educate those excluded from Oxford and Cambridge, **University College London** was the first institution of higher learning in Britain to admit Catholics, Jews, and women. The embalmed body of founder Jeremy Bentham is on display in the South Cloister. *(Main entrance on Gower St. South Cloister entrance through the courtyard. ⊖Warren St. or Goodge St. or Tottenham Crt. Rd.)* Now the administrative HQ of the University of London, **Senate House** was the model for the Ministry of Truth in *1984*—George Orwell worked there as part of the BBC's propaganda unit in WWII. *(At the southern end of Malet St. ⊖Goodge St. or Russell Sq.)*

OTHER BLOOMSBURY SIGHTS. Next to the British Library are the soaring Gothic spires of **St. Pancras Station.** Formerly housing the Midland Grand Hotel, today Sir George Gilbert Scott's facade is a hollow shell awaiting redevelopment as a Marriott. *(Euston Rd. ⊖King's Cross or St. Pancras.)*

CHELSEA

As wealthy as neighboring Belgravia and Kensington, Chelsea boasts a riverside location and a strong artistic heritage. Henry VIII's right-hand man (and later victim) Saint Thomas More was the first big-name resident in the 16th century, but it was in the 19th century that the neighborhood acquired its reputation as an artistic hothouse. **Cheyne Walk** was home to J.M.W. Turner, George Eliot, and Dante Gabriel Rossetti; while Oscar Wilde, James Singer Sargent, James McNeill Whistler, and Bertrand Russell lived on **Tite Street.** Mark Twain, Henry James, T.S. Eliot, William Morris, and, more recently, Mick Jagger, were also Chelsea residents. *(⊖Sloane Sq. From there, buses #11, 19, 22, 211, and 319 run down the King's Rd.)*

THE ROYAL HOSPITAL. Charles II established the Hospital—designed by Christopher Wren—as a retirement community for army veterans in 1692. It remains a military institution, with the uniformed "Chelsea Pensioners" arranged in companies under the command of a retired officer. French cannon from Waterloo guard the open south side of **Figure Court,** named for Grinling Gibbons's statue of Charles II, while the north is divided between the **chapel** and the **Great Hall.** The outhouses harbor a small **history museum.** *(Royal Hospital Rd. ☎ 7881 5246. Open Nov.-Mar. M-Sa 10am-4:30pm, Su 2-4:30pm; Apr. until 7:30pm; Sept. until 7pm; May-Aug. until 8:30pm. Free.)*

CHELSEA PHYSIC GARDEN. Founded in 1673 to provide medicinal herbs, the Physic Garden was the staging post from which tea was introduced to India and cotton to America. Today it remains a living repository of all manner of plants, from opium poppies to leeks. *(66 Royal Hospital Rd., entrance on Swan Walk. ☎ 7352 5646. Open early Apr. to late Oct. W noon-5pm, Su 2-6pm; M-F noon-5pm during Chelsea Flower Show (late May) and Chelsea Festival (mid-June). £5, concessions £3.)*

OTHER CHELSEA SIGHTS. Sloane Square serves as the eastern end of the **King's Road,** until 1829 a private royal route from Hampton Court to Whitehall. The 60s were launched here in 1955 when Mary Quant dropped the miniskirt on an unsuspecting world. In **Carlyle's House,** which remains much as it was during Thomas's lifetime, the historian, writer, and "Sage of Chelsea" entertained Dickens, Tennyson, Eliot, and Ruskin. *(24 Cheyne Row.* ☎ *7352 7087. Open Apr.-Oct. W-F 2-5pm, Sa-Su 11am-5pm; last admission 4:30pm. £3.90, children £1.80.)* Where Cheyne Walk spills onto Chelsea Embankment stands **Chelsea Old Church,** looking remarkably new following post-WWII restoration. The bombs spared the southern chapel, where Saint Thomas More worshipped in the 16th century. Henry VIII is reported to have married Jane Seymour here before the official wedding. *(Old Church St. Open Tu-F 2-5pm. Services Su 8, 11am, 12:15, and 6pm. Free.)*

THE CITY OF LONDON

The City of London **("the City")** is the oldest part of the capital—for most of its 2000 years, this *was* London, the rest merely outlying villages. Following the Great Fire of 1666 and the Blitz of 1940-43, the area underwent a cosmetic rearrangement that left little of its medieval history behind.

▓ MONUMENT. The only non-ecclesiastical Wren building in the City, this Doric pillar topped with a gilded flaming urn is a lasting reminder of the Great Fire. Erected in 1677, the 202 ft. column stands exactly that distance from the bakery on Pudding Lane where flames first broke out. The column offers an expansive view of London; bring stern resolution to climb its 311 steps. *(Monument St.* ❸*Monument.* ☎ *7626 2717. Open 9:30am-5pm; last admission 4:40pm. £2, children £1.)*

TOWER BRIDGE. This is perhaps the most iconic symbol of London—which helps explain why tourists often mistake it for its plainer sibling, London Bridge. Folklore claims that when London Bridge was sold and moved to Arizona, the Yanks thought they were getting Tower Bridge. For a deeper understanding of the history and technology behind the bridge, try the **Tower Bridge Experience,** with its cheesy animation and tour of the Engine Room. Don't expect too much of the view—iron latticework gets in the way. *(Enter Tower Bridge Experience through the west side (upriver) of the North Tower.* ❸*Tower Hill or London Bridge.* ☎ *7940 3985, lifting schedule 7940 3984. Open daily 10am-6pm; last admission 5:30pm. £5, concessions £4.25.)*

GUILDHALL. Dating from 1440, this vast Gothic hall is where the representatives of the City's 102 guilds, from the Fletchers (arrow-makers) to the Information Technologists, meet at the **Court of Common Council,** presided over by the Lord Mayor, who wears traditional robes and is followed by a sword-wielding entourage. The Court is held in public the third Thursday of every month. *(Enter the Guildhall through the low, modern annex.* ☎ *7606 3030. Open daily May-Sept. 10am-5pm; Oct.-Apr. closed Su. Last admission 4:30pm. Occasional tours. Free.)*

THE BARBICAN. In the aftermath of WWII, the Corporation of London decided to develop this bomb-flattened 35-acre plot into a textbook piece of integrated development. At the middle of the resulting concrete labyrinth is the **Barbican Centre** cultural complex. Described at its 1982 opening as "the City's gift to the nation," it incorporates a concert hall, two theaters, a cinema, three art galleries, and cafeterias, bars, and restaurants—if you can find any of them. For more on Barbican events, see p. 137 and p. 139. *(Main entrance on Silk St. From* ❸*Moorgate or Barbican, follow the yellow lines.* ☎ *7638 8891. Open M-Sa 9am-11pm, Su 10am-11pm.)*

ST. MARY-LE-BOW. Another Wren creation, St. Mary's is most famous for its **Great Bell**—true cockneys are born within earshot of the bell-toll. The church was almost entirely rebuilt after the Blitz, but the 11th-century **crypt,** whose bows (arches) gave the church its epithet, survived. Since the 12th century, it has hosted the **Court of Arches,** during which the Archbishop of Canterbury swears in bishops. *(Cheapside.* ❺ *St. Paul's or Mansion House.* ☎ *7246 5139. Open M-F 7:30am-6pm. Free.)*

OTHER SIGHTS. ▧**All Hallows-by-the-Tower** bears its longevity proudly, incorporating a Saxon arch from AD 675 and a Roman pavement in the undercroft "museum." *(Byward St.* ❺*Tower Hill.* ☎ *7481 2928. Church open daily 9am-6pm. Crypt and museum open M-Sa 11am-4pm, Su 1-4pm. Free.)* Dwelling incongruously in the shadow of the Temple Court building are the remains of the 3rd-century Roman **Temple of Mithras,** discovered during construction work in 1954 and shifted up 18 ft. to street level. *(Queen Victoria St.* ❺*Mansion House or Bank.)* **St. Stephen Walbrook** (built 1672-79) is arguably Wren's finest church. The plain exterior gives no inkling of the wide dome that floats above Henry Moore's 1985 freeform altar. *(39 Walbrook.* ❺*Bank or Cannon St.* ☎ *7283 4444. Open M-Th 9am-4pm, F 12:30pm for 1hr. organ concert. Free.)* The most famous modern structure in the City is **Lloyd's of London,** built by Richard Rogers in 1986. With metal ducts, lifts, and chutes on the outside, it wears its heart (and the rest of its internal organs) on its sleeve. *(Leadenhall St.* ❺*Bank.)*

HOLBORN AND CLERKENWELL

Squeezed between the City and the West End, **Holborn's** crush of streets hides many an ancient marvel. The rise, fall, and rise of currently-hip **Clerkenwell** appropriately coincides with the changing role that alcohol has played in the local economy.

▧**THE TEMPLE.** South of Fleet St., this labyrinthine compound encompasses the inns of the **Middle Temple** to the west and the neighboring **Inner Temple** to the east—there was once an Outer Temple, but it's long gone. The Inner Temple was leveled during the Blitz; with the exception of the Tudor **Inner Temple Gateway,** 16-17 Fleet St., all is reconstruction. **Middle Temple Hall,** closed to the public, still has its 1574 hammerbeam ceiling as well as a dining table made from the hatch of Sir Francis Drake's *Golden Hinde. (Between Fleet Sts., Essex St., Victoria Embankment, and Temple Ave./Bouvier St.; numerous passages lead to the Temple.* ❺*Temple or Blackfriars.)* From 1185 until the order was dissolved in 1312, this land belonged to the crusading Knights Templar; the **Temple Church** is sole remnant of this time. Adjoining the round church is a Gothic nave, built in 1240, with an altar screen by Wren. *(☎ 7353 3470. Hours vary depending on the week's services and are posted outside the door of the church for the coming week. Organ recitals W 1:15-1:45pm; no services Aug.-Sept. Free.)* According to Shakespeare's *Henry VI,* the red and white flowers that served as emblems in the Wars of the Roses were plucked in **Middle Temple Garden,** south of the hall. *(Garden open May-Sept. M-F noon-3pm. Free.)*

ST. ETHELDREDA'S. The only pre-Reformation Catholic church in the city, bought back from the Church of England in 1870 after centuries of captivity, is also one of London's most beautiful. Inside, the surprisingly high ceiling swallows up the bustle of the streets, creating an island of calm in the midst of Holborn Circus. *(☎ 7405 1061. Open daily 7:30am-7pm. Free.)*

ROYAL COURTS OF JUSTICE. Straddling the official division between the City of Westminster and the City of London, this sprawling neo-Gothic structure encloses courtrooms and the Great Hall (home to Europe's largest mosaic floor) amid labyrinthine passageways. All courtrooms are open to the public during trials. *(Where the Strand becomes Fleet St.* ❺*Temple or Chancery Ln.* ☎ *7947 6000. Wheelchair accessible. Open M-F 9am-4:30pm; cases are heard 10am-1pm and 2-3:30pm. Free.)*

CLERKENWELL GREEN. Not very green at all—actually just a wider-than-normal street—Clerkenwell Green boasts a few venerable historical associations. Wat Tyler rallied the Peasants' Revolt here in 1381, and Lenin published the Bolshevik newspaper *Iskra* from no. 37a, the Green's oldest building (1737). It now houses the Marx Memorial Library. *(☎ 7253 1485. Open M-Th 1-2pm, book in advance for large groups. Closed Aug.)* Across from this revolutionary hotbed, the Old Sessions House (1782) was formerly the courthouse for the county of Middlesex—note the Middlesex arms on the portico. Reputedly haunted, it's now the enigmatic London Masonic Centre. *(Closed to the public.)*

ST. BARTHOLOMEW THE GREAT. Visitors must enter through a 13th-century arch, disguised as a Tudor house, to reach this Norman gem. William Hogarth was baptized in the 15th-century font, and Ben Franklin worked for a printer in the Lady's Chapel. The tomb near the altar belongs to **Rahere,** who founded both the church and **St. Bartholomew's Hospital** across the street in 1123. *(Little Britain, off West Smithfield. ⊖Barbican. ☎ 7606 5171. Open Tu-F 8:30am-5pm, Sa 10:30am-1:30pm, Su 8:30am-1pm and 2:30-8pm. Free.)*

KENSINGTON AND EARL'S COURT

Nobody took much notice of Kensington before 1689, when the newly crowned William and Mary moved into Kensington Palace and high society tagged along. The next significant date in Kensington's history was 1851, when the Great Exhibition showcased imperial imports and home-grown handicrafts, bringing in enough money to finance a slew of museums and colleges. In Kensington's southwestern corner, Earl's Court is a grimier district, dubbed "Kangaroo Valley" in the 1960s and 1970s for its popularity with Australian expats.

KENSINGTON PALACE. In 1689, William and Mary commissioned Wren to remodel Nottingham House into a proper palace. Parts are still in use as a royal residence—Princess Diana was the most famous recent inhabitant. Inside, the **Royal Ceremonial Dress Collection** displays intricate courtier costumes, with a number of the Queen's demure evening gowns and Di's racier numbers. In the **State Apartments,** Hanoverian economy is evident in the *trompe l'oeil* decoration throughout. *(Western edge of Kensington Gardens; enter through the park. ⊖High St. Kensington or Queensway. ☎0870 752 7777. Open daily Mar.-Oct. 10am-6pm; Nov.-Feb. 10am-5pm. Last admission 30min. before close. £10.80, concessions £8.20, children £7, families £32.)*

HYDE PARK AND KENSINGTON GARDENS. Surrounded by London's wealthiest neighborhoods, giant **Hyde Park** has served as the model for city parks around the world, including New York's Central Park and Paris's Bois de Boulogne. The contiguous **Kensington Gardens** were created in the late 17th century when Kensington Palace became the new royal residence. Officially known as the **Long Water,** the 41-acre **Serpentine** was created in 1730. South of Long Water, some distance from the lake itself, basks the **Serpentine Gallery,** the unlikely venue for contemporary art shows. Running through the southern section of the park, the dirt track of **Rotten Row** stretches west from Hyde Park Corner. Originally the *Route du Roi* or "King's Road," it was the first English thoroughfare lit at night to deter crime. At the northeastern corner of the park, near Marble Arch, proselytizers, politicos, and flat-out crazies dispense their knowledge to bemused tourists at **Speaker's Corner** on Sundays. *(Framed by Kensington Rd., Knightsbridge, Park Ln., and Bayswater Rd. ⊖Queensway, Lancaster Gate, Marble Arch, Hyde Park Corner, or High St. Kensington. ☎7298 2100. Park open daily 5am-midnight. Gardens open dawn-dusk. Both free.)*

ALBERTOPOLIS. The Great Exhibition of 1851 was the brainchild of Prince Albert, Queen Victoria's husband. By the time the exhibition closed a year later, six million people had passed through, and the organizers were left with a £200,000 profit. (Take that, Millennium Dome.) At Albert's suggestion, the cash was used to purchase 86 acres to be dedicated to institutions promoting British arts and sciences. The most famous of these are the **Victoria and Albert Museum** (p. 128), **Science Museum** (p. 130), and **Natural History Museum** (p. 130), and the **Royal Albert Hall,** an all-purpose venue that has hosted a full-length marathon and the first public display of electric lighting, as well as the annual **Proms** (p. 139) concerts. *(Kensington Gore. ⊖South Kensington or High St. Kensington.)* Opposite the hall, His Highness is commemorated by Gilbert Scott's **Albert Memorial**—it's either nightmarish or fairytale, depending on your opinion of Victorian High Gothic. *(Kensington Gore. ☎7495 0916. 45min. Tours Su 2 and 3pm. £3.50, concessions £3.)*

KNIGHTSBRIDGE AND BELGRAVIA

It's hard to imagine that **Knightsbridge,** now home to London's most expensive stores, was once a racy district known for taverns and highwaymen. Neighboring **Belgravia** was catapulted to respectability by the presence of royalty at nearby Buckingham Palace in the 1820s. **Belgrave Square,** the setting for *My Fair Lady,* is now so expensive that the aristocracy has had to sell out to foreign governments.

APSLEY HOUSE. "No. 1, London" was bought in 1817 by the **Duke of Wellington,** whose heirs still occupy the top floor. On display is Wellington's outstanding collection of art, much of it given in gratitude by the crowned heads of Europe following the battle of Waterloo. The majority of the paintings hang in the **Waterloo Gallery,** where the Duke held his annual Waterloo banquet. In the basement, a cabinet is filled with Wellington's medals, while another holds newspaper caricatures from his later political career. *(Hyde Park Corner. ⊖Hyde Park Corner. ☎7499 5676. Open Tu-Su Apr.-Oct. 10am-5pm; Nov.-Mar. 10am-4pm. £4.50, students £3, children £2.30)*

WELLINGTON ARCH. At the center of London's most infamous intersection, Wellington Arch was built in 1825 as the "Green Park Arch." In 1838 it was dedicated to the good duke, and—much to the horror of its architect, Decimus Burton—eight years later was encumbered by a gigantic statue of the man. Wellington's statue was finally replaced in 1910 by the *Quadriga and Peace,* designed by army vet Adrian Jones. Inside the arch, exhibitions on the building's history and the changing nature of war memorials play second fiddle to the viewing platforms. *(Hyde Park Corner. ⊖Hyde Park Corner. ☎7930 2726. Open Apr.-Oct. W-Su 10am-5pm; Nov.-Mar. W-Su 10am-4pm. £3, concessions £2.30, children £1.50.)*

MARYLEBONE AND REGENT'S PARK

Marylebone's most famous resident (and address) never existed. Armchair sleuths come searching for 221b Baker St., fictional home of the fictional Holmes, but find instead the headquarters of the Abbey National bank.

▨ REGENT'S PARK. Perhaps London's most attractive and most popular park, with landscapes ranging from football-scarred fields to Italian-style formal plantings. It's all very different from John Nash's vision of wealthy villas hidden among exclusive gardens; fortunately for us common folk, in 1811 Parliament intervened and guaranteed the space would remain open to all. *(⊖Baker St., Regent's Park, Great Portland St., or Camden Town. ☎7486 7905. Open daily 6am-dusk. Free.)*

MADAME TUSSAUD'S AND THE PLANETARIUM. Back in the 18th century, Mrs. T got her big break with a string of commissions for death masks of guillotined aristocrats, including a freshly beheaded Marie Antoinette. Despite its revolutionary beginnings, the display of waxworks positively fawns over royalty and other more and less worthy celebrities. The **London Planetarium** offers low-budget cinematic spectacle, but little else. *(Marylebone Rd. ⊖Baker St. ☎0870 400 3000. Wheelchair accessible. Open M-F 9:30am-5:30pm, Sa-Su 9am-6pm during July-Aug. daily 9am-6pm. Planetarium shows 2 per hr. Tickets sold at both Madame Tussaud's and Planetarium and valid for both.*

Advance booking highly recommended; £1 extra. Prices depend on day of the week, entrance time, and season. £11-22, concessions £9-18, under 16 £6-17; option to include "Chamber Live" exhibit adds £3.)

THE SOUTH BANK

⬛LONDON EYE. Also known as the **Millennium Wheel,** the 443 ft. London Eye is the biggest observational wheel in the world. Ellipsoid glass "pods" give uninterrupted views from the top of each 30min. revolution; on clear days you can see as far as Windsor. *(Jubilee Gardens. ⊖Waterloo or Westminster. ☎0870 444 5544. Open daily late May to early Sept. 9:30am-10pm; Apr. to late May and rest of Sept. 10:30am-8pm; Jan.-Mar. and Oct.-Dec. 10:30am-7pm. Ticket office in corner of County Hall, open daily 8:30am-6:30pm. Advance booking recommended. £11.50, concessions £9, under 16 £5.75.)*

SHAKESPEARE'S GLOBE THEATRE. In the shadow of Tate Modern, the half-timbered Globe (opened 1997) rises just 700 yd. from where the original burned down in 1613. Arrive in time for a morning tour, given only during the performance season. Tours include the ruins of the **Rose Theatre,** Bankside's first, where both Shakespeare and Marlowe performed. The site was rediscovered in 1989; not much besides the outline is left. *(Bankside. ⊖Southwark or London Bridge. ☎7902 1500. Open daily May-Sept. 9am-noon and 1-4pm (exhibits only); Oct.-Apr. 10am-5pm. £8, concessions £6.50, children £5.50, families £24.)* For performance information, see **Entertainment,** p. 137.

TATE MODERN AND THE MILLENNIUM BRIDGE. Opposite one another on Bankside are the biggest success and most abject failure of London's millennial celebrations. The **Tate Modern** (p. 128), created from the shell of the former Bankside power station, is as visually arresting as its contents are thought-provoking. Built to link the Tate to the City, the striking **Millennium Bridge** was not only completed six months too late for the Y2K festivities, but, following a (literally) shaky debut, closed down in days, reopening only after over a year of delays. It has now been successfully stabilized. *(Queen's Walk, Bankside. ⊖Southwark, Blackfriars, or St. Paul's.)*

SOUTHWARK CATHEDRAL. Though Christians have worshiped here since AD 606, the church of St. Saviour only made cathedral status in 1905. The oldest complete part of the building is the **retrochoir,** separated from the main choir by a 16th-century altar screen. The **north aisle** holds the tomb of John Gower (d. 1408), the "first English poet," while across the 19th-century nave, the **south aisle** bears a window and monument to Shakespeare, whose brother Edward is buried here. The new **Visitor Centre** houses a high-tech exhibition on the area. *(Montague Close. ⊖London Bridge. ☎7367 6700. Open daily 8am-6pm. Exhibition open M-Sa 10am-6pm. Cathedral free. Audioguide £5, concessions £4, ages 5-15 £2.50. Camera permit £1.50.)*

OTHER SIGHTS. ⬛Vinopolis is a Dionysian Disneyland offering patrons an interactive (yes, that means samples) tour of the world's wine regions. *(1 Bank End. ⊖London Bridge. ☎7940 8301. Open M noon-9pm, Tu-Su noon-6pm; last admission 2hr. before close. £12.50, seniors £11.50.)* The **Old Operating Theatre and Herb Garret** is located in the loft of an 18th-century church. The oldest operating theater in the world boasts a fearsome array of primitive surgical instruments. *(9a St. Thomas's St. ⊖London Bridge. ☎7955 4791. Open daily 10:30am-4:45pm. Closed Dec. 12-Jan. 5. £4.25, concessions £3.25, children £2.50, families £11.)* A less authentic horror is the **London Dungeon;** the most effective instrument of torture here is the unbelievably long queue. *(28-34 Tooley St. ⊖London Bridge. ☎7403 7224. Open daily in summer 9:30am-7:30pm; in winter 10am-5:30pm £13.95, concessions £11.25, children £9.95.)*

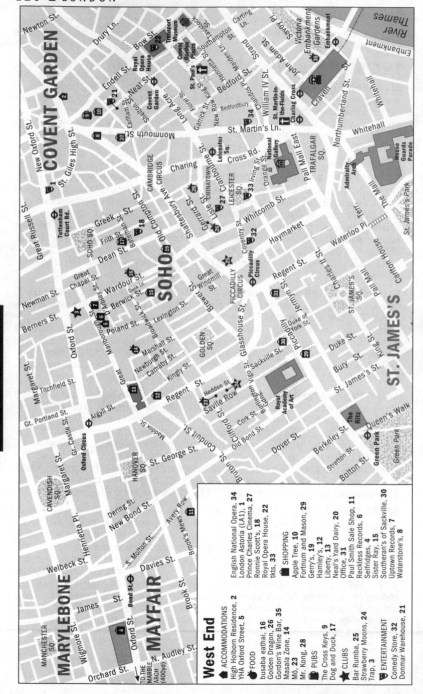

West End

ACCOMMODATIONS
High Holborn Residence, **2**
YHA Oxford Street, **5**

FOOD
busaba eathai, **16**
Golden Dragon, **26**
Gordon's Wine Bar, **35**
Masala Zone, **14**
MÒ, **23**
Mr. Kong, **28**

PUBS
The Cross Keys, **9**
Dog and Duck, **17**

CLUBS
Bar Rumba, **25**
Strawberry Moons, **24**
Trap, **3**

ENTERTAINMENT
Comedy Store, **32**
Donmar Warehouse, **21**

English National Opera, **34**
London Astoria (LA1), **1**
Prince Charles Cinema, **27**
Ronnie Scott's, **18**
Royal Opera House, **22**
tkts, **33**

SHOPPING
Apple Tree, **10**
Fortnum and Mason, **29**
Gerry's, **19**
Hamley's, **12**
Liberty, **13**
Neal's Yard Dairy, **20**
Office, **31**
Paul Smith Sale Shop, **11**
Reckless Records, **6**
Selfridges, **4**
Sister Ray, **15**
Southeran's of Sackville, **30**
Uptown Records, **7**
Waterstone's, **8**

THE WEST END

OXFORD AND REGENT STREETS. Oscar Wilde famously quipped that London's famous shopping strip, **Oxford Street,** is "all street and no Oxford." **Regent Street** is more imposing, though none of John Nash's original Regency arcades have survived. To the north, near Oxford Circus, **Carnaby Street** was at the heart of Swinging London in the 1960s. After that psychedelic high followed 30 years as a lurid tourist trap; now Carnaby swings again for the naughty noughties with an influx of trendy boutiques. (⊖ Oxford Circus.)

MARBLE ARCH. Designed by Nash in 1828 as the front entrance to Buckingham Palace but rendered useless by a spate of palatial extensions, the Marble Arch was moved to the present site as an entrance into Hyde Park. Then new roads cut the arch off, leaving it stranded forlornly on a traffic roundabout. (⊖ Marble Arch.)

MAYFAIR AND ST. JAMES'S

PICCADILLY, BOND STREET, AND SAVILE ROW. Frilly ruffs were big business in the 16th century—one local tailor named his house after these "piccadills," and the name stuck. Clogged with traffic, **Piccadilly** is no longer the preferred address of gentlemen as it was in the late 18th century, but it's still posh with a capital P. (⊖ Piccadilly Circus or Green Park.) Running into Piccadilly is **Old Bond Street,** London's swankiest shopping street; this end is dominated by art and jewelry dealers, while most of the designer boutiques are on **New Bond Street.** (⊖ Bond St. or Green Park.) **Savile Row,** running parallel to Bond St., is synonymous with elegant and expensive tailoring; it's also where the **Beatles** performed their last ever live gig on the roof of No. 3 while filming *Let It Be.* (⊖ Piccadilly Circus.)

ST. JAMES'S PALACE. St. James's, constructed in 1536, is London's only remaining purpose-built palace. The massive gateway is one of the few features remaining. Unless your name starts with HRH, the only part you're likely to get into is the **Chapel Royal.** (Services Oct.-Easter Su 8:30 and 11:30am.) From Easter to September, services are held in the Inigo Jones-designed **Queen's Chapel,** across Marlborough Rd. (Between the Mall and Pall Mall. ⊖ Green Park.)

SOHO

Soho has a history of welcoming all colors and creeds to its streets. Early settlers were led by 17th-century French Huguenots fleeing religious persecution, but these days Soho is less gay Paris, more just gay; a concentration of gay-owned restaurants and bars has turned **Old Compton Street** into the heart of gay London. Former Soho resident **Karl Marx** lived with his wife, maid, and five children while writing *Das Kapital* at 28 Dean St., the two-room flat is marked by a blue plaque.

PICCADILLY CIRCUS. Five of the West End's arteries merge and swirl around Piccadilly Circus, and the entire tourist population of London seems to bask under its lurid neon signs. The **statue of Eros** was dedicated to the Victorian philanthropist Lord Shaftesbury: the god originally pointed his arrow down Shaftesbury Ave., but recent restoration has put his aim significantly off. (⊖ Piccadilly Circus.)

LEICESTER SQUARE. Amusements here range from London's largest cinemas to the **Swiss Centre** glockenspiel, whose atonal renditions of Beethoven's *Moonlight Sonata* are enough to make even the tone-deaf weep. (Rings M-F at noon, 6, 7, 8pm; Sa-Su noon, 2, 4, 5, 6, 7, and 8pm.) Be true to your inner tourist and buy violets from a flower-seller or sit for a caricature. (⊖ Leicester Sq. or Piccadilly Circus.)

LONDON

CHINATOWN. Pedestrianized, tourist-ridden **Gerrard Street,** with scroll-worked dragon gates and pagoda-capped phone booths, is the self-proclaimed heart of this tiny slice of Canton, but gritty **Lisle Street,** one block south, has a more authentic feel. Chinatown is most vibrant during the year's two major festivals: the raucous **Chinese New Year Festival** in February and the **Mid-Autumn Festival** at the end of September. *(Between Leicester Sq., Shaftesbury Ave., and Charing Cross Rd.)*

THE ROYAL OPERA HOUSE. The Royal Opera House reopened in 2000 after a major expansion. During the day, the public is free to wander the ornate lobby of the original 1858 theater as well as the enormous glass-roofed space of **Floral Hall.** From there, take the escalator to reach the **terrace** overlooking the Piazza, with great views of London. *(Enter on Bow St. or through the northeast of the Piazza. ☎ 7304 4000; www.royaloperahouse.org. 1¼hr. backstage tours M-Sa 10:30am, 12:30, and 2:30pm; reservations essential. Open M-Sa 10am-3:30pm; box office M-Sa 10am-8pm. Tours £8, concessions £7.)* For performances at the Opera House, see p. 139.

COVENT GARDEN

On the very spot where, 350 years ago, Samuel Pepys saw the first Punch and Judy show in England, street performers entertain the thousands who flock here summer and winter, rain and shine, Londoner and tourist alike. *(⊖ Covent Garden.)*

ST. PAUL'S. Not to be confused with the famous cathedral, this simple Inigo Jones church is the sole remnant of the original square. Known as "the actor's church," the interior is festooned with plaques commemorating thespians from Vivien Leigh to Tony Simpson. *(On Covent Garden Piazza; enter via King St., Henrietta St., or Bedford St. ☎ 7836 5221. Open M-F 8:30am-4:30pm and Su 11am for morning services.)*

THEATRE ROYAL, DRURY LANE. Founded in 1663, this is the oldest of London's surviving theaters. Charles II met Nell Gwynn here in 1655, and David Garrick ruled the roost in the 18th century. In the 19th century, a corpse and dagger were found bricked up in the wall, a story which now contributes to Drury Lane lore. *(Entrance on Catherine St. ☎ 7850 8791, tours 7240 5357. Tours M-Tu, Th-F 2:15 and 4:45pm; W and Sa 10:15am and noon. £8.50, concessions £6.50.)*

WESTMINSTER

TRAFALGAR SQUARE AND THE STRAND

John Nash designed **Trafalgar Square** in 1820, but it took almost 50 years for London's largest roundabout to take on its current appearance: Nelson arrived in 1843, the lions in 1867. The long-empty **fourth plinth** now holds specially commissioned modern sculpture. Every year the square hosts a giant **Christmas tree,** donated by Norway as thanks for assistance against the Nazis. *(⊖ Charing Cross or Leicester Sq.)*

ST. MARTIN-IN-THE-FIELDS. James Gibbs's 1720s creation is instantly recognizable as the model for countless Georgian churches across Britain and America. It's still the Queen's parish church; look for the royal box left of the altar. Handel and Mozart performed here, and St. Martin's still hosts frequent concerts. The downstairs **crypt** has a life of its own, home to a cafe, bookshop, art gallery, and the **London Brass Rubbing Centre.** *(St. Martin's Ln., at the northeast corner of Trafalgar Sq.; crypt entrance on Duncannon St. ⊖ Charing Cross. ☎ 7766 1100.)*

WHITEHALL

A long stretch of imposing facades housing government ministries, "Whitehall" is synonymous with the British civil service. From 1532 until a fire in 1698, however, it was the home of the monarchy and one of the greatest palaces in Europe. Today all that remains are Inigo Jones's **Banqueting House** and Henry VIII's wine cellars, under the monolithic **Ministry of Defence** and viewable only upon written applica-

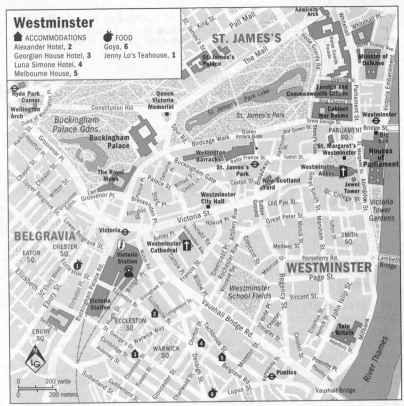

Westminster

🏠 ACCOMMODATIONS
Alexander Hotel, **2**
Georgian House Hotel, **3**
Luna Simone Hotel, **4**
Melbourne House, **5**

🍴 FOOD
Goya, **6**
Jenny Lo's Teahouse, **1**

LONDON

tion. Opposite the Banqueting House, the burnished hussars of the Household Cavalry stand at **Horseguards.** *(Guard changed M-F 11am, Sa 10am. Dismount for inspection daily 4pm.)* Where Whitehall becomes Parliament St., gates mark the entrance to **Downing Street.** No. 10 is the official residence of the Prime Minister, but Tony Blair's family is so big, he's swapped with Chancellor Gordon Brown at No. 11. *(Between Trafalgar Sq. and Parliament Sq. ⊖Westminster, Embankment, or Charing Cross.)*

PARLIAMENT SQUARE

Designed in 1750, Parliament Square rapidly became the focal point for opposition to the government. Today, demonstrators are dissuaded by a continuous stream of heavy traffic, with no pedestrian crossings. Standing opposite the **Houses of Parliament** (p. 109), a bronze Winston Churchill was famously given a turf mohawk during the May 2000 anti-capitalist demonstrations. South of the square rises **Westminster Abbey** (p. 110) while to the west looms the great dome of **Methodist Central Hall,** where the United Nations first met in 1946. *(⊖Westminster.)*

ST. MARGARET'S WESTMINSTER. Literally in Westminster Abbey's shadow, St. Margaret's has been the official church of the House of Commons since 1614. The **Milton Window** (1888), to the right of the main entrance above the North Aisle, shows the poet dictating *Paradise Lost* to his daughters. The **East Window** celebrates the wedding of Henry VIII to Catherine of Aragon. Opposite, the **West Window** commemorates Sir Walter Raleigh, now lying in the chancel. *(⊖Westminster. ☎ 7654 4840. Open M-F 9:30am-3:45pm, Sa 9:30am-1:45pm, Su 2-5pm. Free.)*

OTHER SIGHTS

WESTMINSTER CATHEDRAL. Following Henry VIII's break with Rome, London's Catholic community remained without a cathedral for over three centuries—until 1887, when the Church purchased a derelict prison as the site from which the neo-Byzantine church was to rise. The architect's plan outran its budget, and in 1903, the interior remained incomplete. The three blackened brick domes contrast dramatically with the swirling marble of the lower walls and the magnificence of the side chapels. A lift carries visitors up the 273 ft. **bell tower** for a view of Westminster, the river, and Kensington. *(Cathedral Piazza, off Victoria St. ⊖Victoria. ☎ 7798 9055. Cathedral open daily 7am-7pm. Free, suggested donation £2. Bell Tower open daily Mar.-Nov. 9am-12:30pm and 1pm-5pm; Dec.-Feb. Tu-Sa 9am-12:30pm. £3, concessions £1.50.)*

ST. JAMES'S PARK AND GREEN PARK. The run-up to Buckingham Palace is flanked by two parks. St. James's Park, acquired along with St. James's Palace by Henry VIII in 1531, owes its informal appearance to a landscaping by Nash in 1827. Across the Mall, Green Park is the creation of Charles II; "Constitution Hill" refers not to his interest in politics, but to his daily exercises. *(Open daily 5am-midnight.)*

THE ROYAL MEWS. A working carriage house doubling as a museum, the main attraction is the Queen's collection of conveyances, from the "glass coach" used to carry Diana to her wedding to the four-ton Gold State Coach. Kids will enjoy a chance to get up close to the horses, each named by the Queen herself. *(Buckingham Palace Rd. ⊖St. James's Park or Victoria. ☎ 7766 7302. Wheelchair accessible. Open daily Apr.-July and Sept. 11am-4pm, last admission 3:15pm; Aug.-Sept., 10am-5pm, last admission 4:15pm. £5.50, seniors £4.50, under 17 £3, families £14.)*

GREATER LONDON

NORTH LONDON

CAMDEN TOWN

An island of honest tawdriness in an increasingly affluent sea, Camden Town has thrown off attempts at gentrification thanks to **Camden Market** (p. 134), London's fourth most popular tourist attraction, centered in **Camden Lock Market.**

HAMPSTEAD

Hampstead caught the attention of well-heeled Londoners in the 17th century, when it became fashionable to take the waters at Hampstead Wells on the site of today's **Well Walk.** In the 1930s, Hampstead saw many European avant-garde luminaries in flight from fascism: residents Aldous Huxley, Piet Mondrian, and Sigmund Freud have lent the area an enduring cachet.

HAMPSTEAD HEATH. Hampstead Heath is one of the last remaining traditional commons in England, open to all since at least 1312. **Parliament Hill** is the highest open space in London, with excellent views across the city. Farther north, ▨**Kenwood House** is a picture-perfect 18th-century country estate, designed by

Robert Adams and home to the impressive **Iveagh Bequest** (p. 131) of Old Masters. *(Train to Hampstead Heath or ⊖Hampstead. Bus #210. Heath open 24hr.; be careful after dark. Kenwood House grounds open daily Apr.-Oct. 8am-8:30pm, Oct.-Mar. 8am-4:45pm.)*

KEATS HOUSE. While living here (1818-20), John Keats produced some of his finest work, including *Ode to a Nightingale*. Inside, poems lie scattered about the reconstructed rooms. *(Keats Grove. ⊖Hampstead. ☎7435 2062. Open Apr.-Nov. Tu-Su noon-5pm; Nov.-Mar. noon-4pm. £3, concessions £1.50, under 16 free.)*

EAST LONDON

WHITECHAPEL AND THE EAST END

The boundary between the East End and the City of London is as sharp today as it was when Aldgate and Bishopsgate were real gateways in the wall separating the rich City from the poorer quarters to the east. The best reasons to visit are the vibrant **markets** (p. 134), which draw shoppers from all over.

DOCKLANDS

Countering heritage-obsessed Greenwich across the Thames, brash young Docklands is the largest commercial development in Europe. Until the 1960s, this man-made archipelago was the heart of British commerce, with an endless stream of cargoes from across the empire being loaded and unloaded. In 1981, the London Docklands Development Corporation (LDDC) was founded to redevelop the area. The showpiece is **Canary Wharf,** with Britain's highest skyscraper, the 800 ft., pyramid-topped **One Canada Square.** Under the tower, vast **Canada Place** and **Cabot Square** malls suck in shoppers, while the dockside plaza is lined with pricey corporate feeding troughs. *(⊖/DLR: Canary Wharf.)*

GREENWICH

Seat of the Royal Navy until 1998, Greenwich's position as the "home of time" is intimately connected to its maritime heritage—the Royal Observatory, site of the **Prime Meridian,** was originally founded to produce the accurate star-charts essential to navigation. *(All sights are closest to DLR: Cutty Sark.)*

ROYAL OBSERVATORY GREENWICH. Charles II founded the Royal Observatory in 1675 to find a way of calculating longitude at sea. Though the problem was eventually solved without reference to the sky, the connection lives on—the **Prime Meridian** (marking 0° longitude) started out as the axis along which astronomers' telescopes swung. Next to the meridian, Wren's **Flamstead House** retains its original interior in **Octagon Room.** Climb the **Observatory Dome** to see the 28" scope, constructed in 1893. It hasn't been used since 1954, but you can see the stars at the **Planetarium** in the South Building. *(At the top of Greenwich Park, a steep climb from the National Maritime Museum. A tram leaves the back of the Museum every 30min. on the hr. ☎8312 6565; www.rog.nmm.ac.uk. Open daily 10am-5pm; last admission 4:30pm. Free.)*

ROYAL NAVAL COLLEGE. On the site of Henry VIII's Palace of Placentia, the Naval College was founded by William III in 1694 as the Royal Hospital for Seamen. In 1873 it became the Royal Naval College, but the nautical association ended in 1998 when the University of Greenwich blew in. Mary II had insisted that the new buildings not restrict the view from the Queen's House; Wren responded with two symmetrical wings separated by a colonnaded walkway. Buy a ticket to the **Painted Hall,** which took 19 years to complete, and the simple **chapel.** *(King William Walk. ☎8269 4791. Open daily 10am-5pm, Su chapel 12:30-5pm. Free.)*

LONDON

OTHER GREENWICH SIGHTS. Now part of the National Maritime Museum (p. 131), Inigo Jones's **Queen's House** was commissioned in 1616 by Anne of Denmark, James I's queen, but only completed 22 years later for Charles I's wife, Henrietta Maria. *(Trafalgar Rd., at the foot of Greenwich Park.)* Last of the great tea clippers, the **Cutty Sark** has thoroughbred lines even landlubbers will appreciate—she was the fastest ship of her time, making the round-trip to China in only 120 days. The deck and cabins have been restored to their 19th-century prime, while the hold contains an exhibition on the ship's history and a collection of figureheads. *(King William Walk, by Greenwich Pier. ☎8858 2698. Open daily 10am-5pm. £4.25, concessions and under 16 £3.25, families £10.50.)* Close by the *Cutty Sark*, **Gypsy Moth** is a 54 ft. craft in which 64-year-old Francis Chichester sailed nearly 30,000 solo miles in 1966.

WEST LONDON

■ **KEW GARDENS.** Founded in 1759 by Princess Augusta as an addendum to Kew Palace, the Royal Botanical Gardens have since expanded into a leading botanical research center, thanks in no small part to its living collection of thousands of flowers, fruits, trees, and vegetables from across the globe. The three great **conservatories** and their smaller offshoots house a staggering variety of plants ill-suited to the English climate. Most famous of them is the steamy **Palm House.** The **Temperate House** is the world's largest ornamental greenhouse, although the snazzy **Princess of Wales Conservatory** has a larger area, thanks to its pyramidal structure. The interior is divided into 10 different climate zones, including one devoted entirely to orchids. *(Main entrance and visitors center is at Victoria Gate, nearest the Tube. ☎8332 5000, 24hr. recorded information ☎8332 5655. ⊖Kew Gardens (Zone 3). Tours start at Victoria Gate visitors center. 1hr. walking tours daily 11am and 2pm; free. "Explorer" hop-on-hop-off shuttle makes 35min. rounds of the gardens; 1st shuttle departs daily 11am, last 3:35pm. £3.50, children £1. Open Apr.-Aug. M-F 9:30am-6:30pm, Sa-Su 9:30am-7:30pm; daily Sept.-Oct. 9:30am-6pm; Nov.-Jan. 9:30am-4:15pm; Feb.-Mar. 9:30am-5:30pm. Last admission 30min. before closing. Glasshouses close 5:30pm Feb.-Oct., 3:45pm Nov.-Jan. £7.50, "late entry" (from 45min. before the glasshouses close) £5.50; under 16 free.)*

HAMPTON COURT PALACE. Although a monarch hasn't lived here for 250 years, Hampton Court still exudes regal charm. Cardinal Wolsey built the first palace here in 1514, showing the young Henry VIII how to act the part of a powerful ruler. Henry learned the lesson all too well, confiscating Hampton in 1528, and embarking on a massive building program. In 1689, William and Mary employed Wren to bring the Court up to date, but less than 50 years later George II abandoned it for good. The **palace** is divided into six 45-60min. tour routes, all starting at **Clock Court,** where you can pick up a program of the day's events and an audioguide. In **Henry VIII's State Apartments,** only the massive Great Hall and exquisite Chapel Royal hint at past magnificence. Below, the **Tudor Kitchens** offer insight into how Henry ate himself to a 54" waist. Predating Henry's additions, the 16th-century **Wolsey Rooms** are complemented by Renaissance masterpieces. Most impressive are Wren's **King's Apartments,** restored after a 1986 fire to their original appearance under William of Orange. The **Queen's Apartments** weren't completed until 1734, postponed by Mary II's death. The **Georgian Rooms** were created by William Kent for George II's family. Scarcely less impressive are the **gardens,** with Mantegna's *Triumphs of Caesar* secreted away in the Lower Orangery. North of the palace, the **Wilderness,** a pseudo-natural area earmarked for picnickers, holds the ever-popular **maze,** planted in 1714. Its small size belies its devilish design. *(30min. from Waterloo by train, 24min. from Clapham Junction; 4hr. by boat Apr.-Sept., Westminster Passenger Cruises ☎7930 2062. ☎087 0752 7777; www.hrp.org.uk. Open late Mar. to late Oct. M 10:15am-6pm, Tu-Su 9:30am-6pm; late Oct.-late Mar. closes 4:30pm; last admission 45min. before closing. Gardens open until dusk or 9pm. Palace and gardens £11.80, concessions*

£8.70, children £7.70, families £35; Maze or South Gardens only £3.50, children £2.50; gardens (excluding South Gardens) free. Free admission for worshippers at Chapel Royal services, held Su 11am and 3:30pm. All tours included in the ticket.)

🏛 MUSEUMS AND GALLERIES

London boasts a spectacular set of museums. After a decade of rising museum prices, admission to all major collections is now free indefinitely, in celebration of the Queen's Golden Jubilee.

MAJOR COLLECTIONS

BRITISH MUSEUM

Great Russell St. ☎ 7323 8000. ⊖Tottenham Crt. Rd., Russell Sq., or Holborn. Free tours start 12:30pm at the Enlightenment Desk. 1½hr. Highlights Tour daily 10:30am, 1, and 3pm. Advanced booking recommended. £8, concessions £5. Various other themed tours run throughout the week; check website or info desk for details. Audioguide £3.50. Wheelchair accessible. Great Court open Su-W 9am-6pm, Th-Sa 9am-11pm (winter 9pm). Galleries open daily 10am-5:30pm, selected galleries have extended hours Th-F. Temporary exhibitions around £5, concessions £3.50.

The December 2000 opening of the **Great Court**—Europe's largest covered square—finally restored the museum's focal point, the enormous rotunda of the **Reading Room.** These desks have shouldered the weight of research by Marx, Lenin, and Trotsky, plus most major British writers and intellectuals.

The funny thing about the British Museum is that there's almost nothing British in it. The most famous items in the collection are found in the **Western Galleries.** Room 4 harbors an unrivaled collection of Egyptian sculpture, including the **Rosetta Stone.** Room 18 is entirely devoted to the **Elgin Marbles.** Other highlights include giant Assyrian and Babylonian reliefs, the Roman Portland Vase, and bits from two Wonders of the Ancient World—the **Temple of Artemis** at Ephesus and the **Mausoleum of Halikarnassos.** Just when you thought you'd nailed antiquity, the **Northern Galleries** strike back with eight rooms of mummies and sarcophagi and nine of artifacts from the ancient Near East. Also in the northern wing are the excellent African and Islamic galleries, the giant Asian collections, and the substantially less impressive Americas collection. Treasures excavated from the **Sutton Hoo Burial Ship** fill Room 41. Next door, Room 42 is home to the enigmatic **Lewis Chessmen,** an 800-year-old chess set abandoned in the Outer Hebrides. Collectors and enthusiasts will also enjoy the comprehensive Clock Gallery (Room 44) and Money Gallery (Room 68).

NATIONAL GALLERY

Main entrance on north side of Trafalgar Sq., Westminster. ⊖Charing Cross or Leicester Sq. ☎ 7747 2885. Wheelchair accessible at Sainsbury Wing on Pall Mall East. Open M-Tu and Th-Su 10am-6pm, W 10am-9pm. Special exhibitions in the Sainsbury Wing occasionally open until 10pm. Tours: Start at Sainsbury Wing info desk. 1hr. gallery tours daily 11:30am and 2:30pm, W also 6:30pm; free. Audioguides free, £4 suggested donation. Some temporary exhibitions £5-7, seniors £4-5, students and ages 12-18 £2-3.

The National Gallery was founded by an Act of Parliament in 1824, with 38 pictures displayed in a townhouse; over the years it's grown to hold the burgeoning collection. Numerous additions have been made, the most recent (and controversial) being the massive modern **Sainsbury Wing**—Prince Charles described it as "a monstrous carbuncle on the face of a much-loved and elegant friend." The Sainsbury Wing holds almost all of the museum's large exhibitions as well as the restaurants and lecture halls. If you're pressed for time, head to the **Micro Gallery** in the Sainsbury

LONDON

Wing, where you can design and print out a personalized tour of the paintings you want to see. Its climate-controlled rooms house the oldest, most fragile paintings, including the 14th-century English *Wilton Diptych*, Botticelli's *Venus and Mars*, and the *Leonardo Cartoon*, a detailed preparatory drawing by da Vinci for a never-executed painting. With paintings from 1510 to 1600, the **West Wing** is dominated by the **Italian High Renaissance,** both Roman and Venetian, and the first flowering of German and Flemish art. The **North Wing** spans the 17th century, with an exceptional display of Flemish and Spanish Renaissance works spread over 17 rooms. The **East Wing,** home to paintings from 1700 to 1900, is the most crowded, housing the most famous works and the Impressionist galleries. The focus is primarily on room 45, which features one of Van Gogh's *Sunflowers.*

TATE BRITAIN

Millbank, in Westminster. ❸Pimlico. ☎ 7887 8008. Tours: M-F Art from 1500-1800 11am, 1800-1900 noon, Turner 2pm, 1900-2002 3pm. Sa-Su tours of 1500-2004 at noon and 3pm; all free. Audioguide £3, concessions £2.50. Wheelchair accessible. Open daily 10am-5:50pm, last admission 5pm. Special exhibitions £3-9.50.

Tate Britain now houses an excellent collection of British art including foreign artists working in Britain and Brits working abroad from 1500 to the present. There are four Tate Galleries in England; this is the original, opened in 1897 to house Sir Henry Tate's collection of "modern" British art. It was expanded to include the famed British painter's J.M.W. Turner bequest of 282 oils and 19,000 watercolors. The museum can feel like one big tribute to Turner. The **Clure Gallery** continues to display Turner's prolific collection of hazy British landscapes. The bulk of the museum consists of the **Tate Centenary Development,** rotating exhibits which loosely trace the chronology of art in Britain from 1500 to 2005. The rooms are organized through themed subdivisions such as "British Art and Asia" or "Art and Victorian Society." The annual **Turner Prize** for contemporary art is awarded here; shortlisted works are on the walls from November to mid-January.

TATE MODERN

Bankside, on the South Bank. From Southwark tube, turn left up Union then left on Great Suffolk, then left on Holland. ❸Southwark or Blackfriars. ☎ 7887 8000. Tours meet on gallery concourses; free. Audioguide £2. Open M-Th, Su 10am-6pm, F-Sa 10am-10pm.

Since opening in May 2000, Tate Modern has been credited with single-handedly reversing the long-term decline in British museum-going. The largest modern art museum in the world (until New York's MOMA re-opens in 2005), its most striking aspect is the building itself, formerly Bankside Power Station. The conversion to gallery added a seventh floor, with wraparound views of north and south London, and turned the old **Turbine Hall** into an immense atrium that often overpowers the installations commissioned for it. The Tate groups works according to themes rather than period or artist—the four overarching divisions are **Still Life/Object/Real Life** and **Landscape/Matter/Environment** on Level 3, and **Nude/Action/Body** and **History/Memory/Society** on Level 5—even skeptics admit that this arrangement throws up some interesting contrasts. The thematic display forces visitors into contact with an exceptionally wide range of art. It's now impossible to see the Tate's more famous pieces, which include Picasso's *Nude Woman with Necklace*, without also confronting challenging and invigorating works by less well-known contemporary artists.

VICTORIA AND ALBERT MUSEUM

Main entrance on Cromwell Rd. ☎ 7942 2000. ❸South Kensington. Wheelchair accessible on Exhibition Rd. Open daily 10am-5:45pm, plus W and last F of month until 10pm. Tours meet at rear of main entrance; free. Last F of month also features live performances, guest DJs, late-night exhibition openings, bar, and food.

The V&A is dedicated to displaying "the fine and applied arts of all countries, all styles, and all periods." The subject of a £31 million refit, the vast **British Galleries** hold a series of recreated rooms from every period between 1500 and 1900 that are mirrored by the vast **Dress Collection,** a dazzling array of the finest *haute couture* through the ages. The ground-floor **European** collections range from 4th-century Byzantine tapestry to Alfonse Mucha posters; if you only see one thing, make it the **Raphael Gallery,** hung with six massive paintings commissioned by Pope Leo X in 1515. The **Sculpture Gallery,** home to Canova's *Three Graces* (1814-17) and the voluptuous *Sleeping Nymph* (1820-24), is not to be confused with the **Cast Courts,** a plaster-replica collection of the world's sculptural greatest hits, from Trajan's Column to Michelangelo's *David.* The V&A's **Asian** collections are particularly formidable. Particularly worth experiencing is **Tippoo's Tiger,** the graphically fascinating 1799 model of a tiger eating a man—complete with organ sounds and crunching noises.

In contrast to the geographically laid-out ground floor, the **upper levels** are mostly arranged by material; here you'll find specialist galleries devoted to everything from jewelry to musical instruments to stained glass. Two exceptions to the materially themed galleries are the **Leighton** gallery, with a fresco by the eponymous Victorian painter, and the sprawling **20th-century** collections, a trippy highlight. The six-level **Henry Cole wing** is home to **British** paintings, including some 350 works by Constable and numerous Turners.

OTHER COLLECTIONS

BLOOMSBURY

🏛**BRITISH LIBRARY GALLERIES.** The British Library presents an appropriately stunning display of books and manuscripts, from the 2nd-century *Unknown Gospel* to the Beatles' hand-scrawled lyrics. Other highlights include a Gutenberg Bible, Joyce's handwritten draft of *Finnegan's Wake,* and pages from da Vinci's notebooks. *(96 Euston Rd. ⊖King's Cross. ☎7412 7332. Open M and W-F 9:30am-6pm, Tu 9:30am-8pm, Sa 9:30am-5pm, Su 11am-5pm. Tours M, W, F 3pm, Sa 10:30am and 3pm; £6, concessions £4.50. Tours including reading rooms Tu 6:30pm, Su and Bank Holidays 11:30am and 3pm; £7/£5.50. Reservations recommended. Free.)*

THE CITY OF LONDON

🏛**MUSEUM OF LONDON.** In the corner of the **Barbican** complex (p. 115), this engrossing collection traces London's history from foundation to present day, with a strong selection of Roman and medieval objects and the gold-plated **Lord Mayor's State Coach,** built in 1757. *(London Wall; enter through the Barbican or from Aldersgate. ⊖St. Paul's or Barbican. ☎7600 3699. Wheelchair accessible. Open M-Sa 10am-5:50pm, Su noon-5:50pm; last admission 5:30pm. Audioguides £2. Free.)*

HOLBORN AND CLERKENWELL

🏛**SIR JOHN SOANE'S MUSEUM.** Eccentric architect John Soane gave his imagination free rein when designing this intriguing museum for his personal collection of art and antiquities. Idiosyncratic cupolas cast light on a bewildering panoply of ancient carvings; in the **Picture Room,** multiple Hogarths hang from fold-out panels. *(13 Lincoln's Inn Fields. ⊖Holborn. ☎1405 2107. Open Tu-Sa 10am-5pm, 1st Tu of month also 6-9pm. Tours Sa 2:30pm. £1 donation requested. Tours £3, students free.)*

🏛**THE COURTAULD INSTITUTE GALLERIES.** The Courtauld's outstanding small collection ranges from 14th-century Italian to 20th-century abstraction, focusing on Impressionism; masterpieces include Manet's *A Bar at the Follies Bergères,* van Gogh's *Self Portrait with Bandaged Ear*, and Cézanne's *The Card Players*. *(Somerset House, the Strand.* ⊖ *Charing Cross or Temple.* ☎ *7420 9400. Wheelchair accessible. Open daily 10am-6pm. £6.50, concessions £4; free M 10am-2pm.)*

THE GILBERT COLLECTION. The Gilbert Collection of Decorative Arts opened in 2000 to widespread acclaim. Pick up a free audioguide and magnifying glass as you enter—the latter is invaluable for studying the displays of micromosaics and ornate snuffboxes. *(Somerset House, the Strand.* ⊖ *Charing Cross or Temple.* ☎ *7420 9400; www.gilbert-collection.org.uk. 1hr. tours Sa 2:30pm, £6.50, concessions £6, includes admission. Open daily 10am-6pm. £6.50, concessions £6, children free.)*

KENSINGTON AND EARL'S COURT

■ **SCIENCE MUSEUM.** Dedicated to the Victorian ideal of Progress (with a capital P), this museum focuses on the power of technology. You'll find high-tech displays, priceless historical artifacts, and a few mind-numbing galleries. Most impressive is the **Making of the Modern World,** a collection of pioneering contraptions from "Puffing Billy," the oldest surviving steam locomotive, to the Apollo 10. The exhibits of the **Wellcome Wing** are overshadowed by the curve of the vast **IMAX cinema.** *(Exhibition Rd.* ⊖ *South Kensington.* ☎ *0870 870 4868, IMAX 0870 870 4771. Open daily 10am-6pm. Shows every 75min. 10:45am-5pm. Free. IMAX £7.50, concessions £6.)*

■ **NATURAL HISTORY MUSEUM.** Architecturally the most impressive of the South Kensington museums, this cathedral-like building is home to an outstanding collection of critters, rocks, and other wonders. Highlights include the remarkably realistic T-Rex (complete with bad breath) in the **Dinosaur** exhibit, the engrossing interactive **Human Biology** gallery, and the giant **Mammals** hall. *(Cromwell Rd.* ⊖ *South Kensington.* ☎ *7942 5000. Wheelchair accessible. Open M-Sa 10am-5:50pm, Su 11am-5:50pm; last admission 5:30pm. Free. 45min. highlight tours every hr. 11am-4pm; reserve at the main info desk; free. Special exhibits £5, concessions £3.)*

MARYLEBONE AND REGENT'S PARK

■ **THE WALLACE COLLECTION.** Housed in palatial Hertford House, this is a stunning array of paintings, porcelain, and medieval armor. The **first floor** is home to a world-renowned collection of 18th-century French art as well as the **Great Gallery,** containing 17th-century works. *(Hertford House, Manchester Sq.* ⊖ *Bond St. or Marble Arch.* ☎ *7563 9500; www.wallace-collection.com. Open M-Sa 10am-5pm, Su noon-5pm. Free 1hr. tours W and Sa 11:30am and Su 3pm. Free talks M-F 1pm, occasionally Sa 11:30am.)*

THE SOUTH BANK

■ **IMPERIAL WAR MUSEUM.** Five floors of modern, exciting, respectful warfare education. Massive 15-inch naval guns guard the entrance to the building, formerly the infamous lunatic asylum known as Bedlam. Grab a free **floorplan,** then decide on your battle plan. The best and most publicized display is up on the 3rd floor: the **Holocaust Exhibition** provides an honest and poignant look at all the events surrounding the tragedy. *(Lambeth Rd., Lambeth.* ☎ *7416 5320, recorded info* ☎ *7416 5000.* ⊖ *Lambeth North or Elephant & Castle. Open daily 10am-6pm. Audioguide: £3, concessions £2.50. Free.)*

THE WEST END

■ **LONDON'S TRANSPORT MUSEUM.** Kids and adults will find themselves engrossed in this informative and fun history of London's public transportation. Clamber over dozens of buses to try the Tube simulator. *(Southeast corner of Covent Garden Piazza.* ⊖ *Covent Garden.* ☎ *7565 7299. Wheelchair accessible. Open M-Th and Sa-Su 10am-6pm, F 11am-6pm; last admission 5:15pm. £5.95, concessions £4.50, children free.)*

■ **ROYAL ACADEMY OF ART.** Founded in 1768 as both art school and meeting place for Britain's foremost artists, the Academy holds outstanding exhibitions. It occupies spectacular **Burlington House,** built in 1665, the only survivor of Piccadilly's aristocratic mansions. Anyone can submit a piece for the Summer Exhibition (June-Aug.), held every year since 1769. (⊖Piccadilly Circus or Green Park. ☎7300 8000. Wheelchair accessible. Open Sa-Th 10am-6pm, F 10am-10pm. £7, concessions £6.)

INSTITUTE OF CONTEMPORARY ARTS (ICA). A grand Neoclassical pediment in London's most conservative neighborhood is the last place you'd expect to find Britain's national center for the contemporary arts—at least it's conveniently located for attacking the establishment. (Nash House, the Mall. ⊖Charing Cross or Piccadilly Circus. ☎7930 3647; www.ica.org.uk. Open M noon-11pm, Tu-Sa noon-1am, Su noon-10:30pm; galleries close 7:30pm. Galleries M-F £1.50, Sa-Su £2.50; concessions £1/£1.50. Cinema £6.50, M-F before 5pm £5.50; concessions £5.50/£4.50.)

WESTMINSTER

■ **CABINET WAR ROOMS.** For six tense years, Churchill, his cabinet and generals, and dozens of support staff haunted these underground quarters; the day after the war ended, the rooms were shut up and left undisturbed until their 1981 reopening. Highlights include the room containing the top-secret transatlantic hotline—official word was that it was Churchill's personal loo. (Clive Steps, King Charles St. ⊖Westminster. ☎7766 0130. Open daily Apr.-Sept. 9:30am-6pm; Oct.-Mar. 10am-6pm. Last admission 5:15pm. £7.50, concessions £5.50, under 16 free.)

NORTH LONDON

■ **THE IVEAGH BEQUEST.** A stout collection bequeathed by Edward Guinness, Earl of Iveagh, the Kenwood setting and magnificent pictures make it one of London's finest small galleries. Highlights include works by Rembrandt, Vermeer, Turner, and Botticelli. (Kenwood House. ⊖Hampstead. ☎8348 1286. Open Apr.-Sept. Sa-Tu and Th 10am-6pm, W and F 10:30am-6pm; Oct. until 5pm; Nov.-Mar. until 4pm. Free.)

EAST LONDON

■ **NATIONAL MARITIME MUSEUM.** The NMM's displays cover almost every aspect of seafaring history. Its galleries resemble a nautical theme park—once the kiddies get into the **All Hands** interactive gallery, it'll be hard to get them out. The pride of the naval displays is the **Nelson Room,** which tells the stirring tale of a 12-year-old midshipman's rise through the ranks. (Romney Rd., between Royal Naval College and Greenwich Park. DLR: Cutty Sark. ☎8858 4422. Open daily June to early Sept. 10am-6pm; early Sept. to May 10am-5pm. Last admission 30min. before close. Free.)

■ **WHITECHAPEL ART GALLERY.** Long the sole artistic beacon in an impoverished area and now the forefront of the East End's buzzing art scene, Whitechapel hosts excellent, often controversial, shows of contemporary art. (Whitechapel High St. ⊖Aldgate East. ☎7522 7888. Open Tu-W and F-Su 11am-6pm, Th 11am-9pm. Free.)

SOUTH LONDON

■ **DULWICH PICTURE GALLERY.** Designed by Sir John Soane, this marvelous array of Old Masters was England's first public art gallery. Rubens and van Dyck feature prominently, as does Rembrandt's A Girl at a Window. (Gallery Rd., Dulwich. 10min. from North or West Dulwich rail station, or bus P4 from ⊖Brixton. ☎8299 8700. From West Dulwich station, turn right onto Thurlow Park Rd., then left onto Gallery Rd. and follow the signs for a 15min. walk; from North Dulwich, turn left out of the station and a 10min. walk through Dulwich Village to the Gallery. Wheelchair accessible. Open Tu-F 10am-5pm, Sa-Su 11am-5pm. Tours Sa-Su 3pm; free. £4, seniors £3, students and under 16 free.)

LONDON

▢ SHOPPING

This has always been a trading city, and London's economy is truly international. Thanks to the eclectic taste of Londoners, the range of goods is unmatched.

DEPARTMENT STORES

▨ **Selfridges,** 400 Oxford St. (☎0870 837 7377). ⊖Bond St. The total department store. Covers everything from traditional tweeds to space-age clubwear. 14 eateries, hair salon, bureau de change, and hotel. Open M-W 10am-7pm, Th-F 10am-8pm, Sa 9:30am-7pm, Su noon-6pm. AmEx/MC/V.

▨ **Hamley's,** 188-189 Regent St. (☎7734 3161). ⊖Bond St. 7 floors filled with every conceivable toy and game. Dozens of strategically placed product demonstrations are guaranteed to turn any mummy's darling into a snarling, toy-demanding menace. Open M-F 10am-8pm, Sa 9:30am-8pm, Su noon-6pm. AmEx/MC/V.

Liberty, 210-220 Regent St. (☎7734 1234). ⊖Oxford Circus. Focus on top-quality design and handicrafts. Enormous hat department and a whole hall of scarves. Open M-W 10am-6:30pm, Th 10am-8pm, F-Sa 10am-7pm, Su noon-6pm. AmEx/MC/V.

Fortnum & Mason, 181 Piccadilly (☎7734 8040). ⊖Green Park or Piccadilly Circus. London's smallest, snootiest department store, est. 1707. Famed for its sumptuous food hall. Open M-Sa 10am-6:30pm. AmEx/MC/V.

Harrods, 87-135 Old Brompton Rd. (☎7730 1234). ⊖Knightsbridge. The only thing bigger than the bewildering store is the mark-up on the goods—no wonder only tourists actually shop here. Open M-Sa 10am-7pm. AmEx/MC/V/your soul.

Harvey Nichols, 109-125 Knightsbridge (☎7235 5000). ⊖Knightsbridge. Bond St., Rue St.-Honoré, and Fifth Avenue all rolled up into 5 floors of fashion, from the biggest names to the hippest contemporary unknowns. Open M-Tu and Sa 10am-7pm, W-F 10am-8pm, Su noon-6pm. AmEx/MC/V.

MAJOR CHAINS

As with any large city, London retailing is dominated by chains. Fortunately, local shoppers are picky enough that buying from a chain doesn't mean abandoning the flair and quirky stylishness for which Londoners are famed. Most chains have a flagship on or near **Oxford Street.** Different branches have slightly different hours, but stores are usually open daily 10am-7pm, starting later (noon) on Su and staying open an hour later one night of the week (usually Th). Some of the popular London chains are: ▨Lush, FCUK, Topman/Topshop/Miss Selfridge, Karen Miller, Oasis, Jigsaw, Muji, Marks and Spencer, Sainsbury's, Shellys and UNIQLU.

SHOPPING BY NEIGHBORHOOD

CENTRAL LONDON

OXFORD AND REGENT STREETS. The atmosphere is incredible in the department stores and mainstream chains of Oxford St. and Regent St., London's shopping center. Fashionable boutiques line pedestrian **South Molton Street,** stretching south into Mayfair from Bond St. Tube, and **Foubert's Place,** near youth-oriented Carnaby St. The area also has a number of excellent sale shops.

MAYFAIR. Mayfair's aristocratic pedigree is evident in the scores of high-priced shops, many bearing Royal Warrants to indicate their status as official palace suppliers. **Bond Street** is the location of choice for the biggest names. Less mainstream designers set up shop on **Conduit Street,** where Old Bond St. meets New Bond St.; here you'll find Vivienne Westwood, Alexander McQueen, and Yohji Yamamoto. Cheaper duds abound at **Paul Smith Sale Shop,** 23 Avery Row (⊖Bond St.); find a smallish range of last-season and clearance items from the acknowledged master of modern British menswear. Exclusive **Sotheran's of Sackville Street,** 2-5 Sackville St. (☎7439 6151; ⊖Piccadilly Circus), founded in 1761, has a charming staff and plenty of affordable books, while the ▓**Waterstone's** at 203-206 Piccadilly (☎7851 2400; ⊖Piccadilly Circus), is Europe's largest bookshop.

SOHO. Despite its eternal trendiness, Soho has never been much of a shopping destination. The main exception is the record stores of **D'Arblay Street** and **Berwick Street,** including **Reckless Records,** 26 and 30 Berwick St. (☎7437 3362); **Sister Ray,** 94 Berwick St. (☎7287 8385); and top DJ hangout **Uptown Records,** 3 D'Arblay St. (☎7434 3639; ⊖Oxford Circus). Keeping up the musical theme are the excellent instrument and equipment shops of **Denmark Street.** ▓**Gerry's** (☎7734 2053; ⊖Piccadilly Circus or Leicester Sq.) stocks a staggering selection of beer and liquor.

COVENT GARDEN. Covent Garden is increasingly mainstream, though there are enough quirky shops left to make it worth a look. North of the piazza, **Floral Street** is firmly established as the area's smartest. Ever-popular **Neal Street** is a top destination for funky footwear and mid-priced clubwear, though the fashion focus has shifted to nearby **Shorts Gardens, Earlham Street,** and **Monmouth Street.** A best bet for women's clothing is ▓**Apple Tree,** 51 and 62 Neal St. (☎7836 6088), which offers colorful clothing that verges on punk. Treat your feet at **Office,** 57 Neal St. (☎7379 1896), the largest outlet of London's foremost fashion footwear retailer. ▓**Neal's Yard Dairy** (☎7240 5700) offers an enormous array of British and Irish cheeses.

BLOOMSBURY. Besides intellectuals, Bloomsbury's main commodity is **books.** The streets around the British Museum in particular are crammed with specialist and cut price booksellers, like ▓**Gay's the Word,** 66 Marchmont St. (☎7278 7654. ⊖Russell Sq.). For a blast from the past, the small selection of vintage clothes in ▓**Delta of Venus,** 151 Drummond St. (☎7387 3037; ⊖Warren St. or Euston), is unbeatable, spanning the 1960s to the early 80s. For a blast into the future, head to **Tottenham Court Road** for electronics.

CHELSEA AND KNIGHTSBRIDGE. No serious shopper ignores Chelsea. If **Sloane Square** is too sloaney (read: preppy), the **King's Road,** with one-off boutiques at all price ranges, is all things to all shoppers. The main shopping arteries of **Knightsbridge** are the **Old Brompton Road,** with upmarket chains, and **Sloane Street,** full of exclusive boutiques. **World's End,** 430 King's Rd. (☎7352 6551) gave birth to the Sex Pistols, but has since gone mainstream. ▓**Steinberg & Tolkein,** 193 King's Rd. (☎7376 3660. ⊖Sloane Sq.) offers London's largest collection of vintage clothing.

NOTTING HILL. The best reason to visit Notting Hill is **Portobello Market,** which brings an influx of color and vivacity to an otherwise gentrified area. The "Market" is actually several distinct markets occupying different parts of the street and operating on different days; Saturdays, when all come together in a mile-long row, is the best day to visit. The **antiques market** stretches north along Portobello from Chepstow Villas to Elgin Crescent. (⊖Notting Hill Gate; open Sa 7am-5pm) sells cheapish bric-a-brac, little of it truly rare or very old; the **general market,** from Elgin Cres. to Lancaster Rd. (⊖Westbourne Park or Ladbroke Grove; open M-W 8am-6pm, Th 9am-1pm, F-Sa 7am-7pm) sells food, flowers, and household essentials; and the **clothes market,** north of Lancaster Rd. (⊖Ladbroke Grove; open F-Sa 8am-3pm) has a wide selection of secondhand clothes, New Age bangles, and cheap clubwear. Also in the area is ▓**The Travel Bookshop,** 13-15 Blenheim Cres. (☎7229 5260), the specialist bookshop featured in *Notting Hill,* today besieged by Grantophiles. **Dolly Diamond,** 51 Pembridge Rd. (☎7792 2479; ⊖Notting Hill Gate), allows you to choose "your" look—Jackie O. or Audrey Hepburn?—from a great selection of classic 50s-70s clothes and elegant 20s-40s evening gowns.

LONDON

NORTH LONDON. In **Camden Town,** you'll find hundreds of identical stores flogging the same chunky shoes and leather trousers they've been selling for years. Arrive early and have a game plan—amid the dross there are genuine bargains and incredible finds. The **Camden markets** are located off Camden High St. and Chalk Farm Rd. (⊖Camden Town). The **Stables Market** (most shops open daily) is nearest to Chalk Farm and the best of the bunch, offering good vintage clothes, as well as some of the most outrageous club- and fetish-wear ever made. **Camden Canal Market** (open F-Su) is down the tunnel opposite Camden Lock, and starts out promisingly with jewelry and watches, but degenerates rapidly into clubbing duds and tourist trinkets. **Camden Lock Market** (most stalls open F or Sa-Su), located between the railway bridge and the canal, is arranged around a food-filled courtyard on the Regent's Canal. **The Camden Market** (open F-Su), nearest to Camden Tube and correspondingly the most crowded, offers jeans, sweaters, and designer fakes. Our favorite Camden shop is ▨**Cyberdog/Cybercity,** arch 14 of the Stables Market (☎7482 2842), with unbelievable club clothes for superior life forms. Try on the fluorescent body-armor or steel corsets. Meanwhile in **Islington,** the **Camden Passage,** Islington High St., behind "The Mall" antiques gallery on Upper St., is *the* place for antiques, especially prints. Shops outnumber stalls. (⊖Angel. Most open W and Sa 8:30am-6pm.)

EAST LONDON. In East London, the street-market tradition is alive and well, helped along by large immigrant communities. The **Brick Lane Market** (⊖Shoreditch or Aldgate East; open Su 8am-2pm) has a South Asian flair, with food, rugs, spices, fabric, and sitar strains, while the **Petticoat Lane Market** (⊖Liverpool St., Aldgate, or Aldgate East; open Su 9am-2pm, starts shutting down about noon) has blocks of cheap clothing.

▣ NIGHTLIFE

The West End, and in particular **Soho,** is the scene of most of London's after-dark action. Hundreds of bars and clubs range from the glitzy Leicester Square tourist traps like the Equinox to semi-secret underground hotspots. The coolest new clubs in London, though, are far from the West End—**Brixton,** in South London, has dozens of hot new clubs and attracts serious clubbers from throughout London. The other major nightlife axis is **Shoreditch** and **Hoxton** (collectively known as **Shoho**) in East London; dead until a few years ago, it's now the city's most cutting-edge area, though parts are still pretty deprived. Style and attitude are essential; most bars and clubs here are for posing as much as for getting down. More recently, South London has come to prominence with the cultural rebirth of the South Bank and the thumping nightlife of a recharged Brixton. In North London, **Notting Hill, Camden Town,** and **Islington** offer a sprinkling of nightspots.

PUBS

Pubs might close at 11pm, but they're still an essential part of the London scene. Whether you're looking for a quiet night out or gearing up for festivities, the city has a pub for you. There are hundreds of pubs in London; these are some of our favorites.

▨ **Ye Olde Mitre Tavern,** 1 Ely Ct. (☎7405 4751). Off #8 Hatton Garden. ⊖Chancery Ln. To find the alley where this pub hides, look for the street lamp on Hatton Garden bearing a sign of a bishop's mitre. This classic pub fully merits its "ye olde"—it was built in 1546 by the Bishop of Ely. With dark oak beams and spun glass, the 2 rooms are perfect for nestling up to a bitter. Open M-F 11am-11pm. AmEx/MC/V (£10 min.).

Ye Olde Cheshire Cheese, Wine Office Ct. (☎ 7353 6170; www.yeoldecheshire-cheese.com). By 145 Fleet St. ⊖Blackfriars or St. Paul's. Once a haunt of Johnson, Dickens, Mark Twain, and Theodore Roosevelt. Front open M-Sa 11am-11pm, Su noon-3pm. Cellar Bar open M-F noon-2:30pm, M-Th and Sa 5:30-11pm. Chop Room open M-F noon-9:30pm, Sa noon-2:30pm and 6-9:30pm, Su noon-2:30pm. Johnson Room open M-F noon-2:30pm and 7-9:30pm. AmEx/MC/V (1.5% surcharge).

The Troubadour, 265 Old Brompton Rd. (☎ 7370 1434; www.troubadour.co.uk). ⊖Earl's Court. A combination pub/cafe/deli, each wing is uniquely fantastic. Breakfast all day £3-5, meals £5.50-10. Open daily 9am-midnight. MC/V.

The Jerusalem Tavern, 55 Britton St. (☎ 7490 4281; www.stpetersbrewery.co.uk). ⊖Farringdon. This tiny, ancient pub offers many niches to get your drink on, including a bizarre one-table balcony across from the bar. Specialty ales (£2.40) like elderberry and Suffolk Gold. Pub grub £5-8. Open M-F 11am-11pm, Sa 5-11pm, Su 11am-5pm. MC/V.

Dog and Duck, 18 Bateman St. (☎ 7494 0697). ⊖Tottenham Crt. Rd. The smallest, oldest pub in Soho. The name refers to Soho's previous role as royal hunting grounds. George Orwell supposedly drank here. Open M-Sa noon-11pm, Su noon-10:30pm. Cash only.

The Cross Keys, 31 Endell St. (☎ 7836 5185). ⊖Convent Garden. It's all about ambience at Cross Keys. The deep red lighting inside makes it the darkest pub around. Food served daily noon-2:30pm. Open M-Sa 11am-11pm, Su noon-10:30pm. Cash only.

BARS

An explosion of **club-bars** has invaded the previously forgotten gap between pubs and clubs, offering seriously stylish surroundings and top-flight DJs together with plentiful lounging space. Club-bars open from noon or early evening, allowing you to skip the cover charge by arriving early and staying put.

Na Zdrowie, 11 Little Turnstile (☎ 7831 9669). ⊖Holborn. Hidden in the pub-filled alleyways behind the Holborn Tube station—when you see Pu's Brasserie, look to the left. The name (nah-ZDROVE-yeh) is a Polish toast. Over 65 types of vodka at about £2.10 a shot (add a mixer for 60p). Open M-F 12:30-11pm, Sa 6-11pm. MC/V.

The Market, 240A Portobello Rd. (☎ 7229 6472). ⊖Ladbroke Grove. Look for the strange sculpture above the door. It's consistently the loudest spot on Portobello, and that's saying a lot. Make some friends while downing a cool Cuban punch (£3). Thai food weekdays noon-3pm. Open M-Sa 11am-11pm, Su noon-12:30am. Cash only.

Filthy MacNasty's Whiskey Café, 68 Amwell St. (☎ 7837 6067). ⊖Angel or King's Cross. Shane MacGowan, U2, and the Libertines have all played here. The last two still drop by periodically; Shane just lives here. Live music and occasional literary readings add to the bad-boy-intellectual atmosphere. 14 varieties of whiskey all go for around £2. Bar food mostly £5-6. Open M-Sa noon-11pm, Su noon-10:30pm. Cash only.

NIGHTCLUBS

Every major DJ in the world either lives in London or makes frequent visits. The UK has taken the lead in developing and experimenting with new types of dance music. Even weekly publications have trouble keeping up with the club scene— *Time Out* (W, £2.35), the Londoner's clubbing bible, only lists about half the happenings any given night. The scene revolves around promoters and the nights they organize rather than the clubs themselves; top nights come, go, and move around unpredictably. To stay on top of things, comb through *Time Out*, which also prints the "TOP" pass, giving you discounts on many of the week's shenanigans.

LONDON

Clubs tend to fall into one of two categories: those for dancing, and those for posing. In the former, dress codes are relaxed; jeans, stylish t-shirts, and trainers, though women are expected to make more effort. At posers' clubs, however, dress is crucial. If you're not sure what to wear, call the club beforehand; otherwise, **black and slinky** is usually safe. **Retro** and **theme** nights mean you have to try harder.

Working out how to get home afterwards is crucial; remember that the Tube and regular buses stop shortly after **midnight,** and after **1am** black cabs are rare. If there's no convenient **Night Bus** home, ask the club in advance if they can order a **minicab** for you; otherwise, order your own before you leave. Although it's technically illegal for minicabs to ply for hire, whispered calls of "taxi" or honking horns signal their presence—but there's no guarantee that the driver is reputable or insured. Agree on a price before you get in, and never ride alone.

▧ **Fabric,** 77a Charterhouse St. (☎ 7336 8898; www.fabriclondon.com). ⊖Farringdon. One of London's premier clubs; expect lines. Boasts a vibrating "bodysonic" dance floor that is actually one giant speaker. F Fabric Live (hip-hop, breakbeat, "soundclash;" 9:30pm-5am; £12), Sa (house, techno; 10pm-7am; £15), Su DTPM polysexual night.

▧ **Strawberry Moons,** 15 Heddon St. (☎ 7437 7300; www.strawberrymoons.co.uk). ⊖Piccadilly Circus or Oxford Circus. Loud, eccentric, hip bar/club with theatrical lighting effects. Tu hip-hop, garage, R&B (cover £5, ladies free before midnight); Th Reach for the Stars mixed hits, karaoke (free before 10pm, £5 after); F Body Heat (free before 9pm, £5 9-10pm, £7 after); Sa Fever! chart classics (free before 8pm, 8pm-9pm £5, 9pm-10pm £7, £9 after). Open M and W 5-11pm, Tu and Th-Sa 5pm-3am.

Trap, 201 Wardour St. (☎ 7434 3820; www.traplondon.com). ⊖Oxford Circus or Tottenham Crt. Rd. The coolest new club-bar in town. Tu-W bar and food available, DJ spins R&B; no cover. Th soul, funk, disco. F R&B club night (Th-F £10 after 10pm). Sa *Sintillate* mix (cover £15; £7 before 10pm).

Notting Hill Arts Club, 21 Notting Hill Gate (☎ 7460 4459). ⊖Notting Hill Gate. Excellent place for relaxed grooving: turntables on folding tables, a dance floor, and minimal decoration, this no-frills basement still manages to rock. M cover £4, before 9pm free; Tu-Th £5, before 8pm free; F £6, before 8pm free; Sa-Su £5, before 6pm free. Open M-W 6pm-1am, Th-F 6pm-2am, Sa 4pm-2am, Su 4pm-12:30am.

Tongue&Groove, 50 Atlantic Rd. (☎ 7274 8600; www.tongueandgroove.org). ⊖Brixton. Unself-consciously trendy club-bar so popular and narrow that people dance on the speakers. Do not underestimate the cocktails (£5 doubles). W US house; Th special guests and Euro house; F house-based mix of African, Cuban, and Brazilian vibes; Sa soulful house, jazz breaks, some disco; Su funk and electronica. Cover £2 Th after 11pm; £3 F, Sa after 10:30. Open M-W and Su 7pm-3am, Th-Sa 7pm-5am.

Ministry of Sound, 103 Gaunt St. (☎ 7378 6528; www.ministryofsound.co.uk). ⊖Elephant and Castle. Take the exit for South Bank University. Mecca for serious clubbers worldwide—arrive before it opens or queue all night. No jeans or trainers. F Smoove garage, R&B (10:30pm-5am; cover £13); Sa Rulin US and house (11pm-8am; £17).

Bar Rumba, 36 Shaftesbury Ave. (☎ 7287 6933; www.barrumba.co.uk). ⊖Piccadilly Circus. It has weathered 11 years of London existence, impressive for any club. M This! starts off the week with a bang. Tu Rumba Pa' Ti with salsa-rap and techno-merengue (open 8:30pm-3am, dance class 6:30-8:30; £4, club and class £7); W 70s-80s classics 10pm-3am (£5 students, £3 with flyer before 11pm, £4 with flyer after 11pm); Th drum&bass (open 8:30pm-3am; £6, before 10pm £3); F the hip-hop Get-Down (open 10pm-4am; £8, before 11pm £6); Sa Funk Asylum (open 10pm-6am; £12, before 11pm £7); Su street soul and R&B (8pm-1am; £5, men £3, women free before 10pm).

ENTERTAINMENT

The West End is one of the world's theater capitals, supplemented by an adventurous "Fringe" and a justly famous National Theatre. New bands spring eternal from the fountain of London's many music venues. Whatever you're planning to do, the listings in *Time Out* (W, £2.35) are indispensable.

THEATER

The stage for a dramatic tradition over 800 years old, London theaters maintain unrivaled breadth of choice. At a **West End theater** (a term referring to all the major stages, even outside the West End), you can expect top-quality performers. **Off-West End** theaters tend to present more challenging works, while remaining as professional as their West End brethren. The **Fringe** refers to scores of smaller venues, often just rooms in pub basements. **tkts**, on the south side of Leicester Square, is run jointly by London theaters and is the only place where you can be sure your discount tickets are genuine. You can only buy on the day of the performance, in person and in cash, on a first-come, first-served basis; there's no choice in seating. There's no way of knowing in advance which shows will have tickets, but you can expect a wide range. Noticeboards display what's available; there's a £2.50 booking fee per ticket. (Open M-Sa 10am-7pm, Su noon-3pm. Most tickets £15-25.)

WEST END AND REPERTORY COMPANIES

Shakespeare's Globe Theatre, 21 New Globe Walk (☎ 7401 9919). ⊖Southwark or London Bridge. A faithful reproduction of the original 16th-century playhouse. Opt for backless wooden benches or stand as a "groundling." For tours, see p. 119. Performances mid-May to late Sept. Tu-Sa 7:30pm, Su 6:30pm; June-Sept. also Tu-Sa 2pm, Su 1pm. Box office open M-Sa 10am-6pm, 8pm on performance day. Seats £12-27, concessions £10-24; standing room £5.

Barbican Theatre (☎ 7382 7000), main entrance on Silk St. A huge, futuristic auditorium with steeply raked, forward-leaning balconies. Hosts touring companies and short-run shows, as well as frequent contemporary dance performances. **The Pit** is largely experimental, while **Barbican Hall** houses the London Symphony Orchestra (p. 139). Tickets £7-30, same-day student and senior standbys from 9am.

National Theatre (☎ 7452 3400, box office ☎ 7452 3000; www.nationaltheatre.org.uk), just downriver of Waterloo bridge. ⊖Waterloo or Embankment. At the forefront of British theater since opening under the direction of Laurence Olivier in 1976. Popular musicals and hit plays, which often transfer to the West End, subsidize experimental works. The **Olivier** stage seats 1080, the **Lyttelton** is a proscenium theater, and the **Cottesloe** offers flexible staging for experimental dramas. Box office open M-Sa 10am-8pm. Prices liable to change with shows: Olivier/Lyttelton £10-34, Cottesloe £10-27, standby (1½hr. before curtain) £10 all theaters, standing room £6. Concessions available.

Open-Air Theatre, Inner Circle, Regent's Park (☎ 7486 2431; www.open-air-theatre.org.uk). ⊖Baker St. Bring blankets and waterproofs—performances take place rain or shine. Program runs early-June to early-Sept., and includes 2 Shakespeare plays, a musical, and a children's show. Barbecue before evening shows. Performances M-Sa 8pm; matinees most Th and every Sa 2:30pm. Tickets £8-28; discounts for groups and under 16; student and senior standby £9 1hr. before curtain. Box office open Apr.-May M-Sa 10am-6pm; Jun.-Sept. M-Sa 10am-8pm, Su (only performance days) 10am-8pm.

LONDON

Royal Court Theatre, Sloane Sq. (☎ 7565 5000). ⊖Sloane Sq. Called "the most important theater in Europe," dedicated to new writing and innovative interpretations of classics. Main stage £7.50-32; concessions £9; standing room 1hr. before curtain 10p. Upstairs £12.50-16, concessions £9. M all seats £7.50. Box office open M-Sa 10am-7:45pm, closes 6pm non-performance weeks.

Sadler's Wells, Rosebery Ave. (☎ 7863 8000). ⊖Angel. London's premier dance space, with everything from classical ballet to contemporary tap, plus occasional operas. Box office open M-Sa 9am-8:30pm. Tickets £10-45; student, senior, and child standbys 1hr. before curtain £10-18.50.

MAJOR FRINGE THEATERS

The Almeida, Almeida St. (☎ 7359 4404; www.almeida.co.uk). ⊖Angel or Highbury & Islington. Top fringe in the world. Stars like Kevin Spacey and Nicole Kidman have established acting credentials here. Tickets £6-27.50; concessions standby £10.

Donmar Warehouse, 41 Earlham St. (☎ 7369 1732; www.donmarwarehouse.com). ⊖Covent Garden. Serious contemporary theater. Tickets £14-29; concessions standby £12, 30min. before curtain.

Old Vic, Waterloo Rd. (☎ 7369 1722; www.oldvictheatre.com). ⊖Waterloo. Still in its original 1818 hall (the oldest theater in London), the Old Vic is one of London's most historic and beautiful theaters. For 2004-05 Kevin Spacey is the artistic director, and will be acting as well. Check website for listings. Box office generally M-Th 10am-7pm, F-Sa until 7:30pm.

CINEMA

The heart of the celluloid monster is **Leicester Square** (p. 121), where the latest releases premiere a day before hitting the city's chains. The dominant mainstream cinema chain is **Odeon** (☎ 0870 5050 007; www.odeon.co.uk). Tickets to West End cinemas cost ₤8-11; weekday matinees before 5pm are usually cheaper. For less mainstream offerings, try the ▨**Electric Cinema,** 191 Portobello Rd., for Baroque stage splendor plus a big screen. For an extra special experience, choose a luxury armchair or two-seat sofa. (⊖Ladbroke Grove. ☎ 7908 9696, tickets 7229 8688. Late-night reruns Sa 11pm; classics and recent raves. M ₤7.50, Tu-Su ₤12.50; 2-seat sofa ₤20-30; first 3 rows ₤5-₤10.) ▨**Riverside Studios,** Crisp Rd., shows a wide and extraordinary range of excellent foreign and classic films. (⊖Hammersmith. ☎ 8237 1111. ₤5.50, concessions ₤4.50.) The ▨**National Film Theatre (NFT),** on the South Bank, underneath Waterloo Bridge, promises a mind-boggling array of films—six different movies hit the three screens every evening, starting around 6pm (⊖Waterloo, Embankment, or Temple. ☎ 7928 3232. ₤7.50, concessions ₤5.70). **The Prince Charles Cinema,** Leicester Pl., will let you *Sing-a-long-a-Sound-of-Music*, with Von Trappists dressed as everything from nuns to "Ray, a drop of golden sun." (⊖Leicester Sq. ☎ 7957 4009 or 7420 0000. ₤3-4.)

COMEDY

Capital of a nation famed for its sense of humor, London takes comedy seriously. On any given night, you'll find at least 10 comedy clubs in operation: check listings in *Time Out* or a newspaper. Summertime visitors should note that London empties of comedians in **August,** when most head to Edinburgh to take part in the annual festivals (p. 564); that means **July** provides plenty of comedians trying out material. ▨**Comedy Store,** 1a Oxendon St., the UK's top comedy club and sower of the seeds that gave rise to *Ab Fab, Whose Line is it Anyway?*, and *Blackadder.* Tu Cutting Edge (current events-based satire), W and Su *Comedy Store Players* improv, Th-Sa standup. (⊖Piccadilly Circus. ☎ 0870 060 2340. Shows Tu-Su 8pm, F-Sa also midnight. Book ahead. 18+. Tickets ₤12-15, concessions ₤8.) East London's ⚏Comedy Cafe, 66 Rivington St., merits a health warning: prolonged exposure may lead to uncontrollable laughter. (☎7739 5706. Reserve F-Sa. Doors open 7pm. Show from 9pm, dancing until 1am. Cover W free, Th £5, F £10, Sa £14.)

MUSIC

ROCK AND POP
Birthplace of the Stones, the Sex Pistols, Madness, and the Chemical Brothers, and home to Madonna (sort of) and McCartney, London is a town steeped in rock.

▨ **The Water Rats,** 328 Grays Inn Rd. (☎7837 7269). ⊖King's Cross St. Pancras. Pub-cafe by day, stomping ground for top new talent by night (from 8pm). Oasis was signed here after their 1st London gig. Cover £5-6, with band flyer £4-5.

Brixton Academy, 211 Stockwell Rd. (Ticketweb ☎7771 3000). ⊖Brixton. 1929 ex-theater; sloping floor ensures everyone can see the band. Covers all the bases, from the Pogues to Senegalese stars. 4300 seat capacity. Box office open only on performance evenings. Tickets £15-33.

Dublin Castle, 94 Parkway (☎7485 1773). ⊖Camden Town. 3 bands nightly 8:45-11pm. Doors open 8:30pm. Cover M-Th and Su £5, students £4.50, F-Sa £6/£4.50.

Forum, 9 11 Highgate Rd. (☎7284 1001, box office 7344 0044). ⊖Kentish Town. Turn right out of Tube station, go over the crest of the hill and bear left—you'll see the marquee. Lavish Art Deco theater with great sound and views. Van Morrison, Bjork, Oasis, Jamiroquai, and others have played this 2000-capacity space. Tickets around £12-35.

London Astoria (LA1), 157 Charing Cross Rd. (☎7344 0044). ⊖Tottenham Court Rd. Once a pickle factory, then a strip club and music hall before turning to rock in the 1980s. M-W and Su sees not-quite-big acts and the popular M G-A-Y. Th-Sa club night.

CLASSICAL
Home to four world-class orchestras, three major concert halls, two opera houses, two ballet companies, and more chamber ensembles than you could Simon Rattle your baton at, London is ground zero for serious music—and there's no need to break the bank. To hear some of the world's top choirs for free, head to Westminster Abbey (p. 110) or St. Paul's Cathedral (p. 111) for **Evensong.**

Barbican Hall (see **Barbican Theatre,** p. 137). ⊖Barbican or Moorgate. One of Europe's leading concert halls. The resident **London Symphony Orchestra** plays over 80 concerts a year. Tickets £5-35.

English National Opera, the Coliseum, St. Martin's Ln. (☎7632 8300; www.eno.org). ⊖Charing Cross or Leicester Sq. Known for both innovative productions of the classics and contemporary work. All performances in English. Box office open M-Sa 10am-8pm. Tickets £5-15, under 18 half-price. Standbys on performance days, by phone from 12:30pm or in person at 10am.

The Proms (☎7589 8212), at the Royal Albert Hall (p. 117). This summer season of classical music has been held since 1895, with concerts every night from mid-July to mid-Sept. "Promenade" refers to the tradition of selling dirt-cheap standing tickets, but it's the presence of up to 1000 dedicated prommers that gives the concerts their unique atmosphere. Lines for standing places often start mid-afternoon. Tickets (£5-75) go on sale in mid-May; standing room (£4) from 1½hr. before the concert.

Royal Opera House, Bow St. (☎7304 4000). ⊖Covent Garden. Known as "Covent Garden" to the aficionado, also home to the **Royal Ballet.** Box office open daily 10am-8pm. £100 or more, but standing room and restricted-view upper balcony can be as low as £5. Concessions standby 4hr. before curtain £12.50-15. 67 seats from 10am day of show £10-40.

LONDON

Wigmore Hall, 36 Wigmore St. (☎ 7935 2141; www.wigmore-hall.org.uk). ⊖Oxford Circus. London's premier chamber music venue, in a beautiful setting with excellent acoustics. Occasional jazz. Season Oct.-July; concerts most nights 7:30pm. £3-35.

JAZZ, FOLK, AND WORLD

This isn't Chicago, but top **jazz** clubs still pull in big-name performers. **Folk** (which in London usually means Irish) and **world** music keep an even lower profile, mostly restricted to pubs. International performers occasionally make appearances at major concert halls such as the Barbican and the Wigmore Hall.

▨ **Jazz Café,** 5 Parkway (☎ 7344 0044; www.jazzcafe.co.uk). ⊖Camden Town. Shows can be pricey but the roster of top jazz, hip-hop, funk, and Latin performers (£10-30) explains it. Jazzy DJs spin on club nights following the show F-Sa (cover £8-9, £5 with flyer), until 2am. Awesome jam session open to all Su noon-4pm (cover £3 or £1 with musical instrument). Open M-Th 7pm-1am, F-Sa 7pm-2am, Su 7pm-midnight. MC/V.

606 Club, 90 Lots Rd. (☎ 7352 5953; www.606club.co.uk). Look for the brick arch labeled 606 opposite the "Fire Access" garage across the street; ring the doorbell to be let downstairs. Entrance F-Su with a meal purchase only. Cover £7 M-Th, £9 F, £8 Sa-Su. Reservations recommended. Closing times are for food—music goes until the band goes home. M-W open 7:30pm, 1st band 8-10:30pm, 2nd 10:45pm-1:00am; Th-Sa open 8pm, music 9:30pm-1:30am; Su (vocalists) open 8pm, music 9pm-midnight. MC/V.

Ronnie Scott's, 47 Frith St. (☎ 7439 0747). ⊖Tottenham Court Rd. or Piccadilly Circus. London's oldest and most famous jazz club. 2 bands alternate 4 sets M-Sa, opener at 9:30pm and headline around 11pm. Su brings lesser-known bands (from 7:30pm). Reservations often essential. Food £6-25. Cocktails £7-9. Cover M-Th £15, F-Sa £25, Su £8-12; students M-W £10. Box office open M-Sa noon-5:30pm. Club open M-Sa 8:30pm-3am, Su 7:30-11pm. Cash only.

SOUTH ENGLAND

South England's sprawling pastures unfold with a history that affirms Britain's island heritage while expressing a deep continental link. Early Britons who crossed the Channel settled the counties of Kent, Sussex, and Hampshire, while William the Conqueror left his mark in the form of intimidating castles and inspiring cathedrals, many built around former Roman settlements. Today, Victorian mansions balance atop seaside cliffs and the masts of restored ships spike the skyline, summoning a chorus of voices from England's naval and literary past. Make like a medieval pilgrim in Canterbury, watch out for invading warships on the Cliffs of Dover, or throw your hands up in Fatboy Slim's hometown of Brighton.

HIGHLIGHTS OF SOUTH ENGLAND

BRIGHTON Wander the tacky paradise by day and shimmy at the nightclubs 'til the break of dawn (p. 159).

DOVER Don't miss the famous chalk-white cliffs, either from the commanding headland or aboard the ferry bringing you to port or whisking you away (p. 148).

SOUTH DOWNS WAY Hike through landscape that inspired the "Idea of England," and is strewn with Bronze Age burial mounds (p. 154).

KENT

CANTERBURY ☎ 01227

And specially from every shires ende
Of Engelond to Caunterbury they wende.
—Geoffrey Chaucer, *The Canterbury Tales*

In 1170, three headstrong knights left Henry II's court in France, their motives unknown to history, and traveled to Canterbury to murder Archbishop Thomas Becket under the massive columns of his own cathedral. A decade of routine tension between church and crown had suddenly produced England's best-known martyr. Three centuries of innumerable pilgrims flowed to St. Thomas's shrine, creating the great medieval road between London and Canterbury. Chaucer caricatured this road and the society surrounding it in his ribald *Canterbury Tales*, which have done more to enshrine the cathedral in perpetual memory than its now-vanished bones. Many medieval buildings remain in the northwest half of the city; the south, mostly rebuilt after WWII bombing, is more modern.

SOUTH ENGLAND

SOUTH ENGLAND

South England

North Sea

English Channel

Strait of Dover

River Thames

River Thames

KENT

SUSSEX

SURREY

HAMPSHIRE

Isle of Wight

New Forest

TO CALAIS

TO OOSTEND

TO BOULOGNE

TO DIEPPE

TO BILBAO, LE HAVRE, CHANNEL ISLANDS

20 miles

20 kilometers

Margate
Broadstairs
Ramsgate
Sandwich
Deal
Dover
Folkestone
Canterbury
Sittingbourne
Ashford
Staplehurst
Leeds Castle
Maidstone
Chatham
Southend
Chelmsford
Sissinghurst
Rye
Hastings
Battle
Pevensey
Eastbourne
Seaford
Charleston Farmhouse
Hailsham
Lewes
Brighton
Newhaven
Burgess Hill
Uckfield
Tunbridge Wells
Tonbridge
Sevenoaks
London
Watford
Windsor
Reading
Newbury
Andover
Basingstoke
Winchester
Southampton
Portsmouth
Chichester
Arundel
Littlehampton
Worthing
Crawley
Gatwick
Godalming
Guildford
Farnborough
Aldershot
Heathrow
Alton
Chawton
Petersfield
Austen's Cottage
WealD & Downland Open Air Museum
Goodwood
Petworth House
Pulborough
Amberley
Fishbourne Roman Palace
Havant
Singleton
South Downs
South Way
Cowes
Newport
Carisbrooke Castle
Shanklin
Sandown
Ryde
Ventnor
Lyndhurst
Lymington

M25
M20
M2
M20
M26
A2
A257
A256
A28
A28
A262
A21
A229
A265
A21
A259
A22
A272
A23
A22
A23
A24
A272
A286
A3
A31
A272
A27
A27
M27
M3
A34
A33
A303
A30
A36
A337
A3055
A3054
A20
A25
A127
A12
A4
A420
M4
M3
A257

TRANSPORTATION

Trains: East Station, Station Rd. East, off Castle St., southwest of town. Open M-Sa 6:10am-8:20pm, Su 6:10am-9:20pm. **Connex South** trains from **London Victoria** (1¾hr., 2 per hr., £17.30). **West Station,** Station Rd. West, off St. Dunstan's St. Open M-F 6:15am-8pm, Sa 6:30am-8pm, Su 7:15am-9:30pm. Connex South from **London Charing Cross** and **London Waterloo** (1½hr., 1 per hr., £17.30).

Buses: Bus station, St. George's Ln. (☎472 082). Open M-Sa 8:15am-5:15pm. **National Express** (☎08705 808 080) from **London** (2hr., 2 per hr., £10.50). Book tickets by 5pm. **Explorer** tickets allow 1-day unlimited bus travel in Kent (£6.50, concessions £4.50, families £13.60).

Taxis: Longport Cars Ltd. (☎458 885). Available daily 7am-2am.

Bike Rental: Downland Cycle Hire, West Station (☎479 643; www.downlandcycles.co.uk). Reserve children's bikes in advance. £10 per day, children £7. Bike trailers £7 per day. £25 deposit.

ORIENTATION AND PRACTICAL INFORMATION

Canterbury Center is roughly circular, defined by the eroding medieval city wall. An unbroken street crosses the city from northwest to southeast, changing names from **Saint Peter's Street** to **High Street** to **The Parade** to **Saint George's Street.** Butchery Ln. and Mercery Ln., each only a block long, run north to the **Cathedral Gates.**

Tourist Information Centre: The Buttermarket, 12/13 Sun St. (☎378 100; fax 378 101). Books beds for a £2.50 charge plus a 10% deposit. Open Easter-Christmas M-Sa 9:30am-5:30pm, Su 10am-4pm; Christmas-Easter M-Sa 10am-4pm.

Tours: 1½hr. **guided tours** of the city depart from the TIC. Daily Apr.-Oct. 2pm; July-Sept. also M-Sa 11:30am. £3.75, concessions £3.25, children £2.75, families £10.

Financial Services: Banks on High St., near the big-name department stores. **Thomas Cook,** 9 High St. (☎597 800). Open M-Sa 9am-5:30pm, Su 11am-4pm.

Launderette: 4 Nunnery Flds. (☎452 211). Open M-F 9am-6pm, Sa 9am-4pm, Su 9am-3pm; last wash 30min. before close.

Police: Old Dover Rd. (☎762 055), outside the eastern city wall.

Hospital: Kent and Canterbury Hospital, 28 Ethelbert Rd. (☎766 877).

Internet Access: Dot Cafe (☎478 778; www.ukdotcafe.com), at the corner of St. Dunstan's St. and Station Rd. W. £2 per 30 min. Open M-Sa 10am-7pm, Su 11am-7pm.

Post Office: 29 High St. (☎473 811), across from Best Ln. Open M 8:30am-5:30pm, Tu-Sa 9am-5:30pm. **Post Code:** CT1 2BA.

ACCOMMODATIONS

Canterbury is busy and singles are scarce; always reserve ahead. **B&Bs** cluster around High St. and near West Station. The less expensive ones (£18-20) on **New Dover Road,** half a mile from East Station, fill fast; turn right from the station and continue up the main artery, which becomes Upper Bridge St. At the second roundabout, turn right onto St. George's Pl., which becomes New Dover Rd.

Kipps Independent Hostel, 40 Nunnery Fields (☎786 121), 5-10min. from city center. Fully equipped self-catering kitchen, comfortable lounge with good movie selection, friendly management, and a social atmosphere. Internet access £1 per 30min. Laundry £3. Key deposit £10. Dorms £13; singles £18.50; doubles £32. MC/V. ❷

Let's Stay, 26 New Dover Rd. (☎463 628). Hostel-style lodgings with a delightful Irish hostess. Ask about the origin of the name! Call ahead. £14. Cash only. ❷

Castle Court Guest House, 8 Castle St. (☎/fax 463 441). Quiet B&B a few minutes from Eastgate in the old town. Vegetarian breakfast available. Singles £25, doubles £42-50. 5% discount for *Let's Go* users. Cash only. ❸

YHA Canterbury, 54 New Dover Rd. (☎462 911; canterbury@yha.org.uk), in a lovely house ¾mi. from East Station and ½ mi. southeast of the bus station. Relaxing lounge, laundry and kitchen facilities, and a **bureau de change.** Breakfast included. Lockers £1 plus deposit. Internet £2.50 per 30min. Reception open 7:30-10am and 3-11pm. Book at least 2 weeks ahead in summer. Dorms £16.40, under 18 £12.30. MC/V. ❷

The Pilgrims Hotel, 18 The Friars (☎464 531). Spacious rooms and soft beds for weary pilgrims, plus a well-appointed restaurant and bar. The city-center location is a veritable Canterbury miracle. Singles £49; doubles £69-75; family room £89. AmEx/MC/V. ❹

Camping: Camping & Caravaning Club Site, Bekesbourne Ln. (☎463 216), off the A257, 1½ mi. east of the city center. Showers, laundry, and facilities for the disabled. £5.80; non-member charge £4.75. MC/V. ❶

🍴 FOOD

The Safeway **supermarket,** St. George's Center, St. George's Pl., is four minutes from the town center. (☎769 335. Open M-F 8am-9pm, Sa 8am-8pm, Su 11am-5pm)

🦁 **Marlowe's,** 55 St. Peter's St. (☎462 194). English food with Mexican flair, where colorful menus offset black-and white photos of old Broadway. Choose from 8 toppings for 8 oz. burgers (£6.60) or a veggie dish (£6-9). Open M-Sa 9am-10:30pm, Su 10am-10:30pm. Cash only. ❷

Jacques, 71 Castle St. (☎781 000). "Fresh ingredients cooked with imagination," live music, and candlelit tables. Owner Peter is on hand to attend to every need. Entrees £11-16. Open M-F 11am-2:30pm and 6-9:30pm, Sa 10am-10pm. MC/V. ❸

Cafe des Amis du Mexique, St. Dunstan's St. (☎464 390), just outside the West Gate. Why so much Mexican flavor in Canterbury restaurants? It's a student town, and Mexican goes well with beer. Try the crispy duck confit with *mole* sauce (£10). Cash only. ❷

C'est la Vie, 17b Burgate (☎457 525). Fresh, inventive takeaway sandwiches (£2.40-3.10). 10% student discount before noon and after 2pm. Open M-F 9am-6pm, Sa 9:30am-6pm. Cash only. ❶

👁 SIGHTS

🏛 CANTERBURY CATHEDRAL

Central and conspicuous. ☎ *762 862; www.canterbury-cathedral.org. Cathedral open Easter-Oct. M-Sa 9am-6:30pm, Oct.-Easter M-Sa 9am-5pm; also Su 12:30-2:30pm and 4:30-5:30pm year-round. 3 1¼hr. tours per day; check nave or welcome center for times. Evensong M-F 5:30pm, Sa-Su 3:15pm. £4.50, concessions £3.50. Tours £3.50, concessions £2.50. 40min. audio tour £3, concessions £2.*

Pilgrim contributions funded most of Canterbury Cathedral's wonders, including the early Gothic **nave,** constructed mostly between the 13th and 15th centuries on a site allegedly consecrated by St. Augustine 700 years earlier. The site of **Thomas Becket's shrine,** destroyed by Henry VIII in 1538, is marked by a candle and protected by an impenetrable velvet rope. The **Altar of the Sword's Point** stands where Becket fell—the final murderer broke off the tip of his sword in

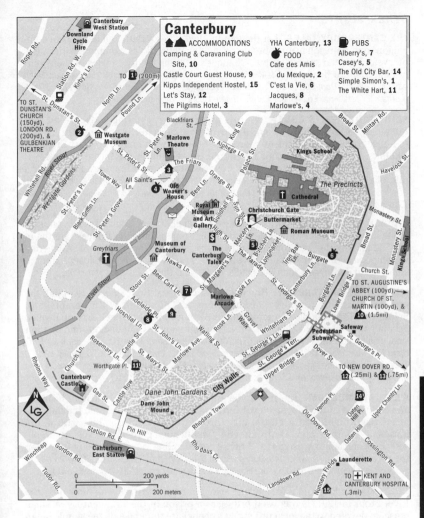

Canterbury

ACCOMMODATIONS
Camping & Caravaning Club Site, 10
Castle Court Guest House, 9
Kipps Independent Hostel, 15
Let's Stay, 12
The Pilgrims Hotel, 3
YHA Canterbury, 13

FOOD
Cafe des Amis du Mexique, 2
C'est la Vie, 6
Jacques, 8
Marlowe's, 4

PUBS
Alberry's, 7
Casey's, 5
The Old City Bar, 14
Simple Simon's, 1
The White Hart, 11

SOUTH ENGLAND

the archbishop's skull—and a 14min. re-creation of the homicide plays just off the cloisters (shown 10am-4pm; 50p). Henry IV, possibly uneasy after having usurped the throne, chose to have his body entombed near Becket's sacred shrine, instead of the usual Westminster Abbey burial. Across from Henry lies Edward, the Black Prince, and the decorative armor he wore at his funeral adorns a nearby wall. The eerily silent **crypt,** billed as a site for quiet reflection, hosts both tourists and funerals.

In a structure plagued by fire and rebuilt time and again, the **Norman crypt,** a huge 12th-century chapel, remains intact. The **Corona Tower** rises above the eastern apse but is not open to visitors. Under the **Bell Harry Tower,** at the crossing of the nave and transepts, perpendicular arches support intricate 15th-century fan vaulting.

OTHER SIGHTS

THE CANTERBURY TALES. Let the gap-toothed Wife of Bath and her waxen companions entertain you in an abbreviated version of the *Tales*, complete with smells of sweat, hay, and general grime. Chaucer's pilgrims tell the stories of their journey into visitors' headsets. *(St. Margaret's St. ☎ 479 227; www.canterburytales.org.uk. Open daily Mar.-June 10am-5pm, July-Aug. 9:30am-5pm, Sept.-Oct. 10am-5pm, Nov.-Feb. 10am-4:30pm. £7, students £6, seniors £5.75, children £5.25, families £22.50.)*

SAINT AUGUSTINE'S ABBEY. Soaring arches and crumbling walls are all that remain of what was once one of the greatest abbeys in Europe, built in AD 598 to house Augustine and the 40 monks he brought with him to convert England. Exhibits and a free audio tour reveal the abbey's history as burial place, royal palace, and pleasure garden. Don't miss St. Augustine's humble tomb under a pile of rocks. *(Outside the city wall near the cathedral. ☎ 767 345. Open daily Apr.-Sept. 10am-6pm; Oct.-Mar. Su and W-Sa 10am-4pm; Nov.-Mar. 10am-4pm. £3.50, concessions £2.60, children £1.80.)*

CHURCH OF SAINT MARTIN. The oldest parish church in England still in use saw the marriage of pagan King Æthelbert to the French Christian Princess Bertha in AD 562, paving the way for England's conversion to Christianity. St. Augustine worshipped here before establishing his own monastery. Here, too, Joseph Conrad slumbers in darkness. *(North Holmes St. ☎ 459 482. Open daily 9am-5pm. Free.)*

MUSEUM OF CANTERBURY. Housed in the medieval Poor Priests' Hospital, the museum spans Canterbury's history from St. Thomas to WWII bombings to beloved children's-book character Rupert Bear. A tongue-in-cheek animated video account of Becket and Henry II's relationship supplies the background to their final grisly encounter. *(Stour St. ☎ 475 200. Open June-Sept. M-Sa 10:30am-5pm, Su 1:30-5pm; Nov.-May M-Sa 10:30am-5pm; last entry 5pm. £3.10, concessions £2.10, family £8.20.) The Museum Passport gives admission to the Museum of Canterbury, the Westgate Museum, and the nearby **Roman Museum**. £5.70, concessions £3.40, families £13.75.)*

WESTGATE MUSEUM. The remainder of medieval Canterbury clusters near the Westgate, one of the few medieval fortifications to survive wartime blitzing. Pilgrims traditionally entered the city through this structure. Just within, the museum—a former prison surrounded by well-tended gardens—keeps armor, old weapons, and a faux prisoner, and offers commanding views of the city from atop the gate. *(☎ 789 576; www.canterbury-museum.co.uk. Open M-Sa 11am-12:30pm and 1:30-3:30pm; last admission 15min. before closing. £1.10, concessions 70p, families £2.60.)*

GREYFRIARS. England's first Franciscan friary, Greyfriars was built over the River Stour in 1267. It was used briefly as a prison in the 19th century. A small museum devoted to the local order and a chapel are found inside the simple building. For a quiet break, walk through Greyfriars's **riverside gardens.** *(6a Stour St.; follow signs from the Westgate gardens. ☎ 462 395. Open Easter-Sept. M-Sa 2-4pm. Free.)*

BEST OF THE REST. A 15th-century Huguenot home on the river, the **Old Weaver's House,** 1 St. Peter's St., features an authentic witch-dunking stool. **Weaver's River Tours** runs 30min. cruises leaving several times a day. *(☎ 07790 534 744; www.canterburyrivertours.co.uk. £5, concessions £4.50, children £4, family £16.)* In the library, the **Royal Museum and Art Gallery,** 18 High St., showcases paintings by locally-born artists of earlier centuries and recounts the history of the "Buffs," one of the oldest regiments of the British Army. *(☎ 452 747. Open M-Sa 10am-6pm. Free.)* Near the city walls to the southwest lie the massive, solemn remnants of the Conqueror's **Canter-**

bury Castle. Outside the walls to the northwest, the vaults of **Saint Dunstan's Church** contain a buried relic said to be the head of Thomas More; legend has it that his daughter bribed the executioner at the Tower of London for it.

🗹 🌊 PUBS AND CLUBS

Simple Simon's, St. Radigunds St. (☎ 762 355). This ale house seems to be the local for half the town. Tu folk, W jazz, Th blues and local bands on F. Open M-Sa 11am-11pm, Su noon-10:30pm. Food served M-Sa 11am-4pm and Su noon-4pm.

The Old City Bar, Oaten Hill Pl. (☎ 766 882). Students and 20-somethings pack into the refurbished pub and beer garden. BBQ (burgers with jacket potato £4.60-5.25) and live music on weekends. Open daily noon-11pm; food served noon-2:30pm.

Casey's, Butchery Ln. (☎ 463 252). A youthful pub lying in a side street near the cathedral, Casey's offers quasi-Irish ambience and traditional food (£6). Open M-Th noon-11pm, F-Sa 11am-11pm, Su noon-10:30pm.

The White Hart, Worthgate Pl. (☎ 765 091), near East Station. Congenial pub with homemade lunch specials and sweets (£4.50-6), plus some of Canterbury's best bitters (£2.30). Enjoy both in the city's largest beer garden. Open daily 10am-11pm.

Alberry's, 38 St. Margaret's St. (☎ 452 378). A stylish wine bar that pours late into the evening. Live music M-Th and Su. Happy hour 5:30-7pm. Open M-W noon-11pm, Th noon-1am, F-Sa noon-2am.

🎵 🌿 ENTERTAINMENT AND FESTIVALS

For up-to-date entertainment listings, pick up *What, Where, When,* free at many pubs. **Buskers,** especially along St. Peter's St. and High St., play streetside Vivaldi while bands of impromptu players ramble from corner to corner, acting out the more absurd of Chaucer's scenes. **Marlowe Theatre,** The Friars, regales contemporary pilgrims with touring London productions. (☎ 787 787. Box office open M-Sa 10am-9pm. Tickets £6.50-22, concessions available.) The **Gulbenkian Theatre,** at the University of Kent, University Rd., west of town on St. Dunstan's St., stages a range of dance, drama, music, and comedy performances, and shows films. (☎ 769 075; www.ken.ac.uk/gulbenkian. Box office open M-F 11am-5pm, Sa-Su 5:30-9pm during term time. Tickets £5-21, £5 rush available from 7pm performance nights.)

In the fall, the **Canterbury Festival** fills two weeks in mid-October with drama, opera, cabaret, chamber music, dance, talks, walks, and exhibitions. (☎ 452 853; box office ☎ 378 188; www.canterburyfestival.co.uk.) In Ashford, five miles southwest of Canterbury, the popular **Stour Music Festival** celebrates Renaissance and baroque music for 10 days at the end of June. The festival takes place at All Saint's Boughton Aluph Church, on the A28 and accessible by rail from West Station. Call the bookings office a month in advance. (☎ 812 740. Tickets £5-14.)

🡢 DAYTRIPS FROM CANTERBURY

▦ SISSINGHURST CASTLE GARDEN

Trains run from Canterbury West to Staplehurst, where buses #4 and 5 run to Sissinghurst. ☎ 01580 710 700; www.nationaltrust.org.uk/sissinghurst. Ticket is occasionally timed. Open mid-Mar. to Oct. M-Tu and F 11am-6:30pm, Sa-Su 10am-6:30pm; last admission 1hr. before close. £6.50, children £3.

A masterpiece of floral design and execution by Vita Sackville-West and her husband, Harold Nicolson—both of Bloomsbury Group fame—Sissinghurst is the most popular garden in a garden-obsessed nation. The eight gardeners maintain the place as close as they can to the original design, a varied array of carved hedges, flower beds and stretches of foliage. After savoring the serenity of the White Garden or the Cottage Garden, visitors may stroll along the moat to forested lakes and lose their way along one of many woodland walks. The staff encourages visitors to come after 4pm, when the sun's light reveals the garden's true beauty.

LEEDS CASTLE

Near Maidstone, 23 mi. west of Canterbury on the A20. Trains run from Canterbury West to Bearsted (1 per hr., £9.70); a shuttle goes from station to castle (£4). Shuttles leave the train station M-Sa 10:35am-2:35pm on the :35's, Su 10:55am-2:55pm on the :55's; and return shuttles leave the castle M-Sa 2-6pm on the hour, Su 2:15-6:15pm on the quarter hour. ☎01622 765 400 or 0870 600 8880. Castle open daily Mar.-Oct. 11am-7:30pm; Nov.-Feb. 10:15am-5:30pm. Grounds open daily Mar.-Oct. 10am-7pm; Nov.-Feb. 10am-5pm; last admission 2hr. before close. Castle and grounds £12.50, concessions £11, children £9, families £39. Call for combined transportation and admission tickets.

Billed as the "Loveliest Castle in the World," Leeds was built immediately after the Norman Conquest and remained a favorite royal playground until Edward VI, Henry VIII's long-sought son, sold it for a song. The ground floor is a quintessential royal Tudor residence. It sharply contrasts with the modern second floor, which was impeccably outfitted according to the tastes of 20th-century owner Olive, Lady Baillie, by the same interior decorator responsible for Jackie Kennedy's White House overhaul. One wing displays an alarming collection of **medieval dog collars.** Outdoors, lose yourself in a **maze** of 2400 yew trees, or the 500 acres of woodlands and gardens hosting black swans and other unusual waterfowl.

DOVER ☎01304

From the days of Celtic invaders to the age of the Chunnel, the white chalk cliffs of Dover have been many a traveler's first glimpse of England. Seen through a telescope, they were the defiant face England presented to would-be invaders from Napoleon to Hitler. Today, the seeming tranquility of the cliffs is belied by the puttering of ferries and the hum of hovercraft, the ambience of a cosmopolitan town dedicated to the business of getting travelers in and out fast. But a walk along the cliffs or an exploration of the magnificent castle will restore any visitor's childhood imaginings of crashing waves and lordly Normans.

◧ TRANSPORTATION

Trains: Priory Station, Station Approach Rd. Ticket office open M-Sa 4:15am-11:20pm, Su 6:15am-11:20pm. Trains (☎08457 484 950) from **Canterbury** (20min., 2 per hr., £4.80) and several **London** stations (2hr., 4 per hr., £20).

Buses: Pencester Road, between York St. and Maison Dieu Rd. (☎01304 240 024). Office open M-Tu and Th-F 8:45am-5:15pm, W 8:45am-4pm, Sa 8:30am-noon. The TIC also sells tickets. **National Express** (☎08705 808 080) from **London,** continuing to the **Eastern Docks** (2¾hr., 23 per day, £10.50). **Stagecoach** (☎08702 433 711) from **Canterbury** (40min., 1 per hr., £2.90) and **Deal** (40min., 1 per hr., £2.40). A bus runs from **Folkestone,** the terminus for Chunnel trains (30min., 2 per hr., £2.20).

Ferries: Eastern Docks sails to **Calais, France** and **Oostend, Belgium;** the TIC offers a booking service. **P&O Stena** (☎08706 000 600; www.posl.com) sail to **Calais** (35 per day, £28); as does **SeaFrance** (☎08705 711 711; www.seafrance.com), 17 per day, £21. The **Seacat** leaves the Hoverport at **Prince of Wales Pier** for Calais (£27). Free bus service leaves Priory Station for the docks 45-60min. before sailing. (See **By Ferry,** p. 29.) The **Channel Tunnel** offers passenger service on **Eurostar** and car transport on **Le Shuttle** to and from the continent. (See **By Chunnel,** p. 29.)

Taxis: Central Taxi Service (☎240 0441). 24hr.

▐ PRACTICAL INFORMATION

Tourist Information Centre: off High St. (☎205 108; www.whitecliffscountry.org.uk), where it divides into Priory Rd. and Biggin St. Multilingual staff sells ferry, bus, and hovercraft tickets and books accommodations for free; after hours call for accommodations list. Open Apr.-May M-F 9am-5:30pm, Sa-Su 10am-4pm; daily June-Aug. 9am-5:30pm; Oct.-Mar. M-F 9am-5:30pm, Sa 10am-4pm.

Tours: White Cliffs Boat Tour (☎271 388; www.whitecliffsboattours.co.uk) sails every hr. from the Marina. £5, children £3, families £14.

Financial Services: Several **banks** are in Market Sq. including **Barclays** in the northwest corner. Open M-Tu 9:30am-4:30pm, W 10am-4:30pm, Th-F 9:30am-5:30pm.

Launderette: Cherry Tree Launderette, 2 Cherry Tree Ave. (☎242 822), off London Rd., past the hostel. Full service available. Open daily 8am-8pm; last wash 7:15pm.

Police: Ladywell St. (☎218 183), off High St.

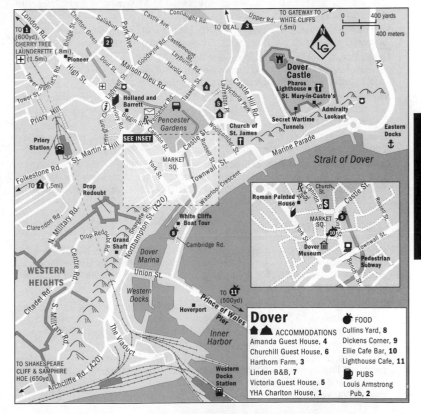

Dover

▲▲ ACCOMMODATIONS
Amanda Guest House, **4**
Churchill Guest House, **6**
Harthorn Farm, **3**
Linden B&B, **7**
Victoria Guest House, **5**
YHA Charlton House, **1**

🍎 FOOD
Cullins Yard, **8**
Dickens Corner, **9**
Ellie Cafe Bar, **10**
Lighthouse Cafe, **11**

🍺 PUBS
Louis Armstrong Pub, **2**

Pharmacy: Superdrug, 33-34 Biggin St. (☎211 477). Open M-Sa 8:30am-5:30pm, Su 10am-4pm.

Hospital: Buckland Hospital, Coomb Valley Rd. (☎201 624), northwest of town. Take bus D9 or D5 from the post office.

Internet Access: En-Route 66 CyberCafe, 8 Bench St. (☎206 633). £2 per 30min. Open daily 9am-7pm.

Post Office: 68 Pencester Rd. (☎241 747), inside Alldays. Open M-F 8:30am-5:30pm, Sa 8:30am-noon. **Post Code:** CT16 1PW.

ACCOMMODATIONS

Rooms are scarce in high season and the ferry terminal makes an unsafe campground. August is especially busy due to the influx of distance swimmers eager to have a crack at the Channel. Cheaper **B&Bs** congregate on **Folkestone Road,** a hike past the train station, and some stay open all night. Pricier B&Bs lie near the city center on **Castle Street,** and more on **Maison Dieu Road.** Most ask for a deposit.

YHA Charlton House, 306 London Rd. (☎201 314). ½ mi. from Priory station; turn left on Folkestone Rd., then left at the roundabout on High St. Lounge, pool table, kitchen, and lockers. Offers discounts on sights. Overflow at **14 Goodwyne Road** (closer to town). Lockout 10am-1pm. Curfew 11pm. Dorms £14.90, under 18 £11.50. MC/V. ❷

Victoria Guest House, 1 Laureston Pl. (☎205 140). Well-traveled hosts extend a friendly welcome. Singles £15-20; doubles £32-54. AmEx (with a 5% surcharge)/MC/V. ❷

Linden Bed & Breakfast, 231 Folkestone Rd. (☎205 449). A ways off, but this plush B&B makes every effort to accommodate—ask about pickup from the train station or docks. Discount vouchers for local sights. Doubles £50. MC/V. ❸

Amanda Guest House, 4 Harold St. (☎201 711). Hall bathrooms are a small price to pay for elegant Victorian light fixtures and marble fireplaces in a house built by the former mayor. July-Aug. doubles £44; Sept.-June £42. Cash only. ❹

Churchill Guest House, 6 Castle Hill Rd. (☎208 365) Large rooms, great views, big beds, and generous amenities. £25-35 per person. MC/V. ❹

Camping: Harthorn Farm (☎852 658), at Martin Mill Station off the A258 between Dover and Deal. 2min. walk from railway station; follow the signs. Open Mar.-Oct. June-Aug. 2-person tent and car £12.50, £15 with electricity; Mar.-May and Sept.-Oct. £10/ £12.50. Hikers and bikers £3; Mar.-May and Sept.-Oct. £2.50. Cash only. ❶

FOOD AND PUBS

Despite (or perhaps because of) the proximity of the Continent, Dover's cuisine remains staunchly English—grease fires rage in the chip shops on **London Road** and **Biggin Street.** Those looking for something healthier should visit **Holland & Barrett,** 35 Biggin St., for **groceries.** (☎241 426. Open M-Sa 9am-5:30pm.)

Ellie Cafe Bar, Market Sq. (☎215 685). Mingle with Dover's cosmopolitan crowd, have a meal (entrees 4.75-5.50) while watching the flat-screen TV, or sip a martini (£3.50) in one of the lounge chairs looking onto Market Sq. Open M-Th 11am-11:30pm, F-Sa noon-midnight, Su noon-10:30pm. Cash only. ❷

Cullins Yard, 11 Cambridge Rd. (☎211 666). This waterside seafood restaurant offers traditional English food. Don't mistake it for a pub, however—everything is exquisitely prepared and priced to match (entrees £6.50-16.80). Open daily from noon, last orders 9pm. MC/V. ❹

Dickens Corner, 7 Market Sq. (☎206 692). The ground floor bustles with channelers wolfing baguettes and sandwiches (£1.50-2.80) or hot lunches (£3-5), while the upstairs tearoom moves at a more refined pace. Open M-Sa 9am-5:30pm. MC/V. ❶

Louis Armstrong Pub, 58 Maison Dieu Rd. (☎204 759). Its presence is indicated only by a weather-beaten picture of Satchmo himself. Live music makes it worth the search. No cover. Open M-Sa 11am-11pm, Su noon-2pm and 7-11pm. Cash only. ❶

The Lighthouse Cafe and Tea Room, the end of Prince of Wales Pier. Gaze at the castle, beaches, and white cliffs as you sip tea ½ mi. offshore, in the closest cafe to France. Worth the visit for the view alone. Open summer daily 10am-5:30pm (check the sign at the start of the pier). Cash only. ❶

🔵 SIGHTS

🔳 **DOVER CASTLE.** The view from Castle Hill Rd., on the east side of town, reveals why sprawling Dover Castle is famed for both its magnificent setting and its impregnability. Overlooking the Pas de Calais, the castle was a natural focal point of Anglo-French conflict, from the Hundred Years' War to WWII, in which the castle trained its guns on German-occupied France. Hitler's missiles destroyed the **Church of St. James,** leaving the ruins crumbling at the base of the hill. Beside **St. Mary-in-Castro's,** a tiled Saxon church, towers the **Pharos lighthouse**—the only extant Roman lighthouse and the tallest remaining Roman edifice in Britain. Climb to the platform of the **Admiralty Lookout** for unsurpassed views of the cliffs and harbor; 20p gets you a binocular look at France. A stroll along the battlements passes by big guns from the various historical periods in which the castle was used—from WWII antiaircraft guns and coastal batteries to a replica trebuchet in the keep yard. The (no longer) 🔳 **Secret Wartime Tunnels** constitute a 3½ mi. labyrinth only recently declassified. Begun in 1803 under the threat of attack by Napoleon, the vast underground burrows descend five stories and served as the base for the WWII evacuation of Allied troops from Dunkirk. The lowest level, not yet open to the public, was intended to house the government should the Cuban Missile Crisis have gone sour. Tours fill quickly and there is usually a long wait; check in at the tunnels first. *(Buses from the town center run daily Apr.-Sept. 1 per hr. (55p); otherwise, scale Castle Hill using the pedestrian ramp and stairs by the first castle sign. Open daily Apr.-June 10am-6pm; daily July-Aug. 9:30am-6:30pm, daily Oct. 10am-5pm; Nov.-Jan. Th-M 10am-4pm, Feb.-Mar. 10am-4pm. £8.50, concessions £6.40, children £4.30, families £21.30.)*

DOVER MUSEUM. This museum depicts Dover's Roman days as the colonial outpost Dubras, and houses a high-tech gallery with the remnants of the oldest ship yet discovered—at 3600 years, it's older than Moses. *(Market Sq. ☎201 066. Open M-Sa 10am-5:30pm; Apr.-Sept. also Su 1pm-5:30pm. £2, concessions 95p, families £5.50.)*

THE WHITE CLIFFS. Covering the surrounding coastline, the white cliffs make a beautiful backdrop for a stroll along the pebbly beach. A few miles west of Dover, the whitest, steepest, and most famous of them all is **Shakespeare Cliff,** traditionally identified as the site of blind Gloucester's battle with the brink in *King Lear.* *(25min. by foot along Snargate St.)* To the east of Dover, past Dover Castle, the **Gateway to the White Cliffs** overlooks the Strait of Dover and serves as an informative starting point for exploration. *(Buses and Guide Friday go to Langdon Cliff at least once per hr. ☎202 756. Open daily Mar.-Oct. 10am-5pm; Nov.-Feb. 11am-4pm.)* Dozens of **cliff walks** lie a short distance from Dover; consult the TIC for trail information. **The Grand Shaft,** a 140 ft. triple spiral staircase, was shot through the rock in Napoleonic times to link the army on the Western Heights with the city center. *(Snargate St. ☎201 066. Open select days throughout year; call for dates.)*

OTHER SIGHTS. Recent excavations have unearthed a remarkably well-preserved **Roman painted house,** New St., off Cannon St. near Market Sq. It's the oldest Roman house in Britain, complete with underground central heating and indoor plumbing. *(☎ 203 279. Open Apr.-Sept. Tu-Su 10am-5pm, last admission 4:30pm. £2, concessions 80p.)* For striking views, take the A20 toward Folkestone to **Samphire Hoe,** a well-groomed park planted in the summer of 1997 with material dug from the Channel Tunnel. The D2 bus to Aycliffe (£1) stops about a 10min. walk from the park, or walk the North Downs Way along the clifftop. (Open daily 7am-dusk.)

▌ DAYTRIP FROM DOVER

DEAL

Trains from Dover Priory arrive in Deal Station (15min., at least 1 per hr., £3.10). The TIC, Deal Library, Broad St., books beds for a 10% deposit and provides the free Deal Historic Town Trails, which details 10 walks in the area. ☎ 01304 369 576. Open M-Tu and Th-Su 9:30am-5pm, W 9:30am-1pm.

Julius Caesar landed here with an invasion force in 55 BC, and Deal's castles represent Henry VIII's 16th-century attempt to prevent similar occurrences. **Deal Castle,** south of town at the corner of Victoria Rd. and Deal Castle Rd., is one of Henry's largest Cinque Ports (anti-pirate establishments that received special privileges from the king in exchange for protecting the shore). A symmetrical maze of corridors and cells is guaranteed to entangle visitors. (☎ 01304 372 762. Open daily Apr.-Sept. 10am-6pm; £3.50, concessions £2.60, children £1.80.)

Walmer Castle, ½ mi. south of Deal via the beachfront pedestrian path or the A258 (and 1 mi. from the Walmer train station), is the best-preserved and most elegant of Henry VIII's citadels. Walmer has been transformed into a country estate which, since the 1700s, has been the official residence of the Lords Warden of the Cinque Ports. Notable Wardens past include the Duke of Wellington (whose famed boots are on display), William Pitt, and Winston Churchill. The most recent warden was the Queen Mother; the beautiful gardens are planted with her favorite flowers. (☎ 01304 364 288. Open daily Mar. 10am-4pm, Apr.-Sept. 10am-6pm; Oct. W-Su 10am-4pm. Last admission 30min. before closing. Closed when Lord Warden is in residence. £5.80, concessions £4.40, children £2.90, families £14. Free and worthwhile 30min. audio tour.) Perhaps the most famous restaurant in Kent, **Dunkerley's Restaurant Bistro ❹,** 19 Beach St., overlooks the sea in Deal. Residents from all over the region flood in to dine on local fish for around £12. (☎ 375 016. Open M 7pm-9:30pm, Tu-Su noon-2:30pm and 7pm-9:30pm. AmEx/MC/V.)

SUSSEX

RYE ☎ 01797

Settled before the Roman invasion, today its sleepy cobblestone streets and half-timbered houses are exceedingly beautiful to look at, but they don't hold much excitement, and most of the town shuts down on Tuesday afternoons. Henry James, a costume-drama favorite, wrote his later novels while living in **Lamb House,** at the corner of West St. and Mermaid St. (Open Apr.-Oct. W and Sa 2-6pm; last admission 5:30pm. £2.75, children £1.30, families £6.90.) Before descending the hill, check out **St. Mary's Church,** at the top of Lion St., a 12th-century parish church that houses one of Britain's oldest working clocks. (☎ 222

SOUTH ENGLAND

430. Open M-F 9am-6pm, Sa 9am-5:30pm, Su 11:40am-5:30pm. ₤2, concessions ₤1.) Around the corner from the church, **Ypres Tower,** built in 1350, was intended to fortify the town against invaders from the sea. The tower now contains the **Rye Museum,** displaying artifacts from Rye's past. (☎226 728. Open Apr.-Oct. M and Th-F 10am-1pm and 2-5pm, Sa-Su 10:30am-1pm and 2-5pm; Nov.-Mar. tower only Sa-Su 10:30am-3:30pm; last admission 3pm. Tower and museum ₤2.90, concessions ₤2.)

Use Rye as a pleasant base for exploring its historical neighbors. **Trains** (☎08457 484 950) arrive at the station off Cinque Port St. from: **Brighton** (2hr., 1 per hr., ₤12.40); **Dover** (1½ hr., 1 per hr., ₤10.40); **Eastbourne** (1hr., 1 per hr., ₤7.10); **London** (1¾hr., 1 per hr., ₤19.20). Local **buses** (☎223 343) stop in the station's carpark. To get to the **Tourist Information Centre** from the station, steer yourself to Cinque Port St. and turn right onto Wish St.; turn left onto the Strand Quay. The oldest part of town is a 5min. hike up **Mermaid Street.** The TIC, in the Heritage Centre, hands out self-guided audio tours, and books rooms for free in person and for a ₤2 charge over the phone. (☎226 696; www.visitrye.co.uk. Open mid-Mar. to Oct. M-Sa 9:30am-5pm, Su 10am-5pm; daily Nov.-Feb. 10am-4pm. Tours ₤2.50, concessions ₤1.50.) Get free **Internet access** at the **library** (☎223 355; 1hr. max.; open M 9:30am-5:30pm, W 10am-5:30pm, Th 9:30am-12:30pm, F 9:30am-6pm, Sa 9:30am-5pm); and the **post office,** 22-24 Cinque Port St. (☎222 163; open M-Tu and Th-F 8:30am-5:30pm, Sa 9am-5:30pm). **Post Code:** TN31 7AA.

The area's only **YHA hostel ❶,** Rye Rd., is in Guestling, 7 mi. south of Rye and 4 mi. north of Hastings. From Rye, head down the A259 past Winchelsea and Icklesham (look for the sign on the right). Alternatively, take bus #711 from Rye to the White Hart in Guestling (M-Sa roughly 2 per hr. until 7:45pm; ₤1.85); from there, the hostel is downhill to the left. You can also take the train to Three Oaks (₤2.90) and follow the signs 1½ mi. (☎1424 812 373. Open daily July-Aug.; May-June and Sept.-Oct. Tu-Sa. Dorms ₤11.80, under 18 ₤8.50. **Camping** by booking only, ₤5.15. MC/V.) For **groceries,** visit **Budgens,** across from the train station. (☎226 044. Open M-Sa 8am-10pm, Su 10am-4pm.) At the bend of one of Rye's most antique streets, **Ye Olde Bell Inn ❶,** 33 The Mint, serves toasted sandwiches (₤2.50-3.25) and other dainties in a cottage garden. (☎223 323. Open M-Sa 11am-11pm, Su 11am-10:30pm.) If you get a sudden craving for sweets, pay a visit to **The Rye Chocolate Shop ❶,** 5a Market Rd., for some real old-fashioned, not-for-lightweights candy. (☎222 522. Open daily 9:30am-5:30pm.)

▣ DAYTRIPS FROM RYE

PEVENSEY

Trains run every hour from Rye and Hastings to Pevensey (£7.10).

William I's march to Battle began from **Pevensey Castle,** a Roman fortress that was already 800 years old when the Norman forces landed. Considered one of the best examples of Roman building in England, the castle has since been reduced to only its original walls, 12 ft. thick and 30 ft. high. (☎01323 762 604. Open daily Apr.-Sept. 10am-6pm; Oct.-Mar. Sa-Su 10am-4pm. ₤3.50, concessions ₤2.80, children ₤1.80.) The best part of Pevensey, however, owes its origins to commerce rather than conquest. The Mint House, on High St. just beyond the castle, was originally a Norman mint, connected to the castle by subterranean tunnels. Henry VIII's physician transformed it into a country retreat. Saleable antiques now fill the old oak-panelled rooms, and the ghost of one denizen's brutally-murdered mistress has been seen in the smallest room of the house. (☎01323 762 337. Open M-F 9am-5pm, Sa 10:30am-4:30pm. ₤1.50, children 50p.)

HASTINGS

Trains arrive from Rye (20min., 2 per hr., £3.90). The TIC, at Queens Sq. and The Stade, signposted from the station, books accommodations for a £1 fee. ☎01424 78 1066; www.hastings.gov.uk. Open M-F 8:30am-6:15pm, Sa 9am-5pm, Su 10am-4:30pm.

Having surrendered its name and identity to a decisive battle (p. 71), Hastings still revels in its 1000-year-old claim to fame. Looming above town, the fragmentary remains of **Hastings Castle,** built by William the Conqueror, mark the spot where the Norman duke's troops camped before confronting Harold II and the Saxons. The castle met its functional demise in the 13th century, when part of the cliff collapsed and took half the fortifications with it. During WWII, homeward-bound Germans finished the job by dropping excess explosives on Hastings. Catch the **1066 Story,** a 17min. film on the famous spat between William and Harold (and Harald of Norway), and visit the castle's moldy dungeons. (Take the West Hill Railway from George St. to the top of the hill. Round-trip 90p. ☎01424 781 111; www.discoverhastings.co.uk. Open daily July 19-Aug. 29 10am-5:30pm; Aug. 30-Sept. 26 10am-5pm; Sept. 27-Oct. 11am-4pm; Nov.-Feb. 13 11am-3:30pm; Feb. 12-Mar. 27 11am-4pm; Mar. 28-July 18 10am-5pm. £3.40, concessions £2.75, children £2.25, families £10.) Before heading back to sea level, duck into St. Clements Caves for the **Smugglers Adventure.** Now more like a theme park, these miles of caves and tunnels were once the nerve center of the Sussex smuggling ring. A ghostly apparition of Hairy Jack is your guide through this spooky lair, full of life-size figures that talk to you if you press their buttons. (☎01424 422 964; www.discoverhastings.co.uk. Open daily Apr.-Sept. 10am-5:30pm; Oct.-Mar. 11am-4:30pm. Last admission 4pm. £5.95, concessions £4.95, children £3.95, families £16.50.) Exhibits on the area's nautical past reside in several charity-run museums among the chippies on the seafront. The **Shipwreck Heritage Centre** is the largest and most notable (☎01424 437 452. Open daily Mar.-Sept. 10am-5pm, Nov.-Feb. 11am-4pm. Suggested donation £1.) Present-day Hastings is packed with tourists and all the amenities that come with them—the town center boasts mainstream shops, and side streets are dotted with traditional pubs and cafes.

BATTLE

Trains run from Hastings (15min., 2 per hr., round-trip £2.60); Battle Abbey is in the center of town, signposted from the train station. The TIC, Battle Abbey, books accommodations. ☎01424 773 721; www.battletown.co.uk. Open daily Apr.-Sept. 9:30am-5:30pm; Oct.-Mar. M-Sa 10am-4pm.

Named after the 1066 action between the Normans and Anglo-Saxons that took place here, the town of Battle makes a fine expedition from Rye. To commemorate his victory in the Battle of Hastings, William built **Battle Abbey** in 1094, spitefully positioning its high altar upon the very spot where Harold fell (p. 71). Little remains apart from the gate and a handsome series of 13th-century common quarters. (☎01424 773 792. Open daily Apr.-Sept. 10am-6pm; Oct.-Mar. 10am-4pm. £5, concessions £3.80, children £2.50, families £12.50.) The battlefield across which duke William's cavalry charged repeatedly is now a pasture marched across by sheep. In summer, you can take a free audio tour of the abbey and walk the **battlefield trail,** a 1 mi. walk through the green hillside.

SOUTH DOWNS WAY

The South Downs Way, perhaps Britain's most famous trail, stretches 99 mi. from Eastbourne west toward Portsmouth and Winchester. It meanders through the rolling hills and livestock-laden greens that typify pastoral England, never far from coastal towns, yet rarely crossing into civilization's domain. The Downs were initially cultivated by prehistoric populations; forts and settlements dot the former paths of Bronze and Iron Age tribes, who were followed by Romans, Saxons, and Normans. Still fertile ground for legend, the windswept slopes and salt-sprayed cliffs of the Downs have borne words as prodigiously as flowers, from William I's *Domesday Book* to A.A. Milne's Pooh Bear stories. The Way is well marked from start to finish, and the walking is moderate enough even for novice hikers, making the South Downs—only recently designated a national park—one of the most accessible and rewarding outdoors experiences England has to offer.

TRANSPORTATION

Trains (☎ 08457 484 950) run to **Eastbourne** from **London Victoria** (1½hr., 2 per hr., £18.50) and **Petersfield** from **London Waterloo** (1hr., 3 per hr., £15.80). From the west, take a train to **Amberley** (via **Horsham**), where the Way greets the River Arun. Eastbourne's helpful **Bus Stop Shop**, Arndale Centre, dispenses info on local buses. From the train station, turn left onto Terminus Rd.; Arndale Centre is on the left. (☎ 01323 416 416. Open M-Sa 9am-5pm.)

Walking the path takes ten days, but public transportation allows for taking it in segments. **Trains** connect **Lewes** to **Southease** (6min., 2 per hr., £1.80); **County Bus** #143 and #21 connects **Eastbourne** to **Lewes** (20min., 2 per day, £1.70). For details, call **Eastbourne Buses** (☎ 01323 416 416) or **Traveline** (☎ 870 608 2608).

Cycling has long been a popular means of seeing the downlands: D.H. Lawrence cycled the Way in 1909 to visit his friend Rudyard Kipling. Cyclists and **horses** have access to most of the trail, but in a number of places their routes diverge from those of the walkers. The **Harvey** map (£9 at the TIC) shows all of them in detail. If you're starting from Eastbourne, **Les Smith Cycles**, 134 Terminus Rd. (☎ 01323 639 056) and **Nevada Bikes**, 324 Seaside (☎ 01323 411 549) are good options. At the other end of the trail, in Winchester, there is **Halford's**, Moorside Rd. (☎ 01962 853 549). The **Cyclists Touring Club** (☎ 0870 873 0060) answers cycling questions. **Audiburn Riding Stables**, Ashcombe Ln., Kingston, conducts guided 1hr. horseback tours. (☎ 01273 474 398. £18, under 16 £15.)

ORIENTATION

Serious hikers will want to begin their exploration in **Eastbourne,** the official start of the Way. Eastbourne's **Beachy Head** (p. 157) is accessible by bus and well signposted from the train station. From the **Winchester** town center (p. 179), at the far other end of the Way, head east on Bridge St., turn right on Chesil St., then left on East Hill. When East Hill splits, take the right fork onto Petersfield Rd. and head for the carpark—signs broadcasting "South Downs Way" should appear at this point. From the midpoint village of **Amberley**, just north of Arundel (p. 166), the Way runs north, parallel to the main road (B2139).

PRACTICAL INFORMATION

Eastbourne is the best place to arrange accommodations and find local services.

Tourist Information Centres:

Brighton: Bartholomew Sq., see p. 159.

Eastbourne: Cornfield Rd. (☎ 01323 411 400). Provides vague but free maps and detailed 1:50,000 Ordnance Survey Landranger maps. Maps #185 and 197-99 are most useful (£5-7). Also sells a number of guides. Open M-F 9am-5:30pm, Sa 9:30am-5pm.

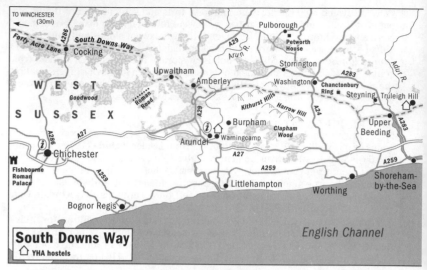

South Downs Way
⌂ YHA hostels

English Channel

Lewes: 187 High St. (☎01273 483 448). Books rooms and sells Ordnance Survey maps and guides. Open M-F 9am-5pm, Sa 10am-5pm; May-Sept. also Su 10am-2pm.

Winchester: The Guildhall, see p. 179.

Guidebooks:

In Print: Paul Millmore's ▓ *South Downs Way (£13)* is the Bible of the Downs. The Eastbourne and Lewes TICs sell *On Foot in East Sussex* (£3.20) and *Along the South Downs Way* (£6), useful for trekkers. *Exploring East Sussex* (£2) lists various guided walks and cycle rides; *The South Downs Way* photocopied edition (£2) has info on accommodations.

Online: The Way also crops up on the Internet. Two websites to try are the South Downs Way Virtual Information Centre (www.vic.org.uk) and the Southeast Walks site (www.southeastwalks.com).

Camping Supplies: Millets: the Outdoors Store, 146-148 Terminus Rd., Eastbourne (☎01323 728 340), stocks camping supplies and Ordnance Survey maps. Open M-Sa 9am-5:30pm, Su 10:30am-4pm. Also many outdoor shops in hiker-friendly Brighton.

Financial Services: All major **banks** are located in the **Eastbourne** town center. Be sure to pick up cash before hitting the trail. **Lloyd's TSB,** 104 Terminus Rd. (☎0845 0723 333). Open M-Tu 9am-5pm, W 10am-5pm, Th-F 9am-5pm, Sa 9am-2pm.

ACCOMMODATIONS

There are few towns along the Way, and **B&Bs** fill quickly. Consider making day-trips; **Brighton** (p. 159) makes a good base, as do **Lewes** (p. 165), **Arundel** (p. 166), and Southcliff Ave. in **Eastbourne.** For a night of comfort before hitting the trail, take a seafront room at **Alexandra Hotel ❸,** King Edward's Parade, in Eastbourne. (☎01323 720 131. Breakfast included. Open Mar.-Dec. June-Sept. £28 per person; Oct.-Dec. and Mar.-Apr. £26. MC/V.) **Camping** on the Way is permitted with the landowner's permission. The following three **YHA hostels** lie along or near the Way, each within a day's walk of the next, and each with a 10am-5pm lockout and 11pm curfew. Be sure to call at least 2 weeks ahead. For other hostels, check the **Accommodations** sections in Brighton (p. 160) or Arundel (p. 166).

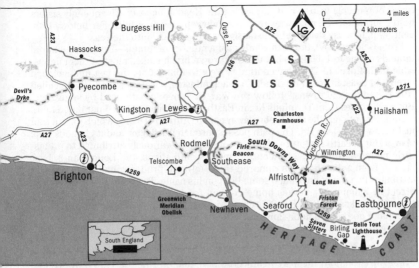

Alfriston: Frog Firle, Alfriston (☎870 423; alfriston@yha.org.uk). 1½ mi. from the Way and from Alfriston, 8 mi. from Eastbourne. Bus #126 passes the front door of the hostel; by foot from Alfriston, turn left from the market cross and pass the village green, then follow the overgrown riverside trail to Lillington footbridge and turn right along the path; the hostel is at the end in a stone house with bovine neighbors. Lockout 11pm-8am. Open daily July-Aug.; Feb.-June and Sept.-Oct. M-Sa; Nov.-Dec. F-Sa. Dorms £10.60, under 18 £7.20. MC/V. ❷

Telscombe: Bank Cottages, Telscombe Village (☎01273 301 357). 2 mi. south of Rodmell, 2 mi. from the Way, 12 mi. west of Alfriston. From Rodmell (p. 158), follow signs directly to hostel. or take bus #123 or 14A and ask to be let off. 18th-century house and cheery staff. Book a week in advance. Lockout 11pm-8am. Open daily Apr.-Sept.; closed Oct.-Mar. Dorms £10.60, under 18 £7.20. MC/V. ❷

Truleigh Hill: Tottington Barn, Truleigh Hill, Shoreham-by-Sea (☎01903 813 419). Halfway along the Way, 10 mi. from Brighton, 4 mi. from Shoreham station. Converted 1930s house with panoramic views and modern facilities. Meals £3.75-5. Open daily July-Aug.; Mar.-June and Sept.-Oct. call 48hr. in advance; closed Nov.-Feb. Dorms £11.80, under 18 £8.50. Lockout 11pm-8am. MC/V. ❷

◪ HIKING THE SOUTH DOWNS WAY

EASTBOURNE TO ALFRISTON

The Victorian seaside city of **Eastbourne,** perched in the shelter of **Beachy Head,** is the path's official starting point. The open-topped bus #3, from Sovereign Harbour and the pier in Eastbourne, brings you to the top of Beachy Head (June-Sept. 1 per hr.; £3, children £1.50), though you can save money and view scenic vistas by asking to be let off at the bottom and climbing it yourself. Make the strenuous ascent and follow the fields upward past wind-bent trees. Mountaineers claim that Beachy Head, 543 ft. above the sea, has the same dizzying effects as alpine ridges. From the top you can view the **Seven Sisters,** a series of chalk ridges carved by centuries of receding waters and surpassing the Head in majesty. The queenly sisters hold court about 4½ mi. away, over a windswept series of hills. Far below, 19th-century lighthouse **Belle Tout** constantly threatens to fall into the sea.

From Beachy Head, the path winds past a number of tumuli—Bronze Age burial mounds dating to 1500 BC—but the overgrown brush makes most of them impossible to distinguish. The Way continues west to **Birling Gap,** the last undeveloped stretch of coast in south England. To reach **Alfriston,** a sleepy 1-road village called "the last of the old towns," follow the Way 4 mi. over a path used by smugglers. Bus #710 comes from Terminus Rd. in Eastbourne (35min., M-Sa 6 per day, £1.60).

Another option is the shorter **bridleway path** to Alfriston (8 mi.) which joins a trail just below East Dean Rd. The path passes through **Wilmington** and its famous **Long Man,** a 260 ft. earth sculpture of mysterious origins. Variously attributed to prehistoric peoples, Romans, 14th-century monks, and aliens, the Long Man is best viewed from a distance. It's rumored that Victorian prudes robbed him of male attributes that might have shed some light on his name. The **Giant's Rest ❷,** on The Street in Wilmington, serves home-cooked food (£5-12) and is a great starting place for walks. (☎01323 870 207. Open M-Sa 11:30am-3pm and 6-11pm, Su noon-10:30pm. Food served noon-2pm and 7-9pm. Cash only.) Going back through Long Man's gate, onto the South Downs Way over Windover Hill, leads to Alfriston.

ALFRISTON TO FORTY ACRE LANE

From Alfriston, join the Way behind the Star Inn, on High St. (the only street), and continue 7 mi. down gentle slopes to Southease. The Way directly crosses Firle Beacon, with a mound at the top said to contain a giant's silver coffin. From Southease, proceed north ¾ mi. to Rodmell. Rodmell's single street contains **Monk's House,** home of Leonard and Virginia Woolf from 1919 until their deaths. The house retains its intimacy and most of the original furnishings. The faithful can retrace the writer's last steps to the River Ouse (1 mi. away), where she committed "the one experience I shall never describe;" her ashes nourish a fig tree in the garden. (☎01372 453 401. Open Apr.-Oct. W and Sa 2-5:30pm. £2.80, children £1.40, families £7.) The **Abergavenny Arms ❷,** Newhaven Rd., (☎01273 472 416) in Rodmell is a good place to fuel up for the 2 mi. hike to the **YHA Telscombe** (p. 157).

The closest that the Way actually comes to **Lewes** (LEW-is) is at the village of **Kingston** to the southwest—where hikers from **Brighton** should pick up the trail. Fortifying pub grub (£7-10) is available at **Juggs Inn ❷** in Lewes (☎01273 472 523. Open M-Sa 11am-11pm, Su noon-10:30pm. Food served noon-2:30pm and 6-9pm). A stone at the parish boundary, called **Nan Kemp's Corner,** feeds one of the more macabre Downs legends: it is said that Nan, jealous of her husband's affection for their newborn, roasted it for him to eat then killed herself here. Continue from Kingston on an 8 mi. stretch to **Pyecombe,** which brings you to **Ditchling Beacon,** the highest point in East Sussex's Downs. The hill was one in a series that relayed the news of the Spanish Armada's defeat to Elizabeth I. If you've come all the way from Telscombe, **YHA Brighton** (p. 161), 2 mi. from Pyecombe, offers a night's rest.

Ambling from Pyecombe to **Upper Beeding** (8 mi.) takes you to **Devil's Dyke,** a dramatic chalk cliff. Local legend says that the Dyke was built by Lucifer himself in a diabolical attempt to let the sea into the Weald and float away all the churches. Climb through fields overrun with crimson poppies to reach the **YHA Truleigh Hill** (p. 157), just 1½ mi. east of Upper Beeding. On the path from Upper Beeding to **Washington** (6¾ mi.) lies the grove of **Chanctonbury Ring**—trees planted in the 18th century around a 3rd-century Roman template, built on a previous Celtic layout.

SOUTH ENGLAND

Completing the 6½ mi. trek from Washington to **Amberley** brings you to a path leading to **Burpham,** from which the **YHA Warningcamp** (p. 166) is 3 mi. away. Full dinner (2 courses £20, 3 courses £30) is served at the **George and Dragon ❺,** in Burpham (☎01903 883 131. Open daily 11am-2:30pm and 6-11pm. Food served noon-2pm and 7-9:30pm. MC/V). The 19 mi. of orchids and spiked rampion fields from Amberley to **Buriton,** passing through **Cocking,** complete the Way to the northwest. Southward, across the River Arun to **Littleton Down,** are views of the Weald and the North Downs. The spire of Chichester Cathedral marks the beginning of **Forty Acre Lane,** the Way's final arm, which touches the West Sussex-Hampshire border.

BRIGHTON ☎01273

The undisputed home of the dirty weekend, Brighton (pop. 180,000) relishes its reputation for the risqué. According to legend, the future King George IV sidled into Brighton around 1784 for some hanky-panky. Having staged a fake wedding with a certain "Mrs. Jones" (Maria Fitzherbert), he headed off to the farmhouse that has since become the Royal Pavilion, and the regal rumpus began. Since then, Brighton has turned a blind eye to some of the more scandalous activities that occur along its shores, as holiday-goers and locals alike peel it off—all off—at England's first bathing beach. Kemp Town (jokingly known as Camp Town), among other areas, has a thriving gay and lesbian population, and the immense student crowd, augmented by flocks of foreign youth purportedly learning English, feeds the notorious clubbing scene of this "London-by-the-Sea."

▄ TRANSPORTATION

Trains: Brighton Station, uphill at the northern end of Queen's Rd. Ticket office open 24hr. Travel center open M-Sa 8:15am-6pm. **Trains** (☎08457 484 950) from: **Arundel** (1¼hr., 1 per hr., £7); **London Victoria** (1hr., 2 per hr., £14.40); **Portsmouth** (1½hr., 2 per hr., £12.80; **Rye** (1¾hr., 1 per hr., £12.40).

Buses: Tickets and info at **One Stop Travel,** 16 Old Steine (☎700 406). Open M-F 8:30am-5:45pm, Sa 9am-5pm; June-Sept. also Su 11am-4:30pm. **National Express** (☎08705 808 080) from **London Victoria** (2-2½hr., 1 per hr., £36).

Public Transportation: Local buses operated by **Brighton** and **Hove** (☎886 200) congregate around Old Steine. The TIC can give route and price information for most buses; all carriers charge £1 in the central area.

Taxis: Brighton Taxis (☎202 020). 24hr.

Bike Rental: Sunrise Cycle Hire, West Pier Promenade, Kings Rd., next to West Pier. (☎748 881.) £12 per day plus £20 refundable deposit. Weekly/monthly hire also available. Open mid-Mar. to mid-Sept. M-Tu and Th-Su 10am-6pm.

▄ ▄ ORIENTATION AND PRACTICAL INFORMATION

Queen's Road connects the train station to the English Channel, becoming **West Street** at the intersection with Western St. halfway down the slope. Funky stores and alternative restaurants cluster around **Trafalgar Street,** which runs east from the train station. The narrow streets of **the Lanes** constitute a pedestrian shopping area by day and the site of Brighton's carousing by night; head east onto North St. from Queen's Rd. to reach them. **Old Steine,** a road and a square, runs in front of the **Royal Pavilion,** while **King's Road** parallels the waterfront.

Tourist Information Centre: 10 Bartholomew Sq. (☎0906 711 2255; www.visitbrighton.com). Enthusiastic staff vends materials on practically every subject, books National Express tickets, and reserves rooms for a £1 charge plus a 10% deposit. Open June-Sept. M-F 9am-5:30pm, Sa 10am-5pm, Su 10am-4pm; Oct.-May M-F 9am-5pm, Sa 10am-5pm, Su 10am-4pm.

Tours: CitySightseeing (☎01789 294 466; www.city-sightseeing.com). 50min. bus tours leave from Brighton pier every 30min. Apr.-Oct., with stops at Royal Pavilion, Railway Station, and Brighton Marina. £6.50, concessions £5.50, children £2.50.

Financial Services: Banks line North St., near Old Steine. **American Express,** 82 North St. (☎712 901). Open M 9am-3:30pm and 4:30pm-5:30pm, Tu-Su 9am-5:30pm.

Disabled Information: Brighton and Hove Federation of Disabled People, 3 Rutland Gardens (☎203 016; www.disabledgo.info).

Gay/Lesbian Information & Services: Lesbian and Gay Switchboard, 6 Bartholomews (☎204 050). Open daily 5pm-11pm. The **TIC** also offers an extensive list of gay-friendly accommodations, clubs, and shops.

Launderette: Bubbles, 75 Preston St. (☎738 556). Open M-Sa 8am-9pm, last wash 7:30pm; Su 9am-7pm, last wash 5:30pm. **KJ,** 116 St. George's Rd. (☎602 421). Open M-F and Su 8am-7pm, Sa 8am-6pm; last wash 1hr. before closing.

Police: John St. (☎0845 607 0999).

Pharmacy: Boots, 129 North St. facing the clock tower (☎207 461). Open M-Sa 8am-7pm, Su 10:30am-5pm.

Hospital: Royal Sussex County, Eastern Rd. (☎696 955).

Internet Access: at the **library,** Church St. (☎296 971), across from the Brighton Museum. Free. 1hr. max. Book ahead. Open M and Th-F 9:30am-5pm, Tu 9:30am-7pm, Sa 9:30am-4pm.

Post Office: 51 Ship St. (☎08457 223 344). **Bureau de change.** Open M-Sa 9am-5:30pm. **Post Code:** BN1 1BA.

▌ ACCOMMODATIONS

Brighton's best budget beds are in its **hostels**; the TIC has a complete list. The city's **B&Bs** and cheaper **hotels** begin at £18-20 and skyrocket from there, and many require two-night minimum stays on summer weekends. Many mid-range B&Bs line **Madeira Place**; shabbier establishments collect west of **West Pier** and east of **Palace Pier.** To the east and running perpendicular to the sea, **Kemp Town** boasts a huge number of B&Bs. Rooms may be cheaper in the **Hove** area, just west of Brighton. Frequent conventions make rooms scarce—book early or consult the TIC.

▓ **Baggies Backpackers,** 33 Oriental Pl. (☎733 740). Go past West Pier along King's Rd.; Oriental Pl. is on the right. Live music, spontaneous parties, and exquisite murals set the mood in this mellow hostel. Talking and singing in the candlelit lounge beats a seedy club-hop. 50 beds in spacious dorms; some doubles. Kitchen and laundry. Key deposit £5. Dorms £12; doubles £30. MC/V. ❷

▓ **Hotel Pelirocco,** 10 Regency Sq. (☎327 055; www.hotelpelirocco.co.uk). Rock-star longings fulfilled at over-the-top, hip-to-be-camp Pelirocco. Each of 19 individually themed swanky rooms (try leopard-print "Betty's Boudoir") houses a PlayStation 2 and private bath. Downstairs bar serves a range of "cult cocktails" until 4am on weekends. Singles £50-58; doubles £90-130. AmEx/MC/V. ❹

Cavalaire Guest House, 34 Upper Rock Gdns. (☎696 899; www.cavalaire.co.uk.) Comfortable rooms, all with TV and CD player, are ideal for a lazy weekend. Wonderful breakfasts, from tropical to vegetarian. No smoking. Internet £5 per hr. Singles from £29; twins and doubles from £70. AmEx/MC/V. ❸

Brighton Backpackers Hostel, 75-76 Middle St. (☎777 717; www.brightonbackpackers.com). Lively, international flavor and great location, despite garishly-colored walls, smoky bedrooms, and moldy bathrooms. Surround-sound speakers and pool table do make the downstairs lounge an all-night party, and satellite TV upstairs furthers the social atmosphere. The quieter annex faces the ocean. Kitchen upstairs. Dorms £15, weekly £80; doubles £25-30. MC/V. ❷

YHA Brighton, Patcham Pl. (☎556 196), 3 mi. north on the London Rd. Take Patcham bus #5 or 5A from Old Steine (stop E) to the Black Lion Hotel (£2). Georgian country house makes a good jumping-off point for the Way (p. 154). Laundry. Breakfast included. Reception closed 10am-1pm. Open daily Mar.-Oct., curfew midnight; Nov.-Feb. Th-Sa, curfew 11pm. Book ahead July-Aug. Dorms £14.90, under 18 £11.60. ❷

Court Craven Hotel, 2 Atlingworth St. (☎607 710), off Marine Parade. A well-decorated gay-friendly guest house in Kemp Town. Clean and elegant, with a bar and deluxe kitchen. Reserve well ahead. Singles £25; doubles £50; prices vary. AmEx/MC/V. ❸

🔪 FOOD

Except for the picks below, the Lanes area is full of suspiciously trendy places waiting to gobble tourist cash. The chippers along the beachfront avenues or north of the Lanes offer better value. Get **groceries** at **Safeway,** 6 St. James's St. (☎570 363. Open M-Sa 8am-9pm, Su 11am-5pm.) Satisfy sugar cravings with **Brighton Rock Candy,** available at any of the multitude of shops claiming to have invented it.

🔲 **Food for Friends,** 17a-18a Prince Albert St. (☎202 310). Large portions and intense flavors in this packed vegetarian joint. Inventive salads and entrees (£8-13) draw heavily on Indian and East Asian cuisines. Open Su-Th 11:30am-10pm, F-Sa 11:30am-10:15pm. MC/V. ❸

🔲 **Nia Restaurant and Cafe,** 87 Trafalgar St. (☎671 371). Generous helpings (£10.75-13.50) are the norm in this cafe near the North Laine. The unique menu offers everything from Japanese cuisine to French pastries to Mediterranean dishes. Open daily 9am-11pm. MC/V. ❸

Bombay Aloo, 39 Ship St. (☎776 038). Indian vegetarian cuisine executed flawlessly for a cultish following. £5 all-you-can-eat meals from 18 steaming and chilled vats (£3.50 from 3:15-5:15pm). Entrees £3-7. Open daily noon-midnight. Sister restaurant at 11a St. James St., across from Safeway, serves meat dishes. MC/V. ❶

One Paston Place, 1 Paston Pl. (☎606 933). Exquisitely prepared French dishes; adventurous eaters can start with veal sweetbreads (£11). Entrees are generally meat-centered and hover around £22. Open Tu-Sa noon-3pm and from 6pm; July-Aug. also Su noon-3pm. AmEx/MC/V. ❺

👓🔪 SIGHTS AND BEACHES

In 1792, Dr. Richard Russell wrote a treatise on the merits of drinking and bathing in seawater to treat glandular disease; thus began the transformation of the sleepy village of Brighthelmstone into a beach town with a decidedly hedonistic bent.

ROYAL PAVILION. Perhaps one oughtn't reduce an entire city to one of its parts, but much of Brighton's present gaudiness may be traced to the construction of the proudly extravagant Royal Pavilion. George IV enlisted architect John Nash to turn an ordinary farm villa into a grandly ornate Chinese/Egyptian fantasy palace topped by Taj Mahal-style domes. Rumor has it that George wept tears of joy upon entering it, proving that wealth does not give one taste. After living there intermittently for several months, Queen Victoria decided to have it demolished—proving

Brighton

▲ ACCOMMODATIONS
Baggies Backpackers, 6
Brighton Backpackers
Hostel, 14
Cavalaire Guest House, 18
Court Craven Hotel, 21
Hotel Pelirocco, 7
YHA Brighton, 2

◆ FOOD
Bombay Aloo, 8
Food for Friends, 13
Nia Restaurant and Cafe, 1
One Paston Place, 22

🍺 PUBS
Fortune of War, 20
Mash Tun, 4
Queen's Arms, 11
Smugglers, 16
Squid, 15

★ CLUBS
The Beach, 19
Candy Bar, 17
Casablanca, 10
Club New York, 3
Event II, 12

SOUTH ENGLAND

that wealth does not deny one taste—until the town offered to buy the royal playground. Enjoy the pavilion from the surrounding parks by renting a deck chair (£1), or take in the view and a sandwich at **Queen Adelaide's Tea Room ❶**. (☎292 880. Open daily Apr.-Sept. 9:30am-5:45pm; Oct.-Mar. 10am-5:15pm. Last admission 4:30pm. £5.95, concessions £4.20, children £3.50, families £15.40. Tours daily 11:30am and 2:30pm, £1.50. Queen Adelaide Tearoom open daily Apr.-Sept. 10am-5pm; Oct.-Mar. 10:30am-4pm.)

THE PIERS. Brighton's unglamorous glitz hits the beach in the form of relatively new **Brighton Pier**, England's fourth-largest tourist attraction. It houses slot machines, video games, and condom dispensers, with a roller coaster and other mildly dizzying rides thrown in for good measure. **Volk's Railway**, Britain's first 3 ft. gauge electric train, shuttles along the waterfront. (☎681 061. Open Apr.-Sept. M-F 11am-5pm, Sa-Su 11am-6pm. £2.40, children £1.20.) The **Grand Hotel**, King's Rd., home to many political conventions, has been rebuilt since a 1984 IRA bombing that killed five but left Margaret Thatcher unscathed. A short walk along the coast past West Pier leads to the smaller residential community of **Hove.**

DOWN BY THE SEA. Brighton's original attraction is, of course, the beach, but those who associate the word "beach" with sand and sun may be sorely disappointed. The weather can be quite nippy even in June and July, and the closest thing to sand here are fist-sized brown rocks. Fortunately, turquoise waters, hordes of bikini-clad beachgoers, and umbrella-adorned drinks allow delusions of the tropics to persist. To visit Telscombe Beach, 4½ mi. east of Palace Pier, follow the sign for "Telescombe Cliffs" at the Telescombe Tavern.

BRIGHTON MUSEUM AND ART GALLERY. More edifying than most of the town's attractions, this recently renovated gallery features paintings, pottery, and Art Deco and Art Nouveau collections, as well as an extensive Brighton historical exhibit that fully explicates the phrase "dirty weekend." In the fine **Willett Collection of Pottery,** postmodern porcelains and Neolithic relics reflect the varied faces of this seaside escape. (Church St., around the corner from the Pavilion. ☎290 900. Open Tu 10am-7pm, W-Sa 10am-5pm, Su 2pm-5pm. Free.)

LANES AND LAINES. Small fishermen's cottages once thrived in the Lanes, an intricate maze of 17th-century streets (some no wider than 3 ft.) south of North St. in the heart of Old Brighton. Now filled with overpriced jewelry shops and restaurants, the Lanes have lost some of their charm. Those looking for fresher shopping opportunities should head to **North Laines,** off Trafalgar St., where alternative merchandise and colorful cafes dominate. On Saturdays, the area is closed to traffic and cafe tables and street performers take over.

OTHER SIGHTS. Although England's largest aquarium has freed its dolphins, many other creatures remain at the touristy **Sea Life Centre.** (Marine Parade, near Palace Pier. ☎604 234. Open daily 9am-6pm; last admission 5pm. £8.50, children £5.50.) For more historical pursuits, head to **St. Nicholas's Church,** on Dyke Rd., which dates from 1370. Its baptismal font is thought to be the most beautiful Norman carving in Sussex. **St. Bartholomew's Church,** on Ann St., was originally called "The Barn" or "Noah's Ark"—one look and you'll see why. This obscure hiccup of Victorian genius rises to 134 ft. (Walk up London Rd. to Ann St.)

🅢 🎵 NIGHTLIFE AND ENTERTAINMENT

For info on hot-and-happening scenes, check *The Punter*, found at pubs, newsagents, and record stores, which details evening events, or *What's On*, a poster-sized flyer found at record stores and pubs. **Gay and lesbian** venues can be found in the latest issues of *Gay Times* (£2.75), available at newsstands; *What's On* also highlights gay-friendly events. The City Council spent £5 million installing surveillance equipment along the seafront and major streets to ensure safety during late-night partying, but still try to avoid walking alone late at night through Brighton's spaghetti-style streets. The Lanes, in particular, can be a bit too deserted for comfort. **Night buses** N97-99 run infrequently but reliably in the early morning, picking up passengers at Old Steine and in front of many clubs, usually hitting each spot twice between 1 and 2:30am (£2.50).

PUBS

J.B. Priestley once noted that Brighton was "a fine place either to restore your health, or...to ruin it again." The city's sea of alcohol provides ample means to achieve the latter. The waterfront between West Pier and Brighton Pier is particularly good for reveling. This is a student town, and where there are students there are cheap drinks. Many pubs offer fantastic specials during the week.

The Mash Tun, 1 Church St. (☎684 951). Alternative pub attracts an eclectic student crowd with "friendly food, tasty barstaff, real music, groovy ales." Sample the dark rum concoction (£2.90). Open M-Sa noon-11pm, Su noon-10:30pm.

Fortune of War, 157 King's Road Arches (☎205 065), beneath King's Rd. by the beach. Evening patrons can relax with their beverage of choice while the sun sets over the Channel. Open M-Sa noon-11pm, Su noon-10:30pm.

Squid, 78 Middle St. (☎727 114). Next door to Brighton Backpackers hostel and linked to Zap Club. Packed with pre-clubbers. Open M-F 4-11pm, Su 3-10:30pm.

Queen's Arms, 7-8 George St. (☎696 873; www.queensarmsbrighton.co.uk). Draws a lively gay and lesbian crowd with a constant stream of live entertainment, including Su night cabaret. Open M-Sa noon-11pm, Su noon-10:30pm.

Olde King and Queen, Marlborough Pl. (☎607 207). This former farmhouse from 1779 offers TV football, a groovy dance floor, a beautiful beer garden, and multiple bars. Open M-Sa 11am-11pm, Su noon-10:30pm.

Smugglers, 10 Ship St. (☎328 439). A pirate's den with a dance beat, with an adjoining jazz club. Bedsteads, 2 dance floors, velvet couches, and vodka-bottle chandeliers make this pub raucous, to say the least. Pints £1.60. Happy hour M-F noon-8pm. Open M-Sa noon-11pm, Su 7:30-10:30pm.

CLUBS

Brighton is the hometown of Norman Cook, better known as Fatboy Slim, and major dance label Skint Records, so it should come as no surprise that Brightonians know a thing or two about dance music. Most clubs are open Monday through Saturday 9pm-2am; after 2am the party moves to the waterfront. Many clubs have student discounts on weeknights and higher covers (£4-10) on weekends.

The Beach, 171-181 King's Rd. Arches (☎722 272). Adds a monstrous big beat to the music on the shore. Drinks and snacks (noon-2pm); the club is open F-Sa 10pm-3am. Cover £5-10, student discounts available; £12 when Fatboy Slim mans the turntables.

Casablanca, 3 Middle St. (☎321 817). One of few clubs in Brighton that regularly offers live jazz, funk, and Latin tunes to a mix of students and late-20-somethings. Dance floor, DJ, and bar upstairs. Headbang, jig, mosh, and grind to bands in the basement. Open M-Sa 10pm-2am. Cover Th-Sa £7.

Event II, at the beach end of West St. (☎732 627). Regularly crammed with a down-from-London crowd looking for thrills. Experienced Brighton clubbers go for less conventional venues, but all agree it's great for a no-surprises good time. Cover from £5; Tu student nights £3. Open Tu and F-Sa 9:30pm-2am.

Candy Bar, 129 St. James's St. (☎662 424). This new midsize venue caters to lesbian clubbers with nightly entertainment. Check billing outside for the week's events. Cover after 9pm M-Th £3, F-Sa £5.

Club New York, 11 Dyke Rd. (☎208 678). A bit off the beaten track—offers a refreshing change of pace from more mainstream, techno-oriented clubs. Upstairs, it's salsa night every night, downstairs plays everything from rock and indie to traditional African beats.

MUSIC, THEATER, AND FESTIVALS

Brighton Centre, King's Rd. (☎0870 900 9100), and **The Dome,** 29 New Rd. (☎709 709; www.brighton-dome.org.uk), host Brighton's biggest events, from Chippendales shows to concerts. (Both offices open M-Sa 10am-5:30pm. TIC also sells tickets.) Local plays and London productions take the stage at the **Theatre Royal** on New Rd., a Victorian beauty with a plush interior. (☎328 488; www.theatreroyalbrighton.co.uk. Tickets £6-20. Open M-Sa 10am-8pm.) **Komedia,** on Gardner St., houses a cafe, bar, theater, comedy club, and cabaret. (☎647 100; www.komedia.co.uk. Tickets £5-8; discounts available. Standby tickets 15min. before curtain. Box office open M-F 10am-10pm, Sa 10am-10:30pm, Su 1pm-10pm.) The **Brighton Festival** (box office ☎709 709), held each May, is one of the largest festivals in England, celebrating music, film, and other art forms. Gays and lesbians celebrate the concurrent **Brighton Pride Festival** (☎730 562) in early August.

⬛ DAYTRIPS FROM BRIGHTON

LEWES. The historic town of Lewes has an appealing location in the Sussex chalklands and makes a perfect jumping-off point for **South Downs Way** trails (p. 154). The views from the flower-strewn ruins of the Norman **Lewes Castle,** High St., 5min. northwest of the train station, merit a visit, as do the small but rich collections of the **Museum of Sussex Archaeology** at the castle's base. (☎01273 486 290. Open Tu-Sa 10am-5:30pm or dusk, Su-M 11am-5:30pm or dusk. Last admission 30min. before closing. £4.30, concessions £3.80, children £2.15, families £11. Admission to the museum comes with a castle ticket.) The 15th-century **Anne of Cleves House Museum,** Southover High St., 15min. from the castle, celebrates Henry VIII Wife #4, the clever woman who not only managed to leave Henry with her head on her shoulders, but got to keep the house as well. (Trains from Brighton's Queen's Rd. station leave for Lewes every 15min., £3.30. ☎01273 474 610. Open Mar.-Oct. Tu-Sa 10am-5pm, Su-M 11am-5pm; Nov.-Feb. Tu-Sa 10am-5pm; £2.90, concessions £2.60, children £1.45, families £7.35. Castle and Museum combination ticket £6/£5.15/£3/£15.) Between Ann of Cleves's House and the Castle lie the ruined walls of **Lewes Priory,** England's oldest Cluniac priory and the site where, after his loss at the battle of Lewes in 1264, Henry III signed the treaty that ended the struggle with his barons and provided for the nation's first Representative Parliament the following year. (☎01273 474610. Entrance by guided tour only.)

THE CHARLESTON FARMHOUSE. Artist Vanessa Bell and her husband Duncan Grant moved into their new home in 1916, transforming the farmhouse into the country retreat of the Bloomsbury group and a center for literary, artistic, and intellectual life in Britain. Artistic influences from further abroad (Italian frescoes and post-Impressionist paintings) decorate the walls. On Fridays, visitors may sneak a peak at Vanessa Bell's studio and take longer guided tours. (East of Lewes, off the A27. Take bus #125 from the Lewes station (6 per day). ☎01323 811 265. Open July-Aug. W-Sa 11:30am-6pm, Su 2-6pm; Apr.-June and Sept.-Oct. W-Su 2-6pm. Last admission 5pm. £6, W and Th only concessions £4.50; connoisseur F £7. Garden only £2.50, children £1.)

ARUNDEL ☎01903

Arundel sits in the shadow of towers and spires, but the town refuses to let them dim its character. Most visitors are drawn by the fairy-tale castle, yet travelers will find that the town's storybook beauty stems less from outlets than from wearisome antique shops and souvenir outlets, and more from the rippling River Arun and the idyllic hillside location. Arundel provides a perfect place from which to explore the surrounding countryside and the **South Downs Way** (p. 154).

▐▄▐▟ TRANSPORTATION AND PRACTICAL INFORMATION

Trains (☎08457 484 950) arrive from: **Brighton** (1hr., 1 per hr., ₤7); **Chichester** (20 min., 2 per hr., ₤3.80); **London Victoria** (1½hr., 2 per hr., ₤17.40); **Portsmouth** (1 hr., 2 per hr. 1 per hr., ₤8.10). Many routes connect at **Littlehampton** to the south or **Barnham** to the west. **Stagecoach Coastline buses** (☎0845 121 0170) stop across from the Norfolk Arms on High St. and just on the town's side of the river, and come from **Littlehampton** (#702, 1-2 per hr.). **South Downs Cycle Hire** is 3 mi. east of Arundel on Blakehurst Farm. (☎889 562. ₤15 per day.) Call **Castle Cars** (☎884 444) for a **taxi.**

The friendly **Tourist Information Centre**, 61 High St., dispenses the free *Town Guide* and information on the South Downs Way. (☎882 268. Open Easter-Oct. M-Sa 10am-6pm; daily Oct.-Easter 10am-3pm.) Other services include: **Lloyds TSB**, 14 High St. (☎717 221; open M-F 9:30am-4:30pm); **police** (☎0845 607 0999), on the Causeway; and the **post office**, 2-4 High St. (☎882 113; open M-F 9am-5:30pm, Sa 9am-12:30pm). **Post Code:** BN18 9AA.

▐▛ ACCOMMODATIONS

B&Bs (₤25-30) are consistent with Arundel's elegance, and priced accordingly. Reserve ahead in summer. The TIC posts an up-to-date list of vacancies.

Arundel House, 11 High St. (☎882 136; arundelhouse@btinternet.com). Recently renovated; offers luxurious rooms in modern minimal decor of dark wood and red glass, offsetting 400-year-old buildings set right in town. All rooms ensuite with Freeview TV and Internet jacks. Doubles £75-95, 2-floor suite £120. MC/V. ❺

Arden House, 4 Queens Ln. (☎882 544). 8 rosy rooms, some with wood-beam ceilings, in a convenient location. Singles £30-40; doubles £48, ensuite £52. Cash only. ❹

The Norfolk Arms, High St. (☎882 101). Luxury awaits in this half hotel, half museum, originally built as a coach house for the duke of Norfolk. Singles £75; doubles £120. AmEx/MC/V. ❺

YHA Warningcamp (☎882 204; fax 882 776), 1½ mi. out of town. Turn right out of the train station, cross the railroad tracks, turn left on the next road, and follow the signs. Family- and group-oriented accommodations in a house with aqua interior. Huge kitchen and laundry facilities. Meals at reasonable prices. Lockout 10am-5pm. Curfew 11pm. Open daily July-Aug.; Sept.-Oct. Tu-Sa; Nov.-Dec. F-Sa; Apr.-June M-Sa. Dorms £13.40, under 18 £9.30. Camping £6.70 per person. MC/V. ❷

Camping: Ship and Anchor Site, Ford Rd. (☎01243 551 262), 2 mi. from Arundel beside the River Arun. Well-kept site with pub and shops nearby. Open March-Oct. Apr.-Sept. £6 per person, children £3; March and Oct. £4.50 per person, children £2. Showers 50p. £1.50 per vehicle. ❶

▐▟ FOOD

Arundel's pubs and tea shops are generally expensive and unremarkable. A few fruit and bread peddlers line High St. and Tarrant St. **Alldays,** 17 Queen St., sells **groceries.** (Open M-Sa 6:30am-11pm, Su 7:30am-11pm.)

White Hart, 12 Queen St. (☎882 374). Serves pub grub and local ales (pints £2.20). Find homemade specials (entrees £9-13) and vegetarian options. Open M-Th 11:30am-3pm and 5pm-11pm, last food orders at 2:30pm and 8:30pm; F-Sa 11:30am-11pm, last food orders at 9pm; Su noon-10:30pm, last food orders at 9pm. ❷

Belinda's, 13 Tarrant St. (☎882 977). Locals frequent this 16th-century tearoom for its large selection of traditional fare. Linger over cream teas (£2), scones (£2.10), and Belinda's famous homemade jam. Open Tu-Sa 9am-5pm, Su 10am-5pm. ❶

Castle Tandoori, 3 Mill Ln. (☎884 224). Dishes out standard, spicy Indian cuisine for about £8 per entree, as well as a buffet lunch (£9) and dinner (£13). Open daily noon-2:30pm and 6-11:30pm. ❸

Tudor Rose (☎883 813), on the corner of High St. and Tarrant St. Visitors can order sandwiches (£3.25-5), roasts (£8), and vegetarian dishes (£4.35-7.95) while inspecting the arms, armor, and other artifacts on the wall. Open daily 9am-6pm. ❷

👁 🌿 SIGHTS AND FESTIVALS

Poised above town like the backdrop of a Disney film, 🔲**Arundel Castle** is lord of the skyline. The castle, hereditary seat of the dukes of Norfolk, was built in the 11th century and restored piecemeal in the 18th and 19th centuries. Winding passages and 131 steps lead to the keep, with views of the town below and the countryside beyond, but don't miss the elegantly carved 18th-century library. Note the death warrant issued against one of the Norfolk dukes by Elizabeth I, and enjoy cream tea (£4) among the flowers in the castle's Tea Garden, near the carpark. (☎882 173. Open Apr.-Oct. Su-F noon-5pm; last entry 4pm. £9.50, concessions £7.50, children £6, families £26.50. Grounds only £4.50.)

Along the river across from the castle, a placard recounts the troubled past of the monks of **Blackfriars,** the Dominican priory whose remains are nearby. Atop the same hill as Arundel Castle, the **Cathedral of Our Lady and St. Philip Howard** (Philip Howard being the aforementioned victim of Elizabeth's excesses) is more impressive for its French Gothic exterior than its fairly standard interior. During the May holiday of **Corpus Christi,** thousands of flowers are laid in a pattern stretching 93 ft. down the center aisle, a tradition dating from 1877. (☎882 297; www.arundelcathedral.org. Open daily summer 9am-6pm; winter 9am-dusk. Free.) At the **Wildfowl and Wetlands Trust Centre,** less than a mile past the castle on Mill Rd., concealed observation blinds permit visitors to "come nose to beak with nature." Over 1000 birds roost on 60 acres. (☎883 355. Open daily summer 9:30am-5pm; winter 9:30am-4:30pm. Last entry 30min. before closing. £5.75, concessions £4.50, children £3.50.)

Right around the August bank holiday, the castle is the centerpiece of the **Arundel Festival,** ten days of musical and Shakespearean shows. The **Festival Fringe** simultaneously offers free or inexpensive events. Tickets for both go on sale six to eight weeks ahead of time. (☎883 690; box office 883 474; www.arundelfestival.org.uk. Tickets up to £20.)

🔲 DAYTRIP FROM ARUNDEL

PETWORTH HOUSE. Situated among acres of sculpted lawns and gardens designed by Capability Brown, Petworth House holds one of the UK's finest art collections. J. M. W. Turner often painted the house and landscape, and many of his works hang alongside canvasses by masters Van Dyck, Bosch, Dahl, and Reynolds. Petworth is also famous for the **Petworth Chaucer,** an early 15th-century manuscript of *The Canterbury Tales,* and the intricate carvings in the legendary **Carving Room.** The 700-acre landscaped park houses England's largest herd of fallow deer. *(Take the train*

10min. to Pulborough and catch bus #1. ☎01798 342 207. House open Apr.-Oct. Sa-W 11am-5:30pm, last entry 5pm. Park open daily 8am-dusk. Tours of House 11am-1pm. House and grounds £7, children £4, families £18. Park only free.)

CHICHESTER   ☎01243

Confined for centuries within eroding Roman walls, the citizens of well-preserved Chichester take pride in their town's position as a center of English culture. The settlement continues to thrive off its markets (cattle, corn, and others), and all roads still lead to the ornate 16th-century Market Cross, but present-day Chichester's tourist appeal relies on more modern attractions. Visitors are lured by one of the country's best theaters, an arts festival, a host of gallery exhibits, and a summer motor-racing spectacular. Timeless attractions such as Chichester's quirky cathedral and the nearby Fishbourne Roman Palace provide permanent delight.

🚆 TRANSPORTATION. Chichester is 45 mi. southwest of London and 15 mi. east of Portsmouth. **Trains** (☎08457 484 950) serve **Southgate station** from: **Brighton** (45min., 3 per hr., £8.30); **London Victoria** via **Horsham** (1¾hr., 2 per hr., £17.40); **Portsmouth** (30min., 3 per hr., £4.90). The **bus station** (☎01903 237 661) is also on Southgate. **National Express** (☎08705 808 080) buses come from **London Victoria** (3¾hr., 2 per day, £16). **Stagecoach Coastline** buses connect Chichester with **Brighton** (#702, 3hr., 2 per hr., £4.60) and **Portsmouth** (#700-701, 1hr., 2 per hr., £4). An **Explorer** ticket grants a day's unlimited travel on buses in southern England from Kent to Salisbury. (£5.25, children £2.60, seniors £3.85, families £10.50). For **taxis,** call **Central Cars of Chichester** (☎0800 789 432).

📋 🎓 ORIENTATION AND PRACTICAL INFORMATION. Four Roman streets named for their compass directions converge at **Market Cross,** the main plaza, and divide Chichester into four quadrants. The **Tourist Information Centre** is at 29a South St.; from the train station, exit left onto Southgate (which becomes South St.). Check the 24hr. computer terminal in the front window for accommodations or use the booking service inside. (☎775 888; www.chichesterweb.co.uk. Open Apr.-Sept. M-Sa 9:15am-5:15pm, Su 11am-3:30pm; Oct.-Mar. M-Sa 9:15am-5:15pm.) **Guided tours** depart from the TIC. (May-Sept. Tu 11am, Sa 2:30pm; Oct.-Apr. Sa 2:30pm only. £2.) Other services include: **HSBC,** at the corner of South St. and East St. (open M-F 9am-5pm, Sa 9:30am-12:30pm); the **police,** Kingsham Rd. (☎0845 607 0999); **Internet access** at **The Internet Junction,** 2 Southgate (☎776 644; £1 per 20min.; open M-F 10am-8pm, Sa 10am-9pm, Su 11am-6pm); and the **post office,** 10 West St., with a **bureau de change** (☎08457 223 344; open M 8:45am-5:30pm, Tu-Sa 9am-5:30pm). **Post Code:** PO19 1AB.

🛏 🍴 ACCOMMODATIONS AND FOOD. B&Bs abound, but cheap rooms are rare, especially on big racecourse weekends (in nearby **Goodwood,** p. 170). Plan on paying at least £20 and expect a 15min. walk from the town center. **Bayleaf ❸,** 16 Whyke Rd., welcomes guests with colorful geraniums and a full English breakfast with vegetarian alternatives. (☎774 330. No smoking.) **University College Chichester ❸,** College Ln., rents out spacious single rooms as B&Bs between June and August. (☎816 070. £25, ensuite £32.) Pitch your tent at **Southern Leisure Centre ❶,** Vinnetrow Rd., a 15min. walk southeast of town. (☎787 715. Clean facilities with showers and laundry. Open Apr.-Oct.; £12.50-14.50, with electricity £14.50-17.50.)

A **market** convenes W and Sa in the parking lot off Market Ave., and East St. Bakeries line North St., while **groceries** chill at **Iceland,** 55 South St. (Open M-Th and Sa 8:30am-6pm, F 8:30am-8pm, Su 10am-4pm.) The town's best eateries line South St. and tend to be expensive. The **Pasta Factory ❷,** 5 South St., rolls out fresh pasta daily; its cannelloni inspire sweet dreams. (☎785 764. Entrees £7-10.) The Francophiles at **Maison Blanc Boulangerie and Patisserie ❶,** 56 South St., fill pastries from eclairs to *passionata* (*pain au chocolat* £1.20) and build sandwiches (*croque monsieur* £3.95). (☎ 539 292. Open M-F 8:45am-5:30pm, Sa 8:45am-6pm.) Upscale **Platters ❹**, 15 Southgate, serves meticulously prepared cuisine in an elegant setting. (☎ 530 430; www.plattersrestaurant.co.uk. Open Tu-Sa noon-2pm and 7-9pm.) The hip pre-theater set dresses sharply to match the interior at **Woodies Wine Bar and Brasserie ❸**, 10 St. Pancras, the oldest wine bar in Sussex. (☎ 779 895. Open M-Sa noon-2:30pm and 6-11pm, Su 6-11pm.) The town's best pubs also congregate around St. Pancras.

◙ **SIGHTS.** Begun in 1091, **Chichester Cathedral,** just west of the Market Cross, is hung with trappings of decorative modernity that link medieval Christianity to the modern Anglican faith. Norman arches frame Reformation stained glass, Queen Elizabeth II and Prince Philip peer from the newly renovated West Front, and Chagall's stained-glass window depicts Psalm 150 with intense colors and detailed symbolism. These are interspersed with older items, including two fine Romanesque sculptures and a Roman mosaic displayed under a floor cutaway. Also in the cathedral is an incredibly rare image of medieval hand-holding in the 14th-century effigies of Earl Fitzalan and his wife, which inspired Larkin's poem "An Arundel Tomb," displayed on a nearby pillar. (☎ 812 482; www.chichestercathedral.org.uk. Open daily summer 7am-7pm; winter 7am-6pm. Tours Apr.-Oct. M-Sa 11am and 2:15pm. Evensong M-Sa 5:30pm, Su 3:30pm. Free lunchtime concerts Tu. £3 requested donation, children £1.50.)

Chichester's other attractions include the **Pallants,** a quiet area with elegant 18th- and 19th-century houses in the quadrant between South St. and East St. **The Pallant House,** 9 North Pallant, is an impeccably restored Queen Anne building, attributed to Christopher Wren, that draws visitors to its collection of 20th-century art, which includes works by Picasso, Cézanne, and Whistler. A packed schedule of temporary exhibitions, concerts, and gallery talks ensures that something interesting happens daily. Renovations, scheduled for completion in spring 2005, will expand the museum to four times its size, adding space and a restaurant. (☎ 774 557; www.pallant.org.uk. Open Tu-Sa 10am-5pm; last admission 4pm. Free tours Sa 3pm. £4, students £2.50, seniors £3, children free.)

🎭🎨 **ENTERTAINMENT AND FESTIVALS.** Located in a residential neighborhood just north of town, the **Chichester Festival Theatre,** Oaklands Park (☎ 781 312), is the cultural center of Chichester. Founded by Sir Laurence Olivier, the internationally renowned venue has attracted such artists as Maggie Smith, Peter Ustinov, and Julie Christie. The newer **Minerva Studio Theatre** is a smaller space for more intimate productions. The **Theatre Restaurant and Cafe** caters to theater-goers from noon on matinee days, and from 5:30pm for evening shows. (*Box office open M-Sa 9 10am-8pm; until 6pm non-performance days. Tickets £15-20; rush seats £6-8, available at 10am day of show.*) During the first two weeks in July, artists and musicians collaborate in one of the finest spells of concentrated creativity in England: the **Chichester Festivities.** (*The box office is at 45 East St. ☎ 780 192; www.chifest.co.uk. Tickets for talks £2-10, concerts £10-30. Open mid-May until festival's end M-Sa 10am-5:30pm.*)

📑 **DAYTRIPS FROM CHICHESTER**

FISHBOURNE ROMAN PALACE. Built around AD 80, possibly by local ruler Togidubnus, the palace is the largest extant domestic Roman building in Britain. Historians believe the original residents possessed wealth of Pompeiian proportions, granted as a reward for their assistance in defeating the Boudiccan uprising. The remains include Britain's oldest mosaic floors and a formal garden replanted according to the original excavated Roman layout. (*About 2 mi. west of the town center;*

follow the signs from the end of Westgate Street. ☎ *01243 785 859. Open daily Aug. 10am-6pm; Mar.-July and Sept.-Oct. 10am-5pm; Feb. and Nov.-Dec. 15 10am-4pm; Dec. 15-Jan. Sa-Su 10am-4pm. Last admission 20min. before closing. £5.20, concessions £4.50, children £2.70.)*

GOODWOOD. Three miles northeast of Chichester, splendid Canalettos, Reynoldses, and Stubbses, as well as a world-famous sculpture collection, vie for attention in the 18th-century seat of the Duke of Richmond. *(☎ 01243 755 040. Open Aug. Su-Th 1-5pm; Apr.-July and Sept.-Oct. Su-M 1-5pm. 5 tours per day. The schedule is irregular; call ahead. £6.50, seniors £6, children £3, under 12 free.)* The rich and famous prefer **Racing at Goodwood,** an equestrian tradition over 200 years old. *(☎ 755 022.)* The plebeian set, on the other hand, choose the rumble of motorcars in late June or early July's famous **Festival of Speed** and September's **Motorcar Revival Race.** *(☎ 755 055.)*

WEALD AND DOWNLAND OPEN AIR MUSEUM. Weald showcases 45 historical buildings of the southeastern countryside that have been transplanted to the site. The mostly medieval structures join exhibits on husbandry, forestry, geology, and society. The museum's great strength is its ability not to induce nostalgia, but to transplant the viewer completely to another living time and place. *(7 mi. north of Chichester off the A286; take bus #56 to Singleton Horse and Groom; ask the driver for a discount on admission. ☎ 01243 811 363. Open daily Mar.-Oct. 10:30am-6pm, last admission 5pm; Nov.-Feb. Sa-Su 10:30am-4pm. £7.50, seniors £6.50, children £4, families £20.)*

HAMPSHIRE

PORTSMOUTH ☎ 023

Don't talk to me about naval tradition. It's nothing but rum, sodomy, and the lash.
—popularly (but falsely) attributed to Winston Churchill

Set Victorian seaside holidays against prostitutes, drunkards, and a bloody lot of cursing sailors, and the 900-year history of Portsmouth (pop. 190,500) will emerge. Henry VIII's *Mary Rose,* which sank in 1545 and was raised 437 years later, epitomizes an incomparable naval heritage in a city that will appeal most to those fascinated by the saga of the Royal Navy. On the seafront, older visitors relive D-Day while fresh faces learn of the days when Britannia ruled the waves.

▐ TRANSPORTATION

Trains: Portsmouth and Southsea Station, Commercial Rd., in the city center. Ticket office open M-Sa 5:40am-8:30pm, Su 6:40am-8:40pm. Travel center open M-F 8:40am-6pm, Sa 8:40am-4:30pm. **Portsmouth Harbour Station,** The Hard, ¾ mi. away at the end of the line, sends ferries to the Isle of Wight. Office open M-F 5:50am-7:30pm, Sa 6am-7:30pm, Su 6:40am-8:10pm. Trains (☎ 08457 484 950) go to both stations from **Chichester** (30min.; 2 per hr.; £4.90, children £2.45) and **London Waterloo** (1¾ hr.; 4 per hour; £21/£10.50).

Buses: The Hard Interchange, The Hard, next to Harbour Station. **National Express** (☎ 08705 808 080) buses arrive from **London Victoria** (2½ hr.; 1 per hour; £18.50, children £9.25) and **Salisbury** (1½ hr., 1 per day, £10/£5).

Ferries: Wightlink (☎ 0870 582 7744) sails to the Isle of Wight from the harbor (15min.; 2-4 per hr.; round-trip £11.20-13.60, children £5.60-6.80). **Hovertravel** (☎ 9281 1000) departs from Clarence Esplanade for Ryde, Isle of Wight (9min.; 2 per hr.; round-trip £12/£6). For services to the Continent, consult **By Ferry,** p. 29.

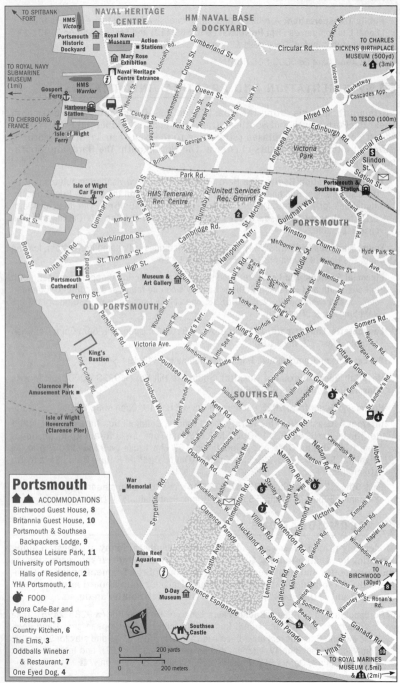

Portsmouth

🏠🏠 ACCOMMODATIONS
Birchwood Guest House, **8**
Britannia Guest House, **10**
Portsmouth & Southsea
 Backpackers Lodge, **9**
Southsea Leisure Park, **11**
University of Portsmouth
 Halls of Residence, **2**
YHA Portsmouth, **1**

🍴 FOOD
Agora Cafe-Bar and
 Restaurant, **5**
Country Kitchen, **6**
The Elms, **3**
Oddballs Winebar
 & Restaurant, **7**
One Eyed Dog, **4**

SOUTH ENGLAND

Public Transportation: A reliable and comprehensive bus system connects the city. **Local bus** companies **First Provincial** (☎9286 2412) and **Stagecoach** (☎01903 237 661) run throughout. Daily pass £2, weekly pass £10.

Taxis: Aqua Cars (☎0800 666 666).

■✱🛈 ORIENTATION AND PRACTICAL INFORMATION

Portsmouth sprawls along the coast for miles—**Portsmouth, Old Portsmouth** (near the Portsmouth and Southsea train station and Commercial Rd.), and the resort community of **Southsea** (stretching to the east) can seem like entirely different cities. Major sights cluster at Old Portsmouth, **The Hard,** and Southsea's **Esplanade.**

Tourist Information Centre: The Hard (☎9282 6722; www.visitportsmouth.co.uk), by the historic ships. Bursting with brochures; the map is worth the £1.20. Books accommodations for a £2 fee. Open daily Apr.-Sept. 9:30am-5:45pm, Oct.-Mar. 9:30am-5:15pm. **Branch: Southsea Offices** (☎832 464) near the Sea Life Centre and Clarence Esplanade.

Tours: Waterbus (☎9282 2584) offers 1hr. guided rides in Portsmouth Harbour, leaving from The Hard. 9:30am-4:30pm. £5, children £2.50.

Financial Services: Banks cluster around the Commercial Rd. shopping precinct, north of Portsmouth and Southsea Station. **Barclay's** can be found at the corner of Commercial Rd. and Swindon St. (☎9230 5858; open M, Tu 9am-5pm; W 9:30am-5pm; Th, F 9am-5pm; Sa 9:30am-4pm.)

Launderette: Laundrycare, 121 Elm Grove. ☎826 245. Open daily 8am-6pm; last wash 4:45pm. Wash £2, dry £1.80.

Police: Winston Churchill Ave. Hampshire hotline ☎0845 454 545.

Hospital: Queen Alexandra Hospital, Southwick Hill Rd. (☎9228 6000). **St. Mary's Hospital,** Milton Rd. (☎9228 6000).

Pharmacy: Superdrug, 1923 Palmerston Rd. ☎812 219. Open M-Sa 8:30am-5:30-pm.

Internet Access: Free at the **library,** Civic Offices, Guildhall Sq.; time may be limited to 30min. (☎9281 9311. Open M-F 9:30am-7pm, Sa 9:30am-4pm, Su noon-4pm.) **The Online Cafe** has 2 locations: 163 Elm Grove (☎9283 1106) and 23 Highland Rd. (☎9286 1221). 50p for 10min. Open M-F 9am-9pm, Sa and Su 10am-9pm.

Post Office: Swindon St. (☎08457 223 344), near the train station. Open M and Th 8:45am-5:30pm, Tu-W and F-Sa 9am-5:30pm. **Post Code:** PO1 1AA.

🛏 ACCOMMODATIONS

Moderately priced **B&Bs** (around £20) clutter **Southsea.** Many are located along Waverley Rd., Clarendon Rd., Granada Rd., and South Parade. If you're arriving via the Portsmouth and Southsea Station, catch one of the frequent buses on Commercial Rd. (#5 and 16). From Portsmouth Harbour, hop aboard any of several buses (#5 and 6) that make the trek from The Hard to South Parade.

🏠 **Portsmouth and Southsea Backpackers Lodge,** 4 Florence Rd. (☎9283 2495). Take any Southsea bus to The Strand. Immaculate rooms. Pan-European crowd and energetic owners. Backpackers have been known to come for 2 days and stay for 2 months. Comfy lounge, satellite TV, kitchen, grocery counter, laundry (£2), and Internet access (£1 per 30min.). Dorms £12; doubles £26, ensuite £29. Cash only. ❶

Birchwood Guest House, 44 Waverley Rd. (☎9281 1337). A touch of quiet elegance in a city of carnivals and sailors. Bright, spacious rooms recently refurbished with aboriginal art. Incredibly personable hosts provide ample breakfasts. Prices vary with season; May-Sept. singles from £30; Oct.-Apr. singles from £20. MC/V. ❸

Britannia Guest House, 48 Granada Rd. (☎814 234). Colorful rooms, oriental carpets, and the owners' maritime interests make this B&B a good diving-in point for Portsmouth. Full English breakfast included. Singles £20; doubles £40-£45. Cash only. ❸

University of Portsmouth Halls of Residence, Langstone Centre, Furze Lane (☎9284 4567). Small, modern rooms in **Rees Hall** are convenient and available mid-July to Sept. Booking ahead is recommended; last-minute arrivals should head directly to Rees Hall (bus #5). Singles with breakfast £29; doubles £49. Cash only. ❸

YHA Portsmouth, Old Wymering Ln., Cosham (☎9237 5661). From Portsmouth, take a bus to Cosham. From Cosham train station, take a right on High St., take Wayte St. left., and cross the roundabout to Medina Rd.; Old Wymering Ln. is on the right after 6 blocks. Has exquisitely detailed woodwork. Lockout 10am-5pm. Ask for key after 11pm. Open Feb. M-F; Mar.-Oct. F-Sa. Dorms £10.60, under 18 £7.20. MC/V. ❶

Camping: Southsea Leisure Park, Melville Rd., Southsea (☎9273 5070). At the eastern end of the seafront, 5-6 mi. from The Hard. Site has toilets, showers, laundry facilities, shop, restaurant-bar, and pool. No reservations needed. 2-person tent £11 per night. ❶

🔆📷 FOOD AND PUBS

Good restaurants assemble along the waterfront, Palmerston Rd., Clarendon Rd., and between the shopping districts in Southsea and on Commercial Rd. There is no shortage of pubs in Portsmouth; the weary sailor can easily find galley fare and a pint, especially near The Hard or along Palmerston. Ethnic foods add spice to the scene on Albert Rd. near the University of Portsmouth student houses. The **Tesco** supermarket is on Crasswell St., just outside town center. (☎839 222. Open 24 hr. from M 7am to Sa 10pm, Su 10am-4pm.)

Agora Cafe-Bar and Restaurant, 9 Clarendon Rd. (☎9282 2617). Serves English breakfasts (£3-5) and light fare by day and Turkish and Greek cuisine (£7.50-9.90) by night to a relaxed crowd. Turkish meats and desserts are particularly worthwhile. Open M-F 9am-4pm and 5:30-11:30pm, Sa 9am-4:30pm and 5:30-11:30pm, 10am-4pm and Su 5:30-11:30pm. Cash only. ❶

Country Kitchen, 59a Marmion Rd. (☎9232 1148). Savory vegetarian and vegan dishes (£2.40-3.95) and guilt-free desserts please the taste buds and the wallet. Great service, too. Open daily 9:30am-5pm. ❶

Oddballs Winebar and Restaurant, 12 Clarendon Rd. (☎9275 5291). Deep wine list and complex, predominantly French dishes (£9-16) made un-intimidating by friendly staff and simple surroundings. Open Tu-Sa noon-11pm, Su noon-10:30pm; food served until 10pm. MC/V. ❸

The Elms, 128 Elm Grove (☎9282 4295). One of the busiest bars in town, this gay and lesbian-friendly establishment features live music on Th and Sa and a rock DJ on F. 18+. Open M-Sa noon-11:20pm, Su noon-11pm. ❶

One Eyed Dog (☎9282 7188), corner of Elm Grove and Victoria Rd. South. This pub/trendy bar draws a steady flow of twentysomethings afternoon and night. The place to sate your thirst (drinks £2-3) but not your hunger (bar snacks only). Cheap beer M nights (£1-2). Open M-Th 4-11pm, F-Sa 1-11pm, Su 4-10:30pm. Cash only. ❶

SOUTH ENGLAND

🕞 SIGHTS

Portsmouth overflows with magnificent ships and seafaring relics. The bulk of sights worth seeing are near The Hard, delighting war buffs, intriguing historians, and looking like some pretty big boats to the rest of the world. In summer, the colorful boardwalk attracts the attention of landlubbers. The sail-shaped Spinnaker Tower, originally intended for millennium festivities, is finally expected to open in the spring of 2005, complete with three observation decks high above the Solent.

🖼 PORTSMOUTH HISTORIC DOCKYARD

In the Naval Yard. Entrance next to the TIC; follow the signs. ☎ 9286 1512 or 9286 1533. Ships open daily Mar.-Oct. 10am-5:30pm; Nov.-Feb. 10am-5pm. Last entry 4:45pm. Each sight £9.70, seniors and children £8. The all-inclusive ticket allows one-time entrance to every site and is valid forever. £15.50, children £12.50.

Historians and armchair admirals will want to plunge head-first into the unparalleled **Historic Dockyard,** which brings together a trio of Britain's most storied ships and a smorgasbord of nautical artifacts. Resurrect the past with these floating monuments to Britannia's mastery of the seas—even the staunchest army man can't help but be awed by the history within these hulls. The five galleries of the **Royal Naval Museum** fill in the temporal gaps between the three ships.

MARY ROSE. Henry VIII's *Mary Rose,* holding court in the harbor, is one of England's earliest warships. Henry was particularly fond of her, but, like many of his women, she died before her time, sunk by the French just after setting sail from Portsmouth in July 1545. Not until 1982 was Henry's flagship raised from her watery grave. The eerie, skeletal hulk was sprayed with a preservative mixture, a 15-year process that should make Mary live forever. The Mary Rose Museum displays thousands of artifacts discovered with the ship, including a collection of 168 longbows meant to be used as shipboard weapons.

HMS VICTORY. Napoleon must be rolling in his spacious tomb to know that Nelson's flagship at Trafalgar is still afloat. In this vessel reside the strongest sentiments of British nationalism, from the plaque on the spot where Nelson fell to the flag code display of his memorable statement, "England Expects That Every Man Will Do His Duty." The *Victory* is still a commissioned warship, the oldest in the world, so espionage laws prohibit the taking of pictures on board. *Victory* can only be seen via guided tour—check your admission ticket for your time slot.

HMS WARRIOR. The HMS *Warrior* provides an intriguing companion to its neighbor the *Victory.* The pride of Queen Victoria's navy and the first iron-hulled warship in the world, *Warrior* never saw battle. Nonetheless, the metaphor-challenged Napoleon III called it "The Black Snake among the Rabbits in the Channel."

ACTION STATIONS. Scale walls, navigate enemy seas, pilot a helicopter, and experience other simulated trials of naval fire in this high-tech new addition to the dockyards. The short Omni film *Command Approved,* played continuously, reveals a "typical" day aboard a Type 23 frigate: missiles and bravado fly as the ship engages in an all-out war with evil modern-day island pirates.

OTHER NAVAL SIGHTS. Portsmouth's museums rarely deal with more than the sea and its inhabitants. **Spitbank Fort,** a peculiar man-made island, protected Portsmouth through two World Wars and remains relatively unscathed. Today, it is available as a day tour and, oddly, a swinging party venue by night. *(☎ 9250 4207; www.spitbankfort.co.uk. 25min. crossing from the Dockyard. Tour Apr.-Oct. Su 2:45pm; call Solent Cruises at ☎ 01983 564 602; £6.95, children £5. Pub nights W-Th at 7:30pm, £17. Party Nights F-Sa at 8pm, £25. Book tours in advance.)* The **Royal Navy Submarine Museum** surfaces in Britain's only walk-on submarine, the HMS *Alliance*. The Gosport ferry regularly crosses from the Harbour train station (£1.80); then follow the signs or take bus #9 to Haslar Hospital. (☎9252 9217. *Open daily Apr.-Oct. 10am-5:30pm, Nov.-Mar. 10am-4:30pm, last admission one hr. before closing. £4.50, concessions £3, families £12.*) The **Royal Marines Museum** chronicles the 400 years over which the British Empire was established, teetered, and was lost. It includes a prodigious display of medals, a jungle tour (beware of scorpions), and an animated marine in drag. (☎9281 9385. *Open daily June-July 10am-5pm; Aug.-May 10am-4:30pm. £4.75, seniors £3.50, children £3.25, families £12.*)

THE BEST OF THE REST

SOUTHSEA. The ⬛D-Day Museum, Clarence Esplanade, leads visitors through life-size dioramas of the June 6, 1944 invasion, sharing perspectives from soldiers as well as the families they left behind. It also houses the Overlord Embroidery, a 272 ft. tapestry that chronologically, though somewhat vaguely, depicts events and scenes from the war surrounding the Overlord operation. (☎9282 7261. *Open daily Apr.-Sept. 10am-5:30pm; Oct.-Mar. 10am-5pm. Last admission 30min. before closing. £5, children and students £3, seniors £3.75, families £13. Admission and special events during the D-Day anniversary week £2.50. Audioguide to the embroidery 50p.*) The imposing **Southsea Castle**, built by Henry VIII at the point of the Esplanade, was an active fortress until 1960. Don't miss the secret underground tunnels. (*Open daily Apr.-Sept. 10am-5:30pm, Oct. 10am-5pm. Last admission 30min. before closing. £2.50, concessions £1.50-1.80, families £6.50.*) The **Blue Reef Aquarium** features sting rays, sharks, displays of exotic coral and fish, and a quintet of eccentric otters whose natural charm makes the rest of the sealife jealous for attention. (☎9287 5222. *Open daily May-Sept. 10am-7pm; Oct.-May 10am-5pm. £6, students and seniors £5, children £4, families £18.*)

CHARLES DICKENS BIRTHPLACE MUSEUM. Charles Dickens was born in Portsmouth in 1812; today his birthplace is an uninspired museum. The only authentic Dickensiana are the couch on which he died (transplanted from Kent) and a lock of his hair. (*393 Old Commercial Rd., ¾ mi. north of Portsmouth and Southsea Station. ☎9282 7261. Open daily Apr.-Oct. 10am-5:30pm; Nov.-Dec. and Feb. 7, Dickens's birthday, 10am-5pm. £2.50, students and children £1.50, seniors £1.80, families £6.50.*)

ISLE OF WIGHT ☎01983

Far more tranquil and sun-splashed than its mother island to the north, the Isle of Wight offers travelers stunning scenery, bright sandy beaches, and peaceful family breaks. The Isle has softened the hardest of hearts through the centuries, from Queen Victoria, who reportedly found much amusement here (and little elsewhere), to Karl Marx, who proclaimed the island "a little paradise."

▛ TRANSPORTATION

Ferries: Wightlink (☎0870 582 7744; www.wightlink.co.uk) ferries frequently from: **Lymington** to **Yarmouth** (30min.; 2 per hr.; round-trip £11.20, children £5.60); **Portsmouth Harbour** to **Fishbourne** (round-trip £11.20/£5.60); **Portsmouth Harbour** to **Ryde** (15min., round-trip £13.60/£6.80). **Red Funnel** ferries (☎023 8033 4010) steam from **Southampton** to **East Cowes** (1 per hr., round-trip £9.80). **Hovertravel** (☎811 000; www.hovertravel.co.uk) sails from **Southsea** to **Ryde** (9min., 2 per hr., round-trip £12/£6).

Public Transportation: Train service on the **Island Line** (☎562 492) is limited to the eastern end of the island, including Ryde, Brading, Sandown, Shanklin, and a few points between. **Buses** by **Southern Vectis** (☎532 373; www.svoc.co.uk) cover the entire island; TICs and travel centers (☎827 005) in Cowes, Shanklin, Ryde, and Newport sell the complete timetable (50p). Buy tickets on board. The **Island Rover** ticket gives you unlimited bus travel (1-day £7.50, children £3.75; 2-day £13/£6.50).

Car Rental: South Wight Rentals, 10 Osborne Rd. (☎864 263), in Shanklin, offers free pickup and drop-off. From £25.50 per day. Open daily 8:30am-5:30pm. **Solent Self Drive,** 32 High St. (☎282 050) in Cowes. £28-£41 per day, £165-£270 per week.

✈ 🛈 ORIENTATION AND PRACTICAL INFORMATION

The Isle of Wight is 23 mi. by 13 mi. and shaped like a diamond, with towns clustered along the coasts. **Ryde** and **Cowes** are to the north, **Sandown, Shanklin,** and **Ventnor** lie along the east coast heading south, and **Yarmouth** is on the west coast. The capital, **Newport,** sits in the center, at the source of the **River Medina.**

Tourist Information Centres: Each supplies an individual town map as well as the free *Isle of Wight Official Pocket Guide.* A **general inquiry service** (☎813 800; www.islandbreaks.co.uk) directs questions to one of the seven regional offices listed below—call the above number first. In winter, TICs tend to close earlier than their posted hours. For accommodations, call the central booking line (☎813 813).

Cowes: Fountain Quay (☎291 914), in the alley next to the ferry terminal for RedJet. Open M-Sa 9am-5pm, Su 10am-4pm; during Cowes week (1st week in Aug.) daily 8am-8pm.

Newport: The Guildhall, High St. (☎823 366), signposted from the bus station. Open year-round M-Sa 9:30am-5:30pm, Su 10am-4pm.

Ryde: Western Esplanade (☎562 905), at the corner of Union St., opposite Ryde Pier and the bus station. Open M-Sa 9:30am-5:30pm, Su 10am-4pm.

Sandown: 8 High St. (☎403 886), across from Boots Pharmacy. Open Apr.-Oct. M-Sa 9:30am-5:30pm, Su 10am-4pm. Call the central line for winter hours.

Shanklin: 67 High St. (☎862 942). Open Apr.-Oct. M-Sa 9:30am-5:30pm, Su 10am-4pm. Call the central line for winter hours.

Ventnor: The Coastal Visitor's Centre, Salisbury Gardens, Dudley Rd. (☎85 54 00). Open Apr.-Oct. M-Sa 9:30am-5pm. Call the central line for winter hours.

Yarmouth: The Quay, signposted from ferry (☎813 818). Open Apr.-Oct. M-Sa 9:30am-5:30pm, Su 10am-4pm. Call the central line for winter hours.

Financial Services: Banks can be found in all major town centers. Fill your pockets in the cities; ATMs are rare in smaller towns.

Police: Hampshire Hotline (☎0845 454 545).

Medical Assistance: St. Mary's Hospital (☎524 081), in Newport. Disabled travelers can seek assistance from **Dial Office** (☎522 823).

Internet Access: Ask the local TIC for the nearest location. **Internet Cafe,** 16-18 Melville St. (☎408 294), off High St. by the pier in Sandown, is your best bet for fast service. £1.50 per 15min. Open Tu-Sa 11am-6pm. **Ryde Library** (☎562 170) free for members, and it only takes 5min. to become one. **Lord Louis Library** (☎823 800) in Newport. Free. Book ahead.

Post Office: Post offices are in every town center. **Post Code:** PO30 1AB (Newport).

🏠 ACCOMMODATIONS

Accommodation prices on Wight range from decent to absurd, often depending on proximity to the shore. Budget travelers should try one of the YHA hostels at either end of the island, look into less-visited areas, or try their luck with the **Accommodation Booking Service** (☎813 813). Campsites are plentiful; check the free *Isle of Wight Camping and Touring Guide,* available from all TICs.

▓ **Claverton House,** 12 The Strand, Ryde (☎613 015). Lavishly appointed bedrooms and flower-scented private bathrooms with thick lavender towels could tempt even the most ardent sightseer to spend the day afloat in the tub, but the sea view from the dining room will lure you out again. £60 for 2 nights. Cash only. ❷

▓ **YHA Totland Bay,** Hurst Hill, Totland Bay (☎752 165), on the west end of the island. Take Southern Vectis bus #7 or 7A to Totland War Memorial; turn left up Weston Rd., and take the 2nd left onto Hurst Hill. Comfortable lodgings in a fantastic location—a lucky few even get sea vistas. Lockout 10am-5pm. Curfew 11pm. Open daily May-Aug.; Mar.-Apr. and Sept.-Oct. Tu-Sa. Dorms £11.80; under 18, £8.50. AmEx/MC/V. ❷

Sentry Mead, at the corner of Madeira Rd. and Cliff Rd., Totland Bay (☎753 212; www.sentry-mead.co.uk). One of the island's premier hotels, this tranquil spot has all the draw of a true country hotel. Tastefully decorated lounge and well-kept garden overlooking the Solent offer an ideal setting for relaxation. "Well-behaved dogs" welcome. £50 per person. English breakfast included. Reception 7:30am-midnight. MC/V.❺

YHA Sandown, The Firs, Fitzroy St., Sandown (☎402 651). Signposted from town center; from the train station, take Station Ave. to Fitzroy St. on the right. Clean dorms, kitchen, and large lounge/dining room. Meals £3.60-5.20. Luggage storage and wet-weather shelter available during lockout (10am-5pm). No curfew. Open daily late Mar. to mid-Sept.; mid-Sept. to Dec. and Mar. W-Su. Dorms £11.80, under 18 £8.50. MC/V. ❷

Seaward Guest House, 14-16 George St., Ryde (☎563 168; seaward@FSBDial.co.uk). Near the hovercraft, bus, and train stations. Friendly proprietor offers airy, pastel rooms and hearty breakfasts. Singles £22; doubles and quads £20 per person, ensuite £24. AmEx/MC/V.❷

Wheatsheaf Hotel, St. Thomas Square, Newport, across from the church (☎523 865; www.wheatsheaf-iw.fsnet.co.uk). Classic 17th-century country inn with inviting pub/restaurant downstairs. Dark wood paneled rooms with TV, telephone, and private bath. English breakfast included. Reception 8am-11:30pm. Singles £45; doubles £65. AmEx/MC/V. ❹

Camping: Beaper Farm Camping Site (☎875 184), between Ryde and Sandown; take bus #7. 150 pitches, 24 electricity hookups, showers, and laundry facilities. Open May-Sept. £2.50-4 per person, children £1-1.30. ❶

◖ FOOD

Wanderers on Wight can begin their hunt for food on the local High St. or Esplanade; these commonly named roads often feature uncommonly excellent restaurants. Locally caught fish is a specialty. *The Official Guide to Eating Out,* free and distributed by TICs, offers additional dining options. Most larger cities have supermarkets, and the island harbors nearly one pub per square mile. In Ryde, feast on exquisite gourmet baguettes and pastries ($1.40-4.70) from the **Baguette Factory ❶,** 24 Cross St. (☎611 115. Open M-Sa 8:30am-4pm.) A night out in Sandown calls for a sampling of the decadent Italian dishes ($7.50-17) served at **La Scala ❹,** 26 High St., in a beautiful rustic cellar, its walls thick with wine bottles. (☎403 778. No children. Open daily 6:15-11:30pm.) **S. Fowler & Co. ❷,** 41-43 Union St., Ryde, buzzes with tourists and locals alike, with plenty of meals under $5, including several vegetarian options. (☎812 112. Open daily 10am-midnight. Food served until 10pm.)

◉ ✿ SIGHTS AND FESTIVALS

Wight's natural treasures are especially prominent in the west, with rolling hillsides, multicolored beaches, and the famous Needles; bus #7, 7A, and 7B to Alum Bay catch breathtaking views while whizzing along cliff roads. Zoos specialize in everything from butterflies to dinosaurs to tigers, and one museum is dedicated to the fine art of smuggling. All these sights are listed in the *Official Pocket Guide* (p. 176) and are bound to delight, but don't miss the following must-sees.

▨ **CARISBROOKE CASTLE.** A marvel for castle-chasers everywhere, Carisbrooke includes one of England's most complete early Norman shell-keeps, which has been sitting proudly atop its earthen motte for 900 years. The interiors are a bit touristy, but are not without their own historical trivia: Charles I fled to Carisbrooke in 1647, where he was captured and imprisoned until his execution. Charles didn't accept his fate lying down—visitors climbing through the ruins can still see the window in which the deposed king got stuck while trying to escape. A museum details the structure's history and includes the **Tennyson Room,** with the Victorian poet laureate's hat, desk, cloak, and funeral pall. William the Conqueror's **Chapel of St. Nicholas** has been restored as a WWII memorial and still holds regular services. *(From Newport, with the bus station on your left, follow Upper St. James St., turn right on Trafalgar St., and bear left onto Castle Rd., which becomes Castle Hill. ☎522 107. Open daily Apr.-Sept. 10am-6pm; Oct.-Mar. 10am-4pm. £5, concessions £3.80, children £2.50, families £12.50.)*

OSBORNE HOUSE. Despite its extravagance, with halls full of paintings and statues of Victoria, Albert and the family, this former royal residence showcases a personal side to Queen Victoria's life that we don't often see. Victoria and Prince Albert commissioned it as a "modest" country home and refuge from affairs of state, and took up occasional residence here beginning in 1846. After Albert died in 1861, it became Victoria's retreat; the mementos and family photographs that decorate the home give it an unusually personal touch. The India Exhibit, featuring the elegant **Durbar Room,** is probably the most spectacular, while the recently opened billiard room may appeal to gambling types. In the Horn Room, nearly all of the furniture is made from antlers. **Horse-and-carriage ride** (£2) through the manicured grounds passes the children's Swiss Cottage; free minibuses follow the same route with less grandeur. *(Take Southern Vectis bus #4 or 5 from Ryde or Newport, respectively. ☎200 022. Open daily Apr.-Sept. 10am-5pm; Oct. Su-Th 10am-4pm; Nov.-Mar. by tour only. House and grounds £8.50, concessions £6.40, under 16 £4.30. Grounds only £5/2.50/3.80.)*

ALUM BAY AND THE NEEDLES. Some of Wight's most striking sights predate both Victorians and Normans. On the western tip of the island, the white chalk Needles jut into the sea. Alum's pleasure park distracts from the bay's natural beauty, but a **chairlift** runs down the mosaic-like cliffs to the famous colored beaches—used by resourceful Victorians for paint pigments. *(Take bus #7, 7A, 7B, or 42 to Alum Bay. ☎532 373. Needles Park (☎0870 458 0022; www.theneedles.co.uk) open Apr.-Oct. 10am-5pm; later in August. Free; car park £3; chairlift round-trip £3.25, children £2.25.)*

WALKING, CYCLING, AND FESTIVALS. Walkers and cyclists enjoy the coastal path stretching from **Totland,** past lighthouses both modern and medieval at **St. Catherine's Point,** to **St. Lawrence** at the southern end of the island. Explore the island's 500 mi. of well-maintained footpaths during the annual **Walking Festival** (☎823 310) in mid-May and **Cycling Festival** (☎823 347) in late September, when participants pace along scenic routes or race over strenuous courses. Wight's most fragrant event is the **Garlic Festival,** which takes place for one weekend in late August. Those weary of bland food can expect over 250 stalls selling garlic beer, garlic ice cream, and garlic prawns. *(☎863 566; www.garlicfestival.co.uk.)* Racing ships speed past the coastline in the regatta that takes place during **Cowes Week** in August. *(☎295 744; www.cowesweek.co.uk.)*

WINCHESTER ☎ 01962

Though best known for its dramatic cathedral and as home to wordsmiths Jane Austen and John Keats, Winchester was a political and population center of early medieval England; both Alfred the Great and William the Conqueror deemed it the center of their kingdoms. Monks painstakingly prepared the Domesday Book for William here (p. 71). During the Great Plague of 1665 the town was also temporary court for Charles II. Though its grandest days have passed, Winchester has recently managed to polish some luster into its old walls.

▊ TRANSPORTATION

North of Southampton, Winchester makes an excellent daytrip from **Salisbury,** 25 mi. west, or **Portsmouth,** 27 mi. south.

Trains: Winchester Station, Station Hill, northwest of the city center. Ticket counter open M-F 6am-8:30pm, Sa 6am-7:30pm, Su 7am-8:30pm. Trains (☎ 08457 484 950) from: **Salisbury** (1hr., 2 per hr., £10.30); **Brighton** (1½hr., 1 per hr., £18); **London Waterloo** (1hr., 3-4 per hr., £20); **Portsmouth** (1hr., 1 per hr., £7.30). Be prepared to change trains at Basingstoke or Fareham.

Buses: Buses stop outside on Broadway near Alfred's statue, or inside the **bus station.** Open M 7:30am-5:30pm, Tu-F 8:30am-5:30pm, Sa 8:30am-12:30pm. **National Express** (☎ 08705 808 080) runs from: **London** via **Heathrow** (1½hr., 7 per day, £12); **Oxford** (2½hr., 2 per day, £6.75); **Southampton** (30min., 12 per day, £2.25). **Hampshire Stagecoach** (☎ 01256 464 501) comes from: **Portsmouth** (#69, 1:50hr., 1 per hr., round-trip £5.30) and **Salisbury** (#68/87, 45min., 6 per day, £4). **Explorer** tickets are available for buses in Hampshire and Wiltshire (£6, children £3, seniors £4.20, families £11.25). **Local buses** (☎ 01256 464 501) stop by the bus and train stations, £2.40 for an all-day pass. Ask for a timetable of Winchester buses at the TIC.

Taxis: Francis Taxis (☎ 884 343) by the market. Handicap-accessible cabs available.

▊ ▊ ORIENTATION AND PRACTICAL INFORMATION

Winchester's main (and commercial) axis, **High Street,** stretches from the statue of Alfred the Great at the east end to the arch of **Westgate** opposite. The city's bigger roads stem off High St., which transforms into **Broadway** as you approach Alfred.

Tourist Information Centre: The Guildhall, Broadway (☎ 840 500; www.winchester.gov.uk), across from the bus station. Stocks free maps, seasonal *What's On* guides, and city guides. **Walking tours** £3, children free. Helpful multilingual staff books accommodations for £3 in person or £5 by phone, plus a 10% deposit. Open May-Sept. M-Sa 9:30am-5:30pm, Su 11am-4pm; Oct.-Apr. M-Sa 10am-5pm.

Financial Services: Major **banks** cluster at the junction of Jewry St. and High St. Further down is the **Royal Bank of Scotland,** 67-68 High St. (☎ 863 322). Open M-Tu, Th-F 9:15am-4:45pm, W 10am-4:45pm.

Launderette: 27 Garbett Rd., Winnall (☎ 840 658). Climb Magdalen Hill, turn left on Winnall Manor Rd., and follow until Garbett Rd. on your left. £2.50 per load. Open M-F 8am-8pm, Sa 8am-6pm, Su 10am-6pm. Last wash 1hr. before close.

Pharmacy: Boots, 35-39 High St. (☎ 852 2020). Open M-Th 8:30am-5:30pm, F-Sa 8:30am-5:45pm, Su 10:30am-4:30pm.

Police: North Walls (☎ 08450 454 545), near the intersection with Middle Brook St.

Hospital: Royal Hampshire County, Romsey Rd. (☎ 863 535), at St. James Ln.

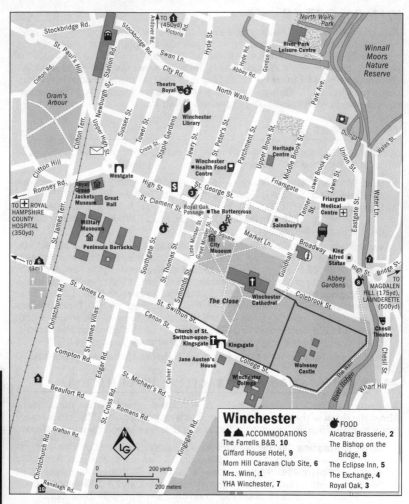

Winchester

♠♣ ACCOMMODATIONS
The Farrells B&B, **10**
Giffard House Hotel, **9**
Morn Hill Caravan Club Site, **6**
Mrs. Winn, **1**
YHA Winchester, **7**

🍴 FOOD
Alcatraz Brasserie, **2**
The Bishop on the Bridge, **8**
The Eclipse Inn, **5**
The Exchange, **4**
Royal Oak, **3**

Internet Access: The **Winchester Library,** Jewry St. (☎853 909). 4 terminals. Free. Open M-Tu and F 9:30am-7pm, W-Th 9:30am-5pm, Sa 9:30am-4pm.

Post Office: 3-4 Upper High St. (☎852 656). Open M-F 8:30am-5:30pm, Sa 9am-12:30pm. **Post Code:** SO23 8UT.

🛏 ACCOMMODATIONS

Winchester's **B&Bs** assemble half a mile southwest of the TIC, near **Ranelagh Road,** at the corner of Christchurch Rd. and St. Cross Rd. Buses #29 and 47 make the journey from the town center twice an hour; #69 runs the same route each hour. Many pubs also offer accommodations, but try to book early. A steady stream of Londoners drives up prices, making Winchester's hostel particularly attractive.

YHA Winchester, 1 Water Ln. (☎08707 706 092). Located in an 18th-century water mill perched atop the rush of the River Itchen. A "simple" hostel, which can mean creative bed arrangements between the mill's roof beams, depending on your room. Kitchen available. Continental breakfast £2.40. Lockout 10am-5pm. Stringent 11pm curfew. Open Mar.-June, Oct. M-Sa; daily July-Sept.; Nov.-Dec. by request due to lack of heat. Dorms £10.60, students £7.60, under 18 £7.20. ❶

The Farrells B&B, 5 Ranelagh Rd. (☎/fax 869 555), off Christchurch Rd., a 10min. walk from town. This 19th-century house feels instantly welcoming, with decades of family photos and vintage Brit-abilia on the wall. £22 per person, with bath £25. ❸

Giffard House Hotel, 50 Christchurch Rd. (☎852 628; www.giffardhotel.co.uk). Leather couches and marble busts adorn the sitting room and conservatory, and a lush red-carpeted staircase leads to luxurious rooms, complete with TVs, private baths, and a chocolate on your pillow. Singles £61; doubles £80-100. ❺

Mrs. Winn, 2 North Hill Close (☎864 926). Comfortable, cheap rooms up the road from the train station. The price of proximity is the dull rumble of coaches. Still, it's tended by hosts with an affection for backpackers and other budget travelers. £15 per person. ❷

Morn Hill Caravan Club Site, Morn Hill (☎869 877), 3 mi. east of Winchester off A31, toward New Forest. Mainly for caravans, so extra facilities are limited. Open Mar.-Nov. Campers £6.20-13.80 per night, tents at warden's discretion; call ahead. ❶

🗆🗹 FOOD AND PUBS

High Street and **Saint George's Street** are home to several food markets, fast-food venues, and tea houses. Restaurants dish out more substantial fare on **Jewry Street,** where you'll find the **Winchester Health Food Centre,** 41 Jewry St. (☎851 113. Open M-F 9:15am-5:45pm, Sa 9am-5:30pm.) If you're looking for **groceries** and fresh food, go to Middle Brook St. off High St., where there is a **Sainsbury's** (☎861 792, open M-Sa 7am-8pm, Su 11am-5pm) and an open-air **market** (Open W-Sa 8am-6pm).

The Eclipse Inn, The Square (☎865 676). Winchester's smallest pub is in a 16th-century rectory the claustrophobic should avoid. Pub grub (£3-7) attracts regulars and, according to tales passed over pints, a ghost or two. Open M-Sa 11am-11pm, Su noon-11pm. Food served daily noon-3pm. ❶

The Bishop on the Bridge, 1 High St. (☎855 111), on the river. Enjoy a meal on the patio or lounge inside on leather chairs. Students flock here and stay into the night. Open Su-Th noon-11pm, F-Sa noon-1am. Food served M-Sa until 9pm, Su until 6pm. ❷

Royal Oak, Royal Oak Passage (☎842 701), next to the Godbegot House off High St. Despite its refurbished gleam, this is yet another pub that claims to be the kingdom's oldest. Descend into the thousand-year-old subterranean foundations and enjoy the locally brewed hogshead cask ale (£1.75) and English cuisine (£4-8). Open daily 11am-11pm. Food served Su-Th noon-9pm, F-Sa noon-7pm. ❶

The Exchange, 9 Southgate St. (☎854 718). The establishment can fill quickly with students and locals, but one can also enjoy the beer garden, tucked away in a quiet corner of the street. Menu includes burgers, sandwiches, and jacket potatoes (all £2-5). Discounts for students and seniors. Open M-Sa 11am-11pm, Su noon-10:30pm. ❷

Alcatraz Brasserie, 24-26 Jewry St. (☎860 047; www.alcatrazuk.com), next to the Theatre Royal. Offers pastas and pizzas (£6-9), as well as innovative salads (£8-9) and meat dishes (£12-17). Marble floors, white tablecloths, and fresh flowers in a quiet setting—perfect for pre-theater. Open M-F 11am-3pm and 6pm-midnight, Sa noon-midnight, Su noon-11pm. ❷

SIGHTS

WINCHESTER CATHEDRAL. Winchester and Canterbury, housing the respective shrines of St. Swithun and St. Thomas Becket, were the two spiritual capitals of medieval England. Winchester cathedral's situation atop peat bogs has forced several reconstructions, rendering the modern structure a stylistic hybrid. Massive Gothic vaults dominate the nave of the longest cathedral in medieval Europe (556 ft.), but the original Norman stonework encloses the transept and accounts for the cathedral's squat and heavy appearance. The oddly Cubist stained glass window is courtesy of Cromwell's window-shattering soldiers. Jane Austen is entombed beneath a humble stone slab in the northern aisle. *(5 The Close. ☎857 200; www.winchester-cathedral.org.uk. Open M-Sa 8:30am-6pm, Su 8:30am-5:30pm. East End closes at 5pm. Suggested donation £3.50, concessions £2.50, children 50p, families £7. Photography permit £2. Free 1hr. tours depart from the west end of the nave daily 10am-3pm on the hour. 1¼hr. tower tours (£3) also available W at 2:15pm, Sa at 11:30am and 2:15pm.)* At the south transept, the lavishly illuminated 12th-century Winchester Bible resides in the **Library,** and the Triforium Gallery contains several relics. *(Open summer M 2pm-4:30pm, Tu-F 11am-4:30pm, Sa 10:30am-4:30pm; winter W and S 11am-3:30pm. £1, concessions 50p, family £2.)* Outside to the south of the cathedral is tiny **St. Swithun's Chapel,** rebuilt in the 16th century, nestled above **Kingsgate.** *(Always open. Free.)*

GREAT HALL. Henry III built his castle here on the remains of a previous fortress of William the Conqueror, and it became a favorite royal haunt. The Great Hall remains, a gloriously intact medieval structure containing a Round Table modeled after King Arthur's. Henry VIII tried to pass the table off as authentic to Holy Roman Emperor Charles V, but the repainted "Arthur," resembling Henry himself, fooled no one. *(At the end of High St. atop Castle Hill. Open daily 10am-5pm. Free.)*

MILITARY MUSEUMS. Through **Queen Eleanor's Garden,** in the Peninsula Barracks, five military museums (the **Royal Hampshire Regiment Museum,** the **Light Infantry Museum,** the **Royal Greenjackets Museum,** the **Royal Hussars Museum,** and the **Gurkha Museum**) tell the stories of several of Britain's great military units. The Royal Greenjackets Museum is the best of the bunch. The heart of the museum is the 276 sq. ft. diorama of the Battle of Waterloo containing 21,500 tiny soldiers and 9600 tiny steeds. *(Between St. James Terr. and Southgate St. ☎828 549. Open M-Sa 10am-1pm and 2-5pm, Su noon-4pm. £2, concessions £1, families £6. Hours for the other 4 museums vary; the Gurkha museum is the only other to charge admission.)*

WOLVESEY CASTLE. Some may find the walk along the river to Wolvesey Castle, once home to the Norman bishop, more enjoyable than the site itself, which has been reduced to barely recognizable remains. The current bishop resides in the newer mansion next door. *(☎252 000. The Close; walk down The Weir on the River Itchen or down to the end of College St. Open daily Apr.-Oct. 10am-5pm. Free.)*

CITY MUSEUM. Galleries of archeological finds, town models, photographs, and interactive exhibits introduce Winchester's past. It began as the Roman city of Venta Bulgarum, then became the capital of Anglo-Saxon England and then a later medieval center for the international textile trade. The Roman gallery includes a rare complete floor mosaic from the local ruins of a Roman villa, and the Anglo-Saxon room holds the 10-century tomb of one of King Cnut's men. *(☎848 269. At Great Minster St. and The Square. Open Apr.-Oct. M-Sa 10am-5pm, Su noon-5pm; Nov.-Mar. Tu-Sa 10am-4pm, Su noon-4pm. Free. 1hr. audio guide £2, under 16 free.)*

WALKS. The Buttercross, standing at 12 High St., is a good starting point for any of several walking routes through town. The statue, portraying St. John, William of Wykeham, and King Alfred, derives its name from the shadow it cast over the 15th-century market to keep butter cool. An ideal walk is along the **River Itchen,** the same taken by poet John Keats; directions and his "Ode To Autumn" are available at the TIC (50p). For a view of the city, including the Wolvesey ruins, climb to **Saint Giles's Hill Viewpoint** at sunset. Pass the Mill and take Bridge St. to the gate marked Magdalen Hill; follow the paths up from there. *The Winchester Walk,* detailing the various possible walking tours of Winchester, is available for 60p at the TIC.

🎭 ENTERTAINMENT AND FESTIVALS

Weekends attract hordes of revelers to bars along **Broadway** and **High Street.** In all its Edwardian glory, **Theatre Royal,** Jewry St. (☎840 440; www.theatre-royal-winchester.co.uk), hosts regional companies and concerts. Late May features the **Homelands Music Festival.** Though it can't compare with Glastonbury's summer music orgy, it draws big names in rock every year. Acquire tickets from the TIC. In early July, the **Hat Fair** (☎849 841; www.hatfair.co.uk), the longest running street theater festival in Britain, fills a weekend with free theater and peculiar headgear.

📷 DAYTRIPS FROM WINCHESTER

🏛 AUSTEN'S COTTAGE

Take Hampshire bus X64 (M-Sa 11 per day, round-trip £5.30), or London and Country bus #65 on Su, from Winchester. Ask to be let off at the Chawton roundabout and follow the brown signs. ☎/fax 01420 83262. Open Mar.-Nov. 11am-4pm., Dec.-Feb. Sa-Su 11am-4pm. £4, students £3, children 50p.

Jane Austen lived in the unassuming village of **Chawton,** 15 mi. northeast of Winchester, from 1809 to 1817. Visitors have come in droves since the recent cinematic fad for adaptations of her novels. It was here, at a tiny wooden table in the dining room of an ivy covered "cottage," that Lizzie Bennett, Emma Woodhouse, and their respective suitors were brought to life. You can still hear the creaking door that warned Austen to hide her writing amid her needlework. Personal letters belongings, and first editions of her books adorn the walls and fill the bookcases.

THE NEW FOREST

20 mi. southwest of Winchester. Take bus #47 to Southampton (round-trip £5) and transfer to bus #56 or 56A to Lyndhurst (round-trip £5.40 or catch a train to Southampton and then a bus to Lyndhurst. ☎023 8028 3444; www.thenewforest.co.uk. Museum open daily 10am-5pm; Aug. until 6pm. £3, children £2, seniors £2.50, families £8.

England's newest National Park was William the Conqueror's 145 sq. mi. personal hunting ground and remains, 1000 years later, an idyllic example of rural England. Wild ponies, donkeys, and deer wander freely alongside winding roads, and the forest is dotted with tiny towns. The **Rufus Stone** (near Brook and Cadnam) marks the spot where William's son was accidentally slain. For the young, pony rides are a popular activity; for the young at heart, pretend to be a cowboy at **Burley Villa Riding School** in New Milton, which offers 2hr. "western riding" tours (☎01425 610 278). The **Museum and Visitor Centre** in Lyndhurst, the forest's largest town, has a list of campsites and other accommodations. Though one can wander into the woods a mere 10min. away, the forest demands a multi-day stay.

SOUTH ENGLAND

Refugee Immigration and the Channel Tunnel

When the $15 billion Channel Tunnel ("Chunnel") was completed in 1994, it was hailed as a tremendous advance in Europe's infrastructure. No longer would ferries or airplanes be needed to cross between England and France—the English Channel could be traversed in a mere 20 minutes. However, it turns out that the Chunnel serves as the most convenient route not only for cargo, but also for refugees who are desperate to find a way onto British soil.

Soon after its completion, refugees from Eastern Europe, the Middle East, and Central Asia began to mass on the French side of the Chunnel, hoping for passage to England. Britain has a well-deserved reputation for being the most hospitable nation in Europe to those fleeing their homes, providing shelter and food vouchers while considering applications for asylum. English is also the only foreign language many refugees know.

For many refugees, the journey begins by paying smugglers to secure passage to the tiny French town of Sangatte, unofficial waiting site for the men hoping to make the hazardous journey to England. (Those who attempt the crossing are almost entirely young males.) Often, they have forfeited their life savings to ride in the backs of trucks—or, if they are lucky, in private cars—across Europe to Sangatte. There they are greeted by Red Cross workers who supervise the camp, providing food and, more often than not, encouragement. Marc Gentilini, president of the French Red Cross, defends his organization's role: "These people have traveled thousands of miles to get here, and it is impossible to make them believe they can't go the last 32 miles."

Refugees pay smugglers for tips on the best ways of getting through the Chunnel—either by hitching rides on freight trains or, more dangerously, on the outside of the Eurostar, which can reach speeds up to 180 mph. They must sneak over fences and past security guards, then onto the trains by sprinting after them or leaping from an overpass. Hidden in the trucks carried on freight trains, on metal ledges under the body of the carriage, or on the sloping roofs of passenger cars, they wait for the train to arrive in England, where they can turn themselves over to the police and ask for asylum. Those who make it must face British social services, waiting in limbo while they apply for asylum. If they are approved, they commonly face xenophobia during the search for positions for which they are overqualified. (Those who can afford a smugglers' passage are often successful professionals or students who end up working in restaurants or as manual labor.)

In November 2001, in an effort to stem the tide of refugees, the French rail service reduced by two-thirds the number of freight trains it sent through the Chunnel. A $9 million investment to improve security, including electric fences and more security personnel, has had some effect—50,000 would-be immigrants were apprehended in 2001. Nevertheless, there is still enough chance of success that people keep trying, occasionally planning mass invasions of the trainyards to overwhelm security forces. As long as the Chunnel affords some hope for a new life, refugees will continue to make their way across by whatever means possible. Despite all the difficulties, England provides a safe haven, far from the wars, political repression, and persecution many of them are fleeing. As Shewan, a migrant from northern Iraq who arrived in England a few years ago, plainly stated, "I feel safe in England. Here I am sure of my life. I know I'm going to stay alive."

Sarah Kerman holds a degree in Literature from Harvard University. She has done some freelance writing and has worked as a writing tutor at the Johns Hopkins Center for Talented Youth.

SOUTHWEST ENGLAND

Idiosyncratic legend and land form the foundation of England's southwest—the counties of Dorset, Devon, Somerset, and Cornwall. King Arthur was allegedly born at Tintagel on Cornwall's northern coast and is said to have battled Mordred on Bodmin Moor. One hamlet purports to be the site of Camelot, another the resting place of the Holy Grail, and no fewer than three small lakes are identified as the grave of Arthur's sword, Excalibur. In a more modern myth, the ghost of Sherlock Holmes still pursues the Hound of the Baskervilles across Dartmoor. Over the years, the southwest has provided refuge for several distinct peoples, whose legacies still float in friendly harbors, kick up along dusty, weathered hiking paths, and make themselves felt in both cuisine and culture. Cornwall was the last stronghold of the Celts in England, while stone circles and excavated artifacts of even older Neolithic communities remain. Farther east, landmarks chronicle other eras, from Salisbury's medieval cathedral and Bath's Roman spas to enigmatic Stonehenge and the fossils of Dorset's Jurassic Coast.

HIGHLIGHTS OF SOUTHWEST ENGLAND

STONEHENGE Puzzle over one of history's most astounding engineering feats and one of the world's great mysteries (p. 191).

BATH Dally in the world of 18th-century pleasure-seekers who rebuilt this Roman spa town with elegant buildings and improper behavior (p. 193).

CHANNEL ISLANDS Explore a world caught halfway between Britain and France, where a Continental feel pervades a world far from anywhere (p. 254).

TRANSPORTATION IN SOUTHWEST ENGLAND

It tends to be easier to get to Somerset, Avon, and Wiltshire than regions farther southwest. **Trains** (☎08457 484 950) offer fast service from London and the north. The region's primary east-west line from **London Paddington** passes through **Taunton** (£41), **Exeter** (£45), and **Plymouth** (£49), ending at **Penzance** (£57). Frequent trains connect London to **Bath, Bristol,** and **Salisbury.** Branch lines connect **St. Ives, Newquay, Falmouth,** and **Barnstaple** to the network. A variety of rail **Rover passes** can be used in the region: the **Freedom of the Southwest Rover** covers Cornwall, Devon, Somerset, and parts of Avon and Dorset (8 days out of 15 £61). The **Devon Rail Rover** is bounded by and includes travel on the Taunton-Exmouth line on the east and the Gunnislake-Plymouth line in the west (3 days out of 7 £24, 8 out of 15 £39.50). The **Cornish Rail Rover** is bounded by the Gunnislake-Plymouth line (£18/£33).

 Buses can be few and far between. **National Express** (☎08705 808 080) runs to major points along the north coast via **Bristol** and to points along the south coast (including **Penzance**) via **Exeter** and **Plymouth.** For journeys within the region, local buses routes are usually less expensive and farther-reaching than trains. **First** is the largest bus company in the area. The comprehensive **Traveline** service (☎0870 608 2608; open daily 7am-5pm) can help plan travel to any destination. **Explorer** and **Day Rambler** tickets (£6, concessions £4.25, families £12.50) allow

185

unlimited travel on all buses within one region. The **Corridor Ticket** (£2.50, children £1.50; £1 more before 8:45am) allows unlimited travel between two points on any route. When traveling to multiple destinations on one route, start at one end and ask the driver for a Corridor ticket to the end of the line, and for the day you'll have unlimited access to all the towns in between. Many tourist destinations are only served by trains and buses seasonally. For off-season transport (Oct.-May), phone Traveline to check routes and schedules.

▨ ⚠ HIKING AND OUTDOORS

Distances between towns in southwest England are so short that you can travel through the region on your own steam. The narrow roads and hilly landscape can make biking difficult, but hardy cyclists will find the quiet lanes and country paths rewarding. Bring along a large-scale Ordnance Survey map (available at TICs; £7) and a windbreaker to shield you from foul weather.

The 630 mi. **South West Coast Path,** England's longest coastal path, originates in Somerset (at Minehead, in Exmoor National Park) and passes through North Devon, Cornwall, and South Devon, ending in Dorset (Poole). Winding past cliffs, caves, beaches, and resorts, it takes several weeks to walk in its entirety. However, as it passes through many towns, is accessible by bus, and features B&Bs and hostels at manageable intervals, so it's perfect for shorter hikes. Many rivers intersect the path, some requiring ferries—check times carefully to avoid being stranded. Some sections of the trail are difficult even for ambitious hikers, so consult tourist offices before you begin. Most TICs sell guides and Ordnance Survey maps covering appropriate sections of the path, which is generally smooth enough to cover by **bike;** rental shops can often suggest three- to seven-day cycling routes.

The path is divided into four parts. The **Somerset and North Devon Coastal Path** extends from Minehead through Exmoor National Park to Bude. The least arduous section, it features the highest cliffs in southwest England and passes the 100 ft. dunes of Saunton Sands and the steep cobbled streets of Clovelly on Hartland Point. The **Cornwall Coast Path,** with some of the most rugged stretches, starts in Bude, where magnificent Cornish cliffs harbor a vast range of birds and marine life, rounds the southwest tip of Britain, and continues along the coast to Plymouth. The **South Devon Coast Path** runs from Plymouth to Paignton, tracing spectacular cliffs, wide estuaries, and remote bays set off by lush vegetation and wildflowers. The final section, the **Dorset Coast Path,** picks up in Lyme Regis and runs to Poole Harbor. For more information, contact the **South West Coast Path Association** (☎01752 896 237) or any local TIC.

WILTSHIRE

SALISBURY ☎01722

A city of busy commercial avenues that suddenly give way to winding back lanes, Salisbury itself is an attraction. Town life spirals outward from the market, overlooked by the towering cathedral spire as it has for centuries. A quick glance down any street reveals facades from the Middle Ages to the industrial period. Meanwhile on the windy plain nearby, awe-inspiring Stonehenge stands its lonely vigil.

Southwest England

TO CHANNEL ISLANDS (see inset)

TO GUERNSEY (80mi), JERSEY (90mi)

Swindon

A4

Avebury

North Wessex Downs

WILTSHIRE

Stonehenge

Old Sarum

Salisbury

A338

R. Avon

A343

Bournemouth

Brownsea

R. Stour

A31

Swanage

Wilton House

A354

Blandford Forum

Poole

Durlston Head

Bath

M4

A350

Frome

Stourhead

A350

Wareham

Corfe Castle

AVON

Cheddar

Cheddar Showcaves

Wookey Hole

Wells

Shaftesbury

Cranborne Chase

DORSET

Dorchester

A35

Weymouth

Isle of Portland

A371

SOMERSET

Glastonbury

Street

R. Brue

Sherborne

A37

Yeovil

Axminster

A35

Lyme Regis

Bristol

R. Severn

Cardiff

WALES

A37

R. Parrett

M5

Lyme Bay

English Channel

Bridgewater

Taunton

A358

Watchet

Minehead

Dunster

A396

Porlock

EXMOOR NATIONAL PARK

R. Exe

M5

Exmouth

Babbacombe Bay

Bristol Channel

Lynton

Lynmouth

A39

A361

Taw

Tiverton

Exeter

Moretonhampstead

Bovey Tracey

Torquay

Paignton

Brixham

Start Bay

Start Point

Morte Point

Ilfracombe

Barnstaple

Castle Drogo

A382

DARTMOOR NATIONAL PARK

Buckland Abbey

A386

Okehampton

DEVON

Tavistock

Yelverton

Plymouth

Cawsand

Bigbury Bay

Bideford

Hartland Point

Clovelly

Tamar

A30

Gunnislake

A38

Whitesand Bay

TO SANTANDER & ROSCOFF

Bude

A39

Boscastle

Tintagel

Camelford

Bodmin Moor

Looe

Polperro

Tintagel Head

Bodmin

Fowey

St. Austell

Dodman Point

Padstow

Newquay

CORNWALL

Truro

Eden Project

St. Agnes Head

Falmouth

Falmouth Bay

Coverack

PENWITH PENINSULA

St. Ives

A30

Helston

The Lizard Peninsula

Morvah

Zennor

St. Just

Penzance

Minack Theater

The Lizard

Sennen Cove

Porthcurno

Land's End

Channel Islands

English Channel

Alderney

Guernsey

Herm

St. Peter Port

Sark

Jersey

St. Hélier

Gorey

TO FRANCE

TO WEYMOUTH

TO POOLE

25 miles

25 kilometers

0

0

10 miles

10 kilometers

SOUTHWEST ENGLAND

▛ TRANSPORTATION

Trains: Station on S. Western Rd., west of town across the River Avon. Ticket office open M-Sa 5:30am-8pm, Su 7:30am-8:45pm. Trains (☎08457 484 950) from most major towns, including: **London Waterloo** (1½hr., 2 per hr., £22-30); **Portsmouth and Southsea** (1½hr., 2 per hr., £11.50); **Southampton** (40min., every hr., £6); **Winchester** (1hr., 2 per hour, £11).

Buses: Station at 8 Endless St. (☎336 855). Open M-F 8:15am-5:30pm, Sa 8:15am-5:15pm. **National Express** (☎08705 808 080) runs from **London** (3hr., 3 per day, £13). Buy tickets at the TIC. **Wilts and Dorset** (☎336 855) runs from **Bath** (#X4, 1 per hr. M-Sa 8am-4pm, £3). An **Explorer** ticket is good for a day's worth of travel on **Wilts and Dorset** buses and some **Hampshire, Provincial, Solent Blue,** and **Brighton & Hove** buses (£6, concessions £4.20, children £3, families £11.50).

Taxis: Cabs cruise by the train station. **505050 Value Cars** (☎505 050) runs 24hr.

Bike Rental: Hayball Cycles, 26-30 Winchester St. (☎411 378). £10 per day, £2.50 overnight, £60 per week; deposit £25. Open M-Sa 9am-5:30pm. For routes and services call the **Walking and Cycling Hotline** (☎623 255).

▟ PRACTICAL INFORMATION

Tourist Information Centre: Fish Row (☎334 956; www.visitsalisbury.com), Guildhall, in Market Sq. National Express ticket service. Books rooms for a 10% deposit. Open June-Sept. M-Sa 9:30am-6pm, Su 10:30am-4:30pm; Oct.-May M-Sa 9:30am-5pm. **City tours** leave Apr.-Oct. 11am and 8pm; June-Aug. 6pm; 1½hr.; £2.50, children £1.

Financial Services: Banks are easily found. **Thomas Cook,** 18-19 Queen St. (☎313 500). Open M-Tu and Th-Sa 9am-5:30pm, W 10am-5:30pm.

Launderette: Washing Well, 28 Chipper Ln. (☎421 874). Open M-Sa 8:30am-5:30am. Wash £3.00, dry £1.40.

Pharmacy: Boots, 51 Silver St. (☎333 233). Open M, Tu 8:45am-5:30pm; W 9am-5:30pm; Th 8:45am-5:30pm; F, Sa 8am-5:30pm; Su 10:30am-4:30pm.

Police: Wilton Rd. (☎411 444).

Internet Access: Starlight Internet Cafe, 1 Endless St. (☎349 359) at Market Sq. £1 per 15min. Open M-Sa 9:30am-8pm, Su 11am-5pm. Also at **YHA Salisbury** (p. 188).

Post Office: 24 Castle St. (☎08457 223 344), at Chipper Ln. **Bureau de change.** Open M-Sa 9am-5:30pm. **Post Code:** SP1 1AB.

▛ ACCOMMODATIONS

Salisbury's proximity to a certain stone circle breeds numerous guesthouses, mostly starting at around £35 per person—ask for an accommodations guide from the TIC. They tend to fill quickly in summer.

YHA Salisbury, Milford Hill House, Milford Hill (☎327 572). Tucked into a cedar grove on the edge of town with 70 beds, 4 kitchenettes, TV lounge, Internet access (£2.50 per 30min.), and cafeteria. Lockout 10am-1pm. The first place to fill in summer; make a reservation. Breakfast included. Dorms £14.90, under 18 £11.60. MC/V. ❷

Matt and Tiggy's, 51 Salt Ln. (☎327 443), up the street from the bus station. A welcoming 450 year-old home with warped floors and ceiling beams, and an overflow house nearby; both are very convenient. Mellow, hostel-style, 2-, 3-, and 4-person rooms; no bunk beds. £3 breakfast deal at Crosskeys restaurant. Dorms £12. Cash only. ❷

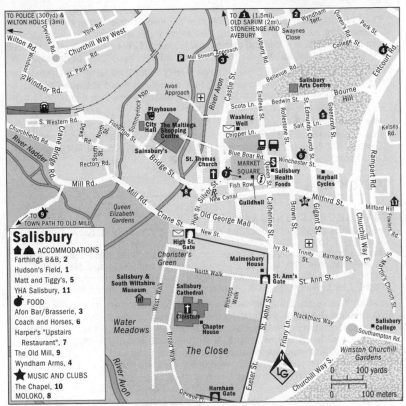

Salisbury

▲▲ ACCOMMODATIONS
Farthings B&B, **2**
Hudson's Field, **1**
Matt and Tiggy's, **5**
YHA Salisbury, **11**
🍴 FOOD
Afon Bar/Brasserie, **3**
Coach and Horses, **6**
Harper's "Upstairs Restaurant", **7**
The Old Mill, **9**
Wyndham Arms, **4**
★ MUSIC AND CLUBS
The Chapel, **10**
MOLOKO, **8**

Farthings B&B, 9 Swaynes Close (☎330 749). A peaceful haven with a gorgeous garden, just a 10min. walk from the city center. May-Sept. singles £27; doubles £55. Oct.-Apr. singles £25; doubles £46; discount for long stays. Cash only. ❸

Camping: Hudson's Field, Castle Rd. (☎320 713). Between Salisbury and Stonehenge, 20min. from city center. Clean and well located. Vehicle curfew 11pm. £4-6. MC/V. ❶

🍴🍽 FOOD AND PUBS

Even jaded pub dwellers can find a pleasing venue among Salisbury's 60-odd watering holes. Most serve food ($4-6) and many offer free live music. **Market Square** in the town center fills on Tuesdays and Saturdays, with vendors hawking everything from peaches to posters. (Open 7am-4pm.) A **Sainsbury's** is at The Maltings. (☎332 282. Open M-Th 8am-8pm, F 8am-9pm, Sa 7:30am-7pm, Su 10am-4pm.)

🍴 **Harper's "Upstairs Restaurant,"** 6-7 Ox Rd., Market Sq. (☎333 118). Inventive English and international dishes (£6-10) make a hearty meal. Try the "Early Bird" dinner (2 generous courses; £8.50 before 8pm). Open M-F noon-2pm and 6-9:30pm, Sa noon-2pm and 6-10pm; June-Sept. also Su 6-9pm. AmEx/MC/V. ❷

🍴 **Coach and Horses,** 39 Winchester St. (☎414 319). Meals (£7-14) and drinks flow nonstop, drawing families during the day and a louder crowd at night to what may be Salisbury's oldest pub, open since 1382. Open M-Sa 11am-11pm. MC/V. ❶

The Old Mill, Town Path (☎327 517), atop the River Nadder at the end of a scenic 15min. stroll along Town Path through the Harnem Water Meadows. The ideal setting for an outdoor drink or a long pub dinner (£12-16) in the 12th-century mill building. Open M-Sa 11am-11pm, Su noon-10:30pm; food served daily noon-2pm, 7-9pm. MC/V. ❷

Afon Bar & Brasserie, Mill Stream Approach (☎552 366), off Castle St. Light lunches (£4-13) and romantic dinners (£10-17) for the smartly-dressed at this mellow spot on the River Avon. Show theater tickets for a free bottle of wine with dinner (M-Th 6:30-7:30pm). Open Tu-Th 11-3pm, 6-11:30pm. ❸

Wyndham Arms, 25 Estcourt Rd. (☎331 026), at the intersection with College St. This loud after-work pub is a perfect place to bump elbows with the locals and down several pints of Hop Back (£2), the renowned and savory local ale. Open M-Th 4:30pm-11pm, F 3-11pm, Sa noon-10pm, Su noon-10:30pm. ❶

◉ SIGHTS

▧ SALISBURY CATHEDRAL

☎555 120. Cathedral open June-Aug. M-Sa 7:15am-8:15pm, Su 7:15am-6:15pm; daily Sept.-May 7:15am-6:15pm. Chapter House open June-Aug. M-Sa 9:30am-5:30pm, Su noon-5:30pm; daily Sept.-May 9:30am-5:30pm. Free tours May-Oct. M-Sa 9:30am-4:45pm, Su 4-6:15pm; Nov.-Feb. M-Sa 10am-4pm. 1½hr. roof and tower tours May-Sept. M-Sa 11am, 2, 3pm; Su 4:30pm. June-Aug. M-Sa also 6:30pm; winter hours vary, so call ahead. £3.80, concessions £3.30, children £2. Roof and tower tour £3, concessions £2.

Salisbury Cathedral, built between 1220 and 1258, rises from its grassy close to a neck-breaking height of 404 ft. as medieval England's highest spire. Its monumental size and ornamental intricacy make the overall visual effect stunning. Built in just 38 years, the cathedral features a singular and weighty design. The bases of the marble pillars bend inward under the strain of 6400 tons of limestone. Nearly 700 years have left the building in need of repair, and scaffolding shrouds parts of the outer walls where the stone is disintegrating. Once inside, head to the wooden tomb of William Longespee, Earl of Salisbury (d. 1226). The chapel houses the oldest functioning mechanical clock, a strange collection of wheels and ropes that has ticked 500 million times over the last 600 years. A tiny stone figure rests in the nave—legend has it that either a boy bishop is entombed on the spot or that it covers the heart of Richard Poore, founder of the cathedral. The incongruously abstract window at the eastern end is dedicated to prisoners of conscience. The best preserved of the four surviving copies of the Magna Carta rests in the **Chapter House** and is still legible (to those who can read medieval Latin). Ask a guide for a complete list of the relief figures in the stunningly detailed friezes.

SALISBURY AND SOUTH WILTSHIRE MUSEUM. The museum houses a mixture of artwork ranging from Turner's watercolors to articles of period fashion and doll houses. The worthwhile Stonehenge exhibit divulges an extensive amount of history. (65 The Close, along the West Walk. ☎332 151. Open July-Aug. M-Sa 10am-5pm, Su 2-5pm; Sept.-June M-Sa 10am-5pm. £4, concessions £3, under 16 £1.50, families £9.50.)

▣ ▧ NIGHTLIFE AND FESTIVALS

The sign outside **The Chapel,** 30 Milford St., states in clear mathematical terms that, as far as dress, "no effort=no entry." Don't wear jeans, tattoos, steel toe-caps or offensive T-shirts, and you might be admitted to the three huge dance floors at a club that advertises itself as one of the UK's best. (☎504 255; www.thechapelnightclub.co.uk. Cover W £2; Th £4, ladies free; F £8, £4 if you're from out of town; Sa £10. Open W 10:30pm-2:30am, Th 10:30pm-2:30am, F-Sa 10:30pm-3am.) **MOLOKO,** 5

Bridge St., is a chain bar, but still one of the most popular in town. Choose from an endless list of vodkas (£2.50-4.50), but try not to spill—up to 200 people pack the tiny space on weekends. (☎507 050. M-Sa noon-midnight, Su 3pm-10:30pm.)

Salisbury's repertory theater company puts on shows at the **Playhouse**, Malthouse Ln., over the bridge off Fisherton St. (☎320 333. Box office open daily 10am-7pm. Tickets £8.50-17; concessions £2 off. Half-price tickets available same day. The **Salisbury Arts Centre**, Bedwin St., offers music, theater, and exhibitions year-round. (☎321 744. Box office open Tu-Sa 10am-4pm. Tickets from £5.) Summertime sees free Sunday **concerts** in various parks; call the TIC for info. The **Salisbury Festival** features dance exhibitions, music, and wine-tasting for two weeks in late May and early June. Contact the Festival Box Office at the Playhouse or the TIC for a program. (☎320 333; www.salisburyfestival.co.uk. Tickets from £2.50.)

🏛 DAYTRIPS FROM SALISBURY

🏛 STONEHENGE

Wilts and Dorset (☎336 855) runs several buses, including daily service from the Salisbury train station (#3, 40min., round-trip £5.25). The first bus leaves Salisbury at 8:45am (Su 10:35am), and the last leaves Stonehenge at 6:20pm (Su 6:55pm). An Explorer ticket (£6) is cheaper than a Salisbury-Stonehenge round-trip; it allows travel all day on any bus, including those stopping by Avebury, Stonehenge's less-crowded cousin (p. 192), and Old Sarum (p. 192). Wilts and Dorset also runs a tour bus from Salisbury (3 per day, £7.50-15). ☎01980 624 715. Open daily June-Aug. 9am-7pm; mid-Mar. to May and Sept. to mid-Oct. 9:30am-6pm; mid-Oct. to mid-Mar. 9:30am-4pm. £5.20, concessions £3.90, children £2.60, families £13.

A half-ruined ring of colossi amid swaying grass and indifferent sheep, Stonehenge has been battered for millennia by the winds whipping across the flat Salisbury plain. The 22 ft. high stones visible today comprise the fifth temple constructed on the site—Stonehenge, it seems, was already ancient in ancient times. The first arrangement probably consisted of an arch and circular earthwork furrowed in 3050 BC that was in use for about 500 years. Its relics are the **Aubrey Holes** (white patches in the earth) and the **Heel Stone** (the rough block standing outside the circle). The next monument used about 60 stones imported from Wales around 2100 BC and marked astronomical directions. The present shape, once a complete circle, dates from about 1500 BC.

The tremendous effort and innovation required to transport and erect the 45-ton stones makes Stonehenge an incomparable monument to human endeavor. As a religious site, it has lain fallow since the Bronze Age, and over the centuries some of the stones have been removed to other building projects. Celtic druids, whose ceremonies took place in forests, did not worship here, but in an era of religious freedom, modern druids claim the site for their own, and are permitted to enter Stonehenge on the summer Solstice to perform ceremonial exercises. In past years, however, new-age mystics have beaten them to the spot; in 1999 this led to conflict with the police and eventual arrests. Recent celebrations have proved considerably more peaceful.

Admission to Stonehenge includes a 30min. audio tour that uses handsets. The effect may be more haunting than the rocks themselves—a bizarre march of tourists who appear engaged in phone calls. Nonetheless, the tour is helpful, and includes arguments between a shepherd and his mother about the stones' origins. English Heritage also offers free guided tours (30min.). From the roadside or from Amesbury Hill, 1½ mi. up the A303, you can get a free, if distant, view of the stones. There are also many walks and trails that pass by; ask at the Salisbury TIC.

OLD SARUM. Old Sarum gets around; it evolved from a Bronze Age gathering place into a Celtic fortress, which was won by the Romans, taken by the Anglo-Saxons, and then the Normans before finally falling into the hands of the British Heritage Society. Civilization left Old Sarum in the 14th century when the church built a new cathedral on the Salisbury plain below, leaving stone ruins of the earlier town strewn across the windswept hill. A detailed crop circle appears annually in the wheat fields below. *(Off the A345, 2 mi. north of town. Buses #3 and 6-9 run every 15min. from Salisbury. ☎975 0700. Open daily Apr.-June 10am-5pm; July-Aug. 9am-6pm; Sept. 10am-5pm; Nov.-Feb. 11am-3pm; Mar. 10am-4pm. £2.80, concessions £2.10, children £1.40.)*

STOURHEAD. When elaborately feathered peacocks casually cross your path, isolated bits of classical sculpture are scattered across the landscape, and the views are unspoiled by any sign of civilization, it is hard to believe you aren't dreaming. Once the estate of a wealthy English banking family, this 18th-century landscape garden consists of carefully proportioned natural and architectural beauty. The garden comes complete with lakes, waterfalls, and stately pleasure domes (18th-century miniature reproductions of Greek temples). *(Trains run to Gillingham station from Salisbury (25 min., every hour, £4). Bus #58A runs between Gillingham station and Stourhead, but service is infrequent. ☎01747 841 152. Open late Mar. to late Sept. M-Tu and F-Su 11am-5pm; Oct. M-Tu and F-Su 11am-4:30pm. Last admission 30min. before close. Garden and house £9.40, children £4.50, families £22.)*

WILTON HOUSE. Declared by James I to be "the finest house in the land," the home of the earls of Pembroke is the quintessential aristocratic country home and setting for numerous films, including *Sense and Sensibility* and *The Madness of King George*. The ornate state apartments resemble Windsor Castle (p. 262), and the grounds are vast and open. The impressive art collection includes the largest assortment of Van Dycks in the world and Rembrandt's celebrated portrait of his mother, which was stolen in 1994 and discovered two years later in the trunk of a London car. Adjoining buildings provide exhibits on domestic arts and on D-Day—the house was an allied headquarters. *(3mi. west of Salisbury on the A30; take bus #60 or 61 (M-Sa every 15min., Su 1 per hr.) ☎746 720; www.wiltonhouse.com. Open daily Mar. 24-Oct. 30 10:30am-5:30pm; last admission 4:30pm. House and grounds £9.75, concessions £8, children £5.50, families £24. Grounds and video only £4.50, children £3.50, family £24.)*

AVEBURY   ☎01672

The tiny village that has grown up within the **stone circle** at Avebury lends an intimate feel to this site, a far cry from the sightseeing mobs storming Stonehenge. Visitors can amble among the megaliths and even picnic in their midst or nap on the soft grass. Dating from 2500 BC, Avebury's sprawling titans are older and larger than their favored cousins at Stonehenge. Built over the course of centuries, the circle has remained true to its original form and a mystery to the archaeologists, mathematicians, and astronomers who have studied it so stubbornly. Just outside the ring, curious and mysterious **Silbury Hill** rises from the ground. Europe's largest manmade mound has stumped researchers; its date of origin, 2660 BC, was only determined by the serendipitous excavation of a flying ant.-Buses #5 and 6 (2 hr., 5 per day, £3.90) run from Salisbury. The **Alexander Keiller Museum** details the history of the stone circle and its environs. (☎539 250. Open daily Apr.-Oct. 10am-6pm; Nov.-Mar. 10am-4pm. £2.50.) **The Circle Restaurant ❷**, just beside the museum, serves sandwiches, soups, and desserts for £3-6. Locate the Avebury **Tourist Information Centre** by following the signs from the bus stop through the carpark. (☎539 425. Open W-Sa 10am-5pm, Su 10am-4pm.)

BEST DAY EVER. It is possible to see Stonehenge, Avebury (p. 192), and Old Sarum (p. 192) in one day—if you get an early start. Head out to Stonehenge on the 8:45am or 10:00am bus, then catch the 11:20am or 12:20pm bus to Amesbury and transfer to an Avebury bus. Take the 2 or 3pm bus back from Avebury and finally, stop off in Old Sarum before you reach Salisbury. Grab a bus timetable from the friendly TIC, and be sure to buy the £6 Explorer ticket.

SOMERSET AND AVON

BATH   ☎ 01225

A place of pilgrimage and architectural masterwork, Bath has been a must-see for travelers since AD 43. The Romans built an elaborate complex of baths to house the curative waters at the town they called Aquae Sulis. In 1701, Queen Anne's trip to the hot springs reestablished the city as a prominent meeting place for artists, politicians, and intellectuals. Bath quickly became a social capital second only to London, its scandalous scene immortalized by authors such as Jane Austen and Charles Dickens. Though damaged in WWII, the city has been painstakingly restored so that today's thoroughfares remain impeccably elegant, with shops and salons laced seamlessly into the fabric of its Georgian architecture.

◧ TRANSPORTATION

Trains: Bath Spa Station, Dorchester St., at the south end of Manvers St. Ticket office open M-Sa 5:45am-8:30pm, Su 8:45am-8:30pm. Travel center open M-F 8am-7pm, Sa 9am-6pm, Su 9:30am-6pm. **Trains** (☎ 08457 484 950) from: **Birmingham** (2hr., every hr., £27); **Bristol** (15min., 3 per hr., £4.80); **Exeter** (1¼hr., 1 per hr., £28); **London Paddington** (1½hr., 2 per hr., £45); **London Waterloo** (2-2½ hr., 2 per day, £21.90); **Salisbury** (1hr., 1 per hr., £10.40); **Plymouth** (2¼., 1 per hr., £45.50).

Buses: Station at Manvers St. (☎ 0870 608 2608). Ticket office open M-Sa 8am-5:30pm. **National Express** (☎ 08705 808 080) from **London** (3½hr., 1 per 1½ hr., £14.50) and **Oxford** (2¼hr., 1 per day, £10.75). **Badgerline** buses sell a **Day Explorer** ticket, good for 1-day unlimited bus travel in the region (£7, concessions £5).

Taxis: Abbey Radio (☎ 444 444).

Boat Rental: Bath Boating Station (☎ 312 900), at the end of Forester Rd., about ½ mi. north of town. Punts and canoes £5.50 per person first hr., £2 each additional hr. Open daily Apr.-Oct. 10am-6pm.

◪ ▯ ORIENTATION AND PRACTICAL INFORMATION

The **Roman Baths,** the **Pump Room,** and **Bath Abbey** cluster in the city center, bounded by York St. and Cheap St. The River Avon flows just east of them, and wraps around the south part of town near the train and bus stations. Uphill to the northwest, historical buildings lie on **Royal Crescent** and **The Circus.**

Tourist Information Centre: Abbey Chambers (☎ 0870 444 6442; www.visitbath.co.uk). Town map and mini-guide 50p, self-guided walking tour £1.20. The free *This Month in Bath* lists events. Books rooms for a £5 charge plus a 10% deposit. Open May-Sept. M-Sa 9:30am-6pm, Su 10am-4pm; Oct.-Apr. M-Sa 9:30am-5pm, Su 10am-4pm.

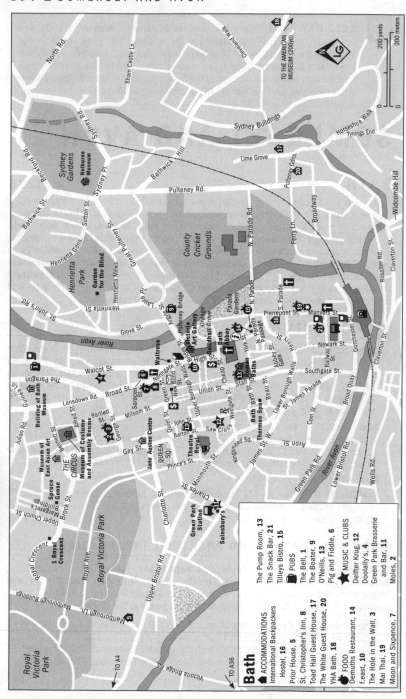

SOUTHWEST ENGLAND

Bath

▲ ACCOMMODATIONS
International Backpackers
Hostel, **16**
Prior House, **5**
St. Christopher's Inn, **8**
Toad Hall Guest House, **17**
The White Guest House, **20**
YHA Bath, **18**

● FOOD
Demuths Restaurant, **14**
f.east, **10**
The Hole in the Wall, **3**
Mai Thai, **19**
Moon and Sixpence, **7**

The Pump Room, **13**
The Snack Bar, **21**
Tilleys Bistro, **15**

🍺 PUBS
The Bell, **1**
The Boater, **9**
O'Neills, **13**
Pig and Fiddle, **6**

★ MUSIC & CLUBS
Delfter Krug, **12**
Doolally's, **4**
Green Park Brasserie
and Bar, **11**
Moles, **2**

Tours: Several companies run tours of the city; try any of the following:

The Mayor's Honorary Guides lead **free walking tours** from the entrance to the Baths daily at 10:30am and 2pm, with additional tours May-Sept. Tu and F-Sa at 7pm. Knowledgeable guides recount the history of the city and point out fascinating architectural features.

Bizarre Bath (☎335 124; www.bizarrebath.co.uk). 90min. tours begin at the Huntsman Inn at N. Parade Passage. The hysterically funny guides impart absolutely no historical facts. Nightly Apr.-Sept. at 8pm. £5, concessions £4.50.

The Great Bath Pub Crawl (☎310 364; www.greatbathpubcrawl.com), meets at the Old Green Tree Pub on Green St., delves into Bath's illicit past, and stops for a few rounds. Apr.-Sept. M-W, Su at 8pm. £5.

Ghost Walk (☎350 512; www.ghostwalksofbath.co.uk), begins its 2hr. tours at 8pm at Nash Bar of Garrick's Head, near Theatre Royal. Apr.-Oct. M-Sa, Nov.-Mar. F. £6, concessions £5. Groups of 10 or more should consider booking a private guide, minimum fee £60.

Mad Max Tours (☎325 900; www.madmaxtours.com). Reservations made through the City of Bath YMCA. Full day begins at 8:45am from the Abbey. Spins through Stonehenge, the Avebury Stone Circles, Castle Combe in the Cotswolds, and Lacock National Trust Village (the backdrop of *Pride & Prejudice* and *Harry Potter*), among other sites. £22.50, entrance to Stonehenge not included. Also offers a half-day tour (1 per day, 2pm) of Stonehenge and Bradford-Upon-Avon. £12.50.

Financial Services: Banks are ubiquitous; most are open M-F 9:30am-5pm, some Sa 9:30am-12:30pm. **Thomas Cook,** 20 New Bond St. (☎492 000). Open M-Tu and Th-Sa 9am-5:30pm, W 10am-5:30pm. **NatWest,** 15 High St. (☎0845 302 1655), across from Guildhall. Open M-Tu and Th-Sa 9am-5pm, W 9:30am-5pm.

Launderette: Spruce Goose, Margaret's Buildings, off Brock St. (☎483 309). Wash £2-3, dry £1.20, soap 60p. Bring £1 coins for washers, 20p coins for dryers. Open M-F and Su 8am-9pm, Sa 8am-8pm; last wash 1hr. before close.

Police: Manvers St. (☎01275 818 181), near the train and bus stations.

Hospital: Royal United Hospital, Coombe Park, in Weston (☎428 331). Take bus #14.

Pharmacy: Boots, 33-35 Westgate St. (☎482 069.)

Internet Access: Central Library, Podium Shopping Centre (☎787 400), above Waitrose. Free. Open M 10am-6pm, Tu-Th 9:30am-7pm, F-Sa 9:30am-5pm, Su 1-4pm. **Ret@iler Internet,** 12 Manvers St. (☎443 181). £1 per 20min. Open M-Sa 9am-9pm, Su 10am-9pm. **Click Internet Cafe,** 13A Manvers St. (☎481 008). £1 per 20min., 2 min. free email check. Open daily 10am-10pm.

Post Office: 21-25 New Bond St. (☎08457 740 740), across from the Podium Shopping Centre. **Bureau de change.** Open M-Sa 9am-5:30pm. **Post Code:** BA1 1AJ.

⌐ ACCOMMODATIONS

Bath's well-to-do visitors drive up prices. **B&Bs** cluster on **Pulteney Road** and **Pulteney Gardens. Marlborough Lane** and **Upper Bristol Road,** west of the city center, offer many quaint options as well.

Prior House, 3 Marlborough Ln. (☎313 587; www.greatplaces.co.uk/priorhouse). Walk 15min. west on Henry St. (which becomes Monmouth St. then Upper Bristol St.) from the bus and train stations. Upon arrival, your hosts will quickly engross you in talk. Continental breakfast included. Doubles £50-55, triple £70. AmEx/MC/V. ❹

YHA Bath, Bathwick Hill (☎465 674). From North Parade Rd., turn left on Pulteney Rd., right on Bathwick Hill, then climb the steep hill (40min.). Bus #18 or 418 from the bus station goes up every 20min. (80p, round-trip £1.20). Secluded Italianate mansion is far but beautiful. Cafe, bar, and kitchen. Laundry (£1.50 wash, 50p dry). Internet access £2.50 per 30min. Book ahead in summer and weekends. Dorms £11.80, under 18 £8.50; doubles £32, ensuite £36. Reception 7:30am-11pm. MC/V. ❷

Toad Hall Guest House, 6 Lime Grove (☎423 254). Make a left off Pulteney Rd. after passing through the overpass. Friendly B&B with 2 spacious doubles (1 can be let as single) and hearty breakfasts. Single £25; doubles £45. Cash only. ❸

St. Christopher's Inn, 9 Green St. (☎481 444; www.st-christophers.co.uk). Convenient location, downstairs bar offers an ideal hangout area for young crowd. Simple and clean bunks. Singles £15; one double £46. Internet access £1 per 20min. Free luggage storage. Discounts available if rooms booked online. AmEx/MC/V. ❷

The White Guest House, 23 Pulteney Gdns. (☎426 075; thewhitehouse@zoom.co.uk). Left off Pulteney Road. Homey B&B with flower-filled patio. Welcoming rooms have TV and bath. Singles £30-35; doubles £46-55. Book ahead in summer. £2 off if you tell them *Let's Go* sent you; 10% off if you stay 3 or more nights. Cash only. ❸

International Backpackers Hostel, 13 Pierrepont St. (☎446 787; www.hostels.co.uk/bath), Up the street from the train station and 3 blocks from the baths. Laid-back backpacker's lair with music-themed suites (beds named after bands or solo artists). Kitchen available. Book ahead in summer. Luggage storage £1 per bag. Internet access £2 per hour. Laundry £2.50. Reception 8am-midnight. Checkout 10:30am. Dorms M-Th, Su £12, F-Sa £13; doubles £35, extra person £17.50. £5 deposit. MC/V. ❷

☐ FOOD

Although restaurants in Bath tend to be expensive, reasonably priced cafes and eateries dot the city, many with outdoor seating. For fruits and vegetables, visit the **market** at Guildhall (☎477 945. Open M-Sa 9am-5:30pm). Next door to Green Park Station, an enormous **Sainsbury's** will satisfy. (☎444 737. Open M-F 8am-10pm, Sa 7:30am-10pm, Su 10am-4pm.) Prepare a picnic with the fresh breads, fruits and vegetables available at **Waitrose** supermarket, in the Podium Shopping Centre on High St., across from the post office. (☎442 550. Open M-F 8:30am-8:30pm, Sa 8am-7pm, Su 11am-5pm.)

🖾 **The Hole in the Wall,** 16-17 George St. (☎425 242; www.theholeinthewall.co.uk). Succulent Anglo-Euro fusion in a casually elegant setting. Lunch and pre-theatre (before 6:30pm) either 2 courses (£9.55) or 3 (£14.95). Dessert £5-6. Open M-Sa noon-2:30pm and 5-10pm, Su 11am-4pm. AmEx/MC/V. ❹

Demuths Restaurant, 2 North Parade Passage (☎446 059; www.demuths.co.uk), off Abbey Green. Exotic vegetarian and vegan dishes like Andalusian tapas (£11.75). Chocolate fudge cake (£4.75) is superb. Lunch £7.50, dinner £11.75. Open M-F, Su 10am-5pm and 6-9pm, Sa 9:30am-5:30pm and 6-9pm. MC/V. ❸

Tilleys Bistro, 3 North Parade Passage (☎484 200; www.tilleysbistro.co.uk). Savor Tilleys French and English creations while relaxing in the elegant and warm atmosphere. Ask to be seated downstairs if there's room. Thorough vegetarian menu available. Entrees £6-10. Open M-Sa noon-2:30pm and 6:30-11pm. MC/V. ❷

f.east, 27 High St. (☎333 500). Fantastic Pan-Asian cuisine from Indonesian satay chicken to Japanese udon. Mod decor and bench seating. Noodles £7-8.90. 10% discount for takeaway. Open M-Sa noon-11pm, Su 5pm-10pm. MC/V. ❷

The Moon and Sixpence, 6a Broad St. (☎460 962). Locals tout the mouth watering "modern international cuisine." Lunch set menu, 2 courses £7.95. Entrees £10-15. Open M-Th noon-2:30pm and 5:30-10:30pm (bar open from noon until close), F-Sa noon-11pm (last table 10:30pm), noon-3pm and 6:30-10pm. AmEx/MC/V. ❸

Mai Thai, 6 Pierrepont St. (☎445 557). Great Thai food at affordable prices. Served in a homey atmosphere. Starters £3.75-5.25. Entrees £4-8. Make reservations for weekends. Open daily noon-2pm and 6-10:30pm. £10 minimum. AmEx/MC/V. ❷

The Snack Bar, 1 Railway St. (☎461 705). Enjoy a full English breakfast (£2.90, served all day), a hot sandwich (£1.90), or a classic dessert like spotted dick with custard (£2) at this conveniently located cafe after arriving in the city from the train or before you grab a bus. Open M-Sa 7am-5:15pm, Su 8:30am-5:15pm. Cash only. ❶

The Pump Room, Abbey Churchyard (☎444 477). Exercises its monopoly over Bath Spa drinking water (50p per glass) in a palatial Victorian ballroom. Breakfast £6. Brunch £8.65. Lunch £6-15. Pricey dinners served July-Aug. (2-3 courses £17.50-19.50). Open daily July-Aug. 8am-9pm; Sept.-June 9:30am-6pm. AmEx/MC/V. ❹

⑥ SIGHTS

A joint ticket is offered to the Baths and Museum of Costume. (£12, children £7.)

THE ROMAN BATHS. In 1880, sewer diggers inadvertently uncovered the first glimpse of what excavation has shown to be an extravagant model of advanced Roman engineering. Bath flourished as a Roman city for 400 years, its hot bubbling springs making the city a pilgrimage site and later the premiere social scene. The **museum** merits the entrance price with its displays on Roman excavation finds and building design, including central heating and internal plumbing. Walkways wind through the impressive remains of the complex, past springs that gurgle up 250,000 gallons a day at 116°F. Computer visuals giving a bird's eye view of the baths, as well complimentary audio guides, offer a more enhanced understanding of the culture and the bathing practice. Read recovered curses that Romans cast into the spring. Tradition held that if a curse floated on the water, it would be visited back upon the curser. The Romans neatly avoided this by writing their ill wishes on lead. *(Stall St. ☎477 785; www.roman-baths.co.uk. Open daily July-Aug. 9am-10pm; Sept.-Oct. and Mar.-June 9am-6pm; Jan.-Feb. and Nov.-Dec. 9:30am-5:30pm. Last admission 1hr. before close. Hourly guided tour included. £9, seniors £8, children £5, families £29.)*

MUSEUM OF COSTUME AND ASSEMBLY ROOMS. The museum hosts a dazzling parade of 400 years of catwalk fashions, from 17th-century silver tissue garments to Jennifer Lopez's racy Dolce&Gabbana jungle-print ensemble. Free audio tours dispel the myth

THE BIG SPLURGE

UP AND AWAY

Bath and southwestern England are covered with brilliant architecture and varied natural landscapes. What better way could there be to admire the elegant geometry of this famous cityscape and its surroundings than from 3000 ft. in the sky? For thrills and unparalleled views, consider taking off in a hot air balloon; you never know just where it will take you, or how much you might be able to see.

A birds-eye view of Bath in a hot-air balloon is an unforgettable experience. Two companies operate balloon flights from Royal Victoria Park. **Ascent Balloon** (☎01761 432 327; www.ascent-balloon.co.uk) is the smaller of the two. It takes four to six people per basket (£129 per person), and offers a special rate for a couple in search of aerial privacy. **Bath Balloons** (☎01225 466 888; www.balnet.co.uk) is part of the larger Ballooning Network and offers a similar experience, topped off with a dose of bubbly. (£125-139 per person. Book 2-3 weeks ahead.)

The most exciting time to go ballooning is during Bath's Balloon Fiesta in mid-May, when dozens of brightly colored balloons linger in the sky like suspended candies. Bristol has an even larger, international balloon festival in August.

of the 18-inch waist of the late 1800s—it was much closer to 21—and offer information on corsets and their political implications. The Dress of the Year exhibit showcases the most important looks of each year since 1963 in rotation. *(Bennett St. ☎477 785; www.museumofcostume.co.uk. Open daily Mar.-Oct. 10am-5pm, Nov.-Feb. 11am-4pm; last admission half hr. before close. £6, concessions £5, children £4, families £16.50).* The museum is in the basement of the **Assembly Rooms**, built to replace an earlier building as fashionable society moved uptown. Here, Bath's visitors were entertained by balls, concerts, and cards. WWII ravaged the rooms, but renovations duplicate the originals in fine detail. *(☎477 785. Open daily 10am-5pm. Free. Rooms are sometimes booked for private functions.)*

BATH ABBEY. Occupying the site where King Edgar was crowned "first king of all England" in 973, the abbey towers over its neighbors at 140 ft. In 1499, Bishop Oliver King commissioned the abbey to replace a Norman cathedral three times its size that had fallen derelict. You can still read the Bishop's rebus, or signature, on the abbey's west facade: look for an olive tree topped by a crown. Inside, the abbey's magnificent ceiling fulfills George and William Vertue's promise to build "the goodliest vault in all England and France." Read about the ways various Brits and others met their ends on the countless memorial plaques. *(Next to the Baths. ☎422 462; www.bathabbey.org. Open Apr.-Oct. M-Sa 9am-6pm, Su 1-2:30pm and 4:30-5:30pm; Nov.-Mar. M-Sa 9am-4pm, Su between services. Requested donation £2.50.) Below the abbey, the Heritage Vaults detail the abbey's Christian history and importance. (Open M-Sa 10am-4pm; last admission 3:30pm. £1.50, children free.)*

THE JANE AUSTEN CENTRE. Austen lived in Bath (at 4 Sydney Pl., among other less fashionable addresses) from 1801 to 1806 and thought it a "dismal sight," although she still decided to set *Northanger Abbey* and *Persuasion* here. The Centre holds nothing that personally belonged to her, but explains Austen's references to Bath and describes the city as it was when she lived here. *(40 Gay St. ☎443 000; www.janeausten.co.uk. Open M-Sa 10am-5:30pm, Su 10:30am-5:30pm. Last complete visit 5pm. £4.65, seniors and students £4.15, children £2.50, under 6 free with adult, families £12.50.)* Tours of the sights in her novels run daily July-Aug. 1:30pm, Sept.-June weekends at 1:30pm from Abbey Churchyard; purchase tickets at the Centre or in front of KC Exchange *(£4.50, concessions £3.50).*

OTHER MUSEUMS AND GALLERIES. Next to Pulteney Bridge, the **Victoria Art Gallery,** Bridge St., holds a diverse collection of works by Old Masters as well as more modern British artists. It houses Thomas Barker's "The Bride of Death"—Victorian melodrama at its sappiest. *(☎477 233; www.victoriagal.org.uk. Open Tu-F 10am-5:30pm, Sa 10am-5pm, Su 2-5pm. Free.)* The handsome **Holburne Museum,** Great Pulteney St., specializes in Georgian art and ceramics. The pride of its collection is Gainsborough's largest oil painting, "The Byam Family." *(☎466 669; www.bath.ac.uk/holburne. Open mid-Feb. to mid-Dec. Tu-Sa 10am-5pm, Su 2:30-5:30pm. £4, children £1.50, seniors £3.50, concessions available.)* The **Museum of East Asian Art,** 12 Bennett St., displays objects dating back to 5000 BC, with an amazing collection of jade and ceramics. Kid friendly. *(☎464 640. Open Tu-Sa 10am-5pm, Su noon-5pm; last admission 4:30pm. £3.50, concessions £1-3, families £8.)* The **American Museum,** Claverton Manor, is worth visiting as much for its breathtaking landscape as for its exhibits featuring transplanted, furnished rooms, including a cozy Revolutionary War-era kitchen. Climb 2 mi. up Bathwick Hill, or take bus #18 or 418 to Bath University. *(☎460 503; www.americanmuseum.org. Open late Mar.-Oct. Tu-Su 2-5:30pm (last entry at 5pm). Gardens and tearoom open Tu-Su noon-5:30pm. £6.50, concessions £5.50, children £3.50, families £17.50.)*

HISTORIC BUILDINGS. Those interested in Bath's architectural history should visit the **Building of Bath Museum,** on the Paragon, which conveys a wealth of information in text-heavy displays. Check out the meticulous model of the city; it took

10,000 hours to perfect its layout at a 1:500 scale. (☎333 895. Open mid-Feb.-Nov. Tu-Su 10:30am-5pm. Last admission 4:30pm. £4, concessions £3, children £1.50, families £10.) In the city's residential northwest corner, Beau Nash's contemporaries John Wood, father and son, made the **Georgian rowhouse** a design to reckon with. Walk up Gay St. to **The Circus,** an oblique tribute to Stonehenge in circumference that has attracted illustrious inhabitants for two centuries; greenish-gray plaques proclaim former residents, including Thomas Gainsborough and William Pitt. Proceed from there up Brock St. to the **Royal Crescent,** a half-moon of 18th-century townhouses. The interior of **1 Royal Crescent** has been painstakingly restored to a near-perfect replica of a 1770 townhouse, authentic down to the last teacup and butter knife. (☎428 126. Open mid-Feb.-Oct. Tu-Su 10:30am-5pm; Nov. Tu-Su 10:30am-4pm. Last admission a half hr. before close. £4, concessions £3.50, families £12.) For stupendous views, climb the 154 steps of **Beckford's Tower,** Lansdown Rd., 2 mi. north of town. Take bus #2 or 702 to Ensleigh; otherwise, it's a 45min. walk. (☎460 705. Open Easter-Oct. Sa-Su 10:30am-5pm. £3, concessions £2, families £6.50.)

THERMAE BATH SPA. This state-of-the-art spa, housed in a modern complex near the Baths, hopes to revive the city's 2000-year-old tradition. The new spa features two natural thermal baths, an open-air roof-top pool, yoga classes, massage treatments, aromatherapy, algae body wraps, and more. The Romans never had it this good—or this expensive. Treatments range from £26-68. (Hot Bath St. ☎331 234. 2hr. in hot baths £17; full day £35. Advanced booking is recommended. Open daily 9am-10pm.)

GARDENS AND PARKS. Consult a map or the TIC's *Borders, Beds, and Shrubberies* brochure to locate the city's many stretches of cultivated green. Next to the Royal Crescent, **Royal Victoria Park** contains one of the finest collections of trees in the country. Its botanical gardens nurture 5000 species of plants from all over the globe. For bird aficionados, there's also an aviary. (Always open. Free.) **Henrietta Park,** laid in 1897 to celebrate Queen Victoria's Diamond Jubilee, was later redesigned as a garden for the blind—only the most fragrant flowers and shrubs were chosen for its tranquil grounds. The **Parade Gardens,** at the base of North Parade Bridge, have lawn chairs and a pleasant green, perfect for relaxing or reading. Check out the messages on the dedication plaques that adorn many of the benches. (☎391 041. Open daily June-Aug. 10am-8pm; Apr. and Sept. 10am-7pm; Nov.-Mar. 10am-4pm. Apr.-Sept. £1.30, children and seniors 65p; Oct.-Mar. free.)

🔲🟦 PUBS AND CLUBS

Luring backpackers to its generous patio, the **Pig and Fiddle,** 2 Saracen St., off Broad St., is the first stop for many pub crawlers. (☎460 868. Open M-Sa 11am-11pm, Su noon-10:30pm.) Friendly and vibrant, **The Bell,** 103 Walcot St., challenges its clientele to talk over the live folk, jazz, blues, funk, salsa, and reggae. Pizzas are baked and served outside in the garden on weekend evenings.(☎460 426. Open M-Sa 11am-11pm, Su noon-10:30pm. Live music M and W evenings, Su lunch.) **The Boater,** 9 Argyle St., isn't the prettiest pub—its galley theme accomplished with tacky high-gloss paint—but the "beer garden" overlooks the river and has a view of the Pulteney Bridge. (☎464 211. Open M-Sa 11am-11pm, Su noon-10:30pm.) **Delfter Krug,** on Sawclose, draws a large weekend crowd with its outdoor seating and lively upstairs club, which plays everything from hip-hop to commercial pop. (☎443 352. Cover £2-5. Open M-Sa noon-2am, Su noon-10:30pm.) Underground **Moles,** 14 George St., pounds out soul, funk, and house, hosting frequent live acts in an intimate setting. (☎404 445. Cover £3-5. Open M-Th 9pm-2am, F-Sa 9pm-4am.) A cafe by day, **Doolally's,** 51 Walcot St., features softer acts by night in its cozy space. (☎444 122. Live music from 8pm. No cover. Open daily 9am-11pm. Su 9am-6pm, all day breakfast.) For jazz, locals favor **Green Park Brasserie and Bar,** a classy bistro in Green Park Station. (☎ 338 565. Open Tu-Su 10:30am-midnight. Live jazz W-Sa 8:30pm, Su 12:30pm.) A former chapel, **O'Neills,** 1 Barton St., now offers the perfect mix of pub and club, alluring patrons of all ages and styles. (☎ 789 106. Cover on W, F, Sa £4-5. Open M-Sa noon-2am, Su noon-10:30pm.)

🎵 🎆 ENTERTAINMENT AND FESTIVALS

In summer, buskers (street musicians) fill the streets with music, and a brass band often graces the Parade Gardens. The magnificent **Theatre Royal,** Sawclose, at the south end of Barton St. (part of Beau Nash's old home), showcases opera and theater. (☎ 448 844. Box office open M-Sa 10am-8pm, Su noon-8pm. Tickets £5-27.)

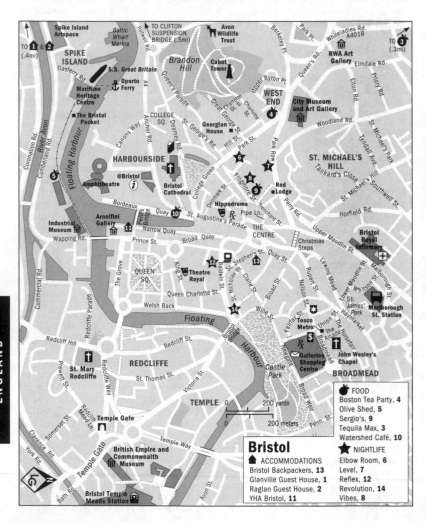

Bristol

🔺 ACCOMMODATIONS
Bristol Backpackers, **13**
Glanville Guest House, **1**
Raglan Guest House, **2**
YHA Bristol, **11**

🍴 FOOD
Boston Tea Party, **4**
Olive Shed, **5**
Sergio's, **9**
Tequila Max, **3**
Watershed Café, **10**

⭐ NIGHTLIFE
Elbow Room, **6**
Level, **7**
Reflex, **12**
Revolution, **14**
Vibes, **8**

SOUTHWEST ENGLAND

Year round, you can take your pick of festivals in Bath. For brochures or reservations, call the **Bath Festivals Box Office**, 2 Church St., Abbey Green. (☎463 362; www.bathfestivals.org.uk has links for each one. Open M-Sa 9:30am-5:30pm.) The renowned **Bath International Music Festival** (May 20-June 5 in 2005) features world-class symphony orchestras, choruses, and jazz bands. The overlapping **Fringe Festival** (☎480 079) celebrates the arts with 190 live performances (May 27-June 12 in 2005). The **Jane Austen Festival**, held at the end of September, features Jane-themed walks, meals, and movies. (Contact the Jane Austen Centre. Tickets £3-10.) Then there's the **Literature Festival** in the first week of March, the **Balloon Fiesta** in mid-May, and the **Film Festival** in late October. Stay abreast of the best events with the weekly *Venue* (£1.20), available at bookstores.

BRISTOL ☎0117

Well-cultured and surprisingly hip, Bristol is Britain's latest success story of urban renewal. Ten years ago, you'd have been hard-pressed to find someone who wanted to visit Bristol, let alone live there. But today, the southwest's largest city (pop. 410, 000) is one of England's fastest-growing communities, and its economy booms while others lag behind. Lucrative opportunities in aerospace, finance, and film animation have eclipsed former fortunes made from shipping and the slave trade, and a population of students and young professionals has reinvigorated the city. For now, this unpretentious city, with its rebuilt city center and hopping nightlife, remains one of Britain's best-kept secrets.

▮ TRANSPORTATION

Trains: Bristol Temple Meads Station. Ticket office open M-Sa 5:30am-9:30pm, Su 6:45am-9:30pm. Trains (☎08457 484 950) from: **Bath** (15min., 4 per hr., £4.80); **Cardiff** (50min., 2 per hr., £7.40); **London Paddington** (1¾hr., 2 per hr., £47 during rush hour, £34 other times); **Manchester** (3½hr., 2 per hr., £39.50). Another station, **Bristol Parkway,** is far, far away—make sure to get off at Temple Meads.

Buses: Marlborough Street Bus Station. Ticket office open M-Sa 7:20am-6pm, Su 9am-6pm. **National Express** (☎08705 808 080) buses arrive from **London** (2½hr., every hr., £14.50) and **Manchester** (5¾hr., 5-7 per day, £28.50) via **Birmingham** (2½hr., £15.50). National Express info shop open M-Sa 7am-8:10pm, Su 7am-9pm.

Public Transportation: First (☎0845 602 0156) buses run in the city. Information desk in Marlborough St. Bus Station. Open M-F 7:30am-6pm and Sa 10am-5:30pm. A **day pass** is £2.80 and an **Explorer** ticket buys 1-day unlimited travel in the Southwest (£7).

Taxis: Bristol Hackney Cabs (☎953 8638) or **Streamline** (☎926 4001).

◢ ▮ ORIENTATION AND PRACTICAL INFORMATION

Bristol is a sprawling mass of neighborhoods. **Broadmead** is the shopping and commerce center, while restaurants and clubs fill the heart of the city along **Park Street** and **Park Row** in the **West End.** The student population to the northeast makes **Whiteladies Road** (follow Queen's Rd. north) another option for restaurants and bars.

Tourist Information Centre: Harbourside (☎0870 444 0654; www.visitbristol.co.uk). From the train station, take bus #8 or 9 (£1) to the City Centre and follow the signs. Books accommodations for a £3 charge plus a 10% deposit. Open daily Mar.-Oct. 10am-6pm; Nov.-Feb. M-Sa 10am-5pm, Su 11am-4pm.

Tours: CitySightseeing (☎01934 830 050; www.bristolvisitor.co.uk) runs bus tours 10am-4:30pm (£7.50, students and children £6.50), and guided walks from the TIC Apr.-Sept. Sa 11am and 2pm (£3.50, children free). **The Bristol Packet** (☎926 8157) begins at Wapping Wharf near the S.S. Great Britain, and also runs various boat tours, including daytrips to Avon Gorge or Bath. Daily in Aug.; Apr.-Sept. Sa-Su. £4-17.50, children £2.50-13, seniors £3.50-16. **Bristol Pirate Walks** (☎07950 566 385) departs from the TIC. Easter-Sept. Tu, Th, Sa 6pm. £3.50, children £1.50.

Financial Services: HSBC, 11 Broadmead (☎08457 404 404). Open M-W and F 9am-5:30pm, Th 9am-7pm, Sa 9:30am-3pm.

Work Opportunities: Locals joke that if you can't find a job in Bristol in two hours, you probably never will. Hundreds of positions in bars, shops, cafes, and hospitals seem perennially vacant. If you don't find something by looking at window ads, the *Evening Post* is a good place to start. The TIC also has a free list of Bristol's employment agencies.

Police: Bridewell St. (☎927 7777).

Pharmacy: Superdrug, 39-43 Broadmead (☎927 9928). Open M-Sa 8:30am-5:30pm, Su 11am-5pm.

Hospital: Bristol Royal Infirmary, Upper Maudlin St. (☎923 0000). Frenchay (☎970 1212), in North Bristol near the M32.

Internet Access: BristolLife, 27/29 Baldwin St. (☎945 9926). £2 per hr. Open M-Sa 10am-8pm, Su 11am-8:30pm.

Post Office: The Galleries, Union St. (☎08457 223 344), on the top floor of the shopping center. Open M-Sa 9am-5:30pm. **Post Code:** BS1 3XX.

ACCOMMODATIONS

A handful of comfortable, cheap, and convenient **B&Bs** lie south of the harbor on **Coronation Road.** Walk west along Cumberland Rd. for 15min., cross the red footbridge and turn right onto Coronation Rd., and walk a few blocks past Deans Ln.

■ **Bristol Backpackers,** 17 St. Stephen's St. (☎925 7900; www.bristolbackpackers.co.uk). This former newspaper building is now a backpacker's dream, in the heart of the city. Internet access £1 per hr. Laundry £1.50. Reception 9am-11:30pm. Photo ID required. Book ahead for weekends. Dorms £14; twins with bunks £42. MC/V. ❷

YHA Bristol, Hayman House, 14 Narrow Quay (☎0870 770 5726). From City Center, across Pero's Bridge. Excellent city-center location, with cafe/bar. Breakfast included. Kitchen. Laundry £3. Internet access 50p per 6min. Reception 24hr. Luggage storage free. Book ahead, especially July-Sept. Dorms £16.40, under 18 £12.30. MC/V. ❷

Glanville Guest House, 122 Coronation Rd. (☎963 1634). Bright, homey lodgings. Book ahead. Singles £20; doubles £30. Family rooms available. Cash only. ❷

Raglan Guest House, 132 Coronation Rd. (☎966 2129). Budget lodgings with comfy beds. Singles £22; doubles and triples £16 per person, with bath £20. Cash only. ❸

FOOD

Plenty of restaurants line **Park Street,** while trendier options crowd **Whiteladies Road.** On Wednesdays, a **farmer's market** takes over Corn St. (Open 9:30am-2:30pm.) Try **Tesco Metro,** on Broadmead, for **groceries.** (☎0845 667 9071. Open M-F 7am-10pm, Sa 7am-8pm, Su 11am-5pm.

Boston Tea Party, 75 Park St. (☎929 8601). An institution and collegiate favorite. Lunch includes homemade soups, sandwiches, and giant salads (£5-6). Relaxed coffee shop offers outdoor seating and funky lounge. Entrees £4-7. Open M 7am-6pm, Tu-Sa 7am-10pm, Su 9am-7pm. AmEx/MC/V. ❶

Tequila Max, 109 Whiteladies Rd. (☎466 144). Mexican at its best, with great enchiladas (£10) and festive decor. W student night has 2-for-1 deals on selected entrees. Open Su-Th noon-2:30pm and 5-11:30pm, F-Sa noon-12:30am. AmEx/MC/V. ❸

Watershed Cafe/Bar, 1 Canons Rd. (☎927 5101; www.watershed.co.uk). Great sandwiches on this riverside location. "Light bites" £3, platters £5-6. Free Internet access. Cafe/bar open M 11am-11pm, Tu-F 9:30am-11pm, Sa 10am-11pm, Su 10am-10:30pm. Food served M-Sa noon-9pm, Su noon-7pm. AmEx/MC/V. ❶

Sergio's, 1-3 Frogmore St. (☎929 1413; www.sergios.co.uk). Flavorful food awaits in this tiny but rowdy Italian eatery. Entrees average £7-14. B.Y.O.B. Takeaway pizza available. Open M-F lunch noon-2:30pm, M-Sa dinner 5:30pm-late. MC/V. ❷

Olive Shed, Princes Wharf (☎929 1960; www.therealolivecompany.co.uk), next to the Industrial Museum. Veggie Mediterranean fare and gourmet seafood. Tapas served all day (£3-5). Entrees £11.50-14.50. Open Tu-Sa 10am-late, Su 10am-5pm. MC/V. ❸

🅖 SIGHTS

@BRISTOL. Opened in 2000 to herald Bristol's cultural renaissance, the three attractions of this modern science center will engross adults as much as kids. **Explore** features interactive exhibits in physics and biology, from a simulation of space flight to the virtual journey of an egg-bound sperm. **Wildwalk** traces the history of life on earth, complete with living specimens and a biodome. The four-story **IMAX,** housed near Wildwalk, shows 3D films on the southwest's largest screen. *(Anchor Rd., Harbourside. ☎0845 345 1235; www.at-bristol.org.uk. Explore and Wildwalk open daily 10am-6pm. IMAX shows every 1¼hr. with evening shows Th-Su. 1 sight £6.50-7.50, concessions £5.50-6, children £4.50-5, families £19-21; 2 sights £11-12/£9.25-9.70/£7.75-8.20/£34.50-36.50; all 3 £16.50/£13.45/£11.45/£52.)*

BRITISH EMPIRE AND COMMONWEALTH MUSEUM. In 1497, the explorer John Cabot set sail from Bristol Harbour for Newfoundland and inaugurated the greatest empire in world history. Using artifacts, spoken testimonies, and documentary footage, the museum presents a variety of perspectives on empire and its legacies, from the impact of colonialism on indigenous peoples and the environment to the experience of modern-day immigrants to Britain. Interactive exhibits bring museum-goers back to when "the sun never set on the British empire," offering challenging and varied cultural perceptions along the way. *(Station Approach, Temple Meads, in a former rail station. ☎925 4980; www.empiremuseum.co.uk. Open daily 10am-5pm. £6.50, concessions £5.50, children £3.95, families £14.)*

CLIFTON SUSPENSION BRIDGE. Isambard Kingdom Brunel, famed engineer of London's Paddington Station, also created the architectural masterpiece that spans the Avon Gorge and offers a breathtaking view of St. Vincent's Rocks. The Visitors Centre explains the finer points of Brunel's genius, which revolutionized Victorian technology, but is closed for renovations slated to end in early 2005. *(Take bus #8 or 9. ☎974 4664; www.clifton-suspension-bridge.org.uk. Bridge always open. Free.)*

S.S. GREAT BRITAIN. Also a Brunel production, this ship was the largest in the world when it was launched in 1843. "The world's first great ocean liner" traveled a million miles in its day, and is undergoing renovation so more of its interior will be open to the public in future months. *(☎929 1843; www.ss-great-britain.com. Open daily Apr.-Oct. 10am-5:30pm; Nov.-Mar. 10am-4:30pm. £6.25, concessions £5.25-3.75.)*

OTHER MUSEUMS. The **City Museum and Art Gallery,** Queen's Rd., covers all the bases from minerals to mummies, including a handsome collection of British ceramics. (☎922 3571. *Open daily 10am-5pm. Free.*) The **Industrial Museum,** Princes Wharf, Wapping Rd., is in a giant warehouse. The ground floor exhibits antique rail and road vehicles manufactured in Bristol, including a horse-drawn fire engine. The first floor displays a mock-up cockpit of a Concorde, used during the airliner's development, and a candid account of Bristol's prominent role in the slave trade. (☎925 1470. *Open Apr.-Oct. M-W and Sa-Su 10am-5pm; Nov.-Mar. Sa-Su 10am-5pm. Free.*) From April to October, you can also visit the **Georgian House,** 7 Great George St., built in 1791, and the **Red Lodge,** Park Row, an Elizabethan home built in 1590. (*Both open M-W and Sa-Su 10am-5pm. Free.*) The **Arnolfini Gallery,** 16 Narrow Quay, exhibits contemporary art. Anticipated reopening in spring 2005. (☎929 9191; *www.arnolfini.org.uk. Open M-W and F-Sa 10am-5pm, Th 10am-9pm, Su noon-5pm. Free.*)

CHURCHES. **John Wesley's Chapel,** 36 The Horsefair, Broadmead, which sits incongruously in the midst of Bristol's shopping district, is the world's oldest Methodist building. Note the chair fashioned from an inverted elm trunk. (☎926 4740. *Open M-Sa 10am-4pm. Free.*) Founded in 1140, the **Bristol Cathedral** is known as a "hall church" because the nave, choir, and aisles are of equal height. The beautiful **Norman Chapter House** was formerly full of the monks' many books. (☎926 4879. *Open daily 8am-6pm. Evensong 5:15pm weekdays, 3:30pm Sa. Free guided tour Sa 11am.*)

BRANDON HILL. Just west of Park St. lies one of the most peaceful and secluded sights in Bristol. Pathways snake through flower beds up the hill to Cabot Tower, a monument commemorating the 400th anniversary of explorer John Cabot's arrival in North America. Ascend the 108 steps for a stunning view. (☎922 3719. *Open daily until dusk. Free.*)

▧ NIGHTLIFE

On weekend nights, virtually the entire city turns out in clubwear, with thousands of university students sustaining the energetic vibe. Bars and clubs cluster around **Park Street** and **Park Row** in the West End, and **Baldwin Street** and **St. Nicholas Street** in the Old City. A handful of gay clubs line **Frogmore Street.**

> **Level,** 24 Park Row (☎961 7348; www.level-bristol.co.uk). Bristol's latest hot zone, this small subterranean club attracts a hip crowd for special events and Sa R&B. M-W student night. Cover £3-8. Open M-Su 9:30pm-2am.

> **Revolution,** St. Nicholas St. (☎929 7197). Any dissent in this completely packed, red-tinted bar drowns in the liquid goodness of exotic vodkas. Live DJs nightly. No cover. Open M-Th 11:30am-1am, F and Sa 11:30am-2am, Su 11:30am-12:30pm.

> **Elbow Room,** 64 Park St. (☎300 242). This relaxed bar features pool tables, moody purple and red lighting, and window seating looking out onto the street. Su live reggae. Open M-Su noon-2am.

> **Vibes,** 3 Frogmore St. (☎934 9076; www.vibesnightclub.co.uk). A new gay venue with neon lights and modern decor. Different rooms play different music, from cheesy pop to hard house. Cover £1-4. Open M-Th 11pm-2am, F-Sa 9pm-3am.

> **Reflex,** 18-24 Baldwin St. (☎945 8891). Throw yourself into a timewarp at this fun 80s bar, complete with Rubik's cube disco lights and air guitar contests. W student night. Cover £1-5. Open M-Tu and Th-Sa 8pm-2am, W 9pm-2am, Su 8pm-12:30am.

♫ ▨ ENTERTAINMENT AND FESTIVALS

Britain's oldest theater, the **Theatre Royal,** King St., was rebuked for debauchery until George III approved the actors' antics. (☎987 7877. Box office open M-Tu 10am-8pm, W 10:30am-8pm, Th-Sa 10am-8pm. Tickets £7-20, students £2 off.) The

Hippodrome, St. Augustine's Parade, presents the latest touring productions and musicals. (Box office open M-Sa 10am-8pm, on non-performance days until 6pm.) In late July, the popular **Bristol Harbour Festival** (☎903 1484) explodes with fireworks, raft races, street performances, live music, hundreds of boats, and a French market. During the **Bristol International Balloon Fiesta** (☎953 5884), the first or second weekend in August, hot-air balloons fill the sky while acrobats and motorcycle teams perform at ground level.

WELLS   ☎01749

Named for the natural springs at its center, Wells (pop. 10,000) is humbled by its magnificent cathedral. Charming, if self-consciously classy, England's smallest city is lined with petite Tudor buildings and golden sandstone shops.

TRANSPORTATION

Trains leave Wells enough alone, but **buses** stop at the **Princes Road Bus Park.** (☎673 084. Ticket office open M-F 9am-4:45pm, Sa 9am-12:45pm.) **National Express** (☎08705 808 080) buses arrive from **London** (3½hr., 1 per day (7pm), £16). **First** runs from **Bath** (☎08456 064 446; #173; 1¼hr.; M-Sa every hr., Su 7 per day; £4) and **Bristol** (☎01934 429 336, #376, 1hr., every hr., £4). If you'll be skipping around in the area, buy a **Day Explorer Pass** (£7; concessions £5). For a taxi, call **Wookey Taxis** (☎678 039). Rent bicycles at **Bike City,** 31 Broad St. (☎671 711. £9 per day, £40 per week. Deposit £50. Open M-Sa 9am-5:30pm.)

PRACTICAL INFORMATION

The **Tourist Information Centre,** Market Pl., at the end of High St., books rooms for a 10% deposit and has bus timetables. Exit left from the bus station, then turn left onto Priory Rd., which becomes Broad St. and eventually merges with High St. (☎672 552; Open daily Apr.-Oct. 9:30am-5:30pm; Nov.-Mar. 10am-4pm.) Other services include: **Thomas Cook,** 8 High St. (☎313 000; open M-W, F-Sa 9am-5:30pm, Th 10am-5:30pm); **work opportunities** at **JobCentre,** 46 Chamberlain St. (☎313 200; open M-Tu and Th-F 9am-5pm, W 10am-5pm); the **police,** 18 Glastonbury Rd. (☎01275 818 181); **Boots** pharmacy, 17-21 High St. (☎01749 673 138; open M-Sa 9am-5:30pm, Su 10:30am-4:30pm); **Wells and District Hospital,** Bath Rd. (☎683 200); **Internet access** at **Microbitz,** Theatre Courtyard, Priory Rd., a PC service center (☎675 467; £2.50 per 30min.; open M-F 9am-5pm), and at Richmond House (see below); and the **post office,** Market Pl. with a **bureau de change** (☎08457 223 344; open M-F 9am-5:30pm, Sa 9am-12:30pm). **Post Code:** BA5 2RA.

ACCOMMODATIONS

Most **B&Bs** offer only doubles and run £22-30, so making Wells a daytrip from Bristol or Bath may be a better option. The closest YHA hostel and campgrounds are 2 and 10 mi. away, respectively, near Wookey Hole and Cheddar (p. 207). At **17 Priory Road ❸,** across the street from the bus station, Mrs. Winter offers warm and spacious rooms with volumes of books lining the shelves. (☎677 300; www.smoothhound.co.uk/hotels/brian.html. Breakfast included. Singles £25; doubles £50; family £25 per person. Cash only.) **Richmond House ❹,** 2 Chamberlain St., promises brass mirrors and an antique fireplace—and that's just the bathroom. From the bus station, follow directions to TIC, but from High St., turn left on Sadler Rd.; Chamberlain St. is the next left. (☎676 438; www.richmondhouse.info. Breakfast included. Free Internet access for guests.)

206 ■ SOMERSET AND AVON

Book ahead in summer. Singles £35; doubles £46-60. Cash only.) **Canon Grange** ❸, Cathedral Green (on Sadler St.), with the Cathedral in its backyard, features inviting, rustic decor with hardwood floors and fluffy quilts. Follow directions to TIC, but from High St., turn left on Sadler. (☎671 800; www.canongrange.co.uk. Doubles £54-57. MC/V.)

🍴 FOOD

Assemble a picnic at the **market** on High St., in front of the Bishop's Palace (open W and Sa), or purchase **groceries** at **Tesco,** across from the bus station on Tucker St. (☎0845 677 9710. Open M 8am-10pm, Tu-Sa 6am-10pm, Su 10am-4pm). At **The Good Earth** ❶, 4 Priory Rd., take great vegetarian soups (£2.15-2.75), quiches (£2.20), and home-cooked pizza (£2 per slice) to go or enjoy them on the backyard patio. (☎678 600. Open M-Sa 9am-5:30pm. MC/V.) A city jail in the 16th century, the **City Arms** ❸, 69 High St., now serves delicious meals including a number of vegetarian options (entrees £7-14) in a flower-filled outdoor veranda. Come nightfall, this is the hottest pub in town. (☎673 916. Restaurant open M-Sa 9am-10pm, Su 9am-9pm; bar M-Sa 10am-11pm, Su noon-10:30pm. AmEx/MC/V, £10 minimum.)

👁 SIGHTS

WELLS CATHEDRAL. The 12th-century church at the center of town anchors a fantastically preserved cathedral complex, with a bishop's palace, vicar's close, and chapter house. The facade comprises one of England's greatest collections of **medieval statues:** 293 figures in all. What really sets Wells apart is the unique feat of engineering known as the **"scissor arches"** at the east end of the nave, which were constructed in the 14th century to prevent the tower from sinking. The church's **astronomical clock** is the second oldest working clock in the world. Watch a group of jousting mechanical knights duke it out every 15min. and share in the frustration of the knight who has consistently lost for the last 600 years. The **Wells Cathedral School Choir,** an institution as old as the building itself, sings services (Sept.-Apr.) Pick up *Music in Wells Cathedral* at the cathedral or TIC. (☎674 483. Open daily Mar.-Sept. 7:15am-8:30pm if there's no concert; Oct.-Feb. until 6pm. Free tours 10, 11am, 1, 2, 3pm. Evensong M-Sa 5:15pm, Su 3pm. Suggested donation £4.50, concessions £3, children £1.50.) Beside the Cathedral, **Vicar's Close** is perhaps Europe's oldest continually inhabited street; most houses date back to 1363. (Always open. Free.)

BISHOP'S PALACE. This palace has been the residence of the Bishop of Bath and Wells for 800 years. The suite of medieval buildings is centered around St. Andrew's Well, and make for great picnics. Bishop Beckynton channeled the flow in the 15th century, and the water still runs through the city streets today. The swans in the moat pull a bell-rope when they want to be fed—the first swan to learn 150 years ago was reliable to the hour; new swans aren't as punctual. Visitors can feed them brown bread (not white—they get sick). (Near the cathedral. ☎678 691; www.bishopspalacewells.co.uk. Open Apr.-Oct. M-F 10:30am-6pm (last entry 5pm), Su noon-6pm (last entry 5pm), often open Sa phone ahead. £4, students £1.50, children £1.)

WELLS AND MENDIP MUSEUM. This museum contains archaeological finds of the Mendip area and remnants of the cathedral's decor. Also on display are the milking pot and bones of an elderly woman believed to be the legendary "Witch of Wookey Hole." (8 Cathedral Green. ☎673 477. Open daily Easter-Oct. 10am-5:30pm; Aug. until 8pm; Nov.-Easter W-M 11am-4pm. £2.50, concessions £2, children £1, families £6.)

SOUTHWEST ENGLAND

⚡ DAYTRIPS FROM WELLS

CHEDDAR

From Wells, take bus #126 or 826; 25min.; M-Sa every hr. (40min. past the hr.), Su 7 per day; round-trip £4.35. Purchase tickets at the base of the hill near the bus stop or at Gough's Cave. ☎742 343; www.cheddarcaves.co.uk. Open daily May to mid-Sept. 10am-5pm; mid-Sept. to Apr. 10:30am-4:30pm. Caves, Jacob's Ladder, and open-top bus £9.50, children £6.50, families £26. Ladder only £3.50, children £2.50. Discount tickets available from the Wells TIC. Cheddar's TIC is at the base of the hill. ☎01934 744 071. Open daily Mar.-Oct. 10am-5pm; Dec.-Easter Su 11am-4pm.

A short journey from Wells brings you to a vale of cheese, in every sense of the word. The town of **Cheddar** lies near a large hill leading to the **Cheddar Gorge,** a miracle of nature/kitschy tourist attraction, complete with colored lights. Carved by the River Yeo (YO), the gorge is perforated by the **Cheddar Showcaves,** limestone hollows that extend deep into the earth. **Gough's Cave,** named for its Victorian discoverer, houses a replica of **Cheddar Man,** a 9000-year-old skeleton (the original is now in the British Museum in London). Informative audio tours have options for adults and children. Down the hill, **Cox's Cave,** the chosen honeymoon spot of J.R.R. Tolkien, features the mercilessly tacky "Crystal Quest," a "fantasy adventure" with wizards and hobgoblins. Admission to the caves includes a ride on an open-top **bus** that travels through the gorge and to the cave entrances (in summer), as well as access to **Jacob's Ladder,** a 274-step lookout over the hills and plains. At the top, a 3 mi. **clifftop gorge walk** has views that outstrip the sights below. **The Cheddar Gorge Cheese Company,** at the hill's base, features cheese-making and cheesetasting. (☎742 810. Open daily 10am-5:30pm. Free.) Those who still feel the need for cheese can stay at the **YHA Cheddar ❷,** ½ mi. from Cheddar Gorge on a residential street. From the bus stop, walk up Tweentown Rd. away from the gorge, turn left on The Hayes, and right at Hillfield. (☎742 494. Kitchen; laundry £1.50. Reception 8-10am and 5-11pm. Lockout 10am-5pm. Open daily July-Aug.; otherwise call 48hr. in advance. Dorms £12, under 18 £8.50. MC/V.)

WOOKEY HOLE

From Wells, take bus #172 or 670, 15min., M-Sa 8 per day, round-trip £2. Caves ☎672 243. Open daily Apr.-Oct. 10am-5pm; Nov.-Mar. 10am-4pm. £8.80, children £5. Papermill ☎01934 672 243. Open daily Apr.-Oct. 10am-5pm; Nov.-Mar. 10:30am-4:30pm. £8.80, children £5.

THE LOCAL STORY

THE WITCH OF WOOKEY HOLE

Immortalized by lore and cloistered in the town's magnificent caves with only her sheep, the infamous "Witch of Wookey" inspired fear and loathing in locals from time immemorial. When a brave monk from nearby Glastonbury made the trek up the hill and into the cave to see if he could resolve—or perhaps, absolve—the woman and the town of their unfortunate situation, he was met by screams and curses as the woman ran away into the chambers of her cavern. As the monk followed her into the darkness, he heard running water and came upon an underground riverbed. Blessing the water, he threw some at the witch. She instantly turned to stone. Fueled by his success, the monk aimed a second volley at the witch's dog, freezing him beside her.

To this day, the witch (along with her mutt) stands, watching over the expansive caves she once called home. Visit the caves and take a tour, where knowledgeable guides (as well as an elaborate system of colored lights) relive the famous battle between witch and monk. Take note of the natural decor of the "rooms" in the witch's home, including its kitchen and parlor (one of the largest natural domes in Europe).

Tours ☎01749 672 243, or check out www.wookey.co.uk for information of daily tours, which run year-round.

Two miles west of Cheddar, the **Wookey Hole Caves** (see **Stoned,** p. 12) are as beautiful as their neighbors and slightly less commercial. A 35min. tour takes visitors into the caves, including chambers that were discovered only after the first cave dives were conducted here in 1935. Admission includes a visit to a working **Papermill,** powered by the River Axe, and an old-style amusement park with **gaudy carnival attractions,** including a family-oriented ghost tour.

GLASTONBURY   ☎01458

The reputed birthplace of Christianity in England, an Arthurian hotspot, and home to England's biggest summer music festival, Glastonbury (pop. 6900) is a quirky intersection of mysticism and pop culture. According to legend, King Arthur, Jesus, Joseph of Arimathea, and Saints Augustine and Patrick all came here. One myth claims Glastonbury Tor is the resting place of the Holy Grail and the spot to which the Messiah will return, another holds that it's the Isle of Avalon, where King Arthur sleeps. Glastonbury's shops do their part to perpetuate the mystical vibe, peddling Celtic trinkets and healing crystals to revelers and believers alike.

◼ TRANSPORTATION. Glastonbury has no train station; **buses** stop at the town hall in the town center. Consult *Public Transport Timetable for the Mendip Area,* free at TICs, for schedules. **First** (☎08706 082 608) buses run to **Bristol** (#376 or 377, 1hr., £2.50-3) via **Wells.** Travel to **Yeovil** (M-Sa #377, 1hr., 1 per day (departs at 9:24pm.); Su #977; 1hr.; every 2 hr.; £5) to connect to destinations in the south, including **Lyme Regis** and **Dorchester.** Travel a full day on all buses with the **Explorer Pass** (£6, concessions £4.25, families £12.50).

◼◼ ORIENTATION AND PRACTICAL INFORMATION. Glastonbury is 6 mi. southwest of Wells on the A39 and 22 mi. northeast of Taunton on the A361. The town is bounded by **High Street** in the north, **Bere Lane** in the south, **Magdalene Street** in the west, and **Wells Road/Chilkwell Street** in the east. The **Tourist Information Centre,** The Tribunal, 9 High St., books rooms for a £3 charge plus a 10% deposit; after hours find the B&B list behind the building in St. John's carpark. (☎832 954; www.glastonburytic.co.uk. Open Apr.-Sept. Su-Th 10am-5pm, F-Sa 10am-5:30pm; Oct.-Mar. Su-Th 10am-4pm, F-Sa 10am-4:30pm.) Other services include: **Thomas Cook,** 42 High St. (☎831 809; open M-Sa 9am-5:30pm); the **police,** 1 West End, in nearby Street (☎01823 337 911); **Moss** pharmacy, 39 High St. (☎831 211. Open M-F 9am-6pm, Sa 9am-5:30pm); **Internet access** at the **library,** 1 Orchard Ct., The Archer's Way, left off of High St. (☎832 148; free; photo ID required; open M and Th-F 10am-5pm, Tu 10am-7pm, Sa 10am-4pm), also at **Galatea's Cafe** (see below); and the **post office,** 35 High St. (☎831 536; open M-F 9am-5:30pm, Sa 9am-1pm). **Post Code:** BA6 9HG.

◼ ACCOMMODATIONS. Single rooms are rare in Glastonbury. Buses stop nearly in front of the **Glastonbury Backpackers ❷,** 4 Market Pl., at the corner of Magdalene St. and High St. Bright blue building with color-themed rooms. A friendly staff and a lively cafe-bar complement the great location. (☎833 353; www.glastonburybackpackers.com. Internet access £2.50 per 30min. Reception 9am-11pm. Kitchen. Dorms £12; doubles £30, with bath £35. MC/V.) Right by the post office, **A. B&B ❸,** 52a High St., offers clean, modern, and spacious rooms. One family room and two twins. (☎832 265. £25 per person. Cash only.) The nearest YHA hostel is the **YHA Street ❶,** The Chalet, Ivythorn Hill St., off the B3151 in Street. Take First bus #376 to Marshalls Elm, and follow the signs 1 mi. (☎442 961. Kitchen. Reception 8:30-10am and 5-11pm. Lockout 10am-5pm. Open daily July-Aug.; May-June Tu-Su; during other months call 48hr. in advance. Dorms £10.60, under 18 £7.20. MC/V.) At **Pilgrims ❷**, 12-13 Norbins Rd., unwind amidst Indian decor in large, cheery rooms near the heart of town. From High St., turn left on the footpath in front of St. John the Baptist Church and follow it as it wraps around the church and becomes Norbins Rd.; the house is down the street on the left. (☎834 722; www.pilgrimsbb.co.uk. £25 per person. Cash only.) Uphill, **Margaret Bernett ❸**, 46 Bove Town, lets a quaint twin room in a small townhouse. The backyard garden rivals the Tor. From the top of High St., turn left and then a quick right onto Bove Town. (☎833 684. Single £23 per person, £20 for two nights; during high season single person must pay doubles price £40. Cash only.)

⌂ FOOD. A **farmer's market** takes place in St. John's carpark, behind the TIC, on the last Saturday of the month. **Heritage Fine Foods,** 34 High St., stocks **groceries.** (☎831 003. Open M-W 7am-9pm, Th-Sa 9am-10pm, Su 8am-9pm.) Find cheap baked goods and sandwiches (£1-5) at **Burns the Bread ❶**, 14 High St. (☎831 532. Open M-Sa 6am-5pm, Su 11am-5pm. Cash only.) The vegetarian and wholefood menu at **Rainbow's End ❶**, 17a High St., changes with the chef's creative whims; if available, try the roasted red pepper and sweet potato flan (£6.50), served with a double portion of salad and garlic potatoes. Soups, salads, and quiches are £3-6. (☎833 896. Open M-Sa 10am-4pm, Su 11am-4pm. Cash only.) At **The Blue Note Cafe ❶**, 4 High St., savor generous portions of hearty specials like spinach and ricotta lasagna (£5.75) in the moody red and beige interior or outdoor courtyard. (☎832 907. Open daily 9:30am-5pm. MC/V.) **Cafe Galatea ❷**, 5a High St., is the best place for late-night veggie fare. Entrees (£7-8.50) play on Mexican, Indian, and Italian themes. (☎834 284. Internet access £ per 30min. Open W-Th 11am-9pm, F 11am-10pm, Sa 10:30am-10pm, Su 10:30am-9pm. MC/V.) While meat may seem foreign to this town, head to **Gigi's ❸**, 2-4 Magdalene St., for a few carnivorous options. Slightly forced Italian decor is forgiven in light of affordable prices (£6-15) and sizable portions. (☎834 612. Open Tu-Th 6-10:45pm, F 6-11pm, Sa-Su noon-2:30pm and 6-11pm. MC/V.)

◎ 📷 SIGHTS AND THE FESTIVAL. Legend holds that Joseph of Arimathea, the Virgin Mary's uncle, traveled with the young Jesus to do business in modern-day Somerset. He later returned in AD 63 to found the massive 📷**Glastonbury Abbey,** on Magdalene St. behind the Town Hall. Though the abbey was destroyed during the English Reformation, the colossal pile of ruins that remains still evokes the grandeur of the original church. The **Lady Chapel** and **Abbot's Kitchen,** coupled with a museum that opened in 1994, help recreate the grandeur and history vested in such sacred ground. Turn left and walk down what was formerly the nave (now a grassy plateau) to reach the **tomb of Arthur and Guinevere.** After a fire damaged the abbey in 1184, the monks needed to raise some cash; fortunately, they "found" Arthur's grave on the south side of Lady Chapel in 1191 and reburied the bodies here, inviting the King and Queen—and the royal treasurer—to attend the ceremony. Near the entrance to the abbey, the **Holy Glastonbury Thorn** blooms every Christmas and Easter. The original thorn, a short walk down Magdelene St. to **Wearyall Hill,** is said to have miraculously sprouted when Joseph of Arimathea drove his staff into the ground. (☎832 267; www.glastonburyabbey.com. Open daily June-Aug. 9am-6pm; Mar.-May and Sept.-Nov. 9:30am-6pm (or dusk if earlier); Dec.-Feb. 10am-dusk. £3.50, concessions £3, children £1.50, families £8.)

A 15min. hike from the base of the 526 ft. **Glastonbury Tor** brings visitors to the huge mound's windy top, a pilgrimage site since the 6th century with breathtaking views of three counties. To reach the Tor, turn right at the top of High St. on Lambrook, which becomes Chilkwell St.; turn left at Wellhouse Ln., and follow the path uphill. The Tor is reputedly the site of the Isle of Avalon, where King Arthur sleeps until his country needs him again. The hill now features a simple tower, built in 1360 as a church. In summer, the **Glastonbury Tor Bus** takes weary pilgrims

SOUTHWEST ENGLAND

from the city center (St. Dunstan's carpark, on Magdalene St.) to a shorter climb on the other side of the Tor, returning them to town via Chalice Well and the Rural Life Museum. *(Tor open all year; free. Hop-on, hop-off bus runs every 30min. (except lunchtimes). Apr.-Oct. 9:30am-5pm. £1, children 50p, free if accompanied by an adult.)*

At the base of the Tor on Chilkwell St., **Chalice Well** is said to be where Joseph of Arimathea washed the holy grail, the cup from which Jesus drank at the last supper. Legend once held that the well ran with Christ's blood; now it's admitted that the red tint comes from rust deposits in the stream. Ancient mystics interpreted the iron-red water's mingling with clear water from nearby **White Well** (which now runs through a cafe across the street) as a symbol of balance between the divine feminine and divine masculine. A tiered garden of climbing vines and "healing" pools now surrounds the fabled spring. *(☎831 154. Open daily Apr.-Oct. 10am-6pm; Feb.-Mar. and Nov. 11am-5pm; Dec.-Jan. 11am-4pm. £2.70, children £1.40, seniors £2.30.)* Down Chilkwell St. from the Chalice Well, the **Rural Life Museum** provides a mildly diverting account of what life was like for a poor Somerset farmer in the 19th century. *(☎831 197. Open Apr.-Oct. Tu-F 10am-5pm, Sa-Su 2-6pm; Nov.-Mar. Tu-Sa 10am-5pm. Free.)*

Glasto's greatest attraction is 5mi. away in Pilton, the site of the annual ⊠**Glastonbury Festival,** undoubtedly the biggest and best of Britain's multitude of summer music festivals. Like a yearly Woodstock, the muddy three-day event takes place at the end of June and features some of the world's biggest bands. *(Tickets are expensive—£105 in 2004—and sell out almost immediately every year. Contact the Glastonbury Festival Office, 28 Northload St. ☎834 596; www.glastonburyfestivals.co.uk.)*

THE DORSET COAST

BOURNEMOUTH ☎01202

Only two centuries old, Bournemouth (pop. 150,000) is an infant among English cities. Once popular for its healing pine scents and curative sea-baths, today the seaside resort lures summer daytrippers with an expansive beach and boardwalk entertainment. Come nightfall, legions of young people swarm its numerous bars and clubs, where the brassy sounds of the grandstand band give way to mainstream tunes and thumping beats.

▐ **TRANSPORTATION.** The **train station** lies on Holdenhurst Rd., 15min. east of the town center. (Travel center open M-F 9am-7pm, Sa 9am-6pm, Su 9am-5pm. Ticket office open M-Sa 5:40am-9pm.) **Trains** (☎08457 484 950) arrive from: **Birmingham** (3hr., every hr., £45.50); **Dorchester** (40min., every hr., £7.70); **London Waterloo** (2hr., 2 per hr., £31.40); **Poole** (10min., 2 per hr., £2.50). **National Express** (☎08705 808 080) buses pull up behind the train station (ticket office open M-Sa 7:30am-6pm, Su 9am-6pm) and serve: **Birmingham** (5-6hr., 3 per day, £33); **Bristol** (3½hr., 1 per day, £13.50); **London** (3hr., every hr., £16; funfare also available when you order online, £1-5); Poole (20 min., 2-3 per hr., £1.50). Tickets are also sold at the TIC. **Wilts and Dorset** (☎673 555) runs local buses, including services to Poole and Southampton. Purchase an **Explorer ticket** (£5.75, children £2.90) for unlimited travel. **United Taxi** (☎556 677) runs 24hr.

▌▐ **ORIENTATION AND PRACTICAL INFORMATION.** The downtown centers around **The Square,** which is flanked by the **Central Gardens** to the northwest and the **Lower Gardens** toward the water. The **Tourist Information Centre,** Westover Rd., sells a 50p map and miniguide and books rooms for a 10% deposit. From the train station turn left on Holdenhurst Rd. and continue straight on Bath Rd., then follow the signs. (☎0906 802 0234; www.bournemouth.co.uk. Open mid-July to Aug. M-Sa 9:30am-7pm, Su 10:30am-5pm; Sept. to mid-July M-Sa 9:30am-5:30pm.) Other services include: **American Express**, 95A Old Christchurch Rd. (☎780 752; open M-Sa 9am-5pm); **work opportunities**, especially seasonal work, at **JobCentre**, 181-187 Old Christchurch Rd. (☎0845 606 0234; open M-Tu and Th-F 9am-5pm, W 10am-5pm); **The Launderette**, 172 Commercial Rd. (☎551 850; wash £2.40, dry £1.50; open M-F 8am-9pm, Sa-Su 8am-8pm; last wash 1hr. before closing); the **police**, Madeira Rd. (☎552 099); **Boots** pharmacy, 18-20 Commercial Rd. (☎551 713; open M-Sa 8:3-am-6pm, Su 10:30am-4:30pm); **Bournemouth Hospital**, Castle Land East, Littledown (☎303 626); **Internet access** at **Cyber College**, 248 Old Christchurch Rd. (☎772 909; £2 per hr., students £1.50 per hr., £1 per hr. after 8pm; open M-Th 10am-midnight, F 10am-1:30pm and 2:30pm-midnight, Sa-Su 11am-11pm); and at the **library**, 22 The Triangle, uphill from City Square (☎454 848; open M 10am-7pm, Tu and Th-F 9:30am-7pm, W 9:30am-5pm, Sa 10am-2pm; free for up to 1hr. per day, 15min. quick access, make reservation for more time); and the **post office**, 292 Holdenhurst Rd. (☎395 840; open 9am-5:30pm). **Post Code:** BH8 8BB.

⌂ ACCOMMODATIONS AND FOOD. Though the hotels in the center of town cater to businessmen and convention-goers, the **East Cliff** neighborhood, 5min. from the train station, bristles with **B&Bs**. Exit left from the station, cross Holdenhurst Rd. to St. Swithuns, and turn left on Frances Rd.; the route is signposted. **Bournemouth Backpackers ❶**, 3 Frances Rd., a friendly independent hostel, fosters a homey environment for overseas travelers with comfy lounges and a barbecue pit. (☎299 491; www.bournemouthbackpackers.co.uk. Kitchen. Reception mid-May to mid-Sept. 8:30-10:30am and 4-7pm; during other months you must book through the website and a 2-night minimum applies. Dorms £11-16 in summer, £9-13 in winter; doubles £30-40/£25-35. Rates highest on Sa; discounted for longer stays. Cash only.) **Lyn-Glary Hotel ❸**, 48 Frances Rd., offers large, airy rooms and a refined decor. (☎551 806; www.bournemouth.uk.com/lynglary. £25 per person. Cash only.) **Kantara ❸**, 8 Gardens View, provides guests with comfortable beds and is a short walk from the train and bus stations. (☎557 260; www.kantaraguesthouse.co.uk. £20 per person. Breakfast £3. MC/V.)

Christchurch Road features diverse food offerings while **Charminster Road** is a center of ethnic cuisine. **Eye of the Tiger ❸**, 207 Old Christchurch Rd., serves delicious Bengali curries for £6-10 and other Tandoori specialties for £6.75-12.95. (☎780 900. Open daily noon-2pm and 6pm-midnight. 10% takeaway discount. MC/V.) For creamy goodness, **Shake Away ❶**, 7 Post Office Rd., provides takeaway and over 120 flavors of milkshakes (£2.25-3.25), from marshmallow to rhubarb. Ask for the student discount. (☎310 105. Open M-F 9am-5:30pm, Su 10am-4:30pm. Cash only.) For an upscale atmosphere at an affordable price, try **Bliss ❷**, 1-15 St. Peter's Rd., which offers a lunch buffet (£4.20, M-Sa noon-3pm). For dinner on weekends, call ahead for a table. (☎319 997. Open Su-Th 11am-1am, F-Sa 11am-4am. MC/V.)

◎ SIGHTS AND BEACHES. The city center holds few interesting attractions. The **Russell-Cotes Art Gallery and Museum**, Russell-Cotes Rd., East Cliff, houses a collection of Victorian art, sculptures, and artifacts. (☎451 858. Open Tu-Su 10am-5pm. Free.) On the corner of Hilton Rd. and St. Peter's Rd., **St. Peter's** parish church holds the remains of Mary Shelley, author of *Frankenstein*. Visitors mostly come for **Bournemouth Beach** (☎451 781), a 7 mi. sliver of shoreline barely wide enough to hold its inflatable slides. Amusements and a theater can be found at **Bournemouth Pier** (50p adults, 25p children; open Apr.-June, Sept.-Oct. 9am-5:30pm, July-Aug. 9am-8:30pm); a short walk takes sunbathers to quieter spots.

SOUTHWEST ENGLAND

Instead of staying in Bournemouth, travel the shore for more stunning sights. A 95 mi. stretch of the Dorset and East Devon coast, dubbed the **Jurassic Coast,** was recently named a World Heritage Site for its famous fossils and unique geology (www.jurassiccoast.com; see also **Lyme Regis,** p. 215). Beautiful **Studland Beach** sits across the harbor, reachable by bus #150 (50min., every hr., round-trip £3). A **nude beach** awaits just down the shore. Take bus #150 or 151 (25min., 2 per hr., £3) to reach the themed landscapes of **Compton Acres,** featuring a stunning Italian garden with Roman statues and a sensory garden designed for the blind. (☎700 110. Open daily Mar.-Oct. 9am-6pm. £6, children £4.) The 1000-year-old **Corfe Castle** is no gently weathered pile of ruins: Parliamentarian engineers were ordered to destroy the castle during the English Civil War. What remains is a testament to its incredible strength. (To get to the castle, travel to Poole (bus #151) or Swanage (#150) to catch bus #142, every hr., round-trip £5.75. ☎418 294. Open daily Apr.-Sept. 10am-6pm; Mar. and Oct. 10am-5pm; Nov.-Feb. 10am-4pm. £4.70, children £2.30, families £11.50.)

🎭 🎪 **ENTERTAINMENT AND FESTIVALS.** Swarms of students and vacationers have revitalized Bournemouth's nightlife. Most start at the roundabout up the hill from **Fir Vale Rd.,** working downhill through the numerous bars on **Christchurch Road.** Club **Slam,** at the top of Fir Vale Rd., is a good place to begin the night. (☎555 129. Tu student night, all drinks £1.50. No cover. Open W-Th, Su 5-11pm; Tu 5pm-2am, Sa-Su 5pm-4am.) Just next door, **Circo** and downstairs club **Elements** attract crowds. (☎311 178. W student night. Cover £3-8. Open M, Th 9pm-2am, W 8pm-2am, F-Sa 8pm-3am.) A mile east of The Square, **The Opera House,** 570 Christchurch Rd., a former theater renovated into two dance floors, is one of the wildest (and cheapest) clubs in town. Take bus #22 from The Square. (☎399 922. Most drinks £1-2. Cover £1-15; Th night is "Hot N' Horny," cover £1-2 before 10pm, £3 after. Open Th-Su 9pm-3am.) In a tradition dating from 1896, 15,000 candles light up the Lower Gardens every summer Wednesday during the **Flowers by Candlelight Festival.** Bournemouth's **Live! Music Festival** (☎451 702; www.bournemouth.co.uk), in late June, hosts free concerts by international performers.

DORCHESTER ☎01305

Every city has its favorite children, but in Dorchester, Thomas Hardy is an only son, and the locals indulge his spirit to no end. Pub regulars will share time-worn stories about the author whose sober statue overlooks the town's main street, and most businesses, from inns to shoe stores, manag to incorporate "Hardy" into their names. The sleepy city that inspired the fictional "Casterbridge" has seen more prosperous times, but the people and landscape remain charming and carry an air of the timelessness that comes from being cemented to the page.

🚍 TRANSPORTATION

Most **trains** (☎08457 484 950) come to **Dorchester South,** off Weymouth Ave. (Ticket office open M-F 6am-8pm, Sa 6:40am-8pm, Su 8:40am-7pm.) Trains run from **Bournemouth** (40min., every hr., £7.70) and **London Waterloo** (2½hr., every hr., £35). Some trains arrive at the unstaffed **Dorchester West,** also off Weymouth Ave., including those from **Weymouth** (15min., 8 per day, £2.70). Dorchester lacks a bus station, but **buses** stop frequently at Dorchester South train station and on Trinity St. **National Express** (☎08705 808 080) serves **Exeter** (2hr., 1 per day, £9.50) and **London** (5hr., 3 per day, £17.50). Tickets are sold at the TIC. **Wilts & Dorset** (☎673 555) bus #184 goes to **Salisbury** via **Blandford** (2hr., 6 per day, £4.50). **First** bus #212 serves **Yeovil** (1½hr., every hr., £3.50), which connects to destinations farther south. **Coach House Travel** (☎267 644) provides local service. For a taxi, call **Coun-**

tyline (☎269 696). Rent **bikes** at **Dorchester Cycles**, 31 Great Western Rd. (☎268 787. £10 per day, £50 per week. Includes helmet, lock, and pump. £100 credit card deposit or passport. Open M-Sa 9am-5:30pm.)

✷ 🛈 ORIENTATION AND PRACTICAL INFORMATION

The intersection of **High West** and **South Street** (which eventually becomes **Cornhill Street**) is the unofficial center of town. The main **shopping district** extends southward along South St. The **Tourist Information Centre**, 11 Antelope Walk, on Trinity St., stocks free town maps, books accommodations for a 10% deposit, and sells Explorer bus tickets for Wilts & Dorset and First buses and general National Express tickets. (☎267 992; www.westdorset.com. Open Apr.-Oct. M-Sa 9am-5pm; May-Sept. also Su 10am-3pm; Nov.-Mar. M-Sa 9am-4pm.) Other services include: **Barclays**, 10 South St. (☎326 730; open M-Tu and Th-F 9:30am-4:30pm, W 10am-4:30pm); **Launderette**, 16c High East St. (wash £2.60-3, dry 20p per 4min.; open daily 8am-8pm); the **police**, Weymouth Ave. (☎251 212); **Boots pharmacy**, 12-13 Cornhill St. (☎264 340; open M-Sa 9am-5:30pm, Su 10am-4pm); **Dorset County Hospital,** Williams Ave. (☎251 150); free **Internet access** at the **library**, Colliton Park, off The Grove (☎224 448; open M 10am-7pm, Tu-W and F 9:30am-7pm, Th 9:30am-5pm, Sa 9am-4pm); and the **post office,** 43 South St., with a **bureau de change** (☎08457 223 344; open M-Sa 9am-5:30pm). **Post Code: DT1 1DH.**

🏠 ACCOMMODATIONS

Large, plush suites await at **The White House ❸,** 9 Queens Ave., off Weymouth Ave. From the train station, exit left onto Station Approach and turn left onto Weymouth Ave.; Queen's Ave. is a few blocks up in Dorchester's posh area, past Lime Close, second house on left. (☎266 714. Singles £25; doubles £40. Cash only.) **Maumbury Cottage ❷,** 9 Maumbury Rd., is close to both train stations. Kind Mrs. Wade lets one single, one double, and one twin and bakes bread for breakfast. (☎266 726. £19 per person. Cash only.) The hotel-style suites at **The King's Arms ❷,** 30 High East St., offer hostel-style value in the center of town. Spacious family rooms sleep four at £12.75 per person. (☎265 353; www.kingsarmsdorchester.com. £6 full English breakfast, £4 continental. All rooms £48. AmEx/MC/V.) Self-catering **YHA Litton Cheney ❶** is 10 mi. west of the city. Take bus #31 to Whiteway, and follow the signs 1½ mi. (☎01308 482 340. Reception 8-10am and 5-10pm. Lockout 10-am-5pm. Curfew 11pm. Open Apr.-Aug. Dorms £10.60, under 18 £7.20. MC/V.) For camping, try **Giant's Head Caravan and Camping Park ❶,** Old Sherborne Rd., in **Cerne Abbas,** 8 mi. north of Dorchester. Head out of town on The Grove and bear right onto Old Sherborne Rd. (☎01300 341 242. Showers, laundry, and electricity. Open Apr.-Sept. £7.50-11 for tent, car, and 2 adults. Cash only.)

🍴 FOOD AND PUBS

The eateries along **High West Street** and **High East Street** provide a range of options. Get your **groceries** at the **market,** in the carpark near South Station (open W 8am-3pm), or at **Waitrose,** in the Tudor Arcade, off South St. (☎268 420; open M-W and Sa 8:30am-7pm, Th-F 8:30am-8pm, Su 10am-4pm). **6 North Square ❸,** serves fresh Dorset seafood and other hearty meals (lunch specials £4.35, dinner entrees £12.50) in a hidden-away spot near the prison. (☎267 679. Open M-Sa 10:30am-2:30pm and 6:30-9:30pm, Su 10:30am-2:30pm cold menu. MC/V.) **The Celtic Kitchen ❶,** 17 Antelope Walk, near the TIC, serves delicious homemade Cornish pasties (£1.70-2.10), from veggie to chicken and tarragon. (☎269 377. Open M-Sa 9am-4pm.

Cash only.) For a spicier option, try **Thai Palace ❸**, with an extensive menu including curries (£7.95-8.95) and seafood. (☎757 188. Open Su-Th noon-2pm and 5:30-11pm, F-Sa noon-2pm and 5:30-11:30pm. MC/V.)

Dorchester barely dabbles in nightlife, but find a good pint among the friendly, alternative crowd at **The Old George**, at the bottom of Trinity St. (☎263 534. DJs and live bands F-Sa. Open M-Th 11am-11pm, F-Sa 11am-midnight, Su noon-10:30pm.) Heed the warning to "duck or grouse" when entering the **King's Arms**, 30 High East St., and then drink and be merry at the historic inn, featured in Hardy's *Mayor of Casterbridge*. (☎265 353. Open M-Sa 11am-11pm, Su noon-10:30pm.) Of Dorchester's two nightclubs, **Paul's**, 27 Trinity St., is popular for R&B and retro nights. (☎268 008. Open Th 10pm-2am, F-Sa 9pm-2am.) Locals favor **Liberty's**, 37-8 High West St., for hip-hop, house, and trance. (☎269 151. Open Th-Sa 10pm-2am.)

🅖 SIGHTS

Dorchester's attractions can't quite compete with the compelling sights in the surrounding hills. East of town, Hardy-related sites hint at the poet-novelist's inspiration for Wessex, a fictional region centered around Dorset. West of town, dramatic remnants of Iron Age and Roman Britain dominate the landscape. Negotiate both areas in a day with a bike or a bus schedule.

Here's the **Thomas Hardy** breakdown: he designed **Max Gate**, 1 mi. southwest of town off Arlington Rd., and lived there from 1885 to his death in 1928, penning *Tess of the D'Urbervilles* and *Jude the Obscure*. (☎262 538. Open Apr.-Sept. M, W, Su 2-5pm. £2.60, children £1.40.) He was christened in **Stinsford Church**, 2 mi. northeast of town in Stinsford Village, and the yard holds his family plot where his first and second wives are buried, though only his heart is buried here—his ashes lie in Westminster Abbey (p. 110). (Take bus #184 (every 2hr., £1) from Trinity St. toward Puddletown; ask to be dropped off near the church. Free.) Finally, he was born in the aptly-named **Hardy's Cottage**, Bockhampton Ln., deep in the woods 3 mi. northeast of Dorchester. (Take bus #184 or 185 and ask to be let off at the Cottage. ☎262 366; open Apr.-Oct. M and Th-Su, 11am-5pm or dusk, whichever comes first. £3.)

On the other side of town, scattered ruins recall Dorchester's status as a neolithic settlement, Celtic stronghold, and Roman city. The most significant of these is **Maiden Castle**, the largest Iron Age fortification in Europe, dating to 3000 BC. The hillfort was protected by a complex tangle of walls and ditches until the Romans seized it in AD 43. Modern visitors can scale what little is left of the ancient ramparts, today patrolled by sheep. Take local shuttle #2 (M-Sa 5 per day, 80p) to Maiden Castle Rd., ¾ mi. from the hill. If it's nice out, opt instead to hike the scenic 2 mi. from the town center down Maiden Castle Rd. (Always open. Free.)

Roman sights within Dorchester are not as impressive, but still merit a visit. Archaeologists have unearthed the complete foundation and mosaic floor of a first-century **Roman Town House** at the back of the County Hall complex. Walk north on The Grove until it intersects with Northernway, where steep stairs lead to the entrance. Just past the South Station entrance sprawls the **Maumbury Rings**, a Bronze Age monument with a grassy, gaping maw used as a Roman amphitheater.

In town, the **Dorset County Museum**, 66 High West St., explores Roman and Hardy history and then some, with a replica of Hardy's study and relics of the city's other keepers—Druids, Romans, and Saxons. (☎262 735. Free audio tour. Open M-Sa 10am-5pm; July-Sept. also Su 10am-5pm. £4.20, concessions £3.20, children free.) For a cuddly experience, head to the Dorset **Teddy Bear Museum**, and learn about the history and development of the Teddy Bear, and see displays on your favorite bears, from Paddington to Pooh, as well as a few who might be new to you, like "Albeart Einstein" and "Abearham Lincoln." *(Antelope Walk.* ☎ *263 200; www.teddybearmuseum.co.uk. Open M-Sa 9:30am-5pm Su 10am-4pm. £3.50, children £2.50, family £10.50.)*

⚑ DAYTRIP FROM DORCHESTER

LYME REGIS

From Dorchester, take First (☎ 01305 783 645) bus #31 from South Station, 1¼hr., every hr., £3.50. The Tourist Information Centre, Guildhall Cottage, Church St., downhill from the bus stop, locates lodgings and stocks walking guides. ☎ *1297 442 138; www.lymeregistourism.com. Open Apr.-Oct. M-Sa 10am-5pm, Su 10am-4pm; Nov.-Mar M-Sa 10am-4pm, Su 10am-2pm. Historian Richard J. Fox conducts 1½hr. walking tours, which leave from Guildhall.* ☎ *1297 443 568. Smugglers' tours Tu and Th 2:30pm. Ghost tours Tu and Th 7:30pm. £3, children £2. Numerous companies on the Cobb run boat tours.*

Known as the "Pearl of Dorset," Lyme Regis (pop. 3500) surveys a majestic sweep of coastline. In 1811, a resident shopkeeper named Mary Anning discovered the first ichthyosaurus fossil a mile west of Lyme Regis. Since then, paleontologist Steve Davies (see **Jurassic Park**, p. 13) has amassed an immense collection of local fossils artfully displayed in the **Dinosaurland Fossil Museum,** Coombe St. (☎ 1297 443 541. Open daily 10am-5pm. ₤4, students and children ₤3, seniors ₤3.50, families ₤12.50.) Davies leads a 2hr. **hunting walk,** which roams the shores in search of fossils; contact Dinosaurland for times. (₤5, children ₤3, seniors ₤4.50.) Lyme Regis is also renowned for **The Cobb,** a 10-20 ft. high manmade seawall that cradles the harbor. In Jane Austen's *Persuasion,* Louisa Musgrove suffers her unfortunate fall on the Cobb's unguarded steps. The **Marine Aquarium** on the Cobb exhibits a small collection of local sea creatures (including a 5 ft. conger eel). (☎ 1297 33106. Open daily Mar.-Oct. 10am-5pm; later in July-Aug. ₤2, concessions ₤1.50.) The **Lyme Regis Museum,** Bridge St., two doors down from the TIC, chronicles Lyme's history. (☎ 1297 443 370. Open Apr.-Oct. M-Sa 10am-5pm, Su 11am-5pm; Nov.-Apr. Sa-Su only. ₤2, concessions ₤1.50, children free.)

Fish and chips sizzle on **Marine Parade** near the Cobb; the seafood (₤5) is excellent at the **Cobb Arms ❷** pub. (☎ 1297 443 242. Open daily 11am-11pm. Food served until 8pm. Cash only.) **Cafe Sol ❶,** 1a Coombe St., fixes tasty baguettes, sandwiches (₤3-3.60), and organic drinks (₤1.40-1.85) on a sunny terrace overlooking the River Lym. (☎ 1297 443 404. Open daily Apr.-Oct. 10am-5pm. Cash only.)

THE HIDDEN DEAL

JURASSIC PARK

Antique souvenirs can cost a pretty penny. But there is one British collectible that is absolutely free: fossils. The beaches surrounding Lyme Regis are littered with specimens ranging from 200 to 65 million years of age. How can Wedgwood compete with a perfectly preserved fish from a prehistoric sea?

The best way to make a fossil find is to join an expert-led tour. Steve Davies, owner of **Dinosaurland Fossil Museum** has decades of experience and the fossils to prove it. He conducts 2hr. fossil-hunting excursions at Black Ven, the mudflow 1 mi. east of Lyme where Mary Anning discovered her famous ichthyosaurus. Because erosion constantly acts on the surrounding cliffs, a new crop of fossils flows down every day, virtually guaranteeing a geological discovery.

The most common fossil-finds are belemnites, squid-like mollusks, and ammonites, beautiful spiral-shelled cephalopods. Some are preserved in iron pyrite, or fool's gold, which gives them a lustrous appearance. Other fossils include shelled creatures like bivalves (oysters) and brachiopods, plant-like crinoids, snails, fishes, and even ichthyosauri.

For tour times, contact Dinosaurland Fossil Museum, Coombe St., Lyme Regis, ☎ *01297 443 541; or consult the chalk board outside the museum doors. £5, children £3.*

DEVON

EXETER
☎ 01392

In 1068, the inhabitants of Exeter earned the respect of William the Conqueror, holding their own against his forces for 18 days. When the wells within the city ran dry, the Exonians used wine for cooking, bathing, and (of course) drinking, which might explain the city's eventual fall. Today, however, the city is on the rise, relishing its status as a busy hub and student center. Restaurants, shops, and wine-bars enclose the magnificent cathedral, and the hum of activity helps visitors forget that this growing city was almost destroyed during WWII.

▆ TRANSPORTATION

Exeter is a convenient gateway to the rest of Devon and Cornwall.

Trains: St. David's Station, St. David's Hill, 15min. from town. Ticket office open M-F 5:45am-8:40pm, Sa 6:15am-8pm, Su 7:30am-8:40pm. Trains (☎ 08457 484 950) from: **Bristol** (1hr., every hr., £16.20); **London Paddington** (2½hr., every hr., £61); **Salisbury** (2hr., every 2hr., £21.70). **Central Station,** Queen St. Ticket office open M-Sa 7:50am-6pm. From **London Waterloo** (3hr., 12 per day, £42).

Buses: Bus station, Paris St. (☎ 427 711). Ticket office open M-F 8:45am-5:30pm, Sa 8:45am-1pm. **Lockers** £1-2. **National Express** (☎ 08705 808 080) buses from **Bristol** (2hr., 5 per day, 10.75) and **London** (4-5hr., 9 per day, 20).

Public Transportation: An **Exeter Freedom Ticket** (£3 per day, £8 per week) allows unlimited travel on city **minibuses**. The **Explorer Ticket** (£6 per day, £16 per week), allows unlimited travel on **Stagecoach** (☎ 427 711) buses.

Taxis: Capital (☎ 433 433).

▐ PRACTICAL INFORMATION

Tourist Information Centre: Civic Centre, Paris St. (☎ 265 700). Books accommodations for a 10% deposit and sells National Express tickets. Open M-Sa 9am-5pm; July-Aug. also Su 10am-4pm.

Tours: The best way to explore is with the City Council's free 1½hr. **themed walking tours** (☎ 265 203), including Murder and Mayhem, Ghosts and Legends, and Medieval Exeter. Most leave from the front of the Royal Clarence Hotel off High St.; some depart from the Quay House Visitor Centre. Apr.-Oct. 4-5 per day; Nov.-Mar. 11am and 2pm.

Financial Services: Thomas Cook, 9 Princesshay (☎ 601 300). Open M-Sa 9am-5:30pm.

Work Opportunities: JobCentre, Clarendon House, Western Way (☎ 474 700), on the roundabout near the TIC. Open M-Tu and Th-F 9am-5pm, W 10am-5pm.

Launderette: Silverspin Cleaning Centre, 12 Blackboy Rd. (☎ 270 067.) Wash £2.20, dry £4. Open daily 8am-10pm.

Internet Access: Central Library, Castle St. (☎ 384 206). Free for the first 30min., then £1.50 per 30min. Open M-Tu and Th-F 9:30am-7pm, W 10am-5pm, Sa 9:30am-4pm, Su 11am-2:30pm.

Pharmacy: Boots, 251 High St. (☎ 432 244). Open M-Sa 8:30am-6pm, Su 10am-4:30pm.

Hospital: Royal Devon and Exeter, Barrack Rd. (☎ 411 611).

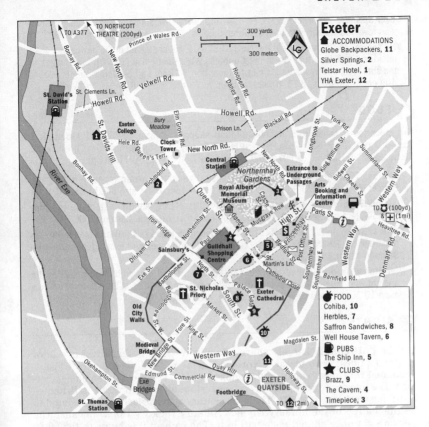

Exeter

🏠 ACCOMMODATIONS
Globe Backpackers, 11
Silver Springs, 2
Telstar Hotel, 1
YHA Exeter, 12

🍴 FOOD
Cohiba, 10
Herbles, 7
Saffron Sandwiches, 8
Well House Tavern, 6

🍺 PUBS
The Ship Inn, 5

⭐ CLUBS
Brazz, 9
The Cavern, 4
Timepiece, 3

Police: Heavitree Rd. (☎08705 777 444).

Post Office: Bedford St. (☎08457 223 344). Bureau de change. Open M-Sa 9am-5:30pm. **Post Code:** EX1 1AH.

🏠 ACCOMMODATIONS

A handful of inexpensive **B&Bs** lie near the **Clock Tower** roundabout north of Queen St., especially on **St. David's Hill** between St. David's Station and the center of town. During April and from July to September, the **University of Exeter** offers a range of accommodations throughout the city, including B&B. (☎215 566. Reservations recommended. Singles 14.50-17.75, with bath 26.50; ensuite doubles 45.50.)

Globe Backpackers, 71 Holloway St. (☎215 521; www.exeterbackpackers.co.uk). Clean, with friendly staff. Self-catering kitchen. Luggage storage £1 per bag. Internet access 5p per min. Towels 50p. Laundry service £3. Key deposit £5. Reception 8am-11pm. Check-out 11am. Dorms £12; doubles £32. Book ahead. MC/V. ❷

Telstar Hotel, 77 St. David's Hill (☎272 466; www.telstar-hotel.co.uk). Family-run B&B with comfortable rooms, many newly renovated. Full breakfast includes fresh fruit salad. Book 1-2 weeks ahead in summer. Singles £25-35; doubles £45-60. MC/V. ❸

SOUTHWEST ENGLAND

Silver Springs, 12 Richmond Rd. (☎494 040; www.silversprings.co.uk). A classy Georgian townhouse near both train stations. Singles £35; doubles £65-70. MC/V. ❹

YHA Exeter, 47 Countess Wear Rd. (☎873 329), 2 mi. southeast of the city center. Take minibus K or T from High St. to the Countess Wear post office (£1.20); follow signs to the spacious, cheery hostel (10min.). Reception 8-10am and 5-10pm. Internet access 50p per 5min. Dorms £13.40, students up to £3 off; under 18 £9.30. MC/V. ❷

🍴 FOOD

Get **groceries** at **Sainsbury's,** in the **Guildhall Shopping Centre.** (☎432 741. Open M-W 8am-6:30pm, Th-F 8am-7pm, Sa 7:30am-6:30pm, Su 10:30am-4:30pm), or **Tesco Metro,** 223-226 High St. (☎607 300. Open M-Sa 7am-10pm, Su 11am-5pm.)

Herbies, 15 North St. (☎258 473). A casual venue for exotic vegetarian delights. Entrees £6-7. Open M-F 11am-2:30pm, Sa 11am-4pm, Tu-Sa also 6-9:30pm. MC/V. ❷

Saffron Sandwiches, 6 South St. (☎670 599). Hearty sandwiches made to order £2.25-3, jacket potatoes £1.10-4:15. Open M-Sa 10am-4pm. Cash only. ❶

Cohiba, 36 South St. (☎678 445). Serves delicious tapas (£4.50) and Mediterranean main dishes (£9-15) with a mellow mix of jazzy Latin tunes and exotic decor. Open M-Sa noon-11pm. MC/V. ❸

Well House Tavern, Cathedral Close (☎310 031). Good pub grub in an annex of the ancient and blue-blood-haunted Royal Clarence Hotel. Open M-Sa 11am-11pm, Su noon-10:30pm. Food served noon-2:30pm. AmEx/MC/V. ❷

👁 SIGHTS

EXETER CATHEDRAL. Largely spared during WWII, this Cathedral is one of England's finest. Two massive Norman towers preside over the West Front, decorated with kings, saints, and a sculpture of St. Peter as a half-naked fisherman. The interior features one of the longest uninterrupted vaults in Britain—a striking sight at over 300 ft. The 16th-century **astronomical clock** is reputed to be the source of the nursery rhyme "Hickory Dickory Dock" because the bishop's cat once chased mice within it. The cathedral is home to the 60 ft. **Bishop's Throne** (made without nails), disassembled and taken to the countryside in 1640 and again during WWII to save it from destruction. The **Minstrels' Gallery** contains carvings of angels playing 14th-century instruments. The Bishop's Palace *library* exhibits a collection of manuscripts known as the **Exeter Book**—the world's richest treasury of early Anglo-Saxon poetry. (☎285 983. *Cathedral open Su-F 8:30am-6:30pm, Sa 8:30am-5:30pm. Library open M-F 2-5pm. Evensong M-F 5:30pm, Sa-Su 3pm. Free guided tours Apr.-Oct. M-F 11am and 2:30pm, Sa 11am, Su 4pm. Requested donation £3.50.)*

THE UNDERGROUND PASSAGES. Nearly 650 years ago, the clergy built underground passages to access the water pipes that delivered clean water to the church community. Not to be outdone, wealthy merchants built their own subterranean piping network. Although the pipes are long since pilfered, visitors can now take a 30min. tour of the incredibly narrow passages (2 ft. by 6 ft.), which contain doors used by Cavaliers during the Civil War to keep out besieging Roundheads. Construction is expected to commence in early 2005 that will close the tunnels for a period; call ahead to ensure that they are open to visitors. *(Romangate Passage, off High St. ☎665 887. Open June-Sept. M-Sa 10am-5pm; Oct.-May Tu-F noon-5pm, Sa 10am-5pm. Closed from 12:50-1:50pm for lunch. Tours every 30min. June-Sept.; last tour 4:30pm. £3.75, families £11, concessions £2.75; Oct.-May £3/£9/£2.)*

THE ROYAL ALBERT MEMORIAL MUSEUM. This museum's thorough exploration of local history, from Roman occupation to WWII attacks, is part of a diverse collection. World culture galleries, amassed largely by local explorers (including Captain Cook), feature everything from totem poles and Egyptian tombs to Polynesian weaponry. The extensive natural history exhibits include rare birds and a stuffed giraffe. *(Queen St. ☎665 858. Open M-Sa 10am-5pm. Free.)*

GARDENS. Upon penetrating the city, William the Conqueror built Rougemont Castle to keep the locals in check. Today, only the castle walls remain, and, due to security at the adjacent court building, tourists can only view the ruins from an awkward angle in the surrounding **Rougemont Gardens.** Follow the path along the castle walls through immaculate flowerbeds to reach the expansive 17th-century **Northernhay Gardens** next door. *(Accessible from Castle St. Open daily dawn-dusk. Free.)*

🕴🏃 NIGHTLIFE AND ENTERTAINMENT

Exeter boasts a growing nightlife, with bars and clubs in the alleys off **High Street** and near **Exeter Cathedral**, and on **Gandy Street**. Black lights and neon disco murals light up **Timepiece**, Little Castle St. (☎493 096; www.timepiece-nightclub.co.uk. Cover £2-5. Open M-W 7pm-1am, Th-Sa 7pm-1:30am, Su 7pm-12:30am.) For a more relaxed scene, head to **The Cavern,** 83-84 Queen St., in a brick cellar, for the best in rock, punk, and local bands. (☎495 370; www.cavernclub.co.uk. Cover £2-5. M-Th 8:30pm-1am, F-Sa 9pm-2am, and Su 8pm-midnight. Cafe open M-Sa 10:30am-4pm.) **Brazz,** 10-12 Palace Gate, is a high-class bar with a big-city feel and fluorescent, two-story aquarium. (☎252 525; www.brazz.co.uk. Open M-F 11am-11pm, Sa noon-11pm, Su noon-10:30pm.) **The Ship Inn,** 1-3 St. Martin's Ln., was once Francis Drake's favorite. (☎272 040. Open M-Sa 11am-11pm, Su noon-10:30pm.)

The professional company at **Northcott Theatre,** Stoker Rd., performs throughout the year. (☎493 493. Box office open M-Sa 10am-6pm, until 8pm on show nights. Tickets £11-15.50, standbys for students £6. Students bookings £2 off M-Th.) Tickets can also be booked at the **Arts Booking and Information Centre,** off High St., which supplies monthly listings of cultural events in the city. (☎211 080. Open M-Sa 9:30am-5:30pm.) The **Exeter Festival,** in the first three weeks of July, features concerts, opera, dance lessons, stand-up comedy, and theater. For tickets, contact the **Festival Box Office,** Civic Centre, Paris St. (☎213 161; www.exeter.gov.uk/festival. Open M-Sa 10am-5pm. Tickets £8-20.)

EXMOOR NATIONAL PARK

Once a royal hunting preserve, Exmoor is among the smallest and most picturesque of Britain's national parks, covering 265 sq. mi. on the north coast of the island's southwestern peninsula. Dramatic sea-swept cliffs fringe moors covered with purple heather where sheep and cattle graze. Wild ponies still roam, and England's last herds of red deer graze in woodlands. Although over 80% of Exmoor is privately owned, the territory is accommodating to respectful hikers and bikers.

⊏ TRANSPORTATION

Traveline (☎0870 608 2608) is the most helpful resource for planning public transport. Exmoor's western gateway is **Barnstaple.** The train station serves Exeter Central and **Exeter St. David's** (1¼hr.; M-Sa 12 per day, Su 5 per day; £10). **National Express** (☎08705 808 080) buses connect **Barnstaple** to **Bristol** (3hr., 1 per

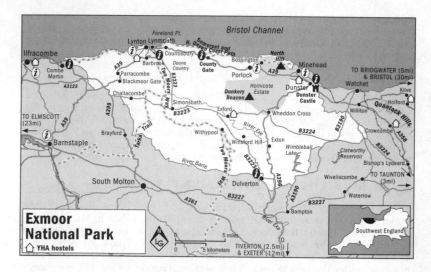

Exmoor National Park
△ YHA hostels

day, $16.50) and **London Victoria** (5½hr., 3-4 per day, $25). To reach **Exeter,** take **First DevonBus** (☎01752 402 060) bus #315 (2¼hr.; M-Sa 4-5 per day, Su 2 per day; $4). To reach **Plymouth,** take #86 (3¼hr.; M-Sa 6 per day, Su 2 per day; $4.50) or the more direct Saturday X85 service (2¾hr., Sa 1 per day, $4.50).

Exmoor's eastern gateway is **Minehead,** accessible via **Taunton,** whose train station connects to bigger cities, including **Exeter St. David's** (25min., every hr., $7.60). To reach Minehead from Taunton, take First bus #28, 928 (Su), or 300 direct (1¼hr.; M-Sa every hr., Su 9 per day; $4) or get off at **Bishops Lydeard** (20min.), then take a **West Somerset Railway** (☎01643 704 996) train to Minehead (1¾hr., Apr.-Oct. 4-8 per day, $10.40). Drivers sell combined bus and train tickets ($12, children $6).

Reaching the outskirts of Exmoor is relatively easy but bus service within the park is erratic. Western Exmoor lies in North Devon, and bus routes are detailed in *North Devon Bus Times;* eastern Exmoor occupies the western part of Somerset and is covered by the *Public Transport Timetable for the Exmoor and West Somerset Area.* Both guides are free at TICs. *Accessible Exmoor,* free from National Park Information Centers (NPICs), provides a guide for disabled visitors.

Nearly all **buses** in the area are run by **First** (☎01752 402 060 in Devon; ☎01823 272 033 in Somerset). Since single fares are about $3-4, it's wise to purchase **First Day Explorer** ($7, children $5) or **First Week Explorer** ($12.50/$7) tickets, which allow unlimited travel on all First buses. First Somerset bus #300 runs east to west along the coast, from Taunton to Barnstaple via Dunster, Minehead, Porlock, Lynton, and Ilfracombe. Listed prices are for off-peak hours (purchased after 8:45am). Devon buses to **Barnstaple** run from: **Ilfracombe** (#3 or 30; 40min.; M-Sa 4 per hr., Su every hr.; $2.10); **Lynmouth** (#309-310, 1hr., M-Sa 3 per day, $2); **Lynton** (#309-310, 1hr., M-Sa every hr., $2.80). Somerset buses to **Minehead** run from: **Barnstaple** (#300, 2¾hr., 1 per day, $4.30). **Dunster** (#15, 28, 39, 300, 398; 10min.; 1-2 per hr.; $1.25); **Ilfracombe** (#300, 2hr., 3 per day, $4.50); **Lynton** (#300, 1hr., 3 per day, $2.80); **Porlock** (#38 or 300; 15min.; M-Sa 9 per day, Su 3 per day; $2).

SOUTHWEST ENGLAND

⑦ PRACTICAL INFORMATION

Both TICs and NPICs stock Ordnance Survey maps (£7), public transport timetables, and the invaluable *Exmoor Visitor* newspaper, which lists events, accommodations, walks, and has a useful map and articles on the area's geography. This information can also be found at www.exmoor-nationalpark.gov.uk.

National Park Information Centers:

Combe Martin: Seacot, Cross St. (☎/fax 01271 883 319), 3 mi. east of Ilfracombe. Open daily July-Aug. 10am-5pm; Apr.-June and Sept. 10am-5pm; Oct. 10am-4pm.

County Gate: (☎01598 741 321), on the A39, Countisbury, 5 mi. east of Lynton. Open daily Apr.-Oct. 10am-5pm.

Dulverton: Dulverton Heritage Centre, The Guildhall, Fore St. (☎01398 323 841). Open daily Apr.-Oct. 10am-5pm; Nov.-Mar. 11am-3pm.

Dunster: Dunster Steep Car Park (☎01643 821 835), 2 mi. east of Minehead. Open daily Apr.-Oct. 10am-5pm; limited openings Nov.-Mar. most school holidays 11am-3pm.

Lynmouth: The Esplanade (☎01598 752 509). Open daily Apr.-Oct. 10am-5pm; Nov.-Mar. Sa-Su 11am-3pm.

Tourist Information Centres: All TICs book accommodations for a 10% deposit.

Barnstaple: The Square (☎01271 375 000). Open M-Sa 9:30am-5pm.

Ilfracombe: The Landmark Seafront (☎01271 863 001). Shares a building with the Landmark Theatre. Open daily Easter-Oct. 10am-5:30pm; Nov.-Easter 10am-4:30pm.

Lynton: Town Hall, Lee Rd. (☎0845 660 3232; www.lyntourism.co.uk). Open daily 9:30am-5pm.

Minehead: 17 Friday St. (☎01643 702 624). Open July-Aug. M-Sa 9:30am-5:30pm, Su 10am-1pm; Sept.-Oct. and Apr.-June M-Sa 9:30am-5pm; Nov.-Mar. M-Sa 10am-4pm.

Porlock: W. End High St. (☎01643 863 150). Open Easter-Oct. M-Sa 10am-5pm, Su 10am-1pm; Nov.-Easter M-F 10:15am-1pm, Sa 10am-2pm.

⌂ ACCOMMODATIONS

Hostels and **B&Bs** (£18-20) fill up quickly; check listings and the *Exmoor Visitor* at the TIC. At busy times, **camping** may be the easiest way to see the park. Most land is private; before pitching a tent, ask the owner's permission. Most of the **YHA hostels** below have daytime lockouts (usually 10am-5pm), and all accept MC/V.

YHA Crowcombe: (☎01984 667 249). A large house in the woods on the Taunton-Minehead Rd., 1½ mi. from Crowcombe Village below Quantock Hills. Take bus #28 or 928 from Taunton toward Minehead, get off at Red Post, and turn onto the road marked "Crowcombe Station;" the hostel is ¾ mi. down, on the right. Kitchen and laundry. Sept.-June. call 48hr. in advance. Dorms £11.50, under 18 £8. ❷

YHA Elmscott: (☎01237 441 367). Bus #319 or X19 from Barnstaple goes to Hartland; from the west end of Fore St. a footpath leads 2½ mi. through The Vale to the hostel. Difficult to find. Kitchen and laundry. Open Easter-Sept. Frequently closed on Su, call ahead. Dorms £10.60, under 18 £7.20. ❶

YHA Exford: Withypoole Rd. (☎01643 831 288), Exe Mead, Exford. Take bus #178 (F), 285 (Su), or Red Bus #295 (June-Sept. only) from Minehead. The hostel is next to the River Exe bridge, in the center of the village. Kitchen and laundry. Curfew 11pm. Open daily July-Aug.; Sept.-June M-Sa. Dorms £11.80, under 18 £8.50. ❷

YHA Lynton: (☎01598 753 237), Lynbridge, Lynton. Take bus #309 or 310 from Barnstaple to Castle Hill Car Park, or #300 from Minehead. Exit left, pass the school, and turn left up Sinai Hill; the hostel is signposted from there (10min. walk). Kitchen and laundry. Sept.-Mar. call 48hr. in advance. Dorms £10.60, under 18 £7.20. ❶

YHA Minehead: (☎01643 702 595), Alcombe Combe, Minehead. Halfway between the town center and Dunster (2 mi. from either), a 3hr. walk to Dunkery Beacon. From Minehead, follow Friday St. as it becomes Alcombe Rd., turn right on Church St. and follow to Manor Rd. (30min. walk). From Taunton, take bus #28 to Minehead or 928 to Alcombe; the bus stops 1 mi. from the hostel. Kitchen and laundry. Open daily July-Aug.; call 48hr. in advance. Dorms £10.60, under 18 £7.20; doubles £28. ❶

Ocean Backpackers, 29 St. James Pl. (☎01271 867 835), Ilfracombe. The alleyway from the bus stop brings you right to the back door. Friendly owners Abbey and Chris provide a laidback atmosphere and run the restaurant next door. All dorm rooms are ensuite. 10min. from nearby surfing at Willicombe. Kitchen and laundry (£2.50). Dorms £11 first night (£1 toward linens), following nights £10, doubles £30. ❷

🎒 🏔 HIKING AND OUTDOORS

With wide-open moorland in the west and wooded valleys in the east, Exmoor has a varied landscape best toured on **foot** or **bike.** The **Exmoor National Park Rangers** (☎01398 323 665) also lead free nature and moorland walks. **NPICs** offer 1½-10 mi. themed walks (£3-5, children and students free; p. 221). **National Trust** leads walks with various focuses, including summer birds, butterflies, deer, and archaeology. (☎01643 862 452. £1-8 per person.) More themed walks are listed in Exmoor Visitor, free at NPICs and TICs. **Heritage Coach Tours** (☎01643 704 204) operates day, half-day, and evening bus tours. **Dulverton Visitors' Center** is open year-round and offer information on all parts of the park (☎01398 323 841).

Although Barnstaple, just outside the park, isn't the only suitable hiking base, it is the largest town in the region, a transport center, and the best place to get gear. Two good points to start woodland traipsings are **Blackmoor Gate,** 11 mi. northwest of Barnstaple, or **Parracombe,** 2 mi. farther northwest. Both are on the Barnstaple-Lynton bus #309 route. The **Tarka Trail** starts in Barnstaple and traces a 180 mi. figure-eight, 31 mi. of which are bicycle-friendly. **Tarka Trail Cycle Hire,** at the Barnstaple train station, is conveniently located at the trailhead. (☎01271 324 202. £9.50 per day, children £4-6. Open daily Apr.-Oct. 9:15am-5pm.)

Only 1 mi. from the park's eastern boundary, **Minehead** is also a good place to start hiking. The busy seaside resort provides plenty of lodging and an informative **nature trail,** beginning on Parkhouse Rd. Other well-marked paths weave through **North Hill.** The 630 mi. **South West Coast Path** (p. 186) starts in Minehead and ends in Poole; the 70 mi. portion running through Exmoor passes through Porlock, Lynmouth, Lynton, Ilfracombe, and Barnstaple. Contact the South West Coast Path Association (☎01752 896 237; www.swcp.org.uk). The trailhead is on Quay St.—follow the signs for "Somerset and North Devon Coastal Path."

Set in wooded valleys 9 mi. along the South West Coast Path from Minehead, **Porlock** offers good hiking and horseback riding. The TIC sells *13 Narrated Walks around Porlock* (£2), which includes a 2 mi. hike to **Weir-Culborne Church,** England's smallest parish church, and an 8 mi. trek to Exmoor's highest point, **Dunkery Beacon.** The TIC also has a list of local stables, including **Burrowhays Farm Riding Stables,** West Luccombe, 1 mi. east of Porlock off the A39. (☎01643 862 463. Open Easter-Oct. M-F and Su. Pony rides £11 per hr., £29.50 per half-day.)

England's "Little Switzerland," the twin villages of **Lynton** and **Lynmouth** sit atop the coast. The **Cliff Railway,** a Victorian-era water-powered lift, shuttles visitors between the two villages. (☎01598 753 486. Open daily July-Aug. 10am-9pm; June and Sept. 10am-7pm; call ahead for times Oct.-May. £1.50, children £1. Bike £3.) **Exmoor Coast Boat Trips,** leads drift-fishing trips and runs to Lee Bay and the Valley of Rocks. (☎01598 753 207. Both trips 1½hr. £9, children £6.) Upstream from the

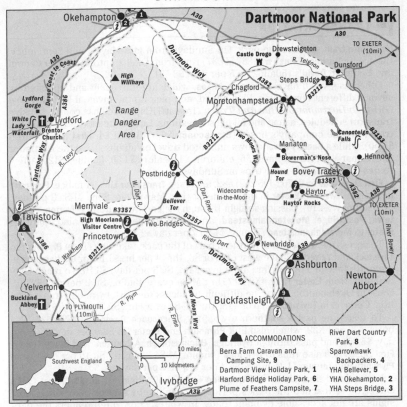

Dartmoor National Park

ACCOMMODATIONS

Berra Farm Caravan and Camping Site, 9
Dartmoor View Holiday Park, 1
Harford Bridge Holiday Park, 6
Plume of Feathers Campsite, 7
River Dart Country Park, 8
Sparrowhawk Backpackers, 4
YHA Bellever, 5
YHA Okehampton, 2
YHA Steps Bridge, 3

harbor, **Glen Lyn Gorge,** Lynmouth Crossroads, showcases the benefits of hydro-electric power on its quirky ravine walk, and recounts the 1952 flood that devastated Lynmouth. (☎01598 753 207. Open Easter-Oct. £3, concessions £2.)

Dunster, a tiny village of cobblestone sidewalks 2½ mi. east of Minehead, is worth a visit for its 14th-century streets, thatched roofs, and **Dunster Castle.** The residence's elaborate interior includes what's reputed to be the oldest bathroom in Somerset, built in 1868. (☎01643 821 314. Open Mar.-Oct. M-W and Sa-Su 11am-5pm; last admission 4:30pm. Gardens open daily 11am-4pm; longer when castle is open. £6.80, children £3.40, families £16.50. Gardens only £3.50/£1.50/£8.)

DARTMOOR NATIONAL PARK

Dartmoor National Park, south of Exmoor and 10 mi. west of Exeter, is a vast, granite-strewn landscape of lush woodlands and looming moors. Granite tors and neolithic rock formations dot the forbidding uplands, while manor homes and country churches occupy more gentle countryside below. Ramblers through the 368 sq. mi. of green hills and gray skies may also find the skeleton of a once-flourishing tin-mining industry and the heavily guarded Princetown prison that inspired the creator of Sherlock Holmes. Dartmoor is most notorious for its rough terrain and harsh climate, mastered only by sheep and wild ponies.

▐ TRANSPORTATION

Only one **train** services the park. On Sundays from late May to mid-September, the scenic **Dartmoor Line** (☎01837 55637) runs from Okehampton to **Exeter Central** and **Exeter St. David's** (50min., Su 5 per day, £3.50).

Otherwise, you'll have to rely on **buses,** which are infrequent and operated by several different companies. Plan ahead, and pick up the invaluable *Discovery Guide to Dartmoor by Bus and Train* (free at TICs), which has comprehensive transport schedules, a map and hiking suggestions. **Explorer** tickets allow unlimited travel on one company's buses (**Stagecoach** £6, children £4; **First** £5, children £3.50), while a **Sunday Rover** allows unlimited travel on all buses and the Dartmoor and Tamar Valley train lines (£5, children £4, seniors £4.50, families £12). A few routes run one or two more trips on Sundays.

First DevonBus (☎01752 495 259) #82, a.k.a. the **Transmoor Link,** connects **Plymouth** in the southwest to **Exeter** in the northeast (late May to late Sept. M-Sa 3 per day, Su 5 per day; £4.10), passing straight through the park and hitting **Yelverton, Princetown, Postbridge, Moretonhampstead,** and **Steps Bridge.** Bus #359 also connects **Exeter** to **Moretonhampstead** (50min., M-Sa 7 per day £2.80).

To access the western and northern part of the park, take a bus from **Plymouth** to **Tavistock** and **Yelverton** in the west (#83 or 86, 1hr., 4 per hr. £3.10) or **Okehampton** in the north (#86 or 118; 1½-2hr.; M-Sa every hr., Su 3 per day) £3.10. To reach Okehampton from **Exeter** take #X9/10 (1hr.; M-Sa every 45min., Su 2 per day £2.70). Once in Okehampton, it can be difficult to access the park by public transportation. Connect in **Tavistock** (#86 or 118; 1hr.; M-Sa every hr., Su 7 per day, £1.70).

To reach the park's southern towns, try **Stagecoach Devon** (☎01392 427 711) buses #39 and X39, which also link **Plymouth** and **Exeter** (M-Sa 9 per day, Su 6 per day; £5.80), and pass through **Ivybridge, Buckfastleigh, Ashburton,** and **Bovey Tracey.** **First** buses X80 also runs to **Ivybridge** (45min., M-Sa 2 per hr., Su 10 per day) from **Plymouth** and **Torquay** (1-1¼hr.; M-Sa 2 per hr., Su 8 per day).

For updated timetables, call **Traveline** (☎0870 608 2608) or any NPIC (p. 224). Once you've reached the park's perimeter, explore by foot or bike, since most sights are not accessible by main roads. In winter, snow often renders the park impassable. **Hitchhikers** report that rides are easy to get, although *Let's Go* does not recommend hitchhiking.

▐ PRACTICAL INFORMATION

All NPICs and TICs stock the indispensable, free *Dartmoor Visitor,* which has a detailed map and listings on events, accommodations, and guided walks (p. 226).

National Park Information Centres: The Princetown NPIC serves as the main visitors center for the entire park, and has free exhibitions about the area.

Haytor: (☎01364 661 520), on the B3387, midway between Bovey Tracey and Whitticombe. Open daily Easter-Oct. 10am-5pm; Nov.-Dec. Sa-Su 10am-4pm.

Newbridge: (☎01364 631 303), in the Riverside carpark. Open daily Easter-Oct. 10am-5pm; Nov.-Dec. Sa-Su 10am-4pm.

Postbridge: (☎01822 880 272), in a carpark off the B3212 Moretonhampstead-Yelverton Rd. Open daily Easter-Oct. 10am-5pm; Nov.-Dec. Sa-Su 10am-4pm.

Princetown (High Moorland Visitor Centre): The Square, Tavistock Rd. (☎01822 890 414), in the former Duchy Hotel. Open daily 10am-6pm.

Tourist Information Centres: The first three TICs listed below are gateways into Dartmoor; the last three are towns whose TICs work in conjunction with the National Park Authority and are staffed by volunteers.

Bovey Tracey: Lower Car Park (☎01626 832 047). Open Easter-Sept. M-F 10am-4pm, Sa 9:30am-3:30pm, Su 10am-noon.

Okehampton: 3 West St. (☎01837 53020), in the courtyard adjacent to the White Hart Hotel. Books accommodations for a 10% deposit. Open Easter-Oct. M-Sa 10am-5pm; Aug. also Su 10am-4pm; Nov.-Easter M and F-Sa 10am-4:30pm.

Tavistock: Town Hall Building, Bedford Sq. (☎01822 612 938). Books accommodations for 10% deposit. Open daily Apr.-Oct. 9:30am-5pm; Nov.-Mar. 10am-4:30pm.

Ashburton: Town Hall, North St. (☎01364 653 426). Open M-Sa 9am-4:30pm.

Buckfastleigh: The Valiant Soldier (☎01364 644 522). Open Apr.-Oct. M-Sa 10:30am-4:30pm.

Moretonhampstead: 11 The Square (☎01647 440 043). Books accommodations, donations requested. Internet access £1.50 for first 20min., then £1 per 15min. Open daily Apr.-Oct. 9:30am-5pm; Nov.-Mar. F-Su 10am-5pm.

▌ACCOMMODATIONS

B&B signs often appear on pubs and farmhouses along the roads, but it's wise to book ahead. In **Okehampton,** a few B&Bs are on **Station Road** between the train station and the town center. **Tavistock,** the largest (and loveliest) town in the area, has more expensive options near the bus station, but they fill up quickly and single rooms are scarce. **Moretonhampstead,** a lively village in the heart of the park, is a convenient place to stay if you want to minimize travel time.

HOSTELS

YHA Bellever (☎01822 880 227), 1 mi. southeast of Postbridge village. Bus #98 from Tavistock stops in front. #82 from Exeter or Plymouth (Oct. Easter Sa-Su only) stops in Postbridge; from there, follow signs and walk west on the B3212 and turn left on Bellever (20-25min. walk). In the heart of the park and very popular. Friendly staff has reams of local knowledge. Kitchen and laundry (£1). Reception 7-10am and 5-10:30pm. Open Mar.-Oct. Dorms £12.50, under 18 £9; family rooms from £36.50. £1 discount for guests who've arrived on foot, bike, or bus. MC/V. ❷

YHA Okehampton, Klondyke Rd. (☎01837 53916). Behind the train station, or a 15min. walk from the town center. From the TIC, turn right on George St., veer right onto Station Rd. just before Simmons Park, and continue uphill and under the bridge. Modern hostel with TV, pool table, and ping pong. Kitchen and laundry. Mountain bike rental £10 per day. Reception July-Aug. 8am-8pm; Sept.-June 8-9am and 5-10pm. Open Feb.-Nov. Dorms £13.40, under 18 £9.30; doubles available. **Camping** available Feb.-Nov. £6.70, under 18 £4.65. MC/V. ❷

YHA Steps Bridge (☎01647 252 435), 1 mi. southwest of Dunsford on the B3212, near the eastern edge of the park. Take bus #359 from Exeter (£2.35), get off at Steps Bridge, and hike up the steep drive. Volunteer run. Kitchen. Reception 7-10am and 5-10pm. Curfew 11pm. Open Apr.-Sept. Dorms £10, under 18 £7. £1 discount for guests who've arrived on foot, bike, or bus. MC/V. ❶

Sparrowhawk Backpackers, 45 Ford St., Moretonhampstead (☎01647 440 318), 5min. from the village center. From the bus carpark, turn left and walk toward the church; at the fork, veer left and turn left onto Ford St. Crisp white bunks in the attic of a former stables. Environmentally conscious owners keep an all-vegetarian kitchen. Dorms £11, children £6; family room £30. Cash only. ❷

CAMPING

Although official **campsites** and **camping barns** exist, many camp on the open moor. Most of Dartmoor is privately owned, so always ask permission. Camping is allowed on non-enclosed moor land more than ¾ mi. from the road or out of sight of inhabited areas. Pitching is prohibited in common areas used for recreation or archaeological sites. Campers may only stay up to two nights in a single spot, and should not build fires in the moors or climb fences or walls unless signs say doing so is permitted. Check www.dartmoor-npa.gov.uk or www.discoverdartmoor.com before heading out, or consult the *Camping and Backpacking with Moor Care and Less Wear* (free at NPICs). When using official campsites, call ahead for reservations, especially in summer. **YHA Okehampton** ❶ also offers camping (p. 225).

Ashburton: River Dart Country Park, Holne Park (☎01364 652 511), ½ mi. off the A38. Follow signs. Lush surroundings and a boating lake. Laundry £2. Open Easter-Sept. Tent or caravan £9.50-16.50 for 2, additional person £4-6. Electricity £2. ❶

Buckfastleigh: Berra Farm Caravan and Camping Site, Colston Rd., (☎01364 642 234), 1½ mi. from town center. Follow the signs for the Otter Park, continue 200 yd. past the entrance, and walk 1 mi. down Old Totnes Rd. 2-person tent £7. ❶

Okehampton: Dartmoor View Holiday Park, Whiddon Down (☎01647 231 545), 5 mi. from town. Head east toward Exeter; stay on the smaller road. Kitchen, laundry and outdoor swimming pool. Open Mar.-Oct. 2-person tent £8.50-11.75. ❶

Princetown: Plume of Feathers Campsite and Camping Barn (☎01822 890 240; www.plumeoffeathers-dartmoor.co.uk), behind the Plume of Feathers Inn, opposite the NPIC. Solid bunks with power showers and access to TV; book 2-3 months in advance. Campground rarely books up. Bunks £5.50-7 per person. Sites £4, children £3. ❶

Tavistock: Harford Bridge Holiday Park (☎01822 810 349), on the River Tavy. From the A386, turn right toward Peter Tavy village. Laundry. Open Mar.-Nov. Tent or caravan £7.25-15 (not all sites have electricity; those that do are more expensive). ❶

🥾🧗 HIKING AND OUTDOORS

Visitors should not underestimate Dartmoor's moody **weather** and treacherous terrain. Ordnance Survey Explorer Outdoor Leisure Map #28 (1:25,000; £7), a compass, and waterproof garb are essential. There is no shelter away from the roads. The **Dartmoor Rescue Group** is on call at ☎999. (See **Wilderness Safety,** p. 52.)

The rugged terrain of Dartmoor, with remnants of the Bronze Age dotting its moorland, offers unparalleled **hiking.** The **National Park Authority** conducts guided walks (1-6hr.; £3-5, free if arriving at starting point by public transport), which are listed in the *Dartmoor Visitor.* Those who would rather trek on their own will find a wealth of information and advice as well as various guidebooks (under £10) at NPICs and TICs. A good option for short hikes is the free *Transmoor Link Bus Walks,* which details four hikes along the #82 Transmoor Link bus route (p. 224). **Dartmoor Way** is a 90 mi. circular route that hits the park's main towns, running through river valleys and rural lakes. The 180 mi. **Tarka Trail** runs from Okehampton to Exmoor National Park in the north (p. 222). The 102 mi. **Two Moors Way** also connects the two parks, running from Lynmouth to Ivybridge.

The area is crowned by several peaks, the highest of which is **High Willhays** (2038 ft.). The peak is accessible only by foot; a 4 mi. hike from Okehampton traverses hilly country and ventures into Dartmoor's danger area. Tiny **Brentor Church** crowns an extinct volcano near Lydford, accessible only by foot. A mile from the village, the 1½ mi. **Lydford Gorge** encompasses lush forests and the whirlpool known as **Devil's Cauldron.** Walk along the top of the gorge to reach the fantastic 90 ft. **White Lady Waterfall.** (☎01822 820 320. Open daily Apr.-Sept. 10am-5:30pm; Oct. 10am-4pm; Nov.-Mar. 10:30am-3pm. £3.80.) A wealth of **Bronze Age structures,** the remains of Neolithic civilization, cluster near Merrivale. The knee-high stone circles, hut circles, burial chambers, and long stone rows date back 3500 years. Merrivale is on the #98 and 172 (summer only) bus routes. Haytor, near Bovey Tracey, features numerous tors, including the massive **Haytor Rocks** and the celebrated ruins at **Hound Tor,** where excavations unearthed the remains of 13th-century huts and longhouses. Venture north (1 mi. from Manaton) to discover the 40 ft. **Bowerman's Nose,** named after the man who first recognized the rock formation's resemblance to the human proboscis. Also near Bovey Tracey is the 220 ft. **Canonteign Falls,** England's highest waterfall. (☎ 01647 252 434. Open daily 10am-6pm or dusk; last admission 1hr. before close. £5.25, seniors £4.75, children £3.30.)

Dartmoor's roads are good for **cycling.** Bookended by Ilfracombe and Plymouth, the 102 mi. **Devon Coast to Coast** winds along rivers and rural countryside. The 11 mi. portion between Okehampton and Lydford is known as **The Granite Way,** and offers traffic-free biking along a former railway line. **Okehampton Cycle Hire** rents bikes. From Fore St., go uphill on North St., which becomes North Rd., then bear left off the main road, continuing downhill to the T junction; follow signs for Garden Centre. (☎ 01837 53248. Open M-F 9am-5:30pm, Sa 9am-4:30pm, Su 10am-4pm. £9.50 per day.) For **horseback riding,** the best bridleways are in the middle of the moor; NPICs can refer you to stables (rides £8-14 per hr.).

 WARNING. The Ministry of Defense often uses parts of the northern moor for **target practice;** consult the Dartmoor Visitor or an Ordnance Survey map for the boundaries of the danger area. Call the military **Freephone** (☎ 0800 458 4868; www.dartmoor-ranges.co.uk) for weekly firing schedules, which are also posted in NPICs; post offices; police stations; and some hostels, campsites, and pubs; and published in Friday's Western Morning News. Danger areas, marked by red-and-white posts, change yearly, so be sure your information is up-to-date. *Let's Go* does not recommend handling any found military debris.

◉ SIGHTS

The harsh Dartmoor landscape stretches across 368 sq. mi. of wide open moorland with Bronze Age burial mounds, knee-high stone rows, and stone circles scattered throughout. Also prevalent are **tors,** which may look manmade, but are actually the result of thousands of years of geological activity. In Dartmoor, "tor" refers to rock structures, originating from the Celtic "tawr" or "tower." Granite pushed to the surface develops cracks over time from the wind; hence the stack-like effect.

CASTLE DROGO. England's youngest castle was built between 1910 and 1930 atop a gorge by tea baron Julius Drewe. Convinced that he was a direct descendant of a Norman who arrived with William the Conqueror, Drewe constructed this granite fortress in the style of his supposed ancestor. From the castle, easy 3-4 mi. hikes go to the **River Teign** and its well-known **Fingle Bridge.** *(Take bus #173 from Moretonhampstead. ☎ 01647 433 306. Open Apr.-Nov. M and W-Su 11am-5:30pm. Grounds open daily 10:30am-5:30pm. £6.20, families £15. Grounds only £3.15.)*

PRINCETOWN PRISON. Dartmoor's maximum-security prison, still in use today, is not a tourist attraction but does have an interesting history. Frenchmen from the Napoleonic Wars and Americans who fought to annex Canada in 1812 once languished within its walls. The bleak moorland surrounding the prison is the setting for Sherlock Holmes's famed escapade, *The Hound of the Baskervilles,* which emerged from an ancient Dartmoor legend of a black dog that stalked a scurrilous aristocrat. The interesting **Prison Museum** nearby features a gallery of weapons made by creative inmates, including a knife made of matchsticks. *(Tavistock Rd. ☎ 01822 892 130. Open daily 9:30am-4:30pm. £2, concessions £1.)*

BUCKLAND ABBEY. A few miles south of Yelverton, this abbey was built by Cistercian monks in 1273 and later bought by Sir Francis Drake, who was born here, and whose drum it still houses—it is said that if ever the drum is lost, England will go to ruins. While the interior is lackluster, the exterior and grounds make for pleasant strolls in Elizabethan gardens. *(Milton Combe Rd. Take Citybus #55 from Yelverton. ☎ 01822 853 607. Open Apr.-Oct. M-W and F-Su 10:30am-5:30pm; Nov.-Mar. Sa-Su 2-5pm. Last admission 45min. before close. £5.30, children £2.60. Grounds only £2.90.)*

TORQUAY ☎ 01803

The largest city in the Torbay resort region and the self-proclaimed "English Riviera," Torquay isn't quite as glamorous as the French original. But the town Agatha Christie called home and where Basil Fawlty ran his madcap hotel does have friendly beaches, abundant palm trees, and stimulating nightlife. Semi-tropical when it doesn't rain, Torquay serves as a base for exploring the sunnier parts of the southwestern English coast.

⚏⚏ TRANSPORTATION AND PRACTICAL INFORMATION. Torquay's **train station** is off Rathmore Rd., near the Torre Abbey gardens. (M-F 7am-5:45pm, Sa 7am-4:45pm, Su 9:40am-5:10pm.) Trains (☎ 08457 484 950) arrive from: **Bristol** (2hr., 6 per day, £21.90); **Exeter** (45min., every hr., £6.90); **London Paddington** (3½hr., 1 per day, £47); **London Waterloo** (4hr., 1 per day, £47); **Plymouth** (1½hr.; every hr.; £8). **Buses** depart from **The Pavilion,** the roundabout where Torbay Rd. meets The Strand. The **Stagecoach** office, next to the TIC, provides information on its buses, which predominate in Torquay. (☎ 664 500. Open June-Aug. M-F 9am-5:30pm, Sa 9am-2pm; Sept.-May M-F 9am-5pm, Sa 9:30am-1:30pm) Bus #85 runs to **Exeter** (1½hr.; M-Sa 2 per hr.; May-Sept. also Su 3 per day; £5.20), as does the more direct #X46 (1hr.; M-Sa every hr., Su 7 per day; £5.20). **First** #X80 and X81 runs to **Plymouth** (1¾hr.; every hr.; £6). **Taxis, Torbay Cab Co.** (☎ 292 292) are on call 24hr.

The **Tourist Information Centre,** Vaughan Parade, arranges theater bookings, discounted tickets for nearby attractions, and accommodations for a 10% deposit. Also sells tickets for the popular **Eden Project** (p. 245). (☎ 0906 680 1268; www.englishriviera.co.uk. Open daily June-Sept. 9:30am-6pm; Oct.-May M-Sa 9:30am-5pm.) **Cruise Tours** (1hr.; £4.50, children £2.50) leave Princess Pier for **Brixham** (Western Lady Ferry Service ☎ 297 292) and **Paignton** (Paignton Pleasure Cruises ☎ 529 147). Buy tickets for both at the booth on Victoria Parade. (Open daily 9am-5pm.) Other services include: **banks** on Fleet St.; **Thomas Cook,** 54 Union St. (☎ 352 100; open M and W-Sa 9am-5:30pm, Tu 10am-5:30pm); **Sparkle Launderette,** 63 Princes Rd., off Market St. (☎ 293 217; wash £3.20, dry 20p per 4min.; open M-F 9am-7pm, Sa 9am-6pm, Su 10am-4pm); the **police,** South St. (☎ 08705 777 444); a **pharmacy, Moss,** 2 Tor Hill Rd. (☎ 213 075; open M-F 9am-6pm, Sa 9am-5pm); **Torbay Hospital,** Newton Rd. (☎ 614 567); free **Internet access** at the **library,** Lymington Rd., beside the Town Hall (☎ 208 300; open M, W, F 9:30am-7pm; Tu 9:30am-5pm; Th 9:30am-1pm; Sa 9:30am-4pm) also at **Microblitz,** 32 Tor Hill Rd. 50p 30min., £1 per hr. (☎ 295 285; open M-F 9:30am-7pm, Sa 9:30am-6pm.); and the **post office,** 25 Fleet St., with a **bureau de change** (open M-Sa 9am-5:30pm). **Post Code:** TQ1 1DB.

⌂⚏ ACCOMMODATIONS AND FOOD. Torquay's numerous hotels and B&Bs get busy during summer, especially in August; book in advance. Find lots of less expensive **beach hotels** on Babbacombe Road, including **Torwood Gardens Hotel ❸,** 531 Babbacombe Rd., where feather pillows promise a good night's rest 5min. from the surf. (☎ 298 408. Apr.-Oct. £25 per person; Nov.-Mar. £22.50. AmEx/MC/V.) Cheaper **B&Bs** line **Scarborough Road, Abbey Road** and **Morgan Avenue.** Well-kept flower boxes and chalk-scrawled poems foster a warm atmosphere at **Torquay Backpackers ❷**, 119 Abbey Rd. From the train station, turn left and walk down Torbay Rd., continuing straight uphill on Shedden Hill Rd., then turn left on Abbey Rd. (☎299 924; www.torquaybackpackers.co.uk. Internet access £1 per 20min. Laundry £3.50. Reception 9am-10pm; shorter hours Oct.-Easter. June-Sept. dorms £12; doubles £28. Oct.-May dorms £10; doubles £24. MC/V.) Continue down Abbey Rd. and turn right at the first street to find **Aries House ❷**, 1 Morgan Ave., where many of the well-furnished rooms are ideal for families. (☎404 926. £16-22 per person. Children half-price in family rooms. Cash only.) A few doors down, amiable Mary Gibbs offers organized and cozy rooms at **Rosemont Guest House ❷**, 5 Morgan Ave. (☎295 475; £16 per person, with bath £17. Cash only.)

Buy **groceries** at **Somerfield**, Union Sq. (☎295 384. Open M-Sa 8:30am-8pm, Su 10am-4pm.) **No. 7 Fish Bistro ❸**, Inner Harbor, Beacon Terr., across from Living Coasts, is the place to splurge for dinner. Superb local seafood (£11-17) in a comfortable setting. (☎295 055; www.no7-fish.com. Open for lunch W-Sa year-round 12:45-1:45pm, for dinner daily July-Sept. 6-9:45pm, June and Oct. M-Sa 7-9:45pm, Nov.-May Tu-Sa 7-9:45pm. AmEx/MC/V.) Locals flock to award-winning **Hanbury's ❷**, Princes St., 2 mi. up Babbacombe Rd., for the sit-down fish and chips (£7-11) and adjoining takeaway. Take bus #32H, 33 or 85 (8min., every 10-30min., £1.10) from The Strand to Princes St. (☎314 616. Open M-Sa noon-1:45pm and 5:30-9:30pm, takeaway open from 4:30pm. MC/V.)

🅰️🅱️ **SIGHTS AND BEACHES.** Opened in 2003 with a spectacular view of the bay, **Living Coasts**, Beacon Quay, is an innovative aviary that recreates the world's coastal environments, from Africa to the Antarctic. (☎202 470. Open daily Apr.-Sept. 10am-6pm; Oct. 10am-5:30pm; Nov.-Mar. 10am-4:30pm. Last admission 1hr. before close. £5.70, seniors and students £4.40, children £4, families £17.50.) To get out of the sun (or rain), head for **Torre Abbey**, The Kings Dr. Founded as a monastery in 1196, and converted into a private mansion in the 16th century. It now houses Torquay's municipal art collection, including William Holman Hunt's pre-Raphaelite masterpiece *The Children's Holiday*. Surrounding gardens and bowling greens add to the charm of the estate. (☎293 593. No stilettos. Open daily Easter-Oct. 9:30am-6pm; last admission 5pm. £3.50, concessions £3, children £1.70, families £7.50.) For information on Agatha Christie's life and a look at Torquay's history, visit the **Torquay Museum**, 529 Babbacombe Rd. (☎293 975. Open M-Sa 9:30am-5:30pm; mid-July to Sept. also Su 1:30-5:30pm. £3, children and students £1.50, concessions £2, families £7.50.) **Princess Theatre**, Torbay Rd., offers another weather-proof option, presenting an array of shows throughout the year. (☎08702 414 120. Tickets £10-30. Open M-Sa 10am-6pm, 10am-8pm with a scheduled show.)

The weather provides a clear distinction between the "English Riviera" and its more established French cousin. Yet spotty skies lend Torquay beaches a beauty of their own, and the slightest hint of sun thrills waiting crowds. **Torre Abbey Sands** draws the hordes, but visitors can reach better beaches by bus. Just southeast of Torquay (bus #200, £1.10), **Meadfoot** features beach huts, deck chairs, and sandy, pebbly shores. Take bus #32 north to slightly rockier **Oddicombe**, hidden under a cove (every 10min., £1.10). Bus #85 heads farther north to peaceful **Watcombe** (15min., every 30min., £1.40) and near-deserted **Maidencombe** (20min., £1.70).

📷🎭 **NIGHTLIFE AND FESTIVALS.** When the sun dips and beaches empty, nightlife options come alive. **Mojo**, Palm Court Hotel, Torbay Rd., is a friendly seaside hangout with Torquay's latest bar hours and dancing after dark. (☎294

882. Live bands F and Su. Sa disco. Open M-Sa 11am-1am, Su 11am-12:30am.) Nightclub **Claires,** Torwood St., lures London's top DJs for hardcore clubbing. (☎292 079. Cover £5. Open F-Su 9pm-2am.) **The Koko Lounge,** 50-54 Union St., hosts a comedy club on Mondays (£5; from 9pm). On other nights, the decadent Romanesque club grooves to rock, dance, and R&B. (☎212 414. Cover £2-5. Open M 8pm-1am, Th 9:30pm-2am, F 9pm-2am, Sa 9:30pm-2am, Su 9:30pm-12:30am.) During the last week of August, Torquay lives the high life during its annual **Regatta** (☎316 618).

PLYMOUTH ☎01752

Immortalized by those hasty to leave it behind—the English fleet that defeated the Spanish Armada in 1588, explorers Sir Francis Drake and Captain Cook, and the Pilgrims—Plymouth is no longer a point of immediate departure. Massive air raids during WWII left the city only the cracked shell of a naval capital, but among its rows of buildings and awkward modern thoroughfares, patches of Plymouth's rich history still merit a day's exploration.

▐ TRANSPORTATION

Plymouth lies on the southern coast between Dartmoor National Park and the Cornwall peninsula, on the London-Penzance train line.

Trains: Plymouth Station, North Rd. Ticket office open M-F 5:20am-8:30pm, Sa 5:30am-7pm, Su 8am-8:30pm. Buses #5 and 6 run to the city center (35p). Trains (☎08457 484 950) arrive from: **Bristol** (2hr., every 30min., £37); **London Paddington** (3½hr., every hr., £49); **Penzance** (2hr., every 30min., £10.70).

Buses: Bretonside Station (☎254 542). Ticket office open M-Sa 8:30am-6pm, Su 9am-5pm. **Lockers** £1-3. **National Express** (☎08705 808 080) to **Bristol** (3hr., 4 per day, £23) and **London** (5-6hr., 7-8 per day, £25). **Stagecoach** bus X38 runs to **Exeter** (1¼-1¾hr., 12-13 per day, £6).

Ferries: Brittany Ferries (☎08703 665 333), at Millbay Docks. Follow signs to "Continental Ferries," 15min. from the town center. Taxi to the terminal £4. Buy tickets 24hr. ahead, though foot passengers may be able to purchase tickets upon arrival. Check in well before departure. To **Roscoff, France** (4-6hr., 12 per week, £58-65) and **Santander, Spain** (18hr., 2 per week, Su and W, £110).

Public Transportation: Citybus (☎222 221) buses from Royal Parade (from £1.10 round-trip).

Taxis: Plymouth Taxis (☎606 060).

✱ ▐ ORIENTATION AND PRACTICAL INFORMATION

The commercial district formed by **Royal Parade, Armada Way,** and **New George Street** is Plymouth's city center. Directly south, the **Hoe** (or "High Place") is a large, seaside park. The **Royal Citadel,** home to many a man in uniform, is flanked by the Hoe to the west and, to the east, **The Barbican,** Plymouth's historic harbor.

Tourist Information Centre: 3-5 The Barbican, shares building with the Mayflower Museum (☎306 330; www.visitplymouth.co.uk). Books accommodations for 10% deposit. Free map. Open M-Sa 9am-5pm; Apr.-Oct. also Su 10am-4pm. **Branch** on Crabtree at the Plymouth Discovery Centre. Open same hours.

Tours: Guide Friday bus tours leave every 30min. from stations near the Barbican and the Hoe. Daily Apr.-Sept.; except mid-Apr. to mid-May Sa-Su only. £6.50, seniors £5.50, children £3, families £15. **Plymouth Boat Cruises** (☎822 797) leave sporadi-

Plymouth

ACCOMMODATIONS
Globe Backpackers, 11
Riverside Caravan Park, 1
Riviera Hotel, 12
Seymour Guest House, 10
YHA Plymouth University, 3

FOOD
Bella Napoli, 9
Fishermans Arms, 13
Tanners Restaurant, 6
Thai House, 7

PUBS
Bar R, 2
Barbican Jazz Cafe, 8
The Union Rooms, 5

NIGHTLIFE
The Two Trees, 4

cally from Phoenix Wharf for short trips around Plymouth Sound (1½hr.; £5, children £2.50, families £11) or longer journeys through the Tamar Valley (4½hr.; £7.50, children £4, families £20).

Financial Services: Banks line Old Town St., Royal Parade, and Armada Way. **Thomas Cook,** 9 Old Town St. (☎612 600). Open M-W and F-Sa 9am-5:30pm, Th 10am-5:30pm, Su 10:30am-4:30pm. **American Express,** 139 Armada Way (☎502 706). Open M and W-Sa 9am-5pm, Tu 9:30am-5pm.

Work Opportunities: JobCentre, Buckwell St. or Hoegate St. (both ☎616 100). Open M-Tu and Th-F 9am-5pm, W 10am-5pm.

Launderette: Hoegate Laundromat, 55 Notte St. (☎223 031). Service wash only. £6.50 per load. Open M-F 8am-6pm, Sa 9am-5pm.

Pharmacy: Boots, 2-6 New George St. (☎266 271). Open M-W and F-Sa 8:30am-6:30pm, Th 8:30am-7pm, Su 10:30am-4:30pm.

SOUTHWEST ENGLAND

Police: Charles Cross (☎08705 777 444), near the bus station.

Hospital: Derriford Hospital (☎777 111). In Derriford, about 5 mi. north of the city center. Take bus #42 or 50 from Royal Parade.

Internet Access: Library (☎305 907), Northhill. Free. ID required. Open M-F 9am-7pm, Sa 9am-5pm.

Post Office: 5 St. Andrew's Cross (☎08457 740 740). **Bureau de change.** Open M-Sa 9am-5:30pm. **Post Code:** PL1 1AB.

ACCOMMODATIONS

B&Bs (£17-20) line **Citadel Road** and its side streets. Rooms tend to be small but cheap. In July and August, self-catering ensuite singles are available at the **YHA at Plymouth University ❸**, 10 Gilwell St. (☎502 401. Reception 8-10am and 5-10pm. £20. Cash only.)

Seymour Guest House, 211 Citadel Rd. East (☎667 002), where Hoegate St. meets Lambhay Hill. Serviceable lodgings with a great location between The Barbican and The Hoe. Singles £20; doubles £36, ensuite £40. Cash only. ❷

Globe Backpackers, 172 Citadel Rd. (☎225 158). Friendly and in a convenient location. Kitchen. Laundry service £3. Reception 8am-11pm. Dorms £11, weekly £66; singles £15; doubles £28; family rooms £45. MC/V. ❶

Riviera Hotel, 8 Elliot St. (☎667 379; www.rivieraplymouth.co.uk), a grand family-run hotel with numerous amenities, including direct dial phones and hair dryers. Breakfast included. Singles £30-35; doubles from £53; family rooms from £57. MC/V. ❸

Riverside Caravan Park, Longbridge Rd., Marsh Mills (☎344 122). Follow Longbridge Rd. 3½ mi. toward Plympton. £2.75-3.75, children £1.25-1.50. Cash only. ❶

FOOD AND PUBS

Sainsbury's is in the Armada Shopping Centre. (☎674 767. Open M-Sa 7am-8pm, Su 10am-4pm.) Find more at **Pannier Market,** an indoor bazaar at the west end of New George St. (☎304 904. Open M-Tu and Th-Sa 8am-5:30pm, W 8am-4:30pm.)

Tanners Restaurant, Finewell St. (☎252 001; www.tannersrestaurant.com), behind St. Andrew's Church. Plymouth's oldest building. Pasta £5-8. 3-course dinner £19. Smart dress. Open Tu-F noon-2:15pm and 7-9:30pm, Sa noon-2pm and 7-9:30pm. MC/V. ❹

Thai House, 63 Notte St. (☎661 600; www.thethaihouse.com). Makes up for Plymouth's dearth of fine dining options with spicy salads and pad thai. Entrees £6-14. Open Tu-Su 6-10:30pm. 15% discount for takeaway. AmEx/MC/V. ❸

Bella Napoli, 41-42 Southside St., The Barbican (☎667 772). A family-run Italian establishment offering fresh fish from the quay. Pasta £7.50-9.75. Veal or fish £11.95-16.95. Open daily 6:30-10:30pm. AmEx/MC/V. ❸

Fishermans Arms, 31 Lambhay St. (☎661 457). Grab some grub at Plymouth's second-oldest pub. Open M-Sa 11am-11pm, Su noon-10:30pm. Food noon-3pm. MC/V. ❶

SIGHTS AND BEACHES

■**NATIONAL MARINE AQUARIUM.** Britain's largest and Europe's deepest tank is home to six sharks at this high-tech aquarium, which also features an immense coral reef tank and Britain's only **giant squid.** (The Barbican. ☎600 301; www.national-aquarium.co.uk. Open daily Apr.-Oct. 10am-6pm; Nov.-Mar. 10am-5pm. Last admission 1hr. before close. £8.75, students and seniors £7.25, children £5.25, families £25.)

THE HOE. Legend has it that Sir Francis Drake was playing bowls on the Hoe in 1588 when he heard that the Armada had entered the Channel. English through and through, he finished his game before hoisting sail to fend off the Spanish ships. Climb 93 spiral steps and leaning ladders to the windy balcony of **Smeaton's**

Tower for a magnificent impression of Plymouth and the Royal Citadel. Originally a lighthouse 14 mi. offshore, the 72 ft. tower was moved to its present site in 1882. Nearby, the **Plymouth Dome** employs plastic dioramas and actors to relate Plymouth's past. (☎603 300; www.plymouthdome.info. Tower open daily Apr.-Oct. 10am-4pm; Nov.-Apr. Tu-Sa 10am-3pm. Dome open daily Apr.-Oct. 10am-5pm; Nov.-Apr. Tu-Sa 10am-4pm. Last entry 1hr. before close. Dome and Tower £6.50, concessions £5.50, children £4, families £16. Dome only £4.75/3.25/£3.75/13; Tower only £2.25, children £1.25.)

PLYMOUTH MAYFLOWER. The museum tells the tale of the *Mayflower* and all you never knew you wanted to know about Pilgrims. (3-5 The Barbican. ☎306 330. Open M-Sa 10am-4pm, Su 11am-3pm; last admission 30min. before close. £2, children £1.)

ST. ANDREW'S CHURCH. St. Andrew's has been a site of Christian meetings since 1087. Three days of bombing in 1941 left it virtually gutted; what visitors can see today is the product of rebuilding and renovation. (Royal Parade. ☎661 414. Open M-F 9am-4pm, Sa 9am-1pm, Su for services only.)

OTHER SIGHTS. The still-in-use **Royal Citadel** may be seen only via a guided tour of its battlements and garrison walls, historic guns, and church, all built 300 years ago by Charles II. (Tours May-Sept. Tu 2:30pm. £3.) At the **Mayflower Steps,** on The Barbican, a plaque and American flag mark the spot from which the Pilgrims set off in 1620. Subsequent departures have been marked as well, including Sir Humphrey Gilbert's journey to Newfoundland, Sir Walter Raleigh's attempt to colonize North Carolina, and Captain Cook's expedition. The blackened shell of **Charles Church**, destroyed by a bomb in 1941, now stands in the middle of the Charles Cross traffic circle as a memorial for victims of the Blitz. The **Plymouth Gin,** 60 Southside St., is England's oldest active gin distillery, at it since 1793. (☎665 292; www.plymouthgin.com. 45min. tours. Open daily Mar.-Dec. 10:30am-4:30pm; Jan.-Feb. Sa 10:30am-3:30pm. Shop open daily 9am-5pm. £5, children free.)

BEACHES. Ferry to **Kingsand** and **Cawsand,** villages with small, pretty slips of sand. **Cawsand Ferry** (☎07833 936 863) leaves from the Mayflower Steps, but sometimes cancels trips due to unfavorable winds. (30min.; 4 per day; £2.50, children £1.)

🎵 🌿 ENTERTAINMENT AND FESTIVALS

Both young and old enjoy the view and atmosphere of the harbor at the traditional pubs along The Barbican. **Barbican Jazz Cafe,** 11 The Parade, strikes the right chord with moody decor and live jazz seven nights a week (☎672 127; www.barbican-jazzcafe.com. Open M-Sa 8pm-2am, Su 8pm-midnight.) Farther inland, Union St. offers a string of bars and clubs. **The Union Rooms,** 19 Union St., is a popular pre-club bar; selected pints, wines and bottles are £1.09-1.99 every day. (☎254 520. Open M-Sa 10am-11pm, Su noon-10:00pm.) Nearby, patrons rock out at **The Two Trees,** 31 Union St. On Sunday karaoke is at 10pm. (Open M-Sa 7pm-2am, Su 3pm-12:30am.) **Bar R,** 2 Sherwell Arcade, North Hill, beyond the City Museum, draws a hip student crowd and an after-work contingent anxious for a pint. (☎669 749. Tu live acoustics. Su "Cheese and Wine" night, £5 bottle of house wine and complimentary cheese. Happy hour daily 7-9pm. Open M-Sa 4:30pm-2am, Su 6pm-1am.)

The **Theatre Royal,** on Royal Parade, has one of the West Country's best stages, featuring ballet, opera, and West End touring companies, including the Royal National Theatre. (☎267 222. Box office open M-Sa 10am-8pm; on non-performance days until 6pm. Tickets £16-44, students £3-5 off M-Th.)

During the August Bank Holiday of every other year (next in 2006), the **Plymouth Navy Days** invites the public to explore the ships and submarines of the city's maximum-security naval base. (☎553 941. Tickets go on sale in late June. Pedestrian ticket £10, children £5; £8/£4 in advance. The **Armed Forces Show** (☎501 750), in the second weekend of July, features exhibitions by the Royal Navy, Army, and Air Force. The **British National Fireworks Championship** explodes in mid-August, while **Powerboat Championships** take place during the last weekend of July.

SOUTHWEST ENGLAND

⏵ DAYTRIPS FROM PLYMOUTH

LOOE AND POLPERRO

Looe is easily reached from Plymouth by train, but fares are expensive. From Plymouth go to Liskeard and from Liskeard, hop on the Plymouth-Penzance line, to Looe (1hr., through-ticket £5.70). Regular buses connect Looe and Polperro, including Hamblys Coaches (☎01503 220 660) and First bus 80A and 81A (☎01752 4020).

Long popular with tourists, the small coastal villages of Looe and Polperro are two of southern Cornwall's most picturesque. The larger of the two, **Looe** is split in half by a wide estuary. Far from the sandy shores and into the sea lies mile-wide **Looe Island**, until recently the only privately owned island in the UK, now under the care of the Cornish Wildlife Trust. **Boat tours** run around the coast and the bay, check for information at the quay. Those who'd rather stay on land should visit the **Discovery Centre**, Millpool, on Looe's west side, which stocks the free *Looe Valley Line Trails from the Track*, a packet of 10 hiking trails. (☎01503 262 777. Open daily Feb.-June and Oct. 10am-4pm; July-Sept. 10am-6pm; Nov.-Dec. 10am-3pm.) The **Tourist Information Centre**, Fore St., East Looe, books rooms for a £2 charge plus a 10% deposit. (☎01503 262 072; www.southeastcornwall.co.uk. Open daily Easter-May and Oct. 10am-2pm; May-Sept. 10am-5pm.)

Polperro was once England's most notorious smuggling bay—the village's proximity to the Channel Islands made it a perfect port for illegal alcohol and tobacco transport. Visit the **Polperro Heritage Museum of Smuggling and Fishing**, which displays photos of smugglers, a sword of a smuggler, stories about smugglers, and also some pictures of a flood. (☎01503 273 005. Open daily Easter-Oct. 10am-6pm; last admission 5:15pm. £1.60, children 50p.) Offshore, the Polperro Boatman's Association runs 30min. **boat trips** to nearby caves. (☎01503 272 476. Tours daily 10am-5pm, weather permitting. £4, children £2). The **Visitors Information Centre**, Talland St., is at end of New St. (☎01503 272 320. Open M-Sa 9:30am-5pm.)

CLOVELLY   ☎01237

Clovelly's torturously steep main street of 170 treacherous cobbled steps has long attracted tourist pilgrimages. To visit Clovelly, privately owned by the Rous family for 700 years, visitors pay a fee that goes toward keeping the village in its time-capsule-like state. After paying the town admission fee, all sights are free. Choose from the restored 1930s **Fisherman's Cottage** (open 9am-4:45pm), making your own pottery (£1.50) at **Clovelly Pottery** (☎431 042; open M-Sa 10am-6pm, Su 10am-5pm), and other crafts-based sights. During the colder months, a short walk east along the shore brings trekkers to a surging **waterfall**, which slows to a stream in warmer months. **Boat trips** from the harbor run to **Lundy Island** (☎431 042. 2 per week, depending on weather; call ahead. 1¼hr. sailing and 6hr. onshore. £25, children £22.50. Island admission £3.50.)

Getting to Clovelly by public transport can be trying. **First bus** #319 connects Clovelly to **Bideford** (40min.; M-Sa 6 per day, Su 2 per day; £2) and continues to **Barnstaple** (1hr., £2.10). On Sundays, the bus also runs from **Bude** (45min.; Su 2 per day; £1.80). The **land rovers** that shuttle visitors between the bottom of Clovelly and the carpark run every 10min. (round-trip £2). The **Clovelly Visitor Centre**, in the carpark, is where visitors pay admission to the village. (☎431 781. Open daily 9am-5:30pm, until 6:30pm July-Aug. £4, children £2.75.)

CORNWALL

Cornwall's version of England surprises most visitors. A rugged landscape of daunting cliffs that cradle sandy beaches, it's no wonder the Celts chose to flee here in the face of Saxon conquest. Today, the westward movement continues in the form of surfers, artists, and vacationers. The ports of Falmouth and Penzance celebrate England's maritime heritage, while stretches of sand around St. Ives and Newquay fulfill many a surfer's fantasies. Cornwall may have England's most precarious economy, visible in the derelict farmhouses and empty mine shafts that dot the countryside, but it's hard to tell in a region so rich in history and good humor, so proud of their past and of their pasty.

TRANSPORTATION

Penzance is the southwestern terminus of Britain's **trains** (☎ 08457 484 950) and the best base from which to explore the region. The main rail line from **Plymouth** to **Penzance** bypasses coastal towns, but connecting rail service reaches **Newquay, Falmouth,** and **St. Ives.** A **Rail Rover** ticket may come in handy (3 days out of 7 £25.50, 8 of 15 £40.50). A **Cornish Railcard** costs £10 per year and saves a third off most fares.

The **First bus** network is thorough, although the interior of Cornwall is more often served by smaller companies. *The Public Transport Guide*, free at bus stations and TICs, compiles every route in the region and is essential reading for smooth travel. Buses run from **Penzance** to **Land's End** and **St. Ives** and from **St. Ives** to **Newquay**, stopping in the smaller towns along these routes. Many buses don't run on Sundays, and often operate only May through September. **Traveline** (☎ 0870 608 2608) can help you get anywhere you want to go. **Explorer** or **Rover tickets** allow unlimited travel on one company's buses and are of excellent value to those making long-distance trips or hopping from town to town. A **First Day South West Explorer** offers unlimited travel on First buses (£7, children and seniors £5, families £15), while a **First Week Explorer** offers a week's unlimited travel all day anywhere in Cornwall (£28). Cyclists may not relish the narrow roads, but the cliff paths, with their evenly spaced hostels, make for easy **hiking.** Serious trekkers can try the famous **Land's End-John O'Groats** route, running from Britain's tip to top.

BODMIN MOOR

Bodmin Moor is high country, containing Cornwall's loftiest points—Rough Tor (1312 ft.) and Brown Willy (1378 ft.). The region is rich with ancient remains, like the stone hut circles that litter the base of Rough Tor. Some maintain that Camelford, at the moor's northern edge, is the site of King Arthur's Camelot, and that Arthur and his illegitimate son Mordred fought each other at Slaughter Bridge, a mile north of town.

THE BIG SPLURGE

CLASSIC CORNWALL

Let's face it: anyone who's seen a James Bond film has fantasized about cruising through the British countryside in a classic sports car. Wind blowing, sunglasses on, nothing reflects the breeding of the English aristocracy or the posh indulgence of the smart set better than a fine day of motoring in a open-top coupe.

Thanks to **Cornwall Classic Car Hire,** you can make your tweed-cap dreams a reality. The family-run business, a few miles off the A30 in mid-Cornwall, began out of a passion for old sports cars and is now one of the most respected car hires in the country. Seven classic sports cars are available for day- to week-long rentals, ranging from the antique 1948 MG TC Midget to the finest of all British sports cars, the sleek 1966 Jaguar E type convertible.

The rentals don't come cheap. The most economical car—the 1974 Triumph Stag convertible—costs £149 per day, while the open-top Jaguar costs £289. For a vastly reduced rate, special "taster-hires" get you the car from 10am to 6pm, and last-minute specials are posted regularly on their website.

Trevelyan, St. Gennys, Bude, Cornwall EX23 0NP. ☎ 084   58 1108; www.cornwallclassiccar-hire.co.uk. Reserve 2-3 months in advance. Prices go up £20-30 on weekends. £500-750 credit card deposit. Insurance and unlimited mileage included.

▐ TRANSPORTATION

The town of **Bodmin** sits at the southern edge of Bodmin Moor, which spreads north to coastal (but non-beach) **Tintagel** and **Camelford**. **Trains** (☎ 08457 484 950) arrive at **Bodmin Parkway** from: **London Paddington** (4hr., 15 per day, £53); **Penzance** (1½hr., every hr., £9.50); **Plymouth** (40min., every per hr., £7.10). The station is open M-F 6:10am-8pm, Sa 6:30am-8am, Su 10:35am-7:40pm. **National Express buses** (☎ 08705 808 080) arrive from **Plymouth** (1½hr., 2 per day, £4.25). **Western Greyhound** (☎ 01637 871 871) #593 runs buses to **Newquay** (1hr., M-Sa 5 per day, £2.70). Access **Camelford** by first hopping the #555 to **Wadebridge** (30min., every hr., £2.20) and then from Wadebridge taking the #594 to Camelford (30min., M-Sa 5 per day, £2). To get to Camelford on weekends, or to reach **Tintagel** and **Boscastle**, take the #555 to Wadebridge (30min., every hr., £2.20) and transfer to #524 (M-Sa 4 per day, Su 3 per day, £2.40). **Hiking** is convenient from Camelford, and is the only way to reach the tors. **Bikes** can be hired in surrounding towns. **Hitchhiking** is dangerous. *Let's Go* does not recommend hitchhiking.

▐ ACCOMMODATIONS

B&Bs can be booked through the Bodmin TIC (p. 236). **Jamaica Inn ❸**, Bolventor, Launceston, in the middle of the moor, is an 18th-century coaching inn that inspired the novel by Daphne du Maurier. Take First bus #X10 (M-Sa 6 per day) from Wadebridge. (☎ 01566 86250; www.jamaicainn.co.uk. Singles £45; doubles £60-80. MC/V.) Just 3 mi. away, **Barn End ❸**, Ninestones Farm, Common Moor, Liskeard, offers doubles. There's no direct bus, but the owners will pick you up from Bodmin or Liskeard if you call ahead. (☎ 01579 321 628. £44. Cash only.) The nearest YHA hostels are in Boscastle (p. 238) and Tintagel (p. 238).

BODMIN   ☎ 01208

The town of Bodmin, the ancient capital of Cornwall, is the last supply stop before venturing out to Arthurian stomping grounds. For hiking or cycling, the 17 mi. **Camel Trail** starts in Padstow and passes through Bodmin on the way to Poley's Bridge, with views of the River Camel, quarries, and tea shops. A former railway track, the trail is mostly smooth and level.

In town, a few sights are of interest. The **Military Museum**, St. Nicholas St., behind Bodmin General Station, displays George Washington's Bible and account book (which reveals a missing $3000), pilfered by the Duke of Cornwall's infantry during the Revolutionary War. The infantry has fought in every major British war since 1702. (☎ 72810. Open M-F 9am-5pm; July-Aug. also Su 10am-4pm. £2.50, children 50p.) Built in 1776, the **Bodmin Jail**, Berrycombe Rd., was the safekeep for the crown jewels and Domesday book during WWII. (☎ 76292. Open Apr.-Oct. Su-F 10am-6pm, Sa 11am-6pm. £3.90, children £2.) In the 1800s, after a harsh winter, men would sell their wives at the **Old Cattle Market**, now the Market House Arcade.

Hidden in Bodmin's forests, the stately 17th-century mansion **Lanhydrock**, was gutted by fire in 1881 and is now encompassed by elaborate formal gardens. Inside, magnificent plaster ceilings portraying scenes from the Old Testament overhang plush Victorian furnishings. From Bodmin, take **Western Greyhound** bus #555 (round-trip £2.20) or walk 2½ mi. southeast of Bodmin on the A38. (☎ 265 950. House open Apr.-Oct. Tu-Su 11am-5:30pm. Gardens open daily mid-Feb. to Oct. 10am-6pm. £7.50, children £3.75. Grounds only £4.20, children £2.10.)

To reach town from the **Bodmin Parkway Station**, 3 mi. away on the A38, take **Western Greyhound** bus #555 (every hr., £2.20) or call **Chris Parnell Taxis** (☎ 75000; £5 between station and town). The **Bodmin General Station**, St. Nicholas St. (☎ 73666), serves **Bodmin & Wenford Railway's** private steam-hauled trains, which run to Bodmin Parkway and Boscarne Junction, 6 mi. away near Wadebridge. (Apr.-Sept. 4-7 per day. Entire route £9, children £5, families £25. Bodmin General to Boscarne Junction £5/£3/£15. Bodmin General to Bodmin Parkway £6/£3.50/£17.50). The **Tourist Information Centre**, Shire Hall, Mount Folly, sells Ordnance Survey maps for £7. (☎76616; www.bodminlive.com. Open Apr.-Oct. M-Sa 10am-5pm; Nov.-Apr. M-F 10am-5pm.) To rent a car, contact **Bluebird Car Hire** (☎07764 154 768), near St. Austell. Other services include: **banks** on Fore St.; the **police** (☎08705 777 444), up Priory Rd.; a **pharmacy, Boots**, 34 Fore St. (☎72836; open M-Sa 9am-5:30pm); and the **post office**, 40 Fore St., in the back of Cost Cutters, (☎08457 740 740; open M-F 9am-5:30pm, Sa 9am-12:30pm). **Post Code:** PL31 2HL.

Friendly Mr. Jeram and precocious canine Ben offer comfortable rooms at **Elmsleigh** ❷, 52 St. Nicholas St., just uphill from the TIC. (☎75976. £18 per person. Cash only.) A mile north of town, camp at the **Camping and Caravaning Club** ❶, Old Callywith Rd., with laundry, showers, and a shop. Head north of town on Castle St., which becomes Old Callywith Rd. (☎73834. Open Mar.-Oct. £3-4.45 per person. Pitch £4.75. Electricity £2.30. Cash only.)

CAMELFORD   ☎01840

Those who imagine Camelot as a pinnacled and pennanted citadel will be disappointed by miniscule Camelford, 13 mi. north of Bodmin. Those who came looking for challenging treks into rugged Bodmin Moor, however, will be duly satisfied. From the center of town, **Rough Tor** (RAO-tor) is a 1¼hr. walk. From the **Tourist Information Centre**, in the North Cornwall Museum, The Clease (☎212 954; open Apr.-Sept. M-Sa 10am-5pm), head downhill, turn left on the main road, and follow it past The Countryman Hotel; a blue plaque marks Rough Tor Rd., which leads to the Tor. The climb is not arduous until the 300 ft. ascent at the top, where stacked granite boulders form steps and passageways. Keep going past the tor, and find your way around an electric fence to climb **Brown Willy**, the highest point in Cornwall, another 1hr. hike. Closer to town (1½ mi. north), tiny **Slaughter Bridge** is inlaid with hunks of petrified wood and marks the site where Arthur supposedly fell. To view it all without moving a muscle, head for ⌖**Moorland Flying Club**, at Davidstow Airfields, 3 mi. from Camelford; a surreal 20min. flight in a two-seat glider through clouds and over harbors will do the job. (☎261 517. Lessons £75 per hr.)

Though several **buses** run to Camelford, most service is indirect. **First** #X10 makes the trip from **Newquay** (1hr., M-Sa 2 per day, £4.) Western Greyhound bus #594 runs from Truro to Bude, stopping at **Wadebridge** (25min., 4 per day, £2.20). The TIC gives good hiking advice.

TINTAGEL   ☎01840

More enjoyable than Camelford, Tintagel, 6 mi. northwest, is a dusty little village just 1 mi. from the magnificent ruins of ⌖**Tintagel Castle**, built by a 13th-century earl on the legendary site of Arthur's birth. Roman and medieval rubble piles atop a headland besieged by the Atlantic, with some chunks having already disappeared into the sea. Below, **Merlin's cave** is worth the climb, but check for low-tide times and be careful on the steep cliffs. Even if you don't buy into the legends, the views are spell-binding. (☎770 328. Open daily Apr.-Sept. 10am-6pm; Oct. 10am-5pm; Nov.-Mar. 10am-4pm.) Inland, **King Arthur's Great Halls of Chivalry**, Fore St., was once headquarters of the Round Table of King Arthur. Millionaire Frederick Thomas Glasscock founded the order following WWI, hoping to spread Arthurian chivalry. Once boasting 17,000 supporters, membership has since fallen to 300. The Great Hall has two rooms: an antechamber with a 10min. light show relating Arthur's story, and the great hall, which houses three (!) Round Tables. (☎770 526. Open daily summer 10am-5pm; winter 10am-dusk. £3, concessions £2.) Escape gaudy homages to Arthur on a 1½ mi. walk through ⌖**St. Nectan's Glen** to a cascading 60 ft. waterfall, a spiritual healing center in times past. From the Visitor Centre, head toward Bossiney for about 1 mi., then follow signs along the footpath to your right; numerous paths lead to the glen. (☎770 760.

SOUTHWEST ENGLAND

Open daily Easter-Oct. 10:30am-6:30pm; Nov.-Easter only F-Su. £2.25, children £1, families £6.) The **Tintagel Visitor Centre**, Bossiney Rd., has a free exhibition that separates fact from fiction in Arthurian lore. The helpful staff also offers hiking and coastal walk suggestions. (☎779 084. Open daily Mar.-Oct. 10am-5pm; Nov.-Feb. 10:30am-4pm.) **Western Greyhound** buses #594 comes from **Camelford** (20min., M-Sa 5 per day, Su the #524 service 3 per day, £1.20). The **YHA Tintagel ❶**, at Dunderhole Point, is ¾ mi. from Tintagel. Head east out of town ¼ mi. past St. Materiana's Church, then follow the footpath to the shore. After 250 yd., look for the chimney. (☎770 6068. Lockout 10am-5pm. Kitchen and laundry £2. Curfew 11pm. Open Easter-Oct. Dorms £10.60, under 18 £7.20. Cash only.)

BOSCASTLE ☎01840

Flanked by two grassy hills, tiny Boscastle is a scenic Cornish village divided by a sparkling river. High cliffs guard the harbor, and climbing the eastern cliff affords expansive sea views. The **National Trust Information Centre**, The Old Forge, Boscastle Harbour, offers hiking suggestions. (☎250 353. Open Apr.-Oct. 10:30am-5pm.) A **Visitor's Centre** in the Cobweb Car Park provides additional information and maps, as well as **Internet access**, £1 per 15min. (☎250 010. Open daily Mar.-Oct. 10am-5pm; Nov.-Feb. 10:30am-4pm.) The Valency Valley above the village invites exploration, with scenic River Valency coursing through wooded vales. From the village car park, a 2½ mi. hike leads to **St. Juliot's Church.** Hikes along the headland cliffs provide spectacular views. In town, the **Museum of Witchcraft** is the largest of its kind. Its collection of artifacts, stories, and newspaper articles explain, chronicle, and defend the occult. Look for the weighing and docking chair used by witchhunters—if the accused weighed less than stacked bibles or floated in water they were considered guilty. (☎250 111. Open Easter-Halloween M-Sa 10:30am-5:30pm, Su 11:30am-5:30pm. £2.50, concessions £1.50, naughty children £1.50.)

Western Greyhound buses #524 and 594 come to Boscastle from **Wadebridge** (1-1½hr.; M-Sa 9 per day, Su 3 per day; £2.40) via **Tintagel** (10min., £1), and from **Bude** (40min.; £2.20). The self-catering **YHA Boscastle Harbour ❶** has an incredible location in the town center, alongside the river. Call ahead, as recent flood damage has closed the hostel for an undetermined length of time. (☎0870 770 5710. Kitchen and laundry £2. Lockout 10am-1pm. Curfew 11pm. Open Apr.-Sept. Dorms £10.60, under 18 £7.20. MC/V.) **Riverside Hotel ❸**, The Bridge, has standard ensuite rooms. (☎250 216. Breakfast included. Singles £22.50-25. MC/V.)

PADSTOW ☎01841

Padstow, enchanting yet unassuming, is the prettiest of the north Cornwall fishing ports. The cobblestoned harbor, cluttered with sailboats and trawlers, overlooks an estuary and sandy beaches. Beyond the ferry point near the TIC, an easy **coastal walk** ascends the cliffs for magnificent ocean views; follow the path past the war memorial to reach more expansive sands and an island-studded bay. Cyclists converge in Padstow for the start of the **Camel Trail** (p. 236) and the **Saints' Way,** which follows the route of the Celtic saints who landed here from Ireland and Wales. **Rent bikes** at **Padstow Cycle Hire,** South Quay, in the carpark. (☎533 533. Open daily mid-July to Aug. 9am-9pm; Sept. to mid-July until 5pm. £8-15 per day. Helmets £1.)

Fishing and boating trips depart from the harbor. **Cornish Bird** operates mackerel, reef, and wreck fishing trips (2-8hr.); anything you catch is yours. Book at **Sport&Leisure,** North Quay. (☎532 639; 532 053 after 6pm. Trips daily Easter-Oct. 9am-5pm. £8-20.) **Ferries** chug across the bay to nearby **Rock,** where visitors will find sailing, waterskiing, windsurfing, and golfing (☎532 239; 10-15min.; daily Easter-Oct.; Nov.-Easter M-Sa; £2, children £1). The **National Lobster Hatchery,** South Quay, across from the bus stop, was built to save the ailing lobster industry from overfishing. Expectant lobster moms are brought here to lay their eggs, and visitors can see the insect-like babies in various stages of development. (☎533 877. Open daily May to mid-Sept. 10am-6pm; mid-Sept. to Apr. M-Sa 10am-4pm. ₤2, concessions ₤1.25, families ₤5.) Numerous nearby beaches are perfect for exploring, surfing, and sunbathing. Take bus #556 (5min.; M-Sa 7 per day, Su 5 per day) to cave-pocked **Trevone Beach.** Bus #556 continues to remote **Constantine Bay** (15min.), with great surfing, and **Porthcothan Beach** (30min.), a relaxing spot for tanning. The professionals at **Harlyn Surf School,** 16 Boyd Ave., teach to all levels at nearby Harlyn Bay. (☎533 076; www.harlynsurfschool.co.uk. Book in advance and meet at Harlyn. Open May-Oct. ₤25 per half-day, ₤50 per day.)

The **Tourist Information Centre,** Red Brick Bldg., North Quay, books rooms for ₤3 plus a 10% deposit. (☎533 449. Internet access ₤1 per 15min. Open daily Apr.-Oct. 9am-5pm; Nov.-Apr. M-F 9:30am-4:30pm.) **Western Greyhound** #555 and 556 go to **Bodmin** from Padstow (45min., every hr., ₤3.90 round-trip) via **Wadebridge.**

Lodgings in Padstow are pleasant but pricey (from ₤30). A short uphill walk from the harbor, the suites at **North Point ❸,** Hill St., have delicate decor and harbor views. (☎532 355. Doubles ₤54-58. Cash only.) Uphill, **Ms. Anne Humphrey ❸,** 1 Caswarth Terr., offers cozy rooms. (☎532 025. Singles ₤25; doubles ₤45. Cash only.) Find a wealth of knowledge at the home of **Peter and Jane Cullinan ❸,** 4 Riverside, along the harbor as you walk into town. The top-floor double has a romantic balcony overlooking the bay. (☎532 383. Doubles ₤50-64. Cash only.) The nearest hostel, the **YHA Treyarnon Bay ❶,** is 4½ mi. from Padstow, on Tregonnan in the small town of Treyarnon. It's off the B3276; take bus #56. (☎0870 770 6076. Open Apr.-Feb. Dorms ₤11.80, under 18 ₤8.50. MC/V.) **Trevean Farm Caravan and Camping Park ❶,** St. Merryn, is 3 mi. outside of town on the B3276. (☎/fax 520 772. Laundry. Open Apr.-Oct. 2-person tent site ₤8-9. Electricity ₤2. MC/V.) Splurge at **St. Petrocs Bistro ❹,** New St., which offers mouthwatering seafood for ₤14-20. (☎532 700. Open daily noon-2pm and 6-9:30pm. MC/V.) Take afternoon tea on 19th-century china at the tiny and intimate **Victorian Tea Room ❶,** 22 Duke St. (☎533 161. All-day breakfast ₤4.50. Open daily Apr.-Oct. 8am-7pm. Cash only.)

NEWQUAY ☎01637

Known as "the new California," Newquay (NEW-key; pop. 20,000) is an incongruous slice of surfer culture in the middle of Cornwall. The town has long attracted riders for its superior waves, and a steady stream of European partiers has transformed the once quiet seaside resort into an English Ibiza, with wet t-shirt contests and dance parties late into the night. Though locals look forward to the end of August when tourist season abates, for now Newquay is keen to maintain its reputation as a favorite summer spot for England's youth.

▮ TRANSPORTATION

The train and bus information centers are at the rail station are on Cliff Rd. (Ticket office open M-F 9am-4pm, Sa 9am-1pm.) All **trains** (☎08457 484 950) come from **Par** (50min.; summer M-F 8 per day, Sa-Su 5 per day; ₤4.50), where they connect to **Penzance** (1½hr., 12 per day, ₤9.50) and **Plymouth** (50min., 15 per day, ₤8.40). **National Express** (☎08705 808 080) buses arrive from **London** (7hr., 2-4 per day, ₤33). Buses travel to Manor Rd. from **St. Austell** (#21, 1hr., every hr., round-trip ₤3.60) and **St. Ives** (#301, 2¼hr., 4 per day, round-trip ₤5.30). Buses 89 and 90 come from **Falmouth** (1½hr.; M-Sa every hr.; round-trip ₤5). Get a **taxi** from **Fleet Cabs** (☎875 000 24hr.).

▮ PRACTICAL INFORMATION

A few blocks toward city center from the train station, the **Tourist Information Centre,** Marcus Hill, has free maps and books accommodations for a ₤3.50 charge plus a 20% deposit. (☎854 020; www.newquay.co.uk. Open June-Sept. M-Sa 9:30am-

5:30pm, Su 9:30am-12:30pm; Oct.-May M-F 9:30am-3:30pm, Sa 9:30am-12:30pm.) **Western Greyhound,** 14 East St., runs **bus tours** to the Eden Project (p. 245) and popular nearby coastal towns. (☎871 871. 5-8hr. Daily tours. £8-15.) Tickets can be booked at the TIC. Other services include: **banks** on Bank St. (most open M-Tu and Th-F 9am-4:30pm, W 10am-4:30pm); **work opportunities** at a very busy **JobCentre,** 32 East St. (☎894 900; open M-Th 9am-5pm, F 10am-5pm); **luggage storage** at **Station Cafe** (£1.50 per item; no overnight storage; open daily Apr.-Oct. 7am-3pm); a **launderette,** 1 Beach Parade, off Beach Rd. (☎875 901; wash £2.30-3, dry 20p per 4min., soap 45p; open M-F 10am-4pm, Sa 10am-3pm; last wash 1hr. before close); the **police,** Tolcarne Rd. (☎08452 777 444); a **Boots pharmacy,** 15 Bank St. (☎872 014; open summer M-F 8am-8pm, Sa 8am-6:30pm; winter M-Sa 9am-5:30pm); **Newquay Hospital,** St. Thomas Rd. (☎893 623); **Internet access** at **Cyber Surf @ Newquay,** 2 Broad St., across from the Somerfield (☎875 497; 7p per min; open in summer M-Sa 10am-10pm, Su noon-8pm, in winter M-Sa 11am-6pm, Su noon-5pm), also at **Tad and Nick's Cafe,** 72-74 Fore St. (☎874 868; 5p per min. Open daily 10am-7pm); and the **post office,** 31-33 East St. (☎08457 223 344; open M 8:45am-5:30pm, Tu-F 9am-5:30pm, Sa 9am-12:30pm). **Post Code:** TR7 1BU.

🏠 ACCOMMODATIONS

B&Bs (£18-20) are near the TIC; numerous **hostels** (£12-16) gather on **Headland Road** and **Tower Road,** near Fistral Beach. Accommodations fill up weeks in advance when surfing competitions come to town; call ahead, especially in summer.

> **The Danes,** 4 Dane Rd. (☎878 130; www.thedanes.co.uk), on Fore St. Clean rooms and beautiful sea views. £22-30 per person. Cash only. ❸

> **Newquay International Backpackers,** 69-73 Tower Rd. (☎879 366; www.backpackers.co.uk). International crowd parties late into the night. Clean dorms. Sauna 50p per 20min. Kitchen and laundry £2.50. Dorms £8.95-14.95; twins £9.95-15.95; ensuite doubles £12.95-18.95. July-Aug. 7-night min. MC/V. ❷

> **Ocean Breeze B&B,** 22 Edgcumbe Ave. (☎850 187), from the train station a right on Cliff Rd. and then right on Edgcumbe. Family-oriented with comfortable rooms. £15-18 per person, £19-22 with breakfast. Cash only. ❸

> **Original Backpackers,** 16 Beachfield Ave. (☎874 668), off Bank St., facing the beach. Kitchen. Laundry £3. Dorms £8-17; closed for part of the winter. MC/V. ❷

> **Together Guest House,** 33 Trebarwith Cres. (☎871 996), a few blocks from the TIC toward the beach. Good value with spacious black-and-white rooms. £23-25. MC/V. ❸

> **Camping: Trenance Chalet and Caravan Park,** Edgcumbe Ave. (☎873 447). A campsite miraculously located in town. From the train station, turn right on Cliff Rd., then right on Edgcumbe and follow it for 10min. Laundry, restaurant, and cafe. Open Easter-Oct. £5-6.50 per person. Electricity 50p. AmEx/MC/V. ❶

🍴🍺 FOOD AND PUBS

Restaurants in Newquay tend to be quick, bland, and costly. Pizza and kebab shops dot town center, catering to late-night stumblers. For a cheap alternative, head to pubs or **Somerfield** supermarket, at the end of Fore St. (☎876 006. Open M-Th and Sa 8am-8pm, F 8am-9pm, Su 11am-5pm; July-Aug. M-F closes 1hr. later.)

> **Ye Olde Dolphin,** 39-47 Fore St. (☎874 262). Newquay's abysmal restaurants count at least one jewel. Meals can be expensive, but take advantage of the specials (6-8pm), including a 3-course meal for £12.45. Open daily 6-11:30pm, also Su lunch. MC/V. ❸

Prego Prego, 4 East St. (☎852 626). A variety of fresh panini (£3) and baguettes (£2.50), from sun-dried tomato and mozzarella to chicken pesto and peppers. Specialty coffees £1-1.65. Open daily 8am-5:30pm. Cash only. ❶

Cafe Irie, 38 Fore St. (☎859 200). Funky cafe serves creative dishes and takes requests; all-day breakfast options (£5 full English). Great tunes and plenty of sofas. Acoustic jams M nights. Open daily June-Sept. 9am-7pm; July-Aug. until midnight (food until 10); winter F-Su 9am-6pm. Cash only. ❶

The Shack, 52 Bank St. (☎875 675). Friendly, family-oriented sit-down with a beach theme and tasty dishes (£3-10), from vegetarian and Caribbean plates to the popular lunchtime Shack Wraps (£3.75-4.25). Open daily Mar.-Sept. 10am-5pm and 6-10pm; Oct.-Feb. 9am-3pm. MC/V. ❷

BEACHES

Atlantic winds descend on **Fistral Beach** with a vengeance, creating what most consider the best surfing in Europe. The shores are less cluttered than the sea, where throngs of wetsuited surfers pile in between the troughs and crests. Ominous skies often forecast the liveliest surf. Lifeguards roam the white sands May through September 10am-6pm. On the bay side, the sands are divided into four beaches: tamer waters at **Towan Beach** and **Great Western Beach** lure throngs of families, while enticing **Tolcarne Beach** and **Lusty Glaze Beach** attract beach-goers of all ages.

Sunset Surf Shop, 106 Fore St., rents surf paraphernalia. (☎877 624. Boards £5-10 per day, £12-25 per 3 days, £25-40 per week. Wetsuits or bodyboards £4-5/£10-12/£20. Open daily Apr.-Oct. 9am-6pm.) **Fistral Surf,** with four branches in Newquay (main one at 19 Cliff Rd.), also rents equipment; call them for surf conditions. (☎850 808. Boards £7 per day, £18 per 3 days, £25 per week. Wetsuits £5/£12-13/£20. Open daily 9am-6pm; July-Aug. 8am-10pm.) Learn the ropes from **West Coast Surfari,** the oldest school in town. Meet at 27 Trebarwith Cres., downhill from the TIC. (☎876 083 or book in surf shops. Lessons £25 per half-day, £35 per day.)

NIGHTLIFE

The party beast stirs at 9pm and roars uncontested through the wee hours. The trail of surfer bars begins on **North Quay Hill** at the corner of Tower Rd. and Fore St. The sheer number of venues and size of the crowds guarantee a good time.

IN RECENT NEWS

CLUBBING WITH CAUTION

Further steps in a region-wide attempt to curb drink spiking and date rape have been taken by one Newquay nightclub. **Sailors** (p. 242) became the first club in Cornwall to install a drink-dispensing machine—similar to a soda or candy dispenser—early in July 2004. The machine allows clubbers looking for bottled drinks to avoid long lines at the bar, and alleviates stress on busy bartenders, as Newquay's beachgoers generally pack clubs to capacity.

The machine, produced by ATM Vending, also promotes drink safety: patrons open drinks themselves, ensuring no tampering. This coincides with the Spike Campaign, inaugurated by Cornish authorities in April 2004. The campaign is being carried by clubs like Sailors, who now use drink mats reminding customers to mind their drinks. Bartenders have also employed the help of "Spike," a green monster atop a bookmark containing contact information—if they pass an unattended drink twice, they will drop in the bookmark to remind patrons how easily someone could compromise their drinks.

Bars UK-wide have also begun selling "alcotops," brightly-colored reusable bottle tops (www.alcotop.co.uk). Clubbers can put the top on when they put down their drinks, dissuading potential spikers whose actions would take much longer and be much more conspicuous.

Central Inn, 11 Central Sq. (☎873 810), in the town center. Outdoor seating facing the busy bustle, crowded all day long. Open summer M-Sa 10:30am-11pm, Su noon-10:30pm; winter M-Sa 11am-11pm, Su noon-10:30pm.

Sailors, 15 Fore St. (☎872 838). An elaborate lighting rig encourages the vibrant dance scene. Tu Porn Squad night, reduced entry in "sexy outfit." Open June-Sept. M-Sa 10pm-2am, Su 10pm-12:30am; Oct.-May Th-Sa 10pm-2am, Su 10pm-12:30am.

Tall Trees, Tolcarne Rd. Park (☎850 313; www.talltreesclub.co.uk). From the train station, walk away from the town center, turn right at Tolcarne Rd., and veer right at what looks like the end. 2 floors and big crowds make the 10min. walk worth it. F-Sa R&B, chart, house, and trance. Cover £2-6, before midnight £1 less. Open mid-Mar. to mid-Sept. M-Sa 9pm-2am; mid-Sept. to mid-Mar. F-Sa only.

Bertie's, East St. (☎870 369). Packs a crowd, especially for M ladies night (ladies free) and Su and Th, when entry before 11pm and drinks are both £1. Cover £5-7. Bar open daily 11am-11pm, Su 11am-10:30pm. Club open daily 9:30pm-2am.

FALMOUTH ☎01326

With the third-deepest natural harbor in the world (after Rio de Janeiro and Sydney), Falmouth (pop. 23,000) has always owed its livelihood to the sea. At the confluence of seven rivers, the port was the perfect entry point into Cornwall for Spanish and French invaders; the 450-year-old twin fortresses of Pendennis and St. Mawes, built by Henry VIII, still eye each other on opposite sides of the bay. Today, the well-to-do port maintains a village-like charm. Hip restaurants and pubs promise a relaxed and enjoyable atmosphere, while the antique ships that often dock in the harbor bring Falmouth's seafaring history to life.

▐ TRANSPORTATION

Trains: Falmouth has 3 unmanned **train stations. Penmere Halt** is near B&Bs; **Falmouth Town** is near the town center; and **Falmouth Docks** is near Pendennis Castle. Buy tickets at **Newell's Travel Agency,** 26 Killigrew St. (☎312 620), next to TIC. Open M-F 9am-5:15pm, Sa 9am-3:45pm. Trains (☎08457 484 950) from: **Exeter** (3-3½hr., 8 per day, £19.90); **London Paddington** (5½hr., 5 per day, £66); **Plymouth** (2hr.; M-Sa 12 per day, Su 7 per day; £10.10); **Truro** (22min., every 1-2hr. £2.70).

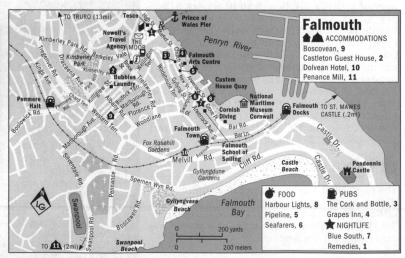

Buses: All buses stop near the TIC. **National Express** (☎08705 808 080) from: **London** (8hr., 2 per day, £33) and **Plymouth** (2½hr., 2 per day, £6). Pick up schedules and tickets at Newell's Travel Agency. **First** bus #7 runs to **Penzance** (1¼hr., 6 per day, round-trip £4.50) via **Helston** (50min., every hr., £3.25), while #89 and 90 go to **Newquay** (1½hr., M-Sa 1 per 2hr., £5.70) via **Truro** (30min., £2.70). **Truronian** (☎01872 273 453) sends buses to the **Lizard Peninsula** (p. 245).

Ferries: Ferries leave from Prince of Wales Pier and Custom House Quay. **St. Mawes Ferry Company** (☎313 201; www.stmawesferry.co.uk) sails to **St. Mawes** (25min.; 2 per hr.; £3.50; students £3, children £2). Runs daily 8:30am-5:15pm, also July-Aug. until 11pm. **Newman's Cruises** (☎01872 580 309) run to **Smugglers Cottage,** up the River Fal (45min.; M-Sa 2 per day; round-trip £6.50, children £3.25). **Enterprise** (☎374 241; www.enterprise-boats.co.uk) makes the idyllic trip to **Truro** (1hr.; May-Sept. M-Sa 5 per day, call for low-season trips; £5; children £2.50).

Taxis: Century Taxis (☎212 000). 24hr.

◼🛈 ORIENTATION AND PRACTICAL INFORMATION

The rail line runs along the highest parts of Falmouth: streets from there to the sea are steep. **The Moor** is Falmouth's main square. The main street extends from there, changing names five times, and covering the commercial area.

The **Tourist Information Centre,** 28 Killigrew St., The Moor, books beds for a 10% deposit. (☎312 300; www.go-cornwall.com. Open Apr.-Sept. M-Sa 9:30am-5:15pm; July-Aug. also Su 10:15am-1:15pm; Oct.-Mar. M-F 9:30am-5:15pm.) Numerous companies run **cruises** (1-2hr., £5-7) on River Fal to the north and Helford River to the southwest. **K&S Cruises** (☎211 056) offers fishing trips (2½ or 4hr., Su-F, £8/16). Other services include: **banks** on Market St.; **Bubbles Laundry,** 99 Killigrew St. (☎311 291; wash £2, dry 20p per 4min., soap £1; open M-F 8am-7pm, Sa 9am-7pm, Su 10am-3pm); the nearest **police** station, in Penryn (☎08452 777 444); **Superdrug** pharmacy, 55 Market St. (318 140; open M-Sa 9am-5:30pm; summer also Su 10am-4pm); **Falmouth Hospital,** Trescobeas Rd. (☎434 700); **Internet access** at the **library,** The Moor (☎314 901; first 30min. free, then 75p per 15min.; open M-Tu and Th-F 9:30am-6pm, Sa 9:30am-4pm), or at **Quench Juice Cafe,** a few doors from the TIC (☎210 634; 50p per 15min.; open M-Sa 9:30am-6:30pm, Su 10:30am-4:30pm); and the **post office,** The Moor (☎08457 740 740; open M-Tu 8:45am-5:30pm, W-F 9am-5:30pm, Sa 9am-12:30pm, with a **bureau de change**). **Post Code:** TR11 3RB.

▮ ACCOMMODATIONS

Western Terrace has a wealth of B&Bs (£15-45 per person), and rooms tend to be high quality. **Avenue Road** and **Melvill Road** sport additional lodgings, while those on **Cliff Road** and **Castle Drive** promise great views for a pretty penny. Most fill up come summer, so be sure to book ahead, especially July-Sept. The swankiest B&B in town, **Dolvean Hotel ❹,** 50 Melvill Rd., lovingly recreates a Victorian home with lacy bedrooms, ornate dining salon, and antique parlor organ. (☎313 658; www.dolvean.co.uk. Singles £40; doubles £70-90. MC/V.) The friendly owners of **Boscovean ❷,** 3 Western Terr., offer lodgings for the best price in town. (☎212 539. Open Apr.-Oct. £15 per person. Cash only.) Guest requests, from veggie breakfasts to a spare umbrella, are met at **Castleton Guest House ❸,** 68 Killigrew St. (☎311 072. Singles £20; doubles £44; family rooms £57. Cash only.) If you're **camping,** the nearest site is **Penance Mill ❶,** 2 mi. away near Meinporth Beach. (☎312 616. Kitchen and laundry. 2-person tent £10.50-13. Electricity £2. Cash only.).

◘ FOOD

Pick up **groceries** at **Tesco,** The Moor. (☎0845 677 9267. Open M-Sa 7am-8pm, Su 10am-4pm.) Falmouth has many options for quality eats, from cheap pasties to outrageously priced lobsters. **Pipeline ❸,** 21 Church St., serves Mediterranean and Cajun fusion (£8-13) amidst playful decor. (☎312 774. Open July-Sept. Tu-Su noon-2pm and 6-10pm; Oct.-June W-Sa noon-2pm and 7-9:30pm, Su breakfast 10am-2pm. MC/V.) With the feel of a coastal cove, **Seafarers ❸,** 33 Arwenack St., serves mouth-watering seafood entrees for £12-20. (☎319 851. Open daily noon-3pm and 6-10pm. Call ahead for reservations. MC/V.) Try the Moby Dick Giant Cod (£6.45) at the delicious fish and chips shop, **Harbour Lights ❶,** Arwenack St. (☎316 934. Open daily 9am-9pm, takeaway until 11:30pm. MC/V, cash only for takeaway orders.)

◉ ◪ SIGHTS AND BEACHES

Opened in 2003, the **National Maritime Museum Cornwall,** Discovery Quay, houses a remarkable collection of famous boats—suspended mid-air in a state-of-the-art gallery—and interactive exhibits on navigation which allow you to prove your own nautical prowess in the radio-controlled sailing simulation. (☎313 388; www.nmmc.co.uk. Open daily 10am-5pm. £6.50, concessions £4.50, families £17.) **Pendennis Castle,** built by Henry VIII to keep French frigates out of Falmouth, now features a walk-through diorama that assaults the senses with waxen gunners bellowing incoherently through artificial fog. (☎316 594. Open daily Apr.-June 10am-5pm; July-Aug. M-F, Su 10am-6pm, Su 10am-5pm; daily Sept. 10am-5pm, Oct.-March 10am-4pm. £4.50, concessions £3.40, children £2.30.) A 25min. ferry across the channel (p. 243) ends among thatched roofs and aspiring tropical gardens in St. Mawes village. **St. Mawes Castle,** 10min. uphill from the ferry drop-off point, is actually a circular battlement built by Henry to blow holes through any Frenchman spared by Pendennis's gunners. Though the tower is worth climbing, Pendennis wins the battle for superior views. (☎270 526. Open daily Apr.-June 10am-5pm, July-Aug. 10am-6pm, Sept. 10am-6pm, Oct. 10am-4pm; Nov.-March M, F-Su 10am-1pm and 2-4pm. £3.20, concessions £2.40, children £1.60. Free 1hr. audio tour.)

　Castle Beach, on Pendennis Head, is pebbly, but great for snorkeling. **Gyllyngvase Beach** and **Swanpool Beach** are both sandy, and have areas suitable for windsurfing.

◪ ♫ NIGHTLIFE AND ENTERTAINMENT

For a small town, Falmouth has a surprisingly vibrant social scene. Friday and Saturday nights, the rowdy crowd at **The Cork and Bottle,** 6-7 Church St. (☎316 909) vies to match an older group at **Grapes Inn** (☎314 704), across the road at 64 Church St. (Both open M-Sa 11am-11pm, Su noon-10:30pm.) The creamy cocktails (£3.95) are delicious at **Blue South,** 35-37 Arwenack St., a sleek surf bar. (☎212 122. Open M-Sa 11am-11pm, Su 11am-10:30pm. During happy hour 5-6pm, 2 cocktails £5.) The town's hottest club, **Remedies,** The Moor, is best on weekends when young crowds groove to hip-hop and Top 40. (☎314 454. Cover Su-M and W free, Tu and Th £3, F £4, Sa £5. Open daily 6pm-2am.) The **Falmouth Arts Centre,** 24 Church St., hosts exhibitions, concerts, theater, and films. (☎212 300. Box office open M-Sa 10am-2pm. Exhibitions free. Theater and concert tickets £5-10.) **Regatta Week,** August 8-14 in 2005, is Falmouth's main sailing event, with boat shows and music performances. The mid-October **Oyster Festival** features oyster tasting, cooking demonstrations, and craft fairs. Contact the TIC for details.

⚡ DAYTRIP FROM FALMOUTH

⛫ THE EDEN PROJECT

Bodelva, St. Austell. The St. Austell railway station is conveniently located on the Plymouth-Penzance line. From the station, Truronian (☎ 01872 273 453) bus T9 runs daily (20min., 13 per day, £2.50); T10 runs from Newquay (50min., M-F 1 per day, Sa 2 per day, Su 1 per day, £4). From the north, take Western Greyhound bus #555 from Padstow (1½hr., 8 per day, £3.50, round-trip £4), which passes through Wadebridge (1hr.) and Bodmin (40min.). Signposted from the A390, A30, and A391. ☎ 01726 811 911; www.edenproject.com. Open daily Apr.-Oct. 9:30am-6pm; Nov.-Mar. 10am-4:30pm. Last admission 1-1½hr. before close. Buy advance tickets at any TIC to avoid lines. £12, seniors £9, students £6, children £5, families £30.

A "living theatre of plants and people," the Eden Project is one of England's most unique and fascinating sights. The millennium project welcomed four million visitors in its first two years. Once a clay mining quarry, the area is now home to three massive biodomes: one open and two covered. Enter the Mediterranean villas of the **Warm Temperate Biome** and breathe in the scent of olive groves and citrus trees. Tickling palm trees hang overhead in the **Humid Tropics Biome,** the world's largest greenhouse, which houses a living rainforest of over 1000 plants. The 30-acre **Roofless Biome** features hemp, sunflowers, tea, and other plants that thrive in a European climate. A fourth biodome, the **Dry Tropics Biome,** is in the works (to be completed by 2006). Don't miss the entertaining "Plant Takeaway" display, a representation of what would befall people should all plants vanish. Those who want to see the natural wonders of the world can do so efficiently; it takes roughly 3-4hr. to walk through all three domes.

THE LIZARD PENINSULA ☎ 01326

The Lizard Peninsula is one of England's least touristed corners. Though its name has nothing to do with reptiles—"Lizard" is a corruption of Old Cornish "Lys ardh," meaning "the high place"—the peninsula does possess a significant outcrop of serpentine rock, so described because of its uncanny resemblance to snake skin. **South West Coastal Path** (p. 186) traces the Lizard around Britain's most southerly point, through dramatic seascapes and lonely fishing villages.

The tiny village of **Lizard** receives somewhat more attention thanks to **Lizard Point,** the southernmost tip of Britain. A short, signposted walk from the village, this windy outcrop remains surprisingly undeveloped save

ON THE MENU

THE PASTY'S PAST

Visitors to Cornwall may be daunted by the mysterious pasty (PASS-tee), its flaky shell encasing a variety of savory or sweet ingredients. According to legend, even the devil had concerns about the piping hot pastry pockets—he dared not venture into Cornwall for fear of being diced and baked into them by housewives.

An important part of Cornish history, pasties were a crucial source of sustenance in mining towns. Baked rock-hard so they wouldn't break if dropped down a mine shaft, pasties provided miners a balanced meal. Their ridged crusts made a perfect grip for dirty fingers, allowing workers to eat the filling and toss the crust later. In large families, the pasty would be filled with different ingredients and marked with initials so that those in the mines could find their favorite flavorings.

Pasties were brought to America in the 19th century by Cornish miners seeking a better life in the tin mines of the mid-west. But no one is certain of the pasty's origin. Some believe it descends from the English star-gazed pie, a similarly shaped sundry stuffed with fish. Others speculate that it traces its origins to invading Vikings. Whatever the source, you need only obey that authority on all things English to satisfy your tastebuds; as Shakespeare writes in *The Merry Wives of Windsor,* "Come, we have a hot pasty to dinner!"

for a 300-year-old lighthouse and the **National Trust Information Centre.** (☎290 230. Open Apr.-Oct. 10am-4pm; mid-June to mid-Sept. until 5pm.) ⊠**Kynance Cove,** 1 mi. northwest of Lizard Point along the coast, is an enchanting sight. Its sandy beach is studded by great masses of rock that create a lively surf. Escape the summer hordes by trekking 3hr. farther northwest to rocky **Mullion Cove,** where steep but climbable cliffs await. **Mullion Island,** 250 yd. off the cove, is home to more seabirds than officials can count. The cove is also accessible from Mullion village, 1½ mi. inland.

Seven miles from Helston in the middle of the peninsula, over 60 satellite dishes make up **Earth Station Goonhilly Satellite Earth Station Experience,** the world's largest satellite station. The site covers an area equivalent to 160 soccer fields. Interactive exhibits allow you to see your head in 3D and send emails to outer space. (☎0800 679 593. Open daily June-Sept. 10am-6pm; Oct. and Apr.-May daily 10am-5pm; Dec. 10am-4pm; Nov.-Dec. and Feb.-Mar. Tu-Su 10am-4pm; late Dec.-early Jan. and early Feb.-mid-Mar. Tu-Su 11am-4pm. Last entry 1hr. before close. £5, concessions £4, children £3.50.) The **National Seal Sanctuary,** Europe's leading marine mammal rescue center and home to sea lions, otters, and seal pups, is 6 mi. from Helston, in the town of Gweek. (☎221 361. Open daily 10am-4pm. £7.50, seniors and children £5.50, students £5.) **Truronian buses** run from Helston to Goonhilly (T2; 20min. M-Sa every 2hr.; T3, Su 20min., 2 per day, round-trip £2.50) and Gweek (T2; 30min.; 2 per day; round-trip £2.30).

The **Tourist Information Centre,** 79 Meneage St., books accommodations for a 10% deposit. (☎565 431; www.go-cornwall.com. Open M-F 10am-1pm and 2-4:30pm, Sa 10am-1pm; Aug. also Sa 2-4:30pm.) Stock up on cash in Helston—elsewhere, **banks** and **ATMs** are rare. The ⊠**YHA Lizard ❷,** a recently refurbished Victorian villa and former hotel, boasts a spectacular cliffside location and comfortable, modern lodgings. (☎291 145. Kitchen and laundry. Reception 8:30-10am and 5-10pm. Open Apr.-Oct. Dorms £13.40, under 18 £9.30. Cash only.) For **campsites,** consult the numerous listings in the free *Go West Guide to Cornwall* and the *Map and Guide to the Lizard Peninsula,* both available at TICs.

PENZANCE ☎01736

Penzance is the very model of an ancient English pirate town: water-logged and swashbuckling. The city's armada of antique shops wages countless raids on tourists, luring them with troves of trinkets. With glorious sunsets and mildly bawdy pubs, it's difficult not to enjoy such an irreverent, fun-loving town.

⌐ TRANSPORTATION

Trains: Station on Wharf Rd., at the head of Albert Pier. Ticket office open M-F 6:05am-8:10pm, Sa 6am-6:10pm, Su 8:15am-5:30pm. Trains (☎08457 484 950) from: **Exeter** (3¼hr., every hr., £19.90); **London** (5½hr., 7 per day, £59); **Newquay** via **Par** (2hr., 8 per day, £10.70); **Plymouth** (2hr., every hr., £10.70); **St. Ives** (via St. Erth: 40-60min., every hr., £2.90).

Buses: Station on Wharf Rd. (☎0845 600 1420), at the head of Albert Pier. Ticket office open M-F 8:30am-4:45pm, Sa 8:30am-3pm. **National Express** (☎08705 808 080) from: **London** via **Heathrow** (8½hr., 7 per day, £33) and **Plymouth** via **Truro** (3hr., 5 per day, £6).

Taxis: Nippy Cabs (☎366 666).

⚡🅩 ORIENTATION AND PRACTICAL INFORMATION

Penzance's train station, bus station, and TIC cluster on **Wharf Road. Market Jew Street** (a corruption of the Cornish "Marghas Yow," meaning "Market Thursday") is laden with bakeries and bookstores. It becomes **Alverton Street,** then **Alverton Road,** before reinventing itself as **the A30,** the road to Land's End.

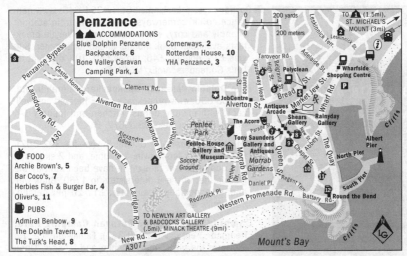

Penzance

▲▲ ACCOMMODATIONS

Blue Dolphin Penzance Backpackers, 6
Bone Valley Caravan Camping Park, 1
Cornerways, 2
Rotterdam House, 10
YHA Penzance, 3

🍴 FOOD
Archie Brown's, 5
Bar Coco's, 7
Herbies Fish & Burger Bar, 4
Oliver's, 11

🍺 PUBS
Admiral Benbow, 9
The Dolphin Tavern, 12
The Turk's Head, 8

Tourist Information Centre: Station Rd. (☎362 207; www.go-cornwall.com), between the train and bus stations. Books beds for a £3 charge plus a 10% deposit. Free Penzance map. Open May-Sept. M-Sa 9am-5:30pm, Su 9am-1pm; Oct.-Apr. M-F 9am-5pm, Sa 10am-1pm.

Tours: Anyone interested in riotous jokes about Neolithic man should try 📷 **Harry Safari** (☎711 427; www.harrysafari.co.uk.), a corny trip through the Cornish wilds. 4hr. Su-F leaves Penzance at 9:30am. £20. **Financial Services: Barclays,** 8-9 Market Jew St. Open M-Tu and Th-F 9am-4:30pm, W 10am-4:30pm, Sa 9am-1:30pm.

Launderette: Polyclean, 4 East Terr. (☎364 815), opposite the train station. Wash £2.20-4, dry 20p per 3min., soap 30p. Open daily 8am-8pm; last wash 7pm.

Police: Penalverne Dr. (☎08705 777 444), off Alverton St.

Pharmacy: Boots, 100-102 Market Jew St. (☎362 135). Open M and W-Sa 8:30am-6pm, Tu 9am-6pm, Su 10am-4pm.

Hospital: West Cornwall Hospital, St. Clare St. (☎874 000).

Internet Access: Penzance Public Library, Morrab Rd. (☎363 954). First 30min. free, then 75p per 15min. Open M-F 9:30am-6pm, Sa 9:30am-4pm. Also at **Penzance Computer Centre,** 76 Market Jew St. (☎333 386). 70p per 15min., and at **Polyclean** (see above). First 15min. free for launderette users; £1.20 per 30min. Available 9am-8pm.

Post Office: 113 Market Jew St. Open M-F 9am-5:30pm, Sa 9am-12:30pm. **Bureau de change. Post Code:** TR18 2LB.

🏠 ACCOMMODATIONS

Penzance's fleet of **B&Bs** (£18-23) mostly gather on **Alexandra Road,** a 10min. walk from the town center. Many buses run from the station to Alexandra Rd. (50p).

📷 **YHA Penzance,** Castle Horneck (☎362 666). Walk 20min. from the train or bus station. 18th-century mansion with spacious dorms. Classy lounge, kitchen, and laundry. At least 16 tickets are reserved for every Minack Theater show (p. 250). Lockout 10am-noon. Dorms £11.50, under 18 £8.25; doubles £27. Camping £5. MC/V. ❷

THE HIDDEN DEAL

BARGAIN BOOTY

The musky scent of age at Penzance's **Antiques Arcade** promises that you're going to buy something really cheap. With two levels of nameless shops selling antique bric-a-brac, this quiet mall has established itself as a premier venue for cheap but reliable antiques, making it popular with dealers for over 15 years.

Straining eyes will discover all sorts of fancy goods of eclectic interest. Common items include Wedgwood dinnerware (from £20), Victorian dressing gowns (£10-40), Newlyn copper, and terra cotta pottery. But other, more exotic pieces abound. In a single display, you're as likely to find a rococo perfume bottle as a porcelain merry-go-round horse or art deco table lamp. Perhaps more importantly, the devoted staff are helpful and unpretentious, as attentive to neophytes as to bona fide collectors. (☎338 121. Open M-Sa 9:30am-5pm.)

Venture downstairs for an even bigger smorgasbord of odds and ends at the Flea Market, where artwork (£5), porcelain plates (20p-£7), jewelry (£2), and small furnishings cover the floors and walls. After you've hoarded souvenirs for yourself, don't forget to pick up the guides to other antique markets. They abound: Cornwall is, after all, one of England's best-kept artistic secrets.

(61-62 Chapel St. ☎363 267. Open M-Sa 10am-5pm.)

Cornerways, 5 Leskinnick St. (☎364 645; www.penzance.co.uk/cornerways), behind the train station. Friendly and cozy, with ensuite rooms. Veggie breakfasts available. Book months ahead for summer. Singles £25; doubles £46; triples £60. 10% discount for Let's Go readers. AmEx/MC/V. ❸

Blue Dolphin Penzance Backpackers, Alexandra Rd. (☎363 836; www.pzbackpack.com). Relaxed and well-kept, with ensuite dorms. Kitchen and laundry £4. Dorms £10; doubles £28. MC/V. ❷

Rotterdam House, 27 Chapel St. (☎/fax 332 362). Friendly Roger lets 1 twin, 1 double, and 2 singles in this quaint house, thought to have been built by the grandfather of the Brontë sisters in 1760. Book well ahead, especially in summer. £17-20 per person. Cash only. ❷

Camping: Bone Valley Caravan Camping Park, Heamoor, Penzance (☎360 313). Family-run site, 1½ mi. from the city center. Kitchen and laundry. Open Mar.-Dec. £3 per person, from £3.50 per pitch. Electricity £1.50. AmEx/MC/V. ❶

FOOD

Expect to pay around £10-15 to dine at one of Penzance's excellent seafood spots along The Quay. The best buys are in coffee shops and local eateries on smaller streets and alleys near Market Jew Street. **Groceries** can be purchased downstairs in the shopping center at **Iceland** (☎361 130. Open M-W 8:30am-6:30pm, Th-F 8:30am-8pm, Sa 8am-6:30pm, Su 10am-4pm.).

Bar Coco's, 12-13 Chapel St. (☎350 222). Relaxed tapas bar with Matissean decor. Tapas £4-7. Mediterranean entrees £8-14. Open M-Sa 10am-11pm. Food served 10:30am-2:30pm and 6:30-10pm. MC/V. ❷

Oliver's, Chapel St. (☎332 555 or 07832 289 956; www.oliverspenzance.co.uk), under the Penzance Art Club. Warm and romantic with candles and a fireplace, this underground restaurant serves modern British and Mediterranean cuisine, entrees £9-14.95. Open Tu-Sa 7-10:30pm. MC/V. ❸

Archie Brown's, Bread St. (☎362 828), above Richard's Archie Brown's Health Food Store. Sunny and artsy, this veggie cafe makes creative meals, like a mushroom burger in pita (£4.75), and homity pie (£5). F all-you-can-eat buffet £10, reserve in advance. Open M-Sa 9:30am-5pm. MC/V. ❷

Herbies Fish and Burger Bar, 56 Causeway Head (☎362 850). Fish made to order and fried to perfection. Cod and chips £3. Open summer M-Sa 11:30am-7pm; winter M-Tu and Th-F 11:30am-2:30pm and 4:15-7pm. Cash only. ❶

⑥ SIGHTS

Penzance features an impressive number of **art galleries,** which crop up every other block. The *Cornwall Gallery Guide* booklet (£1), available at galleries and the TIC, lists the best galleries in Penzance and nearby cities. Archangel St. Michael is said to have appeared to some fishermen on Marazion, just offshore from Penzance, in AD 495—reason enough to build a Benedictine monastery on the spot. Today, **St. Michael's Mount** has a church and castle at its peak and a village at its base; at low tide, visitors can stroll there via a lumpy, seaweed-strewn causeway. The castle's interior is modest (look for a model of the castle made entirely from the corks of champagne bottles), but the grounds are attractive, and the thirty-story views captivating. Appropriate footwear is a must. *(Walk 3 mi. from the TIC to Marazion Sq. or take bus #2, 2A, 2B, 7, 16B, 17B, 300, or 301 (round-trip 1.40). The Mount is accessible by ferry (£1, children 50p) and sometimes by foot (5-10min.); for ferry and tide info, call ☎710 265. Castle ☎710 507. Open Apr.-Oct. M-F, Su 10:30am-5:30pm; July-Aug. also most Sa; Nov.-Mar. M, W, F by tour only, appointment necessary. Last admission 4:45pm. £5.20, children £2.60, families £13. Private gardens £2.50.)* The **Penlee House Gallery and Museum** is internationally known for its impressive collection of Newlyn school art, while the museum upstairs has an eclectic collection of historical artifacts. Look for the 18th-century Scold's Bridle, a menacing warning against loose lips. *(Morrab Rd. ☎363 625; www.penleehouse.org.uk. Open May-Sept. M-Sa 10am-5pm; Oct.-Apr. 10:30am-4:30pm. £2, concessions £1, children free. Sa free.)* The curator of the **Rainyday Gallery,** 116 Market Jew St., compiles the *Cornwall Gallery Guide.* *(☎366 077. Open M-Sa 10am-5pm.)* Another gallery worth a visit is **Badcocks Gallery,** The Strand, Newlyn, for contemporary art, crafts and jewelry *(☎366 159; open M-F 10:30am-5:30pm, Sa 11am-5:30pm).* **Round the Bend,** The Barbican, Battery Rd., is England's only permanent exhibition of contemporary automata. These quirky, often ingenious machines range from the daring to the droll—and most are on sale. *(☎332 211. Open daily Easter-Sept. 11am-5pm. £2.50, children £1.50.)*

ⓐⓝ NIGHTLIFE AND ENTERTAINMENT

The true character of Penzance emerges in its excellent pubs, most of which line Chapel St. **◪Admiral Benbow,** 46 Chapel St., is decorated entirely with paraphernalia culled from local shipwrecks, including a Captain's headboard that dates to the 16th century. *(☎363 448. Open M-Sa 11am-11pm, Su noon-10:30pm.)* **◪The Turk's Head,** 49 Chapel St., dating from the 13th century, is Penzance's oldest pub and was sacked by Spanish pirates in 1595. *(☎363 093. Open M-Sa 11am-3pm and 5:30-11pm, Su noon-3pm and 5:30-10:30pm.)* **The Dolphin Tavern,** The Quay, has the dubious distinction of the being the first place tobacco was smoked in Britain upon Sir Walter Raleigh's return from Virginia. The pub is said to be haunted by at least three ghosts. *(☎364 106. Open M-Sa 11am-11:30pm, Su noon-10:30pm.)*

The Acorn, Parade St., hosts a variety of performances, from jazz bands to comedy clubs to the rather dark productions of **Kneehigh Theatre,** Cornwall's best-known theater. *(☎365 520. Box office open Tu-F 10am-4pm, Sa 10am-3pm. Tickets £3-17.)* Bacchus visits the city the week of June 26 during the pagan **Golowan Festival,** featuring fireworks, and the election of the mock Mayor of the Quay.

▶ DAYTRIP FROM PENZANCE

◪ MINACK THEATRE

9 mi. southwest of Penzance, in the town of Porthcurno. Take First bus #1A from the bus station (30min.; M-Sa 6-9 per day, Su 2 per day; round-trip £2.60), or Sunset Coaches #345 or 346 from YHA Penzance or the TIC (50-60min.; M-F 2 per day, Sa 1 per day). Car access is via the B3283. TIC ☎811 902; www.minack.com. Open daily Apr.-Oct. 9:30am-5:30pm; Nov.-Mar. 10am-4pm. £3, children U16 £1.20, U12 free, seniors £2.20. Ticket office ☎810 181. Open mid-May to Sept. M-F 9:30am-8pm, Sa-Su 9:30am-5:30pm. Performances M-F 8pm, also W and F 2pm. Arrive 1½hr. before curtain. Tickets £6-7.50, children £3-4. £1-2 charge for phone booking.

During warmer months, patrons flock to the stunning open-air ◪**Minack Theatre,** which puts on performances ranging from *Romeo and Juliet* and *Alice Through the Looking Glass* to *Beauty and the Beast.* Hacked into a cliffside at Porthcurno, Minack reportedly appeared in a dream to Rowena Cade, who constructed the surreal amphitheater "with her own hands," literally. The theater's 750 stone seats afford spectacular views of the surrounding waters and have since 1932; on a clear day, visitors can see the Lizard Peninsula, 20 mi. to the southeast.

ST. IVES   ☎01736

As I was going to St. Ives, I met a man with seven wives.
Each wife had seven sacks, each sack had seven cats,
Each cat had seven kits. Kittens, cats, sacks, and wives,
How many were going to St. Ives?

Only one, of course. But medieval St. Ives (pop. 11,400), edged by pastel beaches and azure waters, has attracted visitors for centuries. The cobbled alleyways, colored by overflowing flowerpots, drew a colony of painters and sculptors in the 1920s; today, their legacy fills the windows of countless local art galleries, including a branch of the Tate. Virginia Woolf, too, was bewitched by the energy of the Atlantic at St. Ives: her masterpiece *To the Lighthouse* is thought to refer to the distant Godrevy Lighthouse, disappearing and reappearing in the morning fog.

▉⁊ TRANSPORTATION AND PRACTICAL INFORMATION. Trains (☎08457 484 950) to St. Ives pass through or change at **St. Erth** (15min., every hr., £1.70), though direct service is sometimes available. **National Express** (☎08705 808 080) buses stop in St. Ives (4 per day) between **Plymouth** (3hr.) and **Penzance** (25min.). For Penzance, it's cheaper to take frequent **First** buses (16, 16B, 17B; 40min.; 2 per hr.; round-trip £3). Bus #301 runs July-Aug. from **Newquay** (1¾hr., 4 per day, £4.70). St. Ives is a jumble of alleys and tiny streets. The **Tourist Information Centre,** in the Guildhall, books accommodations for a £3 charge plus a 10% deposit and sells maps (20p). From the bus or train station, walk to the foot of Tregenna Hill and turn right on Street-an-Pol. (☎796 297. Open Easter-Sept. M-Sa 9am-5:30pm, Su 10am-4pm; Oct.-Easter M-F 9am-5pm, Sa 10am-4pm.) **Columbus Walks** run longer 4-8 mi. hikes through the area. (☎07980 149 243. M-Th. £3-7.50.) **Ghost Walks,** which leave from the TIC, provide a spooky overview of town. (☎331 206; www.ghost-hunting.org.uk. 1-1½hr. July-Aug. M-W 8:30 and Tu also 10:15pm; June and Sept. Tu-W 8:30pm; Apr.-May and Oct. Tu 8:30pm. £4, children £2.) Other services include: **banks** along High St., **Barclays** (☎08457 555 555; open M-Tu and Th-F 9:30am-4:30pm, W 10am-4:30pm); **work opportunities** at **JobCentre,** Royal Sq. (☎575 200; open M and W-F 9am-12:30pm and 1:30-4pm, Tu 10am-12:30pm and 1:30-4pm), across from International Backpackers; **Boots pharmacy,** High St. (☎795 072; open

M-Sa 8:30am-8:30pm, Su 9am-4:30pm); free **luggage storage** at the **St. Ives International Backpackers** (see below); **Internet access** at the **library**, Gabriel St., near the TIC (☎795 377. First 30min. free, then £3 per hr. Open Tu-F 9:30am-6pm, until 8pm July-Aug., Sa 9:30am-12:30pm); and the **post office**, Tregenna Pl. (☎795 004; open M-F 9am-5:30pm, Sa 9am-12:30pm), with a **bureau de change. Post Code:** TR26 1AA.

⛺ ACCOMMODATIONS. Expensive **B&Bs** (£20-30) are near the town center on **Parc Avenue** and **Tregenna Terrace**; walk uphill on West Pl., which becomes **Clodgy View** and **Belmont Terrace** (10min.), where cheaper B&Bs offer fine sea views. **St. Ives International Backpackers ❶**, The Stennack, a few blocks uphill from the library, is covered with bright murals, and reception is from a tiki-hut desk. (☎799 444; www.backpackers.co.uk. Internet access £1 per 15min. Dorms £10.95-15.95; twins £28-36. July-Aug. 7 night min. AmEx/MC/V.) **Hobblers House ❸**, on the corner of The Wharf and Court Cocking, near Dive St. Ives, has spacious rooms practically right on the beach. (☎796 439. Open Mar.-Sept. Doubles £50. MC/V.) **Sunrise ❸**, 22 The Warren, downhill from the train and bus station; Mrs. Adams cooks superb breakfasts, including pancakes and kippers. (☎795 407. Singles £26-30; doubles £48-56. MC/V.) For camping or caravaning, **Ayr Holiday Park ❶** is the closest site. Make the 10min. walk to Bullan's Ln. (off The Stennack), turn right onto Bullan Hill, and left onto Ayr Terr. at the top of the road. (☎795 855; www.ayrholidaypark.co.uk. Laundry facilities. £5.30-8.10. AmEx/MC/V.)

🍴📶 FOOD AND PUBS. Get groceries at **Co-op**, Royal Sq., two blocks uphill from the TIC. (☎796 494. Open daily M-Sa 8am-11pm, Su 8am-10:30pm.) For local seafood at reasonable prices, the trendy **Seafood Cafe ❸**, 45 Fore St., can't be beat. Choose your fish raw from the display area (£8.50-15) and select garnishes (£1.45); all meals come with a side potato. (☎794 004. Open daily noon-3pm and 5:30-11pm. MC/V.) Pricier **Porthminster Cafe ❸**, at the end of Porthminster Beach, offers a heavenly view in a relaxed atmosphere. Enjoy pan-fried squid or scallops (£7.50) at tables right on the sand. (☎795 352. Entrees £4.50-16. Open daily noon-4pm and 6-10pm. MC/V.) Back in the town center, **Tides Café ❸**, 4/6 The Digey, serves creative fusion dishes. (☎799 600. Lunch £5-10. Dinner £12-16. Open M-Sa 11am-4pm and 6-10pm. MC/V.) Miniscule **Ferrell & Son Bakery ❶**, at the corner of Fore St. and Bunkers Hill, does its baking onsite; its pasties (£1.60-2.20) and saffron buns (50p) are touted as Cornwall's best. (☎797 703. Open M-Sa 9am-5:30pm. Cash only.)

🏛 GALLERIES AND MUSEUMS. Renowned for its superb lighting, St. Ives was once an artists' pilgrimage site, and the town's art community is still strong. *Cornwall Galleries Guide* (£1) navigates the dozens of galleries littered throughout St. Ives' maze-like alleys. A special ticket offers same-day admission to the Tate and the Barbara Hepworth Museum (£8.50, students £3.90, children and seniors free).

Like its sister, the Tate Modern in London (p. 119), the **Tate Gallery**, on Porthmeor Beach, focuses on abstract art. Exhibits rotate every three months and feature local and international artists. (☎796 226; www.tate.org.uk. Open daily Mar.-Oct. 10am-5:30pm, last admission at 5pm; Nov.-Feb. Tu-Su 10am-4:30pm. Free 1hr. tours M-F 2:30pm. £5.50, students £2.50, children and seniors free.) Under the wing of the Tate, the **Barbara Hepworth Museum and Sculpture Garden**, on nearby Ayr Ln., allows visitors to view the famed 20th-century sculptor's former home, studio, and garden. (Same hours as Tate. £4.25, students £2.25, children and seniors free.) To view works in the St. Ives school style, try **Belgrave Gallery**, 22 Fore St., associated with the Belgrave Gallery London (☎794 888; open M-Sa 10am-1pm and 2-6pm), or **Wills Lane Gallery**, Wills Ln. (☎795 723; open M-Sa 10:30am-5pm).

◪ **BEACHES.** St. Ives's ▨**beaches** are arguably England's finest. Expansive stretches of sand slowly descend into the sea, with shallow shores perfect for romantic strolls. Follow the hill down from the train station to **Porthminster Beach,** a magnificent stretch of golden sand and tame waves. To escape the crowds of toasting flesh, head for quieter **Porthgwidden Beach,** hugged by the jutting arms of the island. **Porthmeor Beach,** below the Tate, attracts surfers but has less appealing sands. Farther east, **Carbis Bay,** 1¼ mi. from very similar Porthminster, is less crowded and easily accessible. Take the train one stop toward St. Erth or bus #17 (5min.; M-Sa 3 per hr.; bus #17B Su every hr.; 70p.)

Beach activities in St. Ives are numerous. **Wind An' Sea Surf Shop,** 25 Fore St., rents surfboards and wetsuits. (☎794 830. £5 per day, £25 per week. £5 deposit. Wetsuit £5. Open daily Easter-Oct. 10am-10pm; Nov.-Easter 10am-6pm.) Open daily 9:30am-6pm, until 10pm July-Aug.) Beginners can start with a lesson at **St. Ives Surf School,** on Porthmeor Beach. (☎07792 261 278. £25 per 2hr., £100 per week. Price includes equipment. Open daily May-Sept. 9am-6pm.) **Dive St. Ives,** 25 The Wharf, offers diving lessons among shipwrecks, reefs, sea anemones, and sometimes even dolphins and sharks. (☎799 229. 3-day course July-Aug. £250; Sept. and June £200. Open daily 9am-8pm; July-Aug. until 10pm.) The less athletically inclined may prefer **boat trips,** which leave from the harbor. **Pleasure Boat Trips** heads to **Seal Island,** a permanent seal colony, and around the bay. (☎797 328. 1¼-2hr. £7, children £5.) Many boat companies head to the famous **Godrevy Lighthouse** (£7). Rent a motor boat from **Mercury Self-Drive** at the harbor. (☎07830 173 878. £8 per 15min., £12 per 30min., £18 per hr. Open daily Easter-Sept. 9am-dusk.)

▨ **NIGHTLIFE.** Beer has flowed at **The Sloop,** on the corner of Fish St. and The Wharf, since 1312. (☎796 584. Open daily 9am-11pm, Su 9am-10:30pm.) Nearby, **The Lifeboat Inn,** Wharf Rd., hosts bands Wednesday and Sunday and karaoke Friday and Saturday. (☎794 123. Open M-Sa 11am-11pm, Su noon-10:30pm.) The Irish **Craic Bar,** The Stennack, inside the Western Hotel, offers acoustic, folk, jazz, and blues in conjunction with next-door **Kettle 'n Wink,** so named for when ale houses hid smuggled brandy in a kettle and customers placed their order by looking at the kettle and winking. (☎795 227. Craic Bar open M-Sa 6-11pm. Kettle 'n Wink open M-Sa 11am-11pm, Su noon-10:30pm.) **Isobar,** at the corner of Street-an-Pol and Tregenna Pl., is St. Ives's busiest club. On Wednesdays, all drinks half price. (☎799 199. Cover W and F £5, Sa £6. Open M-Sa 10-2am, Su noon-1am. Upstairs club open from 10pm.)

PENWITH PENINSULA ☎01736

A largely untouched region of windswept cliffs and sandy shores, Penwith was once the center of Cornwall's mining culture. Derelict copper mines and abandoned tin chimneys are all that remain of this once formidable industry, save for the odd hole in the road where the pavement has collapsed upon an empty shaft. Dotted with Bronze Age structures and bronze beach-goers, Penwith draws visitors for both its history and scenery. From June to September, First bus #300 runs a loop from Penzance, passing through Land's End, Sennen, St. Just, Pendeen, Zennor, and St. Ives (5 per day; hop on, hop off ticket £5.50, children £3.50).

ZENNOR. Legend holds that a mermaid drawn by the singing of a young man in this village returned to the sea with him in tow. On misty evenings, locals claim to see and hear the pair. The immaculate **Old Chapel Backpackers Hostel ❷** is close to gorgeous hiking and 4 mi. from the beaches at St. Ives. Laundry (£1.50 wash, £1 dry) and cafe. (☎798 307; www.backpackers.co.uk/zennor. Continental breakfast

£3, full English £4.50. Showers 20p per 6min. Dorms £12; family rooms £40. Cash only.) Sunset Coach bus #343 from St. Ives en route to Penzance (20min., M-Sa 6 per day); bus #300 runs a similar route June-September (5 per day).

ST. JUST. On Cape Cornwall, 4 mi. north of Land's End, the craggy coast of St. Just (pop. 4000) remains fairly untainted by tourism and is a good base for visiting ancient menhirs and quoits. The one-woman **Tourist Information Centre,** at the library opposite the bus park, books local rooms and carries *Ancient Sites in West Penwith* (£4), outlining good walks from St. Just. (☎788 669. Open June-Sept. M-W 10am-1pm and 2-5pm, F 10am-1pm and 2-6pm, Sa 10am-1pm. **Internet access** available, first 30min. free, 75p per 15min. after.) A mile's walk from the TIC, **Cape Cornwall** was thought to mark the meeting place of the Atlantic Ocean and the English Channel. The cape's hikeable promontory, crowned by a tin-mining chimney, offers superior views. From the Cape, Land's End is a strenuous, 6 mi. walk to the south along the beautiful **South West Coastal Path.** 3 mi. northeast of St. Just in Pendeen, **Geevor Tin Mine** was a working mine until 1990. The site now houses a large museum dedicated to the history of mining. (☎788 662; www.geevor.com. Open Easter-Oct. M-F and Su 10am-5pm; Nov.-Easter Su-F 10am-4pm. Last admission 1hr. before close. £6.50, seniors £6, children £4.50, families £17.50. If traveling by bus, present your ticket for a half-price discount.)

Most routes to Land's End pass through Pendeen and St. Just. **Buses** #17, 17A, 17B come from **Penzance** (45min., every hr., round-trip £2.90) and #300 runs from **St. Ives** (1hr., 5 per day, £3.50). The **YHA Land's End ❷,** Letcha Vean, in Cot Valley, occupies three pristine acres. From the bus station's rear exit, turn left and follow the road as it becomes a footpath leading to the hostel (15min.); a map is posted at the St. Just library. (☎788 437. Reception 8:30-10am and 5-10pm. Open daily May-Sept.; mid-Feb. to Apr. and Oct. Tu-Sa. Dorms £12.50, under 18 £9.25. MC/V.)

▨**SENNEN COVE.** Just 2 mi. from Land's End along the coast, Sennen Cove is a gorgeous mile-long beach, inviting even to those who find the Cornish coastline austere. First **buses** #1 and 1A come from **Penzance** (40min.; M-Sa 7 per day, Su 3 per day; £3.20), while First #300 (2hr., 5 per day) and Sunset Coaches #345 (1hr., M-F 2 per day, Sa 1 per day) come from Penzance (45 min., 3.20) via **St. Just** (20min., round-trip £2.20). All buses stop at both the cove and the town, which lies on higher ground. Find lodgings with enviable views without having to leave the beach at **The Old Success Inn ❹,** on the cove. The adjoining restaurant serves a full menu from bar snacks (£6.75-8.75) to elaborate seafood dishes for £10-12. (☎871 232; www.oldsuccess.com. Restaurant open noon-9:30pm, bar M-Sa 11am-11pm, Su noon-10:30pm. Ensuite singles £31; doubles £88. MC/V.)

LAND'S END. Six kitschy tourist attractions capitalize on England's westernmost point, but none merits the admission fee as views are free. Free fireworks displays Aug. Tu and Th. First buses #1 and 1A go to Land's End from Penzance (55min., every hr., £4) and #300 comes from St. Ives (35min., 5 per day, £4.30 round-trip). For those unafraid of hills and hell-bent drivers, biking affords glimpses of coastlines. The **Visitors Centre** sells tickets for local attractions and dispenses local history. (☎0870 458 0044. Open daily July-Aug. 10am-6pm; Sept.-June 10am-5pm.)

ANCIENT MONUMENTS. Inland on the Penwith Peninsula, some of the least spoiled Stone and Iron Age monuments in England lie along the Land's End-St. Ives bus route. Once covered by mounds of earth, the quoits (also called cromlechs or dolmens) are thought to be burial chambers from 2500 BC. The **Zennor Quoit** is named for the village. The **Lanyon Quoit,** off the Morvah-Penzance road about 3 mi. from each town, is one of the area's most impressive megaliths.

SOUTHWEST ENGLAND

The famous stone near Morvah, on the Land's End-St. Ives bus route, has the Cornish name **Mên-an-Tol**, or "stone with a hole through the middle." The donut is allegedly endowed with curative powers. The best-preserved Iron Age village in Britain is at **Chysauster**, about 4 mi. from both Penzance and Zennor; there's a 2½ mi. footpath off the B3311 near Gulval.

THE CHANNEL ISLANDS

Situated in the waters between England and France, tiny Jersey and Guernsey (as well as the even tinier Alderney, Sark, and Herm) together comprise the 75 square miles known as the Channel Islands. Eighty miles south of England and forty miles west of France, the Islands provide visitors with a fusion of cultures and a touch of (often expensive) elegance. When France acquired Normandy in 1204, the islands declared allegiance to Britain; 2004 thus saw the 800th anniversary of loyalty to the Crown. Their mixed heritage makes for idiosyncratic systems of government and language, all adding up to a singular, insular experience. Soaking up the sun and drinking in the landscapes, however, you soon forget about politics; tucked in a romantic nook or historical cranny, you're worlds away from everywhere.

◪ GETTING THERE

Coming from England, **ferries** are your best bet for getting to the Islands. **Condor Ferries** (☎01202 207 216; www.condorferries.com) runs one early and one late ferry per day to both **Saint Helier, Jersey** and **Saint Peter Port, Guernsey** from three English ports (£32-61, round-trip £50-99): **Weymouth** (near **Dorchester,** p. 212) to Jersey, 3¼hr.; Guernsey, 2hr.; **Poole** (near **Bournemouth,** p. 210) to Jersey 3¾hr.; Guernsey, 2hr. **Portsmouth** (p. 170) is the cheapest, but also the longest; to Jersey, 10½hr.; Guernsey, 7hr. Times, frequency, and ticket prices are affected by both seasons and tides. Check their website for the most up-to-date scheduling or call their general reservation hotline (☎0845 124 2003). Arrive 45min. prior to departure time. ISIC cardholders (p. 14) get a 20% discount; ask before purchasing a ticket.

A WHOLE NEW WORLD. Though part of the UK, Jersey and Guernsey are essentially self-governing nations; you may have to plan your trip as you would a trip to the continent. The British pound is the official currency, but ATMs dish out Jersey or Guernsey pounds. These local pounds are on par with their British counterparts, but are not accepted outside the Channel Islands; you will have to exchange them upon returning to the mainland, possibly losing precious pence to commissions and exchange rates. Another quirk to keep in mind is that your cell phone carrier may recognize you as being in France, in which case your rates will be affected. Pay-as-you-go mobiles from the mainland (p. 44) cannot be topped up here, so your best bet is an international phone card, purchased in the islands.

JERSEY   ☎01534

The largest of the Channel Islands, Jersey's 45 square miles offer a bustling city center (St. Helier), rocky coastlines, sandy beaches, and a gorgeous countryside.

▣ TRANSPORTATION. An elaborate system of **buses** makes local travel painless. **Connex buses** (☎877 772) are based at the station on Weighbridge, St. Helier and travel all over the island. (Open M-F 8am-6pm, Sa-Su 9am-5pm, tickets 85p-£1.60.) **Easylink** (☎721 201) offers a hop-on, hop-off tour service (Su-F from Weighbridge

Terminal). **Explorer** tickets are best if your plans take you all over the island (1 day £7, 3 day £16.50, 5 day £21, one person under 16 free with every ticket). Easylink also offers direct service to sites on any of its four links (single £2).

For a **taxi**, call **Arrow Luxicabs** (☎887 000) or **Yellow Cabs** (☎888 888). **Bike rentals** are also available at **Zebra Car and Cycle Hire**, 9 The Esplanade. (☎736 556; www.zebrahire.com. Open daily 8am-5pm. 1 day bike rental £10).

◪◪ ORIENTATION AND PRACTICAL INFORMATION. The ferry drops you at **Elizabeth Harbor, Saint Helier,** where the majority of the island's city-scene takes place. Exit the Harbor and follow signs to the Esplanade, make a right, and head to the **Tourist Information Centre,** Liberation Square, St. Helier (☎500 700; www.jersey.com). The TIC is stocked with useful pamphlets on cycling and walking tours, as well as maps and updated weather and tide tables. (Open daily 8:30am-7pm). Pick up *Walking in Jersey* and *Cycle Jersey,* both free. **Les Petits Trains** run tours throughout the island offering both English and French commentary (☎07797 777 199. 40min. Single £3.50, round-trip £6; Child £2/2.50, under 5 free. Depart from outside the TIC.) Other services include: **Banks** clustering at the intersection of Conway, New, and Broad St.; **Thomas Cook,** 14 Charing Cross (☎506 900, open M, T, and Th-Sa 9am-5:30pm, W 10am-5:30pm); the **police,** Rougebouillon St. (☎612 612); **Jersey General Hospital,** Gloucester St. (☎622 000), travelers can also call the designated **visitors' doctor** (☎616 833); **Roseville pharmacy,** 7 Roseville St. (☎734 698, open daily 9am-9pm); **Internet access** at **usetheinternet,** 9 Charing Cross (☎733 665, £1 per 15min., open M-F 10am-7pm, Sa 10am-5:30pm, Su 10am-4pm); and the **post office,** Broad St. (☎616 616, open M-F 8:30am-5pm, Sa 8:30am-2pm), with a **bureau de change. Post code:** JE1 1AA.

▮▯ ACCOMMODATIONS AND FOOD. With tourism its biggest industry, the Islands are teeming with accommodation options. Pick up *Open House,* free from the TIC, or contact the Jersey Hospitality Association (☎721 421; www.jerseyhols.com). Be sure to book ahead, as everything fills up quickly in summer.

In St. Helier, pretty and pricey B&Bs line the Havre des Pas, stretching to the beach. Travelers on the cheap will have to head east to coastal St. Martin. The only hostel on the island is the spanking-new 105 bed **YHA Jersey ❷,** La Rue de la Pouclee des Quatre Chemins, Haut de la Garenne, St. Martin. (☎840 100. Take bus #3a from St. Helier, 20 min., every hr.; after 5:45pm take #1 to Gorey and walk ½ mi. up the hill. Open daily Jan.-Nov. 7-10am, 5-11pm; Dec.-Jan. F-Sa only. Dorms £16, under 18 £13; breakfast included. MC/V.) For beautiful views, try the **Seascale Hotel ❸,** Gorey Pier. (☎854 395; www.seascalehotel.com. June-Sept. doubles £58, ensuite with sea view £64; April £50/54; May £54/58. Take bus #1/1a/1b from St. Helier; 2 per hr.; 25 min. AmEx/MC/V.) **Rozel Camping Park ❶,** St. Martin, offers a view of the French coast. (☎856 797; www.jerseyhols.com/rozel. £5.60-8 per person per night, pitch only. Toilets, showers, and laundry. MC/V.)

Jersey offers a range of restaurants that serve up anything from seafood to ethnic. Peer at mosaics and a fountain (and that's just the bathroom) at the **Beach House ❷,** Gorey Pier. Enjoy an extensive menu, from tortilla wraps (£5.95) to salmon (£8.95). Call ahead to reserve an outdoor table. (☎840 450, open Tu-Su 10am-11pm. MC/V.) **City Bar and Brasserie ❷,** 75-77 Halkett Pl., offers sizable portions and free Internet access during your meal from a computer wall-mounted at your table. (☎510 096. Open M-Sa 11:30am-10pm. AmEx/MC/V.) **Signor Sassi ❷,** 33 Broad St., cooks up pizzas (£4.90-7.50) and other favorites. (☎639 333. Open M-Th noon-2:30pm and 5-10pm, F-Sa noon-2:30pm and 5-10:30pm, Su 5-10:30pm. MC/V.)

SOUTHWEST ENGLAND

🆂 **SIGHTS.** Jersey's many worthwhile sights celebrate the island's ever-changing role in the world beyond its waters. The **Jersey Heritage Trust** oversees a large portion of the museums; check out www.jerseyheritagetrust.org. Perhaps the most memorable of Jersey's sights is the gigantic 🅂**Mont Orgueil** castle, Gorey Pier, built in the 13th century to protect the island from the French. Climb to the top for a spectacular panorama, though the views from below are impressive enough. (☎853 292. ₤5.10, concessions ₤4.30. Open daily Apr.-Oct. 10am-6pm; Nov.-Mar. 10am-dusk. Last admission 1hr. before close.) Across from Liberation Square by the St. Helier marina, the 🅂**Maritime Museum** provides a wealth of information with hands-on exhibits, and the renovated-warehouse interior makes you feel as though you've just hopped aboard ship. Enter the "Elements Gallery" to better understand the tides, currents, and winds; try your hand at choosing a sail combination so your small wooden boat can outpace your opponents. (☎811 043. Open daily Apr.-Oct. 10am-5pm, Nov.-Mar. 10am-4pm. ₤5.95, concessions ₤5.10.) The **Jersey War Tunnels,** Les Charrieres Malorey, St. Lawrence, are a fascinating historical experience; one exhibit is housed in what was once an underground German hospital in WWII. (☎860 808. ₤8, concessions ₤4-7. Open daily mid-Feb. to mid-Dec. 9:30am-5:30pm.)

🄳 🄵 **ENTERTAINMENT AND FESTIVALS.** Jersey offers a variety of venues for entertainment. **The Opera House,** Gloucester St., presents the latest in theatre. (Box office ☎511 115. Open M-Sa 10am-6pm, 8pm on show nights, 1 hr. before a show on Su.) Various pubs and clubs offer nightlife options. Locals endorse the **Liquid Club,** on the Waterfront (☎789 346; open W-Su 10pm-2am; cover ₤3-10), and **Cosmopolitan,** The Esplanade. (☎720 289. Open F-Sa, 10pm-2am; cover ₤5.) If visiting during October, take a bite of **Tennerfest** (featured in Guernsey as well), which challenges local restaurants to come up with the best ₤10 menu. Check out www.jersey.com for more on festivals musical, floral and otherwise.

GUERNSEY ☎01481

Smaller in area but bigger on charm, Guernsey bears more obvious evidence of its French roots than Jersey. With cobblestone streets and hillside villas, cultural fusion is preeminent in the island's architecture, cuisine, and speech.

🄴 **TRANSPORTATION. Island Coachways** (☎720 210; www.buses.gg) operate throughout the island, with frequent service to tourist favorites. The bus terminus is on the waterfront, where Quay and South Esplanade converge. Buses #7 and 7a circle the coast (50p, every hr.). Island Coachways also offers themed tours from May-Sept. (like Guernsey in a Day and Fairy Princesses of Pleinmony). Tours generally begin and end at the bus terminus, and depart around 10am. Call for fares and information. For a **taxi,** call **PTR Taxis** (☎07781 133 233). **Quay Cycle Hire,** New Jetty, St. Peter Port, offers **bike rentals** at ₤7 per day, children ₤5. (☎714 146).

🄴 🄵 **ORIENTATION AND PRACTICAL INFORMATION.** A **Tourist Information Centre** awaits you immediately as you exit the ferry; its larger office is located across the harbor on North Esplanade. The TIC has maps as well as the helpful *Naturally Guernsey,* which provides information on the attractions of the island as well as nearby Herm, Sark, and Alderney. The center also books accommodations for a ₤2 charge and a 10% deposit. (☎723 552. www.guernsey-touristboard.com. Open M-F 9am-5pm, Sa 9am-6pm, Su 9:30am-12:30pm.) Other services include: **banks** on High St.; **Thomas Cook,** 22 Le Pollet (☎724 111. Open M-Sa 9am-5:30pm); the **police,** Hospital Ln. (☎725 111); **Princess Elizabeth Hospital,** Le Vauquiedor, St. Martin (☎725 241); **Boots pharmacy,** 26-27 High St.

(☎726 565, open M-Sa 8:30am-9pm); **Internet access** at **Healthxchange,** Albert House, South Esplanade (☎736 837, open M-F 8am-5pm, £1 for first 15min., 75p per 15min. after); and the **post office,** Smith St. (☎711 720, open M-F 8:30am-5pm, Sa 8:30am-noon). **Post Code:** GY1 2JG.

🖪🖰 **ACCOMMODATIONS AND FOOD.** Hotels fill quickly in Guernsey. For lodgings near town and with views of nearby Sark and Herm, try **St. George's Hotel ❸,** St. George's Esplanade, St. Peter Port. (☎721 027. Nov.-Mar. £26.50 per person; Apr.-Oct. £28.50-34. Breakfast included. MC/V.) Further down the road, **La Piette Hotel ❹** is a good deal for those traveling in pairs. (☎710 885. May-Oct. singles £55, doubles £92; Nov.-Apr. singles £52, doubles £88. Breakfast included. MC/V.)

Guernsey will easily satisfy your seafood-tooth. Get fresh fruit and veggies at Peter Hackley and Son's **market,** appropriately on Market St. (☎722 86, open M-Sa 7:30am-5pm). **La Cucina ❷,** North Plantation, above Yugo's Take-Out, serves sandwiches (£4.50-5) with a Mediterranean influence. (☎715 166, open Tu-Sa 11:30am-2:30pm and 7pm-late. Cash only.) **Christies ❸,** Le Pollet, has an airy French bistro feel. (☎726 624. Open daily noon-2:30pm and 6-10:30pm. MC/V.)

🖪 **SIGHTS.** Pull yourself away from Guernsey's wildflowers and beaches long enough to tour 🖪**Hauteville House.** Victor Hugo's home during his exile from France is as nuanced as his writing. The completely preserved home, where he wrote *Les Miserables,* is full of secret passages, hidden inscriptions, and handmade furnishings, all supposedly built by Hugo himself. (☎721 911. Open daily Apr.-June; July-Aug. 10am-5pm; Sept. M-Sa 10am-noon and 2-5pm. £4, concessions £2.) Also worth a visit is the **Castle Cornet** and its museums, right at St. Peter Port. Built in 1204, it has served as a bastion for alternating forces and was most recently handed back to Guernsey in 1947; try your best to navigate your way through the confusing corridors and stairwells. (☎721 657. £6, seniors £4, students and children free. Open daily Apr.-Oct. 10am-5pm, last admission 4:15pm.) A "Venue" ticket (£9, seniors £5) may be purchased for entrance into the Castle as well as the **Fort Grey Shipwreck Museum** and the **Guernsey Museum and Art Gallery.**

Nearby **Herm** (www.herm-island.com) and **Sark** (www.sark.info) are worthwhile daytrips. Pristine beaches await you at Herm, while Sark remains the last feudal state in the Western world. Uncorrupted by cars (transport on the island is left to foot, bicycle, or horse-drawn carriage), Sark's timeless quality is unmatched. If traveling in early July, be sure to check out the annual **Sheep Racing** competition.

🖪🖪 **ENTERTAINMENT AND FESTIVALS.** Shopping in Guernsey, especially along High St., is particularly popular due to the absence of VAT (p. 19). After finding your bargains, plop down for a pint at one of the bars that lines the waterfront. **Ship & Crown,** North Esplanade, is a local favorite (☎721 368, open M-Sa 10am-11:45pm, Su noon-3 and 6-10pm), and **The Albion House Tavern,** Church Sq., is a historic experience in its own right—it's in the *Guinness Book of World Records* as the closest tavern to a church in the British Isles thanks to a protruding gargoyle nearby (☎723 518. Open daily 10:30am-midnight).

Along with **Tennerfest** (p. 257), Guernsey hosts many other competitions and celebrations year-round. Don't miss the **Battle of Flowers** in August, where locals duke it out for the honor of best floral float. (For details, ring Mrs. Marquis at ☎254 473.)

SOUTHWEST ENGLAND

THE HEART OF ENGLAND

The patchwork pastures and half-timbered houses that characterize the countryside west of London are the stuff of stereotypes. The Heart of England contains many of England's most famous attractions: medieval Oxford, Britain's oldest university town; charming Stratford-upon-Avon, Shakespeare's home; and the impossibly picturesque villages of the Cotswolds, scattered among river-riven hills. It takes a resourceful traveler to avoid the touring hordes in this too-perfect landscape, but the region is so rich in history and beauty you are sure to find a quiet little corner of England to call your own, if only for a few hours.

HIGHLIGHTS OF THE HEART OF ENGLAND

OXFORD Admire the gargoyles in a stunning university town, rich in both architectural and bizarre student traditions (p. 263).

WINDSOR Explore one of the world's most sumptuous royal residences, which has housed 40 reigning monarchs (p. 261).

STRATFORD-UPON-AVON Tourist trails honor the Bard's footsteps and the Royal Shakespeare Company venerates his every syllable (p. 275).

ST. ALBANS ☎01727

From the Catuvellauni tribe to the Roman legions, to Norman conquerors, to the warring houses of York and Lancaster, every new administration has wanted to either set St. Albans on fire or make it their magnificent capital—usually a little of both. The Roman soldier Alban was beheaded here for sheltering a priest, making him England's first Christian martyr. Despite his gruesome and premature end, Alban's memory persists in the name of Britain's most significant Roman town.

TRANSPORTATION. St. Albans has two train stations; **City Station,** the main one, is not to be confused with **Abbey Station,** which runs a single schedule local service. **Trains** (☎08457 484 950) enter City Station from **London King's Cross Thameslink** (25min., 4 per hr., round-trip £7.50). To get from City Station to the town center, turn right out of the station onto Victoria Rd., follow the curve and continue straight for about 10min. Avoid the long uphill hike by hopping any "Into Town" bus (65p). **Sovereign** (☎854 732) buses usually stop at both City Station and along St. Peter's St. From **London,** take #797 to Hatfield, Hertford (37min.) and then **UniversityBus** (☎01707 255764) #602 to St. Albans (25min.).

ORIENTATION AND PRACTICAL INFORMATION. Leaving City Station, **Hatfield Road** to the left and **Victoria Street** to the right both lead uphill to the town center; the two streets are intersected perpendicularly by the main drag, which morphs from **St. Peter's Street** to **Chequer Street** to **Holywell Hill** as it descends the slope. The high-columned **Tourist Information Centre,** Market Place, St. Peter's St., has a free map and a sights-filled miniguide, and books your accommodations for £3. (☎864 511; www.stalbans.gov.uk. Open Apr.-Oct. M-Sa 9:30am-5:30pm; July-Sept. also Su 10:30am-4pm; Nov.-Mar. M-Sa 10am-4pm.) Other services include: major **banks** at the beginning of Chequer St.; the **police,** on Victoria St. (☎796 000); **Internet access** at the **library** in The Maltings, across St. Peter's St. from the TIC (☎860 000; open M, W 9:30am-7:30pm, Tu 9:30am-5:30pm, Th 9:30am-1pm, F 10:30am-7:30pm, Sa 9am-4pm); **Maltings pharmacy** at 6 Victoria St. (☎839 335); and the **post office,** 2 Beaconsfield Rd. (☎860 110). **Post Code:** AL1 3RA.

⌖🛏 ACCOMMODATIONS AND FOOD. Reasonable **B&Bs** (£20-40) are scattered and often unmarked. By City Station, **Mrs. Murphy ❸,** 478 Hatfield Rd., adorns rooms with small touches of luxury. (☎842 216. Singles £20; doubles and twins £40; family rooms £40-60. Cash only.) **Mrs. Nicol ❸,** 178 London Rd., opens her beautiful home to guests. (☎846 726; www.178londonroad.co.uk. Satellite TV in all rooms. Singles £30, doubles £50. Cash only.)

Fresh fruit and veggies abound at the famous **market** (W and Sa by the TIC); otherwise head to **Iceland,** 144 Victoria St., for daily staples. (☎833 908. Open M-W 9am-7pm, Th-F 9am-8pm, Sa 8:30am-6pm, Su 10am-4pm.) For lunch, a pint, or pure curiosity's sake, visit **Ye Olde Fighting Cocks ❶,** down Abbey Mill Ln. under the arch by the cathedral. With 7th-century foundations, this bizarre octagonal building may actually be the oldest pub in England. Underground tunnels, used by monks to see the cockfights and later to flee Henry VIII's cronies, run from the cathedral to the pub. (☎865 830. Open M-Sa noon-11pm, Su noon-10:30pm.) Ducks waddle up from the lazy River Ver near the **Waffle House ❷,** St. Michael's St., toward the Roman quarter. Choose from a multitude of creative sweet and savory toppings for £2.40-6.50. (☎853 502. Open Apr.-Oct. M-Sa 10am-6pm, Su 11am-6pm; Nov.-Mar. M-Sa 10am-5pm, Su 11am-5pm.) Hip **Zizzi ❷,** 20 High St., serves pasta and pizza. (☎850 200. Open daily noon-11pm.)

◪ SIGHTS. Built on the foundations of a Saxon parish church, the 1077 Norman design still defines the ▨**Cathedral of St. Alban.** At 227 ft., the medieval nave is the longest in Britain, and the wooden roof one of the largest. Painted while the outcome of the Wars of the Roses was uncertain, the tower ceiling features both the white and red roses of York and Lancaster (p. 72). A shrine to St. Alban stands in defiance of Henry VIII and Cromwell, its fragments at long last reassembled. (☎860 780. M-F, Su 8:30am-5:45pm, Sa 8:30am-9pm. Suggested donation £2.50.)

From the cathedral, walk 10min. down Fishpool St., over the river and uphill as it becomes St. Michael's St. to visit the ▨**Verulamium Museum.** Homes of the rich and poor of Roman Britain have been painstakingly recreated around mosaics and painted wall plasters discovered in the area. (☎751 810. Open M-Sa 10am-5:30pm, Su 2-5:30pm. £3.30, concessions £2.) Barely a block away, the remains of one of the five **Roman theaters** built in England huddles against a backdrop of English countryside; archaeologists still scour the lonely site for artifacts. (☎835 035. Open daily 10am-5pm. £1.50, concessions £1, children 50p.)

Two miles south of St. Albans, The **Gardens of the Rose** in Chiswell Green is the "flagship garden" of the Royal National Rose Society, where over 30,000 roses scale tall buildings and conquer sweeps of field. (☎850 461. Open June-Sept. M-Sa 9am-5pm, Su 10am-6pm. £4, children £1.50, seniors £3.50, families £10.)

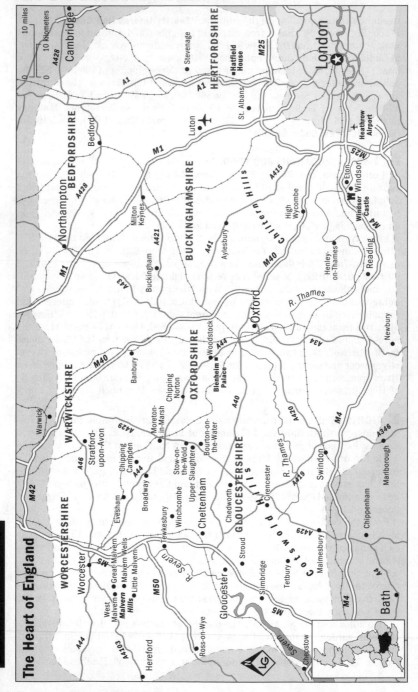

The Heart of England

HEART OF ENGLAND

🎒 DAYTRIP FROM ST. ALBANS

HATFIELD HOUSE

Buses #300 and 301 link St. Albans and Hatfield House (20min., 1-3 per hr., round-trip £3.30). The Hatfield train station, across from the main gate, makes the house easily accessible from other towns. ☎ 01707 262 823. House open daily Easter-Sept. noon-4pm. Hour-long guided tours M-F. House, park, and gardens £7.50, children £4. Park and gardens £4.50, children £3.50. Park only £2, children £1.

Stately 225-room Hatfield House is now owned by the marquesses of Salisbury, but is best-known for its association with **Queen Elizabeth I.** It was here that Lizzy spent her turbulent childhood; here that she was placed under house arrest for suspected treason by her sister, **Queen Mary** (p. 72); and here that she finally ascended the throne and held her first Council of State. Hatfield holds two famous portraits of Elizabeth I, and, though the silk stockings attributed to her are fakes, the gloves are real. Keep an eye out for the queen's 22 ft. long family tree, tracing her lineage to Adam and Eve via Noah, Julius Caesar, King Arthur, and King Lear. All that remains of her original palace is the Great Hall; the rest was razed to make way for the magnificent mansion that dominates the estate today.

WINDSOR   ☎ 01753

The town of Windsor and the attached village of Eton center entirely on Windsor Castle and Eton College, the two famed symbols of the British upper class. In the Middle Ages, residential Windsor fanned out from the castle perimeters, and it is now thick with specialty shops, tea houses, and pubs, all of which wear a certain charm. With the lively community that's developed in the midst of these two iconic institutions, Windsor and Eton have much to offer, particularly to the daytripper.

▐ TRANSPORTATION

Two train stations lie near Windsor Castle, and signs point the way into town. **Trains** (☎ 08457 484 950) pull into **Windsor and Eton Central** from **London Paddington** via **Slough** (40min., 2 per hr., round-trip £7.30). Trains arrive at **Windsor and Eton Riverside** from **London Waterloo** (50min., 2 per hr., round-trip £6.90). **Green Line** buses #701 and 702 arrive at **Central** from London's Victoria Station (1¼hr., 1 per hr., round-trip £6.10).

✱ 🔃 ORIENTATION AND PRACTICAL INFORMATION

Windsor village slopes in a crescent from the foot of its castle. **High Street** spans the hilltop, then becomes **Thames Street** at the statue of Queen Victoria and continues downhill to the river, at which point it reverts to High St.; the main shopping area, **Peascod Street**, meets High St. at the statue. The **Tourist Information Centre,** 24 High St., near Queen Victoria, has free brochures, and a published accommodation guide (£1). (☎ 743 900; www.windsor.gov.uk. Open daily May-Aug. 10am-5:30pm, Sept.-Apr. 10am-4pm. Other services include: the **police**, on the corner of St. Marks Rd. and Alma Rd. (☎ 50600); **Internet access** in the **bureau de change** in Central Station (open M-Sa 9:30am-5:30pm, Su 10am-5pm) or **McDonald's,** 13-14 Thames St.; and the **post office,** 38-39 Peascod St. (open M-F 9am-5:30 pm, Sa 9am-4pm). **Post Code:** SL4 1LH.

ACCOMMODATIONS AND FOOD

Windsor wants for budget accommodations and is best seen as a daytrip from London, but if you decide to stay, the TIC will locate **B&Bs** for a £5 fee; call ☎743 907. The recently refurbished **Clarence Hotel** ❹, 9 Clarence Rd., includes a lounge/bar area, sauna, and spacious rooms. Large windows grace the breakfast room, as well as the rest of the house. (☎864 436. Singles £41-62; doubles £52-72; family rooms £60-89.) **Alma House** ❹, 56 Alma Rd., is located in a quiet neighborhood a few minutes from town. (☎862 983. Singles £50; doubles £65; family rooms £85-90.)

Fast-food joints dominate Thames St. **The Waterman's Arms** ❶, Brocas St., is just over the bridge to Eton, next to the boat house. Founded in 1542, it's still a local favorite, offering cod and chips (£7) and pub classics (£4-7), including roast on Sunday. (☎861 001. Open M-F noon-2pm and 6-9pm, Sa noon-9pm, Su noon-4:30.) Tiny **Crooked House Tea Room** ❷ serves afternoon tea (£7-14) as well as sandwiches (£5-7). (☎857 534. Open M-Sa 10am-5:30pm.)

SIGHTS

WINDSOR CASTLE

☎831 118. Open daily Mar.-Oct. 9:45am-5:30pm; Nov.-Feb. 9:45am-4pm. Last admission 1¼hr. before close. £12, under 17 £6, under 5 free. Audio tours £3.50. Guides £5.

The largest and oldest continuously inhabited castle in the world, Windsor features some of the most sumptuous rooms in Europe and some of the rarest artwork of the Western tradition. It was built high above the Thames by William the Conqueror as a fortress rather than as a residence, and 40 reigning monarchs have since left their own marks. Today, members of the royal family often stay here for weekends and special ceremonies. The Queen is officially in residence for the month of April and one week in June—more than any other building, this is her home. During royal stays, large areas of the castle will be unavailable to visitors, usually without warning. The steep admission prices are lowered on these occasions, but it is wise to call before visiting. Visitors can watch the **Changing of the Guard** in front of the Guard Room at 11am (summer M-Sa; winter alternate days M-Sa). The Guards can also be seen at 10:50am and 11:30am as they march to and from the ceremony through the streets of Windsor.

UPPER WARD. Reach the upper ward through the Norman tower and gate. Stand in the left line to enter the ward past **Queen Mary's Doll House,** a replica of a grand home on a 1:12 scale, with tiny classics in its library handwritten by their original authors, as well as functional plumbing and electrical systems. The opulent **state apartments** are used for ceremonial events and official entertainment. The rooms are ornamented with art from the prodigious **Royal Collection,** including works by Holbein, Reubens, Rembrandt, van Dyck, and Queen Victoria herself. The **Queen's Drawing Room** features portraits of Henry VIII, Elizabeth I, and Bloody Mary, but don't miss smaller embellishments like the silver dragon doorknobs. A fire on the Queen's anniversary in 1992 destroyed the **Lantern Room,** the **Grand Reception Room,** and the stunning **St. George's Hall,** but the rooms are now fully restored.

MIDDLE AND LOWER WARD. The middle ward is dominated by the **Round Tower.** A stroll downhill to the lower ward brings you to **St. George's Chapel,** a 15th-century structure with delicate vaulting and an exquisite wall of stained glass dedicated to the Order of the Garter, England's most elite knighthood. Used for the marriage of Sophie and Prince Edward, the chapel houses the bones of royal ancestors, including the Queen Mother and George III. Ask a guide to explain the accident of history that placed the bones of Charles I and Henry VIII under the same stone until the early 19th century.

OTHER SIGHTS

ETON COLLEGE. Eton College, founded by Henry VI in 1440 as a college for paupers, has ironically evolved into England's preeminent public—which is to say, private—school. Despite its position at the apex of the British class system, Eton has shaped some notable dissident thinkers including Aldous Huxley, George Orwell, and former Liberal Party leader Jeremy Thorpe. The boys still practice many of the old traditions, including wearing tailcoats to class. The 25 houses that surround the quad act as residences for the approximately 1250 students. King's Scholars, selected for scholarships based on exam scores, live in the house known as "College" in the courtyard of College Chapel. *(10-15min. walk down Thames St., across Windsor Bridge, and along Eton High St. ☎671 177. Open daily late Mar. to mid-Apr. and July-Aug. 10:30am 4:30pm; other months 2-4:30pm; schedule depends on academic calendar. Tours daily 2:15 and 3:15pm. £3, under 16 £2.25. Tours £4, under 16 £3.10.)*

LEGOLAND WINDSOR. A whimsical addition to the town, this imaginative amusement park will wow the 11-and-under set with its rides, playgrounds, and circuses. Its Miniland took 100 workers, three years, and 25 million blocks to craft. The replica of the City of London includes a 6 ft. St. Paul's, as well as every other city landmark. *(Tickets available at the Windsor TIC. ☎08705 040 404; www.legoland.co.uk. Open daily mid-July to Aug. 10am-7pm; Apr.-June and Sept.-Oct. 10am-5pm or 6pm. £23, low season £21; children and seniors £20/£19. Shuttle from town center £3, children £1.50.)*

OXFORD ☎01865

Oxford has been home to a near-millennium of scholarship—25 British prime ministers and numerous other world leaders have been educated here. In 1167, Henry II founded Britain's first university, whose distinguished spires have since struck the imaginations of such luminaries as Lewis Carroll and C.S. Lewis. Today, trucks barrel, buses screech, and bicycles scrape past the pedestrians choking the streets. Despite the touring crowds, Oxford has an irrepressible grandeur and pockets of sweet quiet that lift the spirit: the basement room of Blackwell's Bookshop, the impeccable galleries of the Ashmolean, the serene lily ponds of the Botanic Garden, and the perfectly maintained quadrangles of Oxford's 39 colleges.

▄ TRANSPORTATION

Trains: Station on Botley Rd., down Park End. Ticket office open M-F 5:45am-8pm, Sa 6:15am-8pm, Su 7:10am-8pm. Trains (☎08457 484 950) from: **Birmingham** (1¼ hr., 2 per hr., £18); **Glasgow** (7hr., every hr., £70); **London Paddington** (1hr., 2-4 per hr., £14.90); **Manchester** (3¼hr., 1-2 per hr., £38.50).

Buses: Bus Station on Gloucester Green. **Stagecoach** (☎772 250) runs from **Cambridge** (3hr., every hr., £5.99) and operates the **Oxford Tube** (☎772 250) from **London** (1¾hr., 3-5 per hr., £9). The **Oxford Bus Company** runs **CityLink** (☎785 400; www.oxfordbus.co.uk) from: **London** (1¾hr., 3 per hr., £9, students £7); **Gatwick** (2hr., every hr. daytime, £21); **Heathrow** (1½hr, 2 per hr., £14). Stagecoach offers a **Day-Rider ticket** (£2.80); the Oxford Bus Company, a **Freedom ticket**, which gives unlimited travel on all routes in the area (zone) you choose (£2.90-4.20 for 24hr., £9-16 for any 5 days). A **PLUS+PASS** allows for unlimited travel on all Oxford Bus Company, Stagecoach, and Thames Travel buses, covering over 30 routes in the area. (☎785 410; 1 day £5, 7 days £14.)

Public Transportation: The **Oxford Bus Company Cityline** (☎785 400) and **Stagecoach Oxford** (☎772 250) offer swift and frequent service to: Iffley Rd. (#3 or 4, 4A, 4B, 4C, 16B), Banbury Rd. (#2, 2A, 2B, 2D), Abingdon Rd. (#X3, X13, 4, 16, 16A, 35, 35A), Cowley Rd. (#5, 5A, 5B, 5C), and elsewhere. Fares are low (most 60p-£1.40).

Taxis: Radio Taxis (☎242 424). **ABC** (☎770 077). **City Taxis** (☎201 201). All 24 hr.

ORIENTATION AND PRACTICAL INFORMATION

Queen Street becomes **High Street,** and **Cornmarket Street** becomes **St. Aldates** at **Carfax Tower,** the center of the original city. The colleges are all within a mile of one another, mainly east of Carfax along High St. and Broad St. The *Oxford Cycle Map* (free) at the TIC is an excellent guide for cyclists and pedestrians who wish to explore the city.

Tourist Information Centre: 15-16 Broad St. (☎726 871; www.visitoxford.org). A pamphleteer's paradise. The busy staff books rooms for a £4 charge plus a 10% deposit. Visitors' guide and map £1.25, monthly In Oxford guide free, accommodations list £1, restaurant guide free. Job listings, long-term accommodation listings, and entertainment news are posted daily (also available at www.dailyinfo.co.uk). (Open M-Sa 9:30am-5:30pm, Easter-Oct. also Su 10am-3:30pm. Last room booking 4:30pm.)

Tours: The 2hr. official Oxford University **walking tour** (☎726 871) leaves from the TIC and provides access to some colleges otherwise closed to visitors. Daily 11am and 2pm; in summer also 10:30am and 1pm. £6.50, children £3. **Blackwell's** (☎333 606) offers literary walking tours. General tours on Tu 2pm, Th 11am, Sa noon, (£6, concessions £5.50); "Inklings" tours focusing on C.S. Lewis, J.R.R. Tolkien and circle of friends (W, 11:45am), and an Alice and Wonderland tour (F, 2pm), £7, concessions £6.50. **Guided Tours** (☎07810 402 757), 1½hr., depart from outside Trinity College on Broad St. and offer access to some colleges and other university buildings. Daily hourly from 11am-4pm. £6, children £3. The same company runs evening **Ghost Tours,** also leaving from Trinity. 1¼hr. In summer daily 8pm, in winter F-Sa only. £5, children £3. **Bus tour** companies allow hop-on, hop-off access all day. **Guide Friday** (☎790 522) departs from the train station every 10-15min. 9:30am-6pm for a 1hr. tour, (hop on, hop off) at your leisure. £9, concessions £7, children £3.

Budget Travel: STA Travel, 36 George St. (☎792 800). Open M-W and F 9am-6pm, Th 10am-6pm, Sa 10am-5pm, Su 11am-4pm.

Financial Services: Banks line Cornmarket St. **Marks & Spencer,** 13-18 Queen St. (☎248 075), has a **bureau de change** with no commission. Open M-W and F 8:30am-6:30pm, Th 8:30am-7:30pm, Sa 8:30am-6:30pm, and Su 11am-4:30pm. **American Express,** 4 Queen St. (☎207 101). Open M-T and Th-F 9am-5:30pm, W 9:30am-5:30pm, Sa 9am-5pm. **Thomas Cook,** 5 Queen St. (☎447 000). Open M-Sa 9am-5:30pm, Su 11am-4pm. The **TIC** also has a **bureau de change** with no commission.

Launderette: 127 Cowley Rd. Wash £2.60-3.90, dry £2.60. Also 66 Abingdon Rd. Wash £2-3, dryers take 20p and £1 coins. Soap 70p-£1. Open 7am-10pm, last wash 9pm.

Work Opportunities: JobCentre, 7 Worcester St. (☎445 000). Open M-Th 9am-5pm, F 10am-5pm.

Police: St. Aldates and Speedwell St. (☎266 000).

Pharmacy: Boswell's, 1-4 Broad St. (☎241 244). Open M, W 9am-5:30pm, Tu 9:30am-5:30pm, Th-Sa 9am-6pm, Su 11am-5pm.

Hospital: John Radcliffe Hospital, Headley Way (☎741 166). Take bus #10 or 14.

Internet Access: Oxford Central Library, Queen St. (☎815 549), near Westgate Shopping Center. Free. Open M-Th 9:15am-7pm, F-Sa 9:15am-5pm. Also at **Mices,** 118 High St. and 91 Gloucester Green (☎726 364). £1 per 30min. Open M-Sa 9am-11pm, Su 10am-11pm.

Post Office: 102-104 St. Aldates (☎08457 223 344). **Bureau de change.** Open M-Sa 9am-5:30pm. **Post Code:** OX1 1ZZ.

ACCOMMODATIONS

Book at least a week ahead from June to September, especially for singles. **B&Bs** (from £25) line the main roads out of town and are reachable by bus or a 15-45min. walk. Try www.stayoxford.com for options. The 300s on **Banbury Road,** north of town, are accessible by buses #2, 2A, 2B, and 2D. Cheaper B&Bs lie in the 200s and 300s on **Iffley Road** (bus #4, 4A, 4B, 4C, and 16B to Rose Hill), and on **Abingdon Road** in South Oxford (bus #16 and 16A). If it's late, call the **Oxford Association of Hotels and Guest Houses** at one of the following numbers: ☎721 561 (East Oxford), ☎862 138 (West Oxford), ☎244 691 (North Oxford), or ☎244 268 (South Oxford).

Oxford Backpackers Hostel, 9a Hythe Bridge St. (☎721 761), between the bus and train stations. Inexpensive bar, pool table, music, and colorful murals. Passport required. Internet access £1 per 30min. Laundry £2.50. Luggage storage £1 per item. Dorms £13-14, quads £16 per person. MC/V. ❷

YHA Oxford, 2a Botley Rd. (☎727 275). An immediate right from the train station onto Botley Rd. Superb location and bright surroundings. All rooms ensuite. Facilities include kitchen and lockable wardrobes in every room. Lockers £1. Towels 50p. Internet access 50p per 10min. Laundry £3. Full English breakfast included. 4- and 6-bed dorms £19.50 per person, under 18 £14.40; twins £46. £3 student discount. MC/V. ❷

Heather House, 192 Iffley Rd. (☎/fax 249 757), a 10-15min. walk from Magdalen Bridge, or take the bus marked Rose Hill from the bus or train stations or Carfax Tower. Proprietress Vivian offers sparkling, modern rooms. £33-35 per person. MC/V. ❹

Newton House, 82-84 Abingdon Rd. (☎240 561), ½ mi. from town. Take any Abingdon bus across Folly Bridge. Affable proprietor and dark wardrobes await Narnia fans. Recently renovated; all rooms have TV and phone. Singles £36-50, twins and doubles £48-56, ensuite £58-66. AmEx/MC/V. ❹

The Acorn, 260 Iffley Rd. (☎247 998), ¼ mi. east of Heather House. Singles £32; doubles and twins £58, with bath £64; triples £81. MC/V. ❹

Old Mitre Rooms, 4b Turl St. (☎279 821), between Mahogany hair salon and Past Times Stationery. Lincoln College dorms. Open July-Sept. Especially packed during weekends, so book ahead. Singles £30; twins £56; triples £72. MC/V. ❸

Falcon Private Hotel, 88/90 Abingdon Rd. (☎511 122). A great place to nest while exploring Oxford. All rooms ensuite, with an impressive slew of conveniences—TV, phone, hair dryer, alarm clock, and a guest lounge. Singles from £38; doubles and twins from £72; triples from £80. Occasional winter price reductions. AmEx/MC/V. ❹

Camping: Oxford Camping and Caravaning, 426 Abingdon Rd. (☎244 088), behind the Touchwoods camping store. Toilet and laundry facilities. £4.10-5.80. Electricity £2.30. MC/V. ❶

FOOD

The owners of Oxford's bulging eateries know they have a captive market; students fed up with bland college food are easily seduced by a bevy of budget options. The **Covered Market,** between Market St. and Carfax, has fresh produce and deli goods. (Open M-Sa 8am-5pm.) **Gloucester Green Market,** behind the bus station, abounds with tasty treats, well-priced wares, and fabulous trinkets. (Open W 8am-3:30pm.) Get **groceries** at **Sainsbury's,** in the Westgate Shopping Center (Open M-Sa 7am-8pm, Su 11am-5pm.)

HEART OF ENGLAND

TO BLENHEIM PALACE, WOODSTOCK (8mi), STRATFORD-UPON-AVON (60mi), A34 & A44

Oxford

▲▲ ACCOMMODATIONS
The Acorn, **26**
Falcon Private Hotel, **30**
Heather House, **25**
Newton House, **29**
Old Mitre Rooms, **18**
Oxford Backpackers Hostel, **12**
Oxford Camping & Caravaning, **31**
YHA Oxford, **10**

🍴 FOOD
Aquavitae, **28**
Bangkok House, **11**
Chiang Mai, **20**
G&D's Cafe, **5**
Kazbar, **23**
Makan La, **17**
Mick's Cafe, **9**
The Nosebag, **16**

Pierre Victoire Bistrot, **4**
Queen's Lane Coffee House, **19**

🍺 PUBS
The Bear, **21**
The Eagle and Child, **6**
The Head of the River, **27**
The Jolly Farmers, **22**
The Kings Arms, **7**
The Old Bookbinders, **2**
Turf's Tavern, **8**

★ NIGHTLIFE & ENTERTAINMENT
The Bridge, **13**
Duke of Cambridge, **3**
Freud, **1**
KISS, **15**
Park End, **14**
The Zodiac, **24**

HEART OF ENGLAND

University Museum of Natural History and Pitt-Rivers Museum

River Cherwell

Music Meadow

Mesopotamia

S. Parks Rd.

St. Cross Rd.

Holywell Mill Stream

Mansfield Rd.

Great Meadow

Rd.

Parks Rd.

Rhodes House

F

Manor Rd.

St. Cross Rd.

DD

Savile Rd.

J

K

Jowett Walk

Holywell Music Rooms

7

Blackwell's

I

P

Bath Pl.

8

Holywell St.

Sheldonian Theatre

Bodleian Library

Longwall St.

River Cherwell

Addison's Walk

Broad St.

Museum of the History of Science

O

Brasenose Ln.

P

Q

New College Ln.

Magdalen Grove Deer Park

St.

N

St.

Turl St.

R

Radcliffe Camera

T

St. Mary's Passage

St. Mary's

18

S

U

Queens Ln.

St. Edmund Hall

Path along River Cherwell

High St. ("The High")

19

Museum of Oxford

20

21

W

Alfred St.

Bear Ln.

Blue Boar St.

King Edward St.

Oriel St.

Magpie Ln.

V

Peckwater Quad

Merton St.

Rose Ln.

X

Magdalen Bridge Boat Company

Angel Meadow

Magdalen Bridge

Botanic Garden

BB

AA

Dead Man's Walk

Tom Quad

Christ Church Picture Gallery

Z

Christ Church Chapel

Merton Field

Pedestrian Bridges

TO 23 (1mi), 24 (1mi), LAUNDERETTE (450yd)

Cowley Rd.

Bate Collection of Historical Instruments

The Broad Walk

Cricket Ground

CC

Cowley Pl.

Iffley Rd.

St. Aldates

The New Walk

Christ Church Meadow

TO 25 (1mi), 26 (1mi)

27

River Walk

Folly Bridge

28

TO ABINGDON, READING, LONDON, M4, 29, 30, & 31 (1mi)

○ COLLEGES

All Souls College, **T**
Balliol College, **H**
Brasenose College, **S**
Christ Church, **Z**
Corpus Christi College, **AA**
Exeter College, **O**
Hertford College, **P**
Jesus College, **N**
Keble College, **B**
Lincoln College, **R**

Magdalen College, **X**
Harris Manchester College, **K**
Mansfield College, **F**
Merton College, **BB**
New College, **Q**
Nuffield College, **L**
Oriel College, **V**
Pembroke College, **Y**
Queen's College, **U**
Regent's Park College, **C**

Somerville College, **A**
St. Catherine's College, **DD**
St. Cross College, **D**
St. Hilda's College, **CC**
St. John's College, **E**
St. Peter's College, **M**
Trinity College, **I**
University College, **W**
Wadham College, **J**
Worcester College, **G**

HEART OF ENGLAND

Across Magdalen Bridge, cheap restaurants along the first four blocks of **Cowley Road** serve Chinese, Lebanese, and Polish food, as well as fish 'n' chips. Watch out for after-hours **kebab vans,** usually at Broad St., High St., Queen St., and St. Aldates.

Kazbar, 25-27 Cowley Rd. (☎202 920). Mediterranean tapas bar just outside of town. Spanish-style decor and mood lighting create a posh atmosphere. Tasty tapas (£2.20-4.50) like *patatas con chorizo*. Open daily noon-11pm. MC/V. ❶

Pierre Victoire Bistrot, 9 Little Clarendon St. (☎316 616) French cuisine with a cozy, country home feel. Specials change daily, but the chef's whims are certain to satisfy the most discriminating of taste buds. Lunch £5-7; dinner £9-14. Open M-Sa noon-2:30pm and 6-11pm, Su noon-3:30pm and 6-10pm. MC/V. ❸

The Nosebag, 6-8 St. Michael's St. (☎721 033). Cafeteria-style service in a 15th-century stone building. Eclectic menu includes great vegan and vegetarian options and tasty homemade soups for under £8. Indulge in a scrumptious dessert (£1.35-2.75). Open M-Th 9:30am-10pm, F-Sa 9:30am-10:30pm, Su 9:30am-9pm. MC/V. ❷

Makan La, 6-8 St. Michael's St. (☎203 222), underneath The Nosebag, serves Malaysian and European food. Noodle dishes £5. Open M-Th 9:30am-10pm, F-Sa 9:30am-10:30pm, Su 9:30am-9:30pm. AmEx/MC/V. ❶

Chiang Mai, 130a High St. (☎202 233), tucked in an alley; look for the small blue sign. Extensive Thai menu served in a 14th-century home. Try the jungle curry with venison (£8.50). Appetizers £5-7. Entrees £7-10. Open daily noon-2:30pm; M-Th 6-10:15pm, F-Sa 6-10:30pm, Su 6-10pm. Reservations highly recommended. AmEx/MC/V. ❷

Aquavitae, 1 Folly Bridge (☎247 775). Super-sleek Italian eatery with fantastic waterside seating. Entrees £9-17.50. M 6-11pm, Tu-Sa noon-3pm and 6-11pm, also July-Aug. Su noon-3pm and 6-11pm. MC/V. ❹

Bangkok House, 42a Hythe Bridge St. (☎200 705). Fresh flowers and a noisy crowd. Beware: prawn crackers on your table are not complimentary. Entrees £5.50-10. Open M-Sa noon-3pm and 5:30-11pm. AmEx/MC/V. ❷

G&D's Cafe, 55 Little Clarendon St. (☎516 652). Superb ice cream and sorbet (£1.75-4), tasty pizza bagels (£3.45-4.15), and their incongruous intersection—ice cream bagels, all served in a boisterous atmosphere. Open daily 8am-midnight. Cash only. ❶

Queen's Lane Coffee House, 40 High St. (☎240 082). Established in 1654, the Queen's Lane is the oldest coffee house in Europe. Mingle with university students while sampling full English breakfasts (£4.50-5.95) or freshly-made sandwiches (£2.95-4.75). Open daily 7:30am-9:30pm, summer until 10pm. Cash only. ❶

Mick's Cafe, Cripley Rd. (☎728 693), off Botley Rd. next to the train station. A little diner with big breakfasts. Combination platters (£1.20-5) and a distinct ambience draw locals and students. Open M-F 6am-2pm, Sa 7am-1pm, Su 8am-1pm. Cash only. ❶

▶ PUBS

Pubs far outnumber colleges in Oxford; some even consider them the city's prime attraction. Most open by noon, begin to fill around 5pm, and close at 11pm (10:30pm on Sundays). Be ready to pub crawl—many pubs are so small that a single band of celebrating students will squeeze out other patrons, while just around the corner others have several spacious rooms.

■ **Turf's Tavern,** 4 Bath Pl. (☎243 235), off Holywell St. Arguably the most popular student bar in Oxford (they call it "the Turf"), this 13th-century pub is tucked in the alley of an alley, against ruins of the city wall. Bob Hawke, former prime minister of Australia, downed a yard of ale (over 2½ pints) in the record time of 11 seconds here while studying at the university. Choose from 11 ales. Open M-Sa 11am-11pm, Su noon-10:30pm. Hot food served in back room daily noon-7:30pm.

The Kings Arms, 40 Holywell St. (☎242 369). Oxford's unofficial student union. Merry masses head to the back rooms. Open M-Sa 10:30am-11pm, Su 10:30am-10:30pm.

The Bear, 6 Alfred St. (☎728 164). Famous patrons and Oxford students once exchanged their neckties for a free pint. Now over 4500 adorn the walls and ceiling of this tiny pub, established in 1242. Unfortunately, the deal no longer applies. During the day, the clients are older than the neckwear, and the young sit out back. Open M-Sa noon-11pm, Su noon-10:30pm.

The Old Bookbinders, 17/18 Victor St. (☎553 549). Walk up Walton St., left on Jericho St. until Victor St. This crowded little pub provides a neighborhood feel, with old lighters and beer mats, as well as crossword puzzles and cartoons contributing to the decor. Tu quiz night. Open M-Sa until 11pm, Su noon-10pm.

The Jolly Farmers, 20 Paradise St. (☎793 759). One of Oxfordshire's first gay and lesbian pubs. Crowded with students and twentysomethings, especially on weekends; significantly more sedate in summer. Open M-Sa noon-11pm, Su noon-10:30pm.

The Eagle and Child, 49 St. Giles (☎302 925). One of Oxford's most historic pubs, this archipelago of paneled alcoves welcomed C.S. Lewis and J.R.R. Tolkien, who referred to it as "The Bird and Baby." The *Chronicles of Narnia* and *The Hobbit* were first read aloud here. Open M-Sa noon-11pm, Su noon-10:30pm. Food served M-F noon-3:30pm and 5-8pm, Sa-Su noon-4pm.

The Head of the River, Folly Bridge, St. Aldates (☎721 600). Aptly named; outdoor heated seating right on the Thames. Open M-Sa 11:30am-11pm, Su noon-10:30pm. Food served all day.

🅖 SIGHTS

The TIC sells a map (£1.25) and the *Welcome to Oxford* guide (£1) listing the colleges' visiting hours, but those hours can be rescinded without explanation or notice. Some colleges charge admission. Don't bother trying to sneak into Christ Church outside opening hours, even after hiding your backpack and copy of *Let's Go*—bouncers, affectionately known as "bulldogs," in bowler hats and stationed 50 ft. apart, will squint their eyes and kick you out.

CHRIST CHURCH
Just down St. Aldates St. from Carfax. ☎286 573; www.chch.ox.ac.uk. Open M-Sa 9am-12:45pm and 2-5pm, Su noon-5:30pm; last admission 4pm. Chapel services Su 8, 10, 11:15am, and 6pm; weekdays 6pm. £4, concessions £3, families £8.

"The House" has Oxford's grandest quad and its most socially distinguished students, counting 13 past Prime Ministers among its alumni. Charles I made Christ Church his capital for three and a half years during the Civil Wars and escaped dressed as a servant when the city was besieged. Lewis Carroll first met Alice, the dean's daughter, here. Today, the dining hall and Tom Quad serve as shooting locations for *Harry Potter* films. In June, be respectful of irritable undergrads prepping for exams as you navigate the narrow strip open to tourists.

CHRIST CHURCH CHAPEL. The only church in England to serve as both a cathedral and college chapel, it was originally founded in AD 730, by Oxford's patron saint, St. Frideswide, who built a nunnery here in honor of two miracles: the blinding of her troublesome suitor and his subsequent recovery. A stained-glass window (c. 1320) depicts Thomas Becket kneeling moments before being gorily executed in Canterbury Cathedral. A rather incongruous toilet floats in the background of a window showing St. Frideswide's death, and the White Rabbit frets in the stained glass of the hall.

THE BIG SPLURGE

MAGDALEN BRIDGE BOAT COMPANY CRUISES

A traditional pastime in Oxford is punting on the River Thames's many smaller tributaries that snake through the university's grounds. Today, students have combined punting with another local favorite, beer, and created a sport marked more by leisure than exertion. Before venturing out, punters receive a tall pole, a small oar, and an advisory against falling into the river. (Though many an undergrad has cheerfully ignored the warning and tumbled into the river's waters.)

You can take part in this Oxford tradition and try punting (and relaxing) for yourself at **Magdalen Bridge Boat Company,** just under Magdalen Bridge. For a leisurely ride down the river, you can hire a chauffeured punt (£20 per 30min.; fee includes a complimentary bottle of wine). Or, for the more adventurous, try your own hand at the sport (M-F £10 per hr., Sa-Su £12 per hr. £30 deposit. 5 people max. Bring your own wine). Punters have their choice of going south on the River Cherwell, or north along the Isis.

Magdalen Bridge. Follow the signs on the north side of the bridge to the path toward the river. ☎ 202 643. Open daily Mar.-Oct. 9:30am-9pm. Cash only.

TOM QUAD. The site of undergraduate lily-pond dunking, Tom Quad adjoins the chapel grounds. The quad takes its name from Great Tom, the seven-ton bell in Tom Tower that has faithfully rung 101 strokes (the original number of students) at 9:05pm (the original undergraduate curfew) every evening since 1682. Nearby, the fan-vaulted college hall displays portraits of some of Christ Church's most famous alums—Sir Philip Sidney, William Penn, John Ruskin, John Locke, and a bored-looking W.H. Auden in a corner by the kitchen.

OTHER SIGHTS. Through an archway (to your left as you face the cathedral) lie **Peckwater Quad** and the most elegant Palladian building in Oxford. Look here for faded rowing standings chalked on the walls and for Christ Church's library, closed to visitors. Spreading east and south from the main entrance, **Christ Church Meadow** compensates for Oxford's lack of "backs" (the riverside gardens in Cambridge). Housed in the Canterbury Quad, the **Christ Church Picture Gallery** is a noteworthy collection of Italian, Dutch, and Flemish paintings, starring Tintoretto and Vermeer; and also houses cartoons drawn by da Vinci. *(Entrances on Oriel Sq. and at Canterbury Gate; visitors to the gallery only should enter through Canterbury Gate. ☎ 276 172. Open Apr.-Sept. M-Sa 10:30am-1pm and 2-5:30pm, Su 2-5pm; Oct.-Mar. closes at 4:30pm. £2, concessions £1.)*

OTHER COLLEGES

MERTON COLLEGE. Merton's library houses the first printed Welsh Bible. Tolkien lectured here, inventing the Elven language in his spare time. The college's 14th-century **Mob Quad** is Oxford's oldest and least impressive, but nearby **St. Alban's Quad** has some of the university's best gargoyles. Japanese Crown Prince Narahito lived here during his University days. *(Merton St. ☎ 276 310; www.merton.ox.ac.uk. Open M-F 2-4pm, Sa-Su 10am-4pm. Free.)*

UNIVERSITY COLLEGE. Built in 1249, this soot-blackened college vies with Merton for the title of oldest, claiming Alfred the Great as its founder. Percy Bysshe Shelley was expelled for writing the pamphlet *The Necessity of Atheism* but was later immortalized in a prominent monument, to the right as you enter. Bill Clinton spent his Rhodes days here; his rooms at 46 Leckford Rd. are a tour guide's endless source of smoked-but-didn't-inhale jokes. *(High St. ☎ 276 602; www.univ.ox.ac.uk. Open to tours only.)*

ORIEL AND CORPUS CHRISTI COLLEGES. Oriel College (a.k.a. "The House of the Blessed Mary the Virgin in Oxford") is wedged between High St. and Merton

St. and was once the turf of Sir Walter Raleigh. (☎ 276 555; www.oriel.ox.ac.uk. Open to tours only, daily 1-4pm. Free.) South of Oriel, **Corpus Christi College,** the smallest of Oxford's colleges, surrounds a sundialed quad. The garden wall reveals a gate built for visits between Charles I and his queen, who were residents at adjacent Christ Church and Merton colleges during the Civil Wars. (☎ 276 700; www.ccc.ox.ac.uk. Open 1:30-4:30pm.)

ALL SOULS COLLEGE. Only Oxford's best are admitted to this prestigious graduate college. Candidates who survive the admission exams are invited to dinner, where it is ensured that they are "well-born, well-bred, and only moderately learned." All Souls is also reported to have the most heavenly wine cellar in the city. **The Great Quad,** with its fastidious lawn and two spare spires, may be Oxford's most serene. (Corner of High St. and Catte St. ☎ 279 379; www.all-souls.ox.ac.uk. Open Oct.-Apr. M-F 2-4pm; Apr.-Oct. M-F 2-4:30pm. Free.)

THE QUEEN'S COLLEGE. Though the college dates back to 1341, Queen's was rebuilt by Wren and Hawksmoor in the 17th and 18th centuries in the distinctive Queen Anne style. A trumpet call summons students to dinner, where a boar's head graces the table at Christmas. The latter tradition supposedly commemorates an early student who, attacked by a boar on the outskirts of Oxford, choked the animal to death with a volume of Aristotle. Alumni include Edmund Halley, Jeremy Bentham, and the celebrated Mr. Bean. (High St. ☎ 279 120; www.queens.ox.ac.uk. Open to tours only.)

MAGDALEN COLLEGE. With extensive grounds and flower-laced quads, Magdalen (MAUD-lin) is considered Oxford's handsomest college. The college boasts a deer park flanked by the Cherwell and Addison's Walk, a circular path that touches the river's opposite bank. The college's decadent spiritual patron is alumnus Oscar Wilde. (On High St. near the Cherwell. ☎ 276 000; www.magd.ox.ac.uk. Open daily Oct.-March 1pm-dusk; Apr.-June 1-6pm; July-Sept. noon-6pm. £3, concessions £2.)

TRINITY COLLEGE. Founded in 1555, Trinity has a splendid baroque chapel with a limewood altarpiece, cedar latticework, and cherubim-spotted pediments. The college's series of eccentric presidents includes Ralph Kettell, who would come to dinner with a pair of scissors and chop anyone's hair that he deemed too long. (Broad St. ☎ 279 900; www.trinity.ox.ac.uk. Open M-F 10am-noon and 2-4pm, Sa-Su 2-4pm during term, 10am-noon and 2-4pm out of term. £1.50, concessions 75p.)

BALLIOL COLLEGE. Students at Balliol preserve some semblance of tradition by hurling abuse over the wall at their conservative Trinity College rivals. Matthew Arnold, Gerard Manley Hopkins, Aldous Huxley, and Adam Smith were all sons of Balliol's mismatched spires. The interior gates of the college bear lingering scorch marks from the executions of 16th-century Protestant martyrs, and a mulberry tree planted by Elizabeth I still shades slumbering students. (Broad St. ☎ 277 777; www.balliol.ox.ac.uk. Open daily 2-5pm. £1, students and children free.)

NEW COLLEGE. This is the self-proclaimed first *real* college of Oxford; it was here, in 1379, that William of Wykeham dreamed up an institution that would offer a comprehensive undergraduate education under one roof. The bell tower has gargoyles of the Seven Deadly Sins on one side, the Seven Virtues on the other—all equally grotesque. (New College Ln. Use the Holywell St. gate. ☎ 279 555; www.new.ox.ac.uk. Open daily Easter to mid-Oct. 11am-5pm; Nov.-Easter 2-4pm. Easter-Oct. £2, children £1.)

SOMERVILLE COLLEGE. With alumnae including Indira Gandhi and Margaret Thatcher, Somerville is Oxford's most famous once-women's college. Women were not actually granted degrees until 1920—Cambridge held out until 1948.

HEART OF ENGLAND

Today, all of Oxford's colleges are coed except St. Hilda's, which remains women-only. *(Woodstock Rd. From Carfax, head down Commarket St., which becomes Magdalen St., St. Giles, and finally Woodstock Rd. ☎270 600; www.some.ox.ac.uk. Open daily 2-5:30pm. Free.)*

EXETER COLLEGE. Established by the bishop of Exeter in 1314; he set a 14-year limit on schooling for the students, whom he wanted to become priests but not bishops. Esteemed alum J.R.R. Tolkien's bust overlooks the back of the chapel. *(Turl St. ☎279 600; www.exeter.ox.ac.uk. Open daily 2-5pm. Free.)*

OTHER SIGHTS

▓ASHMOLEAN MUSEUM. The grand Ashmolean—the finest collection of arts and antiquities outside London—was Britain's first public museum when it opened in 1683. It showcases sketches by Michelangelo and Raphael, the gold coin of Constantine, and the Alfred Jewel, as well as works by favorites da Vinci, Monet, Manet, van Gogh, Rodin, and Matisse. Check out the stunning Greek pottery, Roman jewelry, and Egyptian artifacts. *(Beaumont St. ☎278 000. Tours £2. Open Tu-Sa 10am-5pm, Su noon-5pm; in summer until 7:30pm on Th. Free.)*

BODLEIAN LIBRARY. Oxford's principal reading and research library has over five million books and 50,000 manuscripts. It receives a copy of every book printed in Great Britain. Sir Thomas Bodley endowed the library's first wing in 1602—the institution has since grown to fill the immense **Old Library** complex, the **Radcliffe Camera** next door, and two newer buildings on Broad St. Admission to the reading rooms is by ticket only. The Admissions Office will issue you a two-day pass ($3) if you are able to prove your research requires the use of the library's books, as well as present a letter of recommendation and a form of identification. No one has ever been permitted to take out a book, not even Cromwell. Well, especially not Cromwell. *(Broad St. ☎277 000. Library open M-F 9am-10pm, Sa 9am-1pm; summer M-F 9am-7pm, Sa 9am-1pm. Tours leave from the Divinity School, in the main quadrangle; in summer M-Sa 4 per day, in winter 2 per day, in the afternoon. Tours £4, audio guide £2.)*

BLACKWELL'S BOOKSTORE. Guinness lists this as the largest four-walled space devoted to bookselling anywhere in the world, with six miles of bookshelves. *(53 Broad St. ☎792 792. Open M and W-Sa 9am-6pm, Tu 9:30am-6pm, Su 11am-5pm.)*

SHELDONIAN THEATRE. This Roman-style auditorium was designed by a teen-aged Christopher Wren. Graduation ceremonies, conducted in Latin, take place in the Sheldonian, as do everything from student recitals to world-class opera performances. *The Red Violin* and *Quills*, as well as numerous other movies, were filmed here. Climb up to the cupola for an excellent view of Oxford's scattered quads. The ivy-crowned stone heads on the fence behind the Sheldonian do not represent emperors: they are a 20th-century study of beards. *(Broad St. ☎277 299. Open roughly M-Sa 10am-12:30pm and 2-4:30pm; in winter, until 3:30pm. £1.50, under 15 £1. Purchase tickets for shows from Oxford Playhouse (☎305 305). Box office open M-Tu and Th-Sa 9:30am-6:30pm or 30 min. before last showing, W 10am-6:30pm. Shows £15.)*

CARFAX TOWER. The tower marks the center of the original city. A hike up its 99 (very) narrow spiral stairs affords a superb overlook from the only present-day remnant of medieval St. Martin's Church. *(Corner of Queen St. and Commarket St. ☎792 653. Open daily Apr.-Oct. 10am-5pm; Oct.-March 10am-3:30pm, weather permitting. £1.50, under 16 75p.)*

THE BOTANIC GARDEN. Green and growing things have flourished for three centuries here in the oldest botanic garden in the British Isles. The path connecting the garden to Christ Church Meadow provides a view of the Thames and cricket grounds on the opposite bank. *(From Carfax, head down High St.; the Garden is at the inter-*

section of High St. and Rose St. ☎ 286 690. Open daily Jan.-Feb. and Nov.-Dec. 9am-4:3-pm, last admission 4:15pm; Mar.-Apr. and Oct. 9am-5pm, last admission 4:15pm; May-Sept. 9am-6pm, last admission 5:15pm; June-Aug. Th until 8pm, last admission 7:15pm. Glasshouses open daily 10am-4pm. £2.50, children free, seniors and students £2.)

THE MUSEUM OF OXFORD. From hands-on exhibits to a murderer's skeleton, the museum provides an in-depth look at Oxford's 800-year history. *(St. Aldates. Enter at corner of St. Aldates and Blue Boar St. ☎ 252 761. Open Tu-F 10am-4pm, Sa 10am-5pm, Su noon-4pm. £2, concessions £1.50, children 50p, under 5 free, families £4.)*

BEST OF THE REST. At **The Oxford Story,** 6 Broad St., a painfully slow-moving ride hauls visitors through dioramas that chronicle Oxford's past. Share the pleasure of a 13th-century student making merry with a wench. *(☎ 728 822. Open daily July-Aug. 9:30am-5pm; Sept.-June M-Sa 10am-4:30pm, Su 11am-4:30pm. 45min. ride. £6.95, students £5.95, seniors £5.75, children £5.25, families £22.50.)* Behind the **University Museum of Natural History,** Parks Rd. *(☎ 272 950; open daily noon-5pm; free)*, the **Pitt-Rivers Museum** has an eclectic archaeological and anthropological collection, including shrunken heads, rare butterflies, and bong-like artifacts. *(☎ 270 927; www.prm.ox.ac.uk. Open M-Sa noon-4:30pm, Su 2-4:30pm. Free.)* The **Museum of the History of Science,** Broad St., features clocks, astrolabes, and Einstein's blackboard. *(☎ 277 280. Open Tu-Sa noon-4pm, Su 2-5pm. Free. Tours £1.50.)* The **Modern Art Oxford,** 30 Pembroke St., hosts international shows. *(☎ 722 733. Tu-Sa 10am-5pm. Su noon-5pm. Free.)* The **Bate Collection of Musical Instruments,** St. Aldates St., rests in the Faculty of Music. *(Before Folly Bridge. ☎ 276 139. Open M-F 2-5pm, also Sa 10am-noon during term time. Free.)*

◧ CLUBS

After happy hour at the pubs, head up **Walton Street** or down **Cowley Road** for late-night clubs and a jumble of ethnic restaurants.

▨ **Freud,** 119 Walton St. (☎ 311 171). Formerly St. Paul's Church. Clash of religion and science provides a surprisingly relaxed atmosphere. Cafe by day, collegiate cocktail bar by night. Open Su-M 11am-midnight, Tu 11-1am, W 11-1:30am, Th-Sa 11am-2am.

The Bridge, 6-9 Hythe Bridge St. (☎ 342 526; www.bridgeoxford.co.uk). Dance to R&B, hip-hop, dance, and cheese on 2 floors. Erratically frequented by big student crowds. Cover £3-7. Open M-Sa 9pm-2am, closed M in summer.

KISS, 36-39 Park End St. (☎ 200 555; www.kissbar.co.uk). Intimate bar conveniently located near several clubs for some pre-dancing cocktails. 2-for-1 drink specials during daily happy hour (7-9:30pm). No cover. Open M-Sa 7pm-2am.

Duke of Cambridge, 5-6 Little Clarendon St. (☎ 558 173). Oxford's choice cocktail lounge, where sophisticated decor gets lost in the buzz of happy hour bliss, half-price cocktails (M-Th, Su 5-8:30pm, F-Sa 5-7:30pm). Cocktails £5.50-6.50; try the Thai cosmo. Smart casual dress. Open M-Sa 5-11pm, Su 5-10:30pm.

The Zodiac, 190 Cowley Rd. (☎ 420 042; www.the-zodiac.co.uk). Big dance floor with nightly themes and the city's best live gigs, including Rage Against the Machine and the Dropkick Murphys. Cover £5-15. Club open W-Th 10:30pm-2am, F 10:30pm-4am, Sa 10:30pm-3am. Box office open Sept.-June M-Sa 1-6pm; July-Aug. Th-Sa only.

Park End, Cantay House, 40 Park End St. (☎ 250 181), is a flashy student and local favorite, cranking out commercial techno and house on three floors. Smart clubwear, please. Cover £3-6. Open Th-Sa 9:30pm-2am.

♫ ENTERTAINMENT

Check *This Month in Oxford* (free at the TIC) for upcoming events. *Daily Information*, posted in the TIC, most colleges, some hostels, and online (www.daily-info.co.uk) provides more listings.

MUSIC. Centuries of tradition give Oxford a quality music scene. Attend a concert or an Evensong service at a college—**New College Choir** is one of the best boy choirs around. Performances at the **Holywell Music Rooms,** on Holywell St., are worth checking out; **Oxford Coffee Concerts** feature famous musicians and ensembles every Su. (☎305 305. Tickets £8.) The **City of Oxford Orchestra,** the professional symphony orchestra, plays a subscription series at the Sheldonian and in college chapels during summer. (☎744 457. Tickets £14-25.) The **New Theatre,** George St., features performances from lounge-lizard jazz to musicals to the Welsh National Opera. (☎320 760. Tickets £10-50, student, senior and child discounts available.)

THEATER. The **Oxford Playhouse,** 11-12 Beaumont St., hosts amateur and professional plays as well as music and dance performances. The playhouse also sells discounted tickets for venues city-wide. (☎305 305; www.oxfordplayhouse.com, www.ticketsoxford.com. Box office open M-Tu and Th-F 9:30am-6:30pm, W 10am-6:30pm, and closes after curtain.) The university itself offers marvelous entertainment; college theater groups often stage productions in gardens or cloisters.

FESTIVALS. The university celebrates **Eights Week** at the end of May, when the colleges enter crews in bumping races and beautiful people sip Pimm's on the banks. In early September, **St. Giles Fair** invades one of Oxford's main streets with an old-fashioned English fun fair. Daybreak on **May Day** (May 1) cues one of Oxford's most celebratory moments: the Magdalen College Choir sings madrigals from the top of the tower beginning at 6am, and the town indulges in morris dancing, beating the bounds, and other age-old rituals of merry men—pubs open at 7am.

▶ DAYTRIP FROM OXFORD

BLENHEIM PALACE

In the town of Woodstock, 8 mi. north of Oxford. Stagecoach (☎772 250) bus #20 runs to Blenheim Palace from Gloucester Green bus station (30-40min., every 30min. 8:15am-5pm, round-trip £3.70). ☎01993 811 091. House open daily mid-Feb. to mid-Dec. 10:30am-5:30pm. Last admission 4:45pm. Grounds open daily 9am-9pm. £12.50, concessions £10, children £7, families £33. Free tours every 5-10min.

The largest private home in England (and one of the loveliest), Blenheim Palace (BLEN-em) was built in honor of the Duke of Marlborough's victory over Louis XIV at the 1704 Battle of Blenheim. The 11th Duke of Marlborough now calls the palace home. His rent is a flag from the estate, payable each year to the Crown on the anniversary of the Battle of Blenheim, Aug. 13—not a bad deal for 187 furnished rooms. High archways and marble floors accentuate the artwork inside, including wall-size tapestries of 17th- and 18th-century battle scenes. Winston Churchill, a member of the Marlborough family, spent his early years here before being shipped off to boarding school; he returned to propose to his wife, and now rests in the nearby churchyard of Bladon village. The grounds consist of 2100 glorious acres, all designed by landscaper "Capability" Brown. Blenheim was recently on display in Kenneth Branagh's 4hr. film *Hamlet* (1996).

STRATFORD-UPON-AVON ☎01789

Shakespeare lived here. This fluke of fate has made Stratford-upon-Avon a major stop on the tourist superhighway. Proprietors tout the dozen-odd properties linked, however remotely, to the Bard and his extended family; shops and restaurants devotedly stencil his prose and poetry on their windows and walls. But, behind the sound and fury of rumbling tour buses and chaotic swarms of daytrippers there still survives a town worthwhile for the grace of the weeping Avon and for the pin-drop silence before a soliloquy in the Royal Shakespeare Theatre.

⌐ HENCE, AWAY!

Trains: Station Rd., off Alcester Rd. Office open M-Sa 6:20am-8:20pm, Su 9:45am-6:30pm. Trains (☎08457 484 950) from: **Birmingham** (50min., every hr., £5); **London Paddington** (2¼hr., 5 per day, £34); **Warwick** (25min., 9 per day, £3.40).

Buses: Riverside Coach Park, off Bridgeway Rd. near the Leisure Centre. **National Express** (☎08705 808 080) from **London** (3hr., 3 per day, £13.50). Tickets at the TIC.

Public Transportation: Local **Stratford Blue** bus #X20 stops on Wood St. and Bridge St. from **Birmingham** (1¼hr.; M-Sa every hr., Su every 1½hr.; £3.50). **Stagecoach** services **Coventry** (2hr., every hr., £3.50) via **Warwick** (20-40min., every hr., £3).

Taxis: Taxi Line (☎266 100).

Bike Rental: Pashley's Store, Guild St. (☎205 057). Mountain bikes £8 per day, £5 per half-day. Open M-F 9am-5pm, Sa 10am-4pm, Su 10am-1pm.

Boat Rental: Theatre Marine, Clopton Bridge (☎07970 289 114), rents rowboats (£4 per 30min., £7 per hr.), motorboats (£8 per 30min., £14 per hr.), and day boats (£45 for up to 6 people). Open daily Apr.-Sept. 10am-7pm.

⁇ WHO IS'T THAT CAN INFORM ME?

Tourist Information Centre: Bridgefoot (☎0870 160 7930; fax 295 262). Provides maps, guidebooks, tickets, and accommodations lists. Books rooms for a £3 charge and a 10% deposit. Open Apr.-Sept. M-Sa 9am-5:30pm, Su 10:30am-4:30pm; Oct.-Mar. M-Sa 9am-5pm. Another **Information Centre** in the Civic Hall, 14 Rother St. (☎299 866). Open daily 9am-5:30pm.

Tours: 2hr. **walking tours** given by Shakespearean actors start at the Royal Shakespeare Theatre (☎403 405) at 10:30am on Sa; also every Th Apr.-Sept. and every Su July-Sept. £6, concessions £5, children free. **Guide Friday City Sightseeing,** Civic Hall, 14 Rother St. (☎299 866) heads to Bard-related houses. Departures every 15min. from Civic Hall. £8, concessions £6, children £3.50. Also offers a bus ticket and admission to any of the Shakespeare Houses (£15/£12/£7), as well as tours to the **Cotswolds** (£17.50/£15/£8) and **Warwick Castle** (£19.50/£14.50/£11; includes castle admission.). Office open daily 9am-5:30pm. **Ghost Walks** (☎292 478) depart from the Swan fountain, Waterside, near the Royal Shakespeare Theatre, Th evenings at 7:30pm. £4, children £2. Advanced booking required.

Financial Services: Barclays, Market Cross (☎08457 555 555), at the intersection of Henley and Bull St. Open M-Tu and Th-F 9:30am-4:30pm, W 10am-4:30pm. **Thomas Cook,** 37 Wood St. (☎293 582). Open M and W-Sa 9am-5:30pm, Tu 10am-5:30pm.

Launderette: Greenhill, Greenhill St. Across from Revital Health Foods. Bring change. Wash £3-5.60; dry 20p; soap £1. Open daily 8am-8pm, last wash 7pm.

Police: Rother St. (☎414 111).

Pharmacy: Boots, 11 Bridge St. (☎292 173). Open M-Sa 8:30am-5:30pm, Su 10:30am-4:30pm.

HEART OF ENGLAND

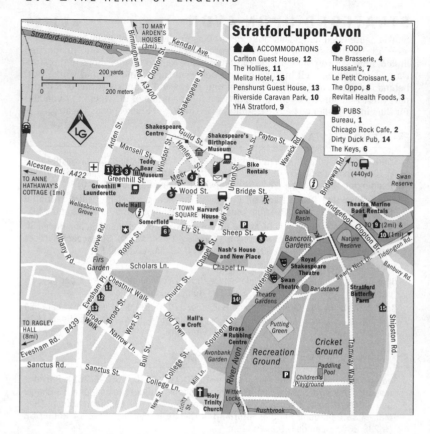

Stratford-upon-Avon

■■ ACCOMMODATIONS
Carlton Guest House, 12
The Hollies, 11
Melita Hotel, 15
Penshurst Guest House, 13
Riverside Caravan Park, 10
YHA Stratford, 9

🍴 FOOD
The Brasserie, 4
Hussain's, 7
Le Petit Croissant, 5
The Oppo, 8
Revital Health Foods, 3

🍺 PUBS
Bureau, 1
Chicago Rock Cafe, 2
Dirty Duck Pub, 14
The Keys, 6

Hospital: Stratford-upon-Avon Hospital, Arden St. (☎205 831), off Alcester Rd. Open 9am-5pm, for minor injuries only.

Internet Access: Central Library, 12 Henley St. (☎292 209). Free. Open M, W-F 9am-5:30pm, Tu 10am-5:30pm, Sa 9:30am-5pm, Su noon-4pm. **Cyber Junction,** 28 Greenhill St. (☎263 400). £2.50 per 30min., £4 per hr.; concessions £2-£3.50. Open M-F 10am-6pm, Sa 10:30am-5:30pm, Su 11am-5pm.

Post Office: 2-3 Henley St. (☎08457 223 344). **Bureau de change.** Open M-Tu 8:45am-5:30pm, W-F 9am-5:30pm, Sa 9am-6pm. **Post Code:** CV37 6PU.

⚓ TO SLEEP, PERCHANCE TO DREAM

B&Bs abound, but singles can be hard to find. Accommodations in the £20-26 range line **Evesham Place, Evesham Road,** and **Grove Road.** Or try **Shipston Road** across the river, a 15-20min. walk from the station.

🛏 **Carlton Guest House,** 22 Evesham Pl. (☎293 548). Spacious rooms and spectacular service make this B&B a great value. Attentive proprietress Sylvia knows all her guests by name. Singles, doubles, twins, and a triple are £20-26 per person. Cash only. ❸

YHA Stratford, Wellesbourne Rd., Alveston (☎297 093), 2 mi. from Clopton Bridge. Follow the B4086 from the town center (35min.), or take bus #X18 or X77 (#618 in the evening) from Bridge St. (10min., every 30min., £1.60). Large, attractive grounds and a 200-year-old building. Breakfast included. Kitchen. Internet access 7p per min. Security on duty after midnight lockout. Dorms £17, under 18 £12.30. MC/V. ❷

Melita Hotel, 37 Shipston Rd. (☎292 432). Upscale B&B with gorgeous garden and retreat-like atmosphere. Guests relax on the sunny patio with less-than-intimidating guard dog Harvey and his new accomplice, terrier Daisy. Singles from £39; doubles £72; triples £98; quads £110-120. AmEx/MC/V. ❹

Penshurst Guest House, 34 Evesham Pl. (☎205 259; www.penshurst.net). Accommodating proprietors take requests, from a vegetarian breakfast to an evening hot chocolate. Singles £22-25; doubles, triples, and quads £21-25 per person. Cash only. ❸

The Hollies, 16 Evesham Pl. (☎266 857). Hosted by a warm proprietress and her daughter. Large rooms, comfortable beds, and a quiet atmosphere make for a relaxing stay. Doubles £40, ensuite £45. MC/V. ❸

Camping: Riverside Caravan Park, Tiddington Rd. (☎292 312), 30min. east of town on the B4086. Sunset views on the Avon, but often crowded. Village pub is a 3-4min. walk. Showers. Open Easter-Oct. Tent and up to 4 people £11. AmEx/MC/V. ❶

◖ FOOD OF LOVE

Baguette stores and bakeries are scattered throughout the town center, while a **Somerfield** supermarket is located in Town Square. (☎292 604. Open M-W 8am-7pm, Th-Sa 8am-8pm, Su 10am-4pm.) The first and third Saturdays of every month, the River Avon's banks welcome a **farmer's market**.

The Oppo, 13 Sheep St. (☎269 980), receives rave reviews from locals. Low 1500s-style ceilings and candles make for a classy-yet-cozy ambience. Try the lasagne (£9), lamb cutlets (£13.50), or grilled goat cheese and tomato salad (£10). Open M-Sa noon-2pm and 5-10pm, Su noon-2pm and 6-9pm. MC/V. ❸

Hussain's, 6a Chapel St. (☎267 506). Stratford's best Indian menu and a favorite of Ben Kingsley. A slew of tandoori prepared as you like it; the chicken tikka masala is fabulous. 3-course lunch £6. Entrees from £6.50. 10% discount for takeaway. Open M-W 5pm-midnight, Th-Su 12:30-2:30pm and 5pm-midnight. AmEx/MC/V. ❷

Le Petit Croissant, 17 Wood St. (☎292 333). Delicious baked treats such as tarts, baguettes, croissants, pasties, and quiches (from 52p). Sandwiches (£1.80-2.50). Open M-Sa 8:30am-6pm. Cash only. ❶

The Brasserie, 59-60 Henley St. (☎205 880). Serves food cafeteria-style, so you can choose from freshly prepared hot and cold selections plus a myriad of irresistible baked goods. Outdoor seating in good weather. Open daily 8am-5:30pm. MC/V. ❷

Revital Health Foods, 8 Greenhill St. (☎292 353). The "Whole Food Takeaway" includes vegan sage and mushroom rolls; potato, cheese, and tomato flan, and "healthy" desserts, like organic vegan chocolate cake (£1-2). Open M-Sa 9am-5:30pm. MC/V. ❶

◣ DRINK DEEP ERE YOU DEPART

Bureau, 1 Arden St. (☎297 641). This pub-by-day's silvered staircase leads to a dance area at night. Various promotions, like £1 drinks M and 2-for-1 drink specials Th. Open M and Th noon-1am, Tu-W and Su noon-midnight, F-Sa noon-2am. Cover M, W-Sa £2-5.

HEART OF ENGLAND

Dirty Duck Pub, Waterside (☎ 297 312). Originally called "The Black Swan," but rechristened by alliterative Americans during WWII. River view outside, huge bust of Shakespeare within. Theater crowds abound, and the actors themselves make frequent entrances. Open M-Sa 11am-11pm, Su noon-10:30pm.

The Keys, Ely St. (☎ 293 909). Low-key locale for a quiet drink with friends, with an open fireplace and comfy lounge. Happy hour daily 5-8pm, includes bottle of wine for £7.50. Open M-Sa noon-11pm, Su noon-10:30pm. Food served noon-3pm and 5:30-9:30pm.

Chicago Rock Cafe, 8 Greenhill St. (☎ 293 344). Popular with locals. W cover bands, Th karaoke, DJs W-Su. Open M-Sa noon-1am, Su noon-12:30pm.

🎭 THE GILDED MONUMENTS

TO BARD...

Stratford's Will-centered sights are best seen before 11am, when the daytrippers arrive, or after 4pm, when the crowds disperse. The five official **Shakespeare properties** are Shakespeare's Birthplace, Mary Arden's House, Nash's House and New Place, Hall's Croft, and Anne Hathaway's Cottage. Opening hours are listed by season: winter (Nov.-Mar.); mid-season (Apr.-May and Sept.-Oct.); and summer (June-Aug.). Diehards should get the **All Five Houses** ticket, which also includes entrance to Harvard House (☎ 204 016; £13, concessions £12, children £6.50, families £29). Those who don't want to visit every shrine can get a **Three In-Town Houses** pass, covering the Birthplace, Hall's Croft, and Nash's House and New Place (£10/8/5/20).

SHAKESPEARE'S BIRTHPLACE. The only in-town sight directly associated with Him includes an exhibit on His father's glove-making, along with the requisite celebration of His life-and-works. Join such distinguished pilgrims as Charles Dickens by signing the guestbook. *(Henley St. ☎ 201 823. Open winter M-Sa 10am-4pm and Su 10:30am-4pm; mid-season M-Sa 10am-5pm and Su 10:30am-5pm; summer M-Sa 9am-5pm and Su 9:30am-5pm. £7.60, concessions £5.50, children £2.60, families £15.)*

SHAKESPEARE'S GRAVE. The least crowded way to pay homage to the institution himself is to visit his little grave inside the quiet, riverside **Holy Trinity Church**—though groups still pack the arched door at peak hours. Rumor has it that Shakespeare was buried 17 ft. underground by request, so that he would sleep undisturbed. A curse on the epitaph (said to be written by the man himself) ensures skeletal safety. The church also harbors the graves of wife Anne and daughter Susanna. *(Trinity St. ☎ 266 316. Entrance to church free, requested donation to see grave £1, students and children 50p. Open year-round Su noon-5pm, Apr.-Sept. M-Sa 8:30am-6pm; Mar. and Oct. M-Sa 9am-5pm; Nov.-Feb. M-Sa 9am-4pm. Last admission 20min. before close.)*

MARY ARDEN'S HOUSE. This farmhouse in Wilmcote, 3 mi. from Stratford, was only recently determined to be the childhood home of Mary Arden (Shakespeare's mother). Originally, historians thought she grew up in the more stately building next door. A brief history recounts how Mary fell in love with Shakespeare, Sr. The house hosts two big events: The **Big Sheep Show** (2nd Su of June) features sheepdogs and sheep, and **Apple Day** (1st Su of Oct.) celebrates cider-making. *(Connected by footpath to Anne Hathaway's Cottage. ☎ 293 455. Open winter M-Sa 10am-4pm and Su 10:30am-4pm; mid-season M-Sa 10am-5pm and Su 10:30am-5pm; summer M-Sa 9:30am-5pm and Su 10am-5pm. £5.70, concessions £5, children £2.50, families £13.50.)*

NASH'S HOUSE AND NEW PLACE. Crazed tourists flock to the home of the first husband of Shakespeare's granddaughter Elizabeth, last of His descendants. Perhaps they're drawn to the fascinating local history collection of **Nash's House.** More likely, they want to see the adjacent **New Place**—Shakespeare's retirement home—and at the time Stratford's finest house. Today only the foundations remain due to a disgruntled 19th-century owner named Gastrell who razed the building to protest taxes. He was run out of town, and, to this day, Gastrells are not allowed in Stratford. *(Chapel St. ☎ 292 325. Open daily in winter M-Sa 11am-4pm; daily in mid-season 11am-5pm; in summer M-Sa 9:30am-5pm and Su 10am-5pm. £3.50, concessions £3, children £1.70, families £9.)* Down Chapel St. from Nash's House, the sculpted hedges, manicured lawn, and abundant flowers of the **Great Garden of New Place** offer a peaceful respite from the mobbed streets. *(Open M-Sa 9am-dusk, Su 10am-dusk. Free.)*

HALL'S CROFT. Dr. John Hall married Shakespeare's oldest daughter Susanna and garnered fame in his own right as one of the first doctors to keep detailed records of his patients. The Croft features an exhibit on Hall and medicine in Shakespeare's time—frogs were a frequent prescription. *(Old Town. ☎ 292 107. Open daily in winter 11am-4pm; daily in mid-season 11am-5pm; summer M-Sa 9:30am-5pm and Su 10am-5pm. £3.50, concessions £3, children £1.70, families £9.)*

ANNE HATHAWAY'S COTTAGE. The birthplace of Shakespeare's wife, about a mile from Stratford in **Shottery,** is the fairy tale, thatched-roof cottage you saw on the travel agent's poster. It boasts very old, original Hathaway furniture and a new hedge maze. Entrance entitles you to sit on a bench He may or may not have also sat on. *(Take the poorly marked footpaths north. ☎ 292 100. Open daily in winter 10am-4pm; mid-season M-Sa 9:30am-5pm and Su 10am-5pm; summer M-Sa 9am 5pm and Su 9:30am-5pm. £5.20, concessions £4, children £2, families £12.)*

...OR NOT TO BARD
Non-Shakespearean sights *are* available (if not particularly exciting) in Stratford.

TEDDY BEAR MUSEUM. The museum boasts thousands of stuffed, ceramic, and painted bears. Though most went to children in Yugoslavia, 12 of the "Diana bears" (left in front of Kensington Palace) rest near the original Fozzie, a gift from Jim Henson. *(19 Greenhill St. ☎ 293 160. Open daily 9:30am-5pm. £2.50, concessions £2, children £1.50, families £7.50.)*

STRATFORD BUTTERFLY FARM. Europe's largest collection of butterflies flutters through tropical surroundings. Less appealing creepy-crawlies—like the Goliath Bird-Eating Spider—hang out in glass boxes in the neighboring room. *(Off Swan's Nest Ln. at Tramway Walk, across the river from the TIC. ☎ 299 288. Open daily summer 10am-6pm; winter 10am-dusk. Last admission 30min. before close. £4.50, concessions £4.)*

HARVARD HOUSE. Period pieces and pewter punctuate this authentic Tudor building. Once inhabited by the mother of the founder of the American university of the same name, the house is now owned by the university. *(High St. ☎ 204 507. Open July-Sept. W-Su noon-5pm; May-June and Oct. W and Sa-Su only. £2.50, children free.)*

RAGLEY HALL. Eight miles from Stratford on Evesham Rd. (A435), Ragley Hall houses the Earl and Countess of Yarmouth. Set in a stunning 400-acre park, the estate has an art collection and a captivating maze. *(Bus #246 (M-Sa 5 per day) runs to Alcester Police Station. Walk 1 mi. to the gates, then ½ mi. up the drive. ☎ 762 090. House open Apr.-Sept. Su, M-Th 11am-6pm; last entry 4:30pm. £7.50, concessions £6.50, children £4.50.)*

⚡ THE PLAY'S THE THING

THE ROYAL SHAKESPEARE COMPANY
The box office in the foyer of the Royal Shakespeare Theatre handles the ticketing for both theaters. Ticket hotline ☎ 0870 609 1110; www.rsc.org.uk. Open M-Sa 9:30am-8pm. Tickets £5-40. Both theaters have £5 standing room tickets; students and under 25 half-price same-day tickets in advance for M-W performances and on the day of the show oth-

erwise. Standby tickets are also available (low season £12, high season £15). **Disabled travelers** *should call in advance to advise the box office of their needs; some performances feature sign language interpretation or audio description.*

One of the world's most acclaimed repertories, the **Royal Shakespeare Company** sells well over one million tickets each year and claims Kenneth Branagh and Ralph Fiennes as recent members. In Stratford, the RSC performs in two connected theaters. The Bard was born on Henley St., died at New Place, sleeps in Holy Trinity, and lives on at the **Royal Shakespeare Theatre,** across from Chapel Ln. on the Waterside. Designs are currently in the works for a major revamping of the flagship stage. The RSC took the shell of burnt-out Memorial Theatre and renovated it as the **Swan Theatre.** A smaller and more intimate space than the attached RST, it resembles Shakespeare's Globe and stages plays by other wordsmiths. The RSC conducts **backstage tours** that cram groups into the wooden "O"s of the theaters. *(☎403 405. 45min. tours M-F 2 per day starting from the RSC foyer, Sa 2 per day from the Swan Theatre; Su 4 per day from the Swan Theatre. Advanced booking recommended. £5, concessions £4.)*

❄ OUR RUSTIC REVELRY

A **traditional town market** is held on Rother St. in Market Place the second and fourth Saturdays of every month. On Sundays from June through August, a **craft market** takes place along the river. (☎267 000. Both open 9am-5pm.) Stratford's biggest festival begins on the weekend nearest April 23, **Shakespeare's birthday.** The modern, well-respected **Shakespeare Birthplace Trust,** Henley St., hosts a **Poetry Festival** every Sunday evening in July and August; past appearances have included Seamus Heaney, Ted Hughes, and Derek Walcott. (☎292 176. Tickets £7-9.50.)

WORCESTER ☎01905

Worcester (WUH-ster) sits over the Severn between Cheltenham and Birmingham, but lacks the former's gentility and the latter's pace. The city's name has been made famous by Worcestershire sauce and Worcester porcelain, and the city itself was the site of the Civil War's final battle and birthplace of the composer Edward Elgar. Beyond the beautiful cathedral, however, Worcester's sights are lackluster.

🚊 TRANSPORTATION. Foregate St. Station, at the edge of the town center on Foregate St., is the city's main train station. (Ticket window open M-Sa 6:10am-7pm, Su 9:10am-4:30pm. Travel center open M-Sa 9:30am-4pm.) **Shrub Hill Station,** just outside of town, serves Cheltenham but has less frequent service to London and Birmingham. (Ticket window open M-Sa 5:10am-9pm, Su 7:10am-9:30pm.) **Trains** (☎08457 484 950) travel to Worcester from: **Birmingham** (1hr., every hr., £5.10); **Cheltenham** (30min., every 2hr., £5.20); **London Paddington** (2½hr., every 1½hr., £25.80). The **bus station** is at Angel Pl. near the Crowngate Shopping Centre. **National Express** (☎08705 808 080) runs from: **Birmingham** (1½hr., 1 per day, £3.50); **Bristol** (5hr., 1 per day, £9.50); and **London** (4hr., 2 per day, £16.50). **First Midland Red West** (☎359 393) is the regional bus company; their **Day Rover** allows unlimited one-day travel within Worcestershire (£4, children £3, families £9.20). **Associated Radio Taxis** is at ☎763 939. **Peddlers,** 46-48 Barbourne Rd., rents **bikes.** (☎24238. £8 per day, £30 per week. Deposit £50. Open M-Sa 9:30am-5:30pm.)

🔳🔁 ORIENTATION AND PRACTICAL INFORMATION. The city center is bounded by the train station to the north and the cathedral to the south. The main street runs between the two, switching names from **Barbourne Road** to **The Tything** to **Foregate Street** to **The Foregate** to **The Cross** to **High Street.** To reach the TIC from Foregate St. station, turn left onto Foregate St. It's a 15min. walk from Shrub Hill:

turn right onto Shrub Hill Rd., then left onto Tolladine Rd. (which later becomes Lowesmoor); continue to St. Nicholas St., which intersects The Foregate. From the bus station, turn left onto **Broad Street** and right onto **The Cross.**

The **Tourist Information Centre,** The Guildhall, High St., sells the *Worcester Visitor Guide* (75p) and books beds for a 10% deposit. (☎726 311. Open M-Sa 9:30am-5pm.) 1½hr. **tours** leave from the TIC. (May-Sept. W 11am and 2:30pm. Oct.-Apr. ghost walks F-Sa 8pm. ₤6, children free.) Other services include: **Barclays,** 54 High St. (☎684 828; open M-Tu and Th-F 9am-5pm, W 10am-5pm, Sa 9am-3pm); **Severn Laun-Dri,** 22 Barbourne Rd. (wash ₤3-4.20, dry ₤1, soap 30p; open daily 9am-8pm; last wash 7pm); the **police,** Castle St. (☎08457 444 888), off Foregate; a **Boots pharmacy,** 72-74 High St. (☎726 868; open M-Sa 8am-6pm, Su 10:30am-4:30pm); **Worcestershire Royal Hospital,** Newtown Rd. Charles Hastings Way (☎763 333; bus #31); free **Internet access** at the **library,** in the City Museum (☎765 312; open M and F 9:30am-8pm, Tu-Th 9:30am-5:30pm, Sa 9:30am-5pm) and at **Coffee Republic,** 31 High St. (₤1 per 20 min; open M-F 7:30am-6:30pm, Sa 8:30am-6:30pm, Su 10am-5pm); and the **post office,** 8 Foregate St., next to the train station, with a **bureau de change** (☎08457 223 344; open M-Sa 9am-5:30pm). **Post Code:** WR1 1XX.

⌂ ACCOMMODATIONS. B&B prices in Worcester are high, as proprietors cater to businessmen or to Londoners weekending in the country. Try your luck on **Barbourne Road,** a 15-20min. walk north from the city center. The nearest **YHA hostel** is 7 mi. away in the town of Malvern, 12min. by train (p. 282). The comfortable **Osborne House ❸,** 17 Chestnut Walk, has TV in every ensuite room, three types of biscuits on the nightstand, and brilliant marmalade. (☎/fax 22296. Singles ₤25-40; doubles ₤45, with bath ₤50; twins ₤40, ensuite ₤45. AmEx/MC/V.) At **The Barbourne ❸,** 42 Barbourne Rd., many of the 24 pink rooms are ensuite; some even have bathtubs. (☎27507. ₤25 per person. AmEx/MC/V.) Its blue counterpart, the nearby **City Guest House ❸,** 36 Barbourne Rd., features comfy beds and friendly service, including welcome trays on arrival. (☎24695. Singles ₤25 per person. AmEx/MC/V.) Riverside **Ketch Caravan Park ❶,** Bath Rd., has toilets and showers. Take the A38 2 mi. south of Worcester or local bus #32, which leaves every 10min. (☎820 430. Open Easter-Oct. ₤8.50 per tent or caravan. Electricity ₤1.75. Showers 20p. Cash only.)

◨▨ FOOD AND PUBS. A **Sainsbury's** is tucked into the Lynchgate Shopping Centre off High St. (☎21731. Open M-Sa 8am-6pm, Su 10:30am-4:30pm.) Look for Indian restaurants and cheap sandwich shops near **The Tything,** at the north end of the city center. The best is just off The Tything: **Monsoon ❷,** 35 Forgate St., delivers well-priced entrees (₤6-9.50) and excellent service. (20% takeaway discount. ☎726 333. Open Su-Th 6pm-midnight, F-Sa 6pm-1am. AmEx/MC/V.) At **Clockwatchers ❶,** 20 Mealcheapen St., farm-fresh sandwiches live up to the address, starting at ₤1.40 for takeaway. (☎611 662. Open M-Sa 8:30am-5pm. AmEx/MC/V.) **Falmouth Pasty Company ❶,** St. Swithin St., serves up piping hot pasties in every conceivable variety, at only ₤1.20 for a small (more than enough), ₤2 for a large (family sized). (☎724 393. Open M-Sa 9am-5pm. Cash only.) For pint-sized entertainment, the pub scene on **Friar Street** is popular. **The Conservatory,** 34 Friar St., has modern decor, a lively crowd, and ales from ₤2-2.50. (☎26929. Open M-Sa 11am-11pm.)

◪ SIGHTS. Worcester Cathedral, founded in AD 680, towers majestically by the River Severn at the southern end of High St. Over the years, the buttresses supporting the central nave have deteriorated, and the central tower is in danger of collapsing. Renovation attempts are perpetually underway, but even steel rods set in the tower's base don't detract from the building's awe-inspiring Norman detail. The **choir** contains intricate 14th-century misericords and King John's tomb; copies of the *Magna Carta* are displayed outside. **Wulston's Crypt** is an entire underground level, with the narrow exit its creepiest attraction. (☎28854. Open daily 7:30am-6pm. Evensong M-F 5:30pm, Su 4pm. Tower open daily 10:30am-4pm. Guided tours £3, book ahead. Tower tours £2, students £1.50, children £1, families £5. Tours Sa; late July also M-F. Suggested donation £3.)

Relive the 1651 Battle of Worcester at the **Commandery,** Sidbury Rd., where visitors can sit in on the trial of Charles I and choose whether to sign the death warrant. (☎361 821. Open M-Sa 10am-5pm, Su 1:30-5pm. £4, concessions £3, families £10.25.) The **Royal Worcester Porcelain Company,** southeast of the cathedral on Severn St., makes the famous blue-, red-, and gold-patterned bone china on which the royal family has been served since George III. Crockery junkies can visit the adjacent **Worcester Museum of Porcelain,** which holds England's largest collection. (☎746 000, tour info 21247. Open M-Sa 9am-5:30pm, Su 11am-5pm. £4, concessions £3.20, under 5 free, families £8.40. Museum tour daily £5.50, families £17. Museum and factory tour M-F £9.30/£7.45/£21.75.) The highlight of the **Worcester City Museum and Art Gallery,** Foregate St., near the post office, north of Foregate train station, is Hitler's clock, found in his office when it was captured by the Worcester Regiment in 1945. (☎25371. Open M-F 9:30am-5:30pm, Sa 9:30am-5pm. Free.)

Three miles south of the train station, **Elgar's Birthplace Museum** is filled with manuscripts and memorabilia. Midland Red West bus #419/420 stops 1 mile away at Crown East Church (10min., 2 per day, round-trip £2.50). Otherwise, walk 6 miles along the Elgar trail. (☎333 224. Open daily 11am-5pm; closed Dec. 23-Feb. 1. £4.50, seniors £4, students £3, children £2.)

▶ DAYTRIP FROM WORCESTER

MALVERN

The Worcestershire Way winds through the Malverns for 45 mi. to Kingsford County Park in the north. Trains (15min., every 30min., £2.80) and Midland Red West buses (40min., 1-2 per hr., £2.75) come from Worcester. The Tourist Information Centre, 21 Church St., by the post office in the town center, assists with advice and pamphlets and books accommodations for a 10% deposit. (☎892 289; fax 892 872. Open daily Easter-Oct. 10am-5pm; Nov.-Easter M-Sa 10am-5pm, Su 10am-4pm.)

The name Malvern refers collectively to the adjacent towns of Great Malvern, West Malvern, Malvern Link, Malvern Wells, and Little Malvern, all of which hug the base and the eastern side of the Malvern Hills. The tops of the Malvern Hills peek over the A4108 southwest of Worcester and offer 8 miles of trails and quasi-divine visions of greenery. **Great Malvern,** a Victorian spa town, was built around the 11th-century **Malvern Priory** on Abbey Rd. Benedictine monks rebuilt the structure in the 15th century, sprucing it up with stained-glass windows. (Suggested donation £1.) On the steep hillside a 20min. hike above town, **St. Ann's Well** supplies the restorative "Malvern waters" that fueled Great Malvern's halcyon days. The beautifully renovated **Malvern Theatres** on Grange Rd., 10min. from the train station, host plays. (☎892 277. Box office open M-Sa 9:30am-8pm. Tickets £10-20.)

The **YHA Hatherly ❶,** 18 Peachfield Rd., in Malvern Wells, has a TV lounge, game room, and member's kitchen. Take Newbury Coaches #675 from Great Malvern or walk 20min. from the train station. (☎569 131. Lockout 10am-5pm. Curfew 11pm. Open daily mid-Feb. to Oct.; Nov.-Dec. F-Sa. £10.60, under 18 £7.20. AmEx/MC/V.)

CHELTENHAM ☎01242

A spa town that grew up in the shadow of Bath, Cheltenham (pop. 110,000) remains a well-to-do urban center. Ever since George III sampled its waters in 1788, the town has flourished as a fashionable place of leisure, evident in its abundance of upscale restaurants, spacious gardens, and trendy boutiques. On weekends, students from the nearby University of Gloucestershire pack dozens of pubs and clubs, energizing the elegant city center with a youthful vibe. Though it has few important sights, Cheltenham continues to draw visitors as the most convenient and cosmopolitan base for visiting the Cotswolds.

⊏ TRANSPORTATION

Cheltenham lies 43 mi. south of Birmingham, on the northeastern outskirts of the Cotswolds. The free *Getting There* pamphlet from the TIC details bus services.

Trains: Cheltenham Spa Station, Queen's Rd., at Gloucester Rd. Ticket office open M-F 5:45am-8:15pm, Sa 5:45am-7pm, Su 8:15am-8:15pm. Trains (☎08457 484 950) from: **Bath** (1½hr., 2 per hr., £11.50); **Birmingham** (45min., 2 per hr., £12.50); **London** (2hr., every hr., £32-41.50); **Worcester** (25min., every 2hr., £5.20).

Buses: Royal Well Coach Station, Royal Well Rd. National Express office open M-Sa 9am-4:45pm. Lockers £1-2. National Express shares another office with Stagecoach on 229 High St. (☎544 120). Open M-Sa 9am-5pm. **National Express** (☎08705 808 080) from: **Bristol** (1¼hr., 3 per day, £6); **Exeter** (4hr., 2 per day, £19); **London** (3hr.,

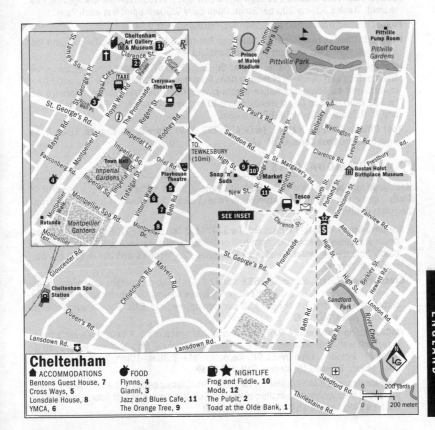

Cheltenham
▲ ACCOMMODATIONS
Bentons Guest House, 7
Cross Ways, 5
Lonsdale House, 8
YMCA, 6

🍴 FOOD
Flynns, 4
Gianni, 3
Jazz and Blues Cafe, 11
The Orange Tree, 9

🍺 ★ NIGHTLIFE
Frog and Fiddle, 10
Moda, 12
The Pulpit, 2
Toad at the Olde Bank, 1

4 per day, £14.50). **Stagecoach** (☎01452 523 928) serves **Gloucester** (40min., every 10 min., £1.70). **Swanbrook Coaches** (☎01452 712 386) runs from **Oxford** (1½hr., 3 per day, £6.50). Buses to **Tewkesbury** leave from High St.

Taxis: Stand by the Royal Well coach station or the Promenade. Free phone in train station. Try **Central Taxis** (☎228 877) or **Starline Taxi** (☎250 250).

ORIENTATION AND PRACTICAL INFORMATION

The heart of Cheltenham is the intersection of pedestrian-only **High Street** and **The Promenade**, the town's central boulevard. The train station is at the western edge of town; walk 20min. or catch bus D or E (5min., every 10min., £1.20).

Tourist Information Centre: Municipal Offices, 77 The Promenade, (☎522 878, accommodations booking ☎517 110; www.visitcheltenham.info). Well-organized staff books accommodations for a 10% deposit and posts B&B vacancies outside after hours. Open M-Tu and Th-Sa 9:30am-5:15pm, W 10am-5:15pm.

Financial Services: Banks are along High St. Most are open M-F 9am-4:30pm, W from 10am, Sa 9am-12:30pm. **Thomas Cook,** 159 High St. (☎847 900. Open M-Sa 9am-5:30pm, Su 11am-5pm.)

Launderette: Soap-n-Suds, 312 High St. (☎513 632), across from the Orange Tree Restaurant. Wash £2-3, dry 20p per 3min. Open daily 7:30am-8pm; last wash 7pm.

Police: Holland House, 840 Lansdown Rd. (☎08450 901 234).

Hospital: Cheltenham General, Sandford Rd. (☎08454 222 222). Follow Bath Rd. southwest from town and turn left onto Sandford Rd.

Internet Access: Smart Space, Regent St. (☎512 515), upstairs from the Everyman Theatre. Free with purchase of food or drink from the cafe. Open M-Sa 9:30am-8:30pm; in Aug. and on non-performance nights closes 6pm. **Central Library,** Clarence St. (☎532 688), next to City Museum. Photo ID required. Open M, W, F 9:30am-7pm, Tu and Th 9:30am-5:30pm, Sa 9:30am-4pm.

Post Office: 225-227 High St. (☎08457 223 344). **Bureau de change.** Open M-Sa 9am-5:30pm. **Post Code:** GL50 1AA.

ACCOMMODATIONS

Standards and prices tend to be high at Cheltenham's **B&Bs** (£25-40). A handful of B&Bs can be found in the **Montpellier** area and along **Bath Road,** a 5min. walk from the town center.

Bentons Guest House, 71 Bath Rd. (☎517 417; fax 527 772). English countryside decor and generous comforts, from hair dryers to towel warmers. Platter-size plates can barely hold the breakfast. Singles £25, ensuite £28; doubles and triples £28 per person. Cash only. ❸

Cross Ways, 57 Bath Rd. (☎527 683; fax 577 226). The proprietor's experience as an interior designer is apparent in this Regency home's sumptuous furnishings. Rooms as comfortable as they are lavish. £30 per person, ensuite £35. Book a few weeks in advance. AmEx/MC/V. ❸

YMCA, Vittoria Walk (☎524 024; www.cheltenhamymca.com). A budget traveler's paradise, with well-kept facilities and a comfortable lounge. Men and women accepted. Breakfast included. Laundry £1.90. Reception M-F 7:30am-10pm, Sa-Su 9am-10pm. Book ahead. Dorms £15; singles £19. MC/V. ❷

Lonsdale House, 16 Montpellier Dr. (☎232 379). Classic bedrooms and a classy dining room. 3rd-floor rooms are smaller; ask to stay on the ground or first floor. Singles £25; doubles £49, ensuite £54-58. AmEx/MC/V. ❸

FOOD

A handful of fruit stands, butchers, and bakeries dot **High Street,** while posh restaurants and cafe-bars line **Montpellier Street** across from Montpellier Gardens. **Tesco,** 233 High St., has it all under one roof. (☎847 400. Open M 8am-midnight, Tu-F 6ammidnight, Sa 6am-10pm, Su 11am-5pm.) A **farmers market** is held the second and last Friday o f the month outside the TIC (9am-3pm) and a Thursday morning **market,** held in the parking lot near Henrietta St., sells fruits, meats, and other wares.

Gianni, 1 Royal Well Pl. (☎221 101), just south of the bus stop on Royal Well Rd. Huge portions of modern Italian food in a fun, lively atmosphere. Try the *penne alla gianni* (£6.95). Appetizers £1.50-7. Pastas £6-8. Entrees £10-14. Open daily noon-3pm and from 6:30pm; last order Su-Th 10:30pm, F-Sa 11pm. AmEx/MC/V. ❸

The Orange Tree, 317 High St. (☎234 232). Creative vegetarian cuisine in a sunny setting. Complement Thai curry or a savory nut roast (both £6.95) with organic beer. Weekend reservations recommended. Open M-Th 10am-9pm, F-Sa 10am-1-pm. MC/V. ❷

Flynns Bar and Brasserie, 16-17 The Courtyard, Montpellier St. (☎252 752). Locals swear by it. Appetizers, like the delicious deep- fried goat cheese filo (£5), are small; entrees are not (£8.50-13). Outdoor seating. Open M-F noon-2:30pm and 6-10:30pm, Sa noon-3pm and 6-10:30pm, Su 1-9pm. AmEx/MC/V. ❷

Jazz and Blues Cafe, 288 High St. (582 346; www.thejazzandbluescafe.com). Relaxed cafe serves up a specialty seafood gumbo (£10.50), and live music Th-Sa. Open M-Sa 9am-5pm and 7-10:30pm, Su 11am-4pm and 7-10:30pm. AmEx/MC/V. ❷

SIGHTS AND FESTIVALS

Cheltenham possesses the only naturally **alkaline water** in Britain—the town was born when George III decided it was good for his health. You, too, can enjoy its diuretic and laxative effects—if "enjoy" is the right word—at the **town hall,** Imperial Sq. (☎521 621. Open M-Sa 9:30am-5:30pm.) The **Pittville Pump Room,** 10min. north of High St. presides over a park designed in its honor. Opened in 1830, the former spa is Cheltenham's finest Regency building. (☎523 852. Open M and W-Su 10am-4pm.) Treatment of the well system is expected to interrupt free tastings in 2005. Call ahead for details. On your way back to town, stop by the **Gustav Holst Birthplace Museum,** 4 Clarence Rd., opposite Pittville Park, to experience the composer's early life in his impeccably restored home. (☎524 846; www.holstmuseum.org.uk. Open Tu-Sa 10am-4pm. £2.50, children and concessions £2, families £7.) The **Cheltenham Art Gallery and Museum,** Clarence St., showcases the Arts and Crafts movement amid a horde of English miscellany, from stuffed pheasants to Victorian tiaras. (☎237 431. Open M-Sa 10am-5:20pm. Free.) Down the Promenade, downtowners sunbathe among exquisite blooms at the **Imperial Gardens.**

The indispensable *What's On* poster, displayed on kiosks and at the TIC, lists concerts, plays, tours, sporting events, and hotspots. The **Cheltenham International Festival of Music** (three weeks in July) celebrates modern classical works. The concurrent **Fringe Festival** organizes jazz, big band, and rock performances. The **International Jazz Festival** takes place at the end of April and the beginning of May, while October heralds the **Cheltenham Festival of Literature.** Full details on these festivals are available from the box office. (Town Hall, Imperial Sq. ☎227 979; www.cheltenhamfestivals.co.uk.) The **National Hunt,** a horseracing event, starts in the winter and will culminate March 15-18 in 2005, causing the population of Cheltenham nearly to double at its peak. (☎513 014, bookings 226 226; www.cheltenham.co.uk.

HEART OF ENGLAND

Tickets sold Sept.-Feb., usually sold out by Feb. Tickets £15-60.) The **Cheltenham Cricket Festival,** the oldest in the country, starts in late July. Inquire about match times at the TIC, or call ☎0117 910 8000. Purchase tickets (£12-15) at the gate.

🎵 NIGHTLIFE

On weekends, Cheltenham springs to life as students and twentysomethings invade its nightspots. Numerous pubs, bars, and clubs line **High Street** east of the Promenade. Popular venues also cluster around **Clarence Street** and the top of **Bath Road.** Many offer reduced covers for students and drink specials.

Frog and Fiddle, 315 High St. (☎701 156). Chill on the big leather couches or play pool and arcade games upstairs. Students make for a laid-back scene. M and W drink special: pints £1.10. Tu curry and a pint £5. Th-F live music and open mike from 9pm. Open M-Sa 11am-11pm, Su noon-10:30pm.

Toad at the Olde Bank, 15-21 Clarence St. (☎230 099). Well-dressed 20-somethings pack the main floor of this club, while others look on from a spacious upstairs balcony. Chart-topping music prevails. Live DJ F-Sa. Cover F-Sa £1-4. Open M-Sa 11am-midnight, Su noon-10:30pm.

The Pulpit, Clarence Parade (☎269 057). Look for yellow signs proclaiming "Scream." This huge converted church fills with a younger crowd on weekends. Open Su-Th noon-11pm, F-Sa noon-midnight.

Moda, 33-35 Albion St. (☎570 583; www.clubmoda.co.uk). Enter from High St. Cheltenham's most stylish nighttime option boasts 3 floors and blasts funky house, R&B, and 70s and 80s music. Cover £2-5, free before 10pm. Open M, W, Th-Sa 9pm-2am.

🎫 DAYTRIP FROM CHELTENHAM

TEWKESBURY

*Stagecoach bus #41 (☎01242 575 606) departs from High St., across from the Tesco Metro, in Cheltenham (25min.; M-Sa every 20-30min., Su every 2hr.; round-trip £3). The **Tourist Information Centre,** in the Town Museum, sells pamphlets (20p) outlining walks through the famous battlegrounds of 1471, the 18th-century alleys, and the heritage trail (40p). ☎01684 295 027. Open M-Sa 9:30am-5pm; Easter-Oct. also Su 10am-4pm.*

Ten miles northwest of Cheltenham, at the confluence of the Rivers Avon and Severn, Tewkesbury is a quiet medieval town with a trove of half-timbered houses. Its most celebrated structure is the stately **abbey** whose Norman tower is the largest in England. The elaborate vaulting of the nave is supported by massive round pillars ("English Romanesque") and illuminated by 14th-century stained glass. First consecrated in 1121, the abbey was reconsecrated after the 1471 Battle of Tewkesbury, when Yorks killed the abbey's monks for attempting to protect refuge-seeking Lancastrians. (☎01684 850 959. Open Apr.-Oct. M-Sa 7:30am-6pm, Su 7:30am-7pm; Nov.-Mar. M-Sa 7:30am-5:30pm, Su 7:30am-7pm. Services Su 8, 9:15, 11am, 6pm. Requested donation £2.) Beside the abbey, the **John Moore Countryside Museum,** 45 Church St., is a merchant's cottage built in 1450 and restored in the 1960s, when developers added modern conveniences to the whole row of 15th-century buildings—the longest in the UK. (☎01684 297 174. Open Apr.-Oct. Tu-Sa 10am-1pm and 2-5pm; Nov.-Mar. Sa and bank holidays 10am-1pm and 2-5pm. £1.25, concessions £1, children 75p, families £3.25.) In the opposite direction, the **Tewkesbury Town Museum,** 64 Barton St., in the same building as the TIC, includes an exhibit on the 1471 battle, the last of the Wars of the Roses. (☎01684 292 901. Open Tu-Sa 10am-1pm and 2-5pm. £1, concessions 75p, children 50p, families £2.50.)

THE COTSWOLDS

The Cotswolds have deviated little from their etymological roots—"Cotswolds" means "sheep enclosure in rolling hillsides." Grazing sheep and cattle roam 800 mi.[2] of vivid, verdant hills, which enfold tiny towns with names longer than their main streets. Saxon villages and Roman settlements, hewn from the famed Cotswold stone, link a series of trails accessible to walkers and cyclists. The Cotswolds are not just for outdoors enthusiasts, however; anyone with an interest in rural England will find something here.

▐ TRANSPORTATION

Public transport to and in the Cotswolds is scarce; planning ahead is a must. The whimsically-named villages of the picturesque "Northern" Cotswolds (Stow-on-the-Wold, Bourton-on-the-Water, Moreton-on-Marsh) are more easily reached via Cheltenham, while the more remote and less touristed "Southern" Cotswolds (Slimbridge and Painswick) are served more frequently from Gloucester.

Train stations in the Cotswolds are few and far between, and service is infrequent. **Moreton-on-Marsh** (open M-Sa 6:30am-1pm) serves trains from **London** (1½hr., every 1-2hr., £21.20) via **Oxford** (30min. 35, £8.20). The same train passes through tiny **Charlbury,** between Moreton-in-Marsh and Oxford. In the Southern Cotswolds, **Cam and Dursley,** (3 mi. from Slimbridge) runs from **Gloucester** (15min., every hr., £3.40) and **London Paddington** (2½hr., 7 per day, £23.80).

It's far easier to reach the Cotswolds by **bus.** The Cheltenham TIC's free *Getting There* pamphlet details service between the town and 27 popular destinations. The free brochure *Explore the Cotswolds by Public Transport,* available at most village TICs, lists bus timetables for the northern, central, and southern regions. Note that schedules vary depending on the day of the week; use the information here only as a guide.

Pulham's Coaches P1 (☎01451 820 369) runs from **Cheltenham** to **Moreton-in-Marsh** (1hr., M-Sa 7 per day, £1.75) via **Bourton-on-the-Water** (35min., £1.65) and **Stow-on-the-Wold** (50min., £1.70). To get to **Lower** and **Upper Slaughter,** ask the driver to drop you at Slaughter Pike, halfway between Bourton-on-the-Water and Stow-on-the-Wold; the villages are half a mile from the road. **Castleway's Coaches** (☎01242 602 949) go from **Cheltenham** to **Broadway** (50min., M-Sa 4 per day, £2) via **Winchcombe** (20min., £1.70). Chipping Camden, north of Broadway, cannot be reached directly from Cheltenham. **First Midland Red** (☎01905 359 393) buses M21 and M22 run there from Moreton-on-Marsh (20min., M-Sa 9 per day, £1.60) via Broadway (5min., M-Sa 5 per day) before terminating in **Stratford** (1hr., M-Sa 8 per day, £2.60).

In the Southern Cotswolds, **Stagecoach** bus #51 runs from Cheltenham to **Cirencester** (40min., M-Sa every hr., £2.25), while **Beaumont Travel** (☎01452 309 770) bus #55 runs there from **Moreton-in-Marsh** (1hr., M-Sa 8 per day, £1.50) via **Stow-on-the-Wold** (40min., £1.30) and **Bourton-on-the-Water** (20min., £1.20). Both buses are covered by a **Cotswold Rover** ticket, which may be purchased from the driver (£4, children £2). Service from Cheltenham to **Gloucester** is frequent on **Stagecoach** bus #94 (30min.; M-F every 10min., Su every 20 min.; £2.10). From Gloucester bus station, **Stagecoach** bus #91 (35min., every hr., £2.50) and **Beaumont Travel** B7 (30min.; 5 per day; £1.80) run to **Slimbridge Crossroads,** a roundabout 1 mile from the village.

The easiest way to explore is by car, but the best way to experience the Cotswolds is on **foot** or **bike. The Toy Shop,** on High St. in Moreton-in-Marsh, rents bikes with lock, map, and route suggestions. (☎01608 650 756. £10 per half-day, £14 per day. Credit card deposit. Open M and W-Sa 9am-1pm and 2-5pm.) **Taxis** are a convenient, if expensive, way of getting from villages to nearby sights that are inaccessible by public transportation. TICs have lists of companies serving their area: **'K' Cars** (☎01451 822 578 or 07929 360 712) is based in Bourton-on-the-Water, while **Cotswold Taxis** (☎07710 117 471) operates from Moreton-in-Marsh. **Coach tours** cover the Cotswolds from Cheltenham, Gloucester, Oxford, Stratford-upon-Avon, Tewkesbury, and other neighboring cities. Try the **Cotswold Discovery Tour,** a full-day bus tour that starts in Bath and visits five of the most scenic and touristed villages. (☎01225 477 101. Apr.-Oct. Tu, Th, Su 9am-5:15pm. £25.)

■♦ ? ORIENTATION AND PRACTICAL INFORMATION

The Cotswolds lie mostly in Gloucestershire, bounded by **Stratford-upon-Avon** in the north, **Oxford** in the east, **Cheltenham** in the west, and **Bath** in the south. The range hardly towers—the average Cotswold hill reaches only 600 ft.—but the rolling hills can make hiking and biking strenuous. The best bases from which to explore are **Cheltenham, Cirencester, Stow-on-the-Wold,** and **Moreton-in-Marsh.**

Tourist Information Centres: All provide maps, bus schedules and pamphlets on area walks, and book beds, usually for a £2 charge plus a 10% deposit.

Bath: See p. 193.

Bourton-on-the-Water: Victoria St. (☎01451 820 211; fax 821 103). Open Apr.-Oct. M-Sa 10am-5pm; Nov.-Mar. M-Sa 9:30am-4:30pm.

Broadway: 1 Cotswold Ct. (☎01386 852 937). Open M-Sa 10am-1pm and 2-5pm.

Cheltenham: See p. 284.

Chipping Campden: Old Police Station, High St. (☎01386 841 206). Open daily Apr.-Oct. 10am-5:30pm; Nov.-Mar. 10am-5pm.

Cirencester: Corn Hall, Market Pl. (☎01285 654 180). Open Apr.-Dec. M 9:45am-5:30pm, Tu-Sa 9:30am-5:30pm; Jan.-Mar. M 9:45am-5pm, Tu-Sa 9:30am-5pm.

Gloucester: 28 Southgate St. (☎01452 396 572; fax 504 273). Open M-Sa 10am-5pm; July-Aug. also Su 11-3pm.

Moreton-in-Marsh: District Council Bldg., High St. (☎01608 650 881; fax 651 542). Open M 8:45am-4pm, Tu-Th 8:45am-5:15pm, F 8:45am-4:45pm, Sa 10am-1pm. Closes 12:30 pm winter Sa.

Stow-on-the-Wold: Hollis House, The Square (☎01451 831 082; fax 870 083). Open Easter-Oct. M-Sa 9:30am-5:30pm; Nov.-Easter M-Sa 9:30am-4:30pm.

Winchcombe: Next to Town Hall, High St. (☎01242 602 925). Open Apr.-Oct. M-Sa 10am-1pm and 2-5pm, Su 10am-1pm and 2-4pm; Nov.-Mar. Sa-Su 10am-1pm and 2-4pm.

⋔ ACCOMMODATIONS

The *Cotswold Way Handbook and Accommodation List* (£2) details **B&Bs,** which usually lie on convenient roads a 5-10min. walk from small villages. If you're not hiking, pick up the cheaper *Cotswolds Accommodation Guide* (50p), which lists B&Bs in or near larger towns. Expect to pay £20-30 per night, unless you stay at one of the YHA hostels, both of which serve meals. **YHA Stow-on-the-Wold ❷,** The Square, is a 16th-century building beside the TIC. Bright rooms with wooden bunks, most ensuite, provide prime village views. (☎01451 830 497; fax 870 102. Kitchen, lounge, and family room with toys. Laundry £3. Reception 8-10am and 5-10pm. Lockout 10am-5pm. Curfew 11pm. Book a month in advance. Open daily mid-Feb. to Oct.; Nov.-Dec. F-Sa. Dorms £13.40, under 18 £9.30; family rooms £45-65. AmEx/MC/V.) The 56-bed **YHA Slimbridge ❶,** Shepherd's Patch, off the A38 and the M5, is a brick cottage 4 mi. from the Cotswold Way. The nearest train station (Cam and Dursley) is 3 mi.; it's easier to take bus #91 or B7 from Gloucester to the Slimbridge Crossroads round-

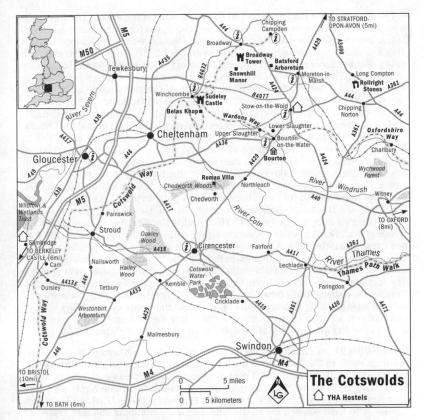

The Cotswolds
⌂ YHA Hostels

about and walk 2 mi. down the village road. (☎0870 770 6036; fax 01453 890 625. Laundry £2.60. Reception 7:15-10am and 5-10:30pm. Curfew 11pm. Open daily mid-July to early Sept.; Oct. to mid-July F-Sa. Closed Dec. Dorms £10.60, under 18 £7.20; twins £25; families £37.50. MC/V.)

Campsites cluster close to Cheltenham, but there are also convenient places to rough it within the Cotswolds. **Moreton-in-Marsh** is one of these; try **Fosseway Farm ❶**, Stow Rd., 5min. out of town toward Stow-on-the-Wold. (☎01608 650 503. Campers' breakfast £3.50. Electricity £2. Laundry £3. £5 per person per night. Caravans with electricity £12. MC/V.) *Camping and Caravaning in Gloucestershire and the Cotswolds* (free at local TICs) lists numerous options.

◪ HIKING

Experience the Cotswolds as the English have for centuries—by treading well-worn footpaths from village to village. Speed-walkers may be able to cruise through numerous towns in a day, but average folk can adequately explore only three or four. To see more than just rolling hills, thatched roofs, and sheep, pick up a free *Cotswold Events* booklet at a TIC. It lists music festivals and antique markets, as well as woolsack races and cheese-rolling opportunities.

HEART OF ENGLAND

TIC shelves strain under the weight of **walking** and **cycling guides.** The *Cotswold Map and Guidebook in One* (£5) is detailed enough to plan bike routes and short hikes. For more intense hiking or biking, the Ordnance Survey Outdoor Leisure Map #45 shows altitudes and more obscure trails (1:25,000; £7). The **Cotswolds Voluntary Warden Service** (☎01451 862 000) conducts free **guided walks,** some with themes (1½-7½hr.). All walks are listed on their website (www.cotswoldsaonb.com) and in the Programme Guide section of the bi-annual Cotswold LION newspaper (free at the TIC); show up at the designated Ordnance Survey point.

Long-distance hikers can choose from a handful of carefully marked trails. B&Bs and pubs lie conveniently within reach of the Cotswold Way and the Oxfordshire Way. The more extensive **Cotswold Way** spans just over 100 mi. from Bath to Chipping Campden, has few steep climbs, and can be done in a week. The trail passes through pasture lands and the remains of ancient settlements. Note that pockmarks and gravel make certain sections unsuitable for biking or horseback riding. Consult the **Cotswold Way National Trail Office** (☎0453 827 004) for details. The **Oxfordshire Way** (65 mi.) runs between the popular hyphen-havens Bourton-on-the-Water and Henley-on-Thames, site of the famed annual regatta. Comprehensive walker's guides can be found in TICs. Amble through ancient pastures while wending from Bourton-on-the-Water to Lower and Upper Slaughter along the **Warden's Way,** a half-day hike. Adventurous souls can continue on to Winchcombe for a total of about 14 mi. The **Thames Path Walk** starts on the western edge of the Cotswolds in Lechlade and follows the Thames 184 mi. to Kingston, near London. The section from the Cotswolds to Oxford is low-impact and particularly peaceful. Contact the **National Trails Office** (☎01865 810 224) for details. Local roads are perfect for **biking;** rolling hills welcome both casual and hardy cyclers. Tiny villages offer little more than pretty houses, so hit a few larger watering holes as well. Parts of the Oxfordshire Way are hospitable to cyclists, if slightly rut-ridden.

WINCHCOMBE. A convenient daytrip before heading farther on, Winchcombe sits 6 mi. north of Cheltenham on the A46 and features the impressive **Sudeley Castle,** a 10min. walk from the town center. Once the manor estate of King Ethelred the Unready, the castle was a prized possession in the Middle Ages, with lush woodland and a royal deer park. Today, the estate is home to Lord and Lady Ashcombe, who have stocked the castle with Tudor memorabilia and maintained 14 acres of prize-winning gardens. The estate's chapel contains the tomb of Henry VIII's Queen #6, Katherine Parr. In summer, Sudeley also holds jousting tournaments and Shakespeare under the stars. (☎01242 602 308; www.sudeleycastle.co.uk. Castle open daily Mar.-Oct. 11am-5pm; last admission 4:30pm. Gardens open daily Mar.-Oct. 10:30am-5:30pm. Castle and gardens £6.85, concessions £5.85, children £3.85. Gardens only £5.50/£4.50/£3.25. All prices £1 more on Su May-Aug.)

BOURTON-ON-THE-WATER. Touted as the "Venice of the Cotswolds," this showpiece village is a popular stop for hikers. The Oxford Way trailhead is here, as is the convergence of other trails, including Warden's, Heart of England, Windrush, and Gloucestershire Ways. Follow signs to the **scale model of Bourton,** a miniature labor of patience. (Open daily mid-Mar. to Oct. 10am-5:15pm.) Between rose-laden gates and dung-strewn fields, **The Cotswold Perfumery,** on Victoria St., features fragrant flowers and a theater equipped with "Smelly Vision," which releases scents as they're mentioned on screen. (☎01451 820 698; www.cotswold-perfumery.co.uk. Open M-Sa 9:30am-5pm, Su 10:30am-5pm. £2, concessions £1.75.)

STOW-ON-THE-WOLD. Historic inns and taverns crowd the Market Square of this self-proclaimed "Heart of the Cotswolds," a more attractive village than Moreton-on-Marsh. Despite such recent developments as a **Tesco** supermarket, Fosse Way (☎01451 807 400; open M-F 6am-midnight, Sa 6am-10pm, Su 10am-4pm), Stow still exudes Cotswold quaintness. A traditional **farmers market** is held the second Thursday of every month from May-Nov. in the Market Square. (☎01453 658 060. Open 9am-2pm.) Three miles downhill, off the A424, **Donnington Trout Farm** lets visitors fish, feed (20p), or eat the trout (£1.50-2). Staff can smoke (in the culinary sense) just about anything, even pigeons. (☎01451 830 873. Open daily Apr.-Oct. 10am-5:30pm; Nov.-Mar. Tu-Su 10am-5pm.) The **YHA hostel** (p. 288) is in the center of town. Ensuite rooms are a perk at the **Pear Tree Cottage** ❹, an old stone house on High St. (☎01451 831 210. Singles £35; doubles £45-50. Cash only.)

THE SLAUGHTERS. Like the proverbial lamb, you can travel to the Slaughters (Upper and Lower), a few miles southwest of Stow. Complete with bubbling stream and centuries-old footbridges, the less-touristed and infinitely more charming Lower Slaughter is connected to its sister village by the Warden's Way. In Lower Slaughter, the **Old Mill,** on Mill Ln., scoops water from the river that flows placidly past; a mill has stood on this spot for 1000 years. (☎01451 820 052. Open daily in summer 10am-6pm; winter 10am-dusk. £1.25, children 50p.)

MORETON-ON-MARSH. With a train station, frequent bus service, and a bike shop, Moreton is a convenient base from which to explore the northern Cotswolds. Little else in the town is of interest. A mile's walk up the road leads to **Batsford Arboretum,** 55 enchanting acres of anti-Cotswold, including a waterfall, a Japanese rest house, trees, and more trees. (☎01386 701 441; www.batsarb.co.uk. Open daily Feb. to mid-Nov. 10am-5pm; mid-Nov. to Jan. Sa-Su 10am-4pm. £5, concessions £4, children £1.) A **Budgen's** supermarket is on High St. near the train station. (☎01608 651 854. Open M-Sa 8am-10pm, Su 10am-4pm.) **Warwick House B&B** ❸, London Rd., offers amazing value with comfortable rooms, a pleasant garden, and free access to a leisure center used by firefighters-in-training. (☎01608 650 773; www.snoozeandsizzle.com. Free pick-up from train station. £21-25 per person. Cash only.) **Blue Cedar House** ❸, Stow Rd., a 5min. walk toward Stow, has welcoming rooms and an airy breakfast area. (☎01608 650 299. Book ahead. Free pick-up from train station. £25 per person, 10% off for 4 nights or more. Cash only.)

BROADWAY. Only 4 mi. southwest of Chipping Campden, restored Tudor, Jacobean, and Georgian buildings with traditional tile roofs rise high on each side of Broadway's main street, giving the town a genteel air. **Broadway Tower,** a 20-40min. uphill hike,

OLYMPICKS OF AULD

Chipping Campden's scenic Dover Hill has hosted the Cotswold Olympicks for almost 400 years. The games were founded by local landowner Robert Dover in 1612 and, although occasionally suspended, their most recent revival in 1963 has carried them into modern times. The light-hearted nature of the activities—like wrestling, Chinese boxing, backsword fighting (exhibition only), and the time-honored shin-kicking (participants are allowed to pad their trousers with hay)—still draws fans in droves.

Where early participants sought escape from oppressive Puritan social norms, today's "athletes" find the tradition, camaraderie, and general mayhem to be the real attraction. The thrill of competition and the ensuing debauchery attracts young and old, respected and "riffraff" alike, and have been chronicled by the likes of Ben Jonson and Shakespeare (see *Merry Wives of Windsor*). Held the Friday after the English Spring Bank Holiday, the games commence at the command of a "Robert Dover" and continue until dusk. Then comes song, dance, and dawn-delaying fun in the town square. Bonfires and fireworks give way to Saturday's Scuttlebrook Wake festivities, which include a parade, the crowning of the May Queen, Morris dancing, and a street fair.

Visit www.stratford-upon-avon.co.uk/ccolymp.htm or ask at Cotswold TICs.

enchanted the likes of poet Dante Gabriel Rossetti, and affords a view of 12 counties. (☎01386 852 390. Open daily Apr.-Oct. 10:30am-5pm; Nov.-Mar. 10:30am-3pm. ₤3.50, concessions ₤3, children ₤2, families ₤10.) **Snowshill Manor,** 2½ mi. southwest of Broadway, was once home to a collector of everything and anything; it now houses about 20,000 random knicknacks. (☎01386 852 410. Open late March to early May Su, M-Th; May-Oct. Su, M-W noon-5pm. ₤7, children ₤3.50.)

CHIPPING CAMPDEN. Years ago, quiet Chipping Campden was the capital of the Cotswold wool trade: the village became a one-time market center ("chipping" means "market"). **Market Hall,** in the middle of the main street, attests to a 400-year history of commerce. The Gothic **Church of St. James,** a signposted stroll from High St. (5min.), is one of the region's prettiest churches. (www.stjameschurchcampden.co.uk. Open Mar.-Oct. M-Sa 10am-5pm, Su 2-6pm; Nov. and Feb. M-Sa 11am-4pm, Su 2-4pm; Dec.-Jan. M-Sa 11am-5pm.) Currently, the town is famous for its **Cotswold Olympic Games** in the first week of June (p. 19). The games take place on **Dovers Hill,** above the town center. From St. Catherine's on High St., turn right onto West End Terr., take the first left, and follow the "public footpath 1 mi. uphill."

CIRENCESTER. One of the larger towns, and sometimes regarded as the capital of the region, Cirencester (SI-ruhn-ses-ter) is the site of Corinium, a once-important Roman town founded in AD 49. Although only scraps of the amphitheater remain, the **Corinium Museum,** Park St., has a formidable collection of Roman paraphernalia. (☎01285 655 611. ₤2.50, concessions ₤1-2.) Cirencester's **Parish Church of St. John Baptist** is Gloucestershire's largest "wool church," meaning it was financed by the wool trade. (☎01285 653 142. Open M-Sa 9:30am-5pm, Su 2:15-5pm. Services M-Sa 3 per day; Su 8, 10, 11:30am, 12:15, 6pm. Donation requested. Gate to the grounds closes at 9pm.) The **world's highest yew hedge** bounds Lord Bathurst's mansion at the top of Park St.; bear right and make a left on Cecily Hill to enter the 3000-acre **Cirencester Park,** whose stately central aisle was designed by Alexander Pope. **Westonbirt Arboretum,** the National Arboretum, stationed 3½ mi. south of nearby Tetbury, features 17 mi. of gorgeous tree-lined paths. (☎01666 880 220. Open daily 10am-8pm or until dusk. ₤7.50, concessions ₤6.50, children ₤1, families ₤15.) **Alexcars** (☎01285 653 985) bus #A1 runs there from Cirencester on summer Saturdays (40min., Apr.-Sept. 2 per day, ₤2.90 round-trip). Otherwise, take the #A1 to Tetbury (45min., M-F 7 per day, ₤1.70) and transfer to **Stagecoach** bus #620 or 628 (7min., M-Sa 5 per day, ₤1.30). An **antique market** opens on Fridays in Corn Hall near the TIC (☎0171 263 6010, open 9am-3pm). (Open 10am-4:30pm.) A cattle market takes place every Tuesday on Tetbury Rd.

CHEDWORTH. Tucked in the hills southeast of Cheltenham, Chedworth contains a well-preserved **Roman Villa,** equidistant from Cirencester and Northleach off the A429. The villa's famed mosaics came to light in 1864 when a gamekeeper noticed tile fragments revealed by clever rabbits. (☎01242 890 256. Open Apr.-Oct. Su, T-Sa 10am-5pm; Mar. and Nov. Su, Tu-Sa 11am-4pm. ₤4.10, children ₤2.) From Cirencester, Beaumont Travel buses reach the villa on weekends, but plan to make a same-day return trip. **The Cotswold Lion** (☎01451 862 000), a bus run by the National Trust, serves the villa from Cirencester, but only on summer weekends (15min., ₤4).

SLIMBRIDGE. Slimbridge, 12½ mi. southwest of Gloucester off the A38, is a dull village with two draws: a pleasant hostel (**YHA Slimbridge,** p. 288) and the largest of seven **Wildfowl & Wetlands Trust** centers in Britain. Sir Peter Scott has developed the world's biggest collection of wildfowl here, with over 180 different species, including all six varieties of flamingos. Unfortunately, it is too far out of the way to be feasible for travelers without a car. (☎01453 891 900; www.wwt.org.uk. Open daily Apr.-Oct. 9:30am-5:30pm; Nov.-Mar. 9:30am-5pm. Last admission 30min. before close. £6.75, concessions £5.50, children £4, families £17.50.)

Six miles southwest of Slimbridge, off the A38 between Bristol and Gloucester, rises massive **Berkeley Castle** (BARK-lay). The stone fortress boasts impressive towers, a dungeon, the cell where King Edward II was murdered, Queen Elizabeth I's bowling green, and a timber-vaulted Great Hall, where barons of the West Country met before forcing King John to sign the *Magna Carta*. (☎01453 810 332. Open Apr.-Sept. W-Sa 11am-4pm, Su 2-5pm; Oct. Su 2-5pm. £7, seniors £5.50, children £4, families £18.50. Tours free and frequent.)

PREHISTORIC REMAINS. Archaeologists have unearthed some 70 ancient habitation sites in the Cotswolds. **Belas Knap,** a 4000-year-old burial mound, stands 1½ mi. southwest of Sudeley Castle. It is accessible from the Cotswold Way or via a scenic 2½hr. walk from Winchcombe; the Winchcombe TIC has a free pamphlet with directions. The **Rollright Stones,** off the A34 between Chipping Norton and Long Compton (a 4½ mi. walk from Chipping Norton), are a 100 ft. wide ring of 11 stones. Consult Ordnance Survey maps (£4-7) or ask at TICs for other sites.

HEREFORD   ☎01432

Near the Welsh border in the scenic Wye River region, Hereford (HAIR-eh-fuhd; pop. 60,000) boasts a storied, centuries-long history as the major market town and agricultural hub of the Wye Valley. Once known for its "white face" cattle, Hereford's modern commercial manifestations are found in the upscale chain stores of High Town, a spacious pedestrian agora that hosts both farmers markets and local entertainment. Meanwhile, good bus and rail connections provide a springboard for westward travel into the Wye Valley on the Welsh-English border (p. 461).

▐ TRANSPORTATION. The **train** and **bus stations** are on Commercial Rd. Trains (☎08457 484 950) arrive from: **Abergavenny** (25min., every hr., £5.80); **Cardiff** (1¼hr., every hr., £12.20); **Chepstow** via **Newport** (1½hr., every hr., £13.70); **London Paddington** (3hr., every hr., £36); and **Shrewsbury** (1hr., 2 per hr., £11.70). **National Express** (☎08705 808 080) runs buses from **Birmingham** (2hr., 1 per day, £6.75) and **London** (4¼hr., 3 per day, £16.50). A convenient bus stop is on Broad St., a few steps past the TIC. **Stagecoach Red and White** buses come from **Abergavenny** (#X4, 1hr., every 2hr., £4.50) and **Brecon** via **Hay-on-Wye** (#39, 1¾hr., M-Sa 6 per day, £5). On Sundays, **Yeoman's** bus #40 takes over the Brecon route (4 per day). For bus info, pick up the *Herefordshire Public Transport Map and Guide* (40p) or the free *Monmouthshire County Council Local Transport Guide* at the TIC. **Rent bikes** from **Phill Prothero Cycles,** Bastion Mews, off Union St. (☎359 478. £10, includes lock, helmet, and repair kit. Open M-W and F 8:30am-5:30pm, Th 8:30am-1pm, Sa 9am-5:30pm.)

▐ PRACTICAL INFORMATION. The **Tourist Information Centre,** 1 King St., in front of the cathedral, books beds for a £1.50 charge plus a 10% deposit. (☎268 430. Open M-Sa 9am-5pm.) **Walking tours** leave from the TIC. (1½hr., mid-May to mid-Sept. M-Sa 11am, Su 2:30pm. £2.) Other services include: **Barclays,** Broad St. (☎422 000. Open M, Tu, Th-F 9am-5pm, W 10am-5pm, Sa 10am-4pm); **Thomas Cook,** St. Peter's St., (☎422 500; open M-Tu and Th-Sa 9am-5:30pm, W 10am-5:30pm); **Coin-op Launder Centre,** 136 Eign St. (☎269 610. Open M-Sa 8am-6pm, Su 8:30am-6pm. Last wash 1hr. before close); the **police** (☎08457 444 888); and the **post office,** 14-15 St. Peter's St. (☎275 221. Open M-F 9am-5:30pm, Sa 9am-4pm.) Post Code: HR1 2LE.

☐☐ ACCOMMODATIONS AND FOOD. Cheap lodgings in Hereford are scarce; your best bet is to walk to the **B&Bs** (from £25) near the T-junction at the end of **Bodenham Road. Bouvrie House ❸,** 26 Victoria St., offers a good location and cheery floral rooms. (☎266 265. Singles £25; doubles £42. Cash only.) The **Holly Tree ❸,** 19-21 Barton Rd., has reasonable prices and is a little further from town center. (☎357 845. No smoking. Doubles £40-44. Cash only.) **Tesco,** Newmarket St., has all your picnic needs covered. (Open 24hr. from M 8am to Sa 10pm.) Or you can stop by the Market Hall Buttermarket for produce and sweets. (Open M-Sa 9am-5:30pm.) At **Cafe@All Saints ❶,** in All Saints Church on High St., try a scone with clotted cream (£1.25). (☎370 415. Open M-Sa 8:30am-5:30pm. MC/V.) Locals and tourist alike relax on cushioned couches amidst cutesy Victorian trinkets at the **Antique Teashop ❶,** 5a St. Peter's St. Decadent pastries (£3) and top-of-the-line teas (£2) allow for thoroughly dignified nibbling and sipping. (☎342 172. Open M-Sa 9:45am-5pm, Su 10:15am-5pm. Cash only.) Sweet and sour pork (£6) complements sweet and sudsy beer at the **Black Lion Inn ❶,** 31 Bridge St., which blends pub atmosphere with Chinese cuisine. (☎343 535. Open M-Th 5:30pm-midnight, F-Sa 5:30pm-12:30am, Su 6pm-midnight. Kitchen closes 30min. before close. MC/V.)

☑☐ SIGHTS AND SHOPPING. The refurbished organ and immense pillars of **Hereford Cathedral** make even the skeptics gasp, as painted vines upon the ceilings and elaborate Romanesque stonework loom dozens of feet above churchgoers. Within is the 13th-century **⊠Mappa Mundi** ("cloth of the world"), which dates from back when the earth was flat and missing half its continents. In the **Chained Library,** 1500 volumes are linked to the shelf by slender chains; the practice was common in 17th century when books were as valuable as small parcels of land. (☎374 200. Cathedral open daily until Evensong. Mappa Mundi and Library open May-Sept. M-Sa 10am-4:15pm, Su 11am-3:15pm; Oct.-Apr. M-Sa. 11am-3:15pm. Cathedral free. Mappa Mundi and Library £4.50, concessions £3.50.) The 17th-century **Old House,** High Town, aptly labeled "the black and white house" on signs around town, is a carefully preserved incarnation of Britain's bourgeois past. (☎260 694. Open Apr.-Sept. Tu-Sa 10am-5pm, Su 10am-4pm; Oct.-Mar. Tu-Sa 10am-4pm. Free.) The slew of cider facts (and vats) housed by the **Cider Museum,** off Pomona Pl., is fascinating, as is the museum's shrine to the dying art of wassailing. Don't let their "What Went Wrong with the Brew" display deter you from the free brandy-tasting. (☎354 207; www.cidermuseum.co.uk. Open Apr.-Oct. M-Sa 10am-5pm; Nov.-Mar. Tu-Sa noon-4pm.; £3, students £2.50.) Hereford's **High Town** area is a network of shop-lined walkways that feature a generic parade of chain stores. Thrifty shoppers may prefer **Chapters,** 17 Union St., where used books, including crime novels and "spine chillers" go for mere pence. (☎352 149. Open M-Sa 9:30am-4:30pm.) **⊠The Dinosaw Market,** 16-17 Bastion Mews, off Union St., promises "things that are not normal," and delivers; an entertaining array of vintage garb, wooden turtles, pink boas, and assorted bric-a-brac fill the store. (☎353 655. Open M-Sa 10am-5:30pm.)

⚑ NIGHTLIFE. Old and young come out to play on weekends in Hereford, but options are few and crowded. **Play,** 51-55 Blueschool St., is a smoky, fabric-draped haunt meant for avid clubbers. Ladies drink free on Monday nights. (☎270 009. Cover £3-5, and cheaper earlier. Open M, Th, Su 9pm-1am, F-Sa 9pm-2am). **Booth Hall,** East St., where St. Peter's St. meets High Town, is a pub that cranks up its music inside while customers sip drinks in the courtyard. (☎344 487. Open M-Sa 11am-11pm, Su 7-10:30pm. Food served M-Sa noon-3pm.)

THE MIDLANDS

Mention "the Midlands," and you'll evoke images grim, urban, and decidedly sunless. But go to the Midlands and you may be surprised by the quiet grandeur of this smokestacked pocket. Warwick's storybook castle and Lincoln's breathtaking cathedral are two of Britain's standout attractions, while the entire towns of Shrewsbury and Stamford are considered architectural wonders. Even Birmingham, the region's oft-maligned center, has its saving graces, among them lively nightlife and the Cadbury chocolate empire. But perhaps Ironbridge and its museums best personify the Midlands; deep in the Severn Valley, this World Heritage Site commemorates the region's innovative role in 18th-century iron production.

HIGHLIGHTS OF THE MIDLANDS

IRONBRIDGE Admire the world's first cast-iron bridge and explore living museums at this monument to Britain's Industrial Revolution (p. 301).

LINCOLN Climb your way to Lincoln's cathedral, once Europe's tallest building and now the stunning centerpiece of this city-on-a-hill (p. 312).

STAMFORD Stroll through the streets of this impeccable stone town on your way to Burghley House, one of Britain's most lavish homes (p. 307).

WARWICK ☎ 01926

Otherwise modest Warwick (WAR-ick) is right to be fiercely proud of her famous castle. Locals boast that it is the UK's biggest tourist attraction, and a walk through its grandiose grounds reveals why. The Great Fire of 1694 has also left the town with a unique architectural heritage, manifest in buildings from both before and after the destruction. Since the city's other sights are limited, Warwick might make a more rewarding daytrip from Birmingham or Stratford-Upon-Avon.

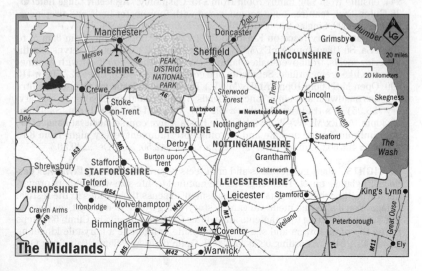

The Midlands

THE MIDLANDS

🖃 🔊 **TRANSPORTATION AND PRACTICAL INFORMATION.** The Warwick **train station** is on Coventry Rd. (Ticket office open M-Sa 5:50am-7:50pm, Su 9:30am-5:40pm.) Trains (☎08457 484 950) run daily from: **Birmingham** (40min., 2 per hr., £3.90); **London Marylebone** (2hr., 1 per hr., £21.90); **Stratford-Upon-Avon** (25min., every 2hr., £3.40). **National Express** (☎08705 808 080) buses stop in Old Square from **London** (3hr., 3 per day, £13.50). **Flightlink** (☎08705 757 747) buses go to Warwick rail station from **Birmingham** (1hr., 1 per day, £6.50) and **Heathrow** (5hr., 3 per day, £23.50) airports; buy tickets at **Co-op Travel,** 15 Market St. (☎410 709; open M and W-F 9am-5:30pm, Tu 9:30am-5:30pm, Sa 9am-5pm). **Local buses** #16 and 18 (3-4 per hr., £2.55-2.85) both stop at Market Pl. from **Coventry** (55min.) and **Stratford** (20min.). **Warwickshire Traveline** (☎414 140) has local bus info. For cabs, try **B&R Cars** (☎771 771). The **Tourist Information Centre,** Court House, Jury St., books rooms for a £2.50 charge plus a 10% deposit and stocks a 50p guided trail map and a free town map. (☎492 212; www.warwick-uk.co.uk. Open daily 9:30am-4:30pm.) **Tours** leave from the TIC (Su 11am, £3). Other services include: **Barclays,** 5 High St. (☎303 000; open M-Tu and Th-F 9:30am-4:30pm, W 10am-4:30pm); a Boots **pharmacy,** Westgate House, 1 Market St. (☎491 927; open M-Th and Sa 8:45am-5:30pm, F 9am-5:30pm); **Warwick Hospital,** Lakin Rd. (☎495 321); the **police,** Priory Rd. (☎410 111); and the **post office,** Westgate House, 45 Brook St. (☎491 061; open M-F 9am-5:30pm, Sa 9am-4pm). **Post Code:** CV34 4BL.

🏠 🍴 **ACCOMMODATIONS AND FOOD.** A stay near the castle can be pricey, but **Emscote Road** (bus X17 runs from Market St. to Emscote frequently) has quality affordable options. From the train station, turn right on Coventry Rd. and left at the Crown & Castle Inn on Coten End, which becomes Emscote Rd. The humorous young proprietor maintains a laid-back atmosphere at **Westham Guest House ❸,** 76 Emscote Rd., 10min. from the Crown & Castle. (☎491 756. Singles £20-22; twins and doubles £38-40, ensuite £40-45; triples and quads from £55. Cash only.) All rooms are ensuite at the gorgeous **Avon Guest House ❸,** 7 Emscote Rd. (☎491 367. www.avonguesthouse.com. Singles £25-30; doubles and twins £48; family rooms £50-80. Cash only.) **Chesterfields ❷,** 84 Emscote Rd., with a sunny breakfast room, offers another cozy option. (☎774 864. Singles from £22; doubles and twins from £44, ensuite from £46; family room from £45. Cash only.) **Agincourt Lodge Hotel ❹,** 36 Coten End, features huge rooms, some with four-poster beds and fireplaces. (☎/fax 499 399. Singles £40-55; doubles £55-75; family rooms £90. MC/V.)

For **groceries,** try **Tesco** on Emscote Rd. (☎307 600. Open 24hr. from 8am M to 10pm Sa, Su 10am-4pm. AmEx/MC/V.) **Fanshawe's ❹,** 22 Market Pl., serves mouthwatering meals, from oven-baked lamb to pan-fried duck. Top it off with gourmet desserts like crème brûlée. Set menu: one course £18, two £20, three £22.50. (☎410 590. Open M-Sa 6pm-10pm. AmEx/MC/V.) The **Crown & Castle Inn ❶,** 2-4 Coventry Rd., has sandwich-and-chips lunch specials (from £2) and an all-you-can-eat carvery (£3.95) in a traditional pub. (☎492 087. Open M-Sa 11am-11pm, Su 11am-10:30pm. AmEx/MC/V.) Warwick Castle hosts a five-course **medieval banquet ❺,** with unlimited wine and ale and ongoing entertainment, every night from 8 to 11pm. (☎406 602. Call for reservations. Jan.-Oct. £42.50; Nov.-Dec. £49.50.)

🔲 **SIGHTS.** Many medievalists and architects regard 14th-century 🗷**Warwick Castle** as England's finest. The dungeons are manned by life-size wax soldiers preparing for battle, while "knights" and "craftsmen" discuss their trades in the festival village. You'll also find medieval games, storytelling by the Red Knight, and events like summer jousting tournaments and winter Christmas festivals. Climb 530 steps to the top of its towers and see the countryside unfold like a fairy-tale kingdom. (☎495 421, 24hr. recording 0870 442 2000. Open daily Apr.-Sept. 10am-6pm; Oct.-

Mar. 10am-5pm. £14.50, children £8.75, seniors £10.50, families £39, weekends and bank holidays 50p-£1 more; mid-Sept. to Apr. £1-2 less. Audio tours £2.95. Warwick Ghosts-Alive brings to life the murder of Sir Fulke Greville, £2.50 extra.) Warwick's less impressive sites include **St. Mary's Church**, Church St., which has a 12th-century Norman crypt containing one of only two surviving ducking stools in England. The church **tower** offers fantastic views of the surrounding area. (☎403 940. Open Apr.-Oct. M-Sa 10am-6pm, Su 12:30-6pm; daily Nov.-Mar. 10am-4:30pm. Last admission 20min. before close. Services Su 8, 10:30am, 6:30pm. Requested donation £1. Tower open daily, last admission 4:30pm. £1.50, children 50p, families £3.50.) In 1571, Elizabeth I gave Lord Leycester the **Lord Leycester Hospital**, 60 High St., to house 12 old soldiers who had fought with him in the Netherlands; today, seven retired veterans live inside. The building's Regimental Museum and Brethren's Kitchen may be more interesting. (☎491 422. Open Easter-Oct. Tu-Su 10am-5pm; Nov.-Easter 10am-4pm. £3.40, concessions £2.90, children £2.40.) The **Warwickshire Museum**, Market Hall, has displays on natural history. (☎412 501. Open Oct.-Apr. Tu-Sa 10am-5pm; May-Sept. Su 11:30am-5pm. Free.)

⚑ DAYTRIP FROM WARWICK

COVENTRY. 12 mi. northeast of Warwick resides Coventry, which deserves a visit if only for its magnificent twin **cathedrals**. Situated poetically beside one another—the destroyed and the resurrected—the newer cathedral, modern in design and decor, towers over the skeleton of the former, both decorated with high stained glass windows. Shards of the old cathedral are visible through the glass "west wall" (actually the south) of the new. (☎7652 1200. Open daily 9am-5:30pm. Requested donation £3. Camera charge £2.) The tourist season commences the first weekend of June during the **Lady Godiva Festival**, which honors Countess Godgifu (who would buy chocolates with a name like that?) of Coventry. Lady Godiva's renowned nude ride through the town is celebrated in an annual parade featuring a modern incarnation. For less scandalous modes of travel, try the **Coventry Transport Museum**, Hales St. The museum displays the largest collection of British cars (400) in the world. (☎7683 2425. Open daily 10am-5pm; last admission 4:30pm. Free.) The **Tourist Information Centre**, 4 Priory Row, books rooms for an 8% deposit. (☎7622 7264. Open M-F 10am-6pm, Sa 9am-5:30pm, Su 11am-5pm.)

BIRMINGHAM ☎0121

Many outside busy "Brum" may grimace at the mention of this industrial heart of the Midlands, a transport hub girdled in ring roads and a mecca for convention-goers. But a walk through Britain's second most populous city (pop. 1 million) will reveal the fruits of focused efforts to overcome an ugly reputation. The third most popular visitor destination for overseas visitors in the UK, Birmingham boasts more canals than Venice and the recently developed Bullring shopping area, Europe's largest retail project. Though offering little in the way of historical interest, the city is quickly defended by loyal "Brummies," whose friendliness is evident amidst both the masses of merchandise-toters and the cliques of night-time clubbers, many of whom are students at the city's university.

☞ TRANSPORTATION

Birmingham is situated along several train and bus lines running between London, central Wales, southwest England, and points north.

Flights: Birmingham International Airport (☎08707 335 511). Free transfer to the Birmingham International train station for connections to New St. Station and London.

Birmingham

⌂ ACCOMMODATIONS
Cook House, **9**
Fountain Court, **10**
Ibis, **12**
Wentworth Hotel, **11**
Woodlands Hotel, **8**

🍎 FOOD
Del Villaggio, **5**

Lasan, **1**
Thai Edge, **4**
Warehouse Cafe, **3**
Wine REPublic, **2**

★ NIGHTLIFE
9 Bar, **7**
Nightingale, **13**
Picasso's, **6**

Trains: New Street Station serves trains (☎ 08457 484 950) from: **Liverpool Lime Street** (1½hr., 1 per hr., £18.60); **London Euston** (2hr., 2 per hr., £35.80); **Manchester Piccadilly** (2hr., 1 per hr., £19.50); **Nottingham** (1¼hr., 3 per hr., £9.70); **Oxford** (1¼hr., 2 per hr., £18). Others pull into **Moor Street** and **Snow Hill** stations. Follow signs to get from New St. to Moor St. Station (10min. walk).

Buses: Digbeth Station, Digbeth High St. **National Express** (☎ 08705 808 080; office open M-Sa 7:15am-7pm, Su 8:15am-7pm) from: **Cardiff** (2½hr., 3 per day, £19); **Liverpool** (3hr., 4 per day, £13); **London** (3hr., 1 per hr., £13); **Manchester** (2½hr., 1 per 2hr., £10.25).

Public Transportation: Information at **Centro** (☎ 200 2700; www.centro.org.uk), in New St. Station. Stocks transit map and bus schedules. Bus and train day pass £5; bus only £2.50, children £1.70. Open M-Tu and F 8:30am-5:30pm, W-Th and Sa 9am-5pm.

Taxis: Blue Arrow (☎ 666 7722).

🔃 PRACTICAL INFORMATION

Tourist Information Centre: The Rotunda, 150 New St. (☎ 202 5099). Books rooms for a 10% deposit and sells theater and National Express tickets. Open M-Sa 9:30am-5:30pm, Su 10:30am-4:30pm.

Financial Services: Banks in the city center. **American Express,** Bank House, 8 Cherry St. (☎644 5533). Open M-Tu and Th-F 9am-5:30pm, W 9:30am-5:30pm, Sa 9am-5pm. **Thomas Cook,** 99 New St. (☎255 2600). Open M-W and F-Sa 9am-5:30pm, Th 10am-5:30pm.

Police: Steelhouse Ln. (☎0845 113 5000).

Pharmacy: Boots, The Bull Ring (☎632 6418), across from New St. station. Open M-F 8am-8pm, Sa 9am-8pm, Su 11am-5pm.

Internet Access: Central Library, Chamberlain Sq. (303 4511), has free access on the 2nd floor, but there's usually a wait. Open M-F 9am-8pm, Sa 9am-5pm. **Ready to Surf,** Corporation St. (☎236 2523). £1 per hr. Open M-Sa 9am-6pm, Su 11-5pm.

Post Office: Big Top, 19 Union Passage (☎643 7051). **Bureau de change.** Open M-Sa 9am-5:30pm. **Post Code:** B2 4TU.

ACCOMMODATIONS

Despite its size, Birmingham has no hostels; the TIC does, however, have good **B&B** listings. Take bus #9, 109, or 139 to busy **Hagley Road** for more options.

Wentworth Hotel, 103 Wentworth Rd. (☎427 2839). From Harborne swimming bath, turn right on Lonsdale Rd. then left on Wentworth Rd. Spacious rooms and a warm atmosphere. Singles £38; doubles £58; family room £65. MC/V. ❹

Ibis, Arcadian Centre, Ladywell Walk (☎622 6010; fax 622 6020), just east of the Hippodrome Theatre. Allure of a good location supplemented by the professional service of a bigger hotel at a smaller price. M-Th £49.95 per room, F Su £45.95. AmEx/MC/V. ❹

Cook House, 425 Hagley Rd. (☎429 1916). Take bus #9 or 139 from Colmore Row (20min.) and ask to stop before the Quantum Pub, then walk back a few minutes. Many rooms in this Victorian home have fireplaces and original furnishings. Singles £20-22, ensuite £28; twins and doubles £38, ensuite £46. Cash only. ❸

Woodlands Hotel, 379/381 Hagley Rd. (☎420 2341). Spacious rooms, many with four-post beds. All ensuite. Singles £50; doubles £66; triples £78; family £88. MC/V. ❹

Fountain Court, 339/343 Hagley Rd. (☎429 1754). Family-run hotel offers ensuite rooms and lounges. Singles M-Th £45, F-Su £35; doubles £55-65. AmEx/MC/V. ❹

FOOD

Birmingham is most proud of **balti,** a Kashmiri-Pakistani cuisine invented by immigrants and cooked in a special pan. Brochures at the TIC map out the city's *balti* restaurants; the best are southeast of the city center in the *"Balti* Triangle." **Groceries** can be purchased from **Sainsbury's,** Martineau Pl., 17 Union St. (☎236 6496; open M-Sa 7am-8pm, Su 11am-5pm). An **Indoor Market** on Edgbaston St. offers fresh produce. (☎622 5449. Open M-Sa 9am-5:30pm.)

Thai Edge, 7 Oozells Sq. (☎643 3993), off Broad St. Bamboo poles and minimalist furniture give this popular Thai restaurant a stylish look. Entrees £6-15. Open M-Th noon-2:30pm and 5:30-11:30pm, F-Sa noon-2:30pm and 5:30-midnight, Su noon-3pm and 6-11pm. AmEx/MC/V. ❸

Warehouse Cafe, 54 Allison St. (☎633 0261), off Digbeth, above the Friends of the Earth office. Birmingham's only vegetarian and vegan establishment. A creative organic menu, including daily specials and lunchtime veggie burgers (£2-4), keeps locals loyal and visitors knocking. Also hosts pricier theme dinners on special nights; call for more info. Open M-Th noon-3pm, F-Sa noon-3pm and 6-9pm. Cash only. ❶

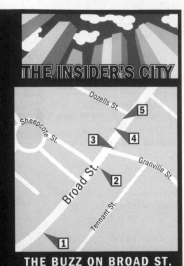

THE BUZZ ON BROAD ST.

Birmingham offers a host of night-life options—vibrant Broad St. has so many that you'll barely have to leave the block.

1 Chic, sassy vodka bar **Revolution,** Broad St. (☎665 6508. Open M-Sa 11:30-2am, Su noon-2am), offers happy hour specials noon-9pm M-Th, Su.

2 Bamboo and leopard print decorate **The Springbok Bar,** 240 Broad St. (☎633 3803. Open M-Th noon-11pm, F-Sa noon-2am, Su noon-10:30pm).

3 Throw back a Guinness at Irish bar **O'Neill's,** Broad St. (☎616 7821. Open M-Tu noon-11pm, W-Sa noon-1am, Su noon-10:30pm.)

4 Sleek **ipanema,** 9 Brindleyplace (☎643 5577. Open M-Sa noon-2am, Su noon-12:30am), offers W jazz classes and Th salsa classes.

5 Enjoy the disco ball and lights at Flare, 55 Broad St. (☎632 5500. Open M-Sa 8pm-2am, Su 8pm-12:30am). Th dance competition. Th-Sa cover £2-5.

Del Villaggio, 245 Broad St. (☎643 4224). Petal-covered tables, cushioned benches, and dim lighting add a romantic element to this modern Italian restaurant. Lunch promotion offers a free glass of the house red or white with any pizza or pasta. Open daily noon-2:30pm and 5-11pm. AmEx/MC/V. ❸

Lasan, James St. (☎212 3664). A posh, cozy restaurant serving modern Indian cuisine. Entrees £7-10. Open M-Sa 6-11pm. AmEx/MC/V. ❷

Wine REPublic, Centenary Sq. (☎644 6464), next to Symphony Hall. Free tapas in outdoor dining area 5:30-6:30pm. Sandwiches, salads, and pastas (£4-7), entrees (£8-15), and over 50 wines. Open M-Sa 11am-11pm, also Su when there's a show. Food served noon-9:30pm. AmEx/MC/V. ❷

🄶 SIGHTS

Birmingham's most significant attractions may be its regenerated shopping districts: **The Mailbox** (☎632 1000. Open M-Sa 10am-8pm, Su 11am-5pm), home to Harvey Nichols and Armani, **Brindleyplace** (☎643 6866; www.brindleyplace.com), along the canals, and the sprawling **Bull Ring** (☎632 1500. Open M-F 9:30am-8pm, Sa 9am-8pm, Su 11am-5pm), recognizable by the architecturally puzzling Selfridges department store that stands at its forefront. **St. Martin's in the Bull Ring,** the site of Birmingham's first parish church, is the heart of the city and worth a stop if you are walking through the Bull Ring (☎643 5428. Open M noon-6pm, Tu-Su 9am-6pm.) The **Birmingham Museum and Art Gallery,** Chamberlain Sq. off Colmore Row, supports **Big Brum,** northern cousin to London's Big Ben. It also houses costumes, pre-Raphaelite paintings, and William Blake's illustrations of Dante's *Inferno.* (☎303 2834. Open M-Th and Sa 10am-5pm, F 10:30am-5pm, Su 12:30-5pm. Free.) The **Barber Institute of Fine Arts,** in the University of Birmingham on Edgbaston Park Rd., displays works by heavyweights like Rubens, Renoir, Matisse, Gauguin, and Degas. (Bus #61, 62, or 63 from the city center. ☎414 7333. Open M-Sa 10am-5pm, Su 2-5pm. Free.) The **National Sea Life Centre,** The Water's Edge, Brindleyplace, is home to over 3000 creatures and has the world's first fully transparent 360° underwater tunnel. (☎643 6777. Open daily 10am-5pm. £9.95, students £7.95, seniors £7.50, children £6.95.) **Thinktank at Millennium Point,** Curzon St., Digbeth, offers an interactive science experience, including the kid-friendly LEGOLab. An IMAX theatre is on the same complex. (☎202 2222. Open daily 11-5pm. £6.95, concessions £5.50, children £4.95, families £18.) Signs point northwest to over 100 shops lining the **Jewellery Quarter,** which hammers out almost all the jewelry in Britain.

CADBURY WORLD. Twelve minutes south of town by rail or bus lies Cadbury World, a cavity-inducing celebration of the chocolate industry. Sniff your way through the story of chocolate's birth in the Mayan rainforests, but be prepared to fend off swarms of schoolchildren. Be sure to snag a few free samples. *(By train from New St. to Bournville, or bus #11A, 11C, 27, and 84 from the city center. ☎ 451 4159. Open daily 10am-3pm; closed M and F Nov.-Feb. £9, concessions £7.20, children £6.80, families £27.60-33, oompa-loompas free. Book tickets in advance.)*

NIGHTLIFE AND ENTERTAINMENT

Birmingham's student population fuels its excellent nightlife venues. Streets beyond the central district can be dangerous. As always, take care at night.

BARS AND CLUBS

Broad Street is lined with trendy cafe-bars and clubs. A thriving gay-friendly scene has arisen in the area around **Essex Street.** Pick up the bimonthly *What's On* to discover the latest hotspots. Clubbers on a budget should grab a guide to public transport's Night Network from the Centro office in New St. Station—**night buses** generally run hourly until 3:30am on Friday and Saturday nights.

9 Bar, 192 Broad St. (☎ 643 5100). The alluringly dark decor of this futuristic warehouse inspires much drinking and posturing, as well as occasional dancing. Dress smart casual. Cover F £1, Sa £3-5. Open F 9pm-2am, Sa 9pm-2am and 2:30-5am for an afterparty.

Picasso's, 200 Broad St. (643 7130). Birdcages, oil paintings, and nude sculptures cultivate an artsy feel. Turns clubby Th-Su 9pm-1am. Dress smart casual. 21+. Open M-W noon-11pm, Th-F noon-1am, Sa noon-2am, Su noon-12:30am. Cover F-Sa £3.

Nightingale, Essex House, Kent St. (☎ 622 1718). 2 frenzied dance floors, 5 bars, jazz lounge, and billiard room attract a mostly gay crowd from all over. Cover varies depending on acts. Dress smart casual. Open Su-Th 5pm-2am, F 5pm-4am, Sa 5pm-7am.

MUSIC AND THEATER

City of Birmingham Symphony Orchestra (☎ 780 3333) plays in superb Symphony Hall, at the ICC on Broad St. Box office open M-Sa 10am-8pm; 10am-6pm if no performance. Su hours depend on concert times. Tickets £5-80; concessions and group discounts; student standbys 1hr. before concerts £3-5.

Hippodrome Theatre, Hurst St. (☎ 0870 730 1234). Once a music hall featuring vaudeville artists, the theater now hosts West End musicals and ballet. M-F 10am-9pm, Sa 9:30am-9pm. Tickets £8.50-34; discounts for students, seniors, groups, and standbys.

Birmingham Repertory Theatre, Centenary Sq. (☎ 236 4455), on Broad St. A less grandiose, but still celebrated, theater hosting dramas, comedies, and new plays. Open M-Sa 9:30am-6pm. Tickets £10-21; discount standby tickets for students and seniors.

The Birmingham Jazz Festival (☎ 454 7020) brings over 200 jazz bands, singers, and instrumentalists to town during the first 2 weeks of July; most events are free, get information for ticketed events from the TIC.

IRONBRIDGE ☎ 01952

Pretty towns shouldn't have deceptively ugly names, though this one could hardly be more apt: the center of Ironbridge is, in fact, a grand 18th-century iron bridge arching 55ft. above the Severn. The bridge owes its existence to Abraham Darby III, the third man of that name to reign over the iron industry that transformed this scenic riverside settlement into the self-proclaimed birthplace of the

Industrial Revolution. Now a World Heritage Site, Ironbridge's 10 museums cluster around a charming tree-lined village whose horizon juxtaposes lingering industrial infrastructure and stunning natural beauty.

▙ TRANSPORTATION. The nearest **train** station is at **Telford,** 20min. from Shrewsbury on the Birmingham-Shrewsbury-Chester line (M-Sa 1-4 per hr., Su 1 per hr.). The only way to reach Ironbridge directly is by **bus.** Timetables are notoriously temperamental; it is essential to call ahead, as the patchy timetables available at TICs often don't agree with schedules posted at bus stops. For bus information, call the TIC, the Telford Travelink (☎200 005) or Traveline (☎0870 608 2608). **Arriva Midlands North** (☎08457 056 005) #96 goes to Ironbridge from **Telford** (15min., M-Sa 6 per day) and **Shrewsbury** (40min.; M-Sa 6 per day, Su 5 per day). Most buses to and from Ironbridge do not run past 5 or 6pm. The Sunday bus from Shrewsbury also stops at **Coalbrookdale, Blists Hill,** and **Coalport.** **Arriva** (☎08456 015 395) runs #99 on the Wellington-Bridgnorth route, stopping at **Ironbridge** and **Coalbrookdale** from **Telford** (25min., M-Sa 16 per day). Arriva #76 (20min., M-Sa 5 per day) and #77 (20min., M-Sa 3 per day) provide service between **Coalbrookdale** and **Coalport** (both home to YHA hostels), stopping at the Ironbridge Museum of the Gorge en route. On weekends and bank holidays, two **Gorge Connect** services (WH1 and WH2, both 1-2 cycles per hr.) shuttle between the various Ironbridge museums; day rovers are a good idea (£3, children £1.50) for all-day travel.

▙ ▟ ORIENTATION AND PRACTICAL INFORMATION. Ironbridge is the name of both the narrow 4 mi. river gorge and the village at the gorge's center. The 10 **Ironbridge Gorge Museums** huddle on the banks of the Severn Valley in an area of 6 sq. mi. Some are difficult to reach without a car—buses run infrequently and stop only at selected points, and bike rental shops are conspicuously absent in town; try **Cycle Adventures** mobile bike hire, which provides free delivery of bikes and helmets for £14 per day (☎07947 131 349; www.cycleadventures.co.uk). Central **Ironbridge** is home to the Iron Bridge and Tollhouse. The Museum of the Gorge is ½ mi. to the west of the village. North of The Museum of the Gorge, in **Coalbrookdale,** are the Coalbrookdale Museum of Iron, the Darby Houses, and Enginuity. Past the Jackfield bridge, 1½ mi. east of Ironbridge village, **Coalport** is home to the Coalport China Museum and the Tar Tunnel. The Blists Hill Victorian Town is ½ mi. north of Coalport. The staff at the **Tourist Information Centre,** in the ground floor of the Tollhouse across the Iron Bridge, provides the free *Ironbridge Gorge Visitor Guide* and book accommodations for a 10% deposit. (☎884 391; www.ironbridge.org.uk. Open M-F 9am-5pm, Sa-Su 10am-5pm.) Ironbridge has **no banks** or **ATMs.** The **post office** is on The Square. (☎433 201. Open M-Tu and Th-F 9am-1pm and 2-5:30pm, W 9am-1pm, Sa 9am-12:30pm.) **Post Code: TF8 7AQ.**

▛▟ ACCOMMODATIONS AND FOOD. The two buildings of the **YHA Ironbridge Gorge ❷** grace the valley's opposite ends, 3 mi. apart. One is in **Coalport,** next to the Coalport China Museum, in a renovated china factory, equipped with laundry facilities, Internet access (50p per 6min.), and a licensed restaurant. (Dorms £13.40, under 18 £9.30, ensuite doubles £34.80.) The more basic one in **Coalbrookdale** inhabits a huge remodeled schoolhouse on a hill, 1mi. from the bridge and TIC. Walk past the Museum of the Gorge and turn right at the roundabout in Coalbrookdale; it's on your right at the turnoff for Paradise St. It has a lounge, games room, kitchen, and laundry. (Dorms £11.80, under 18 £8.50.) Arriva bus #76 reaches both; Coalbrookdale is also a stop on #77. From Shrewsbury or Telford, #96 passes within ½ mi. of each. (☎588 755 for both. Reception closes 10:30pm. Open daily Easter-Oct.; winter weekends. MC/V.)

Otherwise, budget accommodations are scarce. Area **B&Bs** charge upwards of £25 per person, and solo travelers can expect to pay at least £35 for a single room. **The Library House ❹**, Severn Bank, occupies the old village library and greets guests with wine on arrival, earning its Five Diamond Gold status. (☎432 299; www.libraryhouse.com. Singles £55; doubles £65; family rooms £80-85. Cash only.) **Coalbrookdale Villa ❹**, 17 Paradise St., is a stunning Gothic house 10min. from Ironbridge village and only a few steps from the Coalbrookdale museum cluster. Its grassy gardens are home to six pet sheep that the owners refer to as their "eco-friendly lawn-mowers." The kind proprietress provides welcome trays and full breakfasts. (☎433 450. Singles £45; doubles £60-62. Cash only.) Built in the center of Ironbridge village in 1784, **The Tontine Hotel ❸**, The Square, was constructed by the same men responsible for the bridge to accommodate the growing crowds of tourists. Rooms come with color TVs, telephones, and views of the bridge. (☎432 127. Singles £22-36; doubles £40-56. MC/V.) The nearest campsite is the **Severn Gorge Caravan Park ❶**, Bridgnorth Rd., in Tweedale, 3 mi. from Ironbridge and 1 mi. north of the Blists Hill Victorian Town. (☎684 789. 2-person tent sites £11.75. Electricity £4. Showers free.)

At **Peacock's Pantry ❷**, 2-4 The Wharfage, menus feature a huge selection of meals like the "Ironmaster" ploughman's lunch (£5), complete with iron-rich black pudding. (☎433 993. Open daily 11am-5pm. Cash only.) Find lunch and snacks at **Recollections ❷**, 6 Tontine Hill, where Victorian accessories recall the gentrified dimensions of Ironbridge's past. Snacks are £1-3; meals £6-8. (☎432 690. Open daily 11am-5pm. MC/V.) The acclaimed **Ironbridge Brasserie and Wine Bar ❹**, High St., serves classy, vegetarian-friendly bistro fare on a patio with river views. (☎432 743. Entrees £10-15. Open Tu-Th 5-11pm, F-Sa noon-3pm, Su 1-4pm and 6:30-10:30pm. MC/V.) Walk 5min. uphill from Ironbridge toward Madeley for steak-and-kidney pie (£6) at the **Horse and Jockey ❶**, 15 Jockey Bank, said by *Britain Meat* to be the best in the nation. (☎433 798. Open daily noon-2:30pm and 7-11pm. MC/V.)

🏛 **MUSEUMS.** The Ironbridge Gorge Museums are the area's pride and joy, and with good reason: you'd be hard pressed to find a better portrayal of Britain's unique industrial heritage. Spend at least two days to cover them well. If visiting all 10 (or even a significant fraction), buy an **Ironbridge Passport** from any of them, which admits you once to each of the museums (£13.75, seniors £11.50, students and children £8.75, families £42). The major museums are open daily 10am-5pm, while smaller collections such as the Darby Houses have limited hours.

The famous **Iron Bridge,** built in 1779 by Abraham Darby III, spans the River Severn with eye-catching black trusses. A small sign posted on the side of the **Tollhouse** at its southern end lists the fares for every carriage, mule, or child that crosses; even royalty isn't exempt. The TIC occupies the ground floor while the second level houses an exhibit about the bridge's history, including a brief biography of one of its more eccentric funders, John "Iron Mad" Wilkinson, who minted iron coins stamped with his own image. (☎884 391. Open Easter-Oct. M-F 9am-5pm, Sa-Su 10am-5pm. Free.) A 10min. walk from Ironbridge, the **Museum of the Gorge** provides an introduction to the area's history and is a good place to begin a day's exploration. (☎432 405. £2.20, seniors £1.75, students and children £1.15.)

In Coalbrookdale to the northwest, the **Coalbrookdale Museum of Iron** traces the history of the Darby family iron saga. The top floor Great Exhibition recreates the 1851 extravaganza that saw its craft glorified. The massive furnace where Abraham Darby first smelt iron with coke is also on-site. (☎435 960. £5.30/£4.50/£3.40.) Just up the hill, the **Darby Houses** model the quarters of the multiple generations of ironmasters who dwelt there. (☎432 551. £3.10/£2.30/£1.70.) **Enginuity,** just across the courtyard from the Museum of Iron, houses child-friendly hands-on displays that will even teach adults a thing or two. (☎435 905. £5.30/£3.20/£3.20.)

In Coalport to the west, the **Coalport China Museum** and **Jackfield Tile Museum** show the products of other industries; both offer demonstrations and workshops. The Tile Museum is temporarily closed for renovations and was scheduled to reopen in the summer of 2004. (China Museum ☎580 650. £4.50/£4.15/£2.70.) Don a hard hat at the eerie **Tar Tunnel,** where surprised workers first discovered smudgy natural bitumen dripping from the walls. (☎580 827. £1.20/£1.10/70p.) Across the river from the village are the **Broseley Pipeworks,** located in a town of the same name. Here clay pipe-making workshops have been preserved in a state of decrepit authenticity. This is the farthest museum (about 30min. by foot), but one of the most interesting. At the **Blists Hill Victorian Town,** ½ mi. uphill from Coalport, over 40 recreated buildings deliver kitschy antiquity through local craft. Visitors can exchange modern money for Victorian farthings at the local bank, or chat with actors going about their make-believe business. (☎582 050. £8.50/£7.90/£5.30.) Though it's not part of the Ironbridge Passport deal, the **Ironbridge Open Air Museum of Steel Sculpture** is worth a look. Over 60 modern steel sculptures are installed on the 10 acres on Cherry Tree Hill, just uphill from the Museum of Iron. (☎433 152. Open Mar.-Nov. Tu-Su 10am-5pm. £2, concessions £1.50.)

SHREWSBURY ☎01743

Trains, buses, and cars all converge on Shrewsbury—and with good reason. Brightly arrayed hatter's windows, hole-in-the-wall boutiques, and a crooked network of ancient roads make Shrewsbury (SHROWS-bree; pop. 60,000) a haven for those with a weakness for stereotypically English streetscapes. The Severn, the longest river in England, nearly encircles the whole of Shrewsbury, whose location was picked for this natural defense. Roger de Montegomery, second-in-command to William the Conqueror, claimed the area during the 11th century. And immortalized in Shakespeare's Henry IV, the battle of Shrewsbury—between antagonists Prince Hal and Harry Hotspur—reputedly occurred nearby.

◪ TRANSPORTATION

The **train station,** a splendid neo-Gothic building, is at the end of Castle St. (Ticket office open M-Sa 5am-10pm.) **Trains** (☎08457 484 950) run from: **Aberystwyth** (1¾hr.; M-Sa 8 per day, Su 5 per day; £14.70); **London** (3hr., 1-3 per hr., £60); **Swansea** (3½-4hr.; M-Sa 3 per day, Su 2 per day; £15.80); **Wolverhampton** (40min., 2-3 per hr., £7.20); and most of North Wales via **Wrexham General** and **Chester** (1hr.; M-Sa 1 per hr., Su 6 per day; £6.60). The **bus station** is on Raven Meadows, which runs parallel to Pride Hill. (☎244 496. Ticket office open M-F 8:30am-5:30pm, Sa 8:30am-4pm.) **National Express** (☎08705 808 080) arrives from: **Birmingham** (1½hr., 2 per day, £4.75); **Llangollen** (1hr., 1 per day, £3.75); **London** (4½hr., 2 per day, £15.50). **Arriva Midlands** #96 runs from **Telford** via **Ironbridge** (1hr., M-Sa 6 per day). **Taxis** queue in front of the train station; otherwise call **Access Taxis** (☎360 606).

✦ ORIENTATION

The **River Severn** circles Shrewsbury's town center in a horseshoe shape, with the curve pointing south. The town's central axis runs from the train station in the northeast to Quarry Park in the southwest: first **Castle Gates,** the road becomes **Castle Street,** then pedestrian-only **Pride Hill,** then **Shoplatch,** then Mardol Head, and finally **St. John's Hill. St. Mary's Street** and **High Street** branch off from either end of Pride Hill at the center of town, converging to become Wyle Cop before it turns into the English Bridge, crosses the river, and reaches the Abbey. The accessible A5 nearly circles the city at a distance.

🛈 PRACTICAL INFORMATION

The Tourist Information Centre, Music Hall, The Square, across from the Market Bldg, books accommodations for a £1.50 charge (£2 over phone) plus a 10% deposit. (☎281 200; www.shropshiretourism.info. Open May-Sept. M-Sa 9:30am-5:30pm, Su 10am-4pm; Oct.-Apr. M-Sa 10am-5pm.) Historic 1½hr. **walking tours** (☎281 200) from the TIC pass through Shrewsbury's medieval "shutts" (closeable alleys). Special W summer tours feature tea with the mayor. (Daily May-Sept. 2:30pm; Oct. M-Sa; Nov.-Apr. Sa only. £3, children £1.50.) **River King Shrewsbury** (☎343 444; www.river-king.co.uk) offers 45min. cruises along the Severn; 1 per hr. 11am-4pm. Other services include: **Barclays,** 44-46 Castle St., off St. Mary's St. (open M-Tu and Th-F 9am-5pm, W 10am-5pm, Sa 9:30am-3:30pm); **Stidgers Wishy Washy** launderette, 55 Monkmoor Rd., off Abbey Foregate. (☎355 151; self-service Sa only; wash £3, dry 20p per 3min, service £8 per load; open M-Sa 9am-4pm; last wash 1hr. before close); the **police,** Clive Rd. in Monkmoor (☎01743 232 888); Royal **Shrewsbury Hospital,** Mytton Oak Rd. (☎261 138); free **Internet Access** at the **Shrewsbury Library (Shropshire Reference and Information Service),** 1A Castle Gates, just downhill from the main library; (☎255 380 open M, W, F 9:30am-5pm; Tu and Th 9:30am-8pm; Sa 9am-5pm; photo ID required); **Boots pharmacy,** 9-11 Pride Hill (☎351 111; open M-Sa 8:45am-5:45pm); and a **post office,** St. Mary's St., just off Pride Hill (☎08457 740 740; bureau de change. Open M-Sa 9am-5:30pm.) **Post Code:** SY1 1DE.

🛏🍴 ACCOMMODATIONS AND FOOD

Singles are hard to find, so reserve several weeks ahead in summer. Several **B&Bs** (£20-30) lie between **Abbey Foregate** and **Monkmoor Road.** A taxi (from £3.20) lets you skip the considerable hike from the bus and train stations. A charming brick townhouse, **Allandale ❸** hides behind the abbey on Abbey Foregate, and hangs its porch with flower baskets and its walls with charming prints. (☎240 173. £22.50 per person. Cash only.) Comely **Glyndene ❸,** Park Terr., has an elaborate bell-pull and tasteful rooms with TVs. From the bridge, follow the road left of the abbey for both. (☎352 488; www.glyndene.co.uk. £25 per person. Cash only.) **Abbey Lodge ❷,** 68 Abbey Foregate, has standard rooms with TVs on a major road. (☎/fax 235 832. Standard singles £23; doubles with bath £50.) The beautifully decorated **Trevellion House ❸,** 1 Bradford St., off Monkmoor Rd., features quiet, elegant ensuite rooms with wrought-iron beds. (☎249 582. From £22. Cash only.)

Shrewsbury hosts an indoor "Market under the Clock" at the corner of Shoplatch and Bellstone. (☎351 067. Open Tu-W and F-Sa, roughly 9am-4pm.) **Somerfield** has **groceries** at the Riverside Mall, on Raven Meadows near the bus station. (Open M-W and Sa 8am-6pm, Th-F 8am-7pm, Su 10:30am-4:30pm.) Tucked in St. Alkmund's Sq., by Butcher Row, 🌑**The Bear Steps Coffee House ❶** has patio seating next to a shaded park and warns its taller guests to watch their heads when dining indoors, as timbers are lower than 6 ft. The delicious quiche with bread and butter is £5. (☎244 355. Open roughly M-Sa 10am-4pm. Cash only.) Despite its playful name, **Jesters Restaurant ❸,** 14-15 St. Mary's St., keeps it cool with leather armchairs and an inviting bar inside. Light lunches include wraps (crispy duck with green onion £5) while dinner entrees start at £11. (☎358 870. Open M-Sa 11am-late. Food served until 9pm. AmEx/MC/V.) **The Good Life Wholefood Restaurant ❶,** Barracks Passage, off Wyle Cop, serves vegetarian cuisine for low prices. The nutloaves (£2.50) are wonderfully executed. (☎350 455. Open M-F 9:30am-3:30pm, Sa 9:30am-4:30pm) At the **King's Head ❶** pub, Mardol St., try the roast dinner (with potatoes, vegetables, and Yorkshire pudding, £3.50), and admire a medieval painting of the Last Supper. (☎362 843. Open M-Sa 10:30am-11pm, Su noon-11pm. Food served M-F 10:30am-6pm, Sa 10:30am-5pm, Su noon-5pm.)

👁 SIGHTS

Shrewsbury's biggest attraction is its architecture. Tudoresque houses dot the central shopping district and rally in full force at the **Bear Steps,** which start in the alley on High St. across from the Square. **Churches,** many on Saxon foundations, cluster in town center. At the end of Castle St., the riverside acres of **Quarry Park** are filled with expansive grassy lawns along the oft-flooded Severn. At the center of the park, **Dingle Garden** explodes with bright flower arrangements. Shrewsbury also makes a point of honoring its native sons; check out **Darwin's statue** opposite the castle, the colossal **Lord Hill Column** at the end of Abbey Foregate on the tallest Doric column in Europe, and MP **Robert Clive of India** outside Market Sq.

Vivid red sandstone makes **Shrewsbury Castle,** near the train station, stand out. Built out of wood in 1083, the castle has since been replaced by the Great Hall, which now holds the **Shropshire Regimental Museum.** For great views, climb nearby **Laura's Tower,** a summer garden house built in the 1780s as a 21st-birthday present. (☎ 358 516. Museum and tower open daily Easter-Sept. 10am-5pm; Oct.-Easter Tu-Sa 10am-4pm. Grounds open daily Easter-Sept. 9am-5pm; Oct.-Easter M-Sa only. £2, students and children free, seniors £1. Grounds free.) The **Shrewsbury Museum and Art Gallery,** Barker St., off Shoplatch, displays Iron Age log boats and a silver mirror from AD 130, as well as exhibits from later history; try on a Tudor frill collar. (☎ 361 196. Open June-Sept. M-Sa 10am-5pm, Su 10am-4pm; Oct.-Mar. Tu-Sa 10am-4pm; Apr.-May Tu-Sa 10am-5pm. Free.) Beyond the English Bridge, the 919-year-old **Shrewsbury Abbey** holds the remains of a shrine to St. Winefride, a 7th-century princess who was beheaded, then miraculously re-capitated to become an abbess and patroness of North Wales and Shrewsbury. A memorial to local WWI poet Wilfred Owen lies in the garden. (☎ 232 723. Open daily Easter-Oct. 10am-4:45pm; Nov.-Easter 10:30am-3pm.) **St. Mary's Church,** off St. Mary St. near Pride Hill, features a remarkable set of stained-glass windows that illustrate the life of Bernard of Clairvaux in what the church describes as a "medieval strip cartoon." (☎ 357 006. Open M-F 10am-5pm, Sa 10am-4pm. Free.) Shrewsbury hosts an annual **Art Festival** (☎ 07817 167 772) during July, but the mid-August **Flower Show** sees Shrewsbury's population burgeon to 100,000 over 2 days to ogle at the world's longest-running horticultural show. (☎ 234 050; www.shrewsburyflowershow.org.uk. £13, children £6.50.)

🏃 DAYTRIP FROM SHREWSBURY

CRAVEN ARMS
Craven Arms is located 20 mi. south of Shrewsbury on the A49. Easiest access is by bus #435 from Shrewsbury (1 hr., 7 per day.)

20 mi. south of Shrewsbury in Craven Arms, ▨**The Land of Lost Content,** at the corner of Dale St. and Market St., offers a surprisingly fascinating collection of nostalgic Brit-pop culture relics. Named after A.E. Housman's "A Shropshire Lad," the museum holds over 30 displays, among them a clip-on "Roy Roger" tie, diapers trimmed with angel frill, a vial of cod liver oil, and all those childhood belongings you wish you'd never grown out of. (☎ 01588 676 176; www.lolc.org.uk. Open daily Feb.-Nov. 11am-5pm, Dec.-Jan. by appointment. £5, children £2.50.) A few blocks away at the **Secret Hills Shropshire Discovery Centre,** on the corner of School Rd. and the A49, visitors can explore exhibits on local history, including a replica of the Shropshire Mammoth skeleton beneath a grass roof. Four walks network the surrounding area. (☎ 01588 676 000. Open daily Apr.-Oct. 10am-5:30pm; Nov.-Mar. 10am-4:30pm; last admission 1hr. before closing. £4.25, children £2.75)

STAMFORD ☎ 01780

William the Conqueror built a castle at Stamford that was destroyed in a string of nasty sieges and is now the site of a small bus station. Renegade scholars abandoned Oxford in 1333 and came here to found a new school. It foundered, and two years later the rebels sulked home. Despite such pitfalls, this tiny city lures travelers with its high spires, crooked alleys and Norman arches, earning Stamford its reputation as the most splendid stone town in England.

☐ ◪ TRANSPORTATION AND PRACTICAL INFORMATION. Stamford teeters on the edge of Lincolnshire, with Cambridgeshire right below. **Trains** (☎ 08457 484 950) stop at **Stamford Station**, at the southern end of town, from: **Cambridge** (1hr., 1 per hr., £13.30); **Lincoln** (2½ hr., 2 per hr., £17); **London King's Cross** (1hr., 1 per hr., £25.70). **Buses** pass through Sheepmarket, off All Saints' St. (☎ 554 571. Ticket office open M-Sa 9am-5:30pm.) **National Express** (☎ 08705 808 080) makes the trip from **London** (5½hr., 1 per day, £22.50).

To reach the **Tourist Information Centre,** in the Stamford Arts Centre on St. Mary's St., walk straight out of the train station, follow the road as it curves to the right, then take a left on High St. St. Martin's, cross the River Welland, and take a right on St. Mary's St. The TIC gives away a town map, sells the *Town Trail* guide (75p), and books beds for free. (☎ 755 611. Open M-Sa 9:30am-5pm; Apr.-Sept. also Su 11am-4pm.) Other services include: **banks** along High St.: **Lloyd's TSB,** 65 High St. (☎ 0845 072 3333; open M-Tu and Th-F 9am-5pm, W 10am-5pm, Sa 9am-12:30pm); the **police,** North St. (☎ 752 222I; open M-F 9am-5:30pm, Sa 9am-12:30pm); free **Internet access** at the **library,** on High St. (☎ 763 442.; book in advance; open M and W 9am-8pm, Tu and Th-F 9am-5:30, Sa 9am-1pm); and the **post office,** 9 All Saints' Pl. (☎ 08457 223 344). **Post Code:** PE9 2EY.

⌂ ◖ ACCOMMODATIONS AND FOOD. Consider daytripping from Cambridge or Lincoln to avoid Stamford's high prices. Budget **B&Bs** stay on the outskirts; call ahead to get a lift. Try **Birch House ❸,** 4 Lonsdale Rd., 20min. from the train station, where each room is decorated with zest. (☎ 754 876. Singles and doubles £24 per person. Cash only.) **The Candlesticks Hotel ❹,** 1 Church Ln., convenient to the city center, surrounds its gourmet restaurant with elegant, ensuite rooms. (☎ 764 033. Singles £45; doubles and twins £55. AmEx/MC/V.)

For **groceries** hit **Tesco,** 46-51 High St. (☎ 683 000. Open M-W and Sa 7:30am-5:30pm, Th-F 7:30am-6:30pm, Su 10am-4pm.) With delicious baguettes (£2), pastries (75p-£1.65), and hot lunches (£6.75-7.25), **The Central Restaurant ❶,** 7 Red Lion Sq., is the best place to get good, freshly-prepared food at low prices. Includes a restaurant, tea rooms, and an uncannily good bakery. (☎ 763 217. Open M-Th 9:30am-5pm, F-Sa 8am-5pm. AmEx/MC/V with purchases over £5.) Once the Midlands's premier coaching inn, **The George ❷** High St. St. Martin's, is now an upscale wood-panelled hotel and restaurant. (☎ 750 750. Food served noon-10:30pm. AmEx/MC/V.) Savor a pot of tea (95p) and warm your stomach with omelettes and jacket potatoes (£3-6) at **Paddington Station ❶,** Ironmonger St. (☎ 751 110. Open M-Th 9:15am-5pm, F 9:15am-4:30pm, Sa 9:15am-5pm. Cash only.)

◉ ▣ SIGHTS AND ENTERTAINMENT. Stamford's main attraction is ▧**Burghley House,** England's largest Elizabethan mansion. A 1 mi. walk from Stamford along Burghley Park, it is signposted from High St. St. Martin's. Ringed with gardens designed by Capability Brown, the house was the prized creation of William Cecil, Queen Elizabeth I's High Treasurer. The famous **Heaven Room** and infamous **Hell Staircase** display works of Antonio Verrio. Don't miss Burghley's newest addition, a 12-acre **Sculpture Garden** showcasing rare flowers and modern sculpture. (☎752 451; www.burghley.co.uk. House open daily Apr.-Oct. 11am-5pm, last admission 4:30pm; M-Sa by guided tour only. Sculpture Garden open daily 11am-5pm. Park open daily Apr.-Oct. 7am-6pm; low-season until 8pm. £7.80, concessions £6.90, children £3.50. Sculpture garden June-Aug. Sa-Su £3, children 50p. Park free.)

The **Stamford Arts Centre**, St. Mary's St., hosts local productions and national touring companies. (☎763 203. Box office open M-Sa 9:30-8pm, also 1hr. before Su shows.) Begun in 1968, the **Stamford Shakespeare Festival** is based at Elizabethan **Tolethorpe Hall** and attracts over 35,000 each year. (☎756 133; www.stamfordshakespeare.co.uk. June-Aug. in 2005. Tickets £8-16.).

NOTTINGHAM ☎0115

Nottingham (or Snottingham, as the early Anglo-Saxon chronicle has it; pop. 262,000) maintains its age-old tradition, begun by the mythical Robin Hood, of taking from the rich. The modern city uses its favorite rogue to lure tourists to its fluffy attractions. But Nottinghamshire has produced more famed residents than that socially conscious outlaw, including Lord Byron, D.H. Lawrence, and Jesse Boot (whose name appears on pharmacies nationwide).

▐ TRANSPORTATION

Trains: Nottingham Station, Carrington St., south of the city, across the canal. Trains (☎08457 484 950) from: **Lincoln** (1hr., 2 per hr., £6.20); **London St. Pancras** (1¾hr., 2 per hr., £41); **Sheffield** (1hr., 1 per hr., £7.60).

Buses: Broad Marsh Bus Station (☎950 3665), between Collin St. and Canal St. Ticket and info booth open M-F 9am-5:30pm. **National Express** (☎08705 808 080) from **London** (3hr., 8 per day, £15) and **Sheffield** (1½hr., 9 per day., £5.75). **Victoria Bus Station** is at the corner of York St. and Cairn St. **Nottinghamshire County Council Buses** link points throughout the county.

Public Transportation: For short urban journeys, hop on a **Nottingham City Transport** bus (40-90p). All-day local bus passes £2. For public transit info call **Nottinghamshire Buses Hotline** (☎0870 608 2608). Open daily 7am-8pm.

▐ ▐ ORIENTATION AND PRACTICAL INFORMATION

Nottingham is a busy city and its streets are confusing. Its hub is **Old Market Square,** the plaza that spreads before the domed Council House (beware the pigeons).

Tourist Information Centre: 1-4 Smithy Row (☎915 5330), off Old Market Sq. Many reference guides, tour and **job listings,** a free city map, and the free *What's On* entertainment guide. Books rooms (before 4:30pm) for a £3 charge plus a 10% deposit. Open M-F 9am-5:30pm, Sa 9am-5pm; June-Aug. also Su 10am-4pm.

Tours: Nottingham Experience (☎0115 911 5005) leads 30min. tours, leaving from the castle gatehouse. Daily Apr.-Oct. 10am-4pm. £4, concessions £2.50.

Financial Services: American Express, 2 Victoria St. (☎08706 001 060). Open M-Tu and Th-F 9am-5:30pm, W 9:30am-5:30pm, Sa 9am-5pm.

Launderette: Brights, 150 Mansfield Rd. (☎948 3670), near the Igloo hostel. Open M-F 9:15am-7pm, Sa 9:15am-6pm, Su 9:30am-5pm; last wash 1hr. before close.

Police: North Church St. (☎967 0999).

Hospital: Queen's Medical Center, Derby Rd. (☎924 9924).

Internet Access: Nottingham Central Library, Angel Row (☎915 2841). Free. Open M-F 9:30am-7pm, Sa 9am-1pm.

Post Office: Queen St. Open M-Sa 10am-5:30pm. **Post Code:** NG1 2BN.

ACCOMMODATIONS

Moderately priced **guest houses** (£20-25) cluster on **Goldsmith Street,** near Nottingham Trent University.

Igloo, 110 Mansfield Rd. (☎947 5250), on the north side of town. Convenient, and run by a backpacker. TV lounge and kitchen. Curfew 3am. Dorms £13.50. Cash only. ❷

Bentinck Hotel, Station St. (☎958 0285), directly across from the train station. Great location. Clean rooms with TVs, and a late-closing bar downstairs. £19.50 per person, ensuite £23.50. MC/V. ❸

The Lace Market Hotel, 19-31 High Pavement (☎852 3232). Chic, upscale rooms with all the requisite luxuries for a weekend (or weekday) splurge. Flawless service and memorable red-themed interior design. Singles £90; doubles £110-135. AmEx/MC/V. ❺

FOOD AND PUBS

Quick, inexpensive bites are easily found on Milton Street and Mansfield Road. Gaggles of sandwich shops, trendy cafes, and ethnic eateries line Goosegate. Find a **Tesco** supermarket in the Victoria Shopping Centre. (☎980 7500. Open M-Tu and Th-Sa 8am-7pm, W 8am-8pm, Su 11am-5pm.)

The Alley Cafe, 1a Cannon Ct. (☎955 1013), off Long Row West. Low prices and high-quality smoothies and sandwiches (£2.75) in friendly, comfortable vegetarian hideaway. Bar is a hotspot after dinner. Open M-Tu 11am-6pm, W-Sa 11am-11pm. ❶

Ye Olde Trip to Jerusalem, 1 Brewhouse Yard (☎947 3171). This pub, claimant to the title of "Oldest Inn in England," served its first pot of ale in 1189 and served as a staging point for soldiers setting off on the crusades. Known as "The Trip," it's carved into the castle's base. Open M-Sa 11am-11pm, Su noon-10:30pm. Food served M-Sa 11am-6pm, Su noon-6pm. MC/V with purchases over £5. ❶

Hart's, Standard Ct., Park Row (☎911 0666). Braised and glazed variations on English cuisine. Sleek but not snooty. Entrees £11.50-18.50. Pre-theater dinner £18. Open M-Su noon-2pm and 7pm-11pm. AmEx/MC/V. ❹

SIGHTS

GALLERIES OF JUSTICE. This is well put-together interactive museum occupies five subterranean levels below the old Shire Hall. Visitors can explore special exhibitions, like evidence from the 1963 **Great Train Robbery,** before being submitted to the worst of historical English "justice" in the **Crime and Punishment Galleries.** You'll be convicted of trumped-up charges before a merciless judge, then shoved into the dungeons by whip-wielding guards—don't be surprised if you end up in Australia. Return to the side of the righteous in the **Police Galleries,** where exhibits explore the historical and modern role of British coppers. (Shire Hall, High Pavement. ☎952 0558; www.galleriesofjustice.org.uk. Open daily mid-July to Aug. 10am-5pm, Sept. to mid-July Tu-Su 10am-5pm. Last admission 4pm. £7, concessions £6, children £5.25, families £20.)

NOTTINGHAM CASTLE. William the Conqueror put up the original timber structure in 1068, and Henry III had the whole thing redone in stylish gray stone. The ruins of the castle now top a sandstone rise south of the city center. In 1642,

Charles I raised his standard against Parliament here, kicking off the Civil Wars. For its pernicious part in the affair, the castle was destroyed by Parliamentarians. What's left now houses the ■**Castle Museum and Art Gallery,** a collection of historical exhibits, Victorian art, silver, and the regimental memorabilia of the Sherwood Foresters. (☎915 3700. *Open daily 10am-5pm. Admission M-F free; Sa-Su £2, concessions £1, families £5.)* While you're there, check out **Mortimer's Hole,** the underground passageway leading from the base of the cliff to the castle. (☎915 3700. *50min. tours leave from museum entrance M-Sa 11am, 2, 3pm; Su 1 per hr. noon-4pm. £2, concessions £1.)*

THE UNDERGROUND SCENE. Nottingham is riddled with hundreds of caves. As early as the 10th century, dwellers dug homes out of the soft and porous "Sherwood sandstones" on which the city rests. Even in medieval times, the caves were often preferred to more conventional housing—they required no building materials and incurred lower taxes. During WWII many caves were converted to air-raid shelters. Visitors can take a guided tour of one cave complex, surreally situated beneath (and accessed through) the second floor of Broad Marsh Shopping Centre. (☎988 1955. *Open M-Fa 8am-5pm, Sa 11am-4:30pm; last tour 4pm. 40min. guided tour. £4.25, concessions £3.50, families £14. 40min. audio tour. £3.75/2.75/11.50.)*

TALES OF ROBIN HOOD. Cable cars transport visitors through an amusement-park version of Sherwood Forest. Release your inner outlaw at a **medieval banquet** (£35 per person for costume, 4 courses and lots of beer) or at a **medieval murder mystery** (£23.50 per person for three courses) where you can figure out who killed the Sheriff's bride-to-be. *(30-38 Maid Marian Way. ☎ 948 3284. Open daily 10am-5:30pm; last admission 4:30pm. £7, concessions £6, children £5, families £20.)*

NIGHTLIFE AND ENTERTAINMENT

Students crowd the city's thirty-plus clubs and pubs. Live bands, primarily of the punk and indie variety, play to a young crowd on the two floors at **The Social,** 23 Pellham St., where theme nights abound. (☎ 950 5078; www.thesocial.com. Open M-Tu 5pm-11pm, W-F 5pm-2am, Sa 11am-2am.) **Rock City,** 8 Talbot St., hosts local bands and has enough themed nights to accommodate musical tastes from punk to techno. "Loveshack" Fridays are strictly pop, while Saturdays are alternative. (☎ 941 2544; www.rock-city.co.uk. Cover £4-5. Open M-Tu and Th-Sa 8:30pm-2am.) Traditional theater can be found at the **Theatre Royal,** Theatre Sq. (☎ 989 5555.) The **Nottingham Playhouse,** Wellington Circus features more offbeat productions, though it offers its share of Shakespeare as well (☎ 941 9419; tickets £5-25).

DAYTRIPS FROM NOTTINGHAM

◼ NEWSTEAD ABBEY. The ancestral estate of Lord Byron stands north of Nottingham in the village of **Linby.** The sprawling stately home is built around the remnants of a medieval abbey. Byron moved in as a ten-year-old and remained here until forced to sell. Many personal effects remained, including a replica of "Byron's skull cup"—an ancient human cranium unearthed at Newstead in 1806, which the poet coated with silver, inscribed with verse, and filled with wine. The original was reinterred in 1863. Peacocks hold court in the gardens; a sign warns that shiny cars are vulnerable during mating season. *(Buses #737, 747 and 757 travel from Nottingham Victoria Station to the abbey gates (30min., 3 per hr., round-trip £3.50), 1 mi. from the house and grounds. ☎ 01623 455 900; www.newsteadabbey.org.uk. House open daily Apr.-Sept. noon-5pm; last entry 4pm. Grounds open 9am-dusk; last admission 5pm. House and grounds £5, concessions £2.50, under 16 £1.50. Grounds only £2.50, concessions £1.50, families £7.)*

SHERWOOD FOREST. To the north spreads famed Sherwood Forest, considerably thinned since the 13th century. The **Sherwood Forest Visitor Centre** has a small museum, but beware the legions of children armed with mini-archery sets. To escape the crowds, take the signposted 3½ mi. walk, making sure to stop at the "Major Oak," which, at 33 ft. in girth, allegedly served as Robin's hideout. In August, the medieval **Robin Hood Festival** includes a jousting tournament. *(Buses #33 and 36 leave Nottingham Victoria Station (40min., 1 per 1½hr., £5.80). ☎ 01623 823 202. Forest open dawn-dusk. Centre open daily 9am-5:30pm. Free.)*

EASTWOOD. Eastwood native and teacher D. H. Lawrence had his controversial novels banned from the bookshelves; now he's buried in Westminster Abbey. The **D.H. Lawrence Birthplace Museum** celebrates his fame from Lawrence's childhood home. *(8A Victoria St., near Mansfield Rd. ☎ 01773 717 353. Open daily Apr.-Oct. 10am-5pm; Nov.-Mar. 10am-4pm. M-F free, Sa-Su £2, children and concessions £1.20.)* The **Sons and Lovers Cottage,** where young D.H. lived from 1887 to 1891, is free and open by appointment. *(28 Garden Rd. ☎ 01773 717 353.)* Eastwood is 6 mi. west of Nottingham. Rainbow bus #1 (40min., £4.20) leaves often from Nottingham Victoria Station.

THE MIDLANDS

LINCOLN ☎ 01522

Medieval streets climb their cobbled way past half-timbered homes to Lincoln's dominating 12th-century cathedral, a relative newcomer in a town built for retired Roman legionaries in the 1st century. Lincoln does not draw many tourists, but those who do make it will find a bustling marketplace and (after a steep uphill climb to the city's peak) sweeping views of the dusky Lincolnshire Wolds (especially from along Yarborough Rd.). Lincolnshire is also renowned for its sausage, excellent examples of which may be found in the market.

▐ TRANSPORTATION

Lincoln's **Central Station** is on St. Mary's St. (Office open M-Sa 5:45am-7:30pm, Su 10:30am-9:20pm. Travel center open M-Sa 9am-5pm.) **Trains** arrive from: **Leeds** (2hr., 2 per hr., £19); **London King's Cross** (2hr., 1 per hr., £44.50); **Nottingham** (1hr.; M-Sa 2 per hr., Su 7 per day; £6.20). Opposite is **City Bus Station,** Melville St. (Open M-F 8:30am-5pm, Sa 9am-1:45pm.) **National Express** buses come from **London** (5hr., 3 per day, £19) and **Nottingham** (3½hr., 1 per day, £9.50). For information on Lincolnshire bus services, contact the **Lincolnshire Roadcar** station on St. Mark St. (☎ 522 255. Open M-F 8:30am-5pm, Sa 8:30am-4:30pm.)

🌸 🛈 ORIENTATION AND PRACTICAL INFORMATION

Lincoln has an affluent acropolis on **Castle Hill** and a cottage-filled lower town near the tracks. The TIC and major sights lie at the junction of **Steep Hill** and Castle Hill.

Tourist Information Centre: 9 Castle Hill (☎ 873 213; www.lincoln.gov.uk). Books rooms for a £2 charge plus a 10% deposit. Pick up a map (free) and miniguide (50p). Open M-Th 9am-5:30pm, F 9am-5pm, Sa-Su 10am-5pm.

Tours: 1hr. tours depart from the TIC daily July-Aug. 11am and 2:15pm; Sept.-Oct. and Apr.-June Sa-Su only. £3. **Guide Friday** (☎ 522 255) runs hop-on, hop-off bus tours every 30min. 10am-3pm in summer. £6, concessions £5, children £2.50.

Financial Services: Major **banks** line High St. **Thomas Cook,** 4 Cornhill Pavement (☎ 346 400). Open M-Tu and Th-Sa 9am-5:30pm, W 10am-5:30pm.

Pharmacy: Boots, 311-312 High St. (☎ 524 303). Open M-Sa 8:30am-5:45pm, Su 10:30am-4:30pm.

Police: West Parade (☎ 882 222), near the town hall.

Hospital: Lincoln County Hospital, Greetwell Rd., off Greetwell Gate. (☎ 512 512).

Internet Access: Central Library, Free School Ln. (☎ 510 800). Free. Open M-F 9:30am-7pm, Sa 9:30am-4pm. **Sun Cafe,** 7a St. Mary St. (☎ 569 292). £2 per hr. Open M-Sa 9am-6pm, Su noon-5pm.

Post Office: City Sq., Sincil St. (☎ 513 004), just off High St. **Bureau de change.** Open M-F 9am-5:30pm, Sa 9am-5pm. **Post Code:** LN5 7XX.

▐ ACCOMMODATIONS

B&Bs (most £17-20) sprinkle **Carline Road** and **Yarborough Road,** west of the castle. Consult the accommodations list in the window of the branch TIC.

Mayfield Guest House, 213 Yarborough Rd. (☎/fax 533 732). Entrance behind house on Mill Rd., 20min. walk from the station (or bus #7 or 8). Victorian mansion near a windmill with large ensuite rooms and fluffy quilts. Mind the cockatiel. No smoking. Singles £25; doubles £45; twins £46. AmEx/MC/V. ❸

LINCOLN ■ 313

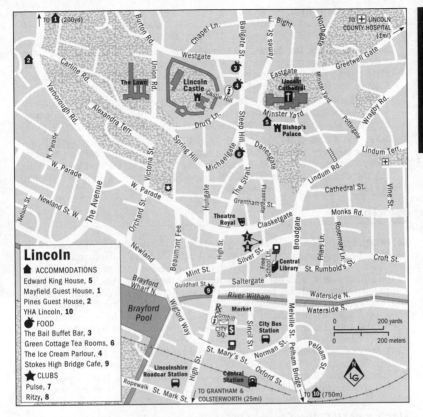

Lincoln

ACCOMMODATIONS
Edward King House, 5
Mayfield Guest House, 1
Pines Guest House, 2
YHA Lincoln, 10

FOOD
The Bail Buffet Bar, 3
Green Cottage Tea Rooms, 6
The Ice Cream Parlour, 4
Stokes High Bridge Cafe, 9

CLUBS
Pulse, 7
Ritzy, 8

Pines Guest House, 104 Yarborough Rd. (☎/fax 532 985), 15min. northwest of the train station; walk or take bus #7 or 8 to Yarborough Rd. Large, thickly carpeted rooms with TVs. The game room has a pool table and bar. Breakfast included. Singles £19, ensuite £30; doubles £38, ensuite £44. Cash only. ❸

Edward King House, Minster Yard (☎528 778), near the Bishop's Palace. Run by the diocese. Views are divine, building immaculate, and city center location miraculous. Continental breakfast included. Singles £22; doubles £43. AmEx/MC/V. ❸

YHA Lincoln, 77 South Park Ave. (☎0870 770 5918). From the station, turn right on Pelham Bridge (becomes Canwick Rd.) and right on S. Park Ave. 46-bed villa. Lockout 10am-5pm. Curfew 11pm. Open Jan.-Oct. Dorms £10.60, under 18 £7.20. MC/V. ❶

FOOD

The **market,** at Sincil St., sells local food, and oddities. (Open M-F 9am-4pm, Sa 9am-4:30pm.) Restaurants, tearooms, and takeaways grace **High Street,** while pubs line **Bailgate Street,** on the other side of the hill.

THE MIDLANDS

■ **The Ice Cream Parlour,** Bailgate St. This tiny, traditional shop scoops out first-rate homemade ice cream and sorbet. A double scoop of orange brandy is £1.90. Open M-Th 10:30am-6pm, F-Su 9:30am-dusk. Cash only. ●

The Green Cottage Tea Rooms, 18 Steep Hill (☎537 909). With 3 tea and coffee menus, a selection of baguettes (£4.80) and pastries (£1.20-2.50), this is an ideal place to rest before the last leg of your ascent up Steep Hill. Open M, W-F, Su 10:30am-4:30pm, Sa 10am-5:30pm; lunch served noon-3pm. Cash only. ●

The Bail Buffet Bar, 14 Bailgate St. (☎546 464). All you can eat from a selection of stews, vegetables, pastas and pizzas for £6. Beef dishes are particularly good. Open for lunch daily noon-2:30pm, dinner Su-Th 5:30-9pm, F-Sa 5:30-10pm. AmEx/MC/V. ●

Stokes High Bridge Cafe, 207 High St. (☎513 825). Busy tearoom in a broad Tudor-style house/bridge, displayed on many a postcard. Watch swans float by on the green canal, or look down on High. St. bustle from three floors above, while nibbling steak pie (£5.75). 2-course lunch special (£4.50) served 11:45am-2pm. Open M-Sa 9am-5pm. Tea served 9:30am-5pm. Cash only. ●

⊚ SIGHTS

■ **LINCOLN CATHEDRAL.** While the rest of Lincoln endured a millennium of rumblings and crumblings in which Roman barricades, bishops' palaces, and conquerors' castles were erected and destroyed, the magnificent cathedral remained king of the hill. Begun in 1072 but not completed for three centuries, it was once the continent's tallest building, taller even than the pyramids of Giza, until the spire toppled. The shimmering Lincolnshire limestone and broad front overwhelm in sheer beauty the castle across the street. Its many endearing features include the imp in the **Angel Choir,** who turned to stone while attempting to chat with seraphim. A treasury room displays sacred silver and a shrine to child martyr Sir Hugh. Rotating exhibits reside in a **library** designed by Christopher Wren. (☎544 544; www.lincolncathedral.com. Open June-Aug. M-Sa 7:15am-8pm, Su 7:15am-6pm; Sept.-May M-Sa 7:15am-6pm, Su 7:15am-5pm. Evensong M-Sa 5:15pm, Su 3:45pm. Tours May-Aug. M-Sa 11am, 1, 3pm; Sept.-Apr. Sa only. Free roof tours M, W, F 2pm; Tu, Th, Sa 11am and 2pm. Library open during exhibitions and by appointment. Cathedral £4, concessions £3, children £1.)

LINCOLN CASTLE. Home to one of four surviving copies of the *Magna Carta*, this 1068 castle was also the house of pain for inmates of Victorian Castle Prison. A cheerful guide leads the "Prison Experience," among other tours. (☎511 068. Open Apr.-Oct. M-Sa 9:30am-5:30pm, Su 11am-5:30pm; Nov.-Mar. M-Sa 9:30am-4:30pm, Su 11am-4:30pm. Last admission 1hr. before close. Tours Apr.-Oct. Sa-Su 11am and 2pm. £3.60, children and concessions £2.10, families £9.30.)

BISHOP'S PALACE. The medieval Bishop's Palace was originally wedged between the walls of the upper and lower Roman cities. Thanks to 12th-century Bishop Chesney, a passageway through the upper city wall links the palatial remains to the cathedral. The palace itself—in Chesney's time the seat of England's largest diocese—is now peacefully ruined, surrounded by vineyards and long views. (☎527 468. Open daily Apr.-June and Sept.-Oct. 10am-5pm, July-Aug. 10am-6pm, Nov.-Mar. M, Th-Su 10am-4pm. £3.50, concessions £2.60, children £1.80, families £8.80.)

▣ ✻ NIGHTLIFE AND FESTIVALS

On the corner of Silver St. and Flaxengate, **Pulse** (☎522 314) has a range of theme nights. Next door, **Ritzy** (☎522 314) is popular, meaning longer lines. Pick up the monthly *What's On* at the TIC, or ask at the cathedral about choral and organ performances. The **Theatre Royal,** Clasketgate near the corner of High St., stages drama and musicals. (☎525 555. Box office open M-F 10am-2pm and 3-5pm, Sa 10am-2pm and 5-6pm. Tickets £7-22.) **The Lawn,** on Union Rd. by the castle, hosts outdoor music and dancing events. (☎560 306. Open Apr.-Sept. M-Th 10am-5pm, F 10am-4:30pm, Sa-Su 10am-5pm; daily Oct.-Mar. 10am-4pm. Free.) Lincoln offers one of Europe's largest **Christmas Markets,** 4 days of Victorian banqueting and fairs in the marketplace. July brings **Medieval Weekend,** a series of events on the castle lawn, and August brings the **Lincoln Early Music Festival.**

▶ DAYTRIPS FROM LINCOLN

GRANTHAM. Young Sir Isaac Newton attended the **King's School** in Grantham and left his signature carved in a windowsill. *(Brook St. ☎01476 563 180. By appointment only. Free, donations accepted.)* The **Grantham Museum** has exhibits on Newton and another of Grantham's progeny, Margaret Thatcher. *(Museum on St. Peter's Hill, by the TIC. ☎01476 568 783. Open M-Sa 10am-5pm; last admission 4:30pm. Free. Grantham is 25 mi. south of Lincoln; 45min. by train (round-trip £8.80). Lincolnshire Roadcar (☎522 255; 1¼hr.; M-Sa 2 per hr., Su less frequent; round-trip £4) bus #1 runs from St. Mark St. station.)*

COLSTERWORTH. Here stands **Woolsthorpe Manor,** Newton's birthplace. Young Isaac scribbled his early musings on the wall, and visitors can still peep at his genius-graffiti. Whether he was actually bonked by one of the apple tree's inspirational fruits is debatable, but this is the site of his "what goes up, must come down" deliberations. The barn contains the **Sir Isaac Newton Science Discovery Centre,** a fantastic hands-on exhibit that clarifies Newtonian ideas for the non-mathematically-inclined. *(Lincolnshire Roadcar, ☎522 255, runs from Grantham (18min., every 2-3hr., round-trip £2.60). ☎01476 860 338. Open Apr.-June and Sept.-Oct. W-Su 1-5pm, July-Aug. W-Su 1-6pm, Mar. and Oct. Sa-Su 1-5pm. Manor £3.60, children £1.80. Discovery Centre free.)*

EAST ANGLIA

Literally England's newest landscape, the fens were drained as late as the 1820s. From Norwich east to the English Channel, the water that once drenched enormous medieval peat bogs was channeled into the maze of waterways known as the Norfolk Broads, now a national park. Continental-style windmills helped maintain the drained fens, and some still mark the marshes. Farther inland, Norman invaders made their way to the elevated mound at Ely, building a cathedral from stone transported by boat across then-flooded fenland; and in a village to the south, renegade scholars from Oxford set up shop along the River Cam in the 15th century.

HIGHLIGHTS OF EAST ANGLIA

CAMBRIDGE Stroll among the colleges (but keep off the grass!) in this picturesque university town, one of the world's best-known reserves of scholarship (p. 316).

ELY CATHEDRAL Gaze skyward at a medieval masterwork, still breathtaking as it towers over former fenland (p. 326).

NORWICH Mind your map in this twisting, wool-trading town, once the largest in Anglo-Saxon England, where markets and festivals have endured for centuries (p. 336).

TRANSPORTATION IN EAST ANGLIA

The major rail operator is **Anglia Railways** (☎ 01603 724 880). A **combined** Plus Pass (about £60), available at stations within East Anglia, entitles you to a week's unlimited travel on all **train** routes in the region. A **regular** Plus Pass allows a week of unlimited travel in either Norfolk or Suffolk (£29). Both zones are covered by their own one- and three-day passes (£9 and £20). All Plus Passes also grant free travel on various lines of the Norwich, Ipswich, and Great Yarmouth **bus** services.

East Anglia's flat terrain and relatively little rainfall pleases **cyclists** and **hikers,** though rental bikes can be difficult to procure outside of Cambridge and Norwich. The area's most popular walking trails are **Peddar's Way,** which runs from Knettishall Heath to Holme and includes the **Norfolk Coast Path** and **Weaver's Way.** TICs in Norwich, Bury St. Edmunds, and several Suffolk villages issue *Peddar's Way and Norfolk Coast Path* and other walking guides.

Harwich (HAR-idge) is a ferry depot for trips to Holland, Germany, and Scandinavia, and **Felixstowe** has ferries to Belgium (see **By Ferry,** p. 29). Call the Harwich **Tourist Information Centre,** Iconfield Park, Parkeston, for ferry details. (☎ 01255 506 139. Open M-F 9am-5pm; Sa-Su 9am-4pm; Oct.-Mar. closed Su.) The Felixstowe TIC is on the seafront. (☎ 01394 276 770. Open daily 9am-5:30pm.)

CAMBRIDGESHIRE

CAMBRIDGE   ☎ 01223

In contrast to museum-oriented, metropolitan Oxford, Cambridge is determined to retain its pastoral academic robes—the city manages, rather than encourages, visitors. No longer the exclusive preserve of upper-class sons, the university has

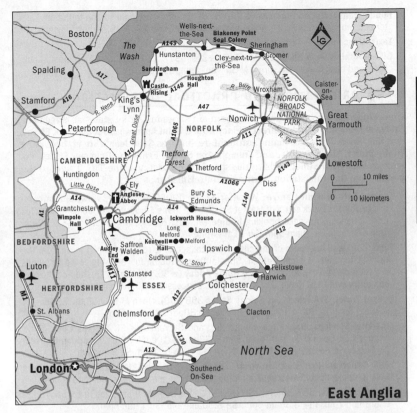

East Anglia

opened its doors to women and state school pupils. Some old upper-crust traditions are slipping, too: now students only bedeck themselves in gown and cravat once a week. At exams' end, Cambridge explodes with Pimms-soaked glee, and May Week (in mid-June, naturally) launches a swirl of cocktail parties and balls.

TRANSPORTATION

Bicycles are the primary mode of transportation in Cambridge, a city which claims more bikes per person than any other place in Britain. On bike or on foot, watch out for confused drivers: a series of one-way streets and countless foreign youths used to riding on the wrong side of the road complicate summer transport.

Trains: Station on Station Rd. Ticket office open daily 5am-11pm. **Trains** (☎08457 484 950) arrive from **London King's Cross** (45min., 3 per hr., £16.40) and **London Liverpool Street** (1¼hr., 5 per hr., £16.40).

Buses: Drummer Street Station. Ticket booth open daily 8:45am-5:30pm; tickets also often available on board. **National Express** (☎08705 808 080) comes from **London** (2hr., 2 per hr., from £9). **Jetlink** runs shuttles from: **Gatwick** (4hr., 1 per hr. £27.50); **Heathrow** (2½hr., 1 per hr., £23.50); and **Stansted** (1hr., 1 per hr., £8.50). **Stagecoach Express** (☎01604 676 060) runs from **Oxford** (3hr., 1 per hr., from £6).

Public Transportation: Cambus (☎423 578) runs from the train station to the city center and around town (£1-2). **Whippet Coaches** (☎01480 463 792) offers daytrips.

Taxis: Cabco (☎312 444) and **Camtax** (☎313 131). Both 24hr.

Bike Rental: Mike's Bikes, 28 Mill Rd. (☎312 591). £10 per day. £50 deposit. Lock, light, and basket included. Open M-Sa 9am-6pm, Su 10am-4pm.

■ ORIENTATION AND PRACTICAL INFORMATION

Cambridge has two main avenues; the main shopping street starts at **Magdalene Bridge** and becomes **Bridge Street, Sidney Street, Saint Andrew's Street, Regent Street,** and **Hills Road.** The other main thoroughfare starts as **Saint John's Street,** becoming **Trinity Street, King's Parade,** and **Trumpington Street.** From the **Drummer Street** bus station, **Emmanuel Street** leads to the shopping district near the TIC. To get to the center from the train station, turn right onto Hills Rd.

Tourist Information Centre: Wheeler St. (☎09065 862 526; www.tourismcambridge.com), 1 block south of Market Sq. Cycling maps £4.30. Books rooms for £3 plus a 10% deposit. Advance booking hotline (at least 5 days; ☎457 581; M-F 9:30am-4pm). Open M-Sa 10am-5pm, Su 11am-4pm.

Tours: 2hr. **walking tours** of the city and a college or 2 (usually King's) leave from the TIC. Call for times. £8, children £4. Special **Drama Tour** in July and Aug. is led by guides in period dress. Tu 6:30pm. £4.50. **Guide Friday** (☎362 444) runs 1hr. hop-on, hop-off **bus tours** every 15-30min. Apr.-Oct. £7.50, concessions £5.50, children £3.

Budget Travel: STA Travel, 38 Sidney St. (☎366 966). Open M-Tu 9:30am-5:30pm, W 9:30am-5pm, Th 10am-5:30pm, F 9:30am-5:30pm Sa 11am-5pm.

Financial Services: Banks line Market Sq. and St. Andrew's St. **Thomas Cook,** 8 St. Andrew's St. Open M-Tu and Th-Sa 9am-5:30pm, W 10am-5:30pm. **American Express,** 25 Sidney St. (☎08706 001 060). Open M-F 9am-5:30pm, Sa 9am-5pm.

Work Opportunities: Blue Arrow, 40 St. Andrews St. (☎323 272). Year-round temp work in domestic and food service. Arrange early for summer jobs—demand is high.

Pharmacy: Boots, 65-67 Sidney St. (☎350 213). Open M 9am-6pm, Tu 8:45am-6pm, W 8:35am-7pm, Th-F 8:35am-6pm, Sa 8:30am-6pm, Su 11am-5pm.

Launderette: Clean Machine, 22 Burleigh St. (☎566 677). Open M-F 9am-8:30pm, Sa-Su 9am-4pm.

Police: Parkside (☎358 966).

Hospital: Addenbrookes, Long Rd. (☎245 151). Take Cambus C1or C2 from Emmanuel St. (£1), and get off where Hills Rd. intersects Long Rd.

Internet Access: International Telecom Centre, 2 Wheeler St. (☎357 358), across from the TIC. £1 for first 33min., then 3-4p per min.; £1 min. As low as 50p per hr. with student ID. Open daily 9am-10pm. **Jaffa Net Cafe,** 22 Mill Rd. (☎308 380). £2 per hr., £5 for 5hr. 10% student discount. Open daily 10am-10pm.

Post Office: 9-11 St. Andrew's St. Open M-Sa 9am-5:30pm. **Post Code:** CB2 3AA.

ACCOMMODATIONS

Rooms are scarce, making prices high and quality low. Most **B&Bs** aren't in the town center, but some around **Portugal Street** and **Tenison Road** that house students during the academic year open to visitors in July and August.

■ **Tenison Towers Guest House,** 148 Tenison Rd. (☎566 511). Fresh flowers grace airy rooms in this impeccable house 2 blocks from the train station. Breakfast includes homemade bread. Singles and doubles £25-28 per person. Cash only. ❸

Warkworth Guest House, Warkworth Terr. (☎363 682). Sunny ensuite rooms near the bus station for those wishing to skip the walk to the city center. Packed lunch on request. Singles from £39-45; doubles £56-62. MC/V. ❹

Home from Home, 78 Milton Rd. (☎323 555). A 20min. walk from city center. Rooms are stocked with biscuits and mini-toiletries. Singles £50, in winter £40; doubles £65/£60; self-catering with kitchens and lounges £350 per week. AmEx/MC/V. ❹

YHA Cambridge, 97 Tenison Rd. (☎354 601; cambridge@yha.org.uk). A relaxed, welcoming atmosphere, though more showers wouldn't hurt. 100 beds. Well-equipped kitchen, laundry, luggage storage, TV lounge, and **bureau de change.** Internet 50p per 7min. £17.50, under 18 £13.50; English breakfast included. MC/V. ❷

Regency Guest House, 7 Regent Terr. (☎329 626; www.regencyguesthouse.co.uk), a 5min. walk from town center. Combines comfortable, elegant accommodations with an excellent location—rare among Cambridge B&Bs. Singles £48; doubles £68. MC/V. ❹

Highfield Farm Camping Park, Long Rd., Comberton (☎262 308; www.highfieldfarm-touringpark.co.uk). Head west on the A603 (3 mi.), then right on the B1046 (1 mi.), or take Cambus #118 (every 45min.) from Drummer St. Flush toilets and laundry. July-Aug. £7.75-10; May-June and Sept. £7.25-9; Apr. and Oct. £7-8.50. Cash only. ❶

🍴 FOOD

Market Square has bright pyramids of cheap fruit and vegetables. (Open M-Sa 9:30am-4:30pm.) Get **groceries** at **Sainsbury's,** 44 Sidney St. (☎366 891. Open M-Sa 8am-10pm, Su 11am-5pm.) Cheap Indian and Greek fare sates hearty appetites. South of town, **Hills Road** and **Mill Road** brim with good, budget restaurants.

Clown's, 54 King St. (☎355 711). Cheerful staff adds the final dash of color to this humming spot—children's renderings of clowns plaster the walls, as do adoring odes by regulars. Serves a variety of pasta and some more northerly European cuisine (£3-6.50). Open daily 7:30am-midnight. Cash only. ❶

Dojo's Noodle Bar, 1-2 Mill Ln. (☎363 471). Whips out comically enormous plates of noodles, some vegetarian, at warp speed. Everything under £6. Open M-Th noon-2:30pm and 5:30-11pm, F-Su noon-4pm and 5:30-11pm. Cash only. ❶

Rainbow's Vegetarian Bistro, 9a King's Parade (☎321 551; www.rainbowcafe.co.uk). Duck under the rainbow sign. A tiny burrow featuring creative vegan and vegetarian fare, all for £7.25. Open Tu-Sa 10am-10pm; last order 9:30pm. Cash only. ❷

Hobbs Pavilion, Park Terrace (☎367 480; www.hobbspavilion.com). A stylish, homey room with a view across Parker's Piece. English fare with an Indian influence (£10-14). Open daily Apr.-Aug. 11am-11pm; Sept.-Mar. noon-3pm and 6-10pm. AmEx/MC/V. ❸

CB1, 32 Mill Rd. (☎576 306). A student-hangout coffee shop where all of the drinks (£1 regular size) are made right on the counter and the walls are crammed with used books for perusal. Internet 4p per min. Open daily 10am-8pm. Cash only. ❶

Restaurant 22, 22 Chesterton Rd. (☎351 880; www.restaurant22.co.uk.). Continually rotating, carefully designed menu is worth the splurge. 8 tables lend an air of exclusivity and require reservations. 4-course dinner £24.50. Open Tu-Sa from 7pm. Food served until 9:45pm. AmEx/MC/V. ❺

Nadia's, 11 St. John's St. (☎568 336). An uncommonly good bakery with divine smells. Flapjacks (90p-£1.20) and sandwiches (£2) are a brunch unto themselves. Takeaway only. Open daily 8am-5pm. Another branch at 16 Silver St. Cash only. ❶

The Little Tea Room, 1 All Saints' Passage (☎319 393), off Trinity St. Hopelessly pretentious, yet the place to be for afternoon tea. Heroic waitstaff navigates 2 tightly packed rooms to serve tip-top teas. Open M-Sa 10am-5:30pm, Su 1-5:30pm. Cash only. ❶

PUBS

King Street has a diverse collection of pubs and used to host the King St. Run, in which contestants stopped at each of the 13 pubs to down a pint (the winner was the first to cross the finish line on his own two feet). Most stay open 11am-11pm (Su noon-10:30pm). The local brewery, Greene King, supplies many of them.

The Mill, 14 Mill Ln. (☎357 026), off Silver St. Bridge. Patrons infiltrate the riverside park on spring nights for punt- and people-watching. In summer, clientele include the odd student and hordes of international youth. Features a rotating selection of real ales.

The Eagle, 8 Benet St. (☎505 020). Cambridge's oldest pub. Watson and Crick rushed in breathlessly to announce their discovery of DNA—the barmaid insisted they settle their 4-shilling tab before she'd serve them a toast. British and American WWII pilots stood on each other's shoulders to burn their initials into the ceiling of the RAF room.

The Anchor, Silver St. (☎353 554). Another undergrad watering hole crowded day and night. Savor a pint while watching amateur punters collide under Silver St. Bridge. Open M-Sa 11am-11pm, Su noon-10:30pm.

King St. Run, King St. (☎328 900). The quintessential college pub packs in the student crowd amid university kitsch. Open M-Sa 11am-11pm, Su noon-10:30pm.

The Free Press, Prospect Row (☎368 337), behind the police station. Named after an abolitionist rag, now popular with locals. No smoking and no cell phones. Open M-F noon-2:30pm and 6-11pm, Sa noon-3pm and 6-11pm, Su noon-3pm and 7-10:30pm.

The Mitre, 17 Bridge St. (☎358 403). Founded in 1754, this pub stands out for its elegance: patrons eat well-presented pub food (£5.25-7.50) beneath gilt mirrors. Food served M-F noon-3pm and 5-8pm, Sa-Su noon-3pm.

 SIGHTS

Cambridge is an architect's fantasia, packing some of England's most breathtaking monuments into less than a single square mile. The soaring **King's College Chapel** and St. John's postcard-familiar **Bridge of Sighs** are sightseeing staples, while more obscure college courts veil undiscovered treats. Most historic buildings are on the **east bank** of the Cam between Magdalene Bridge and Silver St. The manicured gardens, meadows, and cows of the **Backs** lend a pastoral air to the **west bank.**

The **University of Cambridge** has three eight-week terms: Michaelmas (Oct.-Dec.), Lent (Jan.-Mar.), and Easter (Apr.-June). Visitors can gain access to most colleges daily from 9am to 5:30pm, though many close to sightseers during Easter term, and virtually all are closed during exams (mid-May to mid-June); your best bet is to call ahead (☎331 100). If you have time for only a few colleges, **King's, Trinity, Queens', Christ's, Saint John's,** and **Jesus** should top your list. Porters (bowler-wearing ex-servicemen) maintain security. Those who look like undergrads (no backpack, no camera, and definitely no Cambridge sweatshirt) can often wander freely through the grounds after hours. The fastest way to blow your cover is to trample the sacred **grass** of the courtyards, a privilege reserved for the elite. In summer, most undergrads skip town, leaving it to Ph.D. students and mobs of tourists.

KING'S COLLEGE

King's Parade. ☎331 100. Chapel and grounds open M-Sa 9:30am-4:30pm, Su 10am-5pm. Contact TIC for tours. Listing of services and musical events (£1) available at porter's lodge. Evensong 5:30pm most nights. £4, concessions £3, under 12 free.

EAST ANGLIA

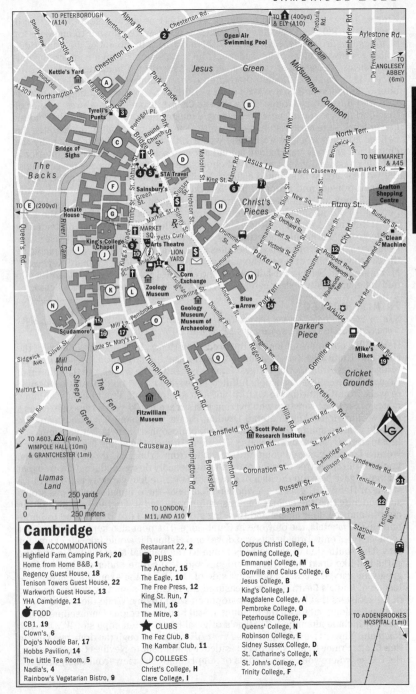

EAST ANGLIA

Cambridge

ACCOMMODATIONS
Highfield Farm Camping Park, **20**
Home from Home B&B, **1**
Regency Guest House, **18**
Tenison Towers Guest House, **22**
Warkworth Guest House, **13**
YHA Cambridge, **21**

FOOD
CB1, **19**
Clown's, **6**
Dojo's Noodle Bar, **17**
Hobbs Pavilion, **14**
The Little Tea Room, **5**
Nadia's, **4**
Rainbow's Vegetarian Bistro, **9**

Restaurant 22, **2**

PUBS
The Anchor, **15**
The Eagle, **10**
The Free Press, **12**
King St. Run, **7**
The Mill, **16**
The Mitre, **3**

CLUBS
The Fez Club, **8**
The Kambar Club, **11**

COLLEGES
Christ's College, **H**
Clare College, **I**

Corpus Christi College, **L**
Downing College, **Q**
Emmanuel College, **M**
Gonville and Caius College, **G**
Jesus College, **B**
King's College, **J**
Magdalene College, **A**
Pembroke College, **O**
Peterhouse College, **P**
Queens' College, **N**
Robinson College, **E**
Sidney Sussex College, **D**
St. Catharine's College, **K**
St. John's College, **C**
Trinity College, **F**

King's College was founded by Henry VI in 1441 as partner school to Eton; it wasn't until 1861 that students from other schools were allowed to compete for scholarships. Ironically, King's is now the most socially liberal of the Cambridge colleges, drawing more of its students from state schools than any other; the college was also the site of student riots in 1968. As a result, Cambridge's best-known college is its least traditional—there are no formal dinners or white-tie balls, and interior corridors are coated with lurid graffiti. Little of this is noticeable to visitors who file into the Gothic **King's College Chapel.** From the southwest corner of the courtyard, you can see where Henry's master mason left off and the Tudors began work—the earlier stone is off-white. The elaborate wall that separates the college grounds from King's Parade was a 19th-century addition; originally the chapel and grounds were hidden behind a row of shops and houses. The interior is a single chamber divided by a carved choir screen. Heralding angels hover against the world's largest fan-vaulted ceiling, described by Wordsworth as a "branching roof self-poised, and scooped into ten thousand cells where light and shade repose." Look for the 15th-century graffiti to the right of the altar and the devilish portrait of a craftsman's estranged wife on the choir screen. Behind the altar hangs Rubens's *Adoration of the Magi* (1639). The canvas has been protected by an electronic alarm since an attack by a crazed chisel-wielder several years ago. Free music recitals often play; schedules are kept at the entrance. As you picnic by the riverbank, think of those who have gone before you: John Maynard Keynes, E. M. Forster, and Salman Rushdie all felt the college's grounds beneath their feet. In mid-June, university degree ceremonies are held in the Georgian **Senate House.**

TRINITY COLLEGE

Trinity St. ☎ *338 400. Chapel and courtyard open daily 10am-5pm. Wren Library open M-F noon-2pm. Easter-Oct. £2, concessions £1, families £4. Nov.-Easter free.*

Henry VIII, not to be outdone by the preceding Henry, intended the College of the Holy and Undivided Trinity (founded 1546) to be the largest and richest in Cambridge. Today Britain's third largest landowner (after the Queen and the Church of England), the college has amply fulfilled his wish. Legend holds that it is possible to walk from Cambridge to Oxford without stepping off Trinity land. The alma mater of Sir Isaac Newton, who lived in E staircase for 30 years, the college has a host of illustrious alumni: literati Dryden, Byron, Tennyson, A. E. Housman, and Nabokov; atom-splitter Ernest Rutherford; philosopher Ludwig Wittgenstein; and Indian statesman Jawaharlal Nehru. The heart of the college, the **Great Court,** is the world's largest enclosed courtyard, reached from Trinity St. through **Great Gate.** Look for the apple tree near the gate: it is supposedly descended from the tree that famously gave Newton the idea of gravity. The castle-like gateway is fronted by a statue of Henry VIII grasping a wooden chair leg—the original scepter was stolen so frequently that the college administration removed it. On the west side of the court stand the dour **chapel** and the **King's Gate tower.** Lord Byron used to bathe nude in the **fountain,** the only one in Cambridge. The poet also kept a bear as a pet (college rules only forbade cats and dogs) and claimed it would take his exams for him. The south side of the court is home to the palatial **Master's Lodge** and the cathedral-like **Great Hall,** where students and deans dine under the hundreds of grotesque carved faces. On the other side of the Hall is the exquisite Renaissance facade of **Nevile's Court.** Newton measured the speed of sound by timing the echo in the cloisters that lead to Sir Christopher's **Wren Library.** While the college's collection has long outgrown the building, it still houses precious manuscripts; those on view include alumnus **A. A. Milne's** original handwritten copies of *Winnie the Pooh* and Newton's own copy of his *Principia.* Pass through the drab, neo-Gothic **New Court** (Prince Charles's former residence), adjacent to Nevile's Court, to get to the Backs, where you can rent **punts** or simply enjoy the view from **Trinity Bridge.**

SAINT JOHN'S COLLEGE. Established in 1511 by Lady Margaret Beaufort, mother of Henry VIII, St. John's centers around a paved plaza rather than a grassy courtyard. The **Bridge of Sighs,** named after the Venetian original, connects the older part of the college with the towering neo-Gothic extravagance of **New Court,** whose silhouette has been likened to a wedding cake. The **School of Pythagoras,** a 12th-century pile of wood and stone thought to be the oldest complete building in Cambridge, hides in St. John's Gardens. No one knows how it got its name. The college also boasts the longest room in the city—the Fellows' Room in Second Court spans 93 ft. and was the site of D-Day planning. *(St. John's St. ☎338 600. Open daily 10am-5:30pm. Evensong 6:30pm most nights. £2, concessions £1.20, families £4.)*

QUEENS' COLLEGE. Founded not once, but twice—by Queen Margaret of Anjou in 1448 and Elizabeth Woodville in 1465—Queens' College has the only unaltered Tudor courtyard in Cambridge. Though rumored to be built on principle alone, the **Mathematical Bridge** has always included screws and bolts. *(Silver St. ☎335 511. Open daily Mar.-Oct. 10am-4:30pm. £1.30.)*

CLARE COLLEGE. Clare's coat-of-arms—golden teardrops ringing a black border—recalls the college's founding in 1326 by thrice-widowed, 29-year-old Lady Elizabeth de Clare. Misery has not laid permanent claim to the college, however: Clare has some of the most cheerful **gardens** in Cambridge. They lie across elegant Clare Bridge. Walk through Wren's **Old Court** for a view of the University Library, where 82 mi. of shelves hold books arranged according to size rather than subject. *(Trinity Ln. ☎333 200. Open daily 10am-4:30pm. £3, under 10 free.)*

CHRIST'S COLLEGE. Founded as "God's-house" in 1448 and renamed in 1505, Christ's has since won fame for its **gardens,** and its association with John Milton and Charles Darwin. Darwin's rooms (unmarked and closed to visitors) were on G staircase in First Court. **New Court,** on King St., is one of Cambridge's most modern structures, with symmetrical concrete walls and dark windows. Bowing to pressure from aesthetically offended Cantabrigians, a wall was built to block the view of the building from all sides except the inner courtyard. *(St. Andrews St. ☎334 900. Gardens open daily term-time 9am-4:30pm, summer 9:30am-noon. Fellows garden open term-time M-F 9:30am-noon and 2-4pm; summer M-F 9:30am-noon. Free.)*

JESUS COLLEGE. Jesus has preserved an enormous amount of medieval work on its spacious grounds. Beyond the high-walled walk called the "Chimny" lies a three-sided court fringed with colorful flowerbeds. Through the arch on the right sit the remains of a gloomy medieval nunnery. *(Jesus Ln. ☎339 339. Courtyard open daily 9am-8pm; open during exams to groups of 3 or fewer.)*

MAGDALENE COLLEGE. Located within a 15th-century Benedictine hostel, Magdalene (MAUD-lin), sometime home of Christian allegorist and Oxford man C. S. Lewis, has retained its religious emphasis. It also retained men-only status until 1988. **Pepys Library,** in the second court, displays the noted statesman and prolific diarist's collections. *(Magdalene St. ☎332 100. Library open Easter-Aug. M-Sa 11:30am-12:30pm and 2:30-3:30pm; Sept.-Easter M-Sa 2:30-3:30pm. Free.)*

SMALLER COLLEGES. Thomas Gray wrote his *Elegy in a Country Churchyard* while staying in **Peterhouse College,** Trumpington St. (☎338 200), the smallest college, founded in 1294. In contrast, the modern medieval brick pastiche of **Robinson College,** across the river on Grange Rd. (☎339 100), is the newest. In 1977, local self-made man David Robinson founded it for the bargain price of £17 million, the largest single gift ever received by the university. **Corpus Christi College,** Trumpington St. (☎338 000), founded in 1352 by the townspeople, contains the oldest courtyard in Cambridge, aptly named Old Court and unaltered since its enclosure. The library, however, maintains the snazziest collection of Anglo-Saxon manuscripts

EAST ANGLIA

in England. Alums include Sir Francis Drake and Christopher Marlowe. The 1347 **Pembroke College,** next to Corpus Christi (☎338 100), harbors the earliest architectural efforts of Sir Christopher Wren and counts Edmund Spenser, Ted Hughes, and Eric Idle among its grads. A chapel designed by Wren dominates the front court of **Emmanuel College,** St. Andrews St. (☎334 200), known as "Emma." John Harvard, benefactor of his own university, studied here; an alum with accomplishments of a different nature is John Cleese. **Gonville and Caius** (KEYs) **College,** Trinity St. (☎332 400), was founded twice, once in 1348 by Edmund Gonville and again in 1557 by John Keys, who chose to take the Latin form of his name, Caius.

MUSEUMS AND CHURCHES

■ **FITZWILLIAM MUSEUM.** A welcome break from academia, the museum fills an immense Neoclassical building, built in 1875 to house Viscount Fitzwilliam's immense and varied collections. Egyptian, Chinese, Japanese, Middle Eastern and Greek antiquities downstairs are joined by a muster of 16th-century German armor. Upstairs, five galleries feature works by Reubens, Monet, and Brueghel. The **Founder's Library** is a must-see, housing an intimate collection of French Impressionists. The drawing room shows William Blake's books and woodcuts. *(Trumpington St. ☎332 900. Open Su noon-5pm, Tu-Sa 10am-5pm. Guided tours Su 2:45pm. Call about lunchtime and evening concerts. Suggested donation £3. Tours £3.)*

OTHER MUSEUMS. Kettle's Yard, at the corner of Castle St. and Northampton St., keeps early 20th-century art. The gallery exhibits rotate, but the house, created in 1956 by Tate curator Jim Ede as "a refuge of peace and order," is a constant. Visitors can wander the house as if it were their own. *(☎352 124. House open Apr.-Sept. Tu-Su 1:30-5 pm; Oct.-Mar. Tu-Su 2-4pm. Gallery open Tu-Su 11:30am-5pm. Free.)* The **Scott Polar Research Institute,** Lensfield Rd., commemorates arctic expeditions with photographic and artistic memorabilia. *(☎336 540. Open Tu-Su 2:30-4pm. Free.)*

CHURCHES. The **Round Church (Holy Sepulchre),** where Bridge St. meets St. John's St., is one of five surviving circular churches in England, built in 1130 (and later rebuilt) on the pattern of the Holy Sepulchre in Jerusalem. *(☎311 602. Open M and Su 1-5pm. Tu-F 10am-5pm, Free.)* **St. Benet's,** a rough Saxon church on Benet St. built in 1050, is the oldest structure in Cambridge. Its spire was knocked down by the Normans. *(☎353 903. Open 7:30am-6:30pm. Free.)* The tower of **Great St. Mary's Church,** off King's Parade, allows the best view of the broad greens and the colleges. Pray that the 12 bells don't ring while you're ascending the 123 tightly packed spiral steps. *(Tower open M-Sa 9:30am-5pm, Su 12:30-5pm. £2, children 75p, families £5.)*

♫ ▒ ENTERTAINMENT AND FESTIVALS

PUNTING. Punting on the Cam is a favored form of hands-on entertainment. Punters take two routes—from Magdalene Bridge to Silver St. or from Silver St. to Grantchester. On the first route (the shorter, busier, and more interesting), you'll pass the colleges and the Backs. To propel your boat, thrust the pole behind the boat into the riverbed and rotate the pole in your hands as you push forward. Be aware that punt-bombing—jumping from bridges into the river alongside a punt, thereby tipping its occupants—is an art form. You can rent at **Tyrell's,** Magdalene Bridge (☎01480 394 941; £12 per hr. plus a £60 deposit), or **Scudamore's,** Silver St. Bridge (☎359 750; M-F £12 per hr. plus a £60 deposit, Sa-Su £15 per hr. plus £70 deposit). Student-punted **tours** (about £10 per person) are another option. Inquire at the TIC for a complete list of companies.

THEATER. The Arts Box Office (☎503 333) handles ticket sales for the **Arts Theatre,** around the corner from the TIC on Pea's Hill, as well as the **ADC Theatre** (Amateur Dramatic Club), Park St., which offers student-produced plays, term-time movies, and the Folk Festival. You can get an earful at the **Corn Exchange,** at the corner of Wheeler St. and Corn Exchange St. across from the TIC, a venue for band, jazz, and classical concerts. (☎357 851. Box office open M-Sa 10am-6pm, until 9pm on performance evenings; Su 6-9pm performance days only. £7.50-24, student standbys half off, day of show only.) The **Cambridge Shakespeare Festival,** in association with the festival at Oxford, features plays through July and August. Tickets are available from the Arts Box Office or at the Corn Exchange (£12, concessions £8).

NIGHTLIFE. At dusk, **evensong** begins in sonorous King's College Chapel, a breathtaking treat for day-worn spirits—not to mention a good way to sneak into the college grounds for free. (M-Sa 5:30pm, Su 3:30pm. Don't forget evensong at other colleges, notably St. John's, Caius, and Clare.) **Pubs** are the core of Cambridge nightlife (p. 320), but clubs are also on the curriculum. Students, bartenders, TIC brochures, and the latest issue of the term-time *Varsity* (20p) are always good sources of information. Small and dim, **The Kambar Club,** 1 Wheeler St., hosts the only indie night in town on Friday, as well as garage, goth, and electronica during the week. (☎842 725. Open M-Sa 10pm-2:30am. Cover £5, students £3.) **The Fez Club,** 15 Market Passage, offers it all from Latin to trance, complete with comfy floor cushions. (☎519 224. Show up early to avoid £2-8 cover. Open M-Th 9pm-2:30am, F-Sa 9pm-3am, Su 8pm-12:30am. Cover M-Th £2-5, F-Sa £6-8, students half sprice M-W; show up early for reduced covers.)

MAY WEEK. In the first two weeks of June, students celebrate the end of the term with May Week, crammed full of concerts, plays, and elaborate balls followed by recuperative riverside breakfasts. The college boat clubs compete in an series of races known as the **bumps.** Crews line up along the river and attempt to ram the boat in front before being bumped from behind. The celebration includes **Footlights Revue,** a collection of comedy skits; performers have included then-undergrads, future *Monty Python* stars John Cleese, Eric Idle, and Graham Chapman.

FESTIVALS. Midsummer Fair, dating from the 16th century, appropriates the Midsummer Common for five days in the third week of June. The free **Strawberry Fair** (www.strawberry-fair.org), on the first Saturday in June, attracts a crowd with food, music, and body piercing. **Summer in the City** and **Camfest** brighten the last two weeks of July with a series of concerts and special exhibits culminating in a huge weekend celebration, the **Cambridge Folk Festival** (☎357 851). Book tickets well in advance (about £38); camping on the grounds is £5-18 extra.

◪ DAYTRIPS FROM CAMBRIDGE

GRANTCHESTER

To reach Grantchester Meadows from Cambridge, take the path following the river. Grantchester village lies 1 mi. from the meadows; ask the way or follow the blue bike path signs (45min. by foot). If you have the energy to paddle your way, rent a punt or canoe. Or hop on Stagecoach Cambus #118 (9-11 per day, round-trip £1.25).

In 1912, poet Rupert Brooke wrote "Grantchester! Ah Grantchester! There's peace and holy quiet there." His words hold true today, as Grantchester is still a mecca for Cambridge literary types. The gentle Cam and swaying seas of grass rejuvenate after the university's bustle. Brooke's home at the **Old Vicarage** is now owned by bad-boy novelist Lord Jeffrey Archer and closed to the public. The weathered and intimate 14th-century **Parish Church of St. Andrew and St. Mary,** on Millway, is not to be missed. The main village pub, the **Rupert Brooke ❷,** 2 Broadway, is a nice place to sit down after a long hike. Boasting a new chef, the pub is striving to improve the reputation of British cuisine, and doing a rather good job of it. (☎840 295. Open daily 11am-11pm. Food served all day (£8-10).) Wend your way to the idyllic ▓**Orchard Tea Gardens ❶**, 45 Mill Way, once a haunt of the "neo-Pagans," a Grantchester offshoot of the famous Bloomsbury Group. Outdoor plays are occasionally performed on summer evenings; ask at the Cambridge TIC. (☎845 788. Light lunches £3-6. Open M-Th 9:30am-6pm, F-Sa 9:30am-7pm.)

ANGLESEY ABBEY

6 mi. northeast of Cambridge on the B1102 (signposted from the A14). Buses #111 and 122 run from Drummer St. (25min., 1 per hr.); ask to be let off at Lode Crossroads. ☎/fax 811 200. House open Apr.-Oct. W-Su and bank holidays 1-5pm. Gardens open 10:30am-5:30pm; last admission 4:30pm. £6.60, children £3.30. Winter Walk Garden Jan.-Mar. and Nov.-Dec. W-Su 10:30am-4:30pm or dusk if earlier. £4.10, children £2.05.

Northeast of Cambridge, 12th-century Anglesey Abbey has been remodeled to house the priceless exotica of the first Lord Fairhaven. One of the niftiest clocks in the known universe sits inconspicuously on the bookcase beyond the library's fireplace, but don't worry if you miss it—there are 55 other timepieces to enjoy along with a multitude of bizarre tokens and trifles. In the 100-acre gardens, trees punctuate lines of clipped hedges and manicured lawns.

WIMPOLE HALL

Bus #175 from Drummer St. (35min., £2). Hall ☎207 257. Open Apr.-Nov. Tu-Th and Sa-Su 1-5pm. £6.60, children £3.20. Home Farm ☎207 257. Open Apr.-Nov. Tu-Th and Sa-Su, as well as F in July, 10:30am-5pm. Farm £5.10, children £3.20. Hall and farm £9/£5.

Cambridgeshire's most elegant mansion lies 10 mi. southwest of Cambridge. The hall holds works by Gibbs, Flitcroft, and Joane; outside, an intricate Chinese bridge crosses a lake set in 60 acres of **gardens** designed by Capability Brown. **Wimpole's Home Farm** brims with Longhorn cattle, Soay sheep, and Tamworth pigs.

AUDLEY END AND SAFFRON WALDEN

Trains leave Cambridge 1 per hr. for Audley End. ☎01799 522 842. House open Apr.-Sept. M and W-Su noon-5pm; Mar. and Oct. W-Su 11am-4pm. Grounds open daily Apr.-Sept. 10am-6pm; Mar. and Oct. 10am-5pm; last admission 1hr. before close. £8.50, concessions £6.40, children £4.30, families £21.30. Grounds only £4.50/£3.40/£2.30/£11.30. Free 15min. talk in the Great Hall. Free 1hr. guided tours, 10 per day. TIC ☎01799 510 444. Open Apr.-Oct. M-Sa 9:30am-5:30pm and Aug. Su 10am-1:30pm; Nov.-Mar. M-Sa 10am-5pm.

The house "too big for a king" proves that even the monarchy has its limits. The magnificent Jacobean hall is but a quarter of Audley End's former size—it once extended down to the river, where part of the Cam was rerouted by Capability Brown. The grand halls display case after case of stuffed critters, including some extinct species. One signposted mile east of Audley End is the old market town **Saffron Walden,** best known for the "pargetting" (plaster molding) of its Tudor buildings and its two mazes, a Victorian hedge maze and an ancient earthen maze. The **Tourist Information Centre** is on Market Sq. Rest at the **YHA hostel ❶**, 1 Myddylton Pl. (☎01799 523 117. Lockout 10am-5pm. Curfew 11pm. Open daily July-Aug.; Apr.-June and Sept. to Oct. Tu-Sa; Mar. F-Sa. £10.60, under 18 £7.20. MC/V.)

ELY ☎01353

The prosperous town of Ely (EEL-ee) was an island until steam power drained the surrounding fenlands in the early 19th century, creating a region of rich farmland. Legend has it that the city got its name when St. Dunstan transformed local monks into eels for their lack of piety. A more likely story claims that "Elig" (Eel Island) was named for the slitherers that once infested the surrounding waters. Ely Cathedral, the "great ship of the fens," is both a destination in its own right and a quiet sanctuary from which to sortie into surrounding Cambridgeshire.

🖅🔃 TRANSPORTATION AND PRACTICAL INFORMATION. Ely is the junction for trains (☎08457 484 950) between London (1¼hr., 2 per hr., £20.10) and various points in East Anglia, including Cambridge (15min., 3 per hr., round-trip £3.70) and Norwich (1hr., 2 per hr., £10.50). Cambus (☎01223 423 554) #X9 arrives at Market St. from Cambridge (30min., 1 per hr., £3.40). Walking from Cambridge to Ely is also possible, a beautiful 17mi. trek through the flat fens that is accessible to novice hikers. Ask at the TIC in Cambridge or Ely for a copy of *The Fen Rivers Way* (£3).

Ely's two major streets—High Street and Market Street—run parallel to the cathedral; the Cromwell House and some shops are on St. Mary's Street. To reach the cathedral and Tourist Information Centre from the train station, walk up Station Rd. and continue up Back Hill. The TIC books rooms for £2 plus a 10% deposit; call at least two days ahead. (☎662 062. Open daily Apr.-Oct. 10am-5:30pm; Nov.-Mar. Su-F 11am-4pm, Sa 10am-5pm.) They also sell a combination ticket, the Passport to Ely, that lets you into Ely Cathedral, Cromwell House, Ely Museum, and the Stained Glass Museum (£11, concessions £8.70, children free). Other services include: the police, Nutholt Ln. (☎01223 358 966); Prince of Wales Hospital, Lynn Rd. (☎652 013); Internet access at the library, 6 The Cloisters, just off Market Pl. (☎616 158; free to search the web, 50p per 10min for email); and the post office, in Lloyd's Chemist on 19 High St. (☎669 946; open M-F 9am-5:30pm, Sa 9am-1pm). Post Code: CB7 4LQ.

🔃🄲 ACCOMMODATIONS AND FOOD. B&B options include The Post House ❸, 12a Egremont St., which has comfortable rooms and a pleasant, homey decor. (☎667 184. Singles £23; doubles £46, ensuite £54. Cash only.) Close to the train station and river and with 16th-century architecture, Mr. and Mrs. Friend-Smith's ❸, 31 Egremont St., lets doubles with views of the garden and the cathedral. (☎663 118. Doubles £52. Cash only.) At Jane's B&B ❸, 82 Broad St., stay in a homey flat complete with kitchen. (☎667 609. £20 per person. Cash only.) Camp among spuds and sugar beets with a cathedral view at Braham Farm ❶, Cambridge Rd., off the A10, 1 mi. from the city center. (☎662 386. £2.50. Electricity £1.50. Cash only.)

Most shops, as they have for centuries, close on Tuesday afternoons in winter. Stock up on provisions at the market in Market Pl. (Open Th and Sa 8am-3pm.) Waitrose Supermarket, Brays Ln., hides behind a Georgian facade. (☎668 800. Open M-Tu and Sa 8:30am-6pm, W-Th 8:30am-8pm, F 8:30am-9pm, Su 10am-4pm.) The Almonry ❷, just off the corner of High St. and Brays Ln., serves basics (£6-7) to the well-heeled in a garden right beneath the cathedral. (☎666 360. Open M-Sa 10am-5pm, Su 11am-5pm. MC/V.) Rubber boots and red suspenders have been replaced with art exhibits at The Old Fire Engine House ❸, 25 St. Mary's St., which bastes, braises, and burnishes the day's local produce. Appropriately enough, smoking is not allowed. (☎662 582. Entrees £15. Open M-Sa 10:30am-5:30pm and 7:30-9pm, Su 12:30-5:30pm. MC/V.) The Steeplegate ❶, 16-18 High St., serves tea and snacks (£2-7) in two rooms built over a medieval undercroft. (☎664 731. Open June-Oct. M-Sa 10am-5pm, Nov.-May M-F 10am-4:30pm and Sa 10am-5pm. MC/V.) The Minster Tavern ❶, Minster Pl., opposite the cathedral to the northwest, is popular for lunch. (☎652 901. Mains £5-6. Open M-F 11am-11pm, Sa noon-10:30pm. AmEx/MC/V.)

🄶 SIGHTS. The towers of massive ▧Ely Cathedral are impossible to miss. The Saxon princess St. Etheldreda founded a monastery on the site in 673; early Norman masons took a century to throw up the nave; and Victorian artists painted the ceiling and completed the stained glass. The present Octagon, an altar topped by the lantern tower, replaced the original tower, which collapsed in 1322. The eight-sided cupola appears to burst into mid-air but is held up by eight stone pillars. In the south transept lies the tomb of the Dean of Ely, Humphrey Tyndall, an eternal PR boost for the monarchy: heir to the throne of Bohemia, Humphrey refused the kingship, declaring that he'd "rather be Queen Elizabeth's subject than a foreign prince." Don't overlook the 215 ft.tiled **floor maze** at your feet. Keep an eye out, too, for the tomb of one of Ely's former bishops, whose pose flaunts his bony corpse. (☎667 735. Open daily Easter-Sept. 7am-7pm; Oct.-Easter M-F 7:30am-6pm, Su 7:30am-5pm. Free guided tours 4 times per day, at 10:45am, 1pm, 2:15pm and 3:15pm. Octagon tours Apr.-Oct. 4 per day; £4, concessions £3.50. West Tower tours Apr.-Oct. One each on Tu, Th, F; call ahead. £3.50/£2.50. Evensong M-Sa 5:30pm, Su 3:45pm. £4.80/£4.20.)

The brilliant **Stained Glass Museum** overlooks the cathedral's nave and details the history of the art form while displaying over a hundred of its finest examples. (☎660 347; www.stainedglassmuseum.com. Open Easter-Oct. M-F 10:30am-5pm, Sa 10:30am-5:30pm, Su noon-6pm; Nov.-Easter M-F 10:30am-4:30pm, Sa 10:30am-5pm, Su noon-4:30pm. Last admission 30min. before closing. £3.50, concessions £2.50, families £7.) At the **brass rubbing center,** visitors can use chalk and paper to rub out the brass engravings in the **cathedral** floor; materials cost £2-6.50. (☎660 345. open M-Sa 10:30am-4pm, Su noon-3pm.) Beautiful monastic buildings around the cathedral are still in use: the **infirmary** houses one of the resident canons, and the **bishop's palace** is a home for disabled children. The other buildings are used by the **King's School,** one of England's older public (read: private) schools.

For an architectural tour of Ely, follow the path outlined in the TIC's free *Eel Trail* pamphlet, which also notes artwork related to the eel. **Ely Museum,** at the Bishop's Gaol on the corner of Market St. and Lynn Rd., tells the story of the fenland city. (☎666 655. Open in summer M-Sa 10:30am-5pm, Su 1-5pm; in winter M-Sa 10:30am-4pm. £3, concessions £2.) **Oliver Cromwell's House,** 29 St. Mary's St., has been retroactively immortalized with wax figures, 17th-century decor, and a "haunted" bedroom. Fish and chips will look positively gourmet after a perusal of Lady Cromwell's recipes. (☎662 062. Open daily Apr.-Oct. 10am-5:30pm; Nov.-Mar. M-F, Su 11am-4pm, Sa 10am-5pm. £3.75, concessions £3.25, children £2.50.)

NORFOLK

KING'S LYNN
☎01553

King's Lynn was one of England's foremost 16th-century ports. Five hundred years later, the once mighty current of the Great Ouse (OOZE; as in slime) River has slowed to a leisurely flow, and the town has slowed its pace to match. The dockside city borrows its Germanic look from trading partners such as Hamburg and Bremen; the earth tones of the flat East Anglian countryside meet with somber red-brick facades. King's Lynn slumbers early and heavily, and the sights can be dry, but the town makes a perfect stopover for hikers exploring the region.

🖪🖬 TRANSPORTATION AND PRACTICAL INFORMATION. Trains (☎08457 484 950) come to the **station** on Blackfriars Rd. from: **Cambridge** (50min., 2 per hr., £8.20); **London King's Cross** (1½hr., 2 per hr., £24.30); **Peterborough** (1¾hr., 2 per hr., £7.60). **Buses** arrive at the **Vancouver Centre** (office open M-F 8:30am-5pm, Sa 8:30am-noon and 1-5pm). **First Eastern Counties** (☎01603 660 553) buses travel from **Norwich** (1½hr., 1 per hr., £6.50) and **Peterborough** (1¼hr., 1 per hr., £6). **National Express** (☎08705 808 080) runs daily from **London** (1 per day, 4hr., £13.00).

The **Tourist Information Centre** in the Custom House, on the corner of King St. and Purfleet St., 10min. from the train station, books rooms for a 10% deposit; take a left out of the station and a right onto Blackfriars St., which becomes New Conduit St. and then Purfleet St. (☎763 044. Open M-Sa 9:30am-5pm, Su 10:15am-4:30pm.) Buy National Express tickets from **West Norfolk Travel,** 2 King St. (☎772 910. Open Apr.-Oct. M-Sa 9:15am-5pm, Su 10am-5pm; daily Nov.-Mar. 10:30am-4pm.) Other services include: the **police,** at the corner of St. James and London Rd. (☎691 211); the **hospital,** on Gayton Rd. (☎613 613); free **Internet access** at the **library** (☎772 568; open M, W, and F 9am-8pm, Tu, Th, and Sa 9am-5pm); and the **post office** (☎08457 223 344) at Baxter's Plain on the corner of Broad St. and New Conduit St. (Open M-F 9am-5:30pm, Sa 9am-12:30pm.) **Post Code:** PE30 1YB.

ⵌ ACCOMMODATIONS AND FOOD. The quayside ⵌ**YHA King's Lynn ❶,** a short walk from the train and bus stations (keep your eyes peeled—it's easy to miss), occupies part of 16th-century Thoresby College, on College Ln., opposite the Old Gaol House. The river view and friendly staff make this your best bet. (☎772 461. No smoking. Lockout 10am-5pm. Curfew 11pm. Open May-Aug.; Apr. and Sept.-Oct. W-Su. Dorms £9.25, under 18 £6.40. MC/V.) **B&Bs** are a hike from city center; the less expensive ones span **Gaywood Road** and **Tennyson Avenue.** Eight gracious rooms comprise Victorian **Fairlight Lodge ❸,** 79 Goodwins Rd. (☎762 234. £19-27 per person. Cash only.) Super-soft beds dominate the (nearly all ensuite) rooms at **Maranatha Guest House ❸,** 115-117 Gaywood Rd., and a pool table livens up the lounge. (☎774 596. Singles £30, doubles £20-25 per person. MC/V.)

King's Lynn restaurants operate on their own time; many close on Sunday. Several supermarkets congregate around the Vancouver Centre. For fresh fruit, visit the markets held at larger **Tuesday Market Place,** on the north end of High St., or at **Saturday Market Place** on the south end. Costumed servers present aromatic Thai dishes (£4-6) at **The Thai Orchid ❸,** 33-39 St. James St. (☎767 013. Open M-Sa noon-2pm and 6-11:30pm, Su noon-2pm and 6-10:30pm. MC/V.) Inexpensive Italian meals (£5-8) await at **Antonio's Wine Bar ❷,** Baxter's Plain, off Tower St. (☎772 324. Open Tu-Sa noon-3pm and 6:30-11pm; last order 9:30pm. MC/V.) Quiet **Archers ❶,** a few steps up Purfleet St. from the TIC, serves varied lunches (£3-6) and teas. (☎764 411. Open M-Tu 9am-4pm, W-Sa 9am-4:30pm. Cash only.)

ⵌⵌ SIGHTS AND ENTERTAINMENT. The sights of King's Lynn are modest, but a **walking tour** is still rewarding. The *King's Lynn Town Walk* guide (30p) is sold at the TIC. The Gaol House is the starting point for 1½hr. guided walks of the town (2pm, 4 days per week; £3, concessions £2.50, children £1). At the **Tales of the Old Gaol House,** Saturday Market Pl., try out the stocks or climb up to the stake for a taste of 17th-century justice. The **Regalia Room** displays the 14th-century King John Cup and other treasures in the undercroft. (☎774 297. Open Apr.-Oct. M-W and F-Sa 10:30am-5pm, Su noon-5pm; Nov.-Mar. M-Tu and F-Sa 10:30am-4pm, Su noon-4pm. £2.50, concessions £2.20, children £1.80.) **St. Margaret's Church,** also on Saturday Market Pl., was built in 1101. Peaceful **Tower Gardens** ensconce Greyfriars Tower on one side of St. James' St., while **The Walks** stretch away on the other side. The **Town House Museum of Lynn Life,** 46 Queen St., leads through medieval, Tudor, Victorian, and 1950s reconstructions. (☎773 450. Open May-Sept. M-Sa 10am-5pm, Su 2pm-5pm; Oct.-Apr. M-Sa 10am-4pm. £1.80, concessions 90p.)

The **Corn Exchange** at Tuesday Market Pl. sells tickets for music, dance, and theater events. (☎764 864. Open M-Sa 10am-6pm; on performance nights also Su 1hr. prior to show. Shows usually 7:30 or 8pm.) Near Tuesday Market Pl., the 15th-century **Guildhall of St. George,** 27-29 King St., is said to be the last surviving building where Shakespeare appeared in one of his own plays. It now hosts the **King's Lynn Arts Centre.** (☎774 725 or 764 864. Open M-F 10am-2pm. Free.) The Guildhall brings the **King's Lynn Festival** to town in the last two weeks of July, offering classical and jazz music, opera, ballet, puppet shows, and films. Get schedules at the Festival Office, 5 Thoresby College, Queen St. (Info ☎767 557, tickets 764 864. Box office open M-Sa 10am-6pm. Tickets £3-10.) The simultaneous free **Festival Too** offers a wide range of bands performing in Tuesday Market Place.

▶ DAYTRIPS FROM KING'S LYNN

SANDRINGHAM. Sandringham has been a royal country retreat since 1862. The Edwardian interior houses halls of weaponry and Spanish tapestries, while the grounds feature neat gardens and a lake. The museum touts the big-game trophies of King George V and royal cars owned by Edward VII in 1900, Prince Charles in 1990, and Princes William and Harry today. George described the site as "dear old Sandringham, the place I love better than anywhere else in the world." Its 600 acres are open to the public when not in use by the royals. Visit during the **flower show** in the last week of July. It's usually closed in June; ask at the King's Lynn TIC. *(10 mi. north of King's Lynn. First Eastern Counties bus #411 arrives from King's Lynn (25 min.; M-Sa 9 per day, Su 1 per hr.; round-trip £3.50). ☎01553 612 908. Open Apr.-Sept. 11am-4:45pm, Oct. 11am-3pm; museum and gardens close Apr.-Sept. 5pm, Oct. 4pm. £6.50, concessions £5, children £4, families £17. Museum and grounds only £4.50/3.50/2.50/11.50.)*

CASTLE RISING. This solid keep, atop a giant mound and ringed by an earthwork bank, sheltered Queen Isabella, "She-Wolf of France," after she plotted the murder of her husband, Edward II. The beautiful view and informative tour make the easy trip worthwhile. *(First Eastern Counties buses run from King's Lynn (#411-413, 15min., M-Sa 17 per day; #415, 15min., Su 11 per day; round-trip £3.20). ☎01553 631 330; www.castlerising.com. Open daily Apr.-Sept. 10am-6pm; Oct. daily 10am-6pm or dusk; Nov.-Mar. W-Su 10am-4pm. Admission and audio tour £3.25, concessions £2.50, children £1.60, families £9.)*

HOUGHTON HALL. Built in the mid-18th century for Robert Walpole, England's first prime minister, Houghton Hall is a magnificent example of Palladian architecture. Rooms were intended to reflect the grandeur of Walpole's office and still include original tapestries, paintings, and "the most sublime bed ever designed." The hall includes one of the world's largest model soldier museums. *(14 mi. northeast of King's Lynn, off the A148 toward Cromer; easily reached by car; otherwise take the X98 bus and ask the driver to stop at Fakenham, then follow signs for a mile. ☎01485 528 569; www.houghtonhall.com. Open mid-Apr. to Sept. W-Th, Su 2-5:30pm; last entry 5pm. £6.50, children £3.)*

THE NORTHERN NORFOLK COAST

The northern Norfolk Coast is a tranquil expanse of British seashore where only the occasional windmill or mansion punctuates untamed beaches, salt marshes, and boggy bays. Those with eight to twelve days to spare can traverse the linked 93 mi. of the **Norfolk Coast Path** and **Peddar's Way** (p. 316). The Peddar's Way, an old Roman road to the coast, begins in **Knettishall Heath Country Park,** extending through **Little Cressingham, North Peckenham,** and the medieval ruins of **Castle Acre,** meeting the Norfolk Coast Path between **Hunstanton** and **Brancaster.** The **Norfolk Coast Path** begins 16 mi. north of King's Lynn at **Hunstanton,** stretches east to **Wells-next-the-Sea** and then **Sheringham** and the **Norfolk Broads** (p. 336), finishing in **Cromer.** The trail and its villages are also fine daytrips. The **Norfolk Coast Hopper,** Norfolk Green Coach #36 (☎0845 300 6116), makes daily stops between Hunstanton and Sheringham (1½hr.; 1 per hr. in summer, fewer in winter; all-day ticket £5).

Non-hikers can see the coast via alternative modes of transportation: **Coastal Voyager** runs sea trips from Southwold (☎07887 525 082; £15 per hr., children £8), and **Skyride Balloons** (☎07000 110 210) offers the best seaviews of all.

The highlight of the coast is ◙**Blakeney Point Seal Colony.** Though accessible by a 4 mi. footpath from Cley-next-the-Sea, the seals would rather their admirers visit by boat; **Temple's Ferry Service** runs trips from Morston Harbor. (☎01263 740 791. 1½hr. £6, children £4.) In Hunstanton, on the Southern Promenade, the **Hunstanton Sea Life Sanctuary and Aquarium** rehabilitates injured and abandoned seals. (☎01485 533 576; www.sealsanctuary.co.uk. Open daily July-Aug. 10am-5pm; Apr.-June, Sept.-Oct. 10am-4pm; Jan.-Mar., Nov.-Dec. 10am-3pm. £6.50, children £4.50.)

For a taste of luxury, visit **Holkham Hall,** 2 mi. west of Wells-next-the-Sea, the Palladian home of the Earl of Leicester. Marvel at the massive marble hall before getting lost in the amusing **Bygones Museum,** which assembles over 4000 knickknacks from the family's past. (☎01328 710 227. Open May.-Sept. M and Th-Su 12-5pm. Hall and museum £10, children £5. Hall only £6.50, children £3.25. Museum only £5/ 2.50.)

The Norfolk Coast is an easy daytrip from **King's Lynn,** though **Hunstanton,** at the western edge, is a more intimate touring base. Buses #410-413 run from Vancouver Centre in King's Lynn to Hunstanton (45min.; M-Sa 2 per hr., Su 1 per hr.; roundtrip £5.10). For details on the Northern Norfolk Coast, maps, and bus schedules, consult the Hunstanton **Tourist Information Centre,** Town Hall, The Green. (24hr. ☎01485 532 610. Open daily Apr.-Sept. 10am-5pm; Oct.-Mar. 10:30am-4pm.) *Walking the Peddar's Way and Norfolk Coast Path with Weavers Way* is a decent guide and accommodations list (£2.70). The **National Trail Office,** 6 Station Rd., Wells-next-the-Sea, has expert advice on hiking the Norfolk Coast Path. (☎01328 711 533. Open daily 9am-5pm.) On the coast, Hunstanton's **YHA hostel ❶,** 15 Avenue Rd., is a 5min. walk from the bus station—take Sandringham Rd. south, then turn right on Avenue Rd. A comfy TV lounge, laundry, and patio await. (☎01485 532 061. Open Apr.-Oct.; Mar. Tu-W. Dorms £11.80, under 18 £8.50. MC/V.)

NORWICH ☎01603

The dizzying streets of Norwich (NOR-idge) wind outward from the Norman castle, past the cathedral, and to the scattered fragments of the 14th-century city wall. Though Norwich retains the hallmarks of an ancient city, a university and active art community ensure that it is also thoroughly modern. Clearly, the hum of "England's city in the country" has not yet abated, with a daily market almost a millennium old still thriving alongside busy art galleries and nightlife.

🚍 TRANSPORTATION

Easily accessible by bus, coach, or train, Norwich makes a decent base for touring both urban and rural East Anglia, particularly the Norfolk Broads.

Trains: Station at the corner of Riverside and Thorpe Rd., 15min. from the city center (bus 40p). Ticket window open M-Sa 4:45am-8:45pm, Su 6:45am-8:45pm. Information desk open M-Sa 9am-7pm, Su 10:15am-5:30pm. **Anglia Railways** (☎08457 484 950) from: **Great Yarmouth** (30min., 2 per hr., £4.20); **London Liverpool Street** (2½hr., 3 per hr., £35.80); **Peterborough** (1½hr., 2 per hr., £12.70).

Buses: Station (☎660 553) on Surrey St., off St. Stephen St., southwest of the castle. Open M-F 8am-5:30pm, Sa 9am-5:15pm. **National Express** (☎08705 808 080) from **London** (3hr., 5 per day, £14). **Cambridge Coach Services** (☎01223 423 900) from

EAST ANGLIA

EAST ANGLIA

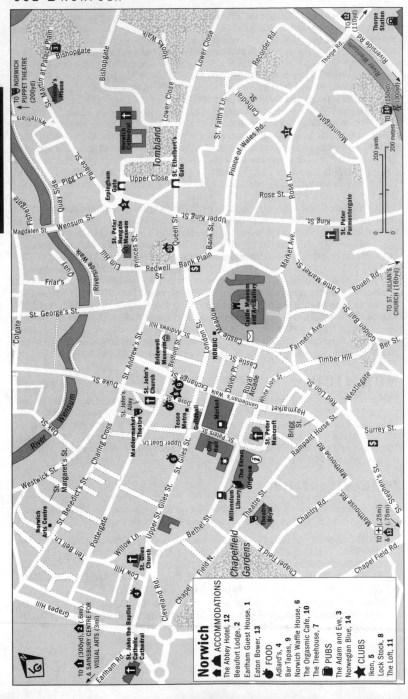

Norwich

▲ ACCOMMODATIONS
The Abbey Hotel, 12
Beaufort Lodge, 2
Earlham Guest House, 1
Eaton Bower, 13

◆ FOOD
Adlard's, 4
Bar Tapas, 9
Norwich Waffle House, 6
The Orgasmic Cafe, 10
The Treehouse, 7

■ PUBS
The Adam and Eve, 3
Norwegian Blue, 14

★ CLUBS
Ikon, 5
Lock Stock, 8
The Loft, 11

Cambridge (#74; 2hr., 4 per day, £12). **First Eastern Counties** (☎08456 020 121) travels to **King's Lynn, Peterborough,** and other Norfolk towns; **Ranger tickets** give 1 day of unlimited travel (£6, children £4, seniors £4.70, families £11.50).

Taxis: Express Taxis (☎767 626). 24hr.

ORIENTATION AND PRACTICAL INFORMATION

Although sights are fairly close together, twisting streets are bound to confuse.

Tourist Information Centre: The Forum, Millennium Plain, Bethel St. (☎727 927; www.norwich.gov.uk). Books rooms for a £3 charge plus a 10% deposit. Open Apr.-Oct. M-Sa 9:30am-6:30pm, Su 10:30am-4:30pm; Nov.-Mar M-Sa 9:30am-6:30pm, Su 10am-5:30pm. Offers 1½hr. **walking tours** Apr.-Oct. £2.50, children £1.

Financial Services: Thomas Cook, 15 St. Stephen's St. (☎241 200). Open M-Tu and Th-F 9am-5:30pm, W 10am-5:30pm, Sa 10am-4pm.

Launderette: Laundromat, 179a Dereham Rd. (☎626 685). Change and soap (20p) available. Open M-Sa 8am-8pm, Su 10am-7pm; last wash 1½hr. before close.

Pharmacy: Boots, Unit 5 Riverside Retail Park (☎662 894). Open M-F 8:30am-8:30pm, Sa 8:30am-6pm, Su 10:30am-4:30pm.

Police: Bethel St. (☎768 769).

Hospital: Norfolk and Norwich University Hospital, Colney Ln., Norwich (☎286 286), at the corner of Brunswick Rd. and St. Stephen's Rd.

Internet Access: Library (☎774 774), next to the TIC. Free access upstairs, and downstairs at 6 "Express Terminals." Open M and W-F 9am-8pm, Tu 10am-8pm, Sa 9am-5pm. Express open M and W-F 9am-9:30pm, Tu 10am-9:30pm, Sa 9am-8:30pm, and Su 10:30am-4:30pm. Otherwise, get a list of cyber cafes at the TIC.

Post Office: Castle Mall (☎08457 223 344). Open M-Sa 9:30am-5:30pm. **Post Code:** NR1 3DD.

ACCOMMODATIONS

Lodgings (£17-20) are located on **Stracey Road,** a 5min. walk from the train station. Turn left onto Thorpe Rd., walk two blocks from the bridge, and go right onto Stracey Rd. Many pleasant **B&Bs** (£18-24) line **Earlham Road** and **Unthank Road,** but they're at least 20min. west of downtown and farther from the train station. More B&Bs are on **Dereham Road;** follow St. Benedict's St., which becomes Dereham.

The Abbey Hotel, 16 Stracey Rd. (☎/fax 612 915), 5min. from the train station up Thorpe Rd. A TV and wash basin await in every quiet room of this clean, yellow building—as do cocoa and biscuits. Singles £22-32; doubles £42-56. Cash only. ❸

Earlham Guest House, 147 Earlham Rd. (☎454 169; www.earlhamguesthouse.co.uk). Take bus #26 or 27 from city center to The Mitre pub or walk 15min across town. Tasteful and clean rooms. No smoking. Singles £26; ensuite doubles £27. AmEx/MC/V. ❸

Beaufort Lodge, 62 Earlham Rd. (☎ 627 928; www.beaufortlodge.com). This newly polished B&B provides plushly carpeted rooms with comfortable furnishings, TV, and more space than you'll know what to do with. Hosts feed you tea, coffee, and cookies after fetching you from the station. No smoking. Singles £45; doubles £55-60. Cash only. ❹

Eaton Bower, 20 Mile End Rd. (☎462 204). Make sure to set your alarm; guests here have a tendency to oversleep in the uncannily comfortable beds. Mornings are greeted with breakfast and classical music overlooking the garden, and every room has a comprehensive folder of maps and brochures. Singles £35; doubles £44-54. Cash only. ❹

⊠ ⊠ FOOD AND PUBS

In the heart of the city, just a stone's throw from the castle, spreads one of England's largest and oldest **open-air markets.** (Open M-Sa roughly 8:30am-4:30pm.) **Tesco Metro** is on St. Giles St. (Open M-Sa 7:30am-8pm, Su 11am-5pm.)

▨ **The Treehouse,** 14 Dove St. (☎ 763 258). Menu has creative vegetarian meals (£6.80) and snacks (£5.20), though huge "snack meals" are deceptively named. Open M-W 10am-4pm, Th-Sa 10am-9pm; food served from 11:30am. Cash only. ❷

Norwich Waffle House, 39 St. Giles St. (☎612 790), serves buttery Belgian waffles smothered in everything from chocolate mousse to tuna and bean sprouts. 2 course lunch just £5.75. Open M-Sa 10am-10pm, Su 11am-10pm. MC/V. ❷

The Orgasmic Cafe, Queen St. (☎ 760 650; www.orgasmic-cafe.com). Go ahead, gasp stylishly as you polish off a meal of freshly baked bread stuffed with salmon, spinach, and *creme fraiche* (£5.50), or one of many inventive pizzas (£7-8). Open M-Sa 10:30am-11pm, Su 11am-10:30pm. Cash only. ❷

Adlard's, 79 Upper Giles St. (☎633 522; www.adlards.co.uk). Norwich's #1 place for haute cuisine. Superbly prepared French-English fusion is well worth the price (entrees £19-21). Decor evokes an airy living room or Parisian cafe. Reserve ahead. Open M 7:30-10:30pm, Tu-Sa 12:30-1:45pm and 7:30-10:30pm. AmEx/MC/V. ❺

Bar Tapas, 16-20 Exchange St. (☎ 764 077). Look for the brightly-colored bull's head. Take your pick of Spanish tapas (from £2.50)—3 make a hearty dinner. Lunch £5, entrees £8.25-12. Open M-W 10am-6pm, Th-Sa 10am-11pm. AmEx/MC/V. ❷

The Adam and Eve, Bishopgate (☎667 423), behind the cathedral at the end of Riverside Walk. Norwich's first pub (est. 1249) is now its most tranquil, hugging the wall around the cathedral yard. Open M-Sa 11am-11pm, Su noon-10:30pm. Cash only. ❶

⊙ SIGHTS

▨ **ORIGINS.** This ultra-interactive history complex, with three floors of exhibits and consoles, will fascinate the whole family. Settlers as diverse as Vikings and WWII American soldiers are treated with equal measures of humor and hard fact. An 18min. film shows the hidden sights of Norfolk and features a 180 degree panoramic screen. *(In the Forum, next to the TIC.* ☎727 922. *Open Apr.-Oct. M-Sa 10am-5:45pm, Su 11am-4:45pm; Nov.-Mar. M-Sa 10am-5:15pm, Su 11am-4:45pm. £6, concessions £4.)*

NORWICH CASTLE MUSEUM AND ART GALLERY. The original castle was built in the early 12th century by the Norman monarch Henry I, intent on subduing the Saxon city. Its current exterior dates from an 1830s restoration, though a recent £12 million refurbishment was the largest in the castle's history. The Castle Museum has a hands-on exhibit, and the archaeology gallery displays relics of Queen Boudicca. From Mar.-Sept. 2005 the museum will host the British Museum's Treasure exhibition. The art gallery contains oil paintings and watercolors. *(☎493 648. Open July-Aug. M-Sa 10am-6pm, Su 1-5pm; Sept.-June M-F 10am-4:30pm, Sa 10am-5pm, Su 1-5pm. £5.25, concessions £4.50, children £3.70.)*

NORWICH CATHEDRAL AND TOMBLAND. The castle and the Norman cathedral dominate Norwich's skyline. The cathedral, built by an 11th-century bishop as penance for having bought his position, features 2-story cloisters (the only ones of their kind in England) and flying buttresses that support the second-tallest spire in the country (315 ft.). Use the mirror in the nave to examine the carved overhead bosses. In summer, the cathedral hosts orchestral concerts and art exhibitions. *(☎764 385. Open daily mid-May to mid-Sept. 7:30am-7pm; mid-Sept. to mid-May 7:30am-6pm.*

Evensong M-F 5:15pm, Sa-Su 3:30pm. Free tours M-F 10:45, 11:30am, 2:15pm. Suggested donation £4.) Like a macabre amusement park, **Tombland,** in front of the Cathedral Park, is the burial site of victims of the Great Plague and now a nightclub hotspot.

BRIDEWELL MUSEUM. This museum displays the history of local industry, recreating an early 19th-century pharmacy, public bar, and tap room, among other common locales of the past. The enchanting medieval building has its own storied history, having served at various times as a merchant's house, mayor's mansion, factory, and prison. *(Bridewell Alley, off St. Andrew's St. ☎615 975. Open Apr.-Sept. Tu-F 10am-4:30pm, Sa 10am-5pm. £2.20, concessions £1.80, families £5.)*

ST. JULIAN'S CHURCH. Julian of Norwich, a 14th-century nun, took up a cell attached to the church and became the first-known woman to write a book in English. Her *Revelations of Divine Love* is based on her mystic visions. *(St. Julian's Alley off Rouen Rd. ☎767 380. Open daily May-Sept. 8am-5:30pm; Oct.-Apr. 8am-4pm. Free.)*

SAINSBURY CENTRE FOR VISUAL ARTS. At the University of East Anglia, 3 mi. west of town on Earlham Rd., this center was destroyed during the English Reformation and restored after WWII. Sir Sainsbury, Lord of the Supermarket, donated his superb collection of art, including works by Picasso, Bacon, and other modern artists, to the university in 1973. The building was designed by Sir Norman Foster. *(Take any university-bound bus, such as #26, and ask for the Constable Terr. stop. ☎456 060; www.uea.ac.uk/scva. Open Tu-Su 11am-5pm, W until 8pm. £2, concessions £1.)*

▐S NIGHTLIFE

Many Norwichian pubs and clubs offer live music. On **Prince of Wales Road,** near the city center, five clubs within two blocks jockey for social position. **The Loft,** on Rose St., is a relaxed, gay-friendly club with live music downstairs on Friday and soul and funk wafting from the loft. (☎623 559. 18+, occasional 16+ nights. Open Th-F 10:30pm-2am, Sa 10pm-3am, Su 9pm-midnight.) **Lock Stock,** on Dove St., with its Sunday night "Exclusive Chilled-out Zone," is another hotspot. (☎629 060. 18+. Open F-Sa 9pm-4am, Su 9pm-2am.) The Riverside has several clubs and bars to choose from, notably, **Norwegian Blue,** in the Riverside Leisure complex, with decor inspired by Scandinavian fjords and IKEA's minimalist style. A 30 ft. waterfall behind the bar splashes over troughs of their 27 different vodkas. (☎618 082. 18+. Open M-Sa noon-11pm, Su noon-10:30pm. Food served until 10pm.) **Ikon,** on Tombland, across from the Maid's Head Hotel, goes retro on Wednesday, party on Friday, and no-nonsense dance on Saturday. (☎621 541. 18+. Cover £1-5. Open W 10pm-2am, F-Sa 9:30pm-2am.) The **City Rail Link** (☎08456 020 121) bus #25 transfers tired partiers between the university and the train station, stopping close to most venues (every 30min. after 11pm; all night Tu-Sa, last bus Su-M 2:30am; 80p-£1.60).

♫ 🌿 ENTERTAINMENT AND FESTIVALS

Norwich offers a rich array of cultural activities. The TIC, as well as many cafes and B&Bs, has information on all things entertaining. Next to the Assembly House on Theatre St., the Art Deco **Theatre Royal** hosts opera and ballet companies, as well as London-based theater troupes such as the Royal Shakespeare Company and Royal National Theatre. (☎630 000. Box office open M-Sa 9:30am-8pm, non-performance days until 6pm. £3-17, concessions available.) The home of the Norwich Players, **Maddermarket Theatre,** St. John's Alley, stages high-quality amateur drama in an Elizabethan-style theater. Adhering to a bizarre tradition, all actors remain anonymous. (☎620 917. Box office open M-Sa 10am-9pm; non-performance days M-F 10am-5pm, Sa 10am-1pm. Tickets £6-8.) The **Norwich Arts Centre,** between Reeves Yard St. and Benedicts St., hosts folk and world music, ballet, and comedy.

EAST ANGLIA

(☎660 352. Box office open M-Sa 9am-10pm. Tickets £4-12.) The **Norwich Puppet Theatre,** St. James, Whitefriars, comes in handy with shows for all ages. (☎629 921. Box office open M-F 9:30am-5pm, Sa 1hr. prior to show. Tickets £5.50, concessions £4, children £3.50.) Ask the TIC about free summer **Theatre in the Parks** (☎212 137).

The **Norfolk and Norwich Festival**—an extravaganza of theater, dance, music, and visual arts—explodes for ten days in mid-May. **Picture This,** in mid-June, offers two weeks of open artists' studios around the county (ask at the TIC). July welcomes the mostly contemporary **LEAP Dance Festival** at the **Playhouse** (☎598 598).

EAST ANGLIA

▶ DAYTRIP FROM NORWICH

NORFOLK BROADS NATIONAL PARK

To reach the Broads, take a train from Norwich, Lowestoft, or Great Yarmouth to the smaller towns of Beccles, Cantley, Lingwood, Oulton Broad, Salhouse, or Wroxham. From Norwich, First Eastern Counties buses go to: Brundell (#704-706; 30min., 2 per hr., round-trip £3), Horning (#54; 30min., 1 per hr., round-trip £4.50); Strumpshaw (#706; 30min., 1 per hr., round-trip £3); Wroxham (#54; 30min., 1 per hr., round-trip £3.50); other Broads towns (#705; M-F 1 per hr.).

Birds and beasts flock to the **Norfolk Broads,** a soggy maze of marshlands, where traffic in hidden waterways conjures the surreal image of sailboats floating through fields. The landscape was formed in medieval times when peat was dug out to use for fuel. Over the centuries, water levels rose and the shallow lakes or "broads" were born. Travel with care, as floods are obviously still frequent.

Among the many **nature trails** that pass through the Broads, **Cockshoot Broad** lets you birdwatch, a circular walk around **Ranworth** identifies the various flora, and **Upton Fen** is popular for its bugs. Hikers can challenge themselves with the 56 mi. **Weaver's Way** between Cromer and Great Yarmouth. The small village of **Strumpshaw** has a popular bird reserve. (☎01603 715 191. Open daily dawn to dusk. £3.25.)

The best way to see the Broads is by boat, and many companies around the bridge in Wroxham rent day launches (£10-14 per hr.). Numerous companies also offer **cruises** around the Broads. **Broads Tours** of Wroxham, on the right before the town bridge, runs river trips and rents day boats. (☎01603 782 207. Boat rentals £11-13 per hr. Open daily 9am-5:30pm. Tours July-Aug. 7 per day; Sept.-June 11:30am and 2pm. £5.50-7.50, children £4.20-5.80.) Certain areas of the Broads are accessible only by car or bike; the pamphlet *Broads Bike Hire,* available at the Wroxham TIC, lists rental shops. A convenient place to rent a cycle is **Camelot Craft** in Wroxham. Follow Station Rd. to the river and take a left onto The Rhond. (☎01603 783 096. £7 per half-day, £10 per day, £45 per week. Open daily 9am-5pm.)

Wroxham, 10min. from Norwich by train, is the best base for information-gathering and preliminary exploration of some of the area's wetlands. To reach the **Wroxham and Hoveton Broads Information Centre** from the train station and bus stop, turn right on Station Rd. and walk about 90 yd. Knowledgeable Broads rangers answer questions and supply maps, guides, and contact information. The office also lists boat rental establishments and campsites throughout the area and books rooms around the park. (☎01603 782 281. Open Apr.-Oct. M-Sa 9am-1pm and 2-5pm.)

SUFFOLK AND ESSEX

BURY ST. EDMUNDS ☎01284

In AD 869, Viking invaders tied the Saxon monarch King Edmund to a tree, used him for target practice, and then beheaded him. Approximately 350 years later, 25 barons met in the Abbey of St. Edmund to swear to force King John to sign the *Magna Carta,* sowing the seeds of democracy in Western Europe. From these two defining moments comes Bury's motto: "shrine of a king, cradle of the law."

Along Crown St. lie the ruins of the 11th-century ⬛Abbey of St. Edmund, one of the few abbey ruins where the rubble core of the walls (and not the cut stones they were once covered with) are exposed. Here, the 25 *Magna Carta* barons met in 1214. (Open until sunset. Free.) Next door, the interior of 16th-century St. Edmundsbury Cathedral is bathed in color; look heavenward and admire the wooden ceiling, and the shields of the *Magna Carta* barons above the High Altar. (☎754 933. Open daily June-Aug. 8:30am-8pm; Sept.-May 8:30am-6pm. Evensong W-Sa 5:30pm, Su 3:30pm. Suggested donation £2. 1 hr. guided tours M-Sa 11am, £3.) The Manor House Museum, bordering the abbey garden, is a must-see if you're cuckoo for clocks. (☎757 076. Open W-Su 11am-4pm. £2.50, concessions £2.) Moyse's Hall Museum, Corn Hill in the marketplace, is devoted to town history. (☎706 183. Open M-F 10:30am-4:30pm, Sa-Su 11am-4pm. £2.50, concessions £2, families £8.) In May, the three-week festival brings music, street entertainment, and fireworks.

Accommodations, budget or otherwise, are hard to come by in Bury. The TIC books B&Bs in town or on nearby farms (£18-25). Tucked between two walls of St. Edmund's Abbey, Park House ❸, 22A Mastow St., lets one room in the best location in town. Reserve well in advance. (☎703 432. Single £25; double £38. Cash only.) Quiet Bury bustles on market days (W and Sa 9am-4pm). The Baxter Court Sandwich Shop ❶, 2 Baxter Ct., behind Marks & Spencer, stuffs large sandwiches. (☎724 411. Open M-Sa 9:30am-4:30pm. Cash only.) The pint-sized Nutshell, Abbeygate at the Traverse, is Britain's smallest pub; ask about their entry in the *Guinness Book of World Records*. (☎764 867. Open M-Sa 11am-11pm, Su noon-10:30pm.)

Bury makes a good daytrip from Norwich or Cambridge, especially if you include a jaunt to Lavenham, Sudbury, or Long Melford. Trains (☎08457 484 950) arrive from: Cambridge (40min., 1 per hr., round-trip £10.40); Felixstowe (1½hr., 1 per hr., £5.70); London (2¼hr., 2 per hr., £27.50). A National Express bus (☎08705 808 080) comes from London (2¼hr., 2 per day, £11.50). Cambus #X11 (☎0870 608 2608) runs from Drummer St. in Cambridge (1hr.; M-Sa 1 per hr., Su 1 per 4hr.; £4). The Tourist Information Centre is on 6 Angel Hill. (☎764 667. Open Easter-Oct. M-Sa 9:30am-5:30pm, Su 10am-3pm; Nov.-Easter M-Sa 10am-4pm.) To reach the TIC from the train station, follow Northgate St. through the roundabout; then turn right onto Mustow St. and walk up to Angel Hill. From the bus station, follow St. Andrew's St. to Brentgovel St., turn right at Lower Baxtel St., and then left onto Abbeygate St. The post office is at 17-18 Cornhill St. (☎08457 223 344; open M-F 9am-5:30pm, Sa 9am-12:30pm). Post Code: IP33 1AA.

🔲 DAYTRIPS FROM BURY ST. EDMUNDS

ICKWORTH HOUSE. 3 mi. southwest of Bury, in the village of Horringer, the capacious home of the Marquis of Bristol is a Neoclassical oddity. Dominated by a 106 ft. rotunda, the opulent state rooms are filled with 18th-century French furniture and numerous portraits, including works of Titian, Velasquez, and Gainsborough. The classical Italian garden is splendid. *(First Eastern Counties buses (#141-144; M-Sa 10 per day, 15min., round-trip £3.10) leave Bury's St. Andrew's Station. ☎01284 735 270. House open late Mar. to Oct. M-Tu, F-Su, and bank holidays 1-5pm. Gardens open daily 10am-5pm. Park open daily 7am-7pm. £6.40, children £2.75. Gardens and park only £2.80/80p.)*

LONG MELFORD. Two Tudor mansions, complete with turrets and moats, grace the village of Long Melford. Melford Hall, the more impressive, has retained much of its original Elizabethan exterior and paneled banquet hall. Peek at the Victorian bedrooms before exploring the colorful gardens. *(☎01787 880 286. Open May-Sept. M and W-Su 2-5:30pm.; Apr. and Oct. Sa-Su 2-5:30pm. £4.50.)* More amusing than stately, Kentwell Hall is filled with authentically costumed guides; visitors are also encouraged to come in Tudor costume. *(☎01787 310 207. Open daily July-Aug. noon-5pm; Mar.-May and Sept.-Oct. Su noon-5pm. £6.95, children £4.45, seniors £5.95.)* Stop by the Long

Melford Church, between the two mansions, erected in 1484 with funding from affluent wool merchants. *(Long Melford is accessible from Bury by H.C. Chambers bus #753, catch it at the bus station. 11 per day, 50min. Round-trip £4.20.)*

COLCHESTER ☎01206

England's oldest recorded town, Colchester (pop. 89,000) has seen its share of the violence that built Britain. A center of power in Celtic Britain, it was the target of Rome's first incursions and the first Roman capital of the island. But the Celts roared back, and Colchester was the first town to fall to the Boudiccan revolt. Romans recaptured the place and built what is now the oldest surviving city wall. Since then things have quieted down, with the exception of the construction of one of William the Conqueror's first castles and the successful siege of that castle by King John in 1216. A pedestrian-only shopping mall now dominates the town.

Colchester Castle houses the dynamic and morbid **Castle Museum,** full of interactive displays. Act out a short scene behind Roman theater masks, try on battle gear, and experience a chilling witch confession in the dungeon. A tour takes you from the depths of the Roman foundations to the heights of the Norman towers. (☎282 939. Open M-Sa 10am-5pm, Su 11am-5pm; last admission 4:30pm. Tours noon-4pm on the hour. Castle £4.50, concessions £2.90. Tours £1.60, children 80p.) Marveling at the fine collection of 18th-century grandfather clocks in ⧉**Tymperleys Clock Museum,** off Trinity St., is a decent way to pass the time. (Open Apr.-Oct. Tu-Sa 10am-1pm and 2-5pm. Free.) Colchester plays host to several smaller museums, all free; visit www.colchestermuseums.co.uk.

Colchester has few offerings for the budget traveler. The cheapest place to stay is in one of the large and spotless rooms at the **Scheregate Hotel ❸,** 36 Osborne St. (☎573 034. Breakfast included. Singles £26-34; doubles £42-48. MC/V.) The **Sainsbury's** is on Priory Walk, off Queen St. (Open M-Sa 8am-6:30pm.) Surprisingly elegant, **The Thai Dragon ❷,** 35 East Hill, has a full lunch for only £5.50. Dinner is pricier (£5-8), but the traditional dishes are quite tasty. (☎863 414. Open M-Sa noon-2:30pm and 6-11pm, Su noon-2:30pm and 6-10:30pm. AmEx/MC/V.)

Colchester is best visited as a daytrip from London or nearby East Anglian towns. **Trains** (☎08457 484 950) pull into **North Station** from **Cambridge** (2½hr., 5 per hr., £12) and **London Liverpool St.** (1hr., 12 per hr., £14.80). North Station lies a good 2 mi. from town (as opposed to Town Station, which nabs local trains); buses frequently make the uphill trip (#1; 80p). **Buses** from **Cambridge** (2½hr., 1 per day, £12) and **London** (2½hr., 3 per day, £12) arrive at the **Bus Authority,** Queen St. (☎282 645), around the corner from the TIC. The **Tourist Information Centre,** 1 Queen St., across from the castle, books rooms for a 10% deposit and leads 2hr. city **tours.** (☎282 920; www.visitcolchester.com. Open Apr.-Oct. M-Tu and Th-Sa 9am-6pm, W 10am-6pm, Su 11am-4pm; Oct.-Mar. M-Sa 10am-5pm. Tours June-Sept. 11:30am; call ahead for dates. £2.50, children £1.25.) **Internet access** at **Compuccino,** 17 Priory Walk, three blocks south of the TIC (☎519 090; £2 per hr.). The **post office** is at 68-70 North Hill (☎08457 223 344; open M-Sa 9am-5:30pm). **Post Code:** CO1 1AA.

NORTHWEST ENGLAND

The decline of heavy industry affected Northwest England as it did the rest of urban Britain, but this region has embraced post-industrial hipness with a fresh youth culture. In the 19th century, coal clouds and sprawling mills revolutionized quiet village life. Prosperity followed where smokestacks led, making the cities of the northwest the world's wool and linen workshops. The last few decades have been difficult, but the cities have met challenges with gritty determination and reenergizing spunk. Today their innovative music and arts scene are world famous: Liverpool and Manchester alone produced four of Q magazine's ten biggest rock stars of the century. Add a large student population and through-the-roof nightlife, and you'll begin to understand the reinvigorated northwest. If you need a break from the frenetic urbanity, find respite in the Peak District to the east and Cumbria to the north, where the Lake District promises stunning crags and waters that send poets into pensive meditation.

NORTHWEST ENGLAND

HIGHLIGHTS OF NORTHWEST ENGLAND

LIVERPOOL Don't miss Liverpool, Beatles fans: virtually every pub, restaurant, and corner claims some connection to the Fab Four (p. 345).

MANCHESTER Revel in the wealth of Manchester nightlife, where trendy cafe-bars morph into late-night venues for dancing and drinking (p. 354).

PEAK DISTRICT AND LAKE DISTRICT Roam the hills, groughs, and moors of urban England's backyard (p. 363), then explore the dramatic mountains and sparkling lakes that inspired Wordsworth, Coleridge, and Romantics everywhere (p. 372).

NORTHWEST CITIES

CHESTER ☎01244

With fashionable stores behind mock-medieval facades, tour guides in Roman armor, and a town crier in full uniform, Chester feels like a theme-park medley of the quintessentially English. Built by Romans, the city was later a base for Plantagenet campaigns against the Welsh—old town law stated that Welshmen wandering the streets after 9pm could be beheaded. Though it once had trading connections throughout continental Europe, silt blocked the River Dee in the 17th century and Chester was left to turn its archaism into a selling point.

◨ TRANSPORTATION

Chester serves as a rail gateway to Wales via the North Wales line. The train stops 10min. northeast of city proper off Hoole Rd., but flashing your ticket gets a free ride into downtown. Buses converge between Northgate St. and Inner Ring Rd. near Town Hall.

339

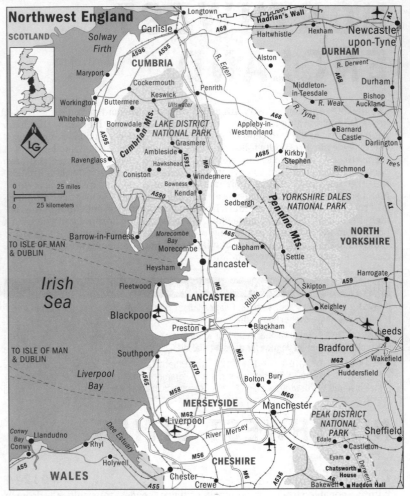

Northwest England

Trains: Station on City Rd. Ticket office open M-Sa 5:30am-12:30am, Su 8am-midnight. Trains (☎08457 484 950) from: **Birmingham** (1¾hr., 1-2 per hr., most indirect, £17.30); **Holyhead** (1½hr., 1-2 per hour, £17.90); **London Euston** (2½hr., 1-2 per hr., £74); **Manchester Piccadilly** (1hr., 1-2 per hr., £9.50). Frequent **Merseyrail** service makes Chester an easy daytrip from **Liverpool** (45min., 2 per hr., £4.15).

Buses: The new station hides near Town Hall off Northgate St. An information stand helps travelers during the day. **National Express** (☎08705 808 080) from: **Birmingham** (2-3hr., 4 per day); **Blackpool** (3½-4hr., 4 per day, £8.25); **London** (5½-10hr., 10 per day, £20); **Manchester** (1¼hr., 5 per day, £5.25). **Huxley Coaches** (☎01948 770 661) bus C56 to Foregate St. from **Wrexham** (1hr.; M-Sa every hr.). **First** buses connect from Liverpool (1½hr., every 20min., £2.20).

Public Transportation: Call ☎602 666 for local bus info (daily 8am-8pm). Routes are scattered amongst 15 *Bus Times* booklets, available free at the TIC. The **Chester women's safe transport service** (☎310 585) operates a women-only bus M-Sa. **Taxis: Radio Taxis** (☎372 372) or **Abbey Taxis** (☎318 318).

✠ 🛈 ORIENTATION AND PRACTICAL INFORMATION

Chester's center is bounded by a **city wall** breached by seven gates. **Chester Cross** is at the intersection of **Eastgate Street, Northgate Street, Watergate Street,** and **Bridge Street,** which together comprise the heart of the downtown commercial district. Beginning just outside the southern walls, a tree-lined path, **The Groves,** follows a mile of the River Dee. North of the walled city lie the bus stop and **Liverpool Road,** which heads toward the hospital and zoo. The train station is on the northwestern edge of town, while the **Roodee** (Chester Racecourse) occupies its southwest edge.

Tourist Information Centre: Town Hall, Northgate St., at the corner of Princess St. (☎402 111; www.chestertourism.com). **Bureau de change. Branch** at the **Chester Visitor Centre,** Vicar's Ln. (☎402 111), opposite the Roman amphitheater. Both book accommodations for a £3 charge and 10% deposit, book National Express tickets, and sell city maps and a city guide with accommodations listings. Pick up *What's On in Chester* (free) for information on upcoming events. Both open May-Oct. M-Sa 9:30am-5:30pm, Su 10am-4pm; Nov.-Apr. M-Sa 10am-5pm, Su 10am-4pm.

Tours: A legionnaire in full armor leads the **Roman Soldier Wall Patrol** (June-Aug. Th-Sa 1:45pm from the Visitor Centre, 2pm from the TIC; £2.50, concessions £2), while ghouls lurk on the **Ghost Hunter Trail** (after 5:30pm, buy tickets at the Dublin Packet pub on Northgate St.; June-Oct. Th-Sa 7:30pm from the TIC; Nov. Sa only; £3.50, concessions £3, families £9). A similar self-guided tour is detailed in **Haunted Chester,** a £1.50 pamphlet sold in bookstores and the TIC. For a run-down of Chester's history, try the **Pastfinder Tour.** (Daily May-Oct. 10:30am and 2:15pm from the Visitor Centre, 10:45am and 2:30pm from the TIC; Nov.-Apr. Sa-Su only. £3, concessions £2.50.) The **Secret Chester** tour, which also departs from the Visitor Center (Tu, Th, and Su 2pm; Sa 10am and 2pm), reveals the secrets of Chester's past by affording access to historic buildings. £4, concessions £3, family £9. Enquiries for the above at ☎402 445. The open-top **Guide Friday** (☎01789 294 466) buses offer hop-on, hop-off service. 4 per hr. £7, concessions £5.50, children £2.50. A more general **Busybus** tour covers Chester and surrounding Cheshire for a half day (☎0870 874 1800; www.busybus.co.uk).

Financial Services: Barclays, St. Werburgh St., in the cathedral complex. Open M-Tu and Th-F 9am-5pm, W 10am-5pm, Sa 9:30am-3:30pm. **Thomas Cook** (☎583 500) has a commissionless **bureau de change** near Chester's Cross on Bridge St. Open M-Tu and Th-Sa 9am-5:30pm, W 10am-5:30pm, Su 11am-4pm.

Launderette: Garden Lane Launderette, 56 Garden Ln. (☎382 694). Wash £2, dry 20p per 3min., soap 50p, service 50p. Open M-Tu and Th-Sa 9am-6pm.

Police: Grosvenor Rd. (☎350 222).

Hospital: Countess of Chester (West Chester) Hospital, Liverpool Rd. (☎365 000). Take bus #40A from the station or #3 from the Bus Exchange.

Internet Access: Library, Northgate St. (☎312 935), beside the Town Hall. Free. Open M and Th 9:30am-7pm, Tu-W and F 9:30am-5pm, Sa 9:30am-4 pm. **i-station,** 4 Rufus Ct. (☎401 680). £2 per 30min. Open M-F 8:30am-10pm, Sa-Su 8:30am-9:30pm.

Pharmacy: Boots, adjacent to the TIC in The Forum Center (☎342 852). Open M-F 8am-6pm, Sa 9am-6pm, Su 11am-4pm.

NORTHWEST ENGLAND

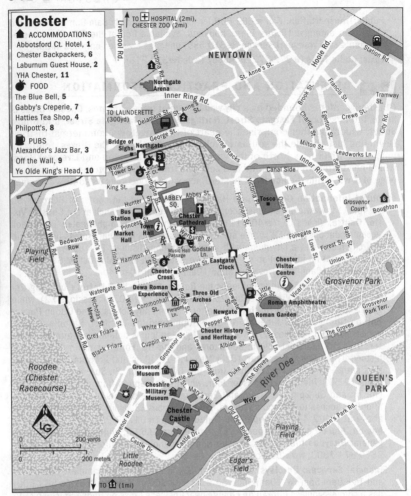

Chester

♠ ACCOMMODATIONS
Abbotsford Ct. Hotel, **1**
Chester Backpackers, **6**
Laburnum Guest House, **2**
YHA Chester, **11**

🍴 FOOD
The Blue Bell, **5**
Gabby's Creperie, **7**
Hatties Tea Shop, **4**
Philpott's, **8**

🍺 PUBS
Alexander's Jazz Bar, **3**
Off the Wall, **9**
Ye Olde King's Head, **10**

Post Office: 2 St. John St. (☎348 315), off Foregate St. **Bureau de change.** Open M-Sa 9am-5:30pm. **Branch** at 122 Northgate St. (☎326 754). Open M-F 9am-5:30pm, Sa 9am-12:30pm. **Post Code:** CH1 2HT.

🏠 ACCOMMODATIONS

B&Bs (from £20) are concentrated on **Hoole Road,** a 5min. walk from the train station (turn right from the exit, climb the steps to Hoole Rd., and turn right over the train tracks), and **Brook Street** (right from the train station exit, then the first left). Bus #53 (6 per hr.) runs to the area from the city center.

YHA Chester, 40 Hough Green (☎680 056; fax 681 204), 1½ mi. from the city center. Cross the river on Grosvenor Rd. and turn right at the roundabout (40min. walk), following the signs pointing toward North Wales. Buses #7 and 16 come from the bus station,

#4 from the train station or £4 cab. Renovated Victorian with laundry (£2 wash, 20p for 3min. dry) and Internet access (50p per 8 min.). Breakfast included. Membership required (£12-14). Reception 7am-10:30pm. Open mid-Jan. to mid-Dec. Dorms £14.90, under 18 £11.50. Twin £33.80, ensuite £37.80. MC/V. ❷

Laburnum Guest House, 2 St. Anne St. (☎/fax 380 313). Four large, ensuite rooms close to town, in a less attractive location. Singles £26; doubles £50. Cash only. ❸

Chester Backpackers, 67 Boughton (☎400 185; www.chesterbackpakers.co.uk), 10min. from the train station. Feels like a laid-back student flat, including a lounge with video collection. Luggage storage, Internet access, kitchen, and laundry. No curfew. Dorms £13; singles £18.50; doubles £30. MC/V. ❷

Abbotsford Court Hotel, 17 Victoria Rd. (☎390 898; fax 380 805). Clean and convenient for both train and city access. Singles £35, doubles £56. AmEx/MC/V.❹

🍴 FOOD

A **Tesco** hides at the end of an alley off Frodsham St. (Open M-Sa 7am-9pm, Su 11am-5pm.) The **market,** in Market Hall at 6 Princess St., counts fruit and vegetables among its bargains. (☎402 340. Open M-Sa 8am-5pm.) On Sundays the town hosts an outdoor **Farmers' Market.** (Open 9:30am-4pm.)

🦿 **Philpott's,** 2 Goss St. (☎345 123), off Watergate St. Philpott's cheery service, pristine counter, and fabulous hand-crafted sandwiches (from £1.60) improve any lunchtime. Takeaway only. Open M-Sa 7:30am-2:30pm. Cash only. ❶

The Blue Bell, 65 Northgate St. (☎317 758). Its name comes from the 'curfew bell' that once rang at 8pm each night to demand that strangers leave the city. Entrees from £11.50, lunch from £5.95, and an award-winning cheese plate for £5.50. Open daily from 11am. Food served noon-2pm and 6-9pm. MC/V. ❹

Gabby's Creperie, Music Hall Passage (☎07811 352 847), just off Northgate St. Design your own savory crepe (from £2.50) or sample one of Gabby's own ingenious offerings—a "squirrel's dream" comes with hazelnuts and hazelnut spread for £2.10. Open M-Sa 11am-5pm, Sa 10am-5pm, Su 11am-4:30pm. Cash only. ❶

Hatties Tea Shop, 5 Rufus Ct. (☎345 173), off Northgate St. A bustling teashop with friendly service and great homemade cakes. "Bumper salad" (with ham, tuna, cheese, and egg) £6.25. Open M-Sa 9am-5pm, Su 11am-4pm. Cash only. ❷

👁 SIGHTS

ARCHITECTURE. Chester's purposefully antiquated architecture is the most striking feature of its city center, though these self-consciously quaint buildings mostly house chain stores and fast-food cafes. Some of the structures do date from the medieval or Tudor eras, however, most notably the 13th-century **"3 Old Arches"** on Bridge St., which are believed to make up the oldest storefront in England. Charming black-and-white painted facades characterize the later **"Magpie"** style—a Victorian phenomenon. Occasional street performers (like classical string septets) grace this much-trafficked area with melodies, and the town crier performs Tu-Sa at noon May through August. Climb the famous **city walls** or the 13th century **rows** of Bridge St., Watergate St., and Eastgate St., where walkways provide access to another tier of storefronts. Some historians theorize that Edward I imported the tiered design from Constantinople, which he visited while crusading. **Northgate,** which offers a fine view of Welsh hills, was rebuilt in 1808 to house the city's jail. The **Bridge of Sighs** is outside the gate; it carried doomed convicts from jail to chapel for their last mass, although a good number attempted escape by jumping into the canal before railings were installed. Cameras stand at the ready before **Eastgate Clock,** the second most photographed timepiece in the world—London's Big Ben ranks first.

CHESTER CATHEDRAL. With roots in the 11th century, the construction (and reconstruction) of Chester Cathedral had a number of stages—the last major one concluded in the 16th century and left the magnificent structure that remains today. One-of-a-kind intersecting stone arches known as **"the crown of stone"** support its main tower, and a choir at the front (where the monks once kept devotions) showcases intricate woodwork full of strange beasts and battle scenes. More elaborate carvings can be found on the **misericords**—literally translated as "mercy seats"—so titled because monks would rest on them during lengthy worship sessions. Art aficionados marvel at the two-century-old **Cobweb painting** in a northern niche, a short-lived artform using caterpillar silk instead of canvas. *(Off Northgate St. ☎324 756. Open daily roughly 8am-6pm. Audio tours £3. Suggested donation £3.)*

ROMAN SIGHTS. The Romans had conquered most of Britannia by AD 43, and Deva (modern-day Chester) was a strategic outpost of considerable importance. The walled city housed the soldiers' barracks and military headquarters, while the "canabae" outside were set up for wicked indulgences like prostitutes and board games. The **Grosvenor Museum,** 27 Grosvenor St., houses a display of artifacts and models that illustrate what Roman life was like for soldiers-in-residence. A connected period house *(No. 20 Castle St.)* displays 3D still-life vignettes of 400 years of high society. *(☎402 008; www.grosvenormuseum.co.uk. Open M-Sa 10:30am-5pm, Su 1-4. Free.)* At the edge of Grosvenor Park, just outside the city wall, specialists daily unearth more of the largest **Roman amphitheater** in Britain. Lions were specially shipped up for the bloody gladiatorial bouts. *(Always open. Free.)* Nearby, the **Roman Garden** provides a great picnic space on shaded grass lined with stunted Roman columns. Off Bridge St., the **Dewa Roman Experience,** Pierpoint Ln., affords a full-immersion encounter with Chester's classical past. Visitors "board" an old galley vessel bound for a recreated version of Britannia. The museum also chronicles the layered archeological exploration of the town. *(☎343 407. Open Feb.-Nov. M-Sa 9am-5pm, Su 10am-5pm; Dec.-Jan. 10am-4pm. £4.25, concessions £2.50.)*

OTHER SIGHTS. Chester Zoo, one of Europe's largest, houses everything from jaguars to otters, as well as human-sized prairie dog tunnels, a "monkey kitchen," and a free-flying bat cave. Check the posted signs to witness action-packed daily animal feedings. *(Take Crosville bus #1 from the Bus Exchange (round-trip £2.80) or M-Sa take First #8 or X8. On Sundays, catch Arriva #411, 412. ☎380 280; www.chesterzoo.org. Open daily summer 10am-6pm, sometimes later; during off-season until 4:30 or 5pm. Last admission 1-1½ hr. before close. £12, concessions £9.50, family £39.50).* The **Chester Military Museum,** in the castle complex, traces Chester's armed forces from medieval archers to contemporary special forces. Learn how 18th recruiting sergeants "enlisted" unsuspecting beer-guzzlers with a well-placed shilling. *(☎327 617; www.chester.ac.uk/militarymuseum. Open M-Su 10am-5pm, last admission 4:30pm. £2, concessions £1).* The history and rehabilitation of the rows, among other smaller exhibits, occupies **Chester History and Heritage** in St. Michael's Church where Bridge St. becomes Lower Bridge St. *(☎402 110. Open M-Th 10am-4pm. Free.)*

🎫 🎵 NIGHTLIFE AND ENTERTAINMENT

Many of the city's 30-odd pubs parrot Olde English decor, and almost all are open M-Sa from noon to 11pm and Sunday from noon to 10:30pm. Watering holes group on **Lower Bridge Street** and **Watergate Street.** Jazz and blues waft into the outdoor courtyard of **Alexander's Jazz Bar,** Rufus Ct., on summer Wednesdays and Thursdays. *(☎340 005. Tu unplugged acoustic. F dancing to latin and funk. Sa live com-*

edy. Cover £2-15. Open M-Sa 10:30am-2am, Su 11am-12:30pm.) Traditionalists head to **Ye Olde King's Head,** 48-50 Lower Bridge St., where an assortment of steins hangs from the beams of a restored 17th-century house that Chester mayor Randal Holme once called home. (☎324 855. Food served all hours.) Situated on what was once a Roman defense ditch, **Off the Wall,** 12 St. John's St., offers 2-meal deals for £5.95 and inexpensive wine (£4.95 per bottle). (☎348 964. Food served daily noon-5pm and from 8pm.)

On sporadic spring and summer weekends, England's oldest **horse races** are held on the **Roodee,** attracting huge and boisterous crowds. If you plan to visit over a race weekend, book far in advance. (☎304 600. Tickets from £4.) The **Chester Summer Music Festival** draws classical musicians to the cathedral in July. (☎320 700. Ticket prices vary.) Check the TIC's free *What's On in Chester* for other events.

LIVERPOOL ☎0151

Much of Britain is quick to belittle once-industrial Liverpool, but Scousers—as Liverpudlians are colloquially known—don't seem to mind much. Their good-humored sort has stood the test of hard knocks and big bombs, and an energized metropolis has emerged. Free museums and many public projects signal a cultural face-lift, but tourists need only walk this edgy city's streets to mine its essence: Liverpool is second only to London in quantity of grade one and two listed buildings; crazed fans sport jerseys for the area's two near-deified football squads; and its streets boast stimulating nightlife and theaters of every hue. Recently named European Capital of Culture 2008, Liverpool's mighty pace shows no signs of waning anytime soon. Oh, yeah—and some fuss is made over the Beatles.

█ TICKET TO RIDE

Trains: Lime Street Station. Ticket office open M-Sa 5am-11:35pm, Su 7:15am-11pm. Trains (☎08457 484 950) from: **Birmingham** (1¾hr., M-Sa every hr., Su 6 per day; £19.20); **London Euston** (3hr., every hr., £85); **Manchester Piccadilly** (1hr., 2-4 per hr., £7.80). The **Moorfields, James Street,** and **Central** stations serve mainly as transfer points to local **Merseyrail** trains, including to **Chester** (45min., 2 per hr., £4.15).

Buses: Norton Street Station receives **National Express** (☎08705 808 080) from: **Birmingham** (3hr., 5 per day, £9.50); **London** (4½-5½hr., 5-6 per day, £20); **Manchester** (1hr., 1-3 per hr., £5.25). Other buses stop at **Queen Square** and **Paradise Street** stations. The 1-day **Mersey Saveaway** can save you a bit of change and is unrestricted during off-peak hours. Sa-Su (£2.10, children £1.60). Valid on ferry and rail also.

Ferries: Liverpool Sea Terminal, Pier Head, north of Albert Dock. Open daily 9am-5pm. The **Isle of Man Steam Packet Company** (☎08705 523 523; www.steam-packet.com) runs ferries from Princess Dock to the **Isle of Man** and **Dublin** (see **By Ferry,** p. 386).

Local Transportation: Private buses cover the city and the Merseyside area. Consult the transport mavens at **Mersey Travel** (☎0870 608 2608; www.merseytravel.gov.uk) in the TIC. Open M and W-Sa 9am-5:30pm, Tu 10am-5:30pm, Su 10:30am-4:30pm.

Taxis: Scouser taxis are cheap, efficient, and amiable. Try **Mersey Cabs** (☎207 2222).

██ HELP!

Liverpool's central district is surprisingly pedestrian-friendly. There are two clusters of museums: on **William Brown Street,** near Lime St. Station and the lovely urban oasis of St. John's Garden, and at **Albert Dock,** on the river. These flank the central shopping district, whose central axis comprises **Bold Street, Church Street,** and **Lord Street** and is largely composed of pedestrian-only walkways and plazas.

Tourist Information Centre: Queen Square Centre, Queen Sq. (☎0906 680 6886; www.visitliverpool.com). Gives away the handy *Visitor Guide to Liverpool and Mersey-side* as well as a huge stock of pamphlets and local events schedules. Books beds for a 10% deposit. Open M and W-Sa 9am-5:30pm, Tu 10am-5:30pm, Su 10:30am-4:30pm. **Branch** at **Albert Dock Centre,** Albert Dock, inside the Maritime Museum (☎0906 680 6886). Open daily 10am-5pm.

Tours: In addition to those listed below, numerous other **bus tours** (from £5) and **walking tours** (£4, concessions £3) run in summer; ask the TIC. The TIC (☎0906 680 6886) also offers guided 2hr. expeditions around and inside **John and Paul's Liverpool homes** through the National Trust. Apr.-Oct. W-Sa. Book in advance. £12.

Phil Hughes (☎228 4565, mobile 07961 511 223). Expert guide runs personalized 3-4hr. Beatles tours with Liverpool highlights for the lucky 8 who fit in his van. Passengers alight at Strawberry Fields and Eleanor Rigby's grave. 1 per day—book in advance. £12; private tours £65.

Magical Mystery Tour (☎ 709 3285; www.caverncitytours.com). A yellow-and-blue bus takes 40 fans to Fab Four sights, leaving the Queens Sq. TIC at 2:10pm and the Beatles Story (p. 350) at 2:30pm. The 2hr. tour is interesting but feels packaged. Purchase tickets in advance at either one of TICs or at the Beatles Story. M-F 1 per day, Sa-Su 2 per day. £11.95, small souvenir included.

The Yellow Duckmarine (☎ 708 7799). Tours that aren't focused on the Beatles (though the company clearly hasn't escaped their influence entirely) in 2 amphibious ex-army vessels. The ticket office is outside of the Beatles Story entrance at the Atlantic Pavilion. Mid-Feb. to Christmas M-F every 1¼hr., Sa-Su every 45min. £10, concessions £9, children £8, families £29.

Financial Services: Banks flood the shopping districts, and ATMs seem to sprout from every last alleyway. **Lloyd's TSB,** 53 Great Charlotte St. (open M-W and F 9am-5pm, Th 10am-5pm) and **HSBC,** 4 Dale St. (open M-F 9:30am-5pm) are 2 options. **American Express,** 54 Lord St. (☎702 4505) has a **bureau de change.** Open M and W-F 9am-5:30pm, Tu 9:30am-5:30pm, Sa 9am-5pm.

Launderette: There are no launderettes downtown, though the **YHA Liverpool** (p. 348) often allows non-residents to use its facilities.

Police: Canning Pl. (☎709 6010). Outpost, 70 Church St. (☎777 4147).

Hospital: Royal Liverpool Hospital, Prescot St. (☎706 2000).

Internet Access: Central Library, William Brown St. (☎233 5835). Free access in the business and reference section on the 2nd fl. Open M-Th 9am-8pm, F 9am-7pm, Sa 9am-5pm, Su noon-4pm. **The Gateway,** 71 London Rd. (☎298 3200. £2.50 per hr. 10p per printout. Open M-Sa 8:30am-6pm.) Also at **Cafe Latténet** in the **International Inn** (p. 348) and McDonald's at Ranelagh and Great Charlotte St. (£1 per 30min.)

Pharmacy: Boots, 18-20 Great Charlotte St. (☎709 4711). Open M-Sa 8:15am-6:15pm, Su 8:15am-4pm.

Post Office: 42-44 Houghton Way (☎08457 740 740), in St. John's Shopping Centre (below the Radio City Tower). **ATM** and **bureau de change.** Open M-Sa 9am-5:30pm. **Post Code:** L1 1AA.

⚑ A HARD DAY'S NIGHT

Your best bets for cheap accommodations lie east of the city center. **Lord Nelson Street** is lined with modest hotels; similar establishments are on **Mount Pleasant,** one block from Brownlow Hill and Central Station. Stay only at places approved by the TIC, and if you need a good night's sleep, consider springing for a single—some hostels host herds of clubbing teens on weekend nights. Demand for beds is highest in early April for the Grand National Race and during the Beatles Convention at the end of August.

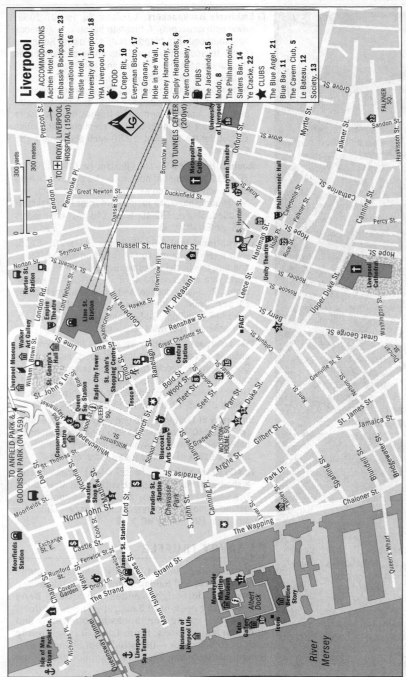

Liverpool

▲ ACCOMMODATIONS
Aachen Hotel, 9
Embassie Backpackers, 23
International Inn, 16
Thistle Hotel, 1
University of Liverpool, 18
YHA Liverpool, 20

● FOOD
La Crepe Rit, 10
Everyman Bistro, 17
The Granary, 4
Hole in the Wall, 7
Honey Harmony, 2
Simply Heathcotes, 6
Tavern Company, 3

🍺 PUBS
The Jacaranda, 15
Modo, 8
The Philharmonic, 19
Slaters Bar, 14
Ye Cracke, 22

★ CLUBS
The Blue Angel, 21
Blue Bar, 11
The Cavern Club, 5
Le Bateau, 12
Society, 13

THE HIDDEN DEAL

THE GRANARY

Wedged into an unassuming corner of Liverpool's business district, **The Granary** might be small, but its barms are most definitely not. A huge variety of breakfast, lunch, and snack foods line all four of its walls in a variety of cases and cabinets, with outrageously low prices advertised conspicuously across every leftover surface.

Toasties (£1 before 11am) come in tried-and-true forms like ham-and-cheese, while lunchtime roasts like pork with apple sauce are £2.29. Toasted teacakes are 40p and huge sandwiches with a kaleidoscope of fillings start from £1.45. A big portion of homemade meat-and-potato "scouse," a dish quite fitting for hungry scousers on lunch break, costs but £1.20.

In a takeaway shop as busy as this one, one would assume that the service would be lacking. The staff here, however, deliver a rare combination of cheerful, efficient service. That's not the only rare combination you'll find here; at the buffet, full of almost 20 different options, you can mix and match eclectic concoctions like ham-and-pineapple rice, potato curry, and tomato paella. A small pot is only 99p, making it possibly the best deal in this entire shop of 'best deals.'

(Drury Ln., between Brunswick St. and Water St. ☎236 6200. Open M-F 7:30am-3:30pm.)

Embassie Backpackers, 1 Falkner Sq. (☎707 1089; www.embassie.com). A first-rate hostel in a gorgeous neighborhood. The friendly staff and owner Kevin are eager to acquaint you with its numerous amenities (laundry, pool table, kitchen, and satellite TV lounge) or chat over free toast and tea. Busy and active on weekends, which see many a guitarist strumming in the basement. Hosts occasional BBQs and clubbing outings, also arranges for the Phil Hughes Beatles tour to pick up from the hostel doors. Reception 24hr. Dorms £13.50 for the 1st night, 12.50 each additional night. Cash only. ❷

Aachen Hotel, 89-91 Mt. Pleasant (☎709 3477; fax 709 1126). Winner of numerous awards, and it's easy to see why. Clean rooms, chatty bar, pool room, and family atmosphere. All rooms have color TVs. Breakfast included. Singles £32-40; twins £46-54; family rooms £68. AmEx/MC/V. ❹

International Inn, 4 South Hunter St. (☎709 8135; www.internationalinn.co.uk), off Hardman St. Clean and fun, this hostel welcomes visitors from all over the world with style and 2-, 4-, 6-, 8-, 10-person ensuite rooms. Pool table, lounge, and kitchen. Internet access £1 per 30min. in the adjoining **Cafe Latténet.** Cafe open M-F 8am-9pm, Sa-Su 9am-5:30pm. Dorms £15, on weekends £16; twins £36. AmEx/MC/V. ❷

YHA Liverpool, 25 Tabley St. (☎709 8888). Pristine, upscale digs on 3 Beatles-themed floors, next to Albert Dock. Suitable rooms for families. Laundry, kitchen, Internet access, currency exchange, and Big Apple Diner. Breakfast included. Membership required. Dorms £16.95-19, under 18 £12.50-14. MC/V. ❷

University of Liverpool. The university conference office (☎794 6440; bookings 794 6453) has information on halls open to travelers. Available mid-June to mid-Sept. Singles £16, with breakfast £18. Cash only. ❷

Thistle Hotel, Chapel St. (☎227 4444). Pleasant hotel, a short walk from downtown Liverpool and Albert Dock. The sophisticated lobby and spacious rooms hide behind a modern concrete facade. Singles £80; doubles from £90. AmEx/MC/V. ❺

◪ SAVOY TRUFFLE

Trendy cafes and budget-friendly Indian restaurants line **Bold Street** and **Hardman Street,** while takeaways crowd near late-night venues and around **Berry Street**—many open until 3am. All-you-can-eat deals (from $4.50) spring from nooks in both trendy and dodgy neighborhoods. From Duke St., a glittering arch over Nelson St.—imported from Shanghai as a recent gift from the People's Republic—marks the entrance to Liverpool's **Chinatown,** the oldest in the world. More upscale restaurants cluster around **Queen Square** and the downtown district. A **Tesco Metro** supermarket is in Clayton Sq., across from St. John's Shopping Centre. (Open M-F 6am-midnight, Sa 6am-10pm, Su 11am-5pm.)

■ **Everyman Bistro,** 5-9 Hope St. in the basement (☎708 9545). A rainbow of tasty sides and main dishes await in myriad neat crocks, generously apportioned. Creamy desserts tempt Everyman and woman alike. Open M-W 11:45am-midnight, Th-F 11:45am-2am, Sa 11am-2am. MC/V. ❷

Simply Heathcotes, 25 The Strand, Beetham Plaza (☎236 3536; www.heathcotes.co.uk). Sloping walls of glass and flickering candles complement French dishes at this suave mecca for young professionals. A 3-course lunch is £15.50, with entrees like Goosnargh duck breast with chicory. Open daily noon-2:30pm, M-F 6-10pm, Sa 6-11pm, Su 6-9:30pm. MC/V. ❹

Honey Harmony, 2 Queen Sq. (☎709 3933; www.honeyharmony.co.uk). Eat your teriyaki seabass stuffed with sun-blushed tomatoes (£10) in a sunken room with a dark red aura and geometric flair. Open M-Th noon-midnight, F-Sa noon-2am. MC/V. ❸

Tavern Company, 4 Queen Sq. (☎709 1070), near the TIC. Mexican BBQ meets upscale wine bar and combines burritos (£8.50) with spirits. Open M-Sa noon-11pm, Su noon-9:30pm. Food served M-Th until 10pm, F-Sa until 10:30pm, Su until 9:30pm. MC/V. ❷

La Crepe Rit, 20-21 The Colonnades, Albert Dock (☎709 9444). Huge glass windows afford views of the docks, while the menu supplies crepe offerings (£3.25-8.50) like the Rose Garden (fruit salad, ice cream, and raspberry sauce). MC/V. ❶

Hole in the Wall, 37 School Ln. (☎709 7733). Considerably larger and brighter than its name would suggest. Serves a huge variety of barms and quiches (both from £2.95). Eat in or takeaway. Open M-Sa 8:30am-5pm. Cash only. ❶

▼ COME TOGETHER

Two of the Liverpool's most notable products—football fans and rock musicians—were born of pub culture, and the city has continued to incorporate these traditions in its pub scene. There's not a spot in Liverpool that's far from a good selection of watering holes; those catering to the younger set cluster between **Slater Street** and **Berry Street,** where £1 (or less!) pints are in plentiful supply.

■ **The Philharmonic,** 36 Hope St. (☎707 2837). John Lennon once said the worst thing about being famous was "not being able to get a quiet pint at the Phil." Non-celebrities can still enjoy a mellow beer in this gorgeous old lounge, where the clientele and the decor are reminiscent of an old boy's club. Don't miss the famous mosaic tiling in the men's bathroom, though women should ask at the bar before checking for themselves. Open M-Sa noon-11pm, Su noon-10:30pm.

Modo, 23-25 Fleet St. (☎709 8832). Bubbling with young professional folks, the curved wooden awning and expansive urban beer garden make this open-air block Liverpool city center on weekend nights. Most drink here first, but a club hides inside down the stairs. Open M-Sa 11:30am-2am, Su noon-12:30am.

The Jacaranda, 21-23 Slater St. (☎708 9424). The site of the 1st paid Beatles gig, the Jac's basement was painted by John and original Beatle Stu Sutcliffe. Peeled plaster has revealed tiny ghost sketches John made in the walls. Live bands and a small dance floor let you kick loose. Open M-Th noon-11pm, F-Sa noon-2am, Su noon-10:30pm.

Slaters Bar, 26 Slater St. (☎708 6990). Youthful queues form outside. Cheap drinks (pints from £1.10). Open M-Sa 11am-2am, Su noon-10:30pm.

THE LOCAL STORY

MEET THE BEATLES

In the summer of 2002, Let's Go interviewed Allan Williams, owner of The Jacaranda Coffee Bar in Liverpool and first manager of the world's favorite mop-heads. Williams r███us with tales of a simpler t███en the Beatles were coffee shop bums, skipping lectures to hang out at The Jac, eating their beloved "bacon-butty" sandwiches, and listening to the music they would come to dominate...when Pete Best kept the beat (not that Ringo interloper) and the group had to be smuggled into Hamburg as "students" (and then deported when a 17-year-old George Harrison was busted for hanging out at 18+ clubs). Here are just a few of his memories.

LG: So tell me how you first met the Beatles.

AW: My wife and I had a coffee bar club... because I was a rock 'n' roll promoter, all the groups used to come to my place, mainly because I let them rehearse for fre█ n the basement... I only knew [the Beatles] as coffee bar layabouts—they were always bumming coffee off of *anybody*... I had complaints about the obscene graffiti that the girls were writing about the groups, and here these lads were from the art school and they could paint. I said, "Will you decorate the ladies' toilets for me?" And the way they decorated them, I'd have preferred the graffiti, to be honest with you. They were just

Ye Cracke, 13 Rice St. (☎709 4171). Where Lennon used to finish off pints; ask about how he later got banned. A grizzled, older crowd frequents the simple bar and beer garden. Open M-Sa noon-11pm, Su noon-10:30pm. Food served until 6pm.

◙ MAGICAL MYSTERY TOUR

With first-rate museums, two dazzling cathedrals, and the twin religions of football and the Beatles, Liverpool's attractions are endowed with spirited heritage and modern vitality. The city center is oozing with theaters and cultural centers, while **Hope Street** to the southeast connects Liverpool's two 20th-century cathedrals. Most other sights are located on or near **Albert Dock,** an open rectangle of Victorian warehouses now stocked with offices, restaurants, and museums.

THE BEATLES STORY. Walk-through recreations of Hamburg, the Cavern Club, and a shiny Yellow Submarine. Trace the rise and—sigh—fall of the band, while helpful timelines and definitions ("mania: mental derangement marked by excitement") keep their legacy in perspective. Audio-taped screeches of real fans and (of course) recordings of the foursome accompany the newfangled audio tour. Avoid popular weekend times. *(Albert Dock. ☎709 1963; www.beatlesstory.com. Open daily 10am-6pm. Last admission 1hr. before close. £8, concessions £5.45, children £5, families £19.)*

LIVERPOOL CATHEDRAL. Begun in 1904 but not completed until in 1978, this vast Anglican cathedral makes up for everything it lacks in age with sheer size. Its towering walls claim a number of superlatives, featuring the highest Gothic arches ever built (107 ft.) and the highest and heaviest (31 tons) bells in existence, as well as an organ with 9765 pipes, second in size only to the one in Royal Albert Hall in London. Take two lifts and climb 108 stairs for awe-inspiring views, or wait below for haunting minor chords capable of rattling windows, heads, and disbelievers. *(Upper Duke St. ☎709 6271. Cathedral open daily 8am-6pm. Tower open daily Mar.-Sept. 11am-5pm, Oct.-Feb. 11am-4pm. £3.25, children £1.50. Cathedral only free.)*

MORE BEATLES. For other Beatles-themed locales, get the **Beatles Map** (£3) at the TIC. To reach **Penny Lane,** take bus #86A, 33, or 35 from Queen's Sq.; for **Strawberry Fields,** take #176 from Paradise St. Souvenir hunters can raid the **Beatles Shop,** 31 Matthew St., canopied with shirts and the best Beatles posters in town. Doors are open "8 Days a Week." *(☎236 8066. Open M-Sa 9:30am-5:30pm, Su 10:30am-4:30pm.)* Right above the shop is the **Matthew Street Gallery,** which holds a number of John Lennon originals. *(☎236 0009. Open M-Sa 10am-5pm, Su 11am-4pm.)*

MERSEYSIDE MARITIME MUSEUM. Liverpool's heyday as a major port has passed, but the six impressive floors of this museum allow you to explore the legacies of adventure and misadventure that have played out upon its corner of the Atlantic and beyond. Collections include relics from the *Titanic.* On the bottom floor is the phenomenal **H.M. Customs and Excise Museum,** with an intriguing array of confiscated goods from would-be smugglers, including a tortoise-turned-mandolin and a teddy bear full of cocaine. In the basement, the **Transatlantic Slavery Gallery** allows visitors to walk through the darkened hull of a recreated slave ship or learn how many (answer: a lot) of Liverpool's street names are connected to the slave trade. *(Albert Dock. ☎478 4499. Open daily 10am-5pm. Free.)*

TATE GALLERY. The Liverpool branch of this legendary institution boasts a collection of favorites (Warhol, Pollock) and lesser-knowns from the 20th century. International artists dominate the ground floor, while the next level shows a rotating collection from the gallery's archives. By prior arrangement, the staff will fit the visually impaired with special gloves and allow them to touch some of the art. *(Albert Dock. ☎702 7400; www.tate.org.uk/liverpool. Open Tu-Su 10am-5:50pm. Free. Suggested donation £2. Special exhibits £4, concessions £3.)*

METROPOLITAN CATHEDRAL OF CHRIST THE KING. Controversially "modern," some would sooner call this oddity of the skyline ugly. A crown of crosses top its reinforced concrete "Lantern Tower" (resembling an upside-down funnel), while inside, bright slivers of stained glass bathe the chapel alcoves in sparkling jewel tones. The bronze Stations of the Cross by sculptor Sean Rice are dramatic, but the immensity of the circular chapel and the welcoming nature are ultimately the spiritual takeaways. *(Mt. Pleasant. ☎709 9222. Open summer M-F 7:30am-6pm, Sa-Su 8:30am-6pm; winter M-F 8am-6pm, Sa 8:30am-6pm, Su 8:30am-5pm. Free.)*

LIVERPOOL AND EVERTON FOOTBALL CLUBS. If you're not here for the Beatles, you're probably here for the football. The rivalry between the city's two main teams is deep and passionate. **Liverpool** and **Everton** offer tours of their grounds (Anfield and Goodison Park, respectively) and tickets to matches when available. Book both in advance.

throwing paint on them as if they were Picassos.

LG: Sort of Pollock-style...
AW: Heh. Yeah...

LG: And how did you become their manager?
AW: I put this big rock 'n' roll show on. They came and saw me the next day and said, "Hey Al? When are you going to do something for us like?" And I said to them, "Look, there's no more painting to be done." And they said, "No, we've got a *group.*" I said, "I didn't know that." And they said, "Well, will you manage us?" By then I had got to know them, and they were quite nice personalities—very witty. And I go, "Oh yeah, this could be fun." And then I managed them.

Williams told us how it was their stint in Hamburg, and not Liverpool, that made the Beatles. He then described his falling out with the group, over (what else?) contract disputes and general rock star ingratitude.

AW: I wrote them a letter saying that they appeared to be getting more than a little swell-headed, and, remember, "I managed you when nobody else wanted to know you. But I'll fix it now so that you'll never ever work again."
LG: Uh-oh.

AW: Heh-heh. So that's my big mistake, yeah. Heh. And on that note, we'll finish.

(Both can be reached by bus #26 from the city center. Liverpool ☎ 260 6677. Everton ☎ 330 2277. Liverpool tour, including entrance to their museum £9, concessions £5.50. Everton tour £8.50/£5. Match tickets usually range £29-32.)

THE MUSEUM OF LIVERPOOL LIFE. Recreated "courts"—enclosed blocks—and basement cellars recall story labor struggles, race relations and "busy, noisy, smoky, money-getting Liverpool." Footage plays from legendary football matches between Liverpool and Everton, while a plaque commemorates Grand National-winning horses and a jukebox lets visitors choose from the numerous hits sung by Liverpool artists. *(Albert Dock. ☎ 478 4080. Open daily 10am-5pm. Free.)*

WALKER ART GALLERY. The massive collection in this stately gallery features a wide range of pieces, including a number of medieval and classical works as well as a variety of impressive post-Impressionist and pre-Raphaelite paintings. *(William Brown St. ☎ 478 4199. Open daily 10am-5pm. Free.)*

THE WILLIAMSON TUNNELS HERITAGE CENTRE. Called "The King of Edge Hill" by some (and the "Mole of Edge Hill" by those more skeptical of his vision), William Josephson kept hundreds of local laborers employed during a post-war depression building huge, multi-level tunnels to nowhere. What little has been excavated can now be toured by visitors with 30min. to spare. *(The Old Stableyard, Smithdown Ln. ☎ 709 6868. Open summer Tu-Su 10am-6pm; winter Th-Su 10am-5pm. Last admission 1hr. before close. £3.50, concessions £3, families £10.)*

OTHER SIGHTS. A small interactive museum below the conservation studios for the National Museum and Galleries of Merseyside, the **Conservation Centre,** Whitechapel, provides insight into the processes of art restoration and preservation. Hands-on exhibits are particularly engaging for children. *(☎ 478 4999. Open M-Sa 10am-5pm, Su noon-5pm. Tours W and Sa 2 and 3pm. Free.)* The **Liverpool Museum,** William Brown St., is currently undergoing renovations to be completed by 2005. It contains a "Treasure House" of prized objects from around the world, a World Cultures Gallery, an extensive Egyptian collection, and a Planetarium. *(Open daily 10am-5pm. Free.)* Housed in a shimmering metallic building, **FACT (Film, Art, Creative Technology),** 88 Wood St., was built as a showcase for the digital arts, showing feature films, cult favorites, digital installations, computer graphics, and even robotics displays. *(☎ 707 4450. Open Tu-W 11am-6pm, Th-Sa 11am-8pm, Su noon-5pm. Screenings run later. Pick up screening schedules from TICs or the FACT lobby. Free. Screenings £3.50-5.50.)* At **Icons,** 17 Colonnades, Albert Dock, silkscreens of Marilyn Monroe and a plethora of Elvis memorabilia find their way into shopping bags. *(☎ 709 1790. Open daily 10am-6pm. Free.)*

♫ HIPPY HIPPY SHAKE

The *Liverpool Echo*, sold daily by street vendors, has up-to-date information, especially the *What's On* section of Friday editions (35p). *Itchy Liverpool* (£3 at TICs) is another useful guide to the nightlife scene. Generally, however, you need only wander near the Ropewalks and you'll find something your style.

    Quiggins, 12-16 School Ln. (☎ 709 2462; open M-Sa 10am-6pm), and the **Palace,** 6-10 Slater St. (☎ 708 8515; open M-Sa 10am-6pm), sell crazy hipster paraphernalia in a collection of stores and have tons of flyers detailing the club scene. Check out posted bills or inquire about gay and lesbian events at **News From Nowhere,** 96 Bold St., a feminist bookshop run by a women's cooperative. (☎ 708 7270. Open M-Sa 10am-5:45pm.)

    On weekend nights, the downtown area overflows with young pubbers and clubbers, especially **Matthew Street, Church Street,** and the area known as the **Ropewalks,** bounded by Hanover St., Bold St., Duke St., and Berry St. Window-shop venues to find what you like, and dress smartly (no trainers) to avoid provoking an army of black-clad bouncers. Avoid wandering into dark alleys, as concentrations of drunken revelers make prime targets for theft. The pricier bars and clubs clustered around **Albert Dock** tend to appeal to a well-groomed 20-something set.

CLUBS AND BARS

Society, 64 Duke St. (☎ 707 3575; www.society.co.uk). Sparing no expense, the owners have revamped their club with a plush Temple Room and exclusive VIP lounge above the steamy dance floor. Decked-out crowds make its theme nights notorious. You too will spare no expense; cover F £7, Sa £10, Su £5. Open F 10:30pm-2am, Sa 10:30pm-4am, Su 10:30pm-1am.

The Cavern Club, 10 Mathew St. (☎ 236 9091). The restored incarnation of this legendary underground Beatles venue still has many of its original brick archways in place. Talented up-and-coming unknowns play here hoping that history will repeat itself. F live music. Cover £2-4 after 9pm. Pub open M-Sa from noon, Su noon-11:30pm. Club open M-W 11am-8pm, Th-Sa 11am-2am, Su 11am-12:30am.

Le Bateau, 62 Duke St. (☎ 709 6508). Friday nights see toxic city and ska, while Saturdays tout funk and indie tunes in the venue's 2 floors. It may be shadowed by its bigger neighbor, Society, but it's far cheaper. Cover £2-4.50. Open F-Sa 10pm-3am.

The Blue Angel, 108 Seel St. (☎ 709 1535). This local dive, better known as the Raz, has an appeal that's less about style and more about unaffected, uninhibited good times. M live music. M sees 70p pints, Tu everything £1, Th 3 for 2 deals. Cover £1-1.50. Open M-Sa 10pm-2am.

Blue Bar, Albert Dock (☎ 702 5835; www.thebluebar.co.uk). Where tanned Brit-flick stars discuss their latest deal while their girlfriends pout. Or vice-versa. Sleek, sparkly, and chill; find (or fake) your inner chic and head on over. Open M-W 11am-12:30am, Th-Sa 11am-2am, Su 11am-12:30am.

MUSIC, THEATER, AND FESTIVALS

⊠ Bluecoat Arts Centre (info line ☎ 709 5297, box office 707 9393), off School Ln. Begun in 1717 as a charity school, Liverpool's performing arts center offers workshops in music, dance, and art. An art-school atmosphere permeates the exhibition spaces, though they house professional work. Open M-Sa 9am-5pm. Box office open M-F 11am-4pm. Gallery open Tu-Sa 10:30am-5pm.

Philharmonic Hall, Hope St. (☎ 709 3789; www.liverpoolphil.com). The **Royal Liverpool Philharmonic,** one of England's better orchestras, performs here along with many others, including jazz and funk bands. Office open for telephone bookings M-Sa 10am-5:30pm, Su noon-5pm; on concert nights, counter is open from 5:30pm until 15min. after the performance begins. Tickets from £15, same-day concessions half-price.

Liverpool Empire Theatre, Lime St. (☎ 0870 606 3536). A variety of dramatic performances, including famed troupes such as the Royal Shakespeare Company. Box office open M-Sa 10am-6pm and before curtain. Tickets from £6-50, concessions available.

Everyman Theatre, 13 Hope St. (☎ 709 4776; www.everymanplayhouse.com). The non-traditional counterpart to its urban partner, Liverpool Playhouse. Box office open M-Sa 10am-6pm and before curtain. Tickets £5-18.

Unity Theatre, 1 Hope Pl. (☎ 709 4988). This socially conscious theater was established in 1937 to support Spanish citizens fighting Franco. Box office open M 1-6pm, Tu-Sa 10:30am-6pm, and 10:30am-8:30pm on show dates.

Festivals: Liverpool hosts numerous conventions and festivals, ranging from the **Mersey River Festival** (mid-June; ☎ 233 3007; www.merseyriverfestival.co.uk) to the **International Street Theatre Festival** (early Aug.; ☎ 709 3334; www.brouhaha.uk.com). At the end of August, a week-long **Beatles Convention** draws Fab Four devotees (☎ 236 9091; www.caverncitytours.com). The TIC stocks a comprehensive list.

MANCHESTER ☎0161

The Industrial Revolution transformed the unremarkable village of Manchester into Britain's second-largest urban area. A center of manufacturing in the 19th century, the city became a hotbed of liberal politics, its deplorable working-class conditions arousing the indignation of everyone from Frederic Engels (who called it "Hell on Earth") to John Ruskin (who called it a "devil's darkness"). Now teeming with electronic beats and post-industrial glitz, Manchester has risen from factory soot to savor its reputation as one of the hippest spots in England. "Madchester" played an instrumental role in the evolution of pop music, especially the New Wave of the 80s. The wide variety of venues throughout the city are where bands like New Order, Joy Division, and Oasis got their starts. Manchester's nightclubs welcome droves of partiers, and though dodgy in parts, the city is undergoing a gradual gentrification and is accessible to the street smart.

▐ TRANSPORTATION

Flights: Manchester International Airport (☎489 3000; ☎090 1010 1000 for arrival information, 50p per call). Trains (15-20min., 4-6 per hr., £3) and buses #44 and 105 run to Piccadilly Station.

Trains: Manchester Piccadilly, London Rd. Travel center open M-Sa 8am-8:30pm, Su 11am-7pm. Trains (☎08457 484 950) from: **Birmingham** (1¾hr., every hr., £19.50); **Chester** (1hr., every hr., £9.50); **Edinburgh** (4hr., 5 per day, £49); **London Euston** (2½-3hr., every hr., £51); **York** (40min., 2 per hr., £16.10). **Manchester Victoria,** Victoria St., mostly serves trains from the west and north. Ticket office open M-Sa 6:30am-10pm, Su 8am-10:15pm. From **Liverpool** (50min., 2 per hr., £7.80). The stations are connected by Metrolink (see below). Additional service to local areas available at the **Deansgate** and **Oxford Road** stations.

Buses: Chorlton Street Coach Station, Chorlton St. Office open M-Th and Sa 7:30am-7pm, F and Su 7:30am-8pm. **National Express** (☎08705 808 080) from: **Birmingham** (2½hr., every hr., £10.25); **Leeds** (1¼hr., every hr., £7); **Liverpool** (55min., every hr., £5.25); **London** (4-5hr., 7-12 per day, £19); **Sheffield** (1½hr., 3 per day, £6.50).

Public Transportation: Piccadilly Gardens is home to about 50 bus stops. Pick up a free route map from the TIC. **Buses** generally run until 11:30pm, some lines until 2:30am on weekends. Office open M-Sa 7am-6pm, Su 10am-6pm. All-day ticket £3.30, £2.95 if purchased before 9:30am. **Metrolink** trams (☎205 2000) link 8 stops in the city center with **Altrincham** in the southwest, **Bury** in the northeast, and **Eccles** in the west (4 per hr., 50p-£4.60). Combined bus and tram ticket £4.50. For more information, call ☎228 7811 (8am-8pm) or visit www.gmpte.gov.uk.

Taxis: Mantax (☎230 333) or **Radio Cars** (☎236 8033).

▣ ▐ ORIENTATION AND PRACTICAL INFORMATION

The city center is an odd polygon formed by **Victoria Station** to the north, **Piccadilly Station** to the east, the canals to the south, and the **River Irwell** to the west. The many byways can be tricky to navigate, but the area is fairly compact, and Mancunians are generally helpful.

Tourist Information Centre: Manchester Visitor Centre, Town Hall Extension, Lloyd St. (☎234 3157). Books accommodations for a £2.50 charge plus a 10% deposit. Distributes the *Manchester Pocket Guide,* the *Greater Manchester Network Map,* and *What's On.* Open M-Sa 10am-5:30pm, Su 10:30am-4:30pm.

Tours: City Sightseeing (☎0871 666 0000) runs hop-on, hop-off bus tours, departing from St. Peter's Sq. Tours daily May-Sept. 10am-4:30pm, every 30-60min.

Budget Travel: STA Travel, 75 Deansgate (☎839 3253). Open M-F 10am-6pm, Sa 10am-5pm.

Financial Services: Thomas Cook, 23 Market St. (☎910 8787). Open M-F 10am-6pm, Sa 9am-5:30pm, Su 11am-5pm. **American Express,** 10-12 St. Mary's Gate (☎833 7303). Open M-F 9am-5:30pm, W open at 9:30am, Sa 9am-5pm.

Work Opportunities: Visa holders can contact **Manpower,** 87-89 Mosley St. (☎236 8891) for work placement.

Police: Bootle St. (☎872 5050).

Crisis Line: Samaritans, 72-74 Oxford St. (☎236 8000; 24hr. 08457 909 090).

Pharmacy: Boots, 32 Market St. (☎832 6533). Open M-W 8am-6pm, Th 8am-8pm, F 8am-6:30pm, Sa 9am-6:30pm, Su 11am-5pm.

Hospital: Manchester Royal Infirmary, Oxford Rd. (☎276 1234).

Internet Access: Central Library, St. Peter's Sq. (☎234 1982). Free. Open M-Tu and Th 10am-7:30pm, W 1-7:30pm, F-Sa 10am-4:30pm. **easyInternet Cafe,** 8-10 Exchange St., (☎839 3500), in St. Ann's Sq. £1 per 40min., £3 per day, £7 per week, 25 days £20. Open M-Sa 7am-11pm, Su 9am-11pm.

Post Office: 26 Spring Gdns. (☎839 0687). Open M-Tu and Th-Sa 8:30am-6pm, W 9am-6pm. **Poste Restante** (☎834 8605) has a separate entrance. Open M-F 6am-1pm, Sa 6am-8:50am. **Post Code:** M2 1BB.

ACCOMMODATIONS

Cheap stays in the city center are hard to find, though summer offers the possibility of decently priced student housing. The highest concentration of budget lodgings is 2-3 mi. south in the suburbs of **Fallowfield, Withington,** and **Didsbury;** take bus #40, 42, or 157. Browse the free *Where to Stay* (at the TIC) for listings.

YHA Manchester, Potato Wharf, Castlefield (☎0870 770 5950; www.yhamanchester.org.uk). Take the metro to G-Mex Station or bus #33 from Piccadilly Gardens toward Wigan to Deansgate. Clean, spacious rooms at the scenic confluence of the city's canals. Friendly staff, good security. Lockers £1-2. Laundry £1.50. Internet access 50p per 6min. Reception 24hr. Breakfast included. Dorms £19.50; doubles £43. MC/V. ❷

THE LOWRY DESIGNER OUTLET

Instead of spending your pounds on King St., home to DKNY, Versace, D&G, Diesel, and Tommy Hilfiger, opt for the **Lowry Designer Outlet** (☎848 1848) in Salford Quays, which peddles high-end designer merchandise at rock-bottom prices. Boyfriends with bags and husbands with prams linger outside the massive outlet's 84 shops, which include a movie theater and food courts.

Proibito (☎877 4287) stocks last year's designer duds at unbelievable prices. Look for DKNY, Guess?, and Calvin Klein jeans for men and women (about £20), Valentino purses (£25-80), as well as pricier Versace, Roberto Cavalli, and D&G items. Perusing the **Karen Millen** store (☎877 8801) may reveal £110 trousers marked down to £10. The **Reiss** outlet (☎877 5051) slashes 30-50% off original prices, charging an average of £30-40 for trendy slacks and shirts. For 20-60% off top-of-the-line shoes and athletic wear, check out the **Nike** outlet (☎877 9100). Deals this good may prove hard to pass up; if you find yourself in need of extra luggage space at the end of the day, head to **Bags, Etc.** (☎877 8387) for purses, totes, and suitcases.

Take the Metrolink to Harbour City Station, cross the pink bridge, and follow signs to the colossal outlet mall, no more than a 10min. walk. Open M-F 10am-8pm, Sa 9am-7pm, Su 11am-5pm.

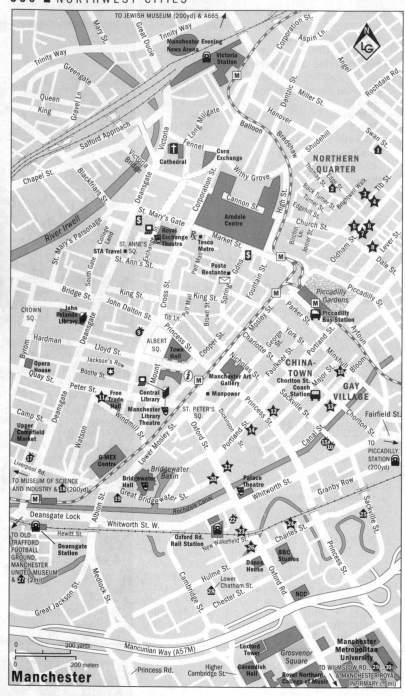

Manchester

Manchester

🏠 ACCOMMODATIONS
Burton Arms, 1
Jurys Inn Manchester, 19
Manchester Backpackers
  Hostel and Guest House, 27
Manchester Conference
  Centre and Hotel, 25
Mill Stone Inn, 2
Student Village, 28
University of Manchester
  Lodgings, 29
YHA Manchester, 18

🍖 FOOD
Camel One, 30
Cornerhouse Cafe, 22
Dimitri's, 17
Gaia, 15
Tampopo Noodle House, 9
Tribeca, 16

⭐ NIGHTLIFE
The Attic, 23
Churchills, 13
Copacabana, 8
Cord, 3
Cruz 101, 12
Dry Bar, 6
Essential, 10
Fab Cafe, 14
The Lass O'Gowrie, 24
Matt and Phred's, 4
Mtwo, 11
Music Box, 21
Night and Day Cafe, 7
Revolution, 26
Simple Bar &
  Restaurant, 5
The Temple, 20

Jurys Inn Manchester, 56 Great Bridgewater St. (☎953 8888). Enormous rooms, luxurious baths, and professional service. A double and single bed in most rooms. Hardly a deal for solo travelers, but a bargain for groups. £79 per room, weekend specials subject to availability. AmEx/MC/V. ❺

Student Village, Lower Chatham St. (☎236 1776). Dorm-style accommodations; groups of 3-7 single rooms share common space, kitchens, and bathrooms. Open mid-June to Sept. Singles £15, students £10. MC/V. ❷

Mill Stone Inn, 67 Thomas St. (☎ 839 0213). Simple but comfortable ensuite rooms conveniently located near Northern Quarter nightlife. Singles £35; twins and doubles £45; triples £60. Book ahead on weekdays. AmEx/MC/V. ❸

NORTHWEST ENGLAND

Manchester Conference Centre and Hotel, Sackville St. (☎955 8000). Modern rooms loaded with amenities including hair dryer, trouser press, and Internet access. Singles M-Th from £65, F-Su from £40; doubles from £75/£60. AmEx/MC/V. ❺

University of Manchester: Call the **University Accommodation Office** (☎275 2888) to find out which dorms are open for lodging during summer (mid-June to mid-Sept.). 3-7 day minimum stay. Reserve a week or more in advance. From £60 per week. MC/V. ❶

Burton Arms, 31 Swan St. (☎/fax 834 3455). Basic rooms above a pub on a busy street. A 15min. walk from both train stations and St. Peter's Sq. £19.50 per person, ensuite £25. AmEx/MC/V. ❸

Manchester Backpackers Hostel and Guest House, 41 and 43 Great Stone Rd. (☎865 9296). From the Old Trafford Metro Station go under the railway to the cricket grounds, make a left at the grounds and follow to the college; make a right. Basic accommodations at a budget price. Dorms £15; twins and doubles £40; triples £51; quads £64. Cash only. ❷

🍴 FOOD

Outwit the pricey **Chinatown** restaurants by eating the multi-course "Businessman's Lunch" offered by most (M-F noon-2pm, $4-8). Better yet, visit **Curry Mile,** a stretch of Asian restaurants on Wilmslow Rd., for quality cuisine. Come evening, hip youths wine and dine in the cafe-bars (p. 359). A **Tesco** supermarket is at 58-66 Market St. (☎911 9400. M-F 6am-midnight, Sa 7am-10pm, Su 11am-5pm.)

🍜 **Tampopo Noodle House,** 16 Albert Sq. (☎819 1966). This spartan noodle house is one of Manchester's favorites. Noodles from Thailand, Malaysia, Indonesia, Vietnam and Japan are well-priced (£4-8), quick, and delicious. Try the Pad Krapow with prawns and chilis. Open daily noon-11pm. Amex/MC/V. ❷

Dimitri's, Campfield Arcade, Tonman St. (☎839 3319). Greek delicacies in a bright place; eat in the outdoor arcade area. Tapas £4.55-6.95, entrees £7.95-12.95. 20% off drinks during happy hour (5-7pm). Open daily 11am-11:30pm. Amex/MC/V. ❸

Gaia, 46 Sackville St. (☎228 1002). Skilled chefs prepare brilliant fusion cuisine with Mediterranean flavor. Renaissance decor features velvet curtains, paintings, and candlelight. Daytime sandwiches and pizzas £4-7. Appetizers £3-5, entrees £9-15. Open M-Th and Su noon-midnight, F-Sa noon-2am. Food served until 10pm. AmEx/MC/V. ❸

Tribeca, 50 Sackville St. (☎236 8300), serves a wide variety of cuisines, from BBQ ribs to bangers and mash. Take your meal on one of the seductively decorated beds downstairs. Entrees £7-13. Two main dishes for £10 noon-3pm daily. Open M, Su noon-12:30am, Tu-Sa noon-2:00am. MC/V. ❸

Cornerhouse Cafe, 70 Oxford St. (☎200 1508). Part of the Cornerhouse Arts Centre; features 1 bar, 3 galleries, 3 arthouse cinemas, and trendy crowds. Create your own panini for £4.75. Other offerings range from gourmet pizza to cajun chicken. Entrees £6-8. Open M-Sa 11am-11pm, Su noon-10:30pm. Hot meals served until 10pm. Bar open M-Sa 9:30am-11pm, Su 12:30-10:30pm. MC/V. ❷

Camel One, 107 Wilmslow Rd. (☎257 2282). A simple eatery with an extensive Indian menu. Banner claims "Voted #1 in England." Kebab sandwiches made to order. Dishes £2-5.50. Open daily 10am-7pm. Cash only. ❶

🅶 SIGHTS

Few of Manchester's buildings are notable—postcards mostly portray the fronts of trams—but an exception is the neo-Gothic **Manchester Town Hall,** at Albert St. Behind the Town Hall Extension, the **Central Library** is the city's jewel. One of the largest municipal libraries in Europe, the domed building has a music and theater library, a language and literature library, and the UK's second-largest Judaica collection. The **Library Theatre Company** (☎236 7110) puts on productions and plays. The **John Rylands Library,** 150 Deansgate, keeps rare books; its most famous holding is the St. John Fragment, a piece of New Testament writing from the 2nd century. The museum is currently closed for renovations and is scheduled to reopen in late 2005. (☎275 3751. Open M-F 10am-5pm, Sa 10am-1pm. Tours W at noon. Free.)

Reopened in June 2002 after a three-year, £35 million renovation, the **Manchester Art Gallery,** on Nicholas St., holds Rossetti's stunning *Astarte Syriaca* among its gigantic collection. (☎235 8888. Open Tu-Su and bank holidays 10am-5pm. Free.) In the **Museum of Science and Industry,** Liverpool Rd., in Castlefield, working steam engines and looms provide a dramatic illustration of Britain's industrialization. (☎832 2244. Open daily 10am-5pm. Museum free. Special exhibits £3-5.) The Spanish and Portuguese synagogue-turned-**Jewish Museum,** 190 Cheetham Hill Rd., traces the history of the city's sizeable Jewish community and offers city tours. (☎834 9879. Open M-Th 10:30am-4pm, Su 10:30am-5pm. £3.95, concessions £2.95, families £9.50.)

Loved and reviled, **Manchester United** is England's reigning football team. The **Manchester United Museum and Tour Centre,** Sir Matt Busby Way, at the Old Trafford football stadium, displays memorabilia from the club's inception in 1878 to its recent trophy-hogging success. (From the Old Trafford Salford Quays Metrolink stop, follow signs. ☎0870 442 1994. Open daily 9:30am-5pm. Tours every 10min., 9:40am-4:30pm. £9, seniors £6, children free, families £25.)

⬛ NIGHTLIFE

CAFE-BARS AND CLUBS

Many of Manchester's excellent lunchtime spots morph into pre-club drinking venues or even become clubs themselves. Manchester's clubbing and live music scene remains a national trendsetter. Centered on **Oldham Street**, the **Northern Quarter** is the city's youthful outlet for live music, its alternative vibe and underground shops attracting a hip crowd. Partiers flock to **Oxford Street** for late-night clubbing and reveling. Don't forget to collect flyers—they'll often score you a discount. **Afflecks Palace**, 52 Church St., supplies paraphernalia from punk to funk; the walls of the stairway are postered with event notices. (☎839 6392. Open M-F 10am-5:30pm, Sa 10am-6pm.) Just up Oldham St., **Fat City** sells hip-hop, reggae, funk, and jazz records as well as passes to clubbing events. (☎237 1181. Open M-Sa 10am-6pm, Su noon-5pm.) At night, streets in the Northern Quarter are dimly lit. If you're crossing from Piccadilly to Swan St. or Great Ancoats St., use Oldham St., where the neon-lit clubs (and their bouncers) provide reassurance. See **Madchester**, p. 26, for plenty more of the best nightlife action.

> **Simple Bar & Restaurant,** 44 Tib St. (☎835 2526). Fuel up here before heading out to the clubs. Open Su-Th 11am-11pm, F-Sa 11am-midnight.

> **Cord,** 8 Dorsey St. (☎832 9494). Where corduroy meets chic. Open M-Sa noon-11pm, Su 3-10:30pm.

> **Dry Bar,** 28-30 Oldham St. (☎236 9840). Cavorting clubbers fill this sultry spot. Cover £2. Open M, W, and Su 9am-midnight, Tu and Th 9am-2am, F-Sa 9am-3am.

THE GAY VILLAGE

Gay and lesbian clubbers will want to check out the Gay Village, northeast of Princess St. Evening crowds fill the bars lining **Canal Street,** in the heart of the area, which is also lively during the day. When weather cooperates, the bars are busy but empty, with patrons flooding the sidewalk tables.

> **Essential,** 8 Minshull St. (☎236 0077), at the corner of Bloom St., off Portland St. Arguably the most popular club in the Gay Village. Dress smart casual. Cover £3-8. Open F 10:30pm-5am, Sa 10:30pm-6am, Su 10:30pm-3am.

> **Cruz 101,** 101 Princess St. (☎950 0101). Fun and sexy cruisers teach a lesson in attitude. Two floors with six bars. Dress smart casual. Cover M, W, Th £2; F £3; Sa £5. Open M and W-Sa 10pm-2am.

TOP TEN LIST

1. Start the night at traditional pub **Lass O'Gowrie**, 36 Charles St. (☎273 6932). Open M-Sa 11am-11pm, Su noon-10:30pm (food served M-Sa noon-7:30pm, Su noon-5pm).

2. The upstairs **Attic,** 50 New Wakefield St. (☎236 6071) grooves to live music. Open M-Sa noon-2am, Su 6pm-midnight. Cover £3-7.

3. Squeeze into **The Temple** (☎278 1610), on Bridgewater St. (literally) for a smoky, intimate drink. Open M-Sa noon-11pm, Su 5-10:30pm.

4. Stop by relaxed **Revolution,** 88-94 Oxford St. (☎237 5377), before hitting the clubs. Open M-Sa 11:30am-2am, Su noon-12:30pm.

5. Loud music and a committed crowd await at **The Music Box,** Oxford Rd. (☎273 3435). Open Th-Sa from 10pm. Cover £5-8.

6. **Mtwo,** Peter St. (☎839 1112) hosts trendy dressers and dancers. Open W-Th 10pm-2am, Sa 9pm-3am. Cover £3-6, free pre-11pm.

7. The crowd at **Fab Café,** 11 Portland St. (☎236 2019) is bright and boisterous. Open M-Th 5pm-2am, F-Sa 3pm-2am, Su 6-10:30pm.

8. **Copacabana,** 5 Dale St. (☎237 3441) serves up sangria and salsa with style. Open Tu and Th 6-11pm, W 6pm-1am, F-Sa 7pm-2am.

9. Start to unwind at the chill **Night and Day Café,** 26 Oldham St. (☎236 1822). Open M-Sa 11am-2am, Su 11am-11pm. Cover £3-5.

10. Close out the night with some relaxing jazz tunes at **Matt and Phred's,** 65 Tib St. (☎831 7002). Three live jazz sets every night. Open M-Sa 5pm-2am.

Churchills, 37 Chorlton St. (☎236 5529). This pub-club in the heart of the Gay Village hosts M Old School themed nights, W drag disco, T, Th karaoke nights, and F-Sa disco dance parties. No cover. Open M-Sa noon-2am, Su noon-12:30am.

🎵 🌿 ENTERTAINMENT AND FESTIVALS

Manchester's many entertainment venues accommodate diverse interests. The **Manchester Evening News (MEN) Arena** (☎930 8000; www.men-arena.com), behind Victoria Station, hosts concerts and sporting events.

Royal Exchange Theatre (☎833 9833) has returned to St. Ann's Sq., a few years after an IRA bomb destroyed the original building. The theater stages traditional and Shakespearean plays and premieres of original works. Box office open M-Sa 9:30am-7:30pm. Tickets £7.25-25.50. Contact regarding concessions.

Bridgewater Hall, Lower Mosley St. (☎907 9000). Manchester's foremost venue for orchestral concerts and home of the Hallé Orchestra. Open M-Sa 10am-8pm, Su noon-6pm. Tickets £7-30.

Palace Theatre, Oxford St. (☎228 6255). Caters to classical tastes in theater, opera, and ballet. Box office open M-Sa 10am-6pm and before curtain.

The Manchester Festival (www.the-manchester-festival.org.uk) runs all summer with dramatic, musical, and multimedia events. For more information, call the city council (☎234 3157). The Gay Village hosts a number of festivals, most notably late August's **Mardi Gras** (☎238 4548), which raises money for AIDS relief.

BLACKPOOL   ☎01253

Recent proposals to clear Blackpool's brassy boulevards of tacky souvenirs just don't seem to get it: tourists flock here for bright lights, simple joys, and cheap thrills, and Blackpool delivers. Penny arcades, 24hr. snooker tables, donkey rides, exotic dancers, tattoo parlors—such frivolities cater to 7.8 million visitors every year. Though it's lost its urbane 19th-century resort status to a more raucous sort, those who can forgive the gaudy hedonism partake in nights of uninhibited fun.

▐ TRANSPORTATION

Buses and trains are regular, but drivers should be warned: it's not uncommon to see 2 or more traffic cops on a single street dispensing fines.

Trains: Blackpool North Station (☎620 385), 4 blocks down Talbot Rd. from North Pier. Booking office open M-F 6:30am-9pm, Sa 6:40am-8:40pm, Su 9:10am-4:40pm. Trains (☎08457 484 950) arrive from: **Birmingham** via **Preston** (2½hr., 1-2 per hr., £29); **Leeds** (2hr., every hr., £13); **Liverpool** (1½hr., every 2 hr., £11.70); **London Euston** via **Preston** (4hr., every hr., £57.10); **Manchester** (1¼hr., 2 per hr., £10.95).

Buses: Station on Talbot Rd. Ticket office open M-Sa 9am-1:15pm and 2-5pm. **National Express** (☎08705 808 080) buses from **Birmingham** (3-4hr., 5 per day, £16), **London** (6½-8hr., 4 per day, £23.50), and **Manchester** (2hr., 4 per day, £5.75).

Public Transportation: Local trains use Blackpool South and Pleasure Beach stations. **Local bus** info is available at Talbot Rd. station. Bus #1 covers the Promenade from North Pier to Pleasure Beach every 20min.; on weekends, **vintage trams** run this route more frequently. A 1-day **Travelcard** (£5, concessions £4.50) buys unlimited travel on trams and local buses; otherwise one ride costs £1.10. 3-day pass £13.

Taxi: Tower Taxi is 24hr. (☎626 262).

⛏ PRACTICAL INFORMATION

Tourist Information Centre: 1 Clifton St. (☎478 222; fax 478 210). Arranges accommodations for £3 plus a 10% deposit, books local shows for £1.50, and sells street maps for £1. (Find the same map in their free accommodations listings.) Open May-Oct. M-Sa 9am-5pm; Nov.-Apr. M-Sa 9am-4:30pm. **Branch** (☎478 222) on the Promenade near the Tower. Open M-Sa 9:30am-5:30pm, Su 10am-4:30pm. A few **iPlus kiosks** scattered throughout town offer up 24hr. computerized information.

Financial Services: Banks are easy to find, especially along Corporation St. and Birley St. Most are open M-F 9am-4:30pm.

Police: Staining Fleetwood (☎852 471).

Hospital: Victoria Hospitals, Whinney Heys Rd. (☎300 000).

Launderette: Albert Road Launderette at the corner of Albert Rd. and Regent Rd. Open M-F 9am-7pm, Sa 9am-4pm, Su 10am-2pm. Last wash 1hr. before closing. Wash £2.40, dry 20p per 5min.

Internet Access: Blackpool Public Library (☎478 080), on Queen St. Free. Open M and F 9am-5pm, Tu and Th 9am-7pm, W and Sa 10am-5pm. **Cafe@Claremont,** Dickson Rd. (☎299 306).

Pharmacy: Boots (☎622 276) at Bank Hey St. and Victoria Rd. Open M-Sa 8:30am-6pm.

Post Office: 26-30 Abingdon St. (☎08457 223 344). **Bureau de change.** Open M-F 9am-5:30pm, Sa 9am-12:30pm. **Post Code:** FY1 1AA.

⛏ ACCOMMODATIONS

With over 2600 guest houses and 96,000 beds, you won't have trouble finding a room, except on weekends during the Illuminations (p. 362), when prices skyrocket. Budget-friendly **B&Bs** dominate the blocks behind the Promenade between the North and Central Piers (£10-20). Pick up the free Bible-sized *Blackpool: So Much Fun You Can Taste It* guide at the TIC for an impressive list.

🏨 **Raffles Hotel,** 73-77 Hornby Rd. (☎294 713; www.raffleshotelblackpool.co.uk), is a 15min. walk from the bus and train stations, 5min. from the Promenade and Tower. From the train or bus station, head toward the ocean along Talbot Rd., turn left on Topping St., left on Church St., right on Regent Rd., and right onto Hornby Rd. Luxuriously decorated rooms include Japanese, Indian and Greek-themed rooms on top levels. Breakfast included. Twins, doubles, and family rooms £24-31 per person. MC/V. ❸

Manor Grove Hotel, 24 Leopold Grove (☎/fax 625 577). Follow the Raffles directions, but turn right at Church St., left onto Leopold Grove, and walk 1 block. Spacious rooms with Internet jacks, TV, phone, and bath. Hearty English breakfast included. £20-21, £6 more for singles, more on weekends. MC/V. ❸

York House, 30 South King St. (☎624 200). Follow Raffles directions, but turn right onto South King St. after the left on Church St. Bay windows, high ceilings, and aristocratic decor. Breakfast included. All rooms with TV and bath. £25 per person. Cash only. ❸

Silver Birch Hotel, 39 Hull Rd. (☎622 125). From either station, head down Talbot Rd. to the ocean, take a left on Market St., pass the Tower, and turn left onto Hull Rd. Maternal proprietress Susan provides decent rooms and warm Irish hospitality. Singles and doubles £13 per person. Breakfast £2. Cash only. ❷

⛏ FOOD

Though waterfront cuisine consists mostly of candy floss and fish and chips, heading off the Promenade should yield some more appetizing alternatives. The **Iceland** supermarket, 8-10 Topping St., is on the same block as the bus station. (☎751 575.

Open M-Sa 8:30am-10pm, Su 10:30am-4pm.) For more exotic flavors, look for the turquoise and yellow **Lagoonda Afro-Caribbean Restaurant ❶**, directly across from the central library, which rewards daring diners who finish the hot jerk with a free beer. (☎293 837. Open Th 7-11pm, F-Sa 7am-midnight, other times for group bookings. Cash only.) The cozy **Coffee Pot ❶**, 12 Birley St., serves big portions; try the roast beef dinner (£4.95), which comes with Yorkshire pudding, boiled potatoes, and two vegetables. (☎751 610. Open daily June-Nov. 8am-6pm; Dec.-May 8am-4:30pm. Cash only.) **Robert's Oyster Bar ❶**, 90 Promenade on the Central Beach, is stocked full of prawns (£1.30) and fresh oysters (6 for £5) for takeaway. (Open roughly 9am-9pm. Cash only.)

🎦 🎵 SIGHTS AND ENTERTAINMENT

No fewer than 36 nightclubs, 38,000 theater seats, several circuses, and a rumbling of roller coasters line the **Promenade,** which is traversed by Britain's first electric tram line. Even the three 19th-century piers are stacked with ferris wheels and chip shops. The only thing the hedonistic hordes don't come for is the ocean.

PLEASURE BEACH. Around 7.8 million people visit this sprawling forty-acre amusement park annually, second in Europe only to EuroDisney. Pleasure Beach is known for its historic wooden roller coasters—the twin-track **Grand National** (c. 1935) is something of a mecca for coaster enthusiasts, and the **Big Dipper** was invented here. Thousands of thrill-seekers line up for the aptly named **Big One** and aren't disappointed as the 235 ft. steel behemoth sends them down a heartstopping 65° slope at 87 mph. Although admission to the themeless park is free, the rides themselves aren't—fortunately, the pay-as-you-ride system means queues are shorter than at other amusement parks. By night, Pleasure Beach features illusion shows, including Las Vegas-style performances. *(Across from South Pier. ☎0870 444 5566. Opening times vary with month and day, but generally 10:30am-9:30pm in summer months. £1-6 per ride. 1-day pass £30, 2-day £45.)*

BLACKPOOL TOWER. When a London businessman visited the 1890 Paris World Exposition, he returned determined to erect Eiffel Tower imitations throughout Britain. Only Blackpool embraced his enthusiasm, and in 1894 the 560 ft. Tower graced the city's skyline. Unfortunately, it looks more like a rusty junkheap find than France's sleek symbol of modernism. The five-story **Towerworld** in its base is a bizarre microcosm of Blackpool's eclectic kitsch with a motley crew of attractions: a neon-blue aquarium, a motorized dinosaur ride, a sprawling jungle gym, arcade games, and a casino. An overly ornate Victorian ballroom hosts sedately dancing senior citizens during the day and live swing band performances at night (8pm). Towerworld's circus, named the UK's best, runs up to four shows per day and features mesmerizing tightrope walking, dance, and stunt acts in a rather gaudy and amateur performance arena. Mooky the Clown was also voted Britain's best. *(☎292 029; www.blackpooltower.co.uk. Open daily May-Oct. 10am-11pm; Nov.-Apr. 10am-6pm. £12, concessions £10. Tickets allow all-day admission.)*

THE ILLUMINATIONS. Blackpool, the first electric town in Britain, consummates its love affair with bright lights in the orgiastic Illuminations. The annual display takes place over 5 mi. of the Promenade from September to early November. In a colossal waste of electricity, 72 mi. of cables light up the tower, the promenade, star-encased faces of Hollywood actors, corporate emblems, and garish placards.

NIGHTLIFE. Between North and Central Piers, Blackpool's famous **Golden Mile** shines with more neon than gold, hosting scores of sultry theaters, cabaret bars, and bingo halls. Rowdy **Syndicate** (☎753 222) brings droves to Church St. Blackpool's most frequented clubs are on the Promenade. **Heaven & Hell** (☎625 118), on Bank Hey St., is one block south of the Tower, and **Waterfront**, 167-170 Promenade (☎292 900), is farther north at the corner of the Promenade and Springfield Rd.

PEAK DISTRICT NATIONAL PARK

Nestled between industrial leviathans Manchester, Nottingham, and Sheffield, the Peak District is one of the most visited National Parks in the world—over 20 million come each year. Yet it's only been popular since 1951, when it was made Britain's first national park; long ago, the entire area was fenced off in bucolic isolation as royal hunting ground, and as recently as 1920 the moorland north of Edale was closed to understandably frustrated urbanites. Though the region can't lay claim to any true mountains, its 555 sq. miles offer a bit of almost everything else. In the **Dark Peak** area to the north, deep groughs (gullies) gouge the soft peat moorland below gloomy cliffs, while friendlier footpaths wind through the rocky hillsides and village clusters to the north. The pastures of the southern **White Peak** region cradle abandoned millstones, willowy duck ponds, and stately country homes in its verdant dales. Transport is best in the south and near outlying cities, but hikers should veer north for a more isolated escape.

☐ TRANSPORTATION

Trains (☎08457 484 950) are scarce in the district: three lines enter its boundaries, but only one crosses the park itself. One line travels from **Derby** to **Matlock**, on the park's southeastern edge (30min., M-Sa 13-14 per day, Su 9 per day, £3.50). Another line runs from **Manchester** to **Buxton** (1hr., every hr., £5.70), but construction will force travelers to connect by bus (free with rail ticket) to Hazel Grove. The **Hope Valley line** (M-F 11 per day, Sa 16 per day, Su 12 per day) goes from Manchester across the park via **Edale** (55min., £6.90), **Hope** (1hr., £7.20), and **Hathersage** (1hr., £7.20), terminating in **Sheffield** (1½hr., £11.20). Both lines from Manchester enter the park at **New Mills**—the Buxton line at Newtown Station and the Hope Valley line at Central Station. A 20min. signposted walk separates the stations.

A sturdy pair of legs is more than sufficient for inter-village journeys between neighboring towns, but the Derbyshire County Council's *Peak District Timetables* (60p) is invaluable for those in search of comprehensive bus information. The timetable includes all routes as well as a large map and information on day-long bus tickets, cycle hire, hostels, TICs, market days, and hospitals. A helpful way to plan regional travel can be found at www.derbysbus.net.

Buses make a noble effort to connect the scattered Peak towns, and **Traveline** (☎0870 608 2608) is a helpful resource. Coverage of many routes actually improves on Sundays, especially in summer. **Trent** (☎01773 712 265) bus TP, the "Transpeak," makes the 3hr. journey between **Manchester** and **Derby,** stopping at **Buxton, Bakewell, Matlock,** and other towns in between (M-Sa 6 per day, Su 5 per day). **First North Staffordshire** (☎01782 207 999) #X18 runs 5 times every day from **Sheffield** to **Bakewell** (45min.), **Buxton** (1¼hr.), and **Leek** (1¾hr.) en route to **Hanley** (2¼hr.). **First South Yorkshire** (☎01709 515 151) #272 and **Stagecoach East Midland** (☎01246 211 007) #273 and 274 reach **Castleton** from **Sheffield** (40-55min.; 15 per day, Su 12 per day). Stagecoach also runs between **Sheffield** and **Buxton** via **Eyam** (#65-66; 1¼hr.; M-Sa 5 per day, Su 3 per day) and from **Bakewell** to **Castleton** (#173; 50min.; M-Sa 5 per day, Su 3 per day). **Bowers Coaches** (☎01298 812 204) #200 runs from **Castleton** to **Edale** (20 min., M-F 3-7 per day) and sometimes continues to

Chapel-en-le-Frith. On weekends it runs as #260 and stops at all the Castleton caverns en route (Sa-Su 7 per day). Ride is free with proof of railway transport. Long distance bus rides come by **National Express** from **London** once a day to: **Bakewell** (4¾hr, ₤19), **Buxton** (5hr., ₤19), and **Matlock** (4½hr, ₤19).

If you're going to use public transport, pick one of the half-dozen bargain day tickets available; they're clearly explained in the *Timetables* booklet, and several have their own brochures at the TIC. The best deal is the **Derbyshire Wayfarer** (₤7.50, concessions ₤3.75, families ₤12), which allows one day of train and bus travel through the Peak District north to Sheffield and south to Derby. Day passes are sold at the Manchester train stations and at National Park Information Centres (NPICs), as well as at local rail stations and on most buses.

🛈 PRACTICAL INFORMATION

Daytime facilities in the Peak District generally stay open all winter due to nearby large cities. Some B&Bs and hostels welcome travelers until December; YHA Edale is open year-round. Most TICs book accommodations for a 10% deposit. The **Peak District National Park Office,** Aldern House, Baslow Rd., Bakewell, Derbyshire (☎01629 816 200; www.peakdistrict-npa.gov.uk) is a useful contact.

National Park Information Centres: All NPICs carry detailed walking guides and provide fun facts on the park.

Bakewell: Old Market Hall (☎01629 813 227; fax 814 782), at Bridge St. From the bus stop, walk a block down Bridge St. with Bath Gardens on your left. Doubles as the TIC, with accommodations booking. Upstairs exhibit on the town's history. Open daily Mar.-Oct. 9:30am-5:30pm; Nov.-Feb. 10am-5pm.

Castleton: Buxton Rd. (☎01433 620 679). From the bus stop, follow the road past the post office into town and head right; the NPIC is along the road that leads to the caverns. Great geological and cultural display in annex. Open daily Apr.-Oct. 9:30am-5:30pm; Nov.-Mar. 10am-5pm.

Edale: Fieldhead (☎01433 670 207; fax 670 216), between the rail station and village; signs point the way from both directions. Open daily Apr.-Oct. 9am-1pm and 2-5:30pm; Nov.-Mar. Sa-Su 9am-1pm and 2-5pm.

Fairholmes: Upper Derwent Valley (☎01433 650 953), near Derwent Dam. Open daily Apr.-Oct. 9:30am-1pm and 2-5pm; Nov.-Mar. Sa-Su 9:30am-1pm and 1-4:30pm.

Tourist Information Centres:

Ashbourne: 13 Market Pl. (☎01335 343 666; fax 300 638). Open Mar.-Oct. M-Sa 9:30am-5pm, Su 10am-4pm; Nov.-Feb. M-Sa 10am-4pm.

Buxton: The Crescent (☎01298 25106). Open daily Mar.-Sept. 9:30am-5pm; Oct.-Feb. 10am-4pm.

Matlock: Crown Sq. (☎01629 583 388). Open daily Mar.-Oct. 9:30am-5pm; Nov.-Feb. 10am-4pm.

Matlock Bath: The Pavilion (☎01629 55082), along the main road. Open daily Mar.-Oct. 9:30am-5pm; Nov.-Feb. Sa-Su 10am-4pm. Hours vary.

🏠 ACCOMMODATIONS

NPICs and TICs distribute park-wide and regional accommodations guides and a Caravaning and camping guide (both free). The *Peak District Visitor's Guide*, with a list of accommodations and attractions, is free from TICs and NPICs. **B&Bs** are plentiful and cheap (₤18-20 in the countryside, ₤20-25 in towns), as are **hostels** (around ₤10). **Bakewell** and **Matlock Bath** are well stocked with B&Bs. Most hostels are not open every day of the week. Many farmers allow **camping** on their land, sometimes for a small fee; remember to ask first and leave the site as you found it.

Peak District National Park

◯ SIGHTS
Axe Edge Moor, **28**
Birchinlee Pasture, **14**
Black Ashop Moor, **13**
Black Hill (1910 ft.), **5**
Blue John Cavern, **21**
Broomhead Moor, **10**

Derwent Moors, **18**
Dick Hill, **2**
Edale Head, **16**
Edale Moor, **17**
Hartington Upper Quarter, **26**
Hobson Moss, **11**
Hope Woodlands, **12**

Jacob's Ladder, **19**
Kinder Low (2087 ft.), **15**
Longsett Moors, **7**
Mam Tor, **20**
Margery Hill (1793 ft.), **9**
Middle Hills, **29**
Peak Cavern, **24**
Raven's Low, **27**
Saddleworth, **3**

Shining Clough Mass, **8**
Shining Tor (1854 ft.), **25**
Speedwell Cavern, **23**
Thor's Cave, **30**
Thurlstone Moor, **6**
Treak Cliff Cavern, **22**
Wessenden Head Moor, **4**
Wessenden Moor, **1**

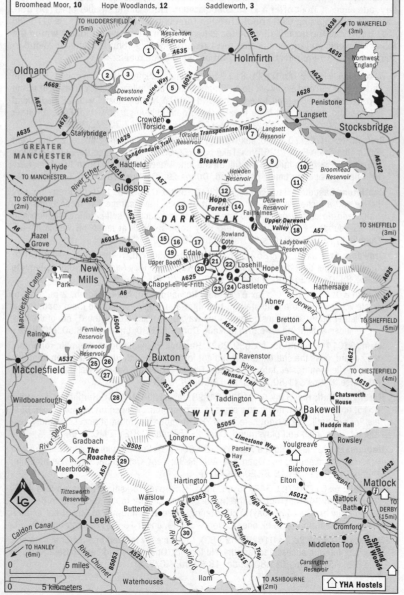

NORTHWEST ENGLAND

YHA HOSTELS

The Peak District has almost 20 hostels, many of which are listed below, but don't let numbers fool you—most fill quickly with school groups, so call ahead to reserve a space. Hostels lie within a day's hike of one another and sell maps detailing routes to neighboring hostels. Alternatively, *Peak District Timetables* (60p at TICs) lists both YHAs and the bus services to them. Unless noted, the hostels serve meals and are phasing out once rigid 10am-5pm lockout and 11pm curfew with keycode access. Most offer a £1 **student discount.** Three of the smaller ones (Bretton, Langsett, and Shining Cliff) book through the central **YHA Diary** office (☎0114 288 4541); only call the hostels directly for general information or for lodging within the following week, and remember that most require booking 48hr. in advance. Membership is generally required and can be purchased in installments.

Bakewell: Fly Hill (☎/fax 01629 812 313), a 5min. walk from the town center. From the bus stop at Rutland Sq., walk up N. Church Street and follow it as it curves right at the top. Follow the signs and take the second right. A homely hostel with 28 beds, kind staff, board games, and huge meals. Open daily July-Aug.; Nov.-Dec. F-Sa; all other times open for group bookings. Dorms £10.60, under 18 £7.20. MC/V. ❶

Bretton: (☎0870 770 5720; fax 0870 770 5682). Self-catering hostel 2½ mi. from Eyam atop Eyam Edge (1250 ft.). Take bus #65-66 to Foolow. Face the pub and follow the sign to Bretton a mile up the hill on the left. A heck of a view. Open July-Aug., flexible openings at other times; call ahead. Dorms £9.30, under 18 £6.70. Cash only. ❶

Castleton: Castleton Hall (☎01433 620 235; fax 01433 621 767). Pretty country house and attached vicarage in the heart of town. The vicarage has nicer rooms with baths and no curfew or lockout. Internet access, spacious self-catering kitchen, and several lounges. Free coffee and tea. Very popular—book at least 2-3 weeks ahead. Open daily Feb.-Dec. Dorms £11.80, under 18 £8.50. MC/V. ❷

Crowden: (☎/fax 01457 852 135), Crowden, Hadfield, Hyde. Take bus #350 to Crowden (3 per day); the hostel is 200 yd. away. Open May-Aug. M-Sa; April Tu-Sa; late Mar. F-Sa. Dorms £10.60, under 18 £7.20. MC/V. ❶

Edale: (☎01433 670 302; fax 670 243), Rowland Cote, Nether Booth, 2 mi. east of Edale village. From the train station, turn right and then left onto the main road; follow it to Nether Booth, where a sign points the way. Buses also stop within ½ mi. of the hostel. Includes a climbing tower. No lockout. Dorms £11.80, under 18 £8.50. MC/V. ❷

Eyam: (☎01433 630 335; fax 639 202), Hawkhill Rd. Walk down the main road from the square, pass the church, and look right for the sign. With turret and oaken door, it's more castle than hostel. Internet access. Open Feb.-Oct. M-Sa; late Oct.-Nov. F-Sa; call otherwise. Dorms £11.80, under 18 £8.50. MC/V. ❷

Hartington Hall: Hall Bank (☎01298 84223; fax 01298 84415), Hartington. From the A515, turn at Ashbowl and follow signs. 131 beds in a 17th-century manor house. Bonnie Prince Charlie once slept here, sans YHA membership. Internet access, laundry, restaurant, TV lounge, and playground. Dorms £15, under 18 £11. MC/V. ❷

Hathersage: Castleton Rd. (☎/fax 01433 650 493). Stone building with white-framed windows and creeping ivy. Open Apr.-Aug. M-Sa; Sept.-Oct. Tu-Sa; otherwise rentable. Dorms £10.60, under 18 £7.20. MC/V. ❶

Langsett: (☎01226 761 548). 5 mi. from Penistone. Yorkshire Traction buses #23, 23a, 24, and 24a stop outside the hostel on their circular routes to and from Barnsley (M-Sa every hr., Su 15 per day). Self-catering. Open daily mid-July to Aug.; Sept. to mid-July most F-Sa; book a week ahead. Dorms £9.30, under 18 £6.70. Cash only. ❶

Matlock: 40 Bank Rd. (☎01629 582 983). Conveniently located in a regional train and bus hub. Internet access and laundry. No lockout. Open daily mid Feb. to Sept.; Nov. to mid-Feb. F-Sa. Dorms £11.80, under 18 £8.50. MC/V. ❷

Ravenstor: (☎01298 871 826), ½ mi. from Millers Dale. Bus #65 and #66 will stop here (both M-Sa 10 per day, Su 7 per day). Internet access, bar, TV, and game room. Open Feb.-Oct. Sa-Su. Dorms £11.80, under 18 £8.50. MC/V. ❷

Shining Cliff: Jackass Ln. (☎07788 725 938), Shining Cliff Woods, 2 mi. from Ambergate. 1 mi. from the road in a pristine forest; call for directions. Trains and buses reach Ambergate. Self-catering; bring a flashlight. Rentable year-round. Dorms £9.30, under 18 £6.20. Cash only. ❶

Youlgreave: Fountain Sq. (☎/fax 01629 636 518). Buses #171 and 172 from Bakewell stop nearby. The building was once used as a village co-operative department store, and men still sleep in a room labeled "Women's Underwear." Open Feb.-Mar. F-Sa; Apr.-Oct. M-Sa; Nov.-Dec. F-Sa. Dorms £11.80, under 18 £8.50. MC/V. ❷

CAMPING BARNS

The 11 YHA-operated, farmer-owned **camping barns** ❶ are simple shelters, providing sleeping platform, water tap, and toilet; bring a sleeping bag and camping equipment. You must book and pay ahead through the **Camping Barns Reservation Office**, 6 King St., Clitheroe, Lancashire BB7 2EP (☎0870 770 8868). You can pay over the phone with a credit card, or they'll hold your reservation for five days while you mail a booking form; forms are available in camping barn booklets, distributed at NPICs and available online at www.yha.org.uk. Barns can be found in: **Abney,** between Eyam and Castleton; **Alstonefield,** between Dovedale and Manifold Valley; **Birchover,** near Matlock off the B5056; **Butterton** (two barns), near the southern end of the park, along the Manifold track; **Edale** village; **Losehill,** near Castleton; **Middleton-by-Youlgreave; Nab End,** in Hollinsclough; **Taddington,** on Main Rd.; and **Underbank,** in Wildboarclough. (All £4 per person.)

⚜ ⚜ HIKING AND OUTDOORS

The central park is marvelous territory for rambling. Settlement is sparser and buses fewer north of Edale in the land of the Kinder Scout plateau, the great Derwent reservoirs, and the gritty cliffs and peat moorlands. From Edale, the **Pennine Way** (p. 396) runs north to Kirk Yetholm, across the Scottish border. Be advised that warm clothing and the customary supplies and precautions should be taken (see **Wilderness Safety,** p. 52). Be respectful, as there are many acres of private land in addition to the 1600 mi. of public rights of way. Ramblers' guidebooks are available at NPICs (p. 364).

The park authority operates 10 **Cycle Hire Centres.** They can be found in **Ashbourne** (☎01335 343 156), on Mapleton Ln.; **Derwent** (☎01433 651 261), near the Fairholmes NPIC; **Hayfield** (☎01663 746 222), on Station Rd. in the Sett Valley; **Middleton Top** (☎01629 823 204), at the visitors center; **Parsley Hay** (☎01298 84493), in Buxton; and **Waterhouses** (☎01538 308 609), in the Old Station Car Park between Ashbourne and Leek on the A523. (Bikes £8.80 per 3hr., £12.80 per day. £20 deposit. Tandem bikes £22 per 3hr., £30 per day. £50 deposit. Helmet included. 10% discount for YHA members, seniors, and Wayfarer ticket holders. Most open daily Apr.-Sept. 9:30am-6pm; Oct.-Mar. call for hours.) *Cycle Derbyshire,* available at NPICs, includes opening hours, locations, and a map with all paths and trails.

CASTLETON ☎01433

For such a small town, Castleton (pop. 705) lays claim to a tremendous amount of natural beauty, and has succeeded in earning itself a fairly predictable level of tourist traffic. Its postcard-perfect streets are lined with ivy-covered stone buildings and hedged gardens. The obvious beauty of the hillsides hide still more, as the semi-precious purple mineral **Blue John** (banded fluorspar) is found only in the

NORTHWEST ENGLAND

local bedrock—and for ridiculous prices in main street shops. These hills are also home to the area's main attraction: four guided caverns. Buses don't serve the caves on weekdays, but on weekends #260 makes a loop between Edale and Castleton (Sa-Su 6-7 per day), stopping at Blue John, Speedwell, and Treak Cliff. The entrances are all within walking distance of one another. As you leave Castleton on Cross St. (which becomes Buxton Rd.), formerly the A625, you'll pass a large sign for Peak Cavern. Road signs for the others appear within 10min.

Although it's not the first on the road out of Castleton, **Treak Cliff Cavern** is the one most worth visiting, with engaging 40min. tours that accentuate the amazing natural features of its caves—deep purple seams of Blue John and frozen cascades of rigid flowstone. The "sculpted" mineral shapes in the stunning **Dream Cave** are reminiscent of melted candle wax. (☎ 620 571; www.bluejohnstone.com. Open daily Easter-Oct. 10am-4:20pm; Nov.-Feb. 10am-3:20pm; Mar.-Easter 10am-4:20pm. Tours every 15-30min. £5.80, seniors £5.20, students and YHA members £5, children £3.20.) Just outside Castleton, in the gorge beneath the castle ruins, **Peak Cavern** features the largest aperture in Britain. Known in the 18th century as the "Devil's Arse," the cavern now features 1hr. tours led by wry-humored guides; Christmastime sees mincemeat pies and live brass bands for generally subterranean merrymaking. (☎ 620 285; www.devilsarse.com. Open daily Easter-Oct. 10am-5pm; Nov.-Easter Sa-Su 10am-5pm; last tour 4pm. £5.50, concessions £4.50, children £3.50.) A joint pass (£10, concessions £8.50, children £6.50) gains access to both Peak Cavern and **Speedwell;** the latter offers boat tours through the underground canals of an old lead mine that culminate at "The Bottomless Pit," a huge underground lake. (☎ 620 512; www.speedwellcavern.co.uk. Tours daily in summer 9:30am-5pm; in winter 10am-3:30pm). **Blue John** is the only cave besides Treak Cliff to offer visitors views of the mineral veins from which it takes its name, but it also involves very steep stair-climbs, and some consider its tours inferior. (☎ 620 638. Open daily in summer 9:30am-5:30pm; in winter 9:30am-dusk.) The caverns are all quite cold, so dress warmly, and screeching school groups convene midday, so go early.

William Peveril, illegitimate son of William the Conqueror, built his 11th-century **Peveril Castle** atop a hill with far-reaching views to survey possible threats to local lead mines. Later used to enforce local hunting rights, the castle sports a keep and crumbling walls open to magnificent rolling horizons. (☎ 620 613. Open daily May-July 10am-6pm; Aug. 10am-7pm; Apr. and Sept.-Oct. 10am-5pm, Nov.-Mar. Th-M 10am-4pm. £2.70, concessions £2, children £1.40, family £6.80.)

Castleton lies 2 mi. west of the **Hope** train station (don't ask for Castleton Station, or you'll end up in a suburb of Manchester), and **buses** arrive from Sheffield, Buxton, and Bakewell (p. 363). Hikers looking for a challenge can set off southward from town on the 26 mi. **Limestone Way Trail** to Matlock. Castleton's **NPIC** (p. 364) stocks maps and brochures on local walks (most under £1). Particularly useful is *Walks around Castleton* (30p), which outlines 2½-9½ mi. hikes. Ramblers preparing for the moors should visit the **Peveril Outdoor Shop,** off the marketplace by the hostel, or one of the town's numerous other outdoors shops. (☎ 620 320. Open M-F 9:30am-5pm, Sa-Su 9:30am-6pm.) The nearest **bank** lies 6 mi. east in **Hathersage;** the Cheshire Cheese Hotel, How Ln., has an **ATM.** The **post office,** How Ln., a few doors down from the bus stop, is in a convenience store. (☎ 620 241. Open M-Tu and F 9am-1pm and 2-5:30pm, W and Sa 9am-12:30pm, Th 9am-12:30pm and 2:15pm-5:30pm.) **Post Code:** S33 8WJ.

The **YHA Castleton,** with a cluster of old stone buildings around a quiet courtyard, is as comfortable as it is comely. It sits in the center of town, on Castle St. next to the castle entrance (p. 366). Those seeking the luxury of a B&B can try ivy-walled **Cryer House ❸,** Castle St., where Mr. and Mrs. Skelton keep two lovely double rooms and a skylit tea shop. (☎/fax 620 244. £49. Cash only.) The **cafe ❶** down-

Don't be left out...

Get your
TRAVEL on.

The International
Student Identity Card

$22 is ALL it takes to SAVE $100's at home and abroad!

save in the U.S. or worldwide

International Student Identity Card
Carte d'étudiant internationale / Carné internacional de estudiante
STUDENT
Studies at / Étudiant à / Est. de Enseñanza
University of California, Berkeley
Name / Nom / Nombre
Debbie Lee
Born / Né(e) le / Nacido/a el
04/29/1982
Validity / Validité / Validez
09/2004 - 12/31/2005
ISIC

Student savings in more than
7,000 locations
across the US &
100 countries
worldwide-
something no other card can offer!

- 1/2 Price Admission
- Reduced Rates
- Accommodations
- Entertainment
- Communications
- Internet

visit www.myISIC.com to find out about discounts
and the benefits of carrying your ISIC.

ISIC

Call or visit ISIC online to purchase your card today:
www.myISIC.com   (800) 474.8214

stairs is one of the prettiest in Castleton, though the town has plenty. It serves four different afternoon teas ($3.10-4) alongside an assortment of sandwiches and baked goods. (Open daily 10am-5pm. Cash only.)

EDALE AND THE NORTHERN DARK PEAK AREA ☎ 01433

The deep dale of the River Noe cradles a collection of hamlets known as **Edale.** The area offers little in the way of civilization besides a church, rail stop, cafe, pub, school, and hostel, but its environs are among the most spectacular in northern England. The northern **Dark Peak** area is wild hill country, with vast moors like **Kinder Scout** and **Bleaklow** left undisturbed by motor traffic. In these mazes, paths are scarce and weather-worn, and the going can be tough through peat bogs. The rare town huddles in the crook of a valley, with provisions and shelter for weary walkers. Less experienced hikers should stick to Edale and southern paths.

On summer weekends Edale brims with hikers and campers preparing to tackle the **Pennine Way** (which begins with a 3- to 4-day stretch through the Peaks; p. 363), or to trek one of the shorter (1½-8½ mi.) trails detailed in the National Park Authority's 8 Walks Around Edale ($1.20). The 3½ mi. path to **Castleton** begins 70 yd. down the road from the TIC and affords a breathtaking view of both the Edale Valley (Dark Peak) and the Hope Valley (White Peak), but requires a good 25min. of uphill walking. A flagstone detour with still more spectacular views runs along the ridge between these valleys to **Mam Tor,** a well-touristed decaying Iron Age fort once home to Celtic worshippers of Brigantia, a fertility goddess. The hill is known locally as the "shivering mountain" for its shale sides; one such shudder left the road below permanently blocked. Cliffs on three sides beckon fearless hang-gliders from near and far. The road detour forces traffic through **Winnat's Pass** to the south, which has steep sides with restricted grazing to allow fantastic rainbows of wildflowers in spring and summer.

Edale lies on the **Hope Valley rail line** and is served by trains every 1-2hr. from **Manchester Piccadilly** (50min.) and **Sheffield** (35min.). Stop at the huge **NPIC** (p. 364) near the train station for weather forecasts and map and compass training. **YHA Edale** (p. 366) is far from town (2 mi.) but not unmanageable for hearty backpackers, though the less athletic can opt for the few B&Bs that line Edale's only real road. Campers can try **Fieldhead ❶,** behind the TIC. (☎ 670 386. $3.50-4 per person, children $2.50-2.75. Cars $1.50. Showers 20p. Cash or check only.)

BAKEWELL ☎ 01629

Light-hued stone homes, a gentle river, and a sophisticated rural feel make Bakewell a postcard country town. Located near several scenic walks through the **White Peaks,** the town is best known as the birthplace of **Bakewell pudding,** allegedly created in the 1860s when a flustered cook at the Rutland Arms Hotel tried to make a tart by pouring an egg mixture over strawberry jam instead of mixing it into the dough (see **Bakewell Pudding,** p. 27). Bakewell's stone buildings line a narrow network of crooked streets and hidden courtyards that converge upon a flowered park at central **Rutland Square.** The River Wye curls around the town edging Riverside Gardens (always open), overhung with willows and spanned by the five graceful arches of a **medieval bridge** (c.1300). On the hill above town, **All Saints Church** is surrounded by tilting gravestones and carved cross fragments. In the south transept, three curious human gargoyles guard the remains of Anglo-Saxon and Norman headstones. Nearby on Cunningham Pl., a 16th-century timber-frame house shelters the **Old House Museum,** which displays regional heritage in the form of a Tudor lavatory, blueprints for a Peak house made of cow dung, and other less excrementitious items. (☎ 813 642; www.oldhousemuseum.co.uk. Open daily Apr.-Oct. 11am-4pm. $2.50, children $1, under 5 free.)

Buses arrive in Rutland Sq. from: **Manchester** via **Buxton** (1¾hr, 6 per day); **Matlock,** site of the nearest train station (#172, R61; 20-50min.; 1-3 per hr.); **Sheffield** (#X18 or 240; 1hr.; M-Sa 13-14 per day, Su 10-12 per day). Bakewell's **NPIC,** at the intersection of Bridge St. and Market St., doubles as a **Tourist Information Centre** (p. 364). Other services include: an **HSBC,** Rutland Sq. (open M-F 9:15-4pm); **camping supplies** at **Yeoman's,** 1 Royal Oak Pl., off Matlock St. (☎815 371; open M-Sa 9am-5:30pm, Su 10am-5pm); the **police,** Granby Rd. (☎812 504); free **Internet access** at **Bakewell Public Library,** Orme Ct. (☎812 267; open M-Tu and Th 9:30am-5pm, W and F 9:30am-7pm, Sa 9:30am-4pm); and a **post office,** in the **Spar** on Granby Rd. (☎815 112; open M-Th 8:30am-6pm, F 9am-5:30pm, Sa 9am-1pm). **Post Code:** DE45 1ES.

The comfy **YHA Bakewell,** on Fly Hill, is a short walk from the TIC (p. 364). **B&Bs** are plentiful considering the village's size, but expect to pay about £20 per person; *Peak District Visitor Guide,* free at the TIC, lists B&Bs in the area. Truly elegant stays await at the **Rutland Arms Hotel ❹,** The Square, which has lodged famous Peak-country pilgrims like Byron, Coleridge, Wordsworth, and Turner. 35 individually decorated rooms feature luxurious beds and satellite TVs. (☎812 812; www.bakewell.demon.co.uk. Full breakfast included. June-Oct. singles £54-59, doubles £88-99; Nov.-May £51-59/81-89. AmEx/MC/V.) Less expensive options lie further from town; **Riverwalk B&B,** Holme Ln., lies a few hundred yards out of town on the A6 towards Buxton over a small bridge. Proximity to the tranquil Wye is a definite plus. (☎812 459. Singles £16.50-18; doubles £44. Cash only.) Entire villages pour into Bakewell's **market,** held since 1330, off Bridge St. (Open M 9am-4pm.) The **Extra Foodstore** peddles **groceries** at the corner of Granby Rd. and Market St. (Open M-Sa 8am-10pm, Su 10am-4pm.) Bakewell has a dense population of cafes, though only a few of them have names that don't include the word "pudding;" even fewer don't have it on the menu. With cheery, lemon-yellow walls and giant cloth sunflowers blooming out of earthenware vases, **The Acorn ❷,** Kings Ct., delivers superior bistro fare in its cozy dining room and adjoining courtyard. Indulgences include the potted Stilton (native to the area) with crusty bread (£3.85) and French lemon tarts with raspberry coulis for £2.90. (☎810 022. Open M-Th 10:30am-5pm, F 10:30am-7pm, Sa 10am-5:30pm, Su 10:30am-5pm. AmEx/MC/V.) Located off a courtyard in the center of town, **The Treeline Cafe ❷,** Diamond Ct., has an airy interior and an outside draped with grapevines that adorn this corner of Bakewell's stone-shadowed streets. The cafe serves an array of daily quiches, paninis, soups, and salads from £3.90. (☎813 749. Open Easter-Oct. M-Sa 10am-5pm, Su 11am-5pm; Nov.-Easter M-W and F-Su 10am-5:30pm. MC/V.)

▶ DAYTRIPS FROM BAKEWELL

■ CHATSWORTH HOUSE

Take bus #179 directly to the house (2 per day) or ask the TIC about other buses that stop close by. ☎01246 582 204; www.chatsworth.org. 1½hr. audio tour £2.50. Guidebooks for house and garden £3 each. Open daily mid-Mar. to late Dec. 11am-5:30pm; last admission 4:30pm. Gardens open daily 11am-6pm; June-Aug. from 10:30am. Last admission 5pm. Mar.-Oct. £9, concessions £7, children £3.50, families £21.50; Nov.-Dec. £10/£8/£4/£24. Gardens only £5.50/£4/£2.50/£13.50.

When the 6th Duke of Devonshire ordered a new set of marble carvings for the fireplaces of his (third) dining room at Chatsworth, he was a bit disappointed with the results; he had "wanted more abandon and joyous expression." Only in a house as magnificent as this one could his complaint seem anything but ridiculous. Once called "the National Gallery of the North," this palatial estate is as much museum as residence, displaying works by Van Dyck, Rembrandt, and Tintoretto. The **Queen of Scots Rooms** in the house, where Mary stayed from 1560 to 1581, cost an

additional $1.50. More impressive still are the sprawling gardens, which brags a hedge maze, a gravity-powered fountain, and a mammoth rock garden on its 105 acres of Elysian environs. Green lawns and sequestered paths will (and should) keep you all day in this "Palace of the Peaks."

HADDON HALL

Haddon Hall is 2 mi. from Bakewell; from town, walk down Matlock St. as it becomes Haddon Rd. and then the A6; a nicer path along the river covers half the distance. Several buses, including #171-172, 179, and TP, stop outside the gate; ask the TIC for details. ☎812 855; www.haddonhall.co.uk. Open daily Apr.-Sept. 10:30am-4:30pm; Oct. Th-Su 10:30am-4pm. £7.25, concessions £6.25, children £3.75, families £19.

Topiaries and award-winning gardens aside, Haddon Hall feels as organic as the winding Wye beneath its turrets. Stone walls seem at home among the scenic sheep-studded countryside; indeed, this "most perfect English house to survive from the Middle Ages" has been a feature for over 800 years, retaining its old world feel thanks to neglect during times of feverish Victorian renovation at other estates. Numerous filmmakers have been charmed by the building's striking crenellated facade and terraced rose gardens; visitors may recognize it as the setting for *The Princess Bride*, Franco Zefferelli's 1996 *Jane Eyre*, and *Elizabeth*. Inadequate wall text makes the $2.50 guide a sound investment.

EYAM

Eyam is 5 mi. north of Bakewell. Take bus #175 from stand D in Bakewell (20min., 3 per day) or #65/66 from Buxton (40min., M-Sa every hr.).

At first glance, Eyam appears an ordinary country hamlet, with curvy cottage-lined streets and a small village green. Closer inspection of these quaint homes, however, reveals somber plaques listing the names of inhabitants who perished in a 17th-century outbreak of the Bubonic plague, during which Eyam underwent a self-imposed quarantine and lost a third of its residents. The first three victims perished in the flower-ringed **Plague Cottages,** Edgeview Rd., and their stories, as well as many others, are told in a series of engaging displays at the **Eyam Museum,** Hawkhill Rd. The museum's collection also includes a number of questionable "home-remedies" (such as drinking hot fat) and touching final letters, many of which were never sent for fear that they would spread the disease. The exhibit concludes with a gift shop selling plastic rats and plague postcards. Yay! (☎01433 631 371. Open Apr.-Oct. Tu-Su 10am-4:30pm; last admission 4pm. $1.50, concessions $1.) **Eyam**

ON THE MENU

BAKEWELL PUDDING

A well-baked Bakewell pudding doesn't have the orderly appearance of many other English pastries. Its rough, oval-shaped crust holds a golden pocket of almondy egg batter spread over jam.

The most popular story of the pudding's invention holds that a 19th-century proprietress of the Rutland Arms Hotel instructed the cook to make a tart. Allegedly, the cook mistakenly put the jam on the bottom instead of the top, the guests loved it, and the rest is history. Others maintain that it was first served to hotel guest Jane Austen in 1811, or that the recipe was actually introduced by an exiled Italian Count.

Today, various parties claim they have possession of the "original recipe," which they store in fireproof vaults for safekeeping. One even threatened to take his competitors to court in order to ensure exclusive selling rights.

The Old Original Bakewell Pudding Shop, Rutland Sq., is undoubtedly the highest profile pudding joint in town. Its restaurant serves Bakewell cream teas (scone, pudding, and tea) for £4.95, while the bakery below sells puddings from £1.15, as well as copies of the recipe which list everything but the secret ingredient. The shop will "Post-a-Pudding" anywhere in the UK for a fee. (☎812 193; www.bakewell-puddingshop.co.uk. Open daily July-Aug. 8:30am-7pm; Sept.-June M-Th 8:30am-6pm, F-Sa 8:30am-8pm, Su 8:30am-7pm.)

Hall, Edgeview Rd., 100 yd. west of the church, traces the owner's family history in a 17th-century manor house. The hall contains a tapestry room, an eight-line love stanza carved into the library window, and a 17th-century pop-up human anatomy textbook. (☎01433 631 976; www.eyamhall.com. Open July-Aug. W-Th and Su 11am-4pm. £4.75, concessions £4.25, children £3.50, families £15.50.) Eyam's **YHA hostel** plants its flag 800m above the town on Hawkhill Rd. (p. 366).

CUMBRIA

LAKE DISTRICT NATIONAL PARK

With some of the most stunning scenery in England, the Lake District owes its beauty to a thorough glacier-gouging during the last ice age. Here, jagged peaks and windswept fells stand in desolate splendor as water trickles through them into serene mountain lakes. The shores are busy, but less packed than one would expect for a region where tourism employs 85% of the population. Though summertime hikers, bikers, and boaters almost equal sheep in number (and with four million sheep, that's quite a feat), there is always some lonely upland fell or quiet cove where your footprints will seem the first for generations.

▐ TRANSPORTATION

Trains: By train, **Oxenholme,** on the West Coast Mainline, is the primary gateway to the lakes. Trains (☎08457 484 950) run to Oxenholme from: **Birmingham** (2hr., every 2 hr., £39.50); **Edinburgh** (2hr., 6 per day, £29); **London Euston** (3½hr., M-Sa 16 per day, Su 11 per day; £62); **Manchester Piccadilly** (1½hr., M-Sa 10 per day, Su 9 per day; £12.50). A branch line covers the 10 mi. to **Windermere** from Oxenholme (20min., every hr., £3.25). Direct service runs to Windermere from **Manchester Piccadilly** (1¾hr., 1 per hr., £12.55).

Buses: National Express (☎08705 808 080) arrives in **Windermere** from **Birmingham** (4½hr., 1 per day, £29) and **London** (7½hr., 1 per day, £27), continuing through **Ambleside** and **Grasmere** to **Keswick. Stagecoach** connects **Keswick** with **Carlisle** (1¼hr.; 2-3 per day). **Stagecoach in Cumbria** is the primary operator in the region. A complete timetable *(The Lakeland Explorer)* is available free from TICs and on board each bus. Major routes include: **"Lakeslink"** bus #555 from **Lancaster** to **Carlisle,** stopping at **Kendal, Windermere, Ambleside, Grasmere,** and **Keswick** (M-Sa 14 per day, Su 7 per day), and the open-top **Lakeland Experience** bus #599 between **Bowness** and **Grasmere** (50min., daily Apr.-Aug. 2-3 per hr.). An **Explorer** ticket offers unlimited travel on all area Stagecoach buses. The 4- and 7-day passes usually save money, even for 2- or 3-day stays. 1-day £8, children £5; 4-day £18/£13; 7-day £25/£17. Explorer tickets may be purchased on buses and at TICs. Also try *Getting Around Cumbria and the Lake District* (free from TICs) or call **Traveline** (☎0870 608 2608).

National Trust Shuttles: On summer Sundays, the National Trust operates free buses to popular sights, some of which are not ordinarily accessible by public transport. Call ☎017687 73780 for more information.

YHA Shuttle: The **YHA Ambleside** provides a minibus service (☎015394 32304) for hikers (or just their packs) between hostels in **Coniston Holly How, Elterwater, Grasmere, Hawkshead, Langdale,** and **Windermere** (2 per day, £2.50; schedules available at hostels), plus a daily service to **Patterdale.** Trips from Windermere train station to Windermere and Ambleside hostels are free. Runs Easter-Oct.

Tours: For those who wish to explore, **Mountain Goat** (☎015394 45161), downhill from the TIC in Windermere, does the climbing for you in off-the-beaten-track, partial- and full-day themed bus tours. £17.50-27.50. Right across the street, **Lakes Supertours**, 1 High St. (☎015394 42751), in the Lakes Hotel, is another option that runs similar half- and full-day tours. £17-27.50.

▶◀ 🛈 ORIENTATION AND PRACTICAL INFORMATION

The Lake District National Park occupies a vast tract of land that fills the heart of Cumbria. The major lakes radiate out from the small town of **Grasmere,** which lies roughly in the park's center. The A591 runs along the north-south axis of the park, joining the towns of **Windermere, Bowness, Ambleside, Grasmere,** and **Keswick.** From these towns smaller thoroughfares radiate out into the rest of the park, making them good, though often crowded places from which to base your travels. **Derwentwater** is one of the most beautiful lakes, **Windermere** is the largest and most developed, and western lakes like **Buttermere** and **Crummock Water** are the most wild.

National Park Information Centres: All dispense information and maps, secure fishing licenses, book accommodations (10% deposit for local; non-local an additional £3 charge), offer guided walks, and often exchange currency. More information at www.lake-district.gov.uk.

National Park Visitor Centre: (☎015394 46601). In Brockhole, between Windermere and Ambleside. Most buses stop here. An introduction to the Lake District with exhibits, talks, films, and special events. Open daily Apr.-Oct. 10am-5pm.

Ambleside Waterhead: (☎015394 32729), on the pier. From town, walk south on Lake Rd. or Borrans Rd. or get off at Waterhead Hotel bus stop. Open daily Easter-Oct. 9:30am-5:30pm.

Bowness Bay: Glebe Rd. (☎015394 42895). Open daily mid-July to Aug. 9:30am-6pm; Apr.-June and Sept.-Oct. 9am-5:30pm; Nov.-Mar. F-Su 10am-4pm.

Coniston: Ruskin Ave. (☎015394 41533), behind the Tilberthwaite Ave. bus stop. Open daily Easter-Oct. 9:30am-5:30pm; Nov.-Easter F-Su 10am-3:30pm.

Glenridding: Main Carpark (☎017684 82414). Open daily Easter-Oct. 9:30am-5:30pm; Nov.-Easter 9:30am-3:30pm.

Grasmere: Redbank Rd. (☎015394 35245). Open daily Easter-Oct. 9:30am-5:30pm; Nov.-Easter F-Su 10am-4pm.

Hawkshead: Main Carpark (☎015394 36525). Open daily July-Aug. 9:30am-6pm; Easter-June and Sept.-Oct. 9:30am-5:30pm; Nov.-Easter Sa-Su 10am-3:30pm.

Keswick: Moot Hall, Market Sq. (☎017687 72645). Open year-round 9:30am-4:30pm.

Pooley Bridge: The Square (☎017684 86530). Open daily Easter-Oct. 10am-5pm.

Seatoller Barn: Borrowdale (☎017687 77294), at the foot of Honister Pass. Open daily Apr.-Oct. 10am-5pm.

🏠 ACCOMMODATIONS

Though **B&Bs** line the streets in many towns, and there's a hostel around nearly every bend, lodgings in the Lake District fill up quickly June through August; reserve well in advance, especially for weekend stays. Hostels, in particular, can be full all summer long; call ahead. TICs and NPICs book rooms. Twenty-six **YHA hostels** provide accommodations in the park, but can differ radically in facilities and style. Reception is often closed 10am-5pm, though public areas and restrooms are usually accessible throughout the day. The **YHA shuttle** travels between the bigger hostels (p. 372). YHA also operates 14 wilderness **camping barns** in the Lakes; for information or reservations call the Keswick NPIC (☎017687 72645). **Campgrounds** are scattered throughout the park. The following is a selection of park hostels; see www.yha.org.uk for more. The Lake District YHAs also run a convenient reservation service; call ☎015394 31117. All of the following accept MC/V).

374 ■ LAKE DISTRICT NATIONAL PARK

Ambleside: Waterhead, Ambleside (☎015394 32304), 1 mi. south of Ambleside on the Windermere Rd. (A591), 3 mi. north of Windermere on the northern shore. Bus #555 stops in front of this mother of all hostels. 245 beds in a refurbished hotel with an amazing view. Distinctive country-club feel—you can even swim off the pier. Books tours, rents mountain bikes, exchanges currency and serves great meals. Be sure to make reservations. Internet access £2.50 per 30min. Dorms £14.40, under 18 £10.30. ❷

Black Sail: Black Sail Hut, Ennerdale, Cleator (☎07711 108450). Splendidly set in remote hills, 3½ mi. from Seatoller. 16 beds. Open daily June-Aug., Apr.-May and Sept.-Oct. Tu-Sa. Dorms £10.60, under 18 £7.20. ❷

Borrowdale: Longthwaite, Borrowdale (☎17687 77257). Take bus #79 from Keswick and then follow signs from Rosthwaite Village. Comfortable riverside hostel. 88 beds. Open daily 7:15-10am, 1-11:30pm. Dorms £11.80, under 18 £8.50. ❷

Buttermere: King George VI Memorial Hostel, Buttermere (☎017687 70245). Turn right at Bridge Hotel from the bus stop, ¼ mi. south of the village on the B5289. Lounges and kitchen. 70 beds. Lockout 10am-1pm. Open daily Apr.-Aug., Sept.-Dec. and Feb.-Mar. Tu-Sa, Jan. F-Sa. Breakfast included. Dorms £14.90, under 18 £11.60. ❷

Cockermouth: Double Mills, Cockermouth (☎/fax 01900 822 561), in the town center, off Fern Bank at Parkside Ave. Converted 17th-century water mill. 26 beds. Open Apr.-Oct. Dorms £9.30, under 18 £7. ❶

Coniston Coppermines: Coppermines House (☎ 015394 41261), 1¼ mi. northwest of Coniston along the Churchbeck River. No need to venture into the hills; the rugged journey to the hostel is itself a scenic challenge. 26 beds in the mine manager's house. Open daily Apr.-Aug., Sept.-Oct. Tu-Sa. Dorms £10.60, under 18 £7. ❷

Coniston Holly How: Far End, Coniston (☎015394 41323), just north of the village at the junction of Hawkshead Rd. and Ambleside Rd. Modernized country house is a good base for walking and water spouts. Curfew 11pm. Open daily Apr. and July-Sept.; May-June, Oct.-Nov., and mid-Jan. to Mar. F-Su. Dorms £11.80, under 18 £8.50. ❷

Derwentwater: Barrow House, Borrowdale (☎017687 77246), 2 mi. south of Keswick on the B5289. Take bus #79, also a Keswick Launch stop. Probably worth the inconvenience to stay in this 90-bed, 200-year-old house with its own waterfall. Open daily Feb. to early Oct.; Jan.-Dec. F-Sa. Dorms £11.80, under 18 £8.50. ❷

Elterwater: (☎015394 37245). On a Great Langdale Valley farm; popular with walkers. Take bus #516 to Elterwater, turn left and follow the road over a stone bridge. Open daily Apr.-Sept.; Feb.-Mar. and Oct.-Dec. Tu-Sa; Jan. F-Sa. £10.60, under 18 £7.20. ❷

Eskdale: (☎019467 23219). In a quiet valley 1½ mi. east of Boot on the Ravenglass-Eskdale railway, adjacent to Hardknot Pass. 50 beds. Open daily July-Aug., Apr.-June M-Sa, Mar. and Sept.-Oct. Tu-Sa. Dorms £10.60, under 18 £7.20. ❷

Grasmere: (☎015394 35316). 2 hostels. **Butharlyp Howe** is 150 yd. up Easedale Rd. 80-bed Victorian house. Internet access. Open Mar.-Oct. Tu-Su; Nov.-Feb. call for availability. Dorms £13, under 18 £9. For **Thorney How** follow Easedale Rd. another ½ mi. and turn right at the fork; the hostel is ¼ mi. down on the left. 48-bed, 350-year-old farmhouse. Dorms £10.60, under 18 £7.20. ❷

Hawkshead: Esthwaite Lodge (☎015394 36293), 1 mi. south of Hawkshead along a well-posted route. Bus #505 from Ambleside stops at the village center. Follow Newby Bridge Rd. to this Regency mansion overlooking Esthwaite Water. Caters to families. 115 beds. Open daily Feb.-Oct.; Nov.-Dec. F-Sa. Dorms £11.80, under 18 £8.50. ❷

Helvellyn: Greenside, Glenridding (☎17684 82269), 1½ mi. from Glenridding on a route toward Helvellyn. Open daily July-Aug.; call 48 hr. in advance year-round for availability. Dorms £10.60, under 18 £7.20. ❷

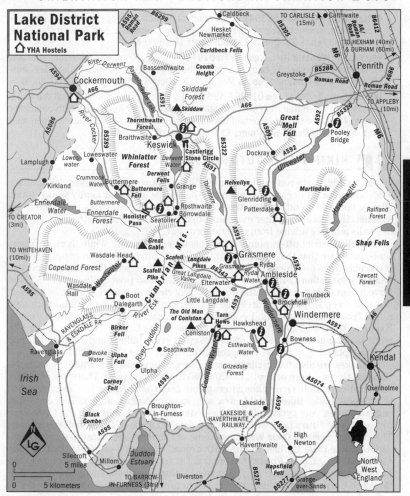

Honister Hause: (☎017687 77267), near Seatoller. Gray building at the summit of Honister Pass, 9 mi. south of Keswick. Bus #77 from Keswick (May-Oct.); #79 stops within 1½ mi. Continue along Honister Pass and follow the signs. 26 beds. Open daily June-Aug.; Apr.-May and Sept.-Oct. M-Tu, F-Su. Dorms £10.60, under 18 £7.20. ❷

Keswick: Station Rd. (☎017687 72484). From the TIC, bear left down Station Rd.; YHA sign on the left. 91 beds in a former hotel with balconies over a river, clean rooms, and a kitchen. Internet access. Curfew 11:30pm. Dorms £11.80, under 18 £8.50. ❷

Langdale: High Close, 1 mi. from Elterwater village. Bookings through Ambleside YHA (p. 375). Old Victorian lodge in a beautiful setting. Open daily Easter-Sept.; call ahead for dates. Dorms £10.60, under 18 £7.20. ❷

Patterdale: (☎017684 82394), ¼ mi. south of Patterdale village, on the A592 to Kirkstone Pass. Internet access. Open daily Apr.-Aug.; Sept.-Oct. and Feb. to Mar. Th-M; Nov. to mid-Feb. F-Sa. Dorms £11.80, under 18 £8.50 ❷

Wastwater: Wasdale Hall, Wasdale (☎019467 26222), ½ mi. east of Nether Wasdale. A climber's paradise; 50 beds in a half-timbered house on the water. Open daily Apr.-Oct.; Nov.-Dec. F-Sa; mid-Feb. to Mar. M, Th-Su. Dorms £10.60, under 18 £7.20. ❷

Windermere: Bridge Ln. (☎015394 43543), ± 2mi. north of Windermere off the A591. Catch the YHA shuttle from the train station. Spacious, 69-bed house with panoramic views of the lake below. Mountain bikes for rent. Internet access £6 per hr. Open daily Feb.-Nov.; early Dec. F-Sa. Dorms £11.80, under 18 £8.50. ❷

🏔 🧗 HIKING AND OUTDOORS

Outdoor enthusiasts run (and walk and climb) rampant in the Lakes. NPICs have guidebooks for all occasions—mountain-bike trails, pleasant family walks, tough climbs, and hikes ending at pubs. Most also offer guided walks throughout the summer. Hostels are another excellent source of information, with large maps on the walls and free advice from experienced staff.

The Lake District offers some of the best **hiking** in Britain. While there are many trails, be aware that they can be hard to follow at times—even on popular routes. If you plan to go on a long or difficult outing, check first with the Park Service, call **weather information** (24hr. ☎017687 75757; YHAs also post daily forecasts), and leave a plan of your route with your B&B proprietor or hostel warden before setting out. Steep slopes and unreliable weather can quickly reduce visibility to only a few feet. A good map and compass are necessities. The Ordnance Survey Explorer Maps #4-7 detail the four quadrants of the Lake District (1:25,000; £7), while Landranger Maps #89-91 and 96-98 chart every hillock and bend in the road for those planning overland or especially difficult routes (1:50,000; £12).

The Lakes are also fine **cycling** country. Several long-distance routes (part of the National Cycling Network; ☎0117 929 0888) traverse the park. There are excellent short routes as well; *Ordnance Survey One Day Cycle Rides in Cumbria* (£10) is a helpful guide. Bike rental is available in many towns, and staffers can often suggest routes. Any cyclist planning an extensive stay should grab the *Ordnance Survey Cycle Tours* (£9), which provides detailed maps of on- and off-trail routes. The circular **Cumbria Cycle Way** tours some of Cumbria's less-traveled areas via a 259 mi. route from Carlisle in the north around the park's outskirts. Pick up *The Cumbria Way Cycle Route* (£4) from a TIC for details. For all travelers in the Lakes but cyclists especially, beware the narrow and stonewalled roads off of the A591. Cars and large buses generally tear around on the winding lanes.

The Lake District is popular for **rock climbing.** Two good sources for climbing information are **Rock & Run**, 3-4 Cheapside, Ambleside (☎15394 33660; open M-Sa 9am-5:30pm, Su 10am-5pm) and the **Keswick Indoor Climbing Wall** (p. 383).

WINDERMERE AND BOWNESS   ☎015394

The largest tourist center in the Lake District, Windermere and its lakeside sidekick, Bowness-on-Windermere (combined pop. 11,000), fill to the gills with vacationers in July and August when sailboats and water-skiers swarm the lake. As transportation hubs and gateways to the rest of the park's natural playgrounds, the two towns offer a tamer take on the region.

📰 🚌 **TRANSPORTATION AND PRACTICAL INFORMATION.** The **train station** and **bus depot** are in Windermere; Bowness, flanking the lake, is an easy 1½ mi. walk south. From the station, turn left onto Victoria Rd., then, staying to the left, follow Crescent Rd. through town to New Rd., which in turn becomes Lake Rd. and leads pierward. **Bus** #599 runs from the station to Bowness pier (3 per hr., £1). For information on getting to Windermere, see p. 372. Try **Windermere Taxis** (☎42355) for a cab, or rent bikes from **Country Lanes Cycle Hire** at the station. (☎015394 44544. £10 per half-day, £15 per day; discounts available with train ticket. Open daily Easter-Oct. 9am-5:30pm.)

The Windermere **Tourist Information Centre**, near the train station, stocks guides to walks (from 40p), books National Express and Stagecoach tickets, arranges accommodations, and changes currency. (☎46499. Open daily July-Aug. 9am-6:30pm; Easter-June and Sept.-Oct. 9am-6pm; Nov.-Easter 9am-5pm.) The **Bowness Bay NPIC** provides similar services and has a display on the Lake District's topology (p. 373). Both towns have **banks.** Windermere services include: **luggage storage** at **Darryl's Cafe**, 14 Church St. (☎42894; £1 per item; open M, Th-Su 8am-6pm); a **launderette** on Main Rd. (wash £2, dry 20p per 4min.; open M-F 8:30am-5:30pm, Sa 9am-5pm); the **police**, Lake Rd. (☎01768 891 999); **Internet access** at **Triarom**, Birch St. (☎44639; £1 per 10min.; open M-Sa 9:30am-5:30pm); and the **post office**, 21 Crescent Rd. (☎43245; open M-F 9:30am-5:30pm, Sa 9am-12:30pm). **Post Code:** LA23 1AA.

◪◳ ACCOMMODATIONS AND FOOD. Windermere and Bowness have a number of **B&Bs**, but booking ahead is still advisable during peak periods. Windermere's **YHA hostel** is 2mi. north of town (p. 376). The best value among Windermere's B&Bs include the motorcyclist- and family-friendly **Brendan Chase** ❷, 1-3 College Rd., with large and attractive rooms in two Edwardian townhouses (☎45638. Singles £25; doubles from £40. Cash only); the warm and well-appointed **Ashleigh Guest House** ❸, 11 College Rd. (☎42292; www.ashleighhouse.com. No smoking; single £30; doubles £46-56. MC/V); and the quiet and homey **Greenriggs** ❷, 8 Upper Oak St. (☎42265. Doubles £50. Cash only). In Bowness, **Laurel Cottage** ❸, St. Martins Pl., is a 400-year-old stone building with a great location just off the main thoroughfare near the pier. (☎45594. No smoking. Singles £27; doubles £58-72. MC/V.) The closest camping is at lovely **Park Cliffe** ❷, Birks Rd., 4½ mi. south of Bowness. Take bus #618 from Windermere station. (☎015395 31344. Open early Mar. to early Nov. £11-12 per tent. AmEx/MC/V.) A smaller but closer option is the **Orrest Head** ❶ campsite above Windermere. (☎42619. No vehicles. £4 per person. Cash only.)

In Windermere, stock up on supplies at **Booths supermarket**, right as you exit the station. (☎46114. Open M-F 8:30am-8pm, Sa 8:30am-7pm, Su 10am-4pm.) For fresh fruit, **Valerie Ann's**, 27b Crescent Rd., vends produce outside its door at market prices. (☎42068. Open daily 9am-5:30pm.) **The Lighthouse** ❷, at the top of Main Rd., sells light fare throughout the day (sandwiches £4), but stays open late as a bar and bistro (entrees £7-13.50. (☎80260. Open daily 9:30am-11:30pm. MC/V.) Bowness has more options for evening dining. Perhaps the two towns' nicest restaurant, and by far the oldest, **The Porthole** ❺, 3 Ash St., stores its amazing wine collection in racks throughout the restaurant. (☎42793. 3-course meal £29-36. Open M-Tu, W-Su 6:30-10:30pm. AmEx/MC/V.) **Jackson's** ❸, St. Martins Pl., serves modern British cuisine at a lower price; a 3-course meal costs £13. (☎46264. Open daily 6-10pm. MC/V.) During the day the **Bowness Kitchen Cafe** ❶, Lake Rd., is great for grabbing a quick bite of lunch. (☎45529. Sandwiches, soups, and pastries £3-5. Open daily Easter-Oct. 9am-6pm; Nov.-Easter 9am-5pm. MC/V.)

◪◳ SIGHTS AND OUTDOORS. A **lake cruise** is a nice way to sample the natural beauty of Windermere's surroundings, and a number of sightseeing boats depart from Bowness pier. **Windermere Lake Cruises** (☎43360) is the main operator, with trips north to Waterhead Pier in Ambleside (30min.; round-trip £6.65, children £3.45) and south to Lakeside (40min., £6.85/£3.55). Nonstop sightseeing cruises are also available (45min., £5/£2.50). On all routes, departures are frequent between April and October, reduced the rest of the year. The **Freedom of the Lake** pass allows unlimited one-day travel (£12, children £6). A cruise to **Lakeside**, at Windermere's southern tip, lets you visit the freshwater **Aquarium of the Lakes** (☎015395 30153; www.aquariumofthelakes.co.uk. Open daily Apr.-Sept. 9am-6pm, Oct.-Mar. 9am-5pm. Last admission 1hr. before closing. £6, children £3.75) or take a ride on the 4 mi. steam-powered **Lakeside and Haverthwaite Railway** (☎015395 31594; Easter-Oct.; £4.50, children £2.25, families 12.60). At the Bowness and Ambleside piers you can buy tickets that combine the lake cruise with one or both of these attractions. Motor and **rowboat rentals** are available at Bowness Pier. (☎40347. Motor boats £12 per hr., rowboats £3 per hr.)

In-town sights are much less remarkable than the lake's offerings, but children and big-time Jemima Puddleduck fans will enjoy **The World of Beatrix Potter,** an indoor recreation of scenes from the author's stories. (☎88444. Open daily Easter-Sept. 10am-5:30pm; Oct.-Easter 10am-4:30pm. £3.90, children £2.90.) At the **Windermere Steamboat Museum,** 1 mi. north of Bowness on Rayrigg Rd., the prized possession is the world's oldest mechanically powered boat, which stands beside other full and scale models. The museum also runs a fairly regular steamboat cruise around the lake that is a bit slower but also more fun than its modern counterparts. (☎45565. Open daily Apr.-Oct. 10am-5pm. Museum £4.25, children £2.25, families £8.50. Cruises £5.50, children £2.50.)

The short but steep climb to **Orrest Head** (1½ mi. round-trip) is moderately difficult, but affords one of the best views in the Lake District; it begins opposite the the TIC on the other side of A591 (signposted).

AMBLESIDE   ☎015394

Set in a valley a mile north of Windermere's waters, Ambleside is an attractive village with convenient access to the southern lakes. It's popular with hikers, who are drawn by its location—or perhaps by its absurd number of outdoors shops. Lake cruises depart from the Waterhead Pier, where you can also rent boats. As in Windermere, most non-lake sights lack luster. At tiny **Bridge House,** off Rydal Rd., bridge and house are one and the same. It shelters a (cramped) **National Trust Information Centre.** (☎32617. Open daily Apr.-Oct. 10am-5pm. Free.) Sports fans should head for the **Homes of Football Photographic Gallery,** 100 Lake Rd., where panoramic photos of urban soccer shrines grace the walls. (☎34440. Open daily 10am-5pm. Free.) At **Adrian Sankey Glass** stop in to see some high-quality glass-blowing. (www.glassmakers.co.uk. Open daily 9am-5:30pm. £1 children 50p.) The **Armitt Ambleside Museum,** Rydal Rd., pays homage to lakeland locals and literary luminaries. (☎31212. Open daily 10am-5pm; last admission 4:30pm. £2.50; children, students and seniors £1.80.) **Trails** extend in all directions from Ambleside. Splendid views of higher fells can be had from the top of **Loughrigg** (a moderately difficult 7 mi. round-trip). An easy mile from town is a pretty wooded area that conceals the **Stockghyll Force** waterfall. Area TICs have guides to these and other walks.

Buses stop on Kelsick Rd. Bus #555 runs within the park to **Grasmere, Windermere,** and **Keswick** (1 per hr.). Bus #505 joins the town to **Hawkshead** and **Coniston** (M-Sa 1 per hr.). **Rent bikes** from **Ghyllside Cycles,** The Slack. (☎015394 33592. £14 per day. Open daily 9am-5:30pm; Nov.-Apr. closed W.) The **Tourist Information Centre** is in the Central Building on Market Cross. It offers services identical to those of the TIC in Windermere (p. 376) and doubles as an NPIC. (☎32582; www.amblesideonline.co.uk. Open daily 9am-5pm.) There's also a **NPIC** at Waterhead (p. 373). Other services include: **banks** on Market Pl.; a **launderette,** across from the bus station on Kelsick Rd. (open M-Sa 10am-6pm); the **police** (☎32218); and the **post office,** Market Pl. (☎32267; open M-F 9am-5:30pm, Sa 9am-12:30pm). **Post Code:** LA22 9BU.

Ambleside's ⬛YHA hostel (p. 373) resides near the steamer pier at Waterhead, a pleasant 1 mi. walk from the town center. Ambleside Backpackers ❷, Old Lake Rd., offers 82 bunks in a comfortable, clean, and airy house. (☎32340. Apr.-Sept. £13.50; Oct.-Mar. £12. Internet access, laundry and well-equipped self-catering kitchen. Dorm and breakfast £14. MC/V.) B&Bs cluster on Church Street and Compston Road, while others line the busier Lake Road leading in from Windermere. Linda's B&B & Bunkhouse ❷, Compston Rd., has four rooms with TV and can alternatively be rented out entirely as a private, hostel-style bunkhouse. (☎32999. £15, with breakfast £20. Cash only.) Compston House ❹, Compston Rd., is a more upscale choice. A New York couple welcome you to their well-furnished and appealing home. (☎32305, www.compstonhouse.co.uk. No smoking. £24-60. MC/V.) Forage for trail snacks at the market on Kelsick Rd. (open W 10am-3:30pm) or at Granny Smith's, Market Pl., where you will find organic fruits and vegetables and other natural foods (☎33145; open M-Sa 8am-5pm, Su 9am-4pm, cash only). Pippin's ❶, 10 Lake Rd., serves great sandwiches, all-day breakfasts, and pizza—plus it's open late. (☎31338. Meals £3-5. Open Su-Th 8:30am-10pm, F-Sa 8:30am-11pm. AmEx/MC/V.) At Lucy's ❸, Church St., a gourmet grocery, restaurant and wine bar make for large evening crowds. (☎31191. Entrees £13-15. Open daily 9am-10pm. MC/V.) The Glass House ❸, Ryndal Rd., serves Mediterranean and modern British cuisine, and is decorated with glass from Adrian Sankey's. (☎32137. Lunch £6.50-8. Dinner £11-15; early-bird special 6:30-7:30pm. Open daily noon-5pm and 6:30-9:30pm; closed Tu in winter. Reserve ahead. MC/V.) One good turn deserves a stop at the Golden Rule ❶, on Smithy Brow, a good local pub that taps local beer. (☎33363. Open daily 11am-11pm. Cash only.)

GREAT LANGDALE VALLEY ☎015394

The spectacular and often mist-filled Great Langdale valley, a horseshoe-shaped glacial scar dominated by the towering Langdale Pikes, begins 3 mi. west of Ambleside. In a grove of trees at the center of the valley, the tiny town of Elterwater, half a mile from its namesake, is happily overwhelmed by its surroundings. This is great hiking country—one possibility is the terrific and only moderately difficult walk connecting Elterwater with Grasmere (4 mi.). Another option is a circuit of the valley beginning from Elterwater village (6 mi.). Hard-core trekkers won't be able to resist the siren song of the Pikes. Several popular ascents begin from the Old Dungeon Ghyll Hotel (see below), at road's end 6 mi. from Ambleside. The path to the summit of the Pike of Blisco is only 2½ mi. (and about 2000 ft. up). Bus #516 travels from Ambleside to the Old Dungeon Ghyll Hotel via Elterwater (M-Sa 6 per day, Su 5 per day). There are two YHA hostels in the area: Elterwater (p. 374), in town, and Langdale (p. 375), beautifully set 1 mi. away. The Britannia Inn ❹, in Elterwater village, has comfortable accommodations right at the bus stop. (☎37210. Doubles £76, £74 in winter. AmEx/MC/V.) Where the road from Ambleside ends, the Old Dungeon Ghyll Hotel ❹, sits encircled by raw wilderness. The O.D.G., as the locals say, is an excellent base for hiking and offers a cozy sanctuary for weary walkers. (☎37272. £42-44 per person, with dinner £60. AmEx/MC/V.)

CONISTON ☎015394

Less touristed than its nearby counterparts, Coniston retains the rustic feel of the region's past. Fells to the north and Coniston Water to the south make it popular with hikers and cyclists. The town is also known for its former resident, Victorian artist-writer-critic John Ruskin. The John Ruskin Museum, on Yewdale Rd., displays a collection of his sketches and photographs, as well as general exhibits on the history and geology of Coniston. (☎41164. Open daily Mar.-Nov. 10am-5:30pm; Dec.-Feb. W-Su 10am-3:30pm. £3.50, children £1.75, seniors £3.20, families £9.) Ruskin's gravestone is in St. Andrew's Churchyard. Pretty Brantwood, Ruskin's 250-acre

NORTHWEST ENGLAND

manor from 1872, looks across the lake at Coniston and the Old Man (p. 380); it holds his art and prose collections. (☎41396. Open daily mid-Mar. to mid-Nov. 11am-5:30pm; mid-Nov. to mid-Mar. W-Su 11am-4:30pm. £5.50, students £4, children £1, families £11.50. Gardens only £3.)

The easiest way to reach Brantwood is by water: the National Trust offers trips on the elegant Victorian steam yacht **Gondola**. (☎35599 for reservations and information. Apr.-Oct. 5 per day. Round-trip £4.80, children £2.80.) The **Coniston Launch** also cruises to Brantwood and offers other excursions. (☎36216. Apr.-Nov. 12 per day. Brantwood round-trip £5.50, children £2.50, families £14.) Hikers can explore the nearby abandoned **Coppermines** area (4½ mi.) in search of the "American's stope"—an old copper mine shaft named in honor of a Yankee who leapt over it twice successfully and survived a 160 ft. fall the third time. Another popular walk is to **Tarn Hows** (from Coniston 5 mi. round-trip; p. 380). The more ambitious can take on the surprisingly feisty 2633 ft. **Old Man** just to the north of town (5 mi. round-trip). The TIC has more information on these and other walks in the area.

Bus #505 travels between Ambleside and Coniston, with some trips originating in Windermere (50min. from Windermere; M-Sa 12 per day, Su 6 per day). Buses stop at the corner of Tilberthwaite and Ruskin Ave. Coniston's **Tourist Information Centre** and **NPIC** are on Ruskin Ave. (p. 373). The town has **no ATM**. Rent a bike at **Summitreks**, 14 Yewdale Rd. (☎41212; £14 per day; open daily 9am-5pm) and mail facilities at the **post office**, Yewdale Rd. (☎41259; open M-F 9am-12:30pm and 1:30-5:30pm, W until 5pm, Sa 9am-noon). **Post Code:** LA21 8DU.

Lodgings are available at Coniston's two **YHA hostels**—**Holly How** (p. 374) or the rugged **Coppermines** (p. 374). The **Beech Tree Guest House ❸**, Yewdale Rd., is a comfortable **B&B** at a decent price. (☎41717. Doubles £46, ensuite £54. Cash only.) Outdoorsfolk will find their ideal hosts in the ice-, rock-, and mineshaft-climbing husband and wife team at **Holmthwaite ❷**, Tilberthwaite Ave. Large rooms and good advice. (☎41231. Single £30; doubles £50. AmEx/MC/V.)

HAWKSHEAD ☎015394

In the hamlet of **Hawkshead,** 4 mi. east of Coniston, you can imagine yourself pulling Wordsworth's hair and passing him notes at the **Hawkshead Grammar School,** Main St., where the poet studied from 1779 to 1787. (☎015394 36735. Open Easter-Oct. M-W, F-Su 10am-12:30pm and 1:30-5pm, Su 1-5pm. £1, children free.) Also on Hawkshead's main street is the **Beatrix Potter Gallery.** Housed in offices once used by her husband, the gallery displays the original sketches and watercolors from her beloved children's stories. (☎36355. Open Apr.-Oct. M-W, Sa-Su 10:30am-4:30pm, last admission 4pm. £3, children £1.50, families £7.50.) Potter lived 2 mi. from Hawkshead on her farm at **Hill Top.** The house, which was featured in many of her stories, remains exactly as she left it. Here you can make like Peter Rabbit and cavort in Mr. McGregor's garden, but be prepared to wait, as lines can be long. Clever bunnies book ahead. (☎36269. Same hours as the Gallery. £4.50, children £3, families £11.) **Tarn Hows,** a pond surrounded by a pine grove, is a peaceful (though popular) picnic spot. This charming scene, 2½ mi. from both Hawkshead and Coniston, is mostly man-made—the trees were planted, the tarn enlarged.

In summer, **bus** #505 stops in Hawkshead on its way between Ambleside and Coniston (M-Sa 12 per day; Su 6 per day). **Mountain Goat** offers a combined boat and bus shuttle to Hill Top from Bowness, as well as a bus from Hawkshead. (☎45164. Apr.-Sept. 8 per day. Round trip from Bowness £6, children £4.) On summer Sundays, the National Trust (☎017687 73780) offers a **shuttle** to Tarn Hows from Coniston and Hawkshead. Get trail advice at the Hawkshead **NPIC** (p. 373).

GRASMERE ☎015394

With a lake and a canonized poet all to itself, the attractive village of Grasmere receives more than its fair share of camera-clicking tourists. The sightseers crowd in at midday to visit sights pertaining to William Wordsworth's life and death, but in the quiet mornings and evenings peace graciously returns. Guides provide 30min. tours of the early 17th-century **Dove Cottage,** where Wordsworth lived with his wife Mary and his sister Dorothy from 1799 to 1808, and which is almost exactly as he left it. Next door, the outstanding **Wordsworth Museum** includes pages of his handwritten poetry and personal opinions on his Romantic contemporaries. The cottage is 10min. from the center of Grasmere down Stock Ln. (☎35544. Open daily mid-Feb. to mid-Jan. 9:30am-5pm. Cottage and museum £6, students and YHA members £4.60, children £3, seniors £5.30. Museum only £4, children £2.) **Wordsworth's grave** is in town at St. Oswald's churchyard.

Another 1½ mi. southeast of Grasmere is **Rydal Mount,** the wordsmith's home from 1813 until his death in 1850. The small hut in which he frequently composed verse lies across the garden terrace facing the water. (Bus #599 stops here. ☎33002. Open daily Mar.-Oct. 9:30am-5pm; Nov.-Feb. W-M 10am-4pm. £4, seniors £3.50, students £3.25, children £1, families £10.) Back in town along Redbank Rd., **Faeryland Grasmere** offers an idyllic spot to get a pot of tea and gaze across the water at the fells, or hire **rowboats** and strike out onto the deep green lake. (£6-15 per person depending on size of group; £20 deposit. Open daily 10am-5:30pm.)

Grasmere is a good place for daffodil-seeking Wordsworthians to begin their rambles. A steep, strenuous scramble (4 mi. round-trip) leads to the top of **Helm Cragg.** The 6 mi. **Wordsworth Walk** circumnavigates the two lakes of the Rothay River, passing the poet's grave. The combined **TIC/NPIC** is on Redbank Rd. (p. 373).

There are two **Grasmere YHA hostel** buildings within a 15min. walk: **Butharlyp How** and **Thorney How** (p. 374). The **Glenthorne Quaker Guest House ❸,** 5 mi. up Easedale Rd., across from the main bus stop, provides lovely views of nearby Silver Howe from clean and spacious rooms. (☎35389; www.glenthorne.org. From £28, full board from £44. Cash only.) **The Harwood ❸,** Red Lion Sq., offers convenient accommodations in the center of town. (☎35248. 2-night minimum stay on weekends. £29.50; £27.50 weeknights. MC/V.) **Sara Arundales ❷,** Broadgate, serves baguettes by day (£4) and transforms into a bistro by night. (☎35266. Dinner £10-11. Open daily 10:30am-4pm and 6-8:30pm. MC/V.) The relatively new **Jumble Room ❸,** Langdale Rd., prepares a number of organic vegetarian and seafood plates. (☎35188. Open Easter-Oct. W-Su 10:30am-4:30pm and 6pm "until food runs out;" Oct.-Easter F-Su same times. MC/V.) The famous **Sarah Nelson's Grasmere Gingerbread Shop ❶,** a staple since 1854, is a bargain at 30p apiece in the tiny Church Cottage, outside St. Oswald's Church. (☎35428. Open Easter-Nov. M-Sa 9:15am-5:30pm, Su 12:30-5:30pm; closes earlier in winter. Cash only.)

KESWICK ☎017687

Sandwiched between towering Skiddaw peak and the northern edge of Derwentwater, Keswick (KEZ-ick) rivals Windermere as the Lake District's tourist capital. However, with an appealing town center and a beautiful lake just a stroll away, Keswick surpasses its competitor in tranquil charm.

🛈 PRACTICAL INFORMATION. For information on how to get to Keswick, see p. 372. The **NPIC** (p. 373) is behind the clock tower in Market Pl. **Keswick Mountain Bikes,** just out of town along Main St. in the Southey Hill Industrial Estate, rents cycles. (☎017687 75202. £10 per half-day, £15 per day. Open daily 9am-5:30pm.) Other services include: **banks** on Main St.; a **launderette,** Main St., right at the mini-roundabout (wash £2.50, dry £1.25; open daily 7:30am-7pm); the **police,** 8 Bank St.,

(☎75448); **Internet access** at **U-Compute,** above the post office (☎72269; £2 per 30min., £3 per hr.; open M-Sa 9am-5:30pm, Su 9:30am-4:30pm); and the **post office,** 48 Main St. (☎72269; open M-F 9am-5:30pm, Sa 9am-1pm). **Post Code:** C84 599.

⌂ ❒ ACCOMMODATIONS AND FOOD. The **Keswick** and **Derwentwater YHA** hostels grace the town (p. 374). The area between Station St., St. John St. (Ambleside Rd.), and Penrith Rd. abounds with **B&Bs.** Better options lie on the far side of the town center, away from the hubbub and closer to the bus station. With a stunning view of the lake and mountains, **Appletrees ❸,** The Heads, makes for a good stay. (☎80400; www.appletreeskeswick.com. No smoking. Singles £29; doubles £52.) Just down the road, **Berkeley Guest House ❸,** The Heads, also has nice views. (☎74222; www.berkeley-keswick.com. No smoking. Singles £27; doubles £38.) Away from the lake but still a good bet, **Badgers Wood ❷,** 30 Stanger St., is vegetarian-friendly, with rooms named after trees. (☎72621. www.badgerswood.co.uk. No smoking. Ensuite £25-26 per person.)

  Sundance Wholefoods, 33 Main St., sells organic **groceries.** (☎74712. Open daily in summer 9am-6pm; in winter about 9am-5pm.) There's also a giant **Co-op** on Main st. next to the launderette. For some meatless treats and generally tasty fare, grab sandwiches and wraps (£3-5) at **Lakeland Pedlar ❶,** on the left at the end of an alley off Main St., across from Sundance Wholefoods. (☎74492. Open daily July-Sept. 9am-8pm; Oct.-Apr. 10am-4pm; May-June M-F 10am-4pm, Sa-Su 9am-5pm.) **Brysons ❶,** 42 Main St., is an excellent bakery with an upstairs tea room. (Open M-Sa 9am-5:30pm, Su 9am-5pm.) For lunch or dinner out in town, the recently opened **Sigi's ❷,** 21 Station St., serves a mix of continental and British cuisine in a classy setting. (☎75159. Lunch £4-8. Dinner entrees £14-16. Open daily 11am-2pm and 6:30-9:30pm.) **Ye Olde Queen's Head,** beside the Lakeland Pedlar, is perfect for unwinding over a pint and playing a game of pool. (☎73333. Happy hour daily 5:30-6:30pm. Open M-Sa 11am-11pm, Su 11am-10:30pm.)

◙ ♫ SIGHTS AND ENTERTAINMENT. The best sight in Keswick is **Derwentwater,** undoubtedly one of the prettiest in this land of lakes. The lapping waves are only a 5min. walk south of the town center along Lake Rd. The **Keswick Launch** sends cruises to other points on the lake, has rowboats and motor boats for hire at the marina (2-person rowboats £6 per hr., 2-person motor boats £13 per hr.), and lands at the start off a handful of trails around the shore. (☎72263. Mid-Mar. to Nov. 6-11 cruises per day, Dec. to mid-Mar. 3 per day. 50min. £5.70, under 16 £2.40.) Right beside the factory where the No. 2 was invented, the **Cumberland Pencil Museum** displays the world's largest pencil and features of the industry's history in the region. The museum lies just out of the town center along Main St. (☎73626. Open daily 9:30am-4pm. £2.50, students £1.75, children £1.25, families £6.25.) The **Keswick Museum and Art Gallery,** in Fitz Park on Station Rd., has an interesting grab-bag of Victorian artifacts. (☎73263. Open Easter-Oct. Tu-W 10am-4pm. Free.) For a break from indoor pursuits, the **Theatre by the Lake** (by the, er, lake) features a surprisingly vibrant year-round program of repertory theater, music, and dance and makes for a nice evening's entertainment. (☎74411. Box office open daily 9:30am-8pm. Discount tickets available.)

⚑ HIKING. A standout 4 mi. amble from Keswick crosses slopeside pastures and visits the **Castlerigg Stone Circle,** a neolithic henge dating back nearly 5000 years. Archaeologists believe it may have been used as a place of worship, astronomical observatory, or trading center. Another short walk hits the beautiful **Friar's Crag,** on the shore of Derwentwater, and **Castlehead,** a viewpoint encompassing town, lakes, and peaks beyond. Both these walks are by-and-large easy on the legs, with only a few moderately tough moments. The more strenuous **Catbells and Newlands**

hike runs 8½ mi. and includes a short passage on the Keswick Launch. Maps and information on these and a wide selection of other walks are available at the NPIC (guides 60p). Climbing enthusiasts can get in a bit of practice before heading for the hills at the **Keswick Indoor Climbing Wall,** a 5min. walk out of town along Main St. Fun for beginners as well, this establishment is run by a keen staff that also leads guided outdoor tours for groups of five or more spanning such pursuits as cycling, climbing, and ghyll scrambling. (☎72000. Open daily 10am-9pm. Climbing wall $4.25, instruction available. Reservations required for outdoor guided tours.)

BORROWDALE ☎017687

One of Lakeland's most beautiful spots, the valley of Borrowdale gracefully winds its way south from the tip of Derwentwater. There are relatively few settlements in this serpentine, tree-filled valley, contributing to its appeal. Postcard-perfect **Ashness Bridge,** in the north, is worth a look, but lies some distance from the main road (and thus from public transportation, though small van tours do tend to stop here). The tiny hamlet of **Rosthwaite** has a few hotels and B&Bs. Towering over all is **Scafell Pike** (3210 ft.), the highest mountain in England, which, along with nearby and nearly as lofty **Scafell** and **Great Gable,** forms an imposing triumvirate with some of the toughest and most rewarding hiking in the lakes. Treks up these peaks begin from **Seatoller,** at the head of the valley, which is home to an **NPIC** (p. 373). Walks to the summits are very strenuous and not to be taken lightly—Scafell Pike is 4 mi. to the top and a 3100 ft. climb; Great Gable is also 4 mi., though not as steep.

Bus #79 runs from Keswick to Seatoller via Rosthwaite (30min., 10-20 per day). Accommodations are scattered throughout the valley. **YHA Borrowdale** (p. 374) is in the valley itself, while **Derwentwater** and **Honister House** are nearby. In Rosthwaite, the friendly **Yew Tree Farm ❸** lies just along a small lane opposite the general store. (☎77675. Breakfast included. Ensuite rooms from $30 per person.) The nearby **Flock-In Tea Room** is the valley's best bet for a quick bite to eat, serving up tasty soups and stews. (Open daily Feb.-Oct. 10am-6pm; Nov.-Jan. 10am-4pm.) Wanderers with heavier purses might try the elegant-yet-laid-back **Scafell Hotel ❹,** which runs a pub with passable grub. (☎77208. $45.50-66.50 per person. MC/V.)

BUTTERMERE VALLEY ☎017687

The dramatic Buttermere Valley encompasses two lakes: Buttermere and Crummock Water. There's a genuine sense of isolation here, and a harsher, less tamed beauty than that found at the more visited lakes. The stark mountains seem to plummet right into the lakes. Miniscule **Buttermere** village consists of only a handful of buildings and lies between the two waters, each just a few minutes' walk away. Good **hikes** range from relatively flat circular walks around Crummock Water (10½ mi.) and Buttermere (5 mi.) to a more challenging trek over the fells that brings you to the neighboring YHA Black Sail and eventually YHA Wastwater (14½ mi.; p. 376). Information on good routes is available at the YHA Buttermere (p. 374). The drive in and out of Buttermere Valley is beautiful on its own; southbound it passes the striking Honister Pass, a big, green half-pipe filled with scattered rocks. **YHA Buttermere** is a mere ¼ mi. south of the village (p. 374), while the uniquely situated **Honister Hause** sits atop Honister Pass (p. 375). Among the few structures in the village itself, the well-appointed and upscale **Bridge Hotel ❹** is the lone accommodation option but a fine choice by any standard. (☎70252; www.bridge-hotel.com. Ensuite from $75, Nov.-Mar. $65. MC/V.) Just up the hill, **Skye Farm ❶** provides basic camping. (☎70222. $5 per person. Cash only.) **Bus** #77/77A serves Buttermere from Keswick. #77A reaches Buttermere via the Honister Pass and, though slower, it is far more scenic. (55min., Apr.-Oct. 8 per day).

ULLSWATER ☎017684

One of Ullswater's delights is that it doesn't reveal its beauty all at once. Around each rocky outcrop or grassy bank, a new corner of the lake is visible. The main settlements, **Glenridding** and **Patterdale**, are on the southern tip of the water, and either can be a departure point for the popular climb up **Helvellyn** (3118 ft.). For those planning the ascent, one possible route begins in Glenridding and takes about five strenuous hours to complete (4 mi.). Departing from the Glenridding Pier, the **Ullswater Steamers** cut across the lake with stops at Howtown and Pooley Bridge. (☎82229; www.ullswater-steamers.co.uk. 15 per day, 3 per day in winter; round-trip from £6.40.) For those who are looking for a walk but are not inclined to get vertical, an outstanding route runs along the lake's eastern shore from Glenridding to Howtown, where you can then catch the steamer for a pleasant ride back. Another Ullswater attraction is **Aira Force**, one of the most accessible waterfalls in the Lakes, just off the A5091 toward Keswick. While Windermere is the place for motorized water sports, Ullswater is great for sailing and paddling around. Ask for Malcolm or Pete at the **Glenridding Sailing Centre**, where sailboats, canoes, kayaks and windsurfers are available for rent. (☎82541. www.lakesail.co.uk. Per day rentals: canoes £45, kayaks £30, sailboats £75, windsurfers £10. Lessons for beginners from £20. Open daily Easter-Oct. 10am-5pm.)

Public transport to Ullswater is limited. The only year-round **bus** service is #108 from **Penrith**, which follows a scenic route along the lake. Sit on the left side for the best views (on the West Coast rail line and connected by bus to Keswick, 5 per day, 40 min., £3.80). Two more services operate seasonal schedules: #517 from **Bowness/Windermere** to **Glenridding** (55min.; Apr.-July Sa-Su 3 per day, daily Aug.) and #208 from **Keswick** to **Patterdale** via Aira Force and Glenridding (35min.; daily Aug., June-July Sa-Su 5 per day). The **YHA shuttle** (p. 372) goes once daily from the southern lakes to Patterdale. A **NPIC** camps out in the main carpark in Glenridding (p. 373), and you'll find plenty of options for resting your head in town. B&Bs include comfortable **Mosscrag ❸**, across the stream from the NPIC (☎82500; www.mosscrag.co.uk; singles £40, ensuite £45; doubles £26, ensuite £30; MC/V), and **Beech House ❷**, on the main road (☎82037; from £20 per person; MC/V). **YHA Helvellyn** is 1½ mi. from Glenridding on the way up the peak (p. 374). **YHA Patterdale** is a basic hostel (p. 376), and Patterdale village has several guest houses, including **Ullswater View ❸**. (☎82175. From £20. AmEx/MC/V.) Upscale hotels dot the lake.

CARLISLE ☎01228

Cumbria's principal (that is, only) city, Carlisle was once nicknamed "The Key of England" for its strategic position in the Borderlands between England and Scotland. Roman Emperor Hadrian, Mary, Queen of Scots, Robert the Bruce, and Bonnie Prince Charlie have all played lord of the land from here. Today, Carlisle remains an ideal stopover for more peaceful border crossings, as well as a good base for examining **Hadrian's Wall** (p. 436).

▐ **TRANSPORTATION.** Carlisle's **train station** is on Botchergate, across from the castle. (Ticket office open M-Sa 4:45am-11:30pm, Su 9am-11:30pm.) **Trains** arrive from: **Edinburgh** (1½hr., every hr., £27); **Glasgow** (1½hr., every hr., £27); **London Euston** (4hr., every hr., £90); **Newcastle** (1½hr.; M-Sa every hr., Su 9 per day; £10.80). Get tickets at the **bus station**, Lonsdale St. (Open M-Sa 8:30am-6:30pm, Su 9:45am-5:30pm.) **National Express** (☎08705 808 080) arrives from **London** (6½hr., 3 per day, £28.50). **Stagecoach in Cumbria** bus #555 travels from **Keswick** in the Lake District (1¼hr., 3 per day, £5). **Bike rental** is available at **Scotby Cycles,** Church St., on the roundabout (☎546 931. £12 per day. £20 deposit. Open M-Sa 9am-5:30pm.)

ORIENTATION AND PRACTICAL INFORMATION. Carlisle's city center is a pedestrian zone formed by the intersection of **English Street** and **Scotch Street**. The **Tourist Information Centre** lies in the middle of the center at the Old Town Hall. To get there from the train station, turn left, going between the massive gatehouses, and walk about three blocks (Botchergate becomes English St.), then cross the Old Town Square. To get to the TIC from the bus station, turn left and then cross Lowther St., and walk through the shopping center. The TIC **exchanges currency** and books rooms. (☎625 600; fax 625 604. Open June-Aug. M-Sa 9:30am-5:30pm, Mar.-May and Sept.-Oct. M-Sa 9:30am-5pm; Nov.-Feb. M-Sa 10am-4pm, Apr.-Aug. Su 10:30am-4pm.) Other services include: **banks** on English St.; the **police** (☎528 191); **Internet access** at @ **Cyber Cafe,** 8-10 Devonshire St. (☎512 308; open M-Sa 8am-10pm, Su 10am-10pm; £3 per hr.), as well as at the **library,** in the Lanes shopping center, across from the TIC (☎607 310; open M-F 9:30am-7pm, Sa 9:30am-4pm; £2 per hr.); and the **post office,** 20-34 Warwick Rd., with a **bureau de change** (☎512 410; open M-Sa 9am-5:30pm). **Post Code:** CA1 1AB.

ACCOMMODATIONS AND FOOD. While Carlisle has no hostels, the **Old Brewery Residences ❷,** Bridge Ln., offers inexpensive college dormitory accommodations in July and August. (☎597 352. £14.50, under 18 £9.50. MC/V.) Running east out of the city, **Warwick Road** and its side streets are scattered with a few **B&Bs.** Top picks include: the relatively large **Cornerways Guest House ❷,** 107 Warwick Rd. (☎521 733; singles £25, ensuite £28; doubles £45/55; MC/V), comfortable **Langleigh House ❸,** 6 Howard Pl. (☎530 440; all rooms ensuite; singles £25; doubles £47.50; cash only), and **Howard Lodge Guest House ❹,** 90 Warwick Rd. (☎529 842; all rooms ensuite; singles £25; doubles £45; cash only).

The fairground interior of **The Market Hall,** off Scotch St., holds fresh fruit, veggies, and baked goods. (Open M-Sa 8am-5pm.) **Casa Romana ❷,** 44 Warwick Rd., is esteemed among many Italian restaurants. Dishes start at £3.20 on the happy hour menu (daily until 7pm), and big pasta dishes are around £10. (☎591 969. Open M-Sa noon-2pm and 5:30pm-10pm). **The Lemon Lounge ❺,** 18 Fisher St., has won a following in town with creative cuisine like strawberries in parma ham salad or sea bass with peaches. (☎546 363. 3-course meal with wine £45-50. Open M-Sa from noon. Call ahead for reservations. AmEx/MC/V.) At night, the Botchergate area gets rowdy, and **Bar Code,** 17 Botchergate, is a popular stop. (☎530 460. Open daily 11am-11pm, F-Sa 11-2am.) Students tend to stay on the far side of the city center where they mix with tourists in **The Boardroom,** Paternoster Row, beside the cathedral. Jukebox tunes and karaoke (Th 8pm) create an upbeat atmosphere. (☎527 695. Open M-Sa 11am-11pm, Su noon-10:30pm. Food served noon-2pm.)

SIGHTS. Built by William II with stones from Hadrian's Wall, **Carlisle Castle** looms in the northwest corner of the city. Mary, Queen of Scots, was imprisoned here until Elizabeth I decided she wanted her a wee bit farther from the border. Hundreds of Scots incarcerated in the dungeons after the 1745 Jacobite rebellion stayed alive by slurping water that collected in the trenches of the dark stone walls. Discover these "licking stones" as you learn about other forms of torture employed against the Scots in the well-preserved castle keep. Admission also grants access to **Cumbria's Military Museum,** which pays tribute to more modern warriors. (☎591 922. Open daily Apr.-Sept. 9:30am-6pm; Oct.-Mar. 10am-4pm. Guided tours June and Sept. 2 per day. £3.80, concessions £2.90, children £1.90. Tours £1.60, children 80p.) The **Tullie House** museum and gallery on Castle St. has exhibits on Hadrian's Wall (p. 436) and other areas of

THE LOCAL STORY

RUMPIES OR STUMPIES?

Like most visitors, Mother Nature seem to have had just a little more fun on the Isle of Man. Loghtan sheep sprout four coiled horns, summer orchids spring from over 17 natural glens, and local scallops, called "queenies," are eminently tasty.

The most famed natural asset, however, is the Manx cat-normal but for its pathetic stump of a tail. How the species lost its rearmost appendage is still debated in delightfully erroneous folklore. One story holds that 9th-century Viking invaders planned to decorate their helmets with cat tails; mother cats, knowing (in their infinite feline wisdom) of the plan, bit off the tails of their infant kittens to foil the covetous soldiers. More popular local wisdom, points even further in the past to Noah's Ark. One frisky cat nearly missed last call for the ark, and when the vessel's doors began to close his tail was caught in the jamb and lost forever.

Three varieties of the Manx puss exist: "Rumpies" are completely tail-less, "stumpies" have the suggestion of a tail-like nub, and "rumpy risers" have a bit of bone or cartilage where the tail should be. Keep an eye peeled, and you might see one, or you can visit the Mann Cat Sanctuary, which hosts a few Manx felines.

(Ash Villa, Main Rd., Santon. 824 195; www.manncat.com. Open W and Su 2pm-5pm.)

borderland history. (☎534 781. Open Nov.-Mar. M-Sa 10am-4pm, Su noon-4pm; Apr.-June and Sept.-Oct. M-Sa 10am-5pm, Su noon-5pm; July-Aug. M-Sa 10am-5pm, Su 11am-5pm. £5.20, concessions £3.60, children £2.60, families £14.50.)

Carlisle's **Cathedral,** Castle St., founded in 1122, contains some fine 14th-century stained glass and the Brougham Triptych, a beautifully carved Flemish altarpiece. Also noteworthy are the carved wooden misericords, seats used by the clergymen so they could rest even while standing at prayer. Because the underside always faced the ground or had a priest in front of it, carpenters had free rein in their carvings, and the results are surprisingly imaginative. Sir Walter Scott married his sweetheart on Christmas Eve, 1797, in what is now called the **Border Regiment Chapel.** (☎548 151. Open M-Sa 7:45am-6:15pm, Su 7:45am-5pm. Evensong M-F 5:30pm. Suggested donation £2.)

ISLE OF MAN   ☎01624

Nearly every inch of this 33 mi. by 13 mi. islet in the middle of the Irish Sea shows its fierce pride by waving, sporting, even tattooing the wheel-like emblem of independence—the Three Legs of Man. Its accompanying motto, which translates to "Whichever Way You Throw Me I Stand," speaks rather aptly to the predicament of the island over the last few millennia, during which it's been thrown around quite a bit. Vikings conquered the island in the 9th century, their rule supplanted by an English-Scottish struggle for control in 1266. The English monarchy prevailed and granted dominion over the island to Lord John Stanley in 1405 in for a tribute of two falcons a year. Self-government was not restored until 1828.

Today, Man controls its own internal affairs while remaining a crown possession. However compromised its version of independence might be, the **Tynwald Court,** established by the Vikings, is the longest-running Parliament in the world. It is still called to session each year on July 5th, in a ceremony held completely in **Manx** (a cousin of Irish and Scottish Gaelic) on Tynwald Hill, site of the original Norse governmental structure. Man takes pride in its unique tail-less **Manx cats** and multi-horned **Manx Loghtan sheep,** as well as its famed local delicacy, the **kipper** (herring smoked over oak chips). The island is best known for its **T.T. Races,** which draw motorcyclists for a fortnight of adrenaline-junkie festivities.

✈ GETTING THERE

Ronaldsway Airport (☎821 600) is 10 mi. southwest of Douglas on the coast road. Buses #1, 1C, 2A, and 2 connect to Douglas (25min., 1-3 per hr.), while others stop at points around the island. **Manx Airlines** has been purchased by **British Airways** (☎0845 773 3377; www.britishairways.com). Flights come from Birmingham, Dublin, Glasgow, London Gatwick, Manchester, and other airports in Britain and Ireland. **British European** (UK ☎01232 824 354, Ireland 1890 925 532; www.britisheuropean.com) also serves the Isle.

Ferries dock at the **Douglas Sea Terminal.** (Travel shop open M-Sa 6:30am-8pm.) The **Isle of Man Steam Packet Company** (☎661 661 or 08705 523 523; www.steampacket.com) runs the only ferries to the isle from: **Belfast** (2¾hr.; Apr.-Oct. 2 per week, usually M and F; July-Aug. also W); **Dublin** (2¾hr., Apr.-Oct. 2-3 per week); **Heysham,** Lancashire (2½-3½hr., 2-5 per day); **Liverpool** (2½hr.; Apr.-Oct. 1-4 per day; Nov.-Mar. 3-4 per week). Fares are highest in summer and on weekends (£28-31, students £19-31, children £14-15; round-trip £50-56/£38-56/£25-28).

⊟ LOCAL TRANSPORTATION

The Isle of Man may have more cars per person than anywhere else in the world except Los Angeles, but it also has an extensive system of public transportation, run by **Isle of Man Transport** (☎663 366; www.gov.im/tourism) in Douglas. Their **Travel Shop,** on Lord St. next to the bus station, has details, including free maps and schedules (☎662 525. Open M-F 8am-5:30pm, Sa 8am-3:30pm.) The Travel Shop and the Douglas TIC sell **Island Explorer tickets,** which provide unlimited travel on most Isle of Man Transport bus and train services, as well as on horse trams (1-day £10, 3-day £21, 5-day £30, 7-day £35; children half-price). Pick up a free copy of the *Isle of Man Transport Timetables* at the TIC for all bus and train info.

Trains: Isle of Man Railways (☎663 366) runs along the east coast from Port Erin to Ramsey (Easter-Oct.; limited service in winter). The 1874 **Steam Railway** runs from Douglas to Port Erin via Castletown. The 1899 **Electric Railway** runs from Douglas to Ramsey. **Groudle Glen Railway** is a 2ft. narrow gauge railway carrying passengers out to Sea Lion Rocks. The **Snaefell Mountain Railway** runs to **Snaefell,** the island's highest peak (2036 ft.); trains #1 and 2 are the oldest in the world.

Buses: Frequent buses connect every hamlet. **Douglas** is the center of the bus empire with a main station on Lord Street.

Tours: Protours, Summer Hill (☎674 301) buses travelers around for full (£16.50) and half days (£7-8), with stops along the way departing from Douglas W and Su. Office on Central Promenade open 45min. before tour departures.

Bicycling: The island's small size makes it easy to navigate by bike. The southern three-quarters of the Isle are covered in challenging hills—manageable, but worthy of Man's reputation as professional terrain. TICs provide a map of 1-day cycle trails.

🛈 PRACTICAL INFORMATION

Manx **currency** is equivalent in value to British currency but not accepted outside the Isle; if you use an ATM on the island, make sure to plan for the fact that it will give you all of your bills in Manx currency. Notes and coins from England, Scotland, and Northern Ireland can be used in Man. Manx coins are reissued each year with different and often bizarre designs—for example, 2002 witnessed the minting of 6 different *Harry Potter* designs. All of these coins

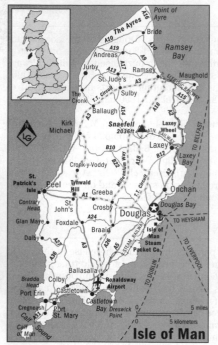

Isle of Man

are available from the Coins Section of the Treasury, located in the Government Office on Bucks Rd. in Douglas. When preparing to leave the island, you can ask for your change in UK tender and usually get it. **Manx stamps** are also unusual (the eagle-eyed will notice that the Queen's head bears no crown); 2004's *Lord of the Rings* stamps are sold in only one other place on earth, New Zealand, where the films were produced. Post offices and newsstands sell Manx Telecom **phonecards,** but mobile phone users on plans from England will likely incur surcharges. The Isle shares Britain's **international dialing code, ☎** 44. In an **emergency,** dial ☎ 999 or 112.

The island-wide **Story of Mann** is a collection of museums and exhibits focused on the island's heritage, including sites in once-capital Castletown, Peel, Ballasalla, and Ramsey. The town of Laxey celebrates the Laxey Wheel, nicknamed Lady Isabella, a 72ft. sesquicentennial waterwheel (the largest in the world), while Cregneash Folk Village recreates Manx crofting life, and the Manx Museum in Douglas institutionalizes the whole affair. You can save money by purchasing a 4-site **Heritage Pass** (£10), available from any of the museums (All sites share the same phone number and website: ☎ 648 000; www.storyofmann.com).

📷 HIKING

In 2004, the first ever **Isle of Man Walking Festival** (☎ 661 177) saw a five-day walking extravaganza around the island, expected to be repeated late June 2005. Diehards trek 31 miles and climb 8,000ft. between Ramsey and Port Erin in the **Manx Mountain Marathon,** Britain's longest one-day race, in early April.

Raad ny Foillan ("Road of the Gull") is a 95 mi. path around the island marked with blue seagull signs. The spectacular 📷**Port Erin to Castletown route** (12 mi.) offers the best of the island's south: beaches, cliffs, splashing surf, and wildlife. **Bayr ny Skeddan** ("The Herring Road"), once used by Manx fishermen, covers the less thrilling 14 mi. land route between Peel in the west and Castletown in the east. It overlaps the **Millennium Way,** which runs 28 mi. from Castletown to Ramsey along the 14th-century Royal Highway, ending one mile from Ramsey's Parliament Sq. *Walks on the Isle of Man,* available at the TIC, gives a cursory description of more than 11 different walks, both long and short, and another pamphlet gives tips on reaching over 17 glens. 12 campsites, with listings at the TIC, dot the isle.

❄ EVENTS

The island's economy relies heavily on tourism, so frequent festivals celebrate everything from jazz to angling. TICs stock a calendar of events; ask for *What's On the Isle of Man* or check out www.isleofman.com. The first two weeks of June turn Man into a merry motorcycling beast for the **T.T. (Tourist Trophy) Races** (www.iomtt.com). The population doubles, the Steam Packet Co. schedules extra ferries at special rates, and Manx Radio is replaced by "Radio T.T." The races were first held on Man in 1907, because restrictions on vehicle speed and road closure were less severe (read: nonexistent) on the island. The circuit consists of 38 mi. of hairpin turns and mountain climbs that top racers navigate at speeds over 120 mph, and the winner's name and make of motorcycle are engraved on the same silver "tourist trophy" that has been used since 1907.

Southern "100" Motorcycle Races (☎822 546) take place over three days in mid-July, bringing more bikers and general good times to Castletown, the self-proclaimed "Road Racing Capital of the World." (July 12-15 in 2004). July also sees the annual **Manx Heritage Festival**, during which new legislation is proclaimed at **Tynwald Fair** (☎685 500). Though this ritual relies on fiercely honored traditions (representatives don wigs and traditional robes), other summer activities are a bit looser in execution. **World Tin Bath Championships** in July, a **Baton Twirling Competition** in August, an **International Chess Tournament** in September, and a **Darts Festival** in April invite Manx natives and visitors alike to revel in idiosyncrasy.

DOUGLAS ☎01624

Grand hotels, a buzzing concrete promenade, and a string of teashops and classier venues remind travelers they aren't too far from the Mainland. In fact, for such a quirky land, the isle's capital is rather standard, despite its glamorous history as smuggling and summering hub for much of Northwest England. Its hub of buses, trains, ferries, and horse-drawn carts, however, easily shuttle tourists to those attractions only Man can provide. Though somewhat uncharismatic, Douglas remains a useful gateway from which to explore the island's more scenic corners.

▐ TRANSPORTATION. Ferries arrive at the **Sea Terminal**, at the southern end of town, where North Quay and The Promenade converge near the bus station. **Isle of Man Transport** (☎663 366), on Banks Circus, runs local trains and buses (see **Local Transportation**, p. 387). Slow but inexpensive horse-drawn **trams** clip-clop down The Promenade between the bus and Electric Railway stations in summer. Stops are posted every 200 yd. (☎663 366. Open daily June-Aug. 9:10am-8:50pm; Sept.-May until 6:30pm.) Motorized **buses** also run along The Promenade, connecting the bus and Steam Railway stations with the Electric Railway (65p). For taxis, call 24hr. **A-1 Radio Cabs** (☎663 344) or **Telecabs** (☎629 191). Several car rental companies are based in Douglas; try **Hertz**, 30 Esplanade (☎621 844); **Athol**, Peel Rd. (☎822 481); or **Mylchreests** (☎08000 190 335), which operates at the Sea Terminal. **Eurocycles**, 8a Victoria Rd., off Broadway, rents **bikes**. (☎624 909. Call ahead in summer. £12 per day. ID deposit. Open M-Sa 9am-5pm.)

▦▌ ORIENTATION AND PRACTICAL INFORMATION. Douglas stretches for 2 mi. along the seafront, from **Douglas Head** to the **Electric Railway** terminal. Douglas Head is separated from town by the **River Douglas**. The ferry and bus terminals lie just north of the river. **The Promenade** curves from ferry terminal to the Electric Railway terminal along the beach, dividing the coastline from the shopping district with a line of Victorian row-houses. Shops and cafes line **The Strand,** a pedestrian thoroughfare that begins near the bus station and runs parallel to The Promenade, turning into Castle St. before terminating at a taxi queue near the Gaiety Theatre. The **Tourist Information Centre,** Sea Terminal Bldg., provides transportation timetables and the worthwhile *What's On* guide. (☎686 766; www.visitisleofman.com. Open daily Easter-Sept. 9:15am-7pm; Oct.-Easter M-F 9:15am-5:30pm.) Other services include: **Lloyds TSB,** 78 Strand St. (08457 301 280; open M-F 9:30am-4:30pm, Sa 9:30am-12:30pm); **Thomas Cook,** 7/8A Strand St. (☎626 288; open M-W and F-Sa 9am-5:30pm, Th 10am-5:30pm); **Broadway Launderette,** 24 Broadway (☎621 511; open M, W, F-Sa 8:30am-5pm, Tu 8:30am-4:30pm, Su 11am-4pm; £3 wash, dry 20p per 5min.); the **police,** Glencrutchery Rd. (☎631 212); **Nobles Isle of Man Hospital,** Westmoreland Rd. (☎642 642); **Internet access** at **Feegan's Lounge,** 8 Victoria St. (☎679 280; £1 per 20min.; open M-Sa 9am-6pm, Su 1pm-5pm), the **library,** 10-12 Victoria St. (☎696 461; M-Sa 9:15am-5:30pm; 75p per 15min., free for students after 4pm), or noisy **Leisure Amusement Centre,** 68-72 Strand St. (☎676 670; open M-Su roughly 9am-9pm); **Boots pharmacy,** 14-22 Strand St. (☎616 120; open M-Sa 8:30am-5:30pm, Su 1-4:30pm); and the **Isle of Man Post,** at the corner of Regent St. and The Strand (☎686 141; open M and W-F 9am-5:30pm, Tu 9:30am-5:30pm, Sa 9am-12:30pm). **Post Code:** IM1 2EA.

⌂◖ ACCOMMODATIONS AND FOOD. Douglas is awash with **B&Bs** and **hotels.** During T.T. Races weeks, they fill a year in advance and raise their rates. The **Devonian Hotel ❷,** 4 Sherwood Terr. on Broadway, is a Victorian-style townhouse conveniently located just off The Promenade. Friendly proprietors accommodate those leaving on early ferries. (☎674 676.; www.thedevonian.co.uk. All rooms with TVs. Singles £20; doubles £36. Cash only.) Just next door, the unmarked **Athol House Hotel ❸,** 3 Sherwood Terr. on Broadway, features elegant rooms with classy pine furniture and TV. Warm host Adrianne greets guests with wine, chocolate, and flowers on arrival. (☎629 356. From £25. Cash only.) The recently refurbished **Glen Mona ❹,** 6 Mona Dr., offers 12 luxurious ensuite rooms with TVs, some with jacuzzis. (☎676 755; www.glenmona-iom.co.uk. Singles £40-70; doubles £60-90. MC/V.) **Grandstand Campsite ❶** is behind the T.T. Races' start and finish line. (☎696 330. Reception M-F 9am-5pm. Open mid-June to Sept., closed the last two weeks of Aug. £8-10 per person. Laundry £2. Showers £1.) It's closed during the T.T. Races and Grand Prix week, but TIC's list 11 other campsites. During the T.T. fortnight, seven makeshift sites open in football fields and public parks.

Grill and chip shops line **Duke Street, Strand Street,** and **Castle Street,** while many of the hotels along **The Promenade** feature classier restaurants. The **Safeway** is on Chester St., behind The Strand. (Open M-W and Sa 8am-8pm, Th-F 8am-9pm, Su 9am-6pm.) At the **Bay Room Restaurant ❶,** in the Manx Museum, diners enjoy tea snacks or hot lunches like Manx mutton broth (£4.25) and Manx seafood medley (£7) amidst selected sculptures from the gallery collection. (☎612 211. Open M-Sa 10am-4:30pm. Cash only.) The dining rooms in **Copperfield's Olde Tea Shoppe and Restaurant ❸,** 24 Castle St., strive for historical ambience. Viking Feasts (£6.75-11.95), Edwardian Extravaganzas (£8.95), and Naughty Nancy's Fancies (95p-£3.75) complete the theme. (☎613 650. Open summer M-Sa 11am-6pm; winter M-Sa 10am-4pm. Cash only.) At **Brendann O'Donnell's ❶,** 16-18 Strand St., Guinness posters and traditional music remind patrons of the Isle's proximity to Ireland. (☎621 566. Open Su-Th noon-11pm, F-Sa noon-midnight. Cash only.)

◖◗ SIGHTS AND ENTERTAINMENT. From the shopping district, signs point to the Chester St. parking garage next to Safeway, where an elevator ride to the 8th floor roof leads visitors across a footbridge to the entrance of the **Manx Museum.** Displays include a 20min. film on the history of the island as well as the

Manx National Gallery of Art. Particularly lively are sections about its days as a Victorian holiday mecca, when it was unofficially known as the Isle of Woman due to its attractive seasonal population. The museum also traces the history of Jewish refugees interned on the island during WWII. (☎648 000. Open M-Sa 10am-5pm. Free.) Past the Villa Marina Gardens on Harris Promenade sits the **Gaiety Theatre,** designed in 1900 and recently restored to something like its former glory. Take a 1½hr. tour to see a Victorian trap system under the stage and other antique machinery. (☎694 555. Box office open M-Sa 10am-4:30pm and 1hr. before curtain. Tours Sa 10:15am. Tickets £10-20, concessions available. Tours £5, children £2.50.) The distant sandcastle-like structure in Douglas Bay is the **Tower of Refuge,** built as an offshore hope for shipwreck survivors, but closed to the general public.

Most of the **clubs** in Douglas are 21+ and some are free until 10 or 11pm, with a £2-5 cover thereafter. Put in a long day (and night) at **The Office,** which has a small dance floor and an ample bar (☎610 763. Su-Th noon-midnight, F-Sa noon-1am. Food noon-8pm.) **Paramount City,** Queen's Promenade, houses two nightclubs: the upstairs **Director's Bar** plays faves from the 50s to the 90s, while the downstairs **Dark Room** pumps chart and dance. (☎622 447. Open F-Sa 10pm-3:30am.)

PEEL ☎01624

Long ago, this "cradle of Manx heritage" played host to the Vikings, whose Nordic pedigree lives on still in Manx blood. The Quayside maintains a rough-and-tumble sailor's edge, while ruins across the harbor loom dark against western sunsets. The most prominent of these relics are the stone towers of **Peel Castle,** which share the skyline of **St. Patrick's Isle** with the stone arches of **St. German's Cathedral** and the excavated tomb of a well-to-do Viking woman nicknamed "The Pagan Lady." The site is reached by a pedestrian causeway from the Quay. A helpful audio tour guides visitors; check out the murder holes and "leper's squint." (Open daily Easter-Oct. 10am-5pm. Last admission 1hr. before close. £3, children £1.50.) Across the harbor on the Quay, the comprehensive ☒**House of Manannan** showcases a panorama of audiovisual displays that usher visitors from a fire-lit Celtic roundhouse to a 30 ft. Viking war ship shored on a recreated indoor beach, culminating at a (fake) blood-splattered fish-gutting table. (☎648 000. Open daily 10am-5pm; last admission 3:30pm. £5, children £2.50.) **Moore's Traditional Curers,** Mill Rd., is the only kipper factory of its kind left in the world (or so it claims). Informal tours let visitors watch kippering in action and even climb up the interior of one of the massive smoking chimneys. (☎843 622; www.manxkippers.com. Shop open M-Sa 10am-5pm. Tours run Apr.-Oct. M-Sa 3:30pm. £2, children £1.) Just down the Quay, the **Leece Museum** exhibits relics from Peel's past. Downstairs is the site of the "Black Hole" prison cell, which now only locks up unfortunate wax figures. (☎845 366. Open Oct.-Easter Tu-Sa noon-4pm; Easter-Sept. W-Su 10am-4pm. Free.)

The **Peel Camping Park ❶,** Derby Rd., is run through the local Town Hall office and has laundry facilities and showers. (☎842 341. Open Easter-Sept. £4 per person.) **Shoprite** grocery store is in the center of town on Michael St. (Open M-F 8am-10pm, Sa 8am-8pm, Su 9am-6pm.) The **Harbour Lights Cafe and Tearoom ❷,** Shore Rd. on the Promenade, offers Manx Kipper Teas (tea, kippers, bread, and teacake). (☎495 197. Kipper tea £7. 3-course supper £25. Open Tu-Su 10am-5pm. Cash only.) "Often licked but never beaten," **Davison's Manx Dairy Ice Cream ❶** next door boasts a huge flavor selection including Turkish Delight and butterscotch honeycomb. (☎844 761. Open daily Apr.-Sept. 10am-9pm; Oct.-Mar. 10am-5pm. Cash only.)

Buses (☎662 525) arrive and depart across the street from the Town Hall on Derby Rd., coming from **Douglas** (#4, 4B, 5A, 6, 6B, X5; 35min.; M-Sa 1-2 per hr., Su 11 per day; £2.80) and **Port Erin** (#8, 55min., M-Sa 3 per day, £3). The **Tourist Informa-**

NORTHWEST ENGLAND

tion Centre is a window in the Town Hall, Derby Rd. (☎842 341. Open M-Th 8:45am-5pm, F 8:45am-4:30pm.) The **post office** is on Douglas St. (☎842 282. Open M-F 9am-12:30pm and 1:30-5:30pm, Sa 9am-12:30pm.) **Post Code:** IM5 1AA.

CREGNEASH
☎01624

The oldest village on the island, Cregneash is known for its open-air museum, which is worth a daytrip from Douglas or Peel and is walkable from Port Erin. The **Cregneash Village Folk Museum** has carefully preserved (and partially recreated) a traditional Manx crofting town, complete with thatched-roof cottages and live demonstrations of blacksmithing and wool dying. Visitors pick their way between roosters as they wander between buildings like **The Karran Farm,** where old women work on gorgeous silk patchwork as they cook rice pudding over a fire. (☎648 000. Open daily Apr.-Oct. 10am-5pm. £3, children £1.50). **Bus** #1 runs to Cregneash from **Douglas** (1¼hr., M-Sa 2 per day) and **Port Erin** (20min., M-Sa 5 per day).

PORT ERIN
☎01624

A quiet city set in a spectacular locale, Port Erin's beauty is all natural. A number of hikes start from the town of Port Erin itself. One of the nicest is the 30min. trail out to **Bradda Head,** which hugs the bay before giving way to a rocky uphill scramble. At the top of the hill, climbers arrive at **Milner's Tower,** a curious structure designed to look like a key. Views of the sea and nearby Calf of Man compensate for the climb up the dimly lit spiral staircase. The trail begins at the Bradda Glen gates off the Promenade, or from the carpark 100 yd. down the road. The **Coronation Footpath,** which begins from the same spots, offers a gentler ascent.

Those particularly charmed by views of the **Calf of Man** can go there on trips that leave daily from Port Erin pier. (☎832 339 or 496 793. Trips depart daily 10:15, 11:30am, 1:45pm in summer, weather permitting; fewer during low season. Book ahead.) For on-land entertainment, **Bellacraine Quad Bike Trails** leads 1½hr. trail rides, including training and refreshments. (☎801 219. £30 per person.)

Port Erin is easily accessible as a daytrip from Douglas or Peel. **Buses** #1 and X2 run to Port Erin from **Douglas** (50min., 2 per hr.) and 2 per day continue all the way to **Cregneash.** Hiking pamphlets are available from the **Tourist Information Centre,** on Station Rd. (☎832 298). **Anchorage Guest House ❸,** Athol Park, has superb the views of the town. (☎832 355; www.anchorageguesthouse.com. Open Feb.-Nov. £22.50-26 per person. AmEx/MC/V.) Returning hikers can treat themselves at **Graingers at Bradda Glen ❸,** at the end of Bradda Close. This cliffside cottage offers local seafood and vegetarian specials (from £9). (☎833 166. Open M 12:30-2:30pm and 5:30-8pm, Tu-Sa noon-3pm and 5:30-8pm, Su noon-4:30pm. Cash only.)

NORTHEAST ENGLAND

Framed by Scotland and the North Sea, this corner of England has always been border country. Hadrian's Wall sketches a history of skirmishes with fierce northern neighbors, and the area's three national parks, some of the most remote countryside in England, retain their frontier ruggedness. No trail tests hikers like the Pennine Way, Britain's first and longest official long-distance path. An extensive network of shorter trails crisscrosses the heather-flecked moors of a Brontëan imagination and the rolling dales beloved by James Herriot. The isolation of the northeast testifies to its agricultural bent; even the main industry (textile manufacturing) sprang from the pervasive presence of sheep. But while the principal urban areas of Yorkshire and Tyne and Wear (including Leeds, York, and Newcastle) grew out of the wool and coal industries and bear the scars to prove it, today their refurbished city centers have turned their energies to accommodating visitors.

HIGHLIGHTS OF NORTHEAST ENGLAND

YORK MINSTER Don't miss this colossal Gothic cathedral, which contains the largest medieval glass window in the world (p. 409).

NATIONAL PARKS Wander the valleys of the **Yorkshire Dales** (p. 404), brave the winds of the **Moors** (p. 415), or seek solitude in rough-hewn **Northumberland** (p. 438).

NEWCASTLE BY NIGHT Sample the famed brown ale of this gritty city, home to crowded dance floors, lively locals, and legendary nightlife (p. 429).

HADRIAN'S WALL Admire the remains of Hadrian's massive construction, which once delineated the northernmost border of the Roman Empire (p. 436).

YORKSHIRE

SHEFFIELD   ☎0114

While Manchester was clothing the world, Sheffield (pop. 530,000) was setting its table, first with hand-crafted flatware, then mass-produced cutlery, and eventually stainless steel (invented here). As 20th-century industry moved elsewhere, economic depression, made globally familiar by *The Full Monty*, set in. Though a dearth of city-center accommodations foils any budget traveler's overnight aspirations, Sheffield, with its three new town squares and numerous art galleries, represents the last bastion of urbanity and nightlife before the Peak District.

🚆 **TRANSPORTATION AND PRACTICAL INFORMATION.** Sheffield lies on the M1 motorway, about 30 mi. east of Manchester and 25 mi. south of Leeds. **Midland Station** (☎08457 221 125) is on Sheaf St., near Sheaf Sq. **Trains** (☎08457 484 950) arrive from: **Birmingham** (1¼hr., 2 per hr., ₤21); **London St. Pancras** (2¼hr., every hr., ₤48); **Manchester** (1hr., 2 per hr., ₤11.40); **York** (1hr., 2 per hr., ₤12.20). The

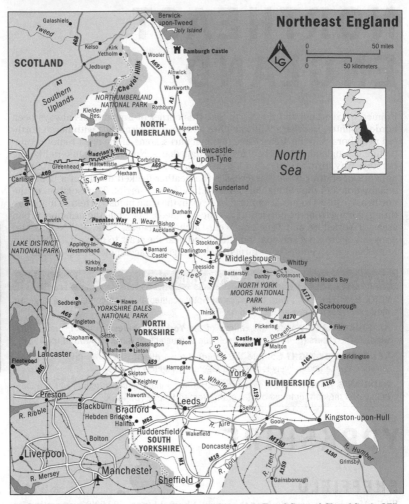

major **bus station** in town is the **Interchange**, between Pond St. and Sheaf St. (☎275 4905. Lockers £1-2. Open M-F 8am-5:30pm.) **National Express** (☎08705 808 080) travels from: **Birmingham** (2½hr., 6 per day, £14.50); **London** (4hr., 8 per day, £14.50); **Nottingham** (1½-2hr., 9 per day., £5.75). The **Supertram**, Sheffield's modern transport system, covers the city. (☎272 8282. Daily pass £2.20, weekly £7.50.)

Sheffield's **Tourist Information Centre**, 1 Tudor Sq., off Surrey St., distributes the free *Visit Sheffield* brochure. (☎221 1900, bookings ☎201 1011. Open M-Sa 10am-1pm and 2:15pm-4pm.) Other services include: **banks** on Pinstone St. and Church St., and **Thomas Cook**, 119 Pinstone St. (☎260 7600; open M-W and F-Sa 9am-5:30pm, Th 10am-5:30pm); the **police**, West Bar Green (☎220 2020); **Northern General Hospital**, Herries Rd. (☎243 4343); **Internet access** at **Matrix** bar, 4 Charter Sq. (☎275 4100; £1.50 per hr., open M-Sa noon-10pm) and **Central Library**, Surrey St.

(☎273 4712; free; open M 10am-8pm, Tu and Th-Sa 9:30am-5:30pm, W 9:30am-8pm); and the **post office,** 9 Norfolk Row (☎281 4713; open M-Tu and Th-F 8:30am-5:30pm, W 9am-5:30pm, Sa 8:30am-3pm). **Post Code:** S1 2PA.

⚑ ⌂ ACCOMMODATIONS AND FOOD. Sheffield doesn't exactly roll out the red carpet, nor even a worn welcome mat, for the budget traveler. If you don't mind the 30min. commute by train, try the **YHA hostel** in **Hathersage** (p. 366). **B&Bs** within Sheffield cost at least £18. **York Villa ❷,** 63 Norfolk Rd., keeps guests in elegant floral rooms in a manse only 5min. from the train station. (☎272 4566. Singles £19, doubles £35. Cash only.) **Rutland Arms ❸,** 86 Brown St., near the train and bus stations, offers clean ensuite rooms above a lively pub. (☎272 9003; fax 273 1425. Singles £21; doubles £30; twin £32, family rooms £42. AmEx/MC/V.) **The Bristol Hotel ❺,** Blonk St., embraces post-industrialism with sand-blasted windows, sparely decorated rooms, talking elevators, and silver shower curtains. (☎220 4000. Singles, twins and doubles £53, triples £63; discounts M-Th. AmEx/MC/V.)

Cheap eats in the city center are hard to come by; head for the student haunts on **Ecclesall Road** or the ubiquitous cafe-bars on **Division Street** and **Devonshire Street,** where clubbers prepare for the evening. The **Spar** supermarket is at the intersection of Division St. and Backfields Alley (☎275 2900. Open daily 24hr.) The minimalist **Showroom Cafe-Bar ❷,** 7 Paternoster Row, draws a black-clad, wine-sipping crowd. Lounge on the couch over great chicken dishes, burgers, and stir-fries (£6.50-12) before watching arthouse flicks next door. Combined film ticket, entree and wine £13.50. (☎249 5479. Open M-W 11am-11pm, Th 11am-midnight, F-Sa 11am-1am, Su 11am-10:30pm. MC/V.) **The Picasso Restaurant and Bar ❹,** upstairs at the Bristol Hotel (p. 395), pays homage to the master of modernity with nouvelle cuisine (£11-12) and colorful furnishings. (☎220 4000. Open M-Sa 9am-11pm, Su 9am-9pm. AmEx/MC/V.)

◙ SIGHTS. Sheffield's cultural reputation has won some vitality from the opening of the **⊠Millennium Galleries,** Arundel Gate. Two of the galleries host small national and international exhibitions. The excellent **Ruskin Gallery** was originally established in 1875 by Victorian critic John Ruskin, intended to show the working class that "life without industry is guilt, and industry without art is brutality." The current gallery merges nature, architecture, and industry. The second permanent gallery celebrates **metalwork.** Stifle that groan of boredom and take a closer look—this isn't shop class. The industrial heritage and the pride of Sheffield reside in its cutlery. (☎278 2600. Open M-Sa 10am-5pm, Su 11am-5pm. Free. Special exhibits usually £4, concessions £3, children £2, families £10.)

The **⊠Graves Gallery,** on Surrey St. above the public library displays post-war British art, Romantic and Impressionist paintings, and houses traveling exhibitions. Particular emphasis on the work of William Roberts (☎278 2600. Open M-Sa 10am-5pm. Free.) The **Site Gallery,** 1 Brown St., showcases contemporary works of media art and photography. (☎281 2077. Open Tu-F and Su 11am-6pm, Sa 11am-5:30pm. Free.) The **Kelham Island Industrial Museum,** Alma St., studies the strong hand of Sheffield's industrial movement. Take bus #53 from the Interchange to Nursery St.; turn left on Corporation St., right on Alma St., and wind 200 yd. through an industrial park to the museum on the right. (☎272 2106. Open M-Th 10am-4pm, Su 11am-4:45pm; last admission 1hr. before close. £3.50, concessions £2.50, children £2, families £8.)

◙ ♫ NIGHTLIFE AND ENTERTAINMENT. Most **clubs** are in the southeastern section of the city, around **Matilda Street;** *Visit Sheffield* has current nightlife listings. **The Leadmill,** 6 Leadmill Rd., plays to almost every taste in three stu-

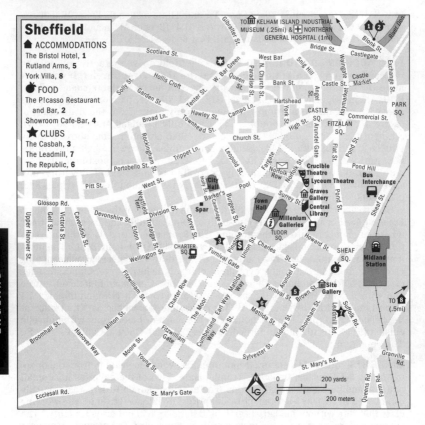

dent-packed rooms. (☎221 2828. Cover £2-5. Open M-F 10pm-2am, Sa 10pm-2:30am.) **The Casbah,** 1 Wellington St., at the corner of Cambridge St., has live rock, indie and punk bands throughout the week, while the DJ and bar upstairs are free of cover. (☎275 6077. Cover £2-5. Open M-Sa 8pm-2am.) **The Republic,** 112 Arundel St., hosts Sheffield's largest party with its Saturday "Gatecrasher" bash. (☎276 6777. Cover M and Th £2-3, F £3-5, Sa £10-15 after 10:30pm. Open M and Th-F 10pm-2am, Sa 10pm-6am.) For nightlife without a backbeat, visit the **Crucible** and **Lyceum Theatres,** both in Tudor Sq. and sharing a box office on Norfolk St., which stage many West End musicals, plays, and dance shows. (☎249 6000. Same-day tickets £7.50.)

PENNINE WAY

The Pennine Peaks arch up the center of Britain from the Peak District to the Scottish border. Britain's first long-distance trail, the 268 mi. **Pennine Way** begins at Edale, crosses the boggy plateau of **Kinder Scout,** passes into the **Yorkshire Dales** at Malham, and reemerges at the 2273 ft. peak of Pen-y-ghent. The northern section crosses the **High Pennines,** a 20 mi. stretch from below Barnard Castle to Hadrian's

Wall, terminating at Kirk Yetholm in Scotland. The rebellious population of this region have erected chapels in defiance of Canterbury, embraced socialism in the face of textile barons, and won public right-of-way access for these very trails.

🔾 HIKING THE PENNINE WAY

Hikers have completed the Way in as few as ten days, but most spend three weeks on the trail. Brief but rewarding forays on well-traveled walkways leave from major towns. The unusual limestone formations in the Yorkshire Dales and the lonely moor of Kinder Scout are Way highlights. The Pennines do not, however, coddle hikers. Sudden storms can reduce visibility to under 20 ft., leave paths swampy, and sink you knee-deep in peat. Those in the know recommend that all save the most hardcore hikers stay away from the Pennines in the winter. Bring a map and compass and know how to use them. Rain gear, warm clothing, and extra food are also essential. (See **Wilderness Safety,** p. 52.) Wainwright's *Pennine Way Companion* (£10), a pocket-sized volume available from bookstores, is a worthwhile supplement to Ordnance Survey maps (£6-8), all available at National Park Information Centres and TICs. Comprehensive coverage of the route comes in the form of two National Trail Guides, *Pennine Way North* and *Pennine Way South*, each £12. Those wishing to see some of the Way without hoofing the whole thing should get hold of the *Pennine Way Public Transport Guide*, free at NPICs.

▐ ACCOMMODATIONS

YHA hostels are spaced within a day's hike (7-29 mi.) of each other. Book online at www.yha.org.uk. Any NPIC or TIC can supply details on trails and alternate accommodations; pick up the *Pennine Way Accommodations Guide* (90p).

YHA HOSTELS
The following hostels are arranged from south to north, with the distance from the nearest southerly hostel listed. Unless otherwise noted, reception is open from 5pm, and breakfast and evening meals are served.

Edale: In the Peak District. See p. 366.

Crowden-in-Longdendale: 15 mi. from Edale in the Peak District. See p. 366.

Mankinholes: 2 mi. outside Todmorden (☎01706 812 340). 2-, 4-, and 6-person rooms. Dorms £10.60, under 18 £7.20. MC/V. ❷

Haworth: Just outside the town. 18 mi. from Mankinholes. See p. 400.

Earby: 13 Birch Hall Ln., Earby (☎01282 842 349), 12 mi. from Haworth. Self-catering. Open Apr.-Oct. Dorms £10.60, under 18 £7.20. MC/V. ❶

Malham: 15 mi. from Earby in the Yorkshire Dales. See p. 405.

Stainforth: 8 mi. from Malham in the Yorkshire Dales. See p. 405.

Hawes: 19 mi. from Stainforth in the Yorkshire Dales. See p. 405.

Keld: 9 mi. from Hawes in the Yorkshire Dales. See p. 405.

Baldersdale: Blackton, Baldersdale (☎0870 770 5684), 15 mi. from Keld in a converted stone farmhouse overlooking Blackton Reservoir. Open daily July-Aug.; Apr.-June and Sept.-Oct. M-F, call ahead to confirm. Dorms £10.60, under 18 £7.20. MC/V. ❶

Langdon Beck: Forest-in-Teesdale (☎01833 622 228), 15 mi. from Baldersdale. Open year-round; call to confirm. Dorms £10.60, under 18 £7.20. MC/V. ❷

Dufton: Redstones, Dufton, Appleby (☎0870 770 5800), 12 mi. from Langdon Beck. Has a small shop. Open daily Apr.-Oct. Dorms £10.60, under 18 £7.20. MC/V. ❶

Alston: The Firs, Alston (☎01434 381 509), 20 mi. from Dufton. Open daily Apr.-Oct.; Sept.-Oct. M-Tu, F-Su. Dorms £10.60, under 18 £7.20. MC/V. ❶

Greenhead: 17 mi. from Alston. See p. 436.

Once Brewed: 7 mi. east of Greenhead. See p. 436.

Bellingham: 14 mi. from Once Brewed in Northumberland. See p. 439.

Byrness: 15 mi. from Bellingham in Northumberland. See p. 439.

CAMPING BARNS

In the High Pennines, the YHA operates six **camping barns,** hollow stone buildings on private farms. Available amenities—electricity, hot water, heating, showers and so on—vary from farm to farm. The telephone numbers below are for confirming arrival times only; to book, call ☎0870 770 6113 or e-mail campbarns-yha@enterprise.net. You can also get information on the YHA website (www.yha.org.uk) and in the free *Camping Barns in England*, available at TICs.

Holwick Barn: Mr. and Mrs. Scott, Low Way Farm, Holwick (☎01833 640 506), 3 mi. north of Middleton-in-Teesdale. Sleeps 20. £6 per person. MC/V. ❶

Witton Barn: Witton Estate, Witton-le-Wear (☎01388 488 322), just off the Weardale Way. Sleeps 15. £5 per person. MC/V. ❶

SOUTH PENNINES

Prepared for bleak and isolated moorlands by *Wuthering Heights*, visitors to the South Pennines may be surprised by the domesticated feel of this landscape. Between the picturesque villages of Hebden Bridge and Haworth, heathery slopes of greenery unfold quietly, patterned into well-cultivated fields and grazed upon by impassive sheep.

▣ TRANSPORTATION

The proximity of the South Pennines to Leeds and Bradford makes **train** transport (☎08457 484 950) fairly easy. **Arriva's** Transpennine Express (☎0870 602 3322) reaches Hebden Bridge directly from Blackpool and Leeds (Several per hr. 7am-9pm M-Sa, every hr. on Su). **Metro's** Airedale Line, from Leeds, stops at **Keighley** (KEETH-lee), 5 mi. north of Haworth. From there, reach Haworth by the **Keighley & Worth Valley Railway's** private steam trains (☎01535 645 214). **Bus** travel will take you through smaller cities. Travel to **Halifax** to get to Hebden Bridge, and Keighley to get to Haworth; both cities are convenient destinations from **Leeds.** Local buses make the half-hour journey from these cities to Hebden Bridge and Haworth; for more information, see below or call **Metroline** (☎0113 245 7676).

TICs have a wide selection of trail guides. The **Worth Way** traces a 5½ mi. route from Keighley to Oxenhope; ride the steam train or Metroline bus back to your starting point. From Haworth to Hebden Bridge, choose a trail from the TIC's *Two Walks Linking Haworth and Hebden Bridge* (50p), which guides visitors along the dark and verdant paths that inspired the Brontë sisters.

HEBDEN BRIDGE   ☎01422

An historic gritstone village sandwiched between two hills, Hebden Bridge lies close to the **Pennine Way** and the circular 50 mi. **Calderdale Way.** Originally a three-farm cluster, the medieval hamlet stitched its way to modest expansion in the booming textile years of the 18th and 19th centuries, and many of the trademark "double-decker" houses of this period are still standing. Today, Hebden Bridge has few sights, but narrow canals, small bridges, friendly locals and an endearingly slow pace of life give the town an allure all its own. Most visitors use it as a starting point for day (or longer) hikes.

One of the most popular hiking destinations is the National Trust's **Harcastle Crags** (☎844 518), a ravine-crossed wooded valley of picture-book greenery known locally as Little Switzerland, 1½ mi. northwest along the A6033; pick up a free guide from the TIC. You can also take day hikes to the villages of **Blackshaw Head, Cragg Vale,** or **Hepstonstall.** Hepstonstall holds the remains of Sylvia Plath and the ruins of the oldest Methodist house of worship in the world. **Calder Valley Cruising** gives horse-drawn boat trips along the Rochdale Canal. (☎845 557. Office open Apr.-Dec. M-F 11am-5pm, Sa-Su 2-5:30pm. 2-3 trips per day in summer. £2.50, concessions £2, children £1.50, families £6.)

Hebden Bridge lies about halfway along the Manchester-Leeds rail line. **Trains** pass through at least hourly, and sometimes as frequently as every 10min. (☎845 476. Manchester £7, Leeds £3.20.) **Buses** stop at the train station and on New Rd. The **Tourist Information Centre,** New Rd., across from New Rd.'s intersection with Hope St., offers the popular *Walks Around Hebden Bridge* (40p) and a mass of other walking guides. (☎843 831. Open mid-Mar. to mid-Oct. M-F 9:30am-5:30pm, Sa 10:15am-5pm, Su 10:30am-5pm; mid-Oct. to mid-Mar. M-F 10am-5pm, Sa-Su 10:30am-4:15pm.) **Internet access** is free at the **library,** at the corner of Cheetham and Hope St. (☎842 151. Open M-F 9am-5:30pm, Sa 9am-12:30pm.) Alternatively, try the **Java Lounge,** 23 Market St. (☎845 740. £1 for 30min. Open M-F 9am-5pm, Sa-Su 10am-5pm. Sometimes closed M and Tu.) The **post office** is on Holme St., off New Rd. (☎842 366. Open M-F 9am-5:30pm, Sa 9am-12:30pm.) **Post Code:** HX7 8AA.

At **Claire McNamee ❷,** 1 Primrose Terr., from the train station, walk through the park and follow the canal to stairs on your left. Up the stairs and a short path brings you to a house with a yellow door. Simple but bright rooms in a house adorned with original works of art by the owners. (☎844 747. Breakfast included. £18. Cash only.) **Angeldale Guest House ❹,** a large Victorian at the north end of Hangingroyd Ln., has lovely, spacious rooms. (☎847 321; www.angeldale.co.uk. Singles £55-59; doubles and twins £23-29.50 per person; family rooms from £46. MC/V.) Purchase **groceries** at the **Coop,** 41 Market St. (☎842 452. Open M-Sa 8am-9pm, Su 10am-4pm.) For award-winning scones (£1.30-1.75), visit the **Watergate Tea Room ❶,** 9 Bridge Gate. (☎842 978. Open daily 10:30am-4:30pm. MC/V.) Satisfying pizzas and pastas (£5-8) are served up at local favorite **Hebdens ❷,** on Hangingroyd Ln., just across the bridge from St. George Sq. Takeaway also available. (☎843 745. Open W-Th 4:30-10pm, F-Sa 5:30-10:30pm, Su 4:30-9:30pm. AmEx/MC/V.)

HAWORTH ☎01535

Haworth's (HAH-wuth) raison d'être stands at the top of its hill—the parsonage that overlooks Brontëland. A cobbled main street milks all association with the ill-fated literary siblings, with numerous tearooms and souvenir shops lining the uphill climb to the Brontë home. The village today wants for wandering heroines, but a moving echo of the windswept moors remains.

◪❼ TRANSPORTATION AND PRACTICAL INFORMATION. The **train station** (☎645 214) only serves the **Keighley and Worth Valley Railway's** private steam trains, which run to and from **Keighley** on weekends all year, and daily during July and August (25min.; call ahead for times; £7, children £3.50). **Metroline** (☎603 284) buses #663-665 and 720 also reach Haworth from **Keighley** (15min., every 15-30min., £1.20-1.40). Bus #500 will take you to and from **Hebden Bridge** (30min., 4-5 per day, £1.20). Or you can pick up a guide from the TIC (50p) and hike there yourself.

The **Tourist Information Centre,** 2-4 West Ln., at Main St.'s breathless summit, provides the useful *Four Walks from the Centre of Haworth* (40p) and the town's mini-guide (35p), and books beds for a 10% deposit. (☎642 329; fax 647 721. Open daily May-Aug. 9:30am-5:30pm; Sept.-Apr. 9:30am-5pm.) The **post office,** 98 Main St., is the only place to **exchange currency.** (☎644 589. Open M-F 9am-1pm and 1:30-5:30pm, Sa 9am-12:30pm.) **Post Code:** BD22 8DP.

⌐⌐◘ ACCOMMODATIONS AND FOOD. Housed in a Victorian mansion, the elegant **YHA Haworth ❶** is a 15min. hike from the train station. (Turn left out of the train station, up Lees Ln.; then turn left on Longlands Dr. ☎642 234. Meals £3-5.25. Open daily mid-Feb. to Oct.; Nov. to mid-Dec. F-Sa. Dorms £11.80, under 18 £8.50. MC/V.) Built by the doctor who attended Charlotte Brontë's death, ▦**Ashmount ❸,** 5min. from the TIC on Mytholmes Ln., has sweeping views and an enchanting, romantic atmosphere. (☎/fax 645 726. Singles £32; doubles £47; triples £60; families £70. MC/V.) ▦**The Old Registry ❸,** 2-4 Main St., has gorgeous themed double rooms. (☎646 503. £65; £75 with whirlpool. MC/V.) For **groceries,** try **Spar Shop** on Station Rd. (☎647 662. Open daily 7am-10:30pm.) Haworth's most popular pub, **The Fleece Inn ❶,** 67 Main St., has a friendly atmosphere that draws crowds of locals. (☎642 172. Open M-Sa 11am-11pm, Su noon-10:30pm. MC/V.) **The Black Bull ❶,** once frequented by the errant Branwell Brontë, is a stone's throw from the TIC. (☎642 249. Open M-Sa 11am-11pm, Su noon-10:30pm. MC/V.) Diverse restaurants line **Mill Hey,** just east of the train station. **Haworth Tandoori ❷,** 41 Mill Hey, a neighborhood favorite, serves a wide selection of curries, biryanis, and vegetarian dishes. (☎644 726. Open daily 5:30pm-midnight. MC/V.)

◙ SIGHTS. Down a tiny lane behind the village church—the site where Charlotte got married and under which all Brontës but Anne are buried—the tasteful ▦**Brontë Parsonage** details the lives of Charlotte, Emily, Anne, Branwell, and their infamously ill-tempered father. Quiet rooms, including the dining room where the sisters penned *Wuthering Heights, Jane Eyre,* and *The Tenant of Wildfell Hall,* contain original furnishings and mementos. (☎642 323; www.bronte.info. Open daily Apr.-Sept. 10am-5:30m; Oct.-Mar. 11am-5pm; closed Jan. £4.80, concessions £3.50, children £1.50, families £10.50.) A footpath behind the church leads uphill toward the pleasant (if untempestuous) **Brontë Falls,** a 2 mi. hike.

LEEDS ☎0113

The stone lions, griffins, and cherubs that adorn its building facades attest to the textile-based prosperity that energized Leeds (pop. 750,000) during the Victorian era. Although most textile jobs have moved overseas, Britain's fourth-largest city has experienced a glamorous economic revival. The birthplace of Marks & Spencer now sports blocks of swanky shops, a dynamic arts scene, extravagant restaurants, and numerous nightlife venues, making this young professionals' hub worth a few days' exploration.

⌐⌐◙ TRANSPORTATION AND PRACTICAL INFORMATION

Trains: City Station, City Sq. Luggage storage £3.50-5. Ticket office open 24hr. Trains (☎08457 484 950) from: **London King's Cross** (2½hr., every hr., £65.20); **Manchester** (1½hr., 4 per hr., £12.10); **York** (30min., 3-4 per hr., £8.10).

Buses: Station on New York St., next to Kirkgate Market. Office open M-W and F 8:30am-5:30pm, Th 9:30am-5:30pm, Sa 9am-4:30pm. Luggage storage £2. **National Express** (☎08705 808 080) serves Leeds from most major cities, including: **Birmingham**

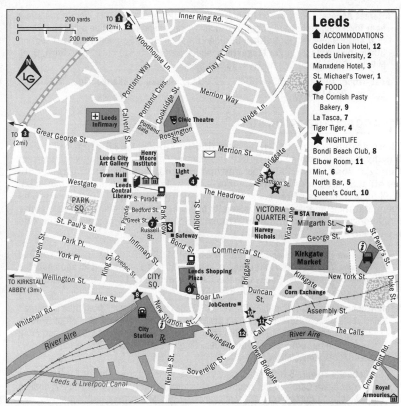

Leeds

🔺 ACCOMMODATIONS
Golden Lion Hotel, 12
Leeds University, 2
Manxdene Hotel, 3
St. Michael's Tower, 1

🍴 FOOD
The Cornish Pasty Bakery, 9
La Tasca, 7
Tiger Tiger, 4

⭐ NIGHTLIFE
Bondi Beach Club, 8
Elbow Room, 11
Mint, 6
North Bar, 5
Queen's Court, 10

($3\frac{1}{4}$hr., 4-6 per day, £20); **Edinburgh** ($7\frac{1}{2}$hr., 2 per day, £33.50); **Glasgow** (6hr., 1 per day, £33.50); **Liverpool** (2hr., every hr., £9.50); **London** (5hr., every hr., £19); **Manchester** (1hr., every hr., £7); **York** (45min., M-Sa every 30min., Su every hr., £3.80). **Metroline** (☎245 7676) runs local buses to **Bradford** (1hr., every 30min., £2) and **Hull** ($1\frac{3}{4}$hr., 7 per day, £3.50).

Taxis: City Cabs (☎246 9999). 24hr.

Tourist Information Centre: Gateway Yorkshire (☎242 5242), in the train station, books rooms for a £2 charge and a 10% deposit; call ☎0800 808 050. Open M 10am-5:30pm, Tu-Sa 9am-5:30pm, Su 10am-4pm.

Budget Travel: STA Travel, 88 Vicar Ln. (☎0870 168 6878). Open M-W and F 9am-6pm, Th 10am-6pm, Su 10am-5pm.

Financial Services: Every conceivable **bank** lies on Park Row. Most open roughly M-F 9am-5:30pm, Sa 9am-1:30pm. **Abbey,** 10 Park Row (☎0845 765 4321). Open M-W and F 9am-5pm, Th 10am-5pm, Sa 9am-4pm.

Work Opportunities: JobCentre, 12-14 Briggate (☎215 5382). Open M-Tu and Th-F 9am-5pm, W 10am-5pm.

Police: Millgarth St. (☎241 3059), north of the bus station.

Pharmacy: Boots, in Leeds City Station (☎242 1713). Open M-F 7am-midnight, Sa 8am-midnight, Su 9am-midnight.

Internet Access: Leeds Central Library, the Headrow (☎247 8911), across the street from Town Hall. Free. ID required. Fills quickly, call ahead to schedule a session. Open M-W and F 9am-8pm, Th 9:30am-5:30pm, Sa 10am-5pm, Su noon-4pm. Last session 30min. before close. **Virgin Megastore,** Albion St. (☎243 8117). £1 per 25min. Open M-W and F 9am-6pm, Th 9am-7pm, Su 10am-5pm.

Post Office: 116 Albion St. (☎08457 223 344). **Bureau de change.** Open M-Sa 9am-5:30pm. **Post Code:** LS2 8LP.

▗ ACCOMMODATIONS

There are no hostels in Leeds, and finding a budget **B&B** often requires a lengthy bus ride into a suburb like Headingly. To get to Headingly's B&B-rich Cardigan Road, (from £30), take any bus toward Headingly from Infirmary St., get off at St. Michael's Church (20min.), and walk 5min. down St. Michael's Ln. Well-located hotels offer weekend discounts; the TIC's free *Visit Leeds* lists them and their specials. The **University of Leeds** ❸ (☎242 4996) offers ensuite single dorm rooms from mid-July to early Sept. £20, £115 per week. Min. two nights' stay. MC/V.

Golden Lion Hotel, 2 Lower Briggate (☎243 6454). This attractive, recently restored hotel pampers guests with room service, satellite TV, and a convenient location near the bus and train stations. Singles weekends £50, weekdays £110; doubles and twins £70/£125; family rooms £80/£125. AmEx/MC/V. ❹

Manxdene Hotel, 154 Woodsley Rd. (☎243 2586), a 15min. walk from the city center. Head east on Great George St., which becomes Clarendon Rd., and turn left on Woodsley Rd. More easily accessible by bus (#56, 63, or 74A from Infirmary St.) or cab (£5). Affordable rooms with standard amenities. Singles £30, ensuite £40; twins and doubles £40/£50. AmEx/MC/V. ❸

St. Michael's Tower, 5-6 St. Michael's Villa, Cardigan Rd. (☎275 5557). One of the least extravagant Cardigan Rd. options, with a lounge and TVs. Singles £25-27, ensuite £33; twins and doubles £40/43, family ensuite £55. MC/V. ❸

▗ FOOD

Butchers and bakers abound at **Kirkgate Market,** off New York St., Europe's largest indoor market. (☎214 5162. Indoor stalls open M-Tu and Th-Sa 9am-5pm, W 9am-2am; outdoor stalls close 30min. earlier.) For posh dining, walk along **Greek Street** between East Parade and Park Row. **Vicar Lane,** north of The Headrow, offers a few less expensive restaurants. Get **groceries** at **Safeway,** Bond St. (☎243 9377). Open M-F 7am-8pm, Sa 8am-8pm, Su 11am-5pm.

Tiger Tiger, 117 Albion St. (☎236 6999). Huge restaurant with open terrace and comfy alcoves make for a chic dining experience. Superb lunch deals offer 1 course for £3. During happy hour, (5-7:30pm) all meals are half price. Open M-Sa noon-2am, Su noon-midnight. AmEx/MC/V. ❶

La Tasca, 4 Russell St. (☎244 2205). Warm and inviting, with a tasteful Spanish theme. Serves tasty tapas (£2-4) and paella (£9) amidst romantic candlelight. Ideal for sharing. Open M-Sa noon-11pm, Su noon-10:30pm. AmEx/MC/V. ❷

The Cornish Pasty Bakery, 54 Boar Ln. (☎242 0121). Hot pockets with assorted fillings 75p-£2, fresh paninis (£1.65-2) and pizza (£1.50-1.70). Open M-Th 8am-8pm, F-Sa 8am-2pm, Su 9am-5pm. Cash only. ❶

◎ ☐ SIGHTS AND SHOPPING

The ⚔Royal Armouries has one of the world's best collections of arms and armor. A war buff's Graceland, the museum features war, tournament, shooting, and self-defense galleries, with interactive battle simulations, recreations of battle scenes, and demonstrations by staff in period dress. Horse events are featured in the menagerie daily at 2pm, and summer weekends often host jousts. Call ahead and bring the kids. From the bus station, walk south under the overpass, veer left at the traffic circle, and turn right at Crow Bridge. Take a left at Armouries Way, just over the bridge. (☎220 1999. Open daily 10am-5pm. Free.)

Leeds's massive **library** and two art museums, clustered adjacent to the Victorian **Town Hall,** form the city's artistic center. The **Leeds City Art Gallery,** on The Headrow, features one the best collections of 20th-century British art outside London. (☎247 8248. Open M-Tu and Th-Sa 10am-5pm, W 10am-8pm, Su 1-5pm. Free.) The adjacent **Henry Moore Institute,** 74 The Headrow, holds excellent sculpture exhibitions. (☎246 7476. Open M-Tu and Th-Su 10am-5:30pm, W 10am-9pm. Free.) The well-maintained ruins of 12th-century **Kirkstall Abbey,** 3 mi. west of the city center on Kirkstall Rd., inspired artist J.M.W. Turner. Take buses #33 or 33A, and get off when you see the abbey on your left. (☎230 5492. Free.)

Leeds is widely known for its shopping, and some of its malls and stores are sights in their own right. For the best town, see **Leeding Fashions,** p. 30.

☒ NIGHTLIFE

Clubbers flock to Leeds to partake in neon nights of commercial dance, house, indie-rock, and hip-hop music. Find up-to-date club listings in the free monthly *Absolute Leeds,* available at the TIC.

Mint, Harrison St. (☎244 3168; www.themintclubleeds.co.uk). Funky house and an inviting dance floor make this club ultra-popular. Open Th-Su 10pm-late. Cover £6-12.

Elbow Room, 64 Call Ln., 3rd/4th fl. (☎245 7011; www.elbow-room.co.uk). Stylish pool hall and bar, with both crowds to get lost in and corner couches to escape to. Pool £5-8 per hr. Cover F-Sa only £3-5, free before 9pm. Open Su 2pm-midnight, M 2pm-2am, Tu-Th noon-2am, F-Sa noon-3am.

Queen's Court, 167-168 Lower Briggate (☎245 9449; www.queens-court.co.uk). Leeds's premier gay club. "Pink Pounder" M 2 floors, 2 DJs, all drinks £1. Cover up to £5. Bar open M-Sa noon-2am, Su noon-midnight;

LEEDING FASHIONS

1 Start out at the **Victoria Quarter** (Open M-Sa 9am-6pm, Su 11am-5pm; www.vqleeds.com), home of the only Harvey Nichols outside London. Recently renovated, the elegant area houses stores from Diesel to Jo Malone, as well as independent favorites.

2 Next head to **The Light,** The Headrow (open M-Sa 9am-6pm, 7pm on Th, Su 11am-5pm. www.thelightleeds.co.uk). Dine, drink, catch a movie (on 1 of their 13 screens), and be sure to stop into some of the retail stores, packed with the latest fashions.

3 For stores of every description, head down Park Row, and you'll find **Leeds Shopping Plaza,** Grosvenor Mall. (Open M-Th 8am-5:45pm, F-Sa 8am-6pm, Su 11am-5pm).

4 The **Corn Exchange,** just off Boar Lane on Call Lane, is a beautiful dome building stacked with everything from vintage to hip trends. (Open M-F 10am-5:30pm, Sa 9:30am-6pm, Su 10:30am-5pm.

club open M 9:30pm-2am, Th-Sa 10:30pm-2am. Food served noon-6pm. Next door, gay-friendly bar **Fibre** (☎08701 200 888) draws a trendy crowd, especially for weekday happy hour 2-for-1 drink specials (5-8pm). Open M-W, Su 11am-midnight, Th 11am-1am, F-Sa 11am-2am.

Bondi Beach Club, Queens Bldg. at City Sq. (☎243 4733). Surfboards, coolers, and a revolving dance floor simulate beach culture in this theme bar. Cover £3-6. "Mental Mondays" offer 2-for-1 drinks from 9-11pm and free drinks from 11pm-2am for £10 cover. Open M and Th 9pm-2:30am, F-Sa 5pm-2:30am.

North Bar, 24 New Briggate (☎242 4540). Crowded bar is a good place to wind down after hitting the clubs. Open M-Tu noon-1am, W-Sa noon-2am, Su noon-10:30pm.

YORKSHIRE DALES

The beauty of the Yorkshire Dales (valleys formed by swift rivers and lazy glacial flows) is enhanced by traces of earlier residents: abandoned castles and stone farmhouses are scattered among the pastures and one-pub hamlets of the region. Bronze and Iron Age tribes blazed "green lanes," footpaths that remain on the high moorland; Romans built roads and stout forts; and 18th-century workers pieced together countless stone walls. As with most British national parks, 99% of the land is privately owned, but most property owners allow hikers to cross their land.

▐ TRANSPORTATION

Skipton is the most convenient place to enter the park. **Trains** (☎08457 484 950) run to Skipton from: **Bradford** (35min., 4 per hr., £4.50); **Carlisle** (2hr., every hr., £13.50); **Leeds** (40min., 2 per hr., £5.40). The **Settle-Carlisle Railway** (☎01729 822 007), one of England's most scenic routes, slices through **Skipton, Garsdale,** and **Kirkby Stephen** (1¾hr., 3-4 per day, £13.40). **National Express** (☎08705 808 080) buses run to **Skipton** from **London** (6hr., 1 per day, £20), **and Leeds** (#537, 1½hr., 2 per day, £4.75).

For non-hikers, getting around the Dales without a car is a challenge. The *Dales Connection* timetable (free at TICs and NPICs) helps clarify public transport. **Traveline** (☎0870 608 2608) also answers transportation questions. Many inter-village **buses** run only a few times per week and tend to hibernate in winter. **Pride of the Dales** (☎01756 753 123) connects **Skipton** to **Grassington** (#72, 30min., every hr., £2.40), sometimes continuing to **Kettlewell** (#72, 1¼ hr, every 2hr., £2.70). **Pennine Bus** (☎01756 749 215) connects **Skipton** to **Malham** (#210, 45min., 2 per day, £3.40) and **Settle** (#580, 40min., every hr., £3.70). Other villages are served less regularly, but **postbuses** run once per day to scheduled towns.

▄▐ ORIENTATION AND PRACTICAL INFORMATION

Sampling the Dales requires several days, a pair of sturdy feet, and careful planning. In the south of the park, **Skipton** serves as a transport hub and provides services not available in the smaller villages. **Grassington** and **Linton,** just north, are scenic bases for exploring southern Wharfedale. **Malham** is a sensible starting point for forays into western Wharfedale and Eastern Ribblesdale. To explore Wensleydale and Swaledale in the north, begin from **Hawes** or **Leyburn.** In addition to the National Park Information Centres listed below, most towns have TICs.

National Park Information Centres: Pick up the invaluable annual park guide, *The Visitor,* and *The Yorkshire Dales Official Guide* (both free), along with numerous maps and walking guides. All NPICs book accommodations for a 10% deposit.

Aysgarth Falls: (☎01969 663 424), in Wensleydale, 1 mi. east of the village. Open daily Apr.-Oct. 10am-5pm; Nov.-Mar. W and F-Su 10am-4pm.

Grassington: Hebden Rd., Wharfedale (☎01756 752 774). Open daily Apr.-Oct. 10am-5pm; Nov.-Mar. W and F-Su 10am-4pm. 24hr. info terminal.

Hawes: Station Yard, Wensleydale (☎01969 667 450). Open daily Apr.-Oct. 10am-5pm; Nov.-Mar. 10am-4pm. 24hr. info terminal.

Malham: Malhamdale (☎01729 830 363), at the southern end of the village. Open daily Apr.-Oct. 10am-5pm; Nov.-Mar. F-Su 10am-4pm.

Reeth: (☎01748 850 252), in the Green. Open daily Apr.-Oct. 9am-5pm; Nov.-Mar. 9:30am-4pm.

Sedbergh: 72 Main St. (☎01539 620 125). Open daily Apr.-Oct. 10am-5pm; Nov.-Mar. Sa-Su 10am-4pm.

🄝 ACCOMMODATIONS

The free *Yorkshire Dales Accommodation Guide* is available at NPICs and TICs. Park officials discourage wild (unofficial) camping; organized campsites abound.

YHA HOSTELS

The Yorkshire Dales area hosts nine **YHA hostels.** Hawes, Keld, and Malham lie on the Pennine Way (p. 396), while Stainforth, Kettlewell, Dentdale, and Grinton Lodge sit a few miles off it. Ingleton, on the western edge of the park, is a good jumping-off point for the Lake District. Kirkby Stephen, north of Hawes, is served by rail, but set a little farther from the hiking trail. Hostel employees will call other YHAs to help you find a bed for the next night. All of the following accept MC/V.

Dentdale: (☎0870 770 5790), Cowgill, on Dentdale Rd., 6 mi. east of Dent, 2 mi. from the Hawes-Ingleton road. A former shooting lodge on the River Dee. Open mid-Mar. to Aug. M-Sa; Sept. to late-Oct. Tu-Sa; Feb. to mid-Mar. and late Oct. to late Nov. F-Sa. Dorms £11.80, under 18 £8.50. ❷

Grinton: Grinton Lodge (☎01748 884 206), ¾ mi. south of town on the Reeth-Leyburn road. Reception from 5pm. Lockout 10am-5pm. Curfew 11pm. Open daily Apr.-Oct.; Feb.-Mar. M-Sa; Nov.-Dec. F-Sa. Dorms £11.80, under 18 £8.50. ❷

Hawes: Lancaster Terr. (☎0870 770 5854), west of Hawes on Ingleton Rd., uphill from town. 54 beds. Curfew 11pm. Open daily Apr.-Aug.; Mar. and Sept.-Oct. Tu-Sa; late Jan. to Feb. and Nov.-Dec. F-Sa. Dorms £10.60, under 18 £7.20. ❶

Ingleton: Greta Tower (☎0870 770 5880), downhill from Market Sq. 58 beds. Reception closed noon-5pm; 11pm curfew. Open daily Mar.-Aug. and late Dec.; Sept.-Oct. M-Sa; Feb. Tu-Sa; Nov. to mid-Dec. F-Su. Dorms £11.80, under 18 £8.50. ❷

Keld: Keld Lodge (☎0870 770 5888), Upper Swaledale, west of Keld village. 38 beds. No smoking. Lockout 10am-5pm. Curfew 11pm. Open daily July-Aug.; Sept.-Oct. Tu-Sa; Apr.-June Tu-Su. Dorms £10.60 under 18 £7.20. ❶

Kettlewell: Whernside House (☎0870 770 5896), in the village center. 43 beds. No smoking. Lockout 10am-5pm. Curfew 11pm. Open daily July-Aug.; June and Sept.-Oct. M-Sa; Feb.-Mar. and late Oct. to mid-Sept. W-Sa. Dorms £10.60, under 18 £7.20. ❶

Kirkby Stephen: Market St. (☎0870 770 5904). In a former chapel, complete with pews and stained glass. 44 beds. Kitchen and laundry. Lockout 10am-5pm. Curfew 11pm. Open daily July-Aug.; Apr.-June and mid-Sept. to Oct. M-Sa; Feb.-Mar. and late Oct. to mid-Sept. W-Sa. Dorms £10.60, under 18 £7.20. ❶

Malham: John Dower Memorial Hostel (☎0870 770 5946). Well-equipped and hiker-friendly. 82 beds. Reception open 11am-5pm. Curfew 11pm. Open daily Feb.-Oct.; late Jan. and Nov. to mid-Dec. Th-Sa. Dorms £11.80, under 18 £8.50. ❷

Stainforth: Taitlands (☎0870 770 6046), 2 mi. north of Settle, ¼ mi. south of Stainforth. Georgian house with a walled garden. Lockout 10am-5pm. Curfew 11pm. Open daily during school holidays; F-Sa otherwise. Dorms £11.80, under 18 £8.50. ❷

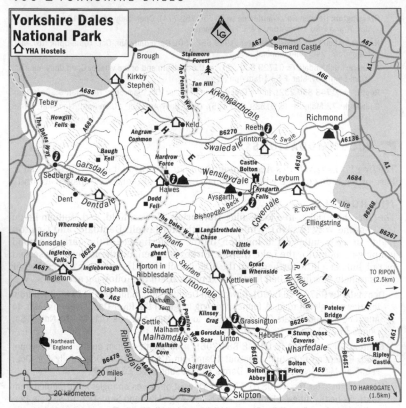

Yorkshire Dales National Park

⌂ YHA Hostels

DALES BARNS

Numerous **Dales Barns,** converted barns split up into hostel-style bunk rooms, cost £5-8 per night. Most have showers, kitchens, and drying rooms. Book weeks ahead, and get specific directions along the trails. **Barden Bunk Barn** ❶ (☎01756 720 330; £9. Cash only.) and **Grange Farm Barn** ❶ (☎01756 760 259; £8, under 18 £6. Cash only.) are a few miles from Skipton. **Hill Top Farm** ❶ (☎01729 830 320; £8. Cash only.) is in Malham. **Craken House Farm** ❶ (☎01969 622 204; £6; rooms £18-20, and offer breakfast (£6); camping £4, 2-person tent £7. Cash only.) stands ½ mi. south of Leyburn. Complete lists are available at TICs.

CAMPING

Campgrounds are difficult to reach on foot, but farmers may let you use their stretches of dale. Ask TICs for a full list of campsites. In Skipton, try **Howarth Farm Camping and Caravan Site** ❶. (☎01756 720 226. £6 per 2-person tent. Cash only.) In Grassington, try **Wood Nook** ❶. (☎01756 752 412. £9 per person, £12 per 2-person tent and car. Electricity £1. MC/V.) Near Hawes, **Bainbridge Ings** ❶ is ½ mi. out of town on the Old Gale back road. (☎01969 667 354. Open Apr.-Oct. 2-person tent and car, £8.50, £1 per extra person, children 50p. Electricity £1.50. Cash only.) **Brompton-on-Swale Caravan Park** ❶ is in Richmond. (☎01748 824 629. Open Apr.-Oct. £11.50 per 2-person tent. MC/V.) In Aysgarth, try **Street Head Caravan Park** ❶. (☎01969 663 472. 2-person tent and car £9. Electricity £2. Cash only.)

🅂 🄼 HIKING AND OUTDOORS

Since buses are infrequent and the scenery breathtaking, hiking remains the best way to see the Dales. The park's seven NPICs can help you prepare for a trek along one of three long-distance footpaths. The challenging 268 mi. **Pennine Way** (p. 396) curls from Gargrave in the south to Tan Hill in the north, passing Malham, Pen-y-ghent, Hawes, Keld, and most of the major attractions of the Dales. The more manageable 84 mi. **Dales Way** runs from Bradford and Leeds past Ilkley, through Wharfedale via Grassington and Whernside, and by Sedbergh on its way to the Lake District; it crosses the Pennine Way near Dodd Fell. The 190 mi. **Coast-to-Coast Walk** stretches from Richmond to Kirkby Stephen.

Authorities encourage visitors to keep to designated trails to avoid falling into hidden abandoned mineshafts. Take a **map** and **trail guide;** stone walls and hills look similar after a while. Don't forget to close gates behind you as you walk. **Ordnance Survey** maps are available for most paths and can be purchased at any NPIC or outdoors supply store (£4.50-8). Outdoor Leisure #2, 21, 30, and 34, and Landranger #91 and 98 are good for specific regions; *Touring Map and Guide* #6 covers the Dales in general. NPICs sell leaflets (£1.20) covering over 30 short

WARNING. Be aware that the Dales are filled with **shake holes:** small, often unmarked depressions, similar to grassy potholes, that indicate underground caverns. They can give way with lethal consequences. Ordnance Survey maps and a compass are essential, especially on smaller, unmarked trails. See **Wilderness Safety,** p. 52, for other important tips.

routes. YHA produces its own leaflets (30p) on day hikes between hostels. **Cyclists** can ask at NPICs about rental stores and buy route cards plotting the **Yorkshire Dales Cycleway,** six 20 mi. routes that connect the Dales (£2.50). Bicycles are forbidden on footpaths. The **Pennine Way/Dales Way Baggage Courier** will cart your pack. (☎ 01729 830 463, mobile 07713 118 862. £5-10 per bag.) If you'd rather not walk at all, ⬛**Cumbria Classic Coaches** runs various trips in vintage coaches. (☎ 01539 623 254; www.cumbriaclassiccoaches.co.uk. £8 per person.)

SKIPTON ☎ 01756

Skipton is most useful as a transfer point or rest stop; once you've gathered your gear, skip town and strike for the Dales. Vacant **Skipton Castle** is the main sight and one of the most complete medieval castles in England. The last surviving Royalist bastion in the north, the castle surrendered to Cromwell's army after a three-year siege. (☎ 792 442. Open Mar.-Sept. M-Sa 10am-6pm, Su noon-6pm; Oct.-Feb. closes 4pm. £5, concessions £4.40, children £2.50.)

Skipton's **train station** is ¼ mi. west of the city center on Broughton Rd. **Buses** stop on Keighley St. between Hirds Yard and Waller Hill, behind Sunwin House. Rent cars from **Skipton Self Drive,** Otley Rd. Garage. (☎ 792 911. From £29 per day, less for longer rentals.) Admire the Dales from the water with **Pennine Cruisers of Skipton,** The Boat Shop, 19 Coach St., which rents dayboats on the Leeds and Liverpool Canal. (☎ 795 478. £75-185 per day, from £430 per week.) **Airborne Adventures** sends hot-air balloons over the Dales from Skipton and Settle twice daily. (☎ 730 166. £185 per person.) The **Tourist Information Centre,** 35 Coach St., books rooms for a 10% deposit. (☎ 792 809. Open daily Apr.-Oct. 10am-5pm, Nov.-Mar. M-Sa 10am-4pm.) Other services include: **HSBC,** 61 High St. (☎ 0845 740 4404; open M-F 9:30am-4:30pm); and the **post office** in a **supermarket** at Sunwin House, 8 Swadford St. (☎ 792 724; open M-F 9am-5:30pm, Sa 9am-1pm). **Post Code:** BD23 1UR.

B&Bs are moderately priced and easy to find—just look along **Keighley Road.** Find canopy beds at **Carlton House ❸**, 46 Keighley Rd. (☎700 921. Singles ₤25; doubles ₤45-50. Cash only.) Nearby, **Westfield Guest House ❷**, 50 Keighley Rd., promises huge breakfasts and huge beds for small prices. (☎790 849. Doubles ₤48-50. Cash only.) Load up on fresh gooseberries and cheese at the **market,** which floods High St. (Open M, W, F-Sa.) **Healthy Life,** 10 High St., near the church, stocks veggie haggis. Upstairs, **Wild Oats Cafe ❶** serves cream tea and sandwiches (₤1-3.50). (☎790 619. Store open M and W-Sa 8:30am-5:30pm, Tu 10am-5pm. Cafe open M-Sa 9:30am-4:45pm. MC/V.) **Bizzie Lizzies ❷**, 36 Swadford St., delivers exceptional fish and chips for ₤5-7. (☎793 189. Open daily 11:30am-9pm. Cash only.)

WHARFEDALE AND GRASSINGTON ☎01756

The valley of Wharfedale, created by the River Wharfe, is best explored using cobbled **Grassington** as a base. Spectacular **Kilnsey Crag** lies 3½ mi. from Grassington toward Kettlewell, through a deep gorge and Bronze Age burial mounds; consult *Wharfedale Walk #8,* available at the NPIC. The **Stump Cross Caverns,** 5 mi. east of Grassington, are adorned with stalagmites and glistening rock curtains. (☎752 780. Dress warmly. Open daily Mar.-Oct. 10am-6pm; Nov.-Feb. Sa-Su 10am-4pm. Last admission 1hr. before close. ₤4.95, children ₤2.75.)

Pride of the Dales **bus** #72 arrives from **Skipton** (M-Sa, every hr., ₤2.40). The **NPIC,** Hebden Rd. (p. 405), stocks the useful *Grassington Footpath Map* (₤1.60) and standard park trail guides (₤1), and leads occasional guided walks from March to October (₤2, children free). Other services include: **outdoor gear** at **The Mountaineer,** Pletts Barn Centre, at the top of Main St. (☎752 266; open daily 9am-5pm); **Barclays,** at the corner of Main St. and Hebden Rd. (☎296 3000; open M-Tu and Th-F 9:30am-3:30pm, W 10am-3:30pm); and the **post office,** 15 Main St. (☎752 226; open M-F 9am-5:30pm, Sa 9am-12:30pm). **Post Code:** BD23 5AD.

Close to the center of Grassington, **Raines Close ❸**, 13 Station Rd., lets comfortable ensuite rooms, some with spectacular views. (☎752 678, www.rainesclose.co.uk. Doubles ₤54-60. MC/V.) Across the street, **Springroyd House ❸**, 8A Station Rd., combines village-center location with clean rooms. (☎752 473. Doubles ₤44-50. Cash only.) Pubs and cafes pack Main Street, including **Lucy Fold Tea Room ❶**, 1 Garr's Ln., off Main St., whose offerings include omelettes, sandwiches, jacket potatoes (all ₤2.75-5). (☎752 414. Open Tu-Su 10:30am-5pm. Cash only.) Visit **Harker's ❶**, 1-3 Main St., for pork pies (95p), traditional Yorkshire curd tarts (₤2 for a large), and other pastries. (☎752 483. Open M-Sa 7:30am-5pm. Cash only.)

MALHAMDALE AND INGLETON

Limestone cliffs and gorges slice the pastoral valley of Malhamdale, creating spectacular natural beauties within easy walking distance of one another. A 3hr. hike from the NPIC will take you past the stunning, stony swath of **Malham Cove,** a massive limestone cliff, to the placid water of **Malham Tarn.** Shuttle buses run from the NPIC to the cove and the tarn (15min., 2 per hr., 50p, children and seniors free). 2 mi. from Malham village is the equally impressive **Gordale Scar,** cut in the last ice age by a glacier. For more, pick up *A Walk in Malhamdale* (#1, ₤1.20), from Malham's **NPIC** (p. 405). The **YHA Malham** (p. 405) is popular with Pennine Way hikers.

North of Malham, the high peaks and cliffs of Ingleborough, Pen-y-ghent, and Whernside form the **Alpes Penninae.** The 24 mi. **Three Peaks Walk,** which connects the Alpes begins and ends in **Horton in Ribblesdale** at the clock of the **Pen-y-ghent Cafe,** a hiker's haunt that serves as the local TIC. (☎01729 860 333. Open Apr.-Oct. M and W-Su 8am-6pm; Nov.-Mar. W-Su 9am-5pm.) **Ingleton** is near the middle of the trek. The village's **Tourist Information Centre,** in the community center carpark, books rooms for a 10% deposit. (☎015242 41049. Open daily Apr.-Oct. 10am-

4:30pm.) The 4½ mi. walk through the **Ingleton Waterfalls** is one of the park's most popular routes. Pick up a leaflet from the TIC or read the Ingleton town trail sign in town center. The **YHA Ingleton** (p. 405) and several **B&Bs** (around £15) on Main St. are good budget options. A 1 mi. walk brings you to **Stacksteads Farm ❶**, Tatterthorne Rd., which offers a bunk barn with 22 beds. (☎015242 41386. Cash only.)

WENSLEYDALE AND HAWES ☎01969

The northerly Wensleydale landscape softens into a broad sash of fertile dairyland. Base your ventures in **Hawes,** which has a **NPIC** (p. 405). Pay 40p at the **Green Dragon Pub** to access the trail to the **Hardrow Force** waterfall, 1 mi. north on the Pennine Way. The **Dales Countryside Museum,** in the same building as the NPIC, chronicles the history of "real Dales people" and books accommodations for a 10% deposit. (☎667 494. Open daily Apr.-Oct. 10am-5pm; Nov.-Mar. 10am-4pm. £3, concessions £2, children free.) The silhouette of **Castle Bolton** graces Wensleydale, and visitors can explore its dungeon and battlements. (☎623 981. Open daily Mar.-Nov. 10am-5pm. £5, children £3.50, families £12.) **B&Bs** (£17-21) line Main St. for those not content with the **YHA Hawes** (p. 405); check the list outside town hall each afternoon. Pubs, takeaways, and a **Barclays** (open M-W and F 9:30am-4:30pm, Th 10am-4:30pm) are also along Main St.

Farther north, **Swaledale** is known for picture-perfect barns and meadows. Also worthwhile are **Aysgarth Falls** to the east—rolling in tiers down the Yoredale Rocks—and the natural terrace of the **Shawl of Leyburn.** Both Aysgarth and Leyburn are served by Pride of the Dales **buses** #156-157 from Hawes to Northallerton (2 hr., every hr., round-trip £2.50). Aysgarth's **NPIC** is in the carpark above the falls (p. 404), and **Leyburn** has a **Tourist Information Centre.** (☎623 069. Open daily Easter-Sept. 9:30am-5:30pm; Oct.-Easter M-Sa 9:30am-4:30pm.)

YORK ☎01904

With a pace suitable for ambling and its tallest building a cathedral, York bears little resemblance to its new American namesake. In AD 71, the Romans founded Eboracum as a military and administrative base for Northern England; the town remained important as Anglo-Saxon "Eoforwic" and Viking "Jorvik." York's history of murder, massacre, and mass-suicide has prompted the title of "most haunted city in the world." But neither its ghostly reputation nor its medieval city walls stop present-day tourist hordes. Modern-day invaders, brandishing zoom lenses, come seeking its collection of rich historical sights—including a monster cathedral—and York manages to put itself on display without sacrificing authenticity.

▆ TRANSPORTATION

Trains: York Station, Station Rd. Travel center open M-Sa 8am-7:45pm, Su 9am-7:45pm. Ticket office open M-Sa 5:45am-10:15pm, Su 7:30am-10:10pm. **Luggage storage** £2-4; open M-Sa 8am-8:30pm, Su 9am-8:30pm. Trains (☎08457 484 950) from: **Edinburgh** (2½hr., 2 per hr., £56); **London King's Cross** (2hr., 2 per hr., £65.50); **Manchester Piccadilly** (1½hr., 3 per hr., £16.10); **Newcastle** (1hr., 4 per hr., £17); **Scarborough** (45min., 2 per hr., £11.40).

Buses: (☎551 400). Stations at Rougier St., Exhibition Sq., the train station, and on Piccadilly. Major bus stop along The Stonebow. **National Express** (☎08705 808 080) from: **Edinburgh** (5½hr., 1 per day, £28.50); **London** (5hr., 4 per day, £22); **Manchester** (2¾hr., 3 per day, £7.75).

Local Transportation: First York (☎622 992, timetables 551 400) has a ticket office on Exhibition Sq. Open M-F 9am-5pm. **Yorkshire Coastliner** (☎0113 244 8976 or 01653 692 556) runs buses from the train station to **Castle Howard** (p. 415).

Taxis: Station Taxis (☎623 332). 24hr. Wheelchair-accessible service available.
Bike Rental: Bob Trotter, 13 Lord Mayor's Walk (☎622 868). From £10 per day. £50 deposit. Open M-W and F-Sa 9am-5:30pm, Th 9:30am-5:30pm, Su 10am-4pm.

ORIENTATION AND PRACTICAL INFORMATION

Today, York's streets present a greater obstacle than the ancient walls ever did. They are winding, short, rarely labeled, and prone to name changes. Fortunately, most attractions lie within the **city walls,** so you can't get too lost, and the towers of the **Minster,** visible from nearly everywhere, provide easy orientation. The **River Ouse** (rhymes with "muse") cuts through the city, curving west to south. The city center lies between the Ouse and the Minster; **Coney Street, Parliament Street,** and **Stonegate** are the main thoroughfares. The **Shambles,** York's quasi-medieval shopping district, lies between Parliament St. and Colliergate.

Tourist Information Centre: Exhibition Sq. (☎621 756; www.york-tourism.co.uk). Books rooms for a £4 charge plus a 10% deposit. *The York Visitor Guide* (£1) has a detailed map. Snickelways of York (£5) is an offbeat self-tour. Open Apr.-Oct. M-Sa 9am-6pm, Su 10am-5pm; Nov.-May M-Sa 9am-5pm, Su 10am-4pm. **Branch** in the train station. Open June-Oct. M-Sa 9am-8pm, Su 9am-5pm; daily Nov.-May 9am-5pm.

Tours: A free 2hr. **walking tour** is offered by the Association of Voluntary Guides (☎630 284; in summer, tours leave at 10:15am, 2:15pm and 6:45pm; in winter, tours leave at 10:15am). Meet in front of the York City Art Gallery; specific times are posted at the TIC. The 1¼hr. **Ghost Hunt of York** (☎608 700) meets at the Shambles daily 7:30pm. £3, children £2. **Guide Friday/City Sightseeing** (☎640 896) leads its familiar hop-on, hop-off bus tours. £7.50, concessions £5, children £3, families £15. Several companies along the **River Ouse** near Lendal, Ouse, and Skeldergate Bridges offer 1hr. **boat cruises,** including **YorkBoat,** Lendal Bridge (☎628 324). Office open M-F 9am-5:30pm. At least 4 trips per day; call ahead. £6.50, seniors £5.50, children £3.30.

Financial Services: Banks abound on Coney St. **Thomas Cook,** 4 Nessgate (☎881 400). Open M, W, F-Sa 9am-5:30pm; Tu 10am-5:30pm. **American Express,** 6 Stonegate (☎676 501). **Bureau de change.** Open M-Tu and Th-F 9am-5:30pm, W 9:30am-5:30pm, Sa 9am-5pm.

Pharmacy: Boots, 5 St. Mary's Sq. (☎635 559). Open M-Sa 9am-5:30pm.

Launderette: Haxby Road Washeteria, 124 Haxby Rd. (☎623 379). £5 per load. Open M-F 8am-5:45pm, Sa 9am-5:15pm, Su 9am-4:15pm; last wash 2hr. before close.

Police: Fulford Rd. (☎631 321).

Hospital: York District Hospital (☎631 313), off Wigginton Rd. Take bus #1 or 18 from Exhibition Sq. and ask for the hospital stop.

Internet Access: Cafe of the Evil Eye, 42 Stonegate (☎640 002). Vends cocktails, coffees, and Internet access (£2 per hr.). **Gateway Internet Cafe,** 26 Swinegate (☎646 446). 50p quick check, £4 per hr.; 20% student discount. **York Central Library,** Museum St., (☎655 631) has 6 free Internet terminals. 30min. max. for non-members. Booking is advisable. Open M-W and F 9am-8pm, Th 9am-5:30pm, Sa 9am-4pm.

Post Office: 22 Lendal St. (☎617 285). **Bureau de change.** Open M-Tu 8:30am-5:30pm, W-Sa 9am-5:30pm. **Post Code:** YO1 8DA.

ACCOMMODATIONS

B&Bs (from £18) are concentrated on the side streets along **Bootham** and **Clifton,** in the Mount area down **Blossom Street,** and on **Bishopthorpe Road,** south of town. Book weeks ahead in summer, when competition for inexpensive beds is fierce; the TICs and the Visitor and Conference Bureau may help.

🞉 **York Backpackers,** 88-90 Micklegate (☎627 720; www.yorkbackpackers.co.uk). A carnival of humanity in an 18th-century mansion. Kitchen, laundry, and TV lounge. Internet access £1 per 20min. "Dungeon Bar" open 5 nights per week, long after the pubs close. Large dorms £13-14; doubles £34. MC/V. ❷

🞉 **Avenue Guest House,** 6 The Avenue (☎620 575; www.avenuegh.fsnet.co.uk), off Clifton on a residential side street. Hosts provide immaculate rooms off an impressive spiral staircase. All rooms with TV. Singles £22; doubles £42, ensuite £50. MC/V.❸

Alexander House, 94 Bishopthorpe Rd. (☎625 016), just outside the city walls, 5min. from the train station. 4 luxurious ensuite doubles adorned with paintings and fresh flowers. Singles £63; doubles £73, £8 discount M-Th in winter. MC/V. ❹

YHA York International, Water End (☎653 147), Clifton, 1 mi. from town. From Exhibition Sq., walk ¾ mi. on Bootham and turn left at Water End; from the train station, follow the river path "Dame Judi Dench" (connects to Water End); or take a bus to Clifton Green and walk ¼ mi. Large TV lounge, giant Connect 4 game set, and dining room with outdoor seating. Breakfast included. Dorms £17, under 18 £12.30; singles £22.50; doubles £43. £3 discount for students and single parents. AmEx/MC/V. ❷

Cornmill Lodge, 120 Haxby Rd. (☎620 566; www.cornmillyork.co.uk). From Exhibition Sq., walk up Gillygate to Clarence St. and then Haxby Rd., or take bus A1 from the station. Quiet vegetarian B&B provides clean rooms with TVs and range of breakfast options. Singles £30-35; ensuite doubles £50-60. MC/V. ❸

Queen Anne's Guest House, 24 Queen Anne's Rd. (☎629 389; www.queen-annesguesthouse.co.uk), a short walk out Bootham from Exhibition Sq. Rooms with floral elegance and TVs; some nearly all bath. Includes regal breakfasts. Singles £24, doubles £46; weekday reductions Oct.-Apr.; discount for Let's Go users. AmEx/MC/V. ❷

Foss Bank Guest House, 16 Huntington Rd. (☎635 548). Walk or take bus #13 from the train station. Comfortable beds in clean rooms by the River Foss. Standard rooms with shower and sink. Doubles are particularly swanky. No smoking. Singles £26; doubles £48, ensuite £54. Discount for Let's Go users. Cash only. ❸

York Youth Hotel, 11-13 Bishophill Senior (☎625 904; www.yorkyouthhotel.com). Well-located hostel catering primarily to groups. Laundry. Key deposit £3. Reception 24hr. Dorms £12-15; singles £25; twins £36-44. AmEx/MC/V. ❷

Camping: Riverside Caravan and Camping Park, Ferry Ln. (☎705 812), Bishopthorpe, 2 mi. south of York off the A64. Take bus #11 or 11Y and ask the driver to let you off at the campsite (2 per hr., round-trip £1.16). July-Aug. and early Sept. £8 per 2-person tent; Apr.-June and mid-Sept. to Oct. £7 per 2-person tent. Cash only. ❶

🞉🞉 FOOD AND PUBS

Greengrocers peddle at Newgate Market between Parliament St. and the Shambles. (Open M-Sa 9am-5pm; Apr.-Dec. also Su 9am-4:30pm.) There are more pubs in the center of York than gargoyles on the Minster's east wall. **Groceries** live in **Sainsbury's,** at the intersection of Foss Bank and Heworth Green. (☎643 801. Open M-Sa 8am-8pm, Su 11am-5pm.)

🞉 **The Blue Bicycle,** 34 Fossgate (☎673 990). Smooth-talking waiters rush flowerpots of fresh bread to your table then follow with carefully-prepared entrees (£16-20) using fresh produce. Open M-Su noon-2:30pm and 6-10pm. AmEx/MC/V. ❹

Oscar's Wine Bar and Bistro, 8 Little Stonegate (☎652 002), off Stonegate. Italianate pub combines a swanky courtyard, lively mood and tasty grub (£6-8). Happy hour M-Su 4pm-11pm, Tu-F 5-7pm. Open M-Sa 11am-11pm, Su noon-10:30pm. AmEx/MC/V. ❷

The Fudge Kitchen, 58 Low Petergate (☎645 596). Over 20 flavors of gooey fudge, from Vintage Vanilla to Banoffee (slices £3-3.50), are made before your eyes by chefs in traditional dress. Open M-Sa 10am-5:30pm, Su 10am-1pm. MC/V. ❶

NORTHEAST ENGLAND

El Piano, 15 Grape Ln. (☎610 676). Latin flavors infuse veggie dishes in this laid-back, colorful locale in a corner of the medieval city. Tapas £2.25-3.75; entrees £6. Open M-Sa 10am-midnight, Su noon-midnight. MC/V. ❷

Ye Olde Starre Inne, 40 Stonegate (☎623 063). Accessed through a tunnel and sunny inner courtyard, the city's oldest pub (licensed since 1644), makes tinglingly good sausages and pies. (£5-7) Open M-Sa 11am-11pm, Su noon-10:30pm. AmEx/MC/V. ❶

🄶 SIGHTS

The best introduction to York is a walk along its **medieval walls** (2½ mi.), especially the northeast section and behind the cathedral. The walls are accessible up stairways by the gates. Beware the tourist stampede, which only wanes in early morning and just before the walls close at dusk.

⊠ YORK MINSTER

You can't miss it. ☎639 347; www.yorkminster.co.uk. Open daily 9am-6pm. Evensong M-Sa 5pm, Su 4pm. Tours 9:30am-3:30pm. £4.50, concessions £3, children free. Combined ticket with Undercroft £6.50, concessions £4.50, children £1.50. Free 1hr. guided tours leave near the entrance every 20min.

Everyone in York converges at the Minster, the largest Gothic cathedral in cubic footage this side of Italy (where they don't even measure things in feet). The cathedral sports an estimated half of all the medieval stained glass in England. The 15th-century **Great East Window,** which depicts the beginning and end of the world in more than a hundred small scenes, is the world's largest medieval stained-glass window. Also world-famous, although nobody seems to know why, is the **Monkey's Funeral,** the fifth pane to the left upon entering the cathedral (look in the bottom right corner). Miles Coverdale translated the first complete printed English Bible here in 1535. The interior of the vast church yawns before the hordes of tourists, but the graceful tombs and detailed stonework fly under the radar of the superlatives with which the place is burdened. York Minster, named for its origins as a humble missionary church, is the gleaming archetype of the English cathedral.

⊠ **CHAPTER HOUSE AND LIBRARY.** If you fancy something a bit less holy, turn to the Chapter House's grotesque medieval carvings. Every minute figure is unique, from mischievous demons to a three-faced woman. Keep an eye out for the tiny Virgin Mary, so small she went unnoticed by Cromwell's idol-smashing thugs. Pick up the safari guide (20p) on your way in to help your hunt. **Minster Library,** designed by Christopher Wren, guards manuscripts at the far corner of the grounds. *(Chapter House open daily 9am-6pm. Library open M-Th 10am-4pm, F 10am-noon. Both free.)*

CENTRAL TOWER. It's a mere 275 steps up to the top of the tower, but ascents are only allowed during a 5min. period every 30min., because the narrow staircase won't allow passing traffic. *(Open daily 9:30am-6:30pm. £2.50, children £1.)*

UNDERCROFT, TREASURY AND CRYPT. Displays narrate how the Minster's central tower began to crack in 1967. Visitors can tour the huge concrete and steel foundations inserted by engineers and remnants of the previously unearthed buildings. Plunge to the **Roman level** to explore the remains of the Roman legionary headquarters, including the site where Constantine was proclaimed emperor. Duck into the **crypt,** not a crypt at all but the altar of the Saxon-Norman church, with the shrine of **St. William** and the 12th-century **Doomstone** upon which the cathedral was built. The **treasury** displays the material wealth of the old archbishops, including Yorkshire silver vessels and the Horn of Ulph. *(Open daily 9:30am-6:30pm. £3, concessions £2, children £1.50. 45min. audio tour included.)*

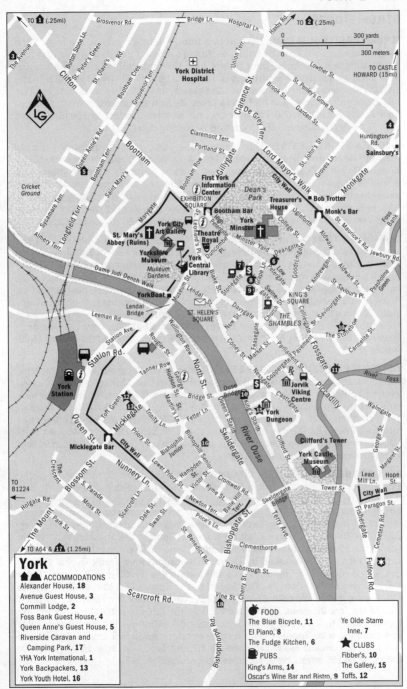

NORTHEAST ENGLAND

York

▲▲ ACCOMMODATIONS
Alexander House, **18**
Avenue Guest House, **3**
Cornmill Lodge, **2**
Foss Bank Guest House, **4**
Queen Anne's Guest House, **5**
Riverside Caravan and
 Camping Park, **17**
YHA York International, **1**
York Backpackers, **13**
York Youth Hotel, **16**

🍎 FOOD
The Blue Bicycle, **11**
El Piano, **8**
The Fudge Kitchen, **6**

🍺 PUBS
King's Arms, **14**
Oscar's Wine Bar and Bistro, **9**

Ye Olde Starre
 Inne, **7**

★ CLUBS
Fibber's, **10**
The Gallery, **15**
Toffs, **12**

OTHER SIGHTS

■ **YORK CASTLE MUSEUM.** Housed in a former debtor's prison, the huge York Castle Museum lives up to its billing as Britain's premier museum of everyday life. Fascinating and extensive, the exhibits were the brainchild of the eccentric Dr. John Kirk, who began collecting items during his house calls from the 1890s to the 1920s. The many themed rooms include **Kirkgate,** an intricately reconstructed Victorian shopping street, and **Half Moon Court,** its Edwardian counterpart. *(Between Tower St. and Piccadilly. ☎650 335; www.york.castle.museum. Open daily 9:30am-5pm except Sept. to mid-July F 10am-5pm. £6, concessions £4.50, children £3.50.)*

■ **JORVIK VIKING CENTRE.** This is one of the busiest places in the city; arrive early or late to avoid lines, or book at least a day ahead. Visitors ride through the York of AD 948 in floating "time cars," past artifacts, painfully accurate smells, and eerily life-like, animatronic mannequins. Built atop a major archaeological site, the museum contains unusually well-preserved Viking artifacts. *(Coppergate. ☎643 211, advance bookings 543 403; www.vikingjorvik.com. Open daily Apr.-Oct. 9am-6pm; Nov.-Mar. 10am-5pm. Last admission 1hr. before close. £7.20, concessions £6.10, children £5.10.)*

CLIFFORD'S TOWER. This tower is one of the last remaining pieces of York Castle and a chilling reminder of one of the worst outbreaks of anti-Jewish violence in English history. In 1190, Christian merchants tried to erase their debts to Jewish bankers by annihilating York's Jewish community. On the last Sabbath before Passover, 150 Jews took refuge in a tower that previously stood on this site and, faced with the prospect of starvation or butchery, committed suicide. Those who did not were massacred. The present tower also affords long views towards the Minster over town. *(Tower St. ☎601 901. Open daily Apr.-Sept. 10am-6pm, Oct. 10am-5pm, Nov.-March 10am-4pm. £2.50, concessions £1.90, children £1.30, families £6.30.)*

YORKSHIRE MUSEUM AND GARDENS. Hidden in ten gorgeous acres of gardens, the Yorkshire Museum presents Roman, Anglo-Saxon, and Viking artifacts, as well as the £2.5 million **Middleham Jewel** (c. 1450 and not for sale), an enormous sapphire set in a gold amulet engraved with the Trinity and the Nativity. In the gardens, children chase pigeons among the ruins of **St. Mary's Abbey,** once the most influential Benedictine monastery in northern England. *(Enter from Museum St. or Marygate. ☎687 687, www.york.yorkshire.museum. Open daily 10am-5pm. £4, concessions £2.50, families £10. Gardens and ruins free.)*

BEST OF THE REST. The **York City Art Gallery,** Exhibition Sq. across from the TIC, shows Continental work, a better selection of English painters (including William Etty, York native and pioneer of the English painted nude), and a spattering of pottery. *(☎551 861. Open daily 10am-5pm; last admission 4:30pm. £2, concessions £1.50. The museum is currently closed for renovations and is expected to reopen in January 2005.)* The **Treasurer's House,** Chapter House St. next to the Minster, built on the site of the Minster's treasurer's residence, holds in 13 rooms the collection of antique furnishings amassed by Edwardian connoisseur Frank Green. Among the period rooms is a medieval hall and a staircase devoted to William III and Mary II. *(☎624 427. Open Apr.-Oct. Su-Th 11am-4:30pm. £4.50, children £2.20, families £11. Tours of the haunted cellar £2, children £1.20. Gardens free.)* The morbidly inclined should try **York Dungeon,** 12 Clifford St. Beat the lines to learn the story of Guy Fawkes and Dick Turpin, or stare at sore-ridden bodies in the plague exhibit and mangled wax figures in the torture exhibit. *(☎632 599. Open daily mid-July to Aug. 10am-6:30pm, Oct and Easter to mid-July 10:30am-6pm, Nov.-Easter 10:30am-5:30pm; last admission 1hr. before closing. £9, concessions £8, children £6-7.)*

NIGHTLIFE AND FESTIVALS

To discover the best of after-hours, consult *What's On* and *Artscene*, available at the TIC, for listings of live music, theater, cinema, and exhibitions. Twilight activities take place in **King's Square** and on **Stonegate**, where barbershop quartets share the pavement with jugglers, magicians, and soapboxers. Next to the TIC, the 250-year-old **Theatre Royal**, St. Leonards Pl., offers stage fare. (☎623 568, 24hr. info 610 041. Box office open M 10am-6pm, Tu-Sa 10am-8pm. £8-17, students £3.50.) The ever-packed **King's Arms**, King's Staith, has outdoor seating along the Ouse. Highwater markers inside the pub glorify past floods (☎659 435; open M-Sa 11am-11pm, Su noon-10:30pm). York's dressy new club, **The Gallery**, 12 Clifford St., has two hot dance floors and six bars. (☎647 947. Smart casual, no trainers or sportswear on weekends. Cover £3.50-8. Open Su-Th 10pm-2am, F-Sa 10pm-3am.) **Toffs,** 3-5 Toft Green, plays mainly dance and house. (☎620 203. No trainers or sportswear on weekends. Cover £3.50-7. Weekly student nights; discount with student ID. Alternative Su 9pm-1am. Open M-Sa 10pm-2am.) **Fibber's,** Stonebow House, the Stonebow, doesn't lie about the quality (usually high) of live music playing nightly at 8pm. (☎466 148. Check *What's On* for events.)

The Minster and local churches host a series of **summer concerts** including July's **York Early Music Festival** (☎658 338). The city recently revived a centuries-old tradition of performing the medieval **York Mystery Plays** (☎635 444) in the nave of the Minster during June and July. Some controversy has surrounded the performances, and a small schedule will be performed in 2005.

DAYTRIP FROM YORK

CASTLE HOWARD

15 mi. northeast of York. Yorkshire Coastliner bus #840 runs to the castle, #842 runs from the castle (40min., both 2 per day, round-trip £4.50); reduced admission with bus ticket. ☎01653 648 333; www.castlehoward.co.uk. Open daily mid-Feb. to Oct. 11am-4:30pm; gardens 10am-6:30pm; 10min. chapel services Sa-Su 5:15pm; last admission 4pm. £9.50, concessions £8.50, children £6.50. Gardens only £6.50/6/4.50.

The domed Castle Howard inspired Evelyn Waugh to write *Brideshead Revisited* and was the scene for the BBC's cinematographic adaptation. Roman busts and portraits of Howard ancestors in full regalia clutter the halls. The **long gallery** is a promenade between enormous windows and shelves stuffed with books. Head to the **chapel** for kaleidoscopic pre-Raphaelite stained glass. More stunning than the castle are its 999 acres of luxurious rose gardens, fountains, and lakes, all roamed by raucous peacocks. From its hilltop, the **Temple of the Four Winds,** offers views of the rolling hills. The **Lakeside Adventure Playground,** provides diversion for kids.

NORTH YORK MOORS

The hilly, heather-clad expanses and cliff-lined coast of the North York Moors have changed little since inspiring Emily Brontë and Bram Stoker. Bleak ridges are cheered in the summertime by large swaths of purple heather, and deep-sided valleys supply the route for superb scenic railways. The region's stunning visual spectrum, ranging from endearing pastoral towns to an impossibly dramatic coastline, makes the North York Moors one of Britain's most visually exciting national parks.

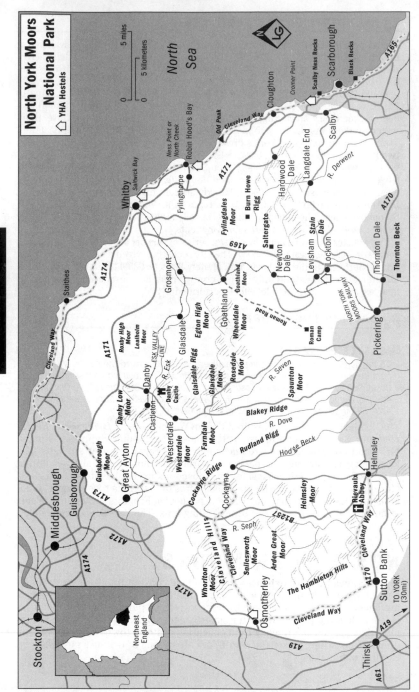

North York Moors National Park

TRANSPORTATION

The primary gateways to the North York Moors are **York** to the south and **Middlesbrough** to the north. Middlesbrough is a short train ride from **Darlington** (30 min., every hr., £3.40), which is on the main London-Edinburgh rail line. The *Moors Explorer* pamphlet, free at TICs and NPICs, covers bus and rail service in glorious detail—service varies by season and is significantly reduced in winter. **Traveline** also provides timetables (☎0870 608 2608).

Three **train** lines serve the park. There is frequent service between **York** and **Scarborough** (45min., 1-2 per hr., £9.30). The scenic **Esk Valley Line** runs from **Middlesbrough** to **Whitby** via **Danby** and **Grosmont** (1½hr., 5 per day, £7.30). The tourist-oriented **North Yorkshire Moors Railway** (reservations ☎01751 472 508, timetables 01751 473 535) links the north and south, chugging from **Pickering** to **Grosmont** (1hr.; 3-7 per day, no service during some low-season times; see p. 422).

Buses run more frequently than trains. To save cash, always ask the driver for daily or weekly passes rather than a single. **Yorkshire Coastliner** (☎01653 692 556) bus #840 travels between **Leeds, York, Pickering,** and **Whitby** (3hr., 5 per day), while #843 runs between **Leeds, York,** and **Scarborough** (3hr., every hr.). **Arriva** bus #93/93A journeys between **Middlesbrough, Whitby, Robin Hood's Bay** (#93 only), and **Scarborough** (2hr., every hr.). **Scarborough and District** (☎01723 503 020) bus #128 covers **Scarborough, Pickering,** and **Helmsley** (1½hr., every hr.). The national park operates the **Moorsbus,** with seasonal routes through the park; schedules are available at all TICs. The Moorsbus runs only on certain days, so make sure to plan. (☎07980 737 589; www.moorsbus.net. Apr.-Oct. Su; daily late July-Aug. All-day pass £2.50.)

ORIENTATION

North York Moors National Park is 30 mi. north of York. Toward the park's southwest corner, appealing **Helmsley** has several excellent sights and good access to hiking, particularly when the **Moorsbus** shuttle is operating (see above). To the east, centrally located **Pickering** is the starting point for the scenic **North Yorkshire Moors Railway,** as well as a sweatless way to take in the views. The **Esk Valley,** cutting across the north of the park and served by another beautiful railway, the **Esk Valley Line,** is good terrain for hikers. The seaside resort towns **Whitby** and **Scarborough** are often flooded with summer vacationers and feel distant from the park. **Robin Hood's Bay,** just south of Whitby, is a small and atmospheric coastal village.

PRACTICAL INFORMATION

The *Moors & Coast* visitor guide (50p), available at any TIC or NPIC, is particularly useful, highlighting the region's events and attractions.

National Park Information Centres:

Danby: The Moors Centre (☎01439 772 737). From the Danby train station, turn left after you pass the gate, and right at the crossroads before the Duke of Wellington Inn; the Centre is ½ mi. ahead on the right. The larger NPIC and an invaluable source of information. Open daily Apr.-Oct. 10am-5pm; daily Mar. and Nov.-Dec. 11am-4pm; Jan.-Feb. Sa-Su 11am-4pm.

Sutton Bank: (☎01845 597 426), 6 mi. east of Thirsk on the A170. Open daily Apr.-Oct. 10am-5pm; Mar. and Nov.-Dec. 11am-4pm; Jan.-Feb. Sa-Su 11am-4pm.

Tourist Information Centres:

Goathland: The Village Store and Outdoor Centre (☎01947 896 207). Open daily Easter-Oct. 10am-5pm; Nov.-Easter M-W and F-Su 10am-4pm.

Great Ayton: High Green Car Park (☎01642 722 835). Open Apr.-Oct. M-Sa 10am-4pm, Su 1-4pm.

THE BIG SPLURGE

DINING ON THE CARS

Possibly the most scenic and lovingly restored rail line in Britain, the North Yorkshire Moors Railway makes for an evocative outing. For the complete experience, try the NYMR's luxurious Pullman dining train. On select days throughout the year, the train is converted into a top-rate restaurant on wheels, serving elaborate five-course dinners in a truly unique setting. With offerings like Contrefilet of Beef Chasseur and Asparagus and Gruyere Tartlets, your craving for something more than pub grub is sure to be satisfied. There are also themed trips, like the Christmas Moorlander and the intriguing Murder Mystery Pullman, a curious evening that involves a murder mystery that unfolds during the ride.

Booking ahead is essential. Dial 01751 472508 for more information or to make reservations. The North Yorkshire Pullman, which serves dinner, runs most Saturdays during the summer; the Moorlander offers a Yorkshire Sunday Lunch more frequently. The Murder Mystery Pullman runs only three times a year. Dinners are £40, lunches £32, and the Murder Mystery will set you back £56.

Such a meal is the perfect way to leave the present behind. The only thing disrupting the sense of travelling back in time is a quick look around the train at one's fellow passengers: the tourists, unfortunately, have not been recreated.

Guisborough: Priory Grounds, Church St. (☎01287 633 801). Open Apr.-Sept. Tu-Su 9am-5pm, Oct.-Mar. W-Su 9am-5pm

Helmsley: Town Hall, Market Pl. (☎01439 770 173), in the town center, right on the main square. Open daily Mar.-Oct. 9:30am-5pm; Nov.-Feb. F-Su 10am-4pm.

Pickering: The Ropery (☎01751 473 791), beside the library, just down the road from the train station. Open Mar.-Oct. M-Sa 9:30am-5pm, Su 9:30am-4pm; Nov.-Feb. M-Sa 10am-4:30pm.

Scarborough: see p. 421.

Whitby: see p. 423.

ACCOMMODATIONS

Local TICs book beds for a small fee and 10% deposit. **B&Bs, hotels,** and **caravan parks** in or near the national park are listed under the appropriate towns.

YHA HOSTELS

The following **YHA hostels** provide lodging in the Moors. Reservations are highly recommended, especially during summer. Clearly named bus stops are rare; tell drivers where you're headed.

Boggle Hole: (☎01947 880 352), Mill Beck, Fylingthorpe. Easy access to the Cleveland Way and Coast to Coast trails. A seaside 19th-century mill, 1 mi. south of Robin Hood's Bay along the beach or, during high tides, cliffs. Reception from 1pm. No curfew. Open daily Feb.-Oct.; Nov. F-Sa. Dorms £10.60, under 18 £7.20. MC/V. ●

Helmsley: (☎/fax 01439 770 433). From Market Pl. take Bondgate Rd., turn left onto Carlton Rd., and left again at Carlton Ln.; hostel is on the left. Lockout 10am-5pm. No curfew. Open daily Apr.-Oct.; Sept.-Nov. call ahead. Dorms £10.60, under 18 £7.20, under 5 free. MC/V. ●

Lockton: The Old School (☎01751 460 376), off the Pickering-Whitby Rd. 2 mi. from the North Yorkshire Moors Railway Station at Levisham. 4 mi. north of Pickering; take Coastliner bus #840 toward Whitby. Self-catering. Reception 8-10am and 5-10pm. Open daily July-Aug.; Apr.-May and Sept. call 48hr. in advance. Dorms £10.60, under 18 £7.20. MC/V. ●

Osmotherley: (☎01609 883 575), Cote Ghyll, Northallerton. Between Stockton and Thirsk, just northeast of Osmotherley. Lockout 11:30pm-7am. Reception open 8am-noon and 1-11pm. Open daily Mar.-Nov.; Feb. F-Sa. Dorms £10.60, under 18 £7.20. Full board £23.50/19.20. MC/V. ●

Scarborough: The White House, Burniston Rd. (☎01723 361 176; fax 500 054), 2 mi. from Scarborough. Take bus #3 from the train station to Scholes Park Rd., then follow Burniston Rd. away from town and turn left just after crossing a small river. In a former mill on a river, 15min. from the sea. Lockout 10am-5pm. Open daily Mar.-Aug.; Sept.-Oct. call ahead. Dorms £10.60, under 18 £7.20. MC/V. ❶

Whitby: (☎01947 602 878). 12th-century stone building near the abbey, atop 199 mossy steps. Moors-bound school groups often fill the place until mid-July; call ahead. Family rooms available. Lockout 10am-5pm. Curfew 11pm. Open daily Apr.-Aug.; Sept.-Oct. M-Sa; Jan.-Mar. and Nov. F-Sa. Dorms £10.25, under 18 £7. MC/V. ❶

CAMPING

The YHA operates four **camping barns** (p. 398) in the Moors: in **Farndale,** Oakhouse farmyard; **Kildale,** on the Cleveland Way; **Sinnington,** on the edge of the park between Pickering and Helmsley; and **Westerdale,** in Broadgate Farm. Reservations must be made in advance; call ☎0870 770 8868 or e-mail campbarns-syha@enterprise.net. All barns £5 per person or less.

⬛🏃 HIKING AND OUTDOORS

Coastal towns aside, hiking is the best way to travel these vast tracts of moor. Wrapping fully around the national park, the 93 mi. **Cleveland Way** is the yellow brick road of the North York Moors. A particularly well-marked and breathtaking portion of the Way is the 20 mi. trail between Whitby and Scarborough (the less eager might only go as far as Robin Hood's Bay, 5½ mi. from Whitby)—hills on one side, tranquil sea on the other, and miles of shoreline cliffs stretching ahead. Ambitious hikers might consider tackling the 79 mi. **Wolds Way,** a stunning coastal hike that extends from Scarborough southward to the sandstone cliffs of Filey, or the shorter and unofficial **White Rose** (37 mi.). The popular **Coast to Coast walk** (192 mi.), begins in St. Bees and terminates in Robin Hood's Bay (right at a pub, of course). Excellent day hikes begin at stations on the park's two scenic **railways,** the Esk Valley Line (p. 417) and the North Yorkshire Moors Railway (p. 422). Trails are not always marked or even visible; hikers should carry a map and compass (see **Wilderness Safety,** p. 52).

The National Park Authority produces a number of guides on the Moors such as the *Walks Around* booklets (£1.90), which detail short (up to half-day) walks starting from villages or points of interest. Before hitting the trails, consult more in-depth books (£3-6) and get advice from tourist officials. The Ordnance Survey Explorer Maps (£7) include eastern and western guides to the park. **Disabled travelers** should pick up the *Easy Going North York Moors Guide* (£4.50) or call ☎01439 770 657 for guidance.

The Moors are steep, and **cycling** around them is a challenge, but the paths along the plateaus are less strenuous. The **Whitby to Scarborough Coastal Railtrail,** with sea views, refreshment stops, and sections for all skill levels, is especially popular. There are also many sections of the **National Cycle Network** that pass through the area; these are well-signed and avoid busy roads. Check out www.sustrans.org.uk for more info. You can rent bikes at **Trailways,** Old Railway Station, in Hawsker, 2 mi. south of Whitby on the A171. (☎01947 820 207; www.trailways.fsnet.co.uk. Open daily Easter-Nov. 10am-6pm; Dec.-Easter call ahead. From £7.80 per day.) TICs and NPICs offer lists of other bike rental stores in the region.

The Moors can be both horribly hot or bitterly cold in the summer. Call the Danby NPIC (☎02187 660 654; see p. 417) for the **weather forecast** before setting out, but be aware that conditions can vary dramatically even within the park, and it is England—bring raingear.

NORTHEAST ENGLAND

HELMSLEY ☎ 01439

Tourist-oriented shops notwithstanding, picturesque Helmsley feels happily stuck in the past. The town centers around the cobbled **Market Place,** site of a Friday market. Built in 1120 to strengthen the Scottish border, **Helmsley Castle** acquired its shattered profile during the Civil War, when Cromwell blew the place in half. (☎770 442. Open daily Apr.-Sept. 10am-6pm; Oct.-Mar. M and Th-Su, 10am-4pm; Nov.-Mar. 10am-1pm and 2-4pm. £4, concessions £3, children £2.) The **Walled Garden** behind the castle contains over a hundred varieties of clematis. (☎771 427. Open Apr.-Oct. daily 10:30am-5pm; Nov.-Mar. F-Su noon-4pm. £3, concessions £2, children free.) **Duncombe Park,** ¾ mi. south of Market Pl. on Buckingham Sq., is a large, landscaped park and nature reserve home to the lavish 18th-century villa of Lord and Lady Feversham. Informative guides point out family portraits, but you may spot the noble twosome in person. (☎770 213. Gardens open Easter-Oct. Su-Th 11am-5:30pm. House open by hourly tour only noon-3:30pm. £6.50, concessions £5, children £3. Gardens only £3.60.)

An enjoyable 3½ mi. walk out of town along the beginning of the Cleveland Way leads to the stunning 12th-century ◾**Rievaulx Abbey** (REE-vo). Established by monks from Burgundy, the abbey was an aesthetic masterpiece until Thomas Mannus, first Earl of Rutland, initiated a swift decay, stripping it of valuables (including the roof). It is now one of the most spectacular ruins in the country. (Moorsbus M8 does stop there, but it runs a very irregular schedule and often not at all. Call ☎01845 597426 for more information. Otherwise, a taxi is the best bet for weary travellers (see below). ☎798 288. Open daily Apr.-Sept. 10am-6pm; Oct.-Mar. 10am-4pm. £4, concessions £3, children £2.) A steep half-mile uphill, the **Rievaulx Terrace & Temples** is a small park that occupies a strip of lawn curving around the abbey far below with 17th-century faux-classical temples at either end. The views of the abbey are captivating and make the terrace worth a look. (☎798 340. Open daily Mar.-Sept. 10:30am-5pm. £3.80, children £2, families £8.)

Helmsley has a comfortable **YHA hostel** (see p. 418) and **B&Bs. Stillworth House ❸,** 1 Church St., lets attractive, large rooms in a Georgian townhouse near the main square. (☎01439 771 072. www.stilworth.co.uk. Ensuite rooms £35 per person.) **Nice Things Cafe ❶,** 10 Market Pl., serves up tasty toasted sandwiches for £4. (☎771 997. Open M-F 9am-5pm, Sa-Su 9am-5:30pm. Hot food until 3:30pm only.) Numerous **pubs** on Market Pl. present many dining alternatives.

Buses stop on Market Pl., where you'll find Helmsley's **Tourist Information Centre** (see p. 418). Auto-less, footsore travelers might choose to catch a **taxi** to the nearby sights (☎770 923; about £5 to Rievaulx). Other services include: **banks,** on Market Pl.; the **police,** Ashdale Rd. (☎01653 692 424, open daily 9am-10am and 6pm-7pm); free **Internet access** at the **library,** in the Town Hall (open Tu 10am-12:30pm, Th 10am-12:30pm and 2-5pm, F 10am-12:30pm, 2-5pm, and 5:30-7pm, Sa 10am-1pm); and the **post office,** Bridge St., just off Market Pl. (open M-Tu and Th-F 9am-12:30pm and 1:30-5:30pm, W and Sa 9am-12:30pm). **Post Code:** YO62 5BG.

PICKERING ☎ 01751

The attractive market town of Pickering is best known as an endpoint of the popular **North Yorkshire Moors Railway,** though it can also serve as a convenient base for exploring the national park. Originally built in fear of Northern invasions, **Pickering Castle** soon became a favorite royal hunting spot. Though not much to look at today, Pickering is one of the best examples of Norman motte-and-bailey castles (p. 82). Remnants of the keep command an excellent view of the countryside. (☎474 989. Open Apr.-Sept. daily 10am-6pm; Oct. M and Th-Su 10am-4pm. £3, concessions £2.30, children £1.50.) The **Parish Church of St. Peter and St. Paul** is a squat Norman building with a 15th-century Gothic spire. Its medieval frescoes are in surprisingly good condition. (Open dawn-dusk. Suggested donation £1.)

NORTHEAST ENGLAND

Pickering's **Tourist Information Centre** is at The Ropery (p. 418). Other services include: **banks,** on Market Pl.; **Internet access** at the **library,** next to the TIC (open M-T and Th 9:30am-5pm, F 9:30am-7:30pm, Sa 9:30am-4:30pm); and the **post office,** 7 Market Pl., inside Morland's Newsagents, **Bureau de change** (☎472 256; open M-F 9am-5:30pm, Sa 9am-1pm). **Post Code:** YO18 7AA.

The nearest hostel to Pickering is the **YHA Old School** in Lockton (see p. 418). Among a number of B&Bs, **Bridge House ❸,** 8 Bridge St., is close to the train station and has a pleasant rear garden beside a stream and three cozy ensuite rooms. (☎477 234. From £27.50.) A small hotel in the town center, **The White Swan Inn ❺,** Market Place, has luxurious rooms and fine food. (☎472 288; www.whiteswan.co.uk. Singles from £80; doubles £55-60 per person. Prices vary by season and time of week. Entrees from £10.) **Wayside Caravan Park ❷,** Wrelton, 2½ mi. down the Pickering-Helmsley road, is well-maintained with beautiful park views. (☎472 608. Open Apr.-Oct. £13 per night.)

SCARBOROUGH ☎01723

Stunningly situated on a hilly peninsula separating two long beaches and dominated by a castle-topped crag, Scarborough has been a popular destination since the mid 1600s. Although it can be quite tacky at times, Scarborough is still a major attraction for English families, especially in the summer. The town has the distinct feel of a seaside resort, with numerous fish and chip shops, a lively boardwalk, and ever-present seagulls giving it a certain charm.

🔄🔀 ORIENTATION AND PRACTICAL INFORMATION. A cliff crowned by Scarborough Castle divides **North Bay** and **South Bay,** each of which is fronted by a long stretch of beach. The **train station** is on **Westborough,** the main shopping street. Regional **buses** arrive and depart from several locations on Westborough; **National Express** services stop behind the train station, and **Arriva** buses in front. The **Tourist Information Centre** is located on Sandside, by the South Bay. (Open daily Easter-Oct. 10am-5pm; Nov.-Easter Su 10am-4pm.) Other services include: **banks** (with many ATMs), along Westborough; the **police** (☎500 300); **Internet access** at **Complete Computing,** 14 Northway (☎500 501; £1 per 15min.; open M-F 9am-5:30pm, Sa 9am-noon) as well as at the **public library** on Vernon Rd. (£1 per hr.); and the **post office,** 11-15 Aberdeen Walk (☎0845 722 3344; open Tu, W, F 9am-5:30pm, M, Th 8:45am-5:30pm, Sa 9am-12:30pm). **Post Code:** YO11 1AB.

🔀🔲 ACCOMMODATIONS AND FOOD. YHA Scarborough is 2 mi. from town (p. 418). Reasonable **B&Bs** (£17-20) can be found along Blenheim Terr., Rutland Terr., and Trafalgar Sq. **Kerry Lee Hotel ❷,** 60 Trafalgar Sq., is welcoming, spotless, and well-priced. (☎363 845. No smoking. From £14 per person, ensuite £16.) Nearby, **Whiteley Hotel ❸,** 99 Queen's Parade, offers attentive service and well-kept ensuite rooms, some overlooking the North Bay. (☎373 514. June-Sept. £23 per person, £25 for rooms facing the sea; Oct.-May £21.50.) Old-fashioned **Parmelia Hotel ❸,** 17 West St., has family-friendly accommodations just south of the town center. (☎361 914. £19.50 per person, with bath £23.) The friendly **Terrace Hotel ❷,** 69 Westborough, welcomes the fatigued just two blocks from the train station. (☎374 937. Singles £20; doubles £17 per person; one night only £2 extra.)

For the cheapest eats, head down Westborough and turn left at St. Helen's Sq. to reach the **Public Market Hall** for an outdoor market. (☎373 579 Open M-Sa about 8am-5:30pm.) You haven't truly been to Scarborough until you've sampled its fish and chips. Many locals swear by **Mother Hubbards ❶,** 43 Westborough, where haddock with chips, bread and butter, and tea or coffee is £5. (☎376 109. Open M-Sa 11:30am-6:45pm.) The **Golden Grid ❷,** 4 Sandside, in an airy dining room along the boardwalk, is more upscale, with a wide range of daily specials and fresh grilled fish that goes well beyond the simple battered haddock. (☎360 922. Cod and chips £5.25. Grilled fish specials £9-16. Open daily 11am-9pm.) Probably Scarborough's best restaurant, **Lanterna ④**, 33 Queen St., serves outstanding Italian cuisine with lots of local seafood. (☎363 616. Entrees £13-20. Open M-Sa 6:30pm-11pm.)

⬛ 🎭 **SIGHTS AND ENTERTAINMENT.** While Scarborough's beach and board-walk amusements occupy many a visitor's time, its other attractions are also worthwhile. Dominating the horizon atop the city's dividing headland, ⬛**Scarborough Castle** was built by Henry II in 1158. A longtime strategic stronghold, the site also served as home to Bronze Age warriors, a Roman signal station, and a Viking fort. Its fascinating history of stubborn sieges is more than matched by tremendous views over town and sea. (☎372 451. Open daily Apr.-Sept. 10am-6pm; Oct. 10am-5pm; Nov.-Mar. W-Su 10am-4pm. £3, children and concessions £2.30; includes 1hr. audio tour.) Just down the hill, the cemetery of 12th-century **St. Mary's Parish Church,** across Church Ln., holds the grave of Anne Brontë. (☎500 541. Open May-Sept. M-F 10am-4pm, Su 1-4pm.) The **Stephen Joseph Theatre,** at the corner of Westborough and Northway right across from the train station, premiered much of Alan Ayckbourn's work, including *How the Other Half Loves*. A wide range of productions are now staged here. (☎370 541; www.sjt.uk.com. Box office open M-Sa 10am-6pm and before curtain.)

NORTH YORKSHIRE MOORS RAILWAY

One of the region's most popular tourist attractions, the steam-pulled North Yorkshire Moors Railway (NYMR) chugs 18 mi. through the heart of the national park. The railway was completed in 1835, and its carriages pulled by horses until 1847, when the first steam engine arrived. Today the NYMR operates as a heritage railway, with brilliantly restored steam engines and carriages, complete with old-fashioned tickets and weathered characters running the railway. Although the whole production is in some ways a tourist trap, it's hard to avoid melting into childish excitement as the train hisses and lurches from station to station, belching steam and smoke the whole way. The train passes superb scenery on its route between **Pickering** and **Grosmont.** Most visitors make a round-trip of it to savor the views, but stations along the way open up some good **hiking;** pick up *Twelve Scenic Walks from the North York Moors Railway* (£2) at any TIC.

Traveling north from Pickering, the railway soon reaches **Levisham,** a pretty village 1½ mi. east of the station. Nearby **Lockton** has a self-catering **YHA hostel** (p. 418). Another stop (by request only), **Newton Dale,** is near many backcountry walks. The most popular stop is **Goathland,** largely because it was the postcard-perfect village featured in the British TV series *Heartbeat*. The train also appeared as the "Hogwarts Express" in the first *Harry Potter* film, so be prepared for aspiring wizards in search of Platform 9¾. The NYMR terminates at **Grosmont,** also a stop on the Whitby-Middlesbrough Esk Valley Line. *(NYMR information: ☎01751 472 508; talking timetable ☎473 535. 3-7 round-trips late daily Mar. to Oct.; Nov.-Dec. most weekends; Jan.-Feb. select holidays. Grosmont to Pickering £10. All-day rover tickets £12, concessions £10.50, children £6, families from £25.)*

WHITBY ☎01947

Straddling a harbor between two desolate headlands, this beautiful seaside resort town has played the muse for many history-makers and literary greats. Here Caedmon sang the first English hymns and Lewis Carroll wrote *The Walrus and the Carpenter* while eating oysters. A former whaling outpost (one of two English ports where the midsummer sun can be seen both rising and setting over the sea), Whitby also inspired Captain James Cook to set sail for Australia in the 18th century. Though it suffers from all of the diversions found in most English beach towns—fish and chip huts, waterfront amusements, and the like—the natural allure of the town and its harbor manage to shine through. Perhaps it's the narrow cobblestone streets, the gentle clanging of the working harbor, or the breathtaking ruins of Whitby Abbey, looming above.

ORIENTATION AND PRACTICAL INFORMATION. Whitby populates the west and east banks of the River Esk, with the North Sea bordering the town to the north. The carcass of Whitby Abbey stands atop 199 steps on the east bank of the river. **Trains** and most **buses** stop at **Station Square,** Endeavour Wharf, on the west side of the river. You can also flag Scarborough-bound buses along **Langborne Rd.** (☎ 602 146. Luggage storage £1. Open M-Sat 8:15-3:45.) Whitby's helpful **Tourist Information Centre** is at Station Sq. across Langborne Rd. (☎ 602 674. Open daily May-Sept. 9:30am-6pm; Oct.-Apr. 10am-12:30pm and 1-4:30pm.) Other services include: **banks,** on Baxter's near the bridge; the **police,** Spring Hill (☎ 603 443); and the **post office,** Langborne Rd., inside the North Eastern Co-Op next to the train station. (☎ 602 327; open M-F 8:30am-5:30pm and Sat 9am-3pm). **Post Code:** YO21 1DN.

ACCOMMODATIONS AND FOOD. The **YHA Whitby,** located on a hilltop right before Whitby Abbey, has incredible views (p. 419). Another hostel, **Whitby Backpackers Harbour Grange ❶,** Church St., has a dockside patio, kitchen, and tidy rooms for a great price. It's 15min. from the TIC—cross the bridge to the east side of the river, walk south on Church St. and look right just after Green Ln. (☎ 600 817. No smoking. Sheets £1. Curfew 11:30pm. Dorms £10.) **B&Bs** gather on the **western cliff,** along Royal Cres., Crescent Ave., Abbey Terr., and nearby streets. The **Ashford Guest House ❸,** 8 Royal Cres., is well-furnished, with ensuite rooms and sea views. (☎ 602 138. No smoking. £24-26 per person.) Camp at the **Northcliffe Caravan Park ❶,** 4 mi. south of town in High Hawkser. Take bus #93 from the bus station (£1), or head south on the A171 and turn onto the B1447. (☎ 880 477. Laundry. Mar.-Oct. £8-12.; closed Nov.-Feb. Showers free.)

The town has a twice-weekly **market** just off of Church St. near the abbey, and a giant **Co-op** between the train station and the TIC to satisfy your grocery needs. (☎ 600 710. Open M-F 8am-10pm, Sa 8am-8pm, Su 10:30am-4:30pm.) According to Whitby locals and travelers alike, **The Magpie Cafe ❷,** 14 Pier Rd., serves the best fish and chips, and the queue that often snakes into the street confirms the claim. (☎ 602 058. Entrees £7-14. Open daily 11:30am-9pm.) For superb food in a relaxed and jovial atmosphere, head to **The Vintner ❸,** 42a Flowergate. Fresh fish specials run £13-15. (☎ 601 166. Open daily 5:30-9:30pm. Lunch served daily 12:00-2:30 except Sunday. Reduced hours Nov.-Mar.) On the east side of the river, **Sanders Yard Restaurant ❶,** 95 Church St., set in a charming courtyard just off the main road, serves tasty vegetarian morsels (sandwiches £3.50) in a funky cafe and tea garden. (☎ 820 228. Open daily 10am-9pm.)

SIGHTS AND ENTERTAINMENT. Enjoying marvelous views of the bay below, the splendid ruins of **Whitby Abbey** sit atop a towering hill buffeted by shrieking winds. Bram Stoker was a frequent visitor to Whitby, and the abbey and graveyard are believed to have inspired *Dracula.* The abbey's nonfictional history commenced in AD 675 but the present structure dates to the 14th century. The textured stone walls, grass-grown nave, and panoramic views of the sea and the town below make this spot a must-see. (☎ 603 568. Open daily Apr.-Sept. 10am-6pm; Oct.-Mar. M and Th-Su 10am-4pm. £4, concessions £3, children £1.90, families £9.50. Free audio tour.) Next to the abbey, the medieval **St. Mary's Church** is filled with a veritable maze of box pews. (☎ 603 421. Open July-Aug. M-Sa 10am-4pm, Su 1-4pm; open winter 11am-2pm. Suggested donation £1.)

NORTHEAST ENGLAND

On Bagdale, **Pannett Art Gallery and Whitby Museum**, in Pannett Park, has model ships, domestic bygones, and a good fossil collection. (☎ 602 908 Open May-Sept. M-Sa 9:30am-5:30pm, Su 2-5pm; Oct.-Apr. Tu 10am-1pm, W-Sa 10am-4pm, Su 2-4pm. Museum £2.50, children £1. Gallery free.) The **Captain Cook Memorial Museum** is at Grape Ln. on the east side of the river. Occupying a historic home where Cook once stayed, the museum contains original letters, drawings, navigational instruments, and lifelike Captain Cook wax figures. (☎ 601 900. Open daily Apr.-Oct. 9:45am-5pm; Mar. Sa-Su 11am-3pm. £3, seniors £2.50, children and students £2.)

Whitby has a small **live music** scene; pubs like the popular **Tab & Spile,** New Quay Rd. (☎ 603 937), across from the train station, have performances most nights starting at 9pm. The town takes particular pride in its **Folk Festival** (☎ 708 424) during the last full week in August, including dance, concerts, and workshops. The *What's On* brochure at the TIC and the *Whitby Gazette* (published Tu and F) list events around town.

ROBIN HOOD'S BAY ☎ 01947

Robin Hood's Bay is a tiny, enchanting town. Stone cottages are set right into a steep valley that plunges down to the sea. The village's only road is so steep and narrow that non-residents are required to park above the town and walk down. The local population gets around by foot on the maze-like stepped alleys that snake through town. While the town can get touristy during summer, but if you stay overnight a sense of peaceful solitude descends on the town. Robin Hood's Bay is 6 mi. south of Whitby; **Arriva** bus #93 stops here en route from Scarborough (40 min.) to Whitby (20 min.). The popular **YHA Boggle Hole** is 1 mi. from town (p. 418). Though the town is easily seen as a daytrip, hotels and B&Bs are also available. One possibility is the **Victoria Hotel ❹,** which offers stunning sea views and spacious rooms on its perch just above the village. (☎ 880 205. No smoking. All rooms ensuite. Singles £45; doubles £72.) Another option is **The Boathouse ❹,** a snug B&B located right in the heart of town at the bottom of the main road with comfortable, airy rooms (☎ 880 099; www.boathouserhb.co.uk. £40 ensuite). At the upper edge of town on the main road, **Candy's Coffee Bar ❶,** Bank Top Rd., serves up scrumptious sandwiches (£1.95) as well as more substantial lunches (£3-5), vegetarian options, and ice cream. (Open daily 9:30am-5:30pm.)

DANBY AND THE ESK VALLEY

The gorgeous Esk Valley cuts across the northern reaches of North York Moors National Park. Outstanding views can be had without leaving the railcars of the **Esk Valley Line** (see p. 417) as they travel between Whitby and Middlesbrough. It's well worth stopping off, however—this is a splendid place for **hiking,** and there are marked trails leaving from almost every station along the rail route. TICs and NPICs can provide further details and literature, such as *Walks in the Esk Valley* (£1.90). At the small town of **Grosmont,** the Esk Valley Line connects with another scenic train journey, the **North Yorkshire Moors Railway** (see p. 422). Farther west in the valley, rolling hills give way to some of the national park's finest moorland. **Danby** is blessed with a scenic setting snuggled in the moors. **The Moors Centre,** the largest of the NPICs (see p. 417), is the best place to research possible routes. *Walks from the Moors Centre* (£1.90) lists excellent nearby walks, among them an easy 30min. jaunt to **Danby Castle,** a roofless jumble of 14th-century stones attached to a working farm. In good weather, an ascent of the 981 ft. **Danby Beacon** affords outstanding views. **The Duke of Wellington Inn ❹,** has convenient accommodations near the train station. (☎ 01287 660 351. From £30 per person.) Another option is the **Danby Mill Farm ❸,** which offers simple, riverside B&B accommodations from £16. Turn right on the main road after leaving the train station. The farm is on the right just after the first bridge. (☎ 01287 660 330). The village of **Castleton** is one stop beyond Danby, and from here the **Esk Valley Walk** (35 mi.) begins winding its way back to the coast. A lovely walk follows its first 2 mi. and ends in Danby.

COUNTY DURHAM

DURHAM ☎0191

The commanding presence of England's greatest Norman Romanesque cathedral lends grandeur to the small city of Durham (pop. 90,000). For 800 years, the Bishops of Durham had absolute authority over the surrounding county, with their own currency, army, and courts. In the 1830s, new rulers—Durham University students—took over the hilltop city. Though the stream of students dries during the summer, hordes of tourists and revelers flow steadily through the narrow streets.

▣ TRANSPORTATION

Durham lies 20 mi. south of Newcastle on the A167 and an equal distance north of Darlington. The **train station** is on a steep hill west of town. (☎232 6262. Ticket office open M-F 6am-9pm, Sa 6am-8pm, Su 7:30am-9pm.) **Trains** (☎08457 484 950) arrive from: **Edinburgh** (2hr., 2-3 per hr., £37); **London King's Cross** (3hr., 2 per hr., £88); **Newcastle** (15min., 3 per hr., £4.10); **York** (45min., 3 per hr., £17). The **bus station** is on North Rd., across Framwellgate Bridge from the city center. (☎384 3323. Office open M-F 9am-5pm, Sa 9am-4pm.) **National Express** (☎08705 808 080) runs from: **Edinburgh** (4½hr., 1 per day, £20); **Leeds** (2½hr., 4 per day, £12.75); **London** (6-7hr., 4 per day, £25). **Go Northern** and **Arriva** run a joint service from the Eldon Sq. station in **Newcastle** (#723, 1hr., 2 per hr., £4). **Arriva** buses serve most local routes. **Rent bikes** at **Cycle Force,** 29 Claypath. (☎384 0319. £12 per day. £35 deposit. Open M-F 9am-5:30pm, Sa 9am-5pm, Su 11am-3pm.)

❄❔ ORIENTATION AND PRACTICAL INFORMATION

The **River Wear** coils around Durham, creating a partial moat crossed by a handful of footbridges. With its cobbled medieval streets, Durham is pedestrian-friendly, though travelers burdened with heavy packs will find its hills challenging. The **Tourist Information Centre,** 2 Millennium Pl., lies just east of the Millburngate Bridge. (☎384 3720. Open M-Sa 9:30am-5:30pm, Su 11am-4pm.) Other services include: **banks** in Market Pl.; the **police,** New Elvet (☎386 4222); free **Internet access** at the **library,** Millennium Pl., right across from the TIC (☎386 4003; open M-F 9:30am-7pm, Sa 9am-5pm); and the **post office,** 33 Silver St. (☎386 0839; open M-Sa 9am-5:30pm). **Post Code:** DH1 3RE.

⌂◖ ACCOMMODATIONS AND FOOD

Durham's accommodations can fill quickly; reserve ahead (especially during university graduation in late June) or take advantage of the TIC's free booking service. Durham lacks hostels, but the large supply of inexpensive and often beautiful **dormitory rooms** is a boon for summer travelers. Others merely tour it, but you can pretend to be lord or lady of Durham Castle in the ▨**University College ❸** dorms. (☎334 4106 or 334 4108; www.durhamcastle.com. Breakfast included. From £25 per person. Doubles £45.) The castle also has a small number of luxurious ensuite rooms, including the fabulous Bishop's Suite, a massive two room affair with 17th-century tapestries on the walls and views of the river. (Bishop's Suite £95, double occupancy £160; ensuite singles £35; ensuite doubles £65.) On a pretty cobbled street behind Durham Cathedral, **St. John's College ❸**, 3 South Bailey, also offers accommodations. (☎334 3877; s.l.hobson@dur.ac.uk. From £23 per person, including breakfast. 2 luxurious ensuite rooms are available, £33). The dorms are available July-Sept. and around Easter and Christmas; contact the **Durham University Conference and Tourism Office** (☎334 2000).

There are inexpensive B&Bs along Gilesgate. Among the most appealing are **Green Grove Guest House ❸**, 99 Gilesgate (☎384 4361; from £20 per person) and **Mrs. Koltai's ❸**, 10 Gilesgate, which is closer to the town center (☎386 2026; £20 per person). **Castle View Guest House ❹**, 4 Crossgate, has comfortable rooms and a well-tended garden. (☎386 8852. All ensuite. Singles £45; doubles £70.) **Camping** is free along the river during festival weekends (F-Su); call the TIC for exact dates.

Fresh produce abounds at the **Indoor Market**, off Market Pl. (Open M-Sa 9am-5pm.) Students congregate over sandwiches or pastas (£2.50-4) in the 16th-century courtyard of **Vennel's ❶**, Saddler St., up a narrow passage from the street, a cool bohemian alcove. (Open daily 9:30am-5pm. Bar open 7:30-11pm.) The busy **Almshouse Cafe and Restaurant ❷**, 10 Palace Green, near the cathedral, serves delicious specials for £4-6. Sandwiches £2. (☎361 1054. Open daily in summer 9am-8pm; in winter 9am-5:30pm. Food served noon-2:30pm and 5:30-8pm.) Dine on Thai cuisine (£10) at **Numjai ❷**, at the northeast corner of the Millburngate Shopping Centre, right on the river. (☎386 2020. Open daily 11:30am-2:30pm and 6-10pm.)

 SIGHTS

DURHAM CATHEDRAL
Crowning the hill in the middle of the city. ☎386 4266; www.durhamcathedral.co.uk. *Open June-Sept. M-Sa 9:30am-8pm, Su 12:30-8pm; Oct.-May M-Sa 9:30am-6pm, Su 12:30-5pm. Tours available June-Sept. Suggested donation £4.*

Built between 1093 and 1133 (and still largely intact), the extraordinary Durham Cathedral stands, in the words of Sir Walter Scott, as "half church of God, half castle 'gainst the Scot." It is considered the finest Norman cathedral in the world. Explanatory panels are sprinkled throughout the cathedral, though a more detailed pamphlet (£1) is also available. The stunning **nave** was the first in England to incorporate pointed arches. At the end of the nave, the beautiful **Galilee Chapel** features 12th-century wall paintings. Nearby is the simple tomb of the Venerable Bede, author of the 8th-century *Ecclesiastical History of the English People*, the first history of England. Behind the choir is the **tomb of Saint Cuthbert**, who died in AD 687 and was buried on Holy Island. When 9th-century Danish raiders sent the island's monks packing, the brothers brought along the saint's body as they fled. After wandering for 120 years, a vision led the monks to Durham, where they built White Church (later the cathedral) to shelter the saint's shrine. Next to the choir, the **Bishop's throne** has been the subject of intense criticism—it stands nearly three inches higher than the Pope's throne at the Vatican. The cathedral's central **tower** reaches 218 ft. and is supported by intricately carved stone pillars. The spectacular view from the top is well worth the dizzying 325-step climb it takes to get there. *(Open mid-Apr. to Sept. M-Sa 10am-4pm; Oct. to mid-Apr. M-Sa 10am-3pm, weather permitting. £2, under 16 £1, families £5.)* The **Monks' Dormitory** off the cloister houses pre-Conquest stones and casts of crosses under an enormous 600-year-old timber roof. *(Open Apr.-Sept. M-Sa 10am-3:30pm, Su 12:30-3:15pm. 80p, children 20p, families £1.50.)* The **Treasures of St. Cuthbert**, also off the

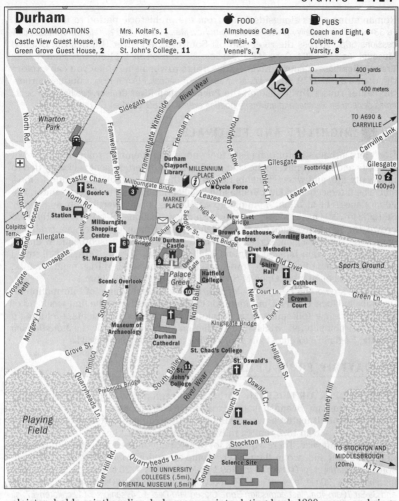

Durham

♠ ACCOMMODATIONS
Castle View Guest House, **5**
Green Grove Guest House, **2**

Mrs. Koltai's, **1**
University College, **9**
St. John's College, **11**

🍎 FOOD
Almshouse Cafe, **10**
Numjai, **3**
Vennel's, **7**

🍺 PUBS
Coach and Eight, **6**
Colpitts, **4**
Varsity, **8**

NORTHEAST ENGLAND

cloister, holds saintly relics, holy manuscripts dating back 1300 years, and rings and seals of the all-powerful Bishops. *(Open M-Sa 10am-4:30pm, Su 2-4:30pm. £2, concessions £1.50, children 50p, families £5.)*

OTHER SIGHTS AND ACTIVITIES

DURHAM CASTLE. Begun in 1072, this fortress was for centuries a key bastion of the county's Prince Bishops (top brass religious royalty). Today it's a splendid residence for university students or summer sojourners. *(Across from the Cathedral. ☎334 3800. Admission by guided tour only. Open daily Mar.-Sept. 10am-12:30pm and 2-4pm; Oct.-Feb. M, W, Sa-Su 2-4pm. £3.50, children £2.50, families £8.)*

BEST OF THE REST. A pleasant afternoon can be spent wandering the horseshoe bend of the River Wear. Along the bank between Framwellgate Bridge and Prebends Bridge, the **Museum of Archaeology** showcases an extensive collection of

Roman stone altars alongside finds from the prehistoric period to the present. *(☎334 1823. Open daily Apr.-Oct. 11am-4pm; Nov.-Mar. M and F-Su 11:30am-3:30pm. £1, concessions 50p.)* Across the river and off South Rd. on Elvet Hill lies the **Oriental Museum**. *(☎334 5694. Open M-F 10am-5pm, Sa-Su noon-5pm. £1.50, concessions 75p.)* **Brown's Boathouse Centres,** Elvet Bridge, rents rowboats in which you can explore the river. *(☎386 3779. £3 per hr., children £2. £5 deposit.)* For a less arduous journey, the center runs a 1hr. cruise on the **Prince Bishop River Cruiser**. *(daily Easter-Sept.; times depend on weather and university boating events. £4.50, children £2.)*

🔲 🎆 NIGHTLIFE AND FESTIVALS

Don't let Durham's historic majesty fool you: in the evening a rollicking crowd of students and locals enlivens the scene. After-hours entertainment is closely tied to university life, and when students depart for the holidays, most nightlife follows suit. The intersection of **Elvet Bridge** and **Saddler Street,** right in the city center, is a good place to be at 10pm. A young crowd fills the popular **Varsity** pub, 46 Saddler St. *(☎384 6704. Open M-Sa 11am-11pm, Su noon-10:30pm.)* Serving a mostly local crowd, the sporty riverside **Coach and Eight,** Bridge House, Framwellgate Bridge, is enormous and has a giant-screen TV to match. *(☎386 3284. Discotheque W and F-Su. Open M-Sa 11am-1am, Su 11am-midnight.)* **Colpitts,** Colpitts Terr., is well suited to live music and offers a more low-key setting. *(☎386 9913. M Irish night, Th folk, and weekend open mics. Open M-Sa noon-11pm, Su noon-10:30pm.)*

The TIC stocks the free pamphlet *What's On,* a great source of information on festivals and local events. Durham holds its **Summer Festival** in the first weekend of July, showcasing folk music, craftsmaking, and other amusements, including a town crier competition *(☎384 3720).* Other major events include the June **Durham Regatta,** England's foremost amateur rowing competition since 1834.

🔁 DAYTRIP FROM DURHAM

BEAMISH OPEN AIR MUSEUM. Perhaps the region's most popular attraction outside of Durham, Beamish is a re-creation of 18th- and early 19th-century life in North England. It features period villages with costumed actors, a farmhouse, a manor house, and an 1825 replica railway. One highlight is the tour into the depths of a former **drift mine.** There's quite a lot to see; plan on spending about four hours in the summer and two in the winter—some attractions only operate in high season. *(8 mi. northwest of Durham on the A693. Go-Northern bus #720 travels from Durham to the museum gates (30min., every hr.). ☎370 4000. Open daily Apr.-Oct. 10am-5pm; Nov.-Mar. Tu-Th and Sa-Su 10am-4pm, last admission 3pm. Closed late Dec. £14, seniors £11, children £7; all visitors £5 in winter.)*

BARNARD CASTLE ☎01833

Twenty miles southwest of Durham along the River Tees, Barnard Castle—the name of both a peaceful market town and its Norman ruins—is the best base for exploring the castles of Teesdale and the peaks of the North Pennine Hills as well as a surprising collection of European masters at the impressive Bowes Museum.

🔁 TRANSPORTATION AND PRACTICAL INFORMATION. To reach Barnard Castle from Durham, take **Go-Northern** bus #723 to Darlington (50min., 2 per hr., £2.60), and then change to **Arriva** bus #75 to Barnard Castle (40min., 2-3 per hr., £3). Just down the road from the main bus stop lies the well-stocked **Tourist Information Centre,** Woodleigh, Flatts Rd. *(☎690 909. Open daily Apr.-Oct. 9:30am-5:30pm;*

Nov.-Mar. M-Sa 11am-4pm.) Other services include: **banks** on Market Pl.; the **police** station, Harmire Rd. (☎637 328); and the **post office**, 2 Galgate, with a **bureau de change** (☎638 247; open M-Sa 9am-5:30pm). **Post Code:** DL12 8BE.

📠🛏 **ACCOMMODATIONS AND FOOD.** Barnard Castle has no hostel, but is blessed with superb **B&Bs**, many of which line Galgate. **Marwood House ❸**, 98 Galgate, offers satellite TV, an exercise room, and a sauna. (☎637 493. From £25. Ensuite £28-30.) Right across the street, **The Homelands ❸**, 85 Galgate, is another excellent choice with more upscale rooms and a lovely rear garden. (☎638 757. Singles £27, with bath £35; doubles with bath £55.) The **Hayloft**, 27 Horsemarket, is an eclectic indoor market jammed with antiques and bric-a-brac, a cafe, and produce. (Open W, F, Sa 11am-5:30pm.) **Stables Restaurant ❶**, in the Hayloft, satisfies with sandwiches and salads (£3), along with other meals for under £4. (☎690 670. Open daily 9am-4:30pm. Cash only.)

🔲 **SIGHTS.** Perched above the River Tees, the remains of **Barnard Castle** sprawl across six acres, including a well-preserved inner keep. (☎638 212. Entrance between the TIC and small church. Open daily Apr.-Sept. 10am-6pm; Oct. 10am-4pm; Nov.-Mar. M and Th-Su 10am-4pm. £3, concessions £2.30, children £1.50. Free audio tour.) Along Newgate, the remarkable ◪**Bowes Museum** was built in the 19th century by John and Josephine Bowes to bring continental culture to England. The gallery now houses the couple's extensive and often curious private collection. Among its many treasures are the largest gathering of Spanish paintings in Britain—El Greco's magnificent Tears of St. Peter among them—and a life-size mechanized silver swan (activated every day at 12:30 and 3:30pm) fancied by Mark Twain. (☎690 606; www.bowesmuseum.org.uk. Open daily 11am-5pm. Tours May-Aug. Tu-Th 2 per day, Sa-Su 1 per day. £6, concessions £5, families £15. Under 16 free.) Dickens fans can follow the **Dickens Drive**, a 25 mi. route that traces the path the famed author took in 1838 while researching for Nicholas Nickleby. Pick up *In the Footsteps of Charles Dickens*, free from the TIC. Overlooking the River Tees, the ruins of 12th-century **Egglestone Abbey,** are a pleasant 3 mi. circular walk along the river to the southeast of town. Arriva bus #79 from Barnard Castle will also drop you there. (Open dawn-dusk. Free.)

Northeast of Barnard Castle on the A688, **Raby Castle** (RAY-bee) is an imposing 14th-century palatial fortress with a deer park. Take Arriva bus #75 (20min., 2 per hr., £1.50) toward Darlington. (☎660 202. Castle open June-Aug. M-F and Su 1-5pm; May and Sept. W and Su 1-5pm. Park and gardens open same days 11am-5:30pm. £7, concessions £6, children £3. Park and gardens only £4, concessions £3.50.)

TYNE AND WEAR

NEWCASTLE-UPON-TYNE ☎0191

The largest city in the northeast, Newcastle (pop. 278,000) has all but shed its image as a faded capital of industry. Although it has rarely been first on tourist itineraries, it's increasingly worth a look: ambitious building efforts—from a restoration of the central historical district to a world-class music hall and an impressive museum of modern art—have lent the city energy and even occasional beauty. Things heat up at night, when locals, students, and tourists throng to Newcastle's (in)famous pubs and clubs. Best of all, perhaps, are the people: Newcastle Geordies are proud of their accent, very proud of their football club, and very, very proud of their brown ale.

▢ TRANSPORTATION

Newcastle is the last English stronghold before the Scottish border. The city lies 1½hr. north of York on the A19 and 1½hr. east of Carlisle on the A69. Edinburgh is straight up the coast along the A1, or through pastures and mountains via the A68.

Trains: Central Station, Neville St. Travel center sells same-day tickets daily 4:25am-9:20pm and advance tickets M-F 7am-7:50pm, Sa 7am-6:50pm, Su 8:40am-7:50pm. Trains (☎08457 484 950) from: **Carlisle** (1½hr., frequent, £11.10); **Durham** (15min., 4 per hr., £4.30); **Edinburgh** (1½hr., frequent, £36); **London King's Cross** (3½hr., every hr., £83).

Buses: St. James Station, St. James Blvd., serves **National Express** (☎08705 808 080) buses from **Edinburgh** (3hr., 4 per day, £13.50) and **London** (7hr., 4 per day, £24). **Haymarket Station,** by the Metro stop, and **Eldon Square Station,** Percy St., are the gateways for local and regional service by **Arriva** (☎261 1779). Ticket office open M-F 7am-5pm, Sa 9am-4pm.

Ferries: International Ferry Terminal, Royal Quays., 7 mi. east of Newcastle. **Fjord Line** (☎296 1313; www.fjordline.no) and **DFDS Seaways** (☎08750 333 000; www.dfds-seaways.co.uk) offer ferry service to **Norway, Sweden,** and the **Netherlands** (see **By Ferry,** p. 29). Bus #327 serves all departures, leaving Central Station and stopping at YHA Newcastle 2½hr. and 1¼hr. before each sailing. Take the Metro to Percy Main, walk 20min. to the quay, or catch a cab (£12).

Public Transportation: Call **Traveline** (☎0870 608 2608) for complete details. The **Metro** subway system runs from the city center to the coast and the airport, as well as to neighboring towns like Gateshead and Sunderland, with only a few strategically located stops in the city center. Tickets are purchased beforehand and checked on board. (Single journeys from 50p). The **DaySaver** allows 1 day of unlimited travel (£3.20). First train around 6am; last around 11:30pm. Local **buses** stop throughout the city, but main terminals are near Haymarket Metro and the Eldon Square Shopping Centre. A **Day Rover,** available at TICs and Metro and bus offices, offers unlimited travel on all Tyne & Wear public transport (£4).

Taxis: Easy to find in the city center and around the train and bus stations, especially plentiful around clubs and bars at night after the metro stops running. **ABC Taxi** (☎232 3636) and **Biker Taxi** (☎276 1192) are two options.

▣ ORIENTATION

The free, full-color map of Newcastle available at the TIC is essential—streets often change direction and name, especially near the river. **Grey's Monument** is the center of the city and useful for orientation. Dedicated to Charles, Earl of Grey, the man responsible for the 1832 Reform Bill and for mixing bergamot into Britain's tea, this 80 ft. stone pillar in **Monument Mall** lies directly opposite **Eldon Square.** The main shopping drag along **Northumberland Street** is nearby. The city of **Gateshead** sits across the Tyne (rhymes with "mine") from Newcastle, and is home to many of the area's attractions.

▤ PRACTICAL INFORMATION

Tourist Information Centre: Newcastle Information Centre, Central Arcade, 132 Grainger St. (☎277 8000). Books rooms for a 10% deposit. Open M-F 9:30am-5:30pm, Sa 9am-5:30 pm; June-Sept. also Su 10am-4pm. **Branch** at Central Station. Open M-F 9:30am-5pm, Sa 9am-5pm.

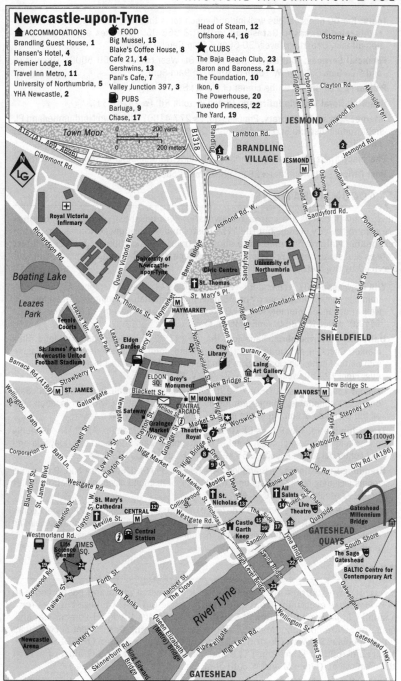

Newcastle-upon-Tyne

ACCOMMODATIONS
Brandling Guest House, 1
Hansen's Hotel, 4
Premier Lodge, 18
Travel Inn Metro, 11
University of Northumbria, 5
YHA Newcastle, 2

FOOD
Big Mussel, 15
Blake's Coffee House, 8
Cafe 21, 14
Gershwins, 13
Pani's Cafe, 7
Valley Junction 397, 3

PUBS
Barluga, 9
Chase, 17

Head of Steam, 12
Offshore 44, 16

CLUBS
The Baja Beach Club, 23
Baron and Baroness, 21
The Foundation, 10
Ikon, 6
The Powerhouse, 20
Tuxedo Princess, 22
The Yard, 19

NORTHEAST ENGLAND

Tours: The TIC offers various walking and coach tours that run June-Sept. £2-6.50. **City-sightseeing Newcastle Gateshead** (☎01708 866 000) operates a popular hop-on, hop-off tour. Departures every 30-60min. from Central Station.

Financial Services: Halifax, 11 New Bridge St. West (☎0870 600 5000). Open M-Tu and F-Sa 9am-5:30pm, W 10am-5:30pm, Th 9am-8pm.

Police: (☎214 6555), at the corner of Market St. and Pilgrim St.

Hospital: Royal Victoria Infirmary, Queen Victoria Rd. (☎232 5131).

Internet Access: City Library, Princess Sq. (☎277 4100), just down Northumberland Pl. from Northumberland St. Free. 2hr. max. Open M-Th 9am-8pm, F and Sa 9am-5pm, Su noon-4pm.

Pharmacy: There are numerous pharmacies along Northumberland St. near the library.

Post Office: 9 Clayton Rd. (☎281 3882), **Post Code:** NE2 4RP.

▐ ACCOMMODATIONS

Inexpensive lodgings are scarce in Newcastle; it's advisable to call ahead. Pickings are slim in the city center, but the YHA hostel and several guest houses are within reasonable walking distance (or a short Metro ride). The biggest cluster of guest houses and small hotels is in residential **Jesmond,** one mile from the city center and serviced by the Metro.

YHA Newcastle, 107 Jesmond Rd. (☎0870 770 5972). Metro: Jesmond. A 20min. walk from city center. Friendly staff and 58 beds in a comfortable townhouse. Often full; call well in advance. Internet access. Curfew 11pm. Open mid-Jan. to mid-Dec. Dorms £11.80, under 18 £8.50. AmEx/MC/V. ❷

University of Northumbria, Sandyford Rd., (☎227 3215, www.unn.ac.uk). Metro: Haymarket. Check in at Claude Gibb Hall. Standard dorm bed-basin-desk combos, some with partial kitchen, in close proximity to the city center. Breakfast included. Open June-Aug. From £22.50; weekends £28.50. MC/V. ❸

Premier Lodge, Quayside (☎0870 990 6530). Metro: Central. This value hotel chain promises comfortable, nondescript rooms with an unbeatable city-center location near all the Quayside action. All rooms ensuite. £56. AmEx/MC/V. ❸

Travel Inn Metro, City Rd. (☎0870 238 3318). Metro: Manors. Another reasonably priced and fairly central chain hotel, a few minutes' walk from both the Quayside and city center. All rooms ensuite. £55 M-Th; £53 F-Sun. AmEx/MC/V. ❸

Brandling Guest House, 4 Brandling Park (☎281 3175). Metro: Jesmond. 9 spacious rooms including family options on a quiet block of Jesmond close to the Metro. Singles from £27; doubles £42. MC/V. ❸

Hansen's Hotel, 131 Sandyford Rd. (☎281 0289; hansen.bookings@btconnect.com). Metro: Jesmond. A 15min. walk from the city center. Small hotel with underwhelming decor but good group rates (discounts for four or more). Internet access. Singles £24; doubles £46. AmEx/MC/V. ❸

◖ FOOD

Every other restaurant in Newcastle has inexpensive pizza and pasta; those in between serve everything from tandoori to veggie burgers. Chinese eateries form a small Chinatown along **Stowell Street** near St. James Blvd.; all-you-can-eat specials under £6 are common. Many of the restaurants lining **Dean Street** serve cheap lunch specials. **Safeway,** Clayton St., is located in the city center. (☎261 2805. Open M-Sa 8am-7pm, Su 11am-5pm.) The **Grainger Indoor Market** is on Grainger St., near the monument. (Open M and W 8am-5pm, Tu and Th-Su 8am-5:30pm.)

NORTHEAST ENGLAND

Bridge St., displays a diverse collection, including a striking array of watercolors and sculpture as well as original pieces by pre-Raphaelite masters. The galleries also host frequent exhibitions, recently featuring the works of Monet, Rembrandt and El Greco. (☎232 7734. Open M-Sa 10am-5pm, Su 2-5pm. Free.)

Newcastle has spearheaded its recent urban renewal with major projects showcasing science, technology, and the arts. The **Life Science Centre,** Times Sq., on Scotswood Rd. by the train station, is a family-friendly hands-on science museum with a motion simulator and 3D movies. (☎243 8210; www.lifesciencecenter.org.uk. Open M-Sa 10am-6pm, Su 11am-6pm; last admission 4pm. £7, concessions £5.50, children £4.50.) Newcastle's recent cultural renaissance manifests itself most clearly, however, along the **Gateshead Quays,** the site of major new development in the city. The **Gateshead Millennium Bridge** is the only rotating bridge in the world, opening like a giant eyelid to allow ships to pass. The bridge is lit by alternating colored spotlights each evening. Best reached by the bridge, the ▧**BALTIC Centre for Contemporary Art,** housed in a completely renovated mid-century grain warehouse, is the largest center for contemporary visual art outside London, with over a square mile of exhibition space. (☎478 1810; www.balticmill.com Open M-W and F-Sa 10am-7pm, Th 10am-10pm, Su 10am-5pm. Free.) Nearby, the organically shaped steel and glass curves of **The Sage Gateshead** are still under construction and set to open in late 2004/early 2005. Once completed, this massive world-class concert hall will provide a permanent home for Northern Sinfonia, the Northumberland regional orchestra, and Folkworks, an agency dedicated to promoting traditional music. Heading south from Newcastle by rail or road, you can't miss the ponderous **Angel of the North,** 5 mi. from the city off the A1. Admired by an estimated 33 million people per year, the striking two hundred-ton steel sculpture is 66 ft. tall and wider than a jumbo jet.

📽 🎵 NIGHTLIFE AND ENTERTAINMENT

Home of the nectar known as brown ale, Newcastle's party scene is legendary throughout Britain. Over a dozen clubs and countless pubs are all packed within about a mile radius. Rowdy Geordie havens line **Bigg Market,** which features one of England's highest concentrations of bars. Be cautious in this area—stocky footballer Paul "Gazza" Gascoigne was beaten up twice here for deserting Newcastle. Beside the river, **Quayside** (KEY-side) attracts a slightly younger crowd and is home to some of the city's most packed clubs. (Note that some Quayside establishments are across the river, in neighboring Gateshead.) For a less heart-stopping, bass-thumping night out, **Osborne Road,** in Jesmond, 1 mi. north of the city center, is increasingly popular with students and locals for traditional bar-hopping. The vibrant gay and lesbian scene centers around **Times Square** in the city's southwest. *The Crack* (monthly; free at record stores) is the best source for music and club listings in Newcastle. No matter what your plans, be sure to finish the night Newcastle-style with a kebab and extra chili sauce.

PUBS

Pubs are generally open Monday to Saturday 11am-11pm and Sunday noon-10:30pm; some are only open evenings. Most offer happy hours until 8pm.

    Chase, 10-15 Sandhill (☎245 0055), Quayside. Neon lights and a fluorescent bar give this hopping pub a trendy rep. The outdoor garden is the place to see and be seen.

    Head of Steam, 2 Neville St. (☎232 4379). Across from Central Station. This split-level venue features the best in live soul, funk, and reggae with packed shows most nights. Local DJs also change things up, going head to head in special mixing contests.

Blake's Coffee House, 53 Grey St. (☎261 5463). A popular, central hangout, with a range of lunch fare (£4-5) and good sandwiches (£2-3). Open M-F 7am-5:30pm, Sa-Su 7am-4pm. Cash only. ❶

Pani's Cafe, 61 High Bridge St. (☎232 4366. www.pani.net). Italian eatery steps from Grey St. with £7-10 dishes and lively music. Open M-Sa 10am-10pm. Cash only. ❷

Valley Junction 397, Archbold Terr. (☎281 6397), in the old station near the Jesmond Metro terminal. Bengali-influenced cuisine served in an antique railway car. The Indian lager Kingfisher (£3.25) blends well with spinach-based paneers (£6-7). Vegan fare available. Open Tu-Sa noon-2pm and 6-11:30pm, Su 6-11:30pm. MC/V. ❷

Big Mussel, 15 The Side, Quayside (☎232 1057; www.bigmussel.co.uk). This busy, 2-level dining room and bar dishes out "casual style and serious seafood." Nice dinners around £10, with £5 lunch specials and early-bird deals. Open M-F noon-2:30pm and 5:30-10:15pm, Sa noon-10pm, Su 5:30pm-10pm. MC/V. ❸

Gershwins, 54 Dean St. (☎261 8100; www.gershwinsrestaurant.co.uk). Cool underground grotto restaurant with faux overhead star lighting. Runs special theater menus and serves continental cuisine with a few notable exceptions (like seared ostrich) for a great price. Full meals run £7-11. Reservations on theater nights. Open M-F noon-2:30 and 5:30pm-11pm, Sa noon-11pm. MC/V. ❸

Cafe 21, 19-21 Queens St. (☎222 0755). Perhaps Newcastle's finest restaurant, serving French cuisine (try the cheddar cheese and spinach soufflé) in an elegant setting near the river. 3-course dinner with wine £27. Reservations requested. Open M-Sa noon-2:30pm, 6-10:30pm. AmEx/MC/V. ❺

👁 SIGHTS

The largely intact **Castle Garth Keep,** at the foot of St. Nicholas St., is all that remains of the 12th-century New Castle. It was constructed on the site of an earlier castle built in 1080 by Robert Curthose, bastard son of William the Conqueror. Oddly enough, the "New Castle" from which the city derives its name is the older Curthose structure. (☎232 7938. Open daily Apr.-Sept. 9:30am-5:30pm; Oct.-Mar. 9:30am-4:30pm. £1.50, concessions 50p.) Just uphill at the corner of Mosley St., the **Cathedral Church of St. Nicholas** is topped with an elegant set of small towers around a double arch, meant to resemble Jesus's crown of thorns. (Open M-F 7am-6pm, Sa 8am-4pm, Su 7am-noon and 4-7pm. Free.) The **Laing Art Gallery,** New

THE LOCA

THE GE

What exactly is
die)? Anyone bo
of Northumberla
Tyne and Wear c
status. But poss
Northerners are c
its origins are d
of the following e

During the Ja
of 1745, Newc
supported King (
ing Hanoverian
deemed "for Gec
bites. In 1815,
son, renowned
inventor of the
tive, invented th
which quickly ga
Northumberla
lamps, and even
became known
1826, Stephens
the Parliamenta
Railways, and hi
the snooty so
began to call all
coal to the Tham

Countless so
als on Geordie c
undecipherabl
proper English. I
die remark "Ah w
telling you "I enjo
singular dialect
mask such poli
however. "Ootsic
translated, "Let u
ter in a civilized
man, like gent
Geordie slang m
accurate sentime

NORTHEAST ENGLAND

Offshore 44, 40 Sandhill (☎261 0921), Quayside. Bearing an uncanny resemblance to a pirate's lair, this riverside pub blasts rock classics amidst treasure chests, candles, and palm trees. Packed by 10pm and popular with the student crowd.

Barluga, 35 Grey St. (☎230 2306). A posh pub with serious class, perfect for an afternoon cocktail or a pre-theater swig.

CLUBS

Opening hours and special events vary with season. Clubs are 18+ unless noted, and most expect sharp streetwear.

Tuxedo Princess, Hillgate Quay (☎477 8899), Gateshead. Perhaps the city's hottest dance club, located on a decommissioned ship under Tyne Bridge and complete with a rotating dance floor. Call for tickets in advance to avoid a ridiculous wait at the door. Cover £4-10. Open M and Th-Sa 8pm-2am.

The Foundation, 57 Melbourne St. (☎261 8985). With a dark and smoky interior, this gutted factory warehouse attracts a flashy crowd. Sa night "Shindig" attracts the country's top DJs. Cover £8-10. Open M and Th 10pm-2, F and Sa 9pm-4am, Su 10pm-3am.

Ikon, 49 New Bridge St. (☎261 2526). Lined with bars, this dance club produces a surging sea of humanity on a nightly basis. Cover £3-7. Open M and W-Sa 10pm-2am.

The Baja Beach Club, Pipewellgate (☎477 6205), Gateshead. Churning out hip-hop hits and pop anthems, this club maintains a huge following thanks in large part to its bikini-clad staff. Cover £2-6. Open M-Sa 9pm-2:15am.

GAY AND LESBIAN NIGHTLIFE

The Powerhouse, Times Sq. (☎261 9755). The only exclusively gay club in all of Northeast England. Ultra-chic black decor. The Purple Lounge upstairs ideal for checking out the talent below. Cover varies (around £5) depending on live acts or theme nights. Open M-F 10:30pm-3am, Sa 10am-4am, Su 10:30am-1am.

Baron and Baroness, Times Sq. (☎233 0414). Rustic wood decor contrasts with its neighbors. 2 levels are filled with alcoves ideal for withdrawing from the crowd. Open M-W noon-11pm, Th and Su noon-midnight, F-Sa 11am-1am. No cover.

The Yard, 2 Scotswood Rd. (☎232 2037). An attractive 2-level bar that eschews the clubby atmosphere of its neighbors, featuring uproarious drag shows Su-M. Open M-Th 1pm-1am, F-Sa noon-1:30am, Su 1pm-12:30am. Cover varies by night.

THEATER

For more refined entertainment, treat yourself to an evening at the lush gilt-and-velvet **Theatre Royal,** 100 Grey St. (☎0870 905 5060; www.theatreroyal.co.uk. Booking office open M-Tu and Th-Sa 9am-8pm, W 10am-8pm) Undoubtedly northern England's premier stage, **The Royal Shakespeare Company** makes a month-long stop at the Theatre Royal each fall, complementing the top-notch array of musicals and other contemporary works. **Live Theatre,** 27 Broad Chare, Quayside, emphasizes local writers and new talent with a dance, music, or theatrical performance almost every night. (☎232 1232; www.live.org.uk. Booking office open M-F 10am-6pm and Sa-Su 2hr. before shows.)

SPORTING EVENTS

St. James' Park, home of the **Newcastle United Football Club,** is a prominent feature of the city skyline (and testament to how seriously the Geordies take their football). Tickets can be hard to come by, but it's worth a shot. (☎201 8400, ticket office ☎261 1571; www.nufc.co.uk.) The **Newcastle Racecourse** in the enormous High Gosforth Park holds a number of top horse-racing events each year and makes for a great day at the track. (☎236 2020.)

NORTHEAST ENGLAND

HADRIAN'S WALL

When Emperor Hadrian ordered that a wall be built in AD 122 to define and guard one of Rome's farthest borders, he was no doubt thinking of what those uncouth blue-tattooed warriors to the north might get up to in the civilized world. Hadrian's unease created a permanent monument on the Roman frontier—first a V-shaped ditch 27 ft. wide, then a stone barrier 15 ft. high and 8-9 ft. thick. Eight years, 17 milecastles (forts), 5500 cavalrymen, and 13,000 infantrymen later, Hadrian's Wall stretched unbroken for 73 mi. from beyond modern-day Carlisle to Newcastle. The years have not been kind, however, to the emperor's massive undertaking. Most of the stones have been carted off and recycled into surrounding structures, and the portions of wall that do remain stand at only half their original height. The highest concentration of ruins is along the western part of the wall, at the southern edge of Northumberland National Park (p. 438).

■ **TRANSPORTATION.** Traveling by car is definitely the best way to see the wall; failing that, **buses** are available. **Stagecoach in Cumbria** sends the **Hadrian's Wall Bus,** a.k.a. #AD122 (who knew public transport had a sense of humor?) from **Carlisle** to **Hexham,** stopping at all the wall's major sights and even offering a guided commentary. (2¼hr., June to mid-Sept. 6 per day, 70p-£4.30; guides July-Aug. Su and M, 3 per day). One daily bus extends to **Newcastle.** Bus #685 runs year-round between **Newcastle** and **Carlisle** via **Hexham, Haltwhistle, Greenhead,** and other wall towns (2hr.; M-Sa 12 per day, Su 4 per day). A **Hadrian's Wall Bus Day Rover ticket,** available from TICs or bus drivers, is a good idea for those planning to make several stops in one day (£6, children £4, families £12). Another option is the **Hadrian's Wall Rail Rover,** a 2-out-of-3-day ticket valid between Sunderland and Carlisle on the Tyne Valley train line and the Tyne & Wear Metro (£12.50, children £6.25).

Trains (☎ 08457 484 950) run frequently between **Carlisle** and **Newcastle,** but stations all lie at least 1½-4 mi. from the wall; be prepared to hike to the nearest stones. Trains depart about every hour and stop at: **Brampton,** 2 mi. from Lanercost and 5 mi. from Birdoswald; **Haltwhistle,** 2 mi. from Cawfields; **Bardon Mill,** 2 mi. from Vindolanda and 4½ mi. from Housesteads; **Hexham** and **Corbridge.**

Make sure to pick up the free and invaluable *Hadrian's Wall Bus and Summer Days Out* brochure. Available at any area TIC or bus, it has timetables and information on accessing the wall using all forms of transportation.

■ **ORIENTATION AND PRACTICAL INFORMATION.** Hadrian's Wall runs 73 mi. between Carlisle to the west and Newcastle to the east, spanning Cumbria, Northumberland, and Tyne and Wear. The towns of **Greenhead, Haltwhistle, Once Brewed, Bardon Mill, Haydon Bridge, Hexham** (the hub of Wall transportation), and **Corbridge** lie somewhat parallel to the wall from west to east. For general information, check the **Hadrian's Wall Information Line** (☎ 01434 322 002; www.hadrianswall.org). Useful publications and accommodation bookings are available at the Hexham **Tourist Information Centre,** at the bottom of the hill across from the abbey on Hallgate Rd. (p. 437), and the **National Park Information Centre** in Once Brewed, on Military Rd. (☎ 01434 344 396 or 344 777. Open daily June-Aug. 9:30am-5:30pm; Apr.-May and Sept.-Oct. 9:30am-5pm; Nov.-Mar Sa-Su 10am-3pm.)

■ **ACCOMMODATIONS.** Both Carlisle and Hexham have a number of B&Bs and make good bases for daytrips to the wall. Other towns near the wall, such as Corbridge and Haltwhistle, also have accommodations. Two hostels lie along the Hadrian's Wall Bus route. **YHA Greenhead ❶,** 16 mi. east of Carlisle, resides in a converted chapel a short walk from the wall. (☎ 0870 770 5842. Lockout 10am-5pm. Open Easter-Oct. Dorms £10.60, under 18 £7.20. MC/V.) **YHA Once Brewed ❷,** Military Rd., Bardon Mill, has a central location—2½ mi. northwest of the Bardon Mill train station, 3 mi. from Housesteads Fort, 1 mi. from Vindolanda, and ½ mi. from the wall itself. (☎0870 770 5980. Laundry. Internet access. Lockout 10am-2pm. Open Apr.-Oct. Dorms £11.80, under 18 £8.50. MC/V.) The isolated **Hadrian Lodge ❷** makes a good base for serious walkers; take a train to Haydon Bridge, then follow the main road uphill for 2½ mi. (☎01434 684 867. Kitchen and laundry. Book in advance. Dorms £15; singles £39.50; doubles £59. AmEx/MC/V.)

◙ **SIGHTS.** All sights listed below are accessible by the Hadrian's Wall Bus. If you have limited money or time, be sure to visit ⊠**Housesteads,** the most complete Roman fort in Britain, 5 mi. northeast of Bardon Mill on the B6318. A half-mile from the road, the well-preserved ruins are set high on a ridge and adjoin one of the best sections of the wall. (☎01434 344 363. Open daily Apr.-Sept. 10am-6pm; Oct.-Mar. 10am-4pm. £3.50, concessions £2.60, children £1.80, families £7.80.) Milecastles and bridges dot the area between Greenhead and **Birdoswald Roman Fort.** The fort itself, 15 mi. east of Carlisle, is the site of recent excavations, and offers views of wall, turret, and milecastle. The interactive **Visitors Centre** introduces the wall and traces Birdoswald's 2000-year history. (☎016977 476 02. Open daily Mar.-Oct. 10am-5:30pm. Museum and wall £3, concessions £2.50, children £1.75, families £7.75.) Constructed of stones "borrowed" from the wall, the **Roman Army Museum** sits at Carvoran, ¾ mi. northeast of Greenhead. It presents impressive stockpiles of artifacts, interactive stations, and a faux Roman Army recruiting video. (☎01697 747 485. Open daily Apr.-Oct. 10am-5:30pm; Feb.-Mar. and Nov. 10am-4pm. £3.30, concessions £2.90, children £2.20; discount with Vindolanda.) **Vindolanda,** 1½ mi. north of Bardon Mill and 1 mi. southeast of Once Brewed, is a fort and civilian settlement predating the wall. Ongoing excavations have revealed hundreds of inscribed wooden tablets that illuminate many details of Roman life. (☎01434 344 277. Same hours as Army Museum. £4.50, concessions £3.80, children £2.90, families £13.) Dramatically situated on the cliffs of Maryport next to the fort, the **Senhouse** museum houses Britain's oldest antiquarian collection, with exhibits on Roman religion and warfare. (☎01900 816 168. Open daily July-Oct. 10am-5pm; Nov.-Mar. F-Su 10:30am-4pm; Apr.-June Tu and Th-Su 10am-5pm. £2.50, children 75p.) From Chollerford, 3 mi. north of Hexham, Britain's best-preserved cavalry fort, **Chesters,** can be reached by a footpath leading ¼ mi. west. The extensive remains of a bath house spot the fort's riverside setting; a museum houses altars and sculptures from the wall. (☎01434 681 379. Open daily Apr.-Sept. 9:30am-6pm; Oct.-Mar. 10am-4pm. £3.50, concessions £2.60, children £1.80.)

In 2003 the **Hadrian's Wall National Trail** was opened, providing a continuous route right along the wall great for long treks and day walks. Alternatively, the recently opened **Hadrian's Cycleway** provides two-wheeled access to all the wall's main attractions without following the actual course of the wall.

HEXHAM   ☎01434

West of Newcastle on the A69, the town of Hexham makes a fine base for exploring Hadrian's Wall, but also has its own sights. The cobbled town center coils around the impressive **Hexham Abbey.** Founded by St. Wilfrid in 637, the Abbey was the first to follow the rule of St. Benedict in England. (☎602 031. Open daily May-Sept. 9:30am-7pm; Oct.-Apr. 9:30am-5pm. Free guided tours June-Sept. Su, Tu, Th 2pm. Suggested donation £2.) Facing the abbey, the substantial 14th-century **Gatehouse Tower** recalls Hexham's turbulent past. More tangible evidence of these troubles can be found in the 14th-century dungeon of the **Border History Museum,** behind Market Pl. (☎652 349. Expected to reopen in 2005.)

Hexham's **train station** is a 10min. walk from the Abbey and the center of town (see **Transportation,** p. 436). The **Tourist Information Centre** stands between the train station and town center, in the carpark facing Safeway. (☎652 220. Open May-Sept. M-Sa 9am-6pm, Su 10am-5pm; Oct.-Apr. M-Sa 9am-5pm.) Other services include: the **police,** Shaftoe Leagues (☎604 111); **General Hospital,** Corbridge Rd. (☎655 655); free **Internet access** at the **library,** Beaumont St., inside Queens Hall (☎652 488; open M and F 9:30am-7:30pm, Tu and W 9:30am-5pm, Sa 9:30am-12:30pm); **banks** along Priestpopple Rd.; **bike rental,** 16-17 St. Mary's Chase (☎601032; £15 per day; open M-Sa 10am-5pm; MC/V); and the **post office,** Priestpopple Rd., in Robbs of Hexham department store (☎602 001; open M-Tu, Th, and Sa 8:30am-5:30pm, W 9am-5:30pm, F 8:30am-6pm). **Post Code:** NE46 1NA.

Allow Patricia and Stuart to welcome you to **West Close House ❸,** Hextol Terr., off Allendale Rd., where little touches like homemade jam complement friendly service, lovely rooms, and a well-tended garden. (☎603 307. From £20 per person. Cash only.) Or try the equally friendly **Laburnum House ❷,** 23 Leazes Crescent, with spacious rooms about 10 minutes from the center of town. (☎601 828. From £18 per person. Cash only). The **YHA Acomb ❶,** 2 mi. from Hexham, tucks backpackers into a converted stable. Take bus #880, 881, or 882 from the Hexham railway station. (☎0870 770 5664. Open Apr.-June and Sept.-Oct. W-Su; daily July-Aug.; Jan.-Mar. F-Sa. Dorms £8.20, under 18 £5.70. Cash only.)

NORTHUMBERLAND

NORTHUMBERLAND NATIONAL PARK

Northumberland National Park's 400 mi.^{2} stretch south from the Cheviot Hills to Hadrian's Wall, marking the site of many skirmishes involving territorial Romans. Great coniferous forests, heathered moorland, grassy hills, and wet bogs all cover this idyllic region. Though visitors are guaranteed some struggle with its public transport network, this least-populated and roughest-edged of England's national parks is blissfully free from tourist legions. You can experience this park with a sense of genuine isolation, often with only a shepherd and his flock in sight.

▐ TRANSPORTATION

Public transportation is limited and requires planning. Bus routes radiate outward from Berwick upon Tweed in the north, and Newcastle in the south. Getting to the area by bus is tricky; getting around the area by bus is nearly impossible. **Bus** #880 runs from **Hexham** to **Bellingham** (45min.; M-Sa 10 per day, Su 3 per day). Bus #416/516 runs from Newcastle to Rothbury via Morpeth (1¼hr.; M-Sa 7 per day, Su 3 per day) and bus #508 goes via Belsay (1½hr., Su only, 2 per day). Change at Morpeth if traveling to Rothbury from **Alnwick.** From **Wooler,** bus #470/473 heads to **Alnwick** (50min., M-Sa 14 per day, Su 2 per day.) and #267/464 to **Berwick** (1hr.; M-Sa 10 per day, Su 3 per day). Bus #710 connects **Wooler** with **Newcastle** and the **Scottish Borders** (W and Sa 1 per day). **National Express's** Newcastle-Jedburgh-Edinburgh bus cuts through the park and stops at **Byrness** (#383; 1 per day). Bus #714 travels from **Gateshead** (across the river from Newcastle) via **Bellingham** to **Kielder/Kielder Water** (2hr.; June-Oct. Su 1 per day). Year-round, **Postbus** #815 journeys from **Hexham** to **Kielder** via **Bellingham** (2½hr., M-Sa 2 per day), while regular bus #814 travels from **Bellingham** to **Kielder** (during school terms M-F 5 per day; school holidays Tu and F 3 per day). For schedules, call **Traveline** (☎ 0870 608 2608), grab the extremely helpful 256-page *Northumberland Public Transport Guide* (£1.20), or opt for the more manageable (and free) *Experience Northumberland by Bus*, available at TICs and bus stations. Though not valid on every service in the area, a single-day **Northeast Explorer** ticket (£6, children £5, families £12), available on participating buses, will save you money for anything more than a single round trip.

ORIENTATION AND PRACTICAL INFORMATION

The park runs from **Hadrian's Wall** (p. 436) in the south up along the Scottish border as far north as the Cheviot foothills. **Bellingham, Rothbury,** and **Wooler** are small towns near the park's eastern edge which offer accommodations and good access to walking routes. In the southwest, just outside the park, the large reservoir of **Kielder Water** is surrounded by England's largest pine forest (the **Kielder Forest**) and is popular for a variety of outdoor pursuits. The A69 moves along the park's southern border while the A68 cuts right through its heart toward Scotland. The Ministry of Defense operates a **Live Firing Range** in the middle of the park south of the Cheviot Hills; walkers should heed the warning signs.

Northumberland National Park operates three **National Park Information Centres (NPICs)** which can advise on hikes and activities and make accommodation bookings. Throughout the warmer months, they often offer ranger-led talks and walks. There are also several **Tourist Information Centres** in the area.

National Park Information Centres:

Ingram: Visitor Centre (☎01665 578 248). Open daily June-Aug. 10am-6pm; Apr.-May and Sept.-Oct. 10am-5pm.

Once Brewed: for Hadrian's Wall; see p. 436.

Rothbury: Church St. (☎01669 620 887). Open daily June-Aug. 10am-6pm; Apr.-May and Sept.-Oct. 10am-5pm; Jan.-Mar. Sa-Su 10am-3pm.

Tourist Information Centres:

Bellingham: Main St. (☎01434 220 616). Open Easter-Oct. M-Sa 9:30am-1pm and 2pm-5:30pm, Su 1-5pm; Nov.-Easter M-F 2-5pm.

Kielder Forest: Visitor Centre (☎01434 250 209), off the C200 in Kielder Castle. Open daily Apr.-Oct. 10am-5pm; Nov.-Dec. F-Sa 11am-4pm.

Tower Knowe (Kielder): Visitor Centre (☎01434 240 436), off the C200. Open daily Apr.-Oct. 10am-6pm, Nov.-Mar. Sa-Su 10am-4pm.

Wooler: Cheviot Centre, 12 Padgepool Pl. (☎01668 282 123). Open Apr.-Oct. M-Sa 10am-5pm, Su 10am-4pm; Nov.-Mar. Sa-Su 10am-4pm.

ACCOMMODATIONS

Bellingham, Rothbury, Wooler, and Kielder Water have **B&Bs** and **hotels.** The following **YHA hostels** offer accommodations in or near the park and accept MC/V.

Bellingham: Woodburn Rd. (☎0870 770 5694). Self-catering cedar cabin along the Pennine Way. Reception from 5pm. Open daily July-Aug.; Apr.-June and Sept.-Oct. Tu-Sa. Dorms £9.30, under 18 £6.50. ●

Byrness: 7 Otterburn Green (☎0870 770 5740). National Express bus #383 (Newcastle-Edinburgh via Jedburgh) will stop here. Basic, self-catering hostel along the Pennine Way. Reception from 5pm. Open Apr.-Sept. Dorms £8.20, under 18 £5.70. ●

Kielder: Butteryhaugh, Kielder Village (☎0870 770 5898), off the C200. Spacious, modern facility. Open daily Apr.-Oct. Dorms £11.80, under 18 £8.50. ●

Wooler: 30 Cheviot St. (☎0870 770 6100). A 5min. walk up Cheviot St. from the bus station. Comfortable hostel with laundry facilities and self-catering kitchen. Reception from 5pm. Open Apr.-Oct. Dorms £10.60, under 18 £7.20. ●

NORTHEAST ENGLAND

◪ HIKING

The **Pennine Way** (p. 396) traverses the park, entering along Hadrian's Wall and passing through Bellingham and the Cheviot Hills before terminating at Kirk Yetholm, Scotland. Another long-distance route crossing the very top of the park is **St. Cuthbert's Way,** which runs through the Cheviot Hills and Wooler on its way between Melrose, Scotland, and Holy Island. Shorter options abound and some good possibilities include walks in the **Simonside Hills,** near Rothbury, and the **Cheviot foothills,** near Wooler. Ordnance Survey produces two Explorer maps, which together cover the entire park and are available at local NPICs and TICs (£13). Among the extensive literature on the park, *Walking the Cheviots* (£8) is one recommended title. The area's isolation is a good reason to walk here, but it's also a good reason to be prepared—maps and proper equipment are essential (see **Wilderness Safety,** p. 52). NPICs and TICs can provide hiking suggestions.

BELLINGHAM AND KIELDER WATER ☎ 01434

With an attractive rural backdrop, modest Bellingham (BELL-in-jum) is a convenient gateway. The Pennine Way passes through; one fine section heads 18 mi. south to Once Brewed, along Hadrian's Wall. Also leaving from town is the easy 3 mi. round-trip walk to **Hareshaw Linn,** a beautiful waterfall in a rocky gorge that has attracted picnickers since Victorian times. Guides (20p) are available at the **TIC** on Main St. (p. 439). In town, the 12th-century **Church of St. Cuthbert** has a rare stone-vaulted roof—so that raiding Border Reivers couldn't burn it down.

Another 10 mi. beyond Bellingham and just outside the park lies **Kielder Water,** a man-made reservoir begun in 1974 that today provides Northeast England with much of its drinking water. Two visitors centers, **Tower Knowe** and **Kielder Castle,** serve the area and are joined by the C200 that runs along the reservoir's western shore. The densely packed **Kielder Forest** surrounds the water and promises great hiking and cycling along its many timber hauling roads, including the popular 26 mi. **Kielder Water Circuit. Kielder Bikes,** just past Kielder Castle, provides good advice on the extensive network of on- and off-road routes. (☎ 250 392. Open daily, daylight hours. Bikes £17.50 per day, £9 for 2 hr.) The **Kielder Water Ferry** *Osprey* departs from Tower Knowe and tours the reservoir, also stopping at the Leaplish Waterside Park. (☎ 250 312. 1¼hr. Apr.-Oct. 5 per day. £5.25, children £3.) The **Hawkhirst Adventure Camp** (☎ 250 217) rents a variety of crafts, although terms and availability vary significantly, so call ahead. The reservoir also offers great trout **fishing** from spots along its shore; be sure to consult the *Northumbrian Water's Angling Guide,* available at TICs, for rules and regulations.

Bellingham and Kielder Water each have YHA hostels (p. 439). The friendly and all-ensuite **Lyndale Guest House ❸,** West View, also boasts a jacuzzi. (☎ 220 361. Singles £25; doubles £50. MC/V.) A number of B&Bs also reside in Kielder Village and Falstone Village—at the northern and southern tips of the water respectively. At the Leaplish Waterside Park the **Reiver's Rest ❶** offers clean dorms and private lodging beside the C200. (☎ 250 312. Dorms £12; doubles £24. Cash only.)

ROTHBURY ☎ 01669

Rothbury, a market town along the River Coquet, is a popular starting point for excursions into the nearby **Simonside Hills.** Rothbury's **NPIC** (p. 439) gives advice on local trails. Among them, the **Sacred Mountain Walk** (9 mi.) rewards those who complete its strenuous climb with some of the finest views in the park. Another popular choice, the **Rothbury Terraces** (2 mi.) follows an old carriage path and passes near **Cragside,** the 19th-century creation of the first Lord Armstrong. (¾ mi. For detailed information on both walks and many others, pick up the free *Roth-*

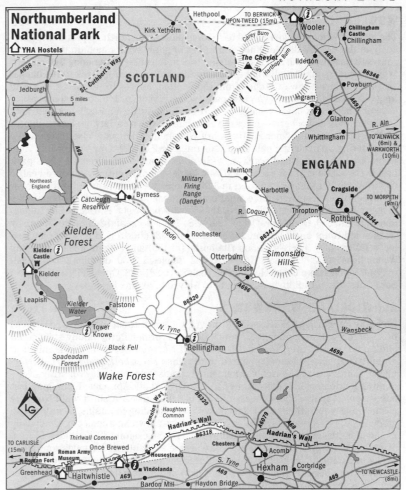

Northumberland National Park. YHA Hostels

bury and Coquetdale: Northumberland National Park at the NPIC.) 1 mi. north of Rothbury on the B6341, Cragside was one of the most advanced houses of its day, with luxuries like electric lighting (powered by its own hydroelectric generator) and a house-wide heating system. The interior is particularly well-preserved, with costumed National Trust guides. (☎ 620 150. Open Apr.-Oct. House open daily 1-5:30pm; last admission 4:30pm. Estate open 10:30am-7pm; last admission 5pm. House and estate £8, children £4. Estate only £5.50/£2.50. June-Oct., bus #508 connects Newcastle and Cragside via Rothbury (5min., Su 2 per day, 70p). Among the **B&Bs** clustered on Rothbury's **High Street** is the **Orchard Guest House ❸**. (☎ 620 684; www.orchardguesthouse.co.uk. Singles from £40; doubles from £58. AmEx/MC/V.) Alternatively, **Katerina's Guest House ❸** has four-post, quilt-covered beds. (☎ 620 691. Doubles from £56. Cash only.) For nourishment, the **Northeastern Coop,** High St., sells **groceries.** (☎ 620 456. Open daily 8am-10pm.) Internet access at **Rothbury Computers,** Town Foot. (☎ 620 070. £2 per 30 min. M-F 9am-5pm, Sa 10am-4pm.)

WOOLER ☎01668

The town of Wooler makes a good base for exploring the northern part of the park, such as the nearby **Cheviot Hills.** A number of short walks include the popular routes to **Humbleton Hill** and a self-guided trail to the ancient **Yeavering Bell** hillfort. More ambitious hikers will want to take on the challenging 7 mi. trek to **The Cheviot** (2674 ft.), whose view stretches from the Scottish border to the North Sea. The long-distance **St. Cuthbert's Way** also pays Wooler a visit (p. 440). 6 mi. southeast of Wooler, **Chillingham Castle** once played host to King Edward I. English eccentricity is now on full display here—the castle is crammed with a variety of bizarre objects collected by current owner Sir Humphry Wakefield. The castle also offers a few self-catering apartments; call ahead for rates. (☎215 359. Open daily July-Aug. noon-5pm; May-June and Sept. M, W-Su noon-5pm. £6, children £3.) In a park beside the castle graze the sixty-odd **Wild Cattle,** the only entirely purebred cattle in the world. Originally enclosed in 1235, the cattle have been inbred for over seven centuries. They resemble other cows, but cannot be herded, are potentially dangerous, and may even kill one of their own if he or she is touched by human hands. (☎215 250. Open Apr.-Oct. M and W-Sa 10am-noon and 2-5pm, Su 2-5pm; by warden-led tours only. 1-1½hr. £4, concessions £3, children £1.50.) Wooler also has a **TIC** (p. 439). There's a good **YHA hostel** (p. 439) and several **B&Bs,** including **Winton House** ❸, 39 Glendale Rd. (☎281 362. Singles £27-30; doubles £40-46. Cash only.) A **Northeastern Coop** is located on High St. (☎281 528. Open daily 8am-10pm.) **Bus** #470 stops in Chillingham en route to Alnwick (20min., 5 per day).

ALNWICK AND WARKWORTH ☎01665

About 31 mi. north of Newcastle off the A1, the small town of **Alnwick** (AHN-ick) bows before the magnificent ◪**Alnwick Castle,** a former Percy family stronghold and now home to the Duke and Duchess of Northumberland. The manicured grounds and stately home appeared in the films *Elizabeth* and *Harry Potter.* Inside, tour some of the richly ornamented rooms, which display an array of the family's heirlooms and artwork. (☎510 777. Open daily Apr.-Oct. 11am-5pm; last admission 4:15pm. £7.50, concessions £7, under 16 free.) A short walk from the castle brings you to the **Alnwick Garden,** with its cascading fountains, beautiful rose gardens and ivy-enclosed walks. (☎511 350; www.alnwickgarden.com. Open daily in summer 10am-6pm; in winter 10am-4pm. £4, concessions £3.75, under 16 free. Joint tickets for both the Castle and Gardens are available. £10, concessions £9.)

The **bus station** is at 10 Clayport St. Buses #505/515/525 connect Alnwick with **Berwick** (1hr.; M-Sa 10 per day, Su 5 per day) and **Newcastle** (1¼hr.; M-Sa 12 per day., Su 8 per day). The **Tourist Information Centre** is at 2 The Shambles, Market Pl. (☎510 665. Open July-Aug. M-Sa 9am-5pm, Su 10am-4pm; reduced hours during off season.) Along Bondgate Without (yes, that's a street name), **Barter Books,** housed in a disused Victorian railway station, provides **Internet access,** but the secondhand bookshop alone is worth visiting. (☎604 888. £1.50 per 15min. Open daily 9am-7pm. Internet access £2 per 30min.) **Bikes** are available for rent at **Alnwick Cycles,** 24 Narrowgate (☎606 738; www.alnwickcycles.co.uk. Open M-Sa 10am-5pm, Su 12:30-4pm. £15 per day, £8 per half-day). The **post office** is at 19 Market St. (☎602 141. Open M-Sa 8:30am-5:30pm.) **Post Code:** NE66 1SS.

Stay with Mrs. Givens and her affectionate mutt at **The Tea Pot** ❸, 8 Bondgate Without. (☎604 473. £20-22 per person, no singles; £1 off with *Let's Go.* Cash only.) Next door at the **Lindisfarne B&B** ❸, 6 Bondgate Without, you'll get just as warm a welcome. (☎603 430. From £20 per person. Cash only.) Grab a quick meal across from the bus station at **The Grapevine** ❶, 1 Market Sq., which offers toasted paninis from £3. (☎604 872. Open M-Sa 8:30am-10pm, Su 10am-5pm.)

Seven miles southeast of Alnwick, the evocative ruins of 12th-century **Warkworth Castle** guard the mouth of the River Coquet. Another Percy bastion, a carving of the family's lion crest still watches over the site where Shakespeare set much of *Henry IV.* (☎711 423. Open daily Apr.-Sept. 10am-6pm; Oct. 10am-4pm; Nov.-Mar. Sa-M 10am-4pm. £3, concessions £2.30, children £1.50.) Carved from the Coquet cliffs, the 14th-century **hermitage** lies a short walk down along the river; the castle staff will ferry you over and a fleet of rowboats is available for rental. (Open Apr.-Sept. W, Su 11am-5pm. £2, concessions £1-1.50.) **Buses** #420, 422, and 518 make frequent trips between Alnwick and Warkworth (25min.).

BERWICK-UPON-TWEED ☎01289

Just south of the Scottish border, Berwick-upon-Tweed (BARE-ick) has changed hands more often than any town in Britain—13 times between 1296 and 1482 alone. The town's history of strife has helped propagate the local legend that Berwick is still at war with Russia: Queen Victoria used her full title in the 1854 declaration of war, "Queen of Great Britain, Ireland, Berwick-upon-Tweed, and the British dominions beyond the sea," but neglected to include Berwick in the peace treaty. Most of the original **Berwick Castle** is buried beneath the train station, although some of the 13th-century fortress still stands beside the river. The town's most substantial sight is the tongue-twisting **Berwick Barracks**, at the corner of Parade and Ravensdowne, which contains the worthwhile **regimental museum** of the King's Own Scottish Borderers. (☎304 493. Open daily Apr.-Sept. 10am-6pm, Oct. 10am-4pm; Nov.-Mar. Th-M 10am-4pm; £3, concessions £2.30, children £1.50.)

Berwick Backpackers ❶, 56-58 Bridge St., is a comfy 6-bed hostel in the middle of town. (☎331 481. Reception 11am-6pm. Dorms from £10; singles £14; ensuite doubles £30. Cash only.) For **B&Bs,** a good choice is the luxurious **Clovelly House ❸**, 58 West St., right in the town center. (☎302 337. £22-28 per person. Cash only.) Friendly **Four North Road ❸,** 4 North Rd., just left up the road a few minutes from the train station is a good option. (☎306 146. From £20 per person. Cash only.) Stock up on foodstuffs at **Somerfield,** Castlegate. (☎308 911. Open M-Sa 8am-8pm, Su 10am-4pm). **Cafe 52 ❷**, 52 Bridge St., serves both lunch (veggie sandwiches £5) and dinner (main dishes £9) and is highly recommended by locals. (☎306 796. Open M-Su 10am-4:30pm and 6:30-10:30pm. Serves food until 9pm. Cash only.)

Berwick is a good transport hub. The **train station** (open M-Sa 6:30am-7:50pm, Su 10:15am-7:30pm) has frequent **rail** service from **Edinburgh** (45min.), **London King's Cross** (4hr.), and **Newcastle** (50min.). From the train station, it's a 5min. walk down Castlegate to the town center. Most **buses** stop at the train station and at the corner of Castlegate and Marygate, at **Golden Square.** Bus #505/515/525 travels from **Newcastle** (2¼hr.; M-Sa 6 per day, Su 5 per day) via **Alnwick** (1hr.). For the Scottish Borders, take bus #23 to **Kelso** (1 hr.; M-Sa 5 per day, Su 3 per day) or #60 to **Galashiels** (1¾hr.; M-F 7 per day, Sa-Su 5 per day) via **Melrose** (1½hr.). The **Tourist Information Centre,** 106 Marygate, books rooms for a 10% deposit. (☎330 733. Open June-Sept. M-Sa 10am-6pm, Su 11am-3pm; Oct.-May M-Sa 10am-3pm, Su 11am-3pm.) Get free **Internet access** at the Berwick **Library,** Walkergate. (☎334 051. Open M and Tu 10am-5:30pm, W and F 10am-7pm, Sa 9:30am-12:30pm.) **Tweed Cycles,** 17a Bridge St., provides **bike rental** and good trail advice. (☎331 476. £12 per day. Open M-Sa 9am-5:30pm.). Across the street from the TIC is the **post office,** 103 Marygate. (☎307 596. Open M-Sa 9am-5:30pm.) **Post Code:** TD15 1BH.

HOLY ISLAND AND BAMBURGH CASTLE ☎01289

10 mi. from Berwick-upon-Tweed, wind-swept ▧**Holy Island,** at low tide connected to the mainland by a causeway, rises just off the coast. Seven years after Northumberland's King Edwin converted to Christianity in AD 627, the missionary Aidan

arrived from the Scottish island of Iona to found England's first monastery. While his wooden structure is long gone, the sandstone ruins of the later **Lindisfarne Priory** still stand in the island's tiny village. (☎389 200. Open daily Apr.-Sept. 10am-6pm; Daily Oct., Feb.-Mar. 10am-4pm; Nov.-Jan. Sa-Su 10am-4pm. £3.50, concessions £2.60, children £1.80.) The hill beyond the priory provides a good view of the remains and will save you a few quid. Tiny **Saint Cuthbert's Island,** marked by a wooden cross 220 yd. off the coast of the priory, is where the famed hermit-saint took refuge when even the monastery proved too distracting. Also on the island, **Lindisfarne Castle** is a 16th-century fort that sits dramatically atop a hill, with a crowded and less inspiring interior of 19th-century furnishings. (☎389 244. Open Apr.-Oct. M-Th and Sa-Su 10:30am-4:30pm, possibly 1½hr. earlier or later depending on tides. £5, children £2.10.) Paths lead beyond the castle and snake along the island's North Sea shore. After returning to the village, try the blend of fermented honey and white wine known as **Lindisfarne Mead,** a syrupy sweet concoction brewed since ancient times. Crossing the 4 mi. seaweed-strewn causeway is possible only at low tide; check the tide tables at a TIC before you go. Irregular bus #477 runs from Berwick to Holy Island (daily in Aug.; Sept.-July some W and Sa). Jim of **Jim's Taxis** can drive you over the causeway before the tide sweeps in. (☎302 814, or mobile ☎07977 143 530. £30 round-trip.) If the waves trap you, the island does have a few accommodations, but they fill up quickly. **The Bungalow ❸,** Chaire Ends, is your best bet, offering real comfort. (☎389 308. Doubles £60. MC/V.)

    Bamburgh Castle, a stunning Northumbrian landmark, straddles a rocky outcropping 25 mi. south of Berwick. The castle's renovation began in the 1890s when it was acquired by the first Baron Armstrong, whose family still resides in its sumptuous interior. The public tour offers a look at one of the largest armories outside London and the ornate, vaulted ceilings of the **King's Hall.** Below the castle and beyond the dunes, sandy beaches make for excellent walks with views of the castle. (☎01668 214 515. Open daily Apr.-Oct. 11am-5pm; last admission 4:30pm. £5, concessions £3.50, children £2.) Reach Bamburgh by **bus** (#411 from Berwick, 45 min.; M-Sa 8 per day, Su 4 per day). Holy Island and Bamburgh Castle can be seen in a single day, though the tides can make scheduling tight.

WALES (CYMRU)

Known to early Anglo-Saxon settlers as foreigners ("waleas") but self-identified compatriots ("cymry"), the people of Wales have always had a fraught relationship with their neighbors to the east. Though inhabitants of the same isle, if many of the nearly 3 million Welsh people had their druthers, they would be floating miles away. Wales clings steadfastly to its Celtic heritage, and the Welsh language endures in conversation, commerce, and literature. As coal, steel, and slate mines fell victim to Britain's faltering economy, Wales turned its economic focus from heavy industry to tourism. Travelers today are lured by miles of dramatic beaches, cliffs, mountains, and brooding castles, remnants of the long battle with England. Against this striking backdrop, the Welsh express their nationalism peacefully in the voting booths and in celebrations of their distinctive culture and language.

TRANSPORTATION

GETTING THERE

Most travelers reach Wales through London. **Flights** to Cardiff International Airport originate within the UK and from a few European destinations. **British Airways** (☎08457 733 377; www.ba.com) flies to Cardiff from Aberdeen and Dublin; the new airline **Air Wales** (UK ☎01792 200 250, Ireland ☎800 665 193; www.airwales.co.uk) connects Cardiff to London, Dublin, Swansea, Plymouth, Newcastle, Jersey, and Amsterdam. **Ferries** criss-cross the Irish Sea, shuttling travelers between Ireland and the docks of Holyhead, Pembroke, Fishguard, and Swansea (see **By Ferry,** p. 38). Frequent **trains** (as often as half-hourly) leave London for the 2hr. trip to Cardiff; call **National Rail** (☎08457 484 950; www.nationalrail.co.uk) or **Arriva Wales** (☎0845 6061 660; www.arrivatrainswales.co.uk) for schedules and prices. **National Express buses** (☎08705 808 080; www.nationalexpress.co.uk) are the slightly slower, cheaper way to get to Wales: a trip from London to Cardiff takes just over 3hr. and costs £15-25.

GETTING AROUND

BY TRAIN

BritRail (US ☎877-677-1066; www.britrail.net) passes are accepted on all trains, except narrow-gauge railways, throughout Wales. The **Freedom of Wales Flexipass,** which allows a certain amount of rail travel as well as daily bus travel for the duration of the pass (4 days in 8 of rail adult £49, child £32; 8 days in 15 of rail £82/£54), is valid on the entire rail network and for most major buses. Pass holders also receive discounts on some narrow-gauge trains, bus tours, and tourist attractions. Call **National Rail** (☎08457 484 950) for information. **Narrow-gauge railways** tend to be tourist attractions rather than actual means of transport, but trainspotters can purchase a **Great Little Trains of Wales Rover** ticket (9 consecutive days on all narrow-gauge railways £55, children £15; ☎01286 870 549; www.greatlittletrainsofwales.co.uk).

BY BUS

The overlapping routes of Wales's numerous bus operators are difficult to navigate. Most are local services; almost every region is dominated by one or two companies. **Cardiff Bus** (☎0870 608 2608; www.cardiffbus.com) blankets the area

WALES

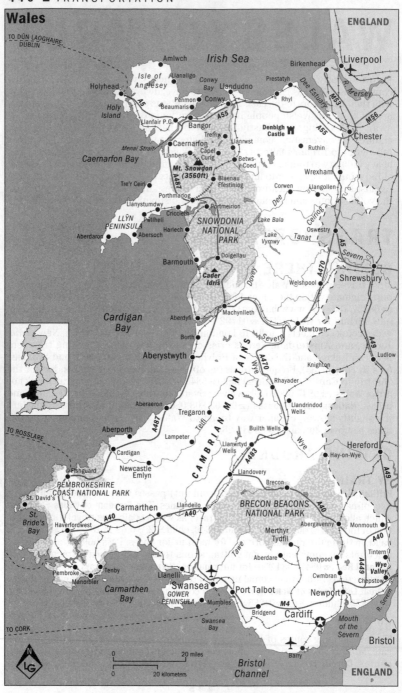

Wales

around the capital. **TrawsCambria** #701, the main north-south bus route, runs from Cardiff and Swansea to Machynlleth, Bangor, and Llandudno. **Stagecoach** (☎0870 608 2608; www.stagecoachbus.com) buses serve routes from Gloucester and Hereford in England west through the Wye Valley, past Abergavenny and Brecon. **First Cymru** (☎0179 258 2233; www.firstgroup.com/ukbus/wales/swwales/home) covers the Gower peninsula and the rest of southwest Wales, including Pembrokeshire Coast National Park. **Arriva Cymru** (☎01492 592 111; www.arriva.co.uk) provides service throughout most of North Wales. Regional public transport guides, available free at Tourist Information Centres (TICs), exist for many areas, but for some you'll have to consult an array of small brochures. The very useful *Wales Bus, Rail, and Tourist Map and Guide* provides information on routes, but not timetables. **Local buses often don't run on Sunday;** some special tourist buses, however, run *only* on summer Sundays. Bus schedules and prices commonly change twice a year, and four changes in a year aren't unusual—confirm in advance to avoid surprises. As always, **Traveline** has the most updated bus information (☎0870 608 2608; www.traveline-cymru.org.uk).

BY FOOT, BICYCLE, AND THUMB

Wales has numerous beautiful and well-marked footpaths and cycling trails; the **Offa's Dyke Path** (p. 462) and the **Pembrokeshire Coast Path** (p. 462) are particularly popular. The **Wales Tourist Board** (☎0871 211 251; www.visitwales.com) maintains the websites **Walking Wales** (www.walking.visitwales.com) and **Cycling Wales** (www.cycling.visitwales.com), provides links to tour operators and other useful sites, and publishes print guides of the same names. The **Countryside Council for Wales** (☎01248 385 500; www.ccw.gov.uk) may also be helpful. *Let's Go* does not recommend **hitchhiking**, but many people choose this form of transport, especially in the summer and in cases of bungled bus schedules.

LIFE AND TIMES

HISTORY

CELTS, ROMANS, AND NORMANS. As the western terminus of many waves of emigration, Wales has been influenced by a wide array of peoples since prehistoric times. Stone, Bronze, and Iron Age inhabitants left their mark on the Welsh landscape in the form of stone villages, earth-covered forts, *cromlechs* (standing stones also known as menhirs and dolmens), and partially subterranean burial chambers. It is the early **Celts,** however, who make Wales most distinct from her neighbors today. The 4th and 3rd centuries BC witnessed two waves of Celtic immigration, the first from northern Europe and the second from the Iberian peninsula. By the time the **Romans** arrived in AD 50, the Celts had consolidated into four main tribes, with links to each other and to Celts in Ireland and Brittany. By AD 59, the Romans had invaded and established a fortress at Segontium (present-day **Caernarfon,** p. 508), across the Menai Straits from **Ynys Môn** (**Isle of Anglesey,** p. 518), the center of druidic, bardic, and warrior life in northern Wales. Although the Romans achieved a symbolic conquest, wily Celtic resistance compelled them to station two of their four legions in Britain along the modern-day Welsh border.

When the Romans departed from Britannia in the early 5th century AD, they left not only towns, amphitheaters, roads, and mines, but also the Latin language and the seeds of Christianity, both of which heavily influenced the development of Welsh scholarship and society. For the next 700 years, the Celts ruled themselves, doing their best to hold invading Saxons, Irish, and Vikings at bay, their efforts per-

IN RECENT NEWS

A QUEEN'S BEST FRIENDS

Everybody's heard of Queen Elizabeth II, but precious few know the entire royal family. Emma, Linnet, Rush, Minnie, Monty, Willow and Holly often go unnoticed, but they regularly shadow the Queen, keeping her company (even on her honeymoon), and scampering through her palaces.

They are the Queen's Welsh corgis—squat dogs with short legs, bobbed tails, perky ears and endearing dispositions. These efficient herders, with origins in South Wales, have long been employed in those hilly environs to round up cattle and sheep. According to legend, however, these dogs had more noble beginnings; ancient woodland fairies supposedly trained corgis (whose name comes from the Welsh "cor" and "ci"—dwarf and dog, respectively) to pull their magical coaches. The history of this royal breed may go back further than the Queen (and even the woodland sprites). In April 2004, a team of Cardiff University researchers unearthed what appeared to be the leg bone of a corgi-like canine on a crannog—a man-made islet—in Llangorse Lake, the hub of the 9th-century Welsh kingdom of Brycheiniog. The Welsh Corgi Club is collaborating with the archaeologists to verify the finding. Regardless of their conclusions, this breed is sure to maintain its royal status in the hearts of British islanders.

haps spearheaded by the legendary **King Arthur.** They were not, in the end, successful; in the 8th century, Anglo-Saxon **King Offa** and his troops pushed what Celts remained in England into Wales and other corners of the island (including Cornwall and Scotland). To make sure they stayed put, Offa built **Offa's Dyke,** a 150 mi. earthwork that marked the first official border between England and Wales and still roughly delineates this line (p. 462). Though Wales consisted of Celtic kingdoms united by language, customary law, a kinship-based social system, and an aristocracy, the kingdoms did not achieve political unity until the time of **Llywelyn ap Gruffydd** in the 13th century, the only Welsh ruler recognized by the English as the Prince of Wales. After his death in 1282, Wales fell to the English.

THE ENGLISH CONQUEST. Within 50 years of William the Conqueror's invasion of England, a quarter of Wales had been subjugated by the **Normans.** The newcomers built a series of castles and market towns, established the feudal system, and introduced a variety of Continental monastic orders. The English **Plantagenet Kings** invaded Wales throughout the 12th century, and in 1282 a soldier of **Edward I** killed Prince Llywelyn ap Gruffydd, ending what was left of Welsh independence. Edward, through sheer trickery, had his son appointed "Prince of Wales," and in 1284 dubbed the Welsh English subjects. To keep these perennially unruly "subjects" in check, Edward constructed a series of massive castles at strategic spots throughout Wales. The magnificent surviving fortresses at **Conwy** (p. 523), **Caernarfon** (p. 508), **Caerphilly** (p. 461), **Harlech** (p. 501), and **Beaumaris** (p. 520) stand as a testament to his efforts.

In the early 15th century, the bold insurgent warfare of **Owain Glyndŵr** (Owen Glendower) temporarily freed Wales from English rule. Reigniting Welsh nationalism and rousing his compatriots to arms, Glyndŵr and his followers captured the castles at Conwy and Harlech, threatened the stronghold of Caernarfon, and convened a national parliament at Machynlleth. With his actions, Glyndŵr created the ideal of a **unified Wales** that has captured the country's collective imagination ever since. Unfortunately, poverty, war, and the plague were ravaging the country, and, despite support from Ireland, Scotland, and France, the rebellion was soon reduced to a series of guerrilla raids. By 1417 Glyndŵr had disappeared into the mountains, leaving only legend to guide his people. Wales placed her hope in Welshborn **Henry VII,** who emerged victorious from the Wars of the Roses and ascended the English throne in 1485 (p. 72), but the Tudors kept none of their campaign promises.

The 1536 **Act of Union** granted the Welsh the same rights as English citizens and returned the administration of Wales to the local gentry, symbolizing full integration with England. The act officially "united and annexed" the country while it secured parliamentary representation. In 1543 **The Courts of Great Session** were established, ruling the land as the high court until 1830. Increased equality came at the price of increased assimilation, and English quickly became the language of the courts, government, and gentry in Wales.

Throughout the 17th century the consolidation of land into large **gentry estates** stratified Welsh society and demonstrated the difficulty of sustaining the booming population on the land. Though certain prominent noblemen supported the parliamentary cause, many Welsh harbored sympathy for the monarchy at the onset of the Civil War. Religious pockets of resistance also grew in response to the efforts of Puritan missionaries; Nonconformists, Baptists, and Quakers all gained footholds during this period.

METHODISM AND THE INDUSTRIAL REVOLUTION. Profound religious shifts changed Welsh society in the 18th and 19th centuries. As the church became more anglicized and tithes grew more burdensome, the Welsh were ripe for the appeal of new Protestant sects. The **Methodist revolution** claimed 80% of the population by 1851. Life centered on the chapel, where people created tight local communities through shared religion, heritage, and language. **Chapel life** remains one of the most distinctive features of Welsh society; the Sabbath closure of stores in parts of Wales (particularly in the north) is but one lasting effect.

The 19th century brought the **Industrial Revolution** to the Isles, and industrialists sought to exploit coal veins in the south and iron and slate deposits in the north of Wales. New roads, canals, and most importantly, **steam railways**, were built to transport these raw materials, and the Welsh population grew from 450,000 to 1.2 million between 1750 and 1851. Especially in the south, soft, pastoral landscapes were transformed into grim mining wastelands, and the workers who braved these dangerous workplaces faced taxing labor, poverty, and despair. Early attempts at unionism failed, and workers turned to violence in order to improve conditions. The discontent was channeled into the **Chartist Movement,** which demanded political representation for all male members of society; its high point was an uprising in Newport in 1839. Welsh society became characterized by two forces: a strongly **leftist political consciousness**—aided by the rise of organized labor—and large-scale **emigration.** Welsh miners and religious groups replanted themselves in America (particularly in Pennsylvania), and in 1865 a group founded **Y Wladfa** (The Colony) in the Patagonia region of Argentina. Rural society was hardly more idyllic, and tenant farmers led the **Rebecca Riots** from 1839 to 1843. Attempts to secure an independent autonomy reached a peak in the Home Rule movement of 1886-1896 but fizzled out due to internal dissent.

The strength of the Liberal Party in Wales bolstered the career of **David Lloyd George,** who rose from being a homegrown rabble-rouser to Britain's Prime Minister (1916-22). But by 1922, the Labour Party had become dominant in industrial communities. Numerous Welshmen went to fight **World War I;** over 35,000 never returned. This enormous loss was compounded by continued emigration and the **economic depression** of the 1930s, resulting in further dissatisfaction.

WALES TODAY

Long home to a distinct culture and a distinct people, Wales now faces the challenges and opportunities of a distinct political entity attached to the one that subjugated it for centuries. The wobbly Welsh **economy** resists any sort of quick fix; the coal and steel industries that fashioned the country during the Industrial Revolution have sharply declined in recent decades, inflicting poverty and unemployment

WALES

in Wales more severe than that endured by the rest of Britain. **Economic rebuilding** is particularly difficult for a nation that has never had diversified industries, especially as it seeks to avoid basing its new economy on low-quality, low-paying jobs. A recent upsurge in **tourism** is promising, however, and visitors are discovering a Wales that outshines its grimy, industrial past. **Cardiff** (p. 454), Welsh capital since only 1955, is currently running for European Capital of Culture 2008 in an attempt to reinvent itself as a center of art and refinement.

MODERN POLITICS. Welsh politics in the late 20th century have been characterized by nationalism and a vigorous campaign to retain one of Europe's oldest living languages. The establishment of Welsh language classes, publications, radio stations, and even a Welsh television channel (known as Sianel Pedwar Cymru, "Channel 4 Wales," or S4C for short), indicates the energy invested in Welsh. In 1967, the **Welsh Language Act** established the right to use Welsh in the courts, while the **1988 Education Reform Act** ensured that all children would be introduced to the language of their forebears. Continuing this trend, the **1993 Welsh Language Act** stipulated that Welsh and English should be regarded as equal in public business.

Nationalist movements emerged in other political arenas as well. Although **Plaid Cymru**—the Welsh Nationalist Party founded in 1925—did not capture a parliamentary seat until 1966, it has since repeatedly demonstrated its political potency. In the 1950s, a **Minister for Welsh Affairs** was made part of the national Cabinet, but Tory rule in the 1980s brought the legitimacy of governing from London into question.

On September 18, 1997, the Welsh voted in favor of **devolution,** but unlike their Scottish counterparts, support for the idea was tepid, with only 50.3% voting "yes" despite major governmental backing. This was still enough to lead to elections for the 60-seat **Welsh Assembly** (held in May 1999), a parliamentary body that now controls Wales's budget. A meager 46% voter turnout saw Labour take home a 28-seat plurality, and Plaid Cymru doing unexpectedly well winning 17 seats in the 1999 elections. But as devolution begins to give the Welsh a taste of their long-sought self-governance, greater independence from Westminster is impeded by the intimate bonds between the two nations: unlike Scotland, Wales shares its educational and legal system with England.

CULTURE AND CUSTOMS

Though Cardiff's cosmopolitan bustle rivals that of other major international cities, the real Wales comes through in its rural towns and villages, where pleasantries are exchanged across garden hedges, locals swap gossip over post office counters, and a visitor can expect to remain anonymous for all of about three minutes. Welsh **friendliness** and **hospitality** seem unfailing; long conversations and cheerful attention tend to be the rule more than the exception. The **Welsh language** (see below) is an increasingly important part of everyday life, and visitors can expect to find road signs, pamphlets, and timetables written both in English and in Welsh. **Nationalism** runs deep in Wales and may surface at unexpected moments: above all, avoid the supreme *faux pas* of calling a Welshman "English" or his country "England."

Wales has long been a country defined by its customs, and **folk culture** has always been at its core. Chances to partake in the distinctly and uniquely Welsh— witnessing an **eisteddfod** (p. 453), listening to a traditional male choir, or tasting homemade baked goods—should not be passed up. Welsh national symbols are the **red dragon,** the **leek,** and the **daffodil. St. David's Day,** the observance of Wales's patron saint, is celebrated March 1 and is one opportunity to see the Welsh **national costume**—a long red cloak and tall black hat. **All Hallow's Eve** (Oct. 31) has traditional significance for the Welsh as the start of the Celtic New Year.

WALES

LANGUAGE

Let me not understand you, then; speak it in Welsh.
—William Shakespeare, Henry IV, Part I

Though modern Welsh borrows from English for vocabulary, as a member of the **Celtic family** of languages, *Cymraeg* is based on a grammatical system more closely related to **Cornish** and **Breton**. After a sharp decline since 1900 (when about 50% of the population spoke Welsh), the language is undergoing a powerful resurgence. Today, more than 26% of people speak the country's mother tongue; just over half of those are native speakers. Welsh-speaking communities are especially strong in the north and west.

Though English suffices nearly everywhere in Wales, it's a good idea to familiarize yourself with the language and avoid the laughter of bus drivers when you try to approximate the name of your destination. Welsh shares with German the deep, guttural **ch** heard in "Bach" or "loch." **Ll**—the oddest Welsh consonant—is produced by placing your tongue against the top of your mouth, as if you were going to say "l" and blowing. If this technique proves baffling, try saying "hl" (hlan-GO-hlen for "Llangollen"). **Dd** is said either like the "th" in "there" or the "th" in "think" (hence the county of Gwynedd is pronounced the same way as Gwyneth Paltrow's first name). **C** and **g** are always hard, as in "cat" and "golly." **W** is generally used as a vowel and sounds either like the "oo" in "drool" or "good." **U** is pronounced like the "e" in "he." Tricky **Y** changes its sound with its placement in the word, sounding either like the "u" in "ugly" or the "i" in "ignoramus." **F** is spoken as a "v," as in "vertigo," and **ff** sounds exactly like the English "f." Emphasis nearly always falls on the penultimate syllable, and there are (happily) no silent letters.

Most Welsh place names are derived from prominent features of the landscape. *Afon* means river, *betws* or *llan* church or enclosure, *caer* fort, *llyn* lake, *mynydd* mountain, and *ynys* island. The Welsh call their land *Cymru* (KUM-ree) and themselves *Cymry* ("compatriots"). Because of the Welsh system of letter mutation, many of these words will appear in usage with different initial consonants. *Let's Go* provides a delicious mouthful of **Welsh Words and Phrases** on p. 815.

THE ARTS

LITERATURE

In Wales, as in other Celtic countries, much of the national literature stems from a vibrant **bardic tradition.** The earliest extant poetry in Welsh comes from 6th-century northern England, where the **cynfeirdd** (early poets), including the influential poet **Taliesin,** composed praiseful oral verse for their patron lords. The *Gododdin*, a series of lays attributed to the poet **Aneirin,** is a celebration of valor and heroism from this period. The 9th-11th centuries brought emotional poetic sagas focusing on pseudo-historical figures, including poet **Llywarch Hen, King Arthur,** and **Myrddin (Merlin).** Ushering in the most prolific period in Welsh literature, 12th-century monastic scribes compiled Middle Welsh manuscripts. Most notable is the **Mabinogion,** a collection of eleven prose tales drawing on mythology and heroic legend. In the 14th century, **Dafydd ap Gwilym** developed the flexible poetic form *cywydd*. Often called the greatest Welsh poet, he turned to love and nature as subjects and influenced the work of later poets such as **Dafydd Nanmor** and **Iolo Goch** well through the 17th century. A growing anglicization of the Welsh gentry in the 18th century led to a decline in the tradition of courtly bards. Poets found their venues mainly at *eisteddfodau* and local poetry competitions.

Modern Welsh literature has been influenced by Bishop William Morgan's 1588 **Welsh translation of the Bible,** which helped standardize Welsh and provided the foundation for literacy throughout Wales. A circle of Welsh romantic

WALES

ON THE MENU

WELSH RABBIT

Switzerland has gooey fondue, Italy hot pizza, and Mexico steaming quesadillas, but none of these are quite as delicious as Wales' contribution to the world of cheese. Take a piece of bread, smear it with a thick concoction of beer, mustard, spices, and, of course, cheese, and then melt it all under high heat until brown and bubbly, and you have a traditional Welsh Rabbit.

Erroneously called and spelled "rarebit" by some, this dish's name has a contested etymology. Some claim it was coined by patronizing Englishmen who considered the Welsh so hopeless that they couldn't even catch a hare for supper—and instead were forced to eat bread and cheese. Another story contends that St. Peter lured the Welsh people out of heaven using a "rabbit" of sorts—a bait of roasted cheese ("caws pobi") to get them outside the pearly gates.

But the Welsh aren't the only ones to have such a dish; older cookbooks contain Scottish and even English rabbit recipes. The instructions for these often call for a "salamander," a large iron slab on a stick (it looks much like a pizza peel) that was heated and then rested just inches above the bread as a rudimentary broiler. Now toaster ovens more often do the trick, and rabbit is common throughout Wales in local cafes and vegetarian hangouts.

poets, **Y Beridd Newydd** (the New Poets), including T. Gwynn Jones and W.J. Gruffydd, developed in the 19th century, while the horrors of WWI produced an anti-romantic poetic voice typified in the work of **Hedd Wyn.** The work of 20th-century Welsh writers (in both Welsh and English) features a compelling self-consciousness in addressing questions of identity and national ideals. The incisive poetry of **R.S. Thomas** treads a fine line between a fierce defense of his proud heritage and a bitter rant against its claustrophobic provincialism, while **Kate Roberts's** short stories and novels, such as *Feet in Chains*, dramatize fortitude in the face of dire poverty. The best-known Welsh writer is Swansea's **Dylan Thomas,** whose emotionally powerful poetry, as well as popular works like *A Child's Christmas in Wales* and the radio play *Under Milk Wood*, describe his homeland with nostalgia, humor, and a bit of bitterness. **Roald Dahl** emerged from Cardiff to spin tales of chocolate fantasy for children (and other types of fantasy for adults). Wales's literary heritage is preserved in the **National Library of Wales** in Aberystwyth (p. 495), which receives (by law) a copy of every Welsh-language book published in the UK.

MUSIC

The Welsh word **canu** means both "to sing" and "to recite poetry," suggesting an intimate historical connection between the sung and the spoken word. Though little Welsh music from before the 17th century has survived, three traditional medieval instruments are known: the **harp,** the **pipe** (hornpipe or bagpipe), and the **crwth,** a six-stringed bowed instrument. The indigenous musical tradition began to disappear when England's 16th-century Tudor court incorporated Welsh harpists; traditional playing died out by the 17th century. The 18th-century rise of chapels led to an energetic singing culture, as Welsh folk tunes were adapted to sacred songs and hymn-writers such as **Ann Griffiths** made their mark. Their works, sung in unison in the 18th century, became the basis for the harmonic **choral singing** of the 19th and 20th centuries, now Wales's best-known musical tradition. While many associate the all-male choir with Wales, both single-sex and mixed choirs are an integral part of social life, and choral festivals like the **cymanfa ganu** occur throughout Wales.

Cardiff's **St. David's Hall** regularly hosts both Welsh and international orchestras. The **Welsh National Opera,** featuring renowned tenor **Bryn Terfel,** has established a worldwide reputation. Modern Welsh composers, including **Alun Hoddinott** and **William Mathias,** have won respect in the classical genre. Young soprano **Charlotte Church** earned international attention with her 1998 debut, *Voice of an Angel.* **Rock music** (in both English and Welsh) is the voice of youth, although the most famous Welsh pop music exports are the no-longer-youthful **Tom Jones** and **Shirley Bassey.** Current bands combine Britpop sounds with a (sometimes fierce) nationalism, led by the **Manic Street Preachers.** Other bands with their share of hits include **Catatonia, Stereophonics,** and the **Super Furry Animals.**

FOOD

Traditional Welsh cooking relies heavily on leeks, potatoes, onions, dairy products, lamb (considered the best in the world), pork, fish, and seaweed. Soups and stews are ubiquitous. **Cawl** is a complex broth, generally accompanied by bread. A wide range of dairy products is also produced in Wales, including the soft, white cheese **Caerphilly. Welsh rabbit** (also called "Welsh rarebit;" see p. 33) is buttered toast topped with a thick, cheesy, mustard-beer sauce. Baked goods tempt most visitors—Wales is famed for unique, tasty **breads. Welsh cakes** are buttery, scone-like treats, studded with currants and golden raisins and traditionally cooked on a bakestone or griddle. The adventurous should sample **laverbread,** a cake-like slab made of seaweed, while the sweet-toothed will love **bara brith** (a fruit and nut bread served with butter), and **teisennau hufen** (fluffy doughnut-like cakes filled with whipped cream). **Cwrw** (beer) is another Welsh staple; **Brains S.A.** is the major brewer in Wales and no rugby game is complete without a can.

FESTIVALS

The most significant of Welsh festivals is the **eisteddfod** (ice-TETH-vod), a competition of Welsh literature (chiefly poetry), music, and arts and crafts. Hundreds of local *eisteddfodau* are held in Wales each year, generally lasting one to three days. The most important of these is the **National Eisteddfod** (Eisteddfod Genedlaethol Cymru; see sidebar). The **International Musical Eisteddfod,** held in Llangollen (p. 530) in July and August, draws folk dancers, singers, and choirs from around the world for performances and competitions.

EISTEDDFOD

The **National Eisteddfod of Wales** is an annual gathering of Welsh writers, musicians and artists that dates back to 1176, when Lord Rhys held a bardic tournament (of sorts) in his castle at Cardigan, awarding a seat at his table to the best poet present. The "Chairing Ceremony" continues today, but you won't hear it called that. It goes by Cadeirio, its Welsh name, as does everything at the festival: Welsh is the only language officially used. In an event known as "talwrn y beirdd" (cockpit of the bards), teams of poets are given a few minutes to compose verse within the strict alliterative and metrical parameters of traditional Celtic forms.

When the festival became affiliated with the neo-Druidic Gorsedd of Bards in the 19th century, it took on an even more Celtic flavor. A year-and-a-day before each festival commences, it is 'proclaimed' by an archdruid attended by a herald a harp-player, and a sword bearer. Many stone circles across Wales mark the locations of past festivals. The event itself is nomadic, taking place in a different location each year and alternating between Northern and Southern sites to diffuse regional tensions. In 2005 the National Eisteddfod's "catchment area" will be in northern Gwynedd.

July 30-Aug. 6 in 2005. For more information, check out www.eisteddfod.org.uk.

SOUTH WALES

South Wales is as enchanting to behold as it is difficult to summarize. The scarred mining fields of its central hills, the idyllic pastorals of its river valleys, and the steady grit and hum of its major ports refuse any common denominator. Today the land seems caught between its rural charms and its growing urban savvy, its English influence and its Welsh heritage. The region's tumultuous social legacy complicates the physical grandeur of its landscapes. Its ragged mountains and stunning coastlines have witnessed countless epics of invasion and oppression. As South Wales works to integrate its history into recent modernization, it plays out a newer and more subtle drama: a feat of balance and reinvention.

HIGHLIGHTS OF SOUTH WALES

VALES AND HILLS Hike the Wye Valley for a fine view of **Tintern Abbey** (p. 463) and proceed north to the stark peaks of **Brecon Beacons National Park** (p. 471).

HAY-ON-WYE Browse the shelves of the small-town literary wonderland that boasts the largest secondhand bookstore in the world (p. 465).

COASTAL RESORTS Explore the coastline of **Pembrokeshire National Park** (p. 484), home to the quaint holiday town of **Tenby** (p. 481) and the majestic **Cathedral of St. David's** (p. 489).

COAL MINING HERITAGE Travel to the hills of **Blaenavon** (recently named a World Heritage Site; p. 468) or the **Rhondda Valley** (p. 461) to discover the industry that fueled the modern industrial world.

CARDIFF (CAERDYDD)   ☎029

Cardiff was once dependent on the outflow of coal from its busy port, but the "Come On, Cardiff!" signs that flutter around the city now speak to the vigor of its reinvention. It calls itself "Europe's Youngest Capital," and seems eager to meet the demands of this title, presenting its rich history along with a spruced-up set of modern sensibilities and a brand-new dynamism. Alongside its impressive traditional monuments are landmarks of a rather different tenor: a towering new stadium by the river and a glitzy bayside cluster of cosmopolitan dining and entertainment venues. Cardiff's three newest buildings have been titled with an eye toward the future (the Plaza, the Stadium, and, most recently, the Centre)— one of many efforts to identify the city as on the brink of a new era. At the same time, tradition—made manifest in the Welsh language and the red dragons emblazoned upon flags and store windows—remains as strong as ever.

⬛ TRANSPORTATION

Trains: Central Station, Central Sq., south of the city center, behind the bus station. Ticket office open M-Sa 5:45am-9:30pm, Su 6:45am-9:30pm. Trains (☎08457 484 950) from: **Bath** (1-1½hr., 1-3 per hr., £11.90); **Birmingham** (2hr., 2 per hr., £21.10); **Bristol** (45min., 3 per hr., £7.20); **Edinburgh** (7-7½hr., 3 per day, £85); **London Paddington** (2hr., 2 per hr., £53.50); **Swansea** (1hr., 2 per hr., £8.10).

Buses: Central Station, on Wood St. National Express booking office and travel center. Show up at least 15min. before closing to book a ticket. Open M-Sa 7am-5:45pm, Su 9am-5:45pm. **National Express** (☎08705 808 080) from: **Birmingham** (2½hr., 8 per

South Wales

SOUTH WALES

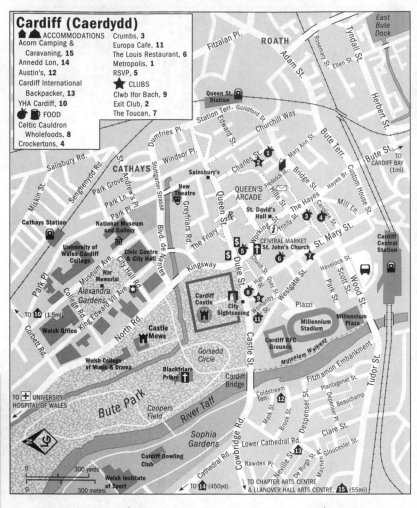

Cardiff (Caerdydd)

▲■ ACCOMMODATIONS
Acorn Camping &
  Caravaning, **15**
Annedd Lon, **14**
Austin's, **12**
Cardiff International
  Backpacker, **13**
YHA Cardiff, **10**

🍴🍺 FOOD
Celtic Cauldron
  Wholefoods, **8**
Crockertons, **4**

Crumbs, **3**
Europa Cafe, **11**
The Louis Restaurant, **6**
Metropolis, **1**
RSVP, **5**

⭐ CLUBS
Clwb Ifor Bach, **9**
Exit Club, **2**
The Toucan, **7**

day, £19); **London** (3½hr., 9 per day, £17); **London Heathrow** (3½hr., 11 per day, £32); **London Gatwick** (5hr., 11 per day, £35.50); **Manchester** (6hr., 8 per day, £25.50). Avoid confusion by picking up timetables at the bus station and a free *Wales Bus, Rail, and Tourist Map and Guide* at the TIC.

Local Transportation: Cardiff Bus, St. David's House, Wood St. (Bws Caerdydd; ☎2066 6444). Office open M-F 8:30am-5pm, Sa 9am-4:30pm. Runs a 4-zone network of green and orange buses in Cardiff and surrounding areas. Stops are often shared with **Stagecoach** and other carriers. Show up at the stop 5-10min. early; schedules can be unreliable, especially on Sundays. Service ends M-Sa 11:20pm, Su 11pm. Fares 65p-£1.55; reduced fares for seniors and children. Week-long **Multiride Passes** available (£16.60, children £10). **City Rider** tickets allow 1-day unlimited travel in the greater Cardiff area and can be purchased from drivers (£3.30, children £2.20, families £6.75). Pick up the free *Guide to Bus Fares* in Cardiff from the bus station or TIC.

Taxis: Castle (☎2034 4344) and **Dragon** (☎2033 3333).

◢◣ ⁊ ORIENTATION AND PRACTICAL INFORMATION

Cardiff Castle is the historical center of the city, though the shops lining Queen St. and The Hayes see much of Cardiff's foot traffic. Further east, the River Taff bounds Bute Park Arboretum, separating residential neighborhoods from downtown and flowing a mile south into Cardiff Bay. The **Civic Centre**, university, and **National Gallery** are just north of the castle, while the small arcades and narrow streets immediately south provide much of the city's cultural fare. Like any city, Cardiff has its unappealing pockets; be cautious at night.

Tourist Information Centre: The Hayes (☎2022 7281; www.visitcardiff.info), in the newly renovated Old Library. Books rooms for a £2 charge plus a 10% deposit. Open M-Sa 10am-6pm, Su 10am-4pm.

Tours: City Sightseeing Cardiff offers a hop-on, hop-off bus tour that departs from the main gate of Cardiff Castle every 30 min. Purchase tickets from the driver, the TIC, or on www.city-sightseeing.com. £7, concessions £5, children £2.50, families £16.50. **Cardiff Waterbus** (☎2048 8842; www.cardiffwaterbus.com) vehicles tour Cardiff Bay, starting in Penarth and passing Mermaid Quay. Reserve ahead for large parties. Call for schedules and prices.

Financial Services: Banks line Queen St. and St. Mary St. **American Express,** 3 Queen St. (☎0870 6001 0601). Open M-F 9am-5:30pm, Sa 9am-5pm. **Thomas Cook,** 16 Queen St. (☎2042 2500) offers commission-free currency exchange. Open M-Th and Sa 9am-5:30pm, F 10am-5:30pm.

Work Opportunities: During popular tourist seasons, and especially in rugby season, local establishments of all sorts look for part-time workers. A keen eye will find signs in many windows and the occasional temp agency. Try **Job Centre Plus,** 64 Charles St. (☎2042 8400). Open M-Tu and Th-F 9am-5pm, W 10am-5pm. Visit the TIC for more information. Employers sometimes post notices on the bulletin board at the Cardiff International Backpacker (p. 458).

Launderette: Drift In, 104 Salisbury Rd. (☎2023 9257), northeast of Cardiff Castle. Open M-F 9am-9pm, Sa 9am-6pm.

Police: King Edward VIII Ave. (☎2022 2111). Open 24hr.

Pharmacy: Boots, 36 Queens St. (☎2023 1291). Open M-Sa 8:30am-6pm.

Hospital: University Hospital of Wales, Heath Park, North Cardiff (☎2074 7747), 3½ mi. from city center.

Internet Access: The **public library,** at Frederick St. and Bridge St. (☎2038 2116) offers free access in 30min. slots. Open M-W and F 9am-6pm, Th 9am-7pm, Sa 9am-5:30pm. Sign up in advance. The TIC provides computers for checking email at £1.50 per 20min. **McDonald's,** 12-14 Queen St. (☎2022 2604), has 4 kiosks. £1 per 30min. Open M-Th 7:30am-11pm, F-Sa 7:30am-midnight, Su 7:30am-9pm. BT public telephones are sometimes accompanied by Internet booths, starting at 10p per min.

Post Office: 2-4 Hill's St. (☎2022 7305), off The Hayes. Open M-Sa 9am-5:30pm. **Bureau de change. Money Gram wiring service. Post Code:** CF10 2SJ.

⌂ ACCOMMODATIONS

Budget accommodation is tough to find in the city center, but the TIC lists reasonable **B&Bs** (£18-20) on the outskirts of Cardiff. B&Bs on lovely **Cathedral Road,** a short ride on bus #32 or a 15min. walk, are often expensive (from £25); better bargains await on side streets. Hotels near the castle are pricey; cheaper ones (around

£20) cluster further out. Between June and September, **Cardiff University Student Housing** lets dorm rooms to documented students (☎2087 4864; summer@cardiff.ac.uk. From £8.50-10 per person, depending on whether stay is over 30 days. Book in advance.) Pick up a free accommodations guide at the TIC.

🏠 **Cardiff International Backpacker,** 98 Neville St. (☎2034 5577). From Central Station, go west on Wood St., turn right onto Fitzhamon Embankment just across the river, then left onto Despenser St.; the hostel is the purple building. This is a backpacker's heaven: drink during happy hour (Su-Th 7pm-9pm) and chill in the comfy lounge (kitchen and classy bar within). Pop up to the rooftop for views of Cardiff and full hammock privileges. Bike rentals £7.50 per day; £5 deposit for helmet and lock. Internet access £1 per 30min. Weekday curfew 2:30am. Dorms £16; doubles £38; triples £48; quads £60. MC/V. ❷

YHA Cardiff, 2 Wedal Rd., Roath Park (☎2046 2303). Take bus #28 or 29 from Central Station (20min., 4-5 per hr., 95p) and get off at Shirley Rd.; Wedal Rd. is directly across the roundabout. Adjacent Roath Gardens offers pleasant streamside walks and tangles of wildflowers. Breakfast included. Internet access 50p per 5min. Reception 7:30am-11pm. Dorms £14.90, under 18 £11.60 extra. MC/V. ❷

Annedd Lon, 157 Cathedral Rd. (☎2022 3349). This 19th century Victorian houses provides a peaceful respite 20min. from the castle. No smoking. Breakfast included. All rooms ensuite. Well-furnished quads (£75-80) and doubles (£50). MC/V. ❸

Austin's, 11 Coldstream Terr. (☎2037 7148; www.hotelcardiff.com). On the banks of the River Taff, 3min. from the castle. Singles £20-25; doubles £35-39. AmEx/MC/V. ❸

Acorn Camping and Caravaning, near Rosedew Farm, Ham Ln. South, Llantwit Major (☎01446 794 024). 1hr. by bus #X91 from Central Station, 15min. walk from the Ham Ln. stop. £6 per person, group discounts available. Electricity £2.75. AmEx/MC/V. ❶

🍴🍺 FOOD AND PUBS

Pubs, chains, and upscale British fare dominate popular, bustling locations like Mill Ln. Caroline St. is a surefire post-club hotspot, with plenty of curried and fried goodies and late hours. (Most open M-W until 3am and Th-Sa until 4am). Corner stalls, pubs, and local bakeries produce Welsh pasties en masse, though more creative and expensive restaurants (£10-20) are nestled between narrow streets directly south of the castle. Greek, Indian, and kebab takeaways with younger clientele congregate on Salisbury St. near the university. And for those on the go, skylit **Central Market** provides produce, mountains of bread, and hot bacon next to barbers, music stores, and inexpensive parakeets (Open daily 10am-4pm.)

🍴 **Europa Cafe,** 25 Castle St. (☎2066 7776), across from the castle, toward the river. Glossy, black stone walls hung with abstract art combine with worn floors to give this offbeat coffee shop a trendy yet comfortable feel (the red plush couch helps with the latter.) Upcoming performers and theme nights are chalked on the wall turned blackboard, and big mochas (£2.30) accompany eclectic books (which you can read for free). M-W 8am-8pm, Th-Sa 8am-11pm, Su noon-6pm. Cash only. ❶

🍴 **Metropolis,** 60 Charles St., (☎2034 4300). Muted, modern interiors and low, rhythmic French music make Metropolis hum with cool. Relax over a 2 course meal (£8, noon-3pm and 6-7pm) and a cigar (£1-10) amidst imaginative architecture. Entrees £8-13. Open M-W noon-11pm, Th noon-midnight, F-Sa noon-2am. Food served M-Sa noon-3pm and 6-11pm. AmEx/MC/V. ❷

🍴 **Celtic Cauldron Wholefoods,** 47-49 Castle Arcade (☎2038 7185). Delivers a bold synthesis of hearty Welsh cuisine and assorted ethnic traditions. Don't be tempted by the pies and cakes in the window; though excellent, they may spoil your appetite for the Glamorganshire sausage, seaweed-based laverbread, and tangy Welsh rarebit (all £5). Open summer M-Sa 8:30am-9pm; winter M-Sa 8:30am-6pm, Su 11am-4pm. MC/V. ❶

SOUTH WALES

The Louis Restaurant, 32 St. Mary St. (☎2022 5722). The "Special Louis 9 Breakfast" can sate the most biting hunger with eggs, bacon, sausage, tomatoes, mushrooms and more. Plenty of seating in clean, bright locale. No smoking. M-Sa 9am-8pm. MC/V. ❶

Crockertons, 10 Caroline St. (☎2022 0088; www.crockertons.co.uk). Touting "urban food," Crockertons uses many local Welsh ingredients and opens its doors onto a street patio, making it feel organic in both a metropolitan and dietary sense. Antipasto (£5), sandwiches (£3). Open M-Sa 7am-7pm, Su 11am-5pm. MC/V. ❶

RSVP, St. John's St. (☎2022 1980). Both restaurant and bar, the newly-renamed RSVP serves high-class fare and, as the name suggests, a generally highbrow clientele. Risotto, lamb, and salad nicoise (£7-11) are classy enough, but wait until "Back to the 70s" hits the bar on Th nights. Open 11am-11pm, F-Sa noon-2am. AmEx/MC/V. ❸

Crumbs Salad Restaurant, 33 Morgan Arcade (☎2039 5007). Set in a winding arcade, this all-vegetarian restaurant has a quaint and homey charm. Prices are cheap and food is simple; mixed salad (£4) and homemade soup (£3.50) can be enjoyed within or taken out (for different prices). M-F 10am-3pm, Sa 10am-4pm. Cash only. ❷

🗻 SIGHTS

🏰 **CARDIFF CASTLE.** Two thousand years have drastically changed these grounds, but the peacocks that now strut the Green still wear crowns (of sorts) suited for the royalty that inspired the castle's extravagance. The Norman Keep or "White Tower," built in 1081 as shelter for the ruling lord in tumultuous times, is an anachronism even within the stone fortress walls. A 19th-century Victorian mansion, designed by William Burges for the 3rd Marquess of Bute, boasts jazzed up medieval mimicry. **Restaurant Undercroft** completes the theme with medieval fixings, including Welsh Cheddar Ploughmans (£4.95) and beer (£2.50) served in a dungeon-like setting fit for Hrothgar himself. Watch out for owls Billy and Floyd during falconry shows. *(Castle St. ☎2087 8100. Open daily Mar.-Oct. 9:30am-6pm; Nov.-Feb. 9:30am-5pm. Last admission 1hr. before close. Adults £6, children and seniors £3.70, students £4.85, family £17.60.)*

NATIONAL MUSEUM AND GALLERY. Popular impressionist paintings do impress, but don't miss the diverse local exhibits, like a room full of carved Celtic crosses and a walk-through display of Wales's indigenous flora and fauna. *(Cathays Park, next to City Hall. ☎2039 7951. Open Tu-Su 10am-5pm. Free. Audio tours, donation requested.)*

CIVIC CENTRE. The Centre is composed of the white Portland stone City Hall and the National Museum, along with the courts and police building. These buildings, constructed while Cardiff's steel and coal wealth still ran high, stand guard around the stately green expanse of Alexandra Gardens. *(Cathays Park. Open to public.)*

🎭 🎵 NIGHTLIFE AND ENTERTAINMENT

CLUBS

After 11pm, the majority of Cardiff's popular downtown pubs stop serving alcohol, and the action migrates to an array of nearby clubs—most located on or around **St. Mary St.** Cardiff's dress code demands black shoes only (many clubs won't let you in without them). After dark, hail a cab if you're leaving the city center. Pick up the *Itchy Cardiff* guide (£3.50), which natives praise for accuracy, from the TIC to get more information about having a fun night out on the town.

🎵 **The Toucan,** 95-97 St. Mary St. (☎2037 2212). An all-female Cuban band, Asian underground artists, and hippie funksters perform at this remarkably comfortable and inviting hangout. Titled the "Best Night Out in Cardiff Bar None" by the *Guardian Guide,* the Tou-

SOUTH WALES

can's low couches and multicolored walls harbor old and young alike, both experienced musicians and clubbing newbies. Music and dancing on the 2nd floor; awesome food and comfy seating on the ground level. Open Tu 6pm-12:30am, W 6pm-1am, Th and Sa 6pm-2am, F 5pm-2am, Su 8pm-12:30pm. Food served until 11pm.

Clwb Ifor Bach (The Welsh Club), 11 Womanby St. (☎2023 2199). 3 worlds collide in the Clwb: floor 1 plays cheesy pop and oldies, especially on W for student night; the middle floor—and the bar—lets you chill to softer music; the top, with low ceilings, rocks out to live bands or hardcore trance. There are drink specials every night, but cover can be hefty (£3-10) for renowned bands. Open M-Th until 2am, F-Sa until 3am. Occasionally open Su and closed M.

Exit Club, 48 Charles St. (☎2064 0101). Where Cardiff's gay crowd dances to chart faves. Miss Diana Manté hosts a drag show on the main floor every Sunday. Many drink here before heading to other clubs. Cover £2-3, free before 9:30pm. Open M-Sa 6pm-1am, Su 6pm-2am.

ARTS

Cardiff is experiencing an artistic renaissance, with an influx of new blood and a renewed interest in Welsh vocal, theatrical, and artistic traditions. With the opening of the Millennium Opera House slated for November 2004, the traditional music scene will catch up with the art galleries and theater. The TIC offers free brochures for local craft shops and art events.

New Theatre, Park Pl. (☎2087 8889; www.newtheatrecardiff.co.uk), off Queen St. Formerly the home of the Welsh National Opera, this pretty theater now hosts musicals and ballets. Box office open M-Sa 10am-8pm. Tickets £8-50. Some student standby tickets available for £5 after 6pm on night of show, all nights except Sa.

St. David's Hall, The Hayes (☎2087 8444). One of Britain's top concert halls; hosts the **BBC National Orchestra of Wales,** with several performances each week, in addition to tribute bands and comedians. Box office open M-Sa 10am-6pm.

Chapter Arts Centre, Market Rd., Canton (☎2030 4400), accessible by the #17 or 18 bus. This red brick building acts as both gallery and venue for film, dance, and drama. Box office open M-F 10am-9pm, Sa 1:30pm-9pm, Su 2pm-9pm.

SPORTS

Millennium Stadium symbolizes Cardiff's renewed commitment to sportsmanship. Rugby matches are played at the Stadium, a 73,000-seater complete with retractable roof. (☎2082 2228; www.cardiff-stadium.co.uk. Open M-Sa 10am-6pm, Su 10am-5pm. Tours £5, children £2.50; book in advance.) Tours depart from the **Millennium Stadium Shop,** located at Entrance 3, Westgate St. (Open M-Sa 10am-6pm, Su 10am-5pm.) In the fall (a.k.a. rugby season), contact the **Welsh Rugby Union** (☎0870 0138600; www.wru.co.uk) for tickets. **Rugby Experience,** on Wood St., by the bus station, peddles "official" rugby paraphernalia; regulars hit nearby pubs with a sudsy Brains S.A. in hand and loads of face paint. (☎2082 2040. Open M-F 9:30am-5:30pm, Sa 9:30am-6pm.) Those who prefer football (soccer) instead find safe haven—and all manner of gear—at **Football Mad** on Union St.(☎2066 4567; www.footballmadshop.co.uk), or join 5-a-side leagues themselves (inquire at ☎2038 9999; £20 per team per game.)

◢ DAYTRIPS FROM CARDIFF

The fairgrounds and sandy beaches of Barry Island attract travelers all year. (Open year-round. Take the train (25 min., 4 per hr., £2.) **Taff Trail** winds from Cardiff Bay through the Taff Valley to the heart of Brecon Beacons National Park (p. 471).

■ **CAERPHILLY CASTLE.** Visitors might find this 30-acre castle site easy to navigate today, but 13th century warriors had to contend with drawbridges, trebuchets, and crossbows (now unloaded and on display) when attacking this menacing stronghold. The Great Hall (70 ft. by 35 ft.) stands in the center; surrounding it are a moat, two parapets, and a lake laid out in a "Chinese Box" system of concentric fortifications. A nearby park (free) offers stunning views of Caerphilly Castle against the surrounding countryside. *(Take the train (20min., M-Sa 2 per hr., £3), or #26 bus. (☎2088 3143). Open daily June-Sept. 9:30am-6pm; Apr.-May 9:30am-5pm; Oct.-Mar. M-Sa 9:30am-4pm, Su 11am-4pm. Last admission 30min. before close. £3, concessions £2.50, families £8.50.)*

MUSEUM OF WELSH LIFE (AMGUEDDFA WERIN CYMRU). Four miles west of Cardiff in **St. Fagan's Park,** this open-air museum occupies more than 100 acres with over 40 buildings—some nearly 500 years old. The Celtic Village and Welsh peasant cottage in particular are full of unexpected strokes of authenticity—interiors that smell like smoke and even a miniature stone pig-house (complete with pigs, in summer). Since no tours are offered, take advantage of the guides and craftsmen stationed around the park. The cart and horse ride (adults £1, children 50p) is fun and worthwhile. *(Buses #32 and 320 run to the museum from Central Station (20min., 1-2 per hr., £2.60). ☎2057 3500. Open daily 10am-5pm. Free. Guidebook £2.)*

LLANDAFF CATHEDRAL. A Celtic cross, one of the oldest Christian relics in Britain, stands outside this 12th-century cathedral, and the Gothic spires upon the bell tower attest to its ancient inspiration. Yet within, the ancient arch over the altar contrasts with a 20th-century concrete version, topped by Christ in Majesty forged from aluminum. Entombed within the premises are St. Dyfrig and St. Teilo, and the triptych of Dante Gabriel Rosetti's Seed of David stands in one corner. Nearby lie the ivy-covered ruins of the **Castle of the Bishops of Llandaff.** Though its luster is somewhat faded—800 years have seen the cathedral turned into a "hog trough" by Cromwell and gutted by a German bomb—Llandaff's grounds still emanate grace and history. *(Take bus #60 or 62 from Central Station to the Black Lion Pub (15min.) and walk up High St., or walk down Cathedral Rd., through Llandaff Fields, and straight on the small, scenic path behind the rugby club. ☎2056 4554. Open daily 7:30am-7pm. Evensong daily 6pm. Free.)*

CASTELL COCH. Lord Bute and his architect William Burges (whose shared appetite for restoration was left unsatisfied by their work at Cardiff Castle) rebuilt the ruins of this 13th century castle in the late 1800s. Their attempt to resurrect a medieval style was ultimately undermined by a sense of Victorian grandeur, and the result looks like something from a fairy tale, complete with spires, latticed gabling, and whimsical decor. Still, the magic of the place is undeniable; in the two-story parlor, the string-pulling Fates look down upon would-be guests, and in the Lady's top-floor bedroom, monkeys frolic overhead and miniature golden castles flank her sink. Unlike many of the other castles near Cardiff, Castell Coch occupies a secluded forest hillside, offering hikers connections to the Taff Trail. *(Take bus #26 or 26a (25min., 1-2 per hr.) from Central Station to Tongwynlais, get off across from the post office, and walk 15min. up Mill St. ☎2081 0101. Open daily Apr.-May 9:30am-5pm; June-Sept. 9:30am-6pm; Oct.-Mar. Su 11am-4pm. £3, concessions £2.50, families £8.50. Audio tour £1. Closed Jan. and first 2 weeks of Feb.*

WYE VALLEY

It's no wonder Wordsworth mused on the tranquility and pastoral majesty that suffuses this once-troubled Welsh-English border territory; it seems untouched by human encroachment and the passage of time. Sheep farms nestle among forests, and walking trails weave through storied castles and abbeys as aimlessly as the meandering Wye moves through its own tranquil valley.

SOUTH WALES

▚ TRANSPORTATION

Chepstow provides the easiest entrance to the valley. **Trains** (☎08457 484 950) run to Chepstow from **Cardiff** (45min., 1-2 per hr., £5.40) and **Newport** (20min., every hr., £4.20). **National Express** (☎08705 808 080) buses go to Chepstow from: **Cardiff** (50min., 13 per day, £4.25); **London** (2½hr., 7 per day, £17); **Newport** (25min., every hr., £2.75). **Stagecoach Red and White** buses #65 and 69 loop between **Chepstow** and **Monmouth** (8-9 per day); bus #69 stops in Tintern. One-day **Network Rider** passes (£4.50, concessions £2, families £9; available on Stagecoach buses), good for travel on all Stagecoach Red and White, Phil Anslow, and Cardiff buses, may save you money. Few buses run on Sunday in the valley. Consult *Discover the Wye Valley by Foot and by Bus* (30p), in area TICs for schedules. **Hitchhikers** try their luck on the A466 in the summer; some stand near the entrance to Tintern Abbey or by the Wye Bridge in Monmouth. *Let's Go* does not recommend hitchhiking.

▚ HIKING

Those who wander the hills that cradle the Wye are rewarded with quiet wooded trails, long romps through open meadows, and stunning vistas of the valley. Two main trails follow the river on either side and are accessible from many different points: the Wye Valley Walk and Offa's Dyke Path. TICs disperse pamphlets and sell Ordnance Survey maps (1:25,000; £8). Campsites are scattered through the area; ask at the Chepstow, Tintern, Hereford, and Powys TICs.

Wye Valley Walk (136 mi.). West of the river, this walk heads north from Chepstow via Hay-on-Wye to Prestatyn along wooded cliffs and farmland, eventually ending in Rhayader. From **Eagle's Nest Lookout,** 3 mi. north of Chepstow, 365 steps descend steeply to the riverbank. At **Symond's Yat Rock,** 15½ mi. north of Chepstow, the hills drop away to a panorama of the Wye's horseshoe bends, 7 counties, and a cliff where peregrine falcons make their nests every spring. When passing Mordiford, an eye turned skyward might serve you well: legend has it the village was once home to a dragon. A popular walk from Chepstow follows the Wye Valley Walk up the Welsh side of the river to Tintern and the Offa's Dyke Path (p. 462) back. The Chepstow TIC offers a guide to this 12 mi. hike for 80p. For more information, consult www.wyevalleywalk.org.

Offa's Dyke Path (177 mi.). East of the river, this beautiful path starts in Sedbury's Cliffs and winds along the Welsh-English border before finishing in Prestatyn, on Wales' northern coast. Built by Saxon King Offa to keep the menacing Welsh at bay, it is Britain's longest archaeological monument, and some of the earthwork (about 20 ft. high) still stands. Join at Chepstow, Monmouth, Bisweir or Redbrook, and follow the yellow arrows and acorn signs. Consult trail maps (available at TICs) before beginning a walk, as some paths change grade suddenly and without warning. Consult the **Offa's Dyke Association,** based halfway up the trail in Knighton (☎01547 528 753).

Royal Forest of Dean. This 27,000 acre forest, once the hunting grounds of Edward the Confessor and Williams I and II, lies just across the English border. Known as the "Queen of Forests," its ancient woods and rolling farmlands provide pleasant hikes. Contact **Forest Service,** Bank St., in Coleford, England, across the river from Monmouth (☎01594 833 057; open M-Th 8:30am-5pm, F 8:30am-4pm) or the **Coleford Tourist Information Centre,** High St. (☎01594 812 388; open M-Sa 10am-5pm). **Forest of Dean Tour Guides** (☎01594 529 358; www.forestofdeantours.org) offers guided tours.

CHEPSTOW (CAS-GWENT)   ☎01291

Established a year after the Battle of Hastings, this town (originally Ceap-stowe, or "marketplace") seems to have forgotten its industrial, ship-building past; sloping gently to the river, Chepstow's walkways wend through modern storefronts.

Though its shopping area offers a pleasant afternoon's diversion, Chepstow's biggest (and best) attraction is **Castell Casgwent,** Britain's oldest datable stone castle. Ferns and flowers spring from its cliffside ruins, which give stunning views through ancient windows. Look for the murder holes above the gate. (☎ 624 065. Open daily 9:30am-6pm, last admission 5:30pm. £3, students £2.50, families £8.50.) Chepstow celebrates its rich history in the **Chepstow Festival,** a three-week spectacular featuring a light show, mock armed battles, and musical and theatrical entertainment. The festival takes place every other year (next in summer 2006; www.chepstowfestival.co.uk), with smaller exhibitions in the odd years. Book accommodations far in advance.

Chepstow's **train station** is on Station Rd., and **buses** stop above the town gate in front of the Somerfield supermarket. Train and bus tickets are bought onboard, except those for bus travel to major cities, which must be purchased at **The Travel House,** 9 Moor St. (☎ 623 031. Open M-Sa 9am-5:30pm.) A **Tourist Information Centre,** on Bridge St., faces the castle. Ask about hikes, book accommodations, or pick up a free copy of *What's On Chepstow.* (☎ 623 772; www.chepstow.co.uk. Open daily Apr.-Oct. 10am-5:30pm; Nov.-Mar. 10am-3:30pm.) Other services include: **Barclays,** Beaufort Sq. (☎ 01633 205 000. Open M-Tu and Th-F 9am-4:30pm, W 10am-4:30pm); **Neptune Laundry Services,** 36 Moor St., near the bus station (☎ 626 372; wash £2.80, dry £1-2, soap 50p; open M-F 8:30am-7pm, Sa 9:15am-5:30pm, Su 10am-4pm); the **police,** Moor St. (☎ 623 993), across from the post office; the **Community Hospital** (☎ 636 637), west of town on St. Lawrence Rd.; free **Internet access** at the **Chepstow Library** on Manor Way in the town center (☎ 635 730; open M, W, F 9am-5:30pm; Tu 10am-5:30pm; Th 9am-8pm; Sa 9:30am-4pm); and the **post office,** Albion Sq. (☎ 622 607; open M-F 9am-5:30pm, Sa 9am-12:30pm.) **Post Code:** NP16 5DA.

Though Chepstow is a more convenient transportation base, nearby Tintern offers cheaper **B&B** accommodations in prettier surroundings. The nearest **YHA hostel** is at **St. Briavel's Castle,** in England (see **Tintern,** p. 463). In Chepstow, **Mrs. Presley ❸,** 30 Kingsmark Ave., has beautiful rooms and includes breakfast, a 10 min. hike from the city proper. (☎ 624 466. £20 per person. Cash only.) The **First Hurdle Guest House ❸,** 9-10 Upper Church St., offers newly refurbished rooms near the castle. (☎ 622 189. Singles £35; doubles £50. AmEx/MC/V.) The **Tesco** on Station Rd. is open 24hr. but closes Sa 10pm-Su 10am and Su 4pm-M 8am.

TINTERN
☎ 01291

One narrow road, the A466, follows the Wye and weaves its way through the small stone houses of Tintern. This welcoming little village, located five miles north of Chepstow, thrives on the tourism brought by ◧**Tintern Abbey,** the center of a 12th century society of Cistercian monks. Hauntingly permanent, its weathered columns that once echoed with prayer now reverberate with the solemnity of nature. The roof opens to the clouds, arches point skyward, and grass sprouts in the transepts; the abbey's tranquility seems even to match the surrounding countryside. And while William Wordsworth once famously drew ascetic inspiration from this "wild secluded scene"—it was his release from "the heavy and the weary weight of all this unintelligible world"—the nearby gift shops and clamor of tour buses suggest that Tintern is not quite as "secluded," or peaceful, as it once was. (☎ 689 251. Open daily June-Sept. 9:30am-6pm; Apr.-May and Oct. 9:30am-5pm; Nov.-Mar. M-Sa 9:30am-4pm, Su 11am-4pm. £3, concessions £2.50, families £8.50. 45min. audio tour £1, plus £5 deposit.) Those interested in the view from "a few miles above" should ask gift shop employees for directions to Monk's Trail, a wooded path that winds through the hills across the river. An uphill hike (roughly 2 mi.) will get you to Devil's Pulpit, a huge stone from which Satan is said to have tempted the monks as they worked in the fields.

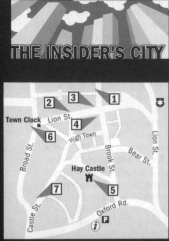

THE INSIDER'S CITY

A VINTAGE DREAM

In late May, the elite of academia pour into Hay-on-Wye in droves to hear scholars and authors discuss their newest books and demonstrate their boundless literary wisdom. But it is old, second-hand books that made this hillside shire into the megalith it is today. Here's a rough guide to the best shops.

1 **Poetry Bookshop,** The Ice House, Brook St. (☎821 812), is the only bookstore in the UK devoted entirely to poetry. Open Apr.-Oct. M-Sa 10am-6pm, Su 11am-5pm.

2 Admire over 500,000 volumes at the original branch of **Richard Booth's Books,** 44 Lion St. (☎820 322), the largest second-hand bookshop in the world. Rifle through the drawers of a room devoted to old postcards to find a century's worth of handwritten notes. Open Apr.-Oct. M-Sa 9am-8pm, Su 11:30am-5:30pm; Nov.-Mar. until 5:30pm.

3 "When a new book is published, read an old one,"

Tintern's **Old Station** lies a mile north of the abbey on the A466, though the Wye River Path is a more scenic and safe route, as the road narrows and sidewalks vanish. The out-of-service train station now holds a series of railway carriages, one of which houses the **Tourist Information Centre,** which offers rides on a model railway. The TIC will book accommodations for a £1 charge. (☎/fax 689 566. Open daily Apr.-Oct. 10:30am-5:30pm.) There are several sights of interest between the abbey and the Old Station on A466. At **The Anchor Tintern** (☎689 207), sample the fruits of a historic cider mill once used by the monks themselves—supposedly the oldest in existence. **Stella's Books** (☎689 755; www.stella-books.com), in the middle of the village proper, stores a selection of over 50,000 obscure old volumes behind its unassuming storefront, including a particularly entertaining array of antiquated children's books. **Parva Farm Vineyard,** just past the Wye Valley Hotel on the A466, produces nearly 4,000 bottles of wine and spicy honey mead a year, and the Dudleys (the owners) let visitors tour the hillside for £1, tasting included. (☎689 636. Open most days 10:30am-6:30pm.)

The nearest **YHA hostel** is **St. Briavel's Castle ❷,** 4 mi. northeast of Tintern across the English border. Once King John's hunting lodge and later a fortress against the pillaging Welsh, this 12th-century castle's enduring medieval character offers a hostel experience unlike any other. Don't miss the 17th-century graffiti marks on one dorm wall. From the A466 (bus #69 from Chepstow; ask to be let off at Bigsweir Bridge) or Offa's Dyke, follow signs for a 2 mi., boot-camp-like, uphill hike from the edge of the bridge. On Wednesdays, bus L12 runs from Monmouth to St. Briavel's. (☎01594 530 272. Lockout 10am-5pm. Curfew 11:15pm. Dorms £11.80, under 18 £8.50. MC/V.) **B&Bs** are strung along the A466 throughout the village, many with river views. At the edge of Tintern, **Holmleigh B&B ❷** has cozy rooms in an old stone house with white gabling and a cliff at its back. Take bus #69 from Chepstow and ask to be let off at the Wye Valley Hotel; it is a 2min. walk back. (☎689 521. From £17.50. Cash only.) **Campers** can use the **field ❶** next to the old train station. (£2.) Near St. Briavel's Castle hostel is the **George Inn Pub ❶,** a 16th-century local favorite, with original timber, low ceilings, and dim lighting straight out of a medieval tale. (☎01594 530 228. Open M-Sa 11:30am-2:30pm and 6pm-11pm, Su noon-2:30pm and 7pm-10:30pm.) **The Moon and Sixpence ❶,** High St., next to the Holmleigh B&B, serves an array of country foods in a pub atmosphere. (☎689 284. Open daily 11am-midnight. Food served until 9pm.)

HAY-ON-WYE (Y GELLI)

☎ 01497

To put it simply, Hay-on-Wye is a town defined by its bookstores. One might even be forgiven for missing the grand vistas surrounding this hillside hideaway, for in Hay everything—its people, its economy, its relentless rhythms—runs on second-hand books. The little village, replete with cobbled alleys and small-town charm, owes its reputation as the world's foremost "Town of Books" (and its world-famous annual Guardian Hay Festival) mainly to Richard Booth, who founded Booth's Books, now the largest second-hand bookstore in the world, in 1961. And while the winding Wye and 2,227 ft. Hay Bluff may astound visitors with natural beauty, Hay's literary charm is even more palpable and seductive.

⌨ TRANSPORTATION AND PRACTICAL INFORMATION. The closest **train station** is in Hereford, England (p. 293). **Stagecoach Red and White** (☎01633 838 856) bus #39 stops at Hay between **Hereford** and **Brecon** (1hr. from Hereford, 45min. from Brecon; M-Sa 7 per day; £3.95-4.40). **Yeoman's** (☎01432 356 202) bus #40 runs the same route 3 per Su (£3.05). The independently run **Tourist Information Centre**, Oxford Rd., in the small shopping center by the bus stop, books beds for a £2 charge and offers Internet access (50p per 15min.) (☎820 144; www.hay-on-wye.co.uk. Open daily Apr.-Oct. 10am-1pm and 2-5pm; Nov.-Mar. 11am-1pm and 2-4pm.) Other services include: **Barclays**, on Broad St. (open M-F 10am-4pm); a **library**, Chancery Ln., with free Internet access (☎820 847. Open M 10am-1pm, 2pm-4:30pm, 5pm-7pm; Th-F 10am-1pm and 2pm-5pm, Sa 9:30am-1pm); a **launderette,** across from the castle (☎820 360; £4 per load, soap 20p; open M-Sa 7am-8pm); and the **post office,** 3 High Town (☎820 536, open M, W, F 9am-1pm and 2-5:30pm, Tu 9am-1pm, Th 9am-5:30pm, Sa 9am-12:30pm). **Post Code:** HR3 5AE.

⌨ ACCOMMODATIONS AND FOOD. The nearest **YHA hostel** is 8 mi. away at Capel-y-Ffin (p. 473). Numerous **B&Bs** occupy the center of town. Delightful stays await at ⛰The Bear ❸, Bear St., a 16th-century coaching inn with low-timbered ceilings, poofy beds, and inviting fireplaces, many of which are closed up and piled high with books. (☎821 302; www.thebear-hay-on-wye.co.uk. Singles £24; twins £48; doubles £58. MC/V.) **Oxford Cottage ❷**, Oxford Rd., provides cozy, sunlit rooms and free run of the kitchen. (☎820 008; www.oxfordcottage.co.uk. £18

demands a sign in front of **Addyman Books,** 39 Lion St. (☎821 136). Relax at one of its upstairs couches or rockers to peruse its various genres. Open daily 9am-5pm.

4 Created as an annex shop to Addyman's Books, **Murder and Mayhem,** 5 Lion St. (☎821 613), specializes in detective fiction, true crime, and horror; painted pistols, menacing daggers, and a hanging gnome complement the theme. Open M-Sa 10:30am-5:30pm, some Su.

5 Hay Castle (☎820 503) is not only the centerpiece of Richard Booth's empire, it also houses photography and other artwork. A 24hr. self-service "honesty bookstore" lines the street-level courtyard (hardcovers 50p, paperbacks 30p). Open daily Apr.-Oct. 9:30am-6pm; Nov.-Mar. 9am-5:30pm.

6 Children will revel in the wide-selection of **Rose's Books** (☎820 031), specialists in out-of-print children's books. Roald Dahl's lesser known works and an illustrated Tolkein's *Bestiary* are sure to tickle your tot. Open daily 9:30am-5pm.

7 **Bookends,** Castle St. (☎821 341) sells all of its volumes for £1 or less, and it's a great place to discover new authors or rediscover old classics. Open Apr.-Oct. Su-W 11am-5:30pm, Th-Sa 9am-8pm; daily Nov.-Mar. 9am-5:30pm.

FROM THE ROAD

THE ENGLISH CANON

I got off my bus on a hot Sunday morning, prepared for a lazy day off. Hay-on-Wye had all the elements of a quiet afternoon's anonymity sleepy cottages, musty bookshops, and, most importantly, few enough people that I was relatively certain not to be distracted from languid hillside snoozing. All I needed was a book. Fortunately I was in Hay-on-Wye. Here, the self-proclaimed King of Hay, Richard Booth, buys books by the ton to stock thousands of shelves.

Window shopping as I went, I strolled Hay's streets looking for a good read-a task appropriately easy for an early Sunday morning (or, as is the case in some Welsh pubs a late Saturday night.) As I entered Booth's Books, the largest second-hand bookstore in the world, I asked the man behind the desk, cardiganed, bespectacled and thumbing an old volume, for a recommendation.

"Why your accent is delightful!" he mused, ignoring my question but clearly noticing my Midwestern twang. "And what brings you here?"

'Anonymity be damned,' I thought, 'I'll just bolt after he finds me a book.' "My name is Matthew. I'm from the States."

"Matthew. Hmm. May I call you Saint Matthew? It isn't everywhere that you'll receive an instant canonization," he said with utter sincerity. I stood confused, nodding noncommittally.

As he got up, he seemed the

per person, £20 on weekends. Cash only.) Camp along the **Wye Valley Walk** or **Offa's Dyke** (p. 462); **Radnor's End Campsite ❶**, on a tiny valley plateau, is closest to town; cross the river via Bridge St. and walk 500 yd. to the right toward Clyro, then turn left into the campsite. (☎820 780. £4.)

Stock up for a picnic along the Wye at **Spar**, 26 Castle St. (☎820 582; open M-Sa 8am-10pm, Sa 8am-7:30pm.) At **The Granary ❷**, Broad St., extravagant salads (£8) accompany "toasties" (£4), tasty cakes (£1.50), and patio seating. Or eat under dried hops in the former wool merchant's building. (☎820 790. Open daily 10am-5:30pm. AmEx/MC/V.) **Oscars ❷**, 17 High Town, offers scones and pastries (£1-1.50) as well as tasty meals and lunch staples like filled baguettes. (☎821 193. Open daily 10:30am-4:30pm. MC/V.) Families are welcome at the **Wheatsheaf Inn ❶**, Lion St., where locals hang out at the bar and game room. (☎820 186. Happy hour M-F 4-6pm. Open M-Sa 11am-11pm, Su 11am-10:30pm. Food served noon-2:30pm, M-F also 6-8pm. MC/V.) Cheaper eats await at **Xtreme Organix ❶**, 10 Castle St., a burger/kebab joint that uses only organic, local meats. (☎821 921. Open daily 9:30am-11pm. MC/V.) Finish up by digging into confections from **The Fudge Shop ❶**, Oxford Rd. by the bus station. (☎821 529. Open daily 10am-5:30pm. AmEx/MC/V.)

🎦 🎋 **SIGHTS AND FESTIVALS.** The exterior of Hay's 13th-century **Norman castle**, scarred by wars, fires, and neglect, no longer houses traditional royalty. Rather, Richard Booth, the self-proclaimed King of Hay, stores just a fraction of his unfathomable number of second-hand books on the first floor. The castle is only secondary to Booth's huge network of stores (many of them "honesty bookshops," where a paybox sits atop outdoor shelves of 30p books), which revived Hay in the 1960s and shaped it into a bibliophile's dream. Other independent stores offer equally delightful selections—some specialize, like the Poetry Bookshop, while others *specialize*, like B&K Books, dedicated to apiculture. To find your dream book, check out our **Insider's City**, pick up the TIC's free *Secondhand & Antiquarian Booksellers & Printsellers* map and brochure, or search over a million titles at www.haybooks.com. The world-renowned, annual 10-day **literary festival** brings the literati to town (recently, Bill Clinton, John Updike, and Richard Starkey—a.k.a. Ringo Starr) to give readings. (May 27th-June 5th in 2005. Book accommodations early. Tickets usually £6, but up to £16 for feature speakers.) For those interested in less cere-

bral pursuits, **Paddles & Pedals,** 15 Castle St., rents canoes and kayaks. (☎820 604. ₤20 per half-day (5 mi.), ₤30 per day (14 mi.). Free pickup.)

ABERGAVENNY (Y FENNI)

☎ 01873

Located on the eastern edge of Brecon Beacons National Park, Abergavenny (pop. 10,000) trumpets itself as the "Gateway to Wales." While bustling, shop-lined pedestrian areas offer all the charms of Welsh village life, savvy visitors realize that the city's real charm lies not within city limits but in its location: Abervagenny is the starting point of many beautiful hikes through the nearby Black Mountains.

TRANSPORTATION. Trains (☎08457 484 950) run from: **Bristol** (1hr., 1-2 per hr., ₤7.80); **Cardiff** (40min., every hr., ₤7.60); **Chepstow** (1¼hr, every 2 hr., ₤8.30); **Hereford** (25min., 2 per hr., ₤5.80); **London** (2¼hr., every hr., ₤53.50); **Newport** (25min., 1-2 per hr., ₤4.80). To get to town, turn right at the end of Station Rd. and walk 5min. along Monmouth Rd. The **bus station** is on Monmouth Rd., by the TIC. **Stagecoach Red and White** (☎01633 838 856) buses roll in from: **Brecon** (#21, 1hr., M-Sa 6 per day, ₤3.50); **Cardiff** (#X3, 1½hr, every hr., ₤4.50); **Hereford** (#X4, 1hr., every hr., ₤4.50). Call **Lewis Taxis** (☎854 140) for inexpensive door-to-door service.

PRACTICAL INFORMATION. The well-stocked **Tourist Information Centre,** Monmouth Rd., across from the bus station, arranges local theater bookings and reserves beds for ₤2. (☎857 588; www.abergavenny.co.uk. Open daily Apr.-Oct. 10am-5:30pm; Nov.-Mar. 10am-4pm.) It shares space with the **National Park Information Centre,** which has helpful maps and useful guidance for hikers. (☎853 254. Open daily Apr.-Oct. 9:30am-5:30pm.) Purchase camping supplies at **Crickhowell Adventure Gear,** 14 High St. (☎856 581. Open roughly M-Sa 9am-1:30pm and 2:30-5:30pm.) Other services include: **banks** along Brecon Rd. and Frogmore St.; the **police** (☎852 273), Tudor St., between Nevill St. and Baker St.; the **hospital** (☎732 732), Nevill Hall, on the A40; **Internet access** at the **Public Library,** Library Sq., Baker St. (☎735 980; free; open M, Tu, F 9:30am-5:30pm; Th 9:30am-8pm; Sa 9:30am-4pm), or **Celtic Computer Systems,** 39 Cross St. (☎858 111; ₤2.50 per 30min.; open M-Sa 9:30am-5:30pm); and the **post office,** St. John's Sq., where

epitome of a bookseller; it was not the worn manuscript or unadventurous wool sweater that gave him away, but rather his tendency to be distracted at every turn, as if each title that caught his eye held both immediate and lasting significance.

Finally, he got to my question. "Interested in books, are you? Well then you must meet Richard." My heart jumped. Richard? Richard the King?

I was then whisked up the castle stairs. Stairs, no doubt, that had born many a traitor's final walk and centuries of regal procession, and were now host to an American, looking for a book in a sea of books, yet oddly adrift.

When I entered, the King was sitting on his somewhat un-royal chair, and conversation was unexpectedly fluid. And then I built up the confidence to ask: "Any good books in this town?" The deadpan reply: "A few...." A ringing phone and a dismissive royal gesture signaled my exit. I was banished, it seemed, bookless and defeated. I walked back to the curious bookseller to thank him.

"You're quite welcome, how delightful of you to come in. Oh," he said with a distracted smile, with a thin novel clasped between his two hands. "Try this one."

Joyfully, I gently cracked its paper spine. A cloth bookmark with "MATTHEW" hand-scrawled on an embroidered border held the place. Another wry, distant smile appeared on the gentleman's face. "For Saint Matthew."

-Matthew Naunheim

Tudor St. turns into Castle St., with a **bureau de change** (☎08457 223 344; open M-F 9am-5:30pm, Sa 9am-12:30pm). **Post Code:** NP7 5EB.

ⓘⓒ ACCOMMODATIONS AND FOOD. B&Bs await on **Monmouth Road,** past the TIC, and **Hereford Road,** 15min. from town. The **Black Sheep Backpackers ❷**, 24 Station Rd., is located across from the train station and offers a colorful basement lounge with kitchen and a full bar upstairs. (☎859 125; www.blacksheepbackpackers.com. Internet access £1 per 15min. Dorms £12; doubles £12-14 per person. Cash only.) The bustling **market** in Market Hall on Cross St. features fresh fruit and vegetables as well as baked goods. Market typically open Tu, F, and Sa 9am-5pm; largest on Tu.) A massive flea market assembles once per month. **Harry's Carvery ❶**, St. John's St., just off of High St., invites culinary creativity with its formidable slew of edible trappings (about £2-3). Try a ciabatta (£2.55) or defy sandwich conventions with a Brie and cranberry foccaccia. (☎852 766. Open M-Su 8:30am-4pm. Cash only.) **Mad Hatters Cafe ❶**, 58 Cross St., serves up pastries (£1-2) and savouries (sandwiches from £2.95) in a pantry-style dining room with a collection of alternative teapots. (☎859 839. Open M-F 9:30am-5:30pm. Cash only.) The elegant dining room at **The Angel Hotel ❹**, 15 Cross St., delivers inventive dishes crafted from local ingredients. Entrees like beef with bernaise (£15) barely leave room for sumptuous desserts (£5). (☎857 121. Open daily noon-2:30pm and 7-10pm. MC/V.)

ⓖ ⛰ SIGHTS AND OUTDOORS. Site of many a medieval intrigue, Abergavenny's **castle** is now reduced to a picturesque, though unremarkable, ruin. A 19th century hunting lodge on the grounds houses the **Abergavenny Museum.** (☎854 282. Open Mar.-Oct. M-Sa 11am-1pm and 2-5pm, Su 2-5pm; Nov.-Feb. M-Sa 11am-1pm and 2-4pm. Grounds open daily 8am-dusk. Grounds free.) The **Borough Theatre,** Cross St., puts on a variety of shows in the center of town. (☎850 805. Box office open Tu-Sa 9:30am-5pm.)

Abergavenny's real attractions hide in the hills that surround it; pick up *Walks from Abergavenny* (£2) from the NPIC for details on hikes in the area. Because almost all of the Black Mountain trails are unmarked, it's crucial to get detailed instructions and an Ordnance Survey Map (£6-7) from the NPIC before heading out. Three major summits are accessible from Abergavenny by foot, though they all require fairly long hikes. **Blorenge** (1833 ft.) is 2½ mi. southwest of town. A path begins off the B4246 or from the TIC, traversing valley woodlands to the upland area; it ascends the remaining 1500 ft. in 4½ mi. (6hr. and 12 mi. round-trip). The trail to the top of **Sugar Loaf** (1955 ft.), 2½ mi. northwest, starts a half-mile west of town on the A40. Many report that it's easy to hitch a ride to the carpark and start hikes from there, though *Let's Go* does not recommend hitchhiking. The path to **Skirrid Fawr** ("the Holy Mountain"; 1595 ft.) lies northeast of town and starts 2 mi. down the B4521. **Pony trekking** can be a wonderful way to enjoy the hills. Local companies include **Grange Trekking Centre** (☎890 215; £18 per half-day, £27 per day) and **Llanthony Riding and Trekking** (☎890 359; £15 per half-day, £28 per day).

🄳 DAYTRIPS FROM ABERGAVENNY

If traveling to the sights near Abergavenny by bus, a **Network Rider** pass (p. 462) is usually cheaper than round-trip tickets.

BIG PIT NATIONAL MINING MUSEUM FOR WALES. Recently named a World Heritage Site, the silent hillsides of Blaenavon, 9 mi. southwest of Abergavenny, bear the weight of years spent at the epicenter of the South Wales coal-mining and iron-production industries. The museum itself, located just next to town, has recently undergone a £7.2 million renovation and now offers visitors the chance to descend a 300 ft. shaft to the subterranean workshops of a 19th century coal mine, where ex-miners share personal experiences as well as broader industrial history. Dress warmly and wear sensible shoes. (Bus X3 (20min., 13 per day) to Pontypool, then #30 (20min., every 2hr.) to Blaenavon. ☎01495 790 311. Open daily mid Feb. to Nov. 9:30am-5pm. Underground tours 10am-3:30pm. Free. Those under 3 ft. 3 in. not admitted underground. Under 16 not admitted without a guardian.)

LLANTHONY PRIORY. All the megaliths in the Black Mountains are said to point toward ruined and relatively untouristed Llanthony Priory. In the 12th century, founder William de Lacy doffed his hunting gear and aristocratic title, rebuilding ancient ruins left at this site so that he could live a more contemplative hermetic life. Visitors can flirt with a life of isolation at the Priory's crumbling arches. (Take Stagecoach Red and White bus X4 (M-Sa 6 per day) or follow the A465 to Llanfihangel Crucorney, where the B4423 begins. Most walk and some hitch the last 6 mi. to the priory, but Let's Go does not recommend hitchhiking. Always open. Free.)

RAGLAN CASTLE. A mere 569 years old, Raglan was the last medieval castle built in Wales. Sir William ap Thomas, its initial owner, constructed it for ostentatious rather than military purposes. Still, the castle withstood an English Civil War siege with admirable fortitude before finally surrendering to Cromwell's troops in 1646. The remaining ruins comprise an impressive network of open-air towers and crumbling staircases that cut striking profiles against the hills beyond. (Take bus #83 from Abergavenny or Monmouth (20min., 6 per day, £4.50) or #60 from Monmouth or Newport (40min. from Newport, 2 per hr., £3-4.20). From the bus stop in Raglan, follow Castle Rd. to where it hits the highway, and cross over the pedestrian path to the road leading up to the Castle. ☎01291 690 228. Open daily June-Sept. 9:30am-6pm; Apr.-May and Oct. 9:30am-5pm; Nov.-Mar. M-Sa 9:30am-4pm, Su 11am-4pm. Last admission 30min. before close. £2.75, concessions £2.25, families £7.75.)

BRECON (ABERHONDDU)   ☎01874

Just north of the mountains, Brecon (pop. 8000) is the best base for exploring the dramatic northern region of Brecon Beacons National Park. Yet the town has an allure all its own: Georgian architecture looms over tiny side streets where a kaleidoscopic cross-section of visitors—student backpackers and long-time residents alike—sip tea and plan hikes through neighboring forests. An even more motley bunch alights in Brecon in August, when the exceptional **Jazz Festival** fills every bed and street corner with the masses assembled to hear luminaries like Branford Marsalis and Van Morrison.

🚍 TRANSPORTATION. Brecon has no bus or train station, but **buses** arrive regularly at **The Bulwark** in the central square. Ask for schedules at the TIC. **National Express** (☎08705 808 080) bus #509 runs from **London** (6hr., 1 per day, £20.50) via **Cardiff** (1¼hr., 1 per day, £3.25). **Stagecoach Red and White** (☎01633 838 856) buses arrive from: **Abergavenny** (#21, 50min., 6 per day, £4.50); **Newport** (#322/509, 2½hr., 1 per day, £4.50); **Swansea** (#63, 1½hr., M-Sa 3 per day, £4-5). Bus #38 comes in from **Hereford** via **Hay-on-Wye** (M-Sa 5 per day, £4.50); on Sundays, **Yeomans** (☎01432 356 202) follows the same route (#40, 3 per day, £4.50).

🛈 PRACTICAL INFORMATION. The **Tourist Information Centre** is located in the Cattle Market carpark, across from Safeway; walk through Bethel Sq. off Lion St. (☎622 485; fax ☎625 256). Open daily 9:30am-5:30pm.) It stocks an abundance of pamphlets, as does the **National Park Information Center** in the same building. **Brecon Cycle Centre,** 10 Ship St., rents mountain bikes and gives advice on maintenance and trails. (☎622 651. £15 per day, £25 per weekend. Open M-Sa 9am-5pm, Su by appointment.) **Bikes and Hikes** (p. 470) also rents equipment and organizes climbing, caving, and other expeditions. (☎610 071. £16 bike rental, £25-35 for assorted activities per day.) Other services include: **Barclays**, at the corner of St. Mary's St. and High St. (☎01633 205 000; open M-Tu and Th-F 9am-4:30pm, W 10am-4:30pm); **Beacons Laundry**, St. Mary's St. (☎07960 979 625; £6 small, £9 large load; open M-Sa 9am-5:30pm); the **police** (☎622 331), Lion St.; free **Internet access** at **Brecon Branch Library**, Ship St. (☎623 346; book ahead; open M and W-F 9:30am-5pm, Tu 9:30am-7pm, Sa 9:30am-1pm); and at **Brecon Cyber Cafe**, 10 Lion St. (☎624 942; £1.25 per 15min., £1 students; open M-Sa 10am-5pm); **Boots pharmacy**, Bethyl Sq. (☎622 917; open M-Sa 9am-5:30pm); and the **post office**, in the Cooperative Pioneer, off Lion St. (☎623 735; open M-F 8:30am-5:30pm, Sa 8:30am-4:30pm). **Post Code:** LD3 7HY.

▐ ACCOMMODATIONS. Mid-August visitors should book far in advance—the Jazz Festival claims every pillow in town. Delightful **Mrs. J. Thomas ❷**, 13 Alexandra Rd. behind the TIC, has traveled to 27 countries, lived in 18, and displays in her sparkling dining room the exotic memorabilia to prove it. Watch out for the tiger rug, head still attached. (☎624 551. Open all year. TV, tea service, breakfast included. £20-22 per person. Cash only.) Pamper yourself at the **George Hotel ❹**, George St., in the town center, a 17th century inn with a Victorian-era restaurant where food is cooked on an open stone kiln. (☎623 421; www.george-hotel.com. Breakfast included. Singles £45; doubles £65-75; family rooms £70. MC/V.) **Mulberry House ❷**, 3 Priory Hill, offers quiet rooms across from the cathedral. (☎624 461. £19 per person. Cash only.) **Bikes and Hikes ❷**, 10 The Struet, near the TIC, lives up to its name: the outdoors-enthusiast owners rent equipment and lead trips. (☎610 071. Dorms £12.50 per person.)

The nearest **YHA hostel** is **Ty'n-y-Caeau** (tin-uh-KAY-uh) **❶**, 3 mi. from Brecon. From the town center, walk down The Watton, continuing to the A40-A470 roundabout. Follow the Abergavenny branch of the A40. Just after the roundabout, take the footpath to the left of Groesffordd (grohs-FORTH), then turn left on the main road. Continue 10-15min., bearing left at the fork; the hostel is on the right. Or take the somewhat longer and more scenic path along the canal path to Brynich, then take a left to Groesffordd. A bus runs from Brecon to Groesffordd with some irregularity; count on walking or taking a cab (£5). The Victorian townhouse has gardens, a TV room, and Internet access. (☎665 270. Open all year. Dorms £10.60, under 18 £7.60. MC/V.) **Camp** at **Brynich Caravan Park ❶**, 1½mi. east of town on the A40, signposted from the A40-A470 roundabout. Canal path provides a prettier walk. (☎623 325; www.brynich.co.uk. Open Easter-Oct. £4.50-5, £10.50-11 for 2 people and car. Prices vary with the season. MC/V.) During the Jazz Festival, additional campsites open on farms.

▐ FOOD. Fill your pack at the **Cooperative Pioneer**, a grocery store off Lion St. (☎625 257. Open M-Sa 8am-9pm, Su 10am-4pm.) **Cegin Cymru ❶** ("Welsh Food Centre"), in the George Inn courtyard, stocks an impressive selection of tinned laverbread and dense clotted cream fudge. (☎620 020. Open Easter-Christmas M-Sa 9am-5pm, Su 10am-4pm. MC/V.) **Pilgrim's Tea Rooms and Restaurant ❶**, makes one feel like high society: sip your cream tea with scones for nibbling (£2.60) in sundappled cathedral gardens, or try the cheesy cauliflower (£4.50) with various salads a la carte. (☎610 610. Open daily 10am-5pm. Cash only.) **St. Mary's Bakery ❶**, 4 St. Mary St., sells yummy baked goods (35p-£1) for great prices. (☎624 311. Open M-F 7am-4pm, Sa 7am-2pm. Cash only.) With sandwiches (from £3) and "Welsh Black" with horseradish, **The Café ❷**, 39 High St., feels like a homestyle production but its home-made cheesecake (£2.20) tastes resoundingly professional. (☎611 191. Open daily 10am-5pm. Cash only.)

⑥ 🎭 **SIGHTS AND FESTIVALS.** As much a museum as a place of worship, **Brecon Cathedral** holds the standards of the Welsh 24th regiment and an impressive art collection. History is literally carved into the stone columns; "mason's marks" are the small designs (crosses, clovers) that illiterate stoneworkers used to label their work. The **Heritage Centre,** in the same hilly grove, details the art of bell-ringing and the history of the cathedral. Look for the gargoyle on the centre's streetside wall; the phallus attached makes it a rare specimen. (Cathedral ☎623 857, Centre ☎625 222. Cathedral open daily 8:30am-6pm. Centre open Mar.-Dec. M-Sa 10:30am-4:30pm, Su noon-3pm.) **Brecknock Museum and Art Gallery,** in the Assize Courthouse near The Bulwark, features a cross-section of Welsh life: walking sticks, milk churns, a smithy, and a two-foot long lovespoon. Don't miss the life-size Victorian Court, complete with barristers and judge. (☎624 121. Open M-F 10am-5pm, Sa 10am-1pm and 2-5pm; Apr.-Sept. also Su noon-5pm. £1, concessions 50p.) At **The Royal Regiment of Wales Museum Brecon,** The Barracks, military paraphernalia commands all available space. (☎613 310; www.rrw.org.uk. Open daily Apr.-Sept. 9am-5pm; Oct.-Mar. M-F 9am-5pm. Last admission 4:15pm. £3, students and children free.) During the second week of August, the **Brecon Jazz Festival** (☎ 611 622; www.breconjazz2004.co.uk) dubs itself "the only festival in Britain bigger than the town itself." Streets are blocked off as thousands converge to appreciate jazz and local brews. Other events include **antique fairs** (last Sa of the month Feb.-Nov.) and **crafts fairs** in Market Hall (3rd Sa of the month Easter-Nov.).

BRECON BEACONS

Brecon Beacons National Park (Parc Cenedlaethol Bannau Brycheiniog) encompasses 520 sq. mi. of red sandstone crags, shaded forests, and breath-taking waterfalls. The park divides into four regions: high mist-cloaked farms and bald peaks of **Brecon Beacons,** where King Arthur's mountain fortress is thought to have once stood; the lush green woods of **Fforest Fawr,** with the spectacular waterfalls of Ystradfellte; the **Black Mountains** to the east, which are correctly described as "Tolkeinesque"; and the remote western ridges of **Black Mountain** (singular), above Upper Swansea Valley. The park, founded in 1957, is not all government land; most is owned by farmers, so take care when trekking. The market towns on the fringe of the park, particularly Brecon and Abergavenny, make pleasant touring bases, but hostels allow easier access to the park's inner regions.

▣ TRANSPORTATION

Getting around Brecon Beacons isn't too difficult; it's getting in with public transport that proves a challenge. The **train** line (☎08457 484 950) from **London Paddington** to South Wales runs via **Cardiff** to **Abergavenny** at the park's southeastern corner and to **Merthyr Tydfil** on the southern edge. The **Heart of Wales** rail line passes through **Llandeilo** and **Llandovery** in the more isolated Black Mountain region, eventually terminating in Swansea. **National Express** (☎08705 808 080) bus #509 runs once a day to **Brecon,** on the northern side of the park, from **London** (£20.50) and **Cardiff** (£3.25). **Stagecoach Red and White** (☎01685 388 216) buses cross the park en route to Brecon from: **Abergavenny** (#21, 50min., 6 per day, £4.50); **Hay-on-Wye** (#38, 45min., M-Sa 5 per day, £2.80-4.10); **Swansea** (#63, 1½hr, 3 per day, £4.50). **Yeomans** (☎01432 356 202) bus #40 runs from **Hay-on-Wye** on Sundays (3 per day, £4-5). Bus #B8 runs between Brecon and Abergavenny once on Sundays. The free *Brecon Beacons: A Visitor's Guide,* available at most TICs, details some bus coverage and describes walks accessible by public transport. The indispensable *Powys City Council Travel Guide* has over 100 pages of bus listings. **Brecon Cycle Centre**

SOUTH WALES

SOUTH WALES

Brecon Beacons National Park

▲ ACCOMMODATIONS

YHA Capel-y-Ffin, 5
YHA Llanddeusant, 1
YHA Llwyn-y-Celyn, 3
YHA Tŷn-y-Caeau, 4
YHA Ystradfellte, 2

(p. 469), among others, rents mountain bikes. **Hitchhikers** say the going is tougher on the A470 than on minor roads, where drivers often stop to enjoy the view. *Let's Go* does not recommend hitchhiking.

🛈 PRACTICAL INFORMATION

Stop at a **National Park Information Centre (NPIC)** before venturing forth, for advice on hiking and biking. Free maps are available, but Ordnance Survey Outdoor Leisure Maps #12 and 13 (1:25,000; £7) are indispensable for serious exploring and for reaching safety in bad weather. The park staff usually conducts guided walks of varying difficulties between April and November.

National Park Information Centres:

Mountain Centre (National Park Visitor Centre in Libanus): (☎01874 623 366; www.breconbeacons.org), in Libanus. Either walk to A470 or take bus #43 to Libanus (7min., M-Sa 6 per day), 5 mi. southwest of Brecon, then walk 1½ mi. uphill; on Su in July-Aug., take a shuttle to the front door (15min., 6 per day) or bus #R6 (15min., 2 per day), both from Brecon. Open daily July-Aug. 9:30am-6pm; Nov.-Feb. 9:30am-4:30pm; Mar.-June and Sept.-Oct. M-F 9:30am-5pm, Sa-Su 9:30am-5:30pm.

Abergavenny: see p. 467.

Brecon: see p. 469.

Craig-y-nos: (☎/fax 01639 730 395), at the Craig-y-nos Country Park. Stagecoach Bus #63, the Swansea-Brecon route (30min. from Brecon, M-Sa 3 per day); ask to be dropped at Craig-y-nos. Open May-Aug. M-F 10am-6pm, Sa-Su 10am-7pm; Mar.-Apr. and Sept.-Oct. M-F 10am-5pm, Sa-Su 10am-6pm; Nov.-Feb. M-F 10am-4pm, Sa-Su 10am-5:30pm.

Llandovery: Kings Rd. (☎01550 720 693). Near Black Mountain; take Heart of Wales train or bus #280 from Carmarthen. Open daily Easter-Sept. 10am-1pm and 1:45-5:30pm; Oct.-Easter M-Sa 10am-1pm and 1:45-4pm, Su 2-4pm.

🏠 ACCOMMODATIONS

The few Brecon B&Bs and hotels are listed in *Mid Wales* and the *Brecon Beacons Guide*. The most comprehensive listing is at www.brecon-beacons.com, which lists guest houses, hostels, cottages, caravans, bunkhouses, farms and campsites.

YHA HOSTELS
Scattered about the park are five **YHA hostels**, including **Ty'n-y-Caeau**, near Brecon (p. 470). The other four are:

Capel-y-Ffin: (kap-EL-uh-fin; ☎01873 890 650), near River Honddu at the eastern edge of the Black Mountains 1.25mi. from Offa's Dyke Path, 8 mi. from Hay-on-Wye. Take Stagecoach Red and White #39 or Yeomans #40 from Hereford to Brecon, stop at Hay, or #20 Newport to Hereford, alight Skirrid Inn. A taxi from Hay (Border Taxis ☎01497 821 266) is £12. The road to the hostel climbs up Gospel Pass past Hay Bluff. From Abergavenny, turn off A465 at Llanfihangel Crucorney to Llanthony; follow signs to Capel-y-Ffin. Horseback-riding trips by Black Mountain Holidays leave from here. (☎01873 890 650; ask for Howard.) Lockout 10am-5pm, daytime access to toilets and bad weather shelter. Curfew 11pm. Open mid-Apr. to Sept., but call 48hr. in advance. Dorms £9.30, under 18 £6.70. Camping £5 per tent. MC/V. ❶

Llanddeusant: (HLAN-thew-sont; ☎01550 740 218), at the foot of Black Mountain near Llangadog village; take the Trecastle-Llangadog road for 9 mi. off the A40. Restricted daytime access 10am-5pm. Curfew 11pm. Open mid-Apr. to Aug.; during other seasons, call 48hr. in advance. Dorms £9.30, under 18 £6.70. MC/V. ❶

Llwyn-y-Celyn: (HLEWN-uh-kel-in; ☎01874 624 261), 7 mi. south of Brecon, 2 mi. north from Storey Arms carpark on the A470. Take Sixty Sixty Bus #43 from Brecon or Merthyr Tydfil (M-Sa every 2hr., Su 3 per day). Close to Pen-y-Fan and the Beacons range. Farm-

SOUTH WALES

house near a nature trail. Lockout 10am-5pm; access to lounges and toilets. Book 2-3 weeks in advance. Curfew 11pm. Open daily Easter-Aug.; Sept.-Oct. Th-M; Nov. and Feb.-Easter F-Su. Dorms £10.60, under 18 £7.60. MC/V. ❶

Ystradfellte: (uh-strahd-FELTH-tuh; ☎01639 720 301), south of the woods and waterfall district, 3 mi. from the A4059 on a paved road; 4 mi. from the village of Penderyn; a 5min. walk from the Porth-yr-Ogof cave. Hard to reach by public transport (the X5 stops 5 mi. away). Small 17th-century cottages. Kitchen. Open Apr.-late September; flexible, call 48hr. in advance. Dorms £9.30, under 18 £6.70. Cash only. ❶

CAMPING

Campsites are plentiful, but often difficult to reach without a car. Check out www.brecon-beacons.com for up-to-date information. Many offer laundry and grocery facilities, and all have parking and showers (£3-6 per tent). Farmers may let you camp on their land if you ask first and leave the site as you found it; be prepared to make a donation toward feeding the sheep. The *Stay on a Farm* guide, available at the TIC, covers all of Wales with nearly 100 different options.

 HIKING

 WARNING. The mountains are unprotected and often difficult to scale. Cloud banks breed storms in minutes. In violent weather, do not take shelter in caves or under isolated trees, which tend to draw lightning. A compass is essential: much of the park is trackless, and landmarks get lost in sudden mists. Never hike alone, and consider registering with the police before setting out. See **Wilderness Safety,** p. 52.

THE BRECON BEACONS

At the center of the park, the Brecon Beacons position the skyline of Brecon against shorn peaks and idyllic farmland. Llangorse Lake, eight miles from Brecon, is the highest natural lake in South Wales, and is home to a crannog (iron-age dwelling) on a man-made island. To the south, the Mountain Centre NPIC outside Libanus (p. 473) houses an exhibit on its history and wildlife. A pamphlet on walks around the center costs £2; these strolls weave through fields of sheep and occasionally stop at churches, ancient monoliths aligned with celestial bodies, and even an Iron Age fort. The most convenient route to the top of **Pen-y-Fan** (pen-uh-VAN; 2907 ft.), the highest mountain in South Wales, begins at **Storey Arms** (a carpark and bus stop 5 mi. south of Libanus on the A470) and offers views of **Llyn Cwm Llwch** (HLIN-koom-hlooch), a 2000 ft. glacial pool in the shadow of neighboring **Corn Du** (CORN-dee) peak. The summit also hosts the remains of an ancient burial cairn. Because this route is the most convenient, it is also the most popular, and many hikers complain about overcrowding and litter on the trail. Most alternate paths are unmarked—consult NPICs (in Brecon, or the Mountain Centre) for recommendations and detailed directions. An arduous ridge path leads from Pen-y-Fan to other peaks in the Beacons.

The touristy **Brecon Mountain Railway,** which departs from Pant Station in Merthyr Tydfil, allows a glimpse of the south side of the Beacons as the narrow-gauge train runs along the Taf Fechan Reservoir north to Pontsticill. (☎01685 722 988. Runs daily from late Mar.-late Oct. 11am-4pm; £7.50, children £3.75, seniors £6.80.)

THE WATERFALL DISTRICT (FOREST FAWR)

Near the southern edge of the park on a limestone outcrop, a well-watered forest erupts with mosses and ferns. The triangle defined by Hirwaun, Ystradfellte, and Pontneeddfechan delineates the forest boundaries, in which rivers tumble through rapids, gorges, and spectacular falls near **Ystradfellte**, about 7 mi. southwest of the Beacons. At **Porth-yr-Ogof** ("Mouth of the Cave"), the River Mellte ducks into a cave at the base of the cliff and emerges as an icy pool. Swimming is decidedly not recommended—the stones are slippery and the pool deepens alarmingly. Exploring any grottoes beyond the main cave without a guide is also ill-advised. Additionally, erosion from water and foot traffic makes even the paths narrow and hard to navigate. Remote but worth the sweat is the **Sgwd yr Eira** waterfall (which means "Fall of Snow" but is also called "The Lady's Fall" because it was allegedly named for one of the 26 daughters of King Brychan) on the River Hepste, a half-mile from its confluence with the Mellte. You can stand behind thundering water in a cliff-face hollow and remain dry as a bone. Follow the marked paths to the falls from Gwaun Hepste. Hikers reach the waterfall district from the Beacons by crossing the A470 near the YHA Llwyn-y-Celyn, climbing Craig Cerrig-gleisiad cliff and Fan Frynych peak, and descending along a rocky Roman road. The route crosses a nature reserve and some of the park's trackless heath.

Between Swansea and Brecon off the A4067, the **Dan-yr-Ogof Showcaves** are one of the Park's most highly promoted attractions. Though their stalagmites and eerie rock formations are quite impressive, their "showcave" status has left them heavily trafficked and saturated with commercial trappings, most notably the grotesque but award-winning "Dinosaur Park"—complete with a "fearsome T-Rex" that looms nearby. (☎01639 730 284, 24hr. info 730 801. Open daily Apr.-Oct., 10am-5pm. £8.50, children £5.80.) From YHA Ystradfellte, 10 mi. of trails pass **Fforest Fawr** on their way to the caves. A **campsite ❶** is nearby. After turning off the A406 for the Showcaves, turn right at the T-junction. (Camping £4 per person. Caravans £10. Electricity free.) Relax at **Craig-y-nos Country Park**, a half-mile away. (☎01639 730 395. Open May-Aug. M-F 10am-6pm, Sa-Su 10am-7pm; Mar.-Apr. and Sept.-Oct. M-F 10am-5pm, Sa-Su 10am-6pm; Nov.-Feb. M-F 10am-4pm, Sa-Su 10am-4:30pm. Free.) **Stagecoach Red and White** #63 (1½hr, 3 per day, £3-4) stops at the hostel, caves, and campsite en route from Brecon to Swansea.

IN RECENT NEWS

THE BEACON

In an age when the euro looms ever larger in the UK, the town of Brecon has gone small, recently introducing its own currency, the beacon. Notes are for local use only, vaguely resemble Monopoly money, and are worth roughly £1. Visitors may not see one while in Brecon, but they have come into widespread use for villagers. The South Powys LETS (Local Exchange Trading System) created the Beacon scheme in 1993, but it has grown significantly in the last years, spurred by increasing competition with the euro. According to the BBC, beacons are just one of a half-dozen LETS currencies in Wales, including the Aber, the Teifi, the Wye, and the Llani.

The idea behind these currencies is to stabilize and strengthen a town's economy by controlling its money supply. The currency is only valid within the participating city, so money stays in the community, protecting small businesses and the local economy as a whole. Supporters also contend that it enables individuals to value goods and services according to community-specific needs rather than national standards, thereby protecting small towns from unfair urban standards. Broader currencies, they claim, tend to drive money toward corporations and capital cities. With the rise of the euro, this continues to be an increasing concern, suggesting a future need for local currencies in towns like Brecon.

THE BLACK MOUNTAINS

Located in the easternmost section of the park, the Black Mountains are a group of long, lofty ridges offering 80 sq. mi. of solitude. Summits like **Waun Fach** (2660 ft.), the highest point, may seem dull and boggy, but the views that ridge walks offer are unsurpassed. Ordnance Survey Outdoor Leisure Map #13 (1:25,000; £7) is essential. **Crickhowell,** on the A40 and Roy Brown's coaches route between Abergavenny and Builth Wells (#82, 25min., 1 every Th)is one of the best starting points for forays into the area, though hikers staying overnight might want to base themselves in the larger town of Abergavenny. You can also explore by bus: Stagecoach Red and White #39 linking Brecon and Hay-on-Wye (p. 469) descends the north side of the Black Mountains. **Gospel Pass,** the park's highest mountain pass, often sees sun above the cloud cover. Nearby, **Offa's Dyke Path** (p. 462) traces the park's eastern boundary. The ridge valleys are studded with churches, castles, and other ruins. There is almost no public transportation along valley routes.

SWANSEA (ABERTAWE)   ☎ 01792

Native son Dylan Thomas's paradoxical assessment of Swansea (pop. 230,000) as "this ugly lovely town," is remarkably resonant. The "ugly" bit is obvious: slab concrete buildings line bustling urban roads, industrial equipment borders the coast, and myriad box houses tuft the hillsides from base to peak in well-defined grids. Yet Swansea is an active city; it hosts colorful cafes and free museums, and embodies a utilitarian charm that its reputation has yet to make known. Farther west, the coastline turns more lovely—an expanse of sandy beaches extends onto the nearby Gower Peninsula, whose shores are only minutes away by bus or car.

⊏ TRANSPORTATION. Swansea has direct connections to most major cities in Britain. At the **train station,** 35 High St., trains (☎08457 484 950) arrive from: **Birmingham** (3½hr., 2 per hr., £32.70); **Cardiff** (1hr., 1-2 per hr., £8.10); **London** (3hr., 1 per hr., £68). The **Quadrant Bus Station** (☎0870 608 2608) is near the Quadrant Shopping Centre and the TIC. **National Express** (☎08705 808 080) runs buses from: **Birmingham** (3½hr., 2 per day, £24); **Cardiff** (1¼hr., 11 per day, £5.75); **London** (4½hr, 3 per day, £19.50). **First Cymru** (☎08706 082 608) buses cover the Gower Peninsula and the rest of southwest Wales; M-Sa a shuttle runs to **Cardiff** (1hr., 2-4 per hr., £7.50). A First Cymru **Day Saver** ticket (£3.10, concessions £1.90, families £5) allows unlimited travel for a day in the area; a £1.40 pass will get you unlimited travel M-Th nights after 7pm. The **Swansea Bay Pass,** purchased on the bus, covers a week of travel on the Peninsula (£12.50, concessions £8.40). **Stagecoach Buses** arrive from smaller towns around Wales, including **Brecon** (1½hr., 3 per day, £4.50). **Data Cabs** (☎474 747) and **Yellow Cab** (☎652 244) offer taxi services. From late July to September, **Cruises** (☎01412 432 224) set sail from Swansea to **Ilfracombe** and other spots on the Bristol Channel (£15-35).

⑫ PRACTICAL INFORMATION. On the north side of the bus station, the **Tourist Information Centre** books rooms for a £2 charge plus a 10% deposit and stocks events calendars and a helpful city map. (☎468 321; www.visitswanseabay.com. Open M-Sa 9:30am-5:30pm, Su 10am-4pm.) Other services include: **Barclays** (☎01633 205 000), The Kingsway (open M-Tu and Th-F 9am-5pm, W 10am-5pm, Sa 9:30am-3pm); **American Express,** 28 The Kingsway (☎455 188; open M-Tu and Th-F 9am-5pm, W 9:30am-5pm, Sa 9am-4pm); the **police** (☎456 999), on Grove Pl. at the bottom of Mt. Pleasant Hill; **Singleton Hospital** (☎205 666), on Sketty Park Ln.; free **Internet access** at the **Swansea Public Library,** Alexandra Rd. (☎516 750; book ahead; photo ID required; open M-W and F 9am-7pm, Th and Sa 9am-5pm) and on the ground floor of Debenham's in the Quadrant Shopping Centre (M-F 9:30am-6pm,

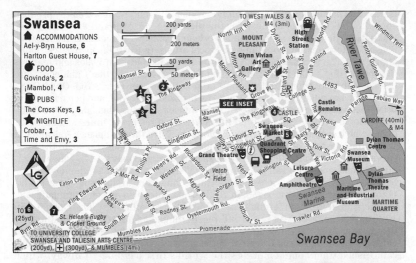

Sa 9am-6pm, (£1.50 per 30min.)); **Co-op pharmacy**, 13 Orchard St. (☎643 527; open M-F 9am-5:30pm, Sa 9am-1pm); and the **post office** with bureau de change, 35 The Kingsway (open M-Sa 9am-5:30pm). **Post Code: SA1 5LF.**

⌂🛏 ACCOMMODATIONS AND FOOD. The closest hostel is the popular **YHA Port Eynon,** an hour out of town by bus (p. 479). Inexpensive **B&Bs** and guest houses line **Oystermouth Road,** along the bay. Frequent buses make downtown access easy. **Ael-y-Bryn House ❻**, 88 Bryn Rd., has bay views and small but well-furnished rooms with TV and tea.(☎/fax 466 707. £20-23 per person. MC/V.) **Harlton Guest House ❼**, 89 King Edward Rd., offers adequate rooms with varying bright color schemes. (☎466 938; www.harltonguesthouse.co.uk. £14 per person. MC/V.) In high season, many travelers **camp** at sites along the Gower Peninsula.

Indian and Chinese takeaways line **St. Helen's Road,** and small cafes, fusion bistros, and trendy restaurants dominate **Oxford Street** and **Wind Street.** The city convenes at the **Swansea Market,** on the other side of the Quadrant Shopping Centre from the bus station, the largest indoor market in Wales. (Open M-Sa 8:30am-5:30pm). Relax at 🏮**Govinda's Vegetarian Restaurant ❶**, 8 Cradock St., a small shrine to tranquility nestled just off The Kingway. Try a salad with a freshly baked roll (£1.35) or an huge platter of vegetables (£6), "prepared in every way imaginable," as you browse brochures for yoga class and vegan toothpaste. (☎468 469. Open Su-Th noon-3pm, F-Sa noon-6pm. Cash only.) Self-described as "Hotter than a chili pepper, smoother than a Latin lover," **¡Mambo! ❷**, 46 The Kingsway, serves tasty Caribbean fare (£6 lunch) in a dining room lit by purple lanterns. (☎456 620. Open 10am-11pm. AmEx/MC/V.) **The Cross Keys ❶**, 12 St. Mary's St., is a sprawling pub, with a menu as large as its beer garden, a full bar to satisfy the barfly, and flashy games to occupy the bar-shy. (☎630 921. Open M-Sa 11am-11:20pm, Su noon-10:30pm. Food served M-Th 11am-8pm, F-Sa 8am-5:30pm, Su noon-6pm. MC/V.)

◖ SIGHTS. The **castle,** reduced to unmemorable ruins by rebel-hero Owain Glyndŵr, lies between Wind St. and The Strand, goes unnoticed by most; cars whiz by feet from its walls, and office buildings usurp its spot in the skyline. It overlooks **Castle Square,** a wide, circular plaza arranged around a two-tiered fountain. The collection at the **Glynn Vivian Art Gallery,** Alexandra Rd., reflects the eclectic tastes of its namesake and largest donor, Richard Glynn Vivian, a wealthy prodigal son who fled Victorian society for the pleasures of travel and art acquisition, amassing an impressive slew of metalwork and Nantgawr porcelain along the way. Seasonal shows feature contemporary local artists. (☎655 006. Open Tu-Su 10am-5pm. Free). The **Swansea Museum,** Victoria Rd., is the oldest in Wales and features the body of Hor, a gilded and mummified Egyptian priest, and the "Cabinet of Curiosities"—an institutionalized celebration of randomness. (☎653 763. Open Tu-Su 10am-5pm; last admission 4pm. Free.) The bronzed, hollowed, and pensive eyes of **Dylan Thomas** gaze seaward at the end of Swansea's marina; this late poet, a demigod of local culture and national literature, inspires many tours named in his honor which shepherd iambic junkies along the **Dylan Thomas Uplands Trail** and **City Centre Trail,** past the poet's favorite haunts. More detailed guidebooks to the trails (from £1.50) are available at the **Dylan Thomas Centre,** Somerset Pl., which venerates Thomas and his "craft of sullen art." Visitors can listen as Thomas breathlessly recites five of his poems, and his more famous portraits hang alongside his notoriously sizeable bar tabs (£8, in 1953). The Centre also presents dramatic, cinematic, and literary performances. (☎463 980, box office 463 892. Open Tu-Su 10:30am-4:30pm. Free.) As in Cardiff, recent rebuilding has transformed the **maritime quarter** from decaying dockland to upscale apartment blocks and outdoor cafes. In the **Maritime and Industrial Museum,** just behind a Leisure Centre, a fully refurbished tram commemorates the world's first passenger railway, which chugged from Swansea to Oystermouth in 1807, powered first by workhorse, then sails to capture bay breezes, then finally conventional methods. (☎ 653 763. Open Tu-Su 10am-5pm. Free. The museum's main building is closed for renovations until Easter 2005, but the passenger railway exhibit is still open next door.)

🎭 🎶 **NIGHTLIFE AND ENTERTAINMENT.** The young folk of Swansea do not go gentle on weekend nights; rather, festivities begin at "pre-club bars" as early as 7pm and rage, rage until 3am. Nightlife centers around **The Kingsway,** where swarms of students club-hop on weekend nights. **Time & Envy,** 72 The Kingsway, marshals the most prestige because of sheer size and numbers. Two doors away yet connected underground, Time aficionados gyrate under 20ft. katanas and a Chinese dragon while those who elect Envy leer from the second floor balcony. (☎653 142. F is £12 all-inclusive members night. Cover £5-7. Open M and W-Th 10pm-2am, F-Sa 10pm-3am.) A short walk away, **Crobar,** Northampton Ln., offers a low-key alternative with white leather booths and a dimly lit second floor obscured by smoke. (☎470 074. Cover from £5. Open F 10pm-3am, S 10pm-4am.) About 5 mi. away, pubs on Gower's Mumbles Rd. are a barfly's magnet (p. 480).

The bimonthly *What's On,* free at the TIC, lists events around town. The **Dylan Thomas Theatre,** along the marina, stages dramas and musicals. (☎473 238. Tickets from £6, concessions from £5.) The **Grand Theatre,** on Singleton St., puts on operas, ballets, concerts, and comedy. (☎475 715. Box office open M-Sa 9:30am-8pm, Su 1hr. before show. Tickets £10-35; same-day concessions available for many less expensive shows.) The **Taliesin Arts Centre,** University College, hosts films, art shows, and dance. (☎296 883. Box office open M-F 10am-6pm, Sa noon-6pm, and before curtain. Get brochures on campus.) In mid-August, the village of Pontardawe, 8 mi. north, floods with international folk and rock musicians for the **Pontardawe International Music Festival** (☎830 200; www.pontardawefestival.com). The **Swansea Festival** (☎411 570, bookings ☎475 715) presents shows, concerts, and family activities. Revelry continues with the **Dylan Thomas Celebration** (☎463 980; www.dylanthomasfestival.com), which includes readings, shows, and lectures that run from Dylan's birthday to the date of his death (Oct. 27th-Nov. 9th).

THE GOWER PENINSULA ☎01792

The 18 mi. Gower Peninsula is rife with unexpected finds. Ancient burial sites, castles, and churches constellate the land; expansive white beaches connect a slate-blue ocean to the flower-covered limestone cliffs that rise above it. Mumbles, its largest city, entrances wide-eyed visitors and nearby Swansea residents alike with its beaches, nightlife, and a lovable seaside demeanor as unassuming as its name.

⌐ TRANSPORTATION. Buses to the peninsula spoke out from Swansea's **Quadrant Station. First Cymru** (☎08706 082 608) buses #2 and 2A leave **Swansea** for Oystermouth Sq. in **Mumbles** (20min., 4 per hr., £1.70) and continue to **Langland Bay** and then **Caswell Bay.** Buses #18 and 18A run to **Oxwich** (40min., 2 per day, £3.10), and lurch through the hills to **Rhossili** via **Port Eynon** (1hr., every 2hr., £3.10). Bus #14 shuttles to **Pennard** (35min., every hr., £3.10). On Sundays, bus travel is more difficult, though buses #48 and 49 run 3 times. The First Cymru **Day Saver** is valid through the Gower and Swansea (£3.10, under 18 £1.90), while the **Gower & City Rider** allows a week's unlimited travel around the Peninsula (£12.50, under 16 £3.50). **A.A. Taxis** (☎360 600) provide on-call transport. The pleasant **Swansea Bikepath and Promenade** traces the coast from Swansea Bay to Mumbles pier.

⚑ PRACTICAL INFORMATION. Mumbles, the largest city on Gower, has the most helpful services. The relocated **Tourist Information Centre** shares space with Mumbles Methodist Church on Mumbles Rd. (☎361 302. Open M-Sa 10am-5pm.) **Gower Guided Walks** (☎07931 932 255; www.gowerguidedwalks.co.uk) offers package deals to those who want to experience the Peninsula by foot. Other services include: **Barclays,** 16 Newton Rd. (☎492 600; open M-Tu and Th-F 9am-4:30pm, W 10am-4:30pm); the **police** (☎456 999), Newton Rd., near Castle St.; free **Internet access** at **Oystermouth Library,** Dunns Ln., a block from the TIC (☎368 380; photo ID required; open M-F 9:30am-5:30pm, Sa 9:30am-5pm; and the **post office,** 522 Mumbles Rd. (☎366 821; open M-F 9am-5:30pm, Sa 9am-12:30pm). **Post Code:** SA3 4DH.

⌂☐ ACCOMMODATIONS AND FOOD. West Gower has less touristy and cheaper accommodations than Mumbles, where **B&Bs** charge upwards of £22 and cluster on **Mumbles Road** and in the **South End** area (a 10min. walk from the TIC); singles are hard to find. Vaunting large bay windows (with large bay views), the gabled **Coast House ❸,** 708 Mumbles Rd., lets you observe schooners over breakfast scones. (☎368 702. Most rooms with TV and bath. Singles £26, doubles from £50.) Behind it, **Rock Villa ❸,** 1 George Bank, offers comparable views, comfortable nooks, and a feeling of familial hospitality. (☎366 794. Doubles and twins £50, ensuite £52. MC/V.) **Glenview Guest House ❹,** 140 Langland Rd., a 10min. walk uphill from the TIC, is an 1870 Victorian belle with luxurious ensuite rooms and extra perks, like views of Underhill Park and a log fire for wintry nights. (☎367 933; fax ☎363 514. Doubles £55-60; twins £65-75; single £45-55; family rooms £65-75; family suite £75-120. Closed Nov. MC/V.) Take bus #14 to reach accommodations in nearby **Bishopston.** To camp at **Three Cliffs Bay Caravan Park ❶,** North Hills Farm, Penmaen, take bus #18 from Swansea. (☎371 218. £6 per person; electricity £1.50. Cash and debit only.) Bus #18A and sometimes #18 run from Swansea to Port Enyon, west of Mumbles and home to the awesome ⊠**YHA Port Eynon ❶.** This former lifeboat house on the beach offers nice rooms, a clean kitchen, and a cozy common area. Learn to surf or enjoy stunning local cliff hikes. (☎390 706; fax 391 623. Reception 8-10am and 5-10pm. Check-in after 5pm. Open Easter-Nov. £11.80, under 18 £8.50. MC/V.) Beachside **camping** is also possible in Port Eynon.

In Mumbles, the **Somerfield** supermarket is at 512 Mumbles Rd. (Open daily 8am-10pm.) The array of freshly harvested options at **The Choice is Yours,** 7 Newton Rd., sells exclusively produce, perfect for cheap snacks or healthy picnic ingredients. (☎367 255. Open M-Sa 8:30am-5:30pm.) Situated on a wooden pier, busy **Verdi's ❶,** Knab Rock, at the southern end of Mumbles Rd., caters to ice cream lovers of every ilk with a variety of traditional (cookies 'n' cream) and distinctive (honeycomb, apple cobbler) flavors. Verdi's restaurant next door serves bistro cuisine. (☎369 135. Single scoop £1.20. Open daily 9am-10pm. MC/V.) **Claude's Restaurant ❷,** 93 Newton Rd., promises "food with flair" and delivers with concoctions like onion and goat cheese tartlets and monkfish with a saffron pancetta infusion (☎366 006; www.claudes.org.uk. Open M-Sa noon-2:30pm and 6-9pm, Su noon-3pm. AmEx/MC/V.) **Madisons ❶,** 620 Mumbles Rd., is a small coffee shop with a big view of the bay serving favorites like omelettes and Welsh rarebit (£2.75). If given a day's notice, they will pack picnic lunches for hikes along the beach or cliffs. (☎368 484. Open daily 8am-10pm. Cash only.)

🔄🏖 **SIGHTS AND BEACHES.** Perched high above Mumbles, the ramparts of 13th century **Oystermouth Castle,** on Castle Ave. off Newton Rd., offer a bird's eye view of labyrinthine streets laced with pastel bungalows and Victorians. (☎368 732. Open Apr. to mid-Sept. daily 11am-5pm. £1.) Further down the peninsula, the 56-acre **Mumbles Hill Nature Reserve** is a steep but worthwhile excursion; hikers find sweeping vistas of Swansea's coastal flats between patches of scrub and natural arbors. The path begins with a staircase by the George Hotel, 10min. from the TIC. Examining the small collection at the **Lovespoon Gallery,** 492 Mumbles Rd., will yield a richer understanding of the heritage of the craft. Make one of these spoons your own, from £5; engraving £6 and 10 days. (☎360 132; www.lovespoons.co.uk. Open M-Sa 10am-5:30pm.)

The Gower Peninsula is strewn with gorgeous beaches, some more friendly to swimmers than others. From Southgate and Pennard, a 30min. walk along the Coast Path brings you to **Three Cliffs,** a secluded, cave-ridden beauty almost completely submerged at high tide. **Langland Bay, Caswell Bay, Oxwich Bay,** and **Port Eynon Bay** are all popular and have received high ratings for their cleanliness and superb views. To reach Langland, walk 45min. along the Bays Footpath that begins around the point of Mumbles Head. Caswell is another 45min., and Oxwich and Port Eynon are several miles beyond; buses #18 and 18A from Swansea will stop if asked. On the peninsula's western tip, green cliffs hug the sweeping curve of ⬛**Rhossili Beach,** whose wide expanse and complete lack of development makes overcrowding unlikely; take bus #18A from Swansea. At low tide, a causeway provides access to the seabird haven **Worm's Head,** a series of serpentine crags that looks like a "wurm"—from the Welsh for dragon—lumbering out to sea. (Call ☎306 534 for details on tides. Worm's Head only approachable 2½hr. either side of low tide). **Llangennith Beach,** north of Rhossili, draws surfers from all over Wales.

🎵🎭 **NIGHTLIFE AND FESTIVALS.** A fishing hole by day, **Mumbles** becomes a watering hole at night. The short stretch of **Mumbles Road** at Mumbles Head is lined with pubs, some of them former haunts of Dylan Thomas. In University of Swansea lingo, to hang out on Mumbles Rd. is to "go mumbling"; to start at one end and have a pint at each pub is to "do the Mumbles Mile." Flower's, Usher's, Buckley's, and Felin Foel are the local real ales. The **Gower Festival** fills the peninsula's churches with string quartets and Bach chorales during the last two weeks of July. (Tickets £5-10; ☎475 715 for booking.) The *What's On* guide, free at the Mumbles TIC, has details.

SOUTH WALES

TENBY (DINBYCH-Y-PYSGOD) ☎01834

Called "the Welsh Riviera," Tenby is neither archetypal Welsh town nor polished seaside resort. The city balances its history as "the little fort of the fishes"—the literal translation of Dinbych-y-Pysgood—with new tourism. And although the novelty shops, chip dives, and humming penny arcades threaten to devalue its charm, the lapping of cerulean waves upon its seaboard and the handsome, multicolored houses overlooking them reinforce its authenticity. Those who avoid July and August—when half of Britain, their children, and their dogs descend upon the town—find less pull from the tourism board and more from the magnetism of warm beaches and an abounding maritime legacy.

▐▔ TRANSPORTATION. The unstaffed **train station** is at the bottom of Warren St. **Tenby Travel,** in the Tenby Indoor Market between High St. and Upper Frog St., books tickets. (☎843 214. Open M-Tu and Th-F 9am-5pm, W and Sa 9am-4pm.) **Trains** (☎08457 484 950) arrive from: **Cardiff** (2½hr., 4 per day, £14.50); **Carmarthen** (45min., 3 per day, £5.40); **Pembroke** (30min., M-Sa 3 per day, Su 2 per day, £3.20); **Swansea** (1½hr., 3 per day, £8.50).

Buses leave from the multi-story carpark on Upper Park Rd., next to Somerfield market. **First Cymru** (☎01792 580 580) arrives from **Haverfordwest** via **Pembroke** (#349; every hr. M-Sa until 7:40pm, Su 3 per day). Or head from **Swansea** to **Carmarthen** (#X11; M-Sa 2 per hr., £3.70) and transfer to **Silcox Coaches** (☎842 189; www.silcoxcoaches.co.uk) bus #333 (1hr., M and W-F 1 per day, Tu and Sa 2 per day). A Silcox Coaches office is in the Town Hall Arcade between South Parade and Upper Frog St. **National Express** (☎08705 808 080) also runs from **Swansea** (#508). First Cymru **FirstDay Saver** (£4) and **FirstWeek Saver** (£12) buy unlimited daily or weekly travel within Pembrokeshire on First buses, while the **West Wales Rover Ticket** (£5) works on all bus lines. **Taxis** congregate near pubs on F and Sa nights; call **Tenby's Taxis** (☎843 678).

▆✶ 🏛 ORIENTATION AND PRACTICAL INFORMATION. The old town is in the shape of a triangle pointing into the bay, with its sides formed by **North Beach** and **South Beach** (which becomes **Castle Beach**), coming to a point at **Castle Hill,** and the train station along the base. From the station, **Warren Street** approaches town, becoming **White Lion Street** and continuing to the promenade overlooking North Beach. From here **Goscar Rock,** a large crag on the beach and Tenby's most postcarded landmark, is visible. Off White Lion, **South Parade** and **Upper Frog Street** lead toward South Beach, while **High Street** and **Crackwell Street** veer off toward the Castle and eventually converge at the harbor. **The Croft** runs along North Beach, and the **Old Wall** runs along South Parade. Overlooking North Beach, the **Tourist Information Centre,** The Croft, has a free accommodations list. (☎842 404. Free town maps. Bookings £2 plus a 10% deposit. Open daily June to mid-July 10am-5:30pm; daily mid-July to Aug. 10am-9pm; Sept.-May M-Sa 10am-4pm.) Other services include: **Barclays,** 18 High St. (the ATM is hidden on Frog St.; open M-W and F 9am-4:30pm, Th 10am-4:30pm); **Washeteria,** Lower Frog St. (☎842 484; wash £1.70-2.60, dry 20p per 5min., soap 20p; open daily 8:30am-9pm; last wash 8:30pm); the **police,** Warren St. (☎842 303), near the church off White Lion St.; **Tenby Cottage Hospital,** Church Park Rd. near Trafalgar Rd. (☎842 040); **Internet access** at **Tenby County Library,** Greenhill Ave. (☎843 934; free; book in advance; open M and W-F 9:30am-1pm and 2-5pm, Tu 9:30am-1pm and 2-6pm, Sa 9:30am-12:30pm), or at **Webb-Computers,** 17 Warren St. (☎844 101; £1 per 15min.; open M-F 9am-5pm, Sa 9am-4pm); **Boots pharmacy,** High St. (☎842 120; open M-Sa 8:30am-6pm, as late as 7pm July-Aug., Su 10am-4pm); and the **post office,** Warren St., at South Parade (☎843 213; open M-F 8:30am-5:30pm, Sa 8:30am-12:30pm). **Post Code:** SA70 7JR.

⌂ ACCOMMODATIONS. On **Warren Street,** outside the town wall near the train station, scads of signs for **B&Bs** (£20-26) line the sidewalks; the side streets of **Greenhill Avenue** and those off the Esplanade and Trafalgar Rd. are almost as well endowed. You can also take a bus to **Saundersfoot** (#352, M-Sa every hr., Su 1-2 per hr. in summer). Overlooking North Beach, **Gwynne House ❸,** Bridge St., shirks the doilies and florid interiors of traditional British guest houses in favor of a relaxed, beach house-like ambience. (☎843 450. Doubles £55, all ensuite. MC/V.) Cheery rooms near South Beach await in the **Blue Dolphin Hotel ❷,** St. Mary's St. (☎842 590. Rooms £19-21 per person, ensuite £25-29. MC/V.) The comfortable ensuite rooms at **Lyndale ❸,** Warren St., may have you spending more time in bed than on the beach. (☎842 836. £25-27.) Campers can head to **Meadow Farm ❶,** at the top of The Croft, overlooking the town. (☎844 829. Open Easter-Sept. £6.)

⌂ FOOD. Tenby has plenty of restaurants, but most are aimed at vacationers and charge accordingly. Lunch specials can soften the blow at nicer eateries, and packing a picnic to take to nearby scenic spots is an appealing and inexpensive option. To put together a meal-to-go, **Tenby Market Hall,** between High St. and Upper Frog St., sells deli goods and baked treats. (Open daily 8:30am-5:30pm; Oct.-June closed Su.) A **Somerfield** supermarket is located on Upper Park Rd. (Open M-Th and Sa 8am-8pm, F 8am-9pm.) Though hidden in an alley connecting Bridge St. and St. Julian's St., a jungle of flowers betrays ◙**Plantagenet House ❹,** Quay Hill. Inside, diners feast by candlelight on butternut squash and coriander potato cakes (£6) in the hearth of the oldest and tallest (39 ft.) medieval Flemish chimney in Wales. This fine establishment specializes in seafoods as rich as its architectural history. (☎842 350. Starters from £4, entrees from £15.50. Open Easter-June M-Sa 6pm-late, July-Aug. noon-3pm and 5pm-late; Sept.-Easter F and Sa 6pm-late. MC/V.) The sandwich crafters at **The Country Kitchen ❶,** Upper Frog St., have turned the filled baguette into a science, with delicious fillings and great prices. (☎843 539. Baguettes from £1.90, sandwiches from £1.40. Open daily June-Aug. 9:30am-3:30pm; Sept.-May 9:30am-3pm. Closing time fluctuates daily. Cash only.) **Pam Pam ❸,** 2 Tudor Sq., offers great food tucked away from the bustle of Tudor Sq., and includes a hefty vegetarian selection, for predictably steep dinner prices (entrees £7-16). Their "light meals menu," however, which runs until 5:30pm, will get you excellent fare for £3-7. (☎842 946. Open daily 11am-10pm. AmEx/MC/V.) **The Ceramic Cafe ❷,** 3 Crackwell St., is the perfect place to kindle any artistic impulses that Tenby's colorful street scenes may have sparked. Bask in creative glory with tempting lunch foods (from £3) as you decorate pottery pieces (£3-35) in this cliffside studio. (☎845 968. Open M-Sa 10am-5pm. MC/V.)

◙ ⌂ SIGHTS AND BEACHES. A sun-bleached **Prince Albert the Good** stands atop Castle Hill looking out over the ruins of the castle and colorful Tenby. On clear days the views reach across Carmarthen Bay, Rhossili Beach's Worm's Head, and the Devon coast. Located in a renovated section of the castle itself, the **Tenby Museum and Art Gallery** presents Tenby's social and artistic heritage. Fascinating for both children and adults, displays recount the tales of "Leekie Porridge," a legendary Tenby pirate whose wax likeness is imprisoned beneath the stairs, and recreate a sea cave full of the seals and puffins for which the Pembroke coast is known. (☎842 809. Open daily Easter-Nov. 10am-5pm; Dec.-Easter M-F 10am-5pm. £2, concessions £1, children £1.50.) The 3 floors of the **Tudor Merchant's House,** on Quay Hill off Bridge St., detail life in a 16th-century Welsh household. The furniture and herb garden reveal much about upper-class living, but so does the garderobe, a three-story latrine whose contents were excavated in 1984 to show what really fueled Tudor Tenby's merchant class. (☎842 279. Open daily Apr.-Sept.

10am-5pm, Oct. 10am-3pm. £2, children £1, families £5.) At night, Tenby's spooks and ghouls share the streets with resort revelers; the 1½hr. **Walks of Tenby** and **Ghost Walk of Tenby** depart from the Lifeboat Tavern in Tudor Sq. at 8pm. (☎845 841. Open daily mid-June to mid-Sept.; mid-Sept. to mid-May M, W, F-Sa, advance booking required. £3.75, concessions £3.50, children £2.75, families £13.)

Promenades and clifftop benches afford marvelous views, but most visitors zip straight to the sand. On sunny days, **North Beach**, below the Croft, and **South Beach**, beyond the Esplanade, swarm with pensioners and naked toddlers. At the eastern tip of Tenby, **Castle Beach** reaches into caves that lure the curious explorer, but only more remote beaches consistently offer escape from oceanside throngs. A variety of inventive **boat excursions** leave from the harbor; check the kiosks at Castle Beach (☎845 400) for the "Seal Safari"—a one-hour jet boat ride to St. Margaret's island and Cathedral Caves (£10, children £6.50)—or the "Special Cruise," a two-hour mystery excursion set against the setting sun (T, Th, Sa-Su 7pm).

DAYTRIPS FROM TENBY

CALDEY ISLAND. Three miles south of Tenby, this largely unspoiled island hosts a diverse community of seabirds, seals, and 20 enterprising Cistercian monks, who produce perfume from indigenous lavender and gorse for the droves that come to see their gorgeous Italianate monastery. Equally fragrant, the chocolate factory inspired by the monks' Belgian roots turns out over 12 tons of sweets a year (bars from 99p). Though the monastery itself is closed to visitors, the island provides other pleasant explorations amidst ivied tree trunks and huge expanses of uncrowded coastline. (Caldey Boats sail from Tenby Harbor. ☎842 296. Cruises 20min. Easter-Oct. 3 per hr. M-Sa 10am-3pm, last round-trip 5pm. Round-trip £8, children £4, seniors £7.)

DYLAN THOMAS BOATHOUSE. Dylan Thomas spent his last four years in the boat house in **Laugharne** (LAN), about 15 mi. northeast of Tenby, happily claiming that he "got off the bus, and forget to get on again." Today, the boathouse contains original furniture (including toys dug up from the garden) and a recreated version of Thomas' writing shed—his "house on stilts high among beaks." Though quite a trek from Tenby by public transport, it's a rewarding pilgrimage for Thomas aficionados, or anyone who likes herons. (Take First Cymru bus #351 to Pendine (50min, every 2hr.) and then transfer to #222, which goes from Pendine to Laugharne (12min., M-Sa 10 per day). ☎01994 427 420; www.dylanthomasboathouse.com. Open daily May-Oct. 10am-5:30pm; Nov.-Apr. 10:30am-3:30pm. £3, concessions £2.25, children £1.50.)

MANORBIER CASTLE. Gerald of Wales, a noted 12th-century transcriber of rural life, was a particular champion of this castle—his birthplace. He referred to it as "the pleasantest spot in Wales," and it's still a contender today. Aside from stunning views (accessible from a dank staircase), the castle offers a few other unexpected finds: a dovecote for harvesting pigeons (for eating), and a set of inexplicably attractive wax figurines (Gerald's likeness is the ugliest of the lot) stands guard throughout the castle and "recreates" 12th-century life. (First Cymru bus #349 shuttles between Tenby, Manorbier, Pembroke, and Haverfordwest (M-Sa every hr., Su 3 per day in summer). ☎01834 317 394. Open daily Easter-Sept. 10:30am-5:30pm. £3, children £1.50, seniors £2.50) Manorbier has a **YHA hostel** (p. 485), as well as numerous **B&Bs.**

CAREW CASTLE. Strange and handsome Carew Castle, 5 mi. northwest of Tenby, is an odd mixture of Norman fortress and Elizabethan manor, where mighty stone towers flank the delicate sills of the somewhat out-of-place windows. Check Coast to Coast, free at most TICs, for events at the castle. (Take Silcox bus #361 from Tenby to the castle (45min., M-Sa 3-4 per day). ☎01646 651 782. Open daily Mar.-Oct. 10am-5pm. Tours at 2:30pm. Castle and mill £1.90, concessions £1.50, families £7.50.)

PEMBROKESHIRE COAST NATIONAL PARK

The 225 mi.^{2} of Pembrokeshire Coast National Park (Parc Cenedlaethol Arfordir Penfro) are divided between long oceanside stretches and scattered inland pockets. The park spans the wooded Gwaun Valley and ancient Celtic ruins deep in the Preseli Hills, but its coastline remains its most compelling draw. The tranquil isolation of intimate coves and the towering permanence of ancient sea cliffs lure serious backpackers and day hikers alike along 186 mi. of coastal trail. While oil refineries and working harbors dot the path as reminders of man's encroachments, sand dunes and wildflower cascades still dominate the scene.

⊏ TRANSPORTATION

The best place to enter the region is **Haverfordwest.** Buses radiate from here to the various coastal regions, which offer a wider variety of accommodation options and prettier surroundings. The rail system is less useful for travelers seeking to make connections around the coast, as Pembroke Docks and Milford Haven end their respective lines. While *Let's Go* does not recommend hitchhiking, hitchers frequent the area. Mountain bikes are an excellent means of transport on the one-lane roads. Do not ride on the coastal path itself; it is illegal and dangerous.

Trains: (☎08457 484 950) arrive from **Cardiff** (3hr., up to 10 per day, £14.50) and **London Paddington** (4½hr., up to 9 per day, £78.50). Also to **Fishguard** on the north coast and **Tenby** and **Pembroke Dock** on the south (change at **Whitland**).

Buses: Consult the bus transport booklets available at all local TICs to sort out the many local providers. **Richards Brothers** (☎01239 613 756) runs from **Haverfordwest** to **Fishguard** (#411, 1½hr., 5 per day) and **St. David's** (#411, 45min., 13 per day, £2.15). **First Cymru** (☎01792 580 580) runs from **Haverfordwest** to **Milford Haven** (#302; 30min.; M-Sa 1-2 per hr., Su 7 per day) and **Tenby** via **Pembroke** (#349; 1½hr., 12 per day). **Silcox Coaches** (☎01646 683 143) teams up with **Taf Valley Coaches** (☎01994 240 908) to run from **Haverfordwest** to **Broad Haven** (#311, 20min., M-Sa 4-7 per day). The **Puffin Shuttle** #400 runs between **St. David's** and **Milford Haven** (3 per day), and the **Strumble Shuttle** #404 connects **St. David's** and **Fishguard** (3 per day). First Cymru's **FirstDay Pass** (£4) will get you unlimited bus transport within Pembrokeshire on their buses, while the more useful West Wales Rover Ticket (£5) works all day on any bus service.

Bike Rental: Voyages of Discovery, Cross Sq. (☎01437 721 911), opposite Lloyd's Bank in St. David's. £10 per half-day, £15 per day. Open daily 8am-7pm.

Other Rentals: A number of **outdoor activity centers** rent canoes, kayaks, ponies, bikes, and various adventure tools; check out *Explore Pembrokeshire,* available at NPICs, for locations. Among the most popular is the excellent **TYF Adventure** (☎01437 721 611 or 0800 132 588; www.tyf.com), with stores in Tenby and St. David's.

🔃 PRACTICAL INFORMATION

The **National Park Information Centers (NPICs)** listed below sell 10 annotated maps covering the coastal path (from 40p each). The indispensable official trail guide is pricey (£13) but detailed and includes color maps. Ask about the guided walks offered by the park. For **weather information,** call any NPIC; in an emergency, contact **rescue rangers** by dialing ☎999 or 112.

National Park Information Centres:

Newport: 2 Bank Cottages, Long St. (☎01239 820 912). Open Apr.-Oct. M-Sa 10am-5:30pm; June-Aug. also Su 10am-1:15pm.

St. David's: The Grove (☎01437 720 392; www.stdavids.co.uk). Doubles as the town TIC. Open daily Apr.-Oct. 9:30am-5:30pm; Nov.-Easter M-Sa 10am-4pm. Closed 2 weeks in Jan.

Tourist Information Centres:

Fishguard: see p. 490.

Haverfordwest: 19 Old Bridge (☎01437 763 110), adjacent to bus stop. Open Apr.-Aug. M-Sa 10am-5:30pm; Sept. 10am-5pm; Oct.-Mar. 10am-4pm.

Milford Haven: 94 Charles St. (☎01646 690 866). Open Apr.-Oct. M-Sa 10am-1pm and 1:30-5pm.

Saundersfoot: The Barbecue, Harbour Car Park (☎01834 813 672). Open daily Apr.-Oct. 10am-5:30pm.

Tenby: see p. 481.

🛏 ACCOMMODATIONS

Many farmers convert fallow fields into summer **campsites** (about £4 per tent); inquire before pitching. While some hostels may allow camping, many prefer not to and have specific quotas (as low as 4 people) on the number of campers they will accommodate, so ask first. Roads between Tenby, Pembroke, and St. David's are home to plenty of **B&Bs** (£15-30), but they can be hard to secure in summer (during school holiday) and buses come only every few hours. Spaced along the coastal path, the park's **YHA hostels,** listed below, are all within a reasonable day's walk of one another. If you plan well ahead (at least 14 days in advance), you can book all of the hostels by calling ☎08702 412 314 or visiting www.yha.org.uk.

Broad Haven: (☎01437 781 688), on St. Bride's Bay off the B4341. Take bus #311 from Haverfordwest to Broad Haven (20min., 4-6 per day) or Puffin bus #400 from St. David's (35min., 3 per day) or Milford Haven (1¼hr., 3 per day). 77 beds. Lockout 10am-1pm. Curfew 11pm. Open mid-Feb. to Oct. Call 48hr. in advance. Dorms £11.80, under 18 £8.50. MC/V. ❷

Manorbier: Skrinkle Haven (☎01834 871 803), a bright, modern building near Manorbier Castle (p. 483). From the train station, walk past the A4139 to the castle, make a left onto the B4585, a right up to the army camp (fear not, it isn't the hostel), and follow the signs. Showers and laundry. Lockout 10am-5pm. Curfew 10pm, keycode access. Open daily Mar.-Oct. Dorms £11.80, under 18 £8.50. MC/V. ❷

Marloes Sands: (☎01646 636 667), near the Dale Peninsula. Take Puffin bus #400 (1¼hr., 3 per day) from St. David's or Milford Haven—ask to be let off at the hostel. A cluster of farm buildings on National Trust Property, with access to a huge and unspoiled beach. A good site for watersports. Lockout 10am-5pm. Curfew 11pm. Open Apr.-Oct. Dorms £8.20, under 18 £5.70. MC/V. ❶

Pen Y Cym: (☎0870 770 5988), near Solvo. Located close to Newgale Beach. Showers and laundry provided. Rated one of the best in Britain. Lockout 10am-4pm. Curfew 11pm. Dorms £13.40, under 18 £9.30. MC/V. ❷

Pwll Deri: (☎0870 770 6004), on breathtaking 300 ft. cliffs around Strumble Head near Fishguard. Lockout 10am-5pm. Curfew 11pm. Open daily mid-July to Aug.; Sept.-Oct. and Apr.-June M and Th-Su. Dorms £9.30, under 18 £6.70. MC/V. ❶

St. David's: (☎01437 720 345), near St. David's Head. Take the 2 mi. path turning right at the Bishop's Palace and look for the red doors. Or, from the A487 (Fishguard Rd.), turn onto the B4583 and follow signs from the golf club. Men stay in the cowshed, women in the stables, with extra rooms in the granary. Lockout 10am-5pm; daytime access to dining hall. Open daily mid-July to Aug.; Sept.-Oct. and Apr. to mid-July W-Su. Dorms £9.30, under 18 £6.70. MC/V. ❶

THE BIG SPLURGE

CRAZY, OR JUST COASTEERING?

You swim from the beach to an isolated islet; huffing all the way, you scramble up a pebbly rockface, and then peer off a 50 ft. crag into roaring blue breakers below. And then you jump.

No, you're not just crazy, you're Coasteering, a sport pioneered on the Pembrokeshire coast in the 1980s. It combines all your favorite beachside activities into one. Swimming, rock scrambling, and even cliff diving are all essential to a fantastic expedition on the cliffs and rock bridges of Wales' southwestern coastline. And with a heart-pounding feat to contemplate (and hopefully execute) every next minute, its sure to tickle your inner adventurer.

TYF in St. David's (p. 489) specializes in this extreme sport, and grades courses on three levels. Blue lines are for beginners: calm seas and light winds ease you onto the cliffs. White lines are a bit choppier, and red lines consist of rough seas meant only for the athletically inclined.

One can expect a £30-40 halfday pricetag, but for the ultimate experience try Presali Venture's £169 weekend. With accompaniments of hiking and surfing, coasteering takes the mainstage. They provide transport from the train station, accommodations, meals, wetsuits, and—most importantly—a trained professional to guide newbies through coasteering's inherent hazards. (☎01348 837 709 for details).

Trefin: (☎01348 831 414), a former school situated in the village of Trefin between St. David's and Fishguard. Bus #411 stops upon request. Just ½ mi. from the coast, near pretty walks. Lockout 10am-5pm. Curfew 11pm, keycode access. Open daily July-Aug.; Sept.-Oct. and Apr.-June Tu-Sa. Dorms £9.30, under 18 £6.70. MC/V. ❶

⚑ 🏔 HIKING AND OUTDOORS

For short hikes, stick to the more accessible **St. David's Peninsula** in the northwest. Otherwise, set out on the 186 mi. **Pembrokeshire Coast Path,** marked with acorn symbols along manageable terrain, which begins in the southeast at Amroth and continues west across old sandstone through Tenby. Bosherton's Lily Ponds, manmade inlets that bloom in early summer, cut inland, but circle around to St. Govan's Head, where worn steps lead to **St. Govan's Chapel.** One myth has it that Sir Gawain retreated here after the fall of Camelot. The waters of the well are said to heal ills and grant wishes, and (supposedly) no mortal can count the steps. From here to the impressive **Elegug Stacks**—offshore pinnacles of rock with the largest seabird colonies of the entire coastline—the path passes natural sea arches (the famous 80 ft. Green Bridge is particularly striking), and limestone stacks. Unfortunately, the stretch from St. Govan's Head to the Stacks (6 mi.) is sometimes used as an artillery range and closed to hikers. Call the **Castemartin Range Office** (☎01646 662 367) or the **Pembroke National Visitor Centre** (☎01646 622 388) for openings or check at the Tenby TIC. For 10 mi. west of the Stacks the coast is permanently off-limits, and the path veers inland to **Freshwater West,** crossing through more industrial areas. Here it passes **Stack Fort,** an imposing circular fortress built in anticipation of a French raid that never took place.

From Freshwater West to **Angle Bay,** the coastline walk covers mild and pretty terrain. It breaks slightly at Milford Haven, where it's intercepted by a channel running over 25 mi. inland. Geologists call it a "ria," or drowned river valley. From the Dale Peninsula, the path passes by the long, clean beaches of **St. Bride's Bay,** where **Marloes Sands** provides a stretch of sand and the **Three Chimneys,** columns of stone shaped by natural erosion, tower. The path curves up to Newgale, and arrives at ancient **St. David's Head,** the site of many Iron Age hill settlements and the oldest named feature on the coast of Wales. The ocean has carved away caves and secluded inlets, leaving a stretch of jagged and awe-inspiring terrain. Past St. David's at Abereiddi, the sea has refilled an old slate quarry to create the beautiful "Blue Lagoon." The final stretch of the Coastal Path, between Newport and the small village of St. Dogmaels, is quite strenuous (its total ascent is equal to that of Mt. Snowdon) but also breathtaking. To explore Pembrokeshire by horseback, contact **Heathertown Riding Centre** (near Tenby; ☎01646 651 025) or **Maesgwynne Riding Stables** (near Fishguard; ☎01348 872 659).

⚲ ISLANDS OFF THE PEMBROKESHIRE COAST

GRASSHOLM. On Grassholm, the island farthest from the shore, 35,000 pairs of gannets raise their young each year. **Dale Sailing Company** runs guided trips around, but not to, the island from Martin's Haven on the Dale Peninsula, often encountering Manx shearwaters and storm petrels. (☎01646 603 110. Fridays, but times vary; call ahead. £20) The company also sails more frequently to the island of **Skomer,** a marine reserve and breeding ground for auks, seals, and puffins. (Open Apr.-Oct. Tu-Su. £7 boat fee, £6 landing fee; children £6 boat fee, no landing fee.)

RAMSEY ISLAND. Owned by the Royal Society for the Protection of Birds, Ramsey Island hosts the largest gray seal colony in Wales and many rare seabirds offshore from St. David's Peninsula. On the east side of the island lurk the **Bitches,** a chain of rocks that have brought countless sailors to doom. **Thousand Islands Expeditions,** Cross Sq., in St. David's, sails from St. Justinian's lifeboat station and goes around the island. (☎01437 721 686 or 0800 163 621. 1½hr. Daily Easter-Nov., weather permitting. £14, children £7; more extensive journeys from £25, children £14.). The adventurous can journey between the Bitches and through the island's sea caves, the longest in Wales, on an inflatable vessel (2hr. tour £30; children £15). **Voyages of Discovery and Ramsey Island Cruises,** Cross Sq., in St. David's, also runs tours as well as trips through rock gorges on specially designed rubber crafts. (☎0800 854 367. Tours from £18, concessions £10.)

PEMBROKE (PENFRO) AND PEMBROKE DOCK ☎01646

In the heart of a county known as "Little England beyond Wales," Pembroke no longer feels like the fierce military stronghold its Norman occupants once fashioned it to be. Battlements that once formed a bastion of anti-Cromwell resistance now offer shade to historical reenactments, and the waters which once served to protect the castle on three sides now harbor swans and hungry picnickers. Pembroke Dock, about 1½ mi. away, lacks its neighbor's ancestry and its charm—the ferry to Rosslare, Ireland, is its greatest attraction. Both towns are stepping stones to the national park, but Pembroke is the more popular place to stay.

◨ TRANSPORTATION. Pembroke's unstaffed **train station** is on Lower Lamphey Rd. at the opposite end of Main St. from the Castle. **Trains** (☎08457 484 950) run from both towns to **Tenby** (20min., 7 per day, £3.10), **Swansea** (2hr.; M-F 6 per day, Sa 7 per day, Su 3 per day; £8.50), and points farther east. In Pembroke, **buses** going east stop outside the Somerfield supermarket; those going north stop at the castle. **National Express** (☎08705 808 080) goes to **Cardiff** via **Swansea** (3¾hr., 3 per day, £12.50) and **London** (6hr., 2 per day, £23.50). In Pembroke Dock, buses stop at the **Silcox Garage.** (☎683 143. Open M-F 9am-5pm, Sa 8:30am-12:30pm). Signal your stop to the bus driver. **First Cymru** (☎01792 580 580) stops in Pembroke and Pembroke Dock between **Tenby** (#349; 40-50min.; M-Sa 11 per day, Su 2 per day, 6 per day in summer, £2.10) and **Haverfordwest** (also #349; 35-40min.; M-Sa 13 per day, Su 4 per day). **Irish Ferries** (☎08705 329 543) and **Stena Line** (☎08705 707 070) send ferries from Pembroke Dock to **Rosslare, Ireland** (see **By Ferry,** p. 29).

ORIENTATION AND PRACTICAL INFORMATION. Pembroke Castle lies up the hill on the western end of **Main Street;** the street's other end (at the train station) fans into five roads from a roundabout. Across the river and to the north is Pembroke Docks. Downhill from Pembroke's town center, the **Tourist Information Centre,** Commons Rd., occupies a former slaughterhouse and has displays on town history and the Pembrokeshire Coastal Path. The staff books accommodations for a £2 charge plus a 10% deposit, sells ferry tickets, and gives away town maps. (☎622 388. Open daily Easter-June 10am-5pm; July-Oct. 10am-5:30pm.) Other services include: **Barclays,** 35 Main St., in Pembroke (open M and W-F 9am-4:30pm, Tu 10am-4:30pm); the Pembroke Dock **police,** 4 Water St. (☎682 121); the Pembroke Dock **hospital,** Fort Rd. (☎682 114); free **Internet access** at the Pembroke **library,** 38 Main St., (☎682 973; open Tu and F 10am-1pm and 2pm-5pm, W and Sa 10am-1pm, Th 10am-1pm and 2-7pm) and at **Dragon Alley,** 63 Main St. (☎621 456; £1 per 15min., £3 per hr.; open M-Tu 10am-7pm, W-Th 10am-9pm, F-Sa 10am-6pm); **Mendus Pharmacy,** 31 Main St. (☎682 370; open M-F 9am-6pm, Sa 9am-5pm); and the **post office,** 49 Main St. (☎682 737; open M-F 9am-5:30pm, Sa 9am-1pm). **Post Code:** SA71 4JT.

ACCOMMODATIONS AND FOOD. The nearest **YHA hostel** is in Manorbier on the bus line between Tenby and Pembroke (p. 485). The few **B&Bs** in Pembroke are scattered, though some reasonable options reside on Main St., and singles are scarce; try to book ahead. Mrs. Willis fosters a vibrant atmosphere at her bright blue **Beech House ❷,** 78 Main St. Look out for the full-feathered peacock on the breakfast room wall. With elegant rooms and delicious home-cooked breakfasts, you'll be amazed you aren't paying more. (☎683 740. £16 per person.) A few doors down, **Woodbine ❸,** Main St., pampers guests with spacious rooms, big wardrobes, and flowers on the window sills. (☎686 338. £22.50 per person.)

Stock up at **Somerfield** market, 6-10 Main St. (Open M-Sa 8am-8pm, Su 10am-4pm.) **Wisebuys,** 19 Main St., is a cut above; an olive bar and assortment of local jams fill many a picnic basket. (☎687 046. Open M-Sa 7am-5:30pm.) **Henry's Gift Shop and Cafe ❶,** 5 Main St., a block from the castle, serves tasty pies, scones, and cakes (from £1) alongside more savory offerings. (☎622 293. Shop open M-Sa 10am-5pm, Su 11am-4pm. Food served M-Sa 10am-4pm. AmEx/MC/V.) Across the Northgate St. bridge is the **Watermans Arms ❶,** 2 The Green, where patrons choose from an extensive curry menu and a lovely balcony with great views of the castle and the swans that float on Mill Pond. (☎682 718. Open daily Easter-Oct. noon-11pm; winter hours vary. Food served noon-10pm.)

SIGHTS. Unpretentious and austere, **Pembroke Castle** shadows Pembroke's Main St. and overshadows much of the town's history. Today, the castle's countless stone chambers invite hours of exploration. Henry VII, founder of the Tudor dynasty, was born in one of the seven massive towers. The Great Keep rises 75 ft. in the air and intrepid visitors ascend over 100 twisted, slippery steps to reach its domed top. Don't miss the underground gloom of "Wogan's Cavern," a huge stone cave that was once a medieval rivergate and paleolithic habitation. (☎684 585; www.pembrokecastle.co.uk. Open daily Apr.-Sept. 9:30am-6pm; Mar. and Oct. 10am-5pm; Nov.-Feb. 10am-4pm. Tours May-Aug. 4 per day. £3, concessions £2, families £8. Tours 50p.) The **Pembroke Glassblowing Studio,** The Commons, is hot—1250° C, to be precise, but only inside the glory holes. Watch craftspeople blow souvenirs from £5. (☎682 482. Open Easter-Oct. M-F 10am-4pm, glassblowing M-F 10:30am-3:30pm.) Located in a beautifully converted Methodist Church, **The Pembroke Antiques Centre,** Wesley Chapel, on Main St., will engross curious browsers and determined purchasers alike. (☎687 017. Open M-Sa 10am-5pm.)

ST. DAVID'S (TYDDEWI)   ☎01437

St. David's is the smallest city in Britain, with the largest cathedral. This enchanting place is little more than a few streets curled around a central village green, but it has been a favored destination among various pilgrims for almost a millennium; in the Middle Ages, two pilgrimages to St. David's were considered equivalent to one trip to Rome, and three summed to a journey to Jerusalem itself.

🚍🚲 TRANSPORTATION AND PRACTICAL INFORMATION. Pick up the Pembrokeshire County Council's *1: Haverfordwest & St. David's Area,* which lists bus services, and *The Pembrokeshire Coastal Bus Service Timetable,* which lists a few more. Both are free at any Pembrokeshire TIC. The **Richards Brothers** (☎01239 613 756) Haverfordwest-Fishguard bus hugs the coast, heading to both towns from St. David's (#411; 50min. from both; M-Sa 6-7 per day from Fishguard, 12 per day from Haverford, Su 2 per day; £2.15). Other buses terminate at St. David's during the week. For a cab, call **Tony's Taxis** (☎720 931).

The **National Park Information Center,** The Grove, doubles as the TIC, and lies at the east end of High St. Check out the stone in the middle of the courtyard—it's positioned to be illuminated by sunlight on St. David's Day each year. (☎720 392; www.stdavids.co.uk. Open daily Easter-Oct. 9:30am-5:30pm; Nov.-Easter M-Sa 10am-4pm.) Other services include: **Barclays,** at High St. and New St. (open M-F 9:30am-4pm); the **police,** High St. (☎720 223); the nearest **hospital** (☎764 545), in Haverfordwest; free **Internet access** at the library, in City Hall, on High St., (open Tu and F 10am-1pm and 2pm-5pm); **St. David's pharmacy,** 13-14 Cross Sq. (☎720 243; open M-F 9am-6:30pm, Sa 9am-4:30pm); and the **post office,** 13 New St. (☎720 283; open M-F 9am-5:30pm, Sa 9am-1pm). **Post Code:** SA62 6SW.

🛏🍴 ACCOMMODATIONS AND FOOD. The **YHA St. David's** (p. 485) lies 2 mi. northwest of town at the foot of a rocky outcrop near St. David's Head. Beautiful **Alandale ❸,** 43 Nun St., is run by Rob and Gloria Pugh, whose genuine warmth is even more memorable than their lovely rooms with cathedral views. (☎720 404. £30.) In the center of town, **The Coach House ❷,** 15 High St., has a cozy lounge and a wide range of simple, clean lodgings, most with TV and bath. The breakfast menu caters to special dietary needs and vegetarians using local, organic items. (☎720 632. £22-24, children ½ price. £10 deposit.)

Pebbles Yard Gallery and Expresso Bar ❶, Cross Sq., has a cafe that serves pitas, salads, and coffee in a trendy loft above the shop. (☎720 122. Open daily 10am-5:30pm.) Across the street is **Chapel Chocolates ❶,** The Pebbles, whose ice cream is so popular, the cathedral has prohibited its consumption inside. Try something wild like Christmas Pudding (cones £1.20), or stick to an impressive array of truffles. (☎720 023; www.chapelchocolates.com. Open daily 10am-5:30pm. AmEx/MC/V.) **Cartref ❷,** 23 Cross Sq., serves up creative Welsh dishes. The Celtic Pie (£7) combines oat and wheatmeal flan with spinach and Welsh cheese. (☎720 422. Open daily Mar.-May 11am-2:30pm and 6:30-8:30pm; June-Aug. 11am-3pm and 6-8:30pm. MC/V.)

👁 SIGHTS. 🔳St. **David's Cathedral,** perhaps the finest in Wales, stands below the village. It dates from the 6th century, when David and his followers lived ascetic lives in picturesque isolation. Pilgrims once flocked to this site; now, modern day "pilgrims" relive the experience, filing past the **reliquary** reputed to hold the bones of St. David, patron saint of Wales, and his comrade St. Justinian. The latter was killed on nearby Ramsey Island but, in saintly conscientiousness, carried his own head back to the mainland. In the St. Thomas Becket chapel, a stained-glass window portrays three surly knights jabbing swords at the martyr. The varied ceilings

SOUTH WALES

are dazzlingly intricate and made of inlaid wood in an elaborate painted design. (☎720 199; www.stdavidscathedral.org.uk. Open M-Sa 8:30am-6pm, Su 12:45-5:45pm, and for evening services. Suggested donation £2, children £1.) Those with an insatiable love for pealing bells are welcome to sit in on a ringer's practice session in the tower. (Su 5:35-5:55pm, W and F 7:45-9pm. Suggested donation £1.)

The **Bishop's Palace,** across a stream from the Cathedral, was built in the 14th century by Bishop Henry Gower, back when it was acceptable for a bishop to have the largest palace in Wales. Now in ruins, the distinctive arched parapets connote the lavishness (and deliberate conspicuousness) of the medieval bishopric. (☎720 517. Open daily June-Sept. 9:30am-6pm; Oct. and Apr.-May 9:30am-5pm; Nov.-Mar. M-Sa 9:30am-4pm, Su 11am-4pm. £2.50, concessions £2, families £7.) A half-mile south of town, the walls of **St. Non's Chapel** mark the birthplace of St. David. Water from the nearby well supposedly cures all ills; take Goat St. downhill and follow the signs. Tours run to **Ramsey Island,** off the coast (p. 487).

FISHGUARD ☎01348

Victim of pirate attacks, star of the film *Moby Dick*, and harbor of the late *Lusitania*, modest Fishguard hasn't let its moments of celebrity go to its head. In fact, it remains deeply enamored of its own maritime history; local legends of smugglers' caves in the nearby Presali hills and versions of the town's claim to be the site of the last invasion of Britain abound in friendly pubs.

☐ TRANSPORTATION. Trains (☎08457 484 950) pull into **Fishguard Harbour,** Goodwick, from **London** via **Bristol, Newport, Cardiff, Swansea,** and **Whitland** (4½hr., 2 per day, £78.50). **Buses** stop at Fishguard Sq., the town center. Ask at the TIC for a free bus and train timetable. From the north, take **Richards Brothers** (☎01239 613 756) buses from **Aberystwyth** to **Cardigan** (#550 or 551, 2hr., M-Sa 10 per day) and then on to **Fishguard** (#412, 45min., M-Sa 12 per day, £3-4). Take **First Cymru** (☎01792 580 580) buses from **Tenby** or **Pembroke** to **Haverfordwest** (#349; 1hr.; M-Sa every hr., Su 2 per day; £2.40) and from **Haverfordwest** to **Fishguard** (#412, 45min., 1-2 per hr.). **Stena Sealink** (☎08705 707 070) runs daily ferries from **Rosslare, Ireland.** (See **By Ferry,** p. 29.) **Town bus** #410 shuttles between Fishguard Harbour and Fishguard Sq. (5min., 2 per hr., 45p), and **Merv's Taxis** (☎875 129) are on call 24hr.

☑ PRACTICAL INFORMATION. The **Tourist Information Centre,** Town Hall, Main St., books buses and ferries, and rooms for a £2 charge plus a 10% deposit. (☎873 484. Open daily Easter-Oct. 10am-5pm.; Nov.-Easter M-Sa 10am-4pm.) Other services include: **Barclays,** across from the TIC (open M-Tu and Th-F 9am-4:30pm, W 10am-4:30pm); the **police,** Brodog Terr. (☎873 225); **Dyfed Launderette and Dry Cleaners,** Brodog Terr. (☎872 140; wash £1.95, dry 60p; open M-Sa 8:30am-5:30pm; last wash 4:30pm); free **Internet access** at the **library,** on High St., one block from Market Sq. (☎872 694; open M, Tu, F 9:30am-1pm and 2pm-5pm, W and Sa 9:30am-1pm, Th 9:30am-1pm and 2pm-6:30pm), or £2 per 30min. at **Ocean Lab** (p. 491); **Boots pharmacy,** Market Sq. (☎872 856; open M-Sa 8:30am-5:30pm); and the **post office,** 57 West St. (☎873 863; open M-F 9am-5:30pm, Sa 9am-12:30pm). **Post Code:** SA65 9NG.

⌂⌂ ACCOMMODATIONS AND FOOD. B&Bs (from £20) on **High Street** in Upper Fishguard and **Vergam Terrace.** The comfortable rooms at **Avon House ❷,** 76 High St., are cheered by the care of the friendly hosts. (☎874 476; www.avonhouse.co.uk. From £18. Cash only.) Near tiny Trefin, **Bryngarw ❸,** Abercastle Rd., 1 mi. off the A487 between St. David's and Fishguard, perches mere feet from a cliff. Take bus #412 from Fishguard Sq. (☎831 211. £28 per person. Cash only.) **Hamilton Guest House and Backpackers Lodge ❷,** 21-23 Hamilton St., is well-kept with a book-lined TV lounge, toast-and-tea breakfasts, sauna, and owner Steve, who knows the area like the back of his hand. (☎874 797; www.fishguard-backpackers.com. Laundry, kitchen, and Internet access. Dorms £12; doubles £30; triples £42; quads £52.) **Y Pantri ❶**, 31 West St., rolls sandwiches, fills baguettes (£1.50), and sells various pasties both savory and sweet (95p) for uncommonly low prices. (☎872 637. Open M-Sa 9am-4:30pm. Cash only.) **The Taj Mahal ❷**, 22 High St., serves a huge variety of quality curries until late. (☎874 593. Entrees from £5. Open M-Su 6-11:30pm, takeaway until midnight. MC/V.) Not your average pub and converted barn, **The Old Coach House ❸**, High St., has a vast menu of British and Italian fare (£4-10) and draws a youthful crowd. (☎875 429. Open M-Sa 11am-11pm, Su noon-10:30pm. Food served noon-2:30pm and 6-9pm. Bookings advisable. AmEx/MC/V.)

🅖 🅙 **SIGHTS AND ENTERTAINMENT.** The **Marine Walk,** a paved path that follows the coastline through woods and along grassy cliffs, has exquisite overlooks of town and sea, and plaques with historical trivia. Ramblers can also see **Goodwick Harbor,** where the ill-fated flagship *Lusitania* began its journey to America.

In a glassy beachside building, the **Ocean Lab,** The Parrog, features a few interactive exhibits for kids and a display on the Ice Age featuring Oscar, one of the largest mammoth skeletons ever found in Europe. (☎874 737. Internet access £2 per 30min. Open daily Easter-Oct. 10am-6pm; Nov.-Mar 10am-4pm.) **Preseli Venture** also offers half- and full-day adventures that include sea kayaking, surfing, and the awesome "coasteering" (see **Crazy or Coasteering?** p. 40. ☎837 709. 18 and over. £39 per half-day. £169 for an all-inclusive weekend.) During the day, sun gluttons dot pebbly **Goodwick Beach.** Inquire at the TIC about hikes into the **Preseli Hills,** ancient grounds speckled with stone circles and a mysterious **standing stone.** If indoor pursuits are more your style, check out the shops near **Upper Fishguard Square.**

Weekend nightlife erupts into a pub scene of festival proportions. **The Old Coach House** (p. 491) is the place to be, but all pubs along **High Street** see some action until 11pm. **The Royal Oak,** West St., at Market Sq., is a pub proud of its history; the infamous "last invasion" surrender treaty was signed here in 1797. It keeps the original table and other artifacts on display while serving up Welsh specialities in huge portions from £10. (☎872 514. Open M-Sa 11am-11pm and Su noon-10:30pm.) Saturday nights, students stumble onto Brynawelon buses that leave the square at 10:30pm, 10:45pm and 11pm for the disco at the **Brynawelon Country Hotel,** nearby in Letterston. (☎840 307. Cover £4. Last hurrah 2am.)

SOUTH WALES

NORTH WALES

The fiercely beautiful mountains of the north have long harbored the most fervent Welsh blood. In the 14th century, Welsh insurgents plotted campaigns against the English from deep within the jagged peaks of Snowdonia. The English King Edward I designed a ring of spectacular fortresses to keep the rebels in the mountains, but Welsh pride never wavered and remains strong despite (or perhaps because of) centuries of union with England. Today, such pride shows itself more in weekend football matches or on signs and menus penned only in Welsh. Yet the north has a kind heart, and villagers are unlikely to let a weary traveler go without food, rest, and a lengthy conversation. To escape the crowds swarming Edward's coastal castles, head to the mountain footpaths, lakes, and hamlets of Snowdonia National Park, which spans most of northwest Wales. To the west, the Llŷn Peninsula beckons with sandy beaches; to the northwest, the Isle of Anglesey is rich in prehistoric remains; and to the east, quiet villages sleep in the Vale of Conwy.

HIGHLIGHTS OF NORTH WALES

SNOWDONIA Scale one of many craggy peaks at **Snowdonia National Park** (p. 510), land of high moors, dark pine forests, and deep glacial lakes.

LLYN PENINSULA Enjoy the unhurried pace of the region amidst the quiet beaches and quiet greenery of **Aberdaron** (p. 507).

CASTLES Admire the fine handiwork of English oppression at **Beaumaris** (p. 520), **Caernarfon** (p. 504), **Conwy** (p. 522), and **Harlech** (p. 501).

ABERYSTWYTH ☎01970

Host to the largest university in Wales, Aberystwyth (ahber-RIST-with) thrives on its youthful vigor. Where 19th-century vacationers once enjoyed the frivolities of resort living, bars now buzz with spirited academics during the school year. Yet even the summer months see the Georgian boardwalk awash with activity as locals thread through shopping districts and take in bayside breezes.

▐▀ TRANSPORTATION

A transport hub for all of Wales, Aberystwyth sits at the end of a rail line running from Birmingham, England.

Trains: Station on Alexandra Rd. Office open M-F 6:20am-5:25pm, Sa 6:20am-3:20pm. Trains (☎08457 484 950) from **Machynlleth** (30min.; M-Sa 9 per day, Su 6 per day; £3.60) and **Shrewsbury** (1¾hr.; M-Sa 7 per day, Su 4-5 per day; £14.70). Machynlleth is the southern terminus of the **Cambrian Coaster** line, which runs from **Pwllheli.** The **Cambrian Coaster Day Ranger** covers travel along the line (£6.60, children £3.30, families £13.20). The **Vale of Rheidol Railway** (☎625 819) arrives from a few mountain sites (p. 496).

Buses: Station on Alexandra Rd., beside the train station. **National Express** (☎08705 808 080) from **London** via **Birmingham** (8hr., 1pm, £25) and a more direct route (7hr., noon, £25). **TrawsCambria** bus #701 from **Cardiff** via **Swansea** (4hr., 2 per

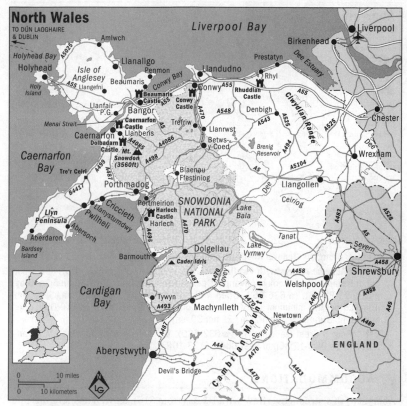

North Wales

day). **Arriva Cymru** (☎08706 082 608) to **Bangor** via **Porthmadog** (#X32, 3½hr.; M-Sa 5 per day), and Machynlleth (#32, 45min., M-Sa 8 per day). **Richard Brothers** (☎01239 613 756) to **Cardigan** via **Synod Inn** (#550/551, 1hr., M-Sa 6 per day); **Arriva Cymru/Summerdale Coaches** (☎01348 840 270) runs the same route twice on Su. **Day Rover** tickets (£5, children £3.70 or £2.50 with paying adult) are valid on most buses in the Ceredigion, Carmarthenshire, and Pembrokeshire area. The **North and Mid-Wales Rover** is valid on buses and trains on the North Wales main line, the Conway Valley, and Cambrian Line (1 day £20, 3 days £30, 7 days £44).

Taxis: Express (☎612 319).

◪ PRACTICAL INFORMATION

Tourist Information Centre: Lisburn House, Terrace Rd. (☎612 125). Books rooms for £2 plus 10% deposit. Open daily July-Aug. 9am-6pm; Sept.-June M-Sa 10am-5pm.

Launderette: Wash 'n' Spin 'n' Dry, 16 Bridge St. (☎820 891). Wash £2.20, dry 20p per cycle, soap 10p. Bring change. Open daily 7am-9pm; last wash 8:30pm.

Banks: Barclays, 26 Terrace Rd. (☎653 353). Open M-Tu and Th-F 9am-5pm, W 10am-5pm.

Police: Blvd. St. Brieuc (☎612 791), at the end of Park Ave.

NORTH WALES

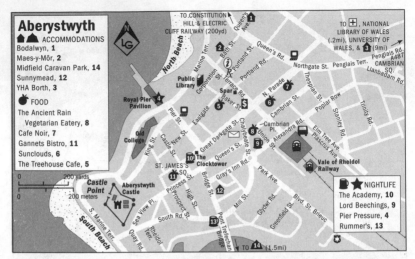

Hospital: Bronglais General Hospital, Caradog Rd., off Penglais Rd. (☎ 623 131).

Internet Access: Aberystwyth Public Library, Corporation St. (☎ 633 703), at the corner of Baker St. Free. Book in advance. Open M-F 9:30am-8pm, Sa 9:30am-5pm. **Biognosis,** 21 Pier St. (☎ 636 953. Open M-Th 10am-6pm, F 10am-4:30pm, Sa 10am-4pm. £3 per hr., minimum £1.50.) **Daton Computers,** Queens Rd. (☎ 610 050; open M-F 9am-5:30pm, Sa 10am-2pm. £1 per 30min).

Post Office: 8 Great Darkgate St. (☎ 632 630). **Bureau de change.** Open M-F 9am-5:30pm, Sa 9am-12:30pm. **Post Code:** SY23 1DE.

🏠 ACCOMMODATIONS

Aberystwyth's streets overflow with B&Bs (from £15), as well as more upscale seaside hotels, especially near the beachfront and on **Bridge Street.**

Sunnymead, 34 Bridge St. (☎ 617 273). Warm yellow-trimmed house holds warm hospitality. £20 per person. MC/V. ❸

Bodalwyn, Queen's Ave. (☎ 612 578; www.bodalwyn.co.uk), near Constitution Hill. The stone Edwardian building offers tasteful, airy ensuite rooms close to the beachfront and city center. Singles £33-38; twins and doubles £55-65; family rooms £65-80. Cash only. Internet access available. Cash only. ❹

Maes-y-Môr, 25 Bath St. (☎ 639 270). Cheap accommodations in a prime location just a block away from the ocean. Rooms have access to a common kitchen. Linens and towels provided. Reception 8am-10pm, ask in the launderette on ground floor. £15. Cash only. ❷

YHA Borth (☎ 871 498), 8 mi. north of Aberystwyth, in an Edwardian house overlooking the ocean. Take the train to Borth, or ride Crosville bus #511 or 512 and ask to stop at the hostel. From the train station, turn right onto the main road and walk 5min. Set near beautiful beaches and often full. Kitchen. Open daily Mar.-Oct. with 48hr. notice; call in advance for other times of the year. Dorms £10.60, under 18 £7.20. MC/V. ❶

NORTH WALES

Midfield Caravan Park (☎612 542), 1½ mi. from town on the A4120, 200 yd. uphill from the A487 junction. From Alexandra Rd., take any bus to Southgate. Lovely site, with a view of town and hills. £6 per person. Electricity £2. Cash only. ❶

🍴 FOOD

Pier Street takeaways are cheap and open Sunday, as are beachside shacks and some sit-down restaurants. **Spar** at 32 Terrace Rd. is open 24hr.

The Ancient Rain Vegetarian Eatery, 13 Cambrian Pl. (☎612 363), at the corner of Union St. A favorite on the alternative cuisine scene, its pancakes (from £2.55) come in flavors like lime-sugar. Vegetarian lunches (like Bread 'n' Brie with Olives) start at £4. Takeaway available. Open M and W-Sa 10am-4pm, Tu 10am-2:30pm. Cash only. ❶

The Treehouse Cafe, 14 Baker St. (☎615 791). Feel wholesome eating your veggie burger (£5.25), your steakburger (£6.20) or even your Asian gravaelox (£7.50)—it's all organic. And so are the crisp veggies and local fruits sold on the ground floor. Open M-Th and Sa 9am-5:30pm, F 9am-7pm. MC/V. ❶

Sunclouds, 25 North Parade (☎617 750). Baguettes and baps usually rule the day, but you'll be glad for the hot, homemade soup with crusty bread (£3) in chilly hours. Open M-Sa 10am-4:30pm. Cash only. ❶

Gannets Bistro, 7 St. James Pl. (☎617 164), across from Market Hall. Run by a former British Airways catering manager—if only airline food were half as good. Entrees are somewhat pricey (£8-14), but lunch specials like seafood ramekin salad (£5) are good deals. Open M-Sa noon-2pm and 6-9:30pm. MC/V. ❸

Cafe Noir, 33 North Parade (☎615 332). Divides its menu into food served "by day" and "by night." Try a large crepe with one of their extravagant combinations (served with salad and a side; £7). Open M-Sa noon-2:30pm and 6-9:30pm. MC/V. ❷

👁 SIGHTS

NATIONAL LIBRARY OF WALES. Occupying a grand classical building that overlooks the bay, this library houses almost every Welsh book or manuscript ever penned and is one of just four libraries in the UK that receives a copy of every piece that is published in Britain. The **Gregynog Gallery** displays the first known Welsh written text (c. 800), the first Welsh printed book (1546), the first Welsh dictionary (1547), the first Welsh map (1573), the first Welsh Bible (1588), and the first Welsh magazine (1735), which managed one issue before folding. Lusty bachelors and gap-toothed "ladies" fill the pages of the oldest surviving manuscript of the *Canterbury Tales*. *(Off Penglais Rd., past the hospital. ☎632 800; www.llgc.org.uk. Reading room open M-F 9:30am-6pm, Sa 9:30am-5pm. Exhibitions open M-Sa 10am-5pm. Free.)*

ELECTRIC CLIFF RAILWAY. At the northern end of the promenade, an electric railcar has been creaking up the steep 430 ft. slope of Constitution Hill since 1896. The Victorian ballroom and bandstand have long since been replaced by the 14 in. lens of the world's largest camera obscura—a contraption that affords a stunning panorama of the coastline. *(☎617 642. Runs daily July-Aug. 10am-6:30pm; mid-Mar. to June and Sept.-Oct. 10am-5:30pm. 6 per hr. Round-trip £2.25, concessions £1.75, children £1. Camera obscura free with rail ride.)*

ABERYSTWYTH CASTLE. Winged Victory flies high above Castle Point, south of the Old College and the site of one of Edward I's many now-decrepit castles. Henry Prince of Wales took this castle with cannons—their first use in Great

NORTH WALES

Britain—but today youngsters and picnickers peacefully overtake what's left of the fortress and share one of the best views in Aberystwyth. *(Always open. Free.)*

PIER. Though it overlooks the many-gabled Victorian townhouses that guard the coastline, Aberystwyth's late 19th-century pier has been overrun by the demands of the tourist trade—it now features a sprawling arcade, a pizza parlor, a nightclub, a pub, and an ice cream shop. At the south end of the promenade, the university's **Old College** is a neo-Gothic structure restored in 1885 as Wales's first university. Prince Charles was drilled in Welsh here before being crowned Prince of Wales. *(Arcade open daily Mar.-Sept. 10am-11pm, Oct.-Feb. 10am-10pm.)*

OTHER SIGHTS. Next to the TIC, the well-maintained **Ceredigion Museum** fills a grand old theater, the Coliseum, and houses two floors of Welsh heritage. *(☎633 088. Open M-Sa 10am-5pm. Free.)* Up Penglais Rd., on the University of Wales campus, the **Aberystwyth Arts Centre** sponsors drama and films in Welsh and English; schedules are available at the TIC. *(☎623 232. Box office open M-Sa 10am-8pm. Cinema most weeknights. Tickets from £4.)*

◪ ▨ PUBS AND CLUBS

Aberystwyth boasts more than 50 pubs, and student swarms keep them buzzing.

▨ **The Academy,** St. James Sq. (☎636 852). This cavernous converted chapel piles bottles of absinthe (£3 per shot) on the organ in the huge game room; barflies grasping Buds flank the 2nd story pulpit to watch the 16 ft. telescreen. Breakfast served all day. Su-Th pints as little as 99p. Open M-Sa noon-11pm, Su noon-10:30pm. Food served noon-3pm and 6-8:30pm.

Rummer's, Pont Trefechan Bridge (☎625 177). A vine-covered riverside beer garden packed with students. Live music Th-Sa of all types. Open M-Tu 7pm-midnight, W-Sa 7pm-1am, Su 7-10:30pm.

Lord Beechings, Alexandra Rd. (☎625 069). Comfortable atmosphere and an enormous array of comfort foods to match (most under £5). Open M-Sa 11am-11pm, Su 11am-10:30pm. Food served W-F and Su noon-3pm, Sa noon-7pm.

Pier Pressure, The Royal Pier, Marine Terr. (☎636 100). Smashed mirrors quake and smashed clubbers shake. Th rocks to 60s-80s; the weekend "Cheese Factory" pulls a young crowd. Cover Th £3, F £4, Sa £5. Open M-W 10pm-1am, Th-Sa 10pm-2am, Su 10pm-midnight.

▨ DAYTRIPS FROM ABERYSTWYTH

DEVIL'S BRIDGE
Trains run from Aberystwyth. (Mid-July to Aug. M-Th 4 per day, F-Su 2 per day; Apr. to mid-July and Sept.-Oct. 2 per day. £11.50, children £2.50.)

Originally built to serve the lead mines, the **Vale of Rheidol Railway** (☎625 819) winds through both working farmland and gorgeous rolling hills. An hour's train ride leads to Devil's Bridge— built by the evil one himself—which is actually three bridges of varying ages built atop one another. The lowest bridge was probably built by monks from the nearby **Strata Florida Abbey** in the 12th century. (☎01974 831 261. Abbey open Apr.-Sept. W-Su 10am-5pm. Grounds open M-Tu, and Oct.-Mar. 10am-4pm. £2.25, concessions £1.75, families £6.25;

Oct.-Apr. grounds free, but exhibits closed.) Catch great views of the bridge and the 300 ft. waterfall by a 10min. walk in the Devil's Punchbowl (£1) or a precipitous 30min. hike down the carved stairs of **Jacob's Ladder** (☎890 233. £2.50, concessions £2, children £1.25.)

MACHYNLLETH ☎01654

Machynlleth (mach-HUN-hleth) is best known for its decidedly brief stint as the capital of Wales. Freedom-fighter Owain Glyndwr set up a short-lived Parliament here back in the 15th century, summoning delegates from across the country and even signing a formal alliance with France against the British. Though the rebellion unraveled, the Celtic pride behind it lives on in Machynlleth's appealing city center (little more than two streets) through the Welsh language and a rich heritage which museums, eateries, and even street signs proudly display.

⊟ TRANSPORTATION. The **train station** (☎702 887), Doll St., receives trains (☎08457 484 950) from: **Aberystwyth** (30min., 11 per day, £3.60); **Birmingham** (2¼hr.; M-F 10 per day, Sa 11 per day, Su 6 per day; £21.30); **Shrewsbury** (1¼hr.; M-F 10 per day, Sa 11 per day, Su 6 per day; £11). The **Cambrian Coaster Day Ranger** covers routes from **Aberystwyth** (£6.60, children £3.30, families £13.20, after 4:30pm £3.70). **Buses** stop by the clock tower. **Arriva Cymru** (☎08706 082 608) buses #32 and X32 pass through Machynlleth as they shuttle between **Aberystwyth** and **Dolgellau** on a north-south route (30min. from both, M-F 9 per day, Sa 8 per day, Su 2 per day). East-west, #28 and #33 provide transport to and from smaller towns.

▚ ORIENTATION AND PRACTICAL INFORMATION. Pentrehedryn Street, Penrallt Street, and **Maengwyn Street** converge at the **clock tower,** which oversees most of Machynlleth's hustle and bustle. From the train station, turn left onto Doll St., veer right at the church onto Penrallt St., and continue until you see the clock tower. The **Tourist Information Centre,** in the Owain Glyndŵr Centre, Maengwyn St., books rooms for a £2 charge plus a 10% deposit. (☎702 401. Open summer M-Sa 9:30am-5:30pm, Su 9:30am-5pm; winter M-Sa 9:30am-5pm, Su 9:30am-4:30pm.) Other services include: **Barclays,** on Penrallt St. beneath the clock tower (open M-W and F 9am-4:30pm, Th 10am-4:30pm); the **police,** Doll St. (☎702 215); the **hospital,** off Maengwn St. (☎702 266); **Nigel's Launderette,** New St. (wash £2.20, dry 20p; open M-Sa 8:30am-8pm, Su 9am-8pm; last wash 30min. before close); **Internet access** at the **Machynlleth Public Library,** Maengwyn St. (☎702 322; free; open M and F 9:30am-1pm and 2-7pm, Tu-W 9:30am-1pm and 2-5pm, Sa 9:30am-1pm. Closed Th and Su.), or at **Celtica** (☎702 702; open daily 10am-6pm) on Aberystwyth Rd. for £1 per hr.; **Rowland's pharmacy,** 8 Pentre Hedyn St. near the clock tower (☎702 237; open M-W and F 9am-5:30pm, Th 9am-12:30pm, Sa 9am-4:30pm); and the **post office,** 51-53 Maengwyn St., inside **Spar** (☎702 323; office open M-Th 8:30am-5:30pm, F 9am-5:30pm, Sa 9am-1pm). **Post Code: SY20 8AF.**

▐◖ ACCOMMODATIONS AND FOOD. Machynlleth lacks hostels, but **YHA Corris ❶,** on Corris Rd., is 15min. away by bus. This eco-friendly hostel occupies a converted school. (☎/fax 761 686. Laundry. Lockout 10am-5pm. Open daily Mar.-Oct.; Jan. to mid-Feb. and Nov. F-Sa. Dorms £10.60, under 18 £7.20. Cash only.) **B&Bs** are expensive and hard to find. **Gwelfryn ❸,** 6 Greenfields Rd., shepherds guests through a flowery front porch to basic rooms. (☎702 532; www.gwelfryn.co.uk. £23.50 per person. Cash only.) Farther outside the city,

OF MOUNTAINS AND MADMEN

Welsh legend holds that whoever spends a night atop Cader Idris will come down a poet, a madman, or not at all. I had been joking, somewhat, when I told my editors that I wanted to spend a night on the peak. We'd all read *The Dark is Rising* sequence, by Susan Cooper, in which Idris figures prominently.

But my first night in Dolgellau, the sky swirled with brooding darkness. The malevolent, magical mountain towered above. A man can easily get stuck at the summit in thick mists like that, and bells in surrounding towns toll for the lost. It was assuredly not a sleep-out opportunity. 'Too bad, such a pity,' I hummed as I tucked myself into the downy blankets of a valley farmhouse.

Shortly thereafter, however, a series of unfortunate coincidences left me temporarily penniless, and camping began looking like a good option. The day was sunny, the trees green, and even Idris looked welcoming. Legends of men swallowed alive by the bottomless lake below, of the hell-hounds racing round the top, of the cairns of long dead kings, and of the malicious Grey King... all seemed quaint little fairytales.

"Well," I thought, "why *not* Idris? No one will bother me there." When I mentioned my plans to a shopkeeper, however, he furrowed his brow. "Good 'eavens m'love," interjected his wife,

Haulfryn ❷ has decent rooms with a lived-in feel. Check out the fish tank and the breakfast nook hung with plates from around the world. (☎702 206. £20. Cash only.) Campers can seek out riverside **Llwyngwern Farm ❶**, off the A487 next to the Centre for Alternative Technology. (☎702 492. Open Apr.-Sept. £8 for two people. MC/V.)

Craft your own menu at **Spar,** 51-53 Maengwyn St. (open M-Sa 7am-11pm, Su 7am-10:30pm), or at the impressive **market** that runs along Maengwyn St., Pentrerhedryon St., and Penrallt St. It dates to 1291, when Edward I granted a charter for weekly markets in the area. (Open W 9:30am-4pm) The ▨**Quarry Shop Cafe and Wholefoods ❶,** 13 Maengwyn St., part of the Centre for Alternative Technology, serves delicious vegan soups, salads (under £3), and rotating daily entrees (from £5) with tasty fruit trifle for dessert. (☎702 339. Cafe five doors from market shop. Open M-Sa 9am-5pm, Th 9am-2pm. Cash only.) Enjoy a mouth-watering assortment of freshly-baked pastries, quiches, and sandwiches at **BJ's ❶,** Maengwyn St., which truly feels like the home kitchen you never had. The Full Welsh Breakfast (£3.95) comes complete with black pudding for venturesome types. (☎703 679. Open M-W and F-Sa 8am-5pm, Th 8am-2pm. Cash only.) Machynlleth pubs don't offer diverse dining options, but tasty dishes are served beside a massive stone hearth at the **Skinners Arms ❷,** 14 Penrallt St., near the clock tower. Entrees in the lounge are £4-9; lighter meals £3-7 at the bar. Come nightfall, it welcomes many a local with tempting brews. (☎702 354. Open M-Tu noon-11pm, W-Sa 11am-11pm, Su noon-10:30pm. Food served M-Sa noon-2pm and 6-8pm. Cash only.)

🖪 **SIGHTS** On a former slate quarry 3 mi. north of town along the A487, the staff of the ▨**Centre for Alternative Technology** have been developing, promoting, and living environmentally-sound lifestyles since 1974. Chug up the 200 ft. cliff via a funicular powered by water imbalances, and then learn about wave, wind, and solar power sources in fascinating outdoor displays. Don't miss the "Mole Hole" (a kiddie favorite) or the "Compost Sampler" which encourages you to touch—and smell—various types of natural fertilizer. Take Arriva bus #34 (5-10min., M-Sa 11 per day, £2.40) to the entrance, or #32 (5min., M-Sa 10 per day) to Pantperthog and walk 200 yd. north across a bridge. (☎705 950. Open daily 10am-5:30pm. Funicular open Apr.-Oct. £7.20, concessions £5.10, children £4.10. Free audio tour.) Further up the A487, the passages of another old slate mine lure tourists to **King Arthur's Labyrinth**—a kitschy celebration of the Arthurian legend on a subterranean riverboat tour. From Machynlleth take bus #32 or 35 toward Dolgellau and ask to be dropped at the Corris Craft Centre. (☎761 584; www.kingarthurslabyrinth.com. Dress warmly. Open daily Apr.-Oct. 10am-5pm; call ahead in winter. £5, concessions £4.45, children £3.50.) From the stately gargoyled clock tower, a 2min. downhill walk along Aberystwyth Rd. (the A487) brings you to **Celtica,** which sports a gift shop and glitzy light and fog. Sadly, the village conveys little real Celtic history. (☎702 702; www.celticawales.com. Open daily 10am-6pm; last entrance 4:40pm. £5.) Located in Y Tabernacl on Penrallt St., the **Museum of Modern Art, Wales,** feels like a big-city gallery; it features Welsh contemporaries' paintings and sculptures. Some evenings, the acoustically renowned performance hall next door fills with music. (☎703 355. Open M-Sa 10am-4pm. Free.) The museum and theater are the center of the late August **Machynlleth Festival,** featuring musical performances and lectures. (☎703 355; www.momawales.org.uk. Tickets £3-15.)

DOLGELLAU ☎01341

Nestled in a deep river valley, Dolgellau (dol-GECTH-lai) seems a quiet refuge from the untamed winds and ethereal mists of the shorn mountain crests which loom above. Yet as one traveler penned about this sleepy town in 1932, "its houses are made of the mountains." The assertion is literal—roughly hewn stone and slate compose Dolgellau's narrow, dignified rows of houses—but it also resonates intangibly. Indeed, culture and history here were shaped by the mountains and the legends they engendered, and today their paths attract hikers of all skill levels.

TRANSPORTATION Buses stop in Eldon Sq. near the TIC, which details all local services in *Gwynedd Public Transport Maps and Timetables.* **Arriva** (☎0870 608 2608) bus #94 (M-Sa 10 per day, Su 7 per day) heads to: **Barmouth** (20min.); **Llangollen** (1½hr.); **Wrexham** (2hr.). Bus #2 heads through the mountains to **Caernarfon** via **Porthmadog** (2¾hr., Su only, 2 per day.). Bus #32 and X32 pass through Dolgellau on their way north to Porthmadog, going to **Machynlleth** (40min., M-Sa 10 per day, Su 2 per day, £2.80) and **Aberystwyth** (1¼hr., M-Sa 6 per day, Su 2 per day), and bus #28 goes to Machynlleth exclusively (40min., M-Sa 9 per day.)

"Idris will'n't be taken lightly. Strange happenings, up on Idris..."

As I set out through the narrow streets of Dolgellau, my gaze was pulled upward. The stern peak—Pen y Gadair—disappeared into mist known locally as the Brenin Llwyd ("breath of the Grey King"). The sun, however, was still bright, and the fog not heavy.

Cader Idris is steeper than it looks, and the climb was long and lonely. Pockets of mist formed vague shapes, then dissipated.

"P'nawn da, Brenin Llwyd!" I said cheerfully. My voice was muted. I swallowed. It was growing dark, and my small sleeping roll was looking inadequate against the chilling wind. I needed some sort of cover. So when I saw the stones rising out of the mists ahead, I smiled triumphantly. Cairns. Perfect, ready-made shelter.

Sleeping in an ancient tomb is not as fun as it sounds. I couldn't sleep. Questions flashed through my head. Why didn't I tell anyone I was coming up here? Are those lichens edible? Where are the public restrooms? I shivered. Cold rocks bit into my back. Gray mist pressed in, and voices on the wind rose and fell in heinous chorus. A lone cry came up from below, and I pressed myself against the rocks. Legends can remind you of their factual roots in a most unsettling manner. More than this I cannot say. Perhaps, if you are brave, or foolhardy...

-Jenny Pegg

🛈 PRACTICAL INFORMATION. The **Tourist Information Centre,** Eldon Sq., by the bus stop, books rooms for a £2 charge plus a 10% deposit. It doubles as a **Snowdonia National Park Information Centre,** with an exhibit on local mountains and trails. (☎422 888. Open summer 9:30am-12:30pm and 1:30-5:30pm, winter 9:30am-12:30pm and 1:30-4:30pm.) Equip yourself with camping and hiking gear and Ordnance Survey maps (£6-7) at **Cader Idris Outdoor Gear,** Eldon Sq., across from the bus stop, or plan an expedition. (☎422 195; fax 423 655; www.cader-idris.co.uk. Open M-Sa 9am-5:30pm; May-Sept. also Su 10am-4pm.) Other services include: **HSBC,** Eldon Sq. (☎525 400; open M-F 9am-4:30pm); **Dolgellau Launderette,** Smithfield St., across from Aber Cottage Tea Room (wash £2.20-3.40, dry £1; no soap; open W-M 9am-7pm; last wash 6:30pm); **police,** Old Barmouth Rd. (☎422 222); Dolgellau and Barmouth District **hospital,** off Penbrynglas (☎422 479); free **Internet access** at the library, Bala Rd. (☎422 771; open M and F 10am-7pm, Tu and Th 10am-5pm, W 10am-1pm, and Sa 10am-noon); **Rowland's Pharmacy,** 3 Eldon Row near the TIC, (☎422 404; open M-Sa 9am-5:30pm, and alternate Su 11am-12pm); and the **post office,** inside **Spar** at Plas yn Dre St. (☎422 466; open M-F 9am-5:30pm, Sa 9am-12:30pm). **Post Code: LL40 1AD.**

🛏🍴 ACCOMMODATIONS AND FOOD. The **YHA Kings** (p. 512) is 4 mi. away. In the town of Dolgellau itself, lodging is scarce and expensive, starting around £22-25. Treat yourself to the refurbished (and 350-year-old) **Aber Cottage ❸,** on Smithfield St. near the bridge, and to its pristine and elegant bedrooms. Breakfast included; al fresco dining available. (☎422 460. Singles £35; doubles £55. Cash only.) Two **B&Bs** with lower rates and spectacular views of the Idris range cling to the hills just north of town. **Arosfyr ❷,** Pen y Cefn, is a working farm with bright, airy rooms and the occasional kitten stalking through the flowers. From the bus stop, cross Smithfield St. bridge, turn left, then right at the school, and follow the steep road until a sign on the right directs you past farm sheds. (☎422 355. £20. Cash only.) Comfortable **Dwy Olwyn ❸** keeps horses and serves big breakfasts. Cross the Smithfield St. bridge, turn right, then left onto the unmarked road after the Kwik Save, and follow the signs 5min. uphill. (☎422 822; www.dwyolwyn.co.uk. Singles £25; doubles £38. Cash only.) **Camping** is available at the deluxe **Tanyfron Caravan and Camping Park ❶,** a 10min. walk south on Arron Rd. onto the A470. (☎/fax 422 638. £7.50 per person, £10 with car. Electricity £2. Cash only.)

Spar market is on Plas yn Dre St. (Open daily 8am-10pm.) Rustic chic and Welsh home cooking await at the **Aber Cottage Tea Room ❸,** Smithfield St., part of the B&B. Patrons unwind in plush chairs and sample an incredible variety of gourmet soups (from £3.50), inventive veggie-bakes (from £7.95), and pastries (from £1.35). (Open daily 10am-5pm. Cash only.) **Popty'r Dref ❶** bakery and delicatessen, Upper Smithfield St., just off Eldon Sq., tempts passers-by with bready aromas and foodstuffs packed to the ceiling. (☎422 507. Pastries £1-2. Open M-F 8am-5pm, Sa 8am-4pm. Cash only.) Duck under the low portal at **Y Sospan ❷,** Queen's Sq., behind the TIC, for sandwiches (from £2.30) and minty lamb steak (£8.95). (☎423 174. Cafe open daily from 9am. Restaurant open F-Sa 6:30-9pm. Cash only.)

🅖 SIGHTS. The free **Quaker Interpretive Centre,** above the TIC and open the same times, details the history of Dolgellau's hotbed of nonconformity, which was home to 45% of all Welsh Quaker emigres to the United States. Once you've gotten yourself oriented, take advantage of Dolgellau's nearby wilderness and head for the hills. The famous **Precipice Walk** (4 mi., 2hr.) follows an easy path revealing vistas of Mawddach Estuary and the huge Idris range. Once restricted to the well-to-do guests of the nearby Caeynwch estate, the **Torrent Walk** (2½mi, 1½hr.) circles along an ancient Roman pathway through woodlands and past waterfalls. Post-rain ventures reward with gushing torrents. The **Llyn Cau, Cader Idris and Tal-y-Llyn Walk** (7mi., 5½hr.) is a strenuous excursion that should only be attempted in good weather. The hard work pays off in panoramas of a glacial lake and native birds from 2617 ft. Mynydd Pencoed. Pick up pamphlets (40p) or *Local Walks Around Dolgellau* (£4) at the TIC; the latter contains 15 hikes for all levels.

CADER IDRIS

Visitors who descend into nearby cities from the misty overpasses near Cader Idris will appreciate its mysterious allure. Even the etymology of the name (translated "Chair of Idris") remains a mystery. One story claims that a national hero named Idris was killed in battle by a host of pillaging Saxons; another maintains that Idris was a giant who kept house here; still others link Idris to King Arthur. Those who flock to this dark mountain care more for its spectacular trails and its desolate, stunning terrain than its mythological origins. This portion of Snowdonia offers scenic walks that are less crowded than those of Mt. Snowdon in the north (all cross privately owned farm and grazing land: be courteous and leave all gates as you found them). The 5 mi. pony track from **Llanfihangel y Pennant** is the longest but easiest path to the summit. After a relatively level initial section, the path climbs steadily through wind-sculpted rocks overlooking the Mawddach estuary and continues over the mountain. The trail from Tŷ Nant is not particularly strenuous and begins at **Tŷ Nant farm,** 3 mi. from Dolgellau. As you ascend, the environs change from hazels and hawthorns to the frost-formed, craggy precipice. Avoid Fox's Path, which ascends Idris from the same place: many accidents occur on its steep scree slope. The **Minffordd Path** (about 3 mi.) is the shortest but steepest ascent. On its way to the summit, it crosses an 8000-year-old oak wood and rises above the lake of **Llyn Cau,** tracing boulders and cairns left by glaciers. One story holds that a young man swimming in the lake was swallowed by a monster and never seen again. Watch out for the Cwn Annwn (Hounds of the Underworld), said to fly around the range's peaks. Allow 5hr. for any of these walks. Booklets (40p) charting each are available at the NPIC. For longer treks, the Ordnance Survey Outdoor Leisure #23 or Landranger #124 maps (£6-7) are essential.

The 9000-acre **Coed-Y-Brenin Forest Park** covers the peaks and valleys around the Mawddach and Eden rivers and is particularly known for its world-class mountain biking trails. Roaming hikers are rewarded with Fallow Deer sightings and a seamless landscape of mosses, ferns, and rare lichen species.The **Karrimor Mountain Bike Trail** features a number of steep climbs and sweeping descents as it traverses 61 mi. of forest roads. The **Red Bull Mountain Biking Trail** labels its rough roads and tumble tracks with daunting names like "Rocky Horror Show" and "Root of all Evil"—challenges meant for experienced riders only. The forest also has trails reserved for hikers and is best entered 7 mi. north of Dolgellau off the A470, near the **Coed-Y-Brenin Visitor Centre.** (☎440 666. Open daily Apr.-Oct. 10am-5pm; Nov.-Mar. Sa-Su 10am-5pm.) Mountaineers and sportsmen will find the town of **Dolgellau** (p. 499) and the **YHA Corris** (p. 497) convenient spots to rest aching limbs.

HARLECH   ☎01766

Reputedly from the Welsh "harddlech," meaning "beautiful slope," Harlech's name says it all. Its steep paved ascent rises above sand dunes and below green ridges, passes tea rooms and inns of High Street (Stryd Fawr) before

NORTH WALES

leading to Harlech's castle, perched over the sea. From its ramparts, clear days grant pristine views of Snowdonia's serrated skyline and the sparkling of Llŷn's town lights at dusk.

TRANSPORTATION. Harlech lies midway on the **Cambrian Coaster** line. The uphill walk to town from the unstaffed **train station** is a challenge; follow the signs until you arrive at a striking sculpture of "Two Kings" from the Mabinogion. **Trains** (08457 484 950) arrive from **Machynlleth** (1¼-1½hr.; M-Sa 7 per day, Su 3 per day; £6.20) and connect to **Pwllheli** and other spots on the **Llŷn Peninsula** (M-Sa 7 per day, Su 3 per day). The **Cambrian Coaster Day Ranger** (£6.60, children £3.30, families £13.20) allows unlimited travel on the Coaster line for a day and is barely more than the single fare from Machynlleth. **Arriva Cymru** (☎0870 608 2608) bus #38 links Harlech to southern **Barmouth** (M-Sa 11 per day £2.15) and northern **Blaenau Ffestiniog** (M-Sa 4 per day), stopping at the carpark on Stryd Fawr and the train station.

ORIENTATION AND PRACTICAL INFORMATION. The castle opens out onto **Twtil;** slightly uphill is the town's major street, **Stryd Fawr** (often called High St.). Near the castle, the **Tourist Information Centre,** Stryd Fawr, doubles as a **National Park Information Centre.** The staff stocks hiking pamphlets and Ordnance Survey maps (£6-7), and books accommodations for a £2 charge plus a 10% deposit. (☎780 658. Open daily Apr.-Oct. 9:30am-5:30pm.) Other services include: **HSBC,** Stryd Fawr (open M-F 9:30-11:30am); the **police,** at the hill's base on the A496 (☎01492 517 171); free **Internet access** at the public library, a posted uphill turn off Ffordd Isaf (☎780 565; open M and F 4:30-7pm, W 10am-1pm); and the **post office,** Stryd Fawr (☎780 231; open M-Tu and Th-F 9:30am-5:30pm, W 9am-12:30pm, Sa 9am-5pm). **Post Code:** LL46 2YA.

ACCOMMODATIONS AND FOOD. Revel in spacious rooms at ⚫Arundel ❷, Stryd Fawr, where breakfast is served on a glassed-in patio with views of the ocean and castle. Walk past the TIC and take a right before the Yr Ogof Bistro. Energetic Mrs. Stein (pronounced "Steen") will pick you up if the climb from the train station isn't appealing. (☎780 637. £16. Cash only.) The closest hostel is **YHA Llanbedr ❶,** originally built as a country guest house and located 4 mi. south of town. Take the train to the Llanbedr stop (10min.) or ride bus #38 and ask to be let off at the hostel. (☎0870 770 5926; fax 770 5927. Open Apr.-Nov. Dorms £10.60, under 18 £7.20. MC/V.) The **Byrdir Guest House ❷,** a former hotel on Stryd Fawr near the bus stop, offers comfortable rooms with TVs and washbasins, and a ground floor bar. (☎ 780 316. From £17.50. Cash only.) **Camp** at **Min-y-Don Park ❶,** Beach Rd., between the train station and the beach. (☎780 286. Laundry £1. Open Mar.-Oct. £9-12 per tent. Showers 20p. Cash only.)

Spar market displays fresh produce outside near the edge of Stryd Fawr's main drag, right before the road curves. (Open daily 8am-8pm.) At ⚫Plâs Cafe ❷, guests linger over afternoon cream teas (£3.50) and sunset dinners (from £7) while enjoying sweeping ocean views. (☎780 204. Open daily Mar.-Oct. 10am-8:30pm; Nov.-Feb. 10am-5:30pm. AmEx/MC/V.) **Yr Ogof Bistro ❸,** Stryd Fawr, has fantastic meat dishes made with lamb and cattle raised on the proprietor's farm. Try the "Boozy Pork" (£9) or go for more traditional £10 steaks. (☎780 888. Open M-Sa 6:30-9:30pm, Su 12:30-2:30pm. MC/V.) The bar at the **Lion Hotel ❷,** off Stryd Fawr above the castle, provides pints in this virtually publess town. Bar snacks are 70p-£3.75, while meals run £6-10. (☎780 731. Open M-F noon-11pm, Sa 11am-11pm, Su noon-10:30pm. Food served until 8:30pm. MC/V.)

🎦 ♫ **SIGHTS AND ENTERTAINMENT.** 🏰**Harlech Castle's** walls, once lapped by the now receded oceans, seem to spring naturally from their craggy perch. One of the "iron ring" fortresses built by Edward I to watch over spirited Welsh troublemakers, it still affords awesome views of blanketing forests, curving coastlines, and ominous mountains, along with a golf course and caravan parks. Spiral scaffolding and rounded windows hint at Harlech's Savoy-inspired design, but rebel Owain Glyndwr's brief occupancy and parliament here suggest a Welsh mettle. (☎780 552. Open daily June-Sept. 9:30am-6pm; Apr.-May and Oct. 9:30am-5pm; Nov.-Mar. M-Sa 9:30am-4pm, Su 11am-4pm. Last admission 30min. before close. £3, concessions £2.50, families £8.50.) Public **footpaths** run from Harlech's grassy dunes to the forested hilltops above the town; get recommendations and directions at the TIC. **Theatr Ardudwy** (☎780 667) occupies a strange cylindrical building on the A496 (called Ffordd Newydd for a stretch) and hosts everything from operas (£20) to dancing Buddhist monks (£10) to popular films (£5).

LLŶN PENINSULA (PENRHYN LLŶN)

With jagged mountains to the east, quiet Anglesey to the north, and choppy seas on three sides, the stunning pastoral scenes of the Llŷn Peninsula seem perfectly out of place. Nonetheless, they have humbled visitors since the Middle Ages, when pilgrims traversed the peninsula on their way to Bardsey Island. The serenity these travelers sought can still be found in Iron Age settlements high on mountains or in *blodau wylltion* (wildflowers) on an afternoon stroll; more prevalent, however, are golden beaches dotted with weekenders—Hell's Mouth is famous for surfing, and Black Sands, near Porthmadog, is a convenient favorite for everything else. The farther west you venture, the more unsullied the Llŷn becomes, and some of its smallest villages have managed to retain some semblance of the serenity that its larger (and less comely) towns have lost.

🚌 TRANSPORTATION

The northern end of the **Cambrian Coaster** (☎08457 489 450) train line runs through **Porthmadog** and **Criccieth** to **Pwllheli,** stopping at smaller towns in between. Trains begin at **Aberystwyth** or Birmingham and require a change at **Machynlleth** for **Porthmadog** (2hr. from Machynlleth; M-Sa 5-7 per day, Su 3 per day) and **Pwllheli** (2hr. from Machynlleth). The **Cambrian Coaster Day Ranger** offers unlimited travel along the line (£6.60 per day, children £3.30, families £13.20).

National Express (☎08705 808 080) bus #545 arrives in **Pwllheli** from **London** via Birmingham, Bangor, Caernarfon, and Porthmadog (10-10½hr., 2 per day, £26.) Bus #380 arrives in **Pwllheli** from **Newcastle-upon-Tyne** via Manchester, Liverpool, and Bangor (12-14hr., 3 per day, £44.50.) **TrawsCambria** bus #701 stops in **Porthmadog** once a day from **Aberystwyth** (2hr.), **Swansea** (6hr.), and **Cardiff** (7hr.). In the other direction, #701 travels from **Porthmadog** to **Bangor** (1hr.). **Express Motors** (☎01286 881 108) bus #1 stops in **Porthmadog** on its winding route between **Blaenau Ffestiniog** (30min.; M-Sa every hr., summer also Su 5 per day) and **Caernarfon** (45-60min.), continuing to **Bangor** (1-1¼hr.; M-Sa 6 per day, Su 3 per day). **Berwyn** (☎01286 660 315) and **Clynnog & Trefor** (☎01286 660 208) run bus #12 between **Pwllheli** and **Caernarfon** (45min.; M-Sa 1 per hr., Su per day).

Several bus companies, primarily **Arriva Cymru** (☎0870 608 2608), serve most spots on the peninsula for about £2. Check bus schedules in the essential *Gwynedd Public Transport Maps and Timetables*, available from TICs and

THE BIG SPLURGE

PORTMEIRION

An Italianate village whose pastel cottages and tropical gardens are perched in the decidedly un-Italianate hills of southern Snowdonia, Portmeirion is the whimsical invention of an extraordinarily wealthy man named William Clough Ellis. Though its appearance is something of an anomaly in these parts, one glance around Portmeirion's glittering fountains and villa facades proves that towns don't need to make sense to be beautiful.

The entire village has been built as a set of rentable portions: each preciously adorned building is actually a suite that guests can let for days (or weeks) at time. Three nights in "The Mermaid," a charming ivy-strewn cottage, go for £345, while a week in one of the condos can cost anywhere from £630 to £1110. Facilities come with self-service kitchens, but Portmeirion's two traditional hotels also offer doubles as low as £135 per night. If you want the deluxe treatment, The Peacock Suite includes a menu of breast of duck, mushroom risotto, and chocolate fondue (£158).

The village of Portmeirion is 3 mi. east of Porthmadog. Bus #98/99 arrives M-Sa 3 times per day. #98 also stops at Minffordd (6-7 per day), a 30min. walk from Portmeirion and a stop on the Cambrian Coaster Line. Village open daily 9:30am-5:30pm. Admission £5.50, children £4.

on some buses. **Arriva** and **Caelloi** (☎01758 612 719) run bus #3 from **Porthmadog** to **Pwllheli** via Criccieth (30-40min.; M-Sa 1-2 per hr., Su 6 per day). Departing from Pwllheli, Arriva buses #8, 17, 17B, and 18 weave around the western tip of the peninsula. A Gwynedd **Red Rover ticket**, available on buses, secures a day of travel throughout the peninsula and Gwynedd and Anglesey counties, and selected journeys to Aberystwyth and distant Wrexham (£4.95, children £2.45).

PORTHMADOG ☎01766

Buses, trains, and cars converge on bustling Porthmadog (port-MA-dock), making it a hub for hikers and beach-bound weekenders. Its principal attraction is the **Ffestiniog Railway**, a narrow-gauge line that departs from Harbour Station on High St. The train is only three seats (and a tiny aisle) wide, but it offers spectacular views and a bumpy 13½ mi. ride into scenic Snowdonia. (☎516 000; www.festrail.co.uk. 2½hr. round trip. June-Aug. 4-10 per day; Apr.-May and Sept.-Oct. 2-4 per day; Nov.-Mar. call for timetables. £14, concessions £11.20, families £28.) At the **Llechwedd Slate Caverns**, visitors can venture into the hollow leftovers of the "other" Welsh mining industry. The site features two underground tours as well as a cluster of exhibits and a recreated Victorian-era mining village (complete with the former residence of the "famous" blind harpist of Meirionydd). Though the **Deep Mine Tour**, complete with a Victorian ghost as your guide, offers a perilous descent on Britain's steepest passenger railway and views of an underground lake, the **Miner's Tramway Tour** is ultimately more stimulating, guiding visitors through expansive "cathedral-like" caves to witness mining demonstrations. John's #142 bus connects the slate mines to the railway station (5min.) and coordinates well with train arrivals and departures (5 per day round-trip). The mines are also accessible by car just off the A70 10mi. south of Betws-y-Coed. Book well in advance (☎830 306. Open daily from 10am. Last tours leave Mar.-Sept. at 5:15pm; Oct.-Feb. 4:15pm. Tours £8.25, concessions £7, children £6.25.)

At the other end of Porthmadog but owned by the Rheilffordd Ffestiniog Railway, across from the train station, the modest **Welsh Highland Railway** (along with Russell, its dogged 1906 locomotive) tries to recapture the glory days of rail travel, reconstructing the atmosphere of a 1920s steam line. Once the longest narrow-gauge line in Wales, the track runs to **Rhyd Ddu**. (Info ☎516 000, timetables available at Harbour Station; www.whr.co.uk. July-Aug. 5 per day; June and Sept. Sa-Su and Tu-Th 5 per day; reduced low-season schedule. Call for exact schedules. £14, children £11.20, families £28.) For a more serious adrenaline rush, try flying a Hovercraft over land or water with **Llŷn Hovercrafts,** just outside of Abersoch. (☎01758 713 527. Open daily Easter-Sept. 10am-5pm; winter by arrangement.) **Ropeworks** operates a network of climbs, trapezes, and swings just off Black Rock Sands. (☎515 316; www.ropeworks.co.uk. Open daily 9:30am-5pm. Advanced booking required. 2hr. session £14, students £12.)

From the **train station,** a right turn on High St. leads to town. **Buses** stop on High St. For travel to the rest of the peninsula, they pick up outside the park. Arriving back, they stop across the street outside the Australia pub (p. 505). **Dukes Taxis** (☎514 799) helps out if you need a lift. **K.K. Cycles,** 141 High St., rents **bikes.** (☎512 310. £2 per hr., £9 per day. Open M-Sa 9am-6pm.) The **Tourist Information Centre,** High St., by the harbor, books rooms for a £2 charge plus a 10% deposit. (☎512 981. Open daily Easter-Oct. 10am-6pm; Nov.-Easter 10am-5pm.) Other services include: **Barclays,** 79 High St. (☎0845 600 0651; open M and W-F 9:30am-4:30pm, Tu 10am-4:30pm); **Internet access** at the **I.T. Centre,** 156 High St. (☎514 944; £1.50 for the first 15min., then 50p per 15min.; open M-F 9:30am-5:30pm, Sa 10am-2pm) or free at the library, Chapel St. (☎514 091; open M 10am-noon and 2-6:30pm, Tu and F 10am-noon and 4-7pm, W 10am-noon and 2-4:30pm, Th and Sa 10am-noon) or the TIC; **Madog Launderette,** 34 Snowdon St. (☎512 121; £2.50 wash, £1 dry; open M-Su 8am-7pm); **Rowland Pharmacy,** 68 High St. (☎513 921; open M-F 9am-5:30pm, Sa 9am-1pm); and the **post office,** at the corner of High St. and Bank Pl., with a **bureau de change** (☎512 010; open M-F 9am-5:30pm, Sa 9am-12:30pm). **Post Code:** LL49 9AD.

The best place to stay in the area is 10min. down High St. (past the railway station, where it becomes Church St.) in neighboring **Tremadog.** National Express #545 (to London) and #380 (to Manchester) and local buses (Arriva #3, 2 per hr.) stop in Tremadog. The first house on the right, best known as Lawrence of Arabia's birthplace, now houses **⧄Snowdon Backpackers Hostel ❷,** complete with TV, fireplace lounge, and kitchen. During the day, the front dining room moonlights as a more upscale cafe. The owners impress with local lore and expert hiking advice. (☎515 354. Continental breakfast included. Laundry £2. Internet access. Apr.-Oct. dorms £13; Nov.-Mar. £12. Twins and doubles £29-33; triples £44-50. AmEx/MC/V.) Signs on **High Street** and **Snowdon Street** in Porthmadog mark hotels and **B&Bs.** A cheaper option is run by **Mrs. G. Williams ❸,** 30 Snowdon St., whose double rooms are bright and cheery. (☎513 968. £20 per person. Cash only.)

Castle Bakery ❶, 105 High St., stocks savory pasties (from 65p), *bara brith* (a Welsh bread; £1.80), sandwiches (£1.60-2.95) and a simple salad bar. (☎514 982. Open daily 8:30am-5pm. Cash only.) At **Jessie's ❶,** 75 High St., select from a huge range of sandwiches from £1.45. (☎512 814. Open M-Sa 9am-5pm; Easter-Sept. also Su 10am-4pm. Cash only.) **The Australia ❶,** 31-33 High St., has good grub (£2-6) and a wide-screen TV. Lore holds that a crew of sailors from Porthmadog abandoned their vessel in Australia, and the Aussies who replaced them frequented this bar once in Wales. (☎510 930. Open M-Sa 11am-11pm, Su noon-10:30pm. Food served daily noon-2:30pm, M-F also 6-8:30pm. MC/V.)

CRICCIETH ☎01766

Above coastal Criccieth (KRIK-key-ith), 5 mi. west of Porthmadog, the remains of **Criccieth Castle** stand on a windy hilltop tucked into Tremadog Bay. Conquered and held by many, both English and Welsh, it has been attacked by more, and its walls still bear the scars of Owain Glyndwr's attempt to scorch

NORTH WALES

this symbol of English hegemony. Little remains, but the site itself is still breathtaking enough to merit exploration. (☎522 227. Open daily June-Sept. 10am-6pm; Oct. 10am-5pm; Apr.-May 10am-5pm. £2.75, concessions £2.25, families £7.75. Nov.-Mar. free, unstaffed, and always open; use side gate.)

B&Bs (£18-25) are scattered **Marine Terrace** and **Marine Crescent,** by the beach near the castle. At **Dan-Y-Castell ❷**, 4 Marine Cres., guests are treated to spacious rooms with ocean views. (☎522 375. £18. Cash only.) **Spar,** 62 High St., stocks basic food items in the center of town. (☎522 410. Open daily 7am-10pm.) Tiny, popular **Poachers Restaurant ❸**, 66 High St., is just a few doors down. The three-course meal (£10.95) is a gastronome's delight; and entrees tend to be seafood- and vegetable-heavy. (☎522 512. Open daily 6-9pm. Reserve ahead. MC/V.) Located just opposite their namesake on 29 Castle St., the **Castell Tea Rooms ❶** occupy a building that has been used as a bakery for over a hundred years. Current baker and proprietor John still bakes a solid array of cakes, pies, and pastries (from £1.10) and serves up basic lunch items. (☎523 528. Open daily 11am-5pm. Cash only.) Though **Cadwalader's ❶** ice cream store has expanded across the Llŷn, its world-famous vanilla is still light and oh-so-creamy. (Open M-F 11am-8pm, Sa-Su 11am-9pm. Cash only.) The beer garden of **Bryn Hir Arms ❶**, 24 High St., is the ideal setting for a relaxed pint, and their downstairs "Bistro Bach" serves upscale pub food for downscale prices. (☎522 493. Open daily Easter-Sept. noon-11pm; Oct.-Easter M-Su noon-11pm. Food served noon-2:30pm and 6-9:30pm. AmEx/MC/V.)

Cambrian Coaster trains arrive from **Pwllheli** and **Machynlleth** via Porthmadog (p. 503). From the station, turn right on High St. for the town center. **Arriva** bus #3 comes from **Porthmadog** and **Pwllheli** (15min.; M-Sa 2 per hr., Su 6 per day). The closest **TIC** is in Porthmadog (p. 504), but most services are right in town. **HSBC** is at 51 High St. (Open M-F 9:15am-11:30pm). The only Internet cafe on the peninsula is **Roots Bookshop,** 46 High St. (☎523 564; 5p per min., open M-Sa 10am-5pm). The **post office** is around the corner from the station. (Open M-Tu and Th-F 9am-5:30pm, W and Sa 9am-12:30pm.) **Post Code: LL52 0BU.**

LLANYSTUMDWY   ☎01766

Just 1½ mi. north of Criccieth, tiny Llanystumdwy (HLAN-ih-stim-doo-ee) was the boyhood home of **David Lloyd George,** British Prime Minister from 1916 to 1922, and the town lovingly ballyhoos its native son at every turn. The **Lloyd George Museum** has become something of a village centerpiece, and its status is well-deserved. It chronicles Lloyd George's life and displays numerous relics from his career, among them his working copy of the Treaty of Versailles and the pen he used to sign it (though a nearby display explains that he preferred writing with "a thick pencil"). Exit the museum, turn right, and follow the path behind it to **Highgate,** George's boyhood home, humble and petite, but well-restored. The cobbler's **workshop** next door features a mannequin fashioned after George's uncle, who tells long-winded family anecdotes on audiotape. A jaunt through the museum carpark and across the street leads to George's solemn **gravesite,** a monolith behind a wrought-iron gate overlooking the gurgling brook in which young George played. (☎522 071. Open daily July-Sept. 10:30am-5pm; Apr.-June M-F 10:30am-5pm; Oct. M-F 11am-4pm. £3, concessions £2, families £7.) Arriva bus #3 stops twice per hr. (20min. from Pwllheli, 15min. from Porthmadog, 4min. from Criccieth).

PWLLHELI   ☎01758

The Cambrian Coaster rail line terminates at Pwllheli (poohl-HEL-ly), 8 mi. west of Criccieth, but there are many buses to aid continued transportation. While the antique shops and touristy stores dominate the main stretches, further afield are two **beaches**—Abererch Beach, dotted with windsurfers and a shallow grade that attracts families, and less known South Beach.

The **train station** hugs the corner of Y Maes and Ffordd-y-Cob at Station Sq. The **bus station** is farther down Ffordd-y-Cob. For **taxis**, call ☎740 999. The **Tourist Information Centre**, Station Sq., books B&Bs for a £2 charge plus a 10% deposit. (☎613 000. Open daily Apr.-Oct. 9am-5pm; Nov.-Mar. M-W and F-Sa 10:30am-4:30pm.) Other services include: **HSBC**, 48 High St. (☎632 700; open M-F 9am-5pm); the **police** (☎701 177); free **Internet access** at **Pwllheli Library**, in Neuadd Dwyfor (the Town Hall, Stryd Penlan; ☎612 089; open M 2-7pm, Tu, Th, and Sa 10am-1pm, W and F 10am-1pm and 2-7pm); and the **post office**, New St., inside a general store (☎612 658; open M-F 9am-5:30pm, Sa 9am-12:30pm). **Post Code:** LL53 5HL.

Bank Place Guest House ❷, 29 High St., is clean, convenient, and well-priced, offering big breakfasts and spacious rooms with TVs. (☎612 103. £16 per person. Cash only.) Area **camping** is good; try **Hendre ❶**, 1½ mi. down the road to Nefyn at Efailnewidd. (☎613 416. Laundry and showers. Open Mar.-Oct. From £10 per tent. Cash only.) Get local pastries (like Welsh cakes and *bara brith*) and produce at the open-air **market** in front of the bus station. (Open W 9am-5pm.) The **Spar** is on Y Maes Sq. (☎612 993. Open daily 8am-10pm.) **Jane's Sandwich Bar ❶**, 55 High St. specializes in paninis and provencettes, filled baguettes grilled in front of you with olive oil and herbs from £1.60-2. (☎614 464. Open M-Sa 7am-2:30pm, Su 8am-2pm. Cash only.) **Taro Deg ❷**, 17 Lon Dywod, near the train station, has an atmosphere to calm even the most frantic rail traveler, complete with sleek minimalist design (☎701 271. Open M-Sa 9am-5pm. MC/V.)

ABERDARON AND TRE'R CEIRI   ☎01758

Once the next-to-last stop on the holy Ynys Enlli (Bardsey Island) pilgrimage, the tiny village of Aberdaron sits steadfast and pensive on the tip of Llŷn Peninsula. In a quiet inlet bounded by steep green hills, its seclusion has allowed Aberdaron to retain some of the small-town serenity that other Llŷn towns have lost. Right next to the ocean, the **Church of Saint Hywyn** has been waging a battle with the tides and winds since medieval times. Thankfully, the 20th century has witnessed the construction of a sturdy seawall as well as the arrival of celebrity vicar **R.S. Thomas**—the other Welsh poet named Thomas—whose experiences working with this rural congregation feature prominently in his works. (Open daily summer 10am-5pm; winter 10am-4pm.) **St. Mary's Well,** 1½ mi. west of town, is also located surprisingly close to the ocean, but lore has it that its water stays fresh even when flooded by high tide. Follow road signs from Aberdaron 2 mi. to **Porthor,** where a beachgoer's footfall causes the "whistling sands" to live up to their name. The **Bardsey Island Trust Booking Office,** in the center of the village, provides information on boats to **Bardsey Island.** Long a religious site—its first monastery was allegedly built in the 6th century—the "Island of Twenty Thousand Saints" was once so holy that three pilgrimages there equaled one to Rome. Because so many holy men made the pilgrimage late in life, the "twenty thousand" in its name allegedly refers to the number of pilgrims buried there. These days, visitors can admire the ruins of the old abbey and observe hundreds of migratory birds. (☎760 667. Trust open Easter-Sept. Sa-Su, weather permitting. Ferries 15-20min., allowing 3½hr. visits; frequency depends on weather and demand. £20, children £10. Longer stays in the island's croglofts and Victorians are available.) A **National Trust information point** occupies the Coast Guard hut overlooking Bardsey at the Uwchmynydd headland.

Bus #17 runs from **Pwllheli** (40min., M-Sa 9 per day); #17B follows a more scenic, coastal route and takes 5min. longer (2 per day). Follow the sign pointing toward Uwchmynydd, or simply head up the hill behind the bus stop to the

NORTH WALES

lovely **Bryn Mor ❷**, where elegant rooms have sea views and TVs. (☎760 344. £22. Cash only.) A small **Spar** provides **groceries.** (☎760 234. Open Apr.-Oct. M-Sa 8am-9pm, Su 9am-9pm; Nov.-Mar. until 5:30pm.) Food has been served since 1300 in the small building now occupied by the **Y Gegin Fawr ❶** ("The Big Kitchen") cafe. Enjoy a "Pilgrim's Lunch" (£4.95) on the creekside patio or in the quaint tea-room. (☎760 359. Open daily July-Aug. 10am-5pm; Easter-June and Sept.-Oct. 10am-5:30pm. Cash only.) The **post office** is inside the Spar market. (Open M-Tu and Th-F 9am-12:30pm and 1:30-5:30pm, W and Sa 9am-noon.) **Post Code:** LL53 8BE.

Tre'r Ceiri (trair-KAY-ree; "Town of the Giants"), on the peninsula's north shore, is Britain's oldest fortress, dating back 4000 years and resting on the easternmost of three mountains known as "The Rivals." Take the Pwllheli-Caernarfon bus #12 to **Llanaelhaearn** (15min.; M-Sa every hr., Su 4 per day), then look for the footpath signposted 1 mi. southwest of town on the B4417 (from the bus stop, go uphill until you hit the B4417, then turn left). At the path's upper reaches, keep to the stony track, a direct uphill route (elevation 1600 ft.). The extensive and well-preserved remains of 150 circular stone huts are clustered within a double defensive wall, which, however strong, fails to protect against the weather; dress warmly.

CAERNARFON ☎01286

Occupied since pre-Roman times and once the center of English government in northern Wales, Caernarfon has witnessed countless struggles for regional political control. It was originally built for English settlers, a legacy that remains visible in a magnificent castle (one of many) built by Edward I. The Welsh have always been eager to claim it for themselves, however, by violence if necessary: during a 1294 tax revolt, they managed to break in, sack the town, and massacre its English inhabitants. Though its streets are lined with modern shops and cafes, Caernarfon feels thoroughly Welsh in character—visitors can hear the town's own dialect used in its flower-bedecked streets and inviting pubs. Caernafon's preserved fortress is widely regarded the most spectacular of Edward I's ring of castles designed to contain and intimidate the rebellious Welsh.

TRANSPORTATION. The nearest **train station** is in **Bangor** (p. 516), though numerous buses coming up from mid-Wales pass through Caernarfon on their way north to Bangor and Anglesey. The central stop is on Penllyn in the city center. **Arriva Cymru** (☎0870 608 2608) buses #5 and 5X come from **Conwy** and **Llandudno** via Bangor (1¾hr. from Llandudno; M-Sa 3 per hr., Su every hr.). **Express Motors** (☎881 108) bus #1 arrives from **Porthmadog** (45-60min.; M-Sa every hr., £2.60) and Arriva bus #32 shares duties on Sundays (6 per day). **Clynnog & Trefor** (☎660 208) and **Berwyn** (☎660 315) run bus #12 from **Pwllheli** (45min.; M-Sa every hr., Su 3 per day). **KMP** (☎870 880) bus #88 runs from **Llanberis** (25min.; M-Sa 1-2 per hr., Su every hr. until 6:50pm). Arriva's **TrawsCambria** bus #701 arrives daily from **Cardiff** (7½hr.). **National Express** (☎08705 808 080) bus #545 arrives daily from **London** via Chester (9hr., 1 per day, £26) or with a change in Birmingham (9½hr., 1 per day, £26). A Gwynedd **Red Rover ticket** earns unlimited bus travel in the county for one day (£4.95, children £2.45). *Gwynedd Public Transport Maps and Timetables* gives info on bus and train routes between major and minor towns.

ORIENTATION AND PRACTICAL INFORMATION. The heart of Caernarfon lies within and just outside the town walls, though the city spreads far beyond. As you face outward from the castle entrance, the TIC is across **Castle**

Ditch Road, which runs past **Castle Square** in one direction and down to the waterfront Promenade in the other. **Castle Street** intersects Castle Ditch Rd. perpendicularly at the castle entrance and leads to **High Street. Bridge Street** spokes north from Castle Square and turns into the heavily trafficked **Bangor Street.**

The **Tourist Information Centre,** Castle St., faces the castle entrance, stocks the free *Visitor's Guide to Caernarfon,* and books accommodations for a £2 charge and a 10% deposit. (☎672 232. Open daily Apr.-Oct. 9:30am-5:30pm; Nov.-Mar. M-Sa 10am-4:30pm.) Get **camping supplies** at **14th Peak,** 9 Palace St. (☎675 124. 10% student discount. Open M-Sa 9am-5:30pm, Su 1-4pm.) Other services include: **banks** in Castle Sq. and down Bridge St.; **Pete's Launderette,** Skinner St., off Bridge St. (☎678 395; open M-Th 9am-6pm, F-Sa 9am-5:30pm, Su 11am-5:30pm; last wash 1hr. before closing); the **police,** Maesincla Ln. (☎673 333, ext. 5242); **Internet access** at the **public library,** at the corner of Bangor St. and Lon Pafiliwn (☎675 944; free; open M-Tu and Th-F 10am-7pm, W 10am-1pm, Sa 9am-1pm) or at the **Dylan Thomas Internet Café,** 4 Bangor St. (☎678 777; £3 per hr.; cash only; wireless Internet access available; open M-Sa 9am-6pm); **Castle Pharmacy,** 1A Castle Sq. (☎672 352; open M-Sa 9am-6:30pm); and the **post office** with bureau de change, Castle Sq. (☎08457 223 344; open M-F 9am-5:30pm, Sa 9am-12:30pm). **Post Code:** LL55 2ND.

⌐ ACCOMMODATIONS. Rooms abound, though cheap ones don't; budget travelers will appreciate ▨**Totter's Hostel ❷,** 2 High St. Friendly Bob and Henryette provide spacious rooms with comfortable wooden bunks; the basement is equipped with a full kitchen, a hand-crafted banquet table, and medieval stone arches. (☎672 963; www.applemaps.co.uk/totters. Dorms £12 per person. MC/V.) **B&Bs** (most around £23-25) line **Church Street** inside the old town wall; those on **St. David's Road,** a 10min. walk from the castle and uphill off the Bangor St. roundabout, are sometimes cheaper. At **Bryn Hyfryd ❸,** St. David's Rd., travelers can sink into flowery bedspreads; one room sports a sun deck, another coast views, and all bath facilities. (☎673 840. Singles £25; doubles £50; family rooms £60. Cash only.) **Marianfa ❸,** St. David's Rd., has a wide variety of spacious rooms with stunning views of the Menai. Ask the proprietress about motorbike and sight-seeing packages. (☎674 815; www.ukworld-int.co.uk/marianfa. Ensuite singles £23; doubles £50. Cash only.) **Camp** at **Cadnant Valley ❶,** Cwm Cadnant Rd. (☎673 196. 2-person tent £7-8.50, with car £10-12, more in summer. Showers and laundry. MC/V.)

◻▨ FOOD AND PUBS. A huge **Safeway** sits on North Road (A487). Take Bangor St. past the roundabout. (Open M-Th 8:30am-10pm, F 8am-10pm, Sa 8am-8pm, Su 10am-4pm.) **Spar,** 29-31 Castle Sq. sells a much smaller selection of **groceries** closer to the center of town. (☎676 895. Open M-Sa 7am-11pm, Su 7am-10:30pm.) On Saturdays and some Mondays, a **market** takes over Castle Sq. (Open 9am-4pm.) **Hole-in-the-Wall Street** is a narrow alleyway known for its dense collection of eateries. Covered with ivy and garlands of light, it lives up to the charming premise of its name. **Stones Bistro ❸,** 4 Hole-in-the-Wall St., near Eastgate, is popular but tucked away, with candlelit tables and local art adorning its walls. The Welsh lamb (£12.95) is served with your choice of a mint, honey, yogurt, pepper, or tomato-garlic sauce. (☎671 152. Open Tu-Sa 6-11pm. AmEx/MC/V.) Climb aboard the **Floating Restaurant ❷,** Slate Quay, where views of strait, castle, and mountains complement an unabashedly nautical menu: "Cast Off" with a starter (from £3.10), venture into "Davy Jones' Locker" with Neptune's Purse (fish and prawns, £6.95), and "Walk the Plank" with a hearty dessert like fudge cake (£2.20). (☎672 896. Open Easter to mid-Sept. 11am-9:30pm. Cash only.) The stout wooden doors of the **Anglesey Arms ❶**

NORTH WALES

open onto the Promenade just below the castle. Relax outdoors with a pint as the sun dips into the shimmering Menai. (☎ 672 158. Live entertainment Fridays. Open M-Sa 11am-11pm, Su noon-10:30pm. MC/V.) Younger crowds flock to **Cofi Roc's** modern decor, on Castle Sq., for tribute bands every Wednesday. (☎ 673 100; www.cofiroc.com. Open daily lunch until late. MC/V.)

🖻 🎧 **SIGHTS AND ENTERTAINMENT.** Built by Edward I to resemble Roman battlements, ◪**Caernarfon Castle** has been called by one resentful Welshman a "magnificent badge of our subjection." Built to resemble the walls of Constantinople, its eagle-crowned turrets, colorfully banded stones, and polygonal towers cost Edward the equivalent of the Crown's annual budget and nearly 17% of his skilled labor force. Its walls withstood a rebel siege in 1404 with only 28 defenders. More recently, the English royalty besieged the castle during Charles' crowning on the slate dais in the courtyard. Summer sees a variety of performances, including scenes from the Welsh epic *The Mabinogi* and reenactments of the American Revolution. Wisecracking docents run hourly tours for £1.50, and a free 20min. video recounts the castle's history every 30min. The **regimental museum** of the Royal Welsh Fusiliers, inside the castle, is huge and worthwhile; medals, uniforms, and helmets accompany rich historical exhibits. Don't miss the Regimental "Goat Major"—each brigade was required to have one—whose gilded horns and headplate have inspired generations of Fusiliers. (☎ 677 617. Open daily June-Sept. 9:30am-6pm; Apr.-May and Oct. 9:30am-5pm; Nov.-Mar. M-Sa 9:30am-4pm, Su 11am-4pm. £4.50, concessions £3.50, families £12.50.) Most of Caernarfon's 13th-century **town wall** survives, and a short stretch between Church St. and Northgate St. is open for climbing during the same hours as the castle.

The remains of a Celtic settlement scatter atop **Twt Hill,** alongside the Bangor St. roundabout; the jutting peak offers an excellent overlook above town and castle. For views of Menai Strait and its surroundings from the water itself, call **Menai Strait Pleasure Cruises** (☎ 672 772), which runs 40min. tours May through October (11:30am-4:30pm, weather and tides permitting; £4, children £2.50). Upon a hill, **Segontium Roman Fort** was once the center for military activity in North Wales. Plundered to its foundations by zealous builders stealing stones for Caernarfon Castle, the fort's grounds are now lackluster rubble, though a museum houses an eclectic display of archaeological excavations. From Castle Sq., follow signs uphill along Ffordd Cwstenin. (☎ 675 625. Museum open Tu-Su 12:30-4:00pm, grounds open daily 10am-4:30pm. Free.)

Six miles south of Caernarfon, peaceful **Parc Glynllifon** is still bordered by the remains of a log fence built to "keep the peasants out and the pheasants in," but visitors are now welcome to wander the manicured lawns and exotic trees. Art galleries and a working steam engine are found near the entrance, but the enormous 19th-century manor and ornate fountain hide deeper in the forest. Take bus #12 south from Caernarfon to the Parc Glynllifon stop (15min., 1 per hour, £1.70 round-trip). (☎ 830 222. Open daily 9am-5pm. £2, children £1, families £5.) **Paradox,** St. Helen's Rd., is a huge nightclub off Castle St.; descend the stairs next to the post office. (☎ 673 100. Cover £2-6. Open F-Sa 10pm-1:30am.)

SNOWDONIA NATIONAL PARK

Amidst the impressive man-made battlements of Edward I in Northern Wales lies the 840 sq. mi. natural fortress of Snowdonia National Park. Known in Welsh as Eryri ("Place of Eagles"), Snowdonia's veiled peaks yield surprisingly diverse terrain—pristine mountain lakes etch outlines of glittering blue onto rolling grasslands, and the desolate cliff-faces of abandoned slate quarries slope into thickly wooded hills. Rock climbing attracts many to Snowdonia

(Tremadog has particularly good courses); Sir Edmund Hillary trained here before attempting Everest. Though these lands lie largely in private hands—only 0.3% belongs to the National Park Authority—endless public footpaths easily accommodate visitors. The second largest of England and Wales's national parks, Snowdonia is also a stronghold of national pride: 65% of its 27,500 inhabitants speak Welsh as their native tongue.

▐ TRANSPORTATION

Trains (☎08457 484 950) stop at larger towns on the park's outskirts, including **Bangor** and **Conwy,** and the Cambrian Coaster line hits **Harlech** and **Dolgellau** in the south. The **Conwy Valley Line** runs across the park from **Llandudno** through **Betws-y-Coed** to **Blaenau Ffestiniog** (1hr. from Llandudno to Blaenau Ffestiniog; M-Sa 7 per day, Su 2-3 per day). **Buses** serve the interior from towns near the edge of the park. *The Gwynedd Public Transport Maps and Timetables* and *Conwy Public Transport Information* booklets, indispensable for travel in the two counties that comprise the park, are both available for free in the region's TICs. **Snowdon Sherpa** buses, usually painted blue, maneuver between the park's towns and trailheads with helpful but irregular service, and will stop at any safe point in the park on request. A Gwynedd **Red Rover ticket** (£4.95, children £2.45) buys unlimited travel for a day on Sherpa buses and all other buses in Gwynedd and Anglesey; a **Snowdon Sherpa Day Ticket** secures a day's worth of rides on Sherpa buses (£3, children £1.50). Most routes run every 1-2hr., but Sunday service is sporadic at best.

Narrow-gauge railway lines let you enjoy the countryside in a few select locations without enduring a hike, though they tend to be fairly pricey. The **Ffestiniog Railway** (p. 504) weaves from **Porthmadog** to **Blaenau Ffestiniog,** where views of pristine mountains give way to the raw cliffs of shingled slate quarries. You can travel part of its route to Minffordd, Penrhyndeudraeth, or Tan-y-bwlch. At Porthmadog, the narrow-gauge rail meets the Cambrian Coaster service from Pwllheli to Aberystwyth; at Blaenau Ffestiniog, it connects with the Conwy Valley Line. The **Snowdon Mountain Railway** and the **Llanberis Lake Railway** make trips from Llanberis (p. 513).

▐ PRACTICAL INFORMATION

TICs and National Park Information Centres (NPICs) stock leaflets on walks, drives, and accommodations, as well as Ordnance Survey maps (£6-7). For details, contact the **Snowdonia National Park Information Headquarters** (☎01766

770 274). The semi-annual booklet put out by the Snowdonia National Park Authority, free at TICs across North Wales, is a good source of information on the park and accommodations. You can also check out www.snpa.co.uk or www.gwynedd.gov.uk.

National Park Information Centres:

Aberdyfi: Wharf Gdns. (☎01654 767 321). Open daily Apr.-Oct. 9:30am-12:30pm and 1:30-5pm.

Betws-y-Coed: The busiest and best stocked. See p. 527.

Blaenau Ffestiniog: Isallt Church St. (☎01766 830 360). Open daily Apr.-Sept. 9:30am-5:30pm.

Dolgellau: see p. 499.

Harlech: see p. 502.

ACCOMMODATIONS

In the high mountains, **camping** is permitted as long as you leave no mess, but the Park Service discourages it because of recent disastrous erosion. In the valleys, the landowner's consent is required to camp. Public campsites dot the roads in peak seasons; check listings below and inquire at NPICs for specific sites. This section lists **YHA hostels** in Snowdonia; **B&Bs** are listed under individual towns. The seven hostels in the mountain area are some of the best in Wales and are marked on the Snowdonia map. All have kitchens, and most offer meals. Keep in mind that YHA now strongly advises you book hostels 48hr. in advance, as many now have unpredictable opening dates in the low season. Book online at www.yha.org.uk.

Bryn Gwynant (☎0870 770 5732), above Llyn Gwynant and along the Penygwryd-Beddgelert Rd., ¾ mi. from the Watkin path. On Su and bank holidays, take Snowdon Sherpa bus S4 from Caernarfon (40min., 5 per day) or Pen-y-Pass (10min., 9 per day). Sherpa summer express #97A comes from Porthmadog or Betws-y-Coed (30min. each way, 3 per day). An old Victorian residence built in the heart of the park. Lockout 10am-5pm. Curfew 11pm. Open Mar.-Oct. Dorms £10.60, under 18 £7.20. MC/V. ❶

Capel Curig (☎0870 770 5746; fax 01690 720 270), 5 mi. from Betws-y-Coed on the A5. Sherpa buses S2 and S3 stop nearby from Llandudno, Betws-y-Coed, and Pen-y-Pass. At the crossroads of many mountain paths; favored by climbers and school kids. Spectacular view of Mt. Snowdon across a lake. Lockout 10am-5pm. Open daily mid-Feb. to Oct.; Nov.-Jan. F-Sa. Dorms £14.40, under 18 £10.80. MC/V. ❷

Idwal Cottage (☎0870 770 5874), just off the A5 at the foot of Llyn Ogwen in northern Snowdonia, 4 mi. from Bethesda. Take Sherpa bus #66 from Bangor (20min., every hr.), changing to S3 at Bethesda (10min.; M-Sa 6 per day, Su 10 per day), which goes to the hostel. On Su, #7 from Bangor stops at the hostel (30min., 2 per day). Lockout 10am-5pm. Curfew 11pm. Open daily Mar.-Nov.; Dec.-Feb. F-Sa. Dorms £11.80, under 18 £8.50. MC/V. ❷

Kings (Dolgellau) (☎0870 770 5900), Penmaenpool, 4 mi. from Dolgellau. Take Arriva bus #28 from Dolgellau (5min.; M-Sa 9 per day, Su 3 per day); the house is a 1 mi. uphill from the bus drop-off. A country house in the Vale of Ffestiniog. Open daily mid-Apr. to Aug.; Sept.-Oct. and Mar.-Apr. F-Sa; rentable Nov.-Mar. Dorms £10.60, under 18 £7.20. MC/V. ❶

Llanberis (☎0870 770 5928), ½ mi. up Capel Goch Rd., with views of Llyn Peris, Llyn Padarn, and Mt. Snowdon; follow signs from High St. Curfew 11pm. Open daily Apr.-Oct.; Nov.-Dec. F-Sa; Jan.-Feb. rentable, March flexible opening. Dorms £11.80, under 18 £8.50. MC/V. ❷

Pen-y-Pass (☎0870 770 5990), in Nant Gwynant, 6 mi. from Llanberis and 4 mi. from Nant Peris. Take Sherpa bus S1 from Llanberis (20min.; late May to Sept. every hr.; Oct. to late May M-Sa 6 per day, Su 9 per day). At the head of Llanberis Pass, 1170 ft. above sea level, it has the highest elevation of any hostel in Wales. Doors open onto a track to the Snowdon summit. Outdoors shop sells supplies and rents hiking boots, waterproofs, and ice axes. Dorms £11.80, under 18 £8.50. MC/V. ❷

Snowdon Ranger (☎0870 770 6038), Llyn Cwellyn. The base for the Ranger Path, one of the grandest Snowdon ascents. Take Sherpa bus S4 from Caernarfon (20min.; M-Sa 8 per day, Su 6 per day). Lockout 10am-5pm. Curfew 11pm. Open daily Easter-Aug.; Sept.-Oct. Tu-Su; Nov.-Mar. F-Su. Dorms £10.60, under 18 £7.20. MC/V. ❶

⚑ OUTDOORS ACTIVITIES

Weather on Snowdonia's mountains shifts quickly, unpredictably, and with a vengeance. No matter how beautiful the weather is below, it will be cold and wet in the high mountains; bring a waterproof jacket and pants, gloves, hat, and wool sweater and peel off layers as you descend. The free *Stay Safe in Snowdonia* is available at NPICs and offers advice and information on hiking and climbing. (See **Wilderness Safety,** p. 52.) Pick up the Ordnance Survey Landranger Map #115 (1:50,000; £6) and Outdoor Leisure Map #17 (1:25,000; £7), as well as individual mountain path guides (40p) at TICs and NPICs. Call **Mountaincall Snowdonia** (☎09068 500 449) for a local three- to five-day forecast.

Snowdonia National Park Study Centre, Plâs Tan-y-Bwlch, Maentwrog, Blaenau Ffestiniog, conducts two- to seven-day courses on naturalist favorites such as botanical painting. (☎01766 590 324. £103-400. Includes accommodation.) **YHA Pen-y-Pass,** Nant Gwynant (p. 513) puts groups in touch with guides for mountaineering, climbing, and water sports. **Beics Eryri Cycle Tours,** 44 Tyddyn Llwydyn, offer trips from Caernarfon for multi-night forays into the park, supplying maps, bikes, accommodation, and luggage transport. (☎01286 676 637. About £60 per night.) **Dolbadarn Trekking** operates out of Llanberis (p. 515). The brave can paraglide off the peaks of Snowdonia with the help of **Snowdon Gliders.** (☎01248 600 330. Call ahead.) Ask park rangers about guided **day-walks.** The less brave can stay indoors for climbing activities at the **Beacon Climbing Centre** (☎01286 650 045. 1½hr. session £40. Open M-F 11am-10pm, Sa-Su 10am-10pm.) or stick to the water on **Llyn Tegid,** Bala, Wales' largest natural lake known for its windsurfing. Myriad other adventures are detailed in *The Snowdon Peninsula: North Wales Activities* brochure, available in TICs and NPICs.

LLANBERIS ☎01286

Beyond its mountain hamlet veneer, Llanberis offers a unique atmosphere blending youthful energy, local pride, and rugged outdoorsmanship. The town's perpetually shifting community of climbers, cyclists, and hikers keeps it lively seven days a week (and most nights as well), while its glassy lake and imposing mountain ranges make for numerous forays for the outdoor adventurers.

🖫🖪 TRANSPORTATION AND PRACTICAL INFORMATION. Situated on the western edge of the park, Llanberis is a short ride from Caernarfon on the A4086. Catch **KMP** (☎870 880) bus #88 from **Caernarfon** (25min.; £1.50, round-trip £2; M-Sa 1-2 per hr., Su every hr. until 7:20pm). KMP #85/86 arrives frequently from **Bangor** (35-50min.; M-Sa 1-2 per hr., Su 7 per day).

The **Tourist Information Centre,** 41b High St., doles out hiking tips and books beds for a £2 charge plus a 10% deposit. It stocks a number of brochures on hikes in Snowdonia, including pamphlets (40p) on the six routes up Mt. Snow-

NORTH WALES

don. (☎870 765. Open daily Easter-Oct. 9:30am-5:30pm; Nov.-Easter W and F-Su 11am-4pm.) Pick up gear, maps, and advice at **Joe Brown's Store**, Menai Hall, High St. (☎870 327. Open summer M-Sa 9am-6pm, Su 9am-5pm; winter M-Sa 9am-5:30pm, Su 9am-5pm.) Other services include: **HSBC**, 29 High St. (open M and W 9:30am-11:30pm, Tu and Th-F 1:30-3:30pm); the bankless **Barclays ATM**, at the entrance to Electric Mountain on the A4086; **Internet access** at **Pete's Eats** (p. 514) and at **Castle Gift Shop**, High St. (☎870 379; 5p per min., min. £1; open M-Su 7am-6pm); and the **post office**, 36 High St. (☎01286 870 201; open M-Tu and Th-F 9am-5:30pm, W and Sa 9am-7:30pm). **Post Code: LL55 4EU.**

⌐⌐ **ACCOMMODATIONS AND FOOD.** During summer weekends, this tiny town is booked full, so make reservations in advance. The quiet and pleasant outskirts of Llanberis harbor tiny ◪**Snowdon Cottage ❸.** With a castle-view garden, sweet-smelling (if cozy) rooms, an "Egyptian" bathroom, a welcoming hearth, and a gracious hostess, staying in may be preferable to outdoorsy pursuits. (☎872 015; £20 per person, £19 for multiple nights. Cash only.) Plenty of sheep and cows keep hostelers company at the **YHA Llanberis** (p. 512), while the **Heights Hotel ❷**, 74 High St., draws a youthful clientele with 21 bunk beds packed into three co-ed dorms. On weekends, half the town crowds into its two ground-floor bars, glass-walled "conservatory" (smoking lounge), and pool room. (☎871 179. June-Aug. dorms £14, with breakfast £17.50; Sept.-May £10/£13. Doubles £50; 3- to 6-person rooms £20 per person. MC/V.) **Pete's Eats** (p. 514) has dorm-style accommodations from £12. Enjoy comfortable, mostly ensuite rooms at the grand **Plas Coch Guest House ❸**, High St. (☎872 122; www.plas-coch.co.uk. Doubles £46-56. Cash only.)

Spar is at the corner of High St. and Capel Goch Rd. (Open M-Sa 7am-11pm, Su 7am-10:30pm.) **Snowdon Honey Farm ❶**, High St., sells a huge selection of its own meads and Celtic wines, as well as honeys, teas, and ice cream. Samples are given with much cheer. (☎870 218. Open daily 7am-6pm. Cash only.) **Pete's Eats ❶**, 40 High St., opposite the TIC, is the place to refuel after a day outdoors—in the evening its counter seems like the heart of the town. Sample a walnut-cheeseburger (£2.20) or so-called super-hot chili (£5.20) with enormous mugs of tea (£1) as you enjoy the culture collision of high chair-bound tots and hip hiker grunge. (☎870 117. Internet access 5p per min., min. 50p. Open Nov.-June 8am-8pm; July-Aug. 8am-9pm. MC/V.) Upscale **Y Bistro ❹**, 45 High St., serves great fish dishes, including monkfish with pancetta and thyme for £15.50. (☎871 278; www.ybistro.co.uk. Open for dinner from 7:30pm; closed some nights, book ahead. MC/V.)

◨ **SIGHTS.** For a small village, Llanberis brims with attractions; most lie near the fork where the A4086 meets High St. Part self-promotion for Edison Energy, part journey to the center of the earth, **Electric Mountain** takes visitors on an informative (and occasionally exciting) underground tour of the Dinorwig power station. Located deep in the heart of a mountain formerly quarried for slate, the station occupies the largest man-made cavern in Europe—St. Paul's Cathedral could fit inside. (☎870 636. Open daily June-Aug. 9:30am-5:30pm; Apr.-May and Sept.-Oct. 10:30am-4:30pm; Nov.-Mar. W-Su 10:40am-4:30pm; closed Jan. 1hr. tour Easter-Sept. £6, concessions £4.50, families £14.) The immensely popular and pricey **Snowdon Mountain Railway** has been letting visitors "climb" Snowdon's summit since 1896, winding along narrow tracks that start from its base station on the A4086. The 2½hr. round-trip allows 30min. at the peak, but one-way tickets are available for those who would like to hike up or down. (☎0870 458 0033; www.snowdonrailway.co.uk. Runs daily

Mar. to early Nov. 9am-5pm; Mar.-May trains do not go to the summit. Weather permitting, misty days afford limited summit views. Single £14, children £11; round-trip £20/£14.)

In nearby **Parc Padarn,** under the tiered cliffs once quarried for slate, the **Welsh Slate Museum** explores the history of the industry and its continued impact with a 3D film, an impressively recreated block of miners' dwellings from various eras, and a series of live displays of slate splitting and finishing. Don't miss the astonishingly large waterwheel. (☎870 630; www.nmgw.ac.uk. Open daily Easter-Oct. 10am-5pm; Nov.-Easter Su-F 10am-4pm. Free.) A short uphill walk takes you to the **Quarry Hospital Visitor Centre.** This old hospital, built by the owner of the mines to deal with health issues "privately," now houses a morbidly fascinating array of factoids and sinister medical implements. (☎870 892. Open Apr.-early Sept. daily 11am-5pm. £1.) The park is also home to the **Llanberis Lake Railway,** which takes a short, scenic route from Gilfach Ddu station at Llanberis through the woods along the lake. (☎870 549; www.lake-railway.co.uk. Open Apr.-Oct. Su-F; July-Aug. also Sa.) The **Woodland and Wildlife Centre,** at the halfway point, is a nice picnic spot. (Railway ☎870 549. 40min. round-trip. Open M-F 11am-4:30pm, Sa-Su 1-4:30pm; schedule at TIC. £4.50, children £1.60. Centre open same hours. Free.) Bolder types can get their feet wet at the **Vivian Diving Center,** with full training for all levels (☎870 889; www.divcvivian.com. Open M-F 10am-5pm, Sa-Su 9am-5:30pm.)

Follow the road into the park until a footbridge to the right leads to **Dolbadarn Castle,** where Prince Llywelyn of North Wales is rumored to have imprisoned his brother for 23 years. Only a single, impressively ragged tower remains.(Always open. Free.) For an eye-level view of the waterfall **Ceunant Mawr,** follow the well-marked footpath from Victoria Terr. by the Victoria Hotel (¾ mi.).

MOUNT SNOWDON AND VICINITY   ☎01286

By far the most popular destination in the park, **Mount Snowdon** is the highest peak in both England and Wales, measuring 3560 ft. The Welsh name for the peak, Yr Wyddfa, meaning "The Burial Place"; comes from a legend holding that Rhita Gawr, a giant cloaked with the beards of the kings he slaughtered, is buried here. Over half a million hikers tread the mountain each year, and it's hardly difficult to see why: in fair weather, the steep green slopes and shimmering lakes tucked beneath the mountain's ragged rock cliffs are stunning. Future hikes were in peril in 1998 when a plot of land that included Snowdon's summit was put up for sale, but celebrated Welsh actor Sir Anthony Hopkins sprang to the rescue, contributing a vast sum to the National Trust to save the pristine peak. Park officers request that hikers stick to the six well-marked trails to avoid damage to Snowdon's ecosystem. The most popular route is the **Llanberis Path** (5 mi.), which begins right outside of town. It is the longest and easiest of the trails, but other paths, like the **Miner's Track** offer far superior views and criss-cross numerous valleys. **The Pyg Track,** which begins in nearby Pen-y-Pass, is a less-frequented gem. Start climbing early in the day to avoid crowds on the trails, and dress warmly on misty days. Trains run up to the summit on the **Snowdon Mountain Railway** (p. 514); a mail box at the top allows you to send postcards from above it all—with a special stamp.

Though Mt. Snowdon is the main attraction in the northern part of the park, experienced climbers cart pick-axes and ropes to the **Ogwen Valley.** There, climbs to **Devil's Kitchen** (Twll Du), the **Glyders** (Glyder Fawr and Glyder Fach), and **Tryfan** all begin from **Llyn Ogwen.** Tryfan's unusual peak has been immortalized in countless National Park posters. Though its elevation has been set at

3010 ft., nobody's quite sure which of two adjacent rocks (nicknamed "Adam" and "Eve") is the actual summit. No trip to the top is complete without performing the famed "jump" (about 3 ft.) between the two crags. Those attempting climbs should pick up the appropriate Ordnance Survey maps and get advice on equipment and supplies at **Joe Brown's Store** (p. 513). Excellent horseback riding is available at the **Dolbadarn Trekking Centre,** High St., Llanberis, whose guides can point out where scenes from *Willow* and *Mortal Kombat: Annihilation* were filmed. (☎870 277; www.dolbadarnhotel.co.uk. ₤15 per hr.)

BANGOR ☎01248

A stronghold of Welsh princes turned university town, Bangor seems neither regal nor academic, but rather a pleasant and convenient coastal hub. With the longest High St. in Wales, Bangor offers shopping and bars crammed until the early hours with University of Wales students.

⌷ TRANSPORTATION. Bangor is the transport depot for the Isle of Anglesey to the west and Snowdonia to the southeast. The **train station** is on Holyhead Rd., at the end of Deiniol Rd. (☎01492 585 151. Ticket office open daily 5:30am-6:30pm; low-season 11:30am-6:30pm.) **Trains** (☎08457 484 950) arrive from: **Chester** (1-1¼hr., 1-2 per hr., ₤13.50); **Holyhead** (30min.; M-Sa 15 per day, Su 10 per day); **Llandudno Junction** (20min., M-Sa 1-2 per hr., Su 10 per day, ₤3.90). The **bus station** is on Garth Rd., a few feet downhill from the town clock. **Arriva Cymru** (☎0870 608 2608) bus #4 arrives from **Holyhead** via **Llangefni** and **Llanfair P.G.** (1¼-1½hr., M-Sa 2 per hr.), while on Sunday #44 makes the trip 6 times. Buses #53, 57, and 58 come from **Beaumaris** (30min.; M-Sa 2-3 per hr., Su 8 per day). Arriva bus #5, 5A, 5B, and 5X journey from **Caernarfon** (25min.; M-Sa every 10-20min., Su every hr.); #5 and 5X continue east to **Conwy** (40min.; M-Sa 2-3 per hr., Su every hr.) and Llandudno (1hr.; M-Sa 2-3 per hr., Su every hr.; ₤1.90). Transfer at **Caernarfon** for the **Llŷn Peninsula,** including Pwllheli and Porthmadog. **TrawsCambria** bus #701 follows the coast all the way from **Cardiff** (7¾hr., 1 per day). **National Express** (☎08705 808 080) buses come from **London** (8½hr., 1 per day, ₤26). For taxi service, try **Ace Taxi** (☎351 324) or **Chubb's Cabs** (☎353 535).

⌷⌷ ORIENTATION AND PRACTICAL INFORMATION. An age-old street plan and roads that don't advertise their names might leave visitors vulnerable to confusion, but Bangor's essential corridor is traced by **Deiniol Road** and **High Street,** which run parallel to each other and sandwich the city. **Garth Road** starts from the town clock on High St. and winds past the bus station, merging with Deiniol Rd. **Holyhead Road** begins its winding ascent at the train station. The **University of Wales at Bangor** straddles both sides of **College Road.**

The **Tourist Information Centre,** Town Hall, Deiniol Rd., a block from the bus station, books rooms for a ₤2 charge plus a 10% deposit and can arrange ferries to Ireland. (☎352 786. Open May-Sept. Tu-Sa 10am-5pm.) Other services include: **banks** on High St.; the **police** (☎370 333), Garth Rd., across from the bus station; the **hospital** (☎384 384); **Internet access** at Java Cafe (p. 517) for ₤1 per 15min. or for free at the **library** across from the TIC (☎353 479; open M-Tu and Th-F 9:30am-7pm, W and Sa 9:30am-1pm); **Boots pharmacy,** 276 High St. (☎362 822; open M-F 8:45am-5:30pm, Sa 8:45am-6pm, Su 11am-5pm); and the **post office,** 60 Deiniol Rd., with a **bureau de change** (☎377 301; open M-F 9am-5:30pm, Sa 9am-12:30pm). **Post Code:** LL57 1AA.

⚑ ⌂ ACCOMMODATIONS AND FOOD. Finding a room in Bangor during graduation festivities (the second week of July) is a nightmarish prospect; book months ahead. The **YHA Bangor ❷**, Tan-y-Bryn, is a half-mile from the town center. Follow High St. to the water and turn right onto the A5122 (Beach Rd.), then right at the sign. Bus #5 (to Llandudno; 2 per hr.) passes the hostel; ask to be dropped off. The rich wood paneling of the entrance hall and wide-beam ceilings betray its former role as 19th-century country estate. Vivien Leigh and Sir Laurence Olivier stayed in what is now Room 6. (☎353 516. Foosball and laundry. Internet access 7p per min. Open daily Apr.-Sept.; Oct. and Mar. Tu-Sa; Nov. and Jan.-Feb. F-Sa. Dorms £11.80, under 18 £8.50. MC/V.) **B&B** options (from £15) in Bangor are solid if not particularly exciting; the most agreeable occupy the townhouses on **Garth Road** and its extensions. **Mrs. S. Roberts ❷**, 32 Glynne Rd., between Garth Rd. and High St., has TVs and 13 choices for breakfast. (☎352 113. £15. Cash only.) Comfortable, if not particularly comely **Dilfam ❷**, is 10min. from the TIC down Garth Rd., all rooms have TVs. (☎353 030. Singles £20; doubles £40, with bath £46. Cash only.) **Dinas Farm ❶**, 3mi. from Bangor on the banks of the River Ogwan, offers camping. Follow the A5 past Penrhyn Castle and turn left off the A5122. (☎364 227. Open Easter-Oct. £3 per person. Electricity £2. Cash only.)

High Street has a surprisingly varied selection of bakeries, pubs, and eateries, as well as a **Kwik Save** supermarket. (Open M-Sa 8am-10pm, Su 10am-4pm.) **Herbs ❷**, 162 High St., has a salad bar (£2.50), cheap lunches (from £3), and interesting combinations like mackerel salad and cranberry with brie (£3.95) in a dining room decorated with mosaics and potted plants. (☎351 249; www.herbsrestaurant.co.uk. Open M-Th 10am-3pm, F-Sa 10am-9pm. AmEx/MC/V.) **Gerrards ❶**, 251 High St., at the clock tower, has bakery fare (2 lunches for £6) in a spacious venue. (☎371 351. Open M-Sa 9am-5pm. Cash only.) Choose between "East" or "West" on the bifurcated menu at the ultra-mellow **Java Restaurant ❷**, up an alley off of High St. near Abbey. Try the smoked chipotle fajitas (£6.95), one of many veggie options, while surfing the web. (☎361 652. Internet access £1 per 15min. Open M-Tu 10am-6pm, W-Sa 10am-10pm. Su 11am-4pm. Hot food served 10am-4pm and 6-10pm. MC/V.)

◙ ⌂ SIGHTS AND ENTERTAINMENT. George Hay Dawkins-Pennant's 19th-century **Penrhyn Castle,** pegs itself as the pinnacle of the short-lived neo-Norman school. The intricate main staircase is full of carved faces and took over 10 years to complete. The house is also home to the largest art collection in Wales after the National Gallery. Its slate-baron owner was on a mission to prove that the material has numerous uses; elaborate slate dressers, a slate billiard table, even a slate canopy bed testify to his quest. Walk up High St. toward the bay, then turn right on the A5122 and go north 1 mi., or catch bus #5 or 5X from town to the grounds entrance (10min.; M-Sa 2 per hr., Su every hr.; 60p); the castle is another mile. (☎353 084. Castle open daily July-Aug. 11am-5pm; late Mar. to June and Sept.-Oct. from noon. Grounds open daily July-Aug. 10am-5pm; late Mar. to June and Sept.-Oct. from 10am. Last admission 30min. before close. £7, children £3.50, families £17.50.)

St. Deiniol's Cathedral, Gwynedd Rd., off High St., has been the ecclesiastical center of this corner of Wales for 1400 years, yet it sits humbly amidst the commercial district. Its unimpressive **Bible Garden** cultivates plants mentioned in the Good Book. (☎353 983. Open M-F 8am-6pm, Sa 10am-1pm, Su for services.) The **Bangor Museum and Art Gallery,** also on Gwynedd Rd., houses an authentic **man-trap**—a snare-like contraption used as an anti-poaching device by insidious landowners—as well as a collection of regional crafts and artifacts. (☎353 368. Open Tu-F 12:30-4:30pm, Sa 10:30am-4:30pm. Free.) Watch tides ebb and flow at the long, onion-domed Victorian **pier** at the end of Garth Rd.

NORTH WALES

The modern **Theatr Gwynedd,** Deiniol Rd., at the base of the hill, houses a thriving troupe that performs in Welsh and English. (☎351 708. Box office open M-F 9:30am-5pm, Sa 10am-5pm, and before curtain. Tickets from £5.) Bangor's students keep clubs buoyant, and many pubs along **High Street** pump up the volume on weekends. Dance your way to happiness (or buy it in liquid form) at **Bliss,** Dean St., off High St. (☎354 977. Cover £3-5. Open W and F-Sa 8pm-1am.) At cover-less **Joop's,** 358/360 High St., friendly bouncers admit a younger crowd. (☎372 040. Open Th-Sa 8pm-1am; last admission 11pm.)

ISLE OF ANGLESEY (YNYS MÔN)

Anglesey is certainly a fair island, but she's rough around the edges—and not just topographically. The island's old name, Môn mam Cymru ("Anglesey, mother of Wales"), indicates roots embedded deeply in its Celtic past; although you won't find spectacular castles or cathedrals, telltale druidic burial sites and tiny chapels dot the rolling farmlands whose granaries have long supported Wales. Anglesey's sense of Welsh heritage, however, is hardly confined to this history: six of every ten islanders speak Welsh as a first language. Much of the coastline has been designated as an Area of Outstanding Natural Beauty, and its stunning landscapes beckon those looking to encounter a bit of history.

▐▀ TRANSPORTATION

Apart from major towns, Anglesey is difficult to explore without a car. **Bangor,** on the mainland, is the best hub for the island. **Trains** (☎08457 484 950) run on the North Wales line to **Holyhead** from Bangor (30min.; M-F 1-2 per hr., Su 13 per day; £5.60); some stop at **Llanfair P.G.** The main **bus** company is **Arriva Cymru** (☎0870 608 2608), whose buses radiate out to most of the island's major towns from the Menai and Britannia bridges. Smaller bus companies fill the gaps. Arriva bus #4 travels north from Bangor to **Holyhead** via **Llanfair P.G.** and **Llangefni** (1¼hr., M-Sa 2 per hr., £3.20); on Sundays, #44 follows a similar route (6 per day). Buses #53, 57, and 58 hug the southeast coast from Bangor to **Beaumaris** (30min.; M-Sa 2 per hr., Su 8 per day; £2.10); some continue to **Penmon** (40min.; M-Sa 12 per day, Su 4 per day). Bus #62 goes to **Amlwch,** on the northern coast, from Bangor (50min.; M-Sa 1-2 per hr., Su 5 per day; £1.75). Bus #42 curves along the southwest coast to **Aberffraw** before continuing north to **Llangefni** (50min. to Aberffraw, 1¼hr. to Llangefni; M-Sa 9 per day, Su 3-5 per day). **Lewis y Llan** (☎01407 832 181) bus #61 travels from **Amlwch** to **Holyhead** (50min.; M-Sa 7 per day, Su 4 per day). Bus #32 shuttles north from **Llangefni** to **Amlwch** (40min.; M-Sa 8 per day, Su 5 per day). The Gwynedd **Red Rover ticket** (£4.95, children £2.45) covers a day's travel in Anglesey and Gwynedd. Pick up the free *Isle of Anglesey Public Transport Timetable* at TICs.

◉ SIGHTS

Various peoples have inhabited Anglesey since prehistory. Burial chambers, cairns, and other remains are scattered on Holyhead and along the eastern and western coasts. Most ancient monuments now lie on farmers' fields, so a map detailing exactly how to reach them is helpful. TICs sell Ordnance Survey Landranger Map #114 (1:50,000; £6) and the more detailed Explorer #262 and 263, each of which covers half of the island (1:25,000; £7). *The Guide to Ancient*

Monuments (£2.95) reveals a comprehensive history of prehistoric relics, while the pamphlet Rural Cycling on Anglesey is a must for bikers (free at TICs).

■ **BRYN CELLI DDU.** The most famous of Anglesey's remains, Bryn Celli Ddu (bryn kay-HLEE thee; "The Mound in the Dark Grove") is a burial chamber dating from the late Neolithic period. From the outside, this 4000-year-old construction looks like any old mound of earth in the middle of a sheep pasture, but a flashlight (bring your own) helps illuminate the etchings on the walls inside. The spiral design on the inner chamber is a reproduction—the original is at the National Gallery in Cardiff. *(Bangor-Holyhead bus #4 sometimes stops at Llandaniel (M-Sa 9 per day); walk 1 mi. from there. Site is signposted of the A4080. Bus #42 to Plas Newydd also comes within 1 mi. of Bryn. Free.)*

PLAS NEWYDD. The 19th-century country home of the Marquess of Anglesey, 2 mi. south of Llanfair P.G., is filled with ornate decor—apparent in the pair of merlins in the saloon. The 58 ft. Rex Whistler *tromp l'oeil* mural in the dining room is a whimsically imagined Mediterranean cityscape (with visions of Wales tucked into its corners); it's the largest painted canvas in Britain. *(Take bus #42 from Bangor to the house (15min.; M-Sa 11 per day, Su 6 per day), or catch #4 to Llanfair P.G. (15min., M-Sa 2 per hr.) and walk. ☎ 01248 714 795. House open Apr.-Oct. M-W and Sa noon-5pm. Garden open 11am-5:30pm. £5, children £2.50. Garden only £3/£1.50.)*

PENMON PRIORY. The late medieval priory of Penmon is the most accessible of Anglesey's sights. It houses two elaborately carved cross stands and Europe's largest dovecote (a set of shoebox-sized nesting holes). From the parking lot, a path leads to 6th-century **St. Seiriol's Well,** reputed to have healing qualities. *(Some buses run directly to the Priory; check timetables. Otherwise, take Arriva Cymru bus #57 or 58 from Beaumaris to Penmon (10-20min.; M-Sa 11 per day, Su 5 per day) and follow the sign to Penmon Point; the priory is an additional 25min. walk on the same road. Free.)*

LLANALLGO. Three sets of remains cluster near the town of Llanallgo, but getting to them requires a bit of effort. Follow the minor road (to the left of the Moelfre road) to the ancient **Lligwy Burial Chamber.** Between 15 and 30 people are entombed in this squat enclosure, covered with a 25-ton capstone. Farther on stand the 12th-century chapel **Hen Capel Lligwy** and the remains of the Roman **Din Lligwy Hut Group.** *(Arriva bus #62 hits Llanallgo on its Bangor-Cemaes route (40min.; M-Sa 1-2 per hr., Su 5 per day). Ask the driver to stop at the roundabout heading to Moelfre.)*

LLANFAIRPWLL... ☎ 01248

Llanfairpwllgwyngyllgogerychwyrndrobwllllantysiliogogogoch (HLAN-vire-poohl-gwin-gihl—ah, never mind), prides itself on having the longest name of any village in the world. Give or take a controversial adjective, the name translates roughly to: "Saint Mary's Church in the hollow of white hazel near the rapid whirlpool and the Church of Saint Tysillio near the red cave." Sights in both New Zealand and Thailand claim longer titles—at 92 and 163 letters, respectively—though these names (one of them packed with extensive reference to "the man with the big knees...known as land eater") bear the tell-tale signs of publicity-seeking embellishment as well. For more information on this otherwise nondescript village's claim to fame, visit the **Tourist Information Centre,** which conveniently adjoins a network of shops and heaps of long-winded commemorative trinkets. (☎ 713 177. Books accommodations for £2 plus a 10%

deposit. (☎713 177. Open Apr.-Oct. M-Sa 9:30am-5:30pm, Su 10am-5pm; Nov.-Mar. M-F 9:30am-1pm and 1:30-5pm, Su 10am-5pm.) Mercifully, the town is known locally as "Llanfairpwll" or "Llanfair P.G."

BEAUMARIS ☎01248

Four miles northeast of the Menai Bridge on the A545, the town of Beaumaris manages to exert its quiet charm without intruding on the lovely country that surrounds it. From its yacht-dotted harbor, nearby Bangor seems as if it belongs to another distant (and far uglier) world entirely. Tall trees and moat-dwelling ducklings now guard once formidable **Beaumaris Castle,** the last and largest of Edward I's Welsh fortresses, which sits in marshland, uncharacteristic of Edward I's "iron ring" castles. It was to be his masterpiece and, though unfinished, is regarded as the most technically perfect castle in Britain. (☎810 361. Open daily June-Sept. 9:30am-6pm; Apr.-May and Oct. 9:30am-5pm; Nov.-Mar. M-Sa 9:30am-4pm, Su 11am-4pm. £3, concessions £2.50, families £8.50.)

Beaumaris Gaol, on Bunkers Hill, presents a fascinating and chilling view of incarceration in Victorian Angelsey. Individual cells feature histories of past occupants and house grim relics from their daily lives, including a system of ropes that allowed female inmates to rock their babies from the working rooms below. Out back, visitors can see the only remaining treadwheel in Britain, which demanded hours of grueling labor from inmates to provide the prison with its advanced plumbing. (☎810 921. Open daily Easter-Sept. 10:30am-5pm. Last admission 4:30pm. £2.50, concessions £1.75, families £8.50.) More charming distractions can be found at the **Museum of Childhood Memories,** 1 Castle St., which displays legions of tin wind-ups, round-eyed dolls, and pea-shooting piggy banks. (☎810 448. Open Easter-Oct. M-Sa 10:30am-5:30pm, Su noon-5pm; Nov.-Easter Sa-Su 10:30am-5pm. Last admission 45min. before close. £3.50, concessions £3, children £2, families £9.50.) Inexpensive 1¼hr. **catamaran cruises** down the Menai Strait and around **Puffin Island** leave from the Starida booth on the pier. (☎810 379 or 810 251. £5, children £4. Weather permitting; call ahead.)

Buses stop on Castle St. The volunteer-run **Tourist Information Centre,** located in Town Hall, on Castle St., provides a free town map and accommodations information. (☎810 040. Open Easter-Oct. M-Th and Sa 10am-4:45pm.) **HSBC** is also on Castle St. (Open M-F 11am-3:30pm.) The **post office** is at 10 Church St. (☎810 320. Open M-Tu and Th-F 9am-5:30pm, W and Sa 9am-12:30pm.) **Post Code:** LL58 8AB.

The closest hostel is the **YHA Bangor** (p. 517). Few of the town's **B&Bs** offer singles; consider sleeping across the strait in Bangor or Caernarfon. Summers are extremely busy. Camping is best at **Kingsbridge Caravan Park ❶,** 1½ mi. from town, toward Llangoed. At the end of Beaumaris's main street, follow the road past the castle to the crossroads. Turn left toward Llanfaes; Kingsbridge is 400 yd. on the right. Arriva buses #57 and 58 running from Bangor stop nearby if you ask. (☎490 636. Open Mar.-Oct. £4-5, £1.50-2 per child. Electricity £2. Cash only.) Cover the basics at **Spar,** 11 Castle St. (Open M-Su 7am-11pm.) Tea shops cluster around the castle; one of the nicest is **Beau's Tea Shop ❶,** 30 Castle St., where stained-glass lamps lend an amber glow. (☎811 010. Open M-Sa 10am-4:30pm, Su 11am-4:30pm. Cash only.) **Sarah's Delicatessen ❶,** 11 Church St., sells delicious gourmet vittles like tongue and local cheeses. (☎811 534. Open M-Sa 9am-5pm. MC/V.)

HOLYHEAD (CAERGYBI) ☎01407

An unattractive town attached to Anglesey by a causeway and a bridge, Holyhead is primarily known as a port for Ireland. **Irish Ferries** (☎08705 171717) and **Stena Line** (☎08705 421 170) operate ferries and catamarans to **Dublin** and its suburb, **Dún Laoghaire.** Foot passengers check in at the terminal adjoining the train station; cars proceed along the asphalt beside the terminal. An walkway, expected by 2005, will provide access to both stations from the town, which lies on the other side of the tracks. Arrive 30min. early and remember your passport. (See **By Ferry,** p. 29.)

St. Cybi's Church, in the center of town between Stanley St. and Victoria Rd., has lovely stained-glass windows and a huge, decorated wood organ. Cromwell used the building as a military headquarters and subsequently wrecked it; it was largely rebuilt in the 17th century. The **Caer Cybi,** a 4th-century Roman defense from sea raiders, surrounds the grounds. (☎763 001. Open daily May-Sept. 11am-3pm; call ahead in low season. Free.) On the far side of town from the ferry terminal, the **Maritime Museum,** Beach Rd., occupies the oldest lifeboat house in Wales and details Holyhead's nautical history. Highlights include surprisingly evocative busts of Hitler and Mussolini carved from whales' ears. (☎764 374. Open Apr.-Oct. Tu-Su 1-5pm. £2, concessions £1.50, children 50p, families £5.) The **Uchedlre Centre,** a former Convent chapel that now serves as an arts facility, overlooks the town from Garreglwyd Rd. Pick up a schedule of exhibits and performances from the shop. (☎763 361; fax 763 341. Open M-Sa 10am-5pm, Su 2-5pm.) If you can, explore the many paths of **Holyhead Mountain** near town. Its North and South Stacks are good for bird-watching, and the lighthouse looks longingly to sea. **Caer y Tŵr** and **Holyhead Mountain Hut Group** sit at the mountain's base. The former is an Iron Age hill fort, the latter a settlement inhabited from 500 BC until Roman times.

Reach Holyhead every hour (Su every 2hr.) by **train** from: **Bangor** (30min., £5.60); **Chester** (1½hr., £18); and **London** (4½-6hr., £89). **Arriva Cymru** (☎0870 608 2608) bus #4 comes from **Bangor** via **Llanfair P.G.** and **Llangefni** (1¼hr., M-Sa 2 per hr., £3.20); on Sundays #44 journeys from **Bangor,** sometimes stopping in **Ysbyty Gwynedd** (1¼hr., 8 per day). **Eurolines/Bus Éireann** #861/871 comes twice daily from **London** (7½hr., £29) via **Birmingham** (4hr.) and #880 comes from **Leeds** (6hr., daily, £29) through **Manchester** (4¾hr.) and **Liverpool** (2½hr.). For a **taxi,** call **Alphacab** (☎765 000). The **Tourist Information Centre,** accessible through Terminal One of the train and ferry station, sells ferry tickets and books rooms for a £2 charge plus a 10% deposit. (☎762 622. Open M-Su 8:30am-6pm.) Other services include: **banks** on Market St.; the **police** (☎762 323); free **Internet access** at the **library,** Newry Fields (☎762 917. Open M 10am-5pm, Tu and Th-F 10am-7pm, W 10am-1pm, and Sa 9:30am-12:30pm) and the **post office,** 13a Stryd Boston, with a **bureau de change** (☎08457 223 344. Open M-F 9am-5:30pm, Sa 9am-12:30pm). **Post Code:** LL65 1BP.

Holyhead **B&Bs** are plentiful and accommodating to passengers at the mercy of boat schedules. Owners may arrange to greet you at unusual times if you call ahead, and "B&B" here often translates to B&PL (beds and packed lunches) for ferry riders. To reach **Orotavia ➋,** 66 Walthew Ave., go up Thomas St., which becomes Porth-y-Felin Rd., and turn right onto Walthew Ave. (not to be confused with nearby Walthew St. or Walthew Ln.); call for a ride from the station if bogged down with bags. (☎760 259; www.orotavia.co.uk. £20. Cash only.) If you are in the mood for something a bit fancier, try pleasant **Yr Hendre ➌,** Porth-y-Felin Rd., across from the park, where the elegant rooms are delightful. (☎762 929; www.yr-hendre.co.uk. Doubles and twins from £50. Cash only.) Down the road from Orotavia, **Witchingham ➋,** 20 Walthew Ave., has a loveable miniature poodle. Call for a ride from the station at any reasonable hour. (☎762 426. £22.50 per person. Cash only.) **Roselea ➋,** 26 Holborn Rd., is the closest B&B to the station and ferries. (☎764 391. Single £25; twins £36; doubles £40. Cash only.) Few Holyhead dining options are noteworthy, but **Market Street** is lined with the typical slew of chippers and bakeries, as well as a **Kwik Save.** (Open M-Sa 8am-8pm, Su 10am-4pm.)

NORTH WALES

CONWY ☎01492

Conwy's impressive stone walls are left over from Edward I's attempt to keep the native Welsh out of his 13th-century castle—another link in his chain of North Wales fortresses. The town bears the obligatory role of tourist mecca, and yet seems to transcend the burden of tourism. Though you may have to muscle your way through castle queues, many other spots cater to visitors; Conwy's elegant narrow streets and pleasant Quayside have come into their own since the 13th century, and now hold an assortment of eclectic attractions.

▌ TRANSPORTATION

Trains: Conwy Station, off Rosehill St. Trains (☎08457 484 950) only stop by request. The station lies on the North Wales line linking Holyhead to Chester. Trains *do* stop at nearby **Llandudno Junction** station, one of the busiest in Wales, which connects to the scenic Conwy Valley line. Ticket office open M-Sa 5:30am-6:30pm, Su 11:30am-6:30pm. Not to be confused with Llandudno proper (a resort town 1 mi. north; p. 525), Llandudno Junction is a 20min. walk from Conwy. Turn left on a side road after exiting the station, walk under a bridge, and climb the stairs to another bridge leading across the estuary to Conwy castle and town. Nearly every bus to Conwy stops at the Junction.

Buses: Buses are the best way to get directly to Conwy, with two main stops on Lancaster Sq. and on Castle St. before the corner of Rosehill St.; check posted schedules. **National Express** (☎08705 808 080) buses come from: **Liverpool** (2¾hr., 1 direct per day, £8.25); **Manchester** (4½hr., 1 direct per day, £13); and **Newcastle** (10hr., 1 direct per day, £44). **Arriva Cymru** (☎0870 608 2608) buses #5 and 5X stop in Conwy as they climb the northern coast from **Caernarfon** via **Bangor** toward **Llandudno** (1-1¼hr.; M-Sa 2 per hr., Su every hr.), and bus #9 leaves from Holyhead and passes through Conwy on the way to Llandudno (1½hr., M-Sa every hr.). Bus #19 crosses Conwy on its **Llandudno-Llanrwst** journey down the Vale of Conwy (15min. from Llandudno, 40min. from Llanrwst; M-Sa 1-2 per hr., Su 10 per day). The free Conwy Public Transport Information booklet is available at the TIC.

▌ ORIENTATION AND PRACTICAL INFORMATION

The town wall has fitted old Conwy into a roughly triangular shape. The castle lies in one corner; **Castle Street,** which becomes **Berry Street,** runs from its foot parallel to the **Quay** and the river beyond it. **High Street** stretches from the Quay's edge to **Lancaster Square,** from which **Rosehill Street** circles back to the castle. In the opposite direction, **Bangor Read** heads northward past the wall.

Tourist Information Centre: (☎592 248), in the same building as the castle entrance. Stocks street maps and books beds for a £2 charge plus a 10% deposit. Open daily June-Sept. 9:30am-6pm; Oct.-Nov. and May 9:30am-5pm, Dec.-Apr. 9:30am-4pm.

Financial Services: Barclays, 23 High St. (☎616 616). Open M-F 10am-4pm.

Police: Lancaster Sq. (☎511 000).

Hospital: In Llandudno off Maesdu Rd. (☎860 066).

Internet Access: Library, Town Hall, Castle St. (☎596 242). Free. Open M and Th-F 10am-5:30pm, Tu 10am-7pm, W and Sa 10am-1pm.

Pharmacy: 24 High St. (☎592 418), open M-Sa 9am-5:30pm).

Post Office: 7 Lancaster Sq. (☎573 990), in The Wine Shop. Open M-Tu 8:30am-5:30pm, W-F 9am-5:30pm, Sa 9am-1:30pm. **Post Code:** LL32 8H7

Taxi: Castle Cars (☎593 398).

ACCOMMODATIONS

Swan Cottage, 18 Berry St. (☎596 840; www.swancottage.btinternet.co.uk), in a 16th-century building near the center of town. One of few B&Bs within the town wall. Cozy rooms with timber ceilings and TVs. £19. Cash only. ❷

Bryn Guest House (☎592 449), at the corner of St. Agnes Rd. and Synchant Pass, outside, flanked by a colorful garden. Singles £25; doubles £46. Cash only. ❸

The Castle Hotel, High St. (☎582 800; www.castlewales.co.uk), in an old coaching inn in the center of town. Its elegant and lavish "character bedrooms" have housed many of Conwy's most illustrious visitors, including William Wordsworth and Thomas Telford. From £40 per person. AmEx/MC/V. ❹

YHA Conwy, Larkhill, Sychnant Pass Rd. (☎593 571), a 10min. uphill walk from the town walls. From Lancaster Sq., head down Bangor Rd., turn left on Mt. Pleasant and right at the top of the hill; it's up a driveway on the left. Self-catering kitchen, laundry (£3), and TV room. Free lockers. Internet access 50p per 6min. Bike rental £6.50 per half-day. Open mid-Feb. to Dec. Dorms £13.40, under 18 £9.30. MC/V. ❷

Glan Heulog, Llanrwst Rd., Woodlands (☎593 845), a 10min. walk from the castle. Go under the arch near the TIC on Rosehill St., down the steps, and across the carpark. Turn right and walk 5min. down Llanrwst Rd. On a hill with TVs, ensuite rooms, and "healthy option" breakfasts. Singles from £25; doubles from £40. MC/V. ❷

Camping: Conwy Touring Park, Llanrwst Rd. (☎592 856), 1 mi. from town. Follow Llanrwst Rd. and signs. Open Easter-Sept. £5-11 per tent. Electricity £1.75-2.80. MC/V. ❶

FOOD

Although fair Conwy fries fish and curries favor with curry flavor, **High Street** is lined with a number of classier (and pricier) restaurants. **Spar** sells **groceries** directly in their midst. (Open daily 8am-10pm.) A weekly **market** fills the train station parking lot every summer. (☎581 924. Open Tu 8:30am-5pm.)

Bistro Conwy, Chapel St. (☎596 326), near the wall close to Bangor Rd. Inspired Welsh fare amidst dried bouquets. Entrees from £13. Open Tu-Su 6:30-9pm. MC/V. ❸

Edward's Hot Carvery, 18 High St. (☎592 443; www.edwardsofconwy.co.uk). Well-deserved accolades hang from the huge meat counter; huge pies (£3) are the specialty of this most awarded butcher in Britain. Open M-Sa 7am-5:30pm. AmEx/MC/V. ❶

Shakespeare Restaurant, High St. (☎582 800), in the Castle Hotel. This award-winning venue puts local foods to exquisite use in daily specials. It's decorated with panels of Shakespeare canvases by Victorian-era artist John Dawson-Watson, who supposedly painted for his keep while here. Open daily 7-9:30pm, Su also lunch. MC/V. ❹

Pen-y-Bryn Tea Rooms, High St. (☎596 445). on High St. Caters to those with a fondness for good tea (Welsh high tea £4) and 16th-century timbered nooks. Open M-F 10am-5pm, Sa-Su 10am-5:30pm. Cash only. ❶

SIGHTS

CONWY CASTLE. Many argue that Conwy is the most magnificent in Edward I's string of 13th-century fortresses. This ominous castle needed no concentric fortifications; parapets joining eight rugged towers sit atop natural rock to make this one of Edward I's most imposing undertakings. It was more intimidating still for the untold Normans who wasted away in the prison, and it was in the chapel that Richard II was betrayed and deposed in 1399. The £1 guided tour is worth it—the guide's ferocious approach to history is ultimately more entertaining than unsettling. (☎592 358. Open daily June-Sept. 9:30am-6pm; Apr.-May and Oct. 9:30am-5pm; Nov.-Mar. M-Sa 9:30am-4pm, Su 11am-4pm. £3.75, concessions £3.25, families £10.75.)

PLAS MAWR. The National Trust has lovingly restored this 16th-century mansion to recall its days as home to merchant Robert Wynn, and the exquisite furnishings and plasterwork prove why it was worth the effort. Don't miss the display on Tudor-era hygiene and its discussion of so-called "pisse prophets." The entrance price includes a free 1hr. audio tour that attempts to psychoanalyze Wynn according to his architectural choices. (☎580 167. Open daily June-Aug. 9:30am-6pm; Apr.-May and Sept. 9:30am-5pm; Oct. 9:30am-4pm. £4.50, concessions £3.50, families £12.50.)

THE SMALLEST HOUSE. When this 380-year-old house was finally condemned for human habitation in 1900, its owner (a strapping 6'3" fisherman) spent years measuring other tiny homes to prove that this one was the smallest in Britain. With a frontage of 6 ft., you can question his taste in housing all you like, but you can't question the legitimacy of his claim. There's (obviously) not much to see here beyond two levels and a small gift stand. (Head down High St. and onto the Quay. ☎593 484. Open daily Aug. 10am-9pm; Easter-July and Sept.-Oct. 10am-6pm. 75p, children 50p.)

TEAPOT MUSEUM. "You'd have to be potty to miss it," proclaims the sign under which two grand British traditions—tea and eccentricity—meet. The one-room museum displays 300 years of teapots—some short, some stout, and most equipped with an inventive spout—Princess Di dispenses through her forehead, Lady Thatcher through the nose, and the Queen through a corgi atop her head. Don't knock over the Humpty Dumpty pot. (Castle St. ☎596 533. Open Easter-Oct. M-Sa 10am-5:30pm, Su 11am-5:30pm. £1.50, concessions £1, families £3.50.)

CONWY MUSSEL CENTRE. In a stylish Mussel Purification Centre on the Quay, a mussel named Melfyn and his band of "Conwy Mussel Men" (and some women, who have actually played a substantial role in the industry) guide visitors through the history of mussel raking in the Conwy estuary, which bears the best mollusks in Britain. A short video and Melfyn's cheerily masochistic cooking suggestions make it worthwhile. (Open daily in summer roughly 10am-5pm; call ahead in winter. Free.)

OTHER SIGHTS AND ENTERTAINMENT. Almost a mile long, the **town wall** was built at the same time as the castle and shielded burghers with its 22 towers and 480 arrow slits. Follow the signs around town to its three entry points. (Always open. Free.) The historian involved in the restoration of 14th-century **Aberconwy House,** Castle St., the oldest home in Conwy, once called it "remarkable simply because it is still standing." While the house has some nice antique pieces, the place is generally as unexciting as his summation implies. (☎592 246. Open Apr.-Oct. M and W-Su 11am-5pm. £2.40, children £1.20.) Preserving a bit of tranquility in the middle of town, **St. Mary's Church** is noteworthy for its stained glass as well as its cemetery, which holds the grave that inspired Wordsworth's "We are Seven." (Hours vary; if the doors aren't open, keys are available from the rectory daily 10am-5pm.) In early July, the **North Wales Bluegrass Festival** brings a bit of Appalachia to Conwy, and many zealous banjo-ers in caravans and tents.

LLANDUDNO ☎ 01492

Around 1850, the Mostyn family envisioned the bucolic town of Llandudno (hlan-DID-no) as a resort town; accordingly, they constructed a city with wide avenues open to sea and sky. Today, Victorian hotels and shores dappled with sunbathers prove the vision's endurance. Llandudno's leisure activities are a big draw—the Great Orme, a massive tor on its own peninsula, lures many to its slopes.

TRANSPORTATION. Llandudno is the northern terminus of several lines of transport. The train station is at the end of Augusta Rd. (Ticket office open M-Sa 8:40am-3:30pm; July-Aug. also Su 10:15am-5:45pm.) Trains (☎ 08457 484 950) arrive on the Conwy Valley line from **Blaenau Ffestiniog** via **Llanrwst** and **Betws-y-Coed** (1¼hr.; M-Sa 6 per day, Su 2 per day; £5.20). On the North Wales line, trains enter **Llandudno Junction,** 1 mi. south of town, from: **Bangor** (20min., 1-3 per hr., £3.90); **Chester** (1hr., 1-4 per hr., £10.80); **Holyhead** (50min., 19 per day). Trains will sometimes stop at Llandudno by request. **National Express** (☎ 08705 808 080) buses hit Mostyn Broadway daily from: **Chester** (1¾hr., £8.25) and **London** (8hr., £24); and twice per day from **Manchester** (4¼hr., £10.75). **Arriva Cymru** (☎ 0870 608 2608) buses #5, 5A, and 5X come from **Bangor** (1hr., 1-3 per hr.); **Caernarfon** (1½hr., 1-3 per hr.); **Conwy** (20min.; M-Sa 2-3 per hr., Su every hr., £1.10). Bus #19 arrives from **Llanrwst** in the Vale of Conwy, passing through Conwy (1hr.; M-Sa 8 per day, Su 10 per day). **Snowdon Sherpa** S2 travels from **Betws-y-Coed** (50min., 3 per day). **Kings Cabs** (☎ 878 156) runs **taxis.** Rent **bikes** at **West End Cycles,** 22 Augusta St., near the train station. (☎ 876 891. £7 per day. £25 deposit. Open M-Sa 9am-5:30pm.)

ORIENTATION AND PRACTICAL INFORMATION. Llandudno is flanked by two pleasant **beaches** with pretty boardwalks; the West Shore is less built up than the North, which is decorated with Victorian promenades and tipped by a long pier. Mostyn St. is the main drag. A left on Augusta St. as you exit the train station leads to the **Tourist Information Centre,** 1-2 Chapel St., which books rooms for a £2 charge plus a 10% deposit. (☎ 876 413; fax 872 722. Open Easter-Oct. M-Sa 9am-5:30pm, Su 10am-4pm; Nov.-Easter M-Sa 9am-5pm.) Other services include: **Barclays,** at the corner of Mostyn St. and Market St. (open M-Tu and Th-F 9:30am-4:30pm, W 10am-4:30pm, Sa 9:30am-3:30pm.); the **police,** Oxford Rd. (☎ 517 171); **General Hospital,** near the Maesdu Golf Course on the West Shore (☎ 860 066); free **Internet access** at the **library,** on Mostyn St. between Lloyd St. and Trinity Sq. (☎ 876 826; open M-Tu and F 9am-6pm, W 10am-5pm, Th 9am-7pm, Sa 9:30am-1pm) and at **Le Moulin Rouge,** (see below); and the **post office,** 14 Vaughn St., with a **bureau de change** (☎ 876 125; open M-F 9am-5:30pm, Sa 9am-12:30pm). **Post Code:** LL30 1AA.

ACCOMMODATIONS AND FOOD Lodging is easy to find in Llandudno, though summer months are extremely popular. Budget travelers should seek out **B&Bs** (£15-19) on **Chapel Street, Deganwy Avenue,** and **St. David's Road.** Conveniently located next to the TIC, **Walsall House ❷,** 4 Chapel St., has questionable carpet designs but cozy rooms, all with TVs. (☎ 875 279; www.walsallhouse.co.uk. £16-£18 per person, £2 more for breakfast. Cash only.) Nearby **Merrydale Hotel ❷,** 6 Chapel St., has simple, cheery rooms (☎ 860 911. £18 per person. Cash only.) At **Burleigh House ❷,** 74 Church Walks, two huge wooden frogs welcome visitors to a townhouse less than a block from the beach. (☎ 875 946. Singles £18; doubles £40, ensuite £43; larger suites £28 per person. Cash only.) The **Empire Hotel ❹,** 73 Church Walks, pampers with down duvets on cast iron beds, satellite TV, marble bathrooms and a poolside cafe with candlelit suppers. (☎860 555; www.empirehotel.co.uk. Singles from £50; doubles from £85. AmEx/MC/V.)

The Fat Cat Cafe-Bar ❶, 149 Mostyn St., offers simple earthtones and non-traditional dishes. (☎871 844. Open M-Sa 10am-11pm, Su 10am-10:30pm. AmEx/MC/V.) Hidden down a set of stairs off of an alley, **The Cocoa House ❷**, George St., aimed to provide the social atmosphere of a pub while serving cocoa instead of alcohol during the temperance movement. These days, the establishment is "fully licensed" and offers creative lunch specials to crowds of locals from £5. (☎876 601. Open daily 10am-4:30pm. Cash only.) For a quick lunch, **Le Moulin Rouge ❶**, 104 Mostyn St., wraps up crisp panini with fillings like bacon, tomato, stilton, and pear in various combinations (£2.85); 20min. free Internet access with purchase of £3 or more. (☎874 111. Open M-Su 8am-5:30pm. Cash only.) **The Cottage Loaf ❷**, Market St., maintains a village tavern atmosphere with a beer garden and serves up really good pub grub. (☎870 762. Entrees from £5.50. Open M-Sa 11am-11pm, Su noon-10:30pm. Food served noon-6pm. Cash only.) Literally hundreds of other options line main streets, including an **ASDA grocer,** wedged between Mostyn Blvd. and Conway Rd. (☎860 068. Open M-F 8am-10pm, Sa 8am-8pm, Su 10:30am-4:30pm.)

◪ **SIGHTS.** Llandudno's pleasant beaches, the Victorian **North Shore** and the quieter **West Shore,** are both outdone by the looming **Great Orme,** a huge nature reserve full of caves, pastures, and some 200 feral Kashmir goats (an in-residence species since the 1890s.) At the 679 ft. summit, even gift shops and coin-op arcades cannot dull the natural wonder atop the flowered hillside. Pick up the free *Walks to the Summit* brochure from the TIC. Those looking for a quicker trip can take the **Great Orme Tramway,** which departs from Church Walks. (☎575 275. 20min. Apr.-Oct. 3 per hr. 10am-6pm. £2.95, children £2.20.) Perhaps the most exciting way to reach the summit, however, is on the **Llandudno Cable Cars** (about 18min. round-trip) as well as spectacular views. They depart from the Happy Valley Gardens. (☎877 205. Open roughly 10am-5pm, weather permitting. Round-trip £5.50, children £2.85.) Halfway up the side of the Great Orme, stop for an engrossing tour of the **Bronze Age Copper Mines.** Visitors lead themselves around narrow, extensive underground passages where prehistoric men once hacked at the ore veins with rocks and animal bones. Their tools were primitive, but the ancient miners dug the so-called "Vivian Shaft" more than 470ft. straight down to sea level more than 4000 years ago. (☎870 447. Open daily Feb.-Oct. 10am-5pm. £4.80, children £3.20, families £13.50. Joint tram ticket £7.60/£5.20/£24.)

Occupying an old warehouse near the TIC, **The Homefront Experience,** New St., off Chapel St., walks visitors through torch-lit corridors and a full-size Anderson bomb shelter, relating the hardscrabble existence of blackout and blitz on the British homefront. (☎871 032; www.homefront-enterprises.co.uk. Open Mar.-Nov. M-Sa 10am-4:30pm, Su 11am-3pm. £3, children £2.) Alice Liddell, muse to Lewis Carroll, spent her childhood summers in Llandudno, and the town has used this connection to justify a low-budget fantasy recreation at **The Alice in Wonderland Centre,** 3-4 Trinity Sq. Dramatic readings accompany creepy mechanized characters and stuffed animals in formal attire. (☎/fax 860 062; www.wonderland.co.uk. Open M-Sa 10am-5pm; Easter-Oct. also Su 10am-4pm. £2.95, children £2.50.)

Eight miles south of Llandudno, 80 acres of twisting, Laburnum-shaded pathways yield the sun-dappled lawns and carp-filled ponds of **Bodnant Gardens.** The cultivated upper terraces give way to a "wilder" river glen downhill in the wooded "Dell." The gardens host plays on summer evenings. (From Llandudno, take Arriva bus #25 (45min., M-Sa 11 per day) to the gates or the Conwy Valley train (M-Sa 6 per day, Su 3 per day) to the Tal-y-Cafn stop, 2 mi. away. ☎01492 650 460. Open daily mid-Mar. to Oct. 10am-5pm; last admission 4:30pm. £5.20, children £2.60.)

🎵📺 NIGHTLIFE AND ENTERTAINMENT. Llandudno's two clubs are a 10min. walk from the town center down Mostyn St. Broadway Boulevard, Mostyn Broadway next to the North Wales Theatre, is a versatile venue with cheap drink deals and a solid mix of chart favorites. (☎879 614. No trainers. Cover £2-6. Open W and F-Sa 9pm-2am, Su 9pm-12:30am; last admission midnight.) A bit farther down Mostyn Broadway and left on Clarence Rd. is Washington, a complex with two venues, Capitol on the first floor and Buzz Club on the second. Capitol is lined with portraits of U.S. presidents and caters to an older set; Buzz is a more traditional dance club. (☎877 974. No trainers. Cover £2-4. Capitol open W-Sa 8pm-1:30am. Buzz open W and F-Sa 8pm-1:30am.) North Wales Theatre, sandwiched between Mostyn Broadway and the Promenade, hosts plays and concerts. (☎872 000; www.nwtheatre.co.uk. Schedules at the TIC. Box office open M-Sa 9:30am-8:30pm, Su 3hr. before curtain. Tickets £6-47, concessions available on certain shows.)

VALE OF CONWY

Technically, much of the Vale of Conwy lies within Snowdonia National Park, but the lush swales, tall canopied conifers, and gurgling streams that greet visitors suggest an ecosystem far gentler than Snowdon's desolate peak. Cyclists take advantage of the scenic terrain because views are glorious and gearchanges infrequent. The excellent *Gwydyr Forest Guide* (£2) details 14 walks that unveil the mossy glens and waterfalls which draw hundreds each summer.

▐ TRANSPORTATION

The single-track, 27 mi. Conwy Valley line (☎08457 484 950) offers unparalleled views. Trains hug the river banks between the seaside resort of Llandudno and the mountain town of Blaenau Ffestiniog, stopping at Llandudno Junction, Llanrwst, and Betws-y-Coed (1hr.; M-Sa 5 per day, Su 3 per day). The North and Mid Wales Rover ticket is good for nearly unlimited bus and train travel as far south as Aberystwyth (1-day £20, 3-day £30, 7-day £44). Most area buses stop at Llanrwst, some also at Betws-y-Coed. The main bus along the Conwy River is Arriva Cymru (☎08706 082 608) #19, which winds from Llandudno and Conwy to Llanrwst (M-Sa 1-2 per hr., Su 10 per day). Sherpa bus #S2 journeys from Llanrwst to Pen-y-Pass via Betws-y-Coed (30min.; M-Sa 7 trips per day, Su 8 per day between Betws-y-Coed and Pen-y-Pass only). Bus #97A connects Betws-y-Coed with Porthmadog (1hr., 3 per day). Routes are constantly changing; consult either the *Gwynedd* or *Conwy County* transport booklets, free at local TICs. Arriva's Explorer pass allows unlimited travel on only its own buses (one day £5, children £3.50; one week £12.50/5.50).

BETWS-Y-COED   ☎01690

At the southern tip of the Vale of Conwy and the eastern edge of the Snowdonia mountains, picturesque Betws-y-Coed (BET-oos uh COYD), has evolved from art colony into a tourist haven. Its main street is crammed with novelty shops, hotels, and outdoor supply stores that coach-tour travelers move through like migratory birds. Yet the town retains its small-town friendliness, and its stunning surroundings overcome this commercialization. Dark green hills rise from the banks of two coursing rivers to frame the town, and nearby meadows are full of grazing sheep oblivious to the highway traffic.

◪ **TRANSPORTATION. Trains** (☎08457 484 950) stop in Betws-y-Coed on the Conwy Valley line (p. 527). **Sherpa** bus #S2, operated by Arriva Cymru, connects Betws-y-Coed with **Pen-y-Pass**, stopping at some area hostels (20min., M-Sa 1-2 per day) and **Llanrwst** (10min., 1-2 per hour), continuing through to **Llandudno** with #19 (1¼hr., 8 per day). **Sherpa** #97A shuttles between **Porthmadog** and Betws-y-Coed (1hr., 3 per day). On Saturdays, Arriva bus #70 runs from **Corwen, Wrecsam,** and **Llangollen** in one direction, and **Llanrwst** and **Llandudno** in the other. Rent **bikes** from **Beics Betws**, up the street behind the post office. (☎710 766; www.bikewales.com. ₤18 per day. Open daily 9:30am-5pm.)

◪◪ **ORIENTATION AND PRACTICAL INFORMATION.** The main (and only real) street is **Holyhead Road** (also the A5). It runs northwest from the River Conwy, slants past the park at the town center (where Station Rd. branches toward the train station), and finally makes a sharp turn to run west out of town toward Swallow Falls. Possibly the busiest **Tourist Information Centre** in North Wales (also a **Snowdonia National Park Information Centre**), the Betws TIC is at the Old Stables, between the train station and Holyhead Rd. A spirited staff provides timetables and information on sights as well as room bookings for ₤2 plus 10% deposit. (☎710 426; www.betws-y-coed.co.uk. Open daily Easter-Sept. 10am-5:30pm; Nov.-Easter 9:30am-12:30pm and 1:30-4:30pm.) From Apr.-Sept., **guided walks** around Betws leave from the TIC. (☎01514 880 052 or 07790 851 333. Duration varies, but usually 6-8 mi. and 5-6hr. By appointment. ₤5.) A number of outdoor stores line Holyhead Rd. Two **Cotswold** outlets are among them, one next to the Royal Oak Hotel, the other south of town. (☎710 234. Both open M-Tu, Th and Su 9am-6, W 10am-6pm, F-Sa 9am-7pm.) The latter houses the upstairs **Cafe Active** which provides **Internet access** at 50p per 15min. (☎710 999. 10p per printout; cash only. Open same as store.) Other services include: an **HSBC** at the southern edge of Holyhead Rd. near the train station (open M 9:15am-2:30pm, Tu-F 9:15am-1pm); the nearby **police** station (☎710 222); and the **post office** inside the Londis, at the T-junction of Holyhead and Station Rd., which **exchanges currency** for no commission (☎710 565; open M-F 9am-5:30pm, Sa 9am-12:30pm). **Post Code:** LL24 0AA.

◪◪ **ACCOMMODATIONS AND FOOD.** Two hostels are located conveniently near town: **YHA Capel Curig** (p. 512) and **YHA Betws-y-Coed ❷**, at the Swallow Falls Complex 2 mi. west of town on the A5. (☎710 796; www.swallowfallshotel.co.uk. Reception 8am-9pm. Call 48hr. ahead. Kitchen, laundry (₤1.50). ₤11.80, under 18 ₤8.50. Cash only.) Most **B&Bs** (from ₤18) cluster along **Holyhead Road**. For a comfy lounge and fine views of riverside lambs, head for **Glan Llugwy ❷**, on the western edge of town, about 10min. from the park. Walk along Holyhead Rd. toward Swallow Falls, or call the kind owners for a lift. They will provide packed lunches or laundry service on request. (☎710 592. Singles from ₤17.50, doubles from ₤33. Cash only.) Lovely **Bryn Llewelyn ❸** is a bit closer to the town center on Holyhead Rd., with large, impeccably clean rooms. (☎710 601; www.bryn-llewelyn.co.uk. No smoking. Singles from ₤20; doubles ₤35-60. Cash only.) 2 minutes past Bryn toward Swallow Falls, check out **Pennant Crafts**, where beautiful pottery designed and fired on the premises sells for less than ₤10. (☎710 224. Open daily Easter-Nov. 9am-5:30pm.) **Riverside Caravan Park ❶** suns itself behind the train station. (☎710 310. Open mid-Mar.-Oct. ₤5.50 per person. Electricity ₤2. Cash only.)

The **Spar** at the northern bend of Holyhead Rd. houses an extensive bakery and sandwich bar. (☎710 324. Open daily 8am-10pm.) A small cafe with hand-painted tables and corkboard art, **Caban-y-Pair ❷**, Holyhead Rd., serves affordable home-cooked food. Soups and sandwiches start at £2.15. (☎710 505. Open June-Oct. M-F 9am-5:30pm, Sa-Su 9am-6:30pm; daily Nov.-May 10am-5pm. Cash only.) A knight guards the door at **Three Gables ❷**, Holyhead Rd., keeping watch over the slew of kitschy treasures that adorn its walls. Try the popular pizza, or sample the Yankee Doodle (steak with pineapple, peas, and chips), from £8. (☎710 328. Open daily Easter-Oct. noon-9:30pm; Nov.-Easter F-Su noon-9:30pm. AmEx/MC/V.)

◪ **SIGHTS.** Betws is known for its eight bridges. Of particular note is Telford's 1815 cast-iron **Waterloo Bridge,** situated at the village's southern end and built the year that battle ensured Napoleon's political demise. The bridge offers good photo-ops from below. A miniature **suspension bridge** spans the Conwy, while **Pont-y-Pair Bridge,** "the bridge of the cauldron," crosses the Llugwy to the north. The first bridge was built in 1475; Inigo Jones may have contributed to building the second, which consists of 11 stone arches hopping from rock to rock. Behind the train station, weathered gravestones surround humble 14th-century **St. Michael's Church.**

Two miles west, signposted off the A5, the swift waters of the Llugwy froth over slanting shelves of rock at **Swallow Falls.** Local lore claims that the soul of an evil 17th-century sheriff is trapped beneath the falls. (Always open. £1.) Sherpa bus #S2 between Betws and Snowdon stops at the falls, as do most #97A buses to Porthmadog (4min., 1-3 per hr.). A half-mile farther along the A5, "the Ugly House," **Tŷ Hyll,** is named for its rough facade, which consists of boulders stacked together without much delicacy (or mortar). Now the house serves as the Snowdonia Society headquarters and houses a display and shop area. (☎720 287. Open daily Apr.-Sept. 9am-5pm; winter hours vary. £1, children free.)

A large portion of Betws-y-Coed's appeal lies in its prime location, and visitors should take advantage of the stunning scenery. Many of the outdoors stores on Holyhead Rd. can arrange excursions, but other private options also abound. The **National Whitewater Centre,** headquartered in nearby Bala, offers river expeditions. (☎01678 521 083, fax 521 158; www.ukrafting.co.uk. £22-100, wetsuit rental £2-5.)

TREFRIW ☎01492

To the south, sleepy Trefriw curves alongside the River Crafnant. **Lake Crafnant,** 3 mi. uphill from town (along the road opposite the Fairy Hotel), is surrounded by some of Snowdonia's highest peaks. North of town, 1½ mi. along the A470, a rust grotto spews the world's only fully licensed medicinal spring water at the **Trefriw Wells Spa,** purportedly discovered by Roman soldiers stationed nearby. A self-guided tour takes visitors into an eerie, copper-toned grotto where booming voiceovers offer a bit of geology and local history. Reach through glimmering stalactites to sample the iron-rich water. In the store on the premises, a month's supply goes for £6.49. (☎640 057. Open daily Easter-Sept. 10am-5:30pm; Oct.-Easter M-Sa 10am-dusk, Su noon-dusk. £3, children £2, families £8.50.)

To reach Trefriw, take Arriva **bus** #19 from Conwy, Llandudno, or Llandudno Junction (M-Sa 1-2 per hr., Su 10 per day). **B&Bs** (from £15) line Trefriw's long main street. The rustic **YHA Rowen ❶**, a white farmhouse halfway between Trefriw and Conwy, is a superb place to rest after the treacherous mile hike uphill from the road; the ascent begins ¼ mi. down from the bus stop, which is served by #19 (20min., every hr.). (☎650 089. Lockout 10am-5pm. Curfew 11pm. Open May-Aug., rentable during other times. Dorms £9.30, under 18 £6.70. Cash only.)

LLANRWST ☎01492

A useful transit town, Llanrwst has several **banks** with **ATMs** that cluster around central Lancaster Sq., marked by the large clocktower. A short walk toward Trefriw leads to **Gwydir Castle,** the 16th-century manor of Sir John Wynne placed "two bowshots above the river Conwy." Peacocks strut the many paths through colorful gardens and sparkling fountains. The manor itself (it earned the title "castle" unofficially and a bit illegitimately) is surprisingly opulent, with strings attached—it claims to be one of the most haunted houses in Wales. When the home was auctioned in 1921, American newspaper giant William Randolph Hearst acquired Lot 88: the wall panels, doorframe, fireplace, and leather frieze of Gwydir's dining room. In 1994, the castle's new owners traced the room to a storage box in a New York museum, re-purchased it, and unpacked Lot 88 to its former glory. (☎641 687. Open daily Easter-Oct. 10am-4:30pm. £3.50, children £1.50.) Stock up on **groceries** at the local **Spar** (open daily 7am-11pm), or at the Tuesday **market.** Connected to town by a 1636 bridge built by Inigo Jones, the 15th-century stone **Tu-Hwnt-i'r-Bont ❶** served once as the court house, but now serves cream teas on the second floor. (Sandwiches from £2.50. Open Easter-Oct. Tu-Su 10:30am-5pm.)

LLANGOLLEN ☎01978

Set in a hollow in the hills near the English border, Llangollen (hlan-GOTH-hlen) hosts the annual International Musical Eisteddfod, an exceptionally popular extravaganza which has drawn over 400,000 performers and competitors since it began in 1947. The town also boasts surrounding natural attractions; hikers head to Horseshoe Pass, and whitewater enthusiasts take in the Dee and its tributaries.

⌷⌷ TRANSPORTATION AND PRACTICAL INFORMATION. For a tourist town, Llangollen can be difficult to reach by public transport. **Trains** (☎08457 484 950) come to **Wrexham,** 30min. away, from **Chester, Shrewsbury,** and **London.** A closer, though less well-served train station is **Ruabon,** from which B&B owners occasionally fetch weary backpackers. To get to Llangollen from Wrexham, take **Bryn Melyn** (☎860 701) bus #X5 (30min., M-Sa 4 per hr., £2.20). Direct service to Llangollen is possible on some buses; **Arriva Cymru** (☎0870 608 2608) bus #94 comes from **Barmouth** (3hr.; M-Sa 7 per day, Su 4 per day; £4.90) and **Dolgellau** (2hr.; M-Sa 8 per day, Su 4 per day; £3.30). Arriva Cymru's bus #70 runs only on weekends, once per day from **Llandudno;** Arriva's #19 runs from Llandudno (2¼hr., 5 per day) on weekdays. **Lloyd's Coaches** (☎01654 702 100) runs #694 the 1st and 3rd Saturdays of the month, which stops at Llangollen between **Chester** and **Machynlleth.**

The **Tourist Information Centre** is in **The Chapel,** a refurbished cultural center on Castle St., a block from the river. Books rooms for a £2 charge plus a 10% deposit. (www.nwt.co.uk. Open daily Easter-Oct. 9:30am-5:30pm; Nov.-Easter 9:30am-5pm.) Activity weekends are available from **Pro Adventure,** 23 Castle St. (☎861 912; www.adventureholiday.com. Open M-Tu 10am-5pm, W-Th 9am-5pm, F 9:30am-5:30pm, Sa 9am-5:30pm, Su 9:30am-5pm. Kayaking £35 per half-day, bike rental £3 per hr.) Other services include: **Barclays,** 9 Castle St., opposite the TIC (☎202 700; open M-Tu and Th-F 10am-4pm, W 10:30am-4pm); **Blue Bay Launderette,** 3 Regent St. (wash £2.20, dry 20p per 5min.; open M-Sa 9am-noon and 12:15-6pm); the **police** (☎01492 517 171, ext. 54940); free **Internet access** at the **library,** upstairs from the TIC (☎869 600; open M 9:30am-7pm, Tu-W 9:30am-5:30pm, F 9:30am-5:30pm, Sa 9:30am-12:30pm); and the **post office,** 41 Castle St., with a **bureau de change.** (☎860 230. Open M-F 9am-5:30pm, Sa 9am-12:30pm.) **Post Code:** LL20 8RU.

ⅡⒸ ACCOMMODATIONS AND FOOD. The **YHA Llangollen ❶,** Tyndwr Hall, Tyndwr Rd., is a Victorian manse 1½ mi. out of town. Follow the A5 toward Shrewsbury, bear right up Birch Hill, and after ½ mi. take a right at the Y-junction. (☎860 330; fax 861 709. Internet access from £1 per 20min. Open mid-Feb. to Oct., rentable other months. Dorms £10.60, under 18 £7.20. MC/V.) **B&Bs** (£20-25) are numerous, especially along **Regent Street.** Once an 18th-century coaching inn, **Poplar House ❸,** 39-41 Regent St., offers rooms with satellite TV and lavish four-course breakfasts. (☎861 772. From £25. Cash only.) The terraced gardens and all-weather tennis court of **Oakmere ❹** promise relaxing evenings. (☎861 126; www.oakmere.llangollen.co.uk. Singles from £38; doubles £55; family room £70. Cash only.) **Campsites** abound; ask at the TIC, or try **Eirianfa Riverside Holiday Park ❶,** 1 mi. from town. on the A5 toward Corwen. (☎860 919. £8-12 per tent. MC/V.)

Spar, 26-30 Castle St., is well-stocked in the center of town. (☎860 275. Open M-Sa 7am-11pm, Su 8am-10:30pm.) Classy cuisine has found a home in comfortable pub-like quarters at the upscale Ⓐ**Corn Mill ❸,** Dee Ln., where the patio hangs low over the river. If the entrees are too expensive (offerings like red bream fillets with coriander-lime dressing run £8-13.25), spend a few pounds on a pint and watch the waterwheel spinning outside. (☎869 555. Open M-Sa noon-11pm, Su noon-10:30pm. Food served noon-9pm. AmEx/MC/V.) At **Maxine's Cafe and Books ❶,** 17 Castle St., thumb through thousands of used volumes in the maze-like warehouse upstairs, and grab a meal at the counter below. The all-day breakfast is £3.95. (☎860 334. Open daily 10am-5pm. Cash only.) **River View Bistro ❷,** at the corner of Dee Ln. and Castle St., caters to chocolate lovers in its Chocolate Cafe section. It offers hot chocolate with flavor twists (£1.95) as well as its specialty cocoa, spiked with brandy (£3.50). (☎860 133. Food served noon-4pm and 6-9pm. Cash only.)

◪ SIGHTS. The sparse ruins of Ⓜ**Castell Dinas Brân** (Crow Castle) lie on a hilltop above town, "to the winds abandoned and the prying stars" as Wordsworth once mused. The panoramic view spans from the peaks of Snowdonia to the English Midlands, and the rolling grassy mounds of the summit are scattered with crumbling archways and walls. Two main paths lead to the castle: a 40min. gravel trail zig-zags directly up the side, while a 1hr. walk follows a pastoral road before ascending more gradually from the other side. Both are reached by an unmarked trail that begins where Wharf Rd. hits Dinbren Rd., just up the hill from the canal bridge. Up Hill St. from the town center, **Plas Newydd** is the former *ferme ornee* (estate in miniature) of two noblewomen who fled Ireland in 1778. While their elopement was quite dramatic, their life in Llangollen was defined by peaceful companionship. As "two of the most celebrated virgins in Europe," the two appealed to the era's intellectuals; Wellington and Sir Walter Scott visited, as did Wordsworth, who penned a poem in their honor. (☎861 314. Open daily Easter-Oct. 10am-5pm; last admission 4pm. Includes audio tour. £3, children £2, families £8.) The ruins of 13th-century **Valle Crucis Abbey** grace a leafy valley, 30min. from Llangollen along Abbey Rd. Its empty arches frame trees, sky, and an unfortunate cluster of caravans next door. (☎860 326. Open daily Apr.-Sept. 10am-5pm; Oct.-Mar. 10am-4pm. £2, concessions £1.50, families £5.50; free in winter.) Both are important landmarks for those interested in the history behind Arthurian legend. Other sites in the area include **Croes Gwenhwyfar** (Guinevere's Cross) and **Eliseg's Pillar.** *Arthurian Llangollen,* outlining links to the myths, is free at TICs.

Eight miles of the gently sloping Dee River Valley greets passengers on the **Llangollen Railway,** with a convenient station where Castle St. hits the highway (A593/A452). The engine stops at Carrog and Berwyn, among other stations, to provide an afternoon's entertainment. (☎860 979. Runs daily Apr.-Oct., 3-7 per day; Nov.-Mar. Sa-Su, 3 per day, but times vary; call ahead.) Aimed at school-children, the **Victorian School Museum** will have everyone cringing at the tiny desks and chalkboards once used to keep children from more exciting pursuits. (☎860 794. Open daily Easter-Oct. 10:30am-4pm. £1.60, children £1.10.)

📷 **FESTIVALS.** Every summer, the town's population of 3000 swells to 80,000 for the **International Musical Eisteddfod** (ice-TETH-vod). From July 5-10 in 2005, the hills (and fields, and streets, and public spaces) will be alive with the singing and dancing of competitors from 50 countries. Book tickets and rooms far in advance through the **Eisteddfod Box Office,** Royal International Pavilion, Abbey Rd. (☎862 000; bookings 862 001; www.international-eisteddfod.co.uk. Open from mid-Mar. M-F 10am-3pm. Tickets £7-50. Unreserved seats and admission to grounds on day of show can be purchased on the fields. £6, children £4.)

NORTH WALES

SCOTLAND

A little over half the size of England but with a tenth the population, Scotland possesses open spaces and wild natural splendor its southern neighbor cannot hope to rival. The craggy, heathered Highlands, the silver beaches of the west coast, and the luminescent mists of the Hebrides elicit any traveler's awe, while farmlands to the south and tiny fishing villages on the eastern shore harbor a gentler beauty. Scotland at its best is a world apart from the rest of the UK. Its people revel in a culture all their own, from the fevered nightlife of Glasgow to the festival energies of Edinburgh to the isolated communities of the Orkney and Shetland Islands. The Scots defended their independence bitterly and heroically for hundreds of years before reluctantly joining with England in 1707. Since the union, they have nurtured a separate identity, retaining control of schools, churches, and the judicial system. In 1999, Scots finally regained a separate parliament, which gave them more power over domestic tax laws and strengthened their national identity. While the kilts, bagpipes, and souvenir clan paraphernalia of the big cities grow tiresome, a visit to the less touristed regions of Scotland will allow you to encounter the inheritors of ancient traditions: a B&B owner speaking Gaelic to her grandchildren, a crofter cutting peat, or a fisherman setting out in his skiff at dawn.

TRANSPORTATION

GETTING THERE

Reaching Scotland from outside Britain is usually easiest and cheapest through London, where the **Scottish Tourist Board,** 19 Cockspur St., SW1 Y5BL (☎0845 225 5121; www.visitscotland.com), stocks brochures and reserves train, bus, and plane tickets.

BY PLANE. British Airways (☎0845 773 3377; www.ba.com) sells a limited number of round-trip tickets starting at £70. **British Midland** (☎0870 607 0555; www.flybmi.com) offers Saver fares from London to Glasgow (from £70 round-trip), but as with any airline, you'll need to book as far in advance as you can (2 weeks if possible) for the cheapest fare. Some of the cheapest fares available with the fewest headaches are **easyJet** (☎0870 600 0000; www.easyjet.com); to Edinburgh from London-Luton, Stansted, or Gatwick; to Glasgow from Luton or Stansted (there are always web-only fares, so prices vary). There's also **Ryanair** (☎0871 246 0000; www.ryanair.com), which flies ridiculously cheaply to Edinburgh from Dublin, and to Glasgow-Prestwick (NOT Glasgow, but an hour away in Prestwick) from London-Stansted and Dublin; and **EUjet** (☎0870 414 1414; www.eujet.com) which flies to Glasgow and Edinburgh from Kent. Scotland is linked by sea (See **By Ferry,** p. 38) to Northern Ireland and the Isle of Man.

BY TRAIN AND BUS. From London, **GNER** runs **trains** (☎08457 225 333; www.gner.co.uk) to **Edinburgh** and **Glasgow,** which can take only 4½-6hr., and fares vary depending on how far in advance you buy (£24-£100). A pricier option is the **Caledonian Sleeper,** run by **Scotrail** (☎0870 606 2031; www.scotrail.co.uk), which leaves London-Euston near midnight and gets to Edinburgh at 7am (£60 for a reclining chair; £95-£125 for a cabin). Although the **bus** from London can take anywhere from 8hr. to 12hr., it may be significantly cheaper than rail travel. **National Express** (☎08705 808 080; www.nationalexpress.com) connects England and Scotland via Glasgow and Edinburgh.

GETTING AROUND

BY TRAIN AND BUS. In the Lowlands (south of Stirling and north of the Borders), train and bus connections are common. In the Highlands, Scotrail and GNER **trains** snake slowly on a few restricted routes, bypassing the northwest almost entirely, and many stations are unstaffed—buy tickets on board. **Buses** tend to be the best way to travel. They're usually more frequent and far-reaching than trains and are always cheaper. **Scottish Citylink** (☎ 08705 505 050; www.citylink.co.uk) runs most intercity routes; **Traveline Scotland** has the best information on all routes and services (☎ 0870 608 2 608; www.travelinescotland.com). Bus service declines in the northwest Highlands and grinds to a halt on Sundays almost everywhere.

A great money-saver is the **Freedom of Scotland Travelpass.** It allows unlimited train travel and transportation on most **Caledonian MacBrayne** ("CalMac") ferries, with discounts on some other ferry lines. Purchase the pass *before* traveling to Britain at any BritRail distributors (see **By Train,** p. 31).

BY BUS TOUR. If you have limited time or if you want to be thrown together with a group of backpackers, a thriving industry of tour companies is eager to whisk you into the Highlands. The two main companies are ◼ **HAGGiS** (☎ 0131 557 9393; www.haggisadventures.com) and **MacBackpackers** (☎ 0131 558 9900; www.macbackpackers.com). Both cater to the young and adventurous with a number of tours departing from Edinburgh, and both run hop-on, hop-off excursions that let you travel Scotland at your own pace (usually within three months). HAGGiS is geared more toward set tours with specific itineraries, run by witty and super knowledgeable local guides, and guarantee accommodation at a few favorite stopping points. MacBackpackers, specializing in tours of the hop-on, hop-off variety, guarantees accommodation at any of the associated, super-social **Scotland's Top Hostels** in Edinburgh, Fort William, Skye, Oban, and Inverness. (See **Bus Tours,** p. 35). **Celtic Connection** (☎ 0131 225 3330; www.thecelticconnection.co.uk) covers Scotland in a variety of five- to twelve-day tours, with one-way, round-trip, or hopon, hop-off options. Other companies, like **Heart of Scotland Tours,** 11 Wellington St. in Edinburgh (☎ 0131 558 8855; www.heartofscotlandtours.co.uk) provide half, one, and two-day bus tours.

BY CAR. Though Southern and Central Scotland are well served by public transportation, travel in the Highlands and Islands may be restricted without a car. Driving gives you the freedom to explore Scotland at your own pace and to access some of its most remote quarters without fear of being stranded by complicated bus services. As in the rest of Britain, driving in Scotland is on the left, seat-belts are required at all times, the minimum age to drive with a valid foreign license is 17, and the minimum age to rent is 21, often higher. In rural areas, roads are often **single-track** or one-lane; both directions of traffic share one lane, and drivers must be prepared to slow to a crawl to negotiate oncoming traffic. Often one car must reverse to a **passing place** (shoulder turn-off) to enable another to pass, as well as to allow same-way traffic to overtake. Many rural roads are also traversed by **livestock** which sounds cute, but should give travelers reason to be wary.

BY BICYCLE. Scotland's biking terrain is scenic and challenging. You can usually rent bikes even in very small towns and transport them by ferry for little or no charge. Fife and regions south of Edinburgh and Glasgow offer gentle country pedaling, and Orkney, Shetland, and the Western Isles are negotiable by bicycle, though strong winds and wet roads are always a threat. In the Highlands, touring is more difficult. Most major roads have only one lane, and locals drive at high speeds; keep your eye out for passing places. Bringing a bike to the Highlands by public transportation can be difficult. Many trains can carry only four or fewer bikes; reservations are essential.

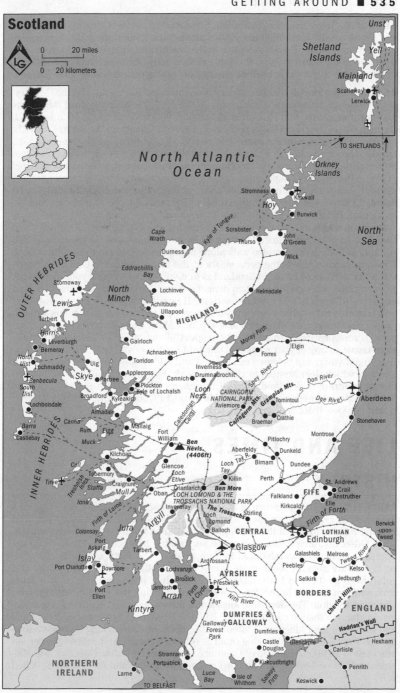

Scotland

SCOTLAND

BY THUMB. Many hitchhike in Scotland, most often in the Highlands and Islands and less so in the more built-up regions around the larger cities. Hitchers report that drivers tend to be most receptive in the least-traveled areas. Far to the northwest and in the Western Isles, the Sabbath is strictly observed, making it difficult or impossible to get a ride on Sundays. *Let's Go* does not recommend hitchhiking.

BY FOOT. Two long-distance footpaths were planned and marked by the Countryside Commission under the Countryside Act of 1967. The **West Highland Way** begins just north of Glasgow in Milngavie and snakes 95 mi. north along Loch Lomond, through Glen Coe to Fort William and Ben Nevis. The **Southern Upland Way** runs 212 mi. from Portpatrick on the southwest coast to Cockburnspath on the east coast, passing through Galloway Forest Park and the Borders. For the most up-to-date information, check www.walkscotland.com. Most Tourist Information Centres (TICs) also distribute simple maps of the Ways as well as a list of accommodations along the routes. For information on these paths, write or call the **Scottish Tourist Board,** 23 Ravelston Terr., Edinburgh EH4 3EU (☎0845 2255 121; www.visitscotland.com). Detailed guidebooks for both are available at most bookstores.

Mountain ranges like the Cuillins, the Torridons, the Cairngorms, Glen Nevis, and Glen Coe have hostels situated in their midst, providing bases for spectacular hillwalking or biking. You can also walk along mainland Britain's highest **cliffs** at Cape Wrath or ramble across the eerie **moors** of the Outer Hebrides. One of the most attractive aspects of hiking in Scotland is that you can often pick your own route. However, the wilds do pose certain dangers: stone markers can be unreliable, and expanses of open heather often disorient. Heavy mists are always a possibility, and blizzards may surprise even in July; never go up into the mountains without proper equipment (see **Wilderness Safety,** p. 52). Many trails (even those in national parks) cross privately owned land; be respectful and, when in doubt, ask permission. Leave a copy of your route and timetable at the hostel or nearest rescue station, and if you're out between mid-August and mid-October, be sure to ask about areas in which deer hunters might be at work. For information on walking and mountaineering in Scotland, consult Poucher's *The Scottish Peaks* (£13), the Scottish Mountaineering Club's *The Munros* (£18), or the introductory Tourist Board booklet, *Walk Scotland.*

LIFE AND TIMES

HISTORY

EARLY TIMES. Little is known of the early inhabitants of Scotland, save that they managed to repel Roman incursions in their land; their fierce raids inspired **Emperor Hadrian** to shield Roman England behind an immense 73 mi. long wall (p. 436). Other invading tribes were more successful, however, and by AD 600 the Scottish mainland was inhabited by four groups. The **Picts,** originally the most powerful, are also the most mysterious—only a collection of carved stones and references to them in Latin histories betray their existence. The Celtic **Scots** arrived from Ireland in the 4th century, transporting the Gaelic language and Christian religion. The Germanic **Angles** and **Saxons** invaded Scotland from northern England in the 6th century. In AD 843, the Scots decisively defeated the Picts and formed a joint kingdom. United by the threat of encroaching **Vikings,** various groups were led by the first king of all Scotland, **Duncan** (later killed by a certain Macbeth in 1040). The House of Canmore ("big-headed," after Duncan's son Malcolm and his well-endowed cranium) reigned over Scotland for 200 years. Allied

SCOTLAND

through marriages with the Norman lords who had come to dominate England, Scotland attained a golden age of growth in the early 12th century under the popular and pious **Kind David I** (1124-1153), who made castles, abbeys, and cathedrals pop up all over the Lowlands. It is perhaps due to this new-found affluence that the successive Scottish monarchs found their independence considerably threatened by the increasingly powerful nation to the south. The 13th century was characterized by an uneasy peace punctuated by periodic skirmishes, as Scottish kings struggled to contain both civil revolts and Scandinavian attacks.

WARRING WITH ENGLAND. King **Alexander III** died in 1286 without an heir, and the ensuing contest over the Scottish crown fueled the territorial ambitions of **Edward I** of England. Edward promptly seized most of Scotland and commenced a long history of English oppression, his not-so-gentle governing hand earning him the nickname "Hammer of the Scots." The **Wars of Independence** bred heroic figures like William Wallace (yes, the *Braveheart* guy) who bravely, and for some time successfully, led a company of Scots against the English. But it was the cunning **Robert the Bruce** who emerged as Scotland's leader, assassinating his way to the throne. Against all odds, Robert led the Scots to victory over Edward II's forces at **Bannockburn** in 1314 and won Scotland her independence. In the next centuries the monarchy set nobles against each other in an attempt to preserve its own waning position, and the Scottish kings frequently capitalized on their **"Auld Alliance"** with France to stave off the English crown.

The reigns of **James IV** (1488-1513) and **James V** (1513-42) witnessed the arrival of both **Renaissance** and **Reformation** (p. 72). Following the death of James V, the infant **Mary, Queen of Scots** (1542-67) ascended to the throne and was promptly sent to France, where she later married the future François II. Lacking a strong ruler during Mary's absence, Scotland was vulnerable to the revolts of the Reformation—nobles and commoners alike were drawn to the appeal of Protestantism, piloted by iconoclastic preacher **John Knox.** In 1560, the monarchy finally capitulated. The Protestant **Scottish Parliament** denied the Pope's authority in Scotland and established the Presbyterian Church as Scotland's new official church.

In 1561, after the death of her husband, staunchly Catholic Mary returned to Scotland. Unpopular amongst Scottish nobles and Protestants, Mary's rule fanned the flames of discontent, and civil war resulted in her forced abdication and imprisonment in 1567. She escaped her Scottish captors only to find another set of shackles across the border, where her cousin Elizabeth I ruled. As Mary languished in an English prison, her son **James VI** was made King. Nine years later, with Catholic Spain a rising threat, Queen Elizabeth made a tentative alliance with the nominally Protestant James (though that didn't stop her from executing his mother in 1587).

UNION WITH ENGLAND. Elizabeth's failure to produce an heir before her death in 1603 left James VI to be crowned **James I of England,** uniting both countries under a single monarch. James ruled from London, while his half-hearted attempts to reconcile the Scots to British rule were tartly resisted. Scottish Presbyterians supported Parliamentarian forces against James's successor **Charles I** during the **English Civil Wars** (p. 73). However, when the Parliamentarians executed Charles, the Scots again shifted alliances and declared the deceased king's son to be King Charles II. **Oliver Cromwell** quickly defeated Charles II (legend has it he hid in a tree to avoid capture, and then fled to France), but in a conciliatory gesture gave Scotland representation in the English Parliament. The Protestant victory of William of Orange over James II in the **Glorious Revolution** (p. 73) and the **War of the Spanish Succession** (1701-1714) convinced Scotland's Presbyterian leaders that its interests were safer with the Anglicans than with longtime ally Catholic France. (That, and the fact that many Scots were impoverished and famine-stricken after defending

THE LOCAL STORY

STONE OF DESTINY

Traveling from the Holy Land to Egypt, Sicily, and Spain before arriving in Ireland in 700 BC, the Stone of Scone (sometimes called "The Stone of Destiny") covered a lot of ground before it began its more recent commute between England and Scotland. The stone gained prominence by its association with the coronation of Scottish kings, but its recent shuttling between the two countries has created a contemporary folklore almost as legendary as the origins of the stone.

On Christmas Day, 1950, Scottish patriot Ian Hamilton hid in Westminster Abbey where the stone had resided since 1296. Intending to steal the 200kg stone and return it to Scotland, he was detected before the heist was completed. Hamilton (later a prominent Scottish MP) convinced the watchman he had been locked in accidentally.

That same night, Hamilton and accomplices entered the abbey and pulled the stone from its stand, breaking it into two pieces in the process. The stone was repaired in a Glasgow workyard and, several months later, carried to the altar at Arbroath Abbey where it was briefly displayed before being returned to Westminster. Or was it? Glasgow councilor Bertie Gray later revealed that the stone was copied and a fake returned. The real deal is now on display at Edinburgh Castle, where it remains heavily guarded.

their independence for four centuries.) The Scottish Parliament was subsumed by England in the **1707 Act of Union.**

THE JACOBITE REBELLION. Scottish supporters of James II (called **Jacobites**) never accepted the Union, and after a series of unsuccessful uprisings, they launched the **"Forty-Five"**—a 1745 rebellion that snared the imaginations of Scots and romantics everywhere. James's grandson Charles (or **Bonnie Prince Charlie**) landed in Scotland, where he succeeded in mustering unseasoned troops from various Scottish clans. From **Glenfinnan** (p. 651), he rallied the troops and marched to Edinburgh, where he kept court and prepared for full rebellion. Unfortunately, on the march to London desertions and the uncertainty of help from France prompted a retreat to Scotland. Modest French support did materialize, and the Jacobites claimed victories at Stirling and Falkirk in 1746. After that, however, the rebellion once again collapsed. Although Charles eventually escaped back to France, his Highland army fell heroically on the battlefield of **Culloden** (p. 643). The English subsequently enacted a harsh new round of oppressive measures: the wearing of hereditary **tartans** and the playing of **bagpipes** were forbidden, speaking **Gaelic** was discouraged, and much of traditional Scottish culture was forcibly forgotten. Sir Walter Scott's novel *Waverley*, written 60 years after the Forty-Five, expresses the next generation's nostalgia for the lost way of life.

ENLIGHTENMENT AND THE CLEARANCES. Despite Jacobite agitation and reactionary English countermeasures, the 18th century proved to be one of the most prosperous in Scotland's history. As agriculture, industry, and trading all boomed, a vibrant intellectual environment and close links to Continental **Enlightenment** thought produced such luminaries as **Adam Smith, David Hume,** and **Thomas Carlyle.**

In the 19th century, although political reforms did much to improve social conditions, economic problems proved disastrous. The Highlands in particular were affected by a rapidly growing population combined with little arable land, archaic farming methods, and the demands of rapacious landlords. The subsequent poverty resulted in mass **emigration,** mostly to North America, and the infamous **Highland Clearances.** Between 1810 and 1820, the Sutherland Clearances, undertaken by the Marquis of Stafford, forcibly and often violently relocated thousands of poor farmers from their lands to the coasts or to smaller landholdings called **crofts,** to make way for expanded sheep ranching. Resistance to the relocations was met with violence—homes were burned and countless people killed. Other Clearances occurred throughout the Highlands, in some cases evicting entire villages, whereupon they were not just relocated to another area in Scotland, but forcibly packed on boats and shipped overseas, populating the globe with McKenzies and Scotts. Meanwhile, the **Industrial Revolution** led to urban growth in southern Scotland—Glasgow grew into a gritty manufacturing metropolis—and increasingly poor living conditions for new industrial laborers.

THE 20TH CENTURY. Scotland, like the rest of Britain, lost countless young men in the Great War and suffered the following economic downturn. In the 1930s, the **Depression** hit Scotland as hard, if not harder, than the rest of the world. The **Home Rule** (or **Devolution**) movement, begun in 1886 and put on hold during WWI, continued agitation for a separate Parliament in Edinburgh. The **Scottish National Party (SNP)** was founded in 1934 on the strength of Scottish nationalist sentiments. Riding this wave of patriotism were the four young tartan-blooded agitators who broke into Westminster Abbey on Christmas of 1950 and liberated the **Stone of Scone** (or "Stone of Destiny"; see sidebar), which previously had been removed from Scotland by Edward I. However successful they were at burglarizing English cathedrals, Home Rulers never managed to score a real victory on the floor of Parliament during the years following WWII. Still, the movement didn't go away; in fact, polls in the 70s indicated as much as three-fourths of Scotland's population favored devolution. Meanwhile, the discovery of North Sea oil gave Scotland an economic boost and incited a new breed of nationalism embodied by the SNP's 1974 political slogan "It's Scotland's Oil!" The crucial **1979 referendum** on devolution, however, failed to win the required proportion of the electorate.

SCOTLAND TODAY

Stands Scotland where it did?
—William Shakespeare, *Macbeth*

CURRENT POLITICS. The May 1997 elections swept the Scottish Conservatives out of power with a landslide victory for Labour and accrued support for the SNP, which based its platform on devolution from England. September 1997 brought a victory for the proponents of home rule; Scottish voters supported **devolution** by an overwhelming 3:1 margin, and the first elections for 129 seats in the new **Scottish Parliament** occurred in 1999. Unlike England, Scotland has adopted a system of proportional representation for elections, allowing the SNP to further extend their influence. Today, Scotland has 72 seats in the United Kingdom's House of Commons and is largely integrated into the British economy. Parliament recently relocated to its new digs at **Holyrood,** Edinburgh (p. 557). Though Edinburgh is able to levy taxes and legislate in other areas, Westminster still controls foreign affairs and fiscal policy. The precise nature of Scotland's relationship with England remains disputed. On the one hand, even the mention of "Bannockburn" still stirs nationalist feeling among Scots, and the last party supporting union with England has been scourged from the Scottish Parliament. On the other, there are many Scottish politicians more closely tied to London than to their own constituents, and three centuries of economic and social intertwining are difficult to combat.

Scotland's **industrial boom** during the World Wars was nurtured during the postwar years by a string of Labour governments who pursued a widespread policy of nationalization of industry. **Thatcherism,** however, removed many of the public-funding props sustaining industries in the north of Britain, and Scotland's workforce was reduced by 20% before the 1980s were a year old. The country faced economic downturn and depression similar to, if not more intense than, that of the industrial meccas of Northern England.

SCOTLAND

SCOTLAND AT CENTURY'S END. Declared **European Capital of Culture** in 1990 and **UK City of Design and Architecture** in 1999, Glasgow's cultural revitalization is an agreeable benefit of the industrial upturn. **Edinburgh,** long a cultural magnet, has recently seen its 55-year-old **International Festival** (and attendant events like **The Fringe** that have come to dominate the festival on their own, see p. 544) make headlines around the world—today, over 15% of the revelers come from overseas. Edinburgh's festival energies peak during August but fuel the economy year round, generating millions of pounds in revenue and thousands of jobs.

Cultural tourism of another form draws droves of heritage-seekers and Celtic devotees to the country each summer. Though the industrial trades still enjoy Scotland's largest workforce, tourism employs more people than any other field in holiday spots like the Highlands and Islands. Still others have turned to new technologies as economic alternatives. On July 5, 1996, **Dolly the sheep** was born in the labs of the Roslin Institute, conceived by Dr. Ian Wilmut. This first successful cloning of a mammal is indicative of a booming interest in **biotechnology.** Scotland also has a stake in **microtechnologies,** producing nearly half of all the superconductors in the UK and earning Central Scotland the nickname "Silicon Glen." As computers and the Internet access filter into the country and trickle down through the social classes, Scotland seems poised to leave its 20th-century woes behind while bringing its older (and more profitable) heritage with it into the new millennium.

CULTURE AND CUSTOMS

The cold, drizzly skies of Scotland loom over some of the warmest people on earth. The Scottish reputation for openness and good nature is well-known and well-founded. Reserve and etiquette is somewhat less important here than in London's urban sprawl; life is generally slower and less frenetic outside—and even within—the densely populated belt running between Glasgow and Edinburgh. But all this is no reason to go forget your manners. As in the few other unharried corners of the world, **hospitality** and **conversation** are highly valued; most Scots will welcome you with geniality and pride, that is, unless you call them English. In certain areas of the Highlands, **nationalism** runs deep and strong; using the (technically) correct "British" will win you no friends. **Religion** and **football,** and the religion of football, are topics best left untouched if you're not prepared to defend yourself—verbally and otherwise. Even the sweetest little old lady can turn out to be a hot-blooded football fanatic.

A WORD ABOUT KILTS. The kilt is not purely a romanticized, Hollywoodized concept, though it's unlikely you'll see very many during your travels. Originally just Highland garb, **tartan** plaids denoted the geographic base of the weaver. Criminalized after the Jacobite rebellion, kilts were revived in the mid-19th-century nostalgia for Highland culture. Today, few Scots still wear their family tartan, though many do own one for use at formal gatherings (and often, sporting events).

KILT IT UP. You don't have to be Scottish to wear a kilt; in fact, it may make men particularly popular with the opposite sex. Hiring a kilt costs about £25, or £30 for the whole nine yards, including kilt, **hose** (socks), **flashes** for the hose (worn facing outwards), **Ghillie Brogues** (shoes), **sgian dubh** (ceremonial dagger, usually false) that goes tucked into the right sock with only the handle showing, **Bonnie Prince Charlie jacket** (a tuxedo-like top), **waistcoat** (vest), and the all-important **sporran**, worn across the front and serving as your only pocket (besides just looking sexy). What goes under is up to you—just keep in mind that all the **bonnie lassies** will be dying to find out.

LANGUAGE

Although the early Picts left no record of their language, settlers in southern Scotland well into the 7th century heard a **Celtic** language related to Welsh. These settlers also transported their native tongues—Gaelic from Ireland, Norse from Scandinavia, and an early form of English (Inglis) brought by the Angles from northern England. By the 11th century, **Scottish Gaelic** (pronounced GAL-ick; Irish Gaelic is GAYL-ick), had subsumed other dialects and become the official language of Scottish law. As the political power of southern Scotland increased, Gaelic speakers migrated to the Highlands and Islands. Inglis, now called **Scots** to differentiate it from its cousin to the south, became the language of the Lowlands and, eventually, of the monarchy. Beginning as a dialectical variation of the English developing in England, Scots (influenced by Flemish, French, and Latin) developed into a distinctive linguistic unit.

While a number of post-1700 Scottish literati, most notably Robert Burns and the contemporary poet Hugh MacDiarmid, have composed in Scots, union with Britain and the political and cultural power of England led to the rise of England's language in Scotland. Today, **standard English** is spoken throughout Scotland, but with a strong Scots influence. In the Highlands, for example, "ch" becomes a soft "h," as in the German "ch" sound. Modern Scottish Gaelic, a linguistic cousin of Modern Irish, is spoken by at least 60,000 people in Scotland today, particularly in the western islands. Recent attempts to revive Gaelic have led to its introduction in the classroom and even on street signs in the Hebrides, assuring that some form of the language will continue to exist in Scotland for years to come. (For a **glossary** of Scottish Gaelic and Scots words and phrases, see the Appendix; for Gaelic **classes**, see p. 63.)

THE ARTS

LITERATURE. Spanning centuries and including composition in three languages—Gaelic, Scots, and English—Scottish literature embodies a complexity of experience. In a nation where stories and myths have long been recounted by fireside, **oral literature** is as much a part of literary tradition as novels. Most medieval Scottish manuscripts have unfortunately been lost—not surprising, as raids on monastic centers of learning were fierce and frequent—effectively erasing pre-14th-century records. **John Barbour** is the best-known writer in Early Scots—his *The Bruce* (c. 1375) preceded Chaucer and favorably chronicled

THE LOCAL STORY

FLIGGITY-FLAG

Scotland's blue flag with its white "X" is one of the oldest flags still used in the world. When St. Andrew (the Apostle called Peter in the Bible) was crucified by the Romans in AD 69, he asked to be hung on an X-shaped cross, as he felt unworthy to be crucified on the same kind of cross on which Christ had suffered. His remains were entombed in Constantinople until AD 370 when St. Rule, directed by divine inspiration, gathered up a tooth, arm bone, kneecap, and some fingers from the resting place of St. Andrew and took them to "the ends of the earth"—a Pictish settlement on the eastern coast of Scotland. The settlement soon became a Christian pilgrimage destination and, when St. Andrews Cathedral (p. 626) was built in the 12th and 13th centuries, the religious center of Scotland.

In 832 AD, an alliance of Picts and Scots fought Northumbrian forces in Lothian for control of the region. As the story goes, the night before the battle, a vision of St. Andrew appeared before the leader of the Picts, and on the battle field the next day, St. Andrew's Saltire—the white X-shaped cross—appeared in the brilliant blue sky. It inspired the Picts and Scots to victory over the Northumbrians. And from that battle onwards, the Saltire became the national emblem of the Scots.

the life of Robert I in an attempt to strengthen national unity. **William Dunbar** (1460-1521) composed in Middle Scots and his work is today considered representative of Scots poetry.

In 1760, **James Macpherson** published the works of **"Ossian,"** supposedly an ancient Scottish bard to rival Homer; Macpherson was widely discredited when he refused to produce the manuscripts that he claimed to be translating. **James Boswell** (1740-95), the biographer of Samuel Johnson (p. 80), composed Scots verse as well as voluminous journals detailing his travels with the good Doctor. "Scotland's National Bard," **Robert Burns** (1759-96), bucked pressure from the south urging him to write in English, instead composing in his native Scots. New Year's Eve revelers owe their anthem to him, though most mouth "Auld Lang Syne" without a clue what it means. **Sir Walter Scott** (1771-1832) was among the first Scottish authors to achieve international accolades for his work. The chivalric *Ivanhoe* is one of the best-known, if sappiest, novels of all time. Scott was also quite nostalgic, and his historic novels (such as *Waverley*) may have single-handedly sparked the 19th-century revival of Highlands culture. **Robert Louis Stevenson** (1850-94) is most famous for his tales of high adventure, including *Treasure Island* and *Kidnapped*, which still fuel children's imaginations. His *Strange Case of Dr. Jekyll and Mr. Hyde* is nominally set in London, but any Scot would recognize Edinburgh's streets. Another of Edinburgh's authorial sons is **Sir Arthur Conan Doyle** (1859-1930), whose *Sherlock Holmes* series is beloved by mystery fans the world over.

Scotland's literary present is as vibrant as its past. A 20th-century renaissance of Scottish Gaelic, particularly the Lowlands ("Lallands") dialect, has had poets—most notably **Hugh MacDiarmid** and **Edwin Morgan**—returning to the language of Burns. James Leslie Mitchell (known as **Lewis Grassic Gibbon;** 1901-1935) had a short but important career—he co-authored *Scottish Scene* with MacDiarmid, a scathing account of what was wrong with their country. **Neil Gunn** (1891-1973) wrote short stories and novels about Highland history and culture. More recent novelists include **Alasdair Gray, Tom Leonard, Janice Galloway,** and **James Kelman,** who won 1995's Booker Prize for his controversial, sharp-edged novel *How Late It Was, How Late.* **Irvine Welsh's** *Trainspotting,* the 1993 novel about Edinburgh heroin addicts and its 1996 film adaptation, have been simultaneously condemned as immoral and hailed as chronicles of a new generation.

ART. Scotland has produced fewer visual artists than it has writers and musicians, but a visit to the extraordinary galleries and museums of Glasgow and Edinburgh indicate the country's fine aesthetic eye. Eighteenth and nineteenth-century portraitists like **Allan Ramsay** and **Sir Henry Raeburn,** and genre painter **David Wilkie** are recognized names in the world of art. As a celebrated participant in both the Arts and Crafts movement (p. 82) and the Art Nouveau scene, Glaswegian artist and architect **Charles Rennie Mackintosh** (1868-1928) considerably boosted Scotland's artistic prestige with his elegant designs, visible in Glasgow's School of Art (p. 589) and the Willow Tea Rooms (p. 587).

MUSIC. The Gaelic music of western Scotland has its roots in the traditional music of Irish settlers; as in Ireland, *ceilidhs* (KAY-lees)—spirited gatherings of music and dance—bring jigs, reels, and Gaelic songs to halls and pubs. Evidence suggests the *clarsach,* a Celtic harp, was the primary medium for musical expression until the 16th century, when the Highlander's **bagpipes** (one of the oldest instruments in the world) and the violin introduced new creative possibilities. Scots musical heritage centers around **ballads,** dramatic narrative songs often performed unaccompanied. The strong folk tradition is evident in the Scottish contribution to popular music: this sound influenced international rock trends, while the country itself produced **The Proclaimers** (whose hit song "I Would Walk (500

Miles)" is still played at dances and gatherings), folk-rockers **Belle and Sebastian,** and Britpop entries **Texas** and **Travis.** Glasgow alone has been a thriving exporter of musical talent since the 80s, generating bands like **Simple Minds** and **Tears for Fears.** Today, Glaswegians are most proud of their stylish rock gods **Franz Ferdinand.**

FOOD AND DRINK

The frequenter of B&Bs will encounter a glorious **Scottish breakfast,** consisting of beans, fried eggs, potato cakes, fried tomato, and a rasher of bacon. In general, however, Scottish cuisine greatly resembles English food. Aside from delicious, buttery **shortbread,** visitors are unlikely to take a shine to traditional dishes, which include **Scotch eggs** (boiled eggs wrapped in sausage, breaded, and fried) and the (in)famous **haggis,** made from a sheep's stomach (see sidebar). Those courageous enough to try it will be rewarded with a zesty, if a bit mushy, delicacy. The truly bravehearted will seek out Scotland's least known specialty, the **fried Mars bar.** Most chip shops will make one for you, but ask around; the crispy exterior and melted interior provide a singular, indulgent joy.

If the food is not for you, Scotland's **whisky** (spelled without the "e") is certainly more welcoming. Scotch whisky is either "single malt" (from a single distillery), or "blended" (a mixture of several different brands). The malts are excellent and distinctive, with flavors and strengths varied enough to accommodate novices and lifelong devotees alike. The blends are the same as those available abroad. Raise a glass yourself at the **distilleries** in Pitlochry (p. 605), the Speyside area (p. 637), or on the Isles of Islay and Jura (p. 619). Due to heavy taxes on alcohol sold in Britain, scotch may be cheaper at home or from duty-free stores than it is in Scotland. The Scots do know how to party: they have the highest alcohol consumption rate in Britain, and, no surprise, are more generous in their licensing laws than in England and Wales—drinks are served later and pubs open longer (often until midnight or later).

SPORTING AND MERRYMAKING

The Scottish are as passionate about **football** as their English neighbors, and the intensity of devotion in Glasgow in particular (see **Pitched Battle,** p. 50) rivals any Mancunian fervor. Scottish **Rugby** takes a close second to football, with three professional league teams, drawing crowds in the thousands. **Golf,** the "tyrannising game" that continues to dominate St.

ON THE MENU

HAGGIS: WHAT'S IN THERE?

The best-known, most distinctive, and, to some, least appealing of Scottish foods, haggis is found everywhere from Edinburgh to the Hebrides. For the uninitiated, haggis is traditionally prepared by filling a sheep's stomach with an oatmeal-based mélange of sheep's liver, heart, lung, and kidney, along with onions, suet, beef, and spices. The stomach bag is then sealed and boiled until it expands to a firm consistency.

The traditional recipe still survives, but local butchers also pride themselves with ground beef-based variations, and vegetarian alternatives are increasingly popular. Haggis now ranges from canned to high cuisine, but its origins remain humble, emerging as a staple of the Scottish diet as early as the 14th century; a 1390 recipe written by one of King Richard II's cooks describes the hearty dish. While a similar recipe appears in early Greek writings, it is more likely that haggis was brought to the British Isles by Scandinavian settlers. The root of the word is related to the Swedish word *hagga,* meaning to chop. After Britain joined the European Union, there were rumblings from the Food Standards Agency over the use of the stomach. Though some recipes allow the use of a jar, local chefs have vowed to retain the ancient culinary tradition, stomach and all.

Andrews, was first invented in 15th-century Scotland (p. 593). The country's over 400 golf courses testify to the persisting influence of this sport. Traditional **Scottish** or **Highland games** originated from competitions under English military oppression, in which participants could use only common objects such as hammers, rounded stones, and tree trunks. Although **"tossing the caber"** may look easy, it actually requires a good deal of talent and practice to chuck an 18 ft., 150 lb. pine trunk. Weekend clan gatherings, bagpipe competitions, and Highland games occur frequently in Scotland, especially in summer; check for events at TICs and in the local newspapers. In addition, the Scottish Tourist Board publishes the annual *Scotland Events*, which details happenings across Scotland.

Each year a slew of festivals celebrate Scotland's distinctive history and culture. June and July's **Common Ridings** in the Borders (p. 565) and the raucous **Up-Helly-Aa'** in Shetland on the last Tuesday in January (p. 694) are among the best known. Scotland is also famous for its New Year's Eve celebration, known as **Hogmanay.** The party goes on all over the country, taking over the streets in Edinburgh and Glasgow (check www.hogmanay.net for events and locations). Above all events towers the **Edinburgh International Festival** (Aug. 15-Sept. 4 in 2004; ☎0131 473 2000; www.eif.co.uk), one of the largest in the world. The concentration of musical and theatrical events in the space of three weeks is dizzying; Edinburgh's cafes and shops stay open all hours and pipers roam the streets. Be sure to catch the **Fringe Festival** (Aug. 8-30 in 2004; ☎0131 226 0000; www.edfringe.com), the much less costly sibling of the International Festival. There are literally hundreds of performances every day, including drama, comedy acts, jazz, and a bit of the bizarre. Travelers planning to travel to Scotland in August should plan well ahead and be sure to swing by Edinburgh.

SCOTLAND

SOUTHERN SCOTLAND

A history of strife distinguishes Southern Scotland, whose changeable landscape includes both vibrant metropolises and serene islands. The Borders region to the southeast contains formidable castles and ruined abbeys commemorating interminable struggles with England, and Dumfries and Galloway in the southwest offer rolling hills and a scenic coastline. Walkers and cyclists enjoy the region's gentle beauty, captured by great Scottish bard Robert Burns. Isolation and tranquility characterize the Isle of Arran, though just eastward lie southern Scotland's true draws: regal Edinburgh and spicy Glasgow. Nearly 80% of all Scots live in the two cities' greater metropolitan areas. A fountainhead of the Enlightenment and Scotland's capital, Edinburgh is easily Britain's most beautiful city and draws enormous crowds each summer during its festivals. Not to be outdone, Glasgow offers formidable art collections and a student-fed, kinetic nightlife.

HIGHLIGHTS OF SOUTHERN SCOTLAND

EDINBURGH AND THE FESTIVAL The world's biggest arts festival explodes across one of the world's great capital cities every August (p. 546).

THE BORDERS Ponder the past at the four Border Abbeys, a ring of evocative medieval ruins with a bloody past, set today amidst silent villages and rolling hills (p. 565).

GLASGOW Survey magnificent architecture, free museums, hundreds of pubs, and Britain's highest concentration of Indian restaurants (p. 581).

ISLE OF ARRAN Delight in "Scotland in miniature," explore Brodick Castle, or take on the challenge of climbing Goatfell (p. 578).

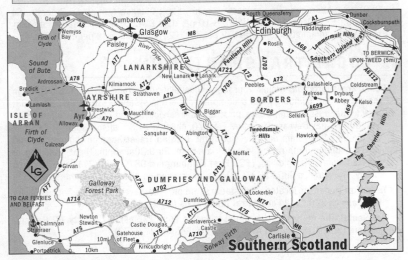

EDINBURGH ☎ 0131

A city of elegant stone amid rolling hills and ancient volcanoes, Edinburgh (ED-in-bur-ra; pop. 500,000) is the jewel of Scotland and easily ranks among Europe's great capitals. Since David I granted it burgh (town) status in 1130, Edinburgh's hilltop citadel has been a site of cultural significance. It was here that the medieval Stuarts created a poetic and musical center for the arts, here that the seeds of the Scottish Reformation were sown, and here that the brilliant intellectuals of the Scottish Enlightenment fostered a heady, forward-thinking atmosphere. Infused with cosmopolitan verve, today's city endures as a cultural beacon, its medieval spires rising above streets lined with rollicking pubs. During August, Edinburgh becomes a performer's mecca, drawing global talent and crowds to its festivals.

■ INTERCITY TRANSPORTATION

Edinburgh lies 45 mi. east of Glasgow and 405 mi. northwest of London on Scotland's east coast, on the southern bank of the Firth of Forth.

Flights: Edinburgh International Airport (☎ 333 1000), 7 mi. west of the city. Lothian's **Airlink** (☎ 555 6363) shuttles between the airport and Waverley Bridge (25min.; every 10-15min. all day, every hr. after midnight; £3, children £2). An **Airsaver** ticket scores a trip on Airlink plus 1 day unlimited travel on Lothian buses (£4.20, children £2.50).

Trains: Waverley Station, in the center of town, lies between Princes St., Market St., and Waverley Bridge. **Luggage storage** £5 per item per day. Free **bike storage** beside Platform 1. Ticket office open M-Sa 4:45am-12:30am, Su 7-12:30am. Trains (☎ 08457 484 950) from: **Aberdeen** (2½hr.; M-Sa every hr., Su 8 per day; £31.60); **Glasgow** (1hr., 4 per hr., £7.80-8.60); **Inverness** (3½hr., every 2hr., £31.60); **London King's Cross** (4¾hr., every hr., £82.70-88.50); **Oban** via Glasgow (4½hr., 3 per day, £25.50); **Stirling** (50min., 2 per hr., £5.30); **Thurso** and **Wick** (7½hr., M-Sa 1 per day, £40.20).

Buses: The modern **Edinbugh Bus Station** is on the eastern side of St. Andrew Sq. Open daily 6am-midnight. Ticket office open daily 8am-8pm. **National Express** (☎ 08705 808 080) from **London** (10hr., 4 per day, £28.50). **Scottish Citylink** (☎ 08705 505 050) from: **Aberdeen** (4hr., at least every hr., £15); **Glasgow** (1hr.; M-Sa 3 per hr., Su 2 per hr.; £3.80); **Inverness** (4½hr., 8-10 per day, £14.70). A combination bus-ferry route via Stranraer goes to **Belfast** (2 per day, £20) and **Dublin** (1 per day, £28).

▣ LOCAL TRANSPORTATION

Public Transportation: Though your feet will usually suffice (and are often faster) within the city center, Edinburgh has a comprehensive bus system. **Lothian** (☎ 555 6363; www.lothianbuses.co.uk) buses provide most services. Exact change required (50p-£1). Buy a 1-day **Daysaver** ticket (M-F £2.70, children £1.80; after 9:30am M-F and all day Sa-Su £1.80) from any driver or in the **Lothian Travelshops** on Hanover St. and Waverley Bridge. Both open M-Sa 8:30am-6pm, Su 9:30am-5pm. **Night buses** cover selected routes after midnight (£2). **First Edinburgh** (☎ 0870 872 7271) also operates locally. **Traveline** (☎ 0800 232 323) has information on all area public transport.

Taxis: Taxi stands are located at all stations and on almost every corner on Princes St. Try **City Cabs** (☎ 228 1211) or **Central Radio Taxis** (☎ 229 2468).

Car Rental: The TIC has a list of rental agencies. From £25 per day. **Thrifty,** 42 Haymarket Terr. (☎ 337 1319), and **Avis,** 100 Dalry Rd. (☎ 337 6363).

Bike Rental: Biketrax, 11 Lochrin Pl. (☎228 6633). Mountain bikes £10 per day. Open M-Sa 9:30am-5:30pm, Su noon-5pm. **Edinburgh Cycle Hire,** 29 Blackfriars St. (☎556 5560), off High St. Organizes cycle tours. Mountain bikes £10-15 per day, £50-70 per week. Open daily 10am-6pm. AmEx/MC/V.

ORIENTATION

Edinburgh is a glorious city for walking. Princes Street is the main thoroughfare in New Town, the northern section of the city. From there you can view the impressive stone facade of the towering Old Town, the southern half of the city. The Royal Mile (Castle Hill, Lawnmarket, High St., and Canongate) is the major road in the Old Town and connects Edinburgh Castle in the west to the Palace of Holyroodhouse in the east. North Bridge, Waverley Bridge, and The Mound connect Old and New Town, with Waverly Station between the city's two parts. Two miles northeast, Leith is the city's seaport on the Firth of Forth.

PRACTICAL INFORMATION

TOURIST AND FINANCIAL SERVICES

Tourist Information Centre: Waverley Market, 3 Princes St. (☎473 3800), on the north side of the Waverley Station complex at street level. Slick, helpful, and often mobbed, the mother-ship of all Scottish TIC's books rooms for a £3 charge plus a 10% deposit; sells bus, museum, tour, and theater tickets; and has excellent free maps and pamphlets. **Bureau de change.** Open July-Aug. M-Sa 9am-8pm, Su 10am-8pm; May-June and Sept. until 7pm; Oct.-Apr. M-W 9am-5pm, Th-Sa 9am-6pm, Su 10am-5pm. In summer, look for the blue-jacketed **Guiding Stars** who wander throughout the city center and can answer questions in several languages.

Budget Travel: STA Travel, 27 Forrest Rd. (☎226 7747). Open M-W and F 10am-6pm, Th 10am-7pm, Sa 10am-5pm.

Financial Services: Banks are everywhere. **Thomas Cook,** 52 Hanover St. (☎226 5500). Open M-Sa 9am-5:30pm. **American Express,** 69 George St. (☎718 2505, call center 08706 001 600). Open M-Tu and Th-Sa 9am-5:30pm, W 9:30am-5:30pm.

LOCAL SERVICES

Camping Supplies: Outdoor Edinburgh, Princes Mall, Waverly Bridge (☎558 7777). All the essentials, but no rentals. Open M-Sa 9am-7pm, Su 11am-6pm.

GLBT Services: Edinburgh has many gay- and lesbian-oriented establishments and events—pick up the *Gay Information* pamphlet at the TIC, or drop by the **Edinburgh Lesbian, Gay, and Bisexual Centre,** 58a-60 Broughton St. (☎478 7069), inside the Sala Cafe-Bar. See also **Gay and Lesbian Nightlife,** p. 562.

Disabled Services: The TIC has info on access to restaurants and sights, and stocks *The Access Guide and Transport in Edinburgh*. **Shopmobility,** The Mound (☎225 9559), by the National Gallery, lends free motorized wheelchairs. Open Tu-Sa 10am-3:45pm.

Public Showers: In the "Superloo" at the train station. Super clean (for a train station). Shower, toilet kit, and towel £3. Toilet 20p. Open daily 4am-12:45am.

Work Opportunities: Each summer hordes of young travelers are employed by festival organizations to help manage bustling offices, set up venues, and help with publicity. During the festival itself jobs open up across the city as bars, hostels and attractions all try to accommodate the burgeoning traffic. Beginning in early Apr., the festival organiza-

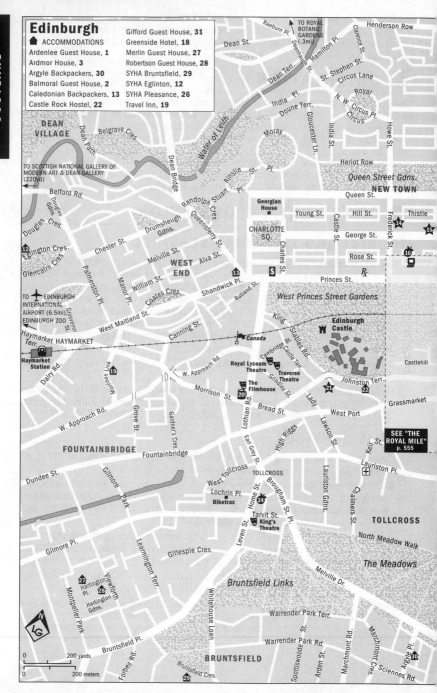

Edinburgh

ACCOMMODATIONS

Ardenlee Guest House, 1
Ardmor House, 3
Argyle Backpackers, 30
Balmoral Guest House, 2
Caledonian Backpackers, 13
Castle Rock Hostel, 22

Gifford Guest House, 31
Greenside Hotel, 18
Merlin Guest House, 27
Robertson Guest House, 28
SYHA Bruntsfield, 29
SYHA Eglinton, 12
SYHA Pleasance, 26
Travel Inn, 19

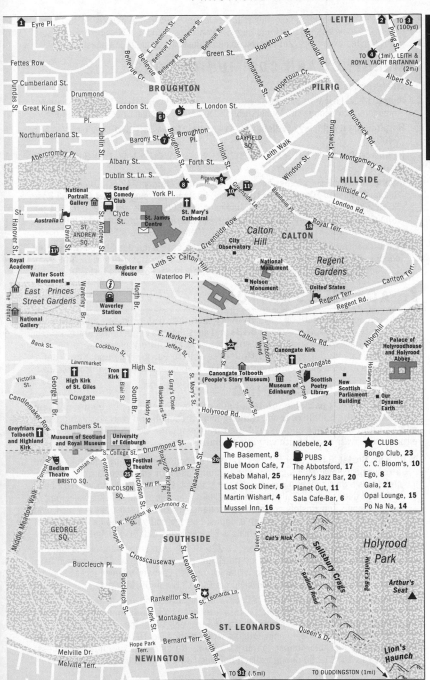

SOUTHERN SCOTLAND

FOOD
The Basement, 8
Blue Moon Cafe, 7
Kebab Mahal, 25
Lost Sock Diner, 5
Martin Wishart, 4
Mussel Inn, 16

Ndebele, 24
PUBS
The Abbotsford, 17
Henry's Jazz Bar, 20
Planet Out, 11
Sala Cafe-Bar, 6

CLUBS
Bongo Club, 23
C. C. Bloom's, 10
Ego, 8
Gaia, 21
Opal Lounge, 15
Po Na Na, 14

tions begin employing office staff and the venues start to hire helpers. In July things really get going as the stages and sets are constructed and establishments of all sorts start to need extra help. Surf to www.edinburghfestivals.co.uk for the latest.

EMERGENCY AND COMMUNICATIONS

Emergency: ☎999 or 112.

Police: 14 St. Leonard's St. (☎662 5000). Blue **police information boxes** are scattered throughout city center, with tourist information and an emergency assistance button.

Hospital: Royal Infirmary of Edinburgh, 41 Lauriston Pl. (☎536 1000, emergencies 536 6000).

Pharmacy: Boots, 101-103 Princes St. (☎225 8331). Open M-W, F-Sa 8am-6pm, Th 8am-7pm, and Su 11am-5pm.

Internet Access: Free **Internet access** at the **Central Library** (242 8000) on George IV Bridge. Open M-Th 10am-8pm, F 10am-5pm, Sa 9am-1pm. **easyInternet Cafe,** 58 Rose St. (☎220 3577), inside Caffe Nero, has hundreds of terminals and great rates. £1 per 30min. Open M-Sa 7am-10pm, Su 9am-10pm. **Internet Cafe,** beside Platform 1, Waverley Station. £1 per 20min. Open M-F 7:30am-9pm, Sa-Su 8:30am-9pm.

Post Office: (☎556 9546), in the St. James Centre beside the Bus Station. **Bureau de change.** Open M-Sa 9am-5:30pm. **Branch** at 46 St. Mary's St. Open M-Tu, Th-F 9am-12:30pm and 1:30-5:30pm, W 9am-1pm, Sa 9am-noon. **Post Code:** EH1 3SR.

⚐ ACCOMMODATIONS

Edinburgh accommodations cater to every kind of traveler. **Hostels** and **hotels** are the only city-center options, while **B&Bs** and **guest houses** begin on the outer edges. It's a good idea to book ahead in summer, and absolutely essential to be well ahead of the game during festival time (late July to early Sept.) and New Year's. Many locals also let their apartments; the TIC's booking service is your hook-up.

HOSTELS AND CAMPING

This backpacker's paradise offers a bevy of convenient hostels, many of them smack-dab in the middle of town, ranging from the small and cozy to the huge and party-oriented. Expect cliques of long-term residents. Several also offer more expensive private rooms with varying amenities.

▨ **High St. Hostel,** 8 Blackfriars St. (☎557 3984). Good facilities, party atmosphere, and a convenient Royal Mile location—this has long been an Edinburgh favorite. Friendly staff leads a daily tour of the city to get you situated. Pool table and movies. 152 beds in 10-bed dorms, co-ed available. With Castle Rock and Royal Mile Backpackers, part of the Scotland's Top Hostels chain (www.scotlands-top-hostels.com), all of which host MacBackpackers groups. No lockable dorms; luggage and valuables lockers. Internet access and laundry. Continental breakfast £1.90. Dorms £10.50-13. AmEx/MC/V. ❶

▨ **Castle Rock Hostel,** 15 Johnston Terr. (☎225 9666). Just steps from the castle, this friendly place has regal views and top-notch lounges. Nightly movies. 220 beds in 8- to 16-bed dorms. No lockable dorms; valuables lockers. Laundry. Internet access 80p per 30min. Continental breakfast £1.90. Dorms £12-13.50. AmEx/MC/V. ❶

Brodies 2, 93 High St. (☎556 6770; www.brodieshostels.co.uk.). New in 2003, this Royal Mile hostel is a sweet deal, with a luxurious common room, spotless and fully equipped kitchen, stainless steel showers and heavenly beds. The wide selection of private rooms includes ideal family lodging. 70 beds in 4- to 10-bed co-ed dorms (1 all female). No lockable dorms; valuables lockers. No smoking. Free Internet access. Dorms £11-16, £17.50 during festival; doubles £34-45; quads from £55. MC/V. ❷

Brodies Backpackers, 12 High St. (☎556 6770; www.brodieshostels.co.uk), under the same management as Brodies 2. Party environment at this small Royal Mile hostel. 56 beds in 16-bed dorms (3 co-ed, 1 all-female) with rustic wooden bunks, stone walls, and tartan spreads. No lockable dorms; valuables lockers. Free Internet access. 24hr. key-card access. Dorms Sept.-July £10.50-16; Aug. £17.50. Weekly £65-89. MC/V. ❶

Edinburgh Backpackers, 65 Cockburn (CO-burn) St. (☎220 2200; www.hoppo.com). Friendly and energetic, with common areas, pool table, ping-pong, and TV. 15% discount at the downstairs Southern Cross cafe. 96 beds in 8- to 14-bed co-ed dorms. Lockable dorms; valuables lockers. Internet access and laundry. Reception 24hr. Check-out 10am. Dorms £13-15.50; Aug. £18. private rooms £44.50-72. MC/V. ❷

Argyle Backpackers, 14 Argyle Pl. (☎667 9991). Take bus #41 from The Mound to Melville Dr., or take a nice 10-min. walk through the park. 2 renovated townhouses with a backyard and cafe. Am alternative to louder city hostels, equipped with private rooms, many with TV. 50 beds in 3- to 8-bed dorms. No smoking. Internet access £1.50 per hr. Lockable dorms; valuables lockers. Dorms £12-15; doubles £34-40. AmEx/MC/V. ❶

Royal Mile Backpackers, 105 High St. (☎557 6120; www.macbackpackers.com). A small spot with community feel, largely due to the many long-term residents. Guests can use amenities at nearby High St. Hostel. 38 beds in 8-bed dorms. No lockable dorms; valuables lockers. Continental breakfast £1.90. Dorms £12-13.50. MC/V. ❶

St. Christopher's Inn, 9-13 Market St. (☎226 1446; www.st-christophers.co.uk), literally across from Waverley Station. A clean and friendly outpost of a chain known for its London hostels. Good security and a discount at downstairs restaurant. 163 beds in 4- to 14-bed co-ed dorms. Lockable dorms; lockers. Internet access, and laundry. Wheelchair accessible. No kitchen. Dorms £15-18; doubles £42-46. MC/V. ❶

City Centre Tourist Hostel, 5 W. Register St. (☎556 8070; www.scotland-hostels.com), shares an entrance with Princes St. East Backpackers but completely separate. Small, comfortable New Town hostel close to Waverley Station. Very clean and without an overpowering party atmosphere. 40 beds in 4- to 10-bed dorms. No lockable dorms; no lockers. Reception 24hr. Dorms £10-18. Cash only. ❷

Caledonian Backpackers, 3 Queensferry St. (☎476 7224; www.caledonianbackpackers.com), at the west end of Princes St. This large, recently renovated hostel has spacious dorms and a great backpackers' bar that stays open late with live music F-Sa, and Tu open mic. 284 beds. Lockable dorms; lockers. 2 kitchens, laundry, and Internet access. Dorms £11-12, £14 during festival; private rooms from £32. MC/V. ❶

SYHA Hostels (www.syha.org.uk). They may not be quite as fun as other hostels, but they're certainly clean, safe, and always well run. All accept MC/V.

    Eglinton, 18 Eglinton Cres. (☎337 1120). An impressive Victorian house near Haymarket Station in the west of the city. 156 beds in 2- to 10-bed dorms. Lockable dorms and lockers. Self-catering kitchen, laundry, and Internet access. Continental breakfast £2.80-3.85. Check-out 10am. Dorms £11.75-18, under 18 £10.50-14. ❷

    Bruntsfield, 7 Bruntsfield Cres. (☎447 2994). Take bus #11, 15-17, or 23. Standard hostel overlooking a park, still relatively close to the city center. 126 beds. Kitchen, laundry, and Internet access. Bag breakfast £1.30. Sony PlayStation £1. Dorms £11.50-16, under 18 £10.50-14. ❷

    International, Central, and Pleasance, Apart from the two permanent hostels, the SYHA turns three University of Edinburgh dorms into hostels during July and August. These are **International,** Kincard's Ct., Guthrie St. (☎0871 330 8519; open July-Aug.) **Central,** Robertson's Close, Cowgate (☎0871 330 8517; open July-Aug.) and **Pleasance,** New Arthur Pl. (☎0871 330 8518; open Aug.). All three offer plain but spacious single rooms, self-catering kitchens on each floor, laundry facilities, Internet access, and in-room phones. £20-22. ❷

Camping: Edinburgh Caravan Club Site, Marine Dr. (☎312 6874), by the Forth. Take bus #8A from North Bridge. Electricity, showers, hot water, laundry, and shop. £4-5 per person, £3 per pitch. Cash only. ❶

HOTELS

Most of the independent city center hotels have stratospheric prices. At the affordable end are budget **chain hotels**—lacking in character, but comfortable, and often very well located. Three sit on prime Old Town real estate: **Grassmarket Hotel ❸**, 94 Grassmarket (☎0870 990 6400; singles £30; MC/V) formerly Premier Lodge, is the most affordable, offering tiny rooms at an unbeatable rate; **Hotel Ibis ❺**, 6 Hunter Sq. (☎240 7000; www.ibishotel.com; £70; AmEx/MC/V); and **Travelodge ❺**, 33 St. Mary's St. are slightly more expensive and luxurious. (☎0870 085 0950; www.travelodge.co.uk. £70, during festival £80. AmEx/MC/V.) **Travel Inn ❹**, 1 Morrison Link, is near Haymarket Station. (☎0870 238 3319; www.travelinn.co.uk. £60 per room. AmEx/MC/V.) The small hotels near Calton Hill, 10min. from Waverley Station, are also worth considering. One option, the **Greenside Hotel ❸**, 9 Royal Terr., is a recently refurbished Georgian building with fine views of the Firth from its top floors. (☎557 0022. Singles £25-65; doubles £45-90. AmEx/MC/V.)

B&BS AND GUEST HOUSES

B&Bs cluster in three well-stocked colonies, all of which you can walk to or reach by bus from the city center. Try Gilmore Pl., Viewforth Terr., or Huntington Gdns. in the **Bruntsfield** district, south from the west end of Princes St. (bus #11, 16, or 17 west/southbound); Dalkeith Rd. and Minto St. in **Newington,** south from the east end of Princes St. (bus #7, 31 or 37 among others); or **Pilrig,** northeast from the east end of Princes St. (bus #11 east/northbound).

▨ **Ardenlee Guest House,** 9 Eyre Pl. (☎556 2838). Take bus #23 or 27 from Hanover St. northbound to the corner of Dundas St. and Eyre Pl. Near the Royal Botanic Gardens, this friendly guest house has big, comfy rooms. £30-40 per person. MC/V. ❸

Merlin Guest House, 14 Hartington Pl., Bruntsfield (☎229 3864), just over 1 mi. southwest of the Royal Mile. Take bus #10 or 27 from Princes St. Comfortable, well-priced rooms. £17-22.50 per person; student discounts in winter. Cash only. ❷

Gifford House, 103 Dalkeith Rd., Newington (☎667 4688), under 2 mi. from the city center. Take bus #33 from Princes St. Enormous rooms and good views of Arthur's Seat. No smoking. Singles £35-65; doubles £55-95; family rooms £80-140. MC/V. ❸

Ardmor House, 74 Pilrig St., Pilrig (☎554 4944). Take bus #11 from Princes St. Off Leith walk, only a short walk from New Town. All rooms ensuite. Excellent Scottish breakfasts. No smoking. Singles £45-85; doubles £60-100. MC/V. ❹

Robertson Guest House, 5 Hartington Gdns., Bruntsfield (☎229 2652). Take bus #10 or 27 from Princes St. Quiet and welcoming, with a nice garden patio. No smoking. £30-35 per person, £40-50 during festival. MC/V. ❸

Balmoral Guest House, 32 Pilrig St., Pilrig (☎554 1857; www.balmoralguesthouse.co.uk). Take bus #11 from Princes St. Wrap yourself in the warm welcome at this well-furnished guest house. No smoking. Singles £30-40; doubles £50-70. MC/V. ❸

◘ FOOD

Edinburgh features an exceptionally wide range of cuisines and restaurants. Of course, if it's traditional fare you're after, the capital won't disappoint, with everything from pub haggis to creative "modern Scottish" at the city's top restaurants. For food on the cheap, many **pubs** offer student and hosteler discounts in the early evening, while fast-food joints are scattered across New Town. Takeaway shops on **South Clerk Street, Leith Street,** and **Lothian Road** have well-priced Chinese and Indian fare, and there's always the option of **groceries** at **Sainsbury's,** 9-10 St. Andrew Sq. (☎225 8400. Open M-Sa 7am-10pm, Su 10am-8pm.)

OLD TOWN

▓ **The City Cafe,** 19 Blair St. (☎220 0125), right off the Royal Mile behind the Tron Kirk. This Edinburgh institution is popular with the young and tightly-clad; a relaxed cafe by day, and a flashy pre-club spot by night. Try the lamb and rosemary burgers (£6). Incredible shakes. Happy hour daily 5-8pm. Open M-Th 11am-11pm, F-Su 11am-10pm; drinks until 1am (3am during festival). MC/V. ❷

▓ **The Elephant House,** 21 George IV Bridge (☎220 5355). In this relaxing ambience Harry Potter and Hogwarts were born on hastily scribbled napkins. A perfect place to chill, chat or pore over the stack of newspapers. Exotic teas and coffees, the best shortbread in the universe, and filling fare for less than £5. Great views of the castle from the back room. Happy hour M-Sa 7-8pm. Live music Th 7pm. Open daily 8am-11pm. MC/V. ❶

The Grain Store, 30 Victoria St. (☎225 7635). Enjoy stone-vaulted ceilings and quiet comfort. The wine menu complements French cuisine prepared with local Scottish produce. 2-course dinner £20. Entrees £18-30. Reservations recommended. Open M-Th noon-2pm and 6-10pm, F-Sa noon-3pm and 6-11pm, Su 6-10pm. AmEx/MC/V. ❹

Kebab Mahal, 7 Nicolson Sq. (☎667 5214). This unglamorous, student-filled hole-in-the-wall will stuff you with authentic Indian Tandoori for under £5. Worth the wait or takeaway. Open M-Th noon-1am, F-Sa noon-2am, Su noon-midnight. AmEx/MC/V. ❶

The Last Drop, 72-74 Grassmarket (☎225 4851). Tourist-friendly pub by the old gallows—hence the name. "Haggis, tatties, and neeps" in carnivore and herbivore versions £5. Student and hosteler discounts until 7pm. Open daily 10am-2am. AmEx/MC/V. ❶

NEW TOWN

The Basement, 10a 12a Broughton St. (☎557 0097). The menu changes daily, with plenty of vegetarian options. Draws a lively mix of locals to its candlelit cavern for Mexican fare Sa-Su and Thai cuisine on W nights. Entrees £5.50-7.50. Reservations recommended. Food served daily noon-10:30pm; drinks until 1am. AmEx/MC/V. ❷

Number One, 1 Princes St. (☎557 6727), underneath the Balmoral Hotel. One of Edinburgh's most exclusive restaurants. Wine and modern Scottish cuisine, including local seafood and seasonal game, round out the trademark 6-course dinner (£41). Book at least 1 week in advance. Open M-Th noon-2pm and 7-10pm, F noon-2pm and 7-10:30pm, Sa 7-10:30pm, Su 7-10pm. AmEx/MC/V. ❺

Lost Sock Diner, 11 E. London St. (☎557 6097). Order a delicious dinner (£4-8) while waiting for your clothes to dry. Open Tu-W 9am-9pm, Th 9am-10pm, F 9am-11pm, Sa 10am-11pm, Su 11am-5pm. Cash (and coins) only. ❷

Mussel Inn, 61-65 Rose St. (☎225 5979; www.mussel-inn.com). Muscle your way in for superior shellfish. Entrees under £10. Open daily noon-10pm. MC/V. ❷

Hadrian's Brasserie, 2 North Bridge (☎557 5000). Given its suave decor and location in the swanky Balmoral Hotel, you might expect to pay more for Hadrian's classic British dishes. All-day 3-course menu £11. Dinner around £14. Open M-Sa 7-10:30am, noon-2:30pm, 6:30-10:30pm; Su 7:30-11am, 12:30-3pm, 6:30-10:30pm. AmEx/MC/V. ❸

ELSEWHERE

▓ **Ndebele,** 57 Home St., Tolcross (☎221 1141; www.ndebele.co.uk), ¾ mi. south from the west end of Princes St. Named for an African tribe, serves generous portions for under £5. Try an avocado, mushroom, and cucumber sandwich (£3) and choose from an array of African and South American drinks. Open daily 10am-10pm. MC/V. ❶

Restaurant Martin Wishart, 54 The Shore, Leith (☎553 3557; www.martinwishart.co.uk), near the Royal Yacht Britannia. An exquisite and imaginative showcase of French cooking. Open Tu-F noon-2pm and Tu-Sa 7-9:30pm. AmEx/MC/V. ❺

👁 📄 SIGHTS AND SHOPPING

TOURS. While a great array of tour companies in Edinburgh tout themselves as "the original" or "the scariest", the most worthwhile of the bunch is ⬛**McEwan's 80/- Edinburgh Literary Pub Tour** (that's "McEwan's eighty shilling"). Led by professional actors, this 2hr., alcohol-friendly crash course in Scottish literature meets outside the Beehive Inn on Grassmarket. (☎226 6665; www.edinburghliterarypubtour.co.uk. Daily June-Sept. 7:30pm; Apr.-May and Oct. Th-Su 7:30pm; Nov.-Mar. F 7:30pm. £8, concessions £6. £1 discount for online booking.) Of the many tours exploring Edinburgh's dark and grisly past, the **City of the Dead Tour,** 40 Candlemaker Row, and its promised one-on-one encounter with the MacKenzie Poltergeist, is the most popular. (☎225 9044. Daily Apr.-Oct. 8:30, 9:15 and 10pm; Nov.-Mar. 7:30 and 8:30pm. £7, concessions £5, children £4.) **Mercat Tours,** leaving from Mercat Cross in front of St. Giles Cathedral, enters Edinburgh's spooky underground vaults, although it, like many of its competitors, relies heavily upon long-winded ghost stories rather than real frights. (☎557 6464. £6.30-9.)

Edinburgh is best explored by foot, but should you begin to tire, several similar hop-on, hop-off open-top bus tours stop at the major sights beginning at Waverley Bridge. **City Sightseeing Edinburgh** buses run most frequently (£7.50, concessions £6.50, children £2.50, families £19.50); others include **Guide Friday, MacTours** and the **Britannia Tour,** which runs to Leith. (General tour bus information ☎220 0770.)

THE OLD TOWN AND THE ROYAL MILE

Edinburgh's medieval center, the fascinating **Royal Mile** defines **Old Town** and passes many classic and worthwhile sights. Once lined with narrow shopfronts and slums towering to a dozen stories, this famous strip is now a playground for the hosteler and local alike, buzzing with bars and attractions. Of course, this also means the cheesy souvenir stores overcrowd the more interesting shops, but treasures can still be found, such as the outstanding ⬛**Royal Mile Whiskies,** 379 High St. Offering a staggering selection of whiskies and ales from every corner of Scotland (and then some), the knowledgeable and down-to-earth staff will help even the most novice drinkers find something to suit them. (☎225 3383; www.royalmilewhiskies.com. Open M-Sa 10am-6pm, Su 12:30-6pm; open until 8pm in Aug.)

⬛**EDINBURGH CASTLE.** Perched atop an defunct volcano, Edinburgh Castle dominates the city skyline. Though there were settlements here long before, the oldest surviving building in the complex is tiny 12th-century **St. Margaret's Chapel,** built by King David I in memory of his mother. The rest of the castle compound arose over the course of centuries of renovation and rebuilding; the most recent additions date to the 1920s. The central **Palace,** begun in the 1430s, was home to Stewart Kings and Queens during the 15th and 16th centuries and contains the room where Mary, Queen of Scots, gave birth to King James VI. It also houses the **Scottish Crown Jewels,** which are older than their counterparts in London. The storied though visually unspectacular Stone of Scone, more commonly known as the **Stone of Destiny** (see p. 45) is also on permanent display. Other highlights of the sprawling compound include the **Scottish National War Memorial** and the **National War Museum of Scotland,** the 15th-century monster cannon **Mons Meg,** and magnificent views all the way to Fife. The **One O'Clock Gun** fires Monday to Saturday. While the castle is most impressive viewed from the outside, a visit is still well worth it. (*Looming over the city center.* ☎225 9846. *Open daily Apr.-Oct. 9:30am-6pm; Nov.-Mar. 9:30am-5pm. Last admission 45min. before close. Free guided tours of the castle depart regularly from the entrance. £9.50, children £2, under 5 free. Excellent audio guide £3.)*

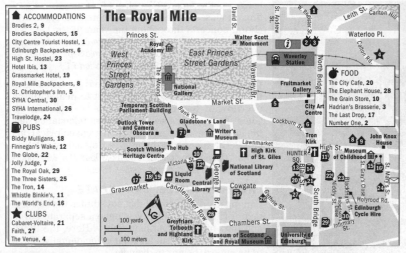

THE ROYAL MILE: CASTLE HILL AND LAWNMARKET

CASTLE HILL. The Scotch Whisky Experience at the **Scotch Whisky Heritage Centre,** 354 Castle Hill, provides a Disney-style 50min. tour through the "history and mystery" of Scotland's most famous export. *(Open daily 9:45am-5:30pm; reduced winter hours. Tours every 15min. £8, concessions £5.50, children £4.25.)* Across the street, the **Outlook Tower** affords city views from a rooftop terrace. Its 150-year-old **camera obscura** captures a moving image of the streets below, while its various illusionary exhibits will certainly entertain. *(Open daily Apr.-June and Sept.-Oct. 9:30am-6pm; July-Aug. 9:30am-7:30pm; Nov.-Mar. 10am-5pm. £6, concessions £4.70, children £3.80.)*

GLADSTONE'S LAND. Staffed with knowledgeable guides, the oldest surviving house on the Royal Mile (c. 1617) has been carefully preserved, with hand-painted ceilings and a fine collection of 17th-century Dutch art. *(477b Lawnmarket. ☎226 5856. Open Apr.-Oct. M-Sa 10am-5pm, Su 2-5pm. £5, concessions £3.75.)*

WRITER'S MUSEUM. Follow the inspirational quotations etched in the pavement to this tribute to literary personae, just off the Royal Mile down Lady Stair's Close. The museum contains memorabilia and manuscripts from to three of Scotland's greatest wordsmiths—Robert Burns, Sir Walter Scott, and Robert Louis Stevenson. *(Lawnmarket. ☎529 4901. Open M-Sa 10am-5pm; during Festival also Su 2-5pm. Free.)*

THE ROYAL MILE: HIGH STREET

HIGH KIRK OF ST. GILES. The kirk is Scotland's principal church, sometimes known as **St. Giles Cathedral.** From its pulpit, reformer John Knox delivered the sermons that drove the Catholic Mary, Queen of Scots, into exile. Spectacular stained-glass windows illuminate the structure, whose crown spire is one of Edinburgh's hallmarks. Most of the present cathedral was built in the 15th century, with restorations and additions ongoing since, but parts of the kirk date as far back as 1126. The 20th-century **Thistle Chapel** honors the Most Ancient and Most Noble Order of the Thistle, Scotland's prestigious chivalric order. St. Giles is flanked on the east by the stone **Mercat Cross,** marking the site of the medieval market (hence, "mercat"), and on the west by the **Heart of Midlothian,** inlaid in the pavement. According to city legend, spitting on the Heart protects you from being

IN RECENT NEWS

PARLIAMENT WOES

Visitors to the palace of Holyrood-house in Edinburgh may notice a rather bizarre-looking modern building across the street. This edifice has already been a symbol, in its short history, of both Scotland's bright future and its deepest misgivings.

With a giant chunk of prime real estate, a team of international architects, and a huge budget, the Scottish Parliament building was to be an exuberant celebration of Scotland's new degree of independence. Then came delays, mishaps, unforeseen costs, and other issues. The just-finished building is three years behind schedule and almost £400 million over budget. Construction problems were at times flat-out embarrassing. In one famous incident, workers received the glass for the building's windows only to find that the plates were too big. Parliament, desperate to avoid further delays and expenditures, ordered that the windows be installed anyway. Architects have complained that the building's quality is being compromised by a "dash to finish" attitude. A panel has already been established to investigate what went wrong.

In the summer of 2004, the building was still swarming with workers. Officials claim that it will be ceremonially opened by the queen on October 9th. This is one stage that is guaranteed to run smoothly, as the queen lives just across the street.

hanged in the square. (Watch out for tour groups spitting en-masse.) The cathedral hosts free organ and choral concerts throughout the year. (Where Lawnmarket becomes High St. ☎225 4363. Open Easter to mid-Sept. M-F 9am-7pm, Sa 9am-5pm, Su 1-5pm; mid-Sept. to Easter M-Sa 9am-5pm, Su 1-5pm. Suggested donation £1.)

TRON KIRK. A block downhill from St. Giles rises the high-steepled Tron Kirk—built to deal with the overflow of 16th-century religious zealots from St. Giles. Today, it houses the Old Town Information Centre, inside the kirk beside an open archaeological dig, and is the focus of Edinburgh's Hogmanay celebrations. (Open daily Apr.-Oct. 10am-5:30pm; Nov.-Mar. noon-5pm; extended hours during Festival. Free.)

THE ROYAL MILE: CANONGATE

Canongate, the steep hill that constitutes the last segment of the Royal Mile, was once a separate burgh and part of an Augustinian abbey. Here, the Royal Mile's furious tourism and, not coincidentally, much of its appeal, begins to dwindle.

CANONGATE KIRK. This 17th-century chapel is where royals used to worship when in residence. Adam Smith, founder of modern economics, lies in the slope to the left of the entrance. Down the hill from his grave, find the famous joint effort of three literary Roberts: Robert Louis Stevenson commemorated a monument erected here by Robert Burns in memory of Robert Fergusson. (Open Apr. to mid-Sept. M-F 9am-7pm, Sa 9am-5pm, Su 1-5pm; mid-Sept. to Mar. M-Sa 9am-5pm, Su 1-5pm. Free.)

SCOTTISH POETRY LIBRARY. A relaxing refuge from the main tourist drag in an award-winning piece of expansive modern architecture, the library treasures a fine collection of Scottish and international poetry. (5 Crichton's Close. ☎557 2876. Open M-F noon-6pm, Sa noon-4pm; during Festival M-F 11am-6pm, Sa 1-5pm. Free.)

HOLYROOD

PALACE OF HOLYROODHOUSE. This Stewart palace at the base of the Royal Mile remains Queen Elizabeth II's official Scottish residence. As a result, only parts of the ornate interior are open to the public, though these still merit a visit. Once home to Mary, Queen of Scots, whose bedchamber is on display, the palace is every bit a royal residence. Dozens of portraits inside the Great Gallery confirm its proud history. On the palace grounds lie the 12th-century ruins of Holyrood Abbey, built by David I in 1128 and ransacked during the Reformation. Only a single doorway remains from the original construction; most of the ruins date from the 13th century. Located in a recently renovated 17th-century schoolhouse near the palace entrance is the **Queen's Gallery**, which displays rotating exhibits from the royal art collection. *(At the bottom of the Royal Mile. ☎556 5100. Open daily Apr.-Oct. 9:30am-6pm; Nov.-Mar. M-Sa 9:30am-4:30pm. Last admission 45min. before close. No admission while royals are in residence (often late May to early July). £8, concessions £6.50, children £4, families £20. Queen's Gallery £5/£4/£3/ £13. Joint £11/£9/£5.50/£27.50. Free audio guide.)*

HOLYROOD SCOTTISH PARLIAMENT BUILDING. The new Scottish Parliament Building (see **Parliament Woes,** left), designed by the late Catalan architect Enric Miralles, is scheduled to open—after years of controversy and massive budget overruns—in October 2004. *(☎348 5000; www.scottish.parliament.uk. Open Tu-Th 9am-7pm; M, F-Su 10am-4pm. Guided tours will be available; check their website for the latest.)*

ELSEWHERE IN THE OLD TOWN

GREYFRIARS TOLBOOTH AND HIGHLAND KIRK. Off George IV Bridge, the 17th-century kirk rests in a quiet churchyard that, while lovely, is estimated to contain 250,000 bodies and has long been considered haunted. A few centuries ago, the infamous body-snatchers Burke and Hare dug up precious corpses here before resorting to outright murder in order to keep the Edinburgh Medical School well-supplied. A far more endearing claim to fame is the loyal pooch Greyfriars Bobby, whose much-photographed statue sits at the southwestern corner of George IV Bridge in front of the kirkyard's gates. *(Beyond the gates atop Candlemakers Row. ☎225 1900. English services 11am, Gaelic services Su 12:30pm. Open Apr.-Oct. M-F 10:30am-4:30pm, Sa 10:30am-2:30pm; Nov.-Mar. Th 1:30-3:30pm. Free.)*

NATIONAL LIBRARY OF SCOTLAND. The library rotates exhibitions from its vast archives, which include a Gutenberg Bible, the last letter of Mary, Queen of Scots, and the only surviving copy of *The Wallace*, a wildly popular epic poem which inspired a certain wildly popular Hollywood movie. *(George IV Bridge. ☎226 4531. Open M-F 9:30am-8:30pm, Sa 9:30am-1pm, Su 2-5pm; during Festival until 8:30pm. Free.)*

THE NEW TOWN

Edinburgh's New Town is a masterpiece of Georgian design. James Craig, a 23-year-old architect, won the city-planning contest in 1767, and his rectangular grid of three parallel streets (**Queen, George,** and **Princes**) linking two large squares (**Charlotte** and **St. Andrew**) reflects the Scottish Enlightenment's belief

THE LOCAL STORY

GREYFRIARS BOBBY

Undoubtedly the most famous resident of the Greyfriars Tolbooth and Highland Kirk's ancient cemetery is a certain John Gray. During the first night following his burial in 1858, Gray's scruffy Skye terrier, Bobby, was seen to lie upon his master's grave. The next night Bobby returned and again held vigil, as he would every night for the next 14 years. As word spread of this extraordinary display of devotion and loyalty, the legend of Greyfriars Bobby became forever a part of Edinburgh lore.

After living to the age of 16, Greyfriars Bobby finally passed away, having spent all but two of his years guarding the tombstone. To honor his loyalty, the city erected a statue of the dog and buried him near his beloved master in the very same kirk.

Over the years this sweet story has found its way into numerous books and even a Disney film. The statue, which sits at the intersection of George IV Bridge and Candlemaker Row, is still the most photographed statue in Scotland. Still, there are those who have their doubts about this touching saga. Some claim that the grave that Bobby so admirably watched over belonged in fact to another John Gray and not his master. Others claim that the dog's real affection was for a nearby bakery. Such spoilsports have been unsuccessful in tarnishing the legend, however, which is still alive and well.

in order. Queen St. and Princes St., the outer streets, were built up on only one side to allow views of the Firth of Forth and the Old Town. Princes St., Edinburgh's main shopping drag, is also home to the venerable **Jenner's,** the Harrod's of Scotland. (☎225 2442. *Open M-Sa 9am-6pm, Su 11am-5pm. AmEx/MC/V.*) On your way out, wander through Charlotte Sq., Edinburgh's most elegant 18th-century plaza.

WALTER SCOTT MONUMENT. Statues of Sir Walter and his dog preside inside the spire of this Gothic "steeple without a church." Climb 287 winding steps past the carved figures of 64 of Scott's most famous characters to reach the top. There you are rewarded with an eagle's-eye view of Princes St., the castle, and the surrounding city. (*Princes St. between The Mound and Waverley Bridge.* ☎529 4068. *Open Mar.-Oct. M-Sa 9am-6pm, Su 10am-6pm; Nov.-Feb. until 3pm. £2.50.*)

GEORGIAN HOUSE. Guides staff each room of this elegantly restored home, which provides a fair picture of how Edinburgh's elite lived 200 years ago during the reign of George III. (*7 Charlotte Sq.* ☎226 3318. *Open daily Mar. and Nov.-Dec. 11am-3pm; Apr.-Oct. 10am-5pm. Last admission 30min. before close. £5, concessions £3.75.*)

CALTON HILL. This somewhat neglected hill at the eastern end of New Town provides a fine view of the city and the Firth of Forth. Climb 143 steps inside the castellated **Nelson Monument,** built in 1807 in memory of the great admiral and the Battle of Trafalgar. (☎556 2716. *Open Apr.-Sept. M 1-6pm, Tu-Sa 10am-6pm; Oct.-Mar. M-Sa 10am-3pm. £2.*) The hilltop grounds are also home to the old **City Observatory** (1818) and the **National Monument** (1822), affectionately known as "Edinburgh's Disgrace." The structure, an ersatz Parthenon designed to commemorate those killed in the Napoleonic Wars, was scrapped when civic coffers ran dry after a mere 12 columns were erected. For all its faults, it does give the town an ancient-looking "ruin"; watch the sun rise between its columns from Waverley Bridge in the spring.

BEYOND THE CITY CENTER

LEITH AND THE BRITANNIA. Two miles northeast of city center, **Leith** stands as Edinburgh's port on the Firth of Forth. Incorporated into the capital in 1920, the area went into steep decline following WWII. Since the 1980s, however, Leith has undergone a revival, its abandoned warehouses replaced (or at least supplemented) by upmarket flats, restaurants, and bars. The most ambitious building projects are along the waterfront; a prime example is the new **Ocean Terminal Shopping Centre.** Moored behind it is one of Edinburgh's top tourist attractions, the ■**Royal Yacht Britannia.** Used by the royal family from 1953 to 1997 (when the government decided it was too expensive and decommissioned it), *Britannia* sailed around the world on state visits and royal holidays before retiring here. Visitors can follow a free audio tour of the entire flagship, which remains exactly as it was when decommissioned. Highlights include the officers' mess, the royal apartments, and the gleaming engine room. (*Entrance on the Ocean Terminal's 3rd fl. Take bus #22 from Princes St. or #35 from the Royal Mile to Ocean Terminal, £1.* ☎555 5566. *Open daily Apr.-Sept. 9:30am-4:30pm; Oct.-Mar. 10am-3:30pm. £8.50, concessions £4.50.*)

DEAN VILLAGE. In the **Water of Leith** valley northwest of the city center, Dean Village was once a busy milling community. Many of the mills remain—some now converted into trendy apartments—and the result is one of the city's most desirable residential areas. The graceful sandstone **Dean Bridge,** a great feat of engineering when it opened in 1832, flies high above the river. A visit to this area might be combined with the **Scottish National Gallery of Modern Art** and **Dean Gallery** (p. 560), both 10min. west of Dean Village along the scenic **Water of Leith Walkway.** *(Walk north on Queensferry St. from the west end of Princes St. Buses #41 and 42 depart from The Mound.)*

CRAIGMILLAR CASTLE. This finely preserved 15th-century castle stands 3½ mi. southeast of central Edinburgh. Mary, Queen of Scots, fled here after the murder of her secretary at Holyroodhouse. While she was here, plans emerged for the murder of her second husband, Lord Darnley. *(Take bus #2, 14 or 32 from Princes St. to the corner of Old Dalkeith Rd. and Craigmillar Castle Rd., then walk 10min. up the castle road. ☎661 4445. Open daily Apr.-Sept. 9:30am-6pm; Oct.-Mar. M-W and Sa 9:30am-4:30pm, Th 9:30am-1pm, Su 2pm-4:30pm. £2.50, seniors £1.90, children 75p.)*

EDINBURGH ZOO. At long last, your search for the world's largest penguin pool has come to an end. You'll find it along with exhibits featuring some 1000 other animals, 2½ mi. west of the city center. The penguins go for a daily waddle around 2:15pm. *(Take bus #12, 26, or 31 westbound from Princes St. ☎334 9171. Open daily Apr.-Sept. 9am-6pm; Oct.-Mar. 9am-4:30pm. £8.50, children and seniors £5.50.)*

GARDENS AND PARKS

HOLYROOD PARK. You can easily visit Edinburgh and remain unaware of the natural wilderness that sits just off the eastern end of the Royal Mile. A true city oasis, Holyrood Park is replete with hills, moorland, and lochs. At 823 ft., ◪**Arthur's Seat,** the park's highest point, affords stunning views of the city and countryside, extending to the Highlands. Considered a holy place by the Picts, Arthur's Seat is probably derived from "Ard-na-Saigheid," Gaelic for "the height of the flight of arrows." Traces of forts and Bronze Age terraces dot the surrounding hillside. From the Palace of Holyroodhouse, the walk to the summit takes about 45min. **Queen's Drive** circles the park and intersects with Holyrood Rd. by the palace.

PRINCES STREET GARDENS. Located directly in the city center and affording fantastic views of Old Town and the castle, this lush park is on the site of now-drained Nor' Loch, where Edinburghers used to drown their accused witches. The Loch has been replaced with an impeccably manicured lawn, stone fountains, winding avenues lined with benches, and enough shady trees to provide shelter from the Scottish "sun." On a fine summer day all of Edinburgh eats lunch here.

ROYAL BOTANIC GARDENS. Edinburgh's herbaceous oasis has plants from around the world. Guided tours wander across the lush grounds and massive greenhouses crammed with orchids, tree ferns, and towering palms. *(Inverleith Row. Take bus #23 or 27 from Hanover St. ☎552 7171. Open daily Apr.-Sept. 10am-7pm; Mar. and Oct. 10am-6pm; Nov.-Feb. 10am-4pm. Free.)*

🏛 MUSEUMS AND GALLERIES

NATIONAL GALLERIES OF SCOTLAND

Edinburgh's four major galleries form an elite group, all excellent collections connected by a free hourly shuttle. (☎624 6200. All open daily 10am-5pm, during festival 10am-6pm, Th until 7pm. All free.)

◪ **NATIONAL GALLERY OF SCOTLAND.** Housed in a grand 19th-century building designed by William Playfair, this compact gallery has a superb collection of works by Renaissance, Romantic, and Impressionist masters including Raphael, Titian, Gauguin, Degas, and Monet. Don't miss the octagonal room, which displays Poussin's entire *Seven Sacraments*. The basement houses a selection of Scottish art. *(On The Mound between the 2 halves of the Princes St. Gardens.)* Reopened in 2003, the **Royal Academy** hosts exhibits from the National Gallery while also running a high-profile show of its own each summer. *(At the corner of The Mound and Princes St.)*

SCOTTISH NATIONAL PORTRAIT GALLERY. Set in an august red brick building, the gallery displays the faces of the famous men and women who have shaped Scotland's history. Military, political and intellectual figures are all represented, including the definitive portraits of wordsmith Robert Louis Stevenson, renegade Bonnie Prince Charlie, and royal troublemaker Mary, Queen of Scots. The gallery also hosts excellent visiting exhibitions. *(1 Queen St., north of St. Andrew Sq.)*

SCOTTISH NATIONAL GALLERY OF MODERN ART. In the west end of town, this permanent collection includes works by Braque, Matisse, and Picasso. The newly-completed landscaping in front of the museum, a bizarre spiral of grass set into a pond, represents the concepts of chaos theory with dirt and greenery. *(75 Belford Rd. Take the free shuttle, bus #13 from George St., or walk along the Water of Leith Walkway.)*

DEAN GALLERY. The newest addition to the National Galleries is dedicated to Surrealist and Dadaist art. The gallery owes much of its fine collection to the landmark sculptor Eduardo Paolozzi, whose towering, three-story statue, *Vulcan*, stands at the main entrance. Other highlights include rotating, high-profile exhibitions and a recreation of Paolozzi's studio loft that overflows with his work. *(73 Belford Rd., across from the Gallery of Modern Art. Special exhibits £3.50.)*

OTHER MUSEUMS AND GALLERIES

MUSEUM OF SCOTLAND AND ROYAL MUSEUM. The superbly designed ▨ **Museum of Scotland,** opened in 1998, traces the whole of Scottish history through an impressive collection of treasured objects and decorative art spanning eight levels. Highlights include the working Corliss Steam Engine and the Maiden, Edinburgh's pre-French Revolution guillotine, used on High St. around 1565. Gallery tours and audio guides in various languages are free. The rooftop terrace provides a 360° view of the city. Less modern and more motley (though still fascinating), the **Royal Museum** has exhibits on natural history, European Art, and Ancient Egypt, to name just a few. Watch the **Millennium Clock** chime every hour, a towering and ghoulish display of mechanized figures that represent the darker periods in the last millennium of human history. *(Chambers St. Museum of Scotland ☎247 4422. Royal Museum ☎247 4219. Both open M and W-Sa 10am-5pm, Tu 10am-8pm, Su noon-5pm. Free.)*

OUR DYNAMIC EARTH. Edinburgh is proud of this glitzy, high-tech lesson in geology. Part amusement park, part science experiment, it appeals mainly to young children. Look for the white tent-like structure next to Holyroodhouse. *(Holyrood Rd. ☎550 7800. Open daily Apr.-Oct. 10am-5pm; July-Aug. 10am-6pm; Nov.-Mar. W-Su 10am-5pm, last entry 1hr. before closing. £9, concessions £6.50, children £5.45, families £24.50.)*

OTHER MUSEUMS. The Museum of Childhood, 42 High St., displays an array of toys, including doll houses, toy soldiers, and trains. *(☎529 4142. Open M-Sa 10am-5pm; during Festival also Su noon-5pm. Free.)* The picturesque **John Knox House,** 43 High St., offers an engaging look at former inhabitants John Knox and James Mossman, and the Protestant-Catholic conflicts that engulfed them. *(☎556 9579. Due to reopen Easter 2005 after a major renovation. Open M-Sa 10am-4:30pm; July-Aug. also Su noon-5pm. £2.25, concessions £1.75, children 75p.)* **Canongate Tolbooth** (c.1591), with a beautiful clock face projecting over the Royal Mile, once served as a prison and gallows for "elite" criminals. Now it houses **The People's Story Museum,** 163 Canongate, an eye-opening look at "the ordinary people of Edinburgh." *(☎529 4057. Open M-Sa 10am-5pm, during Festival also Su 2-5pm. Free.)* Across the street in 16th-century Huntly House, the

Museum of Edinburgh, 142 Canongate, charts the city's advance from prehistory to the present, with a hodgepodge of artifacts such as the original 1638 National Covenant. (☎529 4143. *Open M-Sa 10am-5pm; during Festival also Su 2-5pm. Free.*) **SMALLER ART GALLERIES.** The **City Art Centre,** 2 Market St., houses the city's collection of modern Scottish work and hosts international exhibitions. (☎529 3993. *Open M-Sa 10am-5pm; Su noon-5pm. £5, concessions £3.50.*) Across the street, the **Fruitmarket Gallery,** Market St., shows Scottish and world art. (☎225 2383; *www.fruitmarket.co.uk. Open M-Sa 11am-6pm, Su noon-5pm. Free.*)

🎵 NIGHTLIFE

PUBS

Pubs on the **Royal Mile** tend to attract a mixed crowd of old and young, tourist and local. Students and backpackers gather in force each night in the **Old Town.** Casual pub-goers groove to live music on **Grassmarket, Candlemaker Row, and Victoria Street.** The New Town also has its share of worthy watering-holes, some historical, and most strung along **Rose Street,** parallel to Princes St. Gay-friendly **Broughton Street** is increasingly popular for nightlife, though its pubs are more trendy than traditional. No matter where you are, you'll usually have to start thinking about finishing your drink somewhere between 11pm and 1am, 3am during the Festival.

🎵 **The Tron,** 9 Hunter Sq. (☎226 0931), behind the Tron Kirk. Wildly popular. Students and hostelers get £1 drinks on W nights, burgers and a pint all the time for £4.50. Downstairs is a mix of alcoves and pool tables. Frequent live music. Open M-Sa 11:30am-1am, Su 12:30pm-1am; 8:30am-3am during festival. Food served noon-8pm.

The Globe, 13 Niddry St. (☎557 4670). This backpacker's abode is recommended up and down the Royal Mile. Airs international sports, hosts DJs, and holds quiz nights and karaoke. Open M-F 4pm-1am, Sa noon-1am, Su 12:30pm-1am, 3am during festival.

The Three Sisters, 139 Cowgate (☎622 6801). Loads of space for dancing, drinking, and chilling. Attracts a young crowd to its 3 bars (Irish, Gothic, and Style). Beer garden and barbecue sees close to 1000 pass through on Sa nights. Open daily 9am-1am.

Finnegan's Wake, 9b Victoria St. (☎226 3816). Drink the Irish way with several stouts on tap, road signs from Cork, and live Irish music every weekend. During the summer, broadcasts live Gaelic football and hurling on the big screen. Open daily 1pm-1am.

The Abbotsford, 3 Rose St. (☎225 5276). Probably the most authentic of the Rose St. pubs. Built in 1902, it retains the era's elegant ambience with an ornate wooden bar. Open daily 11am-11pm. Above-average grub served noon-2:30pm and 5:30-10pm.

Jolly Judge, 7 James Ct. (☎225 2669). Hidden down a close just off the Royal Mile, with a great, cozy atmosphere. Open M-Th and Su noon-11pm, F-Sa until midnight.

Biddy Mulligans, 94-96 Grassmarket (☎220 1246). Kick things off early at this Irish-themed pub, which serves big breakfasts. Open daily 9am-1am. Food served until 9pm.

The World's End, 2-8 High St. (☎556 3628), at the corner of St. Mary's St. Traditional and frequented by locals. Pub food in 3 sizes: wee, not so wee, and friggin' huge. Open M-F 11am-1am, Sa-Su 10am-1am.

CLUBS

Edinburgh may be best known for its pubs, but the club scene is none too shabby. It is, however, in constant flux, with venues continuously closing down and reopening under new management—you're best off consulting *The List* (£2.20), a comprehensive biweekly guide to events, available from any local newsagent. Clubs cluster around the city's historically disreputable **Cowgate,** just downhill

EDINBURGH UNIVERSITY PUB CRAWL

Students at the prestigious University of Edinburgh enjoy intellectual rigor and scholarly debates. And beer. Lots and lots of beer. With *Let's Go's* guide to the students' favorite watering holes, you too can follow the path that so many a bright young pupil in this city has identified as the real avenue to enlightenment.

1 Start off at **Sandy Bell's**, where live folk music every night, televised sport, and a tall pint will prime you for the evening ahead. (25 Forrest Rd. ☎225 2751. Open daily 11am-1am.)

2 **Greyfriars Bobby.** Yup, it's a tourist trap. But this pup-named pub is also a favorite with students for a pint and a cheap bar meal. (34 Candlemaker Row. ☎225 8328. Open daily 11am-1am.)

from and parallel to the Royal Mile, and most close at 3am, 5am during the Festival. Smart street-wear is necessary everywhere in Edinburgh.

Cabaret-Voltaire, 36-38 Blair St. (☎220 6176). With a wide range of live music, dance, and art, this innovative club knows how to throw a party. A great, smaller spot with a regular, friendly crowd. Cover free-£15.

Bongo Club, 14 New St. (☎558 7604), off Canongate. Particularly noted for its hip-hop, including the long running and immensely popular Messenger and Headspin nights, which run every other Sa. Cover free-£10.

The Venue, 17-23 Calton Rd. (☎557 3073). It's big. 3 dance floors run the whole musical gamut. Hosts live gigs; call ahead to get the lineup. Cover £2-8.

Faith, 207 Cowgate (☎225 9764). Mockingly located inside an old church, this purple-hued club specializes in R&B. Very popular Su Chocolate. Cover free-£6.

Po Na Na, 43b Frederick St., go down the steps to a yellow cartoon image of a man in a fez. (☎226 2224). Moroccan-themed, with parachute ceilings, red velvet couches, and an eclectic blend of disco, funk, and lounge. Cover £2-5, free before 11pm.

Gaia, 28 King Stables Rd. (☎229 9438). Popular with students. Plays chart, disco, and R&B. Theme nights include the raunchy Tu "Shagtag." Cover £3-4.

Opal Lounge, 51a George St. (☎226 2275). A great New Town spot that attracts a mixed crowd of smartly dressed backpackers, locals and students. DJs spin all day as the restaurant lounge morphs into a club around 9pm. Cover £3-5.

GAY AND LESBIAN NIGHTLIFE

The Broughton St. area of the New Town (better known as the **Broughton Triangle**) is the center of Edinburgh's gay community.

Planet Out, 6 Baxter's Pl. (☎524 0060; www.planetout.8m.com). Prepare for a wild night, especially on M when all drinks are £1.

C.C. Bloom's, 23-24 Greenside Pl. (☎556 9331), on Leith St. A super-friendly, super-fun gay club with no cover. Th and Su karaoke.

Blue Moon Cafe, 36 Broughton St. (☎557 0911), at the corner Barony St. A popular place with great food served until midnight.

Sala Cafe-Bar, 60 Broughton St. (☎478 7069). Formerly known as the Nexus. A relaxed atmosphere with regular live music and an eclectic menu (11am-11pm).

Ego, 14 Picardy Pl. (☎478 7434). Not strictly a gay club, but hosts several gay nights, including **Vibe** (every Tu) and **Blaze** (3 F per month). Cover £2-10.

🎭 ENTERTAINMENT

For all the latest listings, no one knows better than *The List* (£2.20).

THEATER AND FILM

Festival Theatre, 13-29 Nicholson St. (☎529 6000; www.eft.co.uk). Stages predominantly ballet and opera, turning entirely to the Festival in August. Box office open M-Sa 10am-6pm and before curtain. Tickets £8-52.

King's Theatre, 2 Leven St. Promotes serious and comedic fare, musicals, opera, and pantomime. Book through the Festival Theatre.

Royal Lyceum Theatre, 30 Grindlay St. (☎248 4848; www.lyceum.org.uk). The finest in Scottish, English, and international theater. Box office open M-Sa 10am-6pm; on performance nights until 8pm. Tickets £8-20, students half-price.

Traverse Theatre, 10 Cambridge St. (☎228 1404; www.traverse.co.uk). A real launching pad, this theater performs almost exclusively new drama with lots of local Scottish work in the mix. Box office open daily 10am-6pm.

Bedlam Theatre, 11b Bristo Pl. (☎225 9893). A university theater presenting excellent student productions ranging from comedy and drama to F night improv, all in a converted church. A Fringe Festival hotspot. Box office open M-Sa 10am-6pm. Tickets £4-5.

The Stand Comedy Club, 5 York Pl. (☎558 7272; www.thestand.co.uk). Acts every night and all day Su. Special 17-shows-per-day program for the Fringe Festival. Tickets £1-8.

The Filmhouse, 88 Lothian Rd. (☎228 2688). European and arthouse films, though quality Hollywood fare appears as well. Tickets £3.50-5.50. For mainstream cinema, try **Odeon,** 7 Clerk St. (☎667 0971), or **UGC Fountainpark,** Dundee St., Fountainbridge (bus #1, 28, 34, 35; ☎0870 902 0417).

LIVE MUSIC

Thanks to an abundance of university students who never let books get in the way of a good night out, Edinburgh's live music scene is alive and well. Excellent impromptu and professional folk sessions take place at pubs (p. 561), and many of the university houses sponsor live shows—look for flyers near Bristol Sq. Check out *The List* (£2.20). **Ripping Records,** 91 South Bridge (☎226 7010), sells tickets to rock, reggae, and pop performances. Both local and international jazz musicians perform at laid-back **Henry's Jazz Bar,** 8a Morrison St. (☎538 7385. Cover £5. Open

3 With its indoor waterfall, the sleek, trendy, and candlelit **Beluga Bar** is the spot for the stylish scholar set. (30a Chambers St. ☎624 4545. Open daily 9am-1am.)

4 **Oxygen Bar** has been around a while, but still cuts a cool profile with its smart decor spread over multiple levels. (3-5 Infirmary St. ☎557 9997. Open M-Sa 10am-1am, Su 11am-1am.)

5 At the **Brass Monkey,** kick back in the Persian rug-covered and pillow-lined cinema lounge, and enjoy one of Hollywood's finest. (14 Drummond St. ☎556 1961. Open daily 11am-1am.)

6 At the **Pear Tree House,** make the most of the elusive Scottish summer in the peaceful beer garden. (38 West Nicolson St. ☎667 7533. Open daily 11am-midnight, F-Sa until 1am.)

7 A popular, laid-back student hangout, **Negociants** is open late. It's also a great place to cure those late-night munchies—food is served until 2:15am. (45-47 Lothian St. ☎225 6313. Open M-Sa 9am-3am, Su 10am-3am.)

8 Another late night spot that serves food into tomorrow, **Favorit** stays open 24hr. during Festival. (19-21 Teviot Pl. ☎220 6880. Open daily 8am-3am.)

daily 8pm-3am.) **The Venue** (p. 562) and **The Liquid Room,** 9c Victoria St. (☎225 2528; www.liquidroom.com), host rock and progressive shows. **Whistle Binkie's,** 4-6 South Bridge, is a subterranean pub with two live music shows every night. (☎557 5114. Open daily until 3am.) For traditional or folk music, head for **The Royal Oak,** 1 Infirmary St., which hosts free shows every night and welcomes you to join in. (☎557 2976. Open daily until 2am. Live music starts 7pm.)

🌸 FESTIVALS

Edinburgh has special events year-round, but the real show is in August, when it's *the* place to be in Europe. Prices rise, pubs and restaurants stay open later than late (some simply don't close), and street performers have the run of the place. What's commonly referred to as "the Festival" actually encompasses a number of independently organized events. For more information and links to all the separate festivals, check out www.edinburghfestivals.co.uk.

■ EDINBURGH INTERNATIONAL FESTIVAL. Begun in 1947, the **Edinburgh International Festival** attracts the top performers from around the globe, mainly in classical music, ballet, opera, and drama. The most popular single event is the festival's grand finale: a spectacular **Fireworks Concert** with pyrotechnics choreographed to orchestral music. While tickets to some of the headliner acts are made available only months after the previous year's festival, most go on sale in early April, and a full program is published by then. The biggest events do sell out well in advance, though at least 50 tickets for major events are held and sold on the day of the performance at the venue (queue early). Throughout the festival, unsold tickets may be purchased at **The Hub** or at the door an hour prior to showtime. Selected shows are half-price on the day of performance. (*Aug. 14-Sept. 3 in 2005. Bookings can be made by post, phone, fax, web, or in person at The Hub, Edinburgh's Festival Centre, Castlehill, Edinburgh EH1 2NE. ☎473 2000; www.eif.co.uk. Open M-Sa from early Apr.; daily from late July. Tickets £7-57, students and children half-price.*)

■ EDINBURGH FESTIVAL FRINGE. Longer and more informal than the International Festival, the *Guinness Book of World Records* confirms the Fringe as the world's biggest arts festival, showcasing everything from Shakespeare to coconut-juggling dwarves. It began in 1947, when eight theater companies arrived to Edinburgh uninvited, and had to book "fringe" venues to perform. Today, the Fringe Association has its own central office and arguably draws more visitors to Edinburgh than any other event or sight. Anyone who can afford the small registration fee can perform, meaning this orgy of eccentricity attracts a multitude of independent acts—expect both the good and the not-so-good—and guarantees a wild month in Edinburgh year after year. (*Aug. 7-29 in 2005. ☎226 0026; www.edfringe.com. Tickets available online, by phone, in person, or by post at The Fringe Office, 180 High St., Edinburgh EH1 1QS. Open M-F 10am-5pm; during festival daily 10am-9pm. Tickets free to 25.*)

HOGMANAY. The party doesn't stop despite the long, dark winter. The light at the end of the tunnel is the insanity of **Hogmanay,** Edinburgh's traditional New Year's Eve festival, a serious street party with a week of associated events. Hogmanay has deep pagan roots and is observed all over Scotland—it celebrates the turn of the calendar and the return of the sun. It also celebrates the consumption of copious amounts of alcohol. For more information, including how to get tickets, inquire at The Hub or check out www.edinburghshogmanay.org.

OTHER SUMMER FESTIVALS. The following festivities are just a few of the events that take place during the five-week period surrounding the Festival in August. **Military Tattoo** is a magnificent spectacle of military bands, bagpipes, and drums performed before the gates of the castle. (*Tattoo Ticket Sale Office, 33-34 Market St., Edinburgh EH1 1QB. ☎225 1188; www.edintattoo.co.uk. Aug. 5-27 in 2005. Book well in advance. Tickets £9-31.*) One highlight of the **Jazz and Blues Festival** is the free **Jazz on a Summer's Day** in Ross Theatre. (*www.jazzmusic.co.uk. Late July in 2005. Program available in June; bookings by phone, web, or at The Hub. Tickets £5-27.50.*) Charlotte Sq. Gardens host the **International Book Festival,** Europe's largest book celebration, in early and mid-August. (*Scottish Book Centre, 137 Dundee St. ☎228 5444; www.edbookfest.co.uk. Program available mid-June. Tickets £3-9; some free events.*) The **International Film Festival** occurs during the 2nd and 3rd weeks of August. (*Film Festival, The Filmhouse, 88 Lothian Rd. ☎229 2550; www.edfilmfest.org.uk. Box office sells tickets from late July.*)

🔌 DAYTRIPS

SOUTH QUEENSFERRY

From Edinburgh, take First Edinburgh bus #43 from the eastern end of Princes St. (35mins., frequent), or hop a train to nearby Dalmeny.

8 mi. west of central Edinburgh, the town of South Queensferry lies at the narrowest part of the Firth of Forth, where two bridges—the **Forth Road Bridge** and the splendid **Forth Rail Bridge**—cross the waterway. In town center, along High St., the **Queensferry Museum** catalogues the history of the bridges and the community. (☎225 3858. Open M and Th-Sa 10am-1pm and 2:15-5pm, Su noon-5pm. Free.) From Hawes Pier, under the Forth Rail Bridge, the **Maid of the Forth** ferries to Inchcolm Island, site of the wonderfully preserved 12th-century **Inchcolm Abbey.** (Ferry ☎331 4857. Runs daily mid-July to early Sept.; Apr.-June and Oct. Sa-Su. Roundtrip ticket includes admission. £11.50, concessions £9.50, children £4.50.)

Two miles west of South Queensferry stands **Hopetoun House.** Begun around 1700 and designed by Sir William Bruce (also responsible for Holyroodhouse), it offers lovely views of the Forth. (☎0131 331 2451. Open daily Apr.-Sept. 10am-5:30pm; last admission 4:30pm. £6.50, concessions £5.50, children £3.50.) No public transport runs to Hopetoun; take a **taxi** from South Queensferry.

ROSLIN

From Edinburgh, take bus #15A from St. Andrew Sq. (40min.)

The exotic stone carvings of 🔌**Rosslyn Chapel,** in the village of Roslin, 7 mi. south of Edinburgh, raised eyebrows in 15th-century Scotland. Filled with occult symbols, the chapel became important to the Knights Templar and is one of the many British sites claiming to have the Holy Grail stashed somewhere. Its mention in Dan Brown's bestseller *The Da Vinci Code* has recently led thousands of armchair Grail-hunters to its intricately carved walls. The most famous part of the church is the pier known as the **Apprentice Pillar,** supposedly the work of an apprentice killed by the jealous master mason. Outside the chapel, footpaths lead to the ruined **Roslin Castle** in peaceful Roslin Glen. (☎0131 440 2159. Chapel open M-Sa 10am-5pm, Su noon-4:45pm. £5, concessions £4, children £1.)

THE BORDERS

From the time the Roman legions first arrived in the 2nd century until the failure of the Jacobite Rebellion finally cemented English sovereignty, the Borders were caught in a violent tug-of-war between Scotland and England. Present-day Borderers suffer no crisis of identity: grooms wear tartan kilts at their weddings and the blue-and-white-cross of St. Andrew reigns over the Union Jack. Relics of past strife remain in the fortified houses dotting the landscape and the spectacular abbey ruins at Dryburgh, Jedburgh, Kelso, and Melrose. These grim reminders of war stand in contrast to a countryside where fantastic hill paths reward walkers and cyclists and where gentle rivers once inspired the poetry of Sir Walter Scott.

TRANSPORTATION

There are no **trains** in the Borders, but **buses** are frequent. The main travel hub of the Borders is tiny **Galashiels**, or "Gala." (☎01896 752 237. Bus station open M-F 9am-12:30pm and 1:30-5pm. Luggage storage 50p.) **First** (☎01896 752 237) is the largest of several operators. Ask at TICs for the Scottish Borders Council's *Central Borders Travel Guide*, which contains all of the area bus schedules. Schedules can also be obtained by calling **Traveline** (☎0870 608 2608). Inquire about worthwhile day passes. Bus #23 runs from **Berwick** to **Kelso** (1hr.; M-F 5 per day, Sa 6 per day, Su 3 per day), while #60 (M-F 10 per day, Sa-Su 6 per day) goes from Berwick to **Galashiels** (1¾hr.) via **Melrose** (1½hr.). The following routes depart from **Edinburgh:** #62 (every hr.) to **Peebles** (1hr.), **Galashiels** (1¾hr.), **Melrose** (2¼hr.) and **Kelso** (2¾hr.); #29 to **Jedburgh** (2hr.; M-F 5 per day, Sa-Su 3 per day); #30 to **Kelso** (2hr.; M-Sa 9 per day, Su 3 per day). First #131 (1 per day) and **National Express** #383 (1 per day) head from Edinburgh to **Newcastle** via **Galashiels, Melrose,** and **Jedburgh.** Limited-stop bus #95/X95 (8 per day) travels from **Edinburgh** to **Carlisle** (3½hr.) via **Galashiels** (1¼hr.). For additional travel between Borders towns, #68/71 travels from **Galashiels** to **Jedburgh** (1½hr.) via **Melrose** (15min.).

HIKING AND OUTDOORS

The Borders welcome hikers of all levels; take a late afternoon stroll in the hills or wander the wilds for days at a time. The valley of the **River Tweed** cuts through the heart of the region for almost 100 mi., offering many beautiful stretches for a day's trek. At the river's source in the west, the **Tweedsmuirs** provide more difficult terrain. In the north of the Borders the **Moorfoots** and **Lammermuir** hills are well-suited to the country rambler and feature fine panoramic views. In addition to the many short walks that often depart from its towns, two major long-distance paths cross the Borders. Marked by a thistle in a hexagon symbol, the **Southern Upland Way** winds through the region for 82 mi., passing near **Galashiels** and **Melrose** on its route to the sea. **Saint Cuthbert's Way** runs 62 mi. from **Melrose** to Holy Island on the English coast and is marked by a simple cross. The Borders are extensively covered by Ordnance Survey Landranger (#72-75, 79, 80; £6) and Explorer (#330, 331, 336-340, 346; £7) maps, which are a necessity if you plan to strike off the beaten path. Upon arriving in the Borders grab a copy of the superb *Walking the Scottish Borders* (free) at any TIC, which details 30 day walks throughout the area.

The Borders can also cater to both on- and off-trail **bikers.** A number of well-maintained and well-marked trails cross the region including the **Tweed Cycleway,** a 90 mi. route that hugs the Tweed River from Biggar to Berwick, and the **Four Abbeys Cycle Route** that connects the abbeys at Melrose, Dryburgh, Jedburgh, and Kelso. The 250 mi. **Borderloop** and its many side paths will satisfy those looking for a more strenuous route. *Cycling in the Scottish Borders* (free at TIC's) outlines these major routes and 20 shorter trails, lists local cycle shops, and dispenses good advice. The *Scottish Borders* series also offers guides to golfing and fishing.

⌐ ACCOMMODATIONS

TICs can help you find a bed, usually for a 10% deposit. For advance bookings call Scottish Borders Customer Service Centre (☎0870 608 0404). The following **SYHA** hostels in the Borders are strategically dispersed—a fourth is in **Melrose** (p. 567). All have a 10:30am-5pm lockout, and all are only open Apr.-Sept.

Broadmeadows (☎0871 330 8507), 5 mi. west of Selkirk off the A708 and 1¼ mi. south of the Southern Upland Way. The first SYHA hostel (opened 1931), close to the Tweedsmuir Hills. 28 beds. Dorms £10.50, under 18 £8. Cash only. ❶

Coldingham (☎01890 771 298), a 20min. walk from Coldingham at St. Abbs Head, 5min. from the ocean. 40 beds. Dorms £11, under 18 £8.50. MC/V. ❶

Kirk Yetholm (☎0870 004 1132), at the junction of the B6352 and B6401, near Kelso. Bus #81 runs from Kelso (20 min.; M-Sa 7 per day, Su 3 per day). Watch hikers collapse at the end of the Pennine Way. 20 beds. Dorms £10, under 18 £8. Cash only. ❶

MELROSE ☎01896

The loveliest of the region's towns, Melrose draws visitors mainly to its abbey. The town is within convenient reach of Dryburgh Abbey and Abbotsford, Sir Walter Scott's country home. A stop on the **Four Abbeys Cycle Route,** Melrose is also the start of **Saint Cuthbert's Way** and lies near both the **Southern Upland Way** and **Tweed Cycleway,** making it the best base camp for outdoor activities in the Borders. The town's centerpiece, ⊠**Melrose Abbey** dates to the 12th century, though it was later remade in an ornate Gothic style after a particularly harsh thrashing by the English. Search the grounds for the tombstone marking Robert the Bruce's embalmed heart. Among the abbey's many gargoyles, a bagpipe-playing pig and winged cow adorn the south wall. (☎822 562. Open daily Apr.-Sept. 9:30am-6:30pm; Oct.-Mar. M-Sa 9:30am-4:30pm, Su 2-4:30pm. £3.50, seniors £2.50, children £1.20.) Admission to the abbey includes the **Abbey Museum,** which displays objects unearthed from the abbey and regional Roman forts. It also details Sir Walter Scott's life, death, and poetic dishonesty. Come, see, and briskly conquer the one-room **Trimontium Exhibition,** in Market Sq, a quirky jumble of a museum packed to the gills with just about anything relating to Roman Scotland. (☎822 651. Open daily Apr.-Oct. 10:30am-4:30pm. £1.50, concessions £1, families £4.) The Roman fort featured in the museum spanned the three volcanic summits of the **Eildon Hills,** which tower above the town (guided walks to the fort leave from the museum Tu, Th 1:30pm). Legend has it that King Arthur and his knights lie in an enchanted sleep in a cavern beneath the hills and will wake when the country needs saving. (That is, if they're not in Wales, Glastonbury, or any of the other places making similar claims.) The bare peaks are the most distinctive features in the area, and they afford fabulous views of the town to those willing to make the climb. The relatively light **Eildon Hills Walk** (4 mi.) leaves right from the abbey.

Buses to Melrose stop in Market Sq. Beside the River Tweed, **Active Sports,** Annay Rd., **rents bikes** and leads river trips. (☎822 452. Bikes £15 per day. Open daily 9am-9pm. Take the road going out of town past the Abbey and bear left at the fork, heading towards the footbridge over the river.) The **Tourist Information Centre** is across from the abbey on, appropriately, Abbey St. (☎0870 608 0404. Open July-Aug. M-Sa 9:30am-5:30pm, Su 10am-2pm; June and Sept. M-Sa 9:30am-5pm, Su 10am-2pm; Oct. M-Sa 10am-4pm, Su 10am-1pm; Apr.-May M-Sa 10am-5pm, Su 10am-2pm; Nov.-Mar. M-Sa 10am-2pm.) Get free **Internet access** at the **Melrose Library,** Market Sq. (☎823 052; open M and W 10am-1pm and 2:30-5pm, F 2:30-5pm and 5:30-7pm); and send postcards from the **post office,** Buccleuch St. (☎822 040; open M-F 9am-1pm and 2-5:30pm, Sa 9am-12:30pm.) **Post Code:** TD6 9LE.

With a convenient location close to the town center and abbey ruins, the ⬛SYHA Melrose ❶, off High Rd., resembles a stately manor more than a backpackers' abode, with an excellent kitchen, laundry, and Internet access. Some rooms even have views of the Abbey, which is lit at night and makes a haunting spectacle as it looms behind the trees. (☎822 521. Reception 7am-11pm. Curfew 11:30pm. Dorms £10-12, under 18 £8-10. From Market Pl., follow the footpath between the fishmonger and the Ship Inn. Bear right going through the parking lot. MC/V.) Braidwood B&B ❸, Buccleuch St., strikes a good balance between cost and comfort. (☎822 488. From £23 per person. No smoking. Cash only.) Camp at the deluxe Gibson Park Caravan Club Park ❶, off High St., which provides clean facilities in a central location. (☎822 969. Open June-Sept. £4.80. MC/V.) Walters, Market Sq., sells groceries. (Open M-Sa 7am-10pm, Su 8am-10pm.)

⯅ DAYTRIPS FROM MELROSE

⬛ **DRYBURGH ABBEY.** Those with the willingness to walk can reach secluded Dryburgh Abbey, whose serene grounds host extensive ruins and the graves of Sir Walter Scott and WWI Field Marshall Earl Haig. Dryburgh's secluded location sets it apart from the other Border Abbeys, and the sense of tranquility that permeates the crumbling ruins makes it well worth the effort to get there. Its views of the Tweed Valley are among the best around and were favored by Sir Walter. Built in 1150, the abbey was inhabited by Premonstratensian monks for nearly two centuries. When Edward II began removing his English troops from Scotland in 1322, the abbey's monks prematurely rang their bells in celebration. Angry soldiers retraced their steps and set the abbey aflame. If driving, head for Scott's View, north of Dryburgh on the B635. *(From Melrose take bus #67 or 68 (10min., frequent) to St. Boswell's, turn left from the bus station, then follow St. Cuthbert's Way along the River Tweed, eventually crossing a metal footbridge to reach the abbey (30min.). Alternatively, the Four Abbeys Cycle Route connects Melrose and Dryburgh. ☎01835 822 381. Open daily Apr.-Sept. 9:30am-6:30pm; Oct.-Mar. M-Sa 9:30am-4:30pm, Su 2-4:30pm. £3, seniors £2.30, children £1.)*

ABBOTSFORD. Sir Walter Scott wrote most of his Waverley novels in this mock-Gothic estate 2 mi. west of Melrose and died here in 1832. It's easy to picture the writer toiling away in the dark, brooding interior, which has over 9000 rare books in its library as well as a collection of weapons and armor including Rob Roy's gun. Among the estate's other knick-knacks are a lock of Bonnie Prince Charlie's hair and a piece of the gown worn by Mary, Queen of Scots, at her execution. The gardens extend from the house toward the river, and a few peacocks wander about. *(Frequent buses between Galashiels and Melrose stop nearby. Get off at Tweedbank; the house is a 10min. walk. Be sure to tell the driver where you're going. ☎01896 752 043. Open daily June-Sept. 9:30am-5pm; May and Oct. M-Sa 9:30am-5pm, Su 2-5pm. £4.20, children £2.10.)*

THIRLESTANE CASTLE. The ancient seat of the Earls and Duke of Lauderdale, Thirlestane Castle stands 10 mi. north of Melrose on the A68, near Lauder. The defensive walls in the Panelled Room and Library are 13 ft. thick, but the beautiful restoration can't remedy the castle's bloody history—jealous nobles hanged a host of King James III's supporters here in 1482. *(From Melrose or Galashiels, take bus #61 toward Lauder and ask to be let off at the castle. ☎01578 722 430. www.thirlestanecastle.co.uk. Open May-Oct. M-F, Su 10:30am-5pm; last admission 4:15pm. £5.50, families £15.)*

PEEBLES   ☎01721

18 mi. west of Galashiels, Peebles lies beside the River Tweed. The **Tweed Cycleway** passes through town, supplementing the numerous other trails in the area. One excellent short walk departs from the Kingsmeadow car park and sets off for a 5 mi. circular route down and back along the River Tweed. Perched majestically

above a bend in the river, █Neidpath Castle is about 20min. into the walk. The 11 ft.-thick walls of this citadel were breached only once in its long history. Today visitors can climb through and explore its many preserved levels, admiring the view from the top. Inside, batik art depicts the life of Mary, Queen of Scots. (☎720 333. Open May-Sept. M-Sa 10:30am-5pm, Su 12:30-5pm. £3, concessions £2.50, children £1.) The free **Tweeddale Museum and Gallery**, in the Chambers Institute on High St., houses rotating exhibitions and copies of Greek friezes. (☎724 820. Open M-F 10am-noon and 2-5pm; Apr.-Oct. also Sa 10am-1pm and 2-4pm.)

The **Tourist Information Centre** is at 23 High St. (☎0870 608 0404. Open July-Aug. M-Sa 9am-6pm, Su 10am-4pm; June and Sept. M-Sa 9am-5:30pm, Su 10am-4pm; Apr.-May M-Sa 9am-5pm, Su 11am-4pm; Oct. M-F 9:30am-5pm, Su 11am-4pm.) Other services include: **banks** along High St.; **bike rental** at **The Bicycle Works**, 3 High St. (☎723 423; www.thebicycleworks.co.uk; £12 per half-day, £16 per day; open daily 10am-6pm); free **Internet access** at the **library**, High St. (open M, W, F 9:30am-5pm, Tu and Th 9:30am-7pm, Sa 9am-12:30pm); and the **post office,** 14 Eastgate (☎720 119; open M-F 9am-5:30pm, Sa 9am-12:30pm). **Post Code: EH45 8AA.**

Stay with Mrs. O'Hara at the inviting **Rowanbrae ❸**, 103 Northgate (☎721 630; singles £25; doubles from £38; no smoking; cash only), or with Mrs. Mitchell at **Viewfield ❸**, 1 Rosetta Rd., in a room above her wonderful garden. (☎721 232. Singles from £22; doubles from £40. Cash only.) Campers will find comfort at the **Rosetta Caravan Park ❶**, Rosetta Rd., 10min. from town. (☎720 770. Open Apr.-Oct. £5.50 per person, children 50p. Cash only.) Grab your **groceries** at **Somerfield**, Edinburgh Rd. (Open M-Tu and Sa 8am-8pm, W-F 8am-10pm, Su 8am-6pm.) The **Sunflower Restaurant ❷**, 4 Bridgegate, prepares modern Mediterranean cuisine in a classy setting (entrees £12-14), including a daily vegetarian option. (☎722 420. Open M-Sa 9:30am-4pm, W-Sa also 6-9pm, Su 3-7pm. MC/V.)

🔁 DAYTRIPS FROM PEEBLES

TRAQUAIR HOUSE. 12th-century █Traquair House (TRARK-weer), the oldest inhabited house in Scotland, stands 6 mi. east of Peebles and about 1 mi. south of the A72. Remarkably, many original features remain—the interior is still a maze of low-ceilinged rooms, creaky wood floors, and narrow spiral staircases. Present resident Catherine Stuart brews what may be Scotland's finest ale in the 200-year-old brewery and has tastings on summer Fridays, when more visitors than usual find themselves entangled in the hedge maze. *(From Peebles, take bus #62 toward Galashiels to Innerleithen, and walk 1½ mi. There is also a scenic back road running 7 mi. from Peebles to the house; biking is a good option. For a taxi, call ☎01896 831 333. House ☎01896 830 323; www.traquair.co.uk. Open daily June-Aug. 10:30am-5:30pm; Apr.-May and Sept.-Oct. noon-5:30pm. £5.75, concessions £5.30, children £3.20.)*

JEDBURGH   ☎01835

Smack in the heart of Jedburgh (JED-burra; known to locals as "Jethart"), 13 mi. south of Melrose, King David I founded █Jedburgh Abbey on the frontier of his realm. While pillaging Englishmen were successful in sacking the abbey on repeated occasions, much of the magnificent 12th-century structure endures. To appreciate its original grandeur, climb the narrow spiral staircase at the end of the nave for an elevated perspective. (☎863 925. Open daily Apr.-Sept. 9:30am-6:30pm; Oct.-Mar. M-Sa 9:30am-4:30pm, Su 2-4:30pm. £3.50, concessions £2.50, children £1.20.) For the best free view of the abbey, try Abbey Close St. off Castlegate.

The **Mary Queen of Scots House,** down Smiths Wynd on Queen St., stands as a rare example of a 16th-century fortified house. It provides interesting background on the monarch, who visited Jedburgh in 1566. (☎863 331. Open Mar.-Nov. M-Sa 10am-4:30pm, Su noon-4:30pm. £3, concessions £2, children free.) The 19th-century **Jedburgh Castle Jail** looms atop a hill on Castlegate over the original Jethart Castle, which was destroyed in 1409 to prevent the English from taking it. (☎864 750. Open Apr.-Oct. M-Sa 10am-4:45pm, Su 1-4pm. £1.50, concessions £1.) Walkers may enjoy the circular route leaving from the TIC, which temporarily follows **Dere Street,** an old Roman road, before tracing Jed Water back to town (roughly 5 mi.). Cyclists can join the **Four Abbeys Cycle Route** in town or pedal out to the **Borderloop.**

Buses stop on Canongate, near the abbey and next to the **Tourist Information Centre.** The TIC books National Express tickets, books rooms for a 10% deposit, and **exchanges currency** for free. (☎863 435. Open July-Aug. M-Sa 9am-7pm, Su 10am-6pm; June and Sept. M-Sa 9am-6pm, Su 10am-5pm; Oct. M-Sa 9:15am-5pm, Su 10am-5pm; Nov.-Mar. M-Sa 9:30am-4:30pm.) Other services include: **bike rental** at **The Rush,** 39 High St. (☎869 643; £12 per day, £10 per ½ day; open M-F 10am-6pm, Sa 9am-5pm); free **Internet access** at the **library,** Castlegate (open M and F 10am-1pm, 2-5pm, and 5:30-7pm, Tu-Th 10am-1pm and 2-5pm); and the **post office,** 37 High St. (☎862 268; open M-F 9am-5:30pm, Sa 9am-12:30pm). **Post Code:** TD8 6DG.

B&Bs are scattered throughout town. Hard to reach without wheels, Mrs. Lowe's **Windyridge ❷,** 39 Doune Hill, offers panoramic views of castle and abbey from a lovely spot a mile uphill from town. (☎864 404. Singles £22; doubles £46. Cash only.) Family-friendly **Meadhon House ❸,** 48 Castlegate, has a secluded garden right in town. (☎862 504; www.meadhon.com. Singles £32; doubles £45. No smoking. Cash only.) **Craigowen Guest House,** 30 High St., is a cheaper town-center option. (☎862 604. £20 per person. Cash only.) Fun-loving campers can head to **Jedwater Caravan Park ❶,** 4 mi. south of the town center off the A68; watch for signs. (☎869 595. Showers, laundry, fishing, and trampolines. Open Mar.-Oct. 2-person site including car £9. Cash only.) For **groceries,** visit the **Co-op Superstore,** at the corner of Jeweller's Wynd and High St. (☎862 944. Open M-Sa 8am-10pm, Su 9am-6pm.) At **Simply Scottish ❷,** 6-8 High St., well-prepared specials go for £7-10, and a fine 3-course dinner is a steal at £12. (☎864 696. Open M-Th 10am-8:30pm, F-Sa 10am-9pm, Su 11am-8:30pm.)

KELSO ☎01573

The attractive market town of Kelso sits at the meeting of the Tweed and Teviot rivers just a short way from the English border. About 1 mi. from the town center along the Tweed, the Duke and Duchess of Roxburgh reside in the palatial **Floors Castle.** The largest inhabited castle in Scotland, it dates from the 1720s, with vast riverside grounds, stately rooms, and a window for each day of the year. A holly in the gardens marks the site where James II met his noble end—killed while inspecting a cannon. (☎223 333. Open daily Apr.-Oct. 10am-4:30pm; last admission 4pm. £5.75, concessions £4.75, children £3.25.) Sadly, very little remains of **Kelso Abbey,** near Market Sq., another victim of repeated English invasion; the arrow slits on its towers lead historians to believe it may once have been used defensively, and was "slighted" to prevent further subordination. (Open Apr.-Sept. M-Sa 9:30am-6pm, Su 2-6pm; Oct.-Mar. M-Sa 9:30am-4pm, Su 2-4pm. Free.) **Mellerstain House,** one of Scotland's finest Georgian homes, is 6 mi. northwest of Kelso on the A6089. Begun in 1725 by William Adam and completed by his son Robert, the house is noted for its exquisite plaster ceilings and art collection. Take bus #689 (10min.; M-F every hr., Su 8 per day; round-trip £1.20) toward Gordon and ask the driver to drop you near the house. (☎410 225; www.mellerstain.com. Open May-Sept. M, W-F, Su 12:30-5pm. House and gardens £5.50, children free. Gardens only £3.) Those interested in a long walk should try the 13 mi. section of the **Borders Abbeys Way,** running alongside the River Teviot, that joins Kelso to Jedburgh. Cyclists can join the **Four Abbeys Cycle Route** and the **Borderloop** in Kelso.

The **bus station** is on Roxburgh St., near Market Sq. The **Tourist Information Centre,** Market Sq., books rooms for a 10% deposit. (☎0870 608 0404. Open July-Aug. M-Sa 9:30am-5pm, Su 10am-2pm; Apr.-May and Sept.-Oct. M-Sa 10am-5pm, Su 10am-2pm; Nov.-Mar. M-Sa 10am-4pm.) Get free **Internet access** at the **Library,** Bowmont St. (Open M and F 10am-1pm and 2-5pm, Tu, Th 10am-1pm, 2-5pm and 5:30-7pm, W 10am-1pm, Sa 9:30am-12:30pm.) The **post office** is at 13 Woodmarket. (☎224 795. Open M-F 9am-5:30pm, Sa 9am-12:30pm.) **Post Code:** TD5 7AT.

The **SYHA Kirk Yetholm** ❶ (p. 567) is 6 mi. southeast of Kelso. Take the shortcut footpath up the hill from Croft Rd. to reach **Mrs. Ferguson ❸,** 11 King's Croft, offering basic lodgings for a good price. (☎225 480. Singles £25; doubles £44. Cash only.) Closer to town, the relatively large **Bellevue Guest House ❹,** Bowmont St., makes a comfortable touring base. (☎224 588. Singles £35; doubles £52-58. MC/V.) Restock at **Safeway,** Roxburgh St. (☎225 641. Open M-Sa 8am-8pm, Su 9am-6pm.) At **Oscar's ❷,** 35-37 Haymarket, lively music and the early evening menu (until 7pm; entrees £8) makes for the best deal in town. (Open daily 5-10pm.)

DUMFRIES AND GALLOWAY

Dumfries and Galloway see relatively little of the tourism enjoyed to the north and south. Still, this southwest corner of Scotland does possess a few gems, with fine castles and abbeys, stately gardens, and local heroes like Robert the Bruce and Robert Burns. Wise visitors head for the country, where high mountains, dense forest, and 200 mi. of remote coastline supply rugged and rewarding scenery.

▐▌ TRANSPORTATION AND ACCOMMODATIONS

Trains serve Dumfries and Stranraer. Though **buses** reach other towns, service is infrequent. Call **Traveline** (☎0870 608 2608) for schedule information. A **Day Discoverer Ticket,** available on buses, allows unlimited travel in Dumfries and Galloway, and on Stagecoach buses in Cumbria (£5, children £2, family £10). Each town has its own clutch of B&Bs and hotels. The region's three **SYHA hostels** are probably of most interest to walkers; only Minigaff is easily reached by public transport.

Kendoon (☎01644 460 680), 20 mi. from Threave Castle. Near Loch Doon and the Southern Upland Way. Open Apr.-Sept. Dorms £10, under 18 £8. Cash only. ❶

Minigaff (☎01671 402 211), in Minigaff village, across the bridge ½ mi. from Newton Stewart. Accessible by bus from Dumfries, Stranraer, and Kirkcudbright. Popular with hikers and anglers. 36 beds. Open Apr.-Sept. Dorms £10, under 18 £8. MC/V. ❶

Wanlockhead (☎01659 58581), Scotland's highest village, along the Southern Upland Way. 28 beds. Open Apr.-Sept. Dorms £10, under 18 £8. Cash only. ❶

▐▌ HIKING AND OUTDOORS

Dumfries and Galloway only shine once you get outdoors, and with some 1300 mi. of marked trails there is something for everyone. **Merrick** (2765 ft.) in the **Galloway Hills** and **White Coomb** (2696 ft.) in the **Moffat Hills** will provide a challenge for seasoned hikers, along with the region's main draw—the **Southern Upland Way.** Beginning in Portpatrick on the coast of the Irish Sea and snaking 212 mi. clear across Scotland, this long-distance route cuts through Dumfries and Galloway, passing near to each of the region's three SYHA hostels. The official *Southern Upland Way* guide (£16) breaks the route into 15 manageable sections and includes a complete Ordnance Survey map (1:50,000) of its course. In the west, the **Galloway Forest Park** is Britain's largest at over 300 square miles, though its excellent walking, cycling and horseback riding trails can be difficult to reach without a car. The park has three ranger-manned visitor centers: **Clatteringshaws,** 6 mi. west of New Galloway (☎01644 420 285); **Glen Trool,** 12 mi. north of Newton Stewart (☎01671 402 420); and **Kirroughtree,** 3 mi. east of Newton Stewart (☎01671 402 165). All are open daily Apr.-Sept. 10:30am-5pm; Oct. 10:30am-4:30pm. For those more inclined towards a day outing or afternoon walk the free *Walks In and Around* guides detail local routes. Along the coasts and inland, Dumfries and Galloway are popular with serious birdwatchers, particularly around the **Mull of Galloway;** its sea cliffs are home to thousands of marine birds. **Cyclists** will find *Cycling in Dumfries and Galloway* (free at TICs) useful. Both the **#74** and **#7 National Cycle Routes** cross Dumfries and Galloway. Among local routes, the **KM Cycle Trail** runs from Drumlanrig down to Dumfries. The Forest Enterprise puts out a number of leaflets describing on- and off-trail routes in Galloway and other area forests.

DUMFRIES ☎01387

Dumfries (dum-FREEZ, pop. 37,000) hangs its tam on little but the tales of two famous Roberts. In 1306, Robert the Bruce proclaimed himself King of Scotland in Dumfries after stabbing throne-contender Red Comyn at Greyfriars. Beloved Scots-scribbler Robert Burns made Dumfries his home from 1791 until his death in 1796, and the town has devoted many (many) a site to him. Along with these historical claims, the central location and transportation connections make this the unofficial (and unexciting) capital of southwest Scotland.

TRANSPORTATION AND PRACTICAL INFORMATION. The **train station** is on Station Rd. (☎255 115. Open M-Sa 6:35am-7:30pm, Su 10:30am-7:55pm.) Trains (☎08457 484 950) come from: **Carlisle** (40min.; every hr.; £3.50); **Glasgow Central** (1¾hr.; M-Sa 8 per day, Su 2 per day; £10); **London Euston** (change in Carlisle, 5¼hr., 10 per day, £70); **Stranraer** via **Ayr** (3hr., 3 per day, £20.60). **Buses** arrive and depart along Whitesands and #974 runs from **Glasgow** (2hr.; M-Sa 3 per day, Su 2 per day; £6.40). Bus #100 travels from **Edinburgh** (2¾hr., same frequency and price) via **Penicuik** (2¼hr.), while #500/X75 connects Dumfries to **Carlisle** (1hr., 2 per day, £2.40) and **Stranraer** (2¼hr., 8 per day, £5).

The **Tourist Information Centre,** 64 Whitesands Rd., books rooms for a £3 charge plus a 10% deposit and sells National Express tickets. (☎253 862. Open July-Sept. M-Sa 9am-6pm, Su 11am-5pm; Oct.-June M-Sa 9:30am-5pm.) Other services include: **banks** along High St.; free **Internet access** at **Ewart Library,** Catherine St. (☎253 820; open M-W and F 9:15am-7:30pm, Th and Sa 9:15am-5pm); **bike rental** at the **Nithsdale Cycle Center,** 46 Brooms Rd. (☎254 870; £8 per day, 3 days £20. open M-Sa 10am-5pm.); and the **post office,** 7 Great King St., with a **bureau de change.** (☎256 690. Open M-F 8:45am-5:30pm, Sa 9am-12:30pm.) **Post Code:** DG1 1AA.

ACCOMMODATIONS AND FOOD. If your plans call for a night's layover in town, welcoming **Torbay Lodge ❸,** 31 Lover's Walk, is just steps from the train station. (☎253 922; www.torbaylodge.co.uk. From £25 per person. MC/V.) Cheaper abodes lie along **Lockerbie Road,** north of the city across the tracks. Close to the Whitesands bus stop, **The Haven ❷,** 1 Kenmore Terr., is a riverfront home that comes with a kitchen available for use. (☎251 281. Singles £18; doubles £36-40. Cash only.) Find **groceries** at **Somerfield,** Leafield Rd. (Open M-Sa 8am-8pm, Su 9am-6pm.) Plenty of cheap eats line **High Street** and **Whitesands.** Be like Burns and stop for a pint at **The Globe Inn,** 56 High St., one of the poet's favorite haunts. (☎252 335. Open M-W 10am-11pm, Th-Sa 10am-midnight, Su noon-midnight.)

◙ **SIGHTS.** The sights in Dumfries mostly cater to extreme Robert Burns fans. Pick up a free copy of *Dumfries: A Burns Trail* in the TIC for an easy-to-follow walking tour that covers all the major sights. Across the river, the **Robert Burns Centre**, Mill Rd., contains Burns memorabilia, including a cast of his skull; the ten million Burns songs make it worth the small fee. (☎264 808. Open Apr.-Sept. M-Sa 10am-8pm, Su 2-5pm; Oct.-Mar. Tu-Sa 10am-1pm and 2-5pm. £1.55, concessions 80p.) In **St. Michael's Kirkyard,** a marble Burns leans on a plow and gazes at the attractive muse hovering overhead. Burnsmania reaches messianic proportions at the wee **Burns House,** where memorabilia on display includes a tiny box made with wood from the bed the poet died in. (☎255 297. Open Apr.-Sept. M-Sa 10am-5pm, Su 2-5pm; Oct.-Mar. Tu-Sa 10am-1pm and 2-5pm. Free.) The top floor of the **Dumfries Museum,** Church St., has panoramic views from Britain's oldest camera obscura. (☎253 374. Open Apr.-Sept. M-Sa 10am-5pm, Su 2-5pm; Oct.-Mar. Tu-Sa 10am-1pm and 2-5pm. Museum free. Camera obscura £1.55, concessions 80p.)

◪ DAYTRIPS FROM DUMFRIES

▨ **CAERLAVEROCK CASTLE.** 8 mi. southeast of Dumfries, on the B725 just beyond Glencaple, moated and triangular Caerlaverock Castle (car-LAV-rick) is one of Scotland's finest medieval ruins. Though no one is sure whether this strategic marvel was built for Scottish defense or English offense, it was seized by England's Edward I in 1300 and passed around like a hot kipper thereafter. Beyond the castle is a path that runs down to the shore of the Solway Firth (10min.). The mountains of the Lake District rise up in the distance out of the vast flats of the firth, which at low tide is nothing but sand for 20 mi. *(Stagecoach Western Bus #371 runs to the castle from the Loreburn Shopping Centre, off Irish St. in Dumfries (20min.; M-Sa 12 per day, Su 2 per day; round-trip £2.55). ☎01387 770 244. Open daily Apr.-Sept. 9:30am-6:30pm; Oct.-Mar. M-Sa 9:30am-4:30pm, Su 2-4:30pm. £4, concessions £3, children £1.)*

SWEETHEART ABBEY. This abbey, 8 mi. south of Dumfries along the A710, was founded in the late 13th century by Lady Devorguilla Balliol in memory of her husband John. She was later buried here with John's embalmed heart clutched to her breast. Now a splendid, well-preserved ruin, the high arches and central spire of the abbey stand in a rather grisly testament to their love. *(Take MacEwan's bus #372 to New Abbey from Dumfries (15 min.; M-Sa 12 per day, Su 5 per day; round-trip £2.40). ☎01387 850 397. Open daily Apr.-Sept. 9:30am-6:30pm; Oct.-Mar. M-W and Sa 9:30am-4:30pm, Th 9:30am-12:30pm, Su 2-4:30pm. £2, concessions £1.30, children 75p.)*

RUTHWELL CHURCH. Nine miles southeast of Dumfries, the church contains the magnificent 7th-century **Ruthwell Cross,** bearing dense Celtic carvings of vine scrolls and beasts. The Anglo-Saxon poem (and Scotland's oldest surviving fragment of written English), *The Dream of the Rood,* crowds its margins. Call Mrs. Coulthard (☎01387 870 249) to get the key to the church. *(Take a bus to Annan via Clarencefield (30min.; M-Sa every hr., Su every 2hr.; round-trip £2.55) and get off at Ruthwell. Free.)*

DRUMLANRIG CASTLE. 18 mi. north of Dumfries off the A76, Drumlanrig Castle is the home of the Duke of Buccleuch. Surrounded by formal gardens and a large country park, the castle's noted painting collection includes works by Rembrandt and Da Vinci. Take a time out in the classy cafe. *(From Dumfries, Stagecoach Western bus #246 (45min., Su only 2 per day, £2.50) stops 1½ mi. away. ☎01848 331 555; www.buccleuch.com. Castle open by guided tour May-Aug. M-Sa 11am-4pm, Su noon-4pm. Grounds open Easter-Sept. 11am-5pm. £6, concessions £4, children £2; grounds only £3, children £2.)*

CASTLE DOUGLAS ☎ 01556

Between Dumfries and Kirkcudbright, Castle Douglas resembles most other towns in Scotland's southwest. One mile west, however, the 60-acre **Threave Garden** makes a visit worthwhile with peaceful pools surrounded by native and exotic blooms pruned by students of the School of Gardening. Buses #501 and 502 (10 min., 1 per hr.) between Kirkcudbright and Castle Douglas pass the garden turnoff; ask the driver to stop, then walk 15min. (☎ 502 575. Garden open daily 9:30am-sunset. Walled garden and greenhouses open daily 9:30am-5pm. £5, concessions £3.75.) The **Threave Estate Walk** (2½-7½ mi. depending upon detours) meanders pleasantly through the countryside. Leaving from the garden car park, it leads hikers to a number of good bird-watching spots as well as the scenic ruins of 14th-century ⬛**Threave Castle.** A stronghold of the Earls of Douglas and built by Archibald the Grim, this massive tower-castle sits in a commanding position on an island in the River Dee. The Kirkcudbright bus can also drop you off at the roundabout on the A75; from there follow the signs for 30min. beside a one-lane road and then through farmland. Once at the river, ring the ship's bell nearby and a boatman should appear to ferry you across to the castle. (Open daily Apr.-Sept. 9:30am-6:30pm; last boat 6pm. £2.50, concessions £1.90, children 75p.)

MacEwan's buses #501 and 502 zip from **Dumfries** to **Kirkcudbright** via Castle Douglas (40min. from Dumfries, 20min. from Kirkcudbright; 2 per hr.; £3.50). For local lodgings, ask the staff at the **Tourist Information Centre.** (☎ 502 611. Open July-Aug. M-Sa 9:30am-6pm, Su 10am-4pm; Apr.-June M-Sa 10am-5pm, Su 11am-4pm; Sept. M-Sa 10am-4pm, Su 11am-4pm; Oct. M-Sa 10am-4pm.) For a place to crash, try **The Crown Hotel ❸**, 25 King Street (☎ 502 031; www.thecrownhotel.co.uk. Singles £35; doubles £66. Right across from the TIC and the bus station; all ensuite rooms. Cash only.) For **groceries,** the **Co-op Superstore** is along Cotton St. (Open M-Sa 8am-10pm, Su 9am-6pm.) A number of small cafes line **King Street.**

KIRKCUDBRIGHT ☎ 01557

Situated at the mouth of the River Dee, Kirkcudbright (kir-COO-bree) is a quiet town with rows of colorful Georgian homes and interesting sights that refreshingly have nothing to do with Robert Burns. The town's charms attracted a group of artists known as the Glasgow Boys, who took up residence in the 1890s, and Kirkcudbright still fancies itself an artists' colony.

🚍🄸 **TRANSPORTATION AND PRACTICAL INFORMATION. Buses** #501 and 502 travel from **Dumfries** via **Castle Douglas** (1 per hr.), and bus #431 comes from **Gatehouse of Fleet** (20 min.; M-Sa 12 per day, Su 6 per day), beginning on Sunday in **Newton Stewart.** The **Tourist Information Centre,** Harbour Sq., books rooms for a £3 charge. (☎ 330 494. Open July-Aug. M-Sa 9:30am-6pm, Su 10am-5pm; Sept.-June M-Sa 10am-5pm, Su 11am-4pm) Other services include: **Shirley's Launderette,** 20 St. Cuthbert St. (☎ 332 047; wash and dry £5; open M-F 9am-4pm, Sa 9am-1pm); free **Internet access** at the **Library,** High St. (open M 2-7pm, Tu and F 10am-7:30pm, W noon-7:30pm, Th and Sa 10am-5pm); and the **post office,** 5 St. Cuthbert's Pl. (☎ 330 578; open M-F 9am-5:30pm, Sa 9am-12:30pm). **Post Code: DG6 4DH.**

🄵🄲 **ACCOMMODATIONS AND FOOD.** If you plan on spending the night, **Parkview ❷**, 22 Millburn St., is run by warm Mrs. McIlwraith. (☎ 330 056. Singles £19; doubles £38. No smoking. Cash only.) The Georgian townhouse **Number 3 B&B ❸**, 3 High St., is in a perfect location and comes with more luxurious amenities. (☎ 330 881; www.number3-bandb.co.uk. Singles £35; doubles £55. MC/V.) Get **groceries** at **Safeway,** 52 St. Cuthbert St., at Millburn St. (☎ 330 516. Open M-W and Sa 8:30am-6pm, Th-F 8:30am-8pm, Su 10am-5pm.) **The Royal Hotel ❷**, St. Cuthbert St., has an all-you-can-eat seafood lunch buffet (M-Sa noon-2pm; £6.25) and an all-you-can-eat dinner buffet (F-Sa 6:30-9pm, Su noon-3pm; £7.95), though we do not suggest both in one day. (☎331 213. Open daily 10am-9pm.)

◨ **SIGHTS.** Continuing an artistic tradition inaugurated in the 1890s when the Glasgow Boys made Kirkcudbright their home, the **Tollbooth Art Centre,** High St., displays the work of current resident artisans and includes a studio where you can occasionally watch them at work. There's also an interesting video on the history of Kirkcudbright's resident artists. (☎331 556. Open July-Aug. M-Sa 10am-6pm, Su 2-5pm; June and Sept. M-Sa 11am-5pm, Su 2-5pm; Oct.-May M-Sa 11am-4pm. Free.) **MacLellan's Castle,** a 16th-century tower house, dominates the town on Castle St. Sneak into the "Laird's Lug," a secret chamber behind a fireplace from which the laird could eavesdrop on conversations in the Great Hall. (☎331 856. Open daily Apr.-Sept. 9:30am-1pm and 2-6:30pm. £2.20, concessions £1.60, children 75p.) One fine walk in the area departs from the TIC and runs along the coastal headland to Torrs Point (8½ mi. round-trip). **Broughton House,** 12 High St., displays the artwork (mostly carefree girls cavorting amid wildflowers) of E.A. Hornel, who drew inspiration for his later paintings from the years he spent in Japan. The beautiful backyard contains manicured lawns, lily ponds, sundials, and a greenhouse. (☎330 437. Open Apr.-Sept. M-Sa 11am-5pm and Su 1-5pm; Feb.-Mar. and Oct. M-F 11am-4pm. May be closed part of 2005 for renovations—call ahead. £3.50, concessions £2.50.)

STRANRAER ☎01776

On the westernmost peninsula of Dumfries and Galloway, Stranraer (stran-RAHR) provides ferry access to Northern Ireland—and that's about it. Locals have a unique accent, and as most early residents came from Ireland they are often referred to as the Galloway Irish. Four miles east of Stranraer on the A75, the **Castle Kennedy Gardens** includes lovely landscaping between a pair of lochs. Tree-lined walks offer great picnic spots. Buses (#430, 416, and 500) from Stranraer pass the castles; ask the driver to let you off, it's about a mile from the main road. (☎702 024. Open daily Apr.-Oct. 10am-5pm. £3, concessions £2, children £1.) In town, the only sight is the **Castle of St. John,** George St., a 1510 edifice that affords good views of the town. (☎705 088. Open Apr.-Sept. M-Sa 10am-1pm and 2-5pm. Free.)

Friendly **Jan Da Mar Guest House ❷,** 1 Ivy Pl., on London Rd., is just up from the ferry pier. (☎706 194. www.jandamar.co.uk. Singles £18-25; doubles £32-40. Cash only.) The **Harbour Guest House ❸,** 11 Market St., near the west pier, is another good option. (☎704 626. Singles £25-28; doubles £50-60. Cash only.) A **Tesco** is on Charlotte St., near the ferry terminal. (Open M-Sa 7am-8pm, Su 10am-6pm.)

The **train station** is open daily 9:30am-3pm and 4-6:30pm. Trains (☎08457 484 950) arrive from **Ayr** (1¼hr., M-Sa 7 per day, Su 3 per day; £10) and **Glasgow** (2½hr.; M-Sa 4-7 per day, Su 3 per day; £15). **Scottish Citylink** (☎08705 505 050) buses arrive in town at Port Rodie from: **Ayr** (#923; 1½hr., 2 per day, £4.50); **Dumfries** (#500/X75; 2hr.; M-Sa 10 per day, Su 3 per day; £4.50); **Glasgow** (#923, 2½hr., 2 per day, £8.50). **National Express** (☎08705 808 080) runs from: **Carlisle** (2½hr., £15); **London** (10hr., 1 per day, £33); **Manchester** (6hr., 2 per day, £27). **Ferries** travel from Northern Ireland across the North Channel. **Stena Line** (☎08705 707 070) sails from **Belfast** (1¾hr-3¼hr.; 5-7 per day; £14-24, concessions £10-19, children £7-12). Five miles up the coast at **Cairnyan, P&O Ferries** (☎0870 242 4777) arrive from **Larne** (1-1¾hr., 5-8 per day, £18-25). Sea passage is sometimes discounted with a rail ticket.

The **Tourist Information Centre,** 28 Harbour St., books rooms for a 10% deposit. (☎702 595. Open Apr.-Sept. M-Sa 10am-5pm, Su 10am-4pm; Oct.-Mar. M-Sa 10am-4pm.) Other services include: **banks,** throughout the town; free **Internet access** at the **Stranraer Library,** 2-10 N. Strand St. (☎707 400; open M-W and F 9:15am-7:30pm,

Th 9:15am-5pm, Sa 9:15am-1pm and 2-5pm); **bike rental** at the **George Hotel,** 49 George St. (☎702 487; £10 per day; open 24hr.); and the **post office,** in the Tesco on Charlotte St. (☎702 587; open M-F 7am-6pm, Sa 7am-5pm). **Post Code:** DG9 7EF.

WESTERN GALLOWAY

The two peninsulas of Western Galloway extend from Stranraer and are fringed with cliffs, beaches, and great views. Those car-less travelers willing to brave the tricky public transport will find worthwhile stopping places, such as the beautiful and windswept coast around **Sandhead,** south of Stranraer. Take **bus** #407 (20min., M-Sa 10 per day, Su 3 per day). The **Galloway Forest Park** features 300 sq. mi. of hike-able peaks, surrounding Glen Trool (northeast of Stranraer). At the **Mull of Gallo-way,** the southernmost point in Scotland, a lighthouse sits atop amazing sheer cliffs that are home to thousands of sea birds. On a clear day both Northern Ireland and the Isle of Man are visible. **Portpatrick,** 8 mi. southwest of Stranraer, is a low-key seaside town, its rocky coastline fronted by comely pastel buildings. The coast-to-coast **Southern Upland Way** (p. 566) begins here, and there's also a coastal path lead-ing back to Stranraer. Another path runs along the cliffs south of town to the ruins of **Dunskey Castle,** an empty shell perched high above the pounding surf. From the castle, a thin hint of a path leads down to a small cove, where a smuggler's cave, under the castle, can be reached at low tide. **Buses** #358, 367, and 411 serve Port-patrick from Stranraer (25min., M-Sa 16 per day, Su 3 per day). There's a tiny **Tour-ist Information Centre,** on Main St. near the harbor (☎810 717. Open daily May-Sept. 9am-5pm.) The TIC also has **Internet access** (£1 per hr.). The **post office** is just up the street. (Open M-F 9am-1:15pm and 2:15-5:30pm, Sa 9am-12:30pm.) The **Knowe Guest House ❸,** 1 North Cres., has comfortable rooms with harbor views. (☎810 441. No smoking. Singles £20-30; doubles £35-42. MC/V.)

AYRSHIRE

AYR ☎01292

A mildly pleasant seaside town, Ayr (as in fresh sea AIR; pop. 50,000) offers little more than a base for exploring the surrounding area. Locally, most tourists set their sights on Robert Burns's birthplace at Alloway, 3 mi. to the south, though Ayr also possesses the top horse racetrack in Scotland, home to the **Scottish Grand National** in April and the **Ayr Gold Cup** in September. (☎264 179. Call for race dates. Tickets £10-25.) Perhaps the best way to see the coastal islands of the Firth of Clyde is to take a cruise on the **Waverly,** the world's only remaining ocean paddle steamer. Departing from the south side of Ayr's harbor during July and August, the steamer tours many of the nearby islands including the Isle of Arran. (☎0845 130 4647; www.waverlyexcursions.co.uk. Cruises July-Aug. M-W. Full-day tour £25.)

Ayr's **train station** is a 10min. walk from the center of town at the crossroads of Station Rd., Holmston Rd., and Castle Hill Rd. (Open M-Sa 5:30am-11:10pm, Su 8:30am-11:10pm.) Trains (☎08457 484 950) run from **Dumfries** (2 per day, £10.20); **Glasgow** (55min., 2 per hr., £5.30); and **Stranraer** (1½hr.; M-Sa 7 per day, Su 3 per day; £10). The **bus station,** in the town center on Fullerton St. off Sandgate, **stores luggage** (£1) while open. (Open M-F 8:30am-5pm, Sa 9am-1pm.) It receives **Stage-coach Western** (☎613 500) buses from **Glasgow** (1¾hr.; every 30min., £3.15) and **Stranraer** (1¼hr.; 2 per day, £5.70). The **Tourist Information Centre** is nearby at 22 Sandgate. (☎290 300. Open July-Aug. M-Sa 9am-6pm, Su 10am-5pm; Sept.-June

M-Sa 9am-5pm.) Other services include: **banks** on High St.; free **Internet access** at the **Carnegie Library**, 12 Main St. (☎286 385; open M-F 10am-7:30pm, Sa 10am-5pm); **bike rental** at **AMG Cycles**, 55 Dalblair Rd. (☎287 580; £12.50 per day, £35 per week; open M-Sa 9am-5pm, Su noon-4pm); and the **post office**, 65 Sandgate, with a **bureau de change** (☎0845 601 122; open M-Sa 9am-5:30pm). **Post Code:** KA7 1AA.

Among the many **B&Bs** clustered near the beach, the **Tramore Guesthouse ❷**, 17 Eglinton Terr., has Moroccan decor a pebble's toss from the sand. (☎266 019. Singles £22; doubles £38. Cash only.) **Craggallan Guest House ❸**, 8 Queen's Terr., is friendly and comfortable. (☎264 998; www.craggallan.com. £25 per person. MC/V.) The **Safeway** is across from the train station on Castlehill Rd. (☎283 906. Open M-F 8am-10pm, Sa 8am-8pm, Su 9am-5pm.) Probably your best bet for a meal out, **Fouters Bistro ❸**, 2a Academy St., off Sandgate, serves up a mix of Scottish and French cuisine from its subterranean digs. (☎261 391; www.fouters.co.uk. Entrees £10-15. Open Tu-Th noon-2:30pm and 6-9pm, F-Sa noon-2:30pm and 6-10pm.)

🔀 DAYTRIPS FROM AYR

🏰 CULZEAN CASTLE AND COUNTRY PARK

From Ayr take bus #60 (30min., 2 per hr.) to the Culzean stop. The castle is signposted about 1 mi. from the main road. ☎01655 760 274. Castle open daily Apr.-Oct. 10:30am-5pm; last admission 4pm. Park open year-round. Free tours daily July-Aug. 11am and 3:30pm. £9, concessions £6.50, families £23. Park only £5/£3.75/£13.50.

Twelve miles south of Ayr along the A719, Culzean Castle (cul-LANE) perches imposingly on a coastal cliff. According to legend, one of the cliff's caves shelters the Phantom Piper, who plays to his lost flock when the moon is full. The castle's famed oval staircase was designed by Robert Adam; although he drafted nearly 40 blueprints for estate homes and constructed over 20 full-scale castles, his efforts at Culzean are considered his finest. The building's top floor was given to Dwight Eisenhower by the people of Scotland for use during his lifetime—with a presidential budget you can rent his digs for the night (£375; other castle accommodations from £140). Very popular during high season, the castle is surrounded by a 560-acre country park that includes one of the nation's finest walled gardens, an enclosed deer park, and miles of wooded walkways.

At the entrance to the castle and country park, close to the bus stop, the **Glenside Culzean Caravan and Camping Park ❶** provides a great place to pitch your tent, with fresh sea air and views over to the Isle of Arran. (☎01655 760 627. Open Apr.-Oct. Showers and laundry. Car and tent £5.80. Nonmember charge £4.75. MC/V.)

ALLOWAY

From Ayr, take bus #57 M-Sa or #60 Su (10min., every hr.).

3 mi. south of Ayr, the village of Alloway seems to exist solely to ensure that the memory of Robert Burns never dies. Here the **Burns National Heritage Park** encompasses a number of attractions all devoted to the bard, included under a single admission charge. (☎443 700; www.burnsheritagepark.com. £5, concessions £3, children £2.50, families £12. Open daily Apr.-Oct. 9:30am-5:30pm; Nov.-Mar. 10am-5pm.) In 1759 Burns was born under the thatch-roof of **Burns Cottage and Museum**, on the main road, which has succeeded in preserving the era's barnyard smell. (☎01292 441 215.) The **Tam o' Shanter Experience**, Murdochs Lone, presents the life of the poet and a lyrical multimedia reading. (☎01292 443 700.) A short walk from the Experience will bring you to the **Brig o' Doon**, a bridge featured in Burns's "Tam o' Shanter" poem. Also nearby are the **Burns Monument and Gardens** and the ruined **Kirk Alloway**, where, according to Burns, the devil played the bagpipes.

ISLE OF ARRAN ☎ 01770

The glorious Isle of Arran (AH-ren; pop. 4750) justifiably bills itself as "Scotland in Miniature." Gentle lowland hills, majestic Highland peaks, peaceful meadows, and dense forests coexist on an island less than 20 mi. long. Every year thousands of walkers visit Arran for its beautiful and varied terrain, many with their sights set on the isle's popular summits. While the tourist population swells in the summer months, you will still find plenty of room to ramble on your own. In the north, the crags of Goatfell and the Caisteal range overshadow pine-filled foothills. Near the western coast, prehistoric stone circles rise suddenly out of boggy grass. Linked by an excellent transportation network, the eastern coastline winds south from Brodick Castle past Holy Island into meadows and white beaches.

⌸ TRANSPORTATION

To reach Arran, take a **train** (☎ 08457 484 950) to **Ardrossan** from **Glasgow Central** (1hr., 4-5 per day, £4.50), or **bus** #585 from **Ayr** (1hr.; M-Sa 2 per hr., Su 6 per day; £2.75). From Ardrossan, the **CalMac ferry** (☎ 302 166) makes the crossing to **Brodick** on Arran in sync with the train schedule (1hr.; M-Sa 5-6 per day, Su 4 per day; £4.80, bikes £1). There's also a summer ferry service to **Lochranza** on Arran from **Claonaig** on the Kintyre Peninsula (30min.; mid-Apr. to mid-Oct. 8-9 per day; £4.35; bikes £1). The *Area Transport Guide*, distributed free at the TIC and on the ferry, offers more information on these services and contains all bus schedules for the island. **Stagecoach Western** (☎ 302 000; office at Brodick pier) operates a comprehensive **bus** service; a connection to and from every part of the island meets each ferry. Additional services are run by the **Royal Mail Postbus** (☎ 302 507). Available on board, the **Rural Rover Ticket** grants a full day of bus travel. (£3.50, children £2). In high season (Apr.-Oct.), Stagecoach offers half- and full-day **island tours** departing from Brodick pier. (Full-day £7.50, half-day £5.)

▟✴☡ ORIENTATION AND PRACTICAL INFORMATION

The A841 completes a 56 mi. circuit around the Isle of Arran. Ferries from Ardrossan arrive at **Brodick,** on the eastern shore; those from Claonaig arrive at **Lochranza,** in the north. In the southeast of the isle are **Lamlash,** the largest settlement, and the small village of **Whiting Bay. Blackwaterfoot** is the largest town on the sparsely populated western shore. Home to a virgin wilderness of green hills, deep valleys and pine forests, the interior of the island is practically uninhabited. Brodick has the widest range of tourist services. Arran's only **Tourist Information Centre** is across from the ferry pier in Brodick. It books B&Bs for a 10% deposit plus a £3 charge. (☎ 303 774; fax 302 395. Open June-Sept. M-Sa 9am-7:30pm, Su 10am-5pm; Oct.-May M-Th 9am-5pm, F 9am-7:30pm, Sa 10am-5pm.) From April to September, a tourist information desk on the Ardrossan-Brodick ferry answers questions. The island's **police** station (☎ 302 574) is located on Shore Rd. in Lamlash.

▧▨ HIKING AND OUTDOORS

Despite Arran's proximity and excellent connections to Glasgow, swaths of wilderness in the north and southwest remain untouched. The TIC in Brodick stocks information on outdoor pursuits. Ordnance Survey Landranger #69 (£6) and Explorer #361 (£13) maps cover the island in extraordinary detail. Among the available literature, the Forestry Commission produces the small and popular *A Guide to the Forest Walks of The Isle of Arran* (£1), while the more comprehensive *Walking on The Isle of Arran* (£11) sustains travelers planning longer stays with 41 trails. Highlights include the signposted path up popular ⊠**Goatfell,** Arran's highest peak (2866 ft.), which passes forest, heather and a few mountain streams before the final rocky ascent into the clouds (7 mi. round-trip). Beginning on the road between Brodick and Brodick Castle, this hike averages 4-5hr. and only becomes challenging in the final section. The view from the cold and windy peak is worth the last scramble; on a clear day, it stretches from Ireland to the Isle of Mull. For some great mountain scenery without actually climbing one, try the walk up **Glen Rosa.** The easy train remains mostly flat as it follows the glen into the heart of Arran's mountains. From Brodick, head about a mile north, take the left turn onto the string road towards Blackwaterfoot and then take the first right. Another fine walk is the 8 mi. **Cock of Arran** route, which departs from Lochranza and circles the northern tip of the island, passing the ruins of **Lochranza Castle,** and running along miles of beach, from which basking sharks are often seen. Well-marked shorter walks depart from Whiting Bay and north of Blackwaterfoot.

Biking on the hilly island is a rewarding challenge; pedaling part or all of the 56 mi. circuit ringing the island affords splendid views, and traffic is relatively light in most stretches except at the height of summer. Adrenaline junkies will want to try the 11 mi. off-road route between Lamlash and Kilmory, which winds through hilly and wooded terrain. About 300 yd. from Brodick pier along Shore Rd., the expedition leaders at **Arran Adventure** tackle everything from rock climbing to gorge walking and also offer mountain bike rental. (☎302 244; www.arranadventure.com Bikes £15 per day, £45 per week. Open daily Apr.-Sept. 9am-7:30pm.) For **bike rental** elsewhere on Arran inquire at the **Coffee Pot,** Shore Rd., Whiting Bay (☎700 382; £5 per 2 hr., £9 per day, £25 per week; open daily 10am-5pm; July-Aug. until 6pm) or **Blackwaterfoot Garage,** Blackwaterfoot (☎860 277; £8 per day, £20 per week; open Su-F 8:30am-5:30pm, Sa 9am-5pm).

BRODICK ☎01770

Though the town of Brodick itself is not quite a picture-perfect coastal village, it's hard to complain about the setting—a peaceful bay set against a backdrop of rugged mountains. Some 2½ mi. north of town, **Brodick Castle** surveys the harbor. Built on the site of an old Viking fort and the ancient seat of the Dukes of Hamilton, the castle resembles a Victorian manor more than a medieval fortress, and contains a fine collection of paintings and scores of red deer hunting trophies. There's also an impressive jungle-like garden, with walks through groves of giant rhododendrons (in bloom May-June). If you can't manage a visit, look on the back of a Scottish £20 note. (☎302 202. Castle open daily Apr.-Sept. 11am-4:30pm; Oct. 11am-3:30pm; Nov.-Dec. F-Su 11am-3:30pm. Garden open daily 9:30am-sunset. Castle and gardens £7, concessions £5.30. Gardens only £3.50/£2.60/£9.50.) Any northbound bus from Brodick will pass the castle; Stagecoach also operates a vintage castle-bound coach service (Apr.-Sept. 9 per day; round-trip £2, children £1).

Brodick is spread out along **Shore Road,** just north of the ferry pier; take a right with your back to the water. Services include: the only **banks** and **ATMs** on the island along Shore Rd.; a **launderette** at **Collins' Good Food Shop,** Auchrannie Rd., just over the bridge as you head north of town (☎302 427; wash £3.05, dry 35p per 5min.; open M-Tu and Th-Sa 9am-5pm, W 9am-1pm); free **Internet access** at the **Arran Library,** Shore Rd. (open Tu 10am-5pm, Th and F 10am-7:30pm, Sa 10am-1pm); and the **post office,** set back from Shore Rd. on Mayish Rd. (☎302 245; open M-F 9am-5:30pm, Sa 9am-12:45pm; winter closed for lunch). Post Code: KA27 8AA.

As the nexus of island transportation, Brodick is a fine place to spend the night. While the town becomes busy late in the morning with daytrippers pouring off the ferry, things settle down in the evening. Try the spacious, seafront **Glenflorol Guest**

House ❷, Shore Rd. (☎302 707. Singles £20; doubles £40. Cash only.) Nearby and more upscale is **Dunvegan House ❸**, Shore Rd. (☎302 811. www.dunvegan-house.co.uk. No smoking. £30 per person. Cash only.) Another option is sandstone **Carrick Lodge ❸**, a 5min. uphill walk left from the ferry pier. (☎302 550. £28 per person. MC/V.) **Glen Rosa Farm ❶**, just over 2 mi. north of Brodick pier, provides basic camping facilities. (☎302 380. Toilets and cold water. £3.50 per person. Cash only.) The **Co-op** sells **groceries** across from the ferry. (☎302 515. Open M-Sa 8am-10pm, Su 9am-7pm.) A number of bars and inexpensive restaurants line Shore Rd. Travel by car or bus to **Creelers ❹**, along the A841 north of town on the way to the castle, a highly regarded seafood restaurant with fresh fish served in simple style. (☎302 810. Lunch £7.50-9.50. 3-course dinner £25. Open Mar.-Oct. Tu-Sa 12:30-2:30pm and 6-9:30pm, Su 1-3pm and 6-9:30pm; call ahead during winter. MC/V.)

WHITING BAY AND LAMLASH

Southeast Arran is marked by rolling hillsides, swaths of dense forest, and a gentle coastline. **Lamlash** is the largest town on the island and, with a fine natural harbor, a popular sailing center. Just off the coast, **Holy Island** rises dramatically from the water and dominates the Lamlash horizon. Presently owned and inhabited by a group of Tibetan Buddhist monks, the island has an exotic feel to it, with shrines, painted rocks, and Buddhist mottoes sharing the stark hills with herds of wild ponies. The island also provides a number of walking paths including one up **Mulloch Mor** (1030 ft.), the highest point on the island, with splendid views of Arran's mountains and the bright blue sea below. A regular **ferry** (☎600 349) departs Lamlash for Holy Island (15min., May-Sept. 8 per day, round-trip £9) throughout the year, though special arrangements must be made in winter. Farther south, **Whiting Bay**, is a sleepy seaside village stretched along the A841. From a trailhead near the hostel at the southern end of town, two relatively easy walks lead to the **Glenashdale Falls** (1 mi.) and the megalithic stone structures at **Giant's Graves**.

In Lamlash you will find a **Co-op grocery** store along the A841. (Open M-Sa 8am-10pm, Su 9am-7pm.) Just past where the A841 veers from the coast toward Brodick, **◪The Shore B&B ❸**, Shore Rd., has Scandinavian-style lodgings with fantastic views of Holy Island. (☎600 764. No singles. £28-30 per person. MC/V.) The **SYHA Whiting Bay ❶**, at the southern end of Whiting Bay, is a good hostel, right on the coast, next to a bus stop. (☎0870 004 1158. Self-catering kitchen, laundry and Internet access. Open Apr.-Oct. Dorms £10.50-11, under 18 £5-9.50. MC/V.) Helen White offers one ensuite double at the **Craigard B&B ❸**, Shore Rd. (☎700 378. Double £44. Cash only.) Several hotels serve food; **The Coffee Pot ❶**, toward the southern end of town on the coastal road, is a good spot for afternoon tea (£1-3) or a bowl of scrumptious homemade soup. (☎700 382. Open daily 10am-5pm. Cash only.)

LOCHRANZA

Northern Arran is a spectacular land of rich green hillsides, bare peaks and rocky coast. Idyllic **Lochranza**, 14 mi. from Brodick at the island's northern tip, shelters a serene harbor ringed with high hills and guarded by the rubble of a 14th-century **castle.** Pick up the key from the post office and unlock the iron gate to explore the solitary ruins. (Open Apr.-Sept. Free.) The **Isle of Arran Distillery**, at the southern end of town on the road to Brodick, was opened in 1995 but has already achieved international repute with its single malt, which isn't peaty like its Islay counterparts, making it smoother and more palatable to the uninitiated. (☎830 264. Open daily mid-Mar. to Oct. 10am-6pm; last tour 5pm. Tours start at 30min. past the hour and include a wee dram at the end. £3.50, concessions £2.50, under 12 free.) Lochranza also makes a popular base for ramblers, many of whom choose to meander 1 mi. down the coast, where the fishing village of **Catacol Bay** harbors the

Twelve Apostles, a dozen connected white houses that differ only in the shapes of their windows. A number of the northern peaks, including **Caisteal Abhail** (2817 ft.) are within a day's walk. Lochranza has **no banks or ATMs.** There is a **post office** located in **Primrose's,** the local **grocery** store, overlooking the erstwhile castle. (☎830 641. Store open M-F 9:30am-4:30pm, Sa 9am-5pm, Su noon-3pm; post office open M-F 11:30am-2:30pm.) **Post Code:** KA27 8HJ.

While lacking in services and less frequented by bus than its southern neighbors, Lochranza's simple beauty is worth the added effort. Toward the southern end on the main road to Brodick, the **SYHA Lochranza ❶** has 64 beds and two friendly and helpful wardens. (☎0870 004 1140. Open Mar.-Oct. Laundry and Internet access. Curfew 11:30pm. Dorms £10.50-11, under 18 £9. MC/V.) In the former town church across from the castle, Vicki Hudson will welcome you to the **Castlekirk B&B ❸,** which has high, arched ceilings, a lounge with stained-glass windows, and a peaceful ambience. (☎830 202; www.castlekirkarran.co.uk. No smoking. £20-22.50 per person. Cash only.) The top-notch **Apple Lodge ❹,** near the distillery, offers luxurious accommodations, including a suite with full kitchen ideal for longer stays. (☎830 229. No smoking. 3-course dinner £19. From £33 per person. Min. stay 3 days. Cash only.) Near the Apple Lodge, campers can pitch at the **Lochranza Golf Course Caravan and Camping Site ❶.** (☎830 273. Open Apr.-Oct. Toilets, showers, and laundry. £3.70 per person, £2.60 per tent. Cash only.) The restaurant at the **Isle of Arran Distillery ❷** features a daily menu of local Arran produce that ranges from an enormous vegetarian breakfast (£7) to haggis flavored with Arran Malt (£8). (Restaurant open daily mid-Mar. to Oct. 10am-5pm; June-Sept. until 6:30pm. MC/V.) In the evening, the **Lochranza Hotel ❸,** just along from the ferry pier, serves more typical pub grub. (☎830 223. Open daily 11am-9pm. Cash only.)

WESTERN ARRAN

Along the western shore of Arran you will find a handful of tiny settlements separated by miles of coastline. The **Machrie Moor Stone Circle,** a mysterious Bronze Age arrangement of upright stones and boulders, lies at the end of an easy 3 mi. walk. Follow the farm path 1 mi. south of Machrie village along the A841. Another mile south, the trail leading to the **King's Cave** (3 mi.) begins from a Forestry Commission carpark. Passing along coastal cliffs, the walk terminates at the caves where Robert the Bruce allegedly hid before returning to the mainland to claim the throne. From here it is another 2½ mi. south to **Blackwaterfoot,** where you can reconnect with island transportation and find a few places to eat and sleep.

GLASGOW ☎0141

Glasgow (pop. 700,000) is a hip and unpretentious city, in touch with its industrial past, but with a charismatic, cosmopolitan flair. Scotland's largest urban center has reinvented itself many times, retaining the mark of each transformation. Rising to prominence in Queen Victoria's reign, the grand architecture of the period, known as the Glasgow Style and spearheaded by Glaswegian luminary Charles Rennie MacKintosh, still characterizes the city center. But cranes littering the river Clyde and the blackened stones of Glasgow Cathedral recall the city's sooty past as a major industrial hub—once the world's leading shipbuilder and steel producer. Most recently, the daring curves of the multi-million pound Science Centre glint across the river, drawing crowds to Scotland's only IMAX theater. The world-renowned Glasgow School of Art, along with several world-class art museums and collections, give this city a thriving creative pulse. More important for weary travelers is the city's reputation for delectable cuisine, as well as the highest concentration of Indian eateries in the UK. The city's modern dynamism swells at night—fueled by the largest student population in Scotland and football-mad locals.

SOUTHERN
SCOTLAND

⊠ INTERCITY TRANSPORTATION

Glasgow lies on the River Clyde, 40 mi. west of Edinburgh. The M8 motorway links the two cities. Glasgow is the northern end of the M74, connecting with England.

Flights: Glasgow is served by 2 international airports.

Glasgow International Airport (☎887 1111; www.baa.co.uk/glasgow), 10 mi. west in Abbotsinch. Scotland's major airport, served by **KLM, British Airways,** and others. Scottish Citylink bus #905 runs to the airport from Buchanan Station (25min., every 10min. 6am-midnight, £3.40).

Prestwick International Airport (☎02192 511 000; www.gpia.co.uk), southwest of the city center. **Ryanair** flies from here to England and other countries in Europe. Express bus #X77 runs every hour from the terminal building to Buchanan St. (50min., £3.40).

Trains: Bus #88 connects Glasgow's 2 main stations (50p), but it's only a 10min. walk.

Central Station, St. Enoch; U: Gordon St. Open daily 5:30am-midnight. Ticket office open M-Sa 6am-11:25pm, Su 7:10am-11:05pm. Toilets 20p; shower with soap and towel £2; open M-Sa 5am-midnight, Su 6am-midnight. All luggage searched. Trains (☎08457 484 950) from: **Ardrossan** (1hr., 10-12 per day, £4.80); **Carlisle** (1½hr., every hr., £27); **Dumfries** (1¾hr.; M-Sa 7 per day, Su 2 per day; £10.30); **London King's Cross** (5-6hr., every hr., £100); **Manchester** (4hr., every hr., £40); **Stranraer** (2½hr.; M-Sa 8 per day, Su 3 per day; £15.60).

Queen Street Station, beside Millennium Hotel, George Sq. U: Buchanan St. Serves trains from the north and east. Open M-Sa 5am-12:30am, Su 7am-12:30am. Travel center open M-Sa 5:15am-10pm, Su 7am-10pm. Toilets 20p. All luggage scanned. Trains (☎08457 484 950) from: **Aberdeen** (2½hr.; M-Sa every hr., Su 11 per day; £33); **Edinburgh** (50min., 2 per hr., £9); **Fort William** (3¾hr., 2-3 per day, £18.70); **Inverness** (3¼hr., 5 per day, £32.90).

Buses: Buchanan Station, Hanover St. (☎0870 608 2608), 2 blocks north of Queen St. Station. Stables National Express and Scottish Citylink buses. Ticket office open M-Sa 6:30am-10:30pm, Su 7am-10:30pm. Toilets 20p. Luggage storage £2-4 per item. Lockers open daily 6:30am-10:30pm. **Scottish Citylink** (☎08705 505 050) from: **Aberdeen** (3-4½hr., every hr., £16.40); **Edinburgh** (75min., 2-3 per hr., £4); **Perth** (1½hr., every 30min., £6.50); **Inverness** (3½-4½hr., every hr., £15.90); **Oban** (3hr., 2-3 per day, £12.50); **Portree** (6½hr., 4 per day, £22.50). **National Express** (☎08705 808 080) arrives daily from **London** (8-10hr.; every hr.; £29).

⊞ ORIENTATION

George Square is the center of town; the stations and TIC are within a few blocks' radius. Sections of **Sauchiehall Street** (SAW-kee-hall), **Argyle Street,** and **Buchanan Street** are lined with stores and open only to pedestrians, forming busy outdoor shopping districts. **Charing Cross,** in the northwest where Bath St. crosses the M8, can be used as a locator. The vibrant **West End** revolves around **Byres Road** and **Glasgow University,** a mile northwest of George Sq. The city extends south of the **River Clyde** toward Pollok Country Park and the Science Centre.

⊟ LOCAL TRANSPORTATION

Travel Center: Strathclyde Transport Authority, St. Enoch's Sq. (☎0870 608 2608), 2 blocks from Central Station. U: St. Enoch. Immensely useful advice, passes, and Underground maps. Open M-Sa 8:30am-5:30pm. **STA Travel,** 184 Byres Rd. (☎338 6000). Student and budget travel arrangements. Open M-Sa 9am-6pm.

Public Transportation: Glasgow's transportation system includes suburban rail, private local bus services, and the circular **Underground (U)** subway line, a.k.a. the "Clockwork Orange." U trains run every 4-8min. M-Sa 6:30am-11pm, Su 11am-5:30pm. £1, children 50p. **Underground Journey and Season Tickets** are a good deal; bring a photo and ID to the office at St. Enoch station. 10 trips £7.50, children £4; 20 trips £12.50/

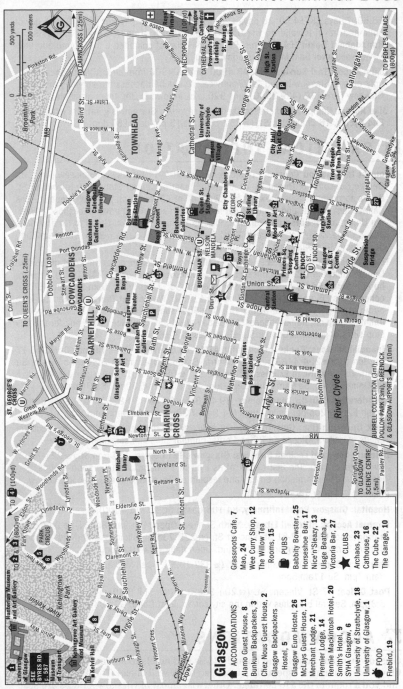

Glasgow

ACCOMMODATIONS

Alamo Guest House, 8
Bunkum Backpackers, 3
Chez Nous Guest House, 2
Glasgow Backpackers Hostel, 5
Glasgow Euro Hostel, 26
McLays Guest House, 11
Merchant Lodge, 21
Premier Lodge, 14
Rennie Mackintosh Hotel, 20
Smith's Hotel, 9
SYHA Glasgow, 6
University of Strathclyde, 18
University of Glasgow, 1

FOOD

Firebird, 19

Grassroots Cafe, 7
Mao, 24
Wee Curry Shop, 12
The Willow Tea Rooms, 15

PUBS

Babbity Bowster, 25
Horseshoe Bar, 17
Nice'n'Sleazy, 13
Uisge Beatha, 4
Victoria Bar, 27

★ **CLUBS**

Archaos, 23
Cathouse, 16
The Cube, 22
The Garage, 10

£6.50; 7 days £8/£4.50; 28 days £25/£13. The **Discovery Ticket** (£1.70) for 1 day of unlimited travel is valid on the Underground after 9:30am M-Sa and all day Su. A **Roundabout Ticket** (£4, children £2) covers 1 day of unlimited Underground and train travel, valid after 9am M-F and all day Sa-Su.

Taxis: Airport Taxi Services (☎848 4900, or dial 4900 from airport freephones) is the only official Glasgow-based 24/7 service. Wheelchair-accessible services available. **Glasgow Taxis LTD** (429 2900) runs 920 taxis in town. 1-3hr. tours available.

Bike Rental: Compact and crisscrossed by bike lanes, Glasgow is great for cycling. **West End Cycles,** 16 Chancellor St. (☎357 1344). £15 per day. £50 deposit.

⁊ PRACTICAL INFORMATION

Tourist Information Centre: 11 George Sq. (☎204 4400; www.seeglasgow.com), off George Sq. south of Queen St. Station, northeast of Central Station. U: Buchanan St. Books accommodations bookings for £2 (local) or £3 (regional) plus 10% deposit, sells CalMac ferry tickets, and arranges car rentals. Also contains a travel bookshop, a Western Union, and a **bureau de change.** Pick up the free *Essential Guide to Greater Glasgow & Clyde Valley* and *Where to Stay.* Open July-Aug. M-Sa 9am-8pm, Su 10am-6pm; Sept.-June M-Sa 9am-7pm, Su 10am-6pm.

Tours: Glasgow City Walk (☎946 4542). Historic 1½hr. tours cover the heart of the city. Departs from the TIC. £5, concessions £4. **Discover Glasgow** (☎248 7644). Hop-on, hop-off **Guide Friday** buses leave from George Sq. 2 per hr. 9:30am-5:30pm. £7.50, concessions £6, under 14 £2.50, families £17.50. **Walkabout Tours** provides day-long audio tours (£5) available at the TIC. **City Sightseeing** (☎204 044) bus tours allow unlimited hop-on, hop-off access with 2-day tickets for the price of 1. Look for the bus stop signs or get on in George Sq. £8, concessions £6.

Financial Services: Banks are plentiful; **ATMs** are on every corner. **Thomas Cook,** 15-17 Gordon St. (☎204 4484), inside Central Station. Open M-Sa 8:30am-5:30pm, Su 10am-4pm. **American Express,** 115 Hope St. (☎08706 001 060). Open July-Aug. M-F 8:30am-5:30pm, Sa 9am-5pm; Sept.-June M-F 8:30am-5:30pm, Sa 9am-noon.

Launderette: Coin-Op Laundromat, 39-41 Bank St. (☎339 8953). U: Kelvin Bridge. Wash £2, dry 20p per 5min. Open M-F 9am-7:30pm, Sa-Su 9am-5pm.

Work Opportunities: Glasgow's tourist influx swells during the summer. To meet the needs of visitors, Glasgow's TIC and other popular sites hire seasonal help.

Bisexual, Gay, and Lesbian Services: Glasgow LGBT Centre, 11 Dixon St. (☎221 7203, www.glgbt.org.uk). The first center of its kind in Scotland, it has support groups, get-togethers, and information on gay and lesbian clubs, bars, and activities in Glasgow.

Police: 173 Pitt St. (☎532 2000).

Hospital: Glasgow Royal Infirmary, 84-106 Castle St. (☎211 4000).

Internet Access: Mitchell Library, North St. Free. Open M-Th 9am-8pm, F-Sa 9am-5pm. **easyInternet Cafe,** 57-61 St. Vincent St. (☎222 2365), adjoining Cafe Nero. £1 buys 40min.-3hr., depending on the demand. Open daily 7am-10:45pm.

Pharmacy: Boots, 200 Sauchiehall St. (☎332 1925). Open M-W and F-Sa 8am-6pm, Th 8am-7pm, Su 11am-5pm.

Post Office: 47 St. Vincent St. (☎204 3688). Open M-F 8:30am-5:45pm, Sa 9am-5:30pm. Several branches within the city center. **Post Code:** G2 5QX.

⌂ ACCOMMODATIONS

Glasgow has four hostels and enough B&Bs and hotels to suit any budget. Places fill up in the summer, especially August, so book well ahead. The TIC can usually find you a room in the £16-20 range. Otherwise, most of Glasgow's B&Bs are scat-

GLASGOW'S "AULD FIRM" FOOTBALL RIVALRY

Red Sox versus Yankees, eat your heart out. England versus Argentina? Think again. Rocky Balboa versus Apollo Creed? Get real. When it comes to sporting rivalries, the 111-year-old contest between the Glasgow Rangers and Glasgow Celtic football clubs puts all other contenders to shame, both for the magnificence of its matchups on the pitch, and for the ferocity of the antagonism it engenders.

On the field of play, the "Auld Firm" rivalry (so named because of the aged status of the clubs involved) has been sublime, with home-grown footballing legends like Jim Baxter and Ally McCoist leading Rangers to Scottish soccer's most ever titles, and top-flight internationals like Sweden's Henrik Larsson carrying Celtic to its current championship form. Since 1891 one of the two clubs has won 86 of 105 possible premier-league titles, their seesawing periods of supremacy infusing nearly every head-to-head match with a sense of urgency rarely witnessed at such a high level of play. 2002 saw the two sides pitted against one another in both of Scotland's Cup competitions, the frenzied excitement of which was surely enough to inspire even the most apathetic of onlookers.

Indeed, off the pitch too, the passion that Auld Firm aficionados expend on the rivalry can scarcely be equaled. A study of any given Rangers-Celtic showdown yields ample proof of their exuberance: the briefest of glances bleacherwards meets with the spectacle of a stadium bedecked in swaths of Rangers blue and Celtic green, and the stands are rocked by songs and chants which repeatedly reverberate from one supporters' section to the other. Oddities also abound, not the least of which is the bewildering sight—unimaginable elsewhere in this normally nationalistic country, but commonplace on the grounds of Celtic Park and Ibrox—of dyed-in-the-wool Scotsmen waving Irish and even *English* flags, in keeping with club ties to Catholic (Celtic) and Protestant (Rangers) movements at home and in Northern Ireland.

Most of the time the rival revels are meant in a spirit of merriment. At times, however, the good fun can turn bad, even ugly. The dark side of the Auld Firm's association with sectarian strife in Ulster is driven home when, nearly every time the sides do battle on the pitch, Unionist Rangers supporters and rival Nationalist Celtic supporters shed each other's blood on the streets of Belfast. A similar style of hooliganism afflicts Scotland itself, where "No Football Colours" signs adorning the doors of Glaswegian pubs don't always succeed in preventing clashes between confrontational fans. And not even an ongoing ban on the sale of alcohol at matches has managed to forestall such appalling exchanges as occurred in March 2002, when Rangers fans directed racist pantomimes at Celtic's French defender Dianbobo Balde, or in September 2001, when a Celtic fan affronted Rangers American midfielder Claudio Reyna by simulating an airplane impacting a building. Perhaps this Mr. Hyde-like side of an otherwise glorious rivalry has contributed to Scottish football's recent money-motivated threat to oust the Auld Firm from its ranks. But whether Rangers and Celtic will surrender a greater share of their revenue for the right to remain in Scotland, or whether they will choose instead to compete in the more lucrative (and more challenging) English leagues, one thing is certain: wherever the clubs choose to vest their future interests, their fortunes will be followed by throngs of fans whose devotion ensures that their rivalry will remain a conspicuous aspect of Scottish culture.

Brian Algra, a former researcher for Let's Go: California, is currently pursuing a doctoral degree in English Literature at the University of Edinburgh.

tered on either side of **Argyle Street** in the university area or east of the Necropolis near **Westercraigs Road.** The universities offer summer housing, but available dorms change from year to year; check at the offices listed below.

HOSTELS

▨ **SYHA Glasgow,** 7-8 Park Terr. (☎332 3004). U: St. George's Cross. Take bus #44 from Central Station, ask for the 1st stop on Woodlands Rd., and follow the signs to the heart of the West End. Once the residence of a nobleman, later an upscale hotel visited by rock stars, now the best hostel in town. All rooms (4-8 beds) ensuite. Newly renovated; TV and game rooms, bike shed, Internet access, laundry, and kitchen; no curfew. June-Sept. dorms £14, under 18 £11.50; Oct- May £12.50/11. MC/V. ❶

Glasgow Euro Hostel (☎222 2828; www.euro-hostels.com). U: St. Enoch, at the corner of Clyde St. and Jamaica St., opposite Central Station. Comfortable, clean, and cool, this is your best bet for budget city-center lodging. All rooms ensuite. Brand new "Osmosis" bar is sleek and great for meeting people. TV lounges, game room, Internet access, laundry, and small kitchen. Breakfast included. Dorms £9.75-18.50. MC/V. ❷

Bunkum Backpackers, 26 Hillhead St. (☎581 4481; www.bunkumglasgow.co.uk). U: Hillhead, just up the hill from Glasgow University and the West End. Not our first choice, but the rooms are spacious and the locale is ideal for a good night's sleep or a trip to the Byres Rd. pubs. Lockers (£10 deposit), laundry (wash £1, dry 20p per 8min.), and kitchen. Dorms £12. Free parking, but call ahead to reserve. MC/V. ❷

Glasgow Backpackers Hostel, 17 Park Terr. (☎332 9099, Oct.-June 0131 220 1869; www.scotlands-top-hostels.com). U: St. George's Cross or Charing Cross. Take bus #44 from Central Station, ask for the 1st stop on Woodlands Rd., and follow the signs for the nearby SYHA hostel. Backpackers hostel is near Kelvingrove Park. Internet access, kitchen. Laundry £2.50. Open July-Sept. Dorms £12; doubles £30. AmEx/MC/V. ❷

UNIVERSITY DORMS

Both universities offer lodgings in several different locations each summer. The TIC's free *Greater Glasgow & Clyde Valley: Where to Stay,* has the best listings.

University of Strathclyde, Office of Sales and Marketing, 50 Richmond St. (☎548 3560; www.rescat.strath.ac.uk), near the campus village. Rooms and B&B available in summer at a number of dorms. Some are shared apartments, others are furnished rooms with 1 small kitchen per floor, laundry, and towels. Book well in advance. Open mid-June to mid-Sept. Singles £20, with breakfast £25-31. Cash only. ❸

University of Glasgow, 3 The Square (☎0800 027 2030; www.cvso.co.uk). Enter from University Ave. and turn right into The Square. Summer housing at several dorms. Office open M-F 9am-5pm. **Cairncross House,** 20 Kelvinhaugh Pl. (☎221 9334), has self-catering rooms off Argyle St., near Kelvingrove Park. Tea, coffee, soap, towels, and linen provided. Breakfast included. Singles and doubles from £23.75. Cash only. ❷

B&BS

McLays Guest House, 268 Renfrew St. (☎332 4796; www.mclays.com). With 3 dining rooms, satellite TV, and phones in each of the 62 rooms, this posh B&B looks and feels more like a hotel. Singles from £24, ensuite £32; doubles £40/£48. MC/V. ❸

Merchant Lodge, 52 Virginia St. (☎552 2424; www.the-merchant-lodge.sagenet.co.uk). Upscale lodgings in the city center. Originally a tobacco store built in the 1800s by traders from the former colonies; still boasts the original stone spiral staircase. Big breakfasts. All rooms ensuite. Singles £36; doubles £56; triples £70. AmEx/MC/V. ❹

Alamo Guest House, 46 Gray St. (☎339 2395; www.alamoguest-house.com), across from Kelvingrove Park. On a quiet West End street. Singles £25; doubles £50. MC/V. ❸

Chez Nous Guest House, 33 Hillhead St. (☎334 2977; www.cheznous-guesthouse.co.uk), just north of Glasgow University, across the street from Bunkum Backpackers. U: Hillhead. An attractive garden and big white sign welcome you to this lovely nook of comfort with convenient access to the West End. Attractive rooms are small but well-kept, and often booked right through the summer; call well in advance. Free parking. Singles £20.50-25; doubles £41-50, ensuite £45. Cash only. ❸

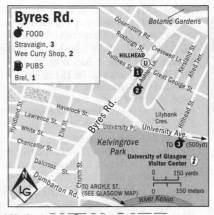

HOTELS

Smith's Hotel, 963 Sauchiehall St. (☎339 7674; www.smiths-hotel.com), a block east of Kelvingrove Park in the West End. Large white building. Free luggage storage for up to a week. Singles £21-36; doubles £38-52; triples £66. MC/V. ❸

Rennie Mackintosh Hotel, 59 Union St. (☎221 0050). This "Mock-Intosh" was inspired, not built, by the famous architect. A standard but central hotel, inexpensive given its location. Ask for a Mackintosh-style room. Breakfast included. Singles £25-30; doubles £25-50. AmEx/MC/V. ❹

Premier Lodge, 10 Elmbank Gdns. (☎0870 990 6312, www.premierlodge.com), right above the Charing Cross underground station. This chain hotel provides clean, comfortable rooms with basic amenities. From £46 per room. AmEx/MC/V. ❸

▣ FOOD

Glasgow is often called the curry capital of Britain, and for good reason. The area bordered by **Otago Street** in the west, **St. George's Road** in the east, and along **Great Western Road, Woodlands Road,** and **Eldon Street** brims with kebab and curry joints. Pick up a handy *Curry Guide to Glasgow* (£1) in the TIC to help you choose. The presence of university students has bred a number of hole-in-the-wall restaurants with excellent food at lower prices. **Byres Road** and **Ashton Lane,** a tiny hard-to-find cobblestone alley parallel to Byres Rd., thrive with cheap, trendy cafes and bistros. Bakeries along **High Street** below the cathedral serve scones for as little as 20p.

▨ **The Willow Tea Rooms,** 217 Sauchiehall St. (☎332 0521; www.willowtearooms.co.uk). U: Buchanan St., upstairs from Henderson Jewellers. A **branch** at 97 Buchanan St. A Glasgow landmark, restored in 1983 to its original design by Charles Rennie Mackintosh. Sample any of the 31 kinds of tea (£1.70 per pot) in this elegant atmosphere, or indulge in a 3-course high tea (£9.50). Open M-Sa 9am-4:30pm, Su noon-4:15pm. MC/V. ❷

▨ **Grassroots Cafe,** 97 St. George's Rd. (☎333 0534). U: St. George's Cross. This gem has the best vegetarian food in town. You can't go wrong here, but the creative handmade pastas (from £6.75) are to die for. Open daily 10am-10pm. AmEx/MC/V. ❷

Firebird, 1321 Argyle St. (☎334 0594). U: Kelvinhall. This is *the* place to be seen, but the prices are unpretentious and the imaginative nosh is outstanding (glazed duck and quince salad; £9.95), especially the house specialty pizzas. Open M-Th 10:30am-midnight, F-Sa 10:30am-1am, Su 11:30am-12:30am. MC/V. ❷

The Wee Curry Shop, 7 Buccleuch St., off Sauchiehall St. (☎353 0777). U: Cowcaddens. Also 23 Ashton Ln. (☎357 5280). U: Hillhead. From the makers of Mother India, a famous local restaurant. The best bang for your buck in this town full of pakora and poori. With short menus and real ingredients, this tiny spot enjoys a large following, so book your table in advance. A 2-course lunch is £4.80. Open M-Sa noon-2:30pm and 5:30-10:30pm. Buccleuch St., cash only. Ashton Ln., MC/V. ❶

Mao, 84 Brunswick St. (☎564 5161; www.cafemao.com). U: St. Enoch. Both floors of this Chinese/Japanese/Southeast Asian hodge-podge are always full. You'll need a pitchfork to get through the heaping portions of noodles. Open M-Th noon-11pm, F-Sa noon-11:30pm, Su 1-10pm. AmEx/MC/V. ❷

Stravaigin, 28 Gibson St. (334 2665), U: Kelvinbridge. Marvelously inventive, Stravaigin has Glasgow's tastiest traditional Scottish cuisine. Their mantra "think globally, eat locally" inspires fresh local seafood, game, and produce with exotic spices, chilies, and sauces (entrees £13-22). Don't miss their award-winning Bloody Marys. Open Tu-Th 5-11pm, F-Sa noon-2:30pm and 5-11pm, Su 5-11pm. AmEx/MC/V. ❸

🔘 SIGHTS

Glasgow is a budget sightseer's paradise, with grand museums, chic galleries, and splendid period architecture. Many of the best sights are part of the **Glasgow Museums** network, whose free collections are scattered across the city. *The List* (£2.20), available from newsagents, reviews current exhibitions and lists galleries.

THE CITY CENTER

▧ **GLASGOW CATHEDRAL AND NECROPOLIS.** The imposing black hulk of the Cathedral is a spectacular example of 13th-century Gothic architecture and a haunting reminder of the stormy Scottish Reformation of the 1560s. The marks and holes in the pillars show where Reformers vandalized the Catholic shrines and destroyed the statues. Neither Scottish Reformers nor Victorians would have been amused by much of the modern stained glass; look for the purple Adam and Eve in the western window, rendered in graphic detail. *(Castle St. ☎552 6891. Open Apr.-Sept. M-Sa 9:30am-6pm, Su 1-5pm; Oct.-Mar. until 4pm. Excellent personal tours of the Cathedral are free, just ask. Organ recitals and concerts held July-Aug. Tu at 7:30pm. Free-£7.)* At the chilling hilltop **Necropolis,** tombstones, statues, and obelisks lie aslant and broken on the ground. A 50 ft. statue of reformer John Knox looms atop the hill. *(Behind the cathedral over the Bridge of Sighs. Be careful after dark. Open 24hr. Free.)*

GEORGE SQUARE. This grand, red-paved landmark has always been the physical, cultural, commercial, and historical center of Glasgow. Named for George III, the square's 80 ft. central column was originally designed to support a statue of His Royal Highness. When the American colonies (Glasgow's closest trading partners) declared independence, Glaswegians replaced the king with a statue of Sir Walter Scott. The author wears his plaid, as always, over the wrong shoulder. Behind its dignified stone facade, the **City Chambers,** on the east side of George Sq., house an elaborate Italian Renaissance interior with more marble than the Vatican. *(☎287 4017. Free 1hr. tours M-F 10:30am and 2:30pm.)* The eclectic **Gallery of Modern Art (GaMA),** Queens St., south of George Sq., occupies a classical-style building that was once the Royal Exchange. *(☎229 1996. Open M-W and Sa 10am-5pm, Th 10am-8pm, F-Su 11am-5pm. Free.)*

ST. MUNGO MUSEUM OF RELIGIOUS LIFE AND ART. The museum surveys every religion from Islam to Yoruba in creative, accessible displays, though its prized possession is Dalí's *Christ of St. John's Cross*. Attractions can be pondered in the serene Japanese Zen Garden—Britain's first. *(2 Castle St. ☎553 2557. Open M-Th and Sa 10am-5pm, F-Su 11am-5pm. Free.)*

MCLELLAN GALLERIES. While the Kelvingrove Gallery and Museum is closed for refurbishment until 2006 (p. 589), over 200 highlights are being showcased at this city center gallery. *(270 Sauchiehall St., look for the big purple awning. ☎565 4137. Open M-Th and Sa 10am-5pm, F and Su 11am-5pm. Free.)*

OTHER CENTRAL SIGHTS. Built in 1471, **Provand's Lordship,** 3-7 Castle St., is the oldest house in Glasgow, and has the squeaky wooden floors to prove it. A collection of antique furniture attempts to transform its musty rooms into a recreation of medieval life, but the comical 19th-century caricatures of street entertainers (on the second floor) steal the show. The garden grows some of Glasgow's finest healing herbs. *(☎553 2557. Open M-Th and Sa 10am-5pm, F and Su 11am-5pm. Free.)* In their enthusiasm for the Industrial Revolution, Glaswegians destroyed most of their medieval past, only to recreate it later on the ground floor of the **People's Palace** on Glasgow Green. *(☎271 2951. Open M-Th and Sa 10am-5pm, F and Su 11am-5pm. Free.)*

THE WEST END

KELVINGROVE PARK, MUSEUM, AND ART GALLERY. Starting one block west of Park Circus, **Kelvingrove Park** is a genteel, wooded expanse on the banks of the River Kelvin, studded with statues and fountains. By day, it is lovely and peaceful, but be cautious at night. Rumored to have been built back to front (the true entrance faces the park, not the street), the spires of the **Kelvingrove Art Gallery and Museum** rise from the park's southwest corner. The museum is closed for renovations until 2006. In the meantime, the collection, including works by Rembrandt, Monet, van Gogh, Renoir, and Cezánne, is on display at the **McLellan Galleries** (p. 589) on Sauchiehall St. *(Open M-Th and Sa 10am-5pm, F and Su 11am-5pm. Free.)*

UNIVERSITY OF GLASGOW. The central spire of the neo-Gothic university towers over University Ave. The best views of the university buildings are from Sauchiehall St. by Kelvingrove Park, or 226 steps up the spire. Pick up *Visiting the University of Glasgow*, free at the TIC, or stop by the **Visitor Centre** for a free map and self-guided tour. *(U: Hillhead. ☎330 5511. Open May-Sept. M-Sa 9:30am-5pm, Su 2-5pm; Oct.-Apr. M-Sa 9:30am-5pm. Free tours M-Sa 2pm. Tower access F 2pm.)* The oldest museum in Scotland, the **Hunterian Museum** includes a death mask of Bonnie Prince Charlie, the 540-year-old University Mace, and a huge coin collection. *(☎330 4221. Open M-Sa 9:30am-5pm. Free.)* Across University St. on Hillhead St., the ⊠**Hunterian Art Gallery** displays 19th-century Scottish art, the world's second-largest Whistler collection, a variety of Rembrandts, Pissarros, Rodins, and an excellent collection of Pre-Raphaelites. Next door is the surprisingly modern reconstructed rooms of the **Mackintosh House.** *(☎330 5431. Open M-Sa 9:30am-5pm; closed during exam period. Gallery free; House £2.50, always free for students, and free for everyone after 2pm.)*

CHARLES RENNIE MACKINTOSH BUILDINGS. Art Nouveau virtuoso Charles Rennie Mackintosh is the most famous Scottish architect and designer, and Glasgow is a permanent exhibition of his work. Consult *Charles Rennie Mackintosh: Buildings & Tours Guide*, free at the TIC or any Mackintosh sight. **The Mackintosh Trail Ticket** (£10) allows unlimited subway access and entrance to all the CRM buildings for one day. Devotees with less time should at least check out the **Glasgow School of Art**, completed in 1898, where Mackintosh fused wrought iron with Scottish Baronial and French influences to create a uniquely modern Glaswegian style. *(167 Renfrew St. ☎ 353 4526. Tours M-F 11am and 2pm, Sa 10:30am; July-Aug. also Sa 11:30am and 1pm, Su 10:30, 11:30am, and 1pm. £3-5.)* The Charles Rennie Mackintosh Society is based in the magnificent **Mackintosh Church.** *(Queen's Cross, 870 Garscube Rd. ☎ 946 6600. Open M-F 10am-5pm; Mar.-Oct. also Su 2-5pm. £2, concessions £1.)*

BOTANIC GARDENS. Colorful gardens stretch along the River Kelvin at the northern end of Byres Rd. The **Main Range** hothouse contains a collection of orchids, ferns, palms, and cacti, while native Scottish species grow outside. A wrought-iron greenhouse, **Kibble Palace** has an elegant fish pond surrounded by Neoclassical statues, but will be closed until 2005 for a makeover. *(Great Western Rd. and Byres Rd.; U: Hillhead. ☎ 337 1642. Gardens open daily 7am-sunset. Kibble Palace and Main Range open daily Apr. to early Oct. 10am-4:45pm; late Oct. to Mar. 10am-4:15pm; Main Range opens Sa 1pm, Su noon. Tours available by reservation. Free.)*

SOUTH OF THE CLYDE

▓ POLLOK COUNTRY PARK AND BURRELL COLLECTION. The **Pollok Country Park** is an expanse of forest paths and colorful flora 3 mi. south of Glasgow. The famous **Burrell Collection** was once the private stash of ship magnate William Burrell, reflecting his diverse tastes: paintings by Cezánne and Degas, European tapestries, Persian textiles, and fine china. *(☎ 287 2550. Open M-Th and Sa 10am-5pm, F and Su 11am-5pm. Tours daily 11am, 2pm. Free.)* Also in the park is the less spectacular **Pollok House,** a Victorian mansion with a small collection of paintings, most notably pieces by El Greco, Goya, and William Blake. *(Take bus #45, 47, 48, or 57 from Jamaica St. (15min., £1.20). ☎ 616 6410. Open daily 10am-5pm. £5, students £3.75; Nov.-Mar. free.)*

GLASGOW SCIENCE CENTRE. The Science Centre is a recent addition to Glasgow's architectural tradition. The UK's only titanium-clad exterior gives it the unmistakable appearance of a giant space-armadillo. The three buildings require three tickets; the first houses Scotland's only **IMAX theater.** *(Open daily 10am-6pm. £5.50, concessions £4.50.)* The second contains hundreds of interactive exhibits. *(Open Tu-Su 10am-5pm. £6.50/£4.50.)* The 417 ft. **Glasgow Tower** is the only building in the world that rotates 360° from the ground up. Built as an airfoil to move with the wind, Scotland's tallest freestanding structure tells the city's story and offers amazing views. *(Open Su-Th noon-6pm, F-Sa noon-8pm. £5.50/£4.50.)* The entire complex cost £75 million—one-tenth the cost of London's Millennium Dome but ten times more successful. *(50 Pacific Quay. U: Cessnock, accessible by Bells Bridge. ☎ 420 5010; www.gsc.org.uk.)*

⬚ SHOPPING

Glasgow's got it all. **Sauchiehall Street** and **Buchanan Street** form a pedestrian-only zone in the heart of downtown, providing excellent shopping opportunities. Glaswegians have been known to remark, "if you go up Sauchie and down Bucky, you will have shopped your heart out." **Princes Square**, 48 Buchanan St., is a high-end shopping mall. Behind Argyle St., **St. Enoch Centre,** 55 St. Enoch Sq., is light and open with many chain stores. The **Buchanan Galleries** shopping center at the end of Buchanan St. opened to protests in 1999 due to its generic appearance, but it remains hugely popular among capitalists and tourists alike.

☑ NIGHTLIFE

Glaswegians have a reputation for partying hard; three universities and the highest student-to-resident ratio in Britain guarantee a kinetic after-hours vibe. *The List* (£2.50), available from newsagents, has detailed nightlife and entertainment listings, while *The Gig* (free at newsstands) highlights the live music scene.

PUBS

You'll never find yourself much more than half a block from a frothy pint in this city. The infamous **Byres Road** pub crawl slithers past Glasgow University, beginning at Tennant's Bar and proceeding toward the River Clyde. Watch for happy hours, but pace yourself for the midnight closing time.

▧ **Uisge Beatha,** 232 Woodlands Rd. (☎564 1596). U: Kelvinbridge. "Uisge Beatha" (ish-ker VAH) is Gaelic for "water of life" (read: whisky), and this pub has over 100 malts (£1.60-30). Savor the national drink as you listen to Gaelic tunes (live Tu-W and Su after 7pm) amidst classic wood furnishings and kilt-clad bartenders. Happy hour daily 4-7pm. Open M-Sa noon-midnight, Su 12:30pm-midnight. Food served M-W noon-5pm, Th-Sa noon-9pm, Su 12:30-3pm.

▧ **Babbity Bowster,** 16-18 Blackfriar St. (☎552 5055). U: Queen St. The perfect place to come for the authentic Glaswegian experience: fewer kilts and less Gaelic music, but more good drinks, and plenty of football talk. Tasty grub offers good value, and the vegetarian haggis (£4.20) isn't half bad. Open M-Sa 10am-midnight, Su 11am-midnight.

Nice'n'Sleazy, 421 Sauchiehall St., Charing Cross rail. (☎333 9637). Sleazy's, as the die-hard alt music crowdsters affectionately call it, features up-and-coming local bands in its cavernous underground belly nearly every night of the week. A colorful hotbed of funk and punk that captures the Glasgow music scene. Open daily 11:30am-11:45pm.

Brel, Ashton Ln. (☎342 4966; www.brelbarrestaurant.com). U: Hillhead. After a long day of sightseeing, nothing beats savoring a fine Belgian beer inside these old stable doors. In summer, people spill out onto the cobblestones of tiny Ashton Street. Try Belgian creations like raspberry beer, cloudy white beer, or "la morte subite"—sudden death beer. Open daily 10am-midnight.

Victoria Bar, 157-159 Bridgegate (☎552 6040). U: St. Enoch/Argyle St. rail. A fine assortment of beer and whisky, guitars strumming in the corner, and a mellow crowd make this a cozy spot to wind down. Open M-Sa 11am-midnight, Su 12:30pm-midnight.

Horseshoe Bar, 17-21 Drury St. (☎221 3051), in an alley off Reinfield St. This horseshoe-shaped Victorian pub has etched mirrors and the longest continuous bar in the UK. Happy hour daily 3-8pm. Karaoke M-Sa from 8pm, Su from 5pm. 3-course lunch (£3; M-Sa noon-2:30pm) or pantry-style dinner (£2.40; M-Sa 3-7:30pm) served upstairs. Open M-Sa 11am-midnight, Su 12:30pm-midnight.

CLUBS

Archaos, 25 Queen St. (☎204 3189). Two-for-one whiskies and student discounts pack in the punters. Sa is the busiest student night. Varied music on the domed 3rd fl.: Th "old school," F "clubby," Sa dance. Cover £3-7. Open Tu and Th-Su 11pm-3am.

The Cube, 34 Queen St. (☎226 8990). Home to some of the longest queues in Glasgow. Swank and ultra cool. Arrive early or know someone important. Tu gay night, W R&B. Cover £8, Th students £6. Open daily from 10:30 or 11pm.

The Garage, 490 Sauchiehall St. (☎332 1120). Look for the yellow truck hanging over the door. Music can be cheesy, but upstairs **Attic** plays indie with an occasional DJ. Cover £2-6, frequent student discounts. Open Sa 10:30pm-3am, Su-F 11pm-3am.

Cathouse, 15 Union St. (☎248 6606; www.glasgowcathouse.co.uk). Grunge and indie please a mostly younger crowd in this 3-floor club. Under-18 rockers can headbang downstairs in the Voodoo Room. Cover £2-5, students £1-3. Open Th-Su 11pm-3am.

🎵 🌿 ENTERTAINMENT AND FESTIVALS

The city's dynamic student population ensures countless film, food, and music events from October to April. **Ticket Centre,** City Hall, Candleriggs, will tell you what's playing at Glasgow's dozen-odd theaters. The free *City Live* guide has great tips. (☎287 5511. Open M-Sa 9:30am-9pm.) Theaters include the **Theatre Royal,** Hope St. (☎332 9000) and the **Tron Theatre,** 63 Trongate (☎552 4267). The **Cottier Theatre,** 935 Hyndland St. (☎357 3868), hosts a variety of musical and theatrical events, from avant-garde plays to opera. The **Royal Concert Hall,** Sauchiehall St., is a frequent venue for the Royal Scottish National Orchestra. (☎353 8000. Box office open M-Sa 10am-6pm.) The **Glasgow Film Theatre,** 12 Rose St., screens both mainstream and sleeper hits. (☎332 8128. Box office open M-Sa noon-9pm, Su 30min. before first film. Screenings £5, concessions £3.50; matinees £4/£3.75.)

During the **West End Festival** (www.westendfestival.co.uk) in late June, the city comes alive with longer bar hours and guest musicians. **Glasgow International Jazz Festival** (☎552 3552; www.jazzfest.co.uk), in the first week of July, draws international jazz greats. Take advantage of the fine dining during 🍴**Gourmet Glasgow,** where for two weeks in July over 50 restaurants and bars offer fixed-price meals and free tastings. Pick up *Gourmet Glasgow,* free at the TIC, or visit www.gourmetglasgow.com.) On the second Saturday of August, over 100 bagpipe bands compete on the Glasgow Green for the **World Pipe Championships** (☎221 5414).

🔲 DAYTRIP FROM GLASGOW

NEW LANARK

To reach New Lanark, you'll need to go through the town of Lanark. Trains from Glasgow Central run to Lanark (55min., every hr., £4.20). Ask for a "New Lanark Day Out" ticket at the train station. (☎08457 484 950. 4 departures and 3 round trips per day. Day round-trip £10.) Drivers will see New Lanark signposted from the M74; head south out of Glasgow.

Thirty miles southwest of Glasgow, in the peaceful Clyde valley, the recreated village of **New Lanark,** a World Heritage Site, allows visitors to experience the utopian dreams of socialist thinker Robert Owen. Founded in 1785, New Lanark was once the most productive manufacturing site in Scotland and a model of progressive working conditions. Owen sent children to school instead of the factory, paid living wages, and founded an Institute for the Formulation of Character. Today, visitors can walk through the restored store (perhaps the first co-op), a millworker's house, and Owen's own surprisingly posh residence. Admission includes the **New Millennium Experience,** a ride through the settlement's colorful history.

The surrounding Clyde valley has lovely hikes—check out displays on the natural wonders at the **Scottish Wildlife Visitor Centre.** (☎665 262. Open Apr.-Sept. M-F 11am-5pm, Sa-Su 1-5pm; Feb.-Mar. and Oct.-Dec. Sa-Su 1-5pm. £1, children 50p.) A 1 mi. walk upstream past the hydropower plant leads to the beautiful **Falls of Clyde.**

New Lanark is an easy daytrip from Glasgow, but a stay at the 🏠**SYHA New Lanark** ❶, Wee Row, Rosedale St., is worth your while. The restored mill workers' lodging has river views, and laundry. All rooms ensuite. (☎666 710. Breakfast included. Reception closed 10:30am-5pm. Curfew 11:45pm. Open Mar.-Oct. Dorms £9.50-12.50, under 18 £5-9.50. MC/V.)

CENTRAL SCOTLAND

Less lofty than the Highlands to the north and more subdued than the cities to the south, central Scotland has draws all its own. The eastern shoulder, curving from Fife to the Highland Boundary Fault along the North Sea, is a calm country-side peppered with centuries-old communities and the odd historical treasure. To the west, the landscape flattens from snow-covered mountains into the plains of the Central Lowlands, endowing the A82 road from Loch Lomond to Glen Coe with some of Scotland's best views. Castles of all vintages and sizes—from proud, ancient Stirling to Macbeth's dark, mystical Glamis—testify to the region's strategic importance, while the remote Inner Hebrides, separated by mountains and a strip of sea, are wrapped in their own enchanting beauty.

HIGHLIGHTS OF CENTRAL SCOTLAND

STIRLING. Admire the 5½ ft. sword of William Wallace and one of Britain's grandest castles in the historic royal seat of Scotland (p. 607).

LOCH LOMOND AND THE TROSSACHS. Explore the bonnie banks of Scotland's first national park, immortalized in the famous ballad (p. 610).

ISLE HOPPING. Pass through the Isle of Mull's pastel, palm-treed **Tobermory** (p. 622) on your way to the melodious caves of the stunning **Isle of Staffa** (p. 623).

ST. ANDREWS   ☎ 01334

Would you like to see a city given over,
Soul and body to a tyrannising game?
If you would, there's little need to be a rover,
For St. Andrews is the abject city's name.
    —Robert F. Murray

The "tyrannising game" of golf overruns the small city of St. Andrews. Driving through the surrounding Fife countryside, with its softly rolling hills and seemingly endless grass, it is not hard to imagine that this landscape provided the inspiration for the first golf courses. But any local will assure you that the town is more than just that. For the last thousand years, what was once Scotland's largest cathedral, now an extensive ruin on the coast, has attracted pilgrims from across Europe; today, a combination of golfers, students, beach bums, castle-hunters, ruin-seekers, and royalty-spotters all converge on its three medieval streets. Even for those not historically inclined, the town is worth spending the night, especially during term-time: thanks no doubt to Scotland's oldest university (founded 1410), tiny St. Andrews has the highest concentration of pubs in the UK.

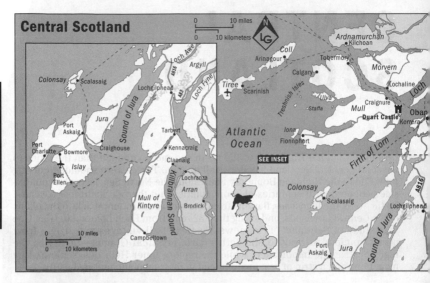

Central Scotland

▣ TRANSPORTATION

Drivers can take the A917, or Fife Coastal Tourist Route from Edinburgh. All **trains** (☎08457 484 590) stop 5 mi. away in **Leuchars** (LU-cars). The London-Edinburgh-Aberdeen stops in Perth, where those coming from Inverness can transfer (1hr., every hr., £8.10). The bus station is on City Rd. (☎474 238). **Buses** (☎01383 621 249) #X59 and X60 come from Edinburgh (2hr., M-Sa 1-2 per hr., £5.70); the #X24 comes in from Glasgow (2½hr., M-Sa every hr., £5.50). From Leuchars, buses #94 and 96 run to St. Andrews (1-2 per hr. 7am-8pm, £1.55). Buses in Fife run reduced service in the evenings and on Sundays; schedules are subject to change. Call Traveline (☎0870 608 2608) for info.

✷ ⑦ ORIENTATION AND PRACTICAL INFORMATION

The three main streets—**North Street, Market Street,** and **South Street**—run nearly parallel to each other, terminating near the cathedral at the town's east end.

Tourist Information Centre: 70 Market St. (☎472 021; www.standrews.co.uk). Ask for the free *St. Andrews Town Map and Guide.* Books accommodations in Fife for a 10% deposit (£3 more elsewhere). **Bureau de change.** Open July-Aug. M-Sa 9:30am-5pm, Su 10:30am-5pm; Sept. M-Sa 9:30am-5pm, Su 11am-4pm; Oct.-Mar. M-Sa 9:30am-5pm; Apr.-June M-Sa 9:30am-5:30pm, Su 11am-4pm.

Financial Services: Royal Bank of Scotland, 113-115 South St. (☎472 181). **Bureau de change.** Open M-Tu, Th-F 9am-5pm, W 9:30am-5pm, Sa 9am-1pm.

Launderette: 14b Woodburn Terr. (☎475 150), outside of town. £5 per load. Open M-Sa 9am-7pm, Su 9am-5pm; last wash 1½hr. before close.

Police: 100 North St. (☎418 700).

Internet Access: Westport, 170 South St., M-W 11am-11pm, Th-Sa 11am-1am, Su noon-10pm. Access is **free** downstairs from the bar, but be a good sport and a have a pint, too.

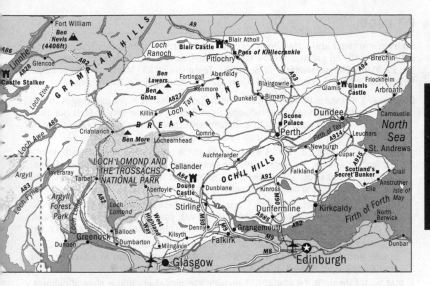

St. Andrews Library, Church Sq. (☎412 685). £1.75 per 30min. Open Tu and Th 9:30am-7pm, M and F-Su 9:30am-5pm.

Hospital: St. Andrews Memorial, Abbey Walk (☎472 327), southeast of town. 24hr. medical attention also available at the **Health Centre,** Pipeland Rd. (☎476 840).

Post Office: 127 South St. (☎08457 223 344). **Bureau de change.** Open M-Sa 10am-5:30pm. **Post Code:** KY16 9UL.

ACCOMMODATIONS

While it is possible to see St. Andrews as a daytrip from Edinburgh, St. Andrews makes an ideal base for visiting the Fife Seaside, and golf enthusiasts will want to headquarter themselves here. St. Andrews has only one hostel, but is packed with delightful B&Bs (£18-29 per person); over 20 line **Murray Park** and **Murray Place** alone. Prices are often cheaper during term time (Oct.-May).

■ **St. Andrews Tourist Hostel,** St. Mary's Pl. (☎479 911), tucked above the Grill House restaurant. From bus station, turn right on City Rd., then left on St. Mary's Pl. Colorfully painted, sparkling clean, spacious common room, and kitchen. Friendly backpacker haven in ideal location. Laundry facilities available. Key deposit £5. Reception 7am-11pm (May-Oct.) Dorms £12; family room £40-48. MC/V. ❷

Brownlees, 7 Murray Pl. (☎473 868; www.brownlees.co.uk). Feel like your own clan lord—each room has its own tartan, all with TV. £25-32 per person. Cash only. ❹

Cameron House, 11 Murray Park (☎472 306). Chat with the owner about golf in this traditionally furnished and very friendly family-run B&B. £25-30. MC/V. ❸

Castlemount, 2 The Scores (☎475 579). Classy and on the coast; castle view from upstairs dining room and from several rooms. Open June-Sept. £30. MC/V. ❸

FOOD

Many restaurants and cafes line the city's main streets, with enough diversity to satisfy virtually all palates and budgets. Those that can stand the smell should try the **I.J. Mellis Cheesemonger**, 149 South St. **Tesco** sits at 130 Market St. (☎413 600. Open M-W 8:30am-7:30pm, Th-F 8:30am-8pm, Sa 8am-7pm, Su 10am-6pm.)

Balaka, 3 Alexandra Pl. (☎474 825). Celebrities and royalty make pilgrimages to this den of gastronomical wonders, including Sean Connery and the King of Malaysia. Best in the UK? *Let's Go* doesn't doubt it. Unparalleled chicken tikka masala (£9.50). M-Th noon-3pm and 6pm-1am, F-Sa noon-1am, Su 5pm-1am. AmEx/MC/V. ❸

Northpoint, 24 North St. (☎473 997). Serves up the best lunch in town. Free-trade coffee, local artwork on the walls, a hip, bustling crowd, and a small and eclectic wine, champagne, and beer list complements the delicious sandwiches; try the baked brie, cranberry chutney, and caramelized onion griddle melt (£4.25). MC/V. ❷

Grill House Restaurant, St. Mary's Pl. (☎470 500), between Alexandra Pl. and Bell St. Conveniently situated downstairs from the hostel, you can order à la carte or take advantage of the 2-course prix-fixe (£12) at this cool mixed-fare spot. AmEx/MC/V. ❸

The Eating Place, 177-179 South St. (☎475 671). Scottish pancakes (under £5)—smaller and less sweet than your average flapjack—served all day in a friendly diner environment. Open M-Sa 9:30am-5pm, Su 11:30am-5pm. MC/V. ❷

P.M.'s, 1-3 Union St. (☎476 425) Late-night, Scottish style. After a night of pubbing, stop by this fish and chip joint, where any candy bar can be deep-fried for an extra 10p. Open M-F and Su 10am-11:30pm, Sa 10am-11pm. Cash only. ❶

 PUBS

After a long day of golf, it's the 19th hole that's most important, and St. Andrews has plenty to choose from. Get a serious lesson in whisky while you stamp your feet to live Scottish music at **Aikman's/The Cellar**, 32 Bell St. Smoky and vivacious, old golfers unwind to the beat upstairs, while young rugby players and lucky travelers sample the weekly rotating ales on the couches downstairs. (☎477 425; www.cellarbar.co.uk. Aikman's open daily 11am-1am; Cellar M-F and Su 6pm-1am, Sa 11am-1am.) The trendy **Gin House**, 116 South St. (next to the Blackfriars ruin) serves up posh martinis with a twist for its lively young hipsters; stop by for "U2sday," when free Baileys and Guinness are dished out whenever a U2 song comes on. (☎473 473; www.ginhouse.co.uk. M-W and Su 10am-midnight, Th-Sa 10am-1am.) **The Victoria**, 1 St. Mary's Pl., offers the lovelorn a place to ease their hearts in deep leather chairs, sometimes with live music, always with drink specials. (☎476 964. Happy hour F-Sa 11pm-midnight. Open M-W 10am-midnight, Th-Sa 10am-1am, Su noon-midnight.) **The Lizard Lounge**, 127 North St., in the basement of the Inn at North St., has happy hour nightly (8-9pm) and live bands most nights. (☎473 387. Open M-W 11am-midnight, Th-Sa 11am-1am, Su noon-midnight.)

SIGHTS AND OUTDOOR ACTIVITIES

GOLF. If you love golf, play golf, or think that you might ever want to play golf, this is your town. The game was such a popular pastime in St. Andrews that Scotland's rulers outlawed the sport three times. At the northwest edge of town, the **Old Course** stretches regally along the **West Sands**, a beach as well manicured as the greens. Mary, Queen of Scots, supposedly played here just days after her husband

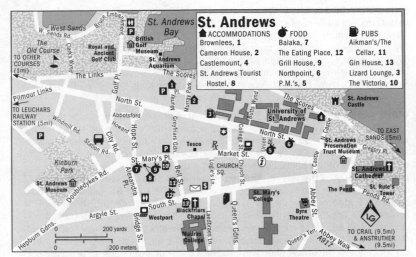

St. Andrews

ACCOMMODATIONS	FOOD	PUBS
Brownlees, 1	Balaka, 7	Aikman's/The
Cameron House, 2	The Eating Place, 12	Cellar, 11
Castlemount, 4	Grill House, 9	Gin House, 13
St. Andrews Tourist	Northpoint, 6	Lizard Lounge, 3
Hostel, 8	P.M.'s, 5	The Victoria, 10

was murdered. Nonmembers must present a handicap certificate or letter of introduction from a golf club. Book at least a year in advance, enter your name into a near-impossible lottery by 2pm the day before you hope to play, or get in line before dawn by the caddie master's hut as a single. (☎466 666. Apr.-Oct. £90 per round; Nov.-Mar. £56.) Call the same number to reserve a time at the less revered **New, Jubilee, Eden,** or **Strathtyrum** courses, or to rent clubs. (£20-45 per round. Club rental £20-30 per day.) The budget option is the nine-hole **Balgove Course** for £7-10. (☎466 666.) The newest and priciest of the Royal & Ancient courses, the **Kingsbarns Golf Links,** farther east along the coast. (☎880 222; www.kingsbarns.com. £125 per round.)

BRITISH GOLF MUSEUM. An endless display of golf paraphernalia, this collection includes examples of the earliest spoons (clubs) and feathers (balls). Enthusiasts will find the exhibits fascinating; others, less so. (Bruce Embankment ☎460 046. Open Apr.-Oct. M-Sa 9:30am-5:30pm, Su 10am-5pm; daily Mar. and Nov. 10am-4pm; Dec.-Feb. 11am-3pm. £4, concessions £3, children £2.)

ST. ANDREWS CATHEDRAL. The haunting, romantic ruins of what used to be Scotland's largest building is still the heart and soul of St. Andrews, especially since its stones now make up most of the facades along South St. The square **St. Rule's Tower** still stands rock solid above the hallowed site where the Greek monk St. Rule buried the relics of St. Andrew, patron saint of Scotland. Climb the tower's 155 steps for a spectacular view of the town, sea, and countryside. The **St. Andrews Cathedral Museum** houses ancient Pictish carvings and modern tombs. (☎472 563. Open daily Apr.-Sept. 9:30am-5:45pm; Oct.-Mar. 9:30am-3:45pm. Cathedral free. Museum and tower £4, seniors £3, children £1.25. Tower only £2.20/£1.60/75p.)

ST. ANDREWS CASTLE. Once the local bishop's residence, the castle features siege tunnels (not for the claustrophobic), bottle-shaped dungeons (not for anyone), and high stone walls to keep out religious heretics. Overrun in 1546 by Reforming Protestants, it's now stormed daily by tourists and school children. For stellar views, descend the path south of the castle fence, where seagulls make their nests in the crags. (On the water at the end of North Castle St. ☎477 196. Free tours daily 11:30am and 3:30pm. Open daily Apr.-Sept. 9:30am-6:30pm; Oct.-Mar. 9:30am-4:30pm. £2.50, seniors £1.90, children £1; joint ticket with cathedral museum £4/£3/£1.25.)

UNIVERSITY OF ST. ANDREWS. Founded in 1410, Scotland's oldest university maintains a well-heeled student body (including young Prince William) and a strong performing arts program. Meander into placid quads through the parking entrances on North St., including **St. Mary's,** where a thorn tree planted in 1728 by Mary, Queen of Scots, still grows. The **official tour** grants access to the building interiors. *(Between North St. and The Scores. Buy tickets from the Admissions Reception, Butts Wynd, beside St. Salvator's Chapel Tower on North St.* ☎*462 245. 1hr. tours mid-June to Aug. M-F 11am and 2:30pm. £4, concessions £3, under 6 free.)*

OTHER SIGHTS AND ACTIVITIES. The baronial **St. Andrews Museum** insists there are religions practiced off the fairways and that golf is but "a small dot" in the town's history. *(Kinburn Park, down Doubledykes Rd.* ☎*412 690 or 412 933. Hours change seasonally so call ahead. Open daily Apr.-Sept. 10am-5pm; Oct.-Mar. 10:30am-4:30pm. Free.)* Reproductions of a olde chemist's shoppe and painful-looking dentistry tools are among artifacts in the tiny **St. Andrews Preservation Trust Museum.** *(North St.* ☎*477 629. Open daily early June to Sept. 2-5pm. Donations welcome.)* The **St. Andrews Aquarium** houses a legion of eels, rays, and orphaned seals near the golf museum. *(The Scores.* ☎*474 786. Open daily 10am-6pm. Seal feeding between 10am and 2pm. £4.50, concessions £3.35-3.85.)* The recently reopened **Byre Theatre** puts on plays year-round. *(Abbey St.* ☎*475 000; www.byretheatre.com. Tickets £5-14. Student discounts available.)* And for beachgoers, the immaculate **West** and **East Sands** on either side of town are perfect for a stroll, but perhaps not a dip; it is the North Sea, after all. *(Free.)*

FIFE SEASIDE ☎01333

"A fringe of gold on a beggar's mantle" is how James II of Scotland described these burghs built among the sheltered bays and farmland of the Kingdom of Fife. Stretching from the Forth Bridge near Edinburgh north along the coast to St. Andrews are the tidy gardens and gabled roofs of the fishing villages in the East Neuk (East Corner) of Fife. Fife has enjoyed a prestigious position in Scotland's history; throughout most of the Middle Ages the Earls of Fife ranked highest among Scottish nobility and the archbishop of St. Andrews made his home here. Today, Fife maintains a quaint, peaceful coastal character. In summer, golfers cram onto the nearly 50 coastal courses. Smaller villages may be seen as daytrips from Edinburgh or St. Andrews; alternately, meandering coastal road A917 (**Fife Coastal Tourist Route**) links villages between the two cities. Drivers will find the ride serene, but non-drivers need not worry: bus service cruises by hourly with frequent stops (#X26; times and rates change seasonally; call **Fife Council's Area Transportation Office** (☎01334 412 902; M-F 9am-5pm). The **Fife Coastal Walk** runs along the shore and allows for walking, hiking, and biking within and between towns.

CRAIL. The oldest and perhaps the prettiest of Fife's villages, Crail developed around a castle built in the 12th century and presents a miniature maze of cobblestone streets and moss-covered stone cottages leading down to a craggy outcropping and sleepy harbor. Crail's **Tourist Information Centre,** 62-64 Marketgate, adjoins a small local history museum. (☎450 869. Open Apr.-Sept. M-Sa 10am-1pm and 2-5pm, Su noon-5pm.) Guided walks of town leave the museum (July-Aug. Su at 2:30pm; 1½-2hr., £3). Visit **Crail Pottery,** 75 Nethergate, for ceramics handmade by a family of master potters, displayed in their 17th-century cottage. (☎451 212; M-F 8am-5pm, Sa-Su 10am-5pm.) In the last week of July, the **Crail Festival** brings concerts, parades, and craft shows from local singers, marchers, and traders.

ANSTRUTHER. The largest of the seaside towns, Anstruther (AN-stoor) lies about 5 mi. west of Crail along the A917 (or 9 mi. southeast of St. Andrews along the B9131). **The Scottish Fisheries Museum,** Shore St., relates the history of the fishing, trade, and smuggling that brought Fife to prominence. (☎310 628. Open Apr.-Oct. M-Sa 10am-5:15pm, Su 11am-4:45 pm; Nov.-Mar. M-Sa 10am-4:30pm, Su 2-4:30pm; last admission 45min. before close. £3.50, concessions £2.50.) 6 mi. off the coast, the stunning mile-long **Isle of May** nature reserve is home to a large population of puffins, kittiwakes, razorbills, guillemots, shags, seals, and if you're lucky, dolphins and whales. Inland from the towering cliffs stand the ruins of Scotland's first lighthouse and the haunted 12th-century **St. Adrian's Chapel,** named after a monk murdered on the lonely island by the Danes in 875. From June to August, weather and tides permitting, the **May Princess** sails from Anstruther to the Isle. (☎310 103. 5hr. round-trip including time to walk ashore. May-Sept. £10, children £7.) Call ahead for sail times, or check with Anstruther's **Tourist Information Centre,** beside the museum (☎311 073. Apr.-June M-Sa 10am-5pm, Su 11am-4pm; July-Mar. M-Sa 10am-5:30pm, Su 11am-5pm.) On the way back from the bay and lighthouse, the **Anstruther Fish Bar and Restaurant ❶,** 44-46 Shore St., is known for serving Scotland's best fish and chips. (☎310 518. Open daily 11:30am-10pm. Cash only.)

(NOT SO) SECRET BUNKER. In the 1950s, the British government built a subterranean shelter halfway between Anstruther and St. Andrews (off the A917) to house British leaders in the case of nuclear war. 24,000 sq. ft. of cheesy displays, strategy rooms, sensory equipment, and even weapons launching systems are tucked away 100 ft. beneath an unassuming Scottish farmhouse. Locals claimed knowledge of the bunker long before the "secret" broke in 1993. Take bus #61 Anstruther-St. Andrews, ask to get off at Strathclyde intersection, walk 1 mi. east on B940, then follow a winding single-track (one lane) road for ½ mi. to the Bunker. (☎310 301. Open daily Apr.-Oct. 10am-5pm. £7, concessions £5.65, children £4.) Free **Internet access** in underground computer room.

ELIE. Don't let the retirement golfing developments along A917 deter you from discovering the sweeping sandy bay of Elie (EEL-y), 5 mi. west of Anstruther. Legend has it that the fishermen of Elie (then the 11th-century burgh of Earlsferry) helped Macduff, Earl of Fife, escape from Macbeth to safety by ferrying him across the Firth to Dunbar. Elie is an ideal spot for watersports and walks along the accessible beaches. Elie still boasts an ancient granary on its accessible pier dating from the 15th century. The picturesque **Ruby Bay,** named for the garnets occasionally found on its red-tinted sands, is an ideal swimming spot for any soul hardy enough to brave the chilly waters. It is worth the short walk to the 18th-century **Lady's Tower,** where Lady Janet Anstruther built an odd stone changing room on the cliffs and sent a bell-ringing servant to warn villagers to keep away when she was swimming, lest some commoner see her in her scanties. **Elie Watersports,** (down Stenton Row, on The Toft) rents and gives instruction on water sports and mountain bikes. (☎330 962; www.eliewatersports.com. £10-£15 per hr.) South Street is home to the oldest houses, including **The Castle** (from the 16th century). While on The Toft, check out the **Ship Inn,** (M-Sa noon-2:30pm, Su 12:30-3pm) a charming bar with rustic outdoor seating just feet from the sea. Try any of the locally caught seafood, or Bob the Butcher's award-winning haggis (£4.50). Delicious barbecues in the beer garden on Sundays (Apr.-Aug., 12:30pm-4pm). If St. Andrews (p. 593) is all booked up, golf at **Elie Sports Club** (☎330 955).

FALKLAND. No other village exudes such a sense of the past as the Royal Burgh of Falkland. With its commanding backdrop of the Lomond Hills, the tiny town is dominated by the Renaissance **Palace,** built by James IV in the beginning of the 16th century to replace the original fortified castle built by the Macduffs (of Shakespeare's *Macbeth*). His grand-daughter, the ill-fated **Mary Queen of Scots,**

CENTRAL SCOTLAND

enjoyed more peaceful days riding, hawking, and hunting the grounds and beautifully maintained **Falkland Gardens**. While admiring the old castle ruins and rosehedges behind the palace, peek into the unceremonious stone **Royal Tennis Court**, said to be the oldest tennis court of its kind in the world. Built in 1539, a club still plays Royal Tennis (versus lawn tennis) here today. (☎01337 857 397. Open Mar.-Oct. M-Sa 10am-5pm, Su 1-4:30pm; last admission 1hr. before close. £7, concessions £5.25, children £3.) To reach Falkland by car, follow the M90, A92, or A912 from the south or the A91 or A912 from the north and west. Public transportation is trickier: take **Stagecoach Fife** buses #36 or 66 from **Glenrothes** (40min., 2-4 per day) or #36 from **Perth** (1hr., 2-4 per day). For more information, call the **Fife Council's Public Transportation Information Line** (☎01592 416 060; M-F 9am-4pm). Though the castle is best seen as a day trip, Falkland's own **Burgh Lodge ❶**, 1 Back Wynd, is a great deal for a night's stay. (☎01337 857 710; www.burghlodge.co.uk. £10 per person, £9 each additional night. MC/V.) Across the street is the **Hayloft Tearoom ❶**, where freshly-baked scones and pastries are all £1 (☎01337 857 590) Cash only.

PERTH   ☎01738

Scotland's capital until 1452, Perth today is a town buzzing with cosmopolitan shops and restaurants and steeped in rich Scottish history. Busy all year round, Perth lives up to its self-promoting titles, "the perfect centre" and the "the fair city," with several beautiful walks in its Kinnoull Hill Wood and convenient access to nearby historical sites like Scone Palace. Travelers on the go might not stay more than an afternoon, but with several main streets of shops and restaurants, the city itself makes a nice stop for a day or two.

🖪 TRANSPORTATION. The **train station** is on Leonard St. (Open M-Sa 6:45am-8:45pm, Su 8:15am-8:25pm.) **Trains** (☎08457 484 950) from: **Aberdeen** (1½hr., 2 per hr., £20.70); **Edinburgh** (1½hr., 2 per hr., £8.50); **Glasgow** (1hr., every hr., £8.50); **Inverness** (2½hr., 8-9 per day, £15.80). The **bus station** is a block away on Leonard St. Ticket office open M-F 7:45am-5pm, Sa 8am-4:30pm. **Scottish Citylink** (☎08705 505 050) buses go from: **Aberdeen** (2hr., every hr., £12.10); **Dundee** (35min., every hr., £3.80); **Edinburgh** (1½hr., every hr., £5.80); **Glasgow** (1½hr., 2 per hr., £6); **Inverness** (2½hr., every hr., £10.80); **Pitlochry** (40min., every hr., £5.30). For more information, call **Traveline** (☎08706 082 608; M-Su 8am-8pm).

🖪 PRACTICAL INFORMATION. The **Tourist Information Centre**, Lower City Mills, books local rooms for £3 plus a 10% deposit. From either station, turn right (north) on Leonard St., turn right then left to South Methven St., and take a left on Old High St. (☎450 600; www.perthshire.co.uk. Open July-Aug. M-Sa 9:30am-6:30pm, Su 11am-5pm; Sept.-Oct. M-Sa 9:30am-5pm, Su 11am-4pm; Nov.-Mar. M-Sa 10am-4pm; Apr.-June M-Sa 9:30am-5:30pm, Su 11am-4pm.) **City Sightseeing** runs **bus tours** in summer, making transport to far-off attractions like Scone Palace and Kinnoull Hill easy. Buy tickets at the TIC or on the bus at the Mill St. stop. (☎629 339. June-Aug. M-Sa every hr. £6.50, seniors and students £4, children £2.) Other services include: **banks; Internet access** across from the TIC at **Gig@Bytes**, 5 St. Paul's Sq. (☎451 580; open M-Sa 10am-6:30pm, Su noon-5pm. £1.50 per 30min.); **police**, Barrack St. (☎621 141); **Superdrug Pharmacy**, 100 High St. (☎639 746); and the **post office**, 109 South St. (☎624 413; open M-Sa 9am-5:30pm). **Post Code:** PH2 8AF.

🖪🖸 ACCOMMODATIONS AND FOOD. The last hostel in Perth closed last year; the nearest option is the **Wester Caputh Independent Hostel** (see *p. 51*). Those with thicker wallets can try one of the numerous B&Bs clustered around **Glasgow**

Road, a 10min. walk from the city center, and on **Pitcullen Crescent,** across the river, with cheaper stays. **Darroch Guest House ❷,** 9 Pitcullen Cres., is one option with friendly, helpful owners (☎616 893. £20-25. AmEx/MC/V.)

An enormous **Safeway supermarket** is located a short drive outside of town on Caledonian Rd. (☎442 422. Open M-Tu and Sa 8am-8pm, W-Th 8am-9pm, F 8am-10pm, Su 9am-6pm.) Restaurants crowd the city's main streets. **Scaramouche ❶,** 103 South St., has a great location and serves cheap, ample portions, and wakes up at night for cheap cocktails and dancing. (☎637 479. Open M-Th 11am-11pm, F-Sa 11am-11:45pm, Su 12:30-11pm. Food served noon-8pm. Cash only.) **Mucky Mulligans,** 97 Canal Cres., hosts live music or DJs Th and Sa. (☎636 705. Occasional cover. Open M-W noon-11:30pm, Th-F noon-1:30am, Sa noon-1am, Su 6-11:30pm.)

🖼🎵 **SIGHTS AND OUTDOOR ACTIVITIES.** In 1559, John Knox delivered a fiery sermon from the pulpit of **St. John's Kirk,** on St. John's Pl., sparking the Scottish Reformation—history has been quieter here since then. (☎638 482. Open for Su services only, 9:30am, 11am.) **The Perth Museum and Art Gallery,** at the intersection of Tay St. and Perth Bridge, chronicles city life and hosts exhibits by local artists. Visitors are invited to try the medieval toilet seat. (Tours M-F in summer by request. Open M-Sa 10am-5pm. Free.) The **Fergusson Gallery,** in the Old Perth Water Works at the corner of Marshall Pl. and Tay St., displays work by local artist J.D. Fergusson. (☎441 944. Open M-Sa 10am-5pm. Free.) **The Perth Theatre,** 185 High St., hosts shows and concerts year-round. (☎621 031. Box office open M-Sa 10am-7:30pm.) The 16th-century home of the Earls of Kinnoull, **Balhousie Castle,** off Hay St., north of the city, now functions as regimental headquarters and houses the **Black Watch Regimental Museum.** It includes weapons, medals, the back-door key to Spandau prison in Berlin, and an occasional real member of the Watch. (☎621 281. Open May-Sept. M-Sa 10am-4:30pm; Oct.-Apr. M-Sa 10am-3:30pm.)

A 20min. walk across the **Perth Bridge** leads to **Kinnoull Hill Woodland Park** and its four nature walks, all of which finish at a magnificent summit with panoramic vistas. Beginners can try the **Tower Walk,** while hikers in better shape might choose the **Nature Walk,** which winds through the thick of the forest. Across the **Queen's Bridge,** near the Fergusson Gallery, the 1 mi. **Perth Sculpture Trail** begins in the Rodney Gardens and surveys 24 pieces of modern art while weaving along the river. **Bell's Cherrybank Centre** is famous for its 900-plus types of heather, but also provides a glossy look at Perth and its native, Arthur Bell, who took up the whisky business and had a library named after him as a reward. Visitors receive free admission to Pitlochry's Blair Athol Distillery (p. 605) and a free dram. Take bus #7 from South St., every 20min., or walk 20min. uphill along Glasgow Rd. (☎482 003. Hours change seasonally; call ahead. Open Apr.-Sept. M-Sa 9am-5pm; June-Sept. M-Sa 9am-5pm and Su noon-5pm; Oct.-Mar. M-F 11am-4pm. £3.)

🔁 DAYTRIPS FROM PERTH

🖼**SCONE PALACE.** Scone (SKOON), less than 3 mi. northeast of Perth on the A93, is a regional jewel. With an impressive collection of china, portrait paintings, ivories, and furniture, as well as the Earl of Mansfield's spectacular orchids, Scone is a fine example of early 19th-century Georgian architecture, but her real treasures lie outside the palace walls. A horticulturalist's utopia awaits in the endless grounds patrolled by showy peacocks and billowing with purple rhododendrons. It was here on the humble **Stone of Scone** (see **Stone of Destiny,** p. 45) where Macbeth, Robert the Bruce, and Charles II were all crowned Kings of Scotland. An entire afternoon could be spent picnicking and

THE HIDDEN DEAL

THE WESTER CAPUTH INDEPENDENT HOSTEL

The **Wester Caputh Independent Hostel,** outside of Dunkeld and Birnam, is everything that a hostel could be and everything that a Scottish countryside experience should be. Surrounded by roses and separated from the scenic River Tay by a raspberry field, this farmhouse is a gem. The friendly managers, Wilma and Roy, make guests feel at home with their cozy fireplace, well-stocked kitchen, old farmhouse decor, and some of Britain's best showers.

Even better than the beds, bathing, and breakfast, however, is the music. Local musicians stop by nightly to play real honest-to-goodness folk tunes on fiddle, guitar, squeezebox, harmonica, and piano; Wilma and Roy always join right in. Hostelers are encouraged, to join in the revelry. Free music and good company make this a required stop for any stay in Perthshire.

Go east out of Dunkeld on the A984 and turn right (heading south) after the church in Caputh. Take the next right going west, and the hostel is the second group of buildings on the right. ☎/fax 01738 710 617 or 710 449. Internet £1 per 15min. Bike rentals £6-10. Laundry £2-4. Dorms £8, with breakfast £10.

viewing the colorful butterfly garden and finding one's way through the **Murray Star Maze.** *(Directly off the A94. Take bus #3 from South St. (every hr.) and tell the driver where you're going, or hop on a bus tour from the TIC. ☎01738 552 300; www.scone-palace.co.uk. Open daily Apr.-Oct. 9:30am-4:45pm. £6.35, seniors and students £5.50, under 16 £3.75. Grounds only £3.25/£2.65/£1.80.)*

GLAMIS CASTLE. Macbeth's purported home, Glamis (pronounced GLAMZ) has been the family home of the Earls of Strathmore for generations; in recent times, it was the childhood playground of the Queen Mum. The castle noses its dozen handsome turrets into the sky 35 mi. northeast of Perth on the A94. Royal watchers will find a treasure trove of stories and artifacts highlighted in a free tour (every 45min. in summer). The original interiors, collections of armor, paintings, and furniture are significant, but the trek to the castle is inconvenient without a car. *(Take Scottish Citylink from Perth to Dundee, then catch Strathtay bus #22 or 22A to Glamis (35min., 5 per day). Call Traveline, ☎0870 608 2608, for updated information. Castle ☎01307 840 393. Open Apr.-Oct. daily 10:30am-5:30pm; Nov.-Mar. call for hours. Last admission 4:45pm. £6.75, concessions £5, children £3.50. Grounds only £3.50/£2.50/ £2.50.)*

DUNKELD AND BIRNAM

☎01350

Huddled amid the forested hills of Perthshire's "Big Tree Country" on either side of the River Tay, the twin medieval towns of Dunkeld (dun-KELD) and Birnam (separated by a short bridge) provide access to one of Scotland's most isolated regions. The area has long welcomed day walkers and ruin-spotters, and local artists energetically contribute to a thriving culture of traditional Scottish folk music.

◪ TRANSPORTATION. The unstaffed **train station** in Birnam is on the Edinburgh-Inverness line. **Trains** (☎08457 484 950) run from: **Edinburgh** (2hr., 5 per day, £9.50); **Glasgow** (1½hr., 5 per day, £17); **Inverness** (1½hr., 5 per day, £15); **Perth** (15min., 5 per day, £5.10). **Scottish Citylink buses** (☎08705 505 050) stop by the Birnam train station carpark from: **Edinburgh** (1½hr., 3 per day, £15); **Glasgow** (2hr., 3 per day, £15); **Inverness** (2hr., 3 per day, £17); **Perth** (22min., 3 per day, £8); **Pitlochry** (20min., 5 per day, £7.50). If you're coming from Perth or Pitlochry, **local buses,** stop at the Birnam House Hotel, are cheaper and may get you closer to your destination. Grab the essential *Highland Perthshire and Stanley Area Local*

Public Transportation Guide (free) from any TIC or call **Traveline** (☎08706 082 608; M-Su 8am-8pm). **Rent bikes** at Dunkeld Bike Hire, Perth Rd., in Birnam. (☎728 744. Bikes £12 per day. £100 deposit. Open daily 9am-5pm.)

⑦ PRACTICAL INFORMATION. Nearly all public transport arrives in Birnam (a popular Victorian vacation spot) but most tourist amenities reside in more historic Dunkeld. The Dunkeld **Tourist Information Centre,** by the fountain in the town center, 1 mi. from the train station, books beds for £3 and a 10% deposit. (☎727 688. Open May-Oct. every day 9:30am-5:30pm; July-Aug. 9:30am-6:30pm.) Other services include: Dunkeld's **Bank of Scotland,** High St. (☎727 759; open M-Tu and Th-F 9am-12:30pm and 1:30-5pm, W 1:30-5pm); **Davidson's Chemists,** 1 Bridge St. M-F 9am-1pm and 2-5:30pm, Sa 9am-1pm and 2-5pm; **Internet access** at the Public Bar of the **Royal Dunkeld Hotel,** Atholl St. (£1 per 10min.); and the **post office,** Bridge St. (☎08457 223 344; open M-W and F 9am-1pm and 2-5:30pm, Th 9am-1pm, Sa 9am-12:30pm). **Post Code:** PH8 0AH.

⌂◖ ACCOMMODATIONS AND FOOD. Aside from the wonderful nearby **Wester Caputh Hostel ❶** (see sidebar), Birnam and Dunkeld have dozens of **B&Bs;** the TIC keeps a list with phone numbers outside its door. The happening **Taybank Hotel ❷,** previously owned by legendary folk musician Dougie Maclean of "Caledonia" fame, is by the Dunkeld Bridge and offers simple rooms themed around Scottish songsters. (☎727 340; www.taybank.com. £17-19 per person; singles £5 extra. MC/V.) The **Waterbury Guest House ❸,** Murthly Terr., in Birnam, is more expensive, but offers lovely ensuite rooms with breakfast and dinner for £60. (☎727 324. £23. AmEx/MC/V.) **Campers** should head for the **Inver Mill Caravan Park ❶,** on the riverside across from Dunkeld and to the north. (☎727 477. Laundry £4. Open Apr.-Oct. £9-11 for 2 people; £1 each additional person. Cash only.)

The **Co-op** supermarket, 15 Bridge St., is in Dunkeld. (☎727 321. Open M-Sa 8am-8pm, Su 9am-6pm.) Don't miss out on a "session" (a wee dram of something local, and a song) at **Maclean's Real Music Bar ❶,** in the Taybank Hotel (see above), where they serve "stovies," or baked potatoes packed with meat or veggies (£3.50), and host casual gatherings of musicians. Spare instruments hang on the walls for you to join in the music-making. (☎727 340. Cover varies. Open daily noon-11pm. MC/V.) For lunch, head to the **Dunkeld Snack Bar ❷,** 5 Atholl St., for fish and chips, or haggis. (☎727 427. Open M-Sa 11am-6pm, Su noon-6pm. MC/V.)

◉◪ SIGHTS AND OUTDOORS. Carefully maintained 18th-century houses line the way to the main attraction, ▨**Dunkeld Cathedral,** High St., just steps from the TIC. A truly peaceful spot, set upon the grand banks of the quiet River Tay, the grassy nave is one of Scotland's most picture-perfect ruins. (Open Apr.-Sept. M-Sa 9:30am-6:30pm, Su 2-6:30pm; Oct.-Mar. M-Sa 9:30am-4pm, Su 2-4pm. Free.) Beatrix Potter spent most of her childhood holidays in Birnam, drawing on her experiences for *The Tale of Peter Rabbit.* The **Beatrix Potter Garden** at the **Birnam Institute,** Station Rd., celebrates her today. (☎727 674; www.birnaminstitute.com. Open M-Sa 10am-4pm, Su 2-4pm. Free.) **The Dunkeld and Birnam Festival,** held the last week of June, includes local paintings, plays, and music. (☎727 688; www.dunkeldandbirnamfestival.org.uk.)

The TIC's *Dunkeld & Birnam Walks* (50p) provides maps of area rambles. Paths lead north from Birnam to the great **Birnam Oak,** remnant of the fabled Birnam Wood in *Macbeth.* The roaring waterfalls of the ▨**Hermitage** tumble 1½ mi. away in a gorge in the middle of the ancient forest. A well-marked ¾ mi. path passes through designated photo-ops. The most strenuous is the **Birnam Hill Walk,** ascends 1000 ft. south of Birnam and rewards with vast panoramas. Birdwatchers will enjoy the **Loch of the Lowes,** a wildlife reserve east of Dunkeld and just south of the A923 (20min. on a path from the TIC). For the past eight years, the Loch has served as a summer home for ospreys who fly all the way from Gambia. (☎727 337. Visitors center open daily mid-July to mid-Aug. 10am-6pm; Apr. to mid-July and mid-Aug. to Sept. 10am-5pm.) To fish, obtain a license (£3-4) from **Kettles**, 15 Atholl St. (☎727 556). Trout season lasts from mid-March to mid-October.

⚡ DAYTRIP FROM DUNKELD AND BIRNAM

THE CATERAN TRAIL. Highland Perthshire, northeast of Dunkeld and Birnam, is home to the spectacular Cateran Trail, a 60 mi. hike past the cairns and ruins lining a loop between the Bridge of Cally, Alyth, Blairgowrie, and the Spittal of Glenshee. The route approximates the "Cateran Brands" trail of medieval cattle rustlers and is well-marked, though visitors are strongly encouraged to equip themselves with Ordnance Explorer Maps 381, 387, and 388 before setting off (available at TICs; £7). Five of the six trails are for beginners, and each ends in a town with several B&Bs. (*Call the Cateran Trail Company (☎0800 277 200) to arrange accommodations—for around £150, they'll cart your pack.*)

LOCH TAY

The most beautiful part of Perthshire is also the most remote. Travelers approaching the Loch from the South should go to **Aberfeldy;** those coming from the North should go to **Killin** for Loch access. Aberfeldy, a low-key base for enjoying the Loch, is accessible by various Perthshire local buses from Pitlochry, Perth, and Dunkeld and Birnam. Schedules vary; **Traveline** (☎08706 082 608) has the most up-to-date information. Towns around Loch Tay may be reached from Aberfeldy by postbus; however, many only run once per day. **Postbus Helpline** (☎01246 546 329) or the Aberfeldy **Tourist Information Centre** can help you plan. (☎01887 820 276. Open July-Aug. M-Sa 9:30am-6:30pm, Su 11am-5pm; Sept.-June M-Sa 9:30am-4:30pm, Su 11am-4pm.) Drivers can reach each of the towns by the A827.

About 5 mi. past Aberfeldy on the southern shore (A827) resides the **Crannog Centre,** a replica of an ancient Celtic loch dwelling. Visitors can listen to the history of Scottish crannogs, walk inside one, and try their best to use the prehistoric tools. (☎01887 830 583. 1hr. tour. Open daily Mar.-Oct. 10am-5:30pm. £4.25, concessions £3.85, children £3.)

On the North shore, midway to Killin, a spectacular single track road takes you off A827 for a scenic route up the side of mighty **Ben Lawers** and around Ben Ghlas to the **Visitor Centre.** (☎01567 820 397. Open daily Easter-Sept. 10am-1pm and 2-5pm.) Those with a car enjoy direct access to the Centre, but beware the flocks of sheep who call the mountain home. Postbus #213 (M-Sa) stops at the bottom of the road that leads to the Visitor Centre on its way from **Aberfeldy** to **Killin.** Continue along the narrow but well-paved road for unparalleled views of the mountains and stop by the tiny village of **Fortingall,** on the northern end of Loch Tay, home to a 3000-year-old yew tree, the oldest living organism in Europe (and perhaps the world) and the supposed birthplace of Pontius Pilate. **Postbuses** arrive from Aberfeldy (#211, 55min., M-Sa 9am). The village of **Killin** has reasonably priced B&Bs and a **SHYA hostel ❶,** one mile outside of town, which, despite 1970s style decor and spartan amenities inside a Victorian townhouse, is a well-located base camp for ramblers. (☎01567 820 546. Open Mar.-Oct. F-Sa. Dorms £9, under 18, £7.50. MC/V.) At the two-room **Breadalbane Folklore Centre** you can discover the secret origin of spiritual Scotland: kelpies, urisks, and faeries. The adjoining **Tourist Information Centre,** by the Falls of Douchart on Main St., which offers information on St. Fillan and the local McGregor clan as well as information on countless walks. (☎01567 820 254. Open July-Aug. daily 9:30am-6:30pm; June and Sept. 10am-6pm; Oct. and Mar.-May 10am-5pm. Folklore Centre £1.55, concessions £1.05.) A 2hr. hike starts from behind the schoolyard on Main St. and leads to a sheep's-eye view of the loch. On the northern end of Main St., go to the **Killin Library** (☎01567 820 571) for free **Internet access; Grant's Laundry** (☎01567 820 235) is the only place in town to wash clothes; **police** are on Main St. (☎01567 820 222). **Postbuses** (each 1 per day) arrive from: **Aberfeldy** (#213, 3hr.); **Crianlarich** (#025, about 45min.); **Tyndrum** (#025, about 45 min.).

PITLOCHRY ☎01796

The small Victorian town of Pitlochry, "gateway to the Highlands," sits where lush lowlands begin to give way to rugged, barren mountains. Pitlochry's beautiful setting has attracted tourists from around the world, transforming the town into a tidy strip of shops selling tacky knick-knacks, wool sweaters, and plush Nessies. Its two distilleries, numerous accommodations, and unparalleled access to walking and hiking routes make it worth a stop on any northbound route.

TRANSPORTATION. Trains (☎08457 484 950) stop near the town center from: **Edinburgh** (2hr., 7 per day, £19.70); **Glasgow** (1¾hr., 7 per day, £19.70); **Inverness** (1¾hr., 9 per day, £13.80); **Perth** (30min., 9 per day, £5). **Scottish Citylink buses** (☎08705 505 050) stop outside the Fishers Hotel on Atholl Rd. from: **Edinburgh** (2hr., 10 per day, £8); **Glasgow** (2½hr., 8 per day, £8); **Inverness** (2hr., every hr., £8.10); **Perth** (40min., every hr., £5). From Perth, Pitlochry is accessible by various local buses; call **Traveline** (☎08706 082 608) for information. Call ahead to rent **bikes** at **Escape Route,** 8 West Moulin Rd. (☎473 859. £9 per half-day, £15 per day.Open Su-F 10am-5pm, Sa 9:30am-5pm.)

PRACTICAL INFORMATION. The **Tourist Information Centre,** 22 Atholl Rd., stocks *Pitlochry Walks* (50p), a must-have map for hikers. (☎472 215. Open June-Aug. M-Sa 9am-7pm, Su 9am-6pm; Sept.-Nov. and Apr.-May M-Sa 9am-6pm, Su 11am-5pm; Nov.-Mar. M-F 9am-5pm, Sa 10am-2pm.) Other services include: the **Royal Bank of Scotland,** 84 Atholl Rd. (☎532 200; open M-Tu and Th-F 9am-5pm, W 9:30am-5pm); the **Pitlochry Launderette,** 3 West Moulin Rd. (☎474 044; wash £3, dry £2; open M-W and F 8:30am-5pm, Th and Sa 9am-5pm); **Lloyds Pharmacy,** 122-124 Atholl Rd. (☎472 414; open Su-M 9:30am-5:30pm, Sa 9:30am-5pm); **Internet access** at the **Computer Services Centre,** 67 Atholl Rd. (☎473 711; £1.50 per 20 min.; open M-F 9am-5:30pm, Sa 9am-12:30pm) or **MG Technologies Internet Cafe,** 26 Bonnethill Rd. (☎474 141; £1.50 per 15min., £2 per 30min.; open daily 9am-5pm); **post office,** 92 Atholl Rd. (open M-F 9am-5:30pm, Sa 1-4pm). **Post Code:** PH16 5AH.

ACCOMMODATIONS AND FOOD. Pitlochry Backpackers ❷, 134 Atholl St., right in the center of town, has dorms, twins, and doubles (some ensuite), plus a friendly staff, cheap bike rentals (£5 per half-day), TV, and pool table. (☎470 044. Curfew 2am. Open Apr.-Oct. £12 per person. MC/V.) Across from the TIC, **Atholl Villa ❸,** 29 Atholl Rd., provides comfortable ensuite rooms, a private carpark, award-winning gardens, and spacious family areas. (☎473 820. £26-40 per person. Cash only.) The **SYHA Pitlochry ❶,** at Knockard and Well Brae Rd., 15min. from town, is more notable for its magnificent views than its standard dorms. From the train and bus stations, turn right on Atholl Rd. then go uphill onto Bonnethill Rd., where the hostel is signposted. (☎472 308. Breakfast £2.20. Internet access £1 per 15min. Laundry £2. Reception open 7am-11am and 5-11:45pm. Curfew 11:45pm. Dorms £10, under 18 £8. MC/V.) Two miles past town on Atholl Rd., camp at **Faskally Caravan Park ❶.** (☎472 007; www.faskally.co.uk. Open mid-Mar. to Oct. £10-12 per tent. Extra for electricity, sauna, pool, and jacuzzi. MC/V.)

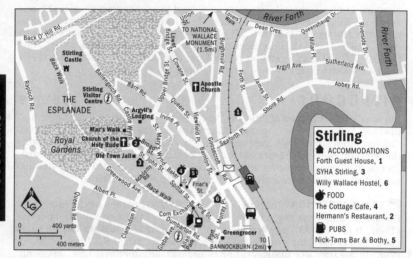

Stirling

♠ ACCOMMODATIONS
Forth Guest House, 1
SYHA Stirling, 3
Willy Wallace Hostel, 6

🍴 FOOD
The Cottage Cafe, 4
Hermann's Restaurant, 2

🍺 PUBS
Nick-Tams Bar & Bothy, 5

On West Moulin Rd., in Pitlochry, the **Pitlochry Co-op** provides **groceries.** (☎474 088. Open daily 8am-10pm.) The 300-year-old **Moulin Inn ❷**, Moulin Sq., in the wee village of Moulin, brews its own "Braveheart Ale" and serves a selection of grub, including various veggie options. (☎472 196. Open Su-Th noon-11pm, F-Sa noon-11:45pm. Food served until 9pm. Free brewery tours M-F 9-4:30pm.) **Ardchoille Fish & Chip Cafe ❶**, 142 Atholl Rd., serves the cheapest eats in town. (☎472 170. Open daily 11am-10pm.) **Victoria's Restaurant and Coffee Shop ❷**, 45 Atholl Rd., has everything from breakfast to dessert. (☎472 670. Open daily 8am-10pm.) End the night with the pub crowd, old and young alike, at **McKays,** on Birnam Pl. just off Atholl Rd. (☎473 888. Open noon-1:30am.)

🎥 🏃 **SIGHTS AND OUTDOORS.** **Hikers** should arm themselves with *Pitlochry Walks* (50p), available at the TIC. For a quick jaunt, take the path over the suspension footbridge in Moulin to the **Pitlochry Dam and Salmon Ladder.** From the observation chamber, watch fish struggle ceaselessly against the current as an electronic fish counter keeps tally. (☎473 152. Open Apr.-Sept. M-F 10:30am-5:30pm. Jul.-Aug. Sa-Su. Observation chamber and dam free; visitor center £2.50, students £1.50, children £1.25.) The opportunistic can get a fishing permit at **Mitchell's of Pitlochry.** (☎472 613. £3-5 per day; £6 for salmon. Open daily Jan.-Oct. 8:30am-6pm, Nov.-Dec. M-Sa 9:30am-5pm.) Observe other unusual processes at the **Heathergems Factory and Visitor Centre,** behind the TIC, where craftsmen cut and polish pressurized heather sprigs into jewelry. (☎473 863. Open daily 9am-5pm.)

Since the word **whisky** comes from an old Gaelic term for "water of life" (*uisge beatha*), Pitlochry just might live forever. At the **Blair Athol Distillery,** a half a mile from the TIC down the main road, enough alcohol evaporates daily to intoxicate the entire town. Kilted guides take you from mashing malt to sampling the wares. (☎482 003; www.discovering-distilleries.com/blairathol. Open Easter-Sept. M-Sa. 9:30am-5pm, tours at 11am, 1pm, 3pm; Jun.-Sept. same times, also Su. noon-5am; Oct. M-F 10am-4pm; Nov.-Dec. M-F tours at 11am, 1pm, 3pm. Last tour 1hr. before closing. £3.) The nearby **Edradour,** Scotland's tiniest distillery, only produces 40 bottles a day but the tour and a sample dram are free. The Edradour is a 2½ mi. walk from Pitlochry, past Moulin along the A924; distilling finishes at 3pm. (☎472 095; www.edradour.co.uk. Open Mar.-Oct. M-Sa 9:30am-5pm, Su noon-5pm.)

⬛ ENTERTAINMENT. The **Pitlochry Festival Theatre**, over the Aldour Bridge, features an array of splendid performances throughout the year. (☎484 600. Tickets £15-20, students and hostelers half-price.) In the recreation fields southwest of town near Tummel Crescent, **Highland Nights** feature local pipe bands and traditional folk dancing. (May-Sept. M 8pm. Tickets available at the gate. £4, concessions £3, children £1.) Pick up the free *What's On in Perthshire* at the TIC for other entertainment ideas.

🔳 DAYTRIPS FROM PITLOCHRY

🔳 **BLAIR CASTLE.** Seven miles north of Pitlochry on the A9, a mile-long palisade of spectacular elm trees lead up to the gleaming white turrets and tall windows which belie the Castle's name: it's certainly more palace than castle, with 30 rooms filled with paintings, weaponry, and luxurious furniture. The grand entrance room is one of the most impressive armories in Scotland, and the great hall is likewise filled with relics from a bellicose past including chain mail, helmets, and lances. The castle grounds, frequented by pedestrians and equestrians alike, are used to train the Duke of Atholl's army, the only private army in Britain. Though they prepared to fight in both the American Revolution and WWI, the farthest the Atholl troops have ever gone is Ireland. *(Take the train to Blair Athol and walk 10min., or hop on bus #26 or 87 from the West End Car Park. ☎481 207; www.blair-castle.co.uk. Open daily Apr.-Oct. 9:30am-4:30pm. £6.70, seniors £5.70, students £4.20, families £17. Grounds only £2.)*

BEN-Y-VRACKIE. The 2757 ft. **Ben-y-Vrackie** provides stellar views of Edinburgh on a clear day. Turn left onto the road directly behind the Moulin Inn in Moulin and follow the curve until you reach a fork. Standing stones can be seen in nearby field. Take the right-hand road northeast to Ben-y-Vrackie. Continue along the left-hand road about 2hr. to **Craigower Hill** for a western view along Loch Tommel and Loch Rannoch to the Glencoe Mountains. A 5 mi. walk from the Pitlochry dam leads to the Pass of Killiecrankie (signposted, and included in *Pitlochry Walks*).

PASS OF KILLIECRANKIE. A few miles north of Pitlochry, right off the A9, the valley of the River Garry narrows into a stunning gorge. In 1689, a Jacobite army slaughtered William III's troops here in an attempt to reinstall James VII of Scotland to the English throne. One soldier, Donald MacBean, preferring to risk the steep fall than to surrender, vaulted 18 ft. across **Soldier's Leap**. The area is home to an intriguing array of wildlife, from the buzzard and the great tit to the primrose and the Devil's Bit. For information or a guided walk, stop at the **National Trust Visitors Centre,** down the path from the pass. *(Elizabeth Yule bus #87 runs from the West End Car Park to the pass in summer (4 per day, £1). ☎473 233. Open daily Apr.-June and Sept.-Oct. 10am-5:30pm, July-Aug. 9:30am-6pm.)*

STIRLING ☎01786

Sitting atop a triangle completed by Glasgow and Edinburgh, it was often said that he who controlled Stirling controlled Scotland. At the 1297 Battle of Stirling Bridge, William Wallace outwitted and overpowered the English army, enabling Robert the Bruce to lead Scotland to independence 17 years later. Despite recent development, this former royal capital certainly hasn't forgotten its heroes; Stirling now swarms with *Braveheart* fans set on recapturing the Scotland of old.

CENTRAL SCOTLAND

⊏ TRANSPORTATION

The **train station** is right in the town center on Goosecroft Rd. (Travel Centre open M-F 6am-9pm, Sa 6am-8pm, Su 8:50am-10pm.) Trains (☎08457 484 950) arrive from: **Aberdeen** (2hr.; M-Sa every hr., Su 6 per day; £30.90); **Edinburgh** (50min., 2 per hr., £5.30); **Glasgow** (40min.; M-Sa 2-3 per hr., Su every hr.; £5.40); **Inverness** (3hr.; M-Sa 4 per day, Su 3 per day; £30.50); **London King's Cross** (5½hr., every hr., £44-84). The **bus station** is also on Goosecroft Rd. (☎446 474. Ticket office open M-Sa 9am-5pm. Luggage storage £1. Open M-Sa 6:30am-10pm, Su 10am-6pm.) **Scottish Citylink** (☎0870 505 050) buses run from: **Fort William** (2¾hr., 1 per day, £14.20); **Glasgow** (40min., 2-3 per hr., £4); and **Inverness** (3¾hr., every hr., £13). **First** (☎01324 613 777) bus M9 runs express to **Edinburgh** (1¼hr., every hr., £4).

🛈 PRACTICAL INFORMATION

The **Tourist Information Centre** is at 41 Dumbarton Rd. (☎475 019. Open July-Aug. M-Sa 9am-7pm, Su 9:30am-6pm; daily Apr.-May and Sept.-Oct. 9am-5pm; Oct.-Mar. M-F 10am-5pm, Sa 10am-4pm.) Next to the castle, the **Stirling Visitor Centre** is high-altitude and high-tech, with exhibits and a 12min. movie on the city's history. They'll exchange your currency for a £3 commission and book you a room for a £3 charge plus a 10% deposit. (☎462 517. Open Apr.-Oct. 9:30am-6pm; Nov.-Mar. 9:30am-5pm.) **Sightseeing Stirling** runs a hop-on, hop-off tour that departs frequently from the train station, traveling to Bannockburn, Stirling Castle, the Wallace Monument and Stirling University. (08707 200 620; £7.50, concessions £6, children £2.50.) Other services include: free **Internet access** at the **library,** Corn Exchange (☎432 107; open M, W, F 9:30am-5:30pm; Tu and Th 9:30am-7pm; Sa 9:30am-5pm); the police (☎456 000); and the **post office,** 84-86 Murray Pl., with a **bureau de change.** (☎465 392; open M-F 9am-5:30pm, Sa 9am-12:30pm). **Post Code:** FK8 2BP.

🛏🍴 ACCOMMODATIONS AND FOOD

The excellent **SYHA Stirling ❷,** St. John St., halfway up the hill to the castle, occupies the shell of the first Separatist Church in Stirling. (☎473 442. 125 beds in 2- to 5-bed dorms. Internet access, laundry and self-catering kitchen. Curfew 2am. Dorms £11.50-13.50, under 18 £9-11.50. MC/V.) At the bright and colorful **Willy Wallace Hostel ❶,** 77 Murray Pl., the warm staff foster a good-times atmosphere. (☎446 773. 54 beds in 6- to 16-bed coed and single-sex dorms. No lockable dorms; no lockers. Internet access, laundry and self-catering kitchen. Dorms £10-12. MC/V.) Near the train station, **Forth Guest House ❸,** 23 Forth Pl., is a comfortable Georgian house with ensuite rooms. (☎471 020. Singles £25-40; doubles £20-45. MC/V.)

Tucked into an alley, **The Greengrocer,** 81 Port St., has the freshest fruits and veggies in town. (☎479 159. Open M-Sa 9am-5:30pm.) Fill your shopping cart at **Iceland,** 5 Pitt Terr. (☎464 300. Open M-F 8:30am-8pm, Sa 8:30am-6pm, Su 10am-5pm.) Find hearty, homemade fare (toasties £3) at **The Cottage Cafe ❶,** 52 Spittal St. (☎446 124. Open Th-Tu 11am-3pm, Th-Sa also 5:30-9pm. Cash only.) In the shadow of the castle, Austrian cuisine at **Hermann's Restaurant ❹,** 58 Broad St., provides a taste of the Alps. (☎450 632. Entrees £12-17. Reservations recommended. Open daily noon-2:30pm and 6-9pm. AmEx/MC/V.) **Nick-Tams Bar & Bothy,** 29 Baker St., is a favorite nighttime hangout, hosting Wednesday live music and Thursday DJs. (☎472 194. Su quiz night. Open Su-Th 11am-midnight, F-Sa 11am-1am. MC/V.)

◎ SIGHTS

█ STIRLING CASTLE. Situated on a defunct volcano and embraced on all sides by the scenic Ochil Hills, Stirling's Castle has superb views of the Forth Valley and prim gardens that belie its turbulent history. The castle's hideous gargoyles glowered over the 14th-century Wars of Independence, a 15th-century royal murder, and the 16th-century coronation of the infant Mary, Queen of Scots; the last military action occurred in 1746, when Bonnie Prince Charlie besieged it while retreating from England. Beneath the cannons pointed at Stirling Bridge lie the 16th-century **great kitchens;** visitors can walk among the recreated chaos of cooks preparing all manor of game for a regal banquet. Near the kitchens, the sloping **North Gate,** built in 1381, is the oldest part of the sprawling complex. Beyond the central courtyard make your way into **Douglas Garden,** which takes its name from the Earl of Douglas who was murdered in 1452 by James II and whose body was dumped here. Free 30min. **guided tours** leave twice an hour from inside the castle gates. (☎450 000. Open daily Apr.-Oct. 9:30am-6pm; Nov.-Mar. 9:30am-5pm; last admission 45min. before close. £8, concessions £6, children £2.) The castle also contains the **Regimental Museum of the Argyll and Sutherland Highlanders,** a fascinating assemblage of a proud military tradition. (Open Easter-Sept. M-Sa 9:30am-5pm; Oct.-Easter 10am-4:15pm. Free.) **Argyll's Lodging,** a 17th-century Earl's mansion below the castle, has been impressively restored. (Open daily Apr.-Sept. 9:30am-6pm; Oct.-Mar. 9:30am-5pm. £3.30, concessions £2.50, children £1.20. Free with castle admission.)

THE NATIONAL WALLACE MONUMENT. This 19th-century tower offers incredible views to those bravehearted enough to climb its 246-step, wind-whipped spiral staircase. Halfway up you can catch your breath to admire William Wallace's actual 5½ ft. sword. (Hillfoots Rd., 1½ mi. from Stirling proper. Sightseeing Stirling runs here, as do local buses #62 and 63 from Murray Pl. ☎472 140; www.nationalwallacemonument.com. Open daily July-Aug. 9:30am-6pm; June 10am-6pm; Sept. 9:30am-5pm; Mar.-May and Oct. 10am-5pm; Nov.-Feb. 10:30am-4pm. £5, concessions £3.75, children £3.25, families £13.25.)

THE OLD TOWN. On **Mar's Walk,** Castle Wynd, an elaborate Renaissance facade is all that was completed of a 16th-century townhouse before its wealthy patron died. Nearby, the stained glass and timbered roof of the **Church of the Holy Rude** witnessed the coronation of James VI and shook under the fire and brimstone of John Knox. (Open daily May-Sept. 11am-4pm; Su service July-Dec. 10am, Jan.-June 11:30am. Organ recitals May-Sept. W 1pm. Donations appreciated.) Next to the church lies 17th-century **Cowane's Hospital,** built as an alms house for poor members of the merchant guild. (Open M-Sa 9am-5pm, Su 1-5pm. Free.) The **Old Town Jail,** St. John St., features somewhat childish but enthusiastic reenactments of prison life. Ascend to the roof for views of the Forth Valley. (☎450 050. Open daily Apr.-Sept. 9:30am-6pm; Oct. and Mar. 9:30am-5pm; Nov.-Feb. 9:30am-4pm. £5.50, concessions £4.25, children £3.65, families £14.65.) Stirling's old **town walls** are some of the best-preserved in Scotland; follow them along the circular **Back Walk.**

BANNOCKBURN. Two miles south of Stirling at **Bannockburn,** a statue of a battle-ready Robert the Bruce overlooks the field where his men decisively defeated the English in 1314, initiating 393 years of Scottish independence. The **Bannockburn Heritage Centre** screens an audiovisual display on the battle. (Take bus #51 or 52 from Stirling Bus Station. ☎812 664. Centre open daily Apr.-Oct. 10am-5:30pm; Feb.-Mar. and Nov.-Dec. 10:30am-4pm. £3.50, children £2.60. Battlefield open year-round.)

▶ **DAYTRIP FROM STIRLING**

DOUNE CASTLE. Perched above a peaceful bend in the river Teith, Doune Castle is an impressively well-preserved 14th-century fortress, one of the earliest castles to be built around a central courtyard. Many of the castle's original rooms are entirely intact, most notably the towering great hall and the kitchen, with a fireplace large enough to roast a herd of cattle. Today, scholars of medieval architecture share the castle with those well-versed in Monty Python; many scenes from *Monty Python and the Holy Grail* were filmed here, and the ticket desk kindly provides coconut shells for eager re-enacters. *(From Stirling, First bus #59 stops in Doune on its way to Callander (25min. every hr.). The castle is a 5min. walk from town; ask the bus driver for directions. ☎ 01786 841 742. Open daily Apr.-Sept. 9:30am-6:30pm; Oct.-Mar. Sa-W 9:30am-4:30pm. £3, concessions £2.30, children £1.)*

THE TROSSACHS ☎ 01877

The most accessible tract of Scotland's wilderness, the mountains and misty lochs of the Trossachs (from the Gaelic for "bristly country") are as popular now as they were under the reign of Queen Victoria. Today, the Trossachs and Loch Lomond form Scotland's first national park, justifiably billed as the "Highlands in miniature." Here you will find long cycle routes winding through dense forest, peaceful loch-side walks, and some of Scotland's more manageable peaks.

By public transport, access to the Trossachs is easiest from **Stirling. First** (☎ 01324 613 777) connects to the region's two main towns, running bus #59 from Stirling to **Callander** (45min., 12 per day, £3) and bus #11 to **Aberfoyle** (45min., 4 per day, £2.50). **Scottish Citylink** also runs a bus from **Edinburgh** to **Callander** via **Stirling** (1¾hr., 1 per day, £8). From **Glasgow,** reach **Aberfoyle** by changing buses at **Balfron.** During the summer, the useful **Trossachs Trundler** (☎ 01786 442 707) travels between **Callander, Aberfoyle,** and the Trossachs Pier at **Loch Katrine;** one daily trip begins and ends in **Stirling** (June-Sept. M and Th-Tu 4 per day; Day Rover £5, concessions £4, children £1.75; including travel from Stirling £7.50/£6/£2.50). **Postbuses** reach some remoter areas of the region; find timetables at TICs or call the **Stirling Council Public Transport Helpline** (☎ 01786 442 707).

The A821 winds through the heart of the Trossachs between **Aberfoyle** and **Callander.** Named the **Trossachs Trail,** this scenic drive passes near majestic **Loch Katrine,** the Trossachs' original lure and the setting of Sir Walter Scott's "The Lady of the Lake." The popular **Steamship Sir Walter Scott** cruises from Trossachs Pier and tours the loch, stopping at **Stronachlachar** on the northwest bank. (☎ 376 316. Apr.-Oct. 11am, 1:45, 3:15pm; W no 11am sailing. £5.90-6.90, children and seniors £4.40-4.90.) At the pier, rent bikes from **Katrinewheelz.** (☎ 376 284. £12 per day.) For a good daytrip, take the ferry to Stronachlachar and then walk or ride back along the 14 mi. wooded shore road to the pier. Above the loch hulks **Ben A'an** (1512 ft.), a reasonable 2 mi. ascent that begins from a carpark a mile along the A821.

Set beside the quiet River Teith, the town of **Callander** makes a good base for exploring the Trossachs and lies close to many outdoor attractions. Dominating the horizon, **Ben Ledi** (2883 ft.) provides a strenuous though not overly challenging trek. A 6 mi. trail up the mountain begins just north of town along the A84. A number of fine walks depart from Callander itself. **The Crags** (6½ mi.) heads up through the woods to the ridge above town, while the popular walk to **Bracklinn Falls** (5 mi.) wanders along a picturesque glen. In Callander, cyclists can join **The Lowland Highland Trail,** a lovely stretch of which runs north to Strathyre along an old railway line. Passing through forest and beside Loch Lubnaig, a side-track from the route runs to **Balquhidder,** where **Rob Roy,** Scotland's legendary patriot, and his family

LOCH LOMOND AND BALLOCH ■ 611

find peace at last under a stone which reads, "MacGregor Despite Them." Callander's **Rob Roy and Trossachs Visitor Centre**, Main St., is a combined TIC and exhibit on the 17th-century local hero. (☎330 342. Open daily June-Aug. 9am-6pm; Sept. 10am-6pm; Mar.-May and Oct.-Dec. 10am-5pm; Jan.-Feb. Sa-Su 11am-4:30pm. Exhibit £3.25, concessions £2.50, children £2.25, families £8.75.) Pick up Ordnance Survey Explorer #378 (£7) or Landranger #57 (£6). Walkers will find the *Walks* pamphlet (£2) useful, and cyclists can consult *Rides around The Trossachs* (£2). Rent bikes at **Cycle Hire Callander**, Aneaster Sq., beside the TIC. (☎331 052. £10 per day, £7 half day. Open daily 9am-6pm. MC/V.)

Aberfoyle is another springboard into the surrounding wilderness. The **Queen Elizabeth Forest Park**, established in 1953 to celebrate her coronation, covers a vast territory from the shore of Loch Lomond to the slopes of the Strathyre Mountains, with Aberfoyle right at its heart. For more information on trails, visit the **Trossachs Discovery Centre**, a TIC right in town. (☎382 352. Open daily July-Aug. 9:30am-6pm; Apr.-June and Sept.-Oct. 10am-5pm; Nov.-Mar. Sa-Su 10am-5pm.) A good walk from town leads to the top of **Doon Hill** (2 mi.), where the ghost of Reverend Robert Kirk is supposedly trapped in an ancient pine. After publishing *The Commonwealth* in 1691, which spoke of the world of elves and pixies, the good reverend was supposedly spirited away by the creatures whose secrets he revealed.

For lodgings, the hidden gem of the region lies 1½ mi. south of Callander at ⬛**Trossachs Backpackers ❷**, Invertrossachs Rd. This hostel's forest-clearing location make it an ideal walking and cycling base. Owners Mark and Janet will pick you up from Callander. Their home features a cable-TV lounge, barbecues, and cycle hire. (☎/fax 331 100. 30 beds in 8-bed dorms and 4- to 6-bed rooms. Lockable dorms; valuables lockers. Laundry, Internet access, and kitchen. Breakfast included. Bikes £12.50 per day, £7.50 ½-day. Dorms £13.50; private rooms £15-30. MC/V.) In Callander itself, **Norwood B&B ❸**, 12 South Church St., is well kept. (☎330 665. Open May-Sept. Singles £22; doubles £38. Cash only.) The **Abbotsford Lodge ❸**, Stirling Rd., is a country cottage with hotel-style facilities. (☎330 066. £21.50-27 per person. MC/V.) In Aberfoyle, Ann and John Epps welcome visitors to **Crannaig House ❹**, Trossachs Rd., with large, spacious rooms. (☎382 276. Singles from £30; doubles £50-60. MC/V.) **Camping** is available at the well-equipped **Trossachs Holiday Park ❶**, 2 mi. south of Aberfoyle on the A81. (☎382 614. Toilets, showers, laundry, and bike rental. Open Mar-Oct. £7-13.50. MC/V.) **Co-op grocery** stores and **banks** are found in both Callander and Aberfoyle, as well as a number of eateries.

LOCH LOMOND AND BALLOCH   ☎01389

Immortalized by the famous ballad, the pristine wilderness surrounding Loch Lomond continues to awe visitors. Britain's largest lake is dotted by some 38 islands. Given their proximity to Glasgow, parts of these bonnie, bonnie banks can get crowded, especially during summer when daytrippers pour into Balloch, the area's largest town. A short walk from the southern tip of the lake, the town sits astride the River Leven and is a convenient transportation hub.

🖪🔃 **TRANSPORTATION AND PRACTICAL INFORMATION.** The Balloch **train station** is on Balloch Rd., across the street from the TIC. **Trains** (☎08457 484 950) arrive from **Glasgow Queen St.** Monday through Saturday, and **Glasgow Central** on Sundays (45min., 2 per hr., £3.50). **Scottish Citylink** (☎08705 505 050) runs frequent buses from **Glasgow** (45min., 7 per day, £3.60) that drop off about 1 mi. from the town center, north of the Balloch roundabout. These buses then continue along the loch's western shore to **Luss** and **Tarbet**. First runs #12/13/313 from **Stirling** via **Balfron** (1½hr., M-Sa 4 per day, £3.80). To reach the eastern side of the loch, take bus #309 from Balloch to **Balmaha** (25min., 7 per day, £1.80). Bus #305 heads for

Luss (15min., 9 per day, £1.50). Balloch's **Tourist Information Centre**, Balloch Rd., is in the Old Station Building. (☎753 533. Open daily Apr.-Sept. 9:30am-6pm.) The **National Park Gateway Centre** sits 1 mi. away along a dirt and gravel road at the Loch Lomond Shores complex, a kind of shopping mall set right on the lake that is often mobbed. (☎722 199. Open daily Apr.-Sept. 9:30am-6:30pm; Oct.-Mar. 10am-5pm.)

⌂ ACCOMMODATIONS. Two miles north of Balloch, the ◨**SYHA Loch Lomond ❷** is one of Scotland's largest hostels, with 160 beds in a stunning 19th-century castle-esque structure. The grandeur of this palatial mansion makes it well worth the effort to get here. From the train station, turn left and follow the main road ¾ mi. to the second roundabout. Turn right, continue 1½ mi., and turn left at the sign for the hostel; it's a short walk up the hill. Or, bus #305 runs from Balloch to the front gates—just be sure to tell the driver where to let you off. (☎850 226. Laundry and Internet access. Entirely self-catering; be sure to bring food with you. Book far in advance. Open Mar.-Oct. Dorms £11.50-13.50, under 18 £9.50-11.50. MC/V.) On Loch Lomond's eastern shore, the **SYHA Rowardennan ❶,** the first hostel along the West Highland Way, overlooks the lake and makes a great base for this more remote region. From Balloch take the bus to Balmaha, and walk 7 mi. along the well-marked way. (☎0870 004 1148. 75 beds. Laundry and basic **groceries.** Curfew 11:30pm. Open Mar.-Oct. Dorms £10.50-12, under 18 £8-9.) **B&Bs** congregate on Balloch Rd., close to the train station and TIC. Across from the train station, **Station Cottages ❸,** Balloch Rd., provides a peaceful and fairly luxurious environment. (☎750 759. Singles £40; doubles £50. MC/V.) The **Lomond Woods Holiday Park ❶,** Old Luss Rd., up Balloch Rd. from the TIC, is an excellent place to pitch your tent. Relax in a spa or sauna and rent mountain bikes at this Club Med of campsites. (☎750 000. 2-person tent £13-18, £2 per extra person. MC/V.)

◨◩ HIKING AND OUTDOORS. Stock up on supplies and information at the TIC or Gateway Centre. Ordnance Survey Explorer #347 and 364 (£7) chart the south and north of the loch, respectively, while Landranger #56 (£6) gives a broader view of the entire region. The long-distance **West Highland Way** runs 95 mi. from Milngavie to Fort William and skirts Loch Lomond's eastern shore. *The West Highland Way* official guide (£15) includes maps for each section of the route. Experienced hikers can try the 7½ mi. portion that runs from Rowardennan to Inversaid, passing through dense oak forests on Lomond's eastern shore. Rising above all, **Ben Lomond** (3195ft.), is the southernmost of Scotland's 284 Munros (peaks over 3000 ft.). A popular walk departs from the 19th-century **Balloch Castle and Country Park,** across the River Leven from the train station, where you will find both a visitors center and park ranger station. (Castle ☎722 230. Open Apr.-Oct.). Outside of **Balmaha,** the strenuous 5 mi. hike up **Conic Hill** rewards hikers with magnificent views of the loch. Visitors can arrange a short boat ride (☎01360 870 214) from Balmaha to the island of **Inchcailloch,** where a 1½ mi. walk circumnavigates a nature preserve. The **Glasgow-Loch Lomond Cycleway** runs 20 mi. from city to lake along mostly traffic-free paths. At Balloch, where the route terminates, **National Cycle Route #7** heads east to the Trossachs while the smaller **West Loch Lomond Cycle Path** wraps around the lake to the west.

At **Loch Lomond Shores,** the region's lakeside visitor complex, the National Park Gateway Centre was designed as a "modern-day castle." Its centerpiece Drumkinnon Tower runs two short films; one explores Loch Lomond's namesake ballad, the other, suited to children, dives into the lake. (☎722 406. Open daily June-Sept. 10am-6pm; Oct.-May 10am-5pm. £5, concessions £3.70.) Across from Drumkinnon Tower, rent bikes or canoes from **Can You Experience,** which also offers guided paddling and cycling tours. (☎602 576. Bikes £15 per day. Canoes £15 per hr. Guided tours Th and Su £18-30. MC/V.) Departing from Loch Lomond Shores and the Bal-

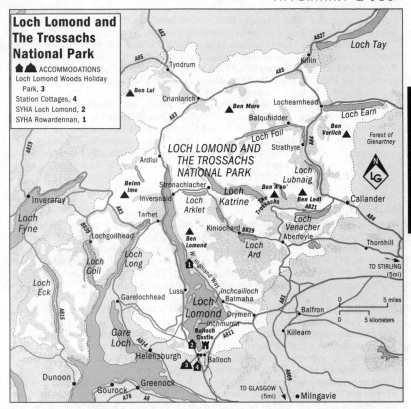

Loch Lomond and The Trossachs National Park

ACCOMMODATIONS
Loch Lomond Woods Holiday Park, 3
Station Cottages, 4
SYHA Loch Lomond, 2
SYHA Rowardennan, 1

loch TIC on the River Leven, 1hr. **Sweeney's Cruises** provide one of the best introductions to the area. (☎752 376. Every hr. 10:30am-5:30pm. £9, children £4.50.) A daily 2½hr. cruise sails to **Luss,** with 30min. ashore (2:30pm, £8.50/£5.20). Avert your eyes (or don't) from the nudist colony on one of the islands.

INVERARAY ☎01499

A pretty town with a splendid lochside setting, Inveraray was completely torn down and rebuilt in the 18th century to make room for the Duke of Argyll's castle. The resulting village has a vaguely regal air to it, but Loch Fyne is still the main attraction. Current home to the Duke and Duchess of Argyll, palatial **Inveraray Castle** is the traditional seat of Clan Campbell. The present building was built by Archibald Campbell, the 3rd Duke of Argyll, replacing an earlier keep as a sign of a more peaceful era in Scottish history, although the castle still bristles with an impressive array of weapons. (☎302 203. Open Apr.-May and Oct. M-Th and Sa 10am-1pm, 2-5:45pm, Su 1-5:45pm; June-Sept. M-Sa 10am-5:45pm, Su 1-5:45pm; last admission 5pm. £5.90, concessions £4.90, children £3.90. Grounds free.) A number of walks (1-2½ mi.) tour the forest and the top of **Dun na Cuaiche,** where you can enjoy a panoramic view. The **Inveraray Jail** welcomes with a "Torture, Death, and Damnation" exhibit. Guests are invited to try the Whipping Table. (☎302 381. Open daily Apr.-Oct. 9:30am-6pm; Nov.-Mar. 10am-5pm. Last admission 1hr. before close. £5.75, concessions £3.75, children £2.80, families £15.70.)

The small, basic **SYHA Inveraray** ❶ is just north of town on Dalmally Rd. Take a left through the arch next to the Inveraray Woollen Mill onto Oban Rd. (☎0870 004 1125. 28 beds in 4- to 6-bed rooms. Self-catering kitchen. Lockout 10:30am-5pm. Curfew 11:30pm. Open Apr.-Sept. Dorms £10.50-11, under 18 £8-8.50. MC/V.) For **B&B,** the loch-side **Old Rectory** ❷, a 5min. walk along the road south from town, has large rooms and a glass-ceilinged breakfast nook. (☎302 280. £16.50-18.50 per person. Cash only.) Cafes and **grocery** stores line Main St.

Scottish Citylink (☎08705 505 050) connects Inveraray with **Glasgow** (1¾hr., 6 per day, £6.90) and **Oban** (1hr., 3 per day, £6.40). The small **Tourist Information Centre,** Front St., books accommodations for a £3 charge plus a 10% deposit. (☎302 063. Open daily July-Aug. 9am-6pm; Nov.-Mar. 10am-3pm; Apr.-June M-Sa 9am-5pm, Su 11am-5pm; Sept.-Oct. M-Sa 9am-5pm, Su noon-5pm .) The **post office** is on Arkland. (☎302 062. Open M-Tu and Th-F 9am-1pm and 2-5:30pm, W 9am-1pm, Sa 9am-12:30pm.) **Post Code:** PA32 8UD.

OBAN   ☎01631

The busiest ferry port on Scotland's west coast, Oban (OH-ben; pop. 8500) welcomes thousands of visitors bound for the Inner Hebrides each year. Though the town lacks notable attractions of its own and teems with tourists during the summer, it makes a fine base for exploring the islands and Argyll countryside. As the sun sets over the blue hills of Mull, the streets of Oban fill with folks strolling along the harbor, chatting with neighbors, or heading to the pub.

⌷ TRANSPORTATION. The **train station** is on Railway Pier. (Ticket office open M-Sa 7:15am-6:15pm, Su 10:45am-6:15pm.) **Trains** (☎08457 484 950) run to Oban from **Glasgow Queen St.** (3hr., 3 per day, £15). **Scottish Citylink** (☎08705 505 050) arrives at the bus stop in front of the train station, from: **Fort William** (1½hr., M-Sa 4 per day, £7.60); **Glasgow** (3hr., M-Sa 6 per day, Su 3 per day; £12.30); and **Inverness** via Fort William (3½hr., M-Sa 3 per day, £12.70).

Caledonian MacBrayne (☎566 688, reservations 08705 650 000) sails from Railway Pier to the Inner Hebrides and the southern Outer Hebrides. Pick up a *Discover* timetable at the ferry station or TIC. Ferries go to: **Craignure, Mull** (45min.; M-Sa 6 per day, Su 5 per day; extra sailings July-Aug.; £3.85); **Lismore** (50min., M-Sa 2-4 per day, £2.65); **Colonsay** (2½hr., 1 per day, £10.90); **Coll** and **Tiree** (2¾hr. to Coll, 3¾hr. to Tiree; 1 per day; £12.30); **Barra** and **South Uist** (5hr. to Barra, 7hr. to South Uist; M and Th-Su 1 per day; £20.20). Passengers should call for times; those with a car should book. Ferry services are reduced during the winter.

From Oban, several operators offer **day tours** to the isles of **Mull, Iona,** and **Staffa.** From April to October, **Bowman's Tours,** across from Railway Pier, runs daily to Mull and Iona and adds Staffa for a bit more. (☎566 809. Mull and Iona £28, children £14. Including Staffa £36/£18.) On Railway Pier, **Turus Mara** operates a day tour that includes Iona, Staffa, and the Treshnish Isles. (☎0800 0858 786. Iona and Staffa £32.50, children £17. Including Treshnish Isles £38.50/£19.50.)

⌷⌷ ORIENTATION AND PRACTICAL INFORMATION. Corran Esplanade runs along the coast north of town, **Gallanach Road** along the coast to the south. Fronting the harbor, **George Street** is the heart of Oban; a block inland, **Argyll Square** is actually a roundabout. The **Tourist Information Centre,** Argyll Sq., inhabits the vaulted interior of an old church and books beds for a £3 charge plus a 10% deposit. (☎563 122. Open July-Aug. M-Sa 9am-8pm, Su 9am-7pm; May-June and Sept. M-Sa 9am-5:30pm, Su 10am-5pm; Oct. M-Sa 9am-5:30pm, Su 10am-4pm; Nov.-Mar. M-F 9:30am-5pm, Sa-Su noon-4pm; Apr. M-F 9am-5pm, Sa-Su 10am-5pm.) Free **Internet access** is available at Corran Halls in the **Oban Library,** Corran Esplanade (open M and W 10am-1pm and 2-7pm, Th 10am-1pm and 2-6pm, F 10am-1pm and 2-5pm, Sa 10am-1pm), and at the TIC (£1 per 12min.). **Boots pharmacy** is on the harbor on the north side of town (34-38 George St., Open M-Sa 8:45am-5:30pm). **Rent bikes** at **Oban Cycles,** 29 Lochside St., off Argyll Sq., across from the Tesco. (☎566 996; www.obancycles.com. £15 per day, £10 per half-day, £55 per week. Open M-F 9am-5:30, Sa 9am-5pm.) There are **post offices** in the nearby **Tesco,** Lochside St. (☎565 676. Open M-Sa 8am-6pm, Su 10am-1pm.) and on Corran Esplanade across town (Open M-F 9am-5:30pm, Sa 9am-1pm). **Post Code:** PA34 4HP.

ACCOMMODATIONS. The waterfront **SYHA Oban ❶,** Corran Esplanade, lies ¾ mi. north of the train station past St. Columba's Cathedral. Enjoy spacious dorms and a self-catering kitchen. (☎0870 004 1144. 84 beds in 6- to 10-bed dorms plus 42 beds in 4-bed ensuite rooms. Laundry and Internet access. Reception until 11:30pm. Curfew 2am. Dorms £10-13, under 18 £8-11.50; private rooms £12.50-15/ £10-13.50. MC/V.) To reach the lively **Oban Backpackers ❷,** 21 Breadalbane St., take George St. away from Railway Pier and bear right at the first fork; the hostel will appear on your right. (☎562 107. 48 beds in 6- to 12-bed single-sex dorms. No lockable dorms; valuables locker. Self-catering kitchen. Breakfast £1.90. Internet access £1 per 30min. Laundry £2.50-£3.50. Curfew 2:30am. Open Apr.-Oct. Dorms £11-12. AmEx/MC/V.) Sprawling **Corran House ❷,** 1 Victoria Cres., sits near the water a half-mile north of the train station. (☎566 040. 36 beds in 2- to 6-bed dorms and 11 private ensuite rooms with TV. No lockable dorms; no lockers. Self-catering kitchen. Breakfast £2.50. Laundry £4.50. Dorms £11; private rooms £15 per person. Cash only.) Eight rooms, all with bath and TV, occupy the bright blue **Maridon House ❷,** Dunuaran Rd., where guests have use of the kitchen. From Argyll Sq., walk to the end of Albany St. and look up. (☎562 670. Singles £22-25, doubles £20-22 per person. MC/V.) For a room with a view head to **The Old Manse Guest House ❸,** one of several high-quality establishments on Dalriach Rd. overlooking the harbor. (☎564 886. Open Mar.-Oct. £24-35 per person. MC/V.) Weary travellers yearning for luxury need look no farther than **The Manor House ❺,** Gallanach Rd., an intimate country house right on the edge of town (☎562 087; www.manorhouseoban.com. £59-78 per person. AmEx/MC/V.)

FOOD AND PUBS. Tesco, Lochside St., covers **grocery** needs. (Open M-Sa 8am-10pm, Su 9am-8pm.) Seafood shops cluster around the ferry terminal on Railway Pier. With a warm and inviting interior, the **Gallery Restaurant ❸,** Argyll Sq., features several local seafood dishes. (☎564 641. Lunch £5-8. Dinner £15-20. Open daily 10am-3pm and 5:30-8:30pm. AmEx/MC/V.) In the summer, **McTavish's Kitchens ❶,** 34 George St., puts on a nightly show of traditional Scottish song and dance in its upstairs restaurant (£4; 8 and 10pm). A downstairs cafeteria serves cheap food throughout the day. (☎563 064. Restaurant open daily noon-2pm and 6-10pm. Cafeteria open daily in summer 9am-10pm; in winter 9am-6pm. MC/V.) **O'Donnell's Irish Pub,** Breadalbane St., draws a younger crowd to its underground digs with a mix of live music, karaoke, and quiz nights. (☎566 159. Open Su-W 2pm-1am, Th-Sa 2pm-2am; reduced off-season hours.) Competing for local drinkers and cheery hostelers, **Markie Dan's,** Victoria Cres., just off Corran Esplanade, has frequent live music, drink specials, and a friendly bar staff. (☎564 448. Open daily 11am-1am.)

SIGHTS. The town's only real tourist draw is the small but renowned **Oban Distillery,** which offers 1hr. tours ending with free samples of the local malt (☎572 004. Open July-Sept. M-F 9:30am-7:30pm, Sa 9:30am-5pm, Su noon-5pm; Apr.-Jun. and Oct. M-Sa 9:30am-5pm; Mar. and Nov. M-F 10am-5pm; Dec.-Feb. M-F 12:30-4pm. Tours every 15 min. in summer; call ahead for reservations. £4). The hilltop Colosseum-esque structure dominating the skyline is **McCaig's Tower.** Commissioned in

CENTRAL SCOTLAND

the 19th century by John Stuart McCaig, it was intended as an art gallery but never completed. Take the steep stairway at the end of Argyll St., then turn left along Ardconnel Rd. and right up Laurel St. (Open 24hr. Free.) North of town, the ivy-eaten ruins of 7th-century **Dunollie Castle,** Oban's oldest building, sit atop a cliff. From town, walk 20min. north along the water until you've curved around the castle then take the path to the right. (Always open. Free.)

◪ DAYTRIPS FROM OBAN

KERRERA. Across the bay from Oban is the beautiful and nearly deserted isle of **Kerrera** (CARE-er-uh) where a no-car policy provides a peaceful habitat for seals and puffins. Ringed by a network of gravel roads, Kerrera makes for great walking and mountain biking. From the ferry landing, turn left and follow the road for 2½ mi. to the southern tip of Kerrera, where tiny ▨**Gylen Castle** stands atop the cliffs in a delightfully isolated spot overlooking lush scenery and a quiet arm of the sea. Enjoy a hearty soup and sandwich (£3) or spend the night in the cozy **Kerrera Bunk-house and Tea Garden ❶,** 2 mi. from the pier near the castle. (☎570 223. Tea Garden open daily Apr.-Sept. 10am-5pm. 10 beds. Self-catering kitchen. Laundry £3. Dorms £10. Cash only.) A **ferry** crosses to Kerrera from a pier 2 mi. south of Oban along Gallanach Rd. Turn the board to the black side to signal the ferryman that you wish to cross. The ferryman also dispenses helpful maps of the island. (☎563 665. 2 per hr. 10:30am-12:30pm and 2-6pm, also M-Sa 8:45am; call ahead in winter. Round-trip £3. Bikes 50p. Maps 20p.)

LOCH ETIVE. Twelve miles northeast of Oban gapes the mouth of Loch Etive. From the **Falls of Lora,** which change direction with the shifting of the tides, to the mountains of Glen Coe, this body of water spans nearly 20 miles. North of **Taynuilt,** the family-run **Loch Etive Cruises** sends tours into otherwise inaccessible country-side. Bring a pair of binoculars to scan the water and shore for seals, otters, red deer, and golden eagles. (☎01866 822 430. May-Sept. M-F, Su 10:30am, noon, and 2pm; Apr. and Oct. Su-F 2pm only. 1½hr. tour £6, children £3, families £13. 3hr. tour £11/5/23.) Both **trains** and Scottish Citylink **buses** traveling from **Oban** to **Glasgow** stop in Taynuilt, and you can call the night before you arrive to arrange a free shuttle from the town to the pier. Monty Python fans can glimpse Castle Aaargh (actually **Castle Stalker**) on Loch Linnhe; cross Connel Bridge at the mouth of Loch Etive and take the A828 10min. from Appin. (Scottish Citylink bus #918 from Oban to Appin passes by; ask the driver. ☎01631 730 234; www.castlestalker.com. Call 1-2 days in advance; visits by appointment only.)

ISLE OF ISLAY ☎01496

Much like the whisky for which it's famous, the Isle of Islay (EYE-luh) demands subtle and mature appreciation. A barely inhabited outpost and a walker's paradise, Islay's real beauty lies in the nuances of its residents' daily lives: the mellow tones of Scottish Gaelic and the intoxicating fumes of some of the world's finest single-malts and newly-cut peat wafting from the island's numerous distilleries.

▉ TRANSPORTATION

Calmac Ferries (☎302 209) leave from **Kennacraig Ferry Terminal,** 7 mi. south of **Tarbert** on the Kintyre Peninsula, sailing either to Port Askaig or to Port Ellen (Port Ellen Terminal 2¼hr.; M-Tu and Th-Sa 3-4 per day, W 2 per day, Su 1-4 per day; £7.75). To reach Kennacraig, take the **Scottish Citylink** (☎08705 505 050) bus that runs between **Glasgow** and **Campbeltown** (Glasgow to Kennacraig 3½hr.; M-Sa 4 per day, Su 1-2 per day). Travelers from **Arran** can catch bus #448 to Kennacraig at the **Claonaig** ferry landing (☎01880 730 253, 20min., M-Sa 3 per day, £2.45) or call a taxi (☎01880 820 220). Every summer Wednesday, a ferry leaves **Oban,** stops on **Colonsay,** and continues to Port Askaig (4hr., £10.85). **British Airways Express** (☎08705 444 000) flies from Glasgow Airport to the Islay Airport between Port Ellen and Bowmore (40min., £75). The comprehensive *Islay and Jura Area Transport Guide* at TICs has more on these services as well as island bus timetables. Most bus schedules follow ferry times quite closely, but call ahead or risk being stranded.

Islay Coaches (☎840 273) operates a few daily buses between Islay towns. Bus #451 connects **Port Ellen** and **Port Askaig** via **Bowmore** (M-Sa about 4 per day, Su 1 per day); #450 runs from **Port Ellen** to **Port Charlotte** via **Bowmore** (M-Sa 3 per day). **Postbuses** (☎01246 546 329) cross the island a few times a day. Many bus times apply to one day only, so read schedules carefully. Purchase single tickets; round trips aren't cheaper, and aren't valid on different bus services. For on-call transportation around the island, contact Carol MacDonald at her 24hr. **Minibus & Taxi Service** (☎302 155, mobile ☎0777 578 2155), which is available for **island tours.**

PORT ELLEN

Port Ellen serves as an immediate signal to those arriving by ferry that life here on Islay is different from that of the mainland. To the west, the windswept **Mull of Oa** drops dramatically into the sea. A short 1½ mi. walk along the Mull of Oa road leads to the solar-powered **Carraig Fhada lighthouse,** which sits across the harbor from town. Beyond the lighthouse lies crescent-shaped **Traigh Bhan,** considered the most beautiful bay on Islay by many locals. A longer trek (about 6 mi.) will bring you to the end of the peninsula and a massive **American Monument,** built to commemorate two ships that sank off this point in 1918, drowning hundreds. Heading east along the A846, you will pass three of Islay's finest distilleries, ☒**Laphroaig** (2 mi.), **Lagavulin** (3 mi.) and **Ardberg** (4 mi.). They're relatively easy to get to, especially with a bike; it's the getting back that may pose a problem. Alternatively, a bus that runs from Port Ellen to Laphroaig, Lagavulin, and finally Ardberg (M-Sa 2-3 per day, more on school days). Past Lagavulin, the ruins of 16th-century **Dunyveg Castle** loom beside the sea. Just past Ardberg you will come across the **Loch an t-Sailein,** known as "Seal Bay" for its breeding colonies. Another 3 mi. east along the A846 from Ardberg, **Kildalton Chapel** holds the miraculously preserved **Kildalton High Cross,** a celtic piece of carved blue stone thought to date from the mid-8th century. This journey is best made by **bicycle,** which you can rent at the **Port Ellen Playing Fields,** in town on the road to Bowmore. (☎302 349 or 07831 246 911. £7 per day, £5 per half-day. Open daily May-Sept. noon-4pm and 6-9pm.) There is a **bank** in town, but **no ATM.** Port Ellen's tiny **Kildalton and Oa Information Point,** Frederick Cres., opposite the **police,** is not an official TIC but stocks bus schedules and leaflets. (☎302 434. Open Mar.-Oct. M-Sa 9:30am-noon; Nov.-Mar. M-Sa 11am-noon.)

If you choose to stay in town, Mr. and Mrs. Hedley's **Trout Fly Guest House ❸,** 8 Charlotte St., has decent rooms close to the ferry. (☎302 204. Singles £21.50; doubles £45. No smoking. Cash only.) Another good option is the simple but comfortable **Mingulay Guest House ❷,** 5 Charlotte St., just past the Trout Fly (☎302 085. From £20 per person. Cash only). Three miles away, the **Kintra Farmhouse B&B ❷** stands in solitary coastal splendor on a working farm. (☎302 051. Open Apr.-Sept. From £18 per person. Cash only.) Kintra also welcomes ☒**camping ❶** in the dunes at the southern end of the **Big Strand** (p. 618), where you can enjoy beach fires. (Toilet and showers. £8 for 2 people and tent.) To reach Kintra from Port Ellen, take the Mull of Oa road 1 mi., then follow the right fork marked "To Kintra." In Port Ellen, **Frederick Crescent** rings the harbor and holds a **Co-op** for **groceries.** (☎302 446. Open M-Sa 8am-8pm, Su 12:30-7pm.) The **Mactaggart Community Cyber**

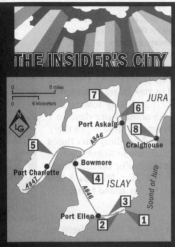

THE WHISKY TRAIL

Islay is renowned for its malt whiskys and boasts seven distilleries; Jura adds one more. The malts are known for their peaty flavor—not surprising; half of Islay is peat bog. The island's clean environment and fresh water supply are ideal for a flourishing whisky trail. What gives each malt its distinctive flavor? A plethora of determinants: water supply, air quality, temperature, the barley—even the shape of the pot-still (large kettle-like distilling structure). Pick up *The Islay and Jura Whisky Trail*, free at TICs, or use our guide:

1 **Ardberg:** (☎302 244), on the southeast coast, 4 mi. from Port Ellen. The peatiest of the island's malts. Ardberg is rapidly emerging as one of Islay's best malts. Tours M-Sa 10:30am and 2:30pm. £2.

2 **Lagavulin:** (☎302 400), 3 mi. from Port Ellen. Check out the massive washbacks that overflow with foam during the fermenting process. Tours M-F 10, 11:30am 11:15am and 2:30pm. £4.

Cafe ❶, 30 Mansfield St., offers diner-style meals (cheeseburger and fries £3.50), satellite TV, and a pool table. (☎302 693. Internet access £1 per 30min. Pool 30p per 30min. Open M-Sa 11am-10pm, Su noon-9pm. Food served until 6pm.)

BOWMORE

Located 10 mi. from both Port Ellen and Port Askaig, Bowmore is Islay's largest town, though it still possesses village charm. Arranged in a grid, the town is centered on **Main Street,** with the 18th-century **Bowmore Round Church** at the top, built perfectly circular to keep Satan from hiding in the corners. (Open daily 9am-6pm. Free.) Diagonally across from the TIC, the **Bowmore Distillery,** School St., is the island's oldest. The coast between Bowmore and Port Ellen is graced by the **Big Strand,** 7 mi. of white-sand beach with waves for **bodysurfing.**

Islay's only **Tourist Information Centre,** Main St., books accommodations for a £3 charge plus a 10% deposit. Ordnance Survey Explorer #352 and #353 (£7) and Landranger #60 (£5) maps cover all of Islay. Pick up *The Isles of Islay, Jura & Colonsay Walks* (£2), which details hikes. (☎810 254. Open May-Aug. M-Sa 9:30am-5pm, Su 2-5pm; Apr. and Sept.-Oct. M-Sa 10am-5pm; Nov.-Mar. M-F 10am-3pm.) Other services include: two **banks** with **ATMs;** a **launderette** in the **Mactaggart Leisure Centre,** School St., where you swim (£2.40) while your clothes take a spin (☎810 767; wash £3.20, dry £1.60; open Tu and F 10:30am-8pm, W and Th 10:30am-9pm, Sa-Su 10:30am-5pm.); **Internet access** at the office of **Ileach** newspaper. Main St. (☎810 355. £1.50 per 30min. Open M-F 10am-4pm, closed for lunch 12:30-1pm.); and the **post office,** Main St. (☎810 366; open M-F 9am-5:30pm, Sa 9am-12:30pm). The post office **rents bicycles** for £10 per day. **Post Code: PA43 7JH.**

Among a flock of similarly priced Bowmore B&Bs, the friendly proprietors of the **Lambeth Guest House ❸,** Jamieson St., offer homey lodgings and good conversation. They also serve a great dinner—ask in advance. (☎810 597. No singles. £20 per person. Cash only.) The waterfront **Harbour Inn ❹,** The Square, offers luxurious (and more expensive) lodging. (☎810 330; www.harbour-inn.com. Singles £65; doubles £95. No smoking. MC/V.) There is a **Co-op** market on Main St. (☎810 201. Open M-Sa 8am-8pm, Su 12:30-7pm.) The Harbour Inn (p. 618) also runs a **restaurant ❺** with a small bar that will serve you a dram of any Islay single-malt whisky. (3-courses £25. Lunch noon-2pm, dinner 6-9pm; bar open 11am-1am. MC/V.)

PORT CHARLOTTE

On the western arm of Islay, across Loch Indaal from Bowmore, Port Charlotte is a quiet village set on a peaceful stretch of the coast. While its rows of white-washed houses are charming, you will find little else in Port Charlotte. The **Museum of Islay Life,** Main St., chronicles a history of Viking raids, clans, and whisky. (☎850 358. Open Apr.-Oct. M-Sa 10am-5pm, Su 2-5pm. ₤2.50, concessions ₤1.50, children ₤1.) 2 mi. back along the A847 toward Bowmore, the ⚡**Bruichladdich Distillery** uses only their original, antiquated equipment, and it's the only distillery on Islay that ages and bottles its whisky on-site.

The basic **SYHA Islay ❶,** above the Wildlife Information Centre was once a distillery. (☎0871 330 8529. 30 beds. Laundry and kitchen. Reception closed 10:30am-5pm. Curfew 11:30pm. Open Apr.-Sept. Dorms ₤10.50, under 18 ₤8.50. MC/V.) There are a couple of **B&Bs** near Port Charlotte, including luxurious **Port Charlotte Hotel ❹,** Main St. The hotel's **restaurant ❺** is equally good with a daily menu featuring local produce. (☎850 360. Singles ₤60; doubles ₤105. 3 courses ₤25. MC/V.) The **Croft Kitchen ❸,** Main St., across from the Museum of Islay Life, lists seafood options on its blackboard menus. (☎850 230. Lunch ₤5-10. Dinner ₤10-15. Open mid-Mar. to mid.-Oct. Th-Tu 10am-8:30pm. MC/V.) The tiny **Spar,** Main St., has basic **groceries.** (Open M-Sa 9am-12:30pm and 1:30-5pm, Su 11:30am-1:30pm.)

ISLE OF JURA ☎01496

Separated from Islay by only a narrow strait, the Isle of Jura ("Deer Island") has somehow grown more wild and isolated during the past century. A census in 1841 showed that 2299 people lived here; today only 150 call the island home. Living in scattered houses along a single-track road on the eastern shore, these hardy souls are outnumbered by deer nearly forty to one. Jura was remote enough to satisfy novelist George Orwell, who penned *1984* here in a cottage free from watchful eyes. The entire center and western coast of this island is uninhabited, offering the adventurous true wilderness. This great **hiking** country includes a series of tough ascents up the three **Paps of Jura** (all over 2400 ft.). The land surrounding **Loch Tarbet** is pristine yet harsh. At the island's northern tip, the **Corryvreckan Whirlpool**—the third largest in the world—churns violently and can be heard from over a mile away. Ordnance Survey Explorer #353 (₤7) and Landranger #361 (₤6) maps cover the island while *Jura: A Guide for Walkers* (₤2) details various hikes.

3 **Laphroaig** (la-FROYG): (☎302 418), 2 mi. from Port Ellen. Its name in Gaelic means "beautiful hollow by the broad bay." Considered by many to be Islay's finest.

4 **Bowmore:** (☎810 441), right in town. The oldest (est. 1779) of Islay's distilleries in full operation and one of the last to malt its own barley. Tours M-F 10:30, 11:30am 10, 11am, 2 and 3pm, Sa 10:30am. £2.

5 **Bruichladdich** (brook-LAD-DIE): (☎850 221), 2 mi. from Port Charlotte. A smoother malt, produced with 19th-century equipment. The only one on the island that bottles its own product. Tours M-F 10:30, 11:30am and 2:30pm; Sa 10:30am and 2:30pm. £3.

6 **Caol Ila** (cool-EE-la): (☎840 207), 1 mi. from Port Askaig. Fine views across the sound and a complimentary swig. Tours by appointment. £4.

7 **Bunnahabhainn** (bunna-HAV-en): (☎840 646). Home to the "Black Bottle," containing all seven of Islay's malts. Tours M-Th 10:30am, 1, and 3pm; F 10:30am. Free.

8 **Jura:** (☎820 240). in Craighouse. Check out the warehouses where the "angels' share" evaporates out of the casks, producing a divine aroma. Produces a vintage label aged at least 36 years. Tours daily 10 and 11am, 2:30pm.

Though the distance between Islay and Jura is short, do not attempt the swim; tidal current sweeps are powerful. The **Jura Ferry** (☎840 681) sends a car and passenger ferry across the Sound of Islay from **Port Askaig** to **Feolin** (5min.; summer M-Sa 13-16 per day, Su 6 per day; in winter M-Sa 12 per day, Su 2 per day; £1.40). During the summer and on weekdays during term, the **Jura Bus Service** (☎820 314 or 820 221) connects Feolin with **Craighouse** and other island points (6-8 per day).

CRAIGHOUSE. Jura's only village is a tiny, one-road settlement 10 mi. north of the ferry landing. At the center of Craighouse, the **Isle of Jura Distillery** (p. 53) employs 28% of the island's working population (12 people). Nearby, a small unmanned **information center** has walking and wildlife guides. There's one hotel and a handful of B&Bs in Craighouse. Up the road from the distillery, **Mrs. Boardman ❷**, 7 Woodside, offers friendly lodgings. The owner also drives a local bus. (☎820 379. £20 per person. Cash only.) The only restaurant in Craighouse is in the **Jura Hotel ❷**, where bar lunches (noon-2pm) and evening meals (7-9pm) average £5-8. The hotel also offers **camping ❶** on its front lawn beside the harbor for those who have returned from the wild. (☎820 243; www.jurahotel.co.uk. From £35 per person. Camping free. Showers and toilet £1. Laundry £3. AmEx/MC/V.) Jura has **no banks**, but both the hotel and the **grocery** store do cash back on purchases. There's also a van run by the Royal Bank of Scotland that functions as a **bank on wheels** and rolls into town for about an hour on Wednesdays at 1pm. Down the road and across from the distillery, the village store sells **groceries** and houses a **post office.** (☎820 230. Store open M-Th 9am-5pm, F-Sa 9am-4:30pm, closed for lunch 1-2pm. Post office open M-Tu and Th-F 9am-12:30pm, W 9-9:30am, Sa 9am-1pm and 2-4:30pm.) **Post Code:** PA60 7XP.

ISLE OF MULL

Even on the brightest of days, mist lingers among the blue hills of Mull, the most accessible of the Inner Hebrides. With towering mountains, remote glens, and miles of untouched coastline, Mull rewards explorers who venture beyond the well-trodden routes. The tiny isles scattered to the east of Mull are attractions themselves (p. 622). Much of Mull's Gaelic heritage has given way to the pressure of English settlers, who now comprise over two-thirds of the population, and to the annual tourist herd (500,000 strong), but life-long locals keep tradition alive.

◪ TRANSPORTATION

CalMac (Craignure Office ☎01680 812 343) runs a ferry from **Oban** to **Craignure** (45min.; M-Sa 6 per day, Su 5 per day; extra sailings July-Aug.; £3.85). Smaller car and passenger ferries run from **Lochaline** on the Morvern Peninsula, north of Mull, to **Fishnish**, on the east coast 6 mi. northwest of Craignure (15min.; M-Sa 13-14 per day, Su 9 per day; £2.40), and from **Kilchoan** on the Ardnamurchan peninsula to **Tobermory** (35min.; M-Sa 7 per day; June-Aug. also Su 5 per day; £3.70). Winter schedules are reduced. **Day tours** run to Mull from **Oban** (p. 614).

Though Mull's public transport is fairly good, be sure to check **bus** times to avoid stranding yourself. **Bowman Coaches** (☎01680 812 313) operates the main bus routes. Bus #496 meets the Oban ferry at **Craignure** and goes to **Fionnphort** (1¼hr.; M-F 4 per day, Sa 3 per day, Su 1 per day; round-trip £9). #495 runs between **Craignure** and **Tobermory** via **Fishnish** (50min.; M-F 6 per day, Sa 4 per day, Su 2 per day; round-trip £6). **R.N. Carmichael** (☎01688 302 220) #494 links **Tobermory** and **Calgary** (45min.; M-F 4 per day, Sa 2 per day; round-trip £3.60). **Postbus** (☎01680 300 321) #187 runs from **Salen,** which lies between Fishnish and Tobermory, to **Ulva Ferry** and **Burg** on the west coast (1hr., M-Sa 2 per day, round-trip £6.50). TICs stock copies of the comprehensive *Mull and Iona Area Transport Guide.*

ORIENTATION

Mull's settlements cling to the sunnier shoreline. Its three main hubs, **Tobermory** (northwest tip), **Craignure** (east tip), and **Fionnphort** (FINN-a-furt; southwest tip), form a triangle bounded on two sides by the A849 and the A848. A left turn off the **Craignure Pier** leads 35 mi. down a single-track road along the southern arm of the island to **Fionnphort.** There, the ferry leaves for **Iona,** a tiny island to the southwest.

HIKING AND OUTDOORS

The Isle of Mull features a range of terrain for walkers, including headland treks, sea-to-summit ascents, and gentle forest strolls. While the coastline has some of the most scenic paths, inland you can trek among mountains and deep glens. Ordnance Survey Landranger #47-49 maps (£6) cover Mull, while *Walking in North Mull* and *Walking in South Mull* (£4 each) highlight individual trails. From Tobermory, a 2 mi. walk departs from the Royal Lifeboat Station at the end of Main St. and follows the shore to a **lighthouse.** Outside of Craignure, **Dun da Ghaoithe Ridge** walk begins just past the entrance to Torosay Castle on the A849. This 11 mi. route ascends 2513 ft., follows a ridge with fabulous views over the Sound of Mull, and finishes on the A848, where you can catch a bus back to town. Popular climbs up **Ben More** (3169 ft.) and **Ben Buie** (2352 ft.) start from the sea. You can also take the bus to **Calgary Bay,** where stretches of beautiful white-sand beach and rocky headland border the bright blue water.

In Tobermory, **Tackle and Books,** 10 Main St., runs 3hr. **fishing trips** that can be suited to experienced anglers or first-time fishermen. (☎302 336. Trips daily Feb.-Oct. Call a day ahead to arrange a sailing. £8-10 per person.)

CRAIGNURE ☎01680

Craignure, Mull's main ferry port, is a tiny town with one nameless street. From the pier, turn left and take your first left again to reach Mull's vintage **steam locomotive,** a narrow-gauge toy of a train that will make you feel like a giant. (☎812 494. Runs mid-Apr. to mid-Oct. 4-10 per day. Round-trip £4, children £3, families £10.75.) The train rolls 1 mi. south to the inhabited **Torosay Castle,** a Victorian mansion with Edwardian artifacts where visitors are urged to sit on the chairs and wander freely. A 1 mi. walk leads from Craignure to the house. (☎812 421. Open daily Apr.-Oct. 10:30am-5pm. Gardens open daily 9am-7pm. £5, concessions £4, children £1.75, families £12.) Further along the coast, spectacular ☒**Duart Castle,** a 700-year-old stronghold, sits 4 mi. from Craignure and remains the seat of the MacLean clan chief. The bus runs to the end of Duart Rd.; it's a 1½ mi. walk to the castle. (☎812 309; www.duartcastle.com. Open daily May-Oct. 10:30am-5:30pm; Apr. Su-Th 11am-4pm. £4, concessions £3.50, children £2.)

Across from the ferry, the **Tourist Information Centre** books rooms for a £3 charge plus a 10% deposit. (☎812 377. Open July-Aug. M-F 8:30am-7pm, Sa-Su 10am-6:30pm; Apr.-June and Sept.-Oct. M-F 8:30am-5:15pm, Sa-Su 10:30am-5:30pm; Nov.-Mar. M-Sa 9am-5pm, Su 10:30am-noon and 3:30-5pm.) The adjoining **CalMac** office is Mull's largest. (Open 1hr. prior to each sailing.) **Rent bikes** at **Kells Gallery and Craft Shop,** near the TIC. (☎812 580. £10 per day. Open Su-F 9:30am-7pm, Sa 9:30am-6:15pm.) The **post office** is in the **Spar.** (☎812 301. Store open M 7:30am-7pm, Tu-F 8:15am-7pm, Sa 9am-6:30pm, Su 10:30am-1pm and 2-7pm. Post office open M-W and F 9am-1pm and 2-5pm, Th and Sa 9am-1pm.) **Post Code:** PA65 6AY.

To reach **Shielings Holiday Campsite ❶** from the ferry terminal, turn left, and take your first left again. Super clean toilet and shower facilities, a TV lounge, boat access, and a variety of permanent tents with gas cookers provide hostel-like accommodation. (☎/fax 812 496. Open Apr.-Oct. 2 people and tent from £10.50, with car from £12; bed in permanent tent £9 per person, bedding £2. Cash only.) **Aon a'Dha ❷,** ½ mi. left of the ferry, has friendly, family-run service at unbeatable prices. (☎812 318. £11 per person, with breakfast £16. Cash only.) Just past the Spar, **MacGregor's Roadhouse ❷** serves up mouthwatering burgers (£6-8) and excellent pizzas (£4.25-9). (☎812 471. Internet access £1 per 15min. Open daily M-Th, Su 8am-8pm, F-Sa 8am-10pm. Food served until 9pm. Cash only.)

TOBERMORY ☎01688

Colorful cafes and pastel houses line the Mediterranean-style harbor village of Tobermory (pop. 1000). Nestled at the foot of steep slopes, Mull's largest town is centered along **Main Street,** which rings the harbor. Just across from the bus stop is the **Tobermory Distillery,** on the opposite side of the harbor from the TIC, which conducts 30min. tours and offers generous swigs of the final product. (☎302 645. Open M-F 10am-5pm. Tours every hr. 11am-4pm. £2.50, children free, seniors £1.) The tiny **Mull Museum,** Main St., chronicles the island's history with local artifacts and folklore. (Open Easter-Oct. M-F 10am-4pm, Sa 10am-1pm. £1, children 20p.) During the last weekend of April, Tobermory hosts the **Mull Music Festival,** while June's **Mendelssohn Festival** celebrates the composer's work, much of which was inspired by the Hebridean Isles. The **Mull Highland Games** feature caber-tossing, hammer-throwing, bagpipes, and *ceilidhs* on the third Thursday of July.

The waterfront **SYHA Tobermory ❶,** on the far end of Main St. from the bus stop, has a kitchen and lounge. (☎302 481. 39 beds. Lockout 10:30am-5pm. Open Mar.-Oct. Dorms £10.50-11.50, under 18 £8-8.50. MC/V.) **B&Bs** line the bay including **Failte Guest House ❸,** 27 Main St., which spoils visitors with comfortable ensuite rooms and great breakfasts. (☎302 495. Singles £25-35; doubles £48-70. MC/V.)

The **Co-op** supermarket, Main St., sits opposite Fisherman's Pier. (☎302 004. Open M-Sa 8am-8pm, Su 12:30-7pm.) Grab fresh fish and chips (£4) from the stall on **Fisherman's Pier ❶.** (Open summer M-Sa 12:30-9pm.) The **Island Bakery and Delicatessen ❶,** 26 Main St., serves sandwiches and pizzas. (☎302 225. Open Apr.-Oct. M-Sa 9am-7:30pm, Su 12:30-4pm; Nov.-Mar. M-Sa 9am-5:30pm. Cash only.)

Tobermory's **Tourist Information Centre,** on the ferry pier across the harbor from the bus stop, sells boat tickets and books rooms for a £3 charge plus a 10% deposit. (☎302 182. Open July-Aug. M-F 9am-6pm, Sa-Su 10am-5pm; May-June M-F 9am-5pm, Sa-Su 11am-5pm; Apr. M-F 9am-5pm, Sa-Su noon-5pm; Sept.-Oct. M-Sa 9am-5pm, Su noon-5pm.) Other services include: a **CalMac** office next to the TIC (☎302 577; open M-F 9am-5:30pm, Sa 9am-4pm); **bike rental** at **Archibald Brown & Son,** 21 Main St. (☎302 020; £8 per half-day, £13 per day; open M-Sa 8:45am-1pm and 2:15-5:30pm); **Clydesdale Bank,** Main St., **the only bank and ATM** on the island (open M-Tu and Th-F 9:15am-4:45pm, W 9:45am-4:45pm) and the **post office,** 36 Main St. (open M-Tu and Th-F 9am-1pm and 2-5:30pm, W and Sa 9am-1pm). **Post Code:** PA75 6NT.

IONA, STAFFA, AND TRESHNISH ISLES

The contemplative isolation and sheer rugged beauty offered by these tiny islands off Mull's west coast make them worth the effort to see. Serene **Iona,** a historic cradle of Christianity, is the largest and most accessible. **Staffa,** one of the world's geological marvels, rises from the sea 8 mi. north of Iona, its towering basalt columns a natural masterpiece. Wildly remote, the **Treshnish Isles** teem with wildlife.

CalMac (Fionnphort Office ☎01681 700 559) sails to Iona from **Fionnphort** (5min., frequent, round-trip £3.60). There are no other direct ferries between the islands; it's easiest to see them by **tour.** During the summer, **Gordon Grant Tours** (☎01681 700 338; www.staffatours.com) run from Fionnphort to Staffa (2½hr., £14) and the Treshnish Isles (5½hr., £27). **The Kirkpatricks** (☎01681 700 358) offer daily cruises to Staffa from Fionnphort and Iona (3hr.; £14, children £7). **Turus Mara** operates tours leaving from the town of **Ulva Ferry** on Mull, including time ashore at each island. (☎08000 858 786. Staffa and Iona £27.50, children £14. Staffa and Treshnish Isles £35/£17.) Day tours also operate from **Oban** (p. 614).

IONA
☎01681

The sacred isle of Iona (pop. 150) beckons travelers with white-sand beaches, brilliant blue waters, and rugged hills. For nearly two centuries after Ireland's St. Columba landed his coracle on this island in AD 563, Iona was one of Europe's most celebrated cradles of Christianity. Distinctive **Iona Abbey** is a 13th-century Benedictine structure on the site of St. Columba's original monastery. Follow signs from the pier to reach the abbey. (☎700 512. Open daily Apr.-Sept. 9:30am-6:30pm; Oct.-Mar. 9:30am-4:30pm. Services daily 9pm, 45min.; M-Sa 2pm, 10min.; M-Th and Sa 9am, F 8:30am, Su 10:30am 20min. £3.30, concessions £2.50, children £1.20.) Adjacent to the abbey, gravestones mark the entrance to a 10th-century chapel. Inside, **St. Columba's Shrine** once contained the possessions of Columba. At the **Columba Centre** in Fionnphort, an exhibition charts the saint's story. (☎700 660. Open daily May-Sept. 10am-5:30pm. Free.) Tiny 12th-century **St. Oran's Chapel** is the oldest ecclesiastical building on the isle. The surrounding burial ground supposedly contains a number of kings, including the pious Macbeth. At the start of the road to the abbey, find the ruins of a 13th-century **nunnery,** one of the better-preserved medieval convents in Britain. Signs lead from the nunnery to the **Iona Heritage Centre,** which tells the story of "the year the potato went away." (☎700 576. Open Easter-Oct. M-Sa 10:30am-4:30pm. £1.90, concessions £1.20.)

Left of the pier, **Ross Finlay** rents **bikes** and runs the island's only **laundry** service. (☎700 357. Bikes £4.50 per half-day, £8 per day. £10 deposit. Laundry £5. Open in summer M-Sa 9:15am-6pm, Su 10:15am-6pm; in winter daily 11am-1pm and 2-4pm.) The **post office** is near the ferry pier. (☎700 515. Open M-Tu and Th-F 9am-1pm and 2-5pm, W 9am-1pm, Sa 9am-12:30pm.) **Post Code: PA76 6SJ.**

On the isle's north end, isolated ▨**Iona Hostel ❷**, about 1½ mi. from the pier, has clean dorms, a lounge, and an open kitchen with postcard-perfect beaches nearby. (☎700 781; www.ionahostel.co.uk. 21 beds in 2- to 6-bed dorms. Dorms £15, children £10.50. Cash only.) The island has scattered **B&Bs** by the pier. Get your **groceries** at the **Spar,** uphill from the ferry. (☎700 321. Open Apr.-Oct. M-Sa 9am-5:30pm, Su 11am-5pm; Nov.-Mar. significantly reduced hours.) The Argyll Hotel's **restaurant ❹** serves fine cuisine, offering a range of organic produce. (3-course dinner with wine £26. Food served 12:30-2pm, 3-5pm, 7-8:30pm. MC/V.)

STAFFA

Sixty million years ago, volcanic activity coupled with the cooling affects of the sea produced the hexagonal basalt columns that have made Staffa famous. Ringed by treacherous cliffs, the 80 acres of soil that blanket this miracle of stone were inhabited by a handful of hardy souls as recently as the late 18th century. All that remains today is a herd of wild sheep and the remnants of a building erected in 1820. At low tide, you can enter ▨**Fingal's Cave** and worship inside its natural basalt cathedral. When rough seas roar into the cavern, the noise reverberates; the pounding of wave against rock so inspired the great composer Felix Mendelssohn that he duplicated its sound in the surging strings of his *Hebrides Overture.*

TRESHNISH ISLES

The Treshnish Isles are a veritable paradise for all kinds of wildlife, especially birds. Unthreatened by humans, the wildlife will tolerate up-close examination on these most isolated isles. Along the cliffs of **Lunga,** birds perch on the islands' only remnant of human inhabitants, a 13th-century **chapel.** Legend holds that monks from Iona buried their library on one of the Treshnish Isles to save it from pillaging during the Reformation. Many have tried digging, as yet without luck.

HIGHLANDS AND ISLANDS

Misty and remote, the Scottish Highlands have long been the stuff of fantasy and romance—heathered outposts doused with the rebellious Scottish spirit. Though active rebellion may have subsided, these sheep-dotted moors, sliced by the narrow lochs of the Great Glen and framed by towering granite mountain ranges maintain a miraculous isolation as one of Europe's last stretches of genuine wilderness. But the Highlands haven't always been so unpopulated. Three centuries ago, almost a third of all Scots lived north of the Great Glen as members of clan-based societies; the cruel 19th-century Clearances (p. 538) emptied the landscape to its present state. But even before the Scots were forcibly removed, earlier populations inhabited these desolate regions. From the Stone Age villages of Orkney and Shetland to Scottish Gaelic road signs lining the Hebridean roads, the remnants of an ancient past here prove more epic and poetic than tartan-clad stereotypes. Get lost in the history, and rack up the best pictures of your entire trip.

HIGHLIGHTS OF THE HIGHLANDS AND ISLANDS

BEN NEVIS Dash up the highest peak in the British Isles, whose 4406 ft. peak hides behind a layer of clouds. On a clear day, you can see all the way to Ireland (p. 648).

ORKNEY AND SHETLAND ISLANDS Seek the unparalleled wealth of ancient ruins set amid sheep, sky, and ocean (p. 680).

ISLE OF SKYE Explore the mighty Cuillin Mountains and misty waters of the most accessible and admired of the Hebrides (p. 655).

NORTHWEST HIGHLANDS Trek far beyond the rail's reaches to find remote sea-lochs splintering rugged mountains (p. 672).

TRANSPORTATION IN THE HIGHLANDS AND ISLANDS

Traveling in the Highlands requires a great deal of planning. Transport services are, as a rule, drastically reduced on Sundays and during the winter, and making more than one or two connections per day on any form of transportation is difficult, even in high season. The *Public Transport Travel Guide* (£1), available from TICs, is absolutely essential. **Trains** (☎08457 484 950), while offering the best views, will only get you so far, and **Scottish Citylink buses** (☎08705 505 050) do not travel far beyond the main rail routes. Citylink offers an unlimited **Explorer Pass** (£39 for 3 days, £62 for 5 days, and £85 for 8 days), which includes a 50% discount on CalMac ferry passages. They also offer 20% discount cards for students, seniors, children, and travelers aged 16-25. Access to more remote and rewarding areas depends on private bus companies, listed in the *Public Transport Travel Guide*. Driving in the Highlands is infinitely more convenient but potentially treacherous (see **By Car**, p. 534). Watch out for livestock. No, seriously.

Most **ferries** are operated by **Caledonian MacBrayne**, known as **CalMac** (☎01475 650 100; www.calmac.co.uk); their free timetable is widely available. Peruse their website for the combination ticket that best suits your trip. Advance booking for cars, which cost significantly more, is highly recommended.

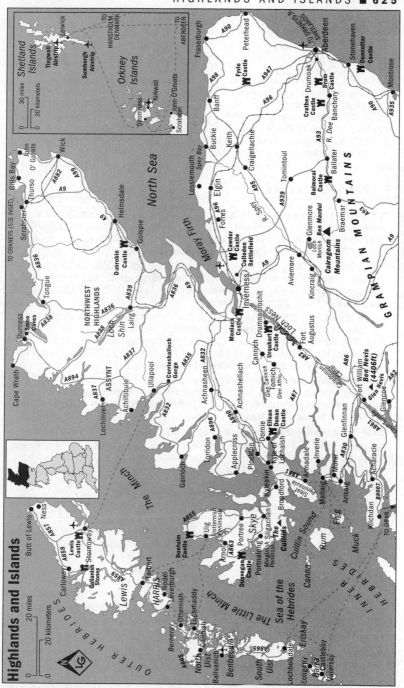

Highlands and Islands

NORTHEASTERN SCOTLAND

ABERDEEN ☎ 01224

Whoever dubbed Aberdeen (pop. 210,000) "The Granite City" wasn't off the mark: most days, the city's buildings—by law a uniform gray—seem to blend with the sky. Though city planners have added lush parks and beach promenades, Aberdeen is still dominated by the 19th-century style of a handful of architects. This melancholy mecca of the North Sea oil industry nevertheless shelters the din of student life and an array of pubs, clubs, and museums. Some visitors use Aberdeen solely as a base for exploring the splendid castles nearby, but those who stay longer realize that this city—Scotland's third-largest—should not be ignored.

▐ TRANSPORTATION

Flights: Aberdeen Airport (☎ 722 331). Stagecoach Bluebird #10 runs to the airport from the bus station (every hr. until 8:40pm, £1.25) and First Aberdeen (☎ 650 065) #27 runs from Guild St. (every hr. until 5:20pm, £1.45). **British Airways** (☎ 08457 733 377) flies from **London Heathrow** and **Gatwick** (11 per day, £30-£105).

Trains: Station on Guild St. Ticket office open M-F 6:30am-7:30pm, Sa 7am-7pm, Su 8:45am-7:30pm. Trains (☎ 08457 484 950) from: **Edinburgh** (2½hr., every hr., £21); **Glasgow** (2½hr., every hr., £28); **Inverness** (2¼hr., every 1½hr., £18.20); **London King's Cross** (7½hr.; 3 per day, 1 sleeper; £90).

Buses: Station on Guild St. (☎ 212 266), next to the train station. Ticket office open M-F 7am-5:45pm, Sa 7am-4:30pm, Su 9:30am-3:30pm. **National Express** (☎ 08705 808 080) from **London** (7 per day, £33). **Scottish Citylink** (☎ 08705 505 050) from **Edinburgh** (4hr., every hr., £15) and **Glasgow** (4hr., every hr., £15). **Stagecoach Bluebird** (☎ 212 266) bus #10 from **Inverness** (4hr., every hr., £9).

Ferries: Aberdeen Ferry Terminal, Jamieson's Quay (☎ 572 615). Turn left (south) at the traffic light off Market St., past the P&O Scottish Ferries building. Open M-F 9am-6pm, Sa 9am-noon. **Northlink Ferries** run to **Kirkwall, Orkney** (5¾hr.; M, W, F 5pm, £32-48) and **Lerwick, Shetland** (12-14hr.; M, W, F, Su 7pm; Tu, Th, Sa 5pm; £43-63).

Local Transportation: First Aberdeen (☎ 650 065) runs public buses. £2 round-trip.

Car Rental: Major car rental companies have offices at the airport and in town. **Arnold Clark Car Hire** (☎ 249 159) is one of the cheapest. 23 and over. Open M-F 8am-6pm, Sa 8am-5pm, Su 11am-5pm. £22 per day, £110 per week.

Taxis: Mairs City Taxis (☎ 724 040). 24hr.

▐ PRACTICAL INFORMATION

Tourist Information Centre: 23 Union St., St. Nicholas House (☎ 288 828; www.agtb.org), in the center of the city. From the bus station, turn right and head east on Guild St., then left on Market St.; take the second left on Union St. Books rooms for a £1.50 charge and 10% deposit. Open M-Sa 9am-5:30pm.

Tours: Grampian Coaches (☎ 650 024) runs various day tours to nearby castles, Royal Deeside, the Whisky Trail, and beyond. July-Sept. £8-12, seniors and children £6-10.

Financial Services: Thomas Cook, Bon Accord Shopping Centre. Open M and W-Sa 9am-5:30pm, Tu 10am-5:30pm, Su noon-5pm.

Launderette: A1, 555 George St. (☎ 621 211). £3.90 per load. Open daily 10am-6pm.

Police: on Queen St. (☎ 386 000).

Hospital: Aberdeen Royal Infirmary, on Foresterhill Rd. (☎ 681 818).

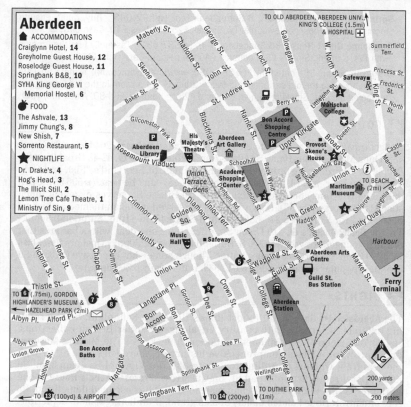

Aberdeen

ACCOMMODATIONS
Craiglynn Hotel, 14
Greyholme Guest House, 12
Roselodge Guest House, 11
Springbank B&B, 10
SYHA King George VI
Memorial Hostel, 6

FOOD
The Ashvale, 13
Jimmy Chung's, 8
New Shish, 7
Sorrento Restaurant, 5

NIGHTLIFE
Dr. Drake's, 4
Hog's Head, 3
The Illicit Still, 2
Lemon Tree Cafe Theatre, 1
Ministry of Sin, 9

Internet Access: free at **Business Point,** in the **Aberdeen Central Library,** on Rosemount Viaduct. (☎652 502.) Open M-Th. 9am-8pm, F-Sa. 9am-5pm. **Costa Coffee,** 31-33 Loch St. (☎626 468). £1.80 per 15min. Open M-W and F-Sa 8:30am-6pm, Th 8:30am-7:30pm, Su 10am-5pm.

Post Office: 48-49 Union St. Open M-Sa 9am-5:30pm. **Post Code:** AB11 6AZ

ACCOMMODATIONS

There are rooms to suit every price range. Reasonable **B&Bs** line the streets near the train station between **Crown Street, Springbank Terrace,** and **Bon Accord Street.** From the bus and train stations, turn south from Guild St. onto College St., then west onto Wellington Pl. which melds into Springbank Terr. Generally, the farther away from Union St., the cheaper the accommodation.

SYHA King George VI Memorial Hostel, 8 Queen's Rd. (☎646 988). A long walk on Union St. and Albyn Pl. or a short ride on bus #14, 15, or 27. Kitchen, smoking lounge, and free parking. Laundry and Internet access (£5 per hr.). Reception 7am-11pm. Lockout 9:30am-1pm. Curfew 2am. Dorms £10-12.50, under 18 £6-11. MC/V. ❷

Roselodge Guest House, 3 Springbank Terr. (☎586 794). Comfortable quarters in a lovely converted home. Rooms with TV. Singles from £20; doubles £34. Cash only. ❸

Springbank Bed & Breakfast, 6 Springbank Terr. (☎592 048). Tidy, quiet, ensuite rooms, run by a hospitable couple. TV. Singles £25; doubles £40. Cash only. ❸

Greyholme Guest House, 35 Springbank Terr. (☎587 081). Tastefully furnished rooms with TVs. Carpark. Singles £25; doubles £40 per person. Cash only. ❸

Craiglynn Hotel, 36 Fonthill Rd. (☎584 050; www.craiglynn.co.uk). A more upscale experience. See the old servants' quarters upstairs or get a room in the old viewing turret facing the sea. Smoking lounge. Singles £42-60; doubles £60-80. AmEx/MC/V. ❹

☐ FOOD

Budget travelers will appreciate the centrally located **Safeway,** 204 Union St. (☎645 483. Open M-Sa 7:30am-10pm, Su 10am-7pm.) ▨**The Ashvale** ❷, 42-48 Great Western Rd., is an Aberdeen institution and 3-time winner of Scotland's "Fish and Chip Shop of the Year" award. The fish and chips (£4.45) can't be beat. (☎596 981. Open daily 11:45am-1am.) **Sorrento Restaurant** ❷, 20 Bridge St. serves excellent lunch specials (2 courses for £5). Hearty dinners are served in Italian-themed ambience: entrees go for £10-12. (☎210 580. Open M-Sa 11:45am-11pm, Su noon-9:30pm.) Trendy **Jimmy Chung's** ❶, 410 Union St., offers the same deal, with a bar area that draws a younger crowd. (☎593 838. Buffet daily noon-2:30pm.) Upstairs **New Shish** ❸, 468 Union St., serves a dinner buffet. Though somewhat expensive (£13; Sa-Su £15), it is popular among locals. (☎643 339. Buffet daily 6:30-10pm.)

◎ SIGHTS

The **Aberdeen Art Gallery,** in Provost Ross's House on Schoolhill, houses rotating exhibits of striking 20th-century art alongside older British collections. (☎523 700. Open M-Sa 10am-5pm, Su noon-3pm. Free.) The **Maritime Museum,** on Shiprow, provides a comprehensive history of Aberdeen's long affair with the sea, from whaling to drilling for oil. (☎337 700. Open M-Sa 10am-5pm, Su noon-3pm. Free.) Just up Broad St. on Guestrow, **Provost Skene's House** is one of the few 17th-century Aberdonian mansions that has escaped demolition. Its rare and mysterious **Painted Gallery** boasts grand, if undistinguished, depictions of the life of Christ, and the house itself functions as a gallery for eclectic collections and shows. (☎641 086. Open M-Sa 10am-5pm, Su 1-4pm. Free.) Across the street, inside the imposing Gothic hulk of **Marischal College,** the **Marischal Museum** provides a glimpse into Northeast Scotland's prehistoric past and into local lad Robert Wilson's collection of Age of Empire booty. (☎274 301. Open M-F 10am-5pm, Su 2-5pm. Free.)

Aberdeen's architecture, though largely uniform, has its interesting features. The gloomiest of turrets looms over **Old Aberdeen** and **King's College,** a short bus ride (#1, 2, 5 or 15) from the city center or a long walk along King St. The **King's College Visitor Centre,** off High St., has an exhibit on the history of **Aberdeen University,** which includes both King's and Marischal Colleges, from its 1495 founding. See how the worst things can come in small packages in the aptly named "Clatter Vengeance" school bell. (☎273 702. Open M-Sa 10am-5pm, Su noon-5pm. Free.) While at King's College, stop at the **Chapel** to see the 16th-century "misery seats," where students were forced to sit in the un-orthopedic chairs for hours. (☎272 137. Open daily 9am-4:30pm. Tours July-Aug. Su 2-5pm. Free.) The 14th-century **St. Machar's Cathedral,** with heraldic ceiling, stained glass, and coffin statues, continues to host religious services. (☎485 908; www.stmachar.com. Open daily 9am-5pm. Services Su 11am and 6pm.) After visiting, take a walk through grassy **Seaton Park,** where the **Brig O' Balgownie**—a gift from Robert the Bruce—spans the River Don.

Though they tend to get lost in the sea of gray, don't miss the city's green spaces, which have won the "Britain in Bloom" award 10 times since 1963. **Duthie Park** (DA-thee), by the River Dee at Polmuir Rd. and Riverside Dr., accessible by bus #16 and 17, is a grassy escape with an extensive rose garden and the **Winter Gardens Hothouse.** (Hothouse open daily May-Aug. 9:30am-7:30pm; Sept. 9:30am-6:30pm; Apr. and Oct. 9:30am-5:30pm. Free.) On the outskirts of town, the **Gordon Highlanders Museum,** St. Lukes, Viewfield Rd., displays the pomp, circumstance, and bloody heroism of the kilted fighting regiment in a 15min. film and detailed exhibit. (Walk down Queens Rd. from the SYHA hostel or take bus #14 or 15 from Union St. ☎311 200; www.gordonhighlanders.com. Open Apr.-Oct. Tu-Sa 10:30am-4:30pm, Su 1:30-4:30pm. ₤2.50, concessions ₤1.50, children ₤1.) Still further (1½ miles beyond the hostel), the aviary, petting zoo, and extensive woodlands of **Hazelhead Park** are worth the quick bus ride (#14 or 15) to the city's edge. Aberdeen's long and sandy **beach** stretches 2 mi. north from the edge of the city. The southern end, accessible via bus #14 or 15, is home to two amusement parks, while the northern end is closer to the fairways. The stretch in between is lined by a long promenade; restless hikers or travelers will appreciate the 2 mi. paved path.

🎭 🎵 NIGHTLIFE AND ENTERTAINMENT

Seagulls aren't the only things to listen to in Aberdeen—five main entertainment venues and other assorted hangouts ensure a steady stream of live music and theater. Obtain tickets and information for all five from the **Aberdeen Box Office,** next to the Music Hall. (☎641 122. Open M-Sa 9:30am-6pm.) **The Music Hall,** on Union St., features pop bands, musicals, and orchestra recitals. (☎632 080; www.musichallaberdeen.com.) **His Majesty's Theatre,** on Rosemount Viaduct, hosts dance, opera, ballet, and theater. (☎641 122; www.hmtheatre.com.) The **Aberdeen Arts Centre,** 33 King St., stages avant-garde and traditional plays year-round. (Tickets ₤3-6, concessions ₤1-2.)

Aberdeen also has a bumping nightlife, courtesy of student throngs forced indoors by the cold weather. Pubs frequently host hip bands in an alcohol-friendly atmosphere. **Langstane Place,** south of Union St., is the place to prowl for dance clubs. Netherkirk Gate also has a number of pubs and clubs. For information on all venues, snag *What's On in Aberdeen* from the TIC or an art gallery.

🏅 **Lemon Tree Cafe Theatre,** 5 West-North St. (☎642 230; www.lemontree.org), near Queen St. Serves food and drink in front of its mainstage, a sure venue for music most nights. Plays and musicals on upstairs stage; tickets £5-9, concessions £2-3. Hours vary depending on show or event; check website or call ahead. Box office open 10am-6pm daily.

Ministry of Sin, 16 Dee St. (☎211 661), a hot dance club in a converted church. Popular late nights, especially Su, with a lively crowd of local students. Drinks as low as £1. Cover £2-4. Open M-Th 11am-midnight, F-Su 10am-3am.

Hog's Head (☎626 490), on Little Belmont St., off Belmont St., has en enormous beer garden crawling with sunshine revellers, and a great bar scene inside when the weather isn't as nice. Show your student ID M from 3pm to closing, and all food and drinks are half price. Open F-Sa 10am-1am, Su-Th 10am-midnight.

The Illicit Still (☎623 123), Guest Row, Broad St., hosts a young crowd, throbbing jukeboxes, plenty of tables and a crowded bar area. Offers full menu until 9pm. Open M-Th 10am-midnight, F-Sa 10am-1am, Su 11am-midnight.

Dr. Drake's, 62 Shiprow (☎596 999; www.drdrakesbar.co.uk). A cozy bar with live music every night. Wait for the doctor himself to step up and play. Occasional drink specials. Open Su-Th 5pm-2am, F-Sa 5pm-3am.

🎇 DAYTRIPS FROM ABERDEEN: THE GRAMPIAN COAST

The dramatic Grampian coast is impressive in any weather. The pounding of the surf on the rugged cliffs make the brilliant hillocks truly dramatic in sunshine or fearsome gales. It is an inspiring little journey from the metropolis of Aberdeen to the stormy coast, and certainly worth it; two of Scotland's most spectacular castles haunt the area.

DUNNOTTAR CASTLE. Dunnottar Castle (dun-AHT-ur) is one of the most magnificent and haunting ruins in Scotland. Braced like a beast against the storm even in ruins, this mighty fortress has seen it all in its bloody, wind-whipped history since it was built in the 14th century. The castle was the backdrop for the Mel Gibson version of *Hamlet*, and has witnessed even more gruesome historical events (like the burning of an entire English garrison by another Mel incarnation, **William Wallace**). At one point the crown jewels of Scotland were guarded here until they were smuggled away during Cromwell's reign. Walk through the haunting chamber on the edge of the cliffs where 167 people were imprisoned in squalor for their religion in 1685. You will kick yourself in the face if you don't visit this clifftop castle; the hike from town alone is worth it for the breathrobbing views. *(Trains (20min., 17-25 per day, £2.90) and Bluebird Northern bus #101 (30min., 2 per hr., round-trip £3.65) connect Aberdeen to Stonehaven. 30min. walk south from town; follow signs. ☎01569 762 173. Open Easter-Oct. M-Sa 9am-6pm, Su 2-5pm; Nov.-Easter M-F 9am-dusk. £3.50, children £1.)*

FYVIE CASTLE. Northwest on the inland A947, 25 mi. from Aberdeen, the 13th-century Fyvie remains amazingly intact despite its cursed status. An ill-tempered ghost called the "Green Lady" (who appears in about 10 other Scottish castles) allegedly still haunts the bedroom of her husband. CBBC TV films "Spook Squad" here. The natural, lived-in interior contains a collection of tapestries and paintings (including a spectacular collection of Raeburns and Gainsboroughs) while the striking exterior is adorned with five turrets—one added by each family that has owned the castle since the 14th century. *(Stagecoach Bluebird (☎01224 212 266) #305 runs from Aberdeen (1hr., every hr.; save money with an all-day Explorer ticket, £9.50). ☎01343 569 164. Open daily July-Aug. 10am-5:30pm; Apr.-June and Sept.-Oct. M-Tu and F-Su noon-5pm. Grounds open daily 9:30am-dusk. £7, concessions £5.25, families £19.)*

ROYAL DEESIDE

Between Aberdeen and Braemar, the River Dee winds through a castle-studded valley of lofty pines and deep, lush glens. With the Cairngorms to the east and the hills of the Highlands to the north and south, the glen caters to royalty and commoners alike. Queen Victoria made this her Scottish retreat, and tourists have followed suit, tracing the **Castle and Victorian Heritage Trails** up and down the valley. If you don't have a car, the efficient **Stagecoach** (☎0870 608 2608) #201 runs every hour between Aberdeen and Braemar (day rover £7, children £3.50), whisking passengers from a stronghold of "Lowland" culture, to the edge of the Highlands.

Thirty minutes down the A93 from Aberdeen is the modest **Drum Castle,** which is pleasantly under-touristed. Drum looks, feels, and actually is ancient; it's been inhabited longer than any other castle in Scotland (from 1323 to 1975) and may have been built as early as 1286. Hop off the bus in Drumoak at the Irvine Arms and walk a mile to the castle and its **Garden of Historic Roses,** a collection of flowers which have been carefully grafted and cultivated over the last four centuries. (☎01330 811 204. Open daily June-Aug. 10am-5:30pm; Apr.-May and Sept. 12:30-5:30pm. Grounds open daily 9:30am-dusk. £7, concessions £5.25, children £1, families £19. Grounds and garden only £2.50/£1.90/£1/£7.)

Crathes Castle, a few miles farther down, is a fine example of a 16th-century tower house, with overhanging turrets and round towers. Grand but not extravagant, the interior contains curiosities like the Horn to Leys, a 1323 gift from Robert the Bruce, and a "trip stair" designed to bungle burglars. Another "Green Lady" allegedly haunts this castle (p. 630), perhaps contributing to the superlative **gardens,** whose blooms deck ingenious alcoves and hedge-lined passages. (☎01330 844 525. Castle open daily Apr.-Sept. 10am-5:30pm; Oct. 10am-4:30pm; last admission 45min. before close. Garden open daily 9am-sunset. ₤7, concessions ₤5.25.)

Another hour along the A93, white **Balmoral Castle and Estate** rests on the southern side of the river, tucked in a valley. The Queen's holiday palace, Balmoral was a gift to Queen Victoria from Prince Albert, who helped design its present form. The traversable landscape is fittingly majestic and worth a stroll, but being a royal hideaway, all but the ballroom (containing rotating exhibits) is closed to the public. (☎01339 742 534; www.balmoralcastle.com. Open daily Apr.-July 10am-5pm. ₤4.50, under 16 ₤1, seniors ₤3.50.) **Pony treks** are another way to see the estate. (Call ahead for 2hr. pony treks starting at 9:30am and 1:30pm. 12 and over. ₤25.)

BRAEMAR ☎013397

Situated on the River Dee, about 60 mi. west of Aberdeen, Braemar is the southern gateway to the Cairngorms. September is the best time to visit: the first Saturday of every September, the town hosts the **Braemar Gathering,** part of the Highland Games. In this 900-year-old tradition, international athletes compete, pipers and dancers entertain, and Her Majesty's military forces take part in such activities as an inter-services Tug of War and Medley Relay Race. (☎01339 755 377; www.braemargathering.org. Tickets ₤12-14. Book in advance.) Brooding 17th-century **Braemar Castle** houses such surprises as a 19th-century fire escape (read: rope and pulley) and Great Lakes Native American artifacts. (☎41219. Open Apr.-Oct. Sa-Th 10am-6pm, also F July-Aug.; last admission 5:30pm. ₤3.50, concessions ₤3, children ₤1.50.) The first full week of July is **Braemar's Gala Week,** complete with a "scenic Barbecue and 4x4 Safaris." (Information available at the TIC.)

The only way into and out of Braemar by public transportation is the **Stagecoach bus** from Aberdeen (2¼hr, every hr.), which stops at Crathie for Balmoral 15min. away. Call **Traveline** (☎08706 082 208) for exact times. Drivers can reach Braemar en route from Perth to Aberdeen or vice versa on the A93. Rent **bikes** and **nordic skis** from the **Mountain Sports Shop,** Invercauld Rd., at the town's eastern edge. (☎41242. Bikes ₤15 per day, skis ₤16. Open M-Th 8:30am-6pm, F-Su 8:30am-7pm.) The **Tourist Information Centre,** on Mar Rd., at the Mews, lists places to sleep and hike. (☎41600. Open daily July-Aug. 9am-6:30pm; June 10am-6pm; Mar.-May M-Sa 10:30am-1:30pm and 2-5:30pm, Su noon-5pm; Nov.-Feb. M-Sa 10:30am-1:30pm and 2-4:30pm, Su noon-5pm.) The **police** station is on Mar Rd. (☎41222.) The **post office** can be found in the **Alldays,** across the street from the TIC (☎08457 223 344; open M-F 9am-noon and 1-5:30pm, Sa 9am-1pm). **Post Code:** AB35 5YQ.

The **Rucksacks Bunkhouse ❶,** 15 Mar Rd., behind the TIC, has space for 26, 10 of whom sleep in the bunkhouse and use their own sleeping bags. Owner Cate runs a clean ship, with a great kitchen. (☎41517. Internet access ₤1 per hr. Laundry service ₤2. Dorms ₤8.50; bunkhouse ₤7. Cash only.) The 64-bed **SYHA Braemar ❷,** 21 Glenshee Rd., occupies a stone house 5min. south of town, surrounded by Scotland's oldest pines. Fear not the 11:30pm curfew—most of Braemar is closed by then anyway. (☎41659. Reception open 7-10:30am and 5-11pm. Check-out 9:30am. June-Aug. dorms ₤10.50, Feb.-May and Sept. ₤10, Oct.-Dec. ₤9.75, Jan. ₤9. MC/V.) Three doors north of the SYHA, the **Callater Lodge ❸,** 9 Glenshee Rd., has light, airy rooms with a reserved, hospitable atmosphere. (☎41275. ₤24-28 per person.) Stock up at the **Alldays** (☎41201; open M-Sa 7:30am-9pm, Su 8:30am-7pm. Cash only.)

ANIMAL FARM

One of the most memorable adventures to be had in the Cairngorms, rain or shine, is at the **Cairngorm Reindeer Centre.** Britain's only reindeer herd was established in 1952 by a Swedish reindeer herder who thought the arctic conditions of the Cairngorm mountains would be ideal for the gentle lichen-eating browsers. The herd has flourished since then, and the unique opportunity to hike up to the free-range herd and interact with them is fantastic. With one of the guides, you will be able to hand-feed grain to the cheeky, awkward-looking yearlings, cows, and impressive Christmas card bulls. For those not able to make the hike up to the herd, there is a paddock behind the visitor's center where reindeer in need of extra care and special feeding are kept. *(Glemore, 6 mi. from Aviemore, toward the ski lift and furnicular. ☎01479 861 228. Open M-Su., 10am-5pm all year round. Visits to the herd daily, 11am all year, and 2:30pm May-Sept. Free-range herd (and hike): Adults £8, children £4. Paddock (behind Centre): £2/£1. Hiking footwear advisable to see the herd.)*

Down the mountain in the lush rolling hills of Kincraig you'll find a very different kind of human interaction with animals at Leault Farm. Neil Ross comes from a long line of shepherds, so it is no wonder that he can direct his regiment of 16 border collies around a flock of

🢂 **HIKING.** The area around Braemar bristles with signposted hikes for all skill levels, centering around the frothy **Linn of Dee.** Along the river, the leisurely **Derry Lodge Walk** promises red deer, red squirrels, and grouse. The more challenging **Lairig Ghru Trail** also starts at the Linn but stretches 20 mi. north to Aviemore. The name means "gloomy pass," which is rather accurate—the path is heartbreakingly desolate as it winds between steep mountainsides and past the often snow-covered **Ben MacDui.** It's also difficult, so don't overestimate your ability or underestimate your need for a map *(Ordnance Survey Outdoor Leisure #43;* ask for other applicable maps at the TIC). To get to the Linn, drive 20min. east of Braemar on the Linn of Dee Rd., or catch the daily **postbus** from the Braemar post office between 1:30pm and 2:30pm (no round trip); check at the TIC. Otherwise, walk or bike the scenic 7 mi. alongside the Linn of Dee Road. Hikers should start early to finish the Lairig Ghru in one day; spend the previous night at the **SYHA Inverey ❶.** The daily postbus stops at the hostel before swinging by the Linn. (☎013397 41969. No showers. Open mid-May to Sept. Dorms £8, under 18 £6.75. MC/V.)

CAIRNGORM MOUNTAINS

☎ **01479**

At the center of the greater Grampian Mountain range stand the awesome Cairngorms. Misty, mighty, and arctic even in summer, these rugged peaks can provide both hard-core "Munro Bagger" expeditions and accessible short day excursions. Though the peaks are bare, covered only with heather, reindeer, and snow for much of the year, the region contains Britain's largest expanse of nature preserves. In addition to winter sports, the Cairngorms offer some of the best hiking, climbing, biking, and horseback riding in the UK.

▰ TRANSPORTATION

The largest town in the Cairngorms, **Aviemore** is conveniently located on the main Inverness-Edinburgh rail and bus lines. The **train station** is on Grampian Rd., just north of the TIC. (☎08457 484 950. Open M-F 7:30am-9:25pm, Sa 7:35am-2:40pm, Su 9:55am-5:35pm.) **Trains** arrive from **Edinburgh** and **Glasgow** (about 2hr. each, 5-8 per day, £32) and **Inverness** (45min., 7-8 per day, £7.20). Southbound **buses** stop at the shopping center north of the train station, northbound buses at the Cairngorm Hotel. **Scottish**

Citylink (☎08705 505 050) runs nearly every hour from: **Edinburgh** (3hr., £12.50); **Glasgow** (3½hr., £12.50); **Inverness** (40min., £4.70). **Kincraig,** 6 mi. south of Aviemore on the A9, is accessible by Scottish Citylink #957 from Perth. For updates and detailed information, call **Traveline** (☎08706 082 608).

The principal path into **Glen More Forest Park,** and the area's prettiest road trip, the **Ski Road** begins south of Aviemore (on the B970) and jogs eastward, merging with the A951. The road passes the sandy beaches of **Loch Morlich** before carrying on to **Glenmore** and ending at the base of mighty **Cairn Gorm** himself. From Aviemore's train station, **Highland Country,** "Munro Bagger" buses #37 and 377 travel the same route, taking in **Kincraig** (10 per day in summer). A similar winter service transports eager skiers.

The **Cairngorm Service Station,** on Aviemore's Main St., rents cars. (☎810 596. £34-42 per day, £185-235 per week. Open M-F 8:30am-5pm.) **Outdoor equipment** is available for rent from **Bothy Bikes,** Grampian Rd., north of the train station. (☎810 111. Half-day £10, full-day £14. Open daily 9am-5:30pm.) Just up the road, across from the **Cairngorm Lodge Youth Hostel** (see below) is **Cairngorm Mountain Bikes and Glenmore Ski Hire,** which acquires brand-new bikes every summer and offers a great all-inclusive ski package. (☎861-253. Bikes £9 per half-day, £15 per full-day. Ski/snowboard equipment, instruction, and liftpass for a day, £56.95.) **Ellis Brigham,** nearby on Grampian Rd., rents skis during the winter and climbing equipment during the summer. (☎810 175. Open M-F 9am-6pm, Sa-Su 8:30am-6pm.) **The Glenmore Shop and Cafe,** just north of the Loch Morlich hostel, rents bikes, skis, snowboards, and even mountainboards downstairs from the cafe area. (☎861 253. Bikes £8 per half-day, £14 per day. Open daily 9am-5pm.)

■❋☊ ORIENTATION AND PRACTICAL INFORMATION

While the Cairngorms themselves are quiet, their largest town, **Aviemore,** is not. Britain's busiest ski village in the winter, the town remains invaluable to tourists in the summer, offering accommodations, amenities, and a prime location for exploring the surrounding region. **Glenmore** offers a more intimate atmosphere, and **Kincraig,** though farther away, sustains visitors with a welcome breath of non-touristed air on the tranquil shores of **Loch Insh.** Nearby but tinier towns like **Boat-of-Garten** also offer places to stay, often at lower rates, and are worth a look.

sheep with just a whistle. Every dog has its own set of commands and waits at attention for a whistle or word that means left, right, quick, slow, and lie down, so that Neil can work half the dogs clockwise around a flock and the other half counterclockwise, in a black and white blur of "thread-the-needle." Neil has individually trained each dog to very high standards- he won the 1995 National Brace Championships, among other herding accolades- and to watch him work his dogs is truly inspiring. His accent is as thick and deep as his pride, and his dogs are as loyal to him as he is to Scotland. Neil won't only mesmerize you with the agility and obedience of his dogs; he'll also tell you about the old days when the area was populated with shepherds instead of tourists and the hills were covered in grass and Blackface sheep instead of heather and four-wheeler tracks. After the herding demonstration you'll have the opportunity to help shear a sheep the old fashioned way, bottle feed orphaned lambs, and watch Neil hone his pups' herding instincts. Leault Farm is a genuine picture of Scottish herding life, and Neil and his family are not only exceptional dog workers but also masters of Highland history and hospitality. *(Leault Farm, Kincraig, 10 min. south of Aviemore on the B9152. ☎01540 651 310. Demonstrations (45 min.) M-F, Su, May-June, noon and 4pm, July-Aug. noon, 2pm, and 4pm, Sept.-Oct. noon and 4pm, Nov.-Apr. call for details. £4.)*

The **Aviemore and Spey Valley Tourist Information Centre,** on Grampian Rd., Aviemore's main artery, books B&Bs for a £3 charge plus a 10% deposit, sells bus tickets, and exchanges currency during high season. (☎810 363. Open July to mid-Sept. M-Sa 9am-6pm, Su 10am-4pm; mid-Sept. to June M-F 9am-5pm, Sa 10am-4pm.) The **Rothiemurchus Estate Visitors Centre** lies near Inveruie, 1 mi. east on the Ski Rd. from Aviemore. (☎812 345. Open daily 9am-5:30pm.) **Glenmore Forest Park Visitors Centre** offers maps and advice on walks west of the mountains. Travelers planning longer walks should stop there. (☎861 220; fax 861 711. Open daily 9am-5pm.) **Kincraig Stores** serves as the **post office.** (☎01540 651 331. Post office open M-Tu and Th-F 9am-1pm. Store open M-Sa 8am-6pm, Su 8:30am-1pm.) Other services include: **police** (☎810 222), Grampian Rd.; **Bank of Scotland,** on Grampian Rd., across from **Tesco** (☎887 240; open M-Tu and Th-F 9am-5pm, W 9:30am-5pm); free **Internet access** at **Aviemore Library,** Grampian Rd. behind the Bank of Scotland (☎811 113; open Tu 2-8pm, W 10am-8pm, F 10am-5pm, closed 12:30-2pm and 5-6pm), or £5 per hr. at **SYHA Aviemore** (see below); and the **post office,** Grampian Rd. (☎811 056; open M-F 9am-5:30pm, Sa 9am-noon). **Post Code:** PH22 1RH.

⚡ ACCOMMODATIONS

Check the TIC's *Aviemore & the Cairngorms* publication for a complete list of seasonal hostels and year-round B&Bs (£15-25).

▨ **Lazy Duck Hostel** (☎821 642; www.lazyduck.co.uk), on Nethy Bridge. Catch Highland Country bus #334 from Aviemore (20min., 8 per day). David (former head of the Independent Backpackers Hostels, Scotland) and Valery run one of the smallest and most charming hostels in Scotland. The cottage sleeps 6-8, and between the loft, the covered garden, wood burning stove, and kitchen, this little escape is pure Highland comfort. Call ahead. Ask Valery for a duck egg breakfast. Dorms £9. Credit cards online only. ❶

Glen Feshie Hostel (☎01540 651 323; glenfeshiehostel@totalise.co.uk), 11 mi. south of Aviemore, 5 mi. from Kincraig. Call ahead for a lift from the station; otherwise it's a 9 mi. walk along Loch-an-Eilein. Homey atmosphere and living quarters close to numerous hikes. Breakfast included. Kate used to run a coastal restaurant; her meals make this hostel stay seem deluxe. Meals £5.50-9.50. Dorms £8. Cash only. ❶

Fraoch Lodge (☎831 331), on Deshar Rd. in Boat of Garten, 6 mi. NE of Aviemore on the A95. Free pickup from Aviemore. Hosts Rebecca and Andrew run a mountaineering outfit from here (www.scotmountain.co.uk) that's busiest in winter; you're apt to find pleasant privacy in summer. Basic kitchen, but opt for outstanding meals by Rebecca with home-grown vegetables instead (£5). Dorms £10; doubles £24. Cash only. ❷

Carrbridge Bunkhouse Hostel (☎841 250), Dalrachny House, Carrbridge. A 10min. walk along a marked footpath from Carrbridge train station. Sparsely done in outdoorsy fashion, but perfect for the serious hiker, nature lover, or bargain hunter. Kitchen, hot showers, and sauna, but bring your own sleep sack. £7. Cash only. ❶

SYHA Aviemore (☎810 345), 100 yd. south of the TIC. The usual SYHA amenities and little to set it apart. 114 beds, 4-8 per room. Breakfast included. Curfew 2am. Dorms £12.25, under 18 £10.75; July-Aug. £1 extra. MC/V. ❷

Insh Hall Lodge (☎01540 651 272), 1 mi. downhill from Kincraig on Loch Insh; bus #957 from Kincraig. Basic, sizeable dorms or B&B. Sauna and gym. Stay 2 nights and use of watersports equipment is free. From £17.50; full board £35.50. Cash only. ❷

SYHA Cairngorm Lodge (☎0870 004 1137), Grampian Rd., Glenmore. Catch a Highland Country Bus (☎811 211) from the Cairngorm Hotel opposite the Rail Station and ask to be dropped off. Newly refurbished with Loch Morlich beach opposite the road. 7 mi. from Aviemore, 2 mi. from Cairn Gorm ski area. Family, double, and dorm rooms all available. £9-12. MC/V. ❷

Aviemore Bunkhouse (☎811 181; www.aviemore-bunkhouse.com), by the Old Bridge Inn on Dalfaber Rd., 200m from TIC. The newest addition to Aviemore's hostels. Although the cinderblock walls are reminiscent of a parking garage, they are sparklingly clean, with new pillows and mattresses. Flexible rooming options. £12. MC/V. ❷

Camping: Glenmore Forest Camping and Caravan Park ❶ (☎861 271), opposite the SYHA Cairngorm Lodge Youth Hostel. Ample space and good facilities, though crowded in summer. Open Dec.-Oct. £4.20-5 per person. **Rothiemurchus Camp and Caravan Park ❶** (☎812 800), 1½ mi. south of Aviemore on Ski Rd. £4 per person.

☐ FOOD

Pubs and restaurants (most with the usual fare) line **Grampian Road** in Aviemore. For **groceries,** the local **Tesco** supermarket is across the street and north of the train station. (☎887 240. Open M-Sa 8am-10pm, Su 9am-6pm. For a trendy experience, try **Cafe Mambo ❷,** 12-13 Grampian Rd., for their burgers (£5-7) and sinful hot chocolate (£1.50). If you've had one too many "fetish" cocktail pitchers (£11.50), stay to dance it off. (☎811 670. Restaurant and bar open Su-W 11am-11pm, Th-Sa noon-1am. Food served until 8:30pm. Club open F-Sa 10pm-1am.) The only ethnic food in town is served (and ready for carry-out for a 10% discount) at **Royal Tandoori ❶,** 50 yd. south of Aviemore's town center at 43 Grampian Rd. Tasty Bangladeshi dishes, open late (by Aviemore standards), and cheap. (☎811 199. Open daily. Lunch noon-2pm, dinner 5pm-11:30pm.)

⚠ ☂ HIKING AND SKIING

The Cairngorms have outdoor activities for every season, keeping the tourism industry afloat year-round. In the winter, the region has Scotland's highest concentration of ski resorts. Outdoors enthusiasts, snowbunnies, and tourists converge at **CairnGorm Mountain** (on the mountain **Cairn Gorm**) for snow skiing. A **funicular railway** replaced the main chairlift in 2000. Sit facing down the mountain for great views on the 5-10min. ride up to **Ptarmigan Centre,** Britain's highest train station (1097m). Catch the peak of **Ben Nevis** to the west from the observation deck. Due to conservation concerns, railway-riders may not set foot outside the Centre. The only way to wander about the peak is to do it the old-fashioned way: hiking up from the bottom. Although a relatively short hike for such a splendid view (around 3 hr. round-trip), certain trails up Cairn Gorm are quite steep and rocky. (*Highland County Bus #37 from Aviemore. ☎861 261; www.cairngormmountain.com. Trains every 15min. Ticket office opens 8:30am, first train up at 10am, last train up at 4:30pm. Funicular £8, concessions £6.50, children £5.*)

Unfortunately for some, the funicular railway does not provide access to the popular peak of **Ben MacDui,** Britain's second highest at 4296 ft. To get there, take the **Northern Corries Path** from the carpark to its terminus, and then navigate an unmarked route to Ben MacDui's peak. Beware, this 7hr. undertaking is suggested only for hikers with some experience. Be prepared for all weather, at any time of year, and bring a stock of food. The still strenuous but shorter **Windy Ridge Trail** reaches the top of Cairn Gorm (3-4hr. round-trip). Before setting out, consult the helpful **Cairngorm Rangers** about trail and weather conditions. (*Office next to the Cairn-Gorm Mountain carpark. ☎861 703. Open daily 9am-5pm, weather permitting; call ahead.*) Other hikes for all skill levels abound. In the ski area, many signposted trails cover Cairn Gorm—all of which leave from the carpark. The Cairngorm Rangers also host free **guided hikes,** usually on Tuesdays. For forest walks, **Glenmore Visitors Centre** has several trails; the most popular is the easy-going 2½-3hr. **Ryovan Trek** through the woods and along **Green Lochen.** (*☎861 220. Open daily 9am-5pm.*) Closer to Aviemore, the daunting but renowned **Lairig Ghru** path heads south through 20 mi. of gloomy valleys to Braemar. This one's only for the bravest of souls, so make sure you have your Ordnance Survey Outdoor Leisure map (#3; £7) and a full day's supply of stamina.

> **SAFETY PRECAUTIONS.** Although the Cairngorms rise only 4000 ft., the weather patterns of the **Arctic tundra** characterize the region. Explorers may be at the mercy of bitter winds and unpredictable mists any day of the year. Many trails are not posted and trekkers must rely on a map and compass. Make sure to use an Ordnance Survey map (Landranger #35 and 36) or, preferably, yellow Outdoor Leisure map #3, both available at the TIC. Explain your route to the staff to find out exactly which maps apply. Be prepared for **sub-freezing temperatures** no matter what the weather is when you set out. Leave a description of your intended route with the police or at the mountain station, and learn the locations of the shelters (known as bothies) along your trail. For more information see **Wilderness Safety**, p. 52.

For skiers, a day ticket at Cairngorm with rail passes costs £25 (concessions £15-18). Several companies run ski schools and rent equipment; pick up a copy of *Scottish Snow* at the Aviemore TIC for details. Down the hill 3 mi. west of the funicular, the interactive **Cairngorm Reindeer Centre** is home to dozens of these majestic creatures. In summer, the **Highland Country** bus service runs from Aviemore to the funicular and Reindeer Centre. Otherwise, you can do the 10 mi. by hoof or bike. The 269 acres of **Highland Wildlife Park** in Kincraig are dedicated to preserving native beasties. Scottish Citylink #957 stops by from Aviemore en route to Edinburgh, Perth, and Pitlochry. (☎01540 651 270; www.kincraig.com/wildlife. Open daily June-Aug. 10am-7pm; Apr.-May and Sept.-Oct. 10am-6pm; Nov.-Mar. 10am-4pm; last admission 2hr. before close. £7; seniors £6, children, students, and disabled £5, families £23.60.) The **Carr Bridge Pony Trekking Centre,** off Station Road in Carrbridge, offers a wonderful way to see the area on horseback with 2hr. treks at 10am and 2pm (£25), a 1 hr. trek at 4:30pm (£15), and a 30min. children's minitrek at 3pm. (☎01479 841 602. Call ahead for reservations and seasonal prices.)

ELGIN   ☎01343

Elgin (whose "g" is pronounced as in Guinness, not gin; pop. 20,000) is a small but relatively urban town halfway between Aberdeen and Inverness, with the charm of rose gardens and ruins but the utility of a general store for the traveler. **Elgin Cathedral** alone warrants a stopover. Once regarded as the most beautiful of Scottish churches (and certainly it was the largest), the cathedral was looted and burned by Wolf of Badenoch in the late 14th century, then further tormented by fire, Edward III, the Reformation, Cromwell, and finally the townspeople who carted off its stones. Half a millennium of neglect has reduced the 200 ft. towers to 90 ft., which still allow a breathtaking view of Elgin and the surrounding country. (☎547 171. Open daily Apr.-Sept. 9:30am-6:30pm; Oct.-Mar. M-W and Sa 9:30am-4pm, Th 9:30am-noon, Su 2-4pm. £2.50, seniors £1.90, children £1.) Next door, all 104 plants mentioned in the Good Book thrive amidst statues of Jesus and Mary in the **Biblical Garden.** (Open daily May-Sept. 10am-7:30pm. Free.) The **Elgin Museum**, 1 High St., in the city center, traces the history of the Moray area from ancient to present times. (☎/fax 543 675. Open Apr.-Oct. M-F 10am-5pm, Sa 11am-4pm, Su 2-5pm. £2, concessions £1, children 50p, families £4.50.)

The **train station** is 5min. south of the city center at the end of South Guildry St. Ticket office open M-Sa 6:15am-9:30pm, Su 10:30am-5:30pm. Station open M-F 8:30am-5pm, Sa 8:30am-12:30pm and 1-6pm. Trains (☎08457 484 950) hail from

HIGHLANDS AND ISLANDS

Aberdeen (1½hr., 10 per day, £11.20) and **Inverness** (45min., 11 per day, £7.40). **Buses** stop behind High St. and the St. Giles Centre. **Stagecoach Bluebird** (☎01343 544 222) bus #10 arrives at the **bus station,** on Alexandra Rd. across from the Town Hall, from **Aberdeen** (2¼hr., every hr., £7) and **Inverness** (1¼hr., 2 per hr., £7). Call **Traveline** (☎08706 082 208) for complete schedules and information. The **Tourist Information Centre,** 17 High St., books accommodations for a £2 charge and 10% deposit. (☎542 666. Open July-Sept. M-Sa 9am-6pm, Su 11am-4pm; Mar. and May-June M-Sa 10am-5pm, Su 11am-3pm; Apr. and Oct. M-Sa 10am-5pm; Nov.-Feb. M-Sa 10am-4pm.) Other services include: free **Internet access** at **Elgin Library** in Cooper Park (☎562 600; open M-F 10am-8pm, Sa 10am-4pm); and the **post office,** with a **bureau de change** (open M-F 8am-8pm, Sa 8am-6pm, Su 10am-5pm) in the large **Tesco** supermarket on Batchen Ln. (☎527 400; open M-F 7:30am-8pm, Sa 7:30am-6pm, Su 10am-5pm). **Post Code:** IV30 1LY.

Elgin may not be worth a stay for the budget traveler, but the town is full of **B&Bs,** especially on the two blocks just north of the train station between **Moss Street, Moray Street,** and **South Guildray Street.** The splendid little **Richmond Bed & Breakfast ❷,** 48 Moss St., has glorious bathrooms (with serious water pressure and heated towel racks), soft linens, and a garden ideal for enjoying the late sunlit hours of the northern summer. (☎542 561. www.milford.co.uk/go/richmondelgin.html. Singles £20; doubles £48, all ensuite. Cash only.) **Auchmillan Guest House ❸,** 12 Reidhaven St. is another good option. (☎549 077. Singles £25-30; doubles £36-40. MC/V.) Grab some cheap, easy grub at **Romak's Tandoori Take Away ❶,** 47 High St. (☎01343 552 266. Open daily 5pm-1am.) **Jimmy Chung's ❶,** 15 Greyfriars St. has a great all-you-can-eat Chinese buffet that hits the spot (and not the pocket). (☎547 788. Open daily 11am-10pm.) Two-course lunches are only £3.25 (noon-2:30pm) at the **Thunderton House ❶** pub, Thunderton Pl. off High St. (☎554 921. Open M-W, Su until 11pm, Th until 11:45pm, F-Sa until 12:30am.)

◪ DAYTRIPS FROM ELGIN

FORRES. Quieter than Elgin and a perennial winner in the cutthroat "Britain in Bloom" competition, the small town of Forres boasts the magnificent **Sueno's Stone,** a richly carved Pictish cross-slab (Scotland's tallest) viewable day and night in a locked glass house. *(Stagecoach Bluebird #10 makes the 30min. trip to this crossroads, halfway between Elgin and Inverness. 2 per hr., £2.40.)*

LOSSIEMOUTH. Secluded Lossiemouth has two sandy, windswept beaches: **East Beach,** connected to the mainland by a footbridge, and **West Beach,** farther from the town center and sporting a lighthouse. Both beaches offer picnic tables and places to get food. Bus #328 connects "Lossie" to Elgin (20min., 13 per day). Halfway to Lossie, stop off at the derelict **Spynie Palace,** once the digs of the Bishops of Moray, which has the largest surviving tower house in Scotland. *(6 mi. north of Elgin on the A941. ☎01343 546 358. Open daily Apr.-Sept. 9:30am-6:30pm; Oct.-Mar. M-Sa 9:30am-4:30pm, Su 2-4:30pm. £2, seniors £1.50, children 75p.)* Campers pitch tents under the watchful lighthouse at **Silver Sands Leisure Park ❶.** *(☎01343 813 262. Open Mar.-Oct. £7.50-12.50 per tent.)*

THE MALT WHISKY TRAIL. The world-famous Speyside area has 57 working distilleries, making it prime territory for indoor as well as outdoor activity. The 62 mi. trail staggers past seven of them, all of which dispense free booze. *(Stagecoach Bluebird bus #10 covers Keith, Elgin, and Forres (all key Speyside stopovers) twice an hour on its way from Aberdeen to Inverness and back. Always tell the driver where you want to go. Bluebird's Day Rover ticket is good for unlimited one-day travel. ☎01343 544 222. £12, children £6.)*

The self-guided whisky trail starts at **Strathisla Distillery,** established in 1786 as the "home and heart" of Chivas Regal, and the Highlands's oldest working distillery. *(10min. north along A96 from the Keith bus or train station. ☎01542 783 044; www.chivas.com. Open Apr.-Oct. M-Sa 10am-4pm, Su 12:30-4pm. £4. No charge—and no drinking—for those under 18.)* If you ask the driver, bus #336 to Glenfiddich (glen-FID-ick) will stop at the **Speyside Cooperage** where visitors can watch casks being hand-made—then on to another tasting session. *(¼ mi. south of Craigellachie on the A941. ☎01340 871 108; www.speysidecooperage.co.uk. Open M-F 9:30am-4:30pm; last admission 4pm. Tours £3, children £1.75, seniors £2.45, families £8.)* The best and only free tour is at **Glenfiddich Distillery** in Dufftown, where bottling is done on the premises. Watch a short video, then walk the rounds with multilingual guides, and end with a generous dram of local origin. *(17 mi. south of Elgin. Take Bluebird bus #336 from Elgin (40min., 6 per day; all-day Explorer ticket £9.50) to the distillery. ☎01340 820 373; www.glenfiddich.com. Open Jan. to mid-Dec. M-F 9:30am-4:30pm; Easter to mid-Oct. also Sa 9:30am-4:30pm and Su noon-4:30pm.)*

TOMINTOUL AND THE SPEYSIDE WAY. Rather than nurse a malt, serious walkers follow the **Speyside Way,** an 84 mi. trail along the river from Buckie at Spey Bay to Aviemore in the Cairngorms. The trail traverses the Highlands's highest village, **Tomintoul,** which began as a village for the evicted Highlanders during the harrowing Clearances, which is surrounded by the rolling hills of the **Glenlivet Estate.** Even here you can't escape the water of life—the famous **Glenlivet Distillery,** Ballindalloch, is a seven-mile hike. *(For Speyside Way information, call the Speyside Way Ranger Service, ☎01340 881 266, and grab a map (£8-9) with the free and indispensable Speyside Way Long Distance Route at the Elgin TIC. For Glenlivet, ☎01542 783 220; www.theglenlivet.com. Open Apr.-Oct. M-Sa 10am-4pm, Su 12:30-4pm. £3, under 18 free.)*

If you're not driving, biking, or long-distance hiking, Tomintoul is difficult to reach. **Roberts Buses** runs from Keith and Dufftown *(☎01343 544 222; #362, Tu and Sa 1 per day)* and Elgin *(#363, Th 1 per day, £4).* The **Tourist Information Centre,** in The Square, dispenses information on various trails and books rooms. *(☎01807 580 285. Open July-Aug. M-Sa 9:30am-6pm, Su 1-6pm; Apr.-June and Sept.-Oct. 9:30am-1pm and 2-5pm.)* Cheap accommodations abound in Tomintoul, including Cathleen Graig's **Alt Na Voir ❷,** with friendly service, good breakfast, and cozy beds. *(Main St., just south of the town center. ☎01807 580 336. £15.)*

THE GREAT GLEN

INVERNESS ☎01463

Inverness is rightfully termed the "hub of the Highlands." The city is not only the main point of access to the region from the rest of the UK; it is also usually the easiest link between points within the region. Downtown Inverness is a bustling neighborhood of shops, pubs, and restaurants, and the surrounding town is filled with accommodations. In short, it is a traveler's town: its location (and proximity to Loch Ness) make it worth a stop before exploring the hills, lochs and castles of the Highland region nearby. The youthful energy of the city makes it a great place to eat well and *ceilidh* the night away.

▐ TRANSPORTATION

Flights: Inverness Airport (☎01667 464 000; www.hial.co.uk), located a few miles east of the city, and accessible by bus (M-Sa every hr.). Planes fly to Edinburgh, Glasgow, London, Dublin, Orkney, and Shetland. **EasyJet** (☎08706 000 000; www.easyjet.co.uk); **British Airways** (☎08457 733 377; www.britishairways.com).

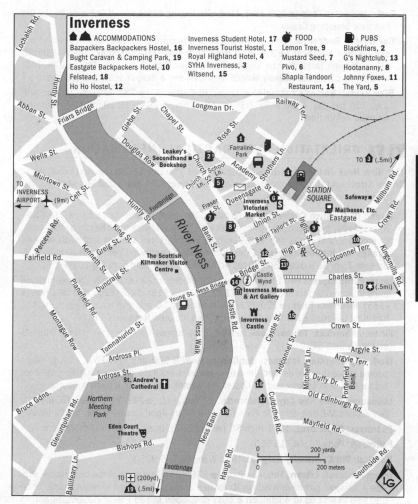

Inverness

♠♠▲ ACCOMMODATIONS
Bazpackers Backpackers Hostel, **16**
Bught Caravan & Camping Park, **19**
Eastgate Backpackers Hotel, **10**
Felstead, **18**
Ho Ho Hostel, **12**

Inverness Student Hotel, **17**
Inverness Tourist Hostel, **1**
Royal Highland Hotel, **4**
SYHA Inverness, **3**
Witsend, **15**

🍴 FOOD
Lemon Tree, **9**
Mustard Seed, **7**
Pivo, **6**
Shapla Tandoori
Restaurant, **14**

🍺 PUBS
Blackfriars, **2**
G's Nightclub, **13**
Hootananny, **8**
Johnny Foxes, **11**
The Yard, **5**

Trains: Station on Academy St., in Station Sq. Travel center open M-Sa 6:30am-8:30pm, Su 9:15am-8:30pm. 24hr. **luggage storage** £2-5. Trains (☎08457 484 950) to: **Aberdeen** (2½hr., 10 per day, £20); **Edinburgh** (3½hr., 11 per day, £33); **Glasgow** (3½hr., 8 per day, £33); **Kyle of Lochalsh** (2½hr., 4 per day, £19); **London** (8hr., 1 per day, £97); **Thurso** (3½hr., 3 per day, £22).

Buses: Farraline Park Bus Station (☎233 371), off Academy St. **Highland Bus and Coach** sells tickets for most companies. Office open M-Sa 8:30am-6:30pm, Su 10am-6:30pm. **National Express** (☎08705 808 080) to **London** (13hr., 1 per day, £35.50). **Scottish Citylink** (☎08705 505 050) to: **Perth** (2½hr., 1 per hr., £11.60); **Edinburgh** (4½hr., 5 per day, £15.90); **Glasgow** (4½hr., 6 per day, £15.90); **Kyle of Lochalsh** (2½hr., 2 per day, £11.40); **London** (10hr., 1 per day, £36); **Thurso** (3½hr., 4 per day, £11.65). Both Citylink and **Rapsons Coaches** (☎01463 222 244) to **Ullapool** (1½hr., M-Sa 2 per day, £7.30).

Taxis: Inverness Taxis (☎220 222). Taxis also line up at the end of Academy St., by the Eastgate Shopping Center.

Car Rental: Budget (☎713 333; www.albacarhire.com) is on Railway Terr., behind the station, and **Europcar** (☎235 337; www.northernvehiclehire.co.uk) has a Telfer St. office, though rates may be slightly higher. **Thrifty,** 33 Harbour Rd. (☎224 466; www.thrifty.co.uk) has delivery service to airport and a fleet of automatic vehicles.

Bike Rental: Barney's convenience store, 35 Castle St. (☎232 249). £7.50 per half-day, £11 per day. Open M-Sa 7:30am-10:30pm, Su 8am-10:30pm, bikes must be returned before dark.

■* ⁊ ORIENTATION AND PRACTICAL INFORMATION

The **River Ness** divides Inverness; most of what you need is on the east bank along **Bridge Street** and the pedestrian area of **High Street.** The train and bus stations are to the north on **Academy Street.**

Tourist Information Centre: Castle Wynd, up the steps toward the castle (☎234 353). Appropriately monstrous, so try not to get lost. The staff helps track Nessie by bus, boat, or brochure, and books non-hostel beds (£3 charge) and **CalMac** ferries. **Bureau de change** and **Internet access** (£1 per 20min., £2.50 per hr.). Open mid-June to Aug. M-Sa 9am-7pm, Su 9:30am-5pm; Sept. to mid-June M-Sa 9am-5pm, Su 10am-4pm.

Tours: Puffin Express (☎717 181; www.puffinexpress.co.uk) runs daily summer minibus tours to John O'Groats and the north (£22, children £15), Skye (£26), and the Orkneys (£55). **Inverness Taxis** (☎220 222) leave from the TIC and give tours to nearby sights, including Culloden Battlefield. Numerous tours hit **Loch Ness** (p. 644).

Financial Services: Thomas Cook (☎882 200), across from the train station. Open M and W-Sa 9am-5:30pm, Tu 10am-5:30pm.

Work Opportunities: Inverness JobCentre (☎888 200 and 888 100), tries to place people where they are needed. Inverness revolves around tourism—in summer, the best bet for jobs is to go knocking on hostel, restaurant, and tourist attraction doors.

Launderette: The New City Launderette, 17 Young St. (☎242 507). Wash £3, dry 20p 5min. Open M-F 8am-8pm, Sa 8am-6pm, Su 10am-4pm; last wash 1hr. before close.

Pharmacy: Super Drug, 1227 High St. (☎232 587). Open M-Sa 8:30am-5:30-pm.

Police: Old Perth Rd. (☎715 555).

Hospital: RNI Community Hospital, Ness Walk. (☎706 935.)

Internet Access: Library, Farraliae Park (☎236 463). Just north of the bus station. Provide a passport picture or a British ID for free access. Call ahead to reserve time, or be prepared to wait up to 45min. on a busy day. Open M and F 9am-7:30pm, Tu and Th 9am-6:30pm, W 10am-5pm, Sa 9am-5pm. **Mailboxes, Etc.,** 24 Station Rd., offers access for £1.95 per 15min., £3 per 30min., and £5 per hr. (☎234 700.)

Post Office: 14-16 Queensgate (☎243 574). Open M-F 9am-5:30pm, Sa 7am-12:30pm. **Post Code:** IV1 1AA.

⁊ ACCOMMODATIONS

▨ **Inverness Tourist Hostel,** 34 Rose St., between the Bus Station, library, and Safeway (☎241 962). Brand-spanking-new with snazzy modern kitchen, leather couches and flat-screen TV to watch that football game in style. Ideal location with the city's amenities, pubs, and shops right outside the door. May-Aug. £11-14, Oct.-Apr. £10. MC/V. ❷

Bazpackers Backpackers Hotel, 4 Culduthel Rd. (☎717 663). Down-home atmosphere and great views of the city from the barbecue area. Kitchen, fireplace, co-ed rooms, and clean bathrooms. No smoking. Reception 7:30am-midnight. Check-out 10:30am. Mid-June to Sept. dorms £9; doubles £14. Oct. to mid-June £8.50/£12. MC/V. ❷

Eastgate Backpackers Hostel, 38 Eastgate (☎718 756; www.eastgatebackpackers.com), in the pedestrian Eastgate Precinct. 38 beds. Relaxed common area with TV and couches. Dorms £9-11; twins £26-30. MC/V. ❷

Witsend, 32 Ardconnel St. (☎239 909). The owners live on the premises, love backpackers, and run a hostel that feels like a B&B. Soak your cares away in the tubs of skylit bathrooms. No smoking and no kitchen, but lots of quiet. Dorms £12; twins £24. ❶

Ho Ho Hostel, 23 High St. (☎221 225; www.hohohostel.force9.com), right in the middle of town. A mecca for backpackers from all over the world for many a year. Single-sex rooms and funky murals painted on the walls. Dorms £10-12. MC/V. ❷

Felstead, 18 Ness Bank. (☎321 634; www.jafsoft.com/felstead/felstead.html). A great location along the eastern bank of the Ness River and 1min. south of the city center. Built by a lucky gambler, this four-star B&B antes up spacious rooms, tartan rugs, and comfortable beds. £28-42 per person. MC/V. ❸

SYHA Inverness, Victoria Dr. (☎231 771). From the train station, turn left on Academy St., go up Millburn Rd., and turn right on Victoria Dr. (10-15min.). With multiple card-swipe checkpoints, this state-of-the-art SYHA has an Orwellian feel. 166 beds. Lockers, kitchen, and TV room. Laundry £1. Internet access £5 per hr. Check-out 10:30am. Curfew 2am. Dorms £11.25-13.75, under 18 £10.75-11.75. MC/V. ❶

Inverness Student Hotel, 8 Culduthel Rd. (☎236 556; www.scotlands-top-hostels.com). 6- to 10-bed dorms and great views. Pub crawl with the friendly staff. Breakfast £1.60. Laundry £2.50. Bikes £6.50 per half-day. Internet access £5 per hr. Reception 6:30am-2:30am. Check-out 10:30am. £10-12. AmEx/MC/V. ❶

Royal Highland Hotel, 18 Academy St. (☎231 926; www.royalhighlandhotel.co.uk), next to the train station. Housed in an historic station-house building with a grand sweeping staircase, this hotel offers unique and luxurious accommodation and is probably the best hotel in Inverness. Singles £75-99; doubles £120-145. AmEx/MC/V. ❺

Camping: Bught Caravan and Camping Park, Bught Ln. (☎236 920). Just off the A82 near the Ness Islands. Open Apr.-Sept. £4.50 per tent, £5.90 per car. Cash only. ❶

FOOD AND PUBS

Inverness is loaded with new restaurants and old pubs. Reach the colossal **Safeway,** Millburn Rd., by going east on Academy St. and following it as it veers north. (☎250 260. Open M-W 8am-10pm, Th-F 8am-11pm, Sa 7:30am-9pm, Su 9am-8pm.) For late night entertainment head to **The Yard,** 28 Church St., a bumping night-spot. Get over the cheesiness, have a drink, and dance the night away to top-40 and early 90s hits. (☎713 005. Open M-F 10am-1am, Sa 10am-12:30am, Su noon-midnight.) After that, try **G's Nightclub,** 21 Castle St., but arrive early—weekend lines are long. (☎233 322. Cover Th-Sa £3-6. Open M-Th and Su until 2am, Sa until 3am.)

Hootananny, 67 Church St. (☎233 651, www.hootananny.com). Certainly the place to be any night of the week, whether you aim to drink whisky and stamp your feet to lively *ceilidh* bands on the 1st floor or groove to live bands with the younger crowd upstairs. Comedy club F-Sa. Open Su-Th noon-midnight, F-Sa noon-1am. ❶

Lemon Tree, 18 Inglis St. (☎241 114), north of High St. Cozy upstairs nook featuring sweet homemade goods and fabulous soups (£1.75). Open M-Sa 8:30am-5:45pm. ❶

HIGHLANDS AND ISLANDS

The Mustard Seed, 16 Fraser St. (☎220 220; www.themustardseedrestaurant.co.uk). Overlooking the river. Creative dishes and excellent "early dinner" deal 6-7pm (£10-13). Open for lunch noon-3pm, dinner 6-10pm. ❸

Pivo, 38-40 Academy St. (☎713 307). A relatively new addition to the Inverness restaurant scene, with a Czech twist. The bar and restaurant combo pulls off the ultra-trendy vibe in an earthy town. Open daily noon-midnight. ❸

Shapla Tandoori Restaurant, 2 Castle Rd. (☎241 919). Perhaps pricier than usual, but the sizzling curries (£5-9) and river views are worth it. Open daily noon-11:30pm. ❷

Johnny Foxes, 26 Bank St. (☎236 577). An Irish bar near the main bridge, which draws a backpacker crowd. M-Sa live music. Su karaoke. Open M-Th 11am-1am, F-Sa 11am-1:30am, Su 12:30pm-midnight. Lunch served noon-3pm. ❶

Blackfriars, 93-95 Academy St. (☎233 881). Purists will take heart: Scottish beer, Scottish whisky, and Scottish folk music (every night but Tu). Open M-W 11am-midnight, Th-Sa 11am-1am, Su 12:30-11pm. Food served noon-7pm. ❶

📷 SIGHTS

With the most popular sights 5 mi. south at the Loch, Inverness nevertheless snares its share of roaming Nessie hunters. The original **Inverness Castle** was built out of wood in the 12th century, suffered a vindictive capture by Mary Queen of Scots, and was rebuilt in stone in 1726 as an army fort, only be blown up by the Jacobites 20 years later. The present castle was built in 1836 and now functions as the courthouse; it is only open to the public during a public trial, but a 40min. **simulation** tries to fill the void by recreating life in 1745, complete with a swearing sergeant recruiting army volunteers. (☎243 363. Open Easter-Nov. M-F 10am-1pm and 2-4pm. £3, concessions £2.70, children £2, families £10.) Down the hill, the **Inverness Museum and Art Gallery,** in Castle Wynd, has an enormous collection of Highland photographs and some archaeological artefacts, as well contemporary art exhibits featuring local artists. (☎237 114. Open M-Sa 9am-5pm. Free.) **Leakey's Secondhand Bookshop,** at the northern end of Church St. in Greyfriar's Hall, claims to be Scotland's largest used book store, and includes many antique prints. (☎239 947. Open M-Sa 10am-5:30pm.) Across the river at Bridge St., **The Scottish Kiltmaker Visitor Centre,** 4-9 Huntly St., demonstrates plaid production and answers such burning questions as "how many pleats make it hang properly?" (☎222 781; www.hector-russell.com. Open mid-May to September M-Sa 9am-9pm, Su 10am-5pm; Oct. to mid-May M-Sa 9am-5pm. £2, concessions £1.)

🎭 🎪 ENTERTAINMENT AND FESTIVALS

Eden Court Theatre, Bishops Rd., stages sophisticated productions, and gives the city a cosmopolitan vibe. (☎234 234; www.eden-court.co.uk. Box office open M-Sa 10am-8:30pm. Tickets £4-35.) Dolphins are sometimes spotted on **Inverness Dolphin Cruises,** especially 3hr. before high tide (tidal information available at TIC). Boats leave from the Shore St. quay, downstream from the city center. (☎717 900. 1½hr. Mar.-Oct. 6 per day. £10, concessions £8, children £7.50, families £36.)

In late July, strongmen hurl cabers (logs) during the **Inverness Highland Games** (☎724 264; www.visithighlands.com. Tickets £3.50, concessions £2), while fife-and-drum bands dominate the **Inverness Tattoo Festival** (☎235 571. £3-5). In August, the **Marymas Fair** recreates 19th-century life with craft stalls and proletarian strife (☎715 760). The **Northern Meeting,** a premier piping competition, comes to Eden Court in early September. (☎234 234; www.eden-court.co.uk. Tickets £12-18.)

◪ DAYTRIPS FROM INVERNESS

Those planning to visit numerous spots in a day should invest in the Highland Country **Tourist Trail Day Rover** tickets, which allow unlimited bus travel for a day to and from Inverness and sights like Culloden Battlefield, Cawdor Castle, Nairn, Fort George, and Castle Stuart. Buses leave from the Inverness bus station or Queensgate. (☎710 555. ₤6.) Car rental is a pricier option (p. 640).

CULLODEN BATTLEFIELD. Five miles east of Inverness on the B9006. Though barren, these fields are rich with history. In 1746, Bonnie Prince Charlie, charismatic but no genius in battle, lost 1200 men in a 40min. bloodbath, ending the Jacobite cause. The complete history is provided by a guide in Jacobite dress. A pretty 1½ mi. south, the stone circles and chambered cairns (mounds of rough stones) of the **Cairns of Clava** recall the Bronze Age. *(Highland Country bus #7 (15min., 4 per day, round-trip £2) leaves from the post office at Queensgate. Visitor Centre ☎01463 790 607. Open daily Feb.-Mar. and Nov.-Dec. 10am-4pm, Apr.-June and Sept.-Oct. 10am-6pm, July-Aug. 9am-7pm. Battlefield free. Centre £3.50, concessions £2.50. Guided tour of the battlefield £5/£3.75.)*

CAWDOR CASTLE. The fairy-tale like castle, complete with drawbridge and garden maze, has been the residence of the Thane of Cawdor's descendants since the 15th century (long after Machabees, the best-known Thane) and is still inhabited for much of the year. The late Lord Cawdor IV detailed its priceless items in a series of witty signs. *(Located between Inverness and Nairn on the B9090, off the A96. Highland Country bus #7 (30min., 4 per day, round-trip £5) leaves from the post office at Queensgate. ☎01667 404 401; www.cawdorcastle.com. Open daily May-Oct. 10am-5pm, last admission 5pm. £6.50, concessions £5.30, children £3.50. Golf £6.)*

MONIACK CASTLE. Built in 1580, the home of the hot-blooded Frasers, 7 mi. west of Inverness, still houses the family and their "fruity passions"—wines, liqueurs, and preserves. Guided tours of the winery run every 20min. and culminate in an unlimited tasting. *(7 mi. west of Inverness on the A862 (Beauly Rd). ☎01463 831 283. Open Mar.-Oct. M-Sa 10am-5pm; Nov.-Feb. 11am-4pm. £2, children free.)*

DUNROBIN CASTLE. The last remnant of aristocracy between Inverness and the northern ferry ports, ◪**Dunrobin Castle** remains the largest house in the Highlands and offers an extravagant interior, elaborate grounds, and a spectacular perch above the sea. Though sections of the mansion date to the 14th century, most of the architecture is Victorian, redesigned at the turn of the 20th, in the Scottish Baronial style. Many of the castle's finest rooms are on display, and the ornate grounds, modeled after Versailles, are dramatically situated. The castle still belongs to the Sutherlands, once the largest landowners in Europe. Its **museum** is worth a look, with a host of collectibles, from animal heads to Pictish stones. Outdoors, the **Falconry Display** allows visitors the opportunity to handle various birds of prey. *(300 yd. north of Dunrobin station, 1½ mi. north of Golspie. Take a train from Inverness (2hr., 2 per day, £11.90) and request the stop. Castle ☎01408 633 177; www.highlandescape.com. Open Apr. to mid-Oct. M-Sa 10:30am-4:30pm, open until 5:50pm June-Aug. Su noon-4:30pm. Last admission 30min. before close. £6, concessions £5.70, children £4.50.)*

Dunrobin is a bit of a long haul from Inverness, and an all-but-impossible daytrip for those without cars. You can, however, bunk for the night at the simple and relatively nearby **SYHA Helmsdale ❶**, in Helmsdale, 12 mi. from the castle and accessible by train and bus from both Dunrobin and Inverness. (☎0143 182 1577. Open Easter-Sept. ₤9.50, under 18 ₤8.)

LOCH NESS ☎01456

Either thousands of tourists embark each year on a foolhardy mission, or the vast and beautiful Loch Ness, 5 mi. south of Inverness, guards its secrets well. In AD 565, St. Columba repelled a savage sea monster as it attacked a monk; whether a prehistoric leftover, giant sea snake, cosmic wanderer, or product of an overactive saintly imagination, the **Loch Ness monster** has captivated the world ever since. Shaped like a wedge, the loch is 700 ft. deep just 70 ft. from its edge. Its bottom caverns extend down so far that no one has definitively determined how vast it really is, or what life exists at its bottom.

The easiest way to see the loch is with one of the dime-a-dozen tour groups, three of which depart from the Inverness TIC. **Jacobite Cruises,** Tomnahurich Bridge, Glenurquhart Rd., whisks you around any number of ways, to Urquhart Castle or on coach and boat trips. (☎01463 233 999. ₤8-20, student discounts, includes castle admission.) **Kenny's Tours** circles the loch on a minibus. (☎01463 252 411. Tours 10:30am-2:20pm and 2:30-5pm. ₤12.75, concessions ₤10.) Multiple **boat cruises** leave Drumnadrochit and tour the sites around Loch Ness for ₤8-20, including **Castle Cruises Loch Ness** (The Art Gallery; ☎450 695) and **Loch Ness Cruises** (Original Loch Ness Visitor Centre; ☎450 395), whose boats are equipped with underwater cameras in case Nessie swims by. **Scottish Citylink** buses from Inverness to the Isle of Skye (#917, 2hr., 5-6 per day) stop at Drumnadrochit, Urquhart Castle, and Fort William (#919, 2hr., 7-9 per day).

In tiny **Drumnadrochit,** 13 mi. south of Inverness on the northwest shore of the loch, not one but two visitor centers expound upon the Nessie legend. The **Original Loch Ness Visitors Centre** (☎450 342; open daily 9am-8pm) falls short, with a monstrous gift shop and a teensy exhibition (₤5, concessions ₤3.50); the **Official Loch Ness Exhibition Centre,** with its 40min. audiovisual display (available in 17 languages) enhanced by smoke and lasers, is the better choice. (☎450 573; www.loch-ness-scotland.com. Open daily July-Aug. 9am-8pm; June and Sept. 9am-6pm; Oct. 9:30am-5:30pm; Nov.-Easter 10am-5:30pm; ₤6, concessions ₤4.50, children ₤3.50.) The Drumnadrochit **Tourist Information Centre,** located on the main road through the village, has all the information you need about tours, transportation, and lodging. (☎01456 459 050. Open June-Sept. M-Sa 9am-6pm, Su 10am-4pm, Oct.-Apr. M-Sa 10am-1:30pm.) Three miles south on the A82 sits ☒**Urquhart Castle** (URK-hart), complete with exhibition center, 10min. film, small display, and gift shop. One of the largest castles in Scotland before it was blown up in 1692 to prevent Jacobite occupation, the ruins now overlook the water of Loch Ness. Most tours from Inverness stop at the ruins and a number of Nessie photos have been fabricated there. The castle is usually packed with tourists during the day, but the ruins are always open after the visitor center closes. (☎450 551. Open June-Aug. daily 9:30am-6:30pm; Apr.-May and Sept. 9:30am-5:45pm; Oct.-Mar. M-Sa 9:30am-3:45pm. ₤5, seniors ₤3.75, children ₤1.20.) The **Great Glen Cycle Route** careens past the loch on its way to Fort William. Eighteen miles down, the River Foyers empties into the loch in a series of idyllic waterfalls.

Near Drumnadrochit within walking distance of Loch Ness, the homey **Loch Ness Backpackers Lodge ❶,** Coiltie Farm House, East Lewiston, features cozy cabin-like rooms, TV room, friendly staff, and a warm fireplace. Entire wall of maps to get you to pubs and vistas, including the hundred foot **Divach Falls,** a lovely hour walk from the hostel. (☎450 807. Continental breakfast ₤2. Internet access ₤1 per 20min. Check-out 10am. Dorms ₤9.50; doubles ₤25.) The more remote **SYHA Loch Ness ❶** stands alone on the loch's western shore, 7½ mi. south of the castle. (☎01320 351 274. Laundry ₤2. Internet access ₤5 per hr. Reserve in advance July-Aug. Open mid-

Mar. to Oct. Dorms £9.50-10.50, under 18 £8.25-9.25.) Both hostels lie on the **Scottish Citylink** bus routes between Inverness and Fort William (#919 and 917, every 2hr., £4.90 from Inverness).

GLEN AFFRIC AND GLEN CANNICH   ☎01456

West of Loch Ness, Glen Affric and Glen Cannich stretch toward the mountains amid one of Scotland's largest indigenous pine forests. Full of hiking opportunities, this remote area has been spared the throngs of tourists attracted by Nessie's tall tales, making it one of the best places to experience Scotland as it used to be.

The main access points for the glens are the villages of **Cannich,** at a turn in the A831, and **Tomich,** farther on; the towns don't offer much but a point of entry. In summer, **Highland Country** (☎01463 233 371) buses run from **Inverness** to **Cannich** (#17; 1hr.; M-F 4 per day, Sa 2 per day), some extending to **Tomich** (M-F 4 per day). Cannich's two **hostels** stand side by side in nearly identical brown buildings, but only the back one is open for now. From the Glen Affric Hotel, head south along the road lined with pine trees, away from the Spar. The antiquated **Glen Affric Backpackers Hostel ❶** (in Cannich) sleeps 70 in mostly double rooms—no bunks. The easygoing wardens are knowledgeable about the area. (☎01456 415 262. £5.) The **Cannich Caravan & Camping Park ❶** rents **caravans** (from £165 per week) and **bikes.** (☎415 364; www.highland-camping.co.uk. Bikes £15 per day. Open Apr.-Oct. £7.50 per day. Pitch £3.50-6.50.) **Slater's Arms ❷,** on the northern end of town, just down the road to Glen Affric, serves standard meals for £4-10. (☎415 215. Open daily 9am-11pm.) The **Spar** next door is the only shop for miles, and contains the Cannich **post office.** (☎415 201. Spar open M-Sa 9am-7pm, Su 10am-6pm. Post office open M-Sa 9am-noon.) **Post Code:** IV4 7LN.

Various walks into Glen Cannich depart from behind the Glen Affric Hotel, beside the bus stop. A 4 mi. walk or bike west on the forest road out of Cannich leads to the trailhead for the popular **Dog Falls Forest Walk** on the eastern edge of the **Glen Affric Caledonian Forest Reserve.** Passing by the waterfall, you'll get a good look at the heart of the 400-year-old pine forest, home to red deer, fox, adders, and otters. For more walks in Glen Affric, pick up *A Guide to Forest Walks and Trails: Glen Affric* (50p), available at Glen Affric Backpackers or any local hotel.

Tomich offers easier access to the more spectacular Glen Affric, including the breathtaking **Plodda Falls Walk.** Walk or bike 6 mi. east on the forest road out of Tomich to reach the trailhead. Your efforts won't go unrewarded—from a restored bridge spanning the gorge or from a viewing platform above, watch the narrow cascades of Plodda Falls crash 100 ft. down into the gorge below. Ordnance Survey Map Landranger #25 will help you navigate successfully. To ease into the wilderness or back to civilization, stay at the birthplace of the Golden Retriever, **The Kennels ❸,** 1 mi. west of Tomich on the road to Plodda Falls. Only one spacious room, but in a convenient location. (☎415 400. £22.50 per person; book far in advance.) The hardy should continue another 3 mi. west to the extremely basic **Cougie Lodge ❶.** (☎415 459. Open Apr.-Sept. Individual rooms £10.) Farther in the same direction, the remote but popular **SYHA Glen Affric ❶,** Alltbeithe, is little more than a cabin buried in the mountains, located where trails to Tomich, Ratagan, and Clunie cross (roughly a 5 mi. hike from end of dirt road). Wind-powered electricity and hot water. Call the SYHA central reservations line (☎08701 553 255). (No phone, showers, laundry, or garbage bin. Open Apr.-Oct. Dorms £10.50, under 18 £8.50.) Bring a sleeping bag when staying at either of these hostels.

FORT WILLIAM AND BEN NEVIS ☎01397

In 1654, General Monck founded the town of Fort William among Britain's highest peaks to keep out "savage clans and roving barbarians." But the town's lofty location on the banks of Loch Linnhe backfired; today thousands of Highlands-bound hikers regularly invade Fort William. Despite these tourist hordes, the town makes an excellent base for exploring some of Scotland's most impressive wilderness. Some will find the touristy buzz of Fort William overwhelming and head for the hills, while others may enjoy stocking up on tartan souvenirs and pub grub with the multitude of hikers.

▐▀ TRANSPORTATION

The **train station** is just beyond the north end of High St. **Trains** (☎08457 484 950) come from **Glasgow Queen St.** (3¾hr.; M-Sa 3 per day, Su 2 per day; £18.50) and **Mallaig** (1½hr.; M-Sa 4 per day, Su 1-3 per day; £7.80) on the magnificent ◪**West Highland Railway.** Built at the turn of the last century, the rail line is a triumph of Victorian engineering, crossing a rugged country of glens, moors, and rivers and skirting some of Scotland's best scenery. The Caledonian overnight sleeper train runs to **London Euston** (12hr., 1 per day, £70-110). **Buses** arrive next to the **Safeway** by the train station. **Scottish Citylink** (☎08705 505 050) travels from: **Edinburgh** (4hr., 3 per day, £16.20); **Glasgow** (3hr., 4 per day, £12.30); **Inverness** (2hr., 7-8 per day, £8.40); **Kyle of Lochalsh** (2hr., 3 per day, £11.20); and **Oban** (1½hr., M-Sa 4 per day, £7.80). Scottish Citylink/Shiel sends a bus to **Mallaig** (1½hr., M-F 1 per day, £6.10).

Highland Country Buses (☎702 373) operates local services. From June to September, #42 departs from the bus station, heading to the SYHA Glen Nevis and the Ben Nevis trailhead (10min.; M-Sa 11 per day, Su 4 per day; £1.30). Bus #45 runs to **Corpach** from the carpark behind the post office (15min.; M-Sa 3 per hr., Su every hr.; £1). **Taxis** queue outside the Tesco on High St.; **Alba Taxi** (☎701 112) is on call late into the night. Rent bicycles at **Offbeat Bikes,** 117 High St. (☎704 008. £10 per half-day, £15 per day, two-seaters £25 per day. Open M-Sa 9am-5:30pm, Su 9am-5pm; closed Su during winter.)

⁊ PRACTICAL INFORMATION

From the bus and train stations, an underpass leads to the north end of **High Street,** Fort William's main pedestrian avenue. The large, bustling **Tourist Information Centre,** Cameron Sq., just off High St., books accommodations for a £3 charge plus a 10% deposit. (☎703 781. Open July-Aug. M-Sa 9am-7pm, Su 10am-6pm; Sept.-Oct. and Mar.-June M-Sa 9am-5pm, Su 10am-4pm; Nov.-Mar. M-Sa 9am-5pm.) **Banks** are on High St. Fort William keeps its droves of hikers well-outfitted with numerous outdoors shops; try **Nevisport,** Airds Crossing, at the north end of High St. (☎704 921. Hiking and climbing boots £4.50-8.50 per day plus deposit. Ski, boot, and pole rental £15-25 per day. Open daily June-Aug. 9am-7pm; Sept.-May M-Sa 9am-3:30pm, Su 9am-5pm.) Find free **Internet access** at the **Fort William Library,** High St., across from Nevisport (open M and Th 10am-8pm, Tu and F 10am-6pm, W and Sa 10am-1pm), or pay an arm and a leg at the **TIC** (£2 per 15 min.). The only place that develops digital pictures and fills your prescription for miles is **Boots Pharmacy,** across from Tesco at the north end of High St. (☎01463 715 555. Open M-F 8:45am-6pm, Sa 8:45am-5:30pm.) The **police** station is at the southern end of High St., past the pedestrian zone, where you'll find the **Lochaber Mountain Rescue Post** (☎999 or 702 361). The **post office,** 5 High St., has a **bureau de change.** (☎702 827. Open M-F 9am-5:30pm, Sa 9am-12:30pm.) **Post Code:** PH33 6AR.

▐▛ ACCOMMODATIONS

Fort William's accommodations fill up quickly in the summer. In town, hostels and **B&Bs** abound, the latter congregating along **Belford Road** and **Achintore Road,** which run from the north and south of town, respectively. Many great accommodations lie just a mile or two outside of Fort William proper along the road through **Glen Nevis.** From the train station, turn left onto Belford Rd. away from the town center. Follow the right fork at the roundabout into Glen Nevis.

Farr Cottage Lodge (☎772 315), on the A830 in Corpach. Take Highland Country bus #45 from Fort William. If you're looking to get wild and woolly, or just hang out with some local characters, this is the place to be. Continental breakfast £2. Dorms £11-12; private rooms £15 per person; cheaper for longer stays. MC/V. ❷

Fort William Backpackers, 6 Alma Rd. (☎700 711, www.scotlands-top-hostels.com). From the train station, turn left onto Belford Rd. then right onto Alma Rd., and bear left at the split. Small and welcoming hostel removed from the hustle below. Watch the sun setting over Loch Linnhe from the back deck. 38 beds in 6- to 8-bed single-sex and co-ed dorms. No lockable dorms; valuables lockers. Internet access and self-catering kitchen. Breakfast £1.90. Laundry £2.50. Curfew 2am. Dorms £11-14. AmEx/MC/V. ❷

The Grange B&B, Grange Rd. (☎705 516). You'll breakfast on fine china in this luxurious Victorian mansion. Open Mar.-Nov. Doubles £74-96. MC/V. ❹

Achintee Farm B&B and Hostel, Achintee Farm (☎702 240), across the river from the Glen Nevis Visitor Centre, 2 mi. from town on the Glen Nevis Rd. Walk or take Highland Country Bus #42, or call ahead and they'll pick you up. This basic farmhouse is ideal for exploring Glen Nevis. The B&B offers large, comfortable rooms. 14 beds in 2- to 5-bed dorms. Lockable dorms; no lockers. Laundry and self-catering kitchen. Dorms £10-12; doubles £25-30 per person. MC/V. ❶

SYHA Glen Nevis (☎702 336), 3 mi. from town on the Glen Nevis Rd. Walk or take Highland Country Bus #42. Upbeat backpacker's hub with ideal location—the front door opens up to the trail to Ben Nevis. 109 beds in 6- to 8-bed single-sex dorms. Laundry, Internet access, and self-catering kitchen. Lockout 9:30am-12:30pm. Curfew 2am. Dorms £10.50-13, under 18 £9-11. MC/V. ❶

Distillery House, North Rd. (☎700 103). From the train station, turn left onto Belford Rd. and continue to the roundabout; the stately white house lies immediately beside the left fork. Fine accommodation in town with a range of rooms. Fully equipped self-catering cottages are ideal for a longer stay. No smoking. Singles £25-45; doubles £40-70; self-catering cottages £40-95. AmEx/MC/V. ❸

Bank Street Lodge, Bank St. (☎700 070, www.bankstreetlodge.co.uk), just off High St. opposite the post office, above the Stables Restaurant. No-frills dorm accommodation right in the middle of town. 43 beds in 4- to 8-bed single-sex dorms. Lockable dorms; valuables locker. Laundry, small kitchen, and TV lounge. Curfew 1am. Breakfast £3.50-5. Dorms £11-12; private rooms from £15. AmEx/MC/V. ❷

Rhu Mhor Guest House, Alma Rd. (☎702 213. www.rhumhor.co.uk). Singles, doubles, and triples with nice mountain views. Open Apr.-Nov. £16-25 per person. MC/V. ❷

Camping: Glen Nevis Caravan & Camping Park (☎702 191), 2½ mi. from town on the Glen Nevis Rd. One of Scotland's most highly acclaimed camping sites amidst the awe-inspiring Nevis Range. Toilets, showers, electricity, and laundry. Reservations July-Aug. Open mid-Mar. to Oct. £1.40-2 per person, £5.20-8.50 per tent and car. Cash only. ❶

🍴🍺 FOOD AND PUBS

Before heading for the hills, pick up a packed lunch (£3) at the **Nevis Bakery,** 49 High St. (☎704 101), across from the TIC, or **groceries** at **Tesco,** at the north end of High St. (open M-Sa 8am-9pm, Su 9am-6pm). **McTavish's Kitchen ❶,** 100 High St., is the Scottish equivalent of a luau in Honolulu: seriously touristy, but fun if you're in the mood. May-Sept. 8-10pm. (☎702 406. Entrees £4-6. Open daily summer 9am-10pm; winter 9am-6pm.) Top-notch seafood awaits at the **Crannog Seafood Restaurant ❸,** superbly situated on the town pier. (☎705 589. Entrees £10-16. Open daily noon-2:30pm and from 6pm.) The lively **Grog & Gruel ❷**, 66 High St., has heaping portions of quesadillas, burgers, and pizzas, with an excellent selection of beer. Try the chocolatey Kelpie, made from seaweed. (☎705 078. Bar meals noon-5pm, restaurant 5pm-9:30pm.) One of Fort William's few hot nightspots, the justifiably popular **Ben Nevis Bar ❶**, 103-109 High St., hosts music at least once a week. (☎702 295. Open Th-Sa 11am-12:15am, Su-W until 11:30pm. Food served noon-10pm.)

🎫 SIGHTS

In Fort William town proper, there's not much in the way of attractions. The **West Highland Museum,** next to the TIC in Cameron Sq., exhibits a few musty displays on local wildlife and the brief but storied Jacobite Rebellion. (☎702 169. Open M-Sa 10am-5pm; July-Aug. also Su 2-5pm; reduced off-season hours. £3, concessions £2, children 50p.) Departing from Fort William's train station, ▨**The Jacobite,** a vintage steam-powered locomotive, travels 42 mi. to Mallaig as part of the **West Highland Railway;** you might recognize it from the *Harry Potter* movies. Heralded as one of "the great railway journeys of the world," the experience does not disappoint. (☎01463 239 026. June-Oct. 1 per day. Round-trip £25, children £14.50.) Two miles outside of town on the A82 to Inverness, the **Ben Nevis Distillery** leads tours that conclude with a dram. (☎700 200. Open M-F 9am-5pm; Mar.-Sept. also Sa 10am-4pm; July-Aug. also Su noon-4pm. £2.) **Fort William Cruises,** on the town pier, operates 1½hr. boat trips on Loch Linnhe. (☎700 714. Apr.-Oct. cruises depart throughout the day. £8, children £5.) It also offers speedboat trips ranging from 1hr. (£15) to a full day trip to the Isle of Mull (£45). In nearby **Corpach, Treasures of the Earth** displays a fine collection of minerals, gemstones, crystals, and fossils. (☎772 283. Open daily July-Sept. 9:30am-7pm; Feb.-Jan. 10am-5pm. £3, children £1.50.)

🥾 🎒 HIKING AND OUTDOORS

GLEN NEVIS. Just outside of Fort William, beautiful Glen Nevis runs southeast into the heart of the mountains. By far the biggest draw to the region and Britain's tallest mountain, **Ben Nevis** (4409 ft.) offers a challenging but manageable hike. One trailhead originates from the Visitor Centre, while another starts opposite the SYHA Glen Nevis (p. 647); the two paths join after 1 mi. While the 8 mi. ascent is challenging for its length rather than its terrain, dramatic weather conditions near the summit can and do prove deadly to the unprepared. Bring food and water, warm and waterproof clothes, and be sure to inform someone of your route. Your planning will prove worthwhile, as the trailside waterfalls and views are breathtaking even in poor conditions. The hike up takes 3-4hr.; the descent 2-3hr. (The round-trip record, set during September's annual **Ben Nevis Race** (www.bennevisrace.com), is an incomprehensible 82min.) Even if you are not planning on tackling Ben Nevis, you should still venture into the glen. The drive up the glacial valley is itself worthwhile and will bring you to some fine day hikes. At the end of Glen Nevis Rd., a popular 3 mi. walk heads to **Nevis Gorge and Steall Falls.** Highland Country Bus #42 stops close to the trailhead, from which a scenic walk passes through a steep rocky gorge and wooded slopes.

Head to the **Glen Nevis Visitor Centre** to stock up on useful information and advice or to get the latest area weather information. (☎705 922. Open daily Apr.-Sept. 9am-5pm.) Walkers will find the Ordnance Survey #7 Pathfinder Guide (£11) useful. Ordnance Survey Explorer #392 (£7) and Landranger #41 (£6) maps-cover the entire area with a specific focus upon Ben Nevis.

AONACH MOR AND THE NEVIS RANGE SKI AREA. Seven miles northeast of Fort William along the A82 on the slopes of **Aonach Mor** (4006 ft.), the **Nevis Range** is Scotland's highest ski area. Throughout the year, the resort's **gondola** propels skiers, hikers, bikers, and sightseers 2150 ft. up into the mountains. (☎705 825. Open July-Aug. Th-F 9:30am-8pm, Sa-W 9:30am-6pm; daily Sept. to mid-Nov. and mid-Dec. to June 10am-5pm. Round-trip £7.80, children £4.90.) During the summer, **Offbeat Bikes** rents downhill cycles at the gondola station, and a network of trails descends from the summit. A number of 2-3 mi. hikes depart from both the base and summit of the gondola. Highland Country buses #41 and 42A travel to Aonach Mor from Fort William's bus station (15min.; M-Sa 4-5 per day, Su 4 per day).

OTHER ACTIVITIES. The **West Highland Way** completes its 95 mi. track in Fort William. Those hungry for more can join the 73 mi. **Great Glen Way,** which runs north all the way to Inverness Castle. Cyclists can take the **Great Glen Cycle Route,** which travels 80 mostly off-road miles from Fort William to Inverness. The free *Cycling in the Forest—The Great Glen* pamphlet breaks the route into 11 manageable sections and includes maps. Numerous adventure sports are offered around Fort William, from canyoning, abseiling (rappelling), and kayaking around the unreal **Inchree Falls** to river rafting and hang gliding in the Glen; ◙**Vertical Descents** is your best outfitter for an adventure. (☎01855 821 593; www.activities-scotland.com)

GLEN COE ☎01855

Stunning in any weather, Glen Coe is best seen in the rain, when a cloak of mist descends upon the valley's innumerable rifts, wreathing the land in a brooding twilight. Only on rare days is the view of its rugged peaks and silvery waterfalls marred by shining sun—the glen records over 100 inches of rain every year. Known for its striking beauty, Glen Coe is infamous as the site of a horrific 1692 massacre, when the Clan MacDonald welcomed a company of Campbell soldiers, henchmen of William III, into their chieftain's home. After enjoying the MacDonalds' hearthside for over a week, the soldiers proceeded to murder their hosts, betraying the sacred trust of Highland hospitality. Every 13th of February, thousands of members of Clan MacDonald from the world over gather as lone bagpipers play throughout the valley in commemoration of the slaughter.

🖃🔃 **TRANSPORTATION AND PRACTICAL INFORMATION.** Essentially a single street, **Glencoe** village rests near the edge of **Loch Leven,** at the mouth of the River Coe and the western end of the Glen Coe valley. The A82 (bound for Glasgow) runs the length of the valley, and **Scottish Citylink** (☎08705 505 050) buses en route from **Fort William** to **Glasgow** (4 per day) are the best way to access the valley directly. **Highland Country** bus #44 serves Glencoe village from Fort William's Middle St. (35min.; M-Sa 9 per day). Buses for Glen Coe all stop along the A82 at the base of Glencoe village and just down from the gas station. For **bike rentals,** head to the **Clachaig Inn,** across the river from the Visitor Centre on the minor road up the valley. (☎811 252. £8 per half-day, £12 per day.)

Before launching into the mountains, stop in at the superb ◙**Glen Coe Visitor Centre,** just off the A82, 1 mi. southeast of Glencoe village. From the village, you can avoid walking along the highway by taking the short trail that starts just up the road from the gas station and passes by the ruins of one of the massacre homesteads. The center has extensive displays on the history and natural features of the area. (☎811 307. Open daily Apr.-Aug. 9:30am-5:30pm; Sept.-Oct. 10am-5pm; Nov.-Feb. M and F-Su 10am-4pm; Mar. 10am-4pm. Exhibit £4.50, concessions £2.95.) The **Spar** market is in Glencoe village. (☎811 367.

Open daily in summer 9am-9pm; reduced winter hours.) The **post office** is just up the road. (Open M-Sa 9am-12:30pm and 1:30-5pm, W and Sa closed afternoons.) **Post Code:** PH49 4HS.

⚑ ACCOMMODATIONS AND FOOD. Many of Glen Coe's accommodations are situated along or just off the minor road that runs roughly parallel to the A82 up the valley, beginning from Glencoe village and reconnecting to the highway after 4 mi. The agreeable **SYHA Glencoe ❶** rests 1½ mi. southeast of Glencoe village on this minor road. (☎811 219. 60 beds in 6- to 8-bed dorms. Laundry, Internet access, and self-catering kitchen. Book in advance. Curfew 11:45pm. Dorms £10-12, under 18 £8.50-10. MC/V.) The family-run **Clachaig Inn ❸** provides comfortable B&B lodging with spectacular views of nearby summits and an attached restaurant. Walk about 3 mi. along the minor road from the village or trace the A82 until the highway and river converge. (☎811 252. £25-40 per person. MC/V.) The Inn's **public bar ❷**, a lively gathering point and traditional trail's-end pub, also serves some of the area's best food (£6-10), with a few vegetarian dishes. (☎811 252. Open Su-Th 11am-11pm, F 11am-midnight, Sa 11am-11:30pm. Food served noon-9pm. Cash only.) For **camping,** head to the **Glen Coe Caravan and Camping Site ❶**, next to the Visitor Centre, which has a wide range of facilities. (☎811 397. Toilets, showers, laundry, and cooking shelters. Open Apr.-Oct. £2.25-4.50 per person.) Beside the River Coe, the **Red Squirrel Campsite ❶**, 1¾ mi. along the minor road from the village, offers more basic camping with a good swimming hole for post-hike refreshment. (☎811 256. £5 per person, 11 and under 50p. Showers 50p.)

⚑ HIKING AND OUTDOORS. Glen Coe features a range of excellent outdoor experiences suited to all interests and abilities. Walkers stroll the floor of the magnificent cup-shaped valley, and climbers head for the cliffs, while, in winter, skiers race down the slopes, and ice-climbers hack their way up frozen waterfalls. Reaching the trailheads—most several miles beyond Glencoe village in the middle of the valley—requires careful planning or a car. With the right timing, you can use the Scottish Citylink **buses** that travel up the A82. For a small fee, most area hostels will also shuttle hikers to the trailheads. However you get there, bring the Ordnance Survey Explorer #384 (£7) map to guide you. The Ordnance Survey #7 Pathfinder Guide (£11) has a number of local hikes and detailed route maps. Low-impact **camping** is permitted in most cases above the valley floor and in the sheltered ridges running perpendicular to the highway.

Among the many options, a number of shorter hikes provide challenging day-trips that stop short of the difficulty found in tackling Glen Coe's most rugged terrain. One 5 mi. trek departs 1 mi. from Glencoe village along the minor road and leads to the summit of the **Pap of Glencoe,** where fantastic views of glen and loch await. In the upper valley, **The Two Passes** route (9 mi.) climbs some 2100 ft., passing through two U-shaped glacial scars. The hike begins from **The Study,** a viewpoint just off the A82 as you move up the road from the large carpark in the valley's center. Departing from that carpark, a 1 mi. trail will lead you to the base of the wooded and boulder-strewn **Lost Valley,** a hidden bowl where Clan MacDonald used to keep stolen cattle. For serious climbing and hiking, ask rangers about route specifics for ascents up the **Three Sisters,** Glen Coe's signature triumvirate of lofty peaks. Another popular choice is the long and difficult traverse of the **Aonach Eagach Ridge;** even locals who have climbed Glen Coe for years have not covered all of its terrain. Over the Pass of Glen Coe just off the A82 you will find ski fields and the **Glen Coe Ski Centre Chairlift.** During the winter, daily lift passes (£17.50, children £9.50) are available. (☎851 226. Open June-Aug. 9:30am-4:30pm, weather permitting. £4, seniors £3, children £2.50, families £11.) When the weather behaves, **Glencoe Cruises & Fishing Trips** (☎811 658) scud across Loch Leven, leaving from the pier in **Ballachulish,** west of Glencoe village.

ROAD TO THE ISLES

As the A830 makes its way from Fort William to Mallaig, it follows the historic Road to the Isles route (Rathad Iarainn nan Eilean). Originally traveled by Hebridean crofters to sell their wares in the larger towns, the road winds around rocky mountains, cuts through shady forests, and skirts shallow lochs. A single lane for much of the route, the drive itself requires as much attention as the scenery. The ▓West Highland Railway (originating in Glasgow; p. 646) runs alongside the road most of the way, providing sublime panoramas at a fast clip (3-4 per day, £8). In summer, "The Jacobite" steam train (p. 648) chugs from **Fort William** to **Mallaig** (via **Glenfinnan** and the famous 21-arched viaduct) in the morning and back in the afternoon, stopping at towns along the way. On a rainy day, you won't miss much by taking the cheaper, more modern version. (☎ 01524 732 100. June-Oct. 1 per day. Round-trip £25, children £14.50. BritRail passes not valid.). **Buses** make the same trip (1½hr.; M-F 1 per day; July-Sept. also Sa; £5.60).

GLENFINNAN. The road runs westward from Fort William along Loch Eil, arriving after 12 mi. at spectacular Glenfinnan, on **Loch Shiel.** Trains often stop for scenic vistas along trestle-bridged **Glenfinnan Viaduct.** A monument recalls August 19, 1745, the day Bonnie Prince Charlie rowed up Loch Shiel and rallied the clans around the **Stewart Standard** (see **The Jacobite Rebellion,** p. 538). Visitors can climb a narrow spiral staircase and squeeze through the hatch at the top, though a knee-high railing is all that lies between you and the drop. The **Visitor Centre** provides the accompanying history lesson and postcards, which you can ponder over a pickle sandwich in the **cafe ❷.** (☎ 01397 722 250. Open daily Apr.-June and Sept.-Oct. 10am-5pm; July-Aug. 9:30am-5:30pm. £2.50, concessions £1.) Walk up the path just behind the Centre for views of monument, viaduct, and loch. If you're feeling lazy, drift on 2hr. **Loch Shiel Cruises** as far as **Acharacle,** at the loch's far shore. Trips depart from the Glenfinnan House Hotel, up the road from the Visitor Centre. (☎ 01687 470 322, www.highlandcruises.co.uk. £10-16, children half-price.)

By **train,** Glenfinnan is 30min. from Fort William (£4) and 50min. from Mallaig (£6); by **bus,** the trips are both 30min. (£3/£5.) ▓**Glenfinnan Sleeping Car ❶,** a vintage railway-car-turned-hostel at the train station, provides unique lodgings. (☎ 01397 722 295. Food served from 8:30am. Linen £2. Dorms £8. Cash only.) For a twilight loch view, opt for pub grub at the **Glenfinnan House Hotel ❷.** (☎ 01397 722 235. Open M-W 11am-midnight, Th-Sa 11am-1am, Su noon-midnight. MC/V.)

ARISAIG AND LOCH MORAR. The road finally meets the west coast at the sprawling settlement of Arisaig. A popular spot for caravans and camping, Arisaig has patches of rocky beach with views of the outer islands. The **HMV Shearwater** (☎ 01687 450 224) operates regular ferries and day cruises from **Arisaig** to **Rum, Eigg,** and **Muck** and sends charter boats to **Skye, Mull,** and **Canna** (p. 652). The trips allow for a few hours on the island of your choice. The **Spar** on Main St. is the only supermarket between Fort William and Mallaig; inside is an **ATM.** (Open M-Sa 8:30am-8pm, Su 9:30am-8pm.) The **Rhu Cafe** in Arisaig is the only place with **Internet access** for miles. (50p per 30 min. M-Sa 9am-6pm, Su 10am-5pm.) Run by volunteers, **The Land, Sea and Island Centre,** 7 New Buildings, is the place to stop before outdoor ventures, with tide tables and other useful amenities. (Open M-Sa 11am-3pm, Su noon-4pm.) For local knowledge and hospitality, stay at **Camus Morar ❸,** a 10min. walk from the A830 in a lochside village halfway between Arisaig and Morar. (☎ 01687 460 007. Singles £20; doubles and twins £15. Cash only.) Three miles south along the A830 from Arisaig, the placid **Camusdarach campsite ❶** sits near the beach. (☎ 01687 450 221. Laundry 50p. £1, £5 per tent. Showers free with £5 key deposit. Cash only.) Across the road and down a short footpath from the campsite are compact white beaches with coves accessible only by foot. Another fine walk westward follows the banks of **Loch Morar,** Britain's deepest freshwater loch (1017 ft.), complete with a monster named Morag, cousin to a certain Nessie.

MALLAIG ☎01687

At the end of the road sits the port town of Mallaig (MAL-egg), where the railway terminates and ferries depart for the Inner Hebrides. **CalMac** (☎08705 650 000) sails from **Mallaig** to **Armadale, Skye** (M-Sa 9 per day; June-Aug. also Su 6 per day; ₤3.05, 5-day round-trip ₤5.25; car ₤16.90/29) and to the **Small Isles. Bruce Watt** (☎462 320) runs ferries and day cruises from Mallaig along Loch Nevis to **Tarbet** and **Inverie** (M, W, F; June to mid-Sept. also Tu and Th; ₤8-15). The only village on the mainland disconnected from all roads, Inverie sits on the wild **Knoydart Peninsula.**

If you're stranded, fill time in town with a visit to **Mallaig Marine World.** (☎462 292. Open Apr.-Oct. M-Sa 9am-6pm, Su noon-6pm; Nov.-Mar. M-Sa 9am-6pm. ₤2.75, concessions ₤2, children ₤1.50, families ₤7.50.) The **Tourist Information Centre** is on the waterfront, just north of the pier. Run by an extremely helpful staff, it has a free telephone for booking and an Internet cafe looking out to the harbor. (☎462 170. Open M-F 10am-5:30pm, Sa 10am-4pm, Su 1:30-4pm.) Other services include: a **Bank of Scotland,** by the train station (☎462 370; open M-Tu and Th-F 9:15am-1pm and 2-4:45pm, W 10am-1pm and 2-4:45pm); **Internet access** at the **TIC** and across the street from the bank in the **Lochaber College Library** (☎460 097; open M 1-5pm, Tu 10am-2pm, W 9:30am-1:30pm, Th 5-8pm, Sa 10am-noon); and the **post office,** in the **Spar** uphill from Sheena's (☎462 419; post office open M-F 9am-5:30pm, Sa 9am-1pm; store M-Sa 8am-10pm, Su 9:30am-9pm). **Post Code:** PH41 4PU.

Sheena's Backpackers Lodge ❶ fills its 12 beds quickly after early train and ferry arrivals. Turn right from the station; the bright, airy hostel is past the bank, above the Tea Garden. (☎462 764. Dorms ₤11. Cash only.) For more private luxury, continue down the street to the **Moorings Guest House ❷,** East Bay, and ask for a harbor view. (☎462 225. ₤16-20. Cash only.) The **Tea Garden ❶** serves a good selection in a pleasant jungle of geraniums. Cash only. Just up the street, the **Marine Hotel ❸,** Station Rd., provides a restful place for ferry stopovers. (☎462 217. ₤28-36 per person. MC/V.) The **Fisherman's Mission ❶,** is a basic cafeteria with cheap, filling grub, like lasagna with chips and peas (₤4). The Mission also has shower facilities. (☎462 086. Open M-F 8:30am-10pm, Sa 8:30am-noon. Food served M-F 8:30am-1:45pm and 5:30-10pm. Cash only.) For delicious seafood, head to the **Fishmarket Restaurant ❷,** which serves up a heaping plate of fish and chips (₤6) in front of the pier. (☎462 299. Open daily noon-9:30pm. Cash only.)

THE INNER HEBRIDES

THE SMALL ISLES ☎01687

The Small Isles rise from the mist as the ferry passes the southern tip of Skye, beckoning wanderers with their utter remoteness. Virtually untouched by tourists and without vehicle-landing facilities, **Rum, Eigg, Muck,** and **Canna** often require their visitors to jump from their ferry to a small dinghy before setting foot on solid land. Those who make the trip are rewarded with a true taste of island life—jalopies and tractors cruise the roads instead of tourist caravans, electricity is provided by generators, and uninterrupted coastline stretches as far as the eye can see.

CalMac (☎462 403) sails from **Mallaig** to **Rum** (₤7.75, 5-day round-trip ₤13.45), **Eigg** (₤5.15/₤9), **Muck** (₤7.90/₤14), **Canna** (₤9.80/₤16.90), and back; call for schedules. Ferries do not allow cars, but are timed to connect with trains from Glasgow and Fort William, and charge £2 per bicycle between any places. Non-landing cruises (5-7hr., £13) also set sail each day, but are excruciating in bad weather. You'll be much happier stepping on land every so often—**Murdo Grant** (☎450 224) sails from Easter to September at 11am from **Arisaig** (p. 651) to: **Rum** (Tu and Th, June-Aug. also Sa-Su. Round-trip £19, children £9); **Eigg** (daily; £15/£6); **Muck** (M, W, F; £15/£6); and in summer to **Canna** by request.

RUM. Rum (often spelled Rhum) is the most striking of the Small Isles, with a mountainous majesty that rivals even neighboring Skye. The largest of the Small Isles, Rum is entirely owned by the National Trust and carefully managed by Scottish Natural Heritage. Deer, highland cattle, feral goats, golden eagles, and migrating Manx shearwater birds are the main inhabitants; the entire human population emigrated in 1826 during the Clearances (p. 538). Today, the grand total of full-time residents has risen to 31, all of whom are SNH employees, student cartographers, geologists, or naturalists. These locals are extremely friendly (and always thrilled to see a new face). The island is covered with well-marked hiking trails; the **Loch Scresort Trail** (6hr. round-trip) is most popular. The real reason to go to Rum, however, is the outrageously opulent ▨**Kinloch Castle**, built in 1901. Dashing playboy George Bullough squandered his family's fortune by importing red Annan stone and 250,000 tons of rich Ayreshire soil for his extravagant summer house and gardens. In summer, take one of the excellent daily tours at 2pm. (☎462 037. Tours £4.) Because ferry daytrips leave very little time, only an overnight stay can do the island justice. Sleep in the castle's former servants' quarters, now **Kinloch Castle Hostel ❷** (☎462 037. Advance booking required. £12 per person. MC/V.) To **camp** on Rum obtain prior permission from the Chief Warden, Scottish Natural Heritage, Isle of Rum, PH43 4RR (☎462 026; pitch £1.50, cash only).

EIGG. The silhouette of Eigg (pop. 78) is easily recognizable by the curious **Sgurr of Eigg** (393m), a pitchstone lava cliff that juts up from the center of the island and into the mist. Eigg shelters the largest human community of the Small Isles amidst vertical cliffs, sandy beaches, green hills and palm trees; the sheltering rock wall of the Sgurr creates a sub-tropical micro-climate. According to local legend, St. Donnan and 52 companions were martyred by the warrior women of the pagan Queen of Moidart at **Kildonnan** in A.D. 617. Almost a thousand years later, the island's entire population (all 395 MacDonalds) were slaughtered by rival MacLeods in **Massacre Cave**. In the summer, ranger John Chester offers weekly **guided walks** from the pier that explore the island's bloody history. (☎482 477. £3. Call in advance to schedule a tour.) A minibus also meets each ferry for a trip across the island to the **Singing Sands**, a perfect beach that sounds out beneath your footsteps (round-trip £3). For **bike hire**, look for the shed just north of the grocery store. (☎482 469. £5 per half-day, £10 per day.) **Glebe Barn ❶** is a hostel with pristine modern comforts, wood burning stove and superb views. (☎482 417. Dorms £9.50-11; doubles £22. Book ahead. Cash only.) For B&B, the best value is **Laig Farm Guest House ❸**, nestled in a private valley with a nearby beach. (☎482 412. £30 per person. Cash only.) The hostel is 1 mi. from the pier, and the guest house is another 3 mi. beyond. For a **taxi**, call ☎482 494.

MUCK AND CANNA. Muck, the teensy (2 mi. by 1 mi.) southernmost isle, is an experiment in communal living. The entire island is a single farm owned by the MacEwens, who handle farming, transport along the Muck 1 road (you can hop aboard the tractor-pulled trailer for a guided tour for £1), and shopping on the mainland. If you intend to stay on the island bring food; supplies are only sporadically available. Or, stay at **Port Mor Guest House ❹**. (☎462 365. Full board £35. Cash only.) Next door is the cozy **Isle of Muck Bunkhouse ❶** (☎642 042. £10.50. Cash only.) A tearoom/craftshop/information center is just up the hill from the pier. The miniature isle of **Canna** (Gaelic for "porpoise") includes the ruins of **St. Columba's Chapel,** a 7th-century nunnery. **Kate's Cottage ❶** is a simple, peaceful converted cottage on the hill over the harbor, with views of Rum and the Cuillins on Skye. (☎ 462 466. £6. Cash only.)

ISLE OF SKYE

Often called the shining jewel in the Hebridean crown, the misty Isle of Skye possesses unparalleled natural beauty—from the serrated peaks of the Cuillin Hills to the Trotternish Peninsula. The island's charms are no secret, as the endless procession of vehicles on the Skye Bridge attests. Most visitors keep to the main roads, and vast swaths of terrain remain unscarred. As elsewhere in the Highlands, the 19th-century Clearances saw entire glens emptied of their inhabitants, and today, northern migration pushes the English population of Skye toward 40%. Nonetheless, the island resists pandering to tourists. Skye has no fast food chains, only four 24hr. ATMs (in Kyle of Lochalsh, Portree, Broadford, and Sligachan), and a strong **Scottish Gaelic** (see **Appendix,** p. 817) influence in its genealogy centers and bilingual signs. Though spotty public transportation may force you to concentrate your travels, Skye's awesome wilds ensure that you won't be disappointed.

▐▀ GETTING THERE

The tradition of ferries carrying passengers "over the sea to Skye" ended with the **Skye Bridge,** which links the island to the mainland's **Kyle of Lochalsh** (toll £5.70 each way). **Trains** (☎ 08457 484 950) to Kyle from **Inverness** (2½hr.; M-Sa 3 per day, Su 2 per day; £14.60). **Scottish Citylink buses** daily from: **Fort William** (2hr., 3 per day, £12); **Glasgow** (6hr., 3 per day, £20); **Inverness** (2hr., 2 per day, £11.40). **Pedestrians** can take either the bridge's 1½ mi. footpath or the **shuttle bus** (2 per hr., £1.70).

From the Outer Hebrides, **Caledonian MacBrayne (CalMac;** ☎ 08705 650 000) ferries sail to **Uig** from **Tarbert** on Harris or **Lochmaddy** on North Uist (1½hr.; M-Sa 1-2 per day; £9, 5-day round-trip £15.25; cars £43/73). Ferries also run to **Armadale** in southwest Skye from **Mallaig** on the mainland. (30min.; M-Sa 4 per day, June-Aug. also Su; £3, 5-day round-trip £5.10; cars £16.50/28.50).

▐▀ LOCAL TRANSPORTATION

To avoid headaches, pick up the handy *Public Transport Guide to Skye and the Western Isles* (£1) at any TIC. The only Sunday buses run to meet the Rassay and Armadale ferries (June-Aug.).

Buses: Buses on Skye are run by different operators; cherish your transport guide, and be careful not to pay twice when making connections, which are infrequent and somewhat pricey (Kyleakin-Uig £8.50; Kyleakin-Armadale £5.50). The only reliable service hugs the coast from Kyleakin to Broadford to Portree on the A87. The **Skye Day Explorer** ticket offers unlimited bus travel for 1 day (£5) or 3 days (£14).

Biking: Cycling is possible and potentially enjoyable, but be prepared for steep hills, nonexistent shoulders, and rain. Most buses will not carry bikes. To **rent** bikes in Kyleakin, try the **Dun Caan Hostel** (☎ 01599 534 087; £10 per day); in Broadford, **Fairwinds Cycle Hire** (☎ 01471 822 270; £7 per day, £5 deposit); in Portree, **Island Cycles** (☎ 01478 613 121; £10-12 per day); and in Uig, **Uig Cycle Hire** (☎ 01470 542311; £12 per day). Reserve ahead, especially in summer.

Car Rental: Kyle Taxi Company (☎01599 534 323) is the cheapest deal in Kyle (starting at £32 per day) and has a low delivery fee if you need it at the ferry in Armadale. **Ewen MacRae** (☎01478 613 269), in Portree. 21+. From £32 per day. £100 credit card deposit.

Tours: Scottish National Heritage and the Highland Council Ranger Service offer free **walking tours** (☎01599 524 270). For the eager and intrepid, the stellar ⬛**MacBackpackers Skye Trekker Tour** (☎01599 534 510), departing from the hostel in Kyleakin, offers a 1-day tour emphasizing the mystical-historical side of the island or a 2-day, eco-conscious hike in the Cuillin Hills. Call ahead. Weekly departure Tu 7:30am. 1-day £15, 2-day £45. For personalized treks, call **A1** (☎01478 611 112) in Portree. £18 per hr.

🎵 🌿 ENTERTAINMENT AND FESTIVALS

Like many of Scotland's isles, Skye's cultural life is vibrant and vigorous, especially since it is the most accessible to visitors. Snag a copy of the weekly *What, Where, and When* leaflet or *The Visitor* newspaper for a list of special events, or consult the TIC. Traditional music in both English and Gaelic is abundant, especially in pubs, and dances—half folk, half rock—take place frequently in village halls, usually after 11pm. In mid-July, **Feis an Eilein** (☎01471 844 207), on the Sleat Peninsula, is a 10-day celebration of Gaelic culture featuring concerts, *ceilidhs*, workshops, and films. Additional revelry can be found at the **Highland Games** (☎01478 612 540), a day of bagpipes and boozing in Portree on the first Wednesday of August, and **Highland Ceilidh,** with *ceilidhs* (p. 542) in Portree, Broadford, and Dunvegan. (☎01470 542 228. June M and W; July-Aug. M-W.)

KYLE OF LOCHALSH AND KYLEAKIN ☎01599

Kyle of Lochalsh ("Kyle" for short) and Kyleakin (Ky-LAACK-in) bookend the Skye Bridge. Kyle, on the mainland, wishes travelers would dally, expressing their wish with the charming slogan "Kyle: Stay a While," but the town is best used en route to Skye. Though Kyleakin is short on conveniences, it operates three hostels and countless tours, making it a backpacker's hub with a boisterous atmosphere.

📞🛈 TRANSPORTATION AND PRACTICAL INFORMATION. The Kyle **train station** is near the pier; the **bus stop** is just to the west. **Highland Country** buses meet incoming trains and head for Kyleakin (every 30min., £1.70). The Kyle **Tourist Information Centre,** overlooking the pier from the hill, has a free phone for accommodations booking. (Open May-Oct. M-Sa 9am-5:30pm.) Other services include: the last **ATM** for miles at Kyle's **Bank of Scotland,** Main St. (☎534 2200; open M-Tu and Th-F 9am-5pm, W 9:30am-5pm); **Internet access** at the chip shop in Kyleakin (open Tu-Sa 5-9:30pm, Su 5-8pm); and the **post office** next door, which sells Citylink bus tickets (☎08457 223 344; open M-F 9am-5:30pm, Sa 9am-12:30pm). **Post Code:** IV40 8AA.

📷 ACCOMMODATIONS. In Kyle of Lochalsh, **Cu'chulainn's Backpackers Hostel ❶,** Station Rd., above a popular pub of the same name, has the usual amenities and especially cozy beds. (☎534 492. Linen 50p. Laundry £2.50. Key deposit £5. Dorms £9. MC/V.) Higher on the price scale is the comfortable **Kyle Hotel ❹,** Main St., which provides traditional Scottish breakfasts. Live music Sa-Su. (☎534 204; www.kylehotel.co.uk. Singles £40-50; doubles £76-110. MC/V.) In Kyleakin, hostels huddle near the pier. The friendly owners of ⬛**Dun Caan Hostel ❶** have renovated a 200-year-old cottage; enjoy a movie in the lounge or concoct a meal spiced with herbs from the garden. (☎534 087; www.skyerover.co.uk. Bike rental £10 per day. No smoking. Book ahead. Dorms £10. MC/V.) The easygoing warden of the **SYHA Kyleakin ❷,** in the large white building on the village green, is a great source for outdoors information. (☎534 585. Laundry. Internet access £5 per hr. Dorms £10-12.50, under 18 £9.50-10.50. MC/V.) Social **Skye Backpackers ❷** next door is a good base. (☎534 510; www.scotlands-top-hostels.com. Internet access £4 per 30min. Laundry £2.50. Curfew 2am. Dorms £11-13. AmEx/MC/V.) For a **B&B**, it's hard to beat **Mrs. Chiffer's ❷** prices, on Olaf Rd., 3 blocks from Skye Backpackers. (☎534 440. £13 per person. Cash only.) An elegant stay awaits at **Ceol-Na-Mara** (KEY-all na MAH-rah) ❸, on South Obbe St. (☎534 443. Doubles £40-44. Cash only.)

🗋🍴 **FOOD AND PUBS.** In Kyle, grab **groceries** at the **Co-op,** up the hill to the west of the Kyle bus station. (☎530 196. Open M-Sa 8am-10pm, Su 10am-6pm.) For a taste of local fish, hop off the train at Kyle and into the **Seafood Restaurant ❸**, in the railway building next to the bay. (☎534 813. Open M-Sa 6-9pm. Cash only.) The amiable staff of the **Pier Coffee Shop ❶** in Kyleakin serve toasties (£2) and breakfast (£4.50) all day long. (☎534 641. Open M-F 9am-8pm, Su 10:30am-8pm. Cash only.) **Cu'chulainn's ❶** in Kyle (see above) offers pub fare in its beer garden. (☎534 492. Open 11am-11pm. MC/V.) Though it lacks numerous restaurants, Kyleakin's nightlife is enlivened by a steady stream of backpackers and tourists. The **King Haakon Bar ❶**, at the east end of the village green, has a free jukebox and frequent live music on weekend nights. (☎534 164. Open M-Th and Sa noon-12:30am, F noon-1am, Su 12:30-11:30pm. Food served 12:30-8:30pm. MC/V.) Live music is also common at **Saucy Mary's,** next door to the SHYA hostel. (Open M-Th 5pm-midnight, F 5pm-1am, Sa 5-11:30pm, Su 5-11pm.) Simple, wholesome food is served at the **Crofters Kitchen ❷**, Alt Ann Abig, on the road toward Broadford, where a two-course lunch costs £6. (☎534 134. MC/V.)

🎯 **SIGHTS.** The **Bright Water Visitor Centre** on the pier in Kyleakin offers a child-oriented look at local history. (☎570 040. Open Apr.-Oct. M-Sa 9am-6pm. Free.) The center also runs 1½hr. trips to **Eilean Ban,** the island under the Skye Bridge, which has an old lighthouse and boasts frequent seal and otter sightings. Departure times vary, so call ahead. (M-Sa 3-4 trips per day. £5, concessions £4, children £3.) Quiet **Kyleakin harbor** lights up in oranges, pinks, and purples during clear sunsets—for the best views, climb up to the memorial on the hill behind the SYHA hostel. A slippery scramble to the west takes you to the small ruins of **Castle Moil.** Cross the little bridge behind the hostel, turn left, follow the road to the pier, and take the gravel path. To stay dry, leave when the tide is lower than the base of the boathouse just east of the pier. According to legend, the original castle on this site was built by "Saucy Mary," who stretched a stout chain across the Kyle Sound and charged ships to come through the narrows. She supposedly flashed those who paid the toll—hence her spicy moniker. (Always open. Free.)

SOUTHERN SKYE   ☎01471

BROADFORD. Situated on a rocky bay 8 mi. west of Kyleakin, Broadford is more road-strip than town, with most amenities and attractions lined up on one side of the A87. The **Tourist Information Centre** sits in the carpark along the bay south of the bus stop. (☎822 361. Open Apr.-Oct. M-Sa 9:30am-5pm, Su 10am-4pm.) Five minutes north on the road is an **ATM** at the **Bank of Scotland.** (☎822 216. Open M-Tu and Th-F 9am-5pm, W 9:30am-5pm.) **Skye Surprises,** by the TIC, combines a **convenience store, petrol station, car rental, launderette,** and **Internet cafe;** look for the hairy Highland cow model out front. (☎822 225; cars from £35 per day; laundry £3.50; Internet access £1 per 30min. Open 24hr.) Broadford also has a **post office.** (☎08457 223 344. Open M-Sa 9am-1pm, M-Tu and Th-F also 2-5:30pm.) **Post Code:** IV49 9AB.

The **SYHA Broadford** ❶ is the only hostel in the area and has views of the harbor and open sea. Head east on the first road north of the bridge and walk ½ mi. (☎822 442. Laundry £2. Reception 7-10am and 5-11pm. Curfew midnight. Open Mar.-Oct. Dorms £10.50-12, under 18 £8.25-9.50. MC/V.) More elaborate accommodation (and views) can be found at the **Dunnollie Hotel** ❹, on the main strip just south of the Co-op. (☎822 253. Singles £55; doubles £75-95. MC/V.) Stock up on **groceries** at the **Co-op**, next to Skye Surprises. (☎822 703. Open M-Sa 8am-10pm, Su 10am-6pm.) **The Fig Tree** ❷, near the post office, serves both lunch and dinner, including Scottish salmon. (☎822 616. Open M-Sa 10:30am-5:30pm and 6:30-9pm. MC/V.)

SLEAT PENINSULA AND ARMADALE. Two miles south of Broadford, the single-lane A851 veers southwest through the foliage of the Sleat Peninsula, dubbed "The Garden of Skye." **Armadale,** 17 hilly miles to the south, sends ferries to Mallaig. Both **Skye-Ways** and **Highland Country** buses run between Armadale and Broadford (4-6 per day, about £3). In town, the **Armadale Castle Gardens** and **Museum of the Isles** unite a disintegrating MacDonald castle, expansive gardens, and an excellent (if somewhat pro-MacDonald) history of the Isles clans. Its **Study Centre** is one of the best places in Scotland for **genealogical research.** (☎844 305; www.clandonald.com. Open daily Apr.-Oct. 9:30am-5:30pm; last admission 5pm. Research from £5 per half-day; first 15min. free. Gardens and museum £4, concessions £3, families £12.) A present-day MacDonald runs the **Flora MacDonald Hostel** ❶, known for lovely views of the Sound. Peter will pick you up at the Armadale ferry, proudly show you his rare Eriskay ponies, and tell you anything you want to know about his ancestor, the hostel's namesake. (☎844 272. Kitchen and TV. Dorms £8. Cash only.) The **SYHA Armadale** ❶ has more rules but a more convenient location, overlooking the water across from the pier. (☎844 260. Lockout 10:30am-5pm. Curfew 11:30pm. Open Apr.-Sept. Dorms £10.50, under 18 £8. MC/V.) North of Armadale at **Ostaig,** the famous Gaelic college **Sabhal Mor Ostaig** ❸ teaches the Gaelic language, promotes Gaelic music, throws Gaelic dances, and hosts Gaelic festivals. They also offer summer courses in—you guessed it—all things Gaelic. Rooms with breakfast are available. (☎844 373; answered in Gaelic. Courses £120-200. Singles £22; twins £18 per person. Cash only.)

◪ **HIKING.** Though southern Skye is sometimes overshadowed by the dramatic Cuillins to the north, its graceful landscape is many an islander's favorite scene. The **Sleat Peninsula** has some of Skye's most verdant terrain, including the **Kinloch Forest** on the Broadford-Armadale bus route. From the Forestry Commission carpark, a footpath traces a lovely circular route past a deserted settlement called **Letir Fura,** from which **Loch na Dal** is visible, clouds permitting (2½hr. round-trip). A popular longer hike (3-3½hr. round-trip) reaches Skye's southernmost tip, the **Point of Sleat,** with its lighthouse and panoramas of the Cuillins to the north. The trailhead begins at the end of the A851, south of **Ardvasar** at the **Aird of Sleat.** An hour's walk rewards with awesome views of western island **Rum** from the watery inlet of **Acairseid an Rubha.** The path is poorly marked; carry Ordnance Survey Landranger Map #32 and consult locals before heading out.

THE CUILLINS AND CENTRAL SKYE ☎01478

Visible from nearly every part of Skye, the Cuillin Hills (COO-leen)—the highest peaks in the Hebrides—dominate central Skye and beckon walkers and climbers. Legend says the warrior Cúchulainn was the lover of the Amazon ruler of Skye, who named the hills for him after the hero returned to Ireland to die. The Kyleakin-Portree road wends its way through the Red Cuillins, which slope dramatically from the road and present a foreboding face to the aspiring hillwalker, meeting the toothed Black Cuillins in Sligachan.

ⁿⁿ ACCOMMODATIONS AND FOOD. Below the mountains at the junction of the A863 to Portree and the A850 to Dunvegan, the village of **Sligachan** (SLIG-a-han) is little more than hotel, pub, and campsite in a jaw-dropping setting. The famous trail through Glen Sligachan departs south from here (p. 658), the best access point to the Cuillins and a true hiker's hub. There are few budget lodgings in town; your best bet is the **Sligachan Hotel ④**, a classic hillwalker's and climber's haunt. (☎650 204. Breakfast included. £30-40 per person; singles £10 more. MC/V.) The hotel's **Seumas' Bar ②** offers a broad selection of beers (try their own ale, Slig 80 Shilling), grub (from seafood gratin to lamb casserole), and nearly every malt in existence. (Live music F-Sa. **ATM** available. Entrees £3-10. Open daily 10:30am-11:30pm. Food served noon-9pm. Cash only.) The **Sligachan Campsite ❶** is across the road. (☎0778 645 3294. Open May-Sept. £4, children £2. Cash only.)

The town of **Glenbrittle** can be reached by Highland Country bus #53 from Portree and Sligachan (M-Sa 2 per day). Expert mountaineers give tips at the **SYHA Glenbrittle ❶**, near the southwest coast, where a jocular atmosphere compensates for spartan quarters. (☎640 278. Open Apr.-Sept. Dorms £10.50-11, under 18 £8.50-9. MC/V.) The **Glenbrittle Campsite ❶** is at the foot of the Black Cuillins. (☎640 404. Open Apr.-Sept. Open daily 8:30am-8:30pm. £4.50, children £2.50. Cash only.)

ⁿⁿ HIKING AND OUTDOORS. The Cuillin Hills are great for experienced hikers but risky for beginners, offering mainly rock climbing. Available at TICs, campsites, and hostels, *Walks from Sligachan and Glen Brittle* (£1) suggests routes. Warm, waterproof clothing and Ordnance Survey Outdoor Leisure Map #8 (1:25,000; £7), also available at the TIC, are essential; see **Wilderness Safety**, p. 52. The pitted peat is always drenched, so expect sopping wet feet. ☒**MacBackpackers Skye Trekker Tour** (p. 655) hikes the gorgeous coastal path from Elgol, camping overnight at Camasunary and moving north through Glen Sligachan the next day. Those with less experience may find this option attractive, as it includes a guide, fellow backpackers, and transport to and from trailheads.

A short but scenic path follows the stream from Sligachan near the campsite to the head of **Loch Sligachan.** After crossing the old bridge, fork right off the main path through the gate and walk upstream along the right-hand bank. The narrow, boggy path leads past pools and mini-waterfalls, in some places tracing the top of a small cliff (3 mi. round-trip). In 1899, a fit (and barefoot!) Gurkha soldier ascended and descended the 2537 ft. **Glamaig** in just 55min. Set aside your ambition, and start the 3½hr. hike only if you feel at ease on steep slopes with unsure footing. A smaller trail branches off the main trail after about 15min. and leads up the ridge between the higher peaks, granting views of the ocean and offshore isles.

Experienced climbers can try to climb **Sgurr nan Gillean Corrie,** to the southwest of Glamaig, towering 3167 ft. above a tiny lake. For more level terrain, take the 8 mi. walk down **Glen Sligachan** through the heart of the Cuillins to the beach of **Camasunary,** with views of the isles of Rum and Muck. From Camasunary, you can hike 5 mi. along the coast to **Elgol.** From there, a sailing trip to **Loch Coriusk** with **Bella Jane Boat Trips** reveals extraordinary panoramas. (☎01471 866 244. Runs Apr.-Oct. M-Sa; for reservations call from 7:30-10am. Round-trip £13; maxi round-trip with 4½hr. on shore £19.) Harder to reach is the gleaming **Spar Cave,** near **Glasnakille,** whose walls glisten with formations such as the "Frozen Waterfall." It is accessible only during low tide, and there are no facilities, so only seasoned cave explorers should attempt it (bring your own flashlight). From Camasunary beach, you can also hike to the loch along a coastal trail that encounters steep rocks at the intimidating "Bad Step" (1½hr.). Elgol is 14 mi. southwest of Broadford on the A881—**postbus** #50B rumbles in from Broadford (M-F 2 per day, Sa 1 per day).

THE MINGINISH PENINSULA ☎01478

Though few make the journey 10 miles west of the Cuillins to the quiet Minginish Peninsula, it offers no less impressive views. **Highland Country Buses** arrive here from **Portree** and **Sligachan** (M-F 4 per day, Sa 1 per day), stopping at **Carbost;** some descend to the **Talisker Distillery** along serene Loch Harport. The 45min. distillery tour is bland, but the whisky isn't: Skye's only malt packs a fiery finish. (Open Apr.-Oct. M-Sa 9:30am-4:30pm; Nov.-Mar. M-F 2-5pm. £4.) Buses continue to **Portnalong,** where there are two hostels. The owner of the **Skyewalker Independent Hostel ❶,** Fiskavaig Rd., may not be Luke's father, but he does own a **post office,** operate several campsites, offer transportation to and from Sligachan, and run the best (and only) licensed **cafe ❶** on the peninsula. (☎640 250 or 0800 027 7059. Dorms £8-9.50. Tents £3. Post office open M and W-Th 9-11am. Cash only.) **Post Code:** IV47 8SL. In a converted cowshed, the rustic **Croft Bunkhouse ❶** sleeps 14 in a gigantic two-tiered platform-style bed—bring a sleeping bag—and sports a ping-pong table and dart board. For longer stays, bothies (stone shelters) with more conventional bunks are also available. (☎640 254. Dorms £7.50; bothies £9. Cash only.) Up the road, the **Taigh Ailean Hotel ❸** delivers both style and comfort. (☎640 271. Breakfast included. From £25 per person. Cash only.)

PORTREE ☎01478

Portree is the jubilant center of Skye, festive no matter what time of year. Named *Port na Righ* (the King's Port) after James V visited in 1540, this cheerful harbor town is Skye's flourishing hub of Gaelic music, arts, and crafts, as well as the island's locus of public transportation. Driven entirely by its guests, Portree caters to visitors' needs with rows of B&Bs, an excellent hostel, delicious food, constant festivals, and lively pubs, without losing any luster.

Buses stop at Somerled Sq. from **Kyle of Lochalsh** (5 per day) and from **Kyleakin** (M-Sa 1-2 per hr.). To reach the **Tourist Information Centre,** Bayfield Rd., from the square, face the Bank of Scotland, turn left down the lane, and left again onto Bridge Rd. The staff explains bus routes and books lodgings for a £3 charge plus a 10% deposit. (☎612 137. Open July-Aug. M-Sa 9am-6pm, Su 10am-4pm; Sept.-Oct. and Apr.-June M-F 9am-5pm, Su 10am-4pm; Nov.-Mar. M-Sa 9am-4pm.) Other services include: the **Bank of Scotland,** Somerled Sq. (open M-Tu and Th-F 9am-5pm, W 9:30am-5pm); a **launderette,** in the basement of the Independent Hostel (☎613 737; open M-Sa 9am-9pm); **Internet access** at the TIC (£1 per 20min.) or free across the street at the **library** (☎612 697); and the **post office,** on Quay Brae by the harbor (☎612 533; open M-Sa 9am-5:30pm). **Post Code:** IV51 9DB.

You can't miss the brightly painted **Portree Independent Hostel ❶,** The Green, which has a prime location, spacious kitchen, and enthusiastic staff. As it's the only hostel in town, advance booking is advised. (☎613 737. Internet access £1 per 20 min. Free towels. Dorms £11; twins £23. MC/V.) For B&B-style hospitality, head to the **Harbor Lodge ❸,** down by the pier. (☎613 332. £22 per person. Cash only.) For higher-end lodgings, **The Portree Hotel ❹,** Somerled Sq., has occupied its corner of the square since 1865. (☎612 511. £35-55 per person. MC/V.) The centrally located **Safeway** is on Bank St. (☎612 845. Open M-Sa 8:30am-8pm, Su 10am-5pm.) 🔲**Cafe Arriba ❷,** Quay Brae, has an imaginative menu that caters to all, from toasties to tahini yogurt falafels. (☎611 830. Open daily 7am-10pm. Takeaway available. MC/V.) **The Granary ❶,** Somerled Sq., sells donuts, filled rolls, and warm bread straight from the oven. (☎612 873. Open M-F 9am-5pm, Sa 9:45am-4:30pm. Cash only.) At the four-star **Bosville Hotel ❷,** Bank St., you can dine on fresh seafood from £6. (☎612 856. Open daily 8am-10pm. Cash only.) For a quiet pint, try the **Caledonian Hotel's** pub on Wentworth St. (☎612 641. Live music F-Sa. Open M-F 11am-1am, Sa 11am-12:30am, Su 12:30-11:30pm.)

NORTHERN SKYE ☎ 01470

Northern Skye is a visibly ancient land, with two scenic roads and miles of pristine shoreline. You can traverse the region blissfully unaware of the thousands of tourists. The northwestern circuit follows the A850 from Portree to haunted Dunvegan Castle, then heads down the A863 along the scenic west coast; the northeastern circuit hugs the A855 around the Trotternish Peninsula past the Old Man of Storr, on through Staffin and Uig, and back to Portree on the A87. From Portree, **postbuses** handle the northwest route (M-Sa 1 per day in the morning); the northeast is covered by **Highland Country** buses on the Portree-Flodigarry Circular route (M-Sa 4-8 per day, June-Sept. also Su 3 per day; Day Rover £5).

TROTTERNISH PENINSULA. The east side of Trotternish is a geological masterpiece of rock punctuated by thundering waterfalls, while the west side has a softer landscape of endless rolling hills. Its rugged peaks and valleys are usually empty, often foggy, and always stunning. Northeast of Portree, the A855 snakes along the east coast of the Trotternish Peninsula past the **Old Man of Storr** and the **Quirang** rock pinnacles. Geologists may enjoy the backstories of these formations, but the rest can stare slack-jawed at one of Mother Nature's most spectacular playing fields. From miles away, the Old Man of Storr seems a towering black stone monolith but it is accessible by a steep hike (1hr. round-trip) that begins in the nearby carpark; ask the bus driver to let you off there. The footpath to the Quirang begins in a carpark on the road from Staffin to Uig. It ascends to the **Prison,** loops upward to the **Needle,** and arrives at the **Table,** a flat grassy promontory (where locals once played shinty an extreme form of field hockey), offering some sweet views (3hr. round-trip). Nearby, **Staffin Bay** abounds with fossils. **Kilt Rock** has lava columns that appear pleated above a rocky base crumbling into the sea. Strong, well-shod walkers can try the challenging but magnificent 12 mi. hike along the **Trotternish Ridge,** which runs the length of the peninsula from the Old Man of Storr to Staffin. The less mighty can take the buses from Portree to Staffin.

DUNVEGAN CASTLE. Dunvegan holds the title of longest-inhabited Scottish castle, occupied since the 13th century. As the ancient (and current) seat of clan MacLeod—one of the few strongholds still owned by a clan chief—it delivers an interesting dose of clan history. The 29th and current chief, John MacLeod of MacLeod, seems to be everpresent; he narrates the informative video, owns a restaurant and an upscale wool shop, and appears throughout Skye on many a glossy poster. Highland Country **bus** #56 (☎ 01478 612 622; M-F 3 per day, Sa 1 per day) runs from Portree to the castle. (☎ 521 206. Open daily Apr.-Oct. 10am-5:30pm; Nov.-Mar. 11am-4pm. £6, children £3.50. Gardens only £4, children £2.50.)

DUNTULM CASTLE. At the tip of the peninsula, the MacDonalds—the MacLeods's peers in nobility—built their own stronghold at Duntulm Castle. According to legend, the house was cursed when a nurse dropped the chief's baby boy from a window, condemning it to its present state of ruin. (Always open. Free.) Near Duntulm at Kilmuir, the highly informative **Skye Museum of Island Life** has preserved a crofter village of 18th-century stone and thatch blackhouses. (☎ 552 206. Open Easter-Oct. M-Sa 9:30am-5:30pm. £1.75, seniors £1.25, children 75p.) Along the same road, **Flora MacDonald's Monument** pays tribute to the Scottish folk hero who sheltered Bonnie Prince Charlie. On a bluff 5 mi. north of **Staffin,** the excellent **Dun Flodigarry Backpackers Hostel** ❶ has a small shop, kitchen, and common area, and is the starting point for many hikes. Take the Staffin bus from Portree and ask to be let off. (☎ 552 212. Internet access £1 per 15min. Dorms £9, twins £12. Cash only.)

UIG ☎01470

Flanking a windswept bay on the peninsula's west coast, the town of Uig (OO-ig) is little more than a ferry terminal and parking lot, acting as the final resting place for long-distance buses from Glasgow and Inverness. **CalMac** runs a **ferry** connecting Uig to **Tarbet, Lewis** (1½ hr.; M-F 3-4 per day, Sa 2 per day; £9, 5-day round-trip £15.25). **Highland Country** buses #57A and 57D also run from **Portree** (M-Sa 3-4 per day, £3). While waiting for a ferry, stop by the **Isle of Skye Brewery**, next to the pier. When not brewing, one of the ten employees will give you a brief tour. (☎542 477. Open M-F 10am-6pm. £2.) The **SYHA Uig ❶** has a fantastic ocean view and is a 30min. walk from the pier. Facing the sea, turn left on the A586; the large white house is up the hill on your left. (☎542 211. Reception closed 10am-5pm. Curfew 11pm. Open Apr.-Oct. Dorms £10.50, under 18 £8.50. MC/V.) Convenient for ferry connections, **Oronsay B&B ❷** is by the pier; all rooms are ensuite, and **bike rental** is available. (☎542 316. Bikes £2 per hr., £12 per day. £16-20 per person. MC/V.) **The Pub at The Pier ❶** serves good grub (meals £5-9) with sides of scenery and an occasional garnish of live music. (☎542 212. Open M-F 11am-midnight, Sa 11am-11:30pm, Su noon-11pm. Food served until 7:45pm. Cash only.)

THE OUTER HEBRIDES

Much of the Outer Hebrides's exposed rock is more than half as old as the planet itself, and a rich sediment of tombs, standing stones, and antiquities lingers from long-gone inhabitants. The culture and customs of the Hebridean people seem equally ancient, rooted in a deep respect for tradition. While television and tourism have diluted old ways of life, you're still more likely to get an earful of Gaelic here than anywhere else in Scotland. On the strongly Calvinist islands of **Lewis, Harris,** and **North Uist,** most establishments close and public transportation ceases on Sundays (though one or two places may assist lost souls with an afternoon pint), while to the south, on **Benbecula, South Uist,** and **Barra,** tight-shuttered Sabbatarianism gives way to Catholic chapels and pictures of the Pope. The extreme seclusion, quiet, and isolation of the islands and their inhabitants make the Western Isles one of Scotland's most undisturbed and unforgettable realms.

🚍 TRANSPORTATION

Caledonian MacBrayne (☎01475 650 100) has a near monopoly over passenger and car **ferries** along major routes. It runs from **Ullapool** to **Stornoway, Lewis** (3½hr.; 2-3 per day; £14, 5-day round-trip £24; car £70/120); from **Uig, Skye** to **Lochmaddy, North Uist** (1¾ hr.; 1-2 per day; £10, 5-day round-trip £16; car £45/75) and to **Tarbert, Harris** (1½ hr.; 1-2 per day; £10, 5-day round-trip £16; car £45/75); and from **Oban** to **Castlebay, Barra** and **Lochboisdale, South Uist** (6½ hr.; 1 per day; £20, 5-day round-trip £35; car £75/125). Plan ahead if you wish to take a car, as capacity is limited. Once in the archipelago, ferries brave rough sounds and infrequent buses cross causeways to connect the islands. If you know ahead of time which areas you will visit, save money on a month's worth of ferry rides by buying an **Island Hopscotch ticket**—you can even bring your bike along for free. Travel options are found at the beginning of the invaluable *Discover Scotland's Islands with Caledonian MacBrayne,* free from TICs. You'll also want to pick up the *Lewis and Harris Bus Timetables* (40p) and *Uist and Barra Bus Timetables* (20p). **Cycling** is popular, though windy hills and sudden rains often wipe out novice riders. Traffic is light, but **hitchhikers** report frequent lifts on all the islands. *Let's Go* does not recommend hitchhiking. Inexpensive **car rental** (from £20 per day) is possible at several places throughout the isles, but vehicles are usually prohibited on ferries. Except in bilingual Stornoway and Benbecula, road signs are in Gaelic only. Although many names are similar in both languages, TICs often carry translation keys, and *Let's Go* lists Gaelic equivalents after English place names where appropriate.

ACCOMMODATIONS

Ferries arrive at odd hours; if you plan to stay near a ferry terminal, try to book a bed ahead. Area TICs book **B&Bs** for a £1.50 charge. **Camping** is allowed on public land in the Hebrides, but freezing winds and sodden ground often make it a miserable experience. Lewis's remote **SYHA Kershader ❷**, Ravenspoint, Kershader, South Lochs, is a standard, if small, hostel, with laundry (£2) and a shop next door in the community center. (☎01851 880 236. Dorms £8.75, under 18 £7.75. MC/V.)

The Outer Hebrides are home to the unique ■**Gatliff Hebridean Trust Hostels ❶** (www.gatliff.org.uk), four 19th-century thatched croft houses turned into simple year-round hostels. The atmosphere and authenticity of these enchantingly remote hostels make them the ideal way to experience the Western Isles. They accept no advance bookings but very seldom turn travelers away. Aside from basic facilities, all provide cooking equipment, range tops, cutlery, crockery, and hot water. Blankets and pillows are provided, but the hostels have coal fires and are not centrally heated—you'll want a good sleeping bag. Most hostels cost £7.50 per person (under 18 £5.50), and **camping** is nearly always £3.75. (Cash only.)

Berneray (Bhearnaraigh): Off North Uist. Frequent buses on the W19 and W17 routes shuttle between the hostel, the Otternish pier (where ferries arrive from Harris), the Lochmaddy pier on North Uist, and the Sollas Co-op food store (30min., M-Sa 6-9 per day, £1). A beautifully thatched and white-washed building near an excellent beach.

Garenin (Na Gearranan): Lewis, 1½ mi. north of Carloway. Buses on the W2 "West Side Circular" route from Stornoway (M-Sa 10-11 per day) go to Carloway, if not Garenin village itself. Free taxi service meets some buses at Carloway. Unsurpassed surroundings.

Howmore (Tobha Mòr): South Uist, about 1hr. north of Lochboisdale by foot. W17 buses from Lochboisdale to Lochmaddy will stop at the Howmore Garage (M-Sa 5-8 per day, £1); from there, follow the sign 1 mi. west from the A865. Overlooks a ruined chapel, and near the rubble that was once Ormiclate Castle.

Rhenigidale (Reinigeadal): North Harris. Take the free minibus from the carpark next to the Tarbert TIC (☎01859 502 221; M-Sa 2 per day; call by 8pm the night before for the morning bus or 3pm for the afternoon). The bus will take your pack if you want to attempt the tough 6 mi. hike along the eastern coast. From Tarbert, take the road toward Kyles Scalpay for 2 mi. and follow the signposted path left to Rhenigidale. The path ascends 850 ft. for stunning views before zig-zagging down steeply (3hr. total). By car, follow the turn-off to Maaruig (Maraig) from the A859, 13 mi. north of Tarbert.

LEWIS (LEODHAS)

With over 20,000 inhabitants, Lewis is the most populous of the Outer Hebridean Islands. More than 8000 people live in Stornoway, the capital and largest town, while other islanders live mainly in crofting settlements strung along the island's west coast. Drifting mists shroud untouched miles of moorland and half-cut fields of peat are occasionally interrupted by archaeological sites, most notably the Callanish Stones. The island is also home to "the most consistent surf in Europe," attracting beach-goers with dramatic swells. The gentle roads of Lewis are good for biking, but check the weather, as a gusty day can affect even strong cyclists. Rent your wheels on a Saturday—virtually everything grinds to a halt on Sunday.

STORNOWAY (STEORNOBHAIGH)   ☎01851

Stornoway is a splash of urban life in the otherwise rural Outer Hebrides. It manages to retain its charm with its castle and museums, however, and is an interesting example of changing times in the farthest reaches of the UK.

▣⚎ TRANSPORTATION AND PRACTICAL INFORMATION. The only things running on Sundays are planes and churchgoers late for service. **CalMac** ferries sail from **Ullapool** (2¾hr., M-Sa 2 per day, June-Aug., 3 per day on W, F; £14, 5-day round-trip £24, with car £69/117). **Buses** operated by **Western Isles Bus** depart from the Beach St. station; pick up a *Lewis and Harris Bus Timetable* (50p). (☎704 327. Luggage storage 20p-£1. Open M-Sa 8am-6pm.) Destinations include **Arnol, Carloway** (Carlabhaigh) and **Callanish** (Calanais; 1hr. M-Sa 4-6 per day); **Port of Ness** (Nis; 1hr., M-Sa 4-6 per day); **Tarbert** (An Tairbeart; M-Sa 5 per day, £3). Car rental is cheaper here than on the mainland: try **Lewis Car Rentals,** 52 Bayhead St., in the center of town (☎703 760), or **Lochs Motors,** across from the bus station. (☎705 857. 21+. £21-25 per day. Open M-Sa 9am-6pm.) Rent bikes at **Alex Dan's Cycle Centre,** 67 Kenneth St. (☎704 025. £10 per day, £30 per week. Open M-Sa 9am-6pm.)

The **Tourist Information Centre** is on 26 Cromwell St. From the ferry terminal, turn left, then right on Cromwell St. (☎703 088. Open Apr.-Oct. M, Tu, Th 9am-6pm and 8-9pm, W and F 9am-8pm, Sa 9am-6pm; Nov.-Mar. M-F 9am-5pm.) From April to October, **Stornoway Trust** (☎704 733) organizes free **walks** through town and country as well as private vehicle tours. Other services include: a **Bank of Scotland,** across from the TIC (☎705 252; open M-Tu and Th-F 9am-5pm, W 10am-5pm); **Thomas Cook,** Cromwell Rd. (☎703 104; open M-W and F-Sa 9am-5:30pm, Th 10am-5:30pm); **Erica's Launderette,** 46 Macaulay Rd., the only one on the island, (☎704 508; £3.50 per load; open M-Tu and Th-Sa 9am-3pm); free **Internet access** at the **Stornoway Library** (☎708 631; open M-Sa 10am-5pm); and the **post office,** 16 Francis St. (open M-F 9am-5:30pm, Sa 9am-12:30pm). **Post Code:** HS1 2AA.

⚎⚎ ACCOMMODATIONS AND FOOD. The best place to lay your head and wax your board is ▨**Fairhaven Hostel ❶,** at the intersection of Francis St. and Keith St., a mecca for wayward kahunas, over the surf shop. From the pier, turn left on Shell St., which becomes South Beach, then right on Kenneth St. and right again onto Francis St. The freshly cooked meals (salmon £8) are a great end to a long day on the water. Surf equipment (wetsuits £10, surf board £10-20) is available for hire as well. (☎705 862; www.hebrideansurf.co.uk. Breakfast £2.50. Dorms £10, full board £20. Cash only.) To get to ▨**Mr. and Mrs. Hill ❷** from the TIC, head north up Church St., turn left on Matheson Rd., and take Robertson Rd., the first street on the right. Enjoy friendly hospitality while snuggling among heaps of pillows and blankets. (☎706 553; £17-19 per person. Cash only.) The **Stornoway Backpackers Hostel ❶,** 47 Keith St., down the road from Fair Haven Hostel, has free tea and coffee to compensate for somewhat lackluster facilities. (☎703 628, www.stornoway-hostel.co.uk. Breakfast included. Dorms £9. Cash only.) The **Laxdale Bunkhouse ❶** sleeps 16 in four modern rooms on the Laxdale Holiday Park campgrounds. (1½ miles from town center. ☎706 966; www.laxdaleholidaypark.com. £9-10 per person. Cash only.) Many **B&Bs** oblige early ferries with a crack-of-dawn breakfast.

Cheap chow is easy to come by in Stornoway, including **groceries** at the **Co-op** on Cromwell St. (☎702 703. Open M-Sa 8am-8pm.) For an unexpected taste of Asia, head to ▨**Thai Cafe ❷,** 27 Church St., where mouthwatering entrees (£4-6) are served in a candlelit setting. (☎701 811. Open M-Sa noon-2:30pm and 5-11pm. Cash only.) The **Bank Street Deli ❶** has everything from curries (£4) to pizza (£3.50); most of the menu is under £2. (☎706 419. Open M-W 11am-11:30pm, Th-F 11am-2am, Sa 11am-11:30pm. Cash only.) The **An Lanntair Gallery ❶** (see below) houses the town's best cafe. (Salmon roll £2.75. Closes 30min. before gallery. Cash only.)

FROM THE ROAD

THE TWO FACES OF STORNOWAY

After the peat and heather of Lewis, Stornoway seemed like a space station on the moon. It was early on a Saturday evening when I arrived, and there were young people on every corner; groups of girls in miniskirts flirted with packs of boys, while laughter and yells echoed from open pub doors over Outkast's "Hey Ya." I changed my clothes and headed out, eager to see what kind of nightlife the Outer Hebrides had to offer. I found myself soberly dumbstruck in a corner, clutching an Irn Bru. Disco balls and black lights revealed flashes of dancing bodies and staggering, drunk old men. I retired early after a few more stops that only further confirmed that Stornoway did indeed have a "vibrant nightlife."

I awoke early the next day to explore. As I admired the peace of the square, a teenage boy whizzed past me on a skateboard and yelled at me in Gaelic; whatever he said, it wasn't flattering.

That evening, I thought I'd attend the 6:30pm Gaelic Presbyterian service. I asked the gentlemen who seemed to be in charge if it would be all right if I sat in; after asking me several times if I knew the service was entirely in Gaelic, he happily gave me the *Bhiobull*, the English King James Bible and an ancient volume of Gaelic verse.

Stepping inside, I realized I was the only female without a hat, and quietly pulled my scarf over my head. An elderly woman beckoned

🔲 **SIGHTS.** The **An Lanntair Gallery**, in the Town Hall on South Beach St., hosts art exhibits and events, with musical and historical evenings. (☎703 307. Open M-Sa 10am-5:30pm. Free.) The **Museum nan Eilean**, Francis St., has fascinating Hebridean exhibitions spanning 9000 years, including an exhibit on the Lewis Chessmen. (☎703 773. Open Apr.-Sept. M-Sa 10am-5:30pm; Oct.-Mar. Tu-F 10am-5pm, Sa 10am-1pm. Free.) Meander the grounds of majestic **Lewis Castle**, northwest of town. Built in the 19th century by an opium smuggler, the castle now shelters a college. The entrance is on Cromwell St., but you can admire it from across the water at the end of N. Beach St.; turn left after the footbridge from New St.

🔲🎆 **NIGHTLIFE AND FESTIVALS.** Don't miss out on Stornoway's vibrant nightlife. **Pubs** and **clubs** crowd the area between Point St., Castle St., and the two waterfronts. There's no better place to watch a big-time sporting event than on the screen at the **Crown Inn**, N. Beach St. (☎703 181. Open M-W 11am-11pm, Th-F 11am-2am, Sa 11am-11:30pm.) **The Heb**, a hip club-bar-cafe, is like nothing you'd ever expect in the Outer Hebrides. (Th-Sa disco from 10pm. 18+. Cover ₤2. Open M-W 11am-8pm, Th 11am-1am, F 11am-2am, Sa 11am-11:30pm.) The **Hebridean Celtic Festival** in mid-July draws top musical talent from all over Scotland and devotees from all over the world. For more information, call ☎07001 878 787.

LEWIS SIGHTS AND SURF

Most of Lewis's biggest attractions, including the Callanish Stones, Dùn Carloway Broch, Gearrannan Blackhouse Village, and the Arnol Blackhouse, line the **west coast** and can be reached via the **W2 bus**, which operates on a circuit beginning at the Stornoway bus station (M-Sa 4 per day in either direction). **Maclennan Coaches** offers a **Day Rover** pass on this route (₤5), or a round-trip ticket to see one, two, or three of the sights from May to October (₤3.50-4.50). Alternatively, travel with **Out and About Tours** (☎612 288; individually designed day tours from ₤20) or **Albannach Guided Tours** (☎830 433; from ₤10), both departing from the TIC.

🔲 **CALLANISH STONES (CALANAIS).** The Callanish Stones, 14 mi. west of Stornoway on the A858, are second only to Stonehenge in grandeur and considerably less overrun. The speckled, greenish-white stones, hewn from three-billion-year-old Lewisian gneiss, form a small circle with five avenues leading outwards. At least one camp of archaeologists believes that prehistoric peoples used Callanish, coupled with two nearby circles, to track the movements of the heavens, employing complex trigonometry. (Always open. Free.) The **Visitor Centre** has a comprehensive exhibit and a short video. (☎621 422. Centre open Apr.-Sept. M-Sa 10am-7pm; Oct.-Mar. 10am-4pm. Exhibit and film £1.75, concessions £1.25, children 75p.) Local writer Gerald Ponting publishes **guides** to Callanish and neighboring sites with explicit directions (40p-£4), available at the Stornoway TIC. Nibble scones at the new age **Callanish Tea House ❶** on the other side of the stones, in the only privately owned blackhouse on the island. (Open M-Sa 9am-6pm. Cash only.)

A mile south of Callanish, postbuses follow the B8011 across the bridge to the island of **Great Bernera** (Bearnaraigh), where the **Bostadh Iron Age House**—one of many—is being excavated from beneath the sands. (Open Tu-Sa noon-4pm. £2, concessions £1, children 50p.) Perhaps more spectacular are the idyllic **white beaches** nearby, but watch out for sheep. Twenty miles farther west stand the surprisingly lush **Glen Valtos** and the expansive beaches at **Timsgarry**, where low tides uncover yards of sand flanked by dozens of deserted islets.

CARLOWAY BROCH (DÙN CHARLABHAIGH).

Five miles north of Callanish along the A858 lies the crofting settlement (a "town" only by local standards) of **Carloway** (Carlabhaigh), dominated by the Iron Age **Carloway Broch.** Dating from the first century BC, this double-walled stone tower is hailed as the most impressive broch in the Western Isles. Once it protected farmers and their cattle from Vikings; now it shelters tourists from high winds. Still, watch your footing: a sudden gust may startle. (Visitor Centre open Apr.-Oct. M-Sa 10am-6pm. Broch always open. Free.) The **Garenin Hebridean Trust Hostel,** 1½ mi. from Carloway (p. 662), stands within the restored **Gearrannan Blackhouse Village,** a worthwhile visit if you haven't seen a traditional croft house. (☎643 416. Open M-Sa 10am-4pm. £2, children £1.)

ARNOL BLACKHOUSE.

Farther north on the A858, beyond **Shawbost,** lies a restored crofter's cottage known as the Arnol Blackhouse. A chimney was intentionally left out of the traditionally thatched roof, as smoke from the peat fire was said to conserve heat by seeping through the thatch. Inhale a hearty lungful inside the cottage, which was a working home until 1960. (☎710 395. Open Apr.-Sept. M-Sa 9:30am-6:30pm; Oct.-Mar. M-Sa 9:30am-4:30pm. £3, seniors £2.60, children £1.)

for me to sit next to her, and winked at me. Phew! I'd felt like an outsider on Saturday night, but here I was the youngest person by 40 years, and certainly the only non-Gaelic-speaking one.

The church was unlike any place of worship I'd ever seen. There was no cross, no altar, no choir, no decoration, no communion, and the service was a somber affair. The congregation sang unaccompanied; the haunting voices reminded me both of Jewish recitations of the Torah and of Buddhist chanting. After the service, the elderly congregation boarded school buses to go back to their crofts outside the city.

I had tea with the woman with whom I had sat during the service. She said she'd grown up in a fishing village and had only moved to her tiny house in Stornoway after her children moved away. I asked her what it had been like moving to the relatively urban Stornoway after growing up in such a remote village. She winked again and showed me the blooming orchid on the windowsill. "This," she whispered, "you can't get 'less you live in Stornoway." My last impressions of Lewis are of resilient, optimistic Mrs. MacLeod, her orchid, and the desolate coast where she'd spent most of her life. My memory of Stornoway is of a quiet struggle between the old life and the new, where Outkast blares on Saturday night and Gaelic psalms are chanted on Sunday.
-Lily Stockman

BUTT OF LEWIS. Besides being the butt of many jokes and terrible puns, the northern-most tip of the Hebrides at the end of the A857 is a "turrible promont'ry" where the Atlantic crashes into the cliffs with deafening ferocity. On your way north you'll pass the village of Galson, where David and Hazel run the **Galson Farm Guesthouse and Bunkhouse** ❶ out of their lovely croft, which sleeps a comfortable eight and has excellent vegetarian options for dinner. (☎ 850 492; www.galson-farm.freeserve.co.uk. Open daily all year; just call ahead. £9. MC/V.)

SURFING. Lewis and Harris are known for their empty blond beaches, pollution-free water, and 5m tides. Warm currents caused by the North Atlantic Drift and long daylight hours further conspire to bring surfers to these places. In Lewis, the most popular surf spot is **Dalmor** beach, near the village of Dalbeg, which has hosted several competitions. The **Port of Ness** is also frequented by some diehards; just around the corner from the **Butt of Lewis,** the island's northernmost point, it makes a great destination for an afternoon. Another option for wave-seekers is **Uig,** the central western area of Lewis. **Kneep Reef** doesn't have much to offer in terms of surf, but the endless deserted beach easily accommodates those who prefer to work on their tans. At **Valtos** or **Europie** beaches, search the sands for Neolithic artifacts and the pink shells fabled to be mermaid fingernails. The best swells migrate according to wind and tidal cycles, so get your information from boarders in the know. At **Hebridean Surf Holidays** (☎ 705 862), on the corner of Keith St. and Francis St. in Stornoway, Derek offers all-inclusive surfing lessons (from £35 per day), or can rent you equipment and transport you to the beach (from £20).

The handy #W2 **bus** route (M-Sa 10-12 per day) runs past Dalbeg and Dalmor beach, while buses operating the W4 route (M-Sa 2-4 per day) from Stornoway and Garynahine pass Kneep Reef and other spectacular surf spots in the Uig district. The Galson Motors bus on the W1 route (M-F 8-9 per day, Sa 6 per day) can whisk you from Stornoway along the northwest coast to the Butt and the Port of Ness.

HARRIS (NA HEARADH)

Harris shares an island with Lewis, but they're entirely different worlds; the two regions split along with the ruling MacLeod clan. The deserted flatlands of Lewis in the north yield to the more rugged and spectacular desolation of Harris's steely gray peaks. Toward the west coast, the Forest of Harris (in fact a treeless, heather-splotched mountain range) descends onto brilliant crescents of yellow sand bordered by indigo waters and *machair*—sea meadows of soft grass and summertime flowers. The A859, or "Golden Road" (named for the king's ransom spent in blasting it from the rock), winds all the way to Harris's southern tip via the desolate east coast, making a harrowing bus trip or grueling bike ride. Small roads branch from Tarbert east to the small fishing community on the island of **Scalpay** (Scalpaigh), connected to Harris by a causeway. Harris is famous for its wool tweed, and although Harris tweed suits are sold for a small fortune in London and New York, the bolts are still woven by locals on hand-operated looms.

HIKING. The imposing rocky stretches and heathered slopes of Harris's hills and mountains provide some of the best hiking in the Hebs. The largest peaks lie within the **Forest of Harris,** whose main entrances are off the B887 to Huisinish Point, at **Glen Meavaig,** and farther west at 19th-century **Amhuinnsuidhe Castle,** 15 mi. from Tarbert. The infrequent summertime #W12 bus from Tarbert serves all of these points (Tu and F 3 per day). An excellent 4hr. hike leads to **Glen Meavaig** from **Ardvourlie** in the north, passing **Loch Bhoisimid;** to reach Ardvourlie, take the #W10 bus from Tarbert or Stornoway (M-Sa 3-4 per day). If you don't have time for exhaustive exploration, hike up **Gillaval** (1554 ft.; at least 1hr.), which overlooks the town and nearby islands; the trails are unmarked, but the best route to the summit is from the east. A pleasant coastal walk follows the shore from **Taobh Tuath** north to **Horgabost.** Take a bus from Tarbert to Taobh Tuath and pick it up again 2hr. later in Horgabost, after trekking along cliffs and sandy beaches. For the most comprehensive walk, try the **Harris Walkway,** a long but light ramble from **Clisham** in the south to **Scaladal** in the north, via Tarbert. Be sure to carry the proper Ordnance Survey map in these remote areas.

TARBERT (AN TAIRBEART)   ☎01859

Tarbert is the main town in Harris, straddling the narrow isthmus that divides the island into North and South. **Ferries** serve Tarbert from **Uig, Skye.** (M, W, F 1 per day; Tu, Th, Sa 2 per day. £9, 5-day round-trip £15.65.) Check with **CalMac** (☎502 444), at the pier in Tarbert, for timetables. Hebridean Transport runs **buses** (☎01851 705 050) from **Leverburgh** and **Stornoway** (45min., M-Sa 3-5 per day, £3) and stop in the carpark behind the TIC. The closest car rental is in Stornoway, Lewis. The island's beguiling remoteness is best enjoyed by **bike;** rent from **Paula Williams.** (☎520 319. £10 per day.) It is easy to lose your bearings in Harris's treeless landscape, and marked trails are scarce; bring a compass and a map.

The **Tourist Information Centre** is on Pier Rd., and now proudly boasts Tarbert's only ATM. (☎502 011. Open Apr. to mid-Oct. M-Sa 9am-5pm, Tu, Th, Sa 7:30-8:30pm; mid-Oct. to Mar. for ferry arrivals.) **Bank of Scotland** is uphill from the pier. (☎502 453. Open M-Tu and Th-F 10am-12:30pm and 1:30-4pm, W 11:15am-12:30pm.) The TIC lists hours for **Internet access** at **Sir E. Scott School library,** a cream-colored building 10min. along the A859 to Stornoway. (☎502 000. £2 per 30min.) The **post office** is on Main St. (☎502 211. Open M-Tu and Th-F 9am-1pm and 2-5:30pm, W 11:15am-12:30pm.) Internet access is also available at the Old Hostel building past the school (£2 for as long as you want). **Post Code:** HS3 3BL.

The well-located **Rockview Bunkhouse ❶,** Main St., is stuffed with beds and is less than 5min. west from the pier. It's run by two postal clerks; you can also check in at the post office. (☎502 211. Dorms £9. MC/V.) Effie MacKinnon keeps a spacious B&B at **Waterstein House ❷,** across from the TIC. (☎502 358. £15 per person. Cash only.) The **Harris Hotel ❹** has a traditional atmosphere and amenities aplenty. (☎502 154. Open Apr.-Oct. £38-45 per person, with dinner £58-63. MC/V.) **A.D. Munro,** Main St., serves Tarbert as grocer, butcher, and baker. (☎502 016. Open M-Sa 7:30am-6pm.) The **Firstfruits Tearoom ❶,** next to the TIC, pours hot drinks in a homey setting. (☎502 439. Open Apr.-Sept. 10:30am-4:30pm. Cash only.) The friendly Harris Hotel **bar ❷** serves food (£5-7) across from the main hotel building. On Sundays, it offers three courses for £21.50. (☎502 154. Bar open M-Tu and Sa 11am-11pm, W-F 11am-midnight. Su dinner 7-8:45pm. MC/V.) Those interested in local history and culture can check out **Evenings of Song, Story, and Slides** at the hotel. (☎502 154. May-Sept. W at 8:30pm. £3.)

RODEL AND LEVERBURGH. Rodel (Roghadal), at Harris's southern tip, is the site of **St. Clement's Church,** which houses three MacLeod tombs. The principal one, built in 1528, portrays the disciples, the Trinity, and MacLeod himself, all hewn from local black gneiss (a granite-like rock). Up the road is **Leverburgh,** where **CalMac** (☎01876 500 337) sails to **Ardmaree, Berneray** (M-Sa 3-4 per day; £4.90, 5-day round-trip £8.30). **Buses** (☎502 441) run from **Tarbert** (45min., M-Sa 7 per day, £3.50). The upscale, funky ▨ **Am Bothan Bunkhouse ❷,** with spacious rooms and a stylish common area, is conveniently located—the bus passes it about ¼ mi. from the pier. (☎520 251, www.ambothan.com. Dorms £13. MC/V.)

HIGHLANDS AND ISLANDS

THE LOCAL STORY

WHISKY GALORE!

During the wartime alcohol rationing of WWII, one lonely outpost on the ▮▮▮ of Scotland had themselves a warm winter.

The sleek 450-foot SS *Politician* ran aground on the rocks near Eriskay on February 5th, 1941, loaded with a curious cargo: 264,000 bottles of Scotland's finest whisky. It was headed for the Mississippi Delta, where forbidden bottles of golden malts would be safe from the bombing raids that had destroyed whisky warehouses in Leith and Glasgow.

The crew survived and made it back to the mainland, but the destroyed ship perched atop the rocks with most of her cargo intact. Curious islanders inspected her and in no time there was a flurry of activity each night as they stealthily salvaged the goods and brought them to safety on Eriskay's welcoming shores. According to one islander, there wasn't a rabbit hole on Eriskay was wasn't packed full of bottles. Another claims he didn't sleep for six weeks because "as soon as you went to bed somebody would come hammering at the door that either had five bottles or he'd be asking for three." The bacchanalia lasted until the spring, when the authorities finally seized the (mostly empty) bottles. The *Polly* was immortalized by Sir Compton MacKenzie's book *Whisky Galore*, a classic movie of the same name, and the isle's only pub, the Am Politician.

THE UISTS (UIBHIST)

Coming from the peak-strewn Highlands, the extreme flatness of the Uists (YOO-ists) is a shock. Save for a thin strip of land along the east coast, these islands are completely level, pocked with so many lochs that it's difficult to distinguish where land ends and water begins. Occasional bursts of sunlight reveal narrow beaches, crumbling blackhouses, wild jonquils, and streams containing some of Europe's best salmon fishing. The islands' tiny population is scattered across small crofts, and the main villages of **Lochmaddy** (Loch nam Madadh) on **North Uist** (Uibhist a Tuath) and **Lochboisdale** (Loch Baghasdail) on **South Uist** (Uibhist a Deas) are pleasant communities that happily greet incoming ferries. The small island of **Benbecula** (Beinn na Faoghla), which possesses the Uists' sole airport, is the stepping stone between the two larger isles. Only intrepid travelers make the trip, but those who do will find that the Uists have a welcoming and laid-back nature.

◗ TRANSPORTATION

CalMac ferries float to **Lochmaddy** from **Uig, Skye** (1¾hr.; 1-2 per day; £9.15, 5-day round-trip £15.65; with car £44/75); they also connect with **Tarbert, Harris** (p. 667). Ferries drift to **Ardmaree, Berneray** from **Leverburgh, Harris** (1¼hr.; M-Sa 3-4 per day; £5, 5-day round-trip £8.60; with car £23.10/£39.50) and to **Lochboisdale** from **Oban** (6¾hr.; M and W-Sa 1 per day; £19.70, 5-day round-trip £33.50; with car £72/£122). The island council also runs the tiny **Sound of Barra Ferry** (☎08151 701 702) from **Eoligarry, Barra** to **Eriskay** (1hr.; M-Sa 4-5 per day, Su 2 per day; £2.50, with car £10). Call ahead to reserve one of the coveted seats.

Pick up the latest bus schedule from the TIC to plan your journey. **Bus** #W17 runs along the main road from Lochmaddy to the airport in **Balivanich** and **Lochboisdale** (M-Sa 5-6 per day, £3.10). #W17 and W19 also meet at least one ferry per day in **Ardmaree** for departures to Harris; W17 and W29 go to **Eriskay** in the south for connections to Barra (5-9 per day). If you arrive on a late ferry, there may not be a bus until the next day. Call ahead to book a B&B that will pick you up or prepare to camp. Get the *Uist and Barra Bus Timetables* (20p) in the Lochmaddy or Lochboisdale TIC and plan ahead. For **car rental,** call **MacLennan's Self Drive Hire,** Balivanich, Benbecula. (☎01870 602 191. 21 and over. From £22 per day. Open M-F 9am-5:30pm, Sa 9am-noon.)

🛈 PRACTICAL INFORMATION

Tourist Information Centres on the piers at **Lochmaddy** (☎01876 500 321. Open Apr.-Oct. M-F 9am-5pm, Sa 9:30am-5:30pm) and **Lochboisdale** (☎01878 700 286. Open Apr.-Oct. M-Sa 9am-5pm) book accommodations and stay open late for ferry arrivals. Lochboisdale has a **Royal Bank of Scotland** (☎01878 700 399. Open M-Tu and Th-F 9:15am-4:45pm, W 10am-4:45pm), Lochmaddy has a **Bank of Scotland** (☎01876 500 323. Open M and Th-F 9:30am-4:30pm, W 10:30am-4:30pm), and Benbecula also has a **Bank of Scotland** (☎01870 602 044. Open M-Tu and Th-F 9am-5pm, W 9:30am-5pm); all have **ATMs** and sometimes close 12:30-1:30pm. Benbecula also has the Uists' sole launderette, **Uist Laundry**, by Balivanich Airport. (☎01870 602 876. Wash £3, dry £2, kilt £8. Open M-F 8:30am-4:30pm, Sa 9am-1pm.) **Internet access** is available at **Cafe Taigh Chearsabhagh**, Lochmaddy (50p donation).

🛏 ACCOMMODATIONS

The only **hostel** near Lochmaddy is the **Uist Outdoor Centre ❶**, which also offers overnight expeditions and courses in rock climbing, canoeing, and water sports from £28 per half day, £48 for a full day. Follow signposts west from the pier for 1 mi. (☎01876 500 480. Bring a sleeping bag and book ahead. Linen £2. Dorms £9.) The other hostels are far from town and require clever navigation if you don't have a car. To reach the excellent **Taigh Mo Sheanair ❶**, in an original croft house near Clachan, take bus #W17 or W18 (20min., 12 per day) from Lochboisdale. The driver can let you off at the Clachan shop on Balishare Rd., from which it's a 1 mi. signposted walk west. (☎01876 580 246. Linen £2. Internet access £1 per hr. Laundry £3. Dorms £10. Camping £4.) Easier to reach but without the creature comforts is the **Gatliff Hebridean Trust Hostel** on **Berneray** (p. 662). Another basic Gatliff Trust Hostel is on South Uist at **Howmore** (p. 662). The bus also passes through **Balivanich,** Benbecula, where the immaculately clean **Taigh-na-Cille Bunkhouse ❷**, 22 Balivanich, just west of the airport, sleeps ten. (☎01870 602 522. Dorms £10-11.)

B&Bs are scattered throughout the island. In Lochmaddy, irresistibly charming Mrs. Morrison mothers you with tea and sweets in her comfortable ▧**Old Bank House ❸**, across the street from the post office by the petrol pumps. (☎01876 500 275. £20 per person. Cash only.) In Lochboisdale, **Mrs. MacLellan's ❷**, Bay View, is above the ferry terminal. (☎01878 700 329. From £18 per person. Cash only.) **Mrs. Johnson ❸** greets guests in the **Old Courthouse.** (☎ 1876 500 358. £18-20, with breakfast £23-25. Cash only.) You can camp almost anywhere, but ask the crofters first.

🍴🍺 FOOD AND PUBS

The cheapest food stores on the islands are the **Co-ops** in **Sollas** (Solas) on North Uist (open M-W and Sa 8:30am-6pm, Th-F 8:30am-7pm) and **Daliburgh** (Dalabrog) on South Uist (☎01878 700 326; open M-Sa 8am-8pm) and **MacLennon's Supermarket** in **Balivanich,** Benbecula (open M-W 9am-6pm, Th-F 9am-8pm, Sa 9am-7pm, Su noon-3pm). For a sit-down supper in either ferry hub, the only option is pub grub (£6-12) at the **Lochmaddy Hotel ❷** (☎01876 500 331) or the **Lochboisdale Hotel ❷.** (☎01878 700 322. Food served noon-2pm and 5:30-9pm.) Across the street from the Lochmaddy Hotel, the **Cafe Taigh Chearsabhagh ❶** sells baked goods and sandwiches for £1-3. (☎01876 500 293. Open M-Sa 10am-5pm.) An upscale restaurant in Benbecula, **Stepping Stone ❸**, provides 5-course meals (£20) in a wooden interior. (☎01870 603 377. Dinner served M-Sa 6-8:45pm.) If you're going out to Bharpa Langass, follow the signs to **Langass Lodge ❸** (☎01876 580 385) for a post-cairn pint. Halfway between Lochmaddy and Clachan, this classy hunting lodge serves superb meals with fresh seafood. (£4-15; MC/V). Down at the bottom of the island chain on the isle of Eriskay (p. 670) is the **Am Politician,** fondly referred to by locals as the "Polly." Grub, tea, coffee, and, as the name of the legendary ship suggests, lost of whisky. (☎01878 720 246. Open M-Sa 11am- "until the patrons go to bed," Su 12:30pm- "until the bartender goes to bed.")

🅶 SIGHTS

The vibrant 🖼**Taigh Chearsabhagh** (tie KEAR-sa-vah) **Museum and Arts Centre** in Lochmaddy is home to a rotating gallery of contemporary Scottish artwork and an extensive photo exhibit on North Uist life. The bright and festive Centre also offers art classes throughout the year and houses artists-in-residence during the summer. The **cafe** (see above) has good eats and the only Internet access in North Uist. (☎01876 500 293. Open daily 10am-5pm. Gallery free. Museum £1, concessions 50p, under 12 free.) Farther west on the A865 are the sweeping beaches at **Sollas,** sea-carved arches and a Victorian folly 5 mi. west at **Scolpaig,** and **Sloc a'Choire,** a spouting cave and hollow arch, at **Tigharry.** It's said that a defiant young lass once hid in the arch rather than marry at her parents' demand; listen carefully and you might still hear her echoing cries. 2 miles past Locheport Rd. on the A867 is the 3000-year-old chambered cairn **Barpa Langass** and nearby stone circle **Pobull Fhinn.** On North Uist's southern tip at **Carinish** lie the ruins of 13th-century **Trinity Temple,** probably the islands' most noteworthy relic. Bus W17 from Lochmaddy swings near Langass and Carinish. Birdwatchers get frustrated by the elusive corncrake at the **RSPB Balranald Reserve** on western North Uist, north of Bayhead, signposted from the A867. (☎01870 620 369. Guided walks May-Aug. Tu 6:30pm and Th 11:30am, £2.50. Take bus #W18 from Lochmaddy; M-Sa, 3-4 per day.)

South Uist has few attractions, most centered around the birthplace of Highlands heroine **Flora MacDonald** in **Milton,** where her striking statue perches on a hill by the A865. The nearby **Kildonan Museum** houses local artifacts and showcases Uist craft producers. (☎01878 710 343. Open Apr.-Oct. M-Sa 10am-5pm, Su noon-5pm. £1, children free.) There are numerous pleasant walks around the Uists; the TIC has several pamphlets to help you find your way. (50p-£2.) On Benbecula, the **Uist Riding School** provides lessons and beach rides. (☎01870 604 283. £10-25.)

SMALLER ISLANDS

BERNERAY (BEÀRNARAIGH). Connected to North Uist's north coast by a causeway, the tiny island of Berneray is a gem. The island is home to the best-equipped 🖼**Gatliff Trust Hostel** and features a gorgeous coast of white sand machair (MA-hur, or sea meadow), a thriving seal population, standing stones, and a friendly human population of 140 that first saw electricity in 1969. Stay with **Donald "Splash" MacKillop** at **Burnside Croft,** where you too can enjoy croft life and help carry a water bucket or two. (☎01876 540 235; www.burnsidecroft.fsnet.co.uk). Berneray is the **ferryport** for Harris arrivals; frequent **buses** #W17 and W19 run from Lochmaddy (30min., M-Sa 6-9 per day, £1).

ERISKAY (EIRIOSGAIGH). Eriskay has a quirky history and is home to the feral Eriskay ponies, but not much else. On February 4, 1941, with wartime alcohol rationing in effect, the S.S. *Politician*—carrying 207,000 cases of whisky to America—foundered on a reef off the isle of Eriskay. Concerned islanders mounted a prompt salvage operation; today the local pub, named after the ship, displays some original bottles (see **Whisky Galore!,** p. 58). Bonnie Prince Charlie first set foot on Scottish soil at **Prince Charles's Bay** in Eriskay. The unique pink flower that grows on the island is said to have been brought by seedlings stuck to the Prince's shoe. Eriskay is connected to South Uist by a causeway; **buses** #W17 and W29 run from Lochboisdale (45min., 10 per day).

BARRA (BARRAIGH)   ☎ 01871

The southern outpost of the Western Isles, Barra is the Hebrides in a nutshell. An unspeakably beautiful composite of moor, machair, and beach, the island is home to over 1000 species of wild plant. On sunny days, the island's colors are unforgettable: sand dunes mottled with yellow and pink wildflowers crown waters wreathed by earthy green kelp. Barra is home to a small number of Gaelic-speaking Scots—most of them MacNeils—who preserve the island's unique culture. The best times to visit are May and early June, when the primroses bloom, or in July during the **Barra Festival,** a celebration of music and craftsmanship. Just four miles wide and eight miles long, Barra is ideal for exploring by bike or on foot.

▤ TRANSPORTATION. **CalMac ferries** (☎ 01878 700 288) sail to **Castlebay** (Bagh A Chaisteil), Barra's main town, from: **Oban** (5hr.; M, W-Th, Sa 1 per day; ₤20, 5-day round-trip ₤35; car ₤75/₤125), **Lochboisdale, South Uist** (1¾hr.; Tu, Th-F, Su 1 per day; ₤6, 5-day round-trip ₤10; car ₤35/₤55), and **Eriskay** (M-Sa 4 per day; ₤5.40, 5-day round-trip ₤10; car ₤17/₤30). Times change frequently, and the schedule is difficult; call the TIC or CalMac for help. **Hebridean Coaches** (☎ 01870 620 345) runs buses #W17 and W29 to Eriskay from **Benbecula** and **Lochboisdale** (M-Sa 5-9 per day).

It is possible to see almost all of Barra in a day, and the best way to do so is by **bike.** To rent from **Castlebay Cycle Hire,** drop by the long wooden shed on the main road. (☎ 810 438. From ₤8 per day. Open daily 10am-1pm.) **Barra Cycle Hire,** on St. Brendan's Rd., also rents bikes. (☎ 810 284. Open daily in summer 10am-5pm.) You can also hop on and off **bus** #W32 as it zooms around the circular island road (☎ 810 262; 90min. circuit; M-Sa 1-2 per hr.) or rent from **Barra Car Hire** (☎ 810 243; 25 and over; from ₤30 per day). If you tire of dry land, try a guided sea-kayaking tour with **Chris Denehy,** and take in the surrounding islands, populated with seals, otters, and eagles. (☎ 810 443. ₤10 per evening, ₤15 per half-day, ₤25 per day.)

▨ PRACTICAL INFORMATION. **Castlebay** is Barra's only town. A helpful **Tourist Information Centre** is around the bend to the east of the pier. They'll find you a B&B for a ₤3 charge plus a 10% deposit, but book ahead—a wedding, festival, or positive weather forecast can fill every bed on the island. (☎ 810 336, www.isleofbarra.com. Open Easter-Oct. M-Sa 9am-5pm, also for late ferries.) Barra has one **ATM,** at the only **bank,** across from the TIC. (☎ 810 281. Open M-F 9:15am-12:30pm and 1:30-4:45pm.) **Internet access** at the **Castlebay School Library,** 10min. west of the Castlebay Hotel. (☎ 810 471. Book ahead. ₤2 per 30min., ₤3.50 per hr. Open M and W 9am-4:30pm, Tu and Th 9am-4:30pm and 6-8pm, F 9am-3:30pm, Sa 10am-12:30pm.) The **post office** is next to the bank. (☎ 810 312. Open M-W and F 9am-1pm and 2-5:30pm, Th 9am-1pm, Sa 9am-12:30pm.) **Post Code:** HS9 5XD.

▥▯ ACCOMMODATIONS AND FOOD. Barra is home to the excellent ▩**Dunard Hostel ❷,** up the hill from the pier and 100 yards to the left. Run by one of the few young couples who've remained on the island past childhood, the hostel is a wonderfully social, truly Hebridean experience. (☎ 810 443. Dorms ₤11. Cash only.) The **Isle of Barra Hotel ❹,** at Tangasdale Beach, overlooks the Atlantic at a picturesque spot; its restaurant serves fresh meals and an unexpectedly good wine list (☎ 810 383. Doubles ₤40-48. MC/V.) Get it all in one place at the **Castlebay Hotel ❹:** comfortable B&B-style accommodations (Singles ₤45; doubles ₤78-85), local salmon or lamb shank (from ₤9) at the **restaurant ❸**, or a drink and live music (summer weekends) at the **bar ❶**. (☎810 223; www.castlebay-hotel.co.uk. Uphill from the harbor. Open daily. Call ahead. Dinner served 5:30-8:30pm. Bar open 11am-midnight. MC/V.) Just below is the **Co-op** food store. (☎810 308. Open M-W and Sa 8:30am-6pm, Th-F 8:30am-7pm.) The cheerful ▇**Cafe Kisimul ❶**, Main St., across from where the boat departs from the pier for the castle, specializes in vegetarian food, but has creative dishes for everyone. (☎810 645. Tu-Th 10am-8pm, F-Sa 10am-10pm, Su noon-8pm, closed M. Cash only.)

▣ **SIGHTS. Kisimul Castle,** medieval bastion of the old Clan MacNeil, floats in stately solitude in the middle of Castle Bay. It was recently leased to Historic Scotland for 1000 years, for ₤1 and one bottle of Talisker whisky per year. Take a motorboat from the pier in front of the TIC to the castle gate; inside awaits one of the oldest self-flushing toilets in the world. (☎810 313. Open Apr.-Oct. M-Sa 9:30am-6:30pm. ₤3.30, concessions ₤2.60, children ₤1.30.) A sampling of island life and Gaelic culture is found at the rotating exhibits of the **"Dualchas" Barra Heritage and Cultural Centre,** near the school. (☎810 413. Open Apr.-Sept. M-Sa 11am-4pm. ₤2, concessions ₤1.50, children ₤1.) The road west from Castlebay passes the brooding, cloud-topped mass of **Ben Tangasdale** before arcing north to an amazing stretch of beach at **Halaman Bay.** From there, the road extends northward past turquoise waters and more white sand. Opposite Allasdale to the north, popular **Seal Bay** makes an excellent picnic spot. A detailed map of Barra can guide you to numerous **standing stones** and **cairns** dotting the hills in the middle of the island.

Farther north in **Eoligarry** is **Cille Bharra Cemetery,** containing "crusader" headstones thought to have served as ballast in the warship of a clan chief. Inside the neighboring **St. Barr's Church,** weave through candlelit shrines, Celtic crosses, and Norman stones. To see the whole island, follow the one-lane A888, which makes a 14 mi. circle around the 1260 ft. slopes of **Ben Heavel,** Barra's highest peak.

▧ **VATERSAY AND MINGULAY.** A short causeway connects Barra to **Vatersay** (Bhatarsaigh; pop. 70), the small, southernmost inhabited island in the Outer Hebrides. The island is home to two shell-sand beaches, just a few hundred yards apart on the narrow isthmus connecting Barra and Vatersay. A monument commemorates the *Annie Jane*, which sank off Vatersay in 1853 while carrying 400 hopeful emigrants to Canada. Buses run to Vatersay from the Castlebay post office by the pier. (M-Sa 3-4 per day). Bird watchers should visit the deserted island of **Mingulay,** still farther south. Call **John MacNeil** to inquire about boat trips from Castlebay in summer. (☎810 449. 2 per week, weather permitting. From ₤20.) **George MacLeod** (☎810 223) at the Castlebay Hotel may be able to arrange similar tours.

THE NORTHWEST HIGHLANDS

The pristine beauty and humbling enormity of Scotland's northwest is irresistible. Spectacularly isolated and sparsely populated, the region's hamlets are threaded with lochs and waterfalls and surrounded by jagged peaks and brooding heather-covered hills. Expanses of mountain and moor stretch along the coast, from the imposing Torridon Hills to Inverpolly near Ullapool, and the sandy beaches and turquoise waters of Durness create a veritable eden of tranquility at the edge of the world. Public transportation is limited where it exists, making access to these awesome natural spectacles difficult, but then that just means fewer tourists.

TRANSPORTATION

Without a car, tramping the northwest coast is tricky in summer and nearly impossible the rest of the year. **Inverness** is the area's main transport hub. Scotrail runs **trains** (☎08457 484 950) from Inverness to **Kyle of Lochalsh** (2½hr., 4 per day, £14) and **Thurso** (3¼hr., 3 per day, £12.50). **Scottish Citylink** (☎08705 505 050) and **Rapson Buses** serve the same routes to **Kyle** (2½hr., 2 per day, £10.60) and **Thurso** (3½hr., 2 per day, £10.50), and also go to **Ullapool**, midway up the northwest coast, where ferries leave for the Outer Hebrides (1½hr., M-Sa 2-4 per day, £6.80). From April to October, the **Northern Explorer Ticket**, available at bus stations, provides transportation on a route looping from Inverness to Ullapool, Durness, Tongue, and Thurso. The ticket covers unlimited travel (3 consecutive days £39; 5 of 10 £62; 8 of 16 £85); otherwise, it's pricey single fares (6hr., 2 per day; Ullapool-Thurso £19). **Postbuses** are another option; consult the public transport guide, or call a local hostel warden. The few locals drive like hell-bats on narrow, winding roads, but pick up any hikers they don't run over. *Let's Go* does not recommend hitchhiking.

DORNIE AND NEAR KYLE ☎01599

Though the tourist mobs rush past to Skye, the region just east of Kyle of Lochalsh is breathtaking in its own right. The made-for-postcard must-see of the area is **Eilean Donan Castle** (EL-len DOE-nin), the restored 13th-century seat of the MacKenzie family and the most photographed monument in Scotland, as well as the setting for the films *Highlander* and James Bond's *The World is Not Enough*. For the best snapshots—those that leave out the unattractive motorway and carpark—station yourself on the bridge 200 yd. west on the A87. (☎555 202. Open daily Apr.-Oct. 10am-5:30pm; Mar. and Nov. 10am-3pm. £4.50, concessions £3.60, families £9.50.) The castle stands beside the A87 between Kyle and Inverness; take a **Scottish Citylink bus** and get off at the sleepy town of **Dornie,** stretched out on Loch Long. If you miss the bus back, stay at the tiny **Silver Fir Bunkhouse ❶**, which sleeps a cozy four, and help yourself to the herbs in the organic garden to spice up your dinner. Turn right at the T-junction in the village. Walk 10min. east along the loch, 200 yd. past the chapel, and look for a blue fence on your left. (☎555 264. Linen £1. £10 per person. Cash only.)

6 mi. north of the A87 at Camuslunie, Killilan, ■**Tigh Iseaball Bunkhouse ❶**, a converted croft cottage, has a lovely setting at the base of a mountain. The owners will pick you up from town and rent you a bike for free if you stay two nights. (☎588 205, www.holidaysinhighlands.com. Dorms £7.50, with breakfast £8.50. Cash only.) The trek to the 370 ft. **Falls of Glomach** is an amazing but tough 1½hr. from Glen Elchig. Farther east, the 3505 ft. **Five Sisters of Kintail** tower above the A87, and, on the other side of the highway, the spectacular **Mam Ratagan pass** leads to secluded Glenelg.

PLOCKTON ☎01599

You may encounter your first Highland traffic jam in Plockton, as cattle and sheep roam the roads freely and find the warmth of road pavement perfect for napping. 6 mi. north of Kyle of Lochalsh, the wee village of Plockton is a coastal gem with palm trees, hand-swept streets, and painted houses all along the tranquil rocky harbor. The **Leisure Marine Office**, on the waterfront, rents canoes, rowboats, paddleboats, and bikes (£5-15 per hr.). Keep your eyes peeled for seals, otter, and the occasional porpoise in the picturesque cove. **Calum's Seal Trips**, at the Main Pier or the Pontoon next to the carpark, are free if no seals show. Signs at both locations indicate the departure point for the next trip. (☎544 306. 1hr. tours daily Apr.-Oct. at 10am, noon, 2, 4pm, and sometimes evenings. £6, children £4.) Several miles north of Plockton is **Craig Highland Farm,** where you can feed and rare breeds of various livestock. (☎544 205. £1.50, children £1. Open daily 10am-dusk.) They also rent out thatched and wood cottages (from £120 per week, MC/V).

Plockton sits on the main Inverness-Kyle of Lochalsh **rail line,** operated by Scotrail, which runs 4 trains per day in each direction. It's also served by the Kyle-Plockton-Ardnarff **postbus service** (#119; 1 per day). Opposite the train station, the **Station Bunkhouse ❶,** 5min. from the waterfront, offers a comfortable hostel. (☎544 235. Dorms £8.50-10. Cash only.) The owners run a basic B&B, the unfortunately-named **Nessun Dorma ❷,** from their house next door. (£15-17; singles £20.)

APPLECROSS

☎01520

The tiny village of Applecross is a magical place to visit; getting there is another story. The direct route, across the harrowing **Bealach na Ba ("Cattle") Pass,** is for the iron-hearted only. At 2054 ft., the steep, single-track Pass is Britain's highest road, punctuated by hairpin turns and livestock with little regard for their own lives and even less for yours. On a clear day, drivers are rewarded with expansive views of Skye and the Small Isles; the rest of the time, vehicles are surrounded by mist and the cliff drop just 5 ft. away is practically invisible. The circuitous **coastal route** is a less death-defying option, offering its own panoramas from above the rocky seashore. A 9500-year-old dwelling in Sand and a Viking lime kiln in Keppoch, along with other pre-historic and natural wonders, are described in the free *Applecross Scenic Walks.* **Mountain & Sea Guides** offers kayaking, rock climbing, and trekking trips. (☎744 394; www.applecross.uk.com. 2hr. session £15, half-day £25, full day £45; 3-day to 1-week trips from £145.) Applecross is served by **postbus** #92 (M-Sa) from **Shieldaig** (11:30am) and **Torridon** (10:30am). The nearest train station is over 17 mi. away in Strathcarron, and catching a bus from there to Shieldaig to meet a connection to Applecross is only possible early in the day.

After a white-knuckle drive on Bealach na Ba Pass, take the left-hand road at the junction and turn right at the red barn to discover the cool and utterly unexpected **Applecross Flower Tunnel Cafe ❶,** a breezy conservatory festooned with flowers and offering jazzy tunes, lattes, and mouth-watering carrot cake. (744 268. Open daily 11am. Cash only.) The best reason to come to Applecross, however, is the ⚿**Applecross Inn ❷,** down the hill on the waterfront. Judith Fish has the right name for the job; with heartwarming Scottish hospitality she serves award-winning local seafood and game. The delightful upstairs **rooms ❸** have sunny ocean views. (☎744 262. Bar-restaurant open 10am-midnight. Rooms £25-35 per person. MC/V.)

TORRIDON

☎01445

North of the Applecross Peninsula lies the Torridon region. The teensy village of Torridon (pop. 230) lies between **Loch Torridon** to the south and the Torridon Hills to the north. Although the town itself doesn't have much to offer, the remote locale draws adventurous hikers to the surrounding peaks. The highest and closest is the challenging **Liathach** (3456 ft.), considered by some the biggest bully in Britain; this small mountaineering community has grown up in its shadow.

From Inverness, **trains** (☎08457 484 950) run to **Achnasheen** (1¼hr.; M-Sa 4 per day, Su 2 per day; £9.30); there, **postbus** #91 (12:10pm) connects to Torridon. Buses do not meet every train; call ☎01463 234 111 to confirm times. **Duncan Maclennan** (☎01520 755 239) shuttle buses connect with the Inverness train at **Strathcarron** (1hr.; June-Sept. M-Sa 12:30pm, Oct.-May M, W, F only; £3). The staff at the **Torridon Countryside Centre,** at the crossroads into Torridon, 100 yd. east of the hostel, possesses an encyclopedic knowledge of the region and sells guides to area walks. (☎791 221. Open daily May-Sept. 10am-6pm.)

At the base of the daunting Liathach, the stark **SYHA Torridon** ❷ offers spartan rooms but has a store with basic **groceries,** and a friendly staff, not to mention rowdy hillwalkers trumpeting their latest exploits. (☎791 284. Open Mar.-Oct. Dorms £10.50-11.50, under 18 £5-9.50. MC/V.) Between the Torridon hostel and the ranger office, the **Torridon Campsite** ❶ is exquisitely located. (☎791 313. £3 per tent. Cash only.) The small **general store** 300 yd. west along the road is your lone bet for supplies. (☎791 400. Open M-Sa 9:30am-6pm, Su 10am-noon and 4-6pm.)

GAIRLOCH ☎01445

Gairloch is spread out over several miles of beautiful coastline. Gairloch is a popular summer resort town, with hotels and B&Bs fully booked in peak season. Just outside the mountains, Gairloch often escapes the rain and fog that cling to the surrounding region. Beyond its wide, sandy beach, the town features a cluttered **Gairloch Heritage Museum,** with such debatable treasures as a carved stone ball ("possibly a symbol of power") and a lighthouse bulb. (☎712 287. Open Apr.-Sept. M-Sa 10am-5pm; in winter by arrangement. £2.50, seniors £2, children 50p.) Horseback riders can get their equestrian fix at the **Gairloch Trekking Centre,** across the road just south of the pier. (☎712 652. £7 per 30min.; lessons available.) Six miles north along the coastal road, the highlight of the area, **Inverewe Gardens,** show flowers from all over the world, grown in a tropical microclimate heated by the passing jetstream. Westerbus runs from Gairloch to the gardens at least once per day during the week (£1); check the timetable at the TIC (p. 675) first. (☎781 200. Garden open daily mid-Mar. to Oct. 9:30am-9pm; Nov. to mid-Mar. 9:30am-5pm. Guided walks mid-Apr. to mid-Sept. M-F 1:30pm. £7, concessions £6.)

Westerbus runs to Gairloch from **Ullapool** (2¼-2¾hr., M-Sa, £4.40). For a £3 charge plus a 10% deposit, the **Tourist Information Centre** books B&Bs in Gairloch and Dundonnell, just east of the Ardessie Gorge. (☎712 130. Open June-Aug. M-Sa 9am-5:30pm, Su 10am-4pm; Sept.-Oct. and Easter-June M-Sa 9am-5pm; Nov.-Easter M-Sa 10am-5pm.) Buy **groceries** at **Mace,** on the A832 just south of its intersection with the B8021. (☎712 242. Open M-F 7:30am-9pm, Sa 8am-9pm.) The cheapest **Internet access** is at **Wordworks,** above the Harbour Centre on Pier Rd. (☎712 712. £1 per hr.). There's also a more expensive connection at the **post office,** 400 yd. west of the A832 on the B8021. (☎08457 223 344. £1 per 15min. Open M-Sa 9am-12:30pm, M-Tu and Th-F also 2-5:30pm.) **Post Code:** IV21 2BZ.

The 12 mi. drive out to the ◪**Rua Reidh Lighthouse** ❶ will reward you with hot showers, delicious food, and incredible views, and you can tell your friends you slept in a lighthouse. (☎771 263; www.ruareidh.co.uk. £9.50-18. From Gairloch take the minor road signposted to Melvaig and follow for 12 mi. to lighthouse. MC/V.) Find a quiet, lochside bed at the **SYHA Carn Dearg** ❶, 2 mi. northwest of town on the B8021. Get off the Gairloch bus at the village of **Strath** and walk toward the sea from there. (☎712 219. Reception 7-10:30am and 5-11:30pm. Curfew 11:30pm. Open mid-May to Sept. Dorms £10, under 18 £9. MC/V.) Just a ½ mi. west of the hostel, campers can pitch at the beachside **Sands Holiday Centre** ❶ (☎712 152; £9-10 per tent). A good meal awaits those who can afford it at **The Old Inn** ❹, a hotel and restaurant just off of the A832 at the south end of town. You'll find a warm atmosphere, fresh local ingredients, an experienced chef, and live music here. (☎712 006. Food served noon-9:30pm. Doubles £70-84. MC/V.)

ULLAPOOL ☎01854

Compared to its neighbors, buzzing Ullapool feels downright cosmopolitan. Though visitors are drawn to its amenities, pubs, and transport links to the Outer Hebrides, Ullapool's retains its charm as a lively seaport on the salty shores of Loch Broom. The area abounds with **hikes** including an excellent ramble through the shaded woodlands of **Ullapool Hill,** where the summit offers impressive views of Glenn Achall (2hr. round-trip). Footpaths are marked with yellow signs and begin 200 yd. northwest of the school on North Rd. and behind the Royal Hotel on Shore St. The SYHA hostel (p. 676) provides free leaflets detailing longer walks that traverse **Scots Pine** and the **Inverpolly Nature Reserve.** Wardens can also suggest how to **cycle** to nearby hostels in **Carbisdale** and **Achiniver.** The **Tourist Information Centre** is on Argyle St. (☎612 135. Open July-Aug. M-Sa 9am-6pm, Su 10am-5pm; Apr.-June and Sept.-Oct. M-Sa 9am-5pm, Su 10am-4pm.) The **Ullapool Museum,** W. Argyle St., uses audiovisual displays to recount local history. (☎612 987. Open Apr.-Oct M-Sa 9:30am-5:30pm; Nov.-Mar. Th-Sa 11am-3pm. £2, concessions £1.50.)

Except for the 1am arrivals, **ferries** from **Stornoway, Lewis** (M-F 2-3 per day; £14, 5-day round-trip £24) are met by **Scottish Citylink** and **Rapsons Coaches** (☎01463 710 555). Buses run from **Inverness** (1½hr., 2 per day, £7.30). **Tim Dearman** (☎01349 883 585) also treks from Inverness (1¾hr., 1 per day, £8.50). **Cal-Mac** (☎612 358) runs a variety of **cruise tours** to Lewis (from £18). Smaller boats conduct wildlife tours (£8-15) to the **Summer Isles** (p. 677); inquire at the pier. **Scotpackers** (see below) runs half- and full-day minibus tours (£10-15, guests £9-13.50). The **post office** is on W. Argyle St. (☎612 228. Open M-Tu and Th-F 9am-1pm and 2-5:30pm, W and Sa 9am-1pm.) **Post Code:** IV26 2TY.

🕮**Scotpackers West House ❶,** W. Argyle St., answers backpacker needs with towering bunks, easy chairs, and a homey lounge. Internet access is free for guests (non-guests £1 per 20min.) and bike rental is £10 per day. (☎613 126; www.scotpackers-hostels.co.uk. Dorms £12. AmEx/MC/V.) The affiliated **Crofton House ❷** has doubles, but phone the hostel first (£30, AmEx/MC/V). The well-situated **SYHA Ullapool ❶,** Shore St., 200 yd. east of the pier, compensates for crowded bunks with outstanding harbor views. (☎612 254. Curfew M-F, Su at midnight; Sa 12:30am. Laundry £2. Bike rental £6-12 per day. Dorms £11.50, under 18 £8.75. MC/V.) The **Ullapool Tourist Hostel ❶,** W. Argyle St., has everything you need in a big white house, plus free coffee, tea, cheap Internet access (£1 per hour), and bikes rentals. (☎613 125. £9.25.) Get the basics at **Costcutter,** across from the post office. (☎M-W 7am-8pm, Th-Sa 7am-10pm, Su 8am-8pm.) At 🕮**The Seaforth ❷,** by the pier, enjoy live music Friday through Sunday and a mouth-watering selection of whiskies. Those fearing prawns or haggis should steer clear. After a meal (£8-13), sample a startlingly distinctive Laphroaig 15-Year-Old. (☎612 122; www.theseaforth.com. Open Su-W 11am-midnight, Th-Sa 11am-1am.) The **Ceilidh Place ❸,** 14 W. Argyle St. (☎612 103), is a hotel, cafe, bar, bookstore, and gallery. In summer, lively Celtic music is performed several nights a week. (AmEx/MC/V.) **Jasmine Tandoori ❶,** West Ln., serves excellent Indian food. (☎613 331. Open daily noon-2pm and 5-11pm.)

🔃 DAYTRIPS FROM ULLAPOOL

🕮**CORRIESHALLOCH GORGE.** Twelve miles south of Ullapool on the A835, the River Broom cascades 150 ft. down the **Falls of Measach** into a menacing gorge. Formed by glacial action, Corrieshalloch slices through the earth like a deep scar. Begin your visit by turning right on the footpath across from the bus stop; about 40 yd. northwest on the path, a short fenced plank thrusts harrowingly over the gorge and serves as a **viewpoint** for the falls upstream to the southeast. Follow the footpath 100 yd. to the **suspension bridge** (built 1867) that balances over the falls. Though it sways unsettlingly with every step, six normal-sized hikers can safely traverse the (oft-inspected) relic. The gorge is easily accessible by any Ullapool-Inverness **bus;** double-check that a return exists before you set out.

ACHILTIBUIE. (Ah-KILL-ta-boo-ee) Northwest of Ullapool lies the **Coigach Peninsula,** whose singular peaks line the horizon. At Achiltibuie, simple beauty awaits those willing to make the trek. A small village caught between coastal waters and towering rock crags, Achiltibuie has a trio of sandy beaches. Off the coast, the lovely **Summer Isles** are so named because local crofters graze their sheep here during high season. The Isles are also home to rock formations and a seal colony.

Tour Achiltibuie from **Ullapool** (p. 675) or on the passenger vessel *M.V. Hectoria* from **Badentarbet Pier,** at the western end of Achiltibuie. (☎01854 622 200. 3½hr. tours with 1hr. ashore Apr.-Oct. M-Sa 10:30am and 2:15pm. £15, children £7.50. 7hr. tour with 4½hr. ashore M-Sa 10:30am. £20/£15.) **Spa Coaches** run from Ullapool (M-F 2 per day, Sa 1 per day; £3.50). If driving, take the A835 north 10 mi. from Ullapool, then head west at the well-marked one-lane road, following it 15 mi. to the coast. On the main road in town, **Achiltibuie Store** sells groceries. (Open M-Sa 9am-5:30pm.) 50 yd. down the road, the **post office** doubles as a TIC. (☎01854 622 200. Open M-Sa 9am-noon; M-W and F also 1-5:30pm.) **Post Code:** IV26 2YG.

The **Hydroponicum** is a self-proclaimed "garden of the future," where produce—including the only native Highland banana—is grown without soil. Get meals made from the freshest, dirt-free ingredients at the **Lily Pond Cafe ❷.** (☎01854 622 202. Hourly tours. Open daily mid-Apr. to Sept. 10am-6pm; June-Aug. also Th-Su 7-9pm. Cafe Easter-Sept. 10am-5pm. £4.75, concessions £3.50, children £2.75. MC/V.) At the **Achiltibuie Smokehouse,** 4 mi. northwest in Altandhu, patrons can watch as fish are slit, sliced, and smoked. Buy your culinary souvenirs here: 200g of smoked Highland eel is only £18. (☎01854 622 353. Open M-Sa 9:30am-5pm. Free.)

The idyllic **SYHA Achininver ❶,** ¼ mi. from a sandy beach and 3 mi. from Achiltibuie, is a short hike from the road. Ask the bus driver to let you off where the hostel is signposted. (☎01854 622 254. Open mid-May to Sept. Dorms £8.75, under 18 £7.50. MC/V.) Mary King runs the **Culross Vegetarian B&B ❸,** combining art and food; peek into the gallery of local works. (☎01854 622 426. Singles £20-25; doubles £30-35. Gallery open M-Sa 10am-5pm; by appointment in winter.) The rooms of the **Summer Isles Hotel ❹,** just up the road from the Hydroponicum, provides views of the islands and offers locally grown food. (☎01854 622 282; www.summerisleshotel.co.uk. Breakfast included. Open Apr.-Oct. £56 per person. MC/V.)

LOCHINVER AND ASSYNT ☎01571

30 mi. up the northwest coast, the unremarkable town of Lochinver is a food-and-petrol outpost for the wild region of Assynt, a breathtaking if desolate region nearly impossible to penetrate without a car. The **Assynt Visitor Centre** on the waterfront in Lochinver serves as a TIC. (☎844 330. Open Easter-Oct. M-Sa 10am-5pm, Su 10am-4pm.) The **Ranger Service** (☎844 654) offers free **guided walks** in summer.

Assynt is known for its treks (8-10hr.) up the imposing mountains of **Suilven** and **Canisp;** though lengthy, these trails are accessible to walkers of all levels. Going south from the Visitor Centre, the second left turn leads to **Glencanisp Lodge,** where a footpath famed for sightings of deer, otter, and golden eagles skirts the River Inver (2hr. round-trip). The shorter **Culaig Wood Walk** (about 1hr. round-trip) starts west of the field near the pier. From the SYHA hostel (p. 678), a **nature trail** crosses the town of **Alt-na-Bradhan** before reaching the striking rock formation at **Clachtoll** (5hr. round-trip). For longer expeditions, buy a good map—Ordnance Survey Landranger #15 is available at the TIC (£6). **Assynt Angling Group** (☎844 257) can recommend fishing holes and the TIC can get you a permit (£5 per day, £25 per week).

The only public transport to enter this forbidding country is the **KSM Motors** bus, which runs once a day from Ullapool (£3). Check with the TIC for times. **Postbus** #123 trundles in from the Lairg train station (M-Sa 12:45pm). A **Royal Bank of Scotland** is at the west end of town, just before the pier. (☎844 215. Open M-Tu and Th-

F 9:15am-12:30pm and 1:30-4:45pm, W from 10am.) The **Spar** supermarket is on the other side of town. (☎844 207. Open M-Sa 8am-6:30pm, Su 9am-5:30pm.) Next door is the **post office**. (☎08457 223 344. Open M and W-F 8am-1pm and 2-5pm, Tu 8:30am-1pm.) **Post Code:** IV27 4SY.

There are a number of decent B&Bs in town; the **Ardglas Guest House ❷**, across the stone bridge, is Lochinver's cheapest, with fine views and spacious rooms. (☎844 257. Singles £15-17; doubles £30-34.) **Hostels** are far but compensate with dramatic locations and great access to hiking and cycling trails. The bare-bones **SYHA Achmelvich ❶**, Recharn, is 3 mi. west on a stunning footpath, or 20min. by the 11:15am postbus. (☎844 480. Reception 7-10:30am and 5-11pm. Open Apr.-Sept. Dorms £8.75, under 18 £7.50. MC/V.) Mr. MacLeod runs the nearby **Achmelvich campsite ❶**, beside a beach that deters swimmers with icy waters. (☎844 393. Tent £7.) Another 13 mi. inland, the heart-rending ruins of **Ardvreck Castle** on Loch Assynt sit opposite the social **Inchnadamph Lodge ❶**, Assynt Field Centre, which has endless amenities. Local deer—including three-horned "Freaky"—lurk nearby, waiting for table scraps. (☎822 218. Breakfast included. Laundry £1.50. Dorms £19.95; doubles £34.) Ullapool-Lochinver buses stop here on request.

DURNESS ☎01971

A quiet village on Scotland's north coast at the turning point of the A838, Durness is a popular stop on tours of the region, and for good reason—even John Lennon made picturesque Durness his summer holiday destination). A mile up the road from the town center, the ◪**Smoo Caves**—deep holes in the limestone—take their name from *smuga*, a Viking word meaning hiding place. Legend claims that the bastard son of a McKay chieftain hid the bodies of 18 murdered men here. When the caverns aren't flooded after heavy rains, you can float via rubber dinghy past the interior waterfall. (☎511 704; ask for Colin. 15min. tours depart from cave entrance daily Apr.-Sept. 10am-5pm. £2.50, children £1.) At the Smoo cave inlet, **Smoo Cave Tours** runs wildlife boat tours, taking in Faraid Head and the Cliffs of Moine Schist, with frequent sightings of gray seals, dolphins, and minke whales. (☎511 704. Easter-Oct. 11-4pm £4, children £2.) Ten minutes west of town, the yellow sands and pure blue water of secluded **Balnakeil Beach** would seem tropical but for the Atlantic winds and the puffin colony. Britain's highest cliffs soar at **Cape Wrath,** 12 mi. west of Durness. From the Cape Wrath Hotel (1½ mi. west down the road from the town center), a ferry crosses to **Kyle of Durness** (☎511 376; 4 per day; round-trip £3.80), where it's met by a **minibus** that completes the trip to Cape Wrath (☎511 287. Round-trip £6.50). **Ferry** and **bus** operate on demand May-Sept. from 9:30am. The Cape may be closed for Royal Air Force training; call ahead.

To reach Durness, hop **postbus** #104 from the **Lairg** train station or #105 from the post office (☎01463 256 228; M-Sa 2 per day). **Postbus** # 136 goes from **Thurso** to **Tongue; Tim Dearman** coaches will shuttle you from Tongue to Durness, but schedules change, so it is wise to call. Tim Dearman coaches also pull in from **Inverness** (5hr., 1 per day, £14) and **Ullapool** (3hr., 1 per day, £8). The **Tourist Information Centre** books B&Bs for a £3 charge plus a 10% deposit. (☎511 259. Open daily Apr.-Oct. 10am-5pm, Nov.-Mar. 10am-1:30pm.) The **post office** is down the road. (☎511 209. Open M-Tu and Th-F 9am-5:30pm, W and Sa 9am-12:30pm.) **Post Code:** IV27 4QF.

The best budget lodgings are provided by the amiable ◪**Lazycrofter Bunkhouse ❶**, whose dull exterior does little justice to its luxurious bunks. (☎511 209 or 511 366; www.durnesshostel.com. Dorms £9.) Simple and right next to Smoo, the **SYHA Durness ❶**, 1 mi. north of town along the A838, has standard bunks but a peat-burning stove and simple charm to set it apart from the average SYHA. (☎511 244. Reception 7-10:30am and 5-11pm. Curfew 11pm. Open Apr.-Sept. Dorms £6.75, under 18 £6. MC/V.) More private respite awaits at **Smoo Falls B&B ❷**, across from the Smoo Caves. (☎511 228. Call ahead Dec.-Jan. No smoking. Singles £25; doubles £36, ensuite £40. Cash only.) **Sango Sands Camping Site ❶** overlooks the sea next to the visitor center. To the south find a beach; to the north, the campground's pub. (☎551 1726. Reception open 9-9:30am and 6-6:30pm. Tent £4. Showers 50p.)

THURSO AND SCRABSTER ☎01847

A big fish in a very, very small pond, **Thurso** (pop. 9000) is considered a veritable Tokyo by the crofters and fishermen of Scotland's desolate north coast. The city has no museums and doesn't seem to care; even the refreshingly frank **Tourist Information Centre**, Riverside Rd., treats the **castle ruins** east of town with casual indifference. (☎892 371. TIC open Apr.-Oct. M-Sa 10am-5pm; June-Sept. also Su 10am-4pm.) Thurso's "urban" character is complemented by one of Europe's best **surfing beaches**, near the castle. Rent wetsuits (£6 per day) and surfboards (£10 per day) at **Harper's**, 57 High St. (☎893 179. Open M-Sa 10am-5pm.) **Scrabster**, 2½ mi. east, is no more than a ferry port for Orkney (p. 680); spend the night in Thurso.

Infectiously friendly ⬛**Sandra's Backpackers Hostel ❶**, 26 Princes St. in Thurso features a kitchenette and dorms with TVs. The owners provide lifts to Scrabster for noon ferry connections. (☎894 575; www.sandras-backpackers.ukf.net. Continental breakfast included. Internet access 75p per 15min. Bike rental £8 per day. Dorms £9; private rooms £25. Cash only.) The **Thurso Youth Club Hostel ❶** is stashed in the echoing halls of a converted mill. From the train station, walk east down Lover's Ln., turn north on Janet St., cross the river, and follow the path to the right. (☎892 964. Continental breakfast and linen included. Open July-Aug. Dorms £8.)

For good eats, **Sandra's Snack Bar and Takeaway ❶**, beneath the hostel, is a happening backpacker hangout with rock-bottom prices. (☎894 575. Open M-F 7:30am-11:30pm, Sa 10am-2am, Su 12:30-10:30pm. 10% discount for hostelers. Cash only.) A more sophisticated menu, including local produce, awaits at **Le Bistro ❷**, 2 Traill St., Thurso, with window seats for people-watchers. (☎893 737. Open M 10am-2:30pm, Tu-F 10am-9pm, Sa 9:30am-4pm and 5:30-9pm.) On Wednesday nights, young and old alike come together at **Commercial ("Comm") Bar**, 1 Princes St. (☎893 366. Open M-Th 11am-midnight, F-Sa 11am-1am, Su noon-11pm.) The **Central Pub**, Traill St., attracts a rowdy crowd in the late afternoons. (☎893 129. Open Su-Th 11am-11:45pm, F-Sa 11am-12:45am.)

JOHN O'GROATS ☎01955

Named for the first man to arrange ferries to the Islands (Jan de Groot, a Dutchman), John O'Groats is known for its position as mainland Britain's northernmost town, and now has been robbed of native charm by a plethora of touristy shops. Don't plan on staying long; the surrounding islands are the real destination. **Wildlife Cruises**, run by **John O'Groats Ferries**, leave the docks daily at 2:30pm in July and August to cruise the rugged waters of Pentland Firth, home to kittiwakes, great black backs, and other animals you've never heard of. (☎611 353. 1½hr. £14, children £7, under 5 free, families £35.) **Dunnet Head**, halfway from John O'Groats to Thurso, is the true northernmost point on the Isle, but **Duncansby Head**, about 2 mi. east of town, has a better view overlooking the Pentland Firth toward Orkney. The **Tourist Information Centre**, Country Rd., by the pier, helps plan escapes to surrounding areas and can arrange accommodations if you miss a ferry. (☎611 373. Open daily June-Aug. 9am-6pm; Apr.-May and Sept.-Oct. 10am-5pm.) To reach town from the **Wick train station**, take **Highland Country** bus #77 (40min.), which also runs to **Thurso** (1hr., M-Sa 5 per day) and passes the hostel. From May to August, John O'Groats Ferries's **Orkney Bus** rides from **Inverness** (daily 2:20pm, June-Aug. also 7:30am; £12). If stuck on the mainland, stay at the simple but practical **SYHA John O'Groats ❶**, 2½ mi. west in Canisbay. (☎0870 004 1129. Reception 7-10am and 5-11:30pm. Curfew 11:30pm. Open Easter-Sept. Dorms £10.50, under 18 £8. MC/V.)

HIGHLANDS AND ISLANDS

ORKNEY ISLANDS

Far removed from the tourist trail, the truly magnificent Orkneys are untouched by time—and unseen by most travelers. Covered by white sand beaches, awesome ocean cliffs, sheep-dotted flatland farms and fog enshrouded hills, Orkney is a remote group of islands well worth the journey for the traveler with a zest for adventure. Home to a mere few thousand residents (mainly fishermen and farmers) and 337 species of birds, the feathered outnumber the flightless 100 to 1. Orcadians have trod the islands for millennia as an independent people, partly Scottish, but also cherishing their inherited Pictish and Viking traditions. The 70-island archipelago retains some of the best-preserved Pictish and Viking villages, monuments, and burial chambers in Europe. Originally part of Norway, the thick Orcadian accent still hints at its Scandinavian roots. Orkney can be difficult to manage without a car and the ferry passages require some time, but each island has enough diversity of rugged landscapes and personalities to make any traveler dumbstruck and thankful that Orkney is well off the beaten path.

Mainland (sometimes called **Pomona**) is Orkney's main island, housing the two largest towns. The alluring capital of **Kirkwall** encases a 12th-century cathedral, still in use, as well as a collection of shops featuring everything from Orkney cheese to cheesy Orkney knick-knacks. Quieter and smaller, **Stromness** invites visitors to wander down wynds to the waterside, where cliffs shelter elderducks and fulmar petrels. The southeastern seaside (actually a string of bridged islands) holds more modern secrets—at low tide, broken prows and sunken sterns rear up along the Churchill Barriers, built by POWs during WWII.

▐ GETTING THERE

Ferries are the main mode of transport between the Orkneys and mainland Scotland. The most budget-friendly option for travelers on foot is the **Pentland Ferry** (☎01856 831 226) from **Gills Bay,** just west of John O'Groats on the A836 (1hr.; 2-4 per day; £10, children £5). Pentland also offers car ferries (£25 per car, £10 per adult). Ferries land at **St. Margaret's Hope** on Orkney. **Causeway Coaches** (☎01856 831 444) runs bus service between there and **Kirkwall** (M-Sa 4 per day). Another provider, **John O'Groats Ferries** (☎01955 611 353; www.jogferry.co.uk) travels from **John O'Groats** to **Burwick, Orkney,** where a free bus takes passengers to Kirkwall. (Ferry 45min., bus 35min.; June-July 3 per day; May 2 per day; Sept. 2 per day; round trips to John O'Groats 45min. after arrival; round-trip £28.) John O'Groats Ferries also offers several ferry-tour packages. Their **Maxi Day Tour** makes stops at most of the major sights, and includes a 2hr. break in Kirkwall (9am-7:45pm, last boarding 8:50am; £35, book ahead); alternatively, try the quicker **Highlights Day Tour,** which hits the same sights but only stops in Kirkwall for 20min. (10:30am-6pm; £32). **Northlink Ferries** (☎0845 600 0449) offers trips from **Scrabster** (west of John O'Groats) to **Stromness** on the posh *Hamnavoe,* which feels more like a hotel lobby than a ferry (1½hr.; M-F 3 per day, Sa-Su 2 per day; £27-33). A bus departs from the **Thurso** rail station for Scrabster before each crossing. Northlink also sails from **Aberdeen** to **Kirkwall** (8hr., round-trip £32-48).

▐ LOCAL TRANSPORTATION

Orkney Coaches (☎01856 870 555; www.rapsons.co.uk) runs between **Kirkwall** bus station and **Stromness Pier Head** (30min., M-Sa 1-2 per hr., £2.20). **Orkney Ferries,** based on Shore St. at the Kirkwall harbor, (☎01856 872 044) is really the only way to island-hop. Some ferries are foot-passengers only (no vehicles), all ferries offer student discounts, and schedules are likely to change; make sure to ask. Passenger and car ferries depart from **Kirkwall** to: **Shapinsay** (45 min.), **Westray & Papa Westray** (1½hr.), **Stronsay** (1½-2hr.), **Eday** (1½hr), and **Sanday** (1½-2hr.). Also from Mainland, ferries depart **Tingwall** to **Rousay, Egilsay, & Wyre** (30-60min.). Ferries leave **Houton** (20min. west of Kirkwall on the A964) to Lyness in the south of **Hoy** (20-45min.), and **Flotta** (45min.). A passenger-only ferry departs from **Stromness** to Moaness in the north of **Hoy** (15min.).

Car rental is by far the most convenient way of getting around Orkney; for rental agencies, try **W.R. Tullock** (☎876 262 Kirkwall office on Castle St., 875 500 Kirkwall Airport; www.okneycarrental.co.uk; 21+; from £34 per day) or **Orkney Car Hire** on Junction Rd. (☎872 866, www.orkneycarhire.co.uk) both in Kirkwall. or **Stromness Car Hire** on John St. (☎850 973; ages 21 and older; from £31 per day, £157 per week; open M-F 8am-6pm, Sa 9am-5pm). **Biking** is an alternative, though the rain and wind can be problematic. You can rent wheels in Kirkwall from **Bobby Cycle Centre,** Tankerness Ln., off Broad St. (☎875 777; www.bobbyscycles.co.uk; £8 per day; open M-F 9am-5pm, Sa 9am-5:30pm) or in Stromness at **Orkney Cycle Hire,** 54 Dundas St. (☎850 255. £8 per day; helmet and map included; open daily 8:30am-9pm). Rates are slightly lower in Kirkwall, and the town has better access to the cool Mainland sights; consider taking the bus from Stromness.

KIRKWALL ☎01856

The bustling center of Orkney is a still just a tiny hub of activity where arts and crafts, music, business, and transportation are most accessible and where travelers feel right at home. Kirkwall is at its best (and most expensive) during the **St. Magnus Festival,** St. Magnus Festival Office, 60 Victoria St., (☎871 445; www.st.magnusfestival.com) which takes place during the third week of June. Musicians from folk singers to the BBC Philharmonic migrate north for the festival and entertain around the clock in the almost 24hr. daylight.

⁊ PRACTICAL INFORMATION. The Kirkwall **Tourist Information Centre,** 6 Broad St., books B&Bs for a £1.50 charge and distributes transport info. (☎872 856. Open May-Aug. M-F 8am-5pm, Sa-Su 9am-4pm; Apr. and Sept.-Oct. M-Sa 10am-4pm, Su 10am-3pm; Nov.-Mar. M-Sa 1-3pm; open for late ferry arrivals.) Guidebooks are also available at **The Orcadian Bookshop** on Albert St. (☎878 888). All inter-island ferry information and bookings are best obtained by walking down to **Orkney Ferries Ltd.,** Shore St. (☎872 044; www.orkneyferries.co.uk.) Other services include: **Bank of Scotland,** 56 Albert St. (☎682 000; open M-Tu and Th-F 9am-5pm, W 9:30am-5pm); **Kelvinator Launderama,** Albert St. (☎872 952; open M-F 8:30am-5:30pm, Sa 9am-5pm); the **police,** Watergate (☎872 241); **Internet access** at **Support Training Limited,** 2 W. Tankerness Ln., one block west of Broad St. (☎873 582; £1 per 10min., £5 per hr.; open M-Tu and Th 9am-5pm, W and F 9am-9:30pm, Sa 10am-5pm), or at the **Kirkwall Hotel,** Harbour St., facing the waterfront (☎872 232; £3 per hr.; most times by request at reception); **Boots** pharmacy, 49-51 Albert St. (☎872 097; open M-Sa 8:30am-5:30pm); and the **post office,** 15 Junction Rd. (☎874 249; open M-Tu and Th-F 9am-5pm, W 9am-4pm, Sa 9:30am-12:30pm). **Post Code:** KW15 1AA.

⁊⁊ ACCOMMODATIONS AND FOOD. A number of hostels, B&Bs and crofthouses can be found by consulting the Orkney Tourist Board's annual publication available around town and at the TIC (www.visitorkney.com). Keep in mind that sometimes the best accommodations are in the most remote areas. Kirkwall's **SYHA hostel ❶** is on Old Skapa Rd. Follow the main pedestrian road south from the TIC for ½ mi. as it evolves from Broad St. into Victoria St. Cross and Union St., heading southwest to Main St., and then High St., where SYHA signs will point you

home. Lodgings are not luxurious, but the warm atmosphere more than compensates. (☎872 243. Reception 7:30-10:30am and 5-11:30pm. Lockout 10:30am-5pm. Curfew midnight. Open Apr.-Oct. Dorms £10.50, under 18 £9.) If you're catching an early ferry out of Kirkwall and want to be right in the town center, try the tidy but miniscule **Peedie Hostel ❶**, 1 Ayre Rd., where you'll have to eat your dinner on your lap. Across the street from the pier. (☎875 477. Dorms £10.) At **Mr. and Mrs. Flett's B&B ❷**, Cromwell Rd., climb a ship's staircase to cozy rooms with views of the harbor and sea. (☎873 160. £16-18 per person.) For a more upscale environment, head to the peaceful **West End Hotel ❹**, Main St. (☎872 368. Singles £42; doubles £58.) Another option is the **Kirkwall Hotel ❹**, Harbour St. (☎872 232. Singles £20-48; double £40-82.) **Camp** at **Pickaquoy Centre Caravan & Camping Site ❶**, on Pickaquoy Rd. just south of the A965. (☎879 900. £7.25 per caravan, £4.90 per tent.) You can pitch a tent almost anywhere on the islands, but always ask the landowner.

Safeway dominates the corner of Broad St. and Great Western Rd. (☎228 876. Open M-F 8am-9pm, Sa 8am-8pm, Su 9am-6pm.) **Buster's Diner ❶**, 1 Mounthoolie Ln., is draped in tacky Americana and cooks up pizza and burgers for under £5— all under the front end of a Ford Mustang. (☎876 717. Open M-F noon-2pm in summer and 4:30-10pm, Sa noon-2am, Su 4-10pm.) Along with cappuccinos and sweet pastries, **Trenabies Cafe ❶**, 16 Albert St., can also fill you up with delicious sandwiches and tatties. (☎874 336. Open M-F 8am-6pm, Sa 9:30am-6pm.) Whether you're downing a Dark Island Ale while watching football or sipping a Highland Park whisky while arguing politics with the locals, **The Bothy Bar ❶** is the place to be. (☎876 000. Su night live folk music. Open M-W 11am-midnight, Th-Sa 11am-1am, Su noon-midnight. Food served until 9:30pm.)

🅖 **SIGHTS.** South of the TIC on Broad St., **St. Magnus Cathedral,** begun in 1137, looms over the town in all its hulking red sandstone glory. (Open Apr.-Sept. M-Sa 9am-6pm, Su 2-6pm; Oct.-Mar. M-Sa 9am-1pm and 2-5pm. Free.) Across Palace Rd. from the cathedral, the **Bishop's and Earl's Palaces** once housed the Bishop of Orkney and his enemy, the wicked Earl Patrick Stewart, but became part of the same complex when the earl was executed for treason. (☎871 918. Both open daily Apr.-Sept. 9:30am-6pm; Oct.-Nov. M-Sa 10am-2pm. £2, seniors £1.50, children 75p. Combination ticket allows entry into both palaces plus Skara Brae, Maes Howe, and the Broch of Gurness. £12/£9/£4.50.)

For a contextual look at the islands' sights, check out the **Orkney Museum,** Broad St., in the center of town. Early photographs and paintings by native son Stanley Cursiter share the house and garden of an Orkney laird, or absentee landowner. (☎873 191. Open Apr.-Sept. M-Sa 10:30am-5pm, Su 2-5pm; Oct.-Mar. M-Sa 10:30am-12:30pm and 1:30-5pm. Free.) The 200-year-old **Highland Park Distillery,** 20min. south of town on Holm Rd. Highland Park, is the world's northernmost whisky distillery and purveyor of acclaimed single malts. Walk to the southern end of Broad St./Victoria St., turn west on Clay Loan, then south on Bignold Park Rd., and take the right fork onto Holm Rd. for a tour, sampling of the wares, and informative (if goofy) video at the Visitor Centre. (☎874 619; www.highlandpark.co.uk. Open Apr.-Oct. M-F 10am-5pm; May-Sept. also Sa-Su noon-5pm, last tour 4pm; Nov.-Mar. shop open M-F 1-5pm, tours 2pm. £3, concessions £2, children £1.50.)

STROMNESS ☎01856

Stromness has been a port of call for centuries, ever since the Vikings first visited its sheltered bay and named it "Hamnavoe." It grew into a prosperous fishing and whaling port, and today it remains a town of narrow cobblestone streets and beautiful open vistas overlooking the bay. The **Pier Arts Centre**, Victoria St., merits a visit to view the work of contemporary Scottish and international artists, as well as a brilliant little collection of 20th-century British artists such as Hepworth, Gabo, Wallis, Frost, and Lanyon. (☎850 209. Open Tu-Sa 10:30am-12:30pm and 1:30-5pm. Free.) The **Stromness Museum**, 52 Alfred St., tackles the history of local boating, as well as a collection of stuffed Orkney birds. (☎850 025. Open daily Apr.-Sept. 10am-5pm; Oct.-Mar. M-Sa 11am-3:30pm. £2.50, concessions £2, children 50p.)

The **Northlink Ferry** runs the *Hamnavoe* from Scrabster to Stromness (p. 680); almost everything you'll need (and almost everything in town) is on **Victoria Street,** which parallels the harbor. The **Tourist Information Centre**, in an 18th-century warehouse on the pier, provides free maps. (☎850 716. Open daily May-Sept. 8:30am-6pm; Oct.-Apr. M-F 9am-5pm, Sa 10am-12:30pm and 1:30-4pm. Open late to meet ferries.) The **Bank of Scotland**, on Victoria St., has the only **bureau de change** in town. (☎862 000. Open M-F 9:45am-12:30pm and 1:30-4:45pm, W from 10:45am.) The **library**, 2 Hellihole Rd., offers free **Internet access**. (☎850 907. Open M-F 2-5pm and 6-8pm, Sa 10am-1pm and 2-5pm.) The **post office** is at 37 Victoria St. (☎850 225. Open M-F 9am-1pm and 2-5:15pm, Sa 9am-12:30pm.) **Post Code:** KY16 3BS.

Perched above the pier, ½ mi. from the TIC, **Brown's Hostel ❶**, 45-47 Victoria St., has an easy-going atmosphere and 14 beds. (☎850 661. £2 key deposit. Dorms £9.50.) **Orca's Hotel ❸**, 76 Victoria St., offers friendly B&B-style service in the middle of town and keeps a stellar restaurant, 🍴**Bistro 76 ❸**, below. (☎/ fax 850 447; www.orcahotel.com. £21-23 per person. Bistro 76 open Tu-Sa 5-11pm.) Pricier accommodations are available at the recently refurbished 100-year-old **Stromness Hotel ❹**, at the Pier Head on Victoria St., which also has two bars and a restaurant. (☎850 289; www.thestromnesshotel.com. May-Sept. £40 per person; Apr. £35; Jan.-Mar. and Oct.-Dec. £29). The **Point of Ness Caravan and Camping Site ❶** is a mile from the pierhead. (☎873 535 or 851 235. Laundry and lounge. Open May to mid-Sept. £7.25 per caravan, £4.90 per tent. Showers 20p.) Across from the pier, **Julia's Cafe & Bistro ❶**, 20 Ferry Rd., has baked goods, vegetarian options and sandwiches (£2-5). Sunlight pours across the bay and into the bay windows. Internet access 50p per 20min. (☎850 904. Open M-Sa 9am-5pm; Easter-Sept. also Su 10am-4pm.)

OTHER MAINLAND SIGHTS ☎01856

Within the scattered mounds in the verdant fields of Orkney lie buried treasure, or 5000-year-old rock structures, at least. The unparalleled Stone Age, Bronze Age, and Viking-era tombs and dwellings around the island are the finest examples of their kind in the world. Although public transportation can be scant, there are tour buses which hit up the four main archaeological sites conveniently located between Kirkwall and Stromness: **Maes Howe Tomb, the Standing Stones of Stenness, the Ring of Brodgar, and Skara Brae.** (See **Orkney Coaches** under Local Transportation.) Reaching these sites by **bicycle** is also an option which many people opt for, but beware the harsh winds and unpredictable weather. Mainland Orkney is characteristically soft rolling farmland, but the coast is packed with sea caves, dramatic cliffs, and riotous seabirds.

If you want guidance, ranger-naturalist Michael Hartley of **Wildabout Tours** squires visitors around Mainland and Hoy in his minibus on half and full-day tours. With encyclopedic knowledge of Orkney, Michael helps visitors envision the islands of millennia past. (☎851 011/850 583; www.orknet.co.uk/wildabout. Tours daily Mar.-Oct. From £10; student and hosteler discounts.) Orkney native John Grieve leads **Discover Orkney Tours,** which crafts trips to meet your interests. (☎872 865. From £10.) John will also take you to the other islands (from £29)—a great way to see them if you lack time or transport. Both guides leave from the TICs in Kirkwall and Stromness; if you arrange ahead, will also pick you up from your ferry, plane, or accommodation. Alternatively, take one of the packaged ferry-and-tour trips (p. 680). The **Orkney Explorer Pass,** for sale at all Historic Scotland sites on Orkney, saves you several pounds on admission to top tourist attractions like Skara Brae and the Broch of Gurness. (£12, concessions £9, child £3.50.)

■ **SKARA BRAE.** Dating back 5000 years, Skara Brae was once a bustling Stone Age village. As the ocean crept farther in, waves gradually consumed the village houses; after approximately 500 years of continuous habitation, the villagers abandoned the settlement. Preserved in sand, the village slept quietly until 1850, when a violent storm ripped out the side of the cliff and revealed nine houses, a workshop, and covered town roads, all in perfect condition. While the visitors center is open only during the day, the site remains accessible until nightfall—a trip at dusk avoids tourists and the admission fee. (19 mi. NW of Kirkwall on the B9056. ☎841 815. Both open daily Apr.-Sept. 9:30am-6:30pm; Skara Brae only, Oct.-Mar. M-Sa 9am-4:30pm, Su 2-4:30pm. Skara Brae and Skaill House £4.50, seniors £3.30, children £1.30.)

RING OF BRODGAR. Six miles east of Skara Brae and 5 mi. northeast of Stromness on the B9055 stands a great circle of vertical slabs of sandstone. The sedimentary sandstones of the Ring of Brodgar may once have witnessed gatherings of local chieftains or burial ceremonies; no two archaeologists agree. Arranged in a 150 yd. circle, the 36 stones used to number 60 and were surrounded by a ditch to ward off dogs and wild predators—now filled in for the safety of visitors. The Ring has stayed true to its heritage as a venue for unusual assemblies—drawn by amber sunsets that silhouette the stones against a blazing sun, a motley crew congregates annually for the summer solstice. (Always open. Free.)

STANDING STONES OF STENNESS. Less than a mile east of the Ring on the B9055, the bern-enclosed Standing Stones of Stenness have been reduced over time to a humble few, but they are still impressive. A solitary monolith directly between the two monuments causes some to argue that Stenness and Brogdar were once part of the same ceremonial process. By 1760 only four of the original 12 stones remained—some suggest that they were knocked down by locals angered by the monument's pagan origins. (Always open. Free.)

MAES HOWE TOMB. Between Kirkwall and Stromness on the A965, this tomb may have held the bones of the area's earliest settlers (from approximately 2700 BC). Vikings arrived mid-12th century and plundered the settlement's treasures; their latter-day carvings constitute the largest collection of runic inscriptions in the world. This site enabled linguists to crack the runic alphabet and translate the profound statements: "This was carved by the greatest rune carver" and "Ingigerth is the most exquisite of women." It is wise to call ahead to reserve a spot in the tour, as they can fill up. (☎761 606; www.maeshowe.co.uk. Open daily Apr.-Sept. 9:30am-6pm; Oct.-Mar. M-Sa 9:30am-4pm, Su 2-4pm. £2.80, seniors £2, children £1.)

BROCH OF GURNESS. Off the A966 on the north coast of the Evie section of Mainland, this broch is the site of a preserved village from the Iron Age, fortuitously unearthed by the ultimate Orcadian Renaissance man, poet and antiquarian Robert Rendall in 1929. The reconstructed Pictish and Viking settlements are worth a stop on the way between towns. (☎751 414. Open Apr.-Sept. M-Su 9:30am-12:30pm and 1:30-6:30pm. £3, concessions £2.30.)

BROUGH OF BIRSAY. At the northwest tip of the mainland, this brough is a mere island at high-tide; in low tide, though, a man-made path atop the wet, rocky ground makes it accessible by foot. Those hoping to see the sights up close should check tidal charts (available at TICs and at Skara Brae, ☎841 815). The island's kirkyard holds a Pictish stone engraving of a crowned royal figure, suggesting that Orcadian kings once ruled from here. Bird-watching is absorbing, but linger too long and the puffins may become your bedfellows. (Open mid-June to Sept.; only accessible during low tide. Free.)

CHURCHILL BARRIERS AND SCAPA FLOW. At the end of the WWWI, the German High Seas Fleet was interned at **Scapa Flow,** the bay south of Houton on Mainland. The German Admiral, von Reuter, ordered all 74 of his ships be scuttled rather than remain in British hands. To the delight of scuba divers from around the world, seven of the wrecks remain. **Scapa Scuba,** Lifeboat House on Dundas St., based in Stromness, offers non-certified "try-a-dive" lessons, equipment, and a dive to the wrecks. They also offer more involved tours for experienced divers. (☎/fax 851 218. £55 per half-day.) If you don't want to get wet, **Roving Eye Enterprises** does the marine work for you via a roaming underwater camera. (☎811 360; www.orknet.co.uk/rov. Tours leave Houton Pier daily. 12:30pm and include a stop at Hoy. £25, children £12.50.) In 1939, German U-boats again entered the straits leading to the **Scapa Flow** naval anchorage during an exceptionally high tide, sinking a warship, killing 800 seamen, and escaping unscathed. The next year, Prime Minister Churchill erected massive barriers to seal the seas from attack. The POWs who built the barriers exhausted over a quarter-million tons of rock, and the barrier's **causeways** now provide access from Mainland to the smaller southeast islands.

SOUTHEAST ISLANDS. Accessible by road from Mainland, this string of islands including Lamb Holm, Burray, and South Ronaldsay, is quiet and full of wonderful craft shops and a charming organic farm hostel. On Lamb Holm, the **Italian Chapel** is all that remains of Camp 60, a prison that held several hundred Italian POWs during WWII. When not at work on the Churchill Barriers, the Italians—using only cement, corrugated iron, and shipwrecked wood—transformed their bare cement hut into a beautiful and brilliant house of worship that is still in use today. (Open daily Apr.-Sept. 9am-10pm; Oct.-Mar. 9am-4:30pm. Occasionally closed F afternoon, the traditional time for Orkney weddings. Free.) During the summer, Causeway Coaches (☎01856 831 444) chugs over the Churchill Barriers from Kirkwall to the pier at St. Margaret's Hope (3-4 per day), on the larger isle of South Ronaldsay. A fantastic tiny 8-bed hostel and organic farm, **Wheems Bothy ❶** stands on the blustery promontory of South Ronaldsay. Mike is a great source of wisdom and Christina runs a treasure of a silk-screen and feltmaking studio. Fresh eggs, produce, and cheese available, depending on the season. Call ahead and they might pick you up. (☎01856 831 537. 50p for heat. Open Apr.-Oct. Dorms £6.50.) The greatest treasure to be found on South Ronaldsay, however, is the family-run ▧**Tomb of the Eagles.** Farther south outside of St. Margaret's Hope in Isbister lies the farm of the Simison family, who own and operate the fantastic visitors center, where you can handle 5000-year-old artifacts, including marvelously intact human skulls and eagle talons. A quarter of a mile from the visitor's center is a bronze-age burnt mound, a stone dwelling with a plumbing system, and beyond that on the dramatic sea cliffs, the spectacular stone age tomb after which the property is named. The optional walk along the cliffs (not for the timid) yields curious seals and nesting seabirds. (☎831 339; www.tomboftheeagles.co.uk. Open Apr.-Oct. 9:30am-6pm; Nov.-Mar. 10am-noon or by appointment. £3.50, children £1.)

ORKNEY CRAFT TRAIL AND ARTISTS STUDIO TRAIL. Founded in the 1990s, the Orkney Craft Industry Association, a group of local artists, weavers, jewelers, woodworkers, and other artisans designed a route connecting their workshops (usually also their homes). The stops include shops of varying price ranges and styles, from **Hoxa Tapestry Gallery** in St. Margaret's Hope (☎831 395), to **Orkney Stained Glass**, on Shapinsay (☎771 276). Brown signs (sometimes faded to orange) direct drivers to hidden hamlets of tradition and creativity.

SMALLER ISLANDS

HOY. Hoy, the second-largest of the Orkney Islands (57 sq. mi.), is enormous both in its loneliness and its grandeur. From the old Norse word "Haey," meaning high island, Hoy is spectacularly hilly in the north and west (more "Highland" in character), while the south and east are lower and more fertile, like the rest of Orkney. Its most famous landmark, the ⊠**Old Man of Hoy**, is a 450 ft. sea stack of sandstone off the west coast of the island. Hikers can take the steep, well-worn footpath from the partially abandoned crofting village of Rackwick, 2 mi. away (3hr. round-trip). The North Hoy Bird Reserve offers respite for guillemots and a host of other species. Dedicated puffin-scouts should see several here during breeding season (late June to early July). The **SYHA Hoy ❶** near the pier and the eight beds of the simple **SYHA Rackwick ❶** farther south, at the start of the path toward the Old Man, offer accommodations and share a telephone number. You will need a sleeping bag at both these hostels. (☎01856 873 535. Hoy open May to mid-Sept. Rackwick open mid-Mar. to mid-Sept. Dorms £7.50, under 18 £6.50.) With only a handful of tiny stores on the island, food and supplies are difficult to procure, especially on Sundays. If you plan to stay over, bring adequate provisions. Next door the tiny isle of Flotta was the home of "that irascible and belligerent Jacobite" James Steward, who murdered Captain James Moore on Kirkwall's Broad St. A strategic military base in both World Wars, Flotta is now a quiet, flat place where you can get a 360-degree view around the isles.

SHAPINSAY. A mere 45min. from Kirkwall, with frequent ferry service, Shapinsay is the most accessible of the outer isles. Mostly wide-open space, Shapinsay's relatively flat landscape is interrupted by **Ward Hill**, the island's highest point at 210 ft. From its peak on a (rare) clear day you can see almost all the Orkney. An excellent example of the Victorian Baronial style, 19th-century **Balfour Castle** was formerly home to the influential lairds of Balfour and is now a posh guest house. Romantics can rent the castle and its chapel for weddings. For those without the curiosity or cash to see inside, the castle is perfectly visible from the ferry. (☎711 282, tours ☎872 856. Tours leave Kirkwall pier May-Sept. Su 2:15pm. £17.) **Burroughston Broch**, an Iron Age shelter, lies 5 mi. north of the ferry pier. Archaeology buffs will be thrilled by the crumbling round home, which was excavated in the 1860s. There are no hostels on Shapinsay, but the award-winning **Girnigoe B&B** (☎711 256), near the beach has rooms in the converted farmhouse. Free transport from ferry.

ROUSAY. Some will argue that Orkney's finest archaeological sights lie not on Mainland, but here on Rousay. Here the **Midhowe Broch and Cairn** has it all covered, including remnants of the Stone, Bronze, and Iron Ages. The **Knowe of Yarso Cairn** stands on a cliff overlooking Eynhallow Sound, and the **Westness Walk** winds past sites from the Neolithic, Pictish, Viking, medieval, and crofting eras. Just above the ferry terminal, a visitor center displays an exhibition on the points of interest in Rousay, and nearby Egilsay and Wyre. Stay at the **Rousay Hostel ❶** on Trumland Farm near the pier; turn left from the ferry port and walk 5min. down the main road. *(☎01856 821 252. Linen £2. Dorms £6.)*

STRONSAY. Seven miles long from hoof to snout, this island is packed with bays and beaches. Along the east coast between Lamb Ness and Odiness is the stunning Vat of Kirbister, a dramatic opening ("gloup") spanned by what is considered the finest natural arch in Orkney. Pictish settlements and an Iron Age fort can also be found on the southeastern bay. **Stronsay Fishmart ❶,** in Whitehall Village, has a cafe and interpretation center. *(☎616 386. £10, with bedding and towel £13. Open all year.)*

EDAY. The peat-covered hills of Eday hide Stone Age field walls, chambered tombs like **Vinquoy** and **Huntersquoy Cairns,** the towering **Stone of Setter,** and, on the Calf of Eday, the remnants of an Iron Age roundhouse. Other than that, the island provides standard, desolate Orkney landscape and little else. **SYHA Eday ❶,** London Bay, is on the main north-south road 4 mi. from the pier. *(☎01857 622 206. Laundry £2. Open Mar.-Oct. Dorms £8, under 18 £7 6. Camping £2.)*

SANDAY. As its name suggests, Sanday's greatest feature is its sweeping white sand beaches. Seal pups can be seen swimming at Otterswick in June, and grey seals are born on the beaches in November. Elusive otters are hard to spy, but their tell-tale tracks can be seen on the sands; five-toed prints and a trailing tail line. Besides boasting all the usual suspects, Sanday also attracts an unusual assortment of vagrant birds, including the hoopie, red-breasted flycatcher, and several types of buntings. The endless Cata Sand is a tidal white sand bay, and at low tide it is a spectacular barefoot walk out to the sea. The unexpected Orkney Angora craft shop in Upper Breckan is home to enormous white fluffy Angora rabbits, who are sheared like sheep every few months for their soft hair which is then hand spun, dyed, and knitted in the shop. *(☎600 421; www.orkneyangora.co.uk. Open daily 1:30pm-5:30pm or by arrangement.)* Dian runs ▓**Ayre's Rock Hostel and Campsite ❶,** one of the best hostels in Scotland. A meticulously kept bunkhouse with two double rooms and a family room, kitchen, towels as big and fluffy as Angora rabbits, and sunsets over the ocean. Internet access in the greenhouse-like family room, 50p per hr. *(☎600 410; www.sanday.co.uk/visitors/accomayer.html. £10, children £5.)*

WESTRAY. The largest of the outer isles is also enormous in island spirit, which makes it one of the most delightful to visit. Just west of Papa Westray, (mama) Westray features ruined **Noltland Castle** and the **Knowe O'Burristae Broch,** along with other ancient rubble and magnificent cliffs. Legend holds that the windowless castle is linked underground to the **Gentlemens' Cave,** which hid supporters of Bonnie Prince Charlie. Bird-watchers rejoice on **Noup Head Reserve,** while budget travelers welcome two top-notch hostels, which make the journey to Westray worthwhile simply for the accommodations. ▓**The Barn ❷,** Chalmersquoy, at the southern end of Pierowall village, is a thirteen-bed hostel in a wonderfully converted stone barn. *(☎01857 677 214. £11.75, children £8.80.)* ▓**Bis Geos Hostel ❶,** 2 mi. west of Pierowall on the edge of the world, so it seems, is a fabulous croft ruin-turned-hostel and cottages, complete with a sauna, laundry machines, Internet access, and heated flagstone floors. If you're lucky, handy-man Raymond might pull up some fresh crabs and lobsters from the ocean cliffs for your dinner. *(☎01857 677 420; www.bisgeos.co.uk. Open May-Sept. Dorms £9.)*

PAPA WESTRAY. "Papay," as the island is known throughout the isles, is home to a mere 60 or so Orcadians. This northern "isle of the priests" once supported an early Christian Pictish settlement. The island lies where the Atlantic Ocean and the North Sea meet, and at the right tidal moments a fearsome tidal race takes place beyond the cliffs at the northern tip. Fly from Kirkwall for £10 (overnight stay required)—if the plane makes a stop at Westray, you can put a certificate for world's shortest commercial flight on your fridge. On the west coast, the **Knap of Howar** is the location of the earliest standing house in northern Europe (c. 3500 BC), built centuries before the pyramids of Egypt. The **Bird Sanctuary** at North Hill sports Europe's largest colony of Arctic terns. Two miles north of the pier, **Beltane House ❶** is open year-round. Hostelers enjoy ensuite dorm rooms while the B&B guests get their own sitting room, but both have access to the only liquor-licensed establishment on the island—a closet full of booze. (☎644 267. Dorms £10; B&B £20 per person.) Bring enough food for at least a day.

NORTH RONALDSAY. Due to the warm Gulf Stream this northern-most island belonging to Orkney is an average of $10°F$ higher than its latitudinal neighbors. The island is not lacking in archaeological wonders, with the **Broch of Burrian**, the **Brae of Stennabreck**, and an unusual standing stone with a hole through it. Better yet, the island's famous **seaweed-eating sheep** graze on the beaches, producing coveted wool; keep you eye out for a seaweed sweater knit from North Ronaldsay yarn. Viciously protective nesting birds are all over—take a cue from them and stay at the solar and wind powered **North Ronaldsay Bird Observatory Hostel ❶**. (☎01857 633 200. Dorms £8, full board £18. Internet access available. Call ahead for a lift from the airport. Airfare to North Ronaldsay is £10 if you stay overnight.)

SHETLAND ISLANDS ☎01595

Shetland and Orkney became part of Scotland in the 15th century, when King Christian I of Denmark and Norway mortgaged them to pay for his daughter's dowry. Though their open landscapes appear similar at first, the island chains diverge in character. Shetland, closer to Norway than Great Britain, seems a country unto itself, looking to a Viking rather than Scottish heritage—an influence still apparent in Nordic craftsmanship, Scandinavian architecture, and festivals like the longship-burning **Up Helly Aa** festival (p. 59). The greatest split may not be genealogical but geological. Shetland's landscape is hauntingly severe, yet the people are memorably jovial and welcoming perhaps because of it. The discovery of oil in the 1970s, combined with their hardy crops and animals (including the Shetland pony), have turned their isolated world into an oasis of relative prosperity.

✈ GETTING THERE

Air travel is the fastest way into the Shetlands, and predictably, the most expensive. However, cheaper flights are available if you stay over a Saturday night in some cases; check with the airline. **British Airways** (☎08457 733 377) flies from **Kirkwall, Orkney** (35min.; 1 per day; round-trip £80-170). BA also flies from: **Inverness** (1½hr., 1 per day; round-trip £124-294); **Aberdeen** (1hr., M-F 3 per day, Sa-Su 2 per day; £80-110); **Edinburgh** (1½hr., 1 per day; £181-250); **Glasgow** (2½hr., M-F 2 per day, Sa-Su 1 per day; £96-200). **Shetland Travelscope** (☎696 644) and **John Leask & Son** (☎693 162; www.leaskstravel.co.uk) can get you tickets and organize your trip. All flights land at **Sumburgh Airport,** on the southern tip of Shetland's Mainland, which also has a visitor's center with a knowledgeable staff, and **Internet access** (£1 per 20min). The airport is 25 mi. (and a hefty £25-35 taxi ride) from **Lerwick,** the islands' capital and largest town. John Leask & Son buses make the journey to Lerwick (1hr.; 6 per day, £2.20). Buses arrive at the **Viking Bus Station** (☎694 100), 5min. from the city center on Commercial Rd.

Ferries are the other means of travel to the Shetlands. Though cheaper, they take far longer than flights. Most ferries arrive at **Holmsgarth Terminal,** a 20min. walk northwest of Lerwick's town center, or the smaller **Victoria Pier,** across

Going abroad?

save now!

Wireless has never been cheaper!

GSM phones starting at

$99

To order, call (858)274-2686
or visit our website

Order with affiliate code: go2004

- ✸ FREE incoming calls
- ✸ No roaming charges
- ✸ Discount international calling rates

International Cell Phones

Get the benefits of a cell phone
at the cost of a calling card.
Say goodbye to payphones and
exorbitant rental fees!

www.telestial.com

Telestial®
Wireless Solutions for Travelers™

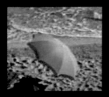  

from the TIC. **Northlink Ferries** (☎01456 000 449; www.northlinkferries.co.uk) arrive from **Aberdeen** (12-14hr.; M, W, F 7pm; Tu, Th, Sa-Su 5pm; $19-30) and **Kirkwall, Orkney** (7¾hr.; Tu, Th, Sa-Su 11:45pm; $26-39). **P&O Smyril Line** (☎690 845, www.smyril-line.com) runs May to mid-Sept. from Lerwick to **Bergen, Norway** (13½hr.; M 11:30pm; $72) and to **Iceland** (31hr., W 2am, $144, with car from $184) via the **Faroe Islands** (13hr., $72). Call ahead for prices and times in low season.

LOCAL TRANSPORTATION

As with Orkney, it is worth renting a car to fully appreciate Shetland; Infrequent public transport makes getting around difficult. Try **Leask & Son** (see above), the more extensive **Bolts Car Hire**, 26 North Rd. (☎693 636, airport branch 01950 460 777; www.boltscarhire.co.uk; 21 and over; $25-35 per day) or **Grantfield Garage**, 44 North Rd. (☎692 709; www.grantfieldgarage.co.uk; 25 and over; $28 per day). Travel between the islands is heavily subsidized; ferries sail to the larger islands nearly every hr., to the smaller islands at least once a day, and no trip costs more than $5. All except those to Fair Isle transport bikes for free. Shetland's main **bus** lines are **John Leask & Son** (☎693 162) and **Whites Coaches** (☎809 443). The TIC stocks the vital *Shetland Transport Timetable* ($1) with bus, ferry, and plane schedules. **Eric Brown's Cycle Hire,** on the second floor of Grantfield Garage, rents touring bikes. (☎692 709. $7.50 per day, $45 per week. Helmets $2. Open M-W 8am-9pm, Th-Sa 8am-10pm, Su 11am-9pm.) Winds and hills can make biking difficult.

Tour companies offer convenient ways of seeing Shetland. Most affordable are the **Leasks Coach Tours,** on the Esplanade in Lerwick. (☎693 162. Mainland tours W, Su $9, Yell and Unst W $25.) Dr. Jonathan Wills runs ◙**Seabirds-and-Seals,** a 3hr. tour which includes cliffs, caves, and wildlife. Tea and coffee served on deck. (☎693 434; www.seabirds-and-seals.com. $30. May-Aug. trips depart from Victoria Pier, Lerwick, at 9:30am, 2pm, and mid-May to mid-July 7:15pm.) **See Shetland Tours** offers pre-arranged and custom-designed itineraries. (☎01595 690 777; ask for Sarah McBurnie. Mainland tours $40, half-day $30; outer islands $30/$55.) Other options include the folklore-oriented **Island Trails** with local Elma Johnson (☎01950 422 408; May-Sept.) and **Shetland Wildlife Tours** (☎01950 422 483).

ORIENTATION AND PRACTICAL INFORMATION

Lerwick is on the eastern coast of Mainland, served by the A970, which runs the island's length. The **Tourist Information Centre,** Market Cross, books beds anywhere in the islands for a $3 charge plus a 10% deposit. (☎693 434; www.visitshetland.com. Open May-Sept. M-F 8am-6pm, Sa 8am-4pm, Su 10am-1pm; Oct.-Apr. M-F 9am-5pm.) Other services include: **Royal Bank of Scotland,** 81 Commercial St. (☎694 520; open M-Tu and Th-F 9:15am-4:45pm, W 10am-4:45pm); free **Internet access** in the left wing of the **Shetland Library,** in the converted church on Lower Hillhead (☎693 868; open M and W-Th 10am-7pm; Tu and F-Sa 10am-

5pm). Send a postcard from the end of the earth at the **post office,** 46-50 Commercial St. (☎08457 223 344; open M-F 9am-5pm, Sa 9am-12:30pm.) **Post Code:** ZE1 0AA.

ACCOMMODATIONS

The community-run 🌑 **SYHA Lerwick ❷,** in the stately Islesburgh House, at King Harald St. and Union St., is perhaps the finest SYHA hostel you'll come across. Excellent modern facilities, a popular cafe with a view of the bowling green and gardens. Bruce, the warden, is the man to talk to about anything Shetland. (☎692 114. Laundry £1. Reception 9am-4:30pm, and 9:45-10:15pm; at other times try the Community Centre next door. Curfew 11:45pm. Open Apr.-Sept. Dorms £11, under 18 £9.50. MC/V.) A mid-range option is the **Glen Orchy Guest House ❹,** 20 Knab Rd., a comfortable B&B overlooking Breiwick Bay that seems more like a hotel. (☎692 031. Singles £43; doubles £68. MC/V.) High-end hotels in town include the indulgent **Kveldsro House ❺,** Greenfield Pl., which boasts (and charges for) a harbor view. (☎692 195. Singles £70; doubles £94. AmEx/MC/V.) Lifelong Shetlander **Mrs. Laurenson ❷,** 4 Sands of Sound, runs a quiet B&B overlooking the ocean, a 20min. walk south from Lerwick. (☎696 799. £20-22.) There are three **campgrounds** on Mainland, but you can pitch almost anywhere with the landowner's permission. **Clickimin Caravan and Camp Site ❶** is closest to the Lerwick ferry terminal; turn left on Holmsgarth Rd. (the A970), go through the roundabout, and turn right on North Lochside. (☎741 000. Showers and laundry, pool, bar, cafe. Reception 8:30am-10pm. Open May-Sept. Pitches £6.20-9.40. MC/V.)

Camping **böds ❶** (Old Norse for "barns") are a very basic alternative. Böds are converted fishing cottages now serving as "camping barns." They are described and pictured in *Shetland Camping Böds*, free at the TIC, or at www.camping-bods.co.uk. Mainland's four böds are available Apr.-Sept.: **Betty Mouat's** near the airport (with hot water and showers), **The Sail Loft** next to the pier in Voe, the **Voe House** in Walls, and **Johnnie Notions** at Hamnavoe, Eshaness, in the extreme northeast. **Grieve House** is on tiny Whalsay, near Lerwick by bus. The **Windhouse Lodge,** on Yell, is better equipped. All böds cost £5 per night and must be booked in advance through the Lerwick TIC. Bring a sleeping bag, camping stove, cooking utensils, and coins for electricity (when available).

FOOD AND PUBS

Inexpensive eats cluster in the center of **Lerwick.** Stock up on **groceries** at **D.G. Leslie's.** (☎693 073. Open M-Sa 8am-7pm, Su 10am-7pm.) Jivin' **Osla's Cafe ❶,** on the Esplanade, specializes in pancakes that are worth a stop, no matter what time of day. (☎696 005. Open M-W 9:30am-7pm, Th-Sa 9:30am-8:30pm, Su 11am-5pm.) Also on the Esplanade, the **Peerie Shop Cafe ❶** serves sandwiches, baked goods, and organic cider in a bright, lively setting. The special hot chocolate is sinful. Funky woollens and crafts sold in next door shop by the same name. (☎692 817. Open M-Sa 9am-6pm.) **Raba ❸,** 26 Commercial Rd., offers traditional Indian cuisine in a traditional atmosphere—the all-you-can-eat Sunday buffet is £8.50. (☎695 554. Open M-Sa noon-2pm and 5pm-midnight, Su noon-11pm) The **Great Wall ❸,** Viking Bus Station, Commercial Rd., serves decent Chinese and Thai food. (☎696 344 for takeaway, ☎693 988 for restaurant. Open M-F noon-2pm and 4:30-11:30pm, Sa noon-11:30pm, Su 1-11:30pm.) For some, Lerwick's most convenient food awaits at the **Islesburgh Community Centre Cafe ❶,** on the first floor of the hostel. (☎692 114. Open M-Th 11am-9pm, F-Sa 11am-5pm.) The **Lounge,** 4 Mounthooly St., is the town's busiest pub; the downstairs is the main hangout each night and the upstairs is thick with smoke and lively Shetland fiddling. Folks bring their own music-makers to the live sessions on Saturday afternoons and some Wednesday nights. (☎692 231. Open M-Sa 11am-1am.) A friendly, eccentric crowd fills **Thule Bar,** near the ferry docks. (☎692 508. Open M-Sa 11am-1am, Su 12:30pm-1am.) **Captain Flint's,** across from the small harbor, has live music and is a popular hangout for locals and backpackers alike. (Open M-Sa 8am-1am, Su 12:30pm-1am.)

SHOPPING

Logically enough, Shetland is one of the best places in the world to buy ▨**Shetland wool.** Huge piles of cheap sweaters (£11-22) collect at the **Judane Shetland Limited Knitwear Factory,** Blackhill Mills, Gremista Industrial Estate, 1½ mi. north of Lerwick on the A970, opposite the factory stack. Just let yourself in and ask if you can buy anything. (☎693 724. Open M-F 8:30am-5pm, Sa 8:30am-3pm.) **Anderson & Co,** in the center of Lerwick at Market Cross, also has warehouse prices. (693 714. Open M-Sa 9am-5pm.) To avoid paying high prices in tourist shops, get bargains upstairs at the **Shetland Woollen Company,** 68 Commercial St., where you can nab leftover sweaters for as low as £5. (☎693 610. Open M-Sa 9am-5pm.) There are also branches in Sandwick, Yell, and Scalloway. **The Spider's Web,** 41 Commercial St., opposite the Queens Hotel, showcases its members' high-quality knitwork. (☎695 246. Open M-Sa 9am-5pm; also Su if there is a cruise ship in port.) On northerly **Unst,** you can simultaneously shop for knits and enjoy apple pie at **NorNova Knitwear** in Muness. (☎01957 755 373. Open daily 10am-4pm.)

MAINLAND SIGHTS

LERWICK. Shetland's capital began as a small fishing town in the 17th century. Weather permitting, you can cruise around the bay on the ▨**Dim Riv,** a full-scale replica of a Viking longship that launches one evening per week in the summer. (☎693 471. Book ahead at the TIC. Cruises £5, children £2.50.) Not much of a sight in itself, the giant pentagonal **Fort Charlotte,** just off Commercial Rd. at the north end of town, offers the best views of Lerwick and its harbor. (Open daily 9am-10pm. Free.) Many a Lerwick youth steals their first kiss up at the **Knab,** a short walk south out of town along Knab Rd. Only a mile west of the city center on Clickimin Rd., the ruins of **Clickimin Broch,** a stronghold from the 4th century BC, loom out of the loch and still look tough enough to repel invaders. (Always open. Free.) Shetland's Norse heritage is on display in longship form at the **Up-Helly-Aa'**

UP HELLY AA

It has been nearly a millennium since the Vikings set sail in their sleek longships to conquer the Shetland Isles, but the wild Norsemen of Lerwick still party like, well, like Vikings. In the endless darkness of the last Tuesday of January, a thousand or so revelers bearing shields and torches bedeck themselves in the sartorial splendor of their Nordic ancestors—animal skins, armor, and horned helmets. The *guizers,* or revelers, elect a Shetlander each year to be the presiding Guizer Jarl (Earl), who organizes the event. On the morning of Up Helly Aa, a proclamation known as "The Bill" is nailed to the Market Cross in the center of Lerwick, which contains the year's best gossip and local humor. That night the guizers march through the streets bearing a meticulously reconstructed 30 ft. Viking longship (galley), which they eventually attack with burning torches to welcome the springtime daylight, singing the traditional song "The Norseman's Home."

The blazing pyre signals just the beginning of the festivities, and the procession then dashes off to the first of a dozen halls where the guizer squads perform with song and dance until dawn. The next day is a public holiday in Lerwick, and the streets are deserted while the town recovers from the previous night's merriment. *(Visitors welcome; call the Lerwick TIC ☎01595 693 434; www.shetland-tourism.co.uk.)*

Exhibition in the **Galley Shed,** Saint Sunniva St., Lerwick. (Open mid-May to Sept. Tu and Sa 2-4pm, Tu and F 7-9pm. ₤3, concessions ₤1.) The **Shetland Museum,** across from the library building on Lower Hillhead, traces local archaeology and crofting and fishing history on a single, well-designed floor. (☎695 057; www.shetland-museum.org.uk. Open M, W, F 10am-7pm, Tu, Th, Sa 10am-5pm. Free.)

SCALLOWAY. Though Scalloway was Shetland's capital in the 17th century and is still a busy fishing port 7 mi. west of Lerwick, there's not much to see here today. The crumbling edifice of **Scalloway Castle** was once home to villainous Earl Patrick Stewart, later becoming the sheriff's headquarters. Get the key from the Shetland Woolen Company (p. 691) or the Scalloway Hotel. (☎01446 793 191. Castle open M-Sa 9:30am-5pm, Su by appointment only. Free.) ◙**Da Haaf Restaurant ❶** North Atlantic Fisheries College, in the harbor, has the best fish and chips on the island without a doubt. Call to reserve a table—locals and tourists alike flock to the spot. (☎880 747. Open M-F 12:30-2pm and 5-8pm.) **John Leask & Son** sends buses from Lerwick (☎693 162; M-Sa 8 per day, round-trip ₤1.20).

JARLSHOF AND SOUTH MAINLAND. At the southern tip of Mainland, southwest of Sumburgh Airport, **Jarlshof** is one of northern Europe's most remarkable archaeological sites. Layers of human settlement have accumulated here from Neolithic times to the Renaissance. In 1896 a storm uncovered the tangle of stone walls and artifacts, some over 4000 years old. (☎460 112. Open daily Apr.-Sept. 9:30am-6:30pm, last admission 6pm. ₤3, seniors ₤2.20, children ₤1.50.) A mile up the road, the **Old Scatness Broch** is the site of ongoing excavation. Remains were discovered in 1975 during airport construction; since then an entire Iron Age village and over 20,000 artifacts have surfaced. A guided tour explains with re-enactments. (☎694 688. Open July to mid-Aug. M-Th 10am-5pm, Sa-Su 10:30am-5:30pm. ₤2, under 16 ₤1.) On nearby **Sumburgh Head,** thousands of gulls, guillemots, and puffins rear their young on steep cliff walls. All South Mainland sights can be reached by the **Leasks bus** that runs to Sumburgh Airport from Lerwick (☎693 162). Four miles north of the airport, the ◙**Croft House Museum,** signposted off the main A970, is the best example of a working croft house, barn, mill, and byre from the 19th century. (☎01950 460 557. Open daily May-Sept. 10am-1pm and 2-5pm. Free.)

NORTH MAINLAND. Also called Northmavine, the northern part of Mainland has the wildest and most deserted coastal scenery in Shetland. At **Mavis Grind,** northwest of Brae, the 100-yard-wide isthmus is flanked by the Atlantic Ocean and the North Sea. Farther northwest stand the imposing volcanic sea-cliffs on ◙**Eshaness.** The standing arch of **Dore Holm** sits in the northwest. ◙**Da Bod Cafe ❷** on the waterfront in Hillswick serves outstanding home-grown vegetarian food, and funds go to the seal and otter sanctuary. (☎01806 503 348. Open May Sa-Su 11am-late, June-Sept. daily 11am-late.) On Sundays, when buses and ferries are rare, **John Leask & Son** runs three different tours of north Mainland. (☎693 162. ₤9.)

🔝 SMALLER ISLANDS

BRESSAY AND NOSS. Hourly ferries (☎980 317; 5min., ₤1.50) sail from Lerwick to Bressay. Hike to the summit of conical **Ward of Bressay,** referred to by natives as "Da Wart" (742 ft.), for a sweeping view of the sea. From Bressay's east coast, 3 mi. past the Lerwick ferry port (follow the "To Noss" signs), dinghies go to the tiny isle of **Noss;** stand at the "Wait Here" sign and wave to flag one down. Great skuas team up with arctic terns to dive-bomb you at the **bird sanctuary;** wave a hat, or stick over your head to ward them off. (National Nature Reserve ☎ 693 345. Mid-May to Aug. Tu-W and F-Su 10am-5pm. Round-trip £3, concessions £1.50. Noss is open to visitors Tu-W and F-Su 10am-5pm; overnight stays are forbidden.)

MOUSA. The tiny, uninhabited island of Mousa, just off the east coast of Mainland, is famous for its 6000 pairs of the miniscule nocturnal Storm Petrels. It also holds the world's best preserved Iron Age **broch,** a 50 ft. drystone fortress that has endured 1000 years of Arctic storms. Flashlights are provided to help you climb the staircase onto the broch's roof. Catch a Sumburgh-bound Leask bus in Lerwick and ask the driver to let you off at the Setter Junction for Sandsayre (round-trip £5); it's a 15min. walk from there to the ferry. (☎ 01950 431 367. Ferry departs mid-Apr. to mid-Sept. M-Th and Sa noon, F and Su 12:30 and 2pm. £7, children £3.50.) On summer weekdays, **Leask Coach Tours** leads tours of Mousa, leaving from the Lerwick Esplanade. (☎ 693 162. M 9:30am and 5:30pm; £12, includes ferry.)

ST. NINIAN'S ISLE. Off the southwest coast of Mainland, an unusual **tombolo**—a beach surrounded on both sides by the sea—links St. Ninian's Isle to Mainland, just outside of **Bigton.** Inhabited from the Iron Age to the late 18th century and site of an early monastery, the isle is now home to a ruined church, rabbits and sheep. It achieved brief fame in 1958 when a hoard of silver was discovered here. The island is difficult to reach: a **bus** bound for Sumburgh departs Lerwick twice a day (noon and 5:40pm) to meet a shuttle that goes to Bigton; the Lerwick-bound bus returns via Bigton (departs Bigton 8am and 1:50pm). In order to visit St. Ninian's in a day—necessary, since there are no accommodations—the carless have to take the noon bus from Lerwick to Bigton, and the 1:50pm bus from Bigton to Lerwick, allowing about 1¼hr. to explore the beach and island.

YELL. The gateway to the Northern Isles, Yell is famous for its otters and its long, uninhabited coastline. If you tire of wildlife-watching, head for the north end of the main road at **Gloup;** a 3 mi. hike from here takes you to the desolate eastern coast. The remains of an **Iron Age fort** on the Burgi Geos promontory have held on to a perfect defensive position—jagged outcroppings face the sea and a 3 ft. ridge leads between cliffs to Mainland. Killer whales are occasionally spotted in **Bluemull Sound** between Yell and Unst. **Ferries** run from Toft on Mainland to Ulsta on Yell (20min., 1-2 per hr., £1.50).

UNST. Unst is home to the northernmost everything in Britain. Its landscape is quite different from Yell; at just 12 mi. long and 5 mi. wide, the island boasts stupendous cliffs and jagged sea stacks. **Muness Castle** was built in the late 16th century. (Free. Open all year.) At **Haroldswick Beach,** gannets dive into the ocean near crumbling, abandoned air-raid shelters. The celebrated bird reserve at **Hermaness** is graced by a pair of black-browed albatrosses and countless puffins. Ferries from Belmont (Unst) and Gutcher (northern Yell) divert routinely to Oddsta on the island of **Fetlar,** where birdwatchers view the crimson-tailed finch. To get to Unst, take a **ferry** from **Gutcher** to **Belmont** (10min., 1-2 per hr., £1.40). A daily **Leask** bus leaves Lerwick at 7:50am (M-F) and 3:45pm (Th) and connects with ferries to Haroldswick on Unst (2¼hr.). The Baltasound **post office** (open M-Tu and F 9am-1pm and 2-5:30pm, W 9am-1pm and 2-4:30pm, Th and Sa 9am-1pm) features Britain's northernmost **Post Code:** ZE2 9DP.

The **Leask** bus stops along the way at **Gardiesfauld Hostel ❶,** in Uyeasound in the south of Unst, where you'll find a gorgeous coastal view. (☎ 01957 755 240. No smoking, no pets, and no alcohol. Dorms £10, under 16 £8, tents £6. Open April-Sept. Cash only.) Only one bus runs by the hostel daily, it's easy to get stranded for the day. Those without private means of transport should consider riding the bus to Unst's main town, **Baltasound,** which has a few **B&Bs.**

HIGHLANDS AND ISLANDS

OTHER ISLANDS. Shetland's outer islands are the most isolated in Britain. **Planes** depart for the islands from **Tingwall** on Mainland, but **ferries** are cheaper. Rooms and transport are hard to find; book several weeks ahead. Bring supplies to last at least a week, as ferries often do not operate in inclement weather. Many ferries run from **Walls, Vidlin,** and **Laxo** on Mainland, which can be reached by bus from Lerwick (generally under 1hr.; consult the *Shetland Transport Timetable*).

Whalsay (pop. 1000) was called "whale island" by the Norse; no wonder, as it is the center of the Shetland fishing industry. The prosperous fishing isle is accessible by bus and ferry from Lerwick and home to coastal walks and stone age relics. The impressive **Symbister House** is one of the best examples of Georgian architecture in the north of Scotland. The **Out Skerries** support 80 hardy fishermen. Planes (☎840 246; M and W-Th 2 per day, £20) arrive from Tingwall, while ferries converge from Lerwick (30min., 2 per hr., £1.40) and Vidlin (1½hr., 10 per week). **Papa Stour's** (pop. 24) frothy coastline features sea-flooded cliff arches, and used to house a colony of "lepers" on the southwest side of the isle. As it turns out, the poor folk simply suffered from terrible malnutrition and vitamin deficiencies from bad diets. A backpackers-style accommodation is available in **Hurdiback ❶** (☎873 229. May-Sept. £10, under 16, £8.50. Cash only.) To get to Papa Stour, fly (Tu only, £16) or sail (☎810 460; book ahead; 7 per week, £2.15) from Tingwall.

Far to the west, rugged **Foula** is home to 40 humans, 2000 sheep, and the highest sheer cliff in Britain (1220 ft.). Barely Scottish, the inhabitants of Foula had their own monarch until the late 17th century, spoke the now-extinct Nordic language of Norn until 1926, and still celebrate Christmas and Easter according to the now-defunct Julian calendar. From April to October, **ferries** (☎753 254) drift from Walls (Tu, Th, and Sa; £2.40) and Scalloway (every other Th, £2.40), while **planes** (☎840 246) fly from Tingwall (1¼hr., 4-5 per week, £21.80).

Fair Isle, midway between Shetland and Orkney, home to the Fair Isle knitting patterns and 70 self-sufficient souls, is billed as the most remote island in Britain. In summer, a **ferry** (☎760 222) braves the North Sea every other Th from Lerwick, and Tuesday and every other Thursday from Grutness (Apr.-Sept., £3). **Planes** (☎840 246) depart from Tingwall (25min.; Apr. to mid-Oct. M, W, F 2 per day; May to mid-Oct. also Sa 1 per day; £38) and Sumburgh (May-Oct. Sa, £38). Unusual but ideal accommodation for birdwatchers is available at the **Bird Observatory Lodge ❸.** (☎760 258; www.fairislebirdobs.co.uk. Open Apr.-Oct. Full board £30-42. Free guided walks.)

🌺 FESTIVALS

Shetland's remoteness, endless daylight in the summer, and endless darkness in the winter make festivals something to look forward to for natives and visitors alike. The TIC is an excellent source for information on the plethora of unique Shetland activities. The **Shetland Folk Festival** (☎741 000; www.sffs.shetland.co.uk), from the 29th of April through the 2nd of May, lures fiddlers from around the world, while the **Shetland Fiddle and Accordion Festival** takes place in Lerwick in mid-October; call the TIC for details. The wild annual **Up Helly Aa Festival** (www.uphellyaa.com), is held in Lerwick the last Tuesday in January (see sidebar). Dating from the Victorian era but with roots in ancient Norse Yule-tide merry-making, the festival exuberantly celebrates Viking heritage, beginning with a review of the year's juiciest gossip and ending with the ceremonial torching of a Viking longship. Shetlanders plan months in advance for this light-bearing event—after the bonfire dies out, blackness settles in again (with only short reprieves of daylight) until late spring. The 2005 **Island Games** will be held in Shetland.

NORTHERN IRELAND

 The phone code for all of Northern Ireland is **028.**

Media headlines screaming about riots and bombs have long overshadowed the typically calm tenor of life in Northern Ireland. In reality, acts of violence and extremist fringe groups are less visible than the division in civil society that sends Protestants and Catholics to separate neighborhoods, separate stores, separate pubs, and often separate schools, with separate, though similar, traditional songs and slang. The 1998 Good Friday Agreement, an attempt to lead Northern Ireland out of its struggles, has itself been a long journey. The Assembly has been suspended a number of times and the lack of progress on various emotional issues continues to frustrate. London has had to take the reins again, while all sides have renewed their efforts to make their country as peaceful as it is beautiful.

Belfast's bursting nightlife gives way to the thatched-cottage fishing villages dotting the strands of the Ards Peninsula, which leads to the rounded peaks of the Mournes and the park retreats of Newcastle. The waterfalls and valleys of the glorious Glens of Antrim lie to the north; nearby, the eighth wonder of the world, the Giant's Causeway, a volcanic staircase, extends out to the Atlantic. The west offers the easily accessible Sperrin Mountains and the tidy-walled farms of the Fermanagh Lake District. Industrial Enniskillen looms just north, though travelers would do well to continue to Derry, a city rich in both political and historical significance. If this brief taste of the North whets your appetite, find expanded coverage in ▣*Let's Go: Ireland 2005.*.

HIGHLIGHTS OF NORTHERN IRELAND

BELFAST. Discover compelling political murals on a black cab tour (p. 700).

GLENS OF ANTRIM. Stroll through tiny villages tucked among the mountains, forests, and lush valleys, then hike along the nearby coast (p. 713).

GIANT'S CAUSEWAY. Marvel at 60-million-year-old volcanic rock formations, the stuff of Irish myth and legend (p. 716).

MONEY. The British pound is legal tender in Northern Ireland. Northern Ireland issues its own bank notes, which are equal in value to their British counterparts, but aren't accepted outside Northern Ireland. All British notes, including Scottish bills, are accepted in the North. Euros are generally not accepted in the North, with the exception of some border towns, where shopkeepers will calculate the exchange rate and add a surcharge.

SAFETY AND SECURITY. Although sectarian violence is now dramatically less common than during the Troubles (p. 697), some neighborhoods and towns still experience turmoil during sensitive political times. It's best to remain cautious during **Marching Season,** July 4-12 (see **Orange Day,** p. 696). August 12, when the

Apprentice Boys march in Derry, is also a testy period. In general, be prepared for transport delays and for shops and services to be closed at these times. Vacation areas such as the Glens and the Causeway Coast are less affected, and overall, Northern Ireland has one of the lowest tourist-related crime rates in the world

Border checkpoints have been removed, and armed soldiers and vehicles are less visible in Belfast and Derry than they once were. **Do not take photographs** of soldiers, military installations, or military vehicles: your film will be confiscated and you may be detained for questioning. Taking pictures of political murals is permissible, though many feel uncomfortable doing so in residential areas. Unattended luggage is always considered suspicious and confiscation-worthy. Hitching is generally unsafe in Northern Ireland. *Let's Go* never recommends hitchhiking.

LIFE AND TIMES

Throughout its turbulent history, the people of Northern Ireland have remained steadfast in their determination to retain their individual cultural and political identities, even at the cost of lasting peace. Many continue to defend the lines that define their differences, along both ideological divisions in the chambers of Parliament an actual city streets. The North's 950,000 Protestants are generally **Unionists,** who want the six counties of Northern Ireland to remain part of the UK; the 650,000 Catholics, however, tend to identify with the Republic of Ireland, not Britain, and many are **Nationalists,** who want the North to join the Republic. The more extreme, and generally working-class, members of either side are known as **Loyalists** and **Republicans,** respectively, or rather, those who throw rocks and those who throw petrol bombs. This brief history surveys the origins of the modern-day troubles (and Troubles) in the North. For cultural and historical context, see p. 722.

A DIVIDED ISLAND. The 17th century's **Ulster Plantation** scattered English and Scottish settlers in the island's northeast, on what had been Gaelic-Irish land. French Protestants sought refuge in Ulster, as did merchants and working-class immigrants from nearby Scotland. Institutionalized religious discrimination limited Catholic access to land ownership and other basic rights, but made the North an attractive destination for Scottish Protestants, who profited from cheap land options. Over 300 years, the Ulster Plantation created a working- and middle-class population that identified with the British Empire and didn't support Home Rule. The **Orange Order**—named for William of Orange, who deposed arch-nemesis Catholic James II in the late 1680s—organized Protestants in local lodges. They ordained July 12th a holiday—**Orange Day**—on which to hold parades celebrating William's victory at the **Battle of the Boyne.** The Order's constituency and radicalism continued to grow despite legislative disapproval, culminating in explosive opposition to the first Home Rule Bill in 1886 (p. 74).

Lawyer and politician **Edward Carson,** with trusty sidekick **James Craig,** advocated against Home Rule and sought to make the British elite better understand the arguments against it. In 1914, when Home Rule seemed likely, Carson held a mass meeting, and Unionists signed the **Ulster Covenant of Resistance to Home Rule.** As Home Rule began to appear imminent, the Unionist **Ulster Volunteer Force** (**UVF;** see p. 727) armed itself. WWI gave Unionists more time to organize and made British leaders realize that the imposition of Home Rule on Ulster would wreak havoc: it would prompt the UVF to pair off against the **Irish Republican Army** (**IRA;** see p. 728), who in turn would fight the governing body. The **1920 Government of Ireland Act** created two parliaments for the North and South. Though the measure went nowhere in the south and was superseded by the **Anglo-Irish Treaty and Civil War,** it became the basis of the Northern government until 1973. The new Parliament met at **Stormont,** near Belfast.

Northern Ireland

The new statelet encompassed only six of the nine counties of Ulster, excluding Catholic Donegal, Monaghan, and Cavan. This arrangement suited the Protestants in the six counties but threatened the Protestant Unionists living elsewhere on the island and the Catholic Nationalists living within the new Ulster. Orange Lodges and other strongly Protestant groups continued to control politics, and the Catholic minority boycotted elections; anti-Catholic discrimination was widespread. **WWII** gave Unionists a chance to show their loyalty—the Republic stayed neutral while the North welcomed Allied troops and airforce bases. Warship-building invigorated Belfast and allowed Catholics to enter the industrial workforce for the first time. Over the following two decades, a grateful British Parliament poured money into loyal little Northern Ireland. Yet discrimination persisted: the Stormont government neglected to institute social reform, and parliamentary districts were unequally drawn to favor Protestants. In 1949, the Republic was officially established and the **Ireland Act** defined the position of Northern Ireland within the UK. As the Republic gained a surer footing, violence (barring the occasional border skirmish) receded on the island.

THE TROUBLES. As time went on the economy grew, but bigotry and resentment festered. The American civil rights movement inspired the 1967 founding of the **Northern Ireland Civil Rights Association (NICRA),** which worked to end anti-Catholic discrimination in public housing. Protestant extremists arose in response, including the acerbic **Reverend Ian Paisley,** whose **Ulster Protestant Volunteers (UPV)** overlapped in membership with the paramilitary UVF, which had been outlawed. The first NICRA march was raucous but nonviolent. However, the second, held in Derry in 1968, was a bloody mess, disrupted by Unionists and then by the water cannons of the **Royal Ulster Constabulary (RUC),** the north's Protestant police force.

John Hume and Protestant **Ivan Cooper** formed a new civil rights committee in Derry, but were overshadowed by Bernadette Devlin's radical, student-led **People's Democracy (PD).** The PD encouraged (and NICRA opposed) a four-day march from Belfast to Derry starting on New Year's Day, 1969. The RUC's physical assault on Derry's Catholic Bogside once the marchers arrived caused the Derry authorities to bar the RUC from the Bogside, making the area **Free Derry.** On August 12, Catholics threw rocks at the annual Apprentice Boys parade along the city walls. The RUC attacked Bogside residents, and a two-day siege ensued. Free Derry remained independent, and the violence proved that the RUC alone could not maintain order. The British Army arrived—and hasn't left yet.

Between 1970 and 1972, concessions and crackdowns were alternately instituted, to little effect. The rejuvenated IRA split: while the "Official" faction faded into insignificance, the **Provisional IRA,** or **Provos** (today's IRA), faltered ideologically but gained guns. In 1970, John Hume founded the **Social Democratic and Labour Party (SDLP),** with the intention of bringing about social change through the support of both Catholics and Protestants; by 1973, it had become the moderate voice of Northern Catholics. But violent strife continued. On January 30, 1972, British troops fired into a crowd of nonviolent protesters in Derry, and 14 Catholics were killed. The British government's reluctance to investigate this **Bloody Sunday** increased Catholic outrage.

Soon after, the British embassy in Dublin was torched, and the IRA bombed a British army barracks. After further bombings in 1973, the Stormont government was replaced by the **Sunningdale Executive,** which split power between Catholics and Protestants. This move was immediately crippled by a massive Unionist work stoppage, and **direct British rule** began. In 1978, 300 Nationalist prisoners began a campaign to have their classification as political prisoners restored. The movement culminated in the ten-man **hunger strike** of 1981. **Bobby Sands** was elected to Parliament from a Catholic district in Fermanagh while leading it. Sands died after 66 days and became a martyr; his face is still seen on murals in the Falls section of Belfast (p. 706). The remaining prisoners officially ended the strike seven months and two days after it began.

The hunger strikes galvanized Nationalists, and support for **Sinn Féin,** the political arm of the IRA, surged. In 1985, British Prime Minister Margaret Thatcher and Taoiseach Garret FitzGerald signed the **Anglo-Irish Agreement,** granting the Republic of Ireland (p. 722) a "consultative role" but no legal authority in the governance of Northern Ireland. Relations between London and Dublin improved, but extremists on both sides were infuriated. In 1992, the **Brooke Initiative** led to the first multiparty talks in the North in over a decade. The **Downing Street Declaration,** issued at the end of 1993 by Prime Minister John Major and Taoiseach Albert Reynolds, invited the IRA to participate in talks if it refrained from violence for three months.

THE 1994 CEASE-FIRE. On August 31, 1994, the IRA announced a complete cessation of violence, while Loyalist guerillas cooperated with their own cease-fire. **Gerry Adams,** Sinn Féin's leader, called for talks with the British government. The peace held for over a year. In February 1995, John Major and Irish Prime Minister John Bruton issued the **joint framework** proposal, which suggested a Northern Ireland Assembly that would include the "harmonizing powers" of the Irish and British governments and the right of the people of Northern Ireland to choose their own destiny. Subsequently, the British government began talks with Loyalists and, for the first time, Sinn Féin. Disarmament was the most prominent problem—both sides refused to put down their guns.

Though the IRA ended their cease-fire on February 9, 1996, with the bombing of a London office building, peace talks persisted. Sinn Féin refused to participate because they could not agree to totally disarm. Their credibility was jeopardized on June 15, 1996, when a blast in Manchester injured more than 200 people.

In October 1996, the IRA bombed the British army headquarters in Belfast, killing one soldier and injuring 30. In early 1997, the IRA tried to influence upcoming British elections with bomb threats; thoroughly angered, John Major condemned Sinn Féin. The Labour party swept the elections and **Tony Blair** became Prime Minister. Sinn Féin also made an impressive showing: Gerry Adams and Martin McGuinness won seats in Parliament, but refused to swear allegiance to the Queen and were subsequently barred from taking their places. The government ended its ban on talks with the still-uncooperative organization, but hopes for a cease-fire were dashed when a prominent Republican's car was bombed; in retaliation, the IRA shot two members of the RUC.

THE GOOD FRIDAY AGREEMENT. On July 19, the IRA announced an "unequivocal" cease-fire to start the following day, and in September 1997, Sinn Féin joined peace talks. The **Ulster Unionist Party (UUP),** the voice of moderate Protestants, joined shortly thereafter. In January 1998, another dozen lives were lost to extremism. After two Protestants were killed in early February, Unionist leaders charged Sinn Féin with breaking its pledge to support peaceful actions and tried to oust party leaders from the talks. Foreign facilitators continued to push for progress.

The delegates approved a draft of the **1998 Northern Ireland Peace Agreement** (the **Good Friday Agreement**) on April 11. The pact asserted that change in the North could come only with the consent of its citizens and declared that the people must determine individually whether to identify as Irish, British, or both. On May 22, in the first island-wide vote since 1918, the Agreement was made law, approved by a resounding majority (71% of the North and 94% of the Republic). It divided the governing of Northern Ireland three ways. The main body is a 108-member **Northern Ireland Assembly;** the second, a **North-South Ministerial Council,** serves as the cross-border authority; and the final strand, the **British-Irish Council,** approaches similar issues on a broader scale, concerning itself with the entirety of the British Isles. On June 25, the UUP and the SDLP won the most seats, while Sinn Féin garnered more support than ever before.

Then, on August 15, a bombing in religiously mixed **Omagh** killed 29 people and injured 382. A splinter group calling itself the **"Real IRA"** claimed responsibility; their obvious motive was to undermine the Good Friday Agreement. Sinn Féin's Gerry Adams unreservedly condemned the bombing. In October, Catholic John Hume and Protestant David Trimble received the Nobel Peace Prize for their participation in the peace process. The coming year, however, was full of disappointments. The formation of the Northern Ireland Assembly was marred by disagreement over disarmament and the release of political prisoners, and it was ultimately assessed as a failure.

CURRENT EVENTS. In December 1999 London returned Home Rule to Northern Ireland after 27 years of British domination. A power-sharing government was formed under the leadership of David Trimble and Seamus Mallon. The IRA's hidden weapon caches remained a central problem and threatened the collapse of the new assembly, whose four parties included the Democratic Unionist Party, the UUP, the Labour Party, and, the source of much controversy, Sinn Féin. In January 2000, Trimble demanded that the IRA put its weapons "beyond use" and predicted a return to British rule if his demands were not met. The IRA's unwillingness to comply hamstrung February peace talks. When the dissident IRA Continuity Group bombed a rural hotel in Irvinestown, the attack was condemned by every Irish political group, including Sinn Féin.

NORTHERN IRELAND

Though the blast injured no one, it was an unwelcome reminder of the past. Britain suspended the power-sharing experiment just 11 weeks after its implementation and reintroduced direct rule.

On May 29, 2000, Britain restored the power-sharing scheme after the IRA promised to begin disarming. In the Republic, **Bertie Ahern** of the Fianna Fail Party scraped out a "no confidence" victory against the opposition Labour Party. Marching Season was a nasty affair, though Blair and Ahern expressed satisfaction over its containment. On July 28, the last political prisoners in **Maze Prison** walked free under the Good Friday provisions, to a mixture of support and outrage.

The story remains the same in the North—political squabbling at the negotiation tables and on the floors of various Parliaments continues, punctuated now and then by bombs or plastic bullets out in the streets. Both sides are making efforts to repair the past—the RUC has been reformed into the **Police Service of Northern Ireland,** and the European Court of Human Rights has recently awarded compensation to the families of IRA fighters lost to the British government's "shoot to kill" policy. The slow path to disarmament points to a safer future—in the spring of 2001, the IRA was still dragging its heels but allowed international diplomats to visit their secret arms dumps. In the June 2001 elections, Loyalist extremists were voted into Parliament in unprecedented numbers, and in July, Catholic schoolchildren in Belfast were targeted by Protestant protesters as they walked to their nearby school. Then, in 2002, the IRA broke new ground by destroying a small payload of their weapons, a concession that proved conducive to peaceful discussion. In 2003, the Assembly was again suspended, though efforts continue to get "ordinary" politics up and running again. In June 2004, the **Bloody Sunday Inquiry** concluded in Derry and a verdict is expected in October.

BELFAST (BÉAL FEIRSTE)

Despite the violent associations conjured by the name Belfast, the capital feels more neighborly than most visitors expect. As the second-largest city on the island and a booming site of mercantile activity for centuries, Belfast (pop. 330,000) stands in stark contrast to the rest of Ireland. Today, its reputation as a thriving artistic center is maintained by renowned writers and an annual arts festival. Such luminaries as Nobel Prize-winner Seamus Heaney and fellow poet Paul Muldoon have given birth to a modern, distinctively Northern Irish literary renaissance that grapples with the area's difficult politics. The Belfast bar scene, a mix of Irish-British pub culture and international trends, entertains locals, foreigners, and a student population as lively as any in the world.

✈ INTERCITY TRANSPORTATION

Flights: Belfast International Airport (☎9442 2448; www.belfastairport.com) in Aldergrove, serves **Aer Lingus** (☎0845 084 4444), **British Airways** (☎0845 850 9850), **British European** (sometimes called **Flybe**) (☎087 0567 6676), and **BMI** (☎0870 607 0555). **Airbus** (☎9066 6630) runs to Laganside and Europa bus stations in the city center (40min.; M-Sa 2 per hr. 5:45am-10:30pm, Su about every hr. 6:15am-9:30pm; £6, round-trip £9). **Belfast City Airport** (☎9093 9093; www.belfastcityairport.com), at the harbor, serves **British European. Trains** run from City Airport **(Sydenham Halt)** to Central Station (M-Sa 25-33 per day, Su 12 per day; £1).

Trains: Infoline ☎9066 6630; www.translink.co.uk. Trains arrive at **Central Station,** East Bridge St. Some also stop at **Botanic Station,** Botanic Ave. in the University area, or **Great Victoria Station,** next to Europa Hotel. To: **Bangor** (33min.; M-F 39 per day, Sa 25 per day, Su 9 per day; £3.10, students £2); **Derry** (2hr.; M-F 9 per day, Sa 6 per day, Su 3 per day; £8.20/£4); **Dublin** (2hr.; M-Sa 9 per day, Su 5 per day; £20).

Buses: Buses to the west, the north coast, and the Republic operate out of **Europa Bus Terminal** (☎9066 6630), off Great Victoria St., behind the Europa Hotel. To: **Derry** (1¾hr.; M-Sa 19 per day, Su 7 per day; £7.50, students £5); **Dublin** (3hr.; M-Sa 7 per day, Su 6 per day; £12/£10). Buses to Northern Ireland's east coast operate out of **Laganside Station** (☎9066 6630), off Donegall Quay.

Ferries: From the ferry terminal, off Donegall Quay, **SeaCat** (☎087 0552 3523; www.seacat.co.uk) sails to: **Isle of Man** (2¾hr.; Apr.-Nov. M, W, F 1 per day); and **Troon, Scotland** (2½hr., 2-3 per day). **Norse Merchant Ferries** (☎087 0600 4321; www.norsemerchant.com) runs to **Liverpool, England** (8hr.). **P&O Irish Ferries** in Larne (☎0870 242 4777) run to **Cairnryan, Scotland. Stena Line** (☎087 0570 7070; www.stenaline.com), up the Lagan River, sails to **Fleetwood, England** and **Stranraer, Scotland.** The docks can be unsafe late at night and early in the morning; take a cab.

🖃 LOCAL TRANSPORTATION

Buses: The red **Citybus Network** (☎9066 6630; www.translink.co.uk) is supplemented by **Ulsterbus's** suburban "blue buses." Travel within the city center £1.20, concessions 60p. 5-day journey passes £6-7.25/£3.75-4.40. 10-day journey passes are £10.50-13/£6-7.25. Citybuses going south and west leave from **Donegall Square East;** those going north and east leave from **Donegall Square West.** To reach Donegall Sq., walk down East Bridge St., turn right on Oxford St., and take a left on May St. The **Centrelink** bus connects Donegall Sq., Castlecourt Shopping Centre, Europa and Laganside Bus Stations, and Central Train Station. Catch buses at any of 24 designated stops. (Every 12min.; M-F 7:25am-9:15pm, Sa 8:30am-9:15pm; £1.10, free with bus or rail ticket.) **Nightlink** buses shuttle the tipsy from Donegall Sq. West to various small towns outside Belfast (Sa 1 and 2am, £3.50). Pay on board or at the Donegall Sq. West kiosk.

Taxis: Value Cabs (☎9080 9080); **City Cab** (☎9024 2000); **Fon a Cab** (☎9033 3333).

Bike Rental: McConvey Cycles, 183 Ormeau Rd. (☎9033 0322; www.mcconvey.com). £10 per day, £40 per week, F-M £20. Panniers £15 per week. £50 deposit. Open M-W and F-Sa 9am-6pm, Th 9am-8pm.

◼ ORIENTATION

City Hall is in **Donegall Square.** A busy shopping district extends north for four blocks to the enormous Castlecourt Shopping Centre. In the eastern part of the shopping district, the **Cornmarket** area shows off characteristically Belfastian architecture and pubs in its narrow entries (small alleyways). The stretch of Great Victoria St. between Europa Station and **Shaftesbury Square** is known as the **Golden Mile** for its highbrow establishments and Victorian architecture. **Botanic Avenue** and **Bradbury Place** (which becomes University Rd.) extend south to **Queen's University,** where student shops and budget accommodations await. In this southern area, the busiest neighborhoods center around **Stranmillis Road, Malone Road,** and **Lisburn Road.** The city center, Golden Mile, and university are quite safe.

Divided from the rest of Belfast by the **Westlink Motorway,** working-class **West Belfast** is more politically volatile than the city center. There remains a sharp division between sectarian neighborhoods: the Protestant neighborhood stretches along **Shankill Road,** just north of the Catholic neighborhood, which is centered on

NORTHERN IRELAND

Falls Road. The two are separated by the **peace line. River Lagan** splits industrial **East Belfast** from Belfast proper. The city's shipyards and docks extend north on both sides of the river as it grows into **Belfast Lough.** During the week, the area north of City Hall is deserted after 6pm. Although muggings are infrequent in Belfast, use taxis after dark, particularly when pubbing in the northeast.

🚹 PRACTICAL INFORMATION

Tourist Information Centre: Belfast Welcome Centre, 47 Donegall Pl. (☎9024 6609; www.gotobelfast.com). Free booklet on Belfast and information on surrounding areas. Books accommodations in Northern Ireland (£2) and the Republic (£3). Open June-Sept. M-Sa 9am-7pm, Su noon-5pm; Oct.-May M-Sa 9am-5:30pm. Irish Tourist Board (Bord Fáilte), 53 Castle St. (☎9032 7888). Books accommodations in the Republic. Open June-Aug. M-F 9am-5pm, Sa 9am-12:30pm; Sept.-May M-F 9am-5pm.

Financial Services: Banks and **ATMs** are plentiful. Most are open M-F 9am-4:30pm. **Thomas Cook,** 10 Donegall Sq. West (☎9088 3800). No commission on cashing traveler's checks. Open M-F 8am-6pm, Sa 10am-5pm. **Belfast International Airport office** (☎9448 4848; www.belfastairport.com) also changes money. Open May-Oct. M-Th 5:30am-8:30pm, F-Sa 5:30am-11pm; daily Nov.-Apr. 6am-8pm.

Luggage Storage: For security reasons, there is no luggage storage at airports, bus stations, or train stations. **Belfast Welcome Centre** (see above) stores luggage for 4hr. (£2) or longer (£4), but not overnight. All 4 **hostels** hold bags during the day for guests.

GLBT Information: Rainbow Project N.I., 33 Church Ln. (☎9031 9030). Open M-F 10am-5:30pm. **Lesbian Line** (☎9023 8668). Open Th 7:30-10pm.

Launderette: Globe Drycleaners & Launderers, 37-39 Botanic Ave. (☎9024 3956). £4.65 for use of machines. Open M-F 8am-9pm, Sa 8am-6pm, Su 2-6pm.

Police: 6-18 Donegall Pass, 65 Knock Rd. (☎9065 0222).

Hospital: Belfast City Hospital, 91 Lisburn Rd. (☎9032 9241).

Internet Access: Belfast Central Library. £1 per 15min., £3 per hr., with photo ID. **Revelations Internet Cafe,** 27 Shaftesbury Sq. (☎9032 0337). £4 per hr., students and hostelers £3 per hr. Open M-F 10am-10pm, Sa 10am-6pm, Su 11am-7pm.

Post Office: Central Post Office, 25 Castle Pl. (☎0845 722 3344). Open M-Sa 9am-5:30pm. **Post Code:** BT1 1BB.

🏠 ACCOMMODATIONS

Nearly all Belfast's budget accommodations are near Queen's University, south of the city center. Walk 10-20min. from Europa Bus Station or any of the train stations, or catch a **Centrelink** bus to Shaftesbury Sq. or, from Donegall Sq. East, **Citybus** #69-71, 83, 84, or 86. Reservations are highly recommended in summer.

HOSTELS AND DORMS

🏅 **Arnie's Backpackers (IHH),** 63 Fitzwilliam St. (☎9024 2867), a short walk from Europa Station. Impressively clean with a library of travel info. No curfew. Dorms £7-9.50. ❶

Belfast Hostel (HINI), 22 Donegall Rd. (☎9031 5435; www.hini.org.uk), off Shaftesbury Sq. Clean and inviting interior. Internet access £1 per 20min. Laundry £3. Reception 24hr. Dorms £8.50-10.50; singles £17-18; triples £33-34. ❶

The Ark (IHH), 18 University St. (☎9032 9626), 10min. from Europa Station on Great Victoria St. Great sense of community: staff of former guest MVPs. Also **books tours** of Belfast (£8) and Giant's Causeway (£18). Internet access £1 per 20min. Weekend luggage storage. Laundry £5. Curfew 2am. Dorms £10; doubles £36. ❶

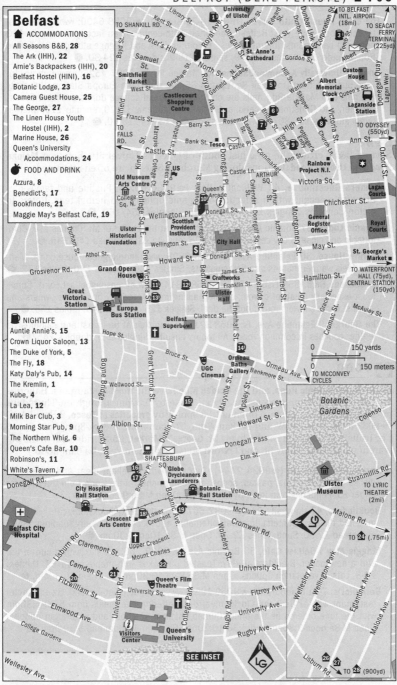

Belfast

▲ ACCOMMODATIONS
All Seasons B&B, 28
The Ark (IHH), 22
Arnie's Backpackers (IHH), 20
Belfast Hostel (HINI), 16
Botanic Lodge, 23
Camera Guest House, 25
The George, 27
The Linen House Youth
Hostel (IHH), 2
Marine House, 26
Queen's University
Accommodations, 24

🍴 FOOD AND DRINK
Azzura, 8
Benedict's, 17
Bookfinders, 21
Maggie May's Belfast Cafe, 19

🍸 NIGHTLIFE
Auntie Annie's, 15
Crown Liquor Saloon, 13
The Duke of York, 5
The Fly, 18
Katy Daly's Pub, 14
The Kremlin, 1
Kube, 4
La Lea, 12
Milk Bar Club, 3
Morning Star Pub, 9
The Northern Whig, 6
Queen's Cafe Bar, 10
Robinson's, 11
White's Tavern, 7

NORTHERN
IRELAND

The Linen House Youth Hostel (IHH), 18-20 Kent St. (☎9058 6400; www.belfasthostel.com), bordering West Belfast. Converted 19th-century linen factory now packs 130 beds into bare rooms. Internet access £2 per hr. Bike and luggage storage 50p. Towels 50p. Laundry £4. Dorms £6.50-9; singles £15-20; doubles £24-30. ❶

Queen's University Accommodations, 78 Malone Rd. (☎9097 4525; www.qub.uc.uk). Take bus #71 from Donegall Sq. East; a 35min. walk from Europa Station. University Rd. runs into Malone Rd.; halls are on the left. Typical college dorms available Easter, summer, and Christmas vacations. Singles UK students £9.20, ensuite £13; international students £10.80/£15.70; non-students £13.40/£18.40. ❷

B&BS

Several B&Bs crowd the area just south of Queen's University, between **Malone Road** and **Lisburn Road.** Options during Marching Season are often restricted.

Camera Guesthouse, 44 Wellington Park (☎9066 0026). Pristine and family-run. Breakfasts delight with a selection of organic options and herbal teas. Caters to dietary concerns. Singles £35, ensuite £45; doubles £54/£60. ❹

Botanic Lodge, 87 Botanic Ave. (☎9032 7682), at the corner of Mt. Charles Ave. Comfortable and close to city center. Singles £25, ensuite £35; doubles £40/£45. ❸

Marine House, 30 Eglantine Ave. (☎9066 2828; www.marineguesthouse.com). Mansion feels warmer than its size first suggests. Singles £40; doubles £50; triples £72. ❹

All Seasons B&B, 356 Lisburn Rd. (☎9068 2814; www.allseasonsbelfast.com). Comfy roost especially great for drivers; secure parking free. Amazingly hospitable owners and super-strength showers round out the deal. Singles £25; doubles £40; triples £55. ❸

The George, 9 Eglantine Ave. (☎9068 3212). Fresh fruit at breakfast and saloon-style leather couches in common room. All rooms ensuite. Singles £25; doubles £45. ❸

◘ FOOD

Dublin Road, Botanic Road, and the **Golden Mile** have the most restaurants. Bakeries and cafes dot shopping areas; nearly all close by 5:30pm, though on Thursdays most of the city center stays open until 8-9pm. Buy **groceries** at **Tesco,** 2 Royal Ave. (☎9032 3270. Open M-W and Sa 8am-7pm, Th 8am-9pm, F 8am-8pm, Su 1-5pm.) For fruits and veggies, visit the lively **St. George's Market,** East Bridge St., in the big warehouse between May St. and Oxford St. (Open F 8am-2pm, Sa 6am-noon.)

▨ Azzura, 8 Church Ln. (☎9024 2444). Tiny cafe with excellent meat and vegetarian dishes. Gourmet pizzas, pastas, soups, and sandwiches arrive warm from the oven for under £5. Peppers grown fresh by the owners. Open M-Sa 9am-5pm. ❶

Bookfinders, 47 University Rd. (☎9032 6677). Stuffy, dusty bookstore/cafe with mismatched dishes, counterculture paraphernalia, and occasional poetry readings. Soup and bread £2.50. Sandwiches £2.20. Open M-Sa 10am-5:30pm. ❶

Maggie May's Belfast Cafe, 50 Botanic Ave. (☎9032 2662). Relax with a cup of tea and a newspaper. Breakfast all day. Toasted pancakes with maple syrup £2. Dinners £4-8. Lots of vegetarian options. Open M-Sa 8am-10:30pm, Su 10am-10:30pm. ❷

Benedict's, 7-21 Bradbury Pl. (☎9059 1999; www.benedictshotel.co.uk). Swanky hotel restaurant with a "Beat the Clock" meal deal, offering fine meals from 5:30-7:30pm with the time ordered as the price. Curried chicken, seafood, and vegetarian options. Open M-Sa noon-2:30pm and 5:30-10:30pm, Su noon-3:30pm and 5:30-9pm. ❸

SIGHTS

Visitors should definitely take a ▧**black cab tour** of the murals of West Belfast, bookable at most hostels. Quality varies; two guaranteed winners are **Original Black Taxi Tours** (passionate; ☎0800 032 2003; £25 for a group of 3) and **Black Taxi Tours** (witty; ☎0800 052 3914; £8 per person). **Mini-Coach** (☎9031 5333) also conducts tours of Belfast (1hr., £8) and the Giant's Causeway (9am-6pm, £16).

DONEGALL SQUARE, CORNMARKET, AND EAST BELFAST

BELFAST CITY HALL. The most impressive piece of architecture in Belfast is, appropriately, its administrative and geographic center. Removed from the crowded streets by a grassy square, City Hall's green copper dome (173 ft.) is visible from nearly any point in the city. Inside, a grand staircase ascends to the second floor, portraits of the city's Lord Mayors somberly line the halls, and glass and marble shimmer in three elaborate reception rooms. At the front entrance, an enormous marble **Queen Victoria** grimaces formidably. The interior of City Hall is accessible only by tour. *(☎9027 0456. 1hr. tours June-Sept. M-F 11am, 2 and 3pm, Sa 2:30pm; Oct.-May M-F 11am and 2:30pm, Sa 2:30pm. Tour times prone to change. Free.)*

LINEN HALL LIBRARY. Originally across the street in the building that became City Hall, this library moved to its current location in 1894. It contains a famous collection of Northern Irish political documents. *(Enter via 52 Fountain St. ☎9087 2214. Free tours available. Open M-F 9:30am-5:30pm, Sa 9:30am-4pm.)*

CORNMARKET ENTRIES. Amidst Cornmarket's modern buildings, relics of old Belfast remain in the tiny entries that connect some of the major streets. **Pottinger's Entry** runs between Ann St. and High St., while, off Lombard St. and Bridge St., **Winecellar Entry** hosts Belfast's oldest pub, **White's Tavern** (p. 708).

ODYSSEY. Belfast's newest mega-attraction is a gigantic center that houses a huge indoor hockey arena, a multiplex cinema and IMAX, and a pavilion of shops, bars, and restaurants—including a Hard Rock Cafe. *(2 Queen's Quay. ☎9045 1055; www.theodyssey.co.uk.)* Also inside is the new ▧**W5 Discovery Centre,** a science complex that beckons geeks of all ages. *(☎9046 7700; www.w5online.co.uk. Open M-Sa 10am-6pm, Su noon-6pm; last admission 5pm. £6, students £4.50, families £17.)*

THE GOLDEN MILE
"The Golden Mile" refers to a strip along **Great Victoria Street** lined with many of Belfast's crown sites. It was once a prime target for IRA bombers.

GRAND OPERA HOUSE. The city's pride and joy was bombed by the IRA, restored to its original splendor, and then bombed again. (See **Entertainment,** p. 706. ☎9024 1919. Office open M-F 8:30am-9pm. Tours begin across the street at the office Sa 11am. £3, seniors, students and children £2.)

CROWN LIQUOR SALOON. The National Trust transformed this popular pub into a showcase of carved wood, gilded ceilings, and stained glass. Snugs fit two to ten. (p. 709. ☎9027 9901.)

QUEEN'S UNIVERSITY AREA

BOTANIC GARDENS. Join birds, bees, and Belfast's student population to bask in the occasional sun at these meticulously groomed gardens behind the university. Visit two 19th-century greenhouses, the toasty **Tropical Ravine,** and the more temperate Lanyon-designed **Palm House.** Don't forget to stop and smell the rose gardens. (☎ 9032 4902. Gardens open daily 8am-dusk. Greenhouses open Apr.-Sept. M-F 10am-noon and 1-5pm, Sa-Su 2-5pm; Oct.-Mar. M-F 10am-noon and 1-4pm, Sa-Su 2-4pm. Free.)

ULSTER MUSEUM. This first-class museum fills its huge display halls with Irish and modern art, local history, antiquities, and the Mummy of Takabuti. The treasure from a Spanish Armada ship that sank off the Causeway Coast in 1588 is also on display. (In the Botanic Gardens, off Stranmillis Rd. ☎ 9038 3000. Open year-round M-F 10am-5pm, Sa 1-5pm, Su 2-5pm. Free, except for certain exhibits.)

WEST BELFAST AND THE MURALS

Separated from the rest of the city by the Westlink motorway, the neighborhoods of West Belfast have historically been at the heart of Northern political tensions. The Catholic area (centered on **Falls Road**) and the Protestant neighborhood (centered on the **Shankill**) are separated by a **peace line**, a grim, gray, seemingly impenetrable wall. It's best to visit the Falls and Shankill during the day, when the many murals can be seen. Visit one neighborhood and then return to the city center before heading to the other, as the area around the peace line can be unsafe. Be discreet if photographing the murals. **It is illegal to photograph military installations;** do so and your film may be confiscated.

THE FALLS. This Catholic neighborhood is much larger than Shankill and houses a younger, growing population. On Divis St., the **Divis Tower**, a high-rise apartment building, was built by optimistic social planners in the 1960s, but soon became an IRA stronghold. The British army still occupies the top floors. Continuing west, Divis St. turns into **Falls Road.** The **Sinn Féin** office is easily spotted: one side plastered with an enormous portrait of Bobby Sands (see **The Troubles,** p. 697) and an advertisement for the Sinn Féin newspaper, An Phoblacht. In the past both the Falls and the Shankill contained many representations of paramilitaries (IRA in the Falls, UVF and UDA in the Shankill). Though these earlier militant murals still remain—including a few that depict the Republican armed struggle in the Lower Falls—more recent murals in both communities have focused on historical and cultural representations. They recall the ancient Celtic heritage of myths and legends and depict The Great Hunger, as Northern Catholics refer to the Famine.

SHANKILL. Shankill Rd. begins at the Westlink and turns into Woodvale Rd. as it crosses Cambrai St. Woodvale Rd. intersects the **Crumlin Road** at the Ardoyne roundabout, and can be taken back into city center. The **Shankill Memorial Garden** honors 10 people who died in a bomb attack on Fizzel's Fish Shop in October 1993; the garden is on Shankill Rd. facing Berlin St. The densely decorated **Orange Hall** sits on the left at Brookmount St. Side streets on the right guide you to the **Shankill Estate** and more murals. Through the estate, the Crumlin Rd. leads back to the city center, past an army base, the courthouse, and the jail, which are linked by a tunnel. The oldest Loyalist murals are found here. The Shankill area is shrinking as middle-class Protestants leave, but a growing Protestant population lives on **Sandy Row**, off Donegall Rd. at Shaftesbury Sq. An orange arch crowned with King William once marked its start. Nearby murals show the Red Hand of Ulster, a bulldog, and William crossing the Boyne.

🎵 ENTERTAINMENT

Belfast's cultural events are covered by the monthly Arts Council Artslink, free at the TIC. More listings appear in the daily Belfast Telegraph (and its Friday arts supplement) and Thursday's Irish News. The **Crescent Arts Centre,** 2 University Rd., supplies general arts information and specific news about its own exhibits and concerts, which take place from September through May. The Centre also

A PRIMER ON THE MURAL SYMBOLS OF WEST BELFAST.
PROTESTANT MURALS. Blue, White, and Red: The colors of the British flag; often painted on curbs and signposts to demarcate Unionist murals and neighborhoods. **The Red Hand:** The crest of Ulster Province, the central symbol of the Ulster flag, which includes a red cross on a white background, used by Unionists to emphasize the separateness of Ulster from the Republic. Symbolizes the hand of the first Norse King, which he supposedly cut off and threw on a Northern beach to establish his primacy. (The crest also appears on Catholic murals which depict the four ancient provinces; evidence of the overlap in heritage.) **King Billy/William of Orange:** Sometimes depicted on a white horse, crossing the Boyne to defeat the Catholic King James II at the 1690 Battle of the Boyne. The Orange Order was later founded in his honor. **The Apprentice Boys:** A group of young men who shut the gates of Derry to keep out the troops of James II, beginning the great siege of 1689. They have become Protestant folk heroes, inspiring a sect of the Orange Order in their name. The slogan "No Surrender," also from the siege, has been appropriated by radical Unionists, most notably the Reverend Ian Paisley. **Lundy:** The Derry leader who advocated surrender during the siege; now a term for anyone who wants to give in to Catholic demands. **Scottish Flag:** Blue with a white cross; recalls the Scottish-Presbyterian roots of many Protestants whose ancestors were part of the Ulster Plantation (see **Cromwell**, p. 726).
CATHOLIC MURALS. Orange and Green: Colors of the Irish Republic's flag; often painted on curbs and signposts in Republican neighborhoods. **The Irish Volunteers:** Republican tie to the earlier (nonsectarian) Nationalists. **Saoirse:** Irish for "Freedom;" the most common term found on murals. **Éireann go bráth:** (erin-go-BRAH) "Ireland forever;" a popular IRA slogan. **Tiocfaidh ár lá:** (CHOCK-ee-ar-LA) "Our day will come." **Slan Abhaile:** (Slawn ah-WAH-lya) "Safe home"; directed at the primarily Protestant RUC police force. **Phoenix:** Symbolizes united Ireland rising from the ashes of British persecution. **Lug:** Celtic god, seen as the protector of the "native Irish" (Catholics). **Green Ribbon:** IRA symbol for "free our POWs." **Bulldog:** Britain. **Bowler Hats:** A symbol for Orangemen.

hosts eight-week courses in yoga, trapeze, writing, trad, and drawing. (☎9024 2338. Classes £36. Open M-Sa 10am-10pm.) **Fenderesky Gallery,** 2 University Rd., in the Crescent Arts building, hosts contemporary shows year-round. (☎9023 5245. Open Tu-Sa 11:30am-5pm.)

Belfast's theater season runs from September to June. The **Grand Opera House,** 2-4 Great Victoria St., hosts opera, ballet, musicals, and plays. (☎9024 1919, 24hr. info 9024 9129; www.goh.co.uk. Open M-W and F-Sa 8:30am-6pm, Th 8:30am-9pm. Tickets from £12.50, student discounts available.) **The Lyric Theatre** plays at 55 Ridgeway St. (☎9038 1081; www.lyrictheatre.co.uk. Box office open M-Sa 10am-7pm. Tickets M-Th £10, F-Sa £12.50.) **The Group Theatre,** Bedford St., brings comedy to Ulster Hall. (☎9032 9685. Box office open M-F noon-3pm. Tickets £4-8.) **Ulster Hall,** Bedford St. (☎9032 3900), hosts everything from classical to pop. Buy tickets at Ticketmaster at Virgin (☎9032 3744). **Waterfront Hall,** 2 Lanyon Pl., is Belfast's newest concert center. (☎9033 4400. Tickets £10-35; student discounts available.)

 FESTIVALS

For three weeks between October and November, over 300 performances of opera, ballet, film, and comedy invade venues across the city during the annual **Queen's University Belfast Festival.** (Box office ☎9066 5577; www.belfastfestival.com.

THE LOCAL STORY

An interview with Danny Devenny, painter of West Belfast murals:

LG: When did murals first appear in the neighborhood?

A: They started in the Loyalist community about the turn of the century. In the Nationalist community, if you had even dared to put a slogan on a wall, you would have been at least beaten up or at worst, put in prison. So, the murals in the Nationalist community didn't appear until well into the late 70s, 80s.

LG: What changed in the 80s?

A: The British recognized that this was a political conflict, and that the people who were arrested and put in prison were doing so for political purposes. Longcash prison was seen as a university of liberation, so people were using the time in prison to educate themselves on history and politics and probably also about the military aspects of a war. The British decided they couldn't have this, so they took away the prisoners' political status. The prisoners were angered, so they refused to comply with the prison regime, which led on to the hunger strikes, as a last resort. During that period people on the outside felt so close to these people that they just defied the British state and painted images on the walls.

LG: How have the murals developed over time?

A: The first murals that went up were about censorship. They were depicting the brutality which the British media were denying was taking place within the prison

For advance schedules, write to: The Belfast Festival at Queens, 25 College Gardens, Belfast BT9 6BS. Tickets sold from mid-September through the festival's end. Tickets £2.50-25.) During the **West Belfast Arts Festival,** in the second week of August, Falls residents celebrate Irish traditional culture through Nationalist festivities. (473 Falls Rd. ☎9028 4028; www.feilebelfast.com.)

🍷🍺 PUBS AND CLUBS

Get current nightlife info from *The List,* available at the TIC, hostels, and restaurants. The city center closes early and is deserted late at night; *Let's Go* suggests starting downtown, moving through Cornmarket, and finishing near the university.

🍺 **Queen's Cafe Bar,** 4 Queen's Arcade (☎9024 9105), between Donegall Pl. and Fountain St. A buzzing, casual, gay-friendly bar in a glitzy shopping arcade off Donegall Pl. Popular with city center workers. Open M-W 11:30am-9pm, Th-Sa 11:30am-11pm.

🍺 **Morning Star Pub,** 17-19 Pottinger's Entry (☎9032 3976), between Ann St. and High St. Look for the Victorian wrought-iron bracket hanging above the entry. Award-winning bar food awaits upstairs. Open M-Sa 11am-11pm, Su noon-6pm.

The Duke of York, 7-11 Commercial Ctr. (☎9024 1062). Old boxing venue turned Communist printing press, which was rebuilt after an IRA bombing in the 60s. Now home to the city's largest selection of Irish whiskeys. 18+. Th trad at 10pm. Sa disco, cover £5. Open M noon-9pm, Tu noon-1am, W noon-midnight, Th-Sa noon-2am.

The Northern Whig, 2 Bridge St. (☎9050 9888; www.thenorthernwhig.com). Occupying the building of its defunct namesake's press, the Whig now serves a mean *mojito* in the heart of Belfast's old printing neighborhood. If staying outside the city, the bar can arrange for reasonable overnight stays in town. Lunch £6. DJ Th 10pm. Live music Su. Food served 10am-9pm. 21+. Bar open M-Tu, Su 10am-11pm, W-Sa 10am-1am.

Katy Daly's Pub, 17 Ormeau Ave. (☎9032 5942). Go straight behind City Hall, heading toward Queen's, and turn left on Ormeau Ave. High-ceilinged, wood-paneled, antique pub with a relaxed crowd. Local bands W. Singers and songwriters Th-Sa.

White's Tavern, 2-4 Winecellar Entry (☎9024 3080), between Lombard and Bridge St.; a left off High St. Belfast's oldest tavern, serving since 1630. Excellent for an afternoon pint. F DJ, live trad Th-Sa. Open M-Sa 11:30am-11pm.

Auntie Annie's, 44 Dublin Rd. (☎9050 1660). Hosts live rock music M-W nights. Downstairs features a more pubby, relaxed vibe (open M-Sa noon-1am, Su 6pm-midnight), while upstairs, darkly-dressed twentysome-things dance and nod to enjoyable indie rock (open Th-Sa 10pm; weekend cover £3-5).

Crown Liquor Saloon, 46 Great Victoria St. (☎9027 9901; www.crownbar.com). This National Trust-owned pub had its windows blown in by a bombing, but the inside feels original. Tourist crowd. Open M-F 8:30am-midnight, Su 12:30-10pm.

Robinson's, 38-40 Great Victoria St. (☎9024 7447). Four floors of themed bars. In the back, renowned **Fibber McGee's** hosts incredible trad sessions nightly at 10:30pm. On the top 2 floors are nightclubs **BT1** and **mezza(nine).** F 80s night. Cover F £5, Sa £8. Open M-Sa 11:30am-1am, Su noon-midnight.

The Fly, 5-6 Lower Crescent (☎9050 9750). Very popular club with insect-friendly decor. 1st floor for pints, 2nd for mingling, 3rd for the test-tube-shot bar with 40 flavors of vodka—from cinnamon to toffee Starburst. Open M-W 7pm-1am, Th-Sa 5pm-1:15am.

La Lea, 48 Franklin St. (☎9023 0200; www.lalea.com), off Bedford St. House music Tu-Su and classy jazz sessions M. Club 21+. Cover £5-10. Open M and W-Su 9:30-2am.

Milk Bar Club, 10-14 Tomb St. (☎9027 8876; www.clubmilk.com). This up and-coming club indulges in cheesy fun. Pop and club hits jam while lines of smiles swing hips at the fluorescent bar. M gay and lesbian night. Open daily 9pm-3am. Cover £3-10.

Kube, 2-6 Dunbar St. (9023 4520; www.kubeonline.com). Kube has won prestigious awards as a cafe-bar and nightclub. Come for great atmosphere in a strictly drug-free environment. Open M-Su 11:30-3am. 18+. Cover Sa £5.

The Kremlin, 96 Donegall St. (☎9080 9700; www.kremlin-belfast.com). Beautiful boys and girls sip and flirt in the bar until they spill onto the dance floor around 10:30pm. Free Internet access upstairs. Doors close at 1am, but the party only heats up inside. F theme night. Free Su-M and before 9pm. Bar open M-Th 4pm-3am, F-Su 1pm-3am.

▶ DAYTRIP FROM BELFAST

ULSTER FOLK, TRANSPORT, AND RAILWAY MUSEUMS

Take the Bangor road (A2) 7 mi. east of Belfast. Buses and trains stop here on the way to Bangor. ☎9042 8428; www.magni.org.uk. Open July-Sept. M-Sa 10am-6pm, Su 11am-6pm; Mar.-June M-F 10am-5pm, Sa 10am-6pm, Su 11am-6pm; Oct.-Feb. M-F 10am-4pm, Sa 10am-5pm, Su 11am-5pm. Folk Museum £5, students and seniors £3, families £14. Transport Museum £5/ £3/£14. Combined admission £6.50/£3.50/£18.

camps. The second batch of murals went up when the prison struggle was resolved, celebrating the IRA people themselves. And with the peace process, I think they purposefully went out to change the style of the murals because in conflict resolution we need to compromise. The murals started to say, "Yes, okay, we're responsible here. Let's find a brighter future." But simultaneously, there was a politicization within our communities, looking at the broader issue: at who we are culturally and at what colonialism has meant. That's why you now have the Celtic imagery going up.

LG: How do you go about painting a mural in West Belfast?

A: You just up and go. No one will stop you and, in fact, people will stop and admire it and discuss it with you, and they'll ask you if you want cigarettes or food. The people in the community are so overwhelmed and overjoyed by the murals in their area that they actually vie with each other [for one].

We're teaching our younger generation about our history. The history taught in the schools was of a totally British bias, so you don't really learn about your own history until you sit down and study, and most of us didn't have that opportunity until we were in prison. We don't want the next generation to have to go to prison to learn about this.

The Ulster Folk and Transport Museums stretch over 176 acres in Holywood. Established by an Act of Parliament in the 1950s, the ⛫**Folk Museum** contains over 30 buildings from the past three centuries and all nine Ulster counties. Most of the buildings are transplanted originals, reconstructed stone by stone on the museum's grounds. The Transport Museum and the Railway Museum are across the road. Inside the **Transport Museum,** horse-drawn coaches, cars, bicycles, and trains chronicle the history of moving vehicles. The hangar-shaped **Railway Museum** displays 25 old railway engines.

COUNTIES DOWN AND ARMAGH

NEWCASTLE AND THE MOURNES

The numerous arcades, joke shops, and waterslide parks of Newcastle's main drag stand in dramatic contrast to the majestic Mourne Mountains rising from the south end of town. On weekends, packs of kids prowl the streets in search of fun, while July and August bring the rest of the family to sunbathe on the beach. With its hostel and numerous B&Bs, Newcastle serves as an inexpensive base for exploring the nearby parks and mountains. No road penetrates the center of the Mournes.

▐ **TRANSPORTATION.** Newcastle's **Ulsterbus** station (☎4372 2296) is at 5-7 Railway St., on Main St. Buses run to: **Belfast** (1¼hr.; M-F 19 per day, Sa 17 per day, Su 10 per day; £5.60, children £2.80); **Downpatrick** (43min., express 20min.; M-F 15 per day, Sa 10 per day, Su 5 per day; £2.70/£1.35); **Dublin** via Newry (3hr.; M-Sa 4 per day, Su 2 per day; £11.70/£5.85); **Newry** (37min.; M-F 12 per day, Sa 7 per day, Su 2 per day; £6/£3). For a **taxi,** call **Donard Cabs** (☎4372 4100). **Rent bikes** at **Wiki Wiki Wheels,** 10b Donard St. (☎4372 3973. £10 per day, £50 per week. ID deposit. Open Jan.-Mar. M-W, F, Su 9:30am-5:30pm; Apr.-Dec. M-Sa 9am-6pm, Su 2-6pm.

▓▐ **ORIENTATION AND PRACTICAL INFORMATION.** Newcastle's main road stretches along the waterfront; initially called **Main Street** (where it intersects **Railway Street**), its name subsequently changes to **Central Promenade** and then **South Promenade.** The **Tourist Information Centre,** 10-14 Central Promenade, is 10min. from the bus station. (☎4372 2222. Open July-Aug. M-Sa 9:30am-7pm, Su 1-7pm; Sept.-June M-Sa 10am-5pm, Su 2-6pm.) **First Trust Bank** is on 28-32 Main St. (☎4372 3476. Open M-F 9:30am-4:30pm, W 10am-4:30pm.) Rent **camping equipment** at **Hill Trekker,** 115 Central Promenade. (☎4372 3842. Open Tu-Su 10am-5:30pm.) **Internet access** is at the **library,** 141-143 Main St. (£1.50 per 30min. Open M-Tu 10am-8pm, W and F 10am-5pm, Sa 10am-1pm and 2-5pm). The **post office** is on 33-35 Central Promenade (☎4372 2651. Open M-W and F 9am-12:30pm and 1:30-5:30pm, Th and Sa 9am-12:30pm.) **Post Code:** BT33.

▐▐ **ACCOMMODATIONS AND FOOD. B&Bs** in this summer resort town are plentiful but pricey; fortunately, there's also a hostel. The Mournes are a free and legal camping alternative. Follow Railway St. toward the water and take a right at the Newcastle Arms to reach **Newcastle Youth Hostel (HINI) ❶,** 30 Downs Rd. Quarters are tight, but such discomforts are appeased by the prime location and well-lit rooms. (☎4372 2133. Dorms £10, under 18 £9; 4-person apartment £40.) Welcoming **Beach House ❹** lodges guests at 22 Downs Rd. (☎4372 2345. Singles £45; doubles £65.) The **camping** is great at **Tollymore Forest Park ❷,** 176 Tullybrannigan Rd., 2 mi. down the A2 or a ride on the "Rural Rover" (10min.; daily 9:10am and 12:25pm; £1.10) from the Ulsterbus station. (☎4372 2428. £13 per tent. Electricity £1.50.)

Junk food venders line the waterfront. 🅜Seasalt ❹, 51 Central Promenade, is a stylish deli-cafe with Mediterranean edge. It transforms into a delicious, reservations-only, three-course bistro on weekend nights. (☎4372 5027; www.seasaltfood.com. Dinner £20. Open Su-W 9am-5pm, Th-Sa 9am-midnight.) Hip Café Mauds ❶, 106 Main St., has excellent views. (☎4372 6184. Open M-Su 9am-9:30pm.) Go to Rooney's ❶, on the corner of Railway St. and Downs Rd., for an exciting fusion menu and romantic table 105. (☎4372 3822. Ostrich £14. New Zealand mussels £5.50. Open Su-Th noon-9pm, F-Sa noon-10pm.)

🅗 HIKING. For a taste of the wilderness surrounding Newcastle, stop by the Tullymore Forest Park, just 2 mi. west of town at 176 Tullybrannigan Rd. A magical entrance lined with gigantic, gnarled trees leads you toward ancient stone bridges and well-marked trails. For more challenging peaks, head to the Mourne Countryside Centre, 87 Central Promenade. A friendly and knowledgeable staff leads hikes and stocks a broad selection of guides and maps of the Mourne mountains. Those planning short excursions can purchase *Mourne Mountain Walks* (£6), which describes 10 one-day hikes. If you're staying overnight, buy the topographical *Mourne Country Outdoor Pursuits Map* for £5. (☎4372 4059. Open M-F 9am-5pm.) The Mourne Heritage Trust, two doors down, is also worth a stop.

Built between 1904 and 1923, the Mourne Wall encircles 12 of the mountains just below their peaks. Walking the 22 mi. wall takes a strenuous 8hr. The Mournes' highest peak, Slieve Donard (2788 ft.), towers above Newcastle. The trail up is wide and well maintained (5hr. round-trip). Donard Park, on the corner of Central Promenade and Bryansford Rd., provides the most direct access to the Mournes from Newcastle; it's convenient to both Slieve Donard and nearby Slieve Commedagh. Follow the dirt path at the back of the car park as it crosses two bridges and eventually joins the Glen River Path (about 1½ mi.) to reach the Mourne Wall. At the wall, turn left for Slieve Donard or right for Slieve Commedagh. Those seeking a more remote trek might try Slieve Bernagh (2423 ft.) or Slieve Binnian (2450 ft.), most easily accessed from Hare's Gap and Silent Valley, respectively. The two craggy peaks, both offering tremendous views, can be combined into a 12 mi. half-day hike.

Wilderness camping is popular. Common spots include the Annalong Valley, the shores of Lough Shannagh, and near the Trassey River. While camping around the Mourne Wall is allowed, camping in forest areas is strictly prohibited due to potential forest fires. Be prepared for weather conditions to change suddenly, and bring warm clothing, as the mountains get cold and windy at night.

ARMAGH (ARD MACHA)

Religious zealotry and violent conflict have long been associated with Armagh. The hilltop fort *Ard Macha* ("Macha's Height") was built in pagan times but supposedly converted to St. Patrick's base of operations in the 5th century. The city has sought to transcend the sectarian scars of its troubled past by emphasizing its role as the ecclesiastical capital of both the Republic and Northern Ireland.

🄴🄽 TRANSPORTATION AND PRACTICAL INFORMATION. From Lonsdale Rd., Ulsterbus runs to Belfast (1¼hr.; M-F 22 per day, Sa 15 per day, Su 7 per day; £6.20) and Enniskillen (2hr.; Sept.-July 2 per day, Oct.-June M-Sa 1 per day; £7.40). English Street, Thomas Street, and Scotch Street comprise Armagh's city center. To the east lies the Mall. West of the city center, two cathedrals sit on neighboring hills. The Tourist Information Centre is at 40 English St. (☎3752 1800. Open M-Sa 9am-5pm; July-Aug. also Su 1-5pm; Sept.-June Su 2-5pm.) Other services include: First Trust bank, English St. (☎3752 2025); Internet access at Armagh Computer World,

43 Scotch St. (☎3751 0002; £3 per hr.; open M-Sa 9am-5:30pm); and the **post office,** 31 Upper English St. (☎084 5722 3344; open M-F 9am-5:30pm, Sa 9am-12:30pm). *Poste Restante* goes to 46 Upper English St. (☎3752 2079). **Post Code:** BT6 17AA.

⌐ ACCOMMODATIONS. Behind the Queen's University campus, **Armagh Youth Hostel (YHANI) ❷** is huge and squeaky clean. From the TIC, turn left twice, follow Abbey St. for two blocks, and cross the parking lot; the hostel entrance is in a small alley. (☎3751 1800. Laundry £3. Reception 8-11am and 5-11pm. Dorms £13; private rooms £14 per person.) Make a right onto Desart Ln., then turn left to reach **Desart Guest House ❸,** 99 Cathedral Rd., a formidable mansion with sunny and plush rooms. (☎3752 2387. Singles £20; doubles £35.) **Maghnavery House ❸,** 89 Gosford Rd., just outside of town, is a converted 19th-century farmhouse perfect for those looking to explore Armagh, Newry, and the Gosford Forest Park. (☎3755 2021; www.maghnaveryhouse.co.uk. Singles £25-30; doubles £40-50.)

⌂⌗ FOOD AND PUBS. Finding an eatery in the city center or near the Shambles Market is easy, though budget options are limited. Buy **groceries** from **Sainsbury's** in the Mall Shopping Centre. (☎3751 1050. Open M-W and Sa 8:30am-8pm, Th-F 8:30am-9pm.) **downstairs@turners ❺,** Armagh's best and most popular restaurant, is tucked away beneath Turner's bar. (☎3752 2719. Salmon £14. Lunch Tu-F and Su noon-3pm. Dinner Th-Sa only 5:30pm-9:30pm.) **Rainbow Restaurant ❷,** 13 Lower English St., is a student hangout during term, serving buffet-style lunches in a cheery location. (☎3752 5391. Lunch from £4. Open M-F 8:45am-5:30pm, Sa 8:45am-9pm.) **Turner's,** 56-57 Upper English St., hosts a mixed twentysomething crowd. (☎3752 2028. Open M-Th and Su 11:30am-11:30pm, F-Sa 11:30am-1am.) Come to cozy **Red Ned's,** 27 Ogle St., for Gaelic football matches and trad every other W. (☎3752 2249. 18+. Open M-Sa 11:30am-1am, Su 12:30pm-midnight.)

◎ SIGHTS. Armagh's cathedrals lord over the city from two opposing hills. To the north, on Cathedral Rd., sits the 1873 Roman Catholic **Cathedral of St. Patrick,** whose imposing exterior clashes with the ultra-modern sanctuary. (☎3752 2802; www.armaghdiocese.org. Open daily until dusk. Free.) To the south is the other **Cathedral of St. Patrick,** or rather, "the Protestant one." Authorities claim that this 13th-century church rests on the site where Patrick founded his main church in AD 445. (☎3752 3142; www.stpatrickscathedralar-magh.com. Open daily Apr.-Oct. 10am-5pm; Nov.-Mar. 10am-4pm. Suggested donation £2.) In the center of town, ▨**St. Patrick's Trian** shares a building with the tourist office. Most exhibits emphasize Patrick's role in Armagh: **Patrick's Testament** introduces the curious to the patron saint's writings. Walk through the **Armagh Story** to learn about the lengthy history of the town. Up College Hill, north of the Mall, the **Armagh Observatory** (☎3752 2928) was founded in 1790 by Archbishop Robinson. Tourists can observe a modern weather station and 1885 refractory telescope.

Two miles west of Armagh on Killylea Rd. (A28), mysterious **Navan Fort** was the capital of the Kings of Ulster for 800 years. Now a grassy mound of dirt, it once held extensive fortifications. Queen Macha is said to have founded the fort, although it is also associated with St. Patrick, who probably chose Armagh as a Christian center because of its proximity to this pagan stronghold. (Open daily dawn-dusk.)

COUNTIES ANTRIM AND DERRY

The A2 coastal road connects the scenic attractions of Co. Antrim and Derry. North of Belfast, stodgy, industrial Larne gives way to lovely seaside villages. The breathtaking scenery of the nine Glens of Antrim then sweeps visitors north to the Giant's Causeway, which spills its geological honeycomb into the ocean off the northern coast. This mid-section of the coast road is a cyclist's paradise. Urban sprawl reappears past the Causeway with the carnival lights of Portrush and Portstewart. The road terminates at Derry, the North's second-largest city.

LARNE (LATHARNA)

Larne is a working town whose significance to tourists lies in its ferries to and from Scotland. **P&O Ferries** (☎ 087 0242 4777; www.poirishsea.com) operates boats from Larne to **Cairnryan and Troon,** Scotland and **Fleetwood,** England. The **train station,** Narrow Gauge Rd., rests adjacent to a roundabout, down the street from the TIC. (☎ 9066 6630. Open Su-F 6:50am-5pm, Sa 8:30am-5:20pm.) The **bus station** is south of town, on the other side of the A8. (☎ 2827 2345. Open M-F 9am-5:15pm.)

Rather than lingering near the ferry port, seek beds down Glenarm Rd., in the more affluent area closer to town. **Inverbann ❷,** 7 Glenarm Rd., has satellite TVs and ensuite rooms. (☎ 2827 2524. ₤18.50 per person.) The **Co-op Superstore** is on Station Rd. by the bus station. (☎ 2826 0737. Open M-W 9am-9pm, Th-F 9am-10pm, Sa 9am-8pm, Su 1-6pm.) The main street is lined with cheap sandwich shops.

To reach town from the harbor, take a right outside of the ferry port. It's a good idea to cab it in the evening, as the route passes through a rough neighborhood. The **Tourist Information Centre,** Narrow Gauge Rd., books rooms. (☎ 2826 0088; www.larne.gov.uk. Open Easter-Sept. M-F 9am-5:15pm, Sa 10am-5pm; Oct.-Easter M-F 9am-5pm.) **Northern Bank,** 19 Main St., has 24hr. **ATMs.**

GLENS OF ANTRIM

During the Ice Age, glaciers sliced through the mountainous coastline northeast of Antrim, leaving nine deep scars in their wake. Over the years, water collected in these valleys, spurring the growth of trees, ferns, and other lush flora not usually found in Ireland. The A2 coastal road connects the mouths of these glens and provides entry to roads inland, allowing weekenders easy access to the area.

Two **Ulsterbus** (Belfast ☎ 9032 0011, Larne 2827 2345) routes serve the glens year-round. Bus #156 from **Belfast** stops in **Larne, Ballygally, Glenarm,** and **Carnlough** (summer M-Sa 6-7 per day, Su 3 per day; low season M-Sa 5-7 per day, Su 1 per day; ₤2.80-5.20) and sometimes continues to **Waterfoot, Cushendall, and Cushendun** (summer M-F 4 per day, Sa-Su 2 per day; low season M-F 2 per day). Bus #150 runs between **Ballymena** and **Glenariff** (M-Sa 5 per day, ₤2.60), then to **Waterfoot, Cushendall,** and **Cushendun** (M-F 5 per day, Sa 3 per day; ₤4.30). The **Antrim Coaster** (#252) goes coastal from **Belfast** to **Coleraine** and stopping at every town along the way (2 per day, ₤7.50). **Cycling** the glens is fabulous from Ballygally to Cushendun; beyond Cushendun, the hilly road makes even motorists groan.

GLENARIFF

Guarded by the village of **Waterfoot,** beautiful, broad Glenariff is 9 mi. up the coast from Glenarm. The glen lies inside large **Glenariff Forest Park,** 4 mi. south of Waterfoot on the Glenariff Rd. (A43). The park's many trails range from half-mile to 5 mi. round-trips. The 3 mi. ◪**Waterfall Trail,** marked by blue triangles, follows the fern-lined Glenariff River from the park entrance to the Manor Lodge. The entrance to **Moyle Way,** a 17 mi. hike from Glenariff to Ballycastle, is directly across from the park entrance. All of the walks begin and end at the carpark, where you'll also find the **Glenariff Tea House ❶,** which has food and free trail maps. (☎2175 8769. Open daily Easter-Sept. 11am-6pm.)

The **bus** between Cushendun and Ballymena (#150) stops at the official park entrance (M-Sa 3-5 per day). If walking from Waterfoot, enter 1½ mi. downhill by taking the road that branches left toward the Manor Lodge Restaurant. About ½ mi. past town toward Larne, **Lurig View B&B ❸,** 38 Lurig View on Glen Rd., provides comfy beds and tasty breakfasts. (☎2177 1618. ₤20 per person.)

CUSHENDALL (BUN ABHANN DALLA)

Cushendall is nicknamed "the capital of the Glens," most likely because its village center consists of *four* shop-lined streets instead of just one. In addition to its commercial significance, Cushendall is also well situated, less than 5 mi. from Glenaan, Glenariff, Glenballyeamon, Glencorp, and Glendun. Grab a bus to the picturesque seaside village of **Cushendun,** 5 mi. north of Cushendall on the A2. In 1954, the National Trust bought the entire minuscule village, a whitewashed and black-shuttered set of buildings lying by a vast beach and perforated by wonderful, murky **caves** carved into red sea cliffs. **Mary McBride's,** 2 Main St. (☎2176 1511), used to be in the *Guinness Book of World Records* as the smallest bar in Europe. The original bar remains but has been expanded to create a lounge.

Ulsterbus (☎9033 3000) #162 runs from **Belfast** (₤6.50) via **Larne** (₤5.50), then north to **Cushendun** (July-Aug. M-F 5 per day, Sa-Su 2 per day; Sept.-June M-F 2 per day). Bus #252 stops everywhere, including Cushendall; #150 stops in **Glenariff. Ardclinis Activity Centre,** 11 High St., **rents bikes** and gives tips on outdoor activities. (☎2177 1340. Bikes ₤10 per day. ₤50 deposit.) The **Tourist Information Centre,** 25 Mill St., is near the bus stop at the Cushendun end of town. (☎2177 1180. Open July-Sept. M-F 10am-1pm and 2-5:30pm, Sa 10am-1pm and 2-4pm; Oct. to mid-Dec. and Feb.-June Tu-Sa 10am-1pm.) **Northern Bank** is at 5 Shore St. (☎2177 1243. Open M 9:30am-12:30pm and 1:30-5pm, Tu-F 10am-12:30pm and 1:30-3:30pm.) The **post office** is inside Spar Market, on Coast Rd. (☎2177 1201. Open M and W-F 9am-1pm and 2-5:30pm, Tu and Sa 9am-12:30pm.) **Post Code:** BT44.

🏠**Glendale ❷,** 46 Coast Rd., has spacious ensuite rooms. (☎2177 1495. ₤18 per person.) West of Cushendun off the A2, guests at 🏠**Drumkeerin,** 201a Torr Rd., may choose between the immaculate all-white **B&B ❸** and the **camping barn ❶.** Owners Mary and Joe also teach **painting courses** and lead **hill walks** and **historical tours.** (☎2176 1554; www.drumkeerinbedandbreakfast.co.uk. Linens ₤2. Camping barn ₤8.50. B&B with bath ₤22 per person.) **Spar Market,** 2 Coast Rd., past Bridge Rd., stocks fruits and veggies. (☎2177 1763. Open daily 7:30am-10pm.) Find fresh sandwiches at **Arthur's ❶,** Shore St. (☎2177 1627. Open daily 10am-5pm.) 🏠**Joe McCollam's (Johnny Joe's),** 23 Mill St. (☎2177 1876), features impromptu ballads, jigs, and limericks, with music on the weekends.

CAUSEWAY COAST

The sea-battered cliffs of the Causeway Coast run from Ballycastle to Portrush. Before yielding to the spectacular Giant's Causeway, they support friendly towns and tower above white, wave-lapped beaches.

BALLYCASTLE

This bubbly seaside town is often the first stop for Causeway-bound tourists. The 🏠**Ould Lammas Fair,** Northern Ireland's oldest and most famous fair, has been held in Ballycastle for 414 years. On the last Monday and Tuesday of August, trad musicians pack pubs and vendors fill the streets. B&Bs and hostels fill up long in advance. **Castle Hostel (IHH) ❶,** 62 Quay Rd., just in town from shore, next to the Marine Hotel, has a relaxed atmosphere. (☎2076 2337; www.castlehostel.com. Dorms ₤8; private rooms

£10.) **Ballycastle Backpackers (IHO) ❶**, North Rd., is also next to the Marine Hotel. (☎2076 3612. Dorms £8; singles £10, ensuite £12.50-15.) **Fragrens ❸**, 34 Quay Rd., is one of Ballycastle's oldest houses. Enjoy the fresh fruit at breakfast. (☎2076 2168. £20 per person.) For **groceries, SuperValu,** 54 Castle St., is a 10min. walk from the hostels. (☎2076 2268. Open M-Sa 8am-10pm, Su 9am-10pm.) **🔲Flash-in-the-Pan ❶**, 74 Castle St., prepares delicious chipper fare. (☎2076 2251. Open Su-Th 11am-midnight, F-Sa 11am-1am.) Large portions and **Internet access** await at **Herald's ❷**, 22 Ann St. (☎2076 9064. Internet access £1 per 30min. Open daily 8am-8pm.) Tourists head for tiny, fire-warmed **House of McDonnell**, 71 Castle St. (☎2076 2975. Sa folk. W, F, Su trad.) **Central Bar**, 12 Ann St., rollicks with piano sing-alongs. (☎2076 3877. W trad, Th karaoke.)

The main street runs perpendicular to the waterfront, starting at the ocean as **Quay Road**, becoming **Ann Street**, and turning into **Castle Street** as it passes the **Diamond**. **Buses** stop at the end of Quay Rd. **Ulstersbus** runs to Belfast (3hr., M-Sa 5-6 per day, £6.50) and **Cushendall** (50min., M-F 1 per day, £3.20). The **Antrim Coaster** also stops here. **Cushleake B&B**, Quay Rd., **rents bikes**. (☎2076 3798. £7 per day.) The **Tourist Information Centre**, 7 Mary St., has 24hr. computerized information outside. (☎2076 2024. Open July-Aug. M-F 9:30am-7pm, Sa 10am-6pm, Su 2-6pm; Sept.-June M-F 9:30am-5pm.) Other services include **First Trust Bank**, Ann St. (☎2076 3326; open M-F 9:30am-4:30pm, W open 10am) and the **post office**, 3 Ann St. (☎2076 2519; open M-Tu and Th-F 9am-1pm and 2-5:30pm, W 9am-1pm, Sa 9am-12:30pm). **Post Code:** BT54.

RATHLIN ISLAND

Just off the coast at Ballycastle, bumpy, boomerang-shaped **Rathlin Island** ("Fort of the Sea") offers the ultimate in escapism for 20,000 puffins, the odd golden eagle, 100 human inhabitants, and four daily ferry loads of tourists. Its windy surface has few trees, but supports a paradise of orchids and purple heather. For a more complete presentation of the island's intertwined history and myths, visit the island's **Boat House Heritage Centre** at the opposite end of the harbor from the ferry. (☎2076 2225; www.moyle-council.org. Open daily May-Aug. 10am-4pm; other months by arrangement. Free.) The **lighthouse** is the best place from which to view birds, but it's accessible only with the warden's supervision. (Call in advance ☎2076 3948.)

Caledonian MacBrayne runs a ferry service from Ballycastle to the island. The small office at the Ballycastle pier, open before each departure, sells tickets. (☎2076 9299. Round-trip £8.60, children £4.30). **Soerneog View Hostel ❶** (SIR-nock; ☎2076 3954; bike rental £7 per day; laundry £3.50; dorms £8) is less secluded than **Kinramer Camping Barn (ACB) ❶**, 4½ mi. from the harbor (☎2076 3948; dorms or camping beds £5). **McCuaig's** is the island's only bar, and apart from the hotel in the evenings, the only restaurant. (☎2076 3974. Food served daily 9am-9pm.)

CARRICK-A-REDE ROPE BRIDGE

Meaning "rock in the road," Carrick-a-rede presents a barrier to migrating salmon returning to their home rivers. Since 1624, fishermen annually cast their nets in the salmon's path, stringing a **rope bridge** between the mainland and the island from April to September to retrieve their haul. Due to depleted salmon populations, fishing has dissipated, but the bridge remains a popular (if somewhat lackluster) tourist attraction, carefully rebuilt by engineers each summer. Crossing the shaky, 48 in. wide, 67 ft. long bridge over the staggering 100 ft. drop to rocks and sea can be a harrowing experience, but it's much safer than it used to be. Wardens are on site during opening hours, and the bridge closes in windy weather. The walk to the bridge leads courageous crossers along the heights of the limestone **Larrybane sea cliffs**, nesting place of the unusual black-and-white razor bill, the quirky brown-and white-bellied guillemot, and the mundane gull. The National Trust's leaflet, available from a warden upon entrance, has a map of the area's geological notables. (☎2076 2178. Bridge open daily Mar.-Sept. 10am-5:15pm; July-Aug. 9:30am-7pm. Tearoom open daily July-Sept. 10am-8pm. Footbridge £2, students £1.)

GIANT'S CAUSEWAY

Advertised as the eighth natural wonder of the world, the ▨**Giant's Causeway** is Northern Ireland's most popular attraction, so don't be surprised to find 2000 other travelers picked the same day to visit. Geologists believe the unique rock formations were formed some 60 million years ago, when molten lava broke through the surface, cooled, and shrank at an unusually steady rate. Composed of over 40,000 perfectly symmetrical hexagonal basalt columns, the sight resembles a large staircase that descends from the cliffs to the ocean's floor below. Several other formations lie beyond the grand Causeway itself: **The Giant's Organ, The Wishing Chair, The Granny, The Camel,** and **The Giant's Boot. Giant's Causeway Visitor Centre** has information on these sights at the pedestrian entrance to the Causeway. (☎ 2073 1855. Open daily May 10am-5:30pm; June 10am-6pm; July-Aug. 10am-7pm; Sept.-Oct. M-F 10am-5pm, Sa-Su 10am-5:30pm.) The Centre runs **Causeway Coaster minibuses** the half-mile to the columns (2min., 4 per hr., £1.20). **Ulsterbus** #172 to Portrush, the #252 Antrim Coaster, the "Causeway Rambler," and the Bushmills Bus all drop visitors at the Visitors Centre.

BUSHMILLS

2 mi. west of the Causeway lies Protestant Bushmills, home to the **Old Bushmills Distillery,** creator of Bushmills Irish Whiskey since 1608 and the oldest licensed whiskey producer in the world. Travelers have been stopping here since ancient days, when it lay on the route to Tara from castles **Dunluce** and **Dunseverick.** When the plant is operating, the tour shows whiskey being thrice-distilled; during the three weeks in July when production stops for maintenance, the far-less-interesting experience is redeemed only by the free sample at its end. Serious whiskey fans should shoulder their way to the front as the tour winds down and volunteer when the guide makes his cryptic request for "help."

DERRY (DOIRE CHOLM CILLE)

Derry became a major commercial port during the Ulster Plantation of the 17th century. Under the English feudal system, the city became the outpost of London's authority, who renamed it Londonderry. (Phone books and such still use this official title, but many Northerners call the city Derry.) The city's troubled history spans from the siege of Derry in 1689, when the now-legendary Apprentice Boys closed the city gates on the armies of King James II, to the civil rights turmoil of the 1960s, when protests over discrimination against Catholics exploded into violence. In 1972, the Troubles reached their pinnacle on Bloody Sunday, when British soldiers shot into a crowd of peaceful protesters. Hearings into the incident were recently held in Derry's Guildhall; a verdict is scheduled for October 2004.

▐▀ TRANSPORTATION

Flights: Eglinton/Derry Airport, Eglinton (☎ 7181 0784). 4 mi. from Derry. Flights to **Dublin, Glasgow, London-Stansted,** and **Manchester.**

Trains: Waterside Station, Duke St. (☎ 7134 2228), on the east bank. Trains to **Belfast** (2½hr.; M-Sa 9 per day, Su 4 per day; £8.60).

Buses: Most stop at the Ulsterbus depot, Foyle St., between the walled city and the river. (☎ 0128 9066 6630). Open 7am-10pm. **Ulsterbus** (☎ 7126 2261) runs #212 to **Belfast** (1½-3hr.; M-Sa 35 per day, Su 6 per day; £8); #275 to **Donegal** (1½hr., M-Sa at noon); #274 to **Dublin** via **Omagh** (4-6 per day, £12.80). **Swilly Buses** (☎ 7126 2017) sends buses to: **Buncrana** (35min.; M-Sa 10 per day, Su 4 per day; £4); **Letterkenny** (1hr.; M-F 12 per day, Sa 12 per day; £6); **Malin Head** (1½hr.; M-F 2 per day, Sa 3 per day; £7.40). **Northwest Busways** (Republic ☎ 077 82619) run to: **Inishowen** and **Buncrana** (M-Sa 9 per day, £2.50); **Malin Head** (2 per day, £4.20).

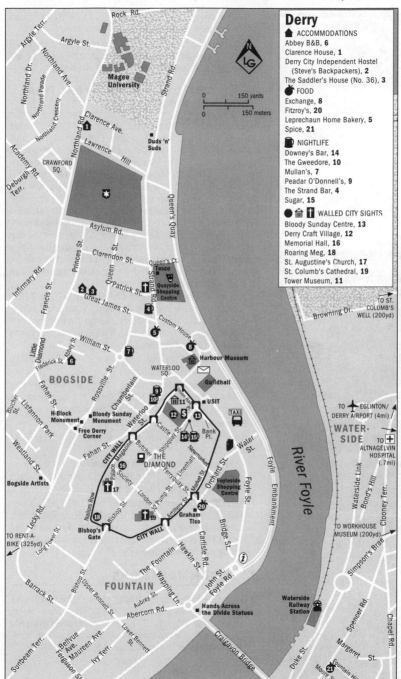

Derry

⌂ ACCOMMODATIONS
Abbey B&B, 6
Clarence House, 1
Derry City Independent Hostel
  (Steve's Backpackers), 2
The Saddler's House (No. 36), 3

🍴 FOOD
Exchange, 8
Fitzroy's, 20
Leprechaun Home Bakery, 5
Spice, 21

🍺 NIGHTLIFE
Downey's Bar, 14
The Gweedore, 10
Mullan's, 7
Peadar O'Donnell's, 9
The Strand Bar, 4
Sugar, 15

● 🏛 ⓘ WALLED CITY SIGHTS
Bloody Sunday Centre, 13
Derry Craft Village, 12
Memorial Hall, 16
Roaring Meg, 18
St. Augustine's Church, 17
St. Columb's Cathedral, 19
Tower Museum, 11

NORTHERN IRELAND

THE BOGSIDE MURALS

1 **The Bloody Sunday Monument** remembers 14 non-violent protesters who died on January 30, 1972 when British soldiers fired into a crowd of civil rights marchers. British-run Widgery Inquiry found no foul play on the part of British troops. Reopened in 1999, a verdict is scheduled for October 2004.

2 The **H-Block Monument** commemorates the 10 lost to the 1981 hunger strike, which grew out of blanket protests, in which no inmates would wear prison uniforms or bathe.

3 Free Derry Corner marks the eastside barrier of the sealed-off Bogside outpost. The painted side of the house is not the original facade. In 1972, British troops were ordered to break the wall down; it was repeatedly rebuilt. A widely recognized symbol of Republican resistance, the monument is untouchable; traffic patterns go around it.

Taxis: Derry Taxi Association (☎ 7126 0247). Also offers tours for around £20.

Bike Rental: Rent-A-Bike, 245 Lone Moor Rd. (☎ 7128 7128; www.happydays.ie), a 20min. walk from the city center. £10 per day, £40 per week. ID deposit.

■✳ 🛈 ORIENTATION AND PRACTICAL INFORMATION

Derry straddles **River Foyle,** just east of the border with Republican Co. Donegal. The city center and university area both lie on the Foyle's western banks. The medieval **walled city,** now Derry's downtown, has a pedestrian shopping district around **Waterloo Street.** In the center of the old city lies the **Diamond,** from which radiate four main streets: **Shipquay Street, Butcher Street, Bishop Street,** and **Ferryquay.** The Catholic **Bogside** neighborhood, which became Free Derry in the 70s, is west of the city walls; most of the Protestant population lives on the Foyle's eastern bank. The train station can be reached from the center by way of **Craigavon Bridge** or a free shuttle at the bus station.

Tourist Information Centre: 44 Foyle St. (☎ 7126 7284; www.derryvisitor.com), in the Derry Visitor and Convention Bureau. Ask for *Derry Tourist Guide, Visitor's Guide,* and free city maps. Books accommodations throughout Northern Ireland.

Bank: Bank of Ireland, Shipquay St. (☎ 7126 4992). Open M-F 9:30am-4:30pm.

Launderette: Duds 'n' Suds, 141 Strand Rd. (☎ 7126 6006). Wash £2, dry £2.50. Open M-F 8am-9pm, Sa 8am-6pm. Last wash 1½hr. before close.

Police: Strand Rd. (☎ 7136 7337).

Hospital: Altnagelvin Hospital, Glenshane Rd. (☎ 7134 5171).

Internet Access: bean-there.com, 20 The Diamond (☎ 7128 1303). £1 per 10min., £2 per 30min. Open M-F 9am-7pm, Sa 10am-6pm, Su 10am-5pm.

Post Office: 3 Custom House St. (☎ 7136 2563). Open M-F 8:30am-5:30pm, Sa 9am-12:30pm. *Poste Restante* letters usually go to the **Postal Sorting Office** (☎ 7136 2577), on the corner of Great James and Little James St. **Post Code:** BT48.

🏠 ACCOMMODATIONS

▨ **Derry City Independent Hostel (Steve's Backpackers),** 44 Great James St. (☎ 7137 7989), 5min. from the city center down Strand Rd. This relaxed hostel offers maps and advice and organizes trips to Giant's Causeway. Free breakfast and Internet access. Dorms £10; doubles £28. ❶

The Saddler's House (No. 36), 36 Great James St. (☎7126 9691; www.thesaddlershouse.com). This Victorian home is an ultimate comfort zone. They also run **The Merchant's House,** 16 Queen St. Both houses singles £30; doubles £45-50. ❹

Abbey B&B, Abbey St. (☎7127 9000 or 079 5817 4289; www.abbeyaccommodation.com). Close to the city center and in the Bogside neighborhood, this B&B greets visitors with coffee and spacious peach rooms. £25. Reduced rates for families. ❸

Clarence House, 15 Northland Rd. (☎7126 5342; www.clarenceguesthouse.co.uk). Wide breakfast offerings and quality rooms stocked with phones, hair dryers, TVs, irons, and bottled water. £27, ensuite £35. Reduced prices for longer stays. ❸

🄲 FOOD

Tesco, in the Quayside Shopping Centre, is a short walk from the walled city along Strand Rd. (Open M-Th 9am-9pm, F 8:30am-9pm, Sa 8:30am-8pm, Su 1-6pm.)

Exchange, Queens Quay (☎7127 3990), down Great James St. toward the River Foyle and a right at the Derry City Hotel. Up-market eatery with private booths and an extensive drink menu. Dinner £8.50-13.75. Open M-Sa noon-10pm, Su 5-9:30pm. ❸

Spice, 162 Spencer Rd. (☎7134 4875), on the east bank. Appetizers £3-4. Daily veggie specials £7.95. Sesame seed pork with ginger dressing £8.50. Seabass with tomato and coriander salsa £11.50. Open daily 12:30-2:30pm and 5:30-10pm. ❸

Fitzroy's, 2-4 Bridge St. (☎7126 6211), next to Bishop's Gate. Modern cafe culture and filling meals, from simple chicken breast to mango lamb. During the day, most meals £4-6. Entrees £7-12. Open M-Tu 10am-8pm, W-Sa 9:30am-10pm, Su noon-8pm. ❷

Leprechaun Home Bakery, 21-23 Strand Rd. (☎7136 3606). Eclairs, buns, cakes, and other confections; sandwiches, salads, and meals (£3-5). Open M-Sa 9am-5:30pm. ❶

👁 SIGHTS

🄼**THE CITY WALLS.** Derry's city walls, 18 ft. high and 20 ft. thick, were erected between 1614 and 1619. They've never been breached, hence Derry's nickname: "the Maiden City." A walk along the top of this mile-long perimeter takes about 20min. The stone tower topping the southeast wall past New Gate was

4 The Rioter: A single rioter holds a bedspring shield against an oncoming British tank during the 1969 Battle of the Bogside.

5 The **Civil Rights Mural** depicts a peaceful protest march of the 1960s. The violent clash between such protestors and the RUC on March 5, 1968 precipitated the Troubles in Northern Ireland.

6 Bloody Sunday Mural: The depicted priest, Edward Daly, helps rush gunshot wound victim Jackie Duddy from the crossfire.

7 Petrol Bomber Mural: A boy with a petrol bomb wears a gas mask to protect himself from gas used by the Royal Ulster Constabulary against Republicans in the 1969 fighting.

8 Death of an Innocent is a portrait of 14-year-old Annette McGavigan, the 100th victim of the Troubles. In 1971 she was caught in crossfire of IRA and British troops on her way home from school, becoming the first child to die because of Derry fighting.

built to protect **St. Columb's Cathedral,** the symbolic focus of the city's Protestant defenders. Stuck in the center of the southwest wall, **Bishop's Gate** was remodeled in 1789 into an ornate triumphal gate in honor of William of Orange.

ST. COLUMB'S CATHEDRAL. Built between 1628 and 1633, this was the first purpose-built Protestant cathedral in Britain or Ireland; all the older ones were confiscated Catholic cathedrals. The original lead-coated wood spire was in disrepair at the time of the Great Siege, so the city's defenders removed its lead and smelted it into bullets and cannonballs. Like many Protestant churches in the North, St. Columba's is bedecked with war banners, including flags from the Crimean War, the World Wars, and two yellow flags captured from the French at the Great Siege. A tiny, museum-like **chapter house** displays the original locks and relics from the 1689 siege. *(London St., off Bishop St. ☎ 7126 7313; www.stcolumbscathedral.org. Open Easter.-Oct. M-Sa 9am-5pm; Nov.-Mar. M-Sa 9am-4pm. Tours £2.)*

TOWER MUSEUM. Derry's top attraction utilizes engaging walk-through dioramas and audiovisual displays to relay Derry's intriguing history, from its days as a mere oak grove, through the siege of 1689, and onward to the Troubles. *(Union Hall Pl. ☎ 7137 2411; www.derry.net/tower. Open July-Aug. M-Sa 10am-5pm, Su 2-5pm; Sept.-June Tu-Sa 10am-5pm. Last admission 4:30pm. £4.20, students and seniors £1.60, families £8.50.)*

THE FOUNTAIN ESTATE. The Protestant Fountain Estate is reached from the walled city by exiting through the left side of Bishop's Gate; it's contained by Bishop St., Upper Bennett St., Abercorn St., and Hawkin St. This small area of 600 residents holds the most interesting Protestant murals.

THE BOGSIDE. This famous Catholic neighborhood is hard to miss—a huge sign west of the city walls at the junction of Fahan St. and Rossville Sq. declares "You Are Now Entering Free Derry." It was originally painted in 1969 on the end of a row house; the houses of the block have since been knocked down, but this end-wall remains, with a frequently repainted but never reworded message. The powerful mural is surrounded by other striking Nationalist artistic creations, and the spot is referred to as **Free Derry Corner.** Nearby, a stone monument commemorates the 14 protesters killed on Bloody Sunday.

🖪 🖷 PUBS AND CLUBS

Mullan's, 13 Little James St. (☎ 7126 5300), on the corner of William and Rossville St. Incredible pub with idiosyncratically lavish decor, from stained-glass ceilings and bronze lion statues to flat-screen TVs. A disproportionate number of women at M night karaoke. W and Th live music, F-Su DJs play house.

Peadar O'Donnell's, 53 Waterloo St. (☎ 7137 2318). Named for the Donegal Socialist who organized the Irish Transport and General Workers Union and took an active role in the 1921 Irish Civil War. Trad nightly. Open M-Sa 11am-1am, Su 7pm-midnight.

The Gweedore, 59-61 Waterloo St. (☎ 7126 3513). The back door has been connected to Peadar's since Famine times. Rock, bluegrass, and funk nightly. Open M-Th 4:30pm-1am, Th-Sa 2pm-1am, Su noon-midnight.

The Strand Bar, 31-35 Strand Rd. (☎ 7126 0494). 4 floors. Th-F live music downstairs; F DJs on every floor. Cover £2-5. Open M-Sa 11:30am-1:30am, Su noon-midnight.

Downey's Bar, 33 Shipquay St. (☎ 7126 0820). Surreal decor attracts a young crowd. 20 purple pool tables and an open ceiling over the bar. Tu-Th live music, F-Sa DJs.

Sugar, 33 Shipquay St., behind Downey's Bar. The newest nightclub in Derry. Big-name DJs drop in on weekends. F and Su 21+, cover £3; Sa 23+, cover £5.

h of Belfast has changed dramatically e the 1994 cease-fires and the 1998 peace eement. Signs of the conflict that engulfed rthern Ireland for 30 years have nearly van ed from the city center, where cozy cafes, anky new bars, and bustling shoppers have placed the army jeeps, battle-scarred build gs, and grim desolation downtown Belfast as once known for. The peace process has een good for business, but take the time to enture just beyond the commercial center, nd you'll find that in many neighborhoods at he front lines of the conflict, the peace divi dend never arrived.

Belfast remains a divided city, and the numerous walls (innocently referred to as 'peace lines') built along the city's internal frontiers are by far the most visible indication of persistent sectarian divisions. The city is a patchwork of single-identity communities; the 2001 census revealed that two-thirds of the city's population live in areas that are either more than 90% Catholic or 90% Protestant. A peace-line marks the dividing line of inter face—the area where a majority Catholic/ nationalist community runs up against a major ity Protestant/Unionist community. Residential segregation has actually increased since the peace process began and in some areas con struction on the walls continues—new ones built and old ones lengthened and heightened, divisions solidified and rigidified amidst the decade-long peace process.

The walls were constructed over the course of the Troubles to separate warring communi ties, prevent attacks, and sometimes create a buffer zone. Many of the peace-lines in place today stand on ground that has been brutally contested for decades. Tensions run high in areas of such close contact, and attacks on the other community are easily launched from the safety of one's own. Long before the modern Troubles began, there was a history of inter face communities building barricades during times of conflict. Riots broke out in Belfast periodically in the first half of the century— during the 1920s with the Anglo-Irish War and subsequent Irish Civil War, and throughout the Depression in the 1930s. In areas affected by the violence, local residents erected barricades to guard their streets from marauding mobs and, in some cases, the security forces.

When parts of Belfast descended into chaos in the late 1960s and early 70s, many communi ties constructed barricades to protect them selves from the violence sweeping the city. In the early years much of this was concentrated in the borderland between Catholic/nationalist Falls and Protestant/Unionist Shankill. British troops arrived in August of 1969, and within a month they assembled the first official peace line between the two areas to try to prevent some of the rioting. The army's wall ran along the same line as some community barricades, replacing and institutionalizing them with a permanent structure. Originally intended to be a temporary response, what began as a simple fence became fortified, elongated, and elevated to the 1½ mile brick wall standing today.

The peace-line solution became an increas ingly acceptable (and sought after) solution to intercommunal conflict at interface areas. Walls, fences, and official roadblocks were constructed throughout Belfast—with community activists from across the divide sometimes working together to lobby for their construction. By the year 2000, the Northern Ireland Office (NIO) Civil Representative's Office reported a total of 27 sep arate walls or fences across the city.

Mysteriously, none of these walls appear on most Belfast maps. Standing next to one, it's hard to imagine how such a dominant and obstructive fixture on the urban landscape could be disre garded. The walls forcefully demarcate not only space but identity as well. As they fortify and contain those within, they identify and guard against those beyond. Some look much like the war wounds they are—looming expanses of cor rugated metal sprayed with graffiti epithets and crowned with thick coils of barbed wire. Others demonstrate the NIO's recent creative efforts to make the walls less of an eyesore—red and yel low brick with discreet security cameras and tasteful wrought iron accessories. Designed to blend more readily into the environment, these new additions achieve a different sense of perma nence. This worries some community members who live in interface areas. In recent debates over whether to build new walls and expand oth ers in flashpoint areas, some have argued that once you begin building walls, they're very hard to take down. Once you go to the effort to make them pretty, the chances they will ever be removed become even more remote.

For the last three years, Brenna Powell has worked at the Stanford Center on Conflict and Negotia tion on projects in partnership with grass-roots organizations in Northern Ireland.

REPUBLIC OF IRELAND (ÉIRE)

Jagged coastal cliffs, thatch-roofed cottages, misty days, and green rolling hills—these are the poetic images of Ireland that dominate the mind. Most travelers don't realize, however, that Ireland is a country on the rise. Poverty and unemployment have historically been widespread, but the EU has brought new life; impressed by the island's recent economic boom, the international media has christened Ireland the "Celtic Tiger." Under an influx of new faces—recent refugees and immigrants have brought Ireland its first-ever population increase—the country's conservatism is slowly cracking. The short-term result is a growing generation gap and disparity between rural and urban areas. Amid the necessary grime of modernization, the lifestyle of the Irish continues unsullied, centering itself around music, sports, and The Pub.

Six of Ulster's nine counties make up Northern Ireland (p. 695), officially a territory of the United Kingdom. Under the 1998 Northern Ireland Peace Agreement, residents of Northern Ireland may choose whether to individually identify themselves as Irish or British, but word choice can still be tricky, as some identify with neither. "Ulster" is a term used exclusively by Protestants in the North. It's best to refer to "Northern Ireland" or "the North" and "the Republic" or "the South." "Southern Ireland" is not a viable term.

For even more detailed coverage of the Emerald Isle, head to your nearest book store for a copy of ⬛Let's Go: Ireland 2005.

HIGHLIGHTS OF THE REPUBLIC OF IRELAND

DUBLIN Relax on the grounds of **Trinity College,** windowshop on **Grafton Street,** then head around the corner to **Temple Bar** for a night of tomfoolery (p. 732).

RING OF KERRY Run the peninsula's circuit (p. 779), and explore the exquisite mountains, lakes, and forests of **Killarney National Park** (p. 780).

GALWAY Down pints of Guinness while enjoying the musical vigor and copious craic of the city's myriad pubs (p. 793).

COUNTY DONEGAL Brush up on your Irish in Ireland's largest gaeltacht (p. 810), and hike past Europe's highest sea cliffs at **Slieve League** (p. 809).

LIFE AND TIMES

A TALE OF IRELAND PAST

ANCIENT HISTORY. Our fragmented knowledge of ancient Irish culture comes from the scant remains of the stone structures left behind. Among these relics are **dolmens,** table-like arrangements of huge stones; **passage tombs** (like **Newgrange,** p. 760); and **stone circles.** This original civilization, which arrived from Britain around 7000 BC, was soon replaced by the **Celts.** Though some Celts may have come as early as 2000 BC, their real migration started in 600 BC. They prospered in farming communities, with regional chieftains and provincial kings ruling territories called túatha. Pagan life was good—or so epics like the Táin would have us believe.

PRICE RANGES>>IRELAND

Our researchers list establishments in order of value from best to worst; our favorites are denoted by the Let's Go thumbs-up (👍). Since the best value is not always the cheapest price, however, we have also incorporated a system of price ranges, based on a rough expectation of what you'll spend. For **accommodations,** we base our range on the cheapest price for which a single traveler can stay for one night. For **restaurants** and other dining establishments, we estimate the average amount a traveler will spend. The table tells you what you'll *typically* find in Ireland at the corresponding price range; keep in mind that no system can allow for every individual establishment's quirks, and you'll typically get more for your money in larger cities. In other words: expect anything.

ACCOMMODATIONS	RANGE	WHAT YOU'RE *LIKELY* TO FIND
❶	under €17/£14	Camping; most dorm rooms, such as HI, HINI, An Óige; other hostels; or a university. Expect bunk beds and communal bath; may have to provide or rent towels and sheets.
❷	€17-26/£14-21	Upper-end hostels or small hotels. May have a private bathroom, or there may be a sink in the room and communal shower in the hall.
❸	€27-41/£22-31	Most B&Bs or a small room with private bath in a hotel. Should have decent amenities, such as phone and TV. Breakfast may be included in the price of the room.
❹	€42-56/£32-46	Similar to 3, but may have more amenities or be in a more touristed area.
❺	above €57/£47	Large hotels or upscale chains. If it's a 5 and it is without the perks you want, you've paid too much.
FOOD	RANGE	WHAT YOU'RE *LIKELY* TO FIND
❶	under €6/£4	Mostly street-corner stands, pizza places, or fast-food joints. Rarely ever a sit-down meal.
❷	€6-10/£4-6	Sandwiches, bar appetizers, or low-priced entrees. May have the option of sitting down or takeaway.
❸	€11-15/£7-10	Mid-priced entrees, possibly with soup or salad. Tip'll add some, since you'll probably have a waiter or waitress.
❹	€16-20/£11-15	A somewhat fancy restaurant or castle. Either way, you'll have a special knife. Few restaurants in this range have a dress code, but some look down on t-shirt and jeans.
❺	above €21/£16	Food with foreign names and a decent wine list. Slacks and dress shirts may be expected.

IRELAND

The Counties of the Republic and Northern Ireland

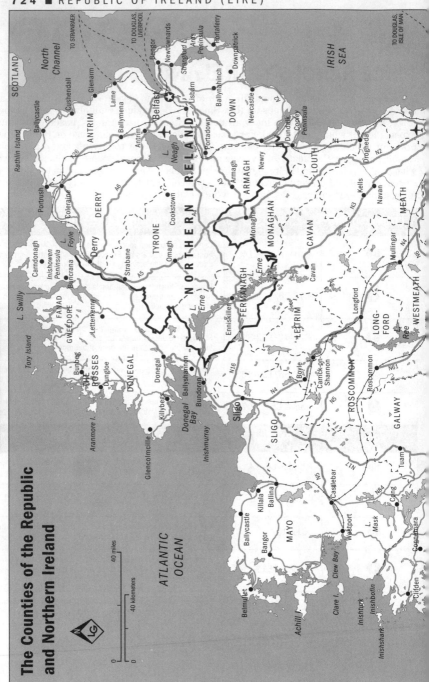

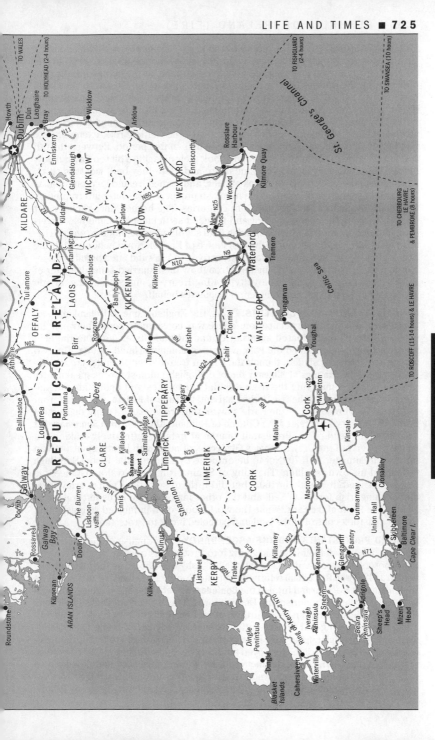

IRELAND

EARLY INVASIONS. Born in Scotland in the early 5th century and kidnapped by Irish pirates, **St. Patrick** was enslaved and forced to tend the pirates' sheep in Ireland. Although he eventually escaped back to Scotland, at the command of a prophetic vision he returned to the Emerald Isle to spread the Gospel to the Celts. Later monks helped St. Patrick bring Christianity to the island; at the same time, they recorded observations of the unfamiliar Celtic culture, with its indigenous writing system found on **ogham stones** and Viking-inspired **round towers. High crosses,** which combine the Christian cross with the Celtic circle, exemplify the melding of Christian and indigenous Celtic beliefs in this period. Between the 6th and 8th centuries, Continental barbarians took their pillaging a bit too far, and new hordes of asylum-seeking monks came to Ireland. Here they built **monastic cities,** illuminated manuscripts like the **Book of Kells,** and earned Ireland its reputation as the "land of saints and scholars." This monkish prosperity was later interrupted by the **Viking** invasions of the 9th and 10th centuries. The hornèd ones raided most frequently along the southern coast and founded settlements at Limerick, Waterford, and Dublin. In 1002, High King **Brian Ború** set off a period of inter-*túath* strife; after his death, chieftains sought the assistance of English Norman nobles to bring peace. Richard de Clare (a.k.a. **Strongbow**) arrived in 1169 and cut a bloody, Anglo-Norman swath through south Leinster. Strongbow then married **Aoife,** daughter of Ború's successor, affirming his loyalty to King Henry II, and with characteristic generosity offered to govern Leinster on England's behalf.

FEUDALISM AND ITS DISCONTENTS. Thus, the English came to Ireland and settled down for a nice, long occupation. There was constant bickering between the Gaelic lords, who dominated agrarian Connacht and Ulster, and the English, whose strongholds included the **Pale,** a fortified domain around Dublin. The two sides were culturally similar, though the Crown fretted over potential cross-pollination: the 1366 **Statutes of Kilkenny** banned English colonists from speaking to, dressing like, or marrying the Irish. Feudal skirmishes and economic decline plagued the island until the rise of the charismatic **Earls of Kildare,** who ruled from 1470 to 1534. Threatened by the Earls' power, the Crown passed more oppressive laws. After Henry VIII created the Church of England, the 1537 **Irish Supremacy Act** declared him head of the Protestant **Church of Ireland**—effectively making the island property of the Crown. **Thomas FitzGerald,** at odds with Henry, sponsored an uprising in Munster in 1579. Not to be outdone by Leinster, the Ulster Earl **Hugh O'Neill** led his own rebellion. The King of Spain promised naval assistance; his Armada arrived in Kinsale in 1601, but did little to stop the English army from demolishing Irish forces. O'Neill and the other major Gaelic lords left Ireland in 1607 in the **Flight of the Earls.** While the world looked on in feigned astonishment, the English took control of the land and parceled it out to Protestants.

PLANTED PROTESTANTS AND THE ASCENDANCY. The English project of dispossessing Catholics of their land and giving it to Protestants (mostly Scottish tenants and laborers, themselves displaced by the English) was known as the **Ulster Plantation.** In 1642, **Owen Roe O'Neill** returned from the Continent to lead the now-landless Irish in an insurrection and formed the **Confederation of Kilkenny,** an uneasy alliance between the Church and Irish and English lords. The concurrent **English Civil Wars** (p. 73) complicated matters even further; **Oliver Cromwell's** victory rendered negotiations between King and Confederation something of a moot point. Once things were settled in England, the Lord Protector turned his attention to Ireland and, following standard procedure, destroyed anything he did not occupy. Catholics were massacred and towns razed as tracts of land were confiscated and doled out to soldiers and Protestant vagabonds. Native Irish could go "to Hell or to Connacht"—both desolate and infertile. By 1660, most Irish land was owned by Protestant immigrants. The Restoration settled things down a bit; Charles II passed the 1665 **Act of Explanation,** requiring Protestants to relinquish one-third of their land to the "innocent papists." The Catholics did not hold their breath for this to happen.

In 1688, Catholic **James II,** driven from England by Protestant **William of Orange** and his **Glorious Revolution** (p. 73), came to Ireland to gather military support. James tried to take Derry in 1689, but a rascally and heroic band of **Apprentice Boys** closed the gates on him and commenced the 105-day **Siege of Derry.** William ultimately emerged victorious and sent his rival into exile on July 12, 1690, at the **Battle of the Boyne.** Many Northern Protestants still celebrate the victory each year on July 12 (called **Orange Day** in honor of the king). At the turn of the 18th century, a set of **Penal Laws** brought further Irish oppression, banning (among other things) the practice of Catholicism. In Dublin and the Pale, the Anglo-Irish garden-partied, gossiped, and constructed their way toward a second London. The term **"Ascendancy"** was coined for them; it described a social class whose elitehood depended upon Anglicanism. **Trinity College** was their quintessential institution. Away from the Ascended nonsense, the Catholic merchant class grew in cities like Galway and Tralee; they were taught in secret **hedge schools** and practiced their religion furtively, using large, flat **Mass rocks** when they couldn't get their hands on altars.

REBELLION AND UNION. The *liberté*-fever inspired by the American and French revolutions was particularly strong among a secret group called the **United Irishmen.** The bloody **Rebellion of 1798** erupted with a furious band of peasants and priests, dashing any hopes England held of making Irish society less volatile by relaxing anti-Catholic laws. With the 1801 **Act of Union,** the Crown abolished Irish "self-government" altogether. The Dublin Parliament died, and "The United Kingdom of Great Britain and Ireland" was born. The Church of Ireland entered into an unequal arranged marriage, changing her name to the "United Church of England and Ireland." Dublin's mad gaiety vanished, the Anglo-Irish gentry collapsed, and agrarian violence and poverty escalated. Union did, however, mean Irish representatives now held seats in the British Parliament. Using their newfound suffrage, Irish farmers elected **Daniel O'Connell** in 1829, forcing Westminster to repeal the anti-Catholic laws that would have barred him from taking his seat. "The Liberator" promptly forced Parliament to allot money for improving Irish living conditions. Unfortunately, O'Connell's crusade for the welfare of his people wasn't enough to protect them from a malicious little fungus.

THE FAMINE AND SOCIAL REFORM. The potato was the wundercrop of the rapidly growing Irish population, and reliance on it had devastating effects when the heroic spud fell victim to fungal disease. During the **Great Famine** (1847-51), an estimated two to three million people died and another million emigrated. The societal structure of surviving Irish peasants was completely reorganized; the bottom layer of truly penniless farmers had been eliminated altogether. Depopulation continued, and **emigration** became a way of life. English injustice fueled the formation of angry young Nationalist groups—in 1858, crusaders supporting a violent removal of the oppressors founded a secret society known as the **Fenians,** while the 1870s saw the creation of the **Land League,** which pushed for further reforms.

In 1870, MP **Isaac Butt** founded the **Irish Home Rule Party.** Home Ruler **Charles Stewart Parnell** was a charismatic Protestant aristocrat with a hatred for everything English. Though he survived implication in the **Phoenix Park murders,** he couldn't beat an 1890 adultery rap; the scandal split all of Ireland into Parnellites and anti-Parnellites. While squabbling politicians let their ideals fall to the wayside, civil society waxed ambitious. The fairer sex established the **Irish Women's Suffrage Federation** in 1911, and Marxist **James Connolly** led strikes in Belfast and Dublin. Meanwhile, various groups (like the **Gaelic Athletic Association** and the **Gaelic League**) tried to revive an essential, unpolluted "Gaelic" culture. Arthur Griffith began a

IRELAND

tiny movement and little-read newspaper, both of which went by the name **Sinn Féin** ("Ourselves Alone"). Thousands of Northern Protestants opposing Home Rule organized a quasi-militia called the **Ulster Volunteer Force (UVF).** Nationalists led by Eoin MacNeill responded by creating the **Irish Volunteers.**

THE EASTER RISING, INDEPENDENCE, AND CIVIL WAR. Summer 1914: Irish Home Rule seemed imminent, and Ulster was ready to go up in flames. Instead, someone shot an Austrian archduke, and the world went up in arms. British Prime Minister Henry Asquith passed a **Home Rule Bill** in return for Irish bodies to fill out the British army; 670,000 Irishmen signed up to fight the Kaiser. Meanwhile, the Fenians and **Padraig Pearse** planned a nationwide revolt for **Easter Sunday, 1916.** A crucial shipment of arms went astray, however, and the uprising fell through. The Pearse group rescheduled their rebellion for the following Monday, April 24; they seized Dublin's **General Post Office** and hunkered down for five days of brawling in the streets. The Crown retaliated—15 "ringleaders" were publicly executed. The Irish grew sympathetic to the rebels and increasingly anti-British. The Volunteers reorganized under Fenian bigwig **Michael Collins,** who brought them to Sinn Féin, and **Éamon de Valera** became the party president. In 1918, the British tried to introduce a draft in Ireland, and the Irish lost what little complacency they had left.

Extremist Irish Volunteers started calling themselves the **Irish Republican Army (IRA)** and became Sinn Féin's military might. Thus the British saw another **War for Independence.** In 1920, British Prime Minister **David Lloyd George** passed the **Government of Ireland Act,** which divided the island into Northern and Southern Ireland. Hurried negotiations then produced the **Anglo-Irish Treaty,** creating a 26-county Irish Free State but recognizing British rule over the northern counties. Everyone split on whether to accept the treaty. A nay-saying portion of the IRA occupied the Four Courts in Dublin and sparked two years of **civil war.** The pro-treaty government won, and Sinn Féin denied the legitimacy of the Free State government and expressed its disapproval by refusing to refer to the country by the official name of **Éire.**

IRELAND TODAY

THE ERA DE VALERA. Under the guidance of **Éamon de Valera,** the government ended armed resistance by Republican insurgents. De Valera founded his own political party, **Fianna Fáil,** won the 1932 election, and held power for much of the next 20 years. In 1937, he and the voters approved a permanent **Irish Constitution** and established the country's legislative structure, consisting of two chambers: the **Dáil** (DAHL) and the **Seanad** (SHA-nud). The Prime Minister is the **Taoiseach** (TEE-shuch), and the **President** is the ceremonial head of state. Ireland stayed officially neutral during WWII (known as **The Emergency**), though many Irish citizens identified with the Allies, and about 50,000 served in the British army. Then, in 1948, the **Republic of Ireland** was officially proclaimed, ending British Commonwealth membership altogether. The Crown, which didn't quite catch all that, recognized the Republic a year later and declared that the UK would maintain control over Ulster until the North consented to join the Republic.

RECENT EVENTS. In the 1960s, increased contact with the rest of the world accelerated economic growth, put the brakes on emigration, and fueled national confidence. Ireland entered the European Economic Community, now the **European Union (EU),** in 1973. In 1985, the **Anglo-Irish agreement** let Éire stick an official nose in Northern negotiations. The Irish broke progressive social and political ground in 1990 by choosing **Mary Robinson** as their female president. The small, leftist **Labour Party** also enjoyed enormous, unexpected success, paving the way for further social reform. In 1993, Taoiseach **Albert Reynolds** declared his top priority was to stop violence in Northern Ireland. A year later he announced a cease-fire agreement between Unionists and the IRA. Fianna Fáil won the June 1997 general election, making **Bertie Ahern**, at 45, the youngest Taoiseach in Irish history. Ahern joined the peace talks that produced the **Good Friday Agreement** in April of 1998. (For the recent status of the Agreement, see p. 699.) In the summer of 2001, the Irish populace defeated the **Nice Treaty**, which was the first step in the addition of 12 new nations to the EU. The referendum shocked Ireland's pro-Treaty government and caused quite a little stir on the Continent. The **euro** was formally introduced into Ireland on January 1, 2002 and the Irish pound (the punt) was dropped.

CULTURE AND CUSTOMS

Although there's little reason to walk on pins and needles when interacting with the Irish, a notoriously friendly and warm people, an awareness of certain customs and practices will save you from accidentally giving insult. In general, avoid **jumping the queue** (patience is a virtue—stay in line and wait your turn), shirking your **responsibilities at the pub** (drinks among small groups are often bought in rounds— observe the golden rule), and making inane references to leprechauns or Lucky Charms. **Conversation** is an art in Ireland, and it's important to distinguish between casual and sensitive issues; abortion, divorce, gay marriage, and the Troubles up North, for instance, are not topics for the pub or the bus stop. Above all, be sensitive, and never, ever, call an Irish person "British."

LANGUAGE AND LITERATURE

HISTORY OF THE IRISH LANGUAGE. The oldest vernacular literature and the largest collection of folklore in Europe are both Irish. The constitution declares Irish the national language of the Republic, yet there are only 60,000 individuals in exclusively Irish-speaking communities, or **gaeltacht** (GAYL-tacht). The most prominent *gaeltacht* are in Connemara, Co. Donegal, the Dingle Peninsula, and the Aran Islands. These geographically disparate communities are further divided by three almost mutually incomprehensible dialects: **Connemara, Donegal,** and the southern **Munster Irish.** Irish reentered the lives of the privileged classes with the advent of the **Gaelic Revival.** In 1893, **Douglas Hyde** (who later became the first president of Éire) founded the **Gaelic League** in order to inspire enthusiasm for the language. Today, it has grown in popularity among native English speakers.

LEGENDS AND FOLKTALES. In early Irish society the **bards'** songs of battles, valor, and lineage were the only record chieftains had by which to make decisions. Poetry and politics of the Druidic tradition were so intertwined that *fili*, trained poets, and *breitheamh*, judges, were often the same people. Poets living in chieftains' households invented the art of verse satire and composed "cycles" of tales narrating the lives of a set of heroes and villains. The most extensive is the **Ulster Cycle**, spinning the adventures of King Conchobar (Conor) of Ulster, his archenemy (and ex-wife) Queen Medbh of Connacht, and his nephew and champion **Cúchulainn** (KOO-hu-lin).

SWIFT, WILDE, AND SHAW. In long-colonized Dublin, **Jonathan Swift** (1667-1745) wrote some of the most marvelous satire in the English language. While he defended the Protestant Church of Ireland, Swift still felt compelled to write about the sad condition of starving Irish Catholic peasants. In the mid-19th century, Dublin's talented young writers often moved on to London to make their names. **Oscar Wilde** (1856-1900) produced many sparklingly witty works, including *The Importance of Being Earnest* (1895). Playwright **George Bernard Shaw** (1856-1950), winner of the 1925 Nobel Prize, was also born in Dublin but moved to London in 1876.

IRELAND

YEATS AND THE REVIVAL. Toward the end of the 19th century, a vigorous and enduring effort known today as the **Irish Literary Revival** took over. The early poems of **William Butler Yeats** (1865-1939) invoked a dreamily rural Ireland of loss and legend, and became the first Irishman to win the Nobel Prize for Literature in 1923. In 1904, Yeats and **Lady Gregory** founded the **Abbey Theatre** in Dublin (p. 752), but conflict arose as to how exactly this new body of "Irish" drama was to be written. A compromise was found in the work of **John Millington Synge,** whose experiences on the Aran Islands led him to write *The Playboy of the Western World* (1907), destroying pastoral myths of "classless" Irish peasantry. The play's premiere was met by protests, as was **Sean O'Casey's** *The Plough and the Star* (1926), which depicted the Easter Rebellion without mythologizing its leaders.

JOYCE, BECKETT, AND RECENT AUTHORS. Ireland's most famous expatriate is **James Joyce** (1882-1941), godfather and patron saint of modernism. Joyce's most accessible writing is the collection of short stories titled *Dubliners* (1914), while his masterwork is generally agreed to be the ground-breaking mock-epic *Ulysses* (1922). Like Joyce, **Samuel Beckett** (1906-89) fled to Paris to pursue his writing career; unlike Joyce, he left most of vernacular Ireland behind. His novels, plays *(Waiting for Godot)*, and bleak prose poems convey a stark pessimism about language, society, and life. Beckett won the Nobel Prize in 1969, but did not accept it on the grounds that Joyce had never received it. After the 1940s, Irish poetry once again commanded widespread appreciation. **Patrick Kavanaugh** (1906-67) debunked a mythical Ireland, while **Paul Muldoon** contributes quirk and confusion to humdrum existence. Notorious wit, playwright, poet, and terrorist **Brendan Behan** created semi-autobiographical works about delinquent life in plays like *The Quare Fellow* (1954). Mild-mannered schoolteacher **Roddy Doyle** won the 1994 Booker Prize for *Paddy Clarke Ha Ha Ha.* Ireland's most famous living poet is **Seamus Heaney,** who won the Nobel Prize for Literature in 1995.

MUSIC

Irish traditional music, or **trad,** is the centuries-old array of dances, melodies, and embellishments that has been passed down through generations of musicians. The tunes can be written down, but trad more often consists of improvisation. Best-selling trad studio artists include **Altan** and the **Chieftains,** but most traditional musicians play before smaller, more intimate audiences of locals. **Pub sessions** typically alternate between fast-paced instrumental music and folk songs.

In Ireland there is surprisingly little distinction between music types—a fine musician uses a variety of sources. The London-based **Pogues** fused rock and trad, and whipped out reels and jigs of drunken, punk-damaged revelry. **My Bloody Valentine** wove shimmering distortions to land themselves on the outskirts of grunge. Ireland's rock musicians have also set their sights on mainstream super-stardom; **U2** is Ireland's biggest rock export, and **Sinéad O'Connor** developed her style in Ireland long before she became a phenomenon in America. In recent years, **The Cranberries, The Corrs,** and **Boyzone** have also achieved success abroad.

MEDIA AND SPORTS

The largest **newspapers** in the Republic are *The Irish Times* and *The Irish Independent. The Times* takes a liberal stance and is renowned for its excellent coverage of international affairs. *The Independent* is more internally focused and often maintains a chatty writing style. Many regional papers offer in-depth local news; the largest is *The Cork Examiner.* **British papers** are also sold throughout Ireland. In 1961, the Republic's national radio service made its first television broadcast, naming itself **Radio Telefís Éireann (RTE).** The government's most recent developments include the start of Irish-language radio and TV stations, called **Telifís na Gaelige,** aimed at promoting the use of Irish in modern media forms.

The Irish take enormous pride in their two native sports: Gaelic football and hurling. In 1884, the **Gaelic Athletic Association (GAA)** was founded to establish official rules and regulations for these and other ancient Irish recreations. **Gaelic football** is like a cross between football and rugby, though it predates them both. As fans like to say, if football is a game, then **hurling** is an art. This fast and dangerous-looking sport was first played in the 13th century and is perhaps best imagined as a blend of lacrosse and field hockey. (The women's version of the game is called **camogie.**) **Football** (or soccer) enjoys nearly as fanatical a following, and the Irish are also fiercely devoted to the football clubs of England. Co. Kildare is well-known as a breeding ground for champion **racehorses.** On the byways of Ulster and in certain places in Cork, the strange, quasi-golf game of **road bowling** sees enthusiastic fans lining the twisty playing fields ("roads," that is).

FOOD AND DRINK

The basics of Irish cuisine are simple: specialties include *colcannon* (a potato dish), Guinness stew, and Irish stew. Loud and long will the Irish bards sing the praises of the man who first concocted **black pudding;** as one local butcher put it, it's "some pork, a good deal of blood, and grains and things—all wrapped up in a tube." **White pudding** uses milk instead of blood. Regional specialties include Cork's **crubeen** (tasty pigs' feet), Dublin's **coddle** (boiled sausages and bacon with potatoes), and Waterford's **blaa** (sausage rolls). Best of all culinary delights is **soda bread,** a heavy white loaf especially tasty when fried. Another indigenous bread is **barm brack,** a spicy mixture of dried fruits and molasses mixed to a lead-like density. **Seafood** can be a real bargain in smaller towns' **chippers.**

People of all ages and walks of life head to **pubs** for conversation, food, drink, music, and **craic** (pronounced "crack"; "a good time"). Most pubs host evening trad sessions, and in rural areas there's always a chance that a *seanachaí* (SHAN-ukh-ee; "traveling storyteller") might drop in. Pubs are generally open Monday through Saturday from 10:30am to 11:30pm (11pm in winter) and Sunday from 12:30 to 2pm and 4 to 11pm. Many pubs, especially in Dublin, are now able to obtain late licenses; others have been granted special "early" permits allowing them to open at 7:30am. **Beer** wins a landslide victory as the drink of choice, and **Guinness** inspires a reverence

ON THE MENU

RISE AND SHINE...

The Emerald Isle is a land of B&Bs, and in each of these homey establishments, the breakfast is just as important as the bed. If you want to be full until the sun goes down, ask for a "full fry." Here's a detailed list of what exactly you'll be eating:

Fried Egg: Traditionally fried on one side only, and cooked until the yolk is slightly runny.

Sausages: Pork scraps squeezed into a tube and tied into small links.

Bacon or Rashers: Thin slices of fried pork. Not as crispy as American bacon, and cured differently. Bacon comes from the pig's belly, rashers from its back.

Black & White Pudding: Unique to Irish Breakfasts, these are slices of thick sausage made from pork, barley, oatmeal, and spices. Black pudding gets its special color and flavor from pig's blood. Every butcher has his own recipe, and flavors vary based on the spices used.

Toast: Slices of white "pan," served with tea.

Brown Bread: Hearty, whole-grain bread, often home-made and seasoned with Guinness, served sliced but not toasted.

Waffles: Criss-cut potatoes, deep-fried. Closer to hash browns than pancakes; using syrup on these is probably a mistake.

Tomatoes: Pronounced to-MAH-tos. Halved and fried.

Mushrooms: Sliced and sauteed. Sometimes used as a vegetarian substitute for meat.

otherwise reserved for the Holy Trinity. Known variously as "the dark stuff," "the blonde in the black skirt," or simply "I'll have a pint, please," it's a rich, dark brew with a head thick enough to stand a match in. **Murphy's** is a similar, slightly creamier Cork-brewed stout. **Irish whiskey,** invented by clever monks, is sweeter than its Scottish counterpart; **Jameson** is popular everywhere. In the west, you may hear locals praise "mountain dew," a euphemism for **poitín** (put-CHEEN), an illegal methanol-based distillation sometimes given to cows in labor that ranges in strength from 115 to 140 proof.

COUNTY DUBLIN

DUBLIN   ☎ 01

In a country known for its rural sanctity and relaxed lifestyle, the international flavor and boundless energy of Dublin (Baile Átha Cliath) stand out. With the whole of Ireland changing at an almost disconcerting pace, the Dublin environs, home to close to a third of the country's population, lead the charge. Fueled by international and rural immigration and the deep pockets of the EU, the city's cultural and economic growth has been all but unstoppable. But while Dublin may seem edgy by Irish standards, it's still relatively friendly for a major city. Not quite as cosmopolitan, but just as eclectic as New York or London, Ireland's capital is home to vibrant theater, music, and literary communities, as well as multiple generations of pubs learning to coexist peacefully. Though their city may not resemble the rustic "Emerald Isle" promoted on tourist brochures, Dublin's residents still embody the charm and warmth that have made their country famous.

✈ INTERCITY TRANSPORTATION

Rail lines, bus lines (both state-run and private), and the national highway system all radiate from Dublin. Because intercity transport is so Dublin-centric, you may find it more convenient to arrange your travel in other parts of the Republic while you're in the capital.

Flights: Dublin Airport (☎814 111; www.aer-rianta.ie). For information on international flights to Dublin, see p. 30. **Dublin buses** #41, 41B, and 41C run from the airport to Eden Quay in the city center (40-45min., 3 per hr., €1.65). The **Airlink shuttle** (☎844 4265) runs non-stop to Busáras Central Bus Station and O'Connell St. (20-25min., 6 per hr. 5:15am-11:30pm, €5), and to Heuston Station (50min., €4.50). **Taxis** to the city center cost €20-25.

Trains: Irish Rail Travel Centre, Iarnród Éireann (EER-ann-road AIR-ann), 35 Lower Abbey St. (☎836 6222; www.irishrail.ie). Open M-F 9am-5pm, Sa 9am-1pm. Purchase tickets in advance at the Travel Centre, at a station 20min. before departure, or over the phone (☎703 4070). Trains to: **Belfast** (☎805 4277); **Cork** (☎805 4200); **Galway** (☎805 4222); **Westport** (☎805 4244); **Killarney/Tralee** (☎805 4266); **Limerick** (☎805 4211); **Sligo** (☎805 4255); **Waterford** (☎805 4233); **Wexford/Rosslare** (☎805 4288). Bus #90 connects Busáras, Connolly, Heuston, and Pearse Stations. Connolly and Pearse are also **DART** stations (p. 736).

Connolly Station, Amiens St. (☎703 2358 or 703 2359), north of the Liffey, close to Busáras. Buses #20, 20A, and 90 head south of the river, and the DART runs to Tara Station on the south quay. Trains to: **Belfast** (2hr.; M-Sa 8 per day, Su 5 per day; €31); **Sligo** (3hr.; 3-4 per day; M-Th and Sa €22, F and Su €30); **Wexford/Rosslare** (3hr., 2 per day, €20).

Heuston Station (☎703 2132, night 703 2131), south of Victoria Quay and west of the city center, a 25min. walk from Trinity College. Buses #26, 51, 79, and 90 run from Heuston to the city center. Trains to: **Cork** (3hr., 6 per day, €50); **Galway** (2¾hr.; 7 per day; €25, F and Su €35); **Kilkenny** (2hr.; M-Th and Sa 5 per day, F 1 per day, Su 4 per day; €23); **Limerick** (2½hr., 9 per day, €38); **Tralee** (4hr., 3-4 per day, €52.50); **Waterford** (2½hr., 4-5 per day, €24.50).

Pearse Station (☎888 0226), just east of Trinity College on Pearse St. and Westland Row. Ticketing open M-Sa 7:30am-10pm, Su 9am-10pm. Receives southbound trains from Connolly Station.

Buses: Busáras Central Bus Station, Store St. (☎836 6111), directly behind the Customs House and next to Connolly Station. Information available at the **Dublin Bus Office,** 59 O'Connell St. (☎872 0000; www.dublinbus.ie). **Bus Éireann** (www.buseireann.ie) window open M-F 9am-5pm and Sa 10:30am-2pm. Buses to: **Belfast** (3hr., 6-7 per day, €18); **Cork** (4½hr., 6 per day, €20.50); **Derry** (4¼hr., 4-5 per day, €17.50); **Donegal** (4¼hr., 4-5 per day, €15); **Galway** (3½hr., 15 per day, €13); **Kilkenny** (2hr., 6-7 per day, €10); **Killarney** (6hr., 5 per day, €20.50); **Limerick** (3½hr., 13 per day, €14.50); **Rosslare** (3hr., 13 per day, €14); **Shannon Airport** (4½hr., 13 per day, €15); **Sligo** (4hr., 4-6 per day, €15); **Waterford** (3hr., 10 per day, €10); **Westport** (5hr., 2-3 per day, €15); **Wexford** (2¾hr.; M-Sa 13 per day, Su 10 per day; €11.50). **PAMBO** (Private Association of Motor Bus Owners), 32 Lower Abbey St. (☎878 8422), provides names and numbers of private operators. Open M-F, call ahead.

Ferries: Bookings online (www.irishrail.ie/rosslare/home), in the Irish Rail office (see **Trains,** p. 732), or over the phone (☎855 0888). **Irish Ferries,** at 2-4 Merrion Row, off St. Stephen's Green. (☎1890 313 131; www.irishferries.com; open M-F 9am-5pm, Sa 9:15am-12:45pm) arrive from **Holyhead** at the **Dublin Port** (☎607 5665). From there, buses #53 and 53A run to Busáras (Every hr., €1.05); **Dublin Bus** also runs buses tailored to ferry schedules (€2.55-3.20). **Stena Line** ferries arrive from Holyhead at the **Dún Laoghaire** ferry terminal (☎204 7777; www.stenaline.com). **Norse Merchant Ferries** (☎819 2999; www.norsemerchant.com) docks at Dublin Port and goes to **Liverpool** (7½hr.; 2 per day; €25-40, with car €105-170). **Isle of Man Steam Packet Company** (UK ☎1800 551 743; www.steam-packet.com) docks at Dublin Port and sends 1 boat per day to Man; rates start at €50, and are cheaper if you're on foot.

▪ ORIENTATION

In general, Dublin is compact, though navigation is made complicated by the ridiculous number of names a street adopts along its way. Streets are usually labelled on the side of buildings at intersections and never on street-level signs. Buying a map with a street index is a smart idea. The most compact is the *EZ Map Guide* (€1.50), which fits easily in a pocket and has excellent detail.

The **River Liffey** forms a natural boundary between Dublin's **North** and **South Sides,** the former claiming most of the hostels and the latter flaunting famous sights and fabulous restaurants. The streets running alongside the Liffey are called **quays** (KEYS); the name of the street changes each block as it reaches a new quay. If a street is split into "Upper" and "Lower," then the "Lower" is the part of the street farther east, closer to the Liffey. The core of Dublin is ringed by **North** and **South Circular Roads,** which enjoy their own assortment of name changes. Most of the city's major sights are located within this area. **O'Connell Street** is the primary link between north and south Dublin. One block south of the river runs **Temple Bar** (a name which usually applies to the area as a whole). **Trinity College** is the nerve center of Dublin's cultural activity; the college touches the northern end of **Grafton Street.** Grafton's southern end opens onto **St. Stephen's Green,** a sizable and famous public park. Merchants on the North Side hawk goods for cheaper prices than those in the more touristed South. **Henry Street** and **Mary Street** comprise a pedestrian shopping zone that intersects O'Connell just after the General Post Office,

IRELAND

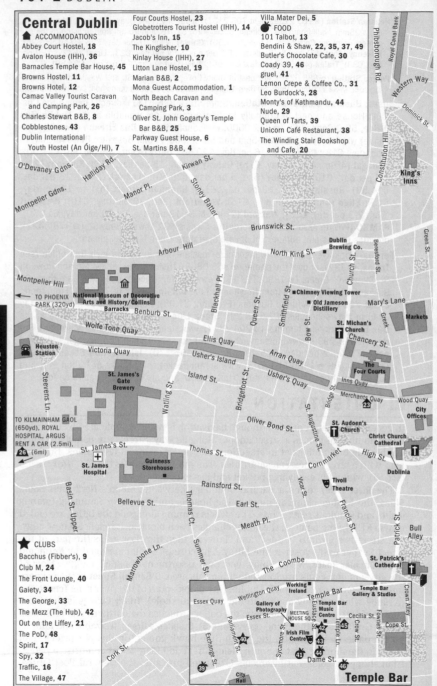

Central Dublin

ACCOMMODATIONS
Abbey Court Hostel, 18
Avalon House (IHH), 36
Barnacles Temple Bar House, 45
Browns Hostel, 11
Browns Hostel, 12
Camac Valley Tourist Caravan and Camping Park, 26
Charles Stewart B&B, 8
Cobblestones, 43
Dublin International Youth Hostel (An Óige/HI), 7
Four Courts Hostel, 23
Globetrotters Tourist Hostel (IHH), 14
Jacob's Inn, 15
The Kingfisher, 10
Kinlay House (IHH), 27
Litton Lane Hostel, 19
Marian B&B, 2
Mona Guest Accommodation, 1
North Beach Caravan and Camping Park, 3
Oliver St. John Gogarty's Temple Bar B&B, 25
Parkway Guest House, 6
St. Martins B&B, 4
Villa Mater Dei, 5

FOOD
101 Talbot, 13
Bendini & Shaw, 22, 35, 37, 49
Butler's Chocolate Cafe, 30
Coady 39, 46
gruel, 41
Lemon Crepe & Coffee Co., 31
Leo Burdock's, 28
Monty's of Kathmandu, 44
Nude, 29
Queen of Tarts, 39
Unicorn Café Restaurant, 38
The Winding Stair Bookshop and Cafe, 20

CLUBS
Bacchus (Fibber's), 9
Club M, 24
The Front Lounge, 40
Gaiety, 34
The George, 33
The Mezz (The Hub), 42
Out on the Liffey, 21
The PoD, 48
Spirit, 17
Spy, 32
Traffic, 16
The Village, 47

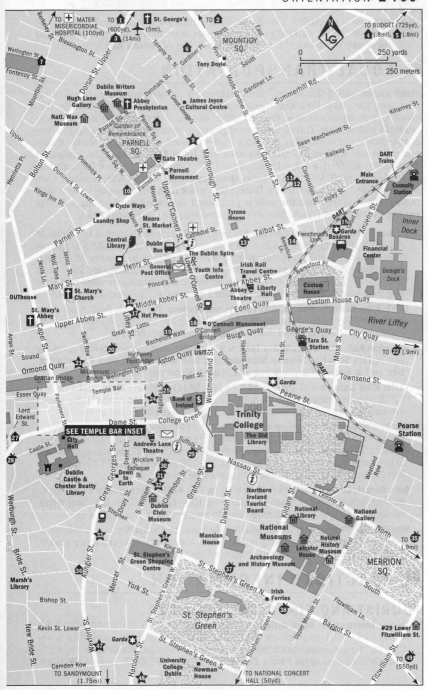

two blocks from the Liffey. The North Side is reputed to be a rougher area, but tourists should avoid walking in unfamiliar areas on either side of the Liffey at night, especially when alone. It is wise to steer clear of **Phoenix Park** after dark.

⌐ LOCAL TRANSPORTATION

Travel passes, called "Ramblers," are designed for people planning to travel a *lot;* each pass has a time limit that requires several trips a day to be worthwhile. Discount tickets are available at the bus office and from city newsagents. Only Irish students with student Travelcards are eligible for student prices. Pick up the free *Main Guide to Dublin Bus Services* leaflet to learn about every variety of special ticket and student discount. **Rambler** and **Travel Wide** passes offer unlimited rides (1 day €7.50; 1 week €18, students €15). Other tickets allow for both bus and suburban rail/DART travel (1-day **short hop** €7.70; weekly €26; monthly €98, students €69). Be warned that a Dublin Bus week runs from Sunday to Saturday inclusive, no matter when the pass is purchased, so a weekly pass bought Friday expires the next day. Dublin Bus months, similarly, are calendar months.

Buses: Dublin Bus, 59 O'Connell St. (☎873 4222; www.dublinbus.ie). Open M 8:30am-5:30pm, Tu-F 9am-5:30pm, Sa 9am-1pm. Buses are cheap (€0.85-3) and run most frequently 8am-6pm (generally every 8-20min., off-peak hours every 30-45min.). Dublin Bus runs a **NiteLink** service to the suburbs (M and W 12:30am and 2am, Th-Sa every 20min. 12:30-4:30am; €4-6; passes not valid). **Wheelchair-accessible buses** are ever more prevalent; check with the Bus Office or online for fully accessible routes.

DART: From **Connolly, Pearse,** and **Tara Street Stations,** the electric DART trains shoot south past **Bray** and north to **Howth** (4-6 per hr. 6:30am-11:30pm, €0.80-1.75). Tickets are sold in the station and must be presented at the end of the trip.

Suburban Rail: From **Connolly Station** trains run northbound and southbound (stopping also at **Tara Street** and **Pearse Stations**), and west to **Mullingar.** From **Heuston Station** west to **Kildare.** Trains are frequent (roughly 30 per day except Su).

Taxis: Blue Cabs (☎802 2222), **ABC** (☎285 5444), and **City Metro Cabs** (☎872 7272) have wheelchair-accessible cabs (call ahead). All 24hr. Alternatively, taxi stands are outside Trinity College, on Lower Abbey St. at the bus station, and on Parnell St.

Car Rental: Argus, 59 Terenure Rd. East (☎490 4444; www.argusrentals.com), also in the tourist office on Suffolk St., and the airport. Economy €50 per day, €220 per week. Ages 25-70. **Budget,** 151 Lower Drumcondra Rd. (☎837 9611; www.budget.ie), and at the airport. Economy from €27 per day, €165-200 per week. Ages 23-75. Be warned that Dublin traffic is heavy, and parking spaces are scarce.

Bike Rental: Cycle Ways, 185-6 Parnell St. (☎873 4748). Rents quality bikes, but no helmets. €20-40 per day. Open M-W and F-Sa 10am-6pm, Th 10am-8pm. **Tony Doyle,** 58 Gardiner St. (☎872 5399), rents bikes to people sticking around the area.

Hitchhiking: Hitchers from Dublin usually take buses to the outskirts where the motorways begin. However, hitchhiking in Co. Dublin and its vicinity is **extremely unsafe,** especially for women. *Let's Go* never recommends hitchhiking.

🔁 PRACTICAL INFORMATION

TOURIST AND FINANCIAL SERVICES

Tourist Information: Main Office, Suffolk St. (☎1850 230 330 or 605 7700, UK ☎0171 493 3201, international ☎669 792 083; www.visitdublin.com). Near Trinity College, in a converted church. Books beds for a €4 charge. **Bus Éireann** has representatives, as does **Argus Rent a Car** (☎605 7701 or 490 4444; open M-F 8:30am-

6pm, Sa 9am-5pm, Su 9am-1pm). Office open M-Sa 9am-5:30pm, July-Aug. also Su 10:30am-3pm. Reservation desks close 30min. earlier. **Northern Ireland Tourist Board:** 16 Nassau St. (☎679 1977 or 1850 230 230), books accommodations in the North. Open M-F 9:15am-5:30pm, Sa 10am-5pm.

Budget Travel: USIT, 19-21 Aston Quay (☎602 1600), near O'Connell Bridge. The place for Irish travel discounts. ISIC, HI, and EYC cards. Photo booths €6. Big discounts, especially for ISIC cardholders and people under 26. Open M-W and F 9:30am-6:30pm, Th 9:30am-8pm, Sa 9:30am-5pm.

Hosteling Organization: An Óige Head Office (Irish Youth Hostel Association/HI), 61 Mountjoy St. (☎830 4555; www.irelandyha.org), at Wellington St. Follow O'Connell St. north, ignoring its name changes. Mountjoy St. is on the left, 20min. from O'Connell Bridge. Book/pay for HI hostels here. Also sells bike and rail package tours. The *An Óige Handbook* lists all HI hostels in Ireland and Northern Ireland. Hugely beneficial membership card valid for the calendar year €20, under 18 €10. Open M-F 9:30am-5:30pm.

Financial Services: Bank branches with **bureaux de change** and **24hr. ATMs** cluster on Lower O'Connell St., Grafton St., and near Suffolk and Dame St. On F evenings, long lines form outside the ATMs, which aren't replenished over the weekends. Most open M-W and F 10am-4pm, Th 10am-5pm.

LOCAL SERVICES

Luggage Storage: Connolly Station. €4-6 per item per day. Open M-Sa 7:40am-11pm. **Heuston Station.** €1.50-5 per item, depending on size. Open daily 6:30am-10:30pm. **Busáras.** €3 per item. Lockers €4-9. Open M-Sa 8am-7:45pm, Su 10am-5:45pm.

Women's Resources: Women's Aid Helpline (☎868 0721 900) offers info on legal matters and support groups (10am-10pm). **Dublin Rape Crisis Centre** (24hr. hotline ☎1800 778 888). **Dublin Well Woman Centre,** 35 Lower Liffey St. (☎872 8051), is a private health center for women. It also runs a clinic (☎660 9860), 67 Pembroke Rd. **Cura,** 30 South Anne St. (☎1850 622 626; Dublin office ☎671 0598), is a Catholic support organization for women with unplanned pregnancies. Open M and W 10:30am-6:30pm, Tu and Th 10:30am-8:30pm, F-Sa 10:30am-2:30pm.

GLBT Resources: Gay Switchboard Dublin is a good resource for events and updates and sponsors a **hotline** (☎872 1055; M-F and Su 8-10pm, Sa 3:30-6pm). **OUThouse,** 105 Capel St. (☎873 4932). Community resource center with drop-in hours M-F noon-6pm.

Launderette: Laundry Shop, 191 Parnell St. (☎872 3541), near Busáras. Open M-F 9:30am-7pm, Sa 9:30am-6:30pm. **All-American Launderette,** 40 South Great Georges St. (☎677 2779). €8 per load. Open M-Sa 8:30am-7pm, Su 10am-6pm.

Work Opportunities: To obtain work through an organization, **Working Ireland,** 26 Eustace St. (☎677 0300; www.workingireland.ie), is a multi-tasking agency that arranges short- and long-term job placement throughout Ireland.

EMERGENCY AND COMMUNICATIONS

Emergency: ☎999 or 112.

Police *(Garda):* Dublin Metro Headquarters, Harcourt Terr. (☎666 9500); Store St. Station (☎666 8000); Fitzgibbon St. Station (☎666 8400); Pearse St. (☎666 9000). **Police Confidential Report Line:** ☎1800 666 111.

Counseling and Support: Tourist Victim Support, 33 Arran Quay (☎878 0870, 24hr. free phone 1800 661 771; www.victimsupport.ie). Open M-Sa 10am-6pm, Su noon-6pm. **Samaritans,** 112 Marlborough St. (☎1850 609 090 or 872 7700). **AIDS Helpline** (☎1800 459 459). Open daily 10am-5pm.

Pharmacy: O'Connell's, 56 Lower O'Connell St. (☎873 0427). Open M-F 7am-10pm, Sa 8am-10pm, Su 10am-10pm. 2 other branches on Grafton St.

Hospital: St. James's Hospital, James St. (☎453 7941). Take bus #123. **Mater Misericordiae Hospital,** Eccles St. (☎830 1122), off Lower Dorset St. Buses #10, 11, 13, 16, 121, and 122.

Internet Access: Free **Internet access** is available at the **central library,** Henry and Moore St., in the ILAC Centre (☎873 4333. Open M-Th 10am-8pm, F-Sa 10am-5pm.) and at **The Internet Exchange,** with branches at Cecila St. (☎670 3000) and Fownes St. in Temple Bar (☎635 1680). €3 per hr. Cecila location open M-F 8am-2am, Sa-Su 10am-midnight; Fownes location open 24hr. **Global Internet Cafe,** 8 Lower O'Connell St. (☎878 0295), 1 block north of the Liffey. €6 per hr., students €5, members €3. Membership €3-6. Open M-F 8am-11pm, Sa 9am-11pm, Su 10am-11pm.

Post Office: General Post Office, O'Connell St. (☎705 7000). Open M-Sa 8am-8pm, Su 10am-6:30pm. Smaller post offices open M-Tu and Th-F 9am-6pm, W 9:30am-6pm. **Post Code:** Dublin 1. Dublin is the only place in the Republic with a post code.

⌐ ACCOMMODATIONS

Dublin has a handful of excellent accommodations, but high demand for lodging keeps less-than-marvelous places open too. Reserve at least a week ahead, particularly for holiday or sporting weekends and during the peak summer season (June-Aug.). Phoenix Park may tempt the desperate, but camping there is a terrible idea, not to mention illegal. Consult Dublin Tourism's *Dublin Accommodation Guide* (€3.50) for more options.

HOSTELS

▨ **Globetrotters Tourist Hostel (IHH),** 46-7 Lower Gardiner St. (☎878 8808; www.townhouseofdublin.com). Pop art, tropical fish, a lush courtyard, and all-you-can-eat Irish breakfast make this mansion feel like a posh B&B. Free Internet access and luggage storage. Towels €6. Dorms €19-22. Singles €60-66.50; doubles €102-110. ❷

▨ **Four Courts Hostel,** 15-17 Merchants Quay (☎672 5839), on the south side of the river, near O'Donovan Rossa Bridge. Bus #748 from the airport stops next door. The friendly staff and relaxed atmosphere of this 250-bed, first-rate hostel compensate for its non-central location. Clean rooms (most with showers), kitchen, and car park. Long-term stays available. Free Internet access in 6min. periods. Continental breakfast included. Laundry €5. Dorms €15-23. Doubles €56-66; family room €23-25. ❶

Jacob's Inn, 21-28 Talbot Pl. (☎855 5660; www.isaacs.ie), 2 blocks north of the Custom House. Clean, spacious rooms all ensuite. Luggage room with individual cages. Bike storage. Wheelchair accessible. Light breakfast included. Lockers €1.50 per night. Towels €2. Lockout 11am-3pm. Dorms €17-25; doubles €65-73. ❷

Abbey Court Hostel, 29 Bachelor's Walk (☎878 0700; www.abbey-court.com), near O'Connell Bridge. Clean, narrow, smoke-free rooms overlook the Liffey. Internet access €2 per 40min. Continental breakfast included at NYStyle cafe next door. Free luggage storage; security box €1. Full-service laundry €8. Dorms €18-29. Doubles €76-88. ❷

Cobblestones, 29 Eustace St. (☎677 5614). A breath of fresh air in the middle of Temple Bar. Snug rooms with large windows and a well-appointed kitchen. Continental breakfast included. Dorms €16-21; doubles €50-55. Discounts mid-week, for groups, and for stays 1 week or longer. ❷

Avalon House (IHH), 55 Aungier St. (☎475 0001; www.avalon-house.ie). Turn off Dame St. onto Great Georges St.; the hostel is a 5min. walk, on the right. Wheelchair accessible. Internet access and kitchen. Light continental breakfast included. Lockers available. Towels €2, deposit €8. Dorms €13-30. Singles €30-37; doubles €56-70. ❶

Kinlay House (IHH), 2-12 Lord Edward St. (☎679 6644), a few blocks from Temple Bar. Slide down oak banisters in the lofty entrance hall, snuggle on soft couches in the TV room, or gaze at Christ Church Cathedral from the window. Internet access €1 per 15min. Continental breakfast included. Free luggage storage. Lockers €2, deposit €5. Laundry €7. Dorms €15-28. Singles €40-50; doubles €52-64, ensuite €56-68. ❷

Browns Hostel, 89-90 Lower Gardiner St. (☎855 0034; www.brownshostelireland.com). Cavernous wine-cellar-turned-kitchen. Closets and A/C in every room; TVs in most. Large, clean, single-sex baths in the basement. Breakfast included. Lockers €1. Blankets €2. Towels €1. Dorms €10-25. ❶

Barnacles Temple Bar House, 19 Temple Ln. (☎671 6277). Right in the hopping heart of Dublin—just a crawl home from the Temple Bar pubs. Lounge with fireplace and TV, and a colorful, well-kept kitchen. All rooms ensuite. Continental breakfast included. Free luggage storage. Laundry €6.50. Dorms €14-26.50. Doubles €65-78. ❶

Litton Lane Hostel, 2-4 Litton Ln. (☎872 8389), off Bachelor's Walk. Former studio for the likes of U2, Van Morrison, and Sinead O'Connor; Warhol-esque silk screens keep things hip. In addition to standard dorms, the hostel has shining new apartments, complete with a separate lounge area, kitchen, bathroom, TV, and laundry facilities. Laundry €5. Key deposit €1. Dorms €15-25; doubles €70-80. 1-bedroom apartments (sleep up to 4), €80-120; 2-bedroom apartments (also sleep up to 4), €130-150. ❷

Dublin International Youth Hostel (An Óige/HI), 61 Mountjoy St. (☎830 4555; www.irelandyha.org), in a converted convent and 18th-century school. O'Connell St. changes names 3 times before the left turn onto Mountjoy St. Recently renovated rooms. Wheelchair accessible. Bureau de change. Internet access €1 per 15min. Car park and buses to Temple Bar. Breakfast included—and served in the chapel. In-room storage. Towels €1. Laundry €5. Dorms €17-18. Doubles €51-57; triples €75-82; quads €92-99. €2 less for An Óige members. ❷

Oliver St. John Gogarty's Temple Bar B&B, 18-21 Anglesea St. (☎671 1822). Fine dorms in an old, well-maintained building above a popular pub. A good location for partiers. Laundry €5. Dorms €18-33; doubles €60-90; triples €93-114. ❷

B&BS AND HOTELS

B&Bs with a green shamrock sign out front are approved by Bord Fáilte; those without haven't been inspected but may be cheaper and better located—establishments with good locations often find that Bord Fáilte's advertising is unnecessary. On the North Side, B&Bs cluster along **Upper Street** and **Lower Gardiner Street,** on **Sheriff Street,** and near **Parnell Square.** Exercise caution when walking through the inner-city at night. There are also several B&Bs outside the city center.

Mona Guest Accommodation, 148 Clonliffe Rd. (☎837 6723). Charming house run for 38 years by Ireland's most endearing proprietress. Homemade brown bread accompanies the full Irish breakfast. Open May-Oct. Singles €35; doubles €66. ❸

Parkway Guest House, 5 Gardiner Pl. (☎874 0469). High-ceilinged, plush-carpeted, tidy rooms. Ask the owner, a hurling veteran, for advice on the city's restaurants and pubs. Irish breakfast included. Singles €35; doubles €52-62, ensuite €60-75. ❸

Charles Stewart B&B, 5-6 Parnell Sq. E. (☎878 0350; www.charlesstewartinn.com). Up O'Connell St. past Parnell St. More hotel than B&B. Birthplace of infamous Oliver St. John Gogarty, close enough to the Dublin Writer's Museum to feel properly literary. Irish breakfast included. Singles €50-63.50; doubles €65-89. Call ahead for specials. ❹

Marian B&B, 21 Upper Gardiner St. (☎874 4129). The McElroys provide fine rooms near Mountjoy Square. Irish breakfast included. Singles €30-32; doubles €54. ❸

IRELAND

The Kingfisher, 166 Parnell St. (☎872 8732; www.clubi.ie/kingfisher). Inn, restaurant, and Internet cafe in one. Clean, compact, modern rooms, uncomplicated food. Irish breakfast included, served until noon. TV/VCR in each room; kitchenettes in some. Singles €45-60; doubles €80-110; triples €165. Discounts in winter. ❹

Browns Hotel, 90 Lower Gardiner St. (☎855 0034; www.brownshotelireland.com). Elegant Georgian building with refurbished rooms. Connected to **Browns Hostel.** Continental breakfast included. Doubles €90-150; triples €110-170. ❺

Villa Mater Dei, 208 Clonliffe Rd., and **St. Martins B&B,** 186 Clonliffe Rd. (☎857 0920). Dedicated owner offers 2 bright, beautiful Victorian houses with modern amenities and lovely gardens. All rooms ensuite with TV. Singles €45; doubles €70. ❹

CAMPING

Most campsites are far from the city center, but camping equipment is available in the heart of the city. **The Great Outdoors,** on Chatham St. off the top of Grafton St., has an excellent selection of tents, backpacks, and cookware. (☎679 4293. 10% discount for An Óige members. Open M-W and F-Sa 9:30am-6pm, Th 9:30am-8pm.) **North Beach Caravan and Camping Park ❶,** in Rush, is accessible by bus #33 from Eden Quay (1hr., 25 per day) and suburban rail. It offers a peaceful, beach-side location in a quiet town outside of Dublin's urban jumble. (☎843 7131; www.northbeach.ie. Kitchen available. Open Apr.-Sept. €8 per person, €4 per child. Electricity €2. Showers €0.50.) Alternatively, try **Camac Valley Tourist Caravan and Camping Park ❶,** Naas Rd., in Clondalkin near Corkagh Park. Take bus #69 (35min., €1.50) to the site. (☎464 0644. Wheelchair accessible. Dogs welcome. Laundry €4.50. €9 per person, €17 per 2 people with car; €20 per caravan. Showers €1.)

🖸 FOOD

Dublin's many **open-air markets** sell fixings fresh and cheap. Vendors hawk fruit, strawberries, flowers, and fish from their pushcarts. The later in the week, the more lively the market. The cheapest **supermarkets** around Dublin are the chain of **Dunnes Stores,** with a full branch at St. Stephen's Green. (☎478 0188. Open M-W and F-Sa 8:30am-7pm, Th 8:30am-9pm, Su noon-6pm.) **Down to Earth,** 73 South Great Georges St., stocks health foods, herbal medicines, and a dozen granolas. (☎671 9702. Open M-Sa 8:30am-6:30pm.) Health food is also available around the city at various branches of **Nature's Way;** the biggest is at the St. Stephen's Green shopping center. (☎478 0165. Open M-W and F-Sa 9am-6pm, Th 9am-8pm, Su noon-6pm.)

🍴 **Unicorn Café Restaurant,** 12B Merrion Court (☎676 2182). Left off Merrion Row, behind Unicorn Market and Cafe. Legendary Italian restaurant serves classic dishes with panache. Entrees €16-25. Open M-Th noon-4pm and 6-11pm, F-Sa noon-4pm and 6-11:30pm. ❹ For those with less time or less money, **Unicorn Food Store and Café,** Merrion Row (☎678 8588), offers food from the same kitchen for a fraction of the price. Sandwiches and panini €4-6. Pastas €5-7. Open daily 8am-7pm. ❷

🍴 **Coady 39,** 39 Dame St. (☎679 0400). Don't let the crystal chandelier or the high ceilings fool you—Coady's will be very kind to your wallet. Dinner plates €7-8.50. Chicken parm and angel-hair pasta €8. Student special (2 slices of pizza and a drink) €5. Open M-Th 7:30am-11pm, F 7:30am-dawn, Sa 8:30am-dawn, Su 8:30am-11pm. ❶

Leo Burdock's, 2 Werburgh St. (☎454 0306), up from Christ Church Cathedral, behind The Lord Edward pub. Real-deal fish and chips in brown paper. A nightly pilgrimage for many Dubliners. Takeaway only. Fish €4-5; chips €2. Open daily noon-midnight. ❶

Queen of Tarts, Dame St. (☎670 7499). This little red gem offers homemade pastries, scones, cakes, and coffee. Excellent granola and fresh fruit €6. Scrumptious sandwiches €5. Breakfast €4-6. Open M-F 7:30am-6pm, Sa 9am-6pm, Su 10am-6pm. ❷

101 Talbot, 101 Talbot St. (☎874 5011), between Marlborough and Gardiner St., through the red doors and upstairs. Casual, airy restaurant serves excellent Italian-Mediterranean food and caters to Abbey Theatre-goers. Handwritten menu changes frequently. Early Bird €21. Entrees €14-20. Open Tu-Sa 5-11pm. ❹

Nude, 21 Suffolk St. Organic, fresh, free-range/free-trade food and modern design. Stroll down the astro-turfed floor to pick up fresh-squeezed juices or incredible smoothies (€2-4), salads (€4), hot panini (€4.50), or pasta (from €5). Picnic bench seating. Great, quick, healthy lunch. Also on Grafton St. above BT2. Open daily 10am-7pm. ❷

The Winding Stair Bookshop and Cafe, 40 Lower Ormond Quay (☎873 3292), near the Ha'penny Bridge. A relaxed cafe overlooking the river sits between 2 floors of an independent bookshop. Flowerboxes and red checkered tablecloths create a homey feel. Crepes €6-7; sandwiches €3-5. Open M-Sa 9:30am-6pm, Su 1-6pm. ❷

gruel, 68 Dame St. (☎670 7119). Keep your eye out for the lowercase "g" sign. Come in for quality organic home-cooking. Their motto: "We gruel, you drool." Lunch is on a weekly rotation, but the popular beef stew (€11) is always on the menu. Huge dinners €6-12. Heavenly brownies €2.40. Open M-Sa 8am-4:30pm, Su 10am-4pm. ❷

Lemon Crepe & Coffee Co., 66 S. William St. (☎672 9004). Squeeze into this tiny, trendy joint for crepes made on the spot. Eat them standing, or grab one of the highly prized tables outside. Savory and sweet crepes €4-6. Open M-W and F 8am-7:30pm, Th 8am-9:30pm, Sa 9am-7:30pm, Su 10am-6:30pm. ❶

Monty's of Kathmandu, 28 Eustace St. (☎670 4911; www.montys.ie), just off Dame St. on the right. Nepalese food with decor to match. Entrees €13-18; try the Sekuwa Chatpate Chicken or the spicy Begum Bahar with an unorthodox mix of chicken and lamb (both €15). Open M-Sa noon-2:30pm and 6-11:30pm, Su 6-11:30pm. ❹

Butler's Chocolate Cafe, 24 Wicklow St. (☎671 0591; www.butlerschocolates.com). Decadence never felt so good. Luxury sweet shop, with branches throughout the city. Signature hot chocolate €2.60. Open M-W and F 8am-7:30pm, Th 8am-9pm. ❶

Bendini & Shaw. 4 **St. Stephen's Green** (☎671 8651); 20 **Upper Baggot Street** (☎660 0131); 1A **Lower Pembroke Street** (☎678 0800); 4 **Lower Mayor Street** (☎829 0275). "Gourmet" sandwich shop. Irish smoked salmon, avocado, and ham salad on a baguette €3.80. Hot dog arrives in a fancy braided pastry bun. Delivery available for orders over €15. All open M-F 7am-5pm, Sa 8am-6pm, Su 9am-5pm. ❷

🅜 PUBLIN

James Joyce proposed that a "good puzzle would be to cross Dublin without passing a pub." When a local radio station once offered £100 to the first person to solve the puzzle, the winner explained that you could take any route—you'd just have to stop in each one along the way. Dublin's watering holes come in all shapes, sizes, specialties, and subcultures. Ask around or check *In Dublin, Hot Press,* or *Event Guide* for music listings. A growing number of places are blurring the distinction between pubs and clubs, with rooms or dance floors opening after certain hours. So pay attention, and hit two birds with one pint. We recommend you begin your expedition at Trinity gates, stroll up **Grafton Street,** teeter to **Camden Street,** stumble to **South Great Georges Street,** then triumphantly drag your soused and sorry self to **Temple Bar.** Start early—say, noon.

IRELAND

THE PERFECT PINT

Bartender Glenn, of a local Dublin Pub, helps Let's Go *resolve the most elusive question of all...*

LG: Tell us, what's the most important thing about pouring a pint?

A: The most important thing is to have the keg as close to the tap as possible. The closer, the better.

LG: And why's that?

A: Well, you don't want the Guinness sitting in a long tube while you wait to pour the next pint. You want to pull it straight out of the keg, without any muck getting in between.

LG: Does stopping to let the Guinness settle make a big difference?

A: Well, you can top it straight off if you want, but you might get too big a head with that. You don't want too small or big a head, so if you stop ¾ of the way, you can adjust the pint until the head is perfect. A true Guinness lover will taste the difference.

LG: Because of the head?

A: No, because of the gas. If you pull the Guinness straight from the tap and get a big head, it means you've gotten too much gas. It kills the taste. That's why you have to tilt the glass.

What you don't want is a window-clean glass; you don't want a glass that you can see through when you're done. Good Guinness leaves a healthy film on the glass. If it doesn't, you didn't get a good Guinness.

GRAFTON STREET AND TRINITY COLLEGE AREA

McDaid's, 3 Harry St. (☎679 4395), off Grafton St. across from Anne St. Center of Ireland's literary scene in the 50s. Incredibly high ceiling, summer patio, and gregarious crowd. Open M-W 10:30am-11:30pm, Th-Sa 10:30am-12:30am, Su 12:30-11pm.

The International Bar, 23 Wicklow St. (☎677 9250), on the corner of South William St. A great place to meet kindred wandering spirits. Excellent improv comedy M; stand-up W and Th; jazz Tu and F; house Su. W-F cover €8. Go early for a seat during the comedy shows. Open M-W 10:30am-11:30pm, Th-Sa 10:30am-12:30am, Su 12:30-11pm.

Bailey, Duke St. (☎670 4939). Sip cocktails on mod white leather bar stools or outside. Open M-Th 12:30-11:30pm, F-Sa 12:30pm-12:30am, Su 12:30-11pm.

Café en Seine, 39-40 Dawson St. (☎677 4567; www.capitalbars.com). An enormous homage to gay Par-ee. The atrium in the back is 4 stories high, and everything in this place feels huge—including the nightly crowds. Live jazz M 10pm-midnight, Su 4-6pm. DJs Th-Sa. Open M-W 9am-1:30am, Th-Sa 9am-3am, Su noon-12:30am.

Dawson Lounge, 25 Dawson St. (☎671 0311), downstairs. The smallest pub in Dublin (only 25 sq. ft., including restrooms and storage) is classy, wood-paneled, and, needless to say, intimate. Open M-W 12:30-11:30pm, Th-Sa 12:30pm-12:30am.

Davy Byrne's, 21 Duke St. (☎677 5217; www.davybyrnespub.com), off Grafton St. Lively, middle-aged crowd fills the pub where Joyce set *Ulysses*'s "Cyclops" chapter. Art-deco bar curves around the airy room. Gourmet pub food served all day. Open M-W 11:30am-11:30pm, Th-Sa 11:30am-12:30am, Su 12:30-11pm.

HARCOURT, CAMDEN, AND WEXFORD STREETS

🖼 **Whelan's,** 25 Wexford St. (☎478 0766). Dark wooden pub in front. Stage venue in back hosts big-name trad, rock, and everything in-between. Live music nightly from 9:30pm (doors open at 8pm); comedy often on W; DJs spin at the popular Fear and Loathing on Wexford St. on Th. Cover €7-15. Lunch (€8-12) served 12:30-2pm. Open late Th-Sa.

The Bleeding Horse, 24 Upper Camden St. (☎475 2705). All sorts of little nooks for private affairs around a tall central bar. Late bar with DJ F-Sa. Open M-W and Su until midnight, Th-Sa until 2am.

The Odeon, Old Harcourt Train Station (☎478 2088). The Odeon has a columned facade and the longest bar counter in Ireland (90 ft. of booze and good times). Everything here is gargantuan, though the upstairs is cozier. Come to be seen. Sa DJ; other nights lounge and dance. Cover €9-10. Open M-W until 11pm, Th 12:30am, F-Sa 2:30am.

AROUND SOUTH GREAT GEORGES STREET

⊠ The Stag's Head, 1 Dame Ct. (☎679 3701). Victorian pub with stained glass, mirrors, and deer heads. The student crowd dons everything from t-shirts to tuxes and spills into the alleys. Excellent pub grub. Entrees €10. Open M-Th 10:30am-11:30pm, F-Su 11am-12:30am. Food served M-F noon-3:30pm and 5-7pm, Sa noon-2:30pm.

Hogan's, 35 S. Great Georges St. (☎677 5904). Draws a fairly attractive crowd, despite its no-frills name and minimalist (but stylish) decor. DJ on the floor or in the basement Th-Su. Latin dance Sa 10pm. Open M-W 12:30pm-11:30pm, Th 12:30pm-1am, F-Sa 12:30pm-2:30am, Su 4-11:30pm.

The Globe, 11 S. Great Georges St. (☎671 1220). Frequented by a laid-back, hip young crowd. Fine spot to relax with a Guinness or a frothy cappuccino. Frequent DJs. Open M-Sa noon-3am, Su 4pm-1am. Rí Rá nightclub attached (see Clublin, p. 750).

TEMPLE BAR

⊠ The Porter House, 16-18 Parliament St. (☎679 8847). Way, way more than 99 bottles of beer on the wall. The country's largest selection of beers plus 10 self-brewed porters, stouts, and ales. Excellent sampler tray (€9) includes stout made with oysters. Fills with a great crowd every night for trad, blues, and rock. Open M-Tu and Th 11:30am-11:30pm, W 11:30am-midnight, F-Sa 11:30am-2:30am, Su 11:30am-11pm.

Brogan's Bar, 75 Dame St. (☎671 1844). Unassuming little spot ignored by tourists despite its location. Spend a night on an internal pub crawl marveling at the impressive collection of Guinness paraphernalia, or just enjoy pint after pint of the "black magic." Open M-W 4-11:30pm, Th 4pm-12:30am, F-Sa 1pm-12:30am, Su 1-11:30pm.

The Foggy Dew, Fownes St. (☎677 9328). Like a friendly village pub but twice as big and loud. Less flash than other Temple Bar pubs. Live rock Su nights. Open M-W 11am-11:30pm, Th 11am-12:30am, F-Sa 11am-1:30am, Su 12:30-11pm.

The Palace, 21 Fleet St. (☎677 9290), behind Aston Quay. This classic, neighborly pub has old-fashioned wood paneling and close quarters; head for comfy seats in the stained-glass, sky-lit back room. Favorite of many a Dubliner. Open M-Th 10:30am-11:30pm, F-Sa 10:30am-12:30am, Su 12:30-11pm.

Messrs. Maguire, Burgh Quay (☎670 5777). Explore this classy watering hole under the spell of homemade brews. Sampler tray of 6 beers €7. Trad M 9:30-11:30pm. Late bar W-Sa. Food served all day. Open M-Tu 10:30am-12:30am, W 11am-1:30am, Th 10:30am-2am, F-Sa 11am-2:30am, Su noon-12:30am.

Oliver St. John Gogarty (☎671 1822), Fleet and Anglesea St. Convivial atmosphere in a traditional but touristed pub. Named for the surgeon and poet who was Joyce's room-mate/nemesis and appeared in Ulysses as Buck Mulligan (see p. 755). Much-sought-after trad daily from 2:30pm. Open daily 10:30am-2am.

Temple Bar Pub, Temple Ln. South (☎672 5286). Sprawling, wheelchair-accessible pub with outdoor beer garden for balmy summer nights. Music daily at 12:30, 5:30, and 8:30pm. Open M-Th 11am-12:30am, F-Sa 11am-1:30am, Su noon-12:30am.

IRELAND

THE BEST OF THE REST

Mulligan's, 8 Poolbeg St. (☎677 5582), behind Burgh Quay off Tara St. Upholds its reputation as one of the best pint-pourers in Dublin. A taste of the typical Irish pub: low-key and "strictly drink." People of all ages gather around the large tables to toast each other. Open M-W 10:30am-11:30pm, Th-Sa 10:30am-12:30am, Su noon-11pm.

Zanzibar (☎878 7212), at the Ha'penny Bridge. Mix of oriental decor and pop culture. Quite the hotspot, but well air-conditioned. Patrons shuttle between the fabulous high-ceilinged bar to the dance floor in back. Live DJ nightly. Cover after 9 or 10pm F €5, Sa €10. Food until 10pm. Open M-F 5pm-2:30am, F-Sa 4pm-2:30am, Su 4pm-1am.

The Celt, 81-82 Talbot St. (☎878 8655). Step out of the city and into Olde Ireland. Small, comfortably worn, and truly welcoming. Nightly trad. Open daily 10:30am-late.

M. Hughes, 19 Chancery St. (☎872 6540), behind Four Courts. Attracts the prosecution and the defense, and is loaded with *Garda* at lunch. Curtained, comfy venue for authentic nightly trad and set dancing M and W-Th around 9:30pm. Join hungover clubgoers and be the first in Dublin to down a Guinness; pub opens at 7am (woo hoo!), closes M-W at 11:30pm, Th-Sa at 12:30am, Su at 11pm.

The Brazen Head, 20 North Bridge St. (☎679 5186), off Merchant's Quay. Dublin's oldest pub, established in 1198, has a cobbled courtyard with beer barrel tables. Nightly trad. Carvery and pub grub menu served 12:30-9pm. Open M-W 10:30am-11:30pm, Th-Sa 10:30am-12:30am, Su 12:30pm-12:30am.

Pravda, 35 Lower Liffey St. (☎874 0090), over the Ha'penny Bridge. Read the Cyrillic on the wall murals and drink Russian vodka. Trendy, popular, gay-friendly, and crowded. Beer garden. DJs Th-Sa. Bar menu daily noon-9pm. Late bar Th-Sa until 1:30am.

◎ SIGHTS

TRINITY COLLEGE. Behind ancient walls sprawls Trinity's expanse of stone buildings, cobblestone walks, and green grounds. The British built Trinity in 1592 as a Protestant seminary that would "civilize the Irish and cure them of Popery." The college became part of the path members of the Anglo-Irish elite trod on their way to high positions. Until the 1960s, the Catholic church deemed it a cardinal sin to attend Trinity; once the church lifted the ban, the size of the student body more than tripled. *Between Westmoreland and Grafton St., in the very center of South Dublin. The main entrance fronts the block-long traffic circle now called College Green. Pearse St. runs along the north edge of the college, Nassau St. to the south. ☎608 1000; www.tcd.ie. Grounds always open. Free.)* Trinity's **Old Library** holds an invaluable collection of ancient manuscripts, including the renowned and beautiful *Book of Kells*. Upstairs, the **Long Room** contains Ireland's oldest harp—the **Brian Ború Harp,** seen on Irish coins—and one of the few remaining **1916 proclamations** of the Republic of Ireland. *(On the south side of Library Sq. ☎608 2320; www.tcd.ie/library. Open June-Sept. M-Sa 9:30am-5pm, Su 9:30-4:30pm; Oct.-May M-Sa 9:30am-5pm, Su noon-4:30pm. €7.50, students and seniors €6.50.)*

GRAFTON STREET. The few blocks south of College Green are off-limits to cars and a playground for pedestrians. Grafton's **street performers** range from string octets to jive limboists.

LEINSTER HOUSE. The Duke of Leinster made his home on Kildare St. back in 1745, when most of the urban upper-crust lived north of the Liffey. By building his house so far south, where land was cheaper, he could afford an enormous front lawn. Today, Leinster House provides chambers for the **Irish Parliament,** or **An tOireachtas** (on tir-OCH-tas). It holds both the **Dáil** (DOIL), which does most of the government work, and the **Seanad** (SHAN-ad), the less powerful upper house.

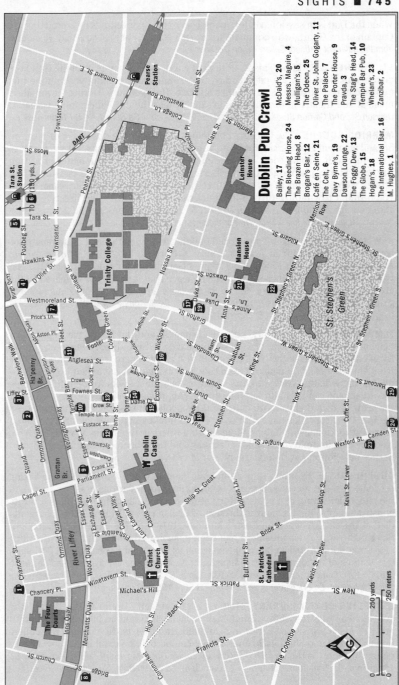

Dublin Pub Crawl

Bailey, 17
The Bleeding Horse, 24
The Brazen Head, 8
Brogan's Bar, 12
Café en Seine, 21
The Celt, 6
Davy Byrne's, 19
Dawson Lounge, 22
The Foggy Dew, 13
The Globe, 15
Hogan's, 18
The International Bar, 16
M. Hughes, 1

McDaid's, 20
Messrs. Maguire, 4
Mulligan's, 5
The Odeon, 25
Oliver St. John Gogarty, 11
The Palace, 7
The Porter House, 9
Pravda, 3
The Stag's Head, 14
Temple Bar Pub, 10
Whelan's, 23
Zanzibar, 2

IRELAND

When the Dáil is in session, visitors can observe the proceedings by contacting the Captain of the Guard, who conducts tours. (☎678 9911. *Passport necessary. Tours leave from the adjacent National Gallery Sa on the hour.)*

ST. STEPHEN'S GREEN. This 22-acre park was a private estate until the Guinness clan bequeathed it to the city. Today, the grounds are teeming with public life: punks, couples, strollers, swans, and a statue of Henry Moore. During the summer, musical and theatrical productions are given near the old bandstand. *(Kildare St., Dawson St., and Grafton St. all lead to it. ☎475 7826. Open M-Sa 8am-dusk, Su 10am-dusk.)*

MERRION SQUARE. The Georgian buildings and elaborate doorways of Merrion Sq. and adjacent **Fitzwilliam Street** feed your architectural longings. After leaving 18 Fitzwilliam St., Yeats took up residence at 82 Merrion Sq. Farther south on **Har'court Street,** playwright George Bernard Shaw and Dracula's creator, Bram Stoker, were neighbors at #61 and #16, respectively. At **#29 Lower Fitzwilliam Street,** you'll find a townhouse-turned-museum that demonstrates the lifestyle of the 18th-century Anglo-Irish elite. *(☎702 6165. Open Tu-Sa 10am-5pm, Su 2-5pm. A short audiovisual show leads to a 25min. tour of the house. €4, concessions €2.)*

NEWMAN HOUSE. This fully restored building was once the seat of **University College Dublin,** the Catholic answer to Trinity. *A Portrait of the Artist as a Young Man* chronicles Joyce's time here. The poet Gerard Manley Hopkins spent the last years of his life teaching classics at the college. The cursory tour is geared to the architectural and the literary. *(85-86 St. Stephen's Green S. ☎716 7422. Admission by guided tour. Open to individuals June-Aug. Tu-F at noon, 2, 3, 4pm; groups admitted throughout the year with advance booking. €5, concessions €4.)*

TEMPLE BAR. West of Trinity, between Dame St. and the Liffey, the Temple Bar neighborhood writhes with activity. In the early 1980s, the Irish transport authority intended to replace the neighborhood with a seven-acre transportation center. Resident artists and nomads raised a row and managed to save their homes. Temple Bar immediately grew into one of Europe's hottest spots for nightlife, forcing the artists and nomads into homelessness. (Ah, the sweet irony of life.) To steer the growth toward ends more cultural than alcoholic, the government-sponsored Temple Bar Properties has spent over €40 million to build a flock of arts-related tourist attractions, with independent coattail-riders springing up as well. Even so, weekend nights tend to be wild, with stag and hen (bachelor and bachelorette) parties pub-hopping with the largely tourist crowd.

DUBLIN CASTLE. Norman King John built the castle in 1204 on top of the Viking settlement; more recently, a series of structures from various eras has occupied the site, culminating in a 20th-century office complex. For the 700 years after its construction, Dublin Castle was the seat of British rule in Ireland. Fifty insurgents died at the castle's walls on Easter Monday, 1916 (see **The Easter Rising,** p. 728). Since 1938, every Irish president has been inaugurated here. Next door, the intricate inner dome of **Dublin City Hall** (designed as the Royal Exchange in 1779) shelters statues of national heroes. *(Dame St., at the intersection of Parliament and Castle St. ☎677 7129. State Apartments open M-F 10am-5pm, Sa-Su and holidays 2-5pm; closed during official functions. €4.50, students and seniors €3.50, children €2. Grounds free.)*

▨ CHESTER BEATTY LIBRARY. Honorary Irish citizen Alfred Chester Beatty was an American rags-to-riches mining engineer who amassed an incredibly beautiful array of Asian art, sacred scriptures, and illustrated texts. He donated the collection to Ireland upon his death, and visitors can peruse the exhibit in a new library behind Dublin Castle. *(☎407 0750; www.cbl.ie. Open May-Sept. M-F 10am-5pm, Sa 11am-5pm, Su 1pm-5pm; Oct-Apr. Tu-F 10am-5pm, Sa 11am-5pm, Su 1pm-5pm. Free.)*

IRELAND

CHRIST CHURCH CATHEDRAL. Sitric Silkenbeard, King of the Dublin Norsemen, built a wooden church on this site around 1038; Strongbow rebuilt it in stone in 1169. Today, stained glass sparkles above the raised crypts, one of which supposedly belongs to Mr. Strongbow and his favorite lutefisk. *(At the end of Dame St., uphill and across from the Castle. A 10min. walk from O'Connell Bride, or take bus #50 from Eden Quay or 78A from Aston Quay. ☎ 677 8099. Open daily 9:45am-5pm except during services. €5, students and seniors €2.50.)*

ST. PATRICK'S CATHEDRAL. The body of Ireland's largest cathedral dates to the 12th century, although much was remodeled in 1864. Jonathan Swift spent his last years as Dean of St. Patrick's, and his crypt is above the south nave. *(From Christ Church, Nicholas St. runs south and downhill, eventually becoming Patrick St. Take bus #49, 49A, 50, 54A, 56A, 65, 65B, 77, or 77A from Eden Quay. ☎ 475 4817; www.stpatrickscathedral.ie. Open daily Mar.-Oct. 9am-6pm; Nov.-Feb. Sa 9am-5pm and Su 10am-3pm. €4.20, students and seniors €3.20, children free.)* **Marsh's Library,** beside the cathedral, is Ireland's oldest public library. A peek inside reveals elegant wire alcoves, an extensive collection of early maps, and occasionally a special exhibit. *(☎ 454 3511. Open M and W-F 10am-12:45pm and 2-5pm, Sa 10:30am-12:45pm. €2.50, students and seniors €1.50.)*

GUINNESS STOREHOUSE. Discover how it brews its black magic and creates the world's best stout. The admirably farsighted Arthur Guinness signed a 9000-year lease on the original 1759 brewery. The Storehouse offers a self-guided tour with multimedia eye-candy and hyper-technical fun. The pilgrimage concludes on the seventh floor of the pint-shaped building, overlooking 64 acres of Guinness, with pints of dark and creamy goodness for all. *Sláinte. (St. James's Gate. From Christ Church Cathedral, follow High St. west through its name changes. Take bus #51B or 78A from Aston Quay or #123 from O'Connell St. ☎ 453 8364; www.guinness-storehouse.com. Open daily 9:30am-5pm; July-Aug. also open 5-9pm. €13.50, students over 18 and seniors €9, students under 18 €7, children 6-12—start them young!—€5, children under 6 free.)*

KILMAINHAM GAOL. A place of bondage and a symbol of freedom—almost all the rebels who fought in Ireland's struggle for independence between 1792 and 1921 spent time here. The jail's last occupant was **Éamon de Valera,** the future leader of Éire. Today, it's a museum that traces the history of penal practices over the last two centuries. *(Inchicore Rd. Take bus #51A from Lower Abbey St., or #68, 69, or 79 from Aston Quay. ☎ 453 5984. Open daily Apr.-Sept. 9:30am-4:45pm, Oct.-Mar. M-F 9:30am-4pm and Su 10am-4:45pm. Tours every 35min. €5, students €2, seniors €3.50. Small museum, separate from tour, free of charge.)*

O'CONNELL STREET. Dublin's biggest shopping thoroughfare starts at the Liffey and leads to **Parnell Square.** At 150 ft., it was once the widest street in Europe. The central traffic islands contain monuments to Irish leaders: **O'Connell's statue** faces the Liffey and O'Connell Bridge; **Parnell's statue** points toward nearby Mooney's pub. One monument you won't see is **Nelson's Pillar,** which stood outside the General Post Office for 150 years. In 1966 the IRA commemorated the 50th anniversary of the Easter Rising by blowing the Admiral out of the water. The recently erected **Dublin Spire** now stands in its place, towering 120m above most everything else in the city. It's the first step in the planned reconstruction of O'Connell St., which, when finished, will return the street to its tree-lined heyday. For now, however, O'Connell St. remains seriously under construction.

GENERAL POST OFFICE. Not just a fine place to send a letter, the Post Office was the nerve center of the 1916 Easter Rising (see **The Easter Rising,** p. 728); Padraig Pearse read the Proclamation of Irish Independence from its steps. When British troops

IRELAND

IN RECENT NEWS

A PINT AND A...

Old habits die hard, and it was widely feared that the Republic of Ireland's ban on smoking in all public places—including pubs—would be met with a wave of the hand and a puff of defiant smoke. But the ban has been an unquestionable success. In the first three months, 97% of pubs, restaurants, and workplaces were shown to be complying with the regulation, thanks in no small part to the €3,000 fine awaiting any violators. A lot of people prefer easy breathing to the eye-watering mystique of a smoke-filled bar.

A few high-profile smokers have made news by violating the restriction: a member of the Dail Eireann lost his seat in a government council after he lit up in the parliament's bar, and Bono of U2 apologized after unintentionally breaking the law with the Red Hot Chili Peppers. But the most vocal critics of the new law have been, predictably, owners of pubs, who fear a loss in clientele. If pub attendance has gone down, it certainly isn't evident in Dublin's raucous Temple Bar, where inside the pubs there's not even a hint of tobacco smoke. But despite the apparent success of the measure, there's no ignoring the older gentleman sitting next to you in the bar, who argues that the taste of Guinness just isn't the same without an accompanying smoke. He may just be right—but now, we'll never know.

closed in, mailbags became barricades. Outside, a number of bullet nicks are still visible. *(O'Connell St.* ☎ *705 7000. Open M-Sa 8am-8pm, Su 10am-6:30pm.)*

CUSTOM HOUSE. Dublin's greatest architectural triumph, the Custom House was designed and built in the 1780s by James Gandon, who gave up the chance to be St. Petersburg's state architect and settled in Dublin. Carved heads along the frieze represent rivers of Ireland; Liffey is the only lady. *(East of O'Connell St. at Custom House Quay, where Gardiner St. meets the river.* ☎ *888 2538. Visitors Centre open mid-Mar. to Nov. M-F 10am-12:30pm, Sa-Su 2-5pm; Nov. to mid-Mar. W-F 10am–12:30pm and Su 2-5pm. €1.)*

FOUR COURTS. On April 14, 1922, General Rory O'Connor seized the Four Courts on behalf of the anti-Treaty IRA; two months later, the Free State government of Griffith and Collins attacked the Four Courts garrison, starting the Irish Civil War (p. 728). The building, also Gandon's work, houses Ireland's highest court. *(Inn's Quay, west of the Custom House.* ☎ *872 5555. Open M-F 9am-4:30pm. Free.)*

■ **ST. MICHAN'S CHURCH.** This modest church, dating from 1095, is best visited for its creepy vaults, which may have inspired Bram Stoker's *Dracula.* *(Church St.* ☎ *872 4154. Open mid-Mar. to Oct. M-F 10am-12:45pm and 2-4:30pm, Sa 10am-12:45pm; Nov. to mid-Mar. M-F 12:30-3:30pm, Sa 10am-12:45pm. Crypt tours €3.50, students and seniors €3, under 16 €2.50. Church of Ireland services Su 10am.)*

OLD JAMESON DISTILLERY. Learn how science, grain, and tradition come together to form liquid gold—whiskey, that is. A film recounts Ireland's spiritual rise, fall, and renaissance; the subsequent tour walks through the creation of the drink, although the stuff's really distilled down the street. The experience ends with a glass of the Irish firewater; be quick to volunteer in the beginning and get to sample a whole tray of different whiskeys. *(Bow St. From O'Connell St., turn onto Henry St. and continue straight as the street dwindles to Mary St., then Mary Ln., then May Ln.; the warehouse is on a cobblestone street on the left. Buses #68, 69, and 79 run from city center to Merchant's Quay.* ☎ *807 2355. Tours daily 9am-5:30pm. €8, concessions €6.25.)*

DUBLIN BREWING COMPANY. For people wanting to see how beer is *actually* made, this microbrewery runs fun, personal tours with plenty of hops to smell and beer to taste. You also get more beer than at the *other* brewery. *(144-146 North King St. From Old Jameson, go up to North King St., turn left, and it's on the left. ☎872 8622; www.dublinbrewing.com. Tours every hr. M-F noon-6pm, and by appointment. €9, students €7.)*

PHOENIX PARK. Europe's largest enclosed public park is most famous for the "Phoenix Park murders" of 1882. The Invincibles, a Republican splinter group, stabbed Lord Cavendish, Chief Secretary of Ireland, and his trusty Under-Secretary 200 yd. from the **Phoenix Column.** A Unionist journalist forged a series of letters linking Parnell to the murderers. The Column, capped with a phoenix rising from flames, is something of a pun—the park's name actually comes from the Irish *Fionn Uísce,* "clean water." Its 1760 acres incorporate the **President's residence** (Áras an Uachtaraín), the US Ambassador's house, cricket pitches, polo grounds, and red deer. The park is peaceful during daylight hours but unsafe at night. *(Take bus #10 from O'Connell St. or #25 or 26 from Middle Abbey St. west along the river.)* The **Dublin Zoo,** one of the very oldest and Europe's largest, is in the park. It contains 700 critters and the **world's biggest egg.** *(Bus #10 from O'Connell St.; #25 or 26 from Wellington Quay. ☎474 8900. Open M-Sa 9:30am-6pm, Su 10:30am-6pm. Last admission at 5pm. Zoo closes at dusk in winter. €12.50, students and seniors €10, children €8.)*

🏛 MUSEUMS AND GALLERIES

NATIONAL GALLERY. This collection of over 2400 canvases includes paintings by Vermeer, Rembrandt, and El Greco. Works by 19th-century Irish artists comprise a major part of the collection. The new **Millennium Wing** houses a 20th-century Irish Art exhibit, a Yeats archive, and a multimedia system exploring many of the museum's rooms in virtual reality. *(Merrion Sq. W. ☎661 5133. Open M-W and F-Sa 9:30am-5:30pm, Th 9:30am-8:30pm, Su noon-5pm. Free guided tours Sa 3pm, Su 2, 3, and 4pm; also daily July-Aug. 3pm. Admission free. Concerts and art classes €6-20.)*

🖼 NATURAL HISTORY MUSEUM. This "museum of a museum" showcases Victorian taxidermy at its strangest, with exotic stuffed animals from the world over. Three creepy skeletons of giant Irish deer greet visitors at the front, and more examples of beautiful classic taxidermy stare out from old Victorian cabinets. The dodo skeleton draws crowds away from Irish parasitic worms. *(Upper Merrion St. ☎677 7444. Open Tu-Sa 10am-5pm and Su 2-5pm. Free.)*

THE NATIONAL MUSEUM OF ARCHAEOLOGY AND HISTORY. The largest of Dublin's museums has extraordinary artifacts spanning the last two millennia. One room gleams with the **Tara Brooch,** the **Ardagh Hoard,** and other Celtic goldwork. Another section is devoted to the Republic's founding years and flaunts the bloody vest of nationalist hero **James Connolly.** *(Kildare St., next to Leinster House. ☎677 7444. Open Tu-Sa 10am-5pm and Su 2-5pm. Guided tours €1.50; call for times. Museum free.)*

COLLINS BARRACKS. Home to the **National Museum of Decorative Arts and History**—the most sophisticated of Dublin's three national museums—the barracks gleam with exhibits that range from the deeply traditional to the subversively multi-disciplinary. The Curator's Choice room shows an assortment of objects in light of their artistic importance, cultural context, and historical significance. *(Benburb St., off Wolfe Tone Quay. Take the Museum Link bus, which leaves from the adjacent Natural History and Archaeology museums once per hr. All-day pass €2.50, one-way €1. Or take buses #25, 66, or 67 from Middle Abbey St. or #90 from Aston Quay. ☎677 7444. Open Tu-Sa 10am-5pm and Su 2-5pm. Guided tours €2; call for times. Museum free.)*

THE NATIONAL LIBRARY. The library chronicles Irish history and exhibits literary goodies in its entrance room. A genealogical research room helps visitors trace even the thinnest twiglets of their Irish family trees. The reading room is quite elegant, with an airy, domed ceiling. *(Kildare St., adjacent to Leinster House.* ☎ *603 0200. Open M-W 10am-9pm, Th-F 10am-5pm, Sa 10am-1pm. Free. Academic reason required to obtain a library card and entrance to the reading room; just "being a student" is usually enough.)*

THE IRISH JEWISH MUSEUM. This museum is in a restored former synagogue and houses a large collection of artifacts, documents, and photographs chronicling the history of the tiny Jewish community in Ireland from 1079 (5 Jews arrived and were sent packing) through later European migrations. *(3-4 Walworth Rd., off Victoria St. South Circular Rd. runs to Victoria St.; from there the museum is signposted.* ☎ *490 1857. Open May-Sept. Tu, Th, and Su 11am-3:30pm; Oct.-Apr. Su 10:30am-2:30pm. Free, donations accepted.)*

DUBLIN WRITERS MUSEUM. Read through placard after placard describing the city's rich literary heritage, or listen to it all on an audio headset tour. Manuscripts, rare editions, and memorabilia blend with caricatures, paintings, a great bookstore, and an incongruous Zen Garden. *(18 Parnell Sq. North* ☎ *872 2077; www.visitdublin.com. Open June-Aug. M-F 10am-6pm, Sa 10am-5pm, Su 11am-5pm; Sept.-May M-Sa 10am-5pm. €6.25, students and seniors €5.25.)*

JAMES JOYCE CULTURAL CENTRE. This museum features Joycenalia ranging from portraits of the individuals who inspired his characters to more arcane fancies of the writer's nephew, who runs the place. Call for information on lectures, walking tours, and **Bloomsday** events. *(35 North Great Georges St.* ☎ *878 8547; www.jamesjoyce.ie. Open Sept.-June M-Sa 9:30am-5pm, Su 12:30-5pm; July-Aug. M-Sa 9:30am-5pm, Su 11am-5pm. Guided tour daily 2pm. Tour €10, students and seniors €9. €5, students and seniors €4.)*

SHAW BIRTHPLACE. This museum serves as both a period piece and a glimpse into G.B. Shaw's childhood. Mrs. Shaw held recitals here, sparking little George's interest in music; her lovely Victorian garden inspired his fascination with landscape painting. *(33 Synge St. Stroll down Camden, make a right on Harrington, and turn left onto Synge St. Convenient to buses #16, 19, or 122 from O'Connell St.* ☎ *475 0854 or 872 2077. Open May-Sept. M-Tu and Th-Sa 10am-5pm, Su 11am-5pm; no tours 1-2pm. Open for groups outside hours by request. €6.25, concessions €5.25, children €3.75.)*

GAELIC ATHLETIC ASSOCIATION MUSEUM. Those intrigued by the world of Irish athletics will appreciate the museum at **Croke Park Stadium.** The GAA museum spells out the rules, history, and heroes of its national sports, with the help of touchscreens and audiovisual displays. *(☎ 855 8176. Museum open M-Sa 9:30am-5pm, Su noon-5pm. Game days open to Cusack Stand ticket-holders only. Last admission 4:30pm. €5, students and seniors €3.50, children €3.)*

▓ CLUBLIN

In Dublin's nightlife war, clubs currently have a slight edge over pub rock venues, though the pubs are fighting back with later hours. As a rule, clubs open at 10:30 or 11pm, but the action really heats up after the 11:30pm pub closings. Most clubs close between 1:30 and 3am, but a few have been known to last until daybreak. To get home after 11:30pm, when Dublin Bus stops running, dancing queens take the **NiteLink bus** (M-W 12:30am and 2am, Th-Sa every 20min. from 12:30am-4:30am; €4), which runs from the corner of Westmoreland and College St. to Dublin's suburbs. **Taxi** stands are located in front of Trinity, at the top of Grafton St. by St. Stephen's Green, and on Lower Abbey St. Be prepared to wait 30-45min. on weekend nights.

▓ **The PoD,** 35 Harcourt St. (☎ 478 0225; www.pod.ie), corner of Hatch St., in an old train station. Spanish-style decor meets hard-core dance music. The truly brave venture upstairs to **The Red Box** (☎ 478 0225), a more intense club with warehouse atmosphere, brain-crushing music, and a crowd at the bar designed to winnow out the weak. Upstairs **Crawdaddy** hosts more low-key events and some world music stars. Often hosts big-name DJs—cover charges skyrocket. Cover €10-20; Th ladies free before midnight; Th and Sa students €5. Open until 3am.

Gaiety, S. King St. (☎679 5622; www.gaietytheatre.com), off Grafton St. Elegant theater shows late-night wild side every F-Sa. 4 bar areas. Best of all worlds with salsa, jazz, swing, latin, and soul. Cover about €10. Open F-Sa 11:15pm-4:15am.

Traffic, 54 Middle Abbey St. (☎873 4800; www.traffic54.net). Nightly DJ spins hip hop, house, or techno from his throne at the end of a long, deep bar. Flanking TVs accompany with flashing images. M-Th and Su nights, 2 cocktails for the price of 1; F-Sa they seem to be 1 for the price of 2. Cover Th €6, F-Sa €8-10; free before 10:30pm. Open M-W noon-11:30pm, Th and Sa noon-2:30am, F 3pm-2:30am, Su noon-1:30am.

Club M, Blooms Hotel (☎671 5622), on Cope St. in Temple Bar, in the big orange building. One of Dublin's largest clubs, attracting a crowd of all ages and styles with multiple stairways and a few bars in back. Cover M-Th and Su €7, ladies free before midnight; F-Sa €12-15. Free tickets often distributed in Temple Bar. Open M-Th 11pm-2:30am, F-Sa 10pm-2:30am, Su 10:30pm-1am.

The Mezz (The Hub), 21-25 Eustace St. (☎670 7655). Live bands rock nightly right inside the entrance—try not to knock over a drum set as you scramble toward the bar. A quiet pub by day, The Mezz turns into a loud bluesy hotspot at night (no cover). It shares the building with **The Hub,** which, as the only 18+ club in Temple Bar, attracts the younger crowd. M gay night, F drum 'n bass, Sa techno, Su funky groove, otherwise mostly house music. Cover M-Th and Su €7, F €10, Sa €13. No cover at The Mezz.

Spy, Powerscourt House (☎677 0014), on South William St. Keep up with the mainstream crowd that packs the downstairs dance club on weekends, or recover from a hard weekend—Sunday Roast features free roast potatoes, live acoustic music, and good company. M gay night. W student night during the school year. Cover F-Sa €8.

Spirit, 57 Mid. Abbey St. (☎877 9999). "Mind" (the basement level): chill-out music, artsy paintings, and a "holistic center" offering airbrush tattoos, tarot card readings, and massage. "Soul" (ground floor): main bar, with colorful lights and a medium-sized dance floor. "Body" (first floor): huge dance floor, pounding beats, and a giant egg-shaped fortress in the middle for the DJs. "Virtue" (top floor): for VIPs only. Cover €10-20. Open Th-Sa 10:30pm-4am. Occasional club nights during the week; call for details.

Bacchus (Fibber's), 80-82 Parnell St. (☎872 2575). No charts here; mostly indie. Houses Ireland's only metal club. Occasional Goth nights. If the darkness, heat, or doom get to be too much, head to the outside deck to cool the hellfires. Weekend cover €7. Open Th-Sa until 2am or later.

The Village, 26 Wexford St. (☎475 8555). Newly renovated 2-floor glittering pub/club. Bands play in separate area Th-Sa from 7-10:30pm (cover €5-15), then DJs come in for chill-out, jungle, and house downstairs. Cover €10 after 11pm. Open Th-Sa until 3am.

GAY AND LESBIAN NIGHTLIFE

▩ **The George,** 89 South Great Georges St. (☎478 2983; www.capitalbars.com). This purple man o' war is Dublin's first and most prominent gay bar. The attached nightclub opens W-Su until 2am. Frequent theme nights and cabaret. Smart outfit a must. Cover €8-10 after 10pm. Open M-Tu 12:30-11:30pm, W-Su 12:30pm-2:30am.

▩ **The Front Lounge,** Parliament St. (☎670 4112). The red velvet seats of this gay bar are filled nightly by a mixed, trendy crowd. Open M and W noon-11:30pm, Tu noon-12:30am, F-Sa noon-2am, Su 4-11:30pm.

Out on the Liffey, 27 Upper Ormond Quay (☎872 2480). The name plays on the more traditional, but still gay, Inn on the Liffey a few doors down. The short hike from the city center ensures a local crowd most nights. Tu game show, F-Sa DJ. No cover. Open M-Tu noon-11:30pm, W-Th 10:30am-12:30am, F-Sa 10:30am-2:30am, Su noon-11:30pm.

IRELAND

♫ ENTERTAINMENT

Whether you fancy poetry or punk, Dublin is equipped to entertain you. The free weekly *Event Guide* is available at the tourist office, Temple Bar restaurants, and the Temple Bar Information Centre. The glossier *In Dublin* (€2.50) comes out every two weeks with feature articles and listings for music, theater, art exhibitions, comedy shows, clubs, museums, and gay venues. *Events of the Week*—a much smaller, free booklet—is jammed with ads, but also has good information buried in it. Check www.visitdublin.com for the latest hotspots.

MUSIC

Dublin's music scene attracts performers from all over the world. Trad is not only a tourist gimmick, but a vibrant and important element of Dublin's music world. Pubs see a lot of musical action, since they provide musicians with free beer and a venue. *Hot Press* (€1.90) has the most up-to-date listings, particularly for rock. Some pubs in the city center have trad sessions nightly, others nearly so: **M. Hughes, Oliver St. John Gogarty,** and **McDaid's** are good bets (see **Publin,** p. 741). The best pub for trad is 🖾**Cobblestones,** King St. North (☎872 1799), in Smithfield. No rock here, but live shows every night, a trad session in the basement, and real live spontaneity. Big-deal bands frequent the **Baggot Inn,** 143 Baggot St. (☎676 1430).

   The **Temple Bar Music Centre,** Curved St. (☎670 9202), has events and concerts virtually every night. The **National Concert Hall,** Earlsfort Terr., provides a venue for classical concerts and performances, hosting nightly shows in July and August and a summer lunchtime series on occasional Tuesdays and Fridays. (☎671 1533. Tickets €8-16; students half-price; summer lunchtime tickets €4-8.) Programs for the **National Symphony** and smaller local groups are available at classical music stores and the tourist office. **Isaac Butt** on Store St. and the **Life** bar on Lower Abbey St. have periodic jazz. Big acts play **Olympia,** 72 Dame St. (☎677 7744), and **Vicar Street,** 99 Vicar St., (☎454 6656), off Thomas St. The stars also perform for huge crowds at the **Tivoli Theatre,** 135-138 Francis St. (☎454 4472); **Croke Park,** Clonliffe Rd. (☎836 3152); and the **R.D.S.** (☎668 0866), in Ballsbridge.

THEATER

There is no true "Theatre District" in Dublin, but smaller theater companies thrive off **Dame Street** and Temple Bar. Box office hours are usually for phone reservations; the window stays open until curtain on performance nights, generally 8pm. Dublin's most famous stage is the 🖾**Abbey Theatre,** founded by Yeats and his collaborator Lady Gregory to promote Irish cultural revival and modernist theater (which proved an interesting combination). Today, the Abbey is Ireland's National Theatre. *(26 Lower Abbey St. ☎878 7222; www.abbeytheatre.ie. Box office open M-Sa 10:30am-7pm. Tickets €15-30; students €9.50. Sa 2:30pm matinees €10.)* The **Peacock Theatre** is the Abbey's experimental downstairs stage. *(☎878 7222. Doors open at 7:30pm. Tickets €12.50-17; Sa 2:45pm matinees €12.50.)*

CINEMA

Ireland's well-subsidized film industry reeled with the arrival of the 🖾**Irish Film Centre,** 6 Eustace St., in Temple Bar. The IFC mounts tributes and festivals, including French and Spanish celebrations and Bloomsday screenings. A variety of classic and European art house films appear throughout the year. You have to be a "member" to buy most tickets. (☎679 3477; www.fii.ie. Weekly membership €1.30; yearly membership €14, students €10. Membership must be purchased at least 15min. before start of show. €6.20, matinees €5.) **The Screen,** D'Olier St. (☎672

5500), also rolls artsy reels. First-run movie houses cluster on O'Connell St., the quays, and Middle Abbey St. The **Savoy**, O'Connell St. (☎874 6000), and **UGC Multiplex**, Parnell St. (☎872 8444), screen major releases for about €7.50.

SPORTS AND RECREATION

Dubliners aren't as sports-crazed as their country cousins, but that's not saying much. Games are still serious business, especially since most tournament finals take place here. The season for **Gaelic football** and **hurling** (see **Sports**, p. 730) runs from mid-February to November. Action-packed and often brutal, these contests will entertain any sports-lover. Games are played in **Croke Park** (Clonliffe Rd., a 15min. walk from Connolly station; buses #3, 11, 11A, 16, 16A, 51A, and 123; tickets €20-60) and on **Phibsborough Road**. Tickets are theoretically available at the turnstiles, but they tend to sell out quickly. For more sports information, check the Friday papers or contact the **Gaelic Athletic Association** (☎836 3222; www.gaa.ie).

🎐 FESTIVALS

BLOOMSDAY. Dublin returns to 1904 each year on June 16, the day of Leopold Bloom's 18hr. journey, which frames the narrative (or lack thereof) of Joyce's *Ulysses*. Festivities are held all week, starting before the big day and, to a lesser extent, continuing after it. The **James Joyce Cultural Centre** (p. 750) sponsors a reenactment of the funeral and wake, and a Guinness breakfast. *(Call ☎878 8547 for info.)*

MUSIC FESTIVALS. The **Festival of Music in Great Irish Houses** (☎278 1528), held during mid-June, organizes concerts of period music in 18th-century homes across the country. The **Feis Ceoil** (☎676 7365) music festival goes trad in mid-March. The **Guinness Blues Festival** (☎497 0381), a three-day extravaganza in mid-July, gets bigger and broader each year. Ask at the tourist office about *fleadhs* (FLAHS), day-long trad festivals that pop up periodically.

ST. PATRICK'S DAY. The half-week leading up to March 17 occasions a city-wide carnival of concerts, fireworks, street theater, and intoxicated madness, celebrating one of Ireland's lesser-known saints. *(☎676 3205.)*

FILM AND THEATRE FESTIVALS. In early March, the **Dublin Film Festival** (☎679 2937; www.iol.ie/dff) brings nearly two weeks of Irish and international movies with a panoply of seminars in tow. The **Dublin Theatre Festival,** a premier cultural event held the first two weeks of October, showcases about 20 works from Ireland and around the world. Tickets may be purchased all year at participating theaters, and, as the festival draws near, at the Festival Booking Office. *(47 East Essex St. ☎677 8439; www.dublintheatrefestival.com. Tickets €13-20, student discounts vary by venue.)*

DUBLIN'S SUBURBS

Strung along the Irish Sea, Dublin's suburbs are a calm alternative to the voracious human tide swarming about the Liffey. The DART, suburban rail, and local buses make the area accessible for afternoon jaunts.

HOWTH (BINN EADAIR)   ☎01

Less than 10 mi. from the center of Dublin, Howth (rhymes with "both") has long been favored by Ireland's literary lasses—it was the childhood home of Yeats's muse Maude Gonne, and the setting for Molly Malone's chapter in *Ulysses*. An affluent Eden dangling from the mainland, the town is becoming an increasingly popular destination; if the sun is shining, expect crowds. The tourist flocks are rewarded with a highlight reel of Ireland: rolling hills, pubs, a literary landscape, fantastic sailing, and a castle.

A great way to experience Howth's heather and seabird nests is on the narrow, 3hr. **cliff walk** that rings the peninsula. At the harbor's end, **Puck's Rock** marks the spot where the devil fell when St. Nessan shook a Bible at him. (It was just that easy.) The nearby **lighthouse,** surrounded by tremendous cliffs, housed Salman Rushdie for a night during the height of the *fatwa.* To reach the trailhead from town, turn left at the DART station and follow Harbour Rd. around the coast for about 20min. Several sights are clustered in the middle of the peninsula; go right as you exit the DART station and then left after ¼ mi. at the entrance to the Deer Park Hostel. Up that road lies the private **Howth Castle,** a charmingly awkward patchwork of materials, styles, and degrees of upkeep. Just offshore, **Ireland's Eye** once provided both a religious sanctuary for monks, whose former presence is visible in the ruins of **St. Nessan's Church,** and a military outlook from one of the coast's many **Martello towers. Ireland's Eye Boat Trips** jet passengers across the water. Find them on the East Pier, toward the lighthouse. (☎087 267 8211. 15min. tours every 30min. 11am-6pm, weather permitting. Round-trip €8, concessions €8.)

The easiest way to reach Howth is by **DART:** take a northbound train to the Howth end of the line (30min., 6 per hr., €1.70). Pay attention when boarding, as the line splits to serve Malahide as well. **Buses** #31 and 31B to Howth leave from Dublin's Lower Abbey St. Turn left out of the DART station and walk toward the harbor on Harbour Rd. Brand new **Ann's Guest Accommodations ❸** is situated where East Pier meets Harbour Rd. Bessie, the owners' friendly dog, leads guests to immaculate modern rooms, and the family shares Howth knowledge accumulated since 1956. (☎832 3197; www.annsofhowth.com. €40-50 per person.) Other **B&Bs** are quite a climb or a short bus ride up Thormanby Rd., but most proprietors will pick guests up at the DART stop. **Gleann na Smól ❸** ("The Valley of the Thrush"), at the end of Nashville Rd. off Thormanby Rd., is an affordable option relatively near the harbor. (☎832 2936. Singles €42; doubles €64.) **Highfield ❸,** Thormanby Rd., is on the left a half-mile past the Church of Assumption. When the weather cooperates, a lovely view of the harbor complements the front bedrooms and the antique-laden dining room. (☎832 3936. All rooms with shower and TV. Doubles €70.)

Maud's ❶, Harbour Rd., is a casual cafe with sandwiches and award-winning ice cream. (☎839 5450. Ice cream €1-4.50. Open 10am-9pm.) Follow the stairs after the Abbey on Abbey Rd. to **Big Blue** and **Cafe Blue ❸,** 30 Church St., for a tasty "Leek and Hake Bake" (€15) and other seafood, steak, and pasta dishes. (☎832 0565. Open Tu-Sa 1:30pm-11pm, Su 12:30-2:30pm. Cafe Tu-Sa noon-9pm.) **The Country Kitchen ❶,** Main St. to the right of the Church, packs fresh sandwiches (€3) for hungry hikers. (☎839 5450. Open M-Sa 8:30am-6pm, Su 9am-1pm.) Top off your cliff walk with a pint and an incredible view of North Howth at **The Summit,** Thornby Rd., and its adjoining nightclub **K2.** (☎832 4615. Open M-Th 11am-11:30pm, F-Sa 11am-12:30am. Club open F-Su. Cover €3 before 11pm, €9 after.)

DÚN LAOGHAIRE ☎01

As one of Co. Dublin's major ferry ports, Dún Laoghaire (dun-LEER-ee) is many tourists' first peek at Ireland. Fortunately, this is as good a place as any to begin your rambles along the coast. Couples stroll down the waterfront on summer evenings, and the whole town turns out for weekly sailboat races.

🖪🖪 TRANSPORTATION AND PRACTICAL INFORMATION. Dún Laoghaire is easily reached on the **DART** from Dublin (€1.40) or southbound **buses** #7, 7A, 8, or (a longer, inland route) 46A from Eden Quay. For those who want to party downtown by night, the 7N **nightbus** departs for Dún Laoghaire from College St. in Dublin. (M-W 12:30 and 2am, Th-Sa every 20min. 12:30-4:30am.) From the ferryport, **Marine Road** climbs up to the center of town. **George's Street,** at the top of Marine Rd., holds most of Dún Laoghaire's shops; many are right at the intersection in the 70's-style **Dún Laoghaire Shopping Centre. Patrick Street,** the continuation of Marine Rd., has some good, cheap eateries. At the ferry terminal, the **tourist office** outfits visitors with maps. (Open M-Sa 10am-1pm and 2-6pm.) Exchange money at the ferry terminal's **bureau de change** (open M-Sa 9am-4pm, Su 10am-4pm), or use the **ATM** at the **Bank of Ireland,** 101 Upper George's St. (☎280 0273; open M-F 10am-4pm, Th 10am-5pm). **Grafton Recruitment,** Upper George's St. (☎284 1818), helps find **work opportunities,** as can **Dún Laoghaire Youth Info Centre,** in the church on Marine Rd. (☎280 9363; open M-F 9:30am-5pm, Sa 10am-4pm). Free **Internet access** is available at the Centre. The **post office** is on Upper George's St. (Open M and W-F 9am-6pm, Tu 9:30am-6pm, Sa 9am-1pm.)

📰🛏 **ACCOMMODATIONS AND FOOD.** The best hostel within walking distance is 🏠**Belgrave Hall ❷,** 34 Belgrave Sq. From the Seapoint DART station, head left down the coast, then zigzag through the intersections: right on Belgrave Rd., left on Eaton Pl., right across from the blue and yellow doors, and left across from Belgrave House. In a splendid, well-maintained old mansion, this top-tier, family-friendly hostel has front rooms with bay views. (☎284 2106. Continental breakfast included. Laundry €7. Dorms €20-25.) Dún Laoghaire is also prime ground for **B&Bs.** Fall off the DART or ferry and you'll find **Marleen ❸,** 9 Marine Rd. (☎280 2456. TV and tea facilities. Full breakfast. Singles €35; doubles €60.) Comfortable **Avondale House ❸,** 3 Northumberland Ave., is around the corner from Dunnes Stores. (☎280 9628. €30 per person.)

Tesco sells **groceries** in the Dún Laoghaire Shopping Centre. (☎280 0668. Open M-W and Sa 8:30am-7pm, Th-F 8:30am-9pm.) The best family restaurant in town is **Bits and Pizzas ❷,** 15 Patrick St. Go early to avoid the wait. (☎284 2411. Pizzas and pasta €7-13. Homemade ice cream €1.85. Open M-W and Sa noon-10:30pm, F noon-11pm, Sa noon-11:30.) **Mia Cucina ❸,** 107 Lower George's St., serves simple Italian meals with fresh seafood. (☎280 5318. Pizzas and pasta €8.50-14. Open M-Th noon-11pm, F-Su noon-midnight.) For home-baked vegetarian fare, head to bohemian **World Cafe ❷,** 56 Lower George's St. (☎284 1024. Open M-Sa 9am-5pm.) The huge glass facade of **40 Foot ❸,** above the harbor on Marine Rd., stretches across the horizon; the bar and kitchen don't disappoint. (☎284 2982; www.40foot.info. Entrees €20-27. M-W 3-course menu €23. Open M-W noon-11:30pm, Th noon-12:30am, F-Sa noon-1:30am, Su noon-11:30pm.)

📷🎭 **SIGHTS AND ENTERTAINMENT.** To reach the 🏰**James Joyce Tower,** Dún Laoghaire's main attraction, take bus #8 from Burgh Quay in Dublin to Sandycove Ave. In September 1904, a young Joyce stayed here for six tense days as a guest of Oliver St. John Gogarty. Joyce later infamized his host in the first chapter of *Ulysses*: the novel opens in and around the tower, with Buck Mulligan playing Gogarty. The tower's museum is a mother load of Joycenalia, displaying his death mask, love letters to Nora, and many editions of *Ulysses*. (☎280 9265. Open Apr.-Oct. M-Sa 10am-1pm and 2-5pm, Su 2-6pm; Nov.-Mar. by appointment. €6, students €5.) At the base of the tower lies another Joyce-blessed site, the 40 ft. **men's bathing place,** where skinny-dipping goes on year-round.

The Dún Laoghaire **harbor** itself is a sight, full of car ferries, fishermen, and yachts cruising in and out of the new marina. Frequent summer-evening **boat races,** usually on Mondays and Thursdays, draw much of the town. The **Irish National Sailing School & Club,** on the West Pier, offers beginner weekend and week-long sailing courses. (☎284 4195; www.inss.ie. €215 per course.) The **Irish Canoe Union** has sum-

IRELAND

mer kayaking courses on area rivers. ($\approx$450 9838 or 087 245 7620. €150 for 4 evening courses and a daytrip.) **Dublin Adventures** ($\approx$087 287 3287) offers canoeing, kayaking trips, and rock climbing. For indoor fun and dance, Dún Laoghaire's best *craic* is at ⚑**Comhaltas Ceoltoiri Éireann** (COLE-tus KEE-ole-tori AIR-run), next door to Belgrave Hall hostel. This is the headquarters of a huge international organization for Irish traditional music; it houses bona fide, non-tourist trad sessions *(seisiúns)* and *céilí* dancing. Of course, pints are also available. ($\approx$280 0295. Year-round F night *céilí* €6. July to mid-Aug. sessions M-Th at 9pm, with informal jam session after.) Next door to the Marina Hostel, ⚑**Purty Kitchen** pub transforms its loft into a nightclub with trad Thursdays, pop Fridays and Sundays, and jazz Saturdays. Pricey dinners and a fabulous wine list are also available. ($\approx$214 7666. Cover €10-12.)

BRAY (BRÍ CHUALAIN) $\approx$01

Although officially located in Co. Wicklow, Bray functions as a suburb of Dublin: the DART and Dublin Bus trundle through the town regularly, bringing flocks of city folk to its beach. Polished but not pretentious, Bray's well-tended gardens and cotton candy-laden seafront manage to stimulate the demanding tourist without sacrificing its small-town charm. Along the beachfront, predictable arcade palaces cater to a crowd of Dublin beachgoers. The **National Sea Life Centre,** on the Strand, hails the dawning of the age of aquariums. ($\approx$286 6939. Open M-F 10am-5pm, Sa-Su 10am-5:30pm. €8.50, concessions €7, children €5.50.) For gorgeous panoramas of the Wicklow Mountains and Bray Bay, hike to the summit of **Bray Head,** high above the south end of the Strand and away from the neon lights. The steep 30min. trail begins after the short paved pedestrian walkway begins to curve up the hill.

Bray is a 40min. **DART** ride from Dublin's Connolly Station (round-trip €3.30). **Buses** #45 and 84 arrive from Eden Quay. To reach **Main Street** from the DART station, take Quinsborough or Florence Rd., which run perpendicular to the tracks. Bray's **tourist office** is the first stop south of Dublin for Wicklow information. The office is downhill on Main St. ($\approx$286 7128. Open July-Aug. M-F 9am-5pm, Sa 10am-4pm; Sept.-June M-F 9:30am-4:30pm, Sa 10am-3pm. Closed M-F 1-2pm.) **B&Bs** line the Strand, but cheaper ones are on **Meath Street** closer to the town center. Anne and Pat Duffy welcome guests to ⚑**Moytura ❸,** 2 Herbert Park, on the right before the fork with King Edward Rd. They provide superb homemade bread and chats on Irish history and literature. ($\approx$282 9827. All rooms ensuite. Singles €40-45; doubles €60-65.) **Campo de' Fiori ❷,** 1 Albert Ave., at the intersection with the Strand, is a humble Italian eatery with a large wine selection, filling pastas, and a courteous staff. ($\approx$276 4257. Pasta €8-16; meat and fish €15-23. Open M and W-Th 5-10:30pm, F-Sa 5-11pm, Su 2-9pm.) **Weary Ass Coffee Shop ❷,** 5 Quinsborough Rd., serves nourishing omelettes and sandwiches for €6. ($\approx$286 2144. Open M-Sa 9am-5pm.) **Clancy's,** on Quinsborough Rd., is a dark, old-time pub with wooden plank tables. ($\approx$286 2362. Trad Tu, Th, F.)

ENNISKERRY AND POWERSCOURT. The **Powerscourt Estate,** in nearby **Enniskerry,** and the tremendous **Powerscourt Waterfall,** a bit farther, both make for convenient daytrips from Bray. Built in the 1730s, the estate has become an architectural landmark. Outside, the terraced **gardens**—displaying everything from Italian opulence to Japanese elegance—justify the high admission. Take an Alpine bus to the Powerscourt garden entrance or #185 to Enniskerry; #44 runs direct from Dublin. ($\approx$204 6000. Open daily 9:30am-5:30pm. House and gardens €8, concessions €7. Gardens only €6/€5.50.) The **falls** are 3½ mi. outside Enniskerry; take a bus from Enniskerry and follow the somewhat cryptic signs from town. The 398 ft. plunge makes this Ireland's tallest (permanent) waterfall—a record challenged by the temporary falls on Hungry Hill in Co. Kerry. Although worth the visit in any season, the falls are most impressive in late spring and after heavy rains. A 40min. walk begins at their base and rambles through quiet, untended woods. (Open daily June-Aug. 9:30am-7pm; Sept.-May 10:30am-dusk. €4.50, students €4.) <

EASTERN IRELAND

Woe betide the unfortunate soul who knows eastern Ireland only through the windows of a westbound bus out of Dublin—the untouristed towns of the east hold many a marvel. Ancient passage tombs in Co. Meath continue to mystify archaeologists, and the lush, mountainous, and sparsely populated terrain of Co. Wicklow is a haven for hikers and beach-lovers. Most major sights are accessible by bus, but traveling here is best accomplished by bike or car.

WICKLOW (CILL MHANTÁIN)   ☎0404

Touted both for its seaside pleasures and as a gateway for aspiring Wicklow mountaineers, Wicklow Town has a wide selection of restaurants and accommodations within walking distance of its pubs. An eager traveler can exhaust the sightseeing potential of the town itself fairly quickly, but there are many afternoons' worth of hiking and cycling in the hills.

◪▤ TRANSPORTATION AND PRACTICAL INFORMATION. The train station is a 15min. walk east of town on Church St. Trains run to Dublin Connolly Station (1¼hr., 3-4 per day, €12.70 round-trip) and to Rosslare via Wexford (2hr., 3 per day, €19 round-trip). Bus Éireann leaves for Dublin from near the gaol at the other end of Main St. (1½hr., 6-9 per day, €6.50). A guided driving tour of Glendalough and the Wicklow mountains leaves daily at 10am. (☎45152. 8½hr. €15.) The tourist office, in Fitzwilliam Sq., provides free maps of town and extensive information on the Wicklow Way. (☎69117. Open June-Sept. M-F 9am-6pm, Sa 9:30am-5:30pm; Oct.-May M-F 9:30am-1pm and 2-5:30pm.) AIB, with its 24hr. ATM, is on the left as you enter town from the train station. (Open M 10am-5pm, Tu-F 10am-4pm.) The Wicklow IT Access Centre, on Main St. across from the AIB, has Internet access. (€6.50 per hr. Open July-Aug. M-Sa 10am-1pm and 2-6pm; Sept.-June M-F 7-10pm.) From the town center, walk down Main St. toward Market Sq., and the post office is on the right. (☎67474. Open M-F 9am-5:30pm, Sa 9:30am-1pm.)

▟ ACCOMMODATIONS. The incredibly helpful, friendly family who runs ▨Wicklow Bay Hostel ❶ treats guests to good beds, clean rooms, and amazing views. From Fitzwilliam Sq., walk toward the river, cross the bridge, and head left until you see a big, yellow building called "Marine House." Call for pick-up from the train station, or more detailed directions. (☎69213; www.wicklowbayhostel.com. Closed Jan. Dorms €13-15; private rooms €16-18.) Next to the gaol, Kilmantin B&B ❸ has bright bedrooms, all ensuite and TV. (☎67373 or 25081. Singles €45; doubles €60.) Evergreen B&B ❸, Friarsfield Rd., is a large home with comfy beds and tasty breakfasts. Turn onto Friar's Hill Rd., downhill from the Grand Hotel, and then right onto Friarsfield Rd. (☎68347. €33.) Several campgrounds grace the area. Pitch your tent at Webster's Caravan and Camping Park ❶ at Silver Strand, 2½ mi. south of town on the coastal road. (☎67615. Open June-Sept. €6-10 per tent. Showers €1.) In Redcross, 8mi. down the N11, River Valley ❶ has cushy campsites. (☎41647. Open Mar.-Sept. €9 per tent. Showers €0.50.)

📵📆 **FOOD AND PUBS.** Greasy takeaway and fresh produce shops line Main St. **Tesco,** out on the Dublin Rd., sells **groceries.** (☎69250. Open M-W and Sa 8:30am-8pm, Th-F 8:30am-10pm, Su 10am-6pm.) Expect fine dining at 🔲**The Bakery Cafe ❸.** Come before 7:30pm on weekdays and indulge with two courses (€24). (☎66770. Irish breakfast €7. Lunch €7-9. Entrees €20-23. Open M-Th 10am-3pm and 6-10pm, F 10am-3pm and 6-11pm, Sa 6-11pm, Su 6-10pm.) **Casapepe ❸** has no-frills Italian fare: pizzas €8-13; pastas, poultry, and fish €11-20. (☎67075. Open daily noon-midnight.) **Philip Healy's ❷,** Fitzwilliam Sq., serves food all day and doubles as a lively hotspot on weekends. (☎67380.) The **Bridge Tavern,** Bridge St., reverberates with trad, local chatter, and clinking pints. (☎67718. Trad daily at 10pm.)

🎦🎪 **SIGHTS AND FESTIVALS.** Wicklow's premier attraction is 🔲**Wicklow's Historic Gaol.** The museum fills nearly 40 cells with audio clips, displays, and interactive activities relating to the gaol, its history, and the messy business of shipping convicts off to Australia. The walls of several cells are covered with prisoners' graffiti. (☎61599. Open daily 10am-6pm; last admission 5pm. Tours 40min., every 10min. €6.50, students and seniors €4.70, children €3.75.) A cliff trail provides superb views en route to 🔲**St. Bride's Head** (a.k.a. **Wicklow Head**), where St. Patrick landed on Travilahawk Strand in AD 432. Cut through the golf course from the **Black Castle** or head out on the coastal road past the clubhouse and find the trailhead in the parking lot on the left; the hike takes over 1hr. At Market Sq., Main St. becomes Summer Hill and then Dunbur Rd., from which beaches extend south to **Arklow.** From Wicklow, the closest strips of sand are **Silver Strand** and **Jack's Hole,** though most people head to larger 🔲**Brittas Bay,** halfway to Arklow.

Beginning the last week of July, Wicklow hosts its annual **Regatta Festival,** the oldest such celebration in Ireland. At night, amicable pub rivalries foster singing competitions and general revelry. The **Wicklow Gaol Arts Festival** livens up mid-July nights with plays and concerts. (☎69117; www.wicklowartsweek.com. Tickets €10-15.) Contact the tourist office for more information.

WICKLOW MOUNTAINS

Carpeted in fragrant heather, the Wicklow Mountains provide a happy home to grazing sheep and scattered villages alike. With summits over 2000 ft. high, this region epitomizes the romantic image of pristine rural Ireland.

GLENDALOUGH (GLEANN DÁ LOCH)   ☎0404

In the 6th century, a vision instructed St. Kevin to give up his life of ascetic isolation and set up a monastery. He offset the workaday austerity of monastic life by choosing one of the most spectacular valleys in Ireland for the site of Glendalough (GLEN-da-lock; "Glen of Two Lakes"). The valley has since become known for its ruins, excellent hikes, and swarms of tourists.

The amiable staff at the **Glendalough Visitors Centre** presents ample information on the valley's intriguing past. The admission fee covers an exhibition, an audiovisual show on the history of Irish monasteries, and occasionally a tour of the ruins. (☎45325. Open daily mid-Mar. to mid-Oct. 9:30am-6pm, mid-Oct. to mid-Mar. 9:30am-5pm; last admission 45min. before closing. Group tours by request; individuals are free to join one in progress. Admission €2.75, students €1.25.) The impressive ruins reflect only a small part of what the monastery looked like in its heyday. A tiny 3 ft. base supports the 100 ft. **round tower** of Glendalough, one of the best-preserved in all of Ireland. The **cathedral,** constructed in a combination of Romanesque architectural styles, was once the largest in the country. In its shadow stands **St. Kevin's Cross,** an unadorned high cross that was carved before the monks had tools to cut holes clean through the stone. The 11th-century **St. Kevin's Church,** whose stone roof remains intact, acquired the misnomer "St. Kevin's Kitchen" because of its chimney-like tower. The **Upper and Lower Lakes** are a rewarding digression from the monastic site. Cross the bridge at the far side of the monastery and head right on the paved path for 5min. to reach the serene Lower Lake. Twenty minutes later, the path hits a **National Park Information Office,** the best source for hiking information (☎45425; open daily May-Aug. 10am-6pm, Sept.-Apr. Sa-Su 10am-dusk.), and the magnificent Upper Lake.

Little Glendalough sits on a tributary of the R756, where the **Glenealo River** pools into the Upper and Lower Lakes. Pilgrims come by car on the R756, on foot along the Wicklow Way, or in buses run by **St. Kevin's Bus Service** from St. Stephen's Green in Dublin (☎01 281 8119; M-Sa 11:30am and 6pm, Su 11:30am and 7pm; round-trip €13) and **Bus Éireann** (☎01 836 6111; daily Apr.-Oct. 10:30am, round-trip 5:45pm; €25, children €12.50). The **post office** is tucked into a row of B&Bs to the left of the Wicklow Heather restaurant.

Cramped Dublin hostels can't possibly compete with the grandeur of ◪**The Glendalough Hostel (An Óige/HI) ❷,** a 5min. walk up the road past the Glendalough Visitors Centre. Prices are a bit high, but good beds, an in-house cafe, and the inspiring Wicklow Mountains backdrop make it the best option in the area. (☎45342. All rooms ensuite. Internet access available. Wheelchair accessible. Picnic lunch €5; Irish or continental breakfast €6.50/€4; dinners €9-11. Towels €1.30. Laundry €5. Dorms €20-22; private rooms €24-25 per person.) One mile up the road, the village of **Laragh** has food options and plenty of **B&Bs.** Tucked into the forest on the road to St. Kevin's Church, **Pinewood Lodge ❸** offers excellent rooms furnished, appropriately, with pinewood. (☎45437. All rooms ensuite. Singles €50; doubles €70.) Laragh's **Wicklow Heather ❸** is family- and vegetarian-friendly and is about the only place in the area open for breakfast. (☎45157. Breakfast €5-10; entrees €13-21; Su 3-course lunch €20. Open M-Th 8:30am-9:30pm, F-Sa 8:30am-10pm, Su 8:30am-9pm.) **Lynham's ❸** piles plates high; the Guinness beef stew (€11.50) is tasty and filling. (☎45345. Entrees €18-23. Open daily 12:30-3pm and 6-9pm.) The attached **Lynham's Pub** lures travelers with cover bands and rock sessions every Wednesday, Thursday, and Saturday. (☎45345. Open daily until midnight.)

THE WICKLOW WAY

Ireland's oldest marked hiking trail (est. 1981) is also its most spectacular. Stretching from Marlay Park at the border of Dublin to Clonegal in Co. Carlow, the 76 mi. Wicklow Way meanders through Ireland's largest highland expanse. As hikers weave over heathered summits and through steep glacial valleys, yellow arrows and signs mark the Way's various footpaths, dirt tracks, and paved roads. Civilization is rarely more than 2 mi. away, but appropriate **wilderness precautions** should still be taken: bring warm, windproof layers and raingear for the exposed hills, and sturdy footwear. Most tourist offices sell the *Wicklow Way Map Guide,* which is the best source of information on the trail and its sights (€5.50; you're not crazy, the map is oriented with north pointing down). Hiking 7-8hr. each day for six days carries backpackers from one end to the other, though there are plenty of attractive abbreviated routes. Numerous side trails make excellent day hikes; *Wicklow Way Walks* (€7.60) outlines several of these loops. An Óige publishes a pamphlet detailing 4-5hr. hostel-to-hostel walks, available at hostels in Wicklow and Dublin. For more information, contact the **National Park Information Office** (☎45425).

Dublin Bus (☎01 873 4222) runs frequently to Marlay Park in **Rathfarnham** (#47A or 47B from Trinity College) and **Enniskerry** (#44 or 185 from Bray). **Bus Éireann** (☎01 836 6111) comes somewhat near the Way farther south, with infrequent service from Busáras in **Dublin** to **Tinahely** and **Shillelagh. St. Kevin's** runs two shuttles daily between Dublin's St. Stephen's Green West, Bray, Roundwood, Laraugh, and Glendalough. (☎01 281 8119. €15 round-trip.) **Bikes** are allowed only on forest tracks and paved sections, but many off-Way roads are equally stunning.

The splendor of the Wicklow Way isn't exactly a well-kept secret—many accommodations take advantage of the endless stream of bodies trekking along. An Óige (☎01 830 4555; www.irelandyha.org) runs a cluster of hostels that lie close to the Way. The superior ⬛**Glendaloch Hostel (An Óige/HI) ➋** is a stone's throw from the Way, by the monastic ruins. (☎0404 45342. Dorms €20-22; doubles €45-48.) **Knockree (An Óige/HI) ➊** is right on the Way, 2 mi. from Powerscourt Waterfall. From Enniskerry, take the right fork of the road leading uphill from the village green and follow the signs to the hostel. (☎01 286 4036. Linen €1.25. Lockout 10am-5pm. Dorms €11-12.) **Camping** is feasible along the Way but requires advance planning. National parklands are fine for low-impact camping, but pitching a tent in state plantations is prohibited. Many **B&Bs** offer camping and pickup if you call ahead; the *Wicklow Way Map Guide* lists about 20.

All hikers should bring food or expect to walk a few miles to a grocery store. Water can be replenished at the hostels and B&Bs along the Way; it is very important to drink plenty of fluid during the strenuous hike to avoid dehydration. When you reach Glencullen or Enniskerry, be sure to make the climb to ⬛**Johnnie Fox's,** Ireland's highest pub at 1200 ft. above sea level. Here, Wicklow Way walkers drink and dine while enjoying the pub's excellent *craic*. The nightly trad and delicious food (entrees €17-22) make the journey worthwhile. (☎01 295 5647. Open M-Sa 10am-11:45pm, Su noon-11pm.)

BOYNE VALLEY

The thinly populated Boyne Valley of Co. Meath hides Ireland's greatest archaeological treasures. Massive passage tombs like Newgrange create subtle bumps in the landscape that belie their cavernous underground chambers. These wonders are older than the Pyramids and at least as puzzling. Celtic High Kings once ruled from atop the Hill of Tara, leaving a healthy dose of mysterious folklore in their wake. Every so often, farmers dig up artifacts from the Battle of the Boyne.

BRÚ NA BÓINNE: NEWGRANGE, KNOWTH, DOWTH   ☎041

Along the curves of the River Boyne, between Slane and Drogheda, sprawls Brú na Bóinne ("Homestead of the Boyne"). The Boyne Valley may not have all the passage tombs in the world—just the biggest and best. There are 40 in this 2500-acre region, each with more than five millennia of history. Neolithic engineers constructed Newgrange, Dowth, and Knowth within walking distance of each other. The work moved at a sluggish pace; it took 80 mega-men ten days to move one kerbstone, and larger mounds took a half-century to build, back when a decent lifespan was just 30 years.

The most impressive of the three main sights for archaeologists, if not for visitors, is **Knowth** (rhymes with "mouth"). The enormous passage tomb, quite unusually, houses *two* burial chambers, back to back, with separate east and west entrances—possibly a nod to the Sun's movement across the horizon. Knowth's carvings are well preserved as prehistoric art goes, with unexplained spirals and etchings adorning the passage. Long-term excavations prevent the general public from entering, but the visitors centre **tour** offers a peek. ⬛**Newgrange** provides the best glimpse at the structure and innards of a spectacular passage tomb. During a massive reconstruction in 1962, archaeologists discovered a roof box over the passage entrance. At dawn on the shortest day of the year (Dec. 21), 17 gilded minutes of sunlight shine through the roof box straight to the back of the 60 ft. passageway, illuminating the burial chamber. Those wishing to see the real event must sign up for a lottery, held every October, but the tour provides a brilliant simulation of the experience. Ongoing excavations have kept **Dowth** (rhymes with "Knowth") closed to the public for several years. To gain admission, get a Ph.D. in archaeology.

Do not try to make your way directly to the sites—a guard minds the gate. Instead, head to the ⬛**Brú na Bóinne Visitors Centre,** across from the tombs near Donore on the south side of the River Boyne, and immediately book a tour. Remember to dress appropriately when visiting—most of the tour takes place outside and Neolithic tombs lack central heating. (☎988 0300. Open June to mid-Sept. 9am-7pm; May 9am-6:30pm; late Sept. 9am-6:30pm; Mar.-Apr. and Oct. 9:30am-5:30pm; Nov.-Feb. 9:30am-5pm. Admission to the Visitors Center only €2.75, seniors €2, students and children €1.50, families €7; center and Newgrange tour €5.50/€4.25/€2.75/ €13.75; center and Knowth, Newgrange, and Knowth €9.75/€7/€4.25/€24.25. Last tour 1½hr. before closing. Last admission to center 45min. before closing.) **Bus Éireann** (☎836 6111) shuttles to Brú na Bóinne from **Dublin** (1½hr., every hr., round-trip €12.70). Several **bus tours** from Dublin include admission to the sights (Bus Éireann Sa-Th, €24.20).

HILL OF TARA ☎046

Home to 142 former Irish Kings, the largest collection of Celtic monuments in the world, and a sacred site for ancient Irish religion, Tara beckons visitors to its flourishing green expanse. From prehistoric times until the 10th century, Tara was the social, political, and cultural heart of Ireland. Many secrets are buried under the 100 acres of grassy mounds, and the grounds are free and open to the public. Don't miss the sacred *Lia Fail* ("Stone of Destiny"), an ancient phallus carved out of rock and used as a coronation stone; the rock was said to roar when the rightful king of Tara placed his hands upon it. The **Mound of Hostages,** the resident burial mound, dates from 2500 BC.

Tara is about 5 mi. east of Navan on the N3. Take any **local bus** from Dublin to **Navan** (1hr.; M-Sa 37 per day, Su 15 per day; €7), and ask the driver to stop at the turnoff, on the left and marked by a small brown sign. From there it's 1 mi. of uphill legwork. The actual buildings—largely wattle, wood, and earth—have long been buried or destroyed; what remains are concentric rings of grassy dunes. They are always open for exploration; to make sense of them, hit the **Visitors Center** in the old church for an excellent guided tour and a slideshow on Tara's history. (☎046 902 5903. Open daily mid-May to mid-June 10am-6pm. Last admission 5:15pm. €2, students €1, seniors €1.25.)

SOUTHEAST IRELAND

A power base for the Vikings and then the Normans, this region has town and street names that ring of the Norse or Anglo-Saxon, rather than the Celtic. The Southeast's most prolific tourist attractions are its beaches, which draw native admirers to the coastline stretching from Kilmore Quay to tidy Ardmore. Historic sights crowd the medieval city of Kilkenny and the cathedral complex at Cashel, while Waterford has resources, nightlife, and grit to match.

KILKENNY (CILL CHAINNIGH) ☎056

Known as both "The Marble City" and the "Oasis of Ireland," Kilkenny is a miniature version of Dublin—it has its own river, a renowned castle, excellent shopping, a tremendous selection of pubs, and a brewery. What it doesn't have are

Dublin's headaches: the traffic is bearable, and everything is within walking distance. A casual stroll down Kilkenny's handsome streets reveals the city's attempt to capitalize on its 15th-century charm.

⫾ TRANSPORTATION

Trains: Kilkenny MacDonagh Station, Dublin Rd. (☎22024). Open M-Sa 7am-8:15pm, Su 9am-1pm and 2:45-9pm. Ticket window open only at departure time. On the main **Dublin-Waterford** rail route (4-6 per day). Trains to: **Dublin** (2hr.); **Thomastown** (15min.); **Waterford** (45min.).

Buses: Kilkenny Station, Dublin Rd. (☎64933 or 051 879 000). Buses also leave from the city center at **The Tea Shop** (p. 763). Buses to: **Cork** (3hr.; M-Sa 3 per day, Su 2 per day; €16); **Dublin** (2hr., 5-6 per day, €10); **Galway** via **Athlone** or **Clonmel** (5hr.; M-Sa 6 per day, Su 3 per day; €19); **Limerick** via **Clonmel** (2½hr.; M-Sa 4 per day, Su 2 per day; €13.30); **Rosslare Harbour** via **Waterford** (2hr.; M-Sa 2 per day, Su 3 per day; €7). **Buggy's Coaches** (☎41264) run from **Kilkenny** to **Ballyragget** (30min., M-Sa 6 per day) and **Castlecomer** (15min., M-Sa 6 per day, €2.50) with stops at the **An Óige hostel** (15min.) and **Dunmore Cave** (20min.). **J.J. Kavanagh's Rapid Express** (☎31106) beats Bus Éireann's prices to **Dublin** (M-Sa 4 per day, Su 2 per day; €6).

Taxis: All companies have a €5.10 min. charge, plus an additional €1.50 per mi. after 3-4 mi. **Paul Butler** (☎087 222 6077); **Frank O'Neill** (☎086 633 4777); **Grab a Cab** (☎086 250 3475). **Castle Cabs** (☎61188) also **stores luggage** for €1.30 per day.

Bike Rental: J.J. Wall Cycle, 88 Maudlin St. (☎21236), will let you buy a cycle and then return it. €15 per day, €80 per week. Open M-Sa 9am-6pm.

✴❼ ORIENTATION AND PRACTICAL INFORMATION

From **MacDonagh Station,** turn left onto burgeoning **John Street** and downhill across the bridge towards the intersection with **High Street** and **the Parade.** Most activity occurs in the triangle formed by **High, Rose Inn,** and **Kieran Streets.**

Tourist Office: Rose Inn St. (☎51500), upstairs in a 1525 pauper house. Provides free maps and sells bus tickets. Open Mar.-Sept. M-F 9am-6pm, Sa 10am-6pm; Oct.-Feb. M-Sa 9am-5pm.

Financial Services: Find **banks** at the intersection of High St. and the Parade. All open M 10am-5pm, Tu-F 10am-4pm.

Launderette: The Laundry Basket (☎70355), top of James St. Full service wash and dry from €5. Dry-cleaning facilities. Open M-F 8:30am-7pm, Sa 9am-5pm.

Police (*Garda*): Dominic St. (☎22222).

Internet Access: Mobile Connections, Rose Inn St. (☎23000). €0.06 per min., €3.60 per hr. Open M-Sa 9am-9pm, Su 2-8pm. **Kilkenny e.centre,** 26 Rose Inn St. (☎60093). €5 per hr., students €4. Open M-Sa 10am-8pm, Su 11am-8pm.

Post Office: High St. (☎21891). Open M and W-Sa 9am-5:30pm, Tu 9:30am-5:30pm, Sa closed 1-2pm.

⌂ ACCOMMODATIONS

▓ **Kilkenny Tourist Hostel (IHH),** 35 Parliament St. (☎63541). Near the popular pubs and next to Smithwick's Brewery. Bright rooms brim with activity: people bustle about in the kitchen and dining room, lounge on couches, and sip Guinness on the front steps. Tons of town info posted in the front hall. Non-smoking. Kitchen open 7am-11pm. Laundry €5. Check-out 10am. 6- to 8-bed dorms €14; 4-bed €16. Doubles €36-40. ❶

▨ **Foulksrath Castle (An Óige/HI),** Jenkinstown (☎67674). On the N77 (Durrow road), 8 mi. north of town. Turn right at signs for Connahy; the hostel is ¼ mi. down on the left. Buggy's Buses run from the Parade M-Sa twice daily (20min., call hostel for times, €2). Housed in a 15th-century castle, Foulksrath is literally a royal accommodation. Enjoy the grand rooftop views, a common room with a fireplace, and paintings by the wonderful, artistic warden. Lock-out 10am-5pm. Dorms €11-12, under 16 €9-10. ❶

Dempsey's B&B, 26 James St. (☎21954). A little old house by the Superquinn supermarket, off High St. Delightful proprietors rent out simple, clean rooms with TVs. Parking €1 per night. Singles €35; ensuite doubles €64-70. ❸

Daly's B&B, 82 John's St. (☎62866). Ferns and other hanging plants greet guests in the sky-lit entrance hall; immaculate, spacious rooms and a large breakfast area lie beyond. Singles €40-45; doubles €68-72. ❸

The Bailey, 13 Parliament St. (☎64337). Excellent B&B rooms conveniently located above Bailey's Pub. Relish breakfast in the delightfully whimsical dining room. Singles €35-50; doubles M-Th €70, F-Su €190. ❸

Nore Valley Park (☎27229). 7 mi. south of Kilkenny between Bennetsbridge and Stonyford, marked from town. Take the New Ross road (R700) to Bennetsbridge, and the signposted right before the bridge. Hot showers, TV room, and a children's play area. Mini-golf (€2.50), go-carts (€1.50), picnic and barbecue areas. Wheelchair accessible. Laundry €5.70. Open Mar.-Oct. Backpackers €6. €2.50 per person, €7 per tent. ❶

Tree Grove Caravan and Camping Park (☎70302). 1 mi. past the castle on the New Ross road (R700). €6.50 per person, €1 per tent. Showers free. ❶

◖ FOOD

Everything in Kilkenny's restaurants is great except the prices, which all hover somewhere in the lower stratosphere. Below are some reasonable options; otherwise, hit the pubs. **Dunnes Supermarket,** Kieran St., sells housewares and food. (☎61655. Open M-Sa 8:30am-10pm, Su 9:30am-7pm.)

▨ **Pordylo's,** Butterslip Ln. (☎70660), between Kieran and High St. Zesty dinners (€17-23) from across the globe, with plentiful vegetarian options. Early bird menu until 7 (2 courses €16). Reservations recommended. Open daily 5:30-11pm. ❹

La Crêperie, 80 John St. Sweet and savory crepes and sandwiches (€2.70-6), fresh salads, and fruit smoothies, all for a great price. Open M-W and Sa 10am-6pm, Th-F 10am-7pm, Su 11am-5pm. ❶

Langton's, 69 John St. (☎65123). The eccentric owner has earned a gaggle of awards for the ever-changing menu of his highbrow restaurant. Full lunch menu with an Irish twist (€10) served daily 12:30-3:30pm; sophisticated dinner menu (2-course €25, 3-course €30) 6-10:30pm. Bar menu (€9-20) served 12:30-9:30pm. ❹

Ristorante Rinuccini, 1 the Parade (☎61575), opposite the castle. Couples enjoy authentic Italian delights and romantic music in this glittering first-rate establishment. Lunch (€9-14) served daily noon-2:30pm; dinner (€13-25) served M-F 6-10:30pm, Sa 5:30-10:30pm, Su 5:30-9:30pm. ❹

The Tea Shop, Patrick St. (☎70051). Excellent little cafe in the city center where travelers grab tasty breakfasts (€6) or sip herbal teas (€1.40) before catching the bus outside. Open M-F 8:30am-6pm, Sa 10am-5pm, Su 10:30am-3pm. ❷

Green Chilli, John St. (☎86990 or 86988), across from La Crêperie. Exquisite Indian food served in a dimly lit, tastefully decorated eatery. Vegetarian dishes €8.50. Carnivorous entrees €13-17. Takeaway €3 less. Open M-Sa 6pm-midnight, Su 5-11pm. ❸

PUBS

Kilkenny's numerous watering holes host a range of live music on most nights, especially in the summer.

■ **The Pump House,** 26 Parliament St. (☎63924). Remains a favorite among locals and hostelers. Loud, convenient, and packed. Downstairs is fairly low-key; ultra-hip upstairs enclave makes you wish you'd packed some Prada. Pool table upstairs €1. M-W summer trad, Su rock and blues.

■ **Tynan's Bridge House Bar** (☎21291), around the corner from the tourist office, on the river. At 300 years old, this is Kilkenny's most original bar. Small, with terrific atmosphere, stained glass, and old spice drawers behind the bar.

Ryan's, Friary St. (☎62281), off High St. No frills, just a good crowd and a beer garden past the rude bathroom signs. Th trad; Sa mongrel mix of trad, blues, and soul.

Anna Conda, Parliament St. (☎71657), near Cleere's. Outstanding trad fills the pub from the low ceilings in front to the high rafters in back. Tall wooden booths and dripping candles in wine bottles add to the atmosphere. New beer garden overlooks the ducks on the Suir. W and F-Su music. No cover.

O'Faoláin's, John St. (☎61018). Throbbing new bar with 3 floors, a 25 ft. ceiling, and a stunning rebuilt Welsh church crafted into the walls. Late bar (W-Sa until 2:30am, M-F and Su until 2am) and dance club (F-Sa; cover €5-10) make for a great place to end the night.

Cleere's, 28 Parliament St. (☎62573). Thespians from the Watergate Theatre across the street converge here during intermission. A black-box theater in back hosts vivacious musical and theatrical acts (occasional cover up to €20). M trad.

Paris, Texas, High St. (☎61822). Not as cheesy as the name. Cool Parisians pack in like cattle at this popular bar; hipster cowpokes shimmy and drink themselves a good time. Trad Tu, W, Su. Blues Th. Steaks and Tex-Mex food (€12-17) served noon-10pm.

Kyteler's Inn, Kieran St. (☎21064). The oldest pub in Kilkenny and the 1324 house of Alice Kyteler, Kilkenny's witch, whose husbands (all 4) had a knack for poisoning themselves on their first anniversaries. The food and drink have since become safer. Trad fills the air W, F, and Su afternoons. F-Sa fiddle away the evening at **Nero's,** a nightclub that burns down the house. Cover €8-12. Open 11pm-2am.

◉ **SIGHTS**

Travelers interested in Kilkennalia, including the city's folkloric tradition, should take a **Tynan Walking Tour.** Besides spinning some animated yarns, the tour is the only way to see the **old city gaol.** Tours depart from the tourist office on Rose Inn St. (☎087 265 1745; www.tynantours.com. 1hr. tours Apr.-Oct. M-Sa 4 per day, Su 2 per day; Nov.-Mar. Sa 3 per day. €6, concessions €5.50.)

■ **KILKENNY CASTLE.** Kilkenny's medieval charm culminates in its 13th-century castle, on the Parade. The 50 yd. **Long Galley,** a spectacle reminiscent of a Viking ship, displays portraits of English bigwigs, giant tapestries, and a beautiful Italian double fireplace. The basement houses the **Butler Gallery** and its modern art exhibits. (☎21450. Castle and gallery open daily June-Aug. 9:30am-7pm; Sept. 10am-6:30pm; Oct.-Mar. 10:30am-12:45pm and 2-5pm; Apr.-May 10:30am-5pm. Castle access by guided tour only. €5, students €2.) Across the street, the internationally recognized **Kilkenny Design Centre** fills the castle's former stables with expensive Irish crafts. (☎22118. Open Apr.-Dec. M-Sa 9am-6pm, Su 10am-6pm; Jan.-Mar. M-Sa 9am-6pm.)

SMITHWICK'S BREWERY. Rumor has it that 14th-century monks, known to be a crafty bunch, once brewed a light ale in the **St. Francis Abbey** on Parliament St. Though the abbey is now in ruins, the industry survives in the yard, at the **Smithwick's Brewery.** Each day 50 free tickets are given out at the security guard station; turn right after the Watergate Theatre and the gate is straight ahead. Collect your ticket and show up at 3pm outside the green doors on Parliament St. for a tour, followed by **two free pints** in the factory's private pub. (☎21014. Tours July-Aug. M-F.)

🄰 🄳 OUTDOORS AND ENTERTAINMENT

Activities in and around Kilkenny are plentiful, especially for outdoors enthusiasts. The **Kilkenny Anglers Club** (☎65220) can set you up for **fishing** on the Nore. If you'd prefer to paddle, call **Go with the Flow River Adventures** (☎087 252 9700) to **canoe** on the river Barrow. The **Kilkenny Golf Club** (☎65400), out Castlecomer Rd., is an 18-hole championship course open to nonmembers.

The tourist office provides a bi-monthly guide to the town's activities; *The Kilkenny People* (€1.30) is a good newsstand source for arts and music listings. The **Watergate Theatre,** Parliament St., stages drama, dance, and opera. (☎61674. Box office open M-F 10am-7pm, Sa 2-6pm, Su 1hr. before curtain. Tickets €10-20, concessions available.) Every August, Kilkenny holds its **Arts Festival,** with daily programs of theater, concerts, and readings by European and Irish artists. (☎52175; www.kilkennyarts.ie. Tickets under €20.) The city's population increases by more than 10,000 when the **Cat Laughs;** held the first weekend in June, this **festival** features international comedy acts.

CASHEL (CAISEAL MUMHAN) ☎062

The town of Cashel lies tucked between a series of mountain ranges on the N8, 12 mi. east of Tipperary town. Legend has it that the devil furiously hurled a rock from high above the plains when he discovered a church was being built in Cashel. The assault failed to thwart the plucky citizens, and today the town sprawls defiantly at the base of the 300 ft. Rock of Cashel.

Dominating the horizon, the ◾**Rock of Cashel,** sometimes called **St. Patrick's Rock,** is a huge limestone outcropping crowned with medieval ruins. Periodic guided tours are informative, if a bit dry; exploring the buildings while in earshot of the guide is a more attractive option. The 1495 burning of the **Cashel Cathedral** by the Earl of Kildare was a highlight of Cashel's illustrious history. When Henry VII demanded an explanation, Kildare replied, "I thought the Archbishop was in it." As any Brit worth his blue blood would, the King made him Lord Deputy. Next to the cathedral, a 90 ft. **round tower,** built just after 1101, is the oldest part of the Rock. The **museum** at the entrance to the castle complex preserves the 12th-century **St. Patrick's Cross.** (Rock open daily mid-June to mid-Sept. 9am-7pm; mid-Mar. to mid-June 9am-5:30pm; mid-Sept. to mid-Mar. 9am-4:30pm. Last admission 45min. before closing. €5, seniors €3.50, students €2.) Smart visitors stop by the **Heritage Center,** on Main St., before heading Rockwards. (☎62511. Open daily May-Sept. 9:30am-5:30pm; Oct.-Apr. M-F 9:30am-5:30pm. Free.) The ◾**Brú Ború Heritage Centre,** below the Rock, hosts wonderful trad and dance. (☎61122. Performances mid-June to mid-Sept. Tu-Sa 9pm. €15, with dinner €40.

All but one of Cashel's **buses** leave from the Bake House on Main St., across from the tourist office; the Dublin bus departs from Feehan's a few doors down. **Bus Éireann** (☎061 33333) serves: **Cork** (1½hr., €12); **Dublin** (3hr., 6 per day, €15); **Limerick** (1hr., 5 per day, €12). **McInerney's** provides **bike rental** near the SuperValu. (☎61225. €10 per day, €60 per week. Open M-Sa 9:30am-5:30pm.) Cashel's **tourist**

office, Main St., splits rent with the **Heritage Center** in City Hall. (☎62511. Open May-Sept. M-F 9:30am-5:30pm, Su 10am-6pm.) The **post office** is on Main St. (☎61418. Open M-F 9am-1pm and 2-5:30pm, Sa 9am-1pm.)

A 5min. walk from town on Dundrum Rd. near the ruins of Hore Abbey, the stunning ✍O'Brien's Farm House Hostel ❶ has an incredible view of the Rock, cheerful rooms, and courteous hosts. (☎61003. Full-service laundry €8-10. Dorms €15. Doubles €45-50. **Camping** €7.50 per person.) Just steps from the Rock, in a quiet residential neighborhood on Dominic St., the sunny rooms of **Rockville House** ❸ are a great bargain. (☎61760. Singles €35; shared rooms €25 per person.) While waiting for the bus, enjoy coffee and light meals at **The Bake House** ❶, across from the tourist office. (☎61680. Open M-Sa 8:30am-5:30pm, Su 10am-5:30pm.) The superior grub (€8) at **Ó'Suilleabáin** ❷ (O'Sullivan's), Main St., makes it the local lunchtime haunt. (☎61858. Food served M-F 11am-2:30pm.) Start your pub-crawling at **Feehan's** (☎61929), where the atmosphere is timeless. If the stars are out, move to the multi-level beer garden at **Mikey Ryan's** (☎61431). Cross over Main St. for some singing and joke-telling at **20 Davern** (☎61121; music M and W), and end the night down the street at lively **Pat and Fox.**

WEXFORD (LOUGH GARMAN) ☎053

Incessant fighting between Gaels, Vikings, and Normans gave birth to Wexford's labyrinth of narrow streets. Park the car and pound the pavement to visit the huddled harbor town's main attractions—its quality pubs and restaurants.

🔲 TRANSPORTATION. From **O'Hanranhan (North) Station** (☎22522), on Redmond Sq., **trains** serve Connolly Station in **Dublin** (2¾hr., 3 per day, €23) and **Rosslare** (15min., 3 per day, €4). **Buses** stop at the train station. If the station office is closed, check **Railway News** (☎24056), across the street, for information. Buses run to **Dublin** (2¾hr., 8-10 per day, €10) and **Rosslare** (20min., 9-12 per day, €3.50); those to and from **Limerick** (4 per day, €16) connect with Irish Ferries and Stena-Sealink sailings. A list of **taxi** companies is posted in the train station. **Hitchhikers** find that the odds of getting a ride are highest around noon or 5-7pm; savvy hitchers make a point of specifying either the Dublin Rd. (N11) or the Waterford Rd. (N25). *Let's Go* does not recommend hitchhiking.

🔳🔲 ORIENTATION AND PRACTICAL INFORMATION. Most of the town's action takes place one block inland, along the twists and turns of **Main Street.** The **Bullring** plaza is near the center of town, a few blocks from where North Main St. changes to South. Another plaza, **Redmond Square,** sits at the northern end of the quays near the train and bus station. The **tourist office** is moving from Crescent Quay to a new location on the waterfront. Contact **Wexford Tourism** (☎52900 or 46506) for updated location and hours. Banks with 24hr. **ATMs** include **AIB** (☎22444) and **Bank of Ireland** (☎21365; both open M 10am-5pm, Tu-F 10am-4pm). The **library** has free **Internet access;** call ahead to reserve a slot. (☎21637. Open Tu 1-5:30pm, W-F 10am-5:30pm.) **Megabytes,** located in the Franciscan Friary, has computers and coffee. (€3 per hr. Open M-Th 9am-7pm, F 9am-5:30pm, Sa 10am-4pm.) Find the **post office** on Anne St. (☎22587. Open M and W-Sa 9am-5:30pm, Tu 9:30am-5:30pm.)

🏠 ACCOMMODATIONS. If your visit coincides with the opera festival, book as far in advance as possible; rooms are often reserved up to a year ahead. Castle views complement immaculate rooms at ✍**The Blue Door** ❸, 18 Lower George St. Look for the crisp white building with flower baskets and a blue door; head downstairs for breakfast. (☎21047. Singles €40-50; doubles €60-80.) ✍**Kirwan House Hos-**

tel (IHH) ❶, 3 Mary St., is a 200-year-old Georgian house right in the heart of town with some slants and creaks in its wooden floors, a barbecue-friendly patio out back, and loads of local information from the staff. (☎21208. Laundry available next door. Dorms €12-14; doubles €34; triples €48.) The **Abbey House** ❸, 34 Abbey St., is a centrally-located, family-run B&B. Enjoy comfy quarters and the dining room with an electric fireplace. (☎24408. Singles €35-40; ensuite doubles €56-62.)

◪▨ **FOOD AND PUBS. Dunnes Store,** Redmond Sq., sells **groceries.** (☎45688. Open M-Tu 9am-8pm, W 9am-9pm, Th-F 9am-10pm, Sa 9am-7pm, Su 10am-7pm.) Relax among old Guinness ads at **The Sky and the Ground** ❸, S. Main St. Scaled-down versions of pricier fare served by the late-night restaurant upstairs (**Heavens Above** ❹; entrees €14-21) are available here until 6pm. Lunch is so good they occasionally sell out the entire menu. (☎21273. Entrees €8.50-10. M-Th and Su live music, typically trad.) **Gusto** ❶, S. Main St., serves high-quality breakfasts (€4-7) and sandwiches, with a slightly sophisticated vibe. Panini (€5.50) are a warm treat. (☎24336. Open M-F 8:30am-5:30pm, Sa 8:30am-5pm, Su 10am-2pm.)

The two halves of **Mooney's Lounge,** Commercial Quay, by the bridge, are Wexford's hot late-night venue. One side opens up for a disco bar after 9:30pm, while the other continues as a pub. (☎21128. Live music F-Su. 18+. Occasional cover €7. Open M-W until 11:30pm, Th-Su until 2:30am.) A classy crowd flocks to **The Centenary Stores,** Charlotte St., off Commercial Quay, a stylish pub and dance club situated in a former warehouse. The patio is great for sunny afternoon pints. (☎24424. Excellent trad Su mornings.) On the corner of Redmond Pl. facing the water, **The Ferryman,** 12 Monck St., is illuminated by ample skylights and faux torches. (☎23877. Carvery lunch served 12:30-3pm.)

◪▣ **SIGHTS AND ENTERTAINMENT.** The remains of the Norman **city walls** run the length of High St. Near the intersection of Abbey St. and Slaney St., **Westgate Tower** is the only one of the wall's original six gates that still stands. It now holds the **Westgate Heritage Centre,** where an excellent 30min. audiovisual show (€3) recounts the town's history. (☎46506. Open M-Sa 10am-6pm, occasional Su during summer.) Next door, the peaceful, overgrown ruins of **Selskar Abbey** mark the site of Henry II's extended penance for his role in Thomas Becket's murder. Enter through the gate by the Heritage Centre. (Open M-F 10am-4pm. Free.) The **Friary Church** (☎22758), on School St., has housed Franciscan monks since 1230.

For detailed information on events throughout the county, pick up *The Wexford People* (€1.50) from any local newsstand or pub. The funky **Wexford Arts Centre,** Cornmarket, presents free visual arts and crafts exhibitions and performances of music, dance, and drama throughout the year. (☎23764. Centre open M-Sa 9am-6pm. Tickets generally €10-18.) The **Theatre Royal,** High St., produces year-round shows, culminating in the internationally acclaimed **Wexford Festival Opera,** held in late October and early November. (☎22400, box office 22144; www.wexfordopera.com. Box office open M-F 9am-5pm.) Wexford's hilly countryside and beaches make for excellent horseback riding. **Shelmalier Riding Stables,** 4 mi. away at Forth Mountain, has riding for both novices and experts. (☎39251. Advanced booking essential). **Boat trips** from Wexford Harbour are another way to explore the area, perfect for those seeking close-up pictures of the **seals** at Raven Point. (☎40564. 30min. tour €7.)

ROSSLARE HARBOUR (ROS LÁIR)   ☎053

Rosslare, best viewed from the deck of a departing ship, is a pragmatic seaside village whose primary function is welcoming voyagers and bidding them *bon voyage* as they depart for France or Wales. **Trains** run from the ferryport to: **Dublin** (3hr., 3 per day, €17.50); **Limerick** (2½hr., 1-2 per day, €17.50) via **Waterford** (1¼hr., €9); and **Wexford** (15min., 3 per day, €4). The **rail office** (☎33592) also houses the bus station. Most **buses** (☎33595) stop by the Kilrane Church and the Catholic church and go to: **Dublin** (3hr., 10-12 per day, €14.50); **Galway** via **Waterford** (4 per day, €23); **Killarney** (M-Sa 5 per day, Su 3 per day; €22) via **Cork** (€19) and **Waterford** (€13); **Wexford** (20min., 13-17 per day, €3.80). **Stena Line** (☎61560, 24hr. info 61505) and **Irish Ferries** (☎33158) both serve the port. **Ferries** shove off for **Wales** (summer 5-6 per day, winter 2 per day), **Britain** (2 per day), and **France** (1 every other day). Trains and buses often connect with the ferries; **Irish Rail** (☎33114) and **Bus Éireann** (☎051 879 000) have desks in the terminal.

Exhausted passengers often take what they can get in town, but better **B&Bs** swamp the N25 just outside of Rosslare. ▨**Mrs. O'Leary's Farmhouse ❷**, off N25 in Kilrane, a 15min. drive from town, stands out from the rest of the rabble. Set on a glorious 100-acre, seaside farm, this well-kept home is a holiday unto itself. A grassy lane leads past dunes of wildflowers to a secluded beach. (☎33134. Call for pickup. €27-30 per person.)

WATERFORD (PORT LÁIRGE) ☎051

A skyline of huge metal silos and harbor cranes greet visitors to Waterford. Fortunately, behind this industrial facade lies a city with ten centuries of fascinating history. The Vikings founded Vadrafjord around AD 914, making it the oldest city in Ireland. Traces of Viking influence persist in Waterford's streets, despite the massive freighters that have replaced the longships.

🖪 TRANSPORTATION. Trains (☎317 889, 24hr. timetable 876 243) arrive at **Plunkett Station,** across the bridge from the Quay, and run to: **Dublin** (2½hr., M-F 5-6 per day, €17-21); **Kilkenny** (40min., 3-5 per day, €8); **Limerick** (2¼hr., M-Sa 2 per day, €15.50); **Rosslare** (1hr., M-Sa 2 per day, €10). The bus station is on the Quay, across from the tourist office. **Buses** (☎879 000) run to: **Cork** (2½hr., 10-13 per day, €14.50); **Dublin** (2¾hr.; M-Sa 10-12 per day, Su 6 per day; €10); **Galway** (4¾hr., 5-6 per day, €18.50); **Kilkenny** (1hr., 1 per day, €8); **Limerick** (2½hr.; M-Th and Su 6 per day, F 7 per day; €14.50); **Rosslare** (1¼hr., 3-5 per day, €12.50). For **taxis,** head to the cab stand on Broad St., or try **7 Cabs** (☎877 777), **Five-0 Cabs** (☎850 000), or **Rapid Cabs** (☎858 585). Waterford's few **hitchers** stand on main routes, away from the city center; others take city buses out to the Crystal Factory before sticking out a thumb. *Let's Go* does not recommend hitchhiking.

🖪🖪 ORIENTATION AND PRACTICAL INFORMATION. Modern Waterford sits on the ruins of the triangular Viking city. The hornéd ones must have had a knack for urban planning, because the area between **the Quay, Parnell Street (the Mall),** and **Barronstrand Street** (Michael and Broad St.) is still hopping, even without the sweet music of falster pibes filling the air. The **tourist office** is on the Quay, across from the bus station. (☎875 823. Open M-F 9am-6pm, Sa 10am-6pm.) **Banks** with 24hr. **ATMs** line the streets. The friendly people at **Youth Information Centre,** 130 the Quay, help with finding **short-term work.** (☎877 328. Open M-F 9:30am-5:30pm.) Find **Internet access** there, or at **Voyager Internet Cafe,** 85 the Quay. (☎843 843. €1.20 per 10min. Open M-Sa 10am-7pm.) The largest of several **post offices** is on the Quay. (☎874 321. Open M and W-F 9am-5:30pm, Tu 9:30am-5:30pm, Sa 9am-1pm.)

🖪 ACCOMMODATIONS. Waterford has no hostels, and most **B&Bs** in the city center are nothing to write home about. Mrs. Ryan invites visitors into her charming home at **Beechwood ❷**, 7 Cathedral Sq. From the Quay, go up Henrietta St.; the B&B is located on a quiet pedestrian street. (☎876 677. Singles €45; doubles €50.)

Avondale House ❹, 2 Parnell St., occupies an old Georgian mansion with plenty of modern luxuries, including TVs, phones, and hair dryers. (☎852 267. Singles €45-60; doubles €70-80.) **The Anchorage** ❹, 9 the Quay, offers upscale accommodations right on the Quay. Each room has TV, phone, and tea/coffee-making facilities. (☎854 302. Singles €45-50; doubles €70-80.)

🄲🄼 **FOOD AND PUBS.** Stock up on cheap **groceries** at **Dunnes Stores** in the City Square Mall. (☎853 100. Open M-W 9am-7pm, Th-F 9am-9pm, Sa 9am-6pm, Su noon-6pm.) At 🄼**Haricot's Wholefood Restaurant** ❷, 11 O'Connell St., the menu of healthy, innovative dishes and vegetarian-friendly meals is constantly changing, with everything made from scratch. (☎841 299. Entrees €9.50. Open M-F 10am-8pm, Sa 10am-6pm.) Candlelit tables set the mood for authentic Italian food at **Emiliano's** ❸, 21 High St. Call ahead for reservations, or arrive before 7pm for the €18 early-bird special. (☎820 333. Pasta €12-13. Entrees €16-24. Open Tu-F 5-10:30pm, Sa-Su 12:30pm and 5-10:30pm.) **Cafe Luna** ❷, 53 John St., is a late-night cafe serving pasta, salads, and sandwiches with a creative twist. Get homemade soup and a half-sandwich for €5. (☎834 539. Most entrees €6-10. Open M-W until midnight, Th-Su until 3:30am.)

The Quays are flooded with pubs, and the corner of John St. and Parnell St. has its share as well. 🄼**Geoff's,** 8 John St., has been one of Waterford's most popular pubs for over a century, yet still manages to feel young and friendly. Locals of all ages drop in for pints and laughs, but go elsewhere for matches—Geoff staunchly refuses to install a television. (☎874 787. Italian-style sandwiches €4-7. Open until 12:30am on weekends. Food served until 9pm.) 🄼**T&H Doolan's,** George's St., has been serving for a respectable 300 years, in an awe-inspiring building with low, low ceilings that have been standing for over 800. Sinéad O'Connor crooned here during her college days. (☎841 504. Pub grub €13-19. Trad nightly 9:30pm. Food served until 9pm.) A small, traditional pub at the corner of Parnell St. and John St., **The Woodman** (☎858 130) shuts down at 12:30am on weekends, so head to the adjoining **Ruby Lounge,** which throbs with chart hits until 2:30am. Get a pre-boogie buzz in the pub's front lounge before 10pm to evade the Th-Sa €8-10 cover.

🄶 **SIGHTS.** To cover all of Waterford's sights in a day requires the swiftness of a Viking raider and the organization of a Norman invader. Buying the **City Pass** from **Waterford Tourism,** 1 Arundel St. (☎852 550), or at the Waterford Crystal Factory, Waterford Treasures, or Reginald's Tower, gets admission to all three for €10.20.

Fancy dinner sets, the Times Square Millennium Ball, and all major sporting trophies have all been handcrafted at the 🄼**Waterford Crystal Factory,** 2 mi. from the city center on N25 (the Cork Rd.). Watch master craftsmen transform molten goo into sparkling crystal, or admire the finished products—and their astronomical prices—in the gallery. To get there, catch the City Imp outside Dunnes on Michael St. and request a stop at the factory (10-15min., every 15-20min., €1.20) or take city bus #3, which leaves across from the Clock Tower every 30min. (☎332 500. Gallery open daily Mar.-Oct. 8:30am-6pm; Nov.-Feb. 9am-5pm. 1hr. tours every 15min. during high season. Tours €7.50, students €3.50. Open daily Mar.-Oct. 8:30am-4pm; Nov.-Feb. M-F 9am-3:15pm.)

To brush up on the 1000-year history of Waterford, head to 🄼**Waterford Treasures** at the Granary, connected to the tourist office. Named the 1999-2000 Ireland Museum of the Year, this €4.5 million project is well worth a visit. The actual artifacts, including the town's written charters, make quite an impressive show. (☎304 500. Open May-Sept. M-Sa 9am-6pm, Su 11am-5pm; Oct.-Apr. M-Sa 10am-5pm, Su 11am-5pm. €6, students €4.50.) At the end of the Quay, **Reginald's Tower** has guarded the city's entrance since the 12th century. Tiny models illustrate the con-

I R E L A N D

tributions Vikings, Normans, and English kings have made to Waterford's growth. (☎873 501. Open daily June-Sept. 9:30am-6pm; Oct.-May Tu-Su 10am-5pm; last admission 45min. before closing. Tours available. €2, seniors €1.25, students €1.)

🎵 🎭 **ENTERTAINMENT AND FESTIVALS.** The tourist office provides an annual list of major events in town; any local newspaper, including the free *Waterford Today*, has more specific entertainment listings. The seasonal **Waterford Show** at City Hall features Irish music, stories, and dance. (☎358 397 or 875 788. Shows July-Aug. Tu-Th and Sa 9pm; May-June and Sept. Tu, Th, Sa 9pm. Tickets €7.) The **Garter Lane Arts Centre,** 22a O'Connell St., supports all different forms of art inside its old Georgian brick. (☎855 038. Centre and box office open M-Sa 10am-6pm; performance nights until 9pm. Tickets €7, concessions €3-5 less.) Waterford's largest festival, the **Spraoi** ("spree"), is held during the August bank holiday weekend, attracting bands from around the globe. (☎841 808; www.spraoi.com.)

SOUTHWEST IRELAND

With a dramatic landscape that ranges from lush lakes and mountains to stark, ocean-battered cliffs, Southwest Ireland is rich in storytellers and history-makers. The humming activity of Cork and the area's frantic pace of rebuilding and growth balance the ancient rhythm of nearby rural villages.

CORK (AN CORCAIGH)   ☎021

In its capacity as Ireland's second-largest city, Cork (pop. 150,000) orchestrates most of the athletic, musical, and artistic activities in the southwest. River quays and pub-lined streets reveal architecture both grand and grimy, evidence of "Rebel Cork's" history of resistance, ruin and reconstruction.

📟 **TRANSPORTATION**

Flights: Cork Airport (☎431 3131), 5 mi. south of Cork on the Kinsale Rd. **Aer Lingus** (☎432 7155), **British Airways** (☎800 626 747), and **Ryanair** (☎01 609 7800) connect Cork to Dublin, Paris, and several English cities.

Trains: Kent Station, Lower Glanmire Rd. (☎450 6766; www.irishrail.ie), in the northeast part of town across the river from the city center. Open M-Sa 6:35am-8pm, Su 7:50am-8pm. Trains to: **Dublin** (3hr.; M-Sa 9 per day, Su 8 per day; €55); **Killarney** (2hr.; M-Sa 7 per day, Su 4 per day; €25.50); **Limerick** (1½hr., 5 per day, €25.50); **Tralee** (2½hr., 3 per day, €30.50).

Buses: Parnell Pl. (☎450 8188), 2 blocks east of Patrick's Bridge on Merchant's Quay. Inquiries desk open daily 9am-6pm. **Bus Éireann** goes to all major cities: **Bantry** (2hr.; M-Sa 7 per day, Su 3 per day; €15); **Dublin** (4½hr.; M-Sa 6 per day, Su 5 per day; €23); **Galway** (4hr., 12 per day, €17); **Killarney** (2hr.; M-Sa 13 per day, Su 11 per day; €13); **Limerick** (2hr., 14 per day, €13.20); **Rosslare Harbour** (4hr., 3 per day, €18.50); **Sligo** (7hr., 5 per day, €23); **Tralee** (2½hr., 12 per day, €14); **Waterford** (2¼hr., M-Sa 13 per day, €14.50). Round-trip fares offer better deals.

Ferries: Ringaskiddy Terminal (☎427 5061), 8 mi. south of the city. Call **Brittany Ferries** (☎437 8401) or **Swansea-Cork Ferries** (☎427 1166).

Bike Rental: Rothar Cycles, 55 Barrack St. (☎431 3133). Return bikes at any other locations approved by the Raleigh Rent-a-Bike program. €20 per day, €80 per week; €25 one-way. €100 deposit or credit card. Open M-F 10am-6pm, Sa 10am-5:45pm.

Southwest Ireland

Hitching: Hitchhikers headed for West Cork and Co. Kerry walk down Western Rd. past the An Óige hostel and the dog track to the Crow's Nest Pub, or they take bus #8. Those hoping to hitch a ride to Dublin or Waterford often stand on the hill next to the train station on the Lower Glanmire Rd. *Let's Go* does not recommend hitchhiking.

ORIENTATION AND PRACTICAL INFORMATION

Downtown Cork is the tip of an arrow-shaped island in the **River Lee.** Before being diverted to create the city's modern moat, the River Lee's present channels once ran straight through the city in grand Venetian fashion. The pavement of horseshoe-shaped **St. Patrick Street** was laid directly over the waterflow, thus the inspiration for its unconventional U-shape. St. Patrick St. becomes **Grand Parade** to the west; to the north it crosses **Merchant's Quay,** home of the bus station. The pedestrian-friendly downtown action concentrates on the vaguely parallel **Paul, St. Patrick,** and **Oliver Plunkett Street.**

Tourist Office: Tourist House, Grand Parade (☎425 5100), near the corner of South Mall, across from the National Monument along the River Lee's south channel. Offers accommodations booking (€4), souvenirs, and a free Cork city guide and map. Open June-Aug. M-F 9am-6pm, Sa 9am-5pm; Sept.-May M-Sa 9:15am-5:15pm.

IRELAND

Cork

▲ ACCOMMODATIONS
Cork International Hostel
(An Óige/HI), **9**
Kinlay House (IHH), **1**
Roman House, **3**
Sheila's Budget Accommodation
Centre (IHH), **4**

🍎 FOOD
Amicus, **8**
Greene's, **5**
Quay Co-op, **15**
Tribes, **13**

🎵 NIGHTLIFE
An Brog, **11**
An Spailpín Fánac, **14**

Bodega, **6**
Franciscan Well Brewery
and Pub, **2**
Half Moon, **7**
Loafer, **17**
The Lobby, **16**
The Old Oak, **12**
The Other Place, **10**

IRELAND

Budget Travel: SAYIT, 76 Grand Parade ($\bf{\varpi}$427 9188), sells Rambler and Eurail tickets, and Ireland Rail Cards. Open M-F 9am-5:30pm, Sa 10am-4pm. **USIT,** Oliver Plunkett St. ($\bf{\varpi}$427 0900). Open M-W and F 9:30am-5:30pm, Th 10am-5:30pm, Sa 10am-2pm.

Financial Services: Banks are easy to find and most have 24hr. **ATMs.**

GLBT Services: The Other Place, 8 South Main St. ($\bf{\varpi}$427 8470; www.gayproject-cork.com). Call M-F 10am-5:30pm. Hosts a gay bar (p. 775). **Gay Information Cork** ($\bf{\varpi}$427 1087). Helpline W and Th-F 10am-1pm and 2-6pm. **Lesbians Inc. (L.Inc.),** White St. ($\bf{\varpi}$480 8600). Consult the *Gay Community News* (GCN) for event information.

Launderette: Duds 'n Suds, Douglas St. ($\bf{\varpi}$431 4799), at the corner of Rutland St. Provides dry-cleaning services and a small snack bar. Wash €4, dry €4.50. Open M-F 8am-9pm, Sa 8am-6pm. Last load in 2hr. before closing.

Police *(Garda)*: Anglesea St. ($\bf{\varpi}$452 2000).

Hospital: Mercy Hospital, Grenville Pl. ($\bf{\varpi}$427 1971). €45 fee for emergency room access. **Cork University Hospital,** Wilton St. ($\bf{\varpi}$454 6400), on the #8 bus route.

Internet Access: 🖳**Web Workhouse,** Winthrop St. ($\bf{\varpi}$427 3090). Lofty, converted warehouse hums with high-speed computers. Tea and coffee available. €1.25-5 per hr. Open 24hr. **Cork City Library** ($\bf{\varpi}$427 7110), across from the tourist office. €1 per 30min. Open M-Sa 9am-5:30pm.

Post Office: Oliver Plunkett St. ($\bf{\varpi}$427 2000). Open M-Sa 9am-5:30pm.

🏚 ACCOMMODATIONS

Most of Cork's **hostels** are excellent and popular, so call ahead. A few terrific **B&Bs** populate **St. Patrick's Hill;** the best ones congregate nearer **Glanmire Road. Western Road,** leading out toward University College, is knee-deep in pricier B&Bs.

🏚 **Sheila's Budget Accommodation Centre (IHH),** 4 Belgrave Pl. ($\bf{\varpi}$450 5562; www.sheilashostel.ie), at Wellington Rd. and York Street Hill. Central location, roomy kitchen, and occasional summertime barbecues in a secluded backyard. All rooms non-smoking and ensuite. 24hr. reception desk doubles as general store and sells breakfast (€3.20). Sauna €2. Bike rental €14. Internet access €1 per 20min. Free luggage storage. Check-out 10am. Dorms €14-17; singles €30; doubles €40-50. ❷

Kinlay House (IHH), Bob and Joan Walk ($\bf{\varpi}$450 8966; www.kinlayhouse.ie), down the alley to the right of St. Anne's (Shandon) Church. Recently renovated, with family-sized rooms and a plush lounge area. Video library and game room. Internet access €1 per 15min. Continental breakfast included. Laundry €7. Free parking. 10- to 14-bed dorms €14-16; singles €30; doubles €45-50; family-sized rooms €20 per person. ❷

Roman House, 3 St. John's Terr., Upper John St. ($\bf{\varpi}$450 3606; www.interglobal.ie/romanhouse), across from Kinlay House. Colorful Roman House is Cork's only B&B catering specifically to gay and lesbian travelers. Walls display proprietor's artwork. All rooms ensuite with TV, oversized armchairs, and hot-pots. Vegetarian breakfast option. Singles €40; doubles €60. ❷

Cork International Hostel (An Óige/HI), 1-2 Redclyffe, Western Rd. ($\bf{\varpi}$454 3289), a 15min. walk from the Grand Parade. Bus #8 stops across the street; turn left and walk about 2 blocks. Immaculate, spacious rooms with high ceilings compensate for the out-of-the-way location of this stately brick Victorian townhouse. All rooms ensuite. Continental breakfast €3.50. Internet access €1 per 10min. Check-in 10:30am-midnight. 10- and 6-bed dorms €17, 4-bed €19; doubles €44. Reduced prices if under 18. ❷

○ FOOD

The **English Market,** accessible from Grand Parade, Patrick St., and Oliver Plunkett St., sells a wide variety of produce fresh from the farms and fisheries of West Cork. **Tesco** on Paul St. is the biggest grocery store in town. (☎427 0791. Open M-W 9am-8pm, Th-F 9am-10pm, Sa 8:30am-8pm, Su noon-6pm.)

▣ **Quay Co-op,** 24 Sullivan's Quay (☎431 7660). Large townhouse windows expose vibrant colors and an energizing, intellectual buzz. A vegan's delight, but no chore for carnivores. A daily menu with excellent soups and desserts. Apricot and yogurt flan €2.50. Specials €7.50. Open M-Sa 9am-9pm. Store open M-Sa 9am-6:15pm. ❷

▣ **Tribes,** Tuckey St. (☎427 6070). Late-night, low-light java shop with south-islander theme. Serves full menu into the wee hours. Global spectrum of coffee blends (€1.80). Teas from black currant to strawberry nettle €1.70. Bronx Burger or Hawaiian bagel sandwich €5.70. Open M-W noon-12:30am, Th-Sa noon-4am. ❶

Amicus, 14A French Church St. (☎427 6455). Artistic and elegant, from the paintings to the creative cuisine: the "Massive Beef Burger" is happily offered next to vegetarian Sicilian curry. Entrees €12-20. Open M-Sa 10am-10:30pm, Su 10am-9:30pm. ❹

Greene's, 48 MacCurtain St. (☎455 2279). Walk through the stone arch past Isaac's Hotel, and look right. Warm colors, grand skylights, stone and wood accents, and exquisite cuisine. Ask for a seat by the window. Entrees €17-30. Open M-Th 6-10pm, F-Sa 6-10:30pm, Su 6-9pm. Early-bird 3-course menu €25, served every night 6-7pm. ❹

◎ SIGHTS

All of Cork's sights can be reached on foot. For guidance, pick up *The Cork Area City Guide* at the tourist office (€1.90).

▣ **UNIVERSITY COLLEGE CORK (UCC).** Built in 1845, UCC's campus is a collection of brooding Gothic buildings, manicured lawns, and sculpture-studded grounds, which make for a fine afternoon walk or picnic along the River Lee. One of the newer buildings, **Boole Library,** celebrates number-wizard George Boole, mastermind of Boolean logic and model for Sherlock Holmes's arch-nemesis Prof. James Moriarty. *(Main gate on Western Rd. ☎490 3000; www.ucc.ie.)*

▣ **FITZGERALD PARK.** Rose gardens, playgrounds, and a permanent parking spot for the ice cream man are all here. Also present are the befuddlingly esoteric exhibitions of the **Cork Public Museum,** which features such goodies as 18th-century toothbrushes and the clothes of James Dwyer, Sheriff of Cork. *(From the front gate of UCC, follow the signposted walkway across the street. ☎427 0679. Will reopen from renovation in late 2004; museum usually open M-F 11am-1pm and 2:15-5pm, Su 3-5pm. M-F students and seniors free, families €3; Sa-Su €1.50.)*

CORK CITY GAOL. This not-to-be-missed museum is a reconstruction of the jail as it appeared in the 1800s, complete with eerily life-like mannequins. Descriptions of Cork's social history accompany tidbits about miserable punishments, such as the "human treadmill" that was used to grind grain. The building also houses an intriguing radio museum. *(Sunday's Well Rd. From Fitzgerald Park, cross the white footbridge at the western end of the park, turn right onto Sunday's Well Rd., and follow the signs. ☎430 5022. Open daily Mar.-Oct. 9:30am-6pm, Nov.-Feb. 10am-5pm. Last admission 1hr. before closing. €6, students and seniors €5, families €15. Admission includes audio tour.)*

ST. ANNE'S CHURCH. Commonly called **Shandon Church,** St. Anne's sandstone-and-limestone-striped steeple inspired the red and white "rebel" flag still flying throughout the county. Notoriously out of sync, the clocks adorning each side of the tower have been held responsible for many Irishmen's tardy arrival at work, and have earned the church its nickname, "the four-faced liar." *(Walk up Shandon St., go right on unmarked Church St., and continue straight.* ☎ *450 5906. Will re-open from renovation in late 2004; usually open June-Sept. M-Sa 10am-5:30pm. €4, students and seniors €3.50, families €12. Group rates available.)*

🗓 🎵 PUBS AND CLUBS

Cork's nightlife has the variety of music and atmosphere you'd expect to find in the Republic's second-largest city. To keep on top of the club scene, check out *List Cork*, a free biweekly schedule of music available at local stores.

🎵 **The Lobby,** 1 Union Quay (☎ 431 9307). Arguably Cork's most famous venue; some of Ireland's biggest folk acts had their first shining moments here. 2 floors overlook the river. Live music every night, from trad to acid jazz; for details check the *Gig Guide*, free at most music stores. Come early for the more popular acts. Occasional cover €5-10.

🎵 **The Old Oak,** Oliver Plunkett St. (☎ 427 6165), across from the General Post Office. Year after year it wins a "Best Traditional Pub in Ireland" award. Packed and noisy. Each section has its own vibe. Bar food served M-F noon-3pm. Bar closes F-Sa 1:45am.

An Spailpín Fánac (on spal-PEEN FAW-nuhk), 28 South Main St. (☎ 427 7949), across from Beamish Brewery. One of Cork's favorite pubs, and one of its oldest (est. 1779). Visitors and locals come for live trad Su nights. Storytelling last Tu of every month.

Half Moon, Academy Ln., on the left side of the Opera House. Cork's most popular dance club. A young, mostly hip crowd fills wide-open spaces. Su nights are the most happening. Strictly 18+. Purchase tickets (€9) from the box office across the street.

An Brog (☎ 427 1392), at the corner of Oliver Plunkett and Grand Parade. Ideal scene for those who crave good alternative rock and want to sport eyebrow rings. Mixed crowd.

Bodega, 46-49 Corn Market St. (☎ 427 2878), off the northern end of Grand Parade and the western end of Paul St. Stone front, wood floors, and a cavernous, pillared main room. An artsy cafe by day with a tasty selection of sandwiches and salads, it transforms into a classy club at night. Great wine selection and an intimate loft.

Franciscan Well Brewery and Pub, 14b North Mall (☎ 421 0130), along the North Quay, just east of Sundays Well Rd. Fantastic Belgian brews. Home-brewed Purgatory Pale Ale and Rebel Red come highly recommended. Backyard beer garden in an open stone courtyard fills in summer. Packed venue for the **October Belgian Beer Festival.**

Loafer, 26 Douglas St. (☎ 431 1612). Cork's favorite gay and lesbian pub fills every night with all age groups. Live bands, lively conversation, the good life.

The Other Place (☎ 427 8470), in a lane off South Main St. Cork's gay and lesbian disco rocks F-Sa 11:30pm-2am. Dance floor and bar/cafe upstairs opens earlier. Attracts a younger set on weekend nights. Cover F €7.50, Sa €10.

🎭 ENTERTAINMENT

Everyman Palace, McCurtain St., hosts the big-name musicals, plays, operas, and concerts. (☎ 450 1673. Box office open M-Sa 10am-6pm, until 7:30pm on show nights. Tickets €10-23.) **The Opera House,** Emmet Pl., next to the river, presents an extensive program of dance and performance art. (☎ 427 0022. Open M-Sa 9am-5:30pm.) From June through September, **hurling** and **Gaelic football** take place every Sunday afternoon at 3pm. For additional details, contact the Gaelic Athletic Association (☎ 439 5368; www.gaa.ie) or consult *The Cork Examiner.* Buy tickets to games at the GAA stadium, **Pairc Uí Chaoimh** (park EE KWEEV). The **Cork Midsummer Festival** (☎ 427 0022; www.corkfestival.ie) enchants visitors from mid-June through the beginning of July. Big-name musicians play for free in local pubs and hotels during the three-day **Guinness Cork Jazz Festival** (☎ 427 8979) in late October.

IRELAND

◪ DAYTRIP FROM CORK

BLARNEY CASTLE. Amidst the idyllic countryside, **Blarney Castle** stands as Ireland's tourism epicenter, home to the celebrated Blarney Stone. Tour the extensive grounds, or bend over backwards to kiss the rock in hopes of acquiring the legendary eloquence bestowed on the smoocher. *(Bus Éireann runs buses from Cork to Blarney M-F 15 per day, Sa 16 per day, Su 10 per day; €4.50 round-trip. ☎438 5252. Open June-Aug. M-Sa 9am-7pm, Su 9:30am-5:30pm; Sept. M-Sa 9am-6:30pm, Su 9:30am-sundown; Oct.-Apr. M-Sa 9am-6pm or sundown, Su 9:30am-5pm or sundown; May M-Sa 9am-6:30pm, Su 9:30am-5:30pm. Last admission 30min. before closing. Castle and grounds €7, seniors and students €5, children €2.50.)*

WEST FROM CORK

From Cork city, westward rambles follow either an inland or coastal route. A coastal **bus** runs to **Skibbereen**, stopping in **Bandon** and **Clonakilty**, and **Rosscarbery** (M-Sa 8 per day, Su 6per day). An inland bus travels to **Bantry** via **Bandon** and **Dunmanway** (M-Sa 7per day, Su 4 per day).

Located in relative isolation at the intersection of R586, R587, and R599, **Dunmanway** (Dún Mánmhai) is one of the few Irish towns that truly prizes tradition over tourism. Of course, it doesn't hurt to have a fabulous hostel like the ◪**Shiplake Mountain Hostel (IHH)** ❶ located in the hills 3 mi. from town. Shiplake's luckiest guests stay in three colorful gypsy caravans, equipped with heat, electricity, and breathtaking views. (☎023 45750; www.shiplakemountainhostel.com. **Bike rental** €6 per day. Breakfasts €2.80-5. Bag lunches €5. Vegetarian entrees €9.50-11. Laundry €3.50. Dorms €11. Singles €16-18; caravans €12.50-13.50 per person. **Camping** €7 per person, €4 per child.) Over the mountains to the northwest, quiet **Ballingeary** (Béal Athán Ghaorthaídh) is the heart of one of western Cork's declining *gaeltachts*.

Every summer the population of upscale **Kinsale** (Cionn tSáile) temporarily quintuples with a flood of tourists. Visitors come to swim, fish, and eat at any of Kinsale's 12 famed and expensive restaurants. **Clonakilty** (Cloch na Coillte; "Clon"), home to Irish hero Michael Collins, lies between Bandon and Skibbereen on N71. The fishing village of **Union Hall** (Breantra) possesses the zany ◪**Ceim Hill Museum,** 3 mi. outside town. (☎028 36280. Open daily 10am-7pm. €4.) Rest your head at legendary ◪**Maria's Schoolhouse Hostel (IHH)** ❶, which offers a 3-course dinner with occasional musical accompaniment on weekend nights. (☎028 33002. Dinner €22. Laundry €7. Dorms €12; singles €30; doubles €45-50.)

The biggest town in western Cork, **Skibbereen** (An Sciobairin; "Skib") is a convenient stop for travelers roaming the coastal wilds. The tiny fishing village of **Baltimore** (Baile Taigh Mór) has traded its pirates for tourists, who come to explore its aquatic offerings and stay in **Rolf's Holiday Hostel** ❶, a 300-year-old complex of stone farmhouses just 10min. from the waterfront. (☎028 20289. Laundry €5. Dorms €13-15; doubles €40; family rooms €55.)

The coastal road continues past the sleepy town of **Schull,** and 15 mi. later, Ireland comes to an abrupt end at spectacular **Mizen Head,** whose cliffs rise 700 ft. above the waves. To reach the **Mizen Vision** museum and the nearby **lighthouse,** you'll have to cross a suspension bridge only slightly less harrowing than the virtual shipwreck that waits inside. The small, windy viewing platform is the most southwesterly point in Ireland. Return to the new **Visitors Centre** to peruse exhibits or indulge in pricey items from the **cafe.** (☎028 35115. Open daily June-Sept. 10am-6pm; daily mid-Mar. to May and Oct. 10:30am-5pm; Nov. to mid-Mar. Sa-Su 11am-4pm. €4.50, students €3.50, under 12 €2.50, under 5 free.)

CAPE CLEAR ISLAND (OILEÁN CHLÉIRE) ☎028

From the ferry landing Cape Clear Island appears desolate and foreboding; the landscape of patchwork fields separated by low stone walls hasn't changed much since Spanish galleons stopped calling here hundreds of years ago. Along with windmills, lighthouses, a castle, and a bird observatory, Cape Clear has **Cléire Goats** (☎39126), home to some of the best-bred furry beasts in Ireland. For €1.50, you can test the owner's claim that his **goat's milk ice cream** is richer and more scrumptious than the generic bovine variety. Experience island lore in early September at Cape Clear's annual **International Storytelling Festival,** which features puppet workshops, music sessions, and a weekend's worth of memorable tales. (☎39116; http://indigo.ie/~stories. €7 per event; all events €30.) Call for the times of **whale- and dolphin-watching** excursions. (☎39172. €10.)

Capt. Cierán O'Driscoll offers **ferry loops** from Cape Clear to **Baltimore** and **Schull.** (☎28138. Mid-June to mid-Sept. 2 per day; single €8, full-loop with lunch €13.) Capt. Molloy ferries directly to **Schull.** (☎28138. 45min.; June 1 per day, July-Aug. 3 per day.; €11.50 round-trip.) Life here is leisurely and hours are approximate—for current opening hours and other information head to the **Information Centre** in the Pottery Shop, on the left just up from the pier. (☎39100. Open June-Aug. 11am-noon and 3-6pm; Sept. 3-5pm.) There are **no banks or ATMs** on the island.

An Óige/HI ❶, Cape Clear's hostel, is a 10min. walk from the pier; follow the main road and keep left. The hostel is in a picturesque stone building with superb views of the harbor. (☎41968. Dorms €15.) Buy **groceries** at **An Siopa Beag** (☎39099), on the pier. The shop also has a small **coffee dock ❶** that peddles takeaway pizzas. (Open Sept.-May M-Th 11am-6pm; daily June-Aug. 11am-6pm.) Multigenerational **Ciarán Danny Mike's ❸**(☎39172) is Ireland's southernmost pub and restaurant. Ciarán (son), Danny (father), and Mike (grandfather) serve soups (€3) and tempting dinners (€10-15). Closer to the pier, **Cotter's Cape Clear Bar ❶** has the simple bar necessities: pub grub and Guinness. (☎39102. Open daily 11am-9pm.) Without a resident *Garda* to regulate after-hours drinking, the Cape Clear fun often rolls on past 3am.

BANTRY (BEANNTRAI) ☎027

According to the big *Book of Invasions,* Ireland's first human inhabitants landed just 1 mi. from here. These days, the invasion racket has died down considerably, but Bantry still has plenty to plunder for the eager explorer. The town's main attraction is the elegant ⚅**Bantry House and Gardens,** a Georgian manor with magnificently restored grounds dramatically perched above the bay. The long and shaded driveway to the house is a 10min. walk from town. If doomed missions and grandiose nobles don't pique your interest, you might take a cruise on one of the **sea trips** that drop you at **Whiddy Island,** where quiet beaches attract birds and their watchers. (☎51739. July-Sept. 5 trips per day. Round-trip €7.) Bantry hosts the **West Cork Chamber Music Festival** during the last week of June and early July. Flex your fervor for seafood during the annual **Bantry Mussel Fair,** held the second weekend in May.

Buses stop outside Julie's Takeaway in Wolfe Tone Sq. **Bus Éireann** heads to **Cork** via **Bandon** and **Bantry** (M-Sa 8 per day, Su 4 per day; €10.50) and **Glengarriff** (M-Sa 3 per day, Su 2 per day; €4). From June to September, buses go twice a day to **Killarney** via **Kenmare** and **Tralee,** and to **Skibbereen. Rent bikes** from **Nigel's Bicycle Shop** on Glengarriff Rd., behind the Quik-Pik, near the Independent Hostel. (☎52657. €12 per day, €50 per week; helmet included. ID or credit card deposit. Open June-Aug. M-Sa 10am-6pm, Sept.-May M-Tu and Th-Sa 10am-5pm.) The **tourist office,** Wolfe Tone Sq., has maps and a **bureau de change.** (☎50229. Open July-Aug. M-Sa 9am-6pm, Su 10am-1pm and 2-5pm; Apr.-June and Sept.-Nov. M-Sa

IRELAND

9:15am-5:15pm.) **AIB** and **Bank of Ireland,** neighbors on Wolfe Tone Sq., both have **ATMs.** (☎50008 and 51377. Both open M 10am-12:30pm and 1:30-5pm, Tu-F 10am-12:30pm and 1:30-4pm.) The **library,** at the top of Bridge St., provides **Internet access** to Co. Cork library cardholders; purchase a card for €2.50 at any participating branch. (☎50460. Open Tu-W and F-Sa 10am-1pm and 2:30-6pm, Th 10am-6pm.) The **post office** is at 2 William St. (☎50050. Open M and W-F 9am-5:30pm, Tu 9:30am-5:30pm, Sa 9am-1pm.)

Bantry Independent Hostel (IHH) ❶ provides bunks, a kitchen, on-street parking, and quiet seclusion. If you're coming in by bus on Glengarriff Rd., save yourself the 8min. walk and ask the driver to let you off at O'Mahoney's Quickpick Food Store. From there, walk up the hill across the road and veer right around the bend. (☎51050. Laundry €5. Open mid-Mar. to Oct. 6-bed dorms €11. Doubles €24.) For delicious toasted sandwiches (€3-4) and a great choice of sweet treats, turn off New St. onto Main St. and follow your nose to **Floury Hands Cafe and Bakery ❶.** (☎52590. Open M-Sa 8am-5:30pm.) **Anchor Bar,** New St. (☎50012), is usually the liveliest of Bantry's pubs, luring the locals with a disco atmosphere on weekends and live music on summer Thursdays.

Bantry is a good place to access **Sheep's Head** (Muintir Bhaire), an alternative for anyone eager to evade the company of camera-toters and the exhaust of tour buses. Walkers and cyclists take advantage of the peaceful roads and the well-plotted **Sheep's Head Way;** information is available at the Bantry tourist office.

BEARA PENINSULA

Beara Peninsula's rugged and desolate landscape offers a haunting canvas for the lonely explorer. Fortunately, the mobs circling the Ring of Kerry usually skip the Beara altogether, missing out on some of the best views of the Iveragh from across the bay. The spectacular **Caha** and **Slieve Miskish Mountains** march down the center of the peninsula, dividing the rocky south from the lush northern shore. The dearth of cars west of the quiet gateway **Glengarriff** makes **cycling** the 125 mi. of **Beara Way** a joy. Many plant themselves at **Murphy's Village Hostel ❶,** in the middle of Glengarriff on Main St., and don't leave until they've sampled Mrs. Murphy's banana chocolate-chip muffins. (☎027 63555. **Internet access** €6.50 per hr. Laundry €6.50. Dorms €13. Singles €25; doubles €35.) The **Healy Pass,** running between **Adrigole** in the south and **Lauragh** in the north, offers stunning views of Co. Cork and Kerry as it winds through some of the highest peaks in Ireland. The curvaceous pass is best explored by car; to enjoy the full effect of the breathtaking scenery it's wisest to travel from south to north.

One of Ireland's largest fishing ports, the commercial hub of **Castletownbere** (Baile Chaisleain Bhearra), on the southern edge of the peninsula, attracts rigs from as far away as Spain. Cyclists often speed through en route to villages farther west and north, though the town occasionally fills with nirvana-seekers heading to the nearby Buddhist center. Castletownbere's seat at the foot of hefty **Hungry Hill** (2245 ft.) makes it a fine launch pad for daytrips up the mountain, but Beara's best scenery is on **Dursey Island,** accessible by Ireland's only cable car.

Castletownbere sends ferries to **Bere Island,** via Murphy's Ferry Service (☎027 75014; www.murphysferry.com; 30min.; June-Aug. 8 per day; Sept.-May 4 per day; round-trip €6) and Bere Island Ferry (☎027 75009; June-Sept. M-Sa 7 per day, Su 5 per day; round-trip €6, with car €20). Peppered with military remnants, the island used to be a British naval base, and the Irish Army still uses it for training. The ferry ride to the island's tiny fishing community is alone worth the journey.

Bus Éireann offers a year-round service to **Cork** via **Glengarriff** (3hr., 1-2 per day, €15.50) and a summer route between Castletownbere and **Killarney** via **Kenmare** (M-Sa 2 per day, €14.10) **Rent bikes** at **Beara Cycles,** Main St. (☎086 101 2026. €9.50

per day, €55 per week. Open M-F 9am-6pm, Su 10am-6pm.) The molehill-sized Castletownbere **tourist office** is behind O'Donoghue's by the harbor. (☎70054. Open June-Sept. M-F 9am-4pm.) The **SuperValu** and the **AIB** across the Square have the **only ATMs** on the peninsula. (☎70015. AIB open M 10am-5pm, Tu and Th-F 10am-4pm, W 10:30am-4pm.) Six miles west on the Allihies road is **Garranes Farmhouse Hostel (IHH) ❶**. The sea views from this clifftop cottage are beautiful. (☎73147. Sauna €3. Laundry €10. Dorms €12; family rooms €14-15 per person.) Seafood lovers head to ⬛**Breen's Lobster Bar ❸**, the Square, for its homemade bread, potato salad, and seafood platters (€10-12), almost large enough for two. (☎70031. Main menu served June-Aug. noon-9pm.)

RING OF KERRY

The term "Ring of Kerry" is generally used to describe the entire **Iveragh Peninsula,** but it more accurately refers to a particular set of roads: N71 from Kenmare to Killarney, R562 from Killarney to Killorglin, and the long loop of N70 west and back to Kenmare. If you don't fancy prepackaged private bus tours departing from Killarney, **Bus Éireann** offers a regular summer circuit (☎064 30011; mid-June to Aug. 2 per day; entire ring in 1 day €18.50), running through all the major towns on the Ring counterclockwise. Another bus runs year-round in the mornings, traveling clockwise from Waterville back to Killarney (1 per day). **Bikers** may find themselves jammed between coach and cliff on narrow, bumpy roads, though traffic can often be avoided by doing the Ring clockwise. A new, signposted bike route avoids main roads and affords better views. Drivers must choose between lurching behind large tour buses and meeting them face-to-face on narrow roads.

KILLARNEY (CILL AIRNE)   ☎064

Only a short walk from some of Ireland's most extraordinary scenery, Killarney manages to celebrate its tourist-based economy without offending the leprechaun-loathing travelers. The town has all the essentials and scads of trinkets, but all that fades in the face of the glorious national park only a few minutes away.

◨ **TRANSPORTATION.** **Kerry Airport** (☎976 4644) is in **Farranfore,** halfway to Tralee on the N22. **Ryanair** (☎01 609 7800; www.ryanair.com) flies to **London Stansted** (2 per day); **Aer Arann Express** (☎1890 462 726; www.aerarannexpress.com) goes to **Dublin** (2-4 per day). **Trains** come into **Killarney Station** (☎31067, inquiries 1850 366 222), off East Avenue Rd. near the intersection with Park Rd. Four trains per day run to: **Cork** (2hr., €20); **Dublin** (3½hr., €52.50); **Limerick** (3hr., €22). The **bus station** (☎30011) is on Park Rd. **Buses** serve: **Cork** (2hr., 11-14 per day, €13.50); **Dingle** (2hr.; M-Sa 8 per day, Su 5 per day; €13); **Dublin** (6hr., 5-6 per day, €20.50); **Galway** via **Tarbert Ferry** (8-9 per day, 2-3 per day; €19-21). Many buses leave from here on the **Ring of Kerry Circuit.** There is also a summer **Dingle/Slea Head** tour (June to mid-Sept. M-Sa 2 per day, €13.50). You'll find several places to **rent bikes** in Killarney, including **O'Sullivans,** Bishop's Ln. (☎31282. €12 per day, €70 per week. Free panniers, locks, repair kits, and maps. Open daily 8:30am-6:30pm.)

◧◪ **ORIENTATION AND PRACTICAL INFORMATION.** Most of Killarney is packed into three crowded streets. **Main Street,** in the center of town, begins at the town hall, then becomes High St. New St. and Plunkett St. head in opposite directions from Main St. **East Avenue Road** connects the train station back to town hall, meeting the **Muckross road,** which leads to Muckross Estate and Kenmare. The **tourist office** is on Beech Rd. (☎31633. Open July-Aug. M-Sa 9am-8pm, Su 10am-1pm and 2:15-6pm; June and Sept. M-Sa 9am-6pm, Su 10am-1pm and 2:15-6pm; Oct.-May M-Sa 9:15am-1pm and 2:15-5:30pm.) Other services include: **AIB,** Main St. (☎31047); **Internet access** at **Killarney Library** (☎32655), at the end of High St. toward New Rd. (Open M-Sa 10am-5pm, Tu and Th until 8pm); and the **post office,** New St. (☎31288; open M and W-F 9am-5:30pm, Tu 9:30am-5:30pm, Sa 9am-1pm).

⚑ ACCOMMODATIONS. With every other house a **B&B,** it's easy to find cushy digs in Killarney. Surrounded by wooded slopes outside town, ◪**Peacock Farms Hostel (IHH) ❶** overlooks Lough Guitane. Take the Muckross Rd. out of town, turn left before the Muckross post office, then go 2 mi. and follow the signs up a steep hill; or call for a ride from the bus station. (☎33557. Organic breakfast €5. Open Apr.-Oct. Dorms €10-12; doubles €28.) The best hostel in town is the immense and immaculate ◪**Neptune's (IHH) ❶,** which provides tours of the area. (☎35255. Tours: Dingle €17.50, Ring of Kerry €16.50, Gap of Dunloe €24. Breakfast €2.50. Free luggage storage; €10 locker deposit. Laundry €7. Dorms €11-16.50; doubles €37-40.) ◪**The Fairview Guest House ❷,** College St., near the bus station, pampers guests in luxurious digs. (☎34164. €35-50 per person for *Let's Go* readers.) **The Súgán (IHH) ❶,** Lewis Rd., is only 2min. from the bus or train station. Ship-like bunk rooms blur the distinction between intimacy and claustrophobia; exuberant staff and impromptu storytelling and music in the common room provide a happy escape. (☎33104. Dorms €15; doubles €35.)

Camping is not allowed in the national park, but excellent campgrounds await nearby. **White Bridge Caravan and Camping Park ❶,** on the Ballycasheen Rd., has laundry, a TV room, and modern showers. (☎31590. €8 per person with tent; 2 person tent with car €18.)

◫◪ FOOD AND PUBS. Food in Killarney is affordable at lunchtime, but prices skyrocket when the sun goes down. ◪**The Stonechat ❸** specializes in veggie meals, but also serves chicken and fish. (☎34295. Lunch €7-9. Dinner €11-14. Open M-Sa 11am-5:30pm and 6:30-10pm.) Homey **Busy B's Bistro ❷,** New St., packs in locals and serves filling, affordable food all day. (☎31972. Sandwiches €3.25-5.50. Entrees €6-10. Open daily 11am-9:30pm.) **Robertino's ❹,** High St., is a great date spot complete with Italian serenades and candlelight. (☎34966. Savory pastas €13.50-15. Pizzas €14.70-20. Meat entrees €18.50-25. Open daily 4-10:30pm.)

Trad is a staple in Killarney's pubs on summer nights, but herds of tourists looking for the next great jig make for a crowded and noisy drinking experience. Several nightclubs simmer from 10:30pm until 2:30 or 3am; most charge €6-8 cover but often offer discounts before 11pm. Patrons both foreign and domestic mingle in the upbeat, comfortable atmosphere of ◪**O'Connor's Traditional Pub,** 7 High St. (☎31115. Trad M-F 9-11:30pm, Su 7-9pm; winter F-Su.) ◪**Courtney's Bar,** Plunkett St., is an excellent club. (☎32689. Frequent live music upstairs June-Aug.)

KILLARNEY NATIONAL PARK

Spanning 37 mi.², a string of forested mountains, and the famous **Lakes of Killarney,** the diverse terrain of Killarney National Park makes for dazzling hiking, biking, and climbing. The park's size demands a map; pick up guides and other printed materials at the Killarney tourist office (p. 779). The most popular destinations in the region are ◪**Ross Castle,** the strikingly complete and completely isolated **Muckross Abbey** (all that's missing is the roof), **Lough Leane, Muckross House** on **Middle Lake,** and the **Gap of Dunloe** just west of the park area and bordered in the southwest by **Macgillycuddy's Reeks,** Ireland's highest mountain range. Killarney National

Park is also a perfect starting point for those walking the spectacular 134 mi. **Kerry Way.** Lucky hikers might spot the indigenous but elusive herd of 850 red deer that is reported to wander the surrounding glens.

THE KERRY WAY

Avoiding the tour bus superhighway that is the Ring of Kerry Rd. doesn't mean writing off the Iveragh entirely; just a stone's throw from the N70, solitude and superior scenery reward walkers along the **Kerry Way.** This well-planned route traverses a wide variety of terrain, from rugged inland expanses to soaring coastal cliffs. Described as an "inner" ring of Kerry, the 135 mi. route follows an assortment of paths—from pastures and old "butter roads" to ancient thoroughfares between early Christian settlements—and crosses the main road just often enough to make daytrips convenient from almost anywhere on the Ring. Look for the wooden posts marked with a yellow walking man and you won't be far off. Those who like their landscapes stark and somewhat rough enjoy the dramatic stretch from **Kenmare** through **Killarney** and northwest to **Glenbeigh.** An especially inspiring stretch of the Way runs between **Waterville** and **Caherdaniel,** filled with views known to elicit a tear or two from even the gruffest pint-puller.

KILLORGLIN TO VALENTIA ISLAND   ☎066

Killorglin (Cill Orglan) lounges on the banks of the River Larne, 13 mi. west of Killarney and in the shadow of Iveragh's mountainous spine. Tourists tend to pass through on their way west to the showier scenery, but what the town lacks in sights it more than makes up for with its annual festival dedicated to he-goats—the ancient **Puck Fair** held in mid-August crowns a particularly virile specimen as King Puck. The town's hostel and B&Bs often fill as early as a year in advance. The bright and bountiful **Laune Valley Farm Hostel (IHH) ❶,** 1¼ mi. from town off the Tralee Rd., beds guests alongside its cows, chickens, dogs, and ducks. (☎976 1488. Wheelchair accessible. Dorms €13-15. Doubles €38-44. **Camping** €7 per person.) **West's Caravan and Camping Park ❶** is 1 mi. east of town on the Killarney Rd. in the shadow of **Carrantoohill,** Ireland's tallest peak. (☎976 1240. Fishing, table tennis, and tennis courts. Laundry €3. Adult and tent €5; car, tent, and 2 adults €15. 2-night caravan rental €75. Showers €2.)

Best known as the birthplace of patriot Daniel O'Connell, **Cahersiveen** (Cathair Saidbhin; CAH-her-sah-veen) is a useful base for exploring nearby archaeological sites and for trips to Valentia Island and the Skelligs. The comfortable **Sive Hostel (IHH) ❶,** 15 East End, Main St., has a welcoming and well-informed staff, comfortable beds, and a third-floor balcony. (☎947 2717. Laundry €7. Dorms €13. Doubles €31-35. **Camping** €7 per person.) Find the freshest seafood at **QC's Chargrill Bar & Restaurant ❹,** Main St. (☎947 2244. Bar menu €4.50-14. Entrees €17-24. Food served 12:30-3pm and 6-9:30pm.)

A welcome escape for travelers sick of dodging tour buses and those that ride them, **Valentia Island's** (Dairbhre) removed location offers stunning views of the mountains on the mainland. A comically short **car ferry** departs every 8min. from **Reenard Point,** 3 mi. west of Cahersiveen, and drops passengers at **Knightstown,** the island's population center. (☎947 6141. April-Sept. M-Sa 8:15am-10pm, Su 9am-10pm. Cars €5 round-trip, pedestrians €1.50, cyclists €2.50) The bridge connecting Valentia to the mainland starts at **Portmagee,** 10 mi. west of Cahersiveen. Valentia has a surprising variety of budget accommodations in and around Knightstown, including the large **Royal Pier Hostel (IHH) ❷.** The clean rooms are cramped, but the more expensive dorms are extremely spacious and have enviable views of the bay. (☎947 6144. Laundry €5. Dorms €18-25; singles €25; doubles with breakfast €35.)

WATERVILLE, SKELLIG ROCKS, AND CAHERDANIEL ☎066

Wedged between the quiet Lough Cussane and crashing Atlantic waves, the traffic in **Waterville** (An Coirean) comes from the tour bus tourists released for a seaside lunch before rumbling on to Sneem. The meditative traveler is left to amble along the shore, which was once treasured by Charlie Chaplin for the liberating anonymity it granted him. **B&Bs** (€25-32) line Main St., but the only hostel in Waterville is ⬛**Peter's Place ❶**, on the southern end of town facing the water. Cheap rates and a candlelit sitting room make up for stiff mattresses and a small bathroom. (☎947 4608. Skellig trips €35. Dorms €12.50; doubles €15.)

About 8 mi. off the shore of the Iveragh Peninsula, the stunning **Skellig Rocks** rise abruptly from the sea. While the multitudes rush around the Ring of Kerry, a detour to the Skelligs is well worth it. As **Little Skellig** comes into view, the jagged rock pinnacles appear snow-capped; increased proximity reveals that they're actually covered with 24,000 pairs of crooning gannets—the largest community in Europe. Boats dock at the larger **Skellig Michael.** Climb the vertigo-inducing 630 stone steps, past many more gannets and puffins, to reach an ancient **monastic settlement.** There is no toilet or shelter on the rock, and the trip is not recommended for young children, the elderly, or those who suffer from serious medical conditions. The fantastic and sometimes soggy **ferry voyage** takes about 1hr., usually departs at 10am from Portmagee, and costs €35. Michael O'Sullivan (☎947 4255) and Mr. Casey (☎947 2437 or 087 239 5470) leave from **Portmagee;** Joe Roddy and Sons (☎947 4268 or 087 120 9924) and Sean Feehan (☎947 9182) depart from **Ballinskelligs.** Seanie Murphy picks up from **Reenard** and **Portmagee** (☎947 6214 or 087 236 2344). Phone ahead to confirm and reserve spaces.

There's little to attract the Ring's droves of travel coaches to **Caherdaniel.** However, the hamlet (two pubs, a grocer, restaurant, and takeaway) does lie near **Derrynane National Park** and miles of beaches ringed by sparkling dunes. Guests have the run of the house at **The Travelers Rest Hostel ❶.** A relaxed sitting room and small dorms make this hostel look and feel more like a B&B. (☎947 5175. Dorms €13; private rooms €16.50.) **Wave Crest Camping Park ❶** perches over the beach 1 mi. east of town. (☎947 5188. Open mid-Mar. to Oct. Laundry €4. €5.50; 2 people with car €17. Showers €1.)

KENMARE (NEIDIN) ☎064

A bridge between the Ring of Kerry and the Beara Peninsula, Kenmare has adapted to a continuous stream of visitors. With colorful houses, misty mountains, and a stone circle steps away from town, it fits the image of the classic Irish town. Tourists fresh off the bus may dilute Kenmare's appeal, but pleasant surroundings overshadow the sweater stalls and postcard stands.

There are plenty of good hikes in the country around Kenmare but few sights in the town itself. The ancient **stone circle,** a 2min. walk down Market St. from the Square, is the largest of its kind (55 ft. diameter) in southwest Ireland. (Always open. €1.50.) The stones are one stop on Kenmare's **tourist trail;** find maps at the tourist office. **The Kenmare Lace and Design Centre,** upstairs next to the heritage center, has demonstrations of the famous Kenmare lace-making technique. (☎42636. Open Mar.-Sept. M-Sa 10am-1pm and 2-5:30pm. Free.)

Buses leave from Brennan's Pub on Main St. to **Killarney** (1hr.; M-Sa 3 per day, Su 1 per day, in winter 2 per day; €7.50) and **Sneem** (35min., June-Aug. M-Sa 2 per day, €6.50). **Rent bikes** at **Finnegan's,** on the corner of Henry St. and Shelbourne St. (☎41083. €12 per day, €75 per week. Open June-Sept. M-Sa 10am-8pm; Oct.-May M-Sa 10am-6:30pm.) The **tourist office** is on the Square. (☎41233. Open June-Sept. M-Sa 9am-6pm, Su 10am-1pm, 2-5pm; Apr.-May and Oct. M-Sa 9am-1pm and 2-5pm.) An **AIB** is at 9 Main St. (☎41010. Open M 10am-5pm, Tu-F 10am-4pm.) The

post office has **Internet access** on the corner of Henry St. and Shelbourne St. (☎41490. €1 per 10min. Open June-Sept. M-F 9am-5:30pm, Sa 9am-1pm; Oct.-May M-F 9am-1pm and 2-5:30pm, Sa 9am-1pm. Computers available June-Aug. M-Sa 8am-8pm; Sept.-May M-Sa 8am-6pm.) Proprietress Maureen runs a tight ship at the excellent ⬛**Fáilte Hostel (IHH)** ❶, at the corner of Henry St. and Shelbourne St. (☎42333. Curfew 1:30am. Open Apr.-Oct. Dorms €12; doubles €32-40; triples €42; quads €56.) ⬛**Kenmare Lodge Hostel** ❶, 27 Main St. has immaculate rooms, a spacious kitchen, and an appreciation for art. (☎40662; www.neidin.net/lodgehostel. Dorms €14-16.) Three miles west of town on the Sneem Rd., the **Ring of Kerry Caravan and Camping Park** ❶ overlooks mountains and a bay. (☎41648. Open Apr.-Sept. Laundry €3.50. 1 person with tent €8; 2 with car and tent €18. Showers €0.50.)

The Pantry, Henry St., has a limited selection of healthy organic goods. (☎42233. Open M-Sa 9:30am-6pm, Su 11am-3pm.) Delicious food (from €13) is served in an old stone townhouse at ⬛**An Leath Phingin** ❹, 35 Main St. (☎41559. Book ahead July-Aug. Open Mar.-Nov. M-Tu and Th-Su 6-9:30pm.) Kerchiefed belles serve up bakery and deli delights at **Jam** ❶ (☎41591. Open M-Sa 8am-5pm.) Kenmare's pubs attract a hefty contingent of tourists, making live music common in summer. Wise visitors follow locals to **The Bold Thady Quill,** in the Landsdowne Arms Hotel, at the top of Main St. (☎41368. Trad W-Su July-Sept.) **Atlantic Bar,** the Square is a relaxed local joint with a lot of character. (☎41094. Su live trad. Sa disco. Food served 9:30-11:30am, 12:30-2:30pm, 5-9pm.)

DINGLE PENINSULA ☎066

For decades, the Dingle Peninsula was the Ring of Kerry's under-touristed neighbor, but word has finally gotten out, and today the tourist blitz encroaches on its spectacular cliffs and sweeping beaches. While Dingle Town is well-connected to Killarney and Tralee, public transport on the peninsula is scarce. The Tralee bus station (☎712 3566) has detailed information. Dingle is best explored by **bike**—the entire western circuit is only a daytrip, while the mountainous northern regions make for more arduous excursions. Maps available in area tourist offices describe the **Dingle Way,** a 95 mi. walking trail that circles the peninsula.

Ventry (Ceann Trá) is home to the ⬛**Celtic and Prehistoric Museum.** (☎915 9191. Open daily Mar.-Nov. 10am-5:30pm; other months call ahead. €5, students and seniors €3.50, children €3, families €14.) Spend the night at ⬛**Ballybeag Hostel** ❷. (☎915 9876; www.iol.ie/~balybeag. Wheelchair accessible. Bike rental €7 per day. Laundry €3. Dorms €14; singles €20.) Nearby, glorious ⬛**Slea Head** (Ceann Sléibhe) presents to the world a face of jagged cliffs and a hemline of frothy waves, featuring soft grassy headlands perfect for afternoon napping.

Appearing like a mirage off the westernmost tip of Ireland, the ghostly ⬛**Blasket Islands** (Na Blascaodaí) occupy a special place in Irish cultural history and in the hearts of all who visit. Whether bathed in glorious sunlight or shrouded in impenetrable mist, the islands' magical beauty and aching sense of eternity explain the disproportionately prolific literary output of the final generation to reside there. **Blasket Island Ferries** bridge the gap between the Blaskets and Dunquin in about 20min. (☎915 4864. Daily Apr.-Oct. every 30min. 10am-5:30pm, weather permitting; round-trip €20.) If rough seas keep you from visiting the islands—or even if they don't—check out the outstanding exhibits at the ⬛**Great Blasket Centre** in Slea Head, just outside of Dunquin on the road to Ballyferriter. (☎915 6444. Open daily July-Aug. 10am-7pm; Easter-June and Sept.-Oct. 10am-6pm. Last admission 45min. before closing. €3.50, students €1.25, families €8.25.)

Right across from the turnoff to the Blasket Centre is **Dunquin's** (Dún Chaoin) **An Óige Hostel (HI) ❶**. (☎915 6121. Reception 9-10am and 5-10pm. Lockout 10am-5pm. Continental breakfast €3. Linen €1.30. Dorms €14-16; doubles €32. Discounts for HI members and during low season.) Toward the pier, the ferry captain's home doubles as the delightful ⊠**Gleann Dearg B&B ❸**. (☎915 6188. Open Mar.-Nov. Singles €30-50; doubles €60-64.) Nearby **Kruger's ❸** is purportedly the westernmost pub in Europe. (☎915 6127. B&B €27 per person.)

DINGLE (AN DAIGEAN) ☎066

Despite the hordes of tourists that flood Dingle with hopes of seeing Fungi the Dolphin, the homegrown spirit of this *gaeltacht* region is still tangible in the quiet streets and alleyways. With fantastic hostels and eateries, an enviable music scene, and easy access to the most isolated highways of its namesake peninsula, this bayside town draws the well-heeled as well as the backpack-laden.

█ TRANSPORTATION. Buses stop by the harbor, on the Ring Rd. behind Super-Valu. **Bus Éireann** runs to: **Ballyferriter** (M-Sa 2-3 per day, €4.80); **Dunquin** (M-Sa 3-5 per day, €4.80); **Tralee** (1¼hr.; M-Sa 6 per day, Su 4 per day; €8.60). For **taxis** try **Cooleen Cabs** (☎087 248 0008) or **Dingle Co-op Cabs** (☎087 222 5777). **Foxy John's,** Main St., rents bikes.(☎915 1316. €10 per day, €50 per week. Open M-Sa 9:15am-8pm, Su 11am-8pm.)

█▊ ORIENTATION AND PRACTICAL INFORMATION. The **R559** heads east to Killarney and Tralee, and west to Ventry, Dunquin, and Slea Head. A narrow road runs north through Conor Pass to Stradbally and Castlegregory. Downtown, **Strand Street** flanks the harbor along the marina, while **Main Street** runs parallel to it uphill. **The Mall, Dykegate Street,** and **Green Street** connect the two, running perpendicular to the water. In the eastern part of town, a roundabout splits Strand St. into **The Tracks,** which continue along the water, **The Holy Ground,** which curves up to meet Dykegate St., and the **Tralee road.**
The **tourist office** is on Strand St. (☎915 1188. Open mid-June to mid-Sept. M-Sa 9am-7pm, Su 10am-5pm; mid-Sept. to mid-June M-Tu and Th-Sa 9:30am-5:30pm.) **AIB** (☎915 1400) and **Bank of Ireland** (☎915 1100) are on Main St., and both have **ATMs.** (Both open M 10am-5pm, Tu-F 10am-4pm.) Find free **Internet access** at the **library** (☎915 1499; call to reserve a slot; open July-Aug. M-Sa 10am-5pm, Th open until 8pm; Sept.-June Tu-Sa 10am-5pm) or at **Dingle Internet Cafe,** Main St. (☎915 2478; €2.60 per 30min.; open May-Sept. M-Sa 10am-10pm, Su 1-8pm; Oct.-Apr. M-Sa 10am-6pm). The **post office** is on Upper Main St. (☎915 1661. Open M-F 9am-5:30pm, Sa 9am-1pm.)

▌ ACCOMMODATIONS. Most of Dingle's hostels are great, but few are close to town. Accommodations in town and along Dykegate and Strand St. fill up fast—always call ahead. ⊠**Ballintaggart Hostel (IHH) ❶**, on N86, is a 25min. walk east of town on the Tralee Rd.; the Tralee bus stops here on request. Built in 1703, this grand stone mansion witnessed the strangling of Mrs. Earl of Cork. Her ghost supposedly haunts the bedchambers, enclosed courtyard, and fire-heated common rooms. The stunning views of Dingle's fields and sparkling bay remain phantom-free. (☎915 1454. Free movie every night. Laundry €6. Dorms €13-20; doubles €48-54; family rooms €65-75. **Camping** €6-7 per small tent, €15 per caravan.) Smack in the middle of town and just a brief stumble from Dingle's finest pubs is the **Grapevine Hostel ❶**, Dykegate St., off Main St. The friendly folks here guide you through the cushy-chaired common room to close but comfy bunk rooms. (☎915 1434. Dorms €14-16.) Look out onto Main St. or opt for creepy and gaze upon the old graveyard behind **Ashe's B&B ❸,** Lower Main St. The rooms are tastefully decorated with soft cream colors and antique bureaus. (☎915 0989. All rooms ensuite and TV. Singles €35-60; doubles €60-80.)

🍴🍺 **FOOD AND PUBS.** Dingle is home to a wide range of eateries, from doughnut stands to gourmet seafood restaurants. **SuperValu,** the Holy Ground, stocks **groceries.** (☎915 1397. Open June-Aug. M-Sa 8am-10pm, Su 8am-9pm; Sept.-Apr. M-Sa 8am-9pm, Su 8am-7pm.) The menu at perpetually busy **Homely House Cafe ❷,** Green St., is divided into "Just a little hungry," "Pretty darn hungry," and "HUNGRY!!!". (☎915 2431. Entrees €4-9.50. Open July-Aug. M-Sa noon-9:30pm; Sept.-June M-Sa noon-5:30pm.) **Midi ❸,** Green St., boasts "Mediterranean food with a touch of the Orient," with vegetarian options upstairs. (Jamaican fish curry €12.50. Entrees €12.50-15; pizzas with salad €9-12.50. Open Tu-Su 5pm until late.) Ex-pat New Yorker brothers Kieran and Sean of **Murphy's Ice Cream ❶,** Strand St., scoop Ireland's only truly homemade ice cream (from €2.30), whipping up inventive, slightly alcoholic creations. (☎915 2477. Open daily June-Sept. 11am-6:30pm and 7:30-10:30pm; mid-Mar. to May 10:30am-6pm. Shoeboxes and whiskey bottles line the walls at **⊠Dick Mack's,** Green St., the quintessentially Irish dual-business pub: the proprietor leaps between the bar and the leather-tooling bench at "Dick Mack's Bar, Boot Store, and Leather Shop." Frequent spontaneous sing-alongs indicate enduring local support.

📷🎭 **SIGHTS AND FESTIVALS.** When **Fungi the Dolphin** was first spotted in Dingle Bay in 1983, the townspeople worried about the effect he would have on the bay's fish population. To say he is now welcome is an understatement, as he single-flipperedly brings in droves of tourists and plenty of cash to his exploiters. **Dolphin Trips** leave to see him from the pier between 10am and 7pm in the summer. (☎915 2626. 1hr. €12, children 2-12 €6. Free if Fungi gets the jitters and doesn't show.) Watching the antics from the shore east of town is a cheaper, squintier alternative. **Sciúird Archaeology Tours** will take you on a whirlwind bus tour of the area's ancient spots. (☎915 1606 or 915 1937. 3hr. 2 per day. €15. Book ahead.) The **Dingle Regatta** hauls in salty dogs on the third Sunday in August. In mid-August, try your luck at the **Dingle Races.**

TRALEE (TRÁ LÍ) ☎066

As the economic and residential capital (pop. 20,000) of Co. Kerry, Tralee's gruff exterior may come as a bit of a shock to those arriving from smaller hamlets on the peninsula. Still, large storefronts line the city's main streets, and quality pubs serve bar food and trad. Ireland's second-largest museum makes the history of Kerry come to life, and a stroll through the city's famed gardens is a true pleasure. The town gets mobbed during the last week of August for the annual **Rose of Tralee,** a centuries-old pageant that has Irish eyes glued to their TVs.

🚆 **TRANSPORTATION. Trains** (☎712 3522) run to: **Cork** (2½hr.; M-Sa 5 per day, Su 3 per day; €26); **Dublin** (4hr.; M-Sa 4 per day, Su 3 per day; €52.50); **Galway** (5-6hr., 3 per day, €52.50); **Killarney** (40min., 4 per day, €7.50); **Waterford** (4hr., M-Sa 1 per day, €41.50) **Buses** (☎712 3566) go to: **Cork** (2½hr., 13 per day, €14.50); **Dingle** (1¼hr.; July-Aug. M-Sa 6 per day, Su 5 per day; Sept.-June M-Sa 4 per day, Su 2 per day; €8.80); **Galway** direct (M-Sa 8 per day, Su 7 per day; €19.50) or via **Tarbert Ferry** (M-Sa 2 per day, €19.50); **Killarney** (40min.; June-Sept. M-Sa 15 per day, Su 11 per day; Oct.-May M-Sa 13 per day, Su 10 per day; €6.70); **Limerick** (2¼hr.; M-Sa 9 per day, Su 8 per day; €13.50). **Rent bikes** from **O'Halloran,** 83 Boherboy. (☎712 2820. €12 per day, €60 per week. Open M-Sa 9:30am-1pm and 2-6pm.)

IRELAND

■ ⚡ **ORIENTATION AND PRACTICAL INFORMATION.** Tralee's streets are hopelessly knotted; arm yourself with free maps from the tourist office. The main avenue—variously called **the Mall, Castle Street,** and **Boherboy,** as it passes the **Square**—has stores and restaurants along its roughly east-west path. **Edward Street** connects this main thoroughfare to the stations. Wide **Denny Street** runs south to the **tourist office,** in Ashe Memorial Hall. (☎712 1288. Open July-Aug. M-Sa 9am-7pm, Su 9am-6pm; May-June and Oct. M-Sa 9am-6pm; Nov.-Apr. M-F 9am-5pm.) **AIB,** Denny St. (☎712 1100), and **Bank of Ireland** (☎712 1177), a few doors down, have **ATMs** throughout town. (Both open M 10am-5pm, W 10:30am-4pm, Tu and Th-F 10am-4pm.) **Millennium,** Ivy Terr., offers **Internet access.** (☎712 0020. €3 per hr. Open M-Sa 10am-6pm.) The **post office** is on Edward St. (☎712 1013. Open M and W-F 9am-5:30pm, Tu 9:30am-5:30pm, Sa 9am-1pm.)

🏠 ⌂ **ACCOMMODATIONS AND FOOD.** Rows of pleasant **B&Bs** line the area where Edward St. becomes Oakpark Rd.; others can be found along Princes Quay, close to the park. Tralee's hostels can barely contain the August festival-goers—reserve ahead. Spotless dorms at **Westward Court (IHH) ❷,** Mary St., are all ensuite and fully armed, with bureaus, desks, and quality showers. (☎718 0081. Wheelchair accessible. Continental breakfast included. Laundry €7. Curfew 3am. Dorms €17; singles €25; doubles €46.) Though slightly pricier than the average hostel, **The Whitehouse Budget Accommodation and B&B ❷,** Boherboy, stretches a few extra euros to the extreme. Enjoy hardwood floors and a downstairs pub with pool tables and a big-screen TV. (☎712 9174 or 710 2780. Wheelchair accessible. Th trad, Sa DJ. Dorms €19; singles €30; doubles €50.) **Woodlands Park Campground ❶,** Dan Spring Rd., is a national award-winner. (☎712 1235. Laundry wash €4.50. Open Apr.-Sept. 2-person tent with car €16.50, without car €14. Showers €1.)

Tesco, the Square, sells **groceries.** (☎712 1110. Open M-Sa 8am-10pm, Su 10am-8pm.) **Tequilas ❸,** Barrack Ln., serves delightfully fresh Tex-Mex fare under the saddles and stirrups hanging overhead. (☎712 4820. Starters €3.50-9. Entrees €10.50-20. Open M-F noon-2:30pm and 5:30-10:30pm, Sa-Su 5-10:30pm.) **O'Riordans ❷,** 9 Russel St., near Rock St., is a busy little kitchen cafe that does a mean full Irish breakfast. (☎710 2759. Breakfast €4.50-7. Soup and sandwich classics €3-7.50. Open M-Sa 8am-5pm, Su 9am-5pm.) JP and Mike act as personal drinking consultants at ▓**Seán Óg's,** 41 Bridge St. (☎712 8822. Trad M-Th and Su.) Across the street, **Abbey Inn** draws an edgy crowd with live rock most weekends. When U2 played here in the late 70s, the manager made them sweep the floors to pay for their drinks because he thought they were so bad. (☎712 3390. Live music Th; DJ other nights. Food 9am-9:30pm. Open M-Sa until 2:30am, Su 1am.)

◎ ▓ **SIGHTS AND FESTIVALS.** Tralee is home to Ireland's second-largest museum, ▓**Kerry the Kingdom,** Denny St., which displays large-scale dioramas and special exhibits. (☎712 7777. Open Jan-Mar. Tu-F 10am-4:30pm; Apr.-May and Sept.-Dec. Tu-Sa 9:30am-5:30pm; daily June-Aug. 9:30am-5:30pm. Last admission 4:30pm. €8, students €6.50, children €5. Free audioguides.) Across the way, another from the ranks of Ireland's "second largests"—the **Town Park,** in this case—blooms in summer with the **Rose of Tralee.** Just down the Dingle Rd., is the **Blenneville Windmill and Visitors Centre,** the largest operating windmill in the British Isles. (☎712 1064. Open daily Apr.-Oct. 10am-6pm. €5, students €4, children €3, families €13.) Lovely lasses of Irish descent flood the town during the last week of August for the beloved **Rose of Tralee Festival,** which culminates in a "personality" contest to earn the coveted title "Rose of Tralee." Rose-hopefuls or spectators can call the Rose Office in Ashe Memorial Hall (☎712 1322; www.roseoftralee.com).

LIMERICK (LUIMNEACH) ☎061

Despite a thriving trade in off-color poems, Limerick has long endured a bad reputation associated with its recent industrial developments. However, the Republic's third-largest metropolis is now a city on the rise, with a vibrant arts scene, top-quality museums, and a well-preserved 12th-century cathedral.

TRANSPORTATION. Trains (☎315 555) run to: **Cork** (2½hr.; M-Sa 6 per day, Su 5 per day; €19.50); **Dublin** (2hr.; M-Sa 10 per day, Su 7 per day; €36.50); **Tralee** (3hr.; M-Sa 5 per day, Su 3 per day; €21.50). Buses arrive and depart from **Colbert Station** (☎313 333), off Parnell St. **Bus Éireann** sends buses to: **Cork** (2hr., 14 per day, €13.20); **Dublin** (3½hr., 13 per day, €14.50); **Galway** (2hr., 14 per day, €13.20); **Kilkenny** (1½hr., 3 per day, €14.50); **Killarney** (2½hr.; M-Sa 6 per day, Su 3 per day; €13.50); **Tralee** (2hr., 8 per day, €13.20). A **local bus** network runs from the city center to the suburbs (M-Sa 2 per hr. 7:30am-11pm, Su 1 per hr. 10:30am-11:20pm; €1.10). **Top Cabs** (☎417 417) goes to most places in the city for under €5 and to Shannon airport for about €20. **Emerald Alpine,** 1 Patrick St., **rents bikes.** (☎416 983. €70-100 per week. Credit card number as deposit. Return to any participating Raleigh location for additional €25. Open M-F 9:15am-1pm and 2-5:30pm, Sa 9:15am-5:30pm.)

ORIENTATION AND PRACTICAL INFORMATION. Limerick's streets form a no-frills grid pattern, bounded by the **Shannon River** to the west and the **Abbey River** to the north. The city's most active area lies in the blocks around **O'Connell Street** (which becomes Patrick St., then Rutland St. to the north, and the Crescent to the south). The city itself is easily navigable by foot, but the preponderance of one-way streets makes it a nightmare for drivers. The **tourist office** is in the space-age glass building on Arthurs Quay. From the station, follow Davis St. as it becomes Glentworth; turn right on O'Connell St., then left at Arthurs Quay Mall. (☎361 555; www.shannonregiontourism.ie. Open July-Aug. M-F 9am-6pm, Sa-Su 9:30am-5:30pm; Sept.-June M-F 9:30am-5:30pm, Sa 9:30am-1pm.) **Banks** line O'Connell St. Just uphill, **Euro@Surf,** Todds Bow, has **Internet access.** (☎404 040. €1 per hr; €2 per 3 hr. Open M-Sa 10am-10pm, Su noon-8pm.) The **post office** is on Lower Cecil St., off O'Connell St. (☎315 777. Open M-Sa 9am-5:30pm, Tu from 9:30am.)

ACCOMMODATIONS. The last of Limerick's hostels left in 2002; scour the area around O'Connell St. for other accommodations. One of the better **B&B** values found in the city is **Alexandra House B&B ❸,** O'Connell St., several blocks south of the Daniel O'Connell statue. Most rooms come with TV and tea-making facilities. (☎318 472. Full Irish breakfast included. Singles €30; shared rooms €25-30 per person.) **Cherry Blossom Budget Accommodation ❶,** O'Connell St., next to Alexandra House, is Limerick's newest kid on the block; the energetic proprietress aims to fill the gap created when the hostels fled town. (☎469 449. €20-25.)

FOOD AND NIGHTLIFE. Forage for **groceries** at **Tesco** in Arthurs Quay Mall. (☎412 399. Open M-W and Sa 8:30am-8pm, Th-F 8:30am-10pm, Su noon-6pm.) If the delicious crepes (€12.50) and "succulent crab meat" sandwiches (€6.95) at **Furze Bush Cafe Bistro ❷,** on the corner of Catherine St. and Glentworth St., don't impress, perhaps the eccentric interior will. (☎411 733. Open June-Aug. M-Sa 10am-5pm; Sept.-May M-W 10:30am-5pm, Th-Sa 10:30am-5pm and 7-10pm.) **Dolan's ❷,** 4 Dock Rd., is a friendly little pub that doubles as a spirited restaurant out back. (☎314 483. Lunch menu €6-10 served 3-9pm.) Limerick's vegetarian headquarters is **The Green Onion ❸,** Rutland St., with high molded ceilings in the converted Old Town Hall. After 6pm, dinner prices fly high (€13.70-25), but the "all-day" lunch menu (€8.95-15.70) offers simpler and cheaper options. (☎400 710. Open M-Sa noon-10pm.)

A wide range of musical options caters to the city's diverse pub crowd and its immense student population. It's worth a Shannon-side walk from the city center to hear the nightly trad played for rambunctious local patrons at **Dolan's,** Dock Rd. (☎314 483; www.dolanspub.com). **The Warehouse** nightclub is in the same building. Alternatively, join the classy crowd on the quay-side patio of the **Locke Bar and Restaurant,** Georges Quay (☎413 733). Or head inside where owner Richard Costello, a former member of Ireland's national rugby team, joins in trad sessions several nights a week. Limerick's insatiable army of students keeps dozens of nightclubs thumping from 11:30pm until 2am nightly. **The Granary,** inside The Trinity Rooms, on Michael St. plays hip-hop, funk, and soul. (☎417 266. Cover €7-9.)

◙ **SIGHTS.** Departing from the tourist office, **walking tours** roam either the northern, sight-filled King's Island region or the more downtrodden locations of Frank McCourt's memoirs. (☎318 106. Island tour daily 11am and 2:30pm. *Angela's Ashes* tour M-F 2:30pm, Sa and Su by appointment. Both €8.) The fascinating ▨**Hunt Museum,** in the Custom House, displays Ireland's largest collection of art and artifacts outside Dublin's National Museum. Browse through drawers to find surprises like the world's smallest jade monkey. (☎312 833; www.huntmuseum.com. Open M-Sa 10am-5pm, Su 2-5pm. €6, concessions €4.75, children €3.) The Visitors Center of **King John's Castle** has vivid exhibits and a video on the castle's gruesome past. Outside, the mangonel—used to catapult pestilent animal corpses into enemy castles—is a particularly convincing testament to perverse military tactics. The underground archaeological dig and slideshow are of particular interest. (☎360 788. Open daily Mar.-Oct. 9:30am-5:30pm; Nov.-Feb. 10:30am-4:30pm. Last admission 4:30pm. €7, concessions €5.60, children €4.20.)

WESTERN IRELAND

Ask any publican—he will probably agree that the west is the "most Irish" part of Ireland. Western Ireland's gorgeous desolation and enclaves of traditional culture are now its biggest attractions. Though poor for farming, the land from Connemara north to Ballina is a boon for hikers and cyclists. Galway, long a bustling seaport, is currently a haven for young ramblers. The Cliffs of Moher, the mesmerizing moonscape of the Burren, and a reputation as the center of the trad music scene attract travelers to Co. Clare.

DOOLIN (DUBH LINN) ☎065

Something of a shrine to traditional Irish music, the little village of Doolin draws thousands of travelers to its pubs for *craic* that will go straight from your tappin' toes to your Guinness-soaked head. Most of Doolin's 200-odd residents run its accommodations and pubs; others split their time between farming and wondering how so many visitors end up in their small corner of the world. However, serious sessions at ▨**McDermott's,** Upper Village, prove that Doolin's trad is more than a tourist trap. Local foot-traffic heads this way around 9:30pm nightly, and remains at a standstill until closing; a 9:20pm arrival may win you a seat. (☎707 4328. Food served until 9:30pm.) The busiest and most touristed of Doolin's three pubs is

O'Connor's (☎707 4168), Lower Village, which serves drink and song nightly at 9:30pm all year. McGann's, Upper Village, also gathers a summer following. (☎707 4133. Music nightly at 9:30pm in summer; Th-Su 9:30pm in winter.)

Barbell-shaped Doolin is made up of two villages about 1 mi. apart. Close to the shore is Lower Village, connected to Upper Village by Fisher Street/Roadford. Buses stop at the Doolin Hostel and Rainbow Hotel—purchase advance tickets at the hostel. Route #15 runs to Kilkee and Dublin via Ennis and Limerick (2 per day); #50 goes to the Cliffs of Moher (15min.) and to Galway (1½hr.) via towns in the Burren (summer M-Sa 3-4 per day, Su 2 per day; low season M-Sa 1 per day). The Doolin Bike Store, outside the Aille River Hostel, rents bikes. (☎707 4260. €10 per day. Open daily 9am-8pm.) The nearest ATM is in Ennistymon, 5 mi. southeast. A traveling bank comes to the Doolin Hostel once a week (Th 10:30am). The nearest post office is in Ennistymon, but stamps are sold at the hostel.

Tourists pack Doolin in the summer, so book early. Musicians often stop by ▓Aille River Hostel (HIH) ❶, Main St., halfway between the villages, to warm up before gigs. The hostel has a friendly, laid-back atmosphere in a gorgeous location: the Aille River gurgles around a tiny wildflower island where an unofficial beer garden assembles just before hostelers head to the pubs. (☎707 4260. Internet access free for guests. Wash free, dry €2. Dorms €12; doubles ensuite €27-30. Camping €6.) The friendly young proprietress of ▓Doolin Cottage ❷, next to the Aille, keeps the rooms spotless and bright. Choose between fully fry or yogurt and honey for breakfast. (☎707 4762. Rooms ensuite €25. Open Mar.-Nov.)

Doolin's few restaurants are excellent but pricey; be grateful that all three pubs serve quality grub. The Doolin Deli ❶, Lower Village, is the only place to go for food under €5. It packages filling sandwiches (€2.50), bakes scones (€0.90), and stocks groceries. (☎707 4633. Takeaway only. Open June-Sept. M-Sa 8:30am-9pm, Su 9:30am-8pm.) The "cafe" part of The Doolin Cafe ❹, Upper Village, refers to the casual atmosphere, not the excellent, upscale food. The early-bird special (5:30-7pm) is pricey, but still an outstanding value, with four gourmet courses for €24.50. (☎707 4795. Open daily 5:30-10pm, also Sa-Su noon-3pm.)

CLIFFS OF MOHER ☎065

Plunging 700 ft. straight down to the open sea, the ▓Cliffs of Moher draw more gawkers on a good July day than many counties see all year. The majestic headland affords views of Loop Head, the Kerry Mountains, the Twelve Bens, and the Aran Islands. Some adventurous visitors climb over the stone walls and trek along an officially closed clifftop path for more spectacular views and a greater intimacy, with potential falls. Warning: Winds can be extremely strong at the top of the Cliffs, and blow a few tourists off every year; Let's Go strongly discourages straying from the established paths. The seasonal tourist office houses a bureau de change and a tea shop. (☎708 1171. Open daily May-Sept. 9:30am-5:30pm.) To reach the cliffs, head 3 mi. south of Doolin on R478, or hop on the Bus Éireann Galway-Cork bus (summer 2-3 per day). From Liscannor, Liscannor Ferries sails directly under the cliffs. (☎708 6060. 1¾hr., 2-3 per day, €20.)

THE BURREN ☎065

Entering the Burren's magical 100 mi.² landscape is like happening upon an enchanted fairyland. Lunar limestone stretches culminate in secluded coves where dolphins often cavort. Mediterranean, Alpine, and Arctic wildflowers peek brightly from cracks in mile-long rock planes, while 28 of Ireland's 33 species of butterfly flutter by. Geologists are baffled by the huge variety of flora and fauna coexisting in the area; their best guess points vaguely to the

IRELAND

end of the Ice Age. The best way to see the Burren is to **walk** or **cycle**, but be warned that the dramatic landscape makes for exhausting climbs and thrilling descents. Tim Robinson's meticulous maps (€6.95) detail the **Burren Way,** a 26 mi. hiking trail from Liscannor to Ballyvaughan; *Burren Rambler* maps (€2.55) are also extremely detailed. **Bus** service in the Burren is some of the worst in the Republic. **Bus Éireann** (☎682 4177) connects Galway to towns in and near the Burren a few times a day during the summer, but infrequently during the winter. **Buses** stop at: the Doolin Hostel in **Doolin,** Burke's Garage in **Lis-doonvarna** (Lios Dún Bhearna), Linnane's in **Ballyvaughan** (Baile Uí Bheacháin), and The Ould Plaid Shawl in **Kinvara** (Cinn Mhara). Other infrequent buses run from Burren towns to **Ennis** (Inis). Based in **Lahinch** (Leacht Uí Chonchúir), Gerard Hartigan gives an enthusiastic **minibus tour** of the Burren and the Cliffs of Moher. (☎086 278 3937. 4½hr. €14.)

ARAN ISLANDS ☎099

On the westernmost edge of Co. Galway, isolated from the mainland by 20 mi. of swelling Atlantic, lie the spectacular Aran Islands *(Oileán Árann).* The green fields of Inishmore, Inishmaan, and Inisheer are hatched with a maze of limestone walls—the result of centuries of farmers piling the stone that covered the islands to clear the fields for cultivation. With a landscape as moody as the Irish weather, the majestic, mythical Arans have always sparked the imaginations of both Irishmen and foreigners. Little is known of the earliest islanders, whose tremendous but mysterious cliff-peering forts seem to have been constructed by the secret designs of the limestone itself. Early Christians flocked here seeking seclusion; the ruins of their churches and monasteries now pepper the islands. Even today, Irish is the first language of the islands, and despite the hundreds of tourists pouring off the ferries each summer day, the islands have maintained a character that continues to make them the highlight of the western coast.

▛ TRANSPORTATION

Three ferry companies (all with booths in the Galway tourist office) operate boats to the Aran Islands. **Island Ferries** (☎091 561 767 or 568 903; www.aranislandferries.com), has main offices in the Galway tourist office and on Forster St., close to Eyre Sq. One ferry sails to **Inishmore** (Apr.-Oct. 4 per day, Nov.-Mar. 2 per day) and another to **Inishmaan** via **Inisheer** (2 per day); both depart from **Rossaveal,** several miles west of Galway (round-trip €19, students €15). A bus runs from Galway's Kinlay House B&B to the ferryport (departs 1½hr. and 1hr. before sailings; €5, students €4). **Queen of Aran II** is the only ferry company based on the islands, but it only runs to **Inishmore** (☎566 535 or 534 553; www.queenofaran2.com; 4 per day; round-trip €19, students €14). Queen of Aran boats also leave from Rossaveal, with a bus departing from Kinlay House (1¼hr. before sailings; €6, students €5). **O'Brien Shipping/Doolin Ferries** runs a daily service in the summer, and 3 times per week in the low season. (Doolin ☎065 707 1710, Galway 091 567 676. **Galway** to any island, round-trip €20-25. **Doolin** to **Inishmore** round-trip €32, to **Inishmaan** €28, and to **Inisheer** €25. Student discount €5 for advance tickets.) The Island Ferries and Queen of Aran boats serving Inishmore are fairly reliable and leave daily. Traveling to or between the Islands can be difficult, to say the least—purchase all of your tickets before setting sail.

INISHMORE (INIS MÓR)

The archaeological sites of Inishmore, the largest and most touristed of the islands, include dozens of ruins and churches and the amazing Dún Aengus fort. Crowds radiate from Kilronan Pier, at the island's center, and lose themselves amid countless species of wildflowers, 7000 mi. stone walls, and harrowing cliffs.

🖅🖬 **TRANSPORTATION AND PRACTICAL INFORMATION.** Roving minibuses leave from the pier. (€10 per 2-3hr.) Aran Bicycle Hire rents bikes. (☎61132. €10 per day. €10 deposit. Open daily June-Aug. 9am-7pm; Sept.-Aug. 9am-5pm.) The Kilronan tourist office sells the *Inis Mór Way* map (€2), stores luggage (€1), and changes money. (☎61263. Open daily June 10am-6pm, July-Sept. 10am-6:45pm, Oct.-Mar. 11am-5pm, Apr.-May 10am-5pm.) The post office is uphill from the pier. (☎61101. Open M-F 9am-1pm and 2-5pm, Sa 9am-1pm.)

🖬🖸 **ACCOMMODATIONS AND FOOD.** Many minibuses make stops at **hostels** and **B&Bs** that are farther away; ask at the tourist office for more information. The dorms at 🖬**Kilronan Hostel ❶,** adjacent to Tí Joe Mac's pub, are small but bright and immaculate. It is centrally located and has a helpful staff. (☎61255. Bike rental €10. Dorms €16, all ensuite.) **Mainistir House (IHH) ❶,** 1 mi. from "town," has a magazine-filled sitting room with big windows looking out to the sea. (☎61169. Bike rental €10 per day. Laundry free. Dorms €15.) Cook Joel prepares legendary 🖬**dinners ❸,** far and away the best deal on the island. Fill up for days on magnificent, mostly vegetarian buffets. Eight-person tables are arranged to encourage conversation with fellow travelers or locals in search of epicurean bliss. (8pm; reserve ahead. €12.) **The Artist's Lodge ❶** is cozy and inviting, with an impressive video collection and crackling fire. Take the turnoff across from Joe Watty's pub on the main road, walk a bit, and look right. (☎61457. Dorms €12.)

The **Spar** market, up the main road, functions as an unofficial community center. (☎61203. Open summer M-Sa 9am-8pm, Su 9am-6pm; winter M-Sa 9am-8pm, Su 10am-5pm.) If the Mainistir House is full, try **Tigh Nan Phaid ❷,** in a thatched building at the turnoff to Dún Aengus, which specializes in home-cooked bread and home-smoked fish. (Open daily 11am-5pm.) For a perfect lunch, **The Man of Aran Restaurant,** just past Kilmurvey Beach to the right, serves wonderfully fresh, organic lunches in a historic setting. (☎61301. Toasties €3.20. Lunch daily 12:30-3:30pm; dinners in summer.) Locals and hostelers savor their pints at popular **Tí Joe Mac,** overlooking the pier. (☎61248. Frequent sessions during summer; W during winter.) Despite its name, **The American Bar,** across from the Aran Sweater Market, is an Irish pub through and through. (☎61130. Food served until 5pm.)

🖬🖢 **SIGHTS AND ENTERTAINMENT.** The time-frozen island, with its labyrinthine stone wall constructions, rewards wandering visitors who take the day to cycle or walk around its hilly contours. The **Inis Mór Way** is a mostly paved route that makes a great bike ride, circling past a majority of the island's sights. The tourist office's maps of the Way (€2) purportedly correspond to yellow arrows that mark the trails, but the markings are frustratingly infrequent and can vanish in fog; it's best to invest in a **Robinson map** for serious exploring or simply follow the crowds and hope for the best. If you only have a few hours, high-tail it to the island's most famous monument, the magnificent 🖬**Dún Aengus,** 4 mi. west of the pier at Kilronan. The fort's walls are 18 ft. thick and form a semicircle around the sheer drop of Inishmore's northwest corner. **Be very careful:** strong winds have been known to blow tourists off the cliffs. The **Black Fort** *(Dún Dúchathair),* 1 mi. south of Kilronan over eerie terrain, is larger than Dún Aengus, a millennium older, and greatly underappreciated. Uphill from the pier in Kilronan, the new, expertly designed ⬛Aran Islands Heritage Centre provides a fascinating introduction to the islands' monuments, geography, history, and peoples. (☎61355. Open daily June-Aug. 10am-7pm; Apr.-May and Sept.-Oct. 11am-4pm. Exhibit or film only €3.50, students €3. Combined admission €5.50/€5.) Finish the day at the Halla Rónáin with ⬛Ragus, a stunningly energetic display of traditional Irish music, song, and dance that costs almost twice as much in Dublin. Tickets are available at the door or from **Aran Fisherman Restaurant**. (☎61515; www.ragustheshow.com. Shows at 2:45 and 9pm. €13.)

INISHMAAN (INIS MEÁIN)

Despite recent dramatic changes on the other two islands, Inishmaan remains a fortress, quietly resisting the tourist hordes invading from Doolin and Galway. Even residents of Inishmore report that stepping onto Inishmaan is like stepping 20 years into the past. The *Inishmaan Way* (€2) describes a 5 mi. walking route that passes all of the island's sights. The thatched cottage where John Synge wrote is 1 mi. down the main road. A bit farther is 7th-century **Dún Chonchúir** (Connor Fort), and at the western end of the road is **Synge's Chair,** where the writer came to reflect and compose. The landscape gets even more dramatic when the coastline comes into view. To the left of the pier, the ruins of 8th-century **Cill Cheannannach** church were a burial ground until the mid-20th century. Entering the **Knitwear Factory,** near the island's center, is uncannily like stepping into a Madison Ave. boutique. The company sells sweaters internationally to upscale clothiers, but visitors get them right off the sheep's back at half the price—expect to pay €90 for an Aran sweater. (☎73009. Open M-Sa 10am-5pm, Su 10am-4pm.) For **tourist information,** as well as the chance to buy a variety of local crafts, try the **Inishmaan Co-op.** (☎73010. Open M-F 10am-5pm, Sa 11am-4pm, Su noon-3pm.) **Mrs. Faherty** runs a **B&B ❸,** signposted from the pier, and provides an enormous dinner. (☎73012. Dinner €12. Open mid-Mar. to Nov. Singles €30-35; doubles €55.) Otherwise, gorgeous **Tigh Congaile ❸** is on the right side of the first steep hill from the pier. (☎73085. Singles €35; shared rooms €30 per person.) Its **restaurant ❸** serves seafood. (Lunch under €7, dinner from €16. Open daily June-Sept. 10am-7pm.) **Padraic Faherty's** thatched pub is the center of island life and serves a small selection of grub until 6:30pm.

INISHEER (INIS OÍRR)

The Aran Islands have been described as "quietness without loneliness," but Inishmaan can get pretty lonely, and Inishmore isn't always quiet. Inisheer, the smallest isle, is the perfect compromise. On clear days, when the island settles into an otherworldly peacefulness, daytrippers wonder if these few square miles hold the key to the pleasures of a simpler life. The **Inis Oírr Way** covers the island's major attractions on a 4 mi. path. The first stop is in town at **Cnoc Raithní,** a bronze-age burial mound from 2000 BC. Walk along the shore to the overgrown graveyard of **St. Cavan's Church** *(Teampall Chaomhain).* Farther east along the water, a grassy track leads to majestic **An Loch Mór,** a 16-acre inland lake brimming with wildfowl. The ring fort **Dún Formna** is perched above the lake. Past the lake and back onto the seashore lies the **Plassy Wreck,** a sunken ship that washed up on Inisheer in 1960. The walk back to town passes the remains of 14th-century **O'Brien Castle,** razed by Cromwell in 1652. On the west side, **Tobar Einne,** St. Enda's Holy Well, is believed to have curative powers. ⬛Aras Eanna screens films, organizes art exhibits, and runs workshops and a cafe. (☎75150. Open daily 10am-5pm. Gallery free. Tickets €3-7.)

Rothair Inis Oírr rents bikes. (☎75033. €9 per day, €40 per week.) Free **Internet access** is available at the **Inisheer Co-op Library,** a beige building up the road from the pier and past the beach. (☎75008. Open Tu, Th, Sa 2:30-5pm.) The **Brú Hostel (IHH) ❶,** visible from the pier, is spacious with great views. (☎75024. Breakfast €4-

6.50. Laundry €5. Dorms €13; private rooms €17.) **The Mermaid's Garden ❸**, on the other side of the beach and signposted from the airstrip, rents lovely, big rooms and serves a wonderful selection of breakfasts. (☎75062. €30 per person; €80 per family.) The **Ionad Campála Campground ❶** offers camping near the beach. (☎75008. Open July-Aug. €8 per tent. Showers €2.) **Tigh Ruairí**, an unmarked white pub-shop on the main road, has **groceries**. (☎75002. Shop open daily July-Aug. 9am-8pm; Sept.-June M-Sa 10am-6pm, Su 10:30am-2pm.) **Fisherman's Cottage ❷** serves organic, island-grown meals. (☎75053. Soup and bread €2.50. Dinners €12.70. Open daily 11am-4pm and 7-9:30pm.) **Tigh Ned's** pub, next to the hostel, caters to a young set; the dim pub at **Ostan Hotel** (☎75020), up from the pier, is as crowded as a place on Inisheer can get.

GALWAY (GAILLIMH)   ☎091

Welcome to the fastest-growing city in Europe. In the past few years, Co. Galway's reputation as Ireland's cultural capital has brought flocks of young Celtophiles to Galway city. Mix more than 13,000 local university students, a large population of twenty-something Europeans, and waves of international backpackers, and you have a college town brimming with *craic*.

TRANSPORTATION

Trains: Station on Eyre Sq. (☎561 444). Open M-Sa 9am-6pm. Trains to **Dublin** (3hr., 4-5 per day, €25-35) via **Athlone** (€11-14); transfer at Athlone for all other lines.

Buses: Station on Eyre Sq. (☎562 000). **Bus Éireann** heads to: **Belfast** (7hr., M-Su 2-3 per day, €28); the **Cliffs of Moher** (late May to mid-Sept. M-Sa 3-4 per day, Su 1-2 per day; €12.50) via **Ballyvaughan** (€8.80); **Cork** (4½hr., 13 per day, €17.50); **Donegal** (4hr., 4 per day, €15.20); **Dublin** (4hr., 14 per day, €13). Private coach companies specialize in Dublin-bound buses: **Citylink** (☎564 163) from Supermac's, Eyre Sq. (14 per day, last bus 5:45pm; €14); **Michael Nee Coaches** (☎095 51082) from Forester St. through **Clifden** to **Cleggan**, meeting the **Inishboffin** ferry (M-Sa 2-4 per day, €8.90); **P. Nestor Coaches** (☎797 144) from the Forster St. car park (5-7 per day, €10-12). **City buses** (☎562 000) leave from the top of Eyre Sq. (every 20min., €1.20) and head to every neighborhood. Commuter tickets €12 per week, students €10.

Taxis: The biggest companies are **Big O Taxis** (☎585 858) and **Cara Cabs** (☎563 939). 24hr. taxis wait around Eyre Sq. and near the tourist office. **Black Cabs** (☎569 444) are cheaper than taxis, but must be called, not hailed.

Bike Rental: Mountain Trail Bike Shop, Middle St. (☎569 888). €10 per day, €75 per week. €40 deposit. Open daily 9:30am-5:30pm.

Hitching: Hitchers usually wait on the Dublin Rd. (N6) scouting rides to Dublin, Limerick, or Kinvara. Most catch bus #2, 5, or 6 from Eyre Sq. to this main thumb-stop. University Rd. leads drivers to Connemara via N59. *Let's Go* does not recommend hitchhiking.

ORIENTATION AND PRACTICAL INFORMATION

Buses and trains stop at **Eyre Square**, a central block of lawn and monuments. B&Bs huddle northeast of the square along **Prospect Hill**; the town's commercial zone stretches in the other direction. **Station Road**, a block east of Williamsgate St., leads into the pedestrian-only heart of Galway, filled with shops and cafes. Fewer tourists venture over the bridges into the more bohemian **left bank** of the Corrib, home to great music and some of Galway's best pubs. The pubs along **the docks** in the southeast of the city are largely fishermen hangouts. When weather permits, guitar players and lusty paramours lie by the river along the **Long Walk**.

IRELAND

Tourist Office: Forster St. (☎537 700). Stocks Aran info and books accommodations for a €4 charge. **Bureau de change.** Open daily 9am-5:45pm.

Budget Travel: SUSIT, Mary St. (☎565 177). Open May-Sept. M-F 9:30am-5:30pm, Sa 10am-3pm; Oct.-Apr. M-F 9:30am-5:30pm, Sa 10am-1pm.

Financial Services: Bank of Ireland, 19 Eyre Sq. (☎563 181). **AIB,** Lynch's Castle, Shop St. (☎567 041). Both have 24hr. **ATMs.** Both open M-F 10am-4pm, Th 10am-5pm.

Work Opportunities: Contact **FAS** (☎534 400; www.fas.ie; open M-F 9am-5pm) or the **Galway Peoples' Resource Centre** (☎564 822 or 562 688; open M-F 9am-5pm).

Police (Garda): Mill St. (☎538 000).

Hospital: University College Hospital, Newcastle Rd. (☎524 222).

Internet Access: Fun World, Eyre Sq. (☎561 415). €5 per hr. Open M-Sa 10am-11pm, Su 11am-11pm.

Post Office: 3 Eglinton St. (☎534 727). Open M and W-Sa 9am-5:30pm, Tu 9:30am-5:30pm.

ACCOMMODATIONS

In the last few years, the number of accommodations in Galway has tripled; it now approaches one thousand. It is still wise to call at least a day ahead in July and August and on weekends.

HOSTELS AND CAMPING

▨ **Salmon Weir Hostel,** 3 St. Vincent's Ave. (☎561 133). Not as impressively stacked or spacious as some of its brethren, but extremely homey, with a friendly, laid-back vibe. Free tea and coffee. Laundry €6. Curfew 3am. Dorms €9-15; doubles €35. ❶

▨ **Sleepzone,** Bóthar na mBán (☎566 999; www.sleepzone.ie), northwest of Eyre Sq. A bit sterile, but beautiful, new, and fully loaded—huge kitchen, common room with flat-screen TV, calm terrace, and car park. Bare floors make it a bit noisy. Free **Internet access** for guests; nonresidents €1 per 15 min. Wheelchair accessible. Dorms €18-22. Singles €50; doubles €30. Weekends €2-10 more. Nov.-Apr. €2-17 less. ❷

Barnacle's Quay Street House (IHH), Quay St. (☎568 644; www.barnacles.ie). Bright, spacious rooms in the eye of the Quay St. storm. Perfect for post-pub-crawl returns, but that same convenience can make front rooms quite noisy. No alcohol allowed on premises. Excellent security. All rooms ensuite. Internet access €1 per 15 min. Light breakfast included. Dorms €15-22. Twin/double €53. Rates lower in low season. ❷

Kinlay House (IHH), Merchants Rd. (☎565 244), off Eyre Sq. Huge and well located, with a plethora of services. Aran Island Ferry bus departs from out front. Discounts for booking with their Cork or Dublin locations. Bureau de change. Wheelchair accessible. Small breakfast included. Laundry €7. Dorms €16-21; singles €45; doubles €52. ❷

Archview Hostel, Dominick St. (☎586 661). Archview prides itself on being "not the flashiest, but the friendliest," a claim that rings true with the genuine community atmosphere. The hostel's location near some of Galway's best music spots compensates for the longer walk from the station (about 15min.). Internet access €5 per hr. Dorms €10. Long-term stays €50 per week. ❶

Camping: Salthill Caravan and Camping Park (☎523 972). Beautiful bay location ½ mi. west of Salthill, 1hr. along the shore from Galway. Open Apr.-Oct. €6 per person. ❶

B&BS

▨ **St. Martin's,** 2 Nun's Island Rd. (☎568 286), on the west bank of the river at the end of O'Brien's Bridge. The gorgeous back garden spills into the river. Located near Galway's best pubs, and just across the river from the main commercial district. All rooms ensuite. Singles €35; doubles €70; large family room €30 per person. ❸

Galway

ACCOMMODATIONS
Adria House, **26**
Archview Hostel, **22**
Ashford Manor, **6**
Barnacle's Quay St. Hostel, **17**
Kinlay House (IHH), **11**
Salmon Weir Hostel, **3**
Salthill Caravan and Camping Park, **27**
San Antonio, **1**

Sleepzone, **2**
St. Joseph's, **12**
St. Martin's, **13**

FOOD
Anton's, **25**
The Home Plate, **7**
Java's, **9**
McDonagh's, **19**
Pierre's, **18**
Tulsi, **15**

NIGHTLIFE
The Blue Note, **21**
Busker Browne's, **16**
The Crane, **20**
Cuba, **5**
GPO, **8**
The Hole in the Wall, **4**
The King's Head, **14**
Roisín Dubh, **23**
Skeffington Arms, **10**
Zulus, **24**

University College-Galway

University College Hospital

University Rd.

Riverside Sports Ground

Waterside St.

St. Bridget's Pl.

Bóthar na mBán

Prospect Hill

Waterside St.

Town Hall

Courthouse

St. Vincent's Ave.

St. Frances St.

Woodquay

St. Brendan's Ave.

Eyre St.

Rosemary Ave.

Bóthar Irwin

St. Patrick's Church

TO (100yd)

Salmon Weir Bridge

Cathedral of Our Lady

Gaol Rd.

River Corrib

Galway Advertiser

Eglinton Canal

Canal Rd.

NUNS ISLAND

FAS

St. Mary's Rd.

St. Helens St.

Presentation Rd.

New Rd.

Mill St.

Galway Peoples' Resource Centre

Nuns Island St.

Nora Barnacle House

Bowling Green

Upper Abbeygate

Market St.

Lynch's Castle

Williamsgate

Eglinton St.

William St.

Kennedy Park

EYRE SQ.

SuperValu

Medieval Wall

EDWARD SQ.

Victoria Pl.

Forster St.

Station Rd.

SUSIT

St. Nicholas

Lombard St.

Shop St.

Zhivago

Abbeygate St. Lwr.

Merchants Rd.

TO (1mi)

Garda

O'Brien's Br.

Bridge St.

Upper Cross St.

High St.

Middle St.

Mainguard St.

Quay St.

An Taibhdhearc

Lower Cross St.

Mountain Trail Bike Shop

Queen St.

Lough Atalia Rd.

Henry St.

Lower Dominick

Druid Theatre

Flood St.

New Dock St.

Dock Rd.

Raleigh Row

William St. W.

Upper Dominick

Wolfetone Br.

City Museum

Spanish Parade

Spanish Arch

Dock St.

Commercial Dock

Sea Rd.

Munster Ave.

Father Burke Park

Father Griffin Rd.

Claddagh Quay

River Corrib

The Long Walk

Old Dock

CLADDAGH

Claddagh Hall

St. Nicholas Rd.

Fairhill

Nimmo's Pier

Father Griffin Rd.

St. Dominick St.

South Park

Galway Bay

Beach Ct.

Father Burke Rd.

TO SALTHILL (.6mi), ATLANTAQUARIUM (.5mi), & (1mi)

Grattan Rd.

N

LG

0 — 300 yards
0 — 300 meters

IRELAND

Ashford Manor, 7 College Rd. (☎563 941), by Lynfield House. Classy, if pricey, B&B with TV, direct-dial phone, and hair dryer in each room. Ample parking. Big breakfast selection. €55, low season €30. ❹

San Antonio, 5 Headford Rd. (☎564 934), a few blocks north of Eyre Sq. Bright rooms with single beds. Backpacker-friendly. €32, without breakfast €25. ❷

Adria House, 34 Beach Ct. (☎589 444; www.adriaguesthouse.com). On a quiet cul-de-sac off Grattan Rd., between the city center and Salthill. Home to a dynamic duo of owners. €25-50 per person, prices highest July-Aug. ❹

St. Joseph's, 24 Glenard Ave. (☎522 147), Salthill. Small B&B with the lowest prices around. €19 with continental breakfast, €23 with full Irish breakfast. ❷

🗀 FOOD

The east bank has the greatest concentration of restaurants. **SuperValu** is located in the Eyre Sq. mall. (☎567 833. Open M-W and Sa 9am-6:30pm, Th-F 9am-9pm, Su noon-5pm.) On Saturday mornings, an █**open market** vends cheap pastries, ethnic foods, and fresh fruit, as well as jewelry and artwork, in front of St. Nicholas Church. (Open 8am-5pm.)

██ **Anton's** (☎582 067). Just over the bridge near the Spanish Arch and a 3min. walk up Father Griffin Rd. Self-consciously hip eateries on the other side of the river could learn a lot from this hidden treasure: Anton's lets the food do all the talking. Scrambled eggs with smoked salmon €4.50. Open M-F 8am-6pm. ❶

██ **Java's,** Abbeygate St. (☎567 400). Hip, dimly lit cafe. The New York-style bagel sandwiches are excellent (€2.75-6.25), as are the brownies. As reliable as Irish rain—only closes early Christmas Eve. Open M-Sa noon-3am, Su 1pm-3am. ❶

McDonagh's, 22 Quay St. (☎565 001). Fish and chip madness—locals and tourists alike line up and salivate at this century-old institution. Takeaway fish fillet and chips €6.70. Open daily noon-midnight; takeaway M-Sa noon-midnight, Su 5-11pm. ❷

The Home Plate, Mary St. (☎561 475). Diners enjoy massive helpings on tiny wooden tables. Quaint and vegetarian-friendly, with curry dishes and sandwich variations big enough to share (but good enough to inspire indulgence). The vegetarian wrap (€8.85) is fantastic. Entrees €7-10. Open M-Sa noon-8pm. ❷

Tulsi, Buttermilk Walk (☎564 831), between Middle and High St. This award-winning restaurant serves Ireland's best Indian food. Open daily noon-3pm and 6-10pm. ❸

Pierre's, 8 Quay St. (☎566 066). This is where you take the woman you love. An oasis of quiet amidst the din of Quay St. The raspberry mousse floating in a chocolate cup is divine. 3-course meal €22.90. Open M-Sa 6-10:30pm, Su 6-10pm. ❹

👁 🎵 SIGHTS AND ENTERTAINMENT

Rededicated as John F. Kennedy Park, **Eyre Square** has a small collection of monuments around its grassy common stand. Across the river to the south of Dominick St., **Claddagh** was an Irish-speaking, thatched-cottage fishing village until the 1950s. Stone bungalows replaced the cottages, but a bit of the small-town appeal and atmosphere still persists. The famous Claddagh rings, traditionally used as wedding bands, are mass-produced today. The **Nora Barnacle House,** 8 Bowling Green, is the home of James Joyce's life-long companion. (☎564 743. Open mid-May to mid-Sept. W-F 10am-1pm and 2-5:30pm. Last admission 5pm. Mid-Sept. to mid-May by appointment only. €2.50.) By the river, the **Long Walk** makes a pleasant stroll, leading to the **Spanish Arch.** If you're pressed for time, half- or full-day group **tours** may be the best way to see the sights of Galway; hop-on, hop-off **buses** line up outside the tourist office (most €11, students €9) and cruise the city. **Bus Éireann** (☎562 000), **Healy Tours** (☎770 066), **Lally Tours** (☎562 905), and **O'Neachtain Tours** (☎553 188) depart for Connemara and the Burren from various points in the city (€20-25, students €15-20).

The free *Galway Advertiser* provides entertainment listings. For tickets to big events throughout Ireland, head to **Zhivago** on Shop St. (☎509 960. Open June-Sept. M-Sa 9am-9pm, Su 10am-6pm; Oct.-May M-W and Sa 9am-6pm, Th-F 9am-9pm, Su noon-6pm. €1.90 booking fee.) Festivals rotate through Galway all year long, with the greatest concentration during the summer months. Reservations for accommodations during these weeks are essential. Ireland's biggest film festival—the **Galway Film Fleadh**—is a jumble of films, lectures, and workshops in early July. (☎569 777; www.galwayfilmfleadh.com.) For two crazed weeks in mid-July, the largest **arts festival** in Ireland reels in famous trad musicians, theater troupes, and filmmakers. (☎583 800; www.galwayartsfestival.ie.) The gates go up on the **Galway Races** at the end of July.

🎭🎷 PUBS AND CLUBS

With approximately 650 pubs and 70,000 people, Galway maintains a healthily low person-to-pub ratio. Music is alive and well—whether alternative rock, live trip-hop, or some of the country's best trad. Very broadly speaking, **Quay Street** and **Eyre Square** pubs cater to tourists, while locals stick to trad-oriented **Dominick Street.** Between midnight and 12:30am, the pubs drain out and the tireless go dancing.

- 🎵 **Roisín Dubh** ("The Black Rose"), Dominick St. (☎586 540). Intimate, bookshelved front hides one of Galway's hottest live music scenes. Some folk and blues, much rock and acoustic, and frequent trad sessions. Cover €5-23, none most weekends.

- 🎵 **Zulus,** Raven's Terr. (☎581 204). Galway's first gay bar. Approximately 95% male, but all are welcome to join in the fun at this colorful, welcoming place. Lively local banter and laughter ricochet off the walls until late.

- **The Blue Note,** 3 William St. West (☎589 116). Where all the cool kids go. Twenty-something hipsters amass to dance to the hottest chart-toppers. Galway's best bet for turntable music, with top-notch guest DJs. Occasional indie films in the winter.

- **The King's Head,** High St. (☎566 630). Like visitors to the city itself, pubbers come into King's Head expecting to spend the night, but fall in love and end up living there instead. Upstairs music varies from trad to rock. Su jazz brunch 1-3pm.

NO WORK, ALL PLAY

GALWAY OYSTER FESTIVAL

Fifty-three years ago this September, the anxious manager of the Great Southern Hotel stood in the lobby of his near-empty hotel lamenting the fall tourism slowdown. In a conversation with his head chef later that day, Collins noted that oysters had just come into season. Suddenly, he was struck by the idea of initiating a festival to herald the oyster season, and so the Galway International Oyster festival was born.

A year later, with support from local businesses and the Guinness Brewing Company, 34 guests attended the first annual festival. Today, over ten thousand locals and tourists consume tens of thousands of oysters. The AA Travel Guide has called the festival one of "Europe's Seven Best," and the London Times proclaimed the festival one of the "Twelve Greatest Shows on Earth."

The weekend's festivities commence with the Pearl Contest, in which one local belle is selected as the "pearl." In addition to a gala ball, parade, and much oyster tasting, the centerpiece of the festival is the Guinness World Oyster-Opening Championship, which challenges competitors to open thirty oysters using only a knife and cloth. The current world record, set in 1977, stands at 1 minute 3 seconds.

Oyster lovers and aspiring pearls can get more information and tickets at www.galwayoysterfest.com.

The Hole in the Wall, Eyre St. (☎565 593). This large pub fills up fast with a beat-seeking college crowd year-round. Booths for intimate groups, small beer garden for overflow flirtation. Quality of music varies, but *craic* is a constant.

Cuba, on Prospect Hill, right past Eyre Sq. Far and away the best club. Upstairs provides wonderfully varied but danceable live music. Cover €5-10.

Busker Browne's, Upper Cross St. (☎563 377), in an old nunnery. Get thee to this upscale bar that packs a professional crowd onto wall-to-wall couches. If the first 2 floors don't impress, head to the fantastic 3rd fl. ▨ **Hall of the Tribes,** easily the most spectacular lounge in Galway. Su morning excellent live jazz downstairs.

The Crane, 2 Sea Rd. (☎587 419), a bit beyond the Blue Note. A friendly, musical pub well known as the place to hear trad in Galway. 2 musicians quickly become 6, 6 become 10, 10 become 20. Trad every night and Su 1-4pm.

Skeffington Arms (☎563 173), across from Kennedy Park. A multi-storied hotel pub with 6 different bars and an intricately carved wooden interior. Suspended walkways overlook the rear. A well-touristed, multi-generational pub crawl unto itself. DJs F-Sa.

GPO, Eglinton St. (☎563 073). A student favorite during term; Most evenings feature some form of house, techno, hip hop, or chart music. Frequent theme nights including W 80s night. Cover €6; pick up a free membership to lower the charge to €4.

CONNEMARA (CONAMARA)

Connemara, a thinly populated region of northwest Co. Galway, extends a lacy net of inlets and islands into the Atlantic Ocean. Rough inland mountains, desolate stretches of bog, and rocky offshore islands are among Ireland's most arresting and peculiar scenery. Driving west from Galway City, the relatively tame and developed coastal strip stretching to Rossaveal suddenly gives way to the pretty fishing villages of Roundstone and Kilkieran. Farther west, Clifden, Connemara's largest town, draws the largest crowds and offers the most tourist services. Ancient bogs spread between the coast and the rock-studded green slopes of the two major mountain ranges, the **Twelve Bens** and the **Maamturks.** Northeast of the Maamturks is **Joyce Country,** named for a long-settled Connemara clan. Ireland's largest *gaeltacht* also stretches along the Connemara coastline, and Irish-language radio (Radio na Gaeltachta) broadcasts from Costelloe.

Cycling is a particularly rewarding way to absorb the region. The 60 mi. routes from Galway to Clifden (via Cong) and Galway to Letterfrack are popular despite fairly challenging dips and curves toward their ends. The seaside route through Inverin and Roundstone to Galway is another option. In general, the dozens of loops and backroads in north Connemara make for beautiful and worthwhile riding. **Hiking** through the boglands and along the coastal routes is also popular—the **Western Way** footpath offers dazzling views as it winds 31 mi. from Oughterard to Leenane through the Maamturks. **Buses** serve the main road from Galway to Westport, stopping in Clifden, Oughterard, Cong, and Leenane. N59 from Galway to Clifden is the main thoroughfare; R336, R340, and R341 make more elaborate coastal loops. **Hitchers** report that locals are likely to stop; *Let's Go* does not recommend hitchhiking.

CLIFDEN (AN CLOCHÁN) ☎095

The town of Clifden is a cluster of buildings sandwiched between a small cliff and a pair of modest peaks. Socially, Clifden serves as a buffer between the built-up southern half of Co. Galway and pristine northern Connemara. During the off season (Sept.-May), the town is quiet, but tourists flood in during the summer months.

🖃🖪 TRANSPORTATION AND PRACTICAL INFORMATION. Bus Éireann leaves from the library on Market St. to: **Galway** via **Oughterard** (2hr.; mid-June to Aug. M-Sa 6 per day, Su 2 per day; Sept.-May 1-3 per day; €9) and **Westport** via **Leenane** (1½hr., late June-Aug. M-Sa 1 per day). **Michael Nee** (☎51082) buses run from the courthouse to **Cleggan** (mid-June to Aug. 3 per day, Sept.-May 3 per week; €6) and **Galway** (2hr., 2 per day, €13). **C&P Hackney** (☎21309 or 086 859 3939) and **Joyce's** (☎21076 or 22082) are taxi services. **Rent bikes** from **Mannion's**, Bridge St. (☎21160 or 21155. €15 per day, €70 per week; deposit €20. Open daily 9:30am-6pm.)

The **tourist office,** Galway Rd., has information on all of Connemara. (☎21163. Open June M-Sa 10am-6pm; July-Aug. M-Sa 9:30am-6pm, Su 10am-6pm; Sept.-Oct. M-Sa 10am-4:50pm; Mar.-May M-Sa 10am-5pm.) **AIB** is in the Square. (☎21129. Open M-F 10am-12:30pm and 1:30-4pm, M until 5pm.) For **Internet access,** try **Two Dog Cafe,** Church St. (☎22186. €1.90 per 15min., students €1.40. Open M-Sa 10:30am-5pm.) The **post office** is on Main St. (☎21156. Open M-F 9:30am-5:30pm, Sa 9:30am-1pm.)

🖪🖪 ACCOMMODATIONS AND FOOD. B&Bs (from €25) litter the streets; reservations are necessary in July and August. 🖪**White Heather House ❸,** the Square has a great location, panoramic views from most rooms, and an Irish breakfast in the mornings. (☎21655. Singles €25-30; doubles €60.) **Clifden Town Hostel (IHH) ❶,** Market St., has great facilities, spotless rooms, and a quiet atmosphere close to the pubs. Despite the modern decor, stone walls remind guests that the house is 180 years old. (☎21076. Dorms €13-15; doubles €32-34; triples €45; quads €55-60.)

Clifden has a surprising variety of culinary options, ranging from family-run kitchens to pub fare, aspiring gourmet cooking to Chinese and fast food. **O'Connor's SuperValu,** Market St., sells **groceries.** (☎21182. Open M-Sa 9am-8pm, Su 10am-6pm.) **Cullen's Bistro & Coffee Shop ❸,** Market St., is a family establishment that cooks up hearty meals (thick Irish stew €14.50) and tempting homemade desserts. (☎21983. Open daily 11am-10pm.) **Walsh's ❶,** Market St., is a busy bakery with a large seating area and food for under €5. (☎21283. Open June-Sept. M-Sa 8:30am-6pm, Su 9am-6pm; Oct.-May M-Sa 8:30am-6pm.) Revelers sit on the floor when the chairs and pool tables fill up at **Malarkey's,** Church St. (☎21801), or join in the music at **Mannion's Bar and Lounge,** Market St. (☎21780).

🖪 SIGHTS. The 10 mi. **Sky Road** provides a lovely route for hiking, biking, or a scenic drive. The trail loops around west of town, ascending to dizzying heights. A mile down Sky Rd. **Clifden Castle** was once home to Clifden's founder, John D'Arcy. Farther out, a peek at the bay reveals the boggy spot near Ballyconneely where US pilots John Alcock and Arthur Brown landed the first nonstop transatlantic flight. One of the nicer ways to get acquainted with Connemara is to hike south to the **Alcock and Brown monument,** situated just off the Ballyconnelly Rd., 3 mi. past Salt Lake and Lough Fadda.

INISHBOFIN (INISH BÓ FINNE) ☎095

Seven miles from the western tip of Connemara, Inishbofin, the "island of the white cow," has gently sloping hills (flat enough for pleasant cycling) scattered with rugged rocks and near-deserted sandy beaches. Days on Inishbofin are best spent meandering through the island's four stone- and wildflower-strewn peninsulas; most items of historical interest are on the southeast peninsula. **Knock Hill** affords spectacular views of the island. **Bishop's Rock,** a short distance off the

IRELAND

mainland, becomes visible at low tide. The ragged northeast peninsula is fantastic for **bird watching:** gulls, cornets, shags, and a pair of peregrine falcons fish among the cliffs and coves. Inishbofin provides a perfect habitat for the **corncrake,** a bird that's near extinction everywhere except in Seamus Heaney's poems. Two pairs of these rare birds presently call Inishbofin home.

Ferries leave for Inishbofin from **Cleggan,** a tiny village with stunning beaches 10 mi. northwest of Clifden. Two **ferry companies** serve the island. **Malachy King** operates the **Island Discovery** and the **Galway Bay,** which comprise the larger, steadier, and faster of the two fleets. (☎44642. 40min.; July-Aug. 3 per day, Apr.-June and Sept.-Oct. 2 per day; €15 round-trip, students €12, children €7.50. Purchase tickets at the pier in Clifden or on the boat.) The **M.V. Dún Aengus/Queen of Aran** runs year-round. (☎45806. 45min.; July-Aug. 3 per day, Apr.-June and Sept.-Oct. 2 per day, Nov.-Apr. 1 per day; €15 round-trips. Purchase tickets onboard.) **Bike rental** is available at the Inishbofin pier. (☎45833. €8 per day.) To sort out a stay, call ahead or visit the **Community Resource Centre** (☎45861) to the left of the pier on the main road. The pleasant staff provides maps (€1.20-4.50), updated information on services, and limited **Internet access.**

Kieran Day's excellent ▨**Inishbofin Island Hostel (IHH) ❶** is a 15min. walk from the ferry landing; take a right at the pier and head up the hill. The hostel is the yellow building. (☎45855. Linen €1. Laundry €6. Dorms €10. Private rooms €30-35. **Camping** €6 per person.) The **Emerald Cottage ❷,** a 10min. walk west from the pier, welcomes guests with home-baked goodies. (☎45865. Singles €25; doubles €50.) **Cloonan's Store,** in front of the Community Centre, sells picnic items. (☎45829. Open M-Sa 11am-1pm and 3-5pm, Su noon-3pm.) Near the pier, **Day's Pub** (☎45829) serves food from noon to 5pm. **Murray's Pub** (☎45804), 15min. west of the pier, is great for conversation, slurred or otherwise.

CONNEMARA NATIONAL PARK ☎095

Connemara National Park occupies 8 mi.² of mountainous countryside and is home to a number of curiosities, including hare runs, orchids, and roseroot. The far-from-solid terrain of the park is composed of bogs thinly covered by a screen of grass and flowers. Guides lead free walks through the bogs (July-Aug. M and F at 10:30am) and offer several children's programs on Tuesdays and Thursdays. The ▨**Visitors Centre** and its adjoining museum team up with perversely funny anthropomorphic peat and moss creatures to teach visitors the differences between hollows, hummocks, and tussocks. Follow this with the dramatic 25min. slide show about the park, which elevates the battle against opportunistic rhododendrons to epic scope. (☎41054. Open June-Aug. 9:30am-6:30pm, Mar.-May and Sept. 10am-5:30pm. €2.75, students €1.25.) The **Snuffaunboy Nature** and **Ellis Wood Trails** are easy 20min. hikes teeming with wildflowers; the former features alpine views while the latter submerges walkers in an ancient forest. For the more adventurous, trails lead from the back of the Ellis Wood Trail and 10min. along the **Bog Road** onto ▨**Diamond Hill,** a 2hr. hike that rewards climbers with views of bog, harbor, and forest, or, depending on the weather, impenetrable mist. (Diamond Hill has been closed for erosion control; call ahead to confirm opening.) Hikers often base themselves at the **Ben Lettery Hostel (An Óige/HI) ❶,** which overlooks postcard-quality stretches of scenery in Ballinafad. The turnoff from N59 is 8 mi. east of Clifden. (☎51136. Dorms €12.) A hike from this remote but friendly hostel through the park to the Letterfrack hostel can be made in a day. A tour of all 12 Bens takes hardy walkers 10hr. **Cycling** the 40 mi. loop through Clifden, Letterfrack, and Inagh valley is breathtaking, but only appropriate for strong bikers.

WESTPORT (CATHAIR NA MART) ☎098

In lovely Westport, palm trees and steep hills lead to quaint, busy streets filled with brightly colored pubs, cafes, and shops. Visitors would be well-advised to follow the river's lead and head to the Quay for a sunset pint. Book your bed in advance or you might have some trouble; tourists flock to Westport like hungry seagulls to harbor feed.

▣ ▨ TRANSPORTATION AND PRACTICAL INFORMATION. Trains leave **Altamont Street Station** (☎25253 or 25329) to **Dublin** via **Athlone** (M-Th and Sa-Su 4 per day, F 2 per day; €21.50-25). **Buses** leave Mill St. on the Octagon for **Achill, Ballina, Castlebar,** and **Galway.** For a **taxi,** call **Brendan McGing** (☎25529). **Rent bikes** from **Sean Sammon,** James St. (☎25471. €10 per day. Open M-Sa 10am-6pm, Su by prior arrangement.) **Bridge Street** and **James Street** are the town's parallel main drags. At one end the streets are linked by **The Mall** and the **Carrowbeg River.** At the other end, **Shop Street** connects **the Octagon** to the **Town Clock. High Street** and **Mill Street** lead out from the Town Clock, the latter into **Altamount Street,** where the Railway Station lies beyond a long stretch of B&Bs. The **tourist office** is on James St. (☎25711. Open daily 9am-5:45pm.) **Bank of Ireland** is at North Mall and has an **ATM.** (☎25522. Open M-F 10am-4pm.) For **Internet access,** try **Dunning's Cyberpub,** the Octagon. (☎25161. €1.30 per 10min., €7.60 per hr. Open daily 9am-11:30pm.)

▨ ▣ ACCOMMODATIONS AND FOOD. Award-winning Irish breakfasts and hospitality have kept travelers coming back to ▨**Altamont House ❸,** Altamont St., for 37 years. (☎25226. Rooms €30, ensuite €33.) The chandeliers in the foyer of ▨**Roscaoin House ❸,** Altamont St., invite guests to well-appointed ensuite rooms, a beautiful back garden, and free Internet access. (☎28519. Doubles €75-80). Peruse local art while waiting for a table at ▨**McCormack's ❷,** Bridge St. Locals praise the exemplary sandwiches and salads. (☎25619. Open M-Tu and Th-Sa 10am-5pm.) ▨**Matt Molloy's,** Bridge St., is owned by the flautist of the Chieftains. Officially, trad sessions occur nightly at 9:30pm; informally, any time of the day is deemed appropriate. (☎26655.) A run-down exterior hides the vibrant **Henehan's Bar,** Bridge St., and its beer garden. (☎25561. Music Th-Su nights in summer, F-Sa in winter.)

◩ ◪ SIGHTS AND HIKING. The commercial exploitation of **Westport House** (☎25430 or 27766) must be a bitter pill for Lord Altamont, its elite inhabitant. The **grounds** there are beautiful, but now charge an entrance fee. It's a 45min. walk from town; from the Octagon, ascend the hill and bear right, then follow the signs to the Quay. More interesting is the **Clew Bay Heritage Centre** at the end of the Quay, which is crammed with historical artifacts. The Centre also provides a **genealogical service.** (☎26852. Open daily July-Sept. 11:30am-5:30pm; Oct. and June M-F 11am-5pm. €3, students €1.50, under 15 free.)

Conical **Croagh Patrick** rises 2510 ft. over Clew Bay. The summit has been revered as a holy site for thousands of years; it was considered most sacred to Lug, the Sun God and one-time ruler of the Túatha de Danann. After arriving here in AD 441, St. Patrick prayed and fasted for 40 days and 40 nights, argued with angels, and then banished snakes from Ireland. The barefoot pilgrimage to the summit originally ended on St. Patrick's feast day, March 17, but the death-by-thunderstorm of 30 pilgrims in AD 1113 moved the holy trek to Lughnasa—**Lug's holy night** on the last Sunday in July—when the weather is slightly more forgiving. Others climb the mountain just for the exhilaration and incredible views. The round-trip hike takes 4hr., but be forewarned: the terrain can be quite steep, and the footing unsure. Well-shod climbers start their excursion from the 15th-century **Murrisk**

Abbey; pilgrims and hikers also set out for Croagh Patrick along the Tóchar Phádraig, a path from **Ballintubber Abbey.** The new and useful **Croagh Patrick Information Centre** (☎64114), at the foot of the mountain on the Pilgrim's Path off R395, offers tours, showers, luggage storage, food, and directions to the summit.

ACHILL ISLAND (ACAILL OILÉAN) ☎098

Two decades ago, Achill (AK-ill) Island was Co. Mayo's most popular holiday destination. Its popularity has dwindled, but Ireland's biggest little island remains one of its most beautiful and personable. Ringed by glorious beaches and cliffs, Achill's interior consists of a couple of mountains and more than a few bogs. The town of **Achill Sound,** the gateway to the island, has the most amenities of any nearby settlement, but **Keel** has more promising nightlife. West of Keel, the seaside resorts of **Pollagh** and **Dooagh** form a flat strip along Achill's longest beaches and serve as brief stopovers on the way to Achill's more westerly (and more potent) vistas at Keem Bay and Croaghaun Mountain. **Cycling** the Atlantic drive is a great way to see the island. The **Achill Seafood Festival** fills the second week in July, and, during the first two weeks of August, Achill hosts the **Scoil Acla** (☎45284), a festival of trad and art.

Achill Sound's strategic location at the island's entrance accounts for its high concentration of shops and services, but practicality isn't the only reason to stop here. Stay for the internationally famous stigmatic and faith healer who holds services at **Our Lady's House of Prayer,** about 20 yd. up the hill from the town's main church. (Open for prayer daily 9:30am-7pm.) The healer draws thousands to the attention-starved town each year, but local opinions remain polarized. About 6 mi. south of Achill Sound—turn left at the first crossroads—two ruined buildings stand in close proximity. The ancient **Church of Kildavnet** was founded by St. Dympna after she fled to Achill to escape her father's incestuous intentions. Nearby, a lonely and crumbling 16th-century tower house with memories of better days calls itself the remains of **Kildavnet Castle,** once owned by Grace O'Malley, Ireland's favorite medieval pirate lass.

Buses run infrequently over the bridge linking Achill Sound, Dugort, Keel, and Dooagh to **Westport, Galway,** and **Cork** (June-Aug. M-Sa 1-3 per day; Sept.-May M-Sa 2 per day), and to **Sligo, Enniskillen,** and **Belfast** (June-Aug. 2-3 per day; Sept.-May 2 per day). If the buses are too infrequent, call for a **taxi** (☎087 243 7686), "no matter how short the trip". Hitchers report relative success during July and August, but cycling is more reliable and *Let's Go* doesn't recommend hitchhiking. The island's **tourist office** is beside the Esso station in Cashel, on the main road from Achill Sound to Keel. (☎098 47353. Open M-F 10am-1pm and 2-5pm.)

Rent bikes at the **Achill Sound Hotel.** (☎45245. €9 per day, €40 per week. Deposit €50. Open daily 9am-9pm.) Other Achill Sound services include: a **Bank of Ireland ATM** (but **no bank**); a **pharmacy** (☎45248; open M-Sa 9:30am-1pm and 2-6pm); and a **post office** with a **bureau de change** (☎45141; open M-F 9:30am-12:30pm and 1:30-5:30pm). The **Wild Haven Hostel ❶,** a block past the church, has polished wood floors and antique furniture. (☎45392. Linen €1.30. Dorms €15; private rooms €20 per person. **Camping** €5.) **SuperValu** sells groceries. (☎45211. Open M-Sa 9am-7pm.) Just before the bridge to town, **Alice's Harbour Bar ❷** flaunts gorgeous views, a stonework homage to the deserted village, and a boat-shaped bar, as well as a brand-new disco that spins Top 40 hits on summer weekends. (☎45138. Lunch menu €2.50-8; dinner €9-17. Food served noon-8pm. Disco cover €7.)

BALLINA (BÉAL AN ÁTHA) ☎096

Ballina (bah-lin-AH) is a fisherman's mecca; armies in olive-green waders invade the town each year during the salmon season (Feb.-Sept.). The town is also a good base for hikes through the bird-rich **Belleek Woods** surrounding **Belleek Castle,** or the **Ox Mountains** to the east. The **Western Way** footpath begins in the Ox Mountains and ends in Connemara. It then meets the **Sligo Way**, which continues toward Sligo. Tourist offices sell complete guides to both trails. Back in town, behind the railway station, is the **Dolmen of the Four Maols**, a.k.a. the "Table of the Giants." The dolmen, which dates from 2000 BC, is said to be the burial site of four Maols who murdered Ceallach, a 7th-century bishop.

Every Saturday night, almost everyone within a 50 mi. radius, from sheep farmers to students, descends on the town for urban *craic*. **Murphy Bros.**, Clare St. (☎22702), pours pints for twentysomethings amidst dark wood furnishings. **Gaughan's**, O'Rahilly St. (☎70096), has been pulling the best pint in town since 1936. Ballina's most popular nightclub, **The Music Box**, at the top of O'Rahilly St., plays Top 40 hits. (☎72379. Cover €7-9. Open Th-Su 11:30pm-2:30am.) A mixed crowd enjoys live music at **The Loft**, Pearse St. (☎21881. Live music W-Su.)

Ballina's **train station** is on Station Rd. (☎71818). Trains go to **Dublin** via **Athlone** (M-Su 3 per day, €25). The nearby **bus station** (☎71800; open M-Sa 7:30am-9:30pm) sends **buses** to: **Dublin** via **Mullingar** (4hr., 6 per day, €12.10); **Galway** via **Westport** (2hr.; M-Sa 6 per day, Su 4 per day; €11.50); **Sligo** (2hr., M-Sa 3-4 per day, €10.75) The **tourist office**, Cathedral Rd., is on the river by St. Muredach's Cathedral. (☎70848. Open May-Sept. M-Sa 10am-1pm and 2-5:30pm.) An **AIB** is on Pearse St. (☎21144. M 10am-5pm, Tu-F 10am-4pm.) **Moy Valley Resources** offers **Internet access** in the same building as the tourist office. (☎70905. €2.50 per 15 min., €9 per hr. Open M-Sa 9am-1pm and 2-5:30pm.)

Much to the budget traveler's chagrin, there are no hostels in Ballina, but **B&Bs** (€25-40) line the main approach to town. **Lismoyne House ❸**, Kevin Barry St., next to the bus station, has stately rooms with high ceilings and big bathtubs. (☎70582. €35 per person.) **Belleek Camping and Caravan Park ❶** is 2 mi. from Ballina toward Killala on R314, behind the Belleek Woods. (☎71533. Laundry €3. Open Mar.-Oct. 1-person tent €7.) Pick up **groceries** at the **Quinnsworth** supermarket, Market Rd. (☎21056. Open M-W and Sa 8:30am-7pm, Th-F 8:30am-9pm, Su noon-6pm.) Takeaway is cheap and lard-soaked; fortunately, most Ballinalian restaurants are attached to pubs and serve similar menus in the pub at a cheaper price. **Cafolla's ❷**, just up from the upper bridge, is one of the town's two unique Irish diners, serving everything from eggs and toast to curry burgers and tongue-tingling milkshakes. (☎21029. Open daily 10am-midnight.)

SLIGO (SLIGEACH) ☎071

A cozy town with the sophistication of a city, present-day Sligo often gets lost in a haze of Yeats nostalgia. The town's thriving nightlife is as diverse as any in Ireland, running the gamut from traditional bars and musical pubs to modern, trendy clubs. The Yeats Memorial Building and countless other landmarks remember the bygone days of the wordsmith.

▐▀ TRANSPORTATION

Trains: McDiarmada Station, Lord Edward St. (☎69888). Open M-Sa 7am-6:30pm, Su 20min. before departures. To: **Dublin** via **Carrick-on-Shannon** and **Mullingar** (3hr., 4-5 per day, €25.50).

Buses: McDiarmada Station, Lord Edward St. (☎60066). Open M-F 9:15am-6pm, Sa 9:30am-5pm. To: **Belfast** (4hr., 2-3 per day, €24); **Derry** (3hr., 4-7 per day, €15); **Donegal** (1hr., 3-7 per day, €11); **Dublin** (3-4hr., 4-5 per day, €15); **Galway** (2½hr., 4-6 per day, €12.50); **Westport** (2½hr., 1-4 per day, €14.50).

Taxis: Cab 55 (☎42333); **Finnegan's** (☎77777 or 41111). €5 for first 2½ mi.

Bike Rental: Flanagan's Cycles, Market Sq. (☎44477, after hours 62633). Rental and repairs. €13 per day, €60 per week; deposit €50. Open M-Sa 9am-6pm.

ORIENTATION AND PRACTICAL INFORMATION

To reach the main drag from the station, take a left on Lord Edward St. and follow it onto Wine St., then turn right on O'Connell St. at the post office. More shops, pubs, and eateries beckon from **Grattan Street.** To get to the river, continue down Wine St. and turn right just after the Yeats Building onto idyllic **Rockwood Parade,** a waterside walkway where swans and locals take their feed.

Tourist Office: Northwest Regional Office, Temple St. (☎61201), at Charles St. From the station, turn left along Lord Edward St. and follow the signs. Information on the entire Northwest. Open July-Aug. M-F 9am-6pm, Sa 10am-4pm, Su 10am-2pm; Sept.-May M-F 9am-5pm; June M-F 9am-5pm, Sa 10am-3pm.

Financial Services: AIB, the Mall (☎42157). 24hr. **ATM.** Open M 10am-5pm, Tu-F 10am-4pm.

Launderette: Keady's, Pearse Rd. (☎69791). Full-service from €8. Open M-Sa 9am-6pm.

Police (Garda): Pearse Rd. (☎42031).

Internet: Cygo Internet Cafe, 19 O'Connell St. (☎40082). €6.50 per hr., students €5.25 per hr. Open M-Sa 10am-7pm.

Post Office: Wine St. (☎59266). Open M and W-Sa 9am-5:30pm, Tu 9:30am-5:30pm.

ACCOMMODATIONS

There are plenty of high-quality hostels in Sligo, but they often fill up quickly, particularly in mid-August when summer school is in session.

Eden Hill Holiday Hostel (IHH), (☎43204) off Pearse Rd. A 20min. trek from the bus station. Turn right at the Marymount sign before the Esso station and take another quick right after 1 block. Recently renovated to supplement its Victorian charm with modern comforts, this clean hostel offers respite from the clamor of town. Showers only hot a few hours each day. Laundry €6. Dorms €14. Private rooms €18. ❶

Pearse Lodge, Pearse Rd. (☎61090). Comfortable, colorful rooms, all ensuite, tea and coffee, hair dryers, and a basket of welcoming chocolates. Even more exciting is breakfast; a cornucopia of international options delights every palate. French toast and bananas, bagels with cream cheese, and the omnipresent full Irish are but a few of the enticing choices. Singles €35. ❹

The White House Hostel (IHH), Markievicz Rd. (☎45160). Take the 1st left off Wine St. after Hyde Bridge; reception in the brown house. Convenient to the heart of town, with a view of the water. Key deposit €7. Dorms €12.50. ❶

FOOD

Tesco Supermarket is on O'Connell St. (☎62788. Open M-Tu and Sa 8:30am-7pm, W-F 8:30am-9pm, Su 10am-4pm.) **Kate's Kitchen,** Castle St., has pâté and other delicacies. (☎43022. Open M-Sa 9am-6:30pm.) The demands of international visitors have inspired culinary development. Grab *Discover Sligo's Good Food,* free at many hostels and bookstores, for new listings.

Bar Bazaar, 34 Market St. (☎44749). An alternative spot to sip fantastic coffee concoctions. Chill in the cozy back room, with funky lanterns and board games. Open M-F 9:30am-6pm, Sa 10am-6pm. ❶

Coach Lane, Lord Edward St. (☎62417). Excellent service and amazing food blend local sensibilities with international flair. A meal might start with a goat cheese purse (€6.50), followed by monkfish sauteed in Chardonnay (€24), tiramisu (€5.20), and a hefty bill. Open daily 5:30-9:45pm. ❹

Castro's, 10-11 Castle St. (☎48290). A painting of Fidel graces the cheery walls of this patriotic Cuban-Irish cafe. Spicy tortilla wraps (€6) are a welcome break from standard sandwich fare. Open M-Sa 9am-6pm. ❷

Fiddler's Creek, Rockwell Parade (☎41866). New and popular "pubstaurant." Dinners are pricey (veggie menu €12; entrees €13-24), but a casual atmosphere prevails. Lunch noon-3pm. Dinner 6-9:30pm. Pub 21 and over. Open daily noon-1am. ❹

🔲📷 PUBS AND CLUBS

Over 70 pubs crowd Sligo's main streets, filling the town with live music during the summer. Events and venues are listed in *The Sligo Champion* (€1.50). Many pubs post signs restricting their clientele to 18+ and check IDs vigilantly.

Shoot the Crows, Grattan St. Owner Ronin holds court at the hippest destination for Sligo pint-seekers. Dark fairies dangle from the ceiling as weird skulls and crazy murals look on in amusement. Music Tu and Th 9:30pm; frequent impromptu sessions.

McLaughlin's Bar, 9 Market St. (☎44209). A true musician's pub, where all manner of song may break out in an evening, from trad to folk and grunge. Small and pleasantly gritty. Open M-Th 4-11:30pm, F-Sa 4pm-12:30am, Su 7am-11:30pm.

Garavogue (☎40100), across the river from the footbridge. Spacious, modern pub with outdoor patio overlooking the river. Dress to impress on weekends. Live music Th. DJs F and Sa. Jazz Su. Open M-W 11:30am-12:30am, Th-Su 11:30am-2am.

McLynn's, Old Market St. (☎60743). 3 generations in the making, with a 4th up and coming. Excellent spot for weekend trad, with owner/fiddler Donal leading the music Th-Su. Open M-W 4-11:30pm, Th-Sa 4pm-1am, Su 7-11pm.

Hargadon Bros., O'Connell St. (☎70933). Open fires, old Guinness bottles, and *poitín* jugs in a maze of dark and intimate nooks. The only music here is the clinking of glasses. Open M-Th 10:30am-11:30pm, F-Sa 10:30am-12:30am, Su 5-11pm.

🟢 SIGHTS

The Model Arts Centre and Niland Gallery, on the Mall, holds an impressive collection of modern Irish art in an elegant, airy space. (☎41405. Open Tu-Sa 10am-5:30pm; June-Oct. also Su noon-5:30pm. Free.) Well-preserved, 13th-century **Sligo Abbey** stands on Abbey St. (☎46406. Open daily Apr.-Oct. 10am-6pm; Nov.-Mar. call for weekend openings. Last admission 45min. before closing. Tours available on request. Admission €2, students and children €1.) The **Sligo County Museum** preserves small reminders of Yeats, including pictures of his funeral. (Open June-Sept. Tu-Sa 10:30am-12:30pm and 2:30-4:50pm; Oct.-May 10:30am-12:30pm. Free.) The Yeats Society displays information on their main man in the **Yeats Memorial Building** on Hyde Bridge. (☎42693. Open daily 10am-4:30pm. Free.) The **Sligo Art Gallery,** in the same building, rotates contemporary Irish art with an exhibit on northwest Ireland in October. (☎45847. Open M-Sa 10am-5:30pm.)

I R E L A N D

◗ DAYTRIPS FROM SLIGO

DRUMCLIFFE. Yeats composed the epitaph that was to be placed on his gravestone a year before his 1939 death in France. His wife didn't carry out his dying wish (to be buried in France, disinterred a year later, and buried next to Benbulben) until nine years later. The grave is in **Drumcliffe's** churchyard, 4 mi. northwest of Sligo off the N15. The church projects an informative animated feature on Drumcliffe's pre-Yeatsian significance as a 6th-century Christian site.

BENBULBEN. Farther north of Drumcliffe, **Benbulben Mountain,** rich in mythical associations, protrudes from the landscape like the keel of a foundered boat. St. Columcille founded a monastery on the peak in AD 547, and it continued to be a major religious center until the 16th century. The 1729 ft. climb is inevitably windy, and the summit can be extremely gusty. If you can keep from being blown away, standing at the 5000 ft. drop at the mountain's edge can be a humbling and beautiful experience. Signs on Drumcliffe Rd. guide travelers to Benbulben; for detailed directions to the trails, ask at the Drumcliffe gas station.

NORTHWEST IRELAND

Northwest Ireland consists entirely of Co. Donegal (DUN-ee-gahl). Among Ireland's counties, Donegal is second to Cork in size and second to none in glorious wilderness. Its landscape contrasts sharply with that of Southern Ireland, replacing lush, smooth hillsides with jagged rocks and bald, windy cliffs. Donegal's *gaeltacht* is the largest sanctuary of the living Irish language in Ireland, a legacy of the county's historic resistance to cultural and political Anglicization and a testament to its relative distance from the Irish tourism machine; be assured that you'll encounter fewer camera-toting tourists here than anywhere else in the country.

DONEGAL TOWN (DÚN NA NGALL) ☎074 97

A gateway for travelers heading to more isolated destinations in the north and northwest, this sometimes sleepy town ignites on weekends, and everything awakens when festivals arrive. The town swells with tourism in July and August, but manages to do so without losing its charm—somehow this "fort of the foreigner" keeps a full invasion at bay while still providing splendid scenery, and a smile.

▐ TRANSPORTATION

Buses: Bus Éireann (☎21101; www.buseireann.ie) runs to: **Derry** (M-Sa 6 per day, Su 3 per day; €10.30); **Dublin** (M-Th and Sa 5 per day, F 7 per day, Su 6 per day; €13.35); **Galway** (M-Sa 4 per day, Su 3 per day; €13.35); **Sligo** (3-7 per day, €9.80). **McGeehan's Coaches** (☎074 95 46150) go to **Dublin** via **Enniskillen** and **Cavan;** also to **Ardara, Glencolmcille, Glenties, Killybegs** and **Dungloe** (3 per day). Both stop outside the Abbey Hotel on the Diamond; timetables posted in the lobby.

Taxis: McCallister (☎087 277 1777) and **Michael Gallagher** (☎087 417 6600).

Bike Rental: The Bike Shop, Waterloo Pl. (☎22515), 1st left off the Killybegs Rd. from the Diamond. Bikes €10 per day, €60 per week. Open M-Sa 10am-6pm.

✈ ℹ ORIENTATION AND PRACTICAL INFORMATION

The center of town is called **the Diamond,** a triangle bordered by Donegal's main shopping streets. Three roads extend from the Diamond: the **Killybegs Road, Main Street,** and **Quay Street** (the **Ballyshannon Road**).

Tourist Office: Quay St. (☎21148; www.donegaltown.ie). Facing away from the Abbey Hotel, turn right; the tourist office is outside the Diamond on the Ballyshannon/Sligo Rd., next to the quay. There are few tourist offices in the county; it's wise to stop here for information and maps before heading north. Open July-Aug. M-Sa 9am-6:30pm, Su 10am-2pm; Sept.-Oct. and Easter-June M-Sa10am-6pm.

Financial Services: AIB (☎21016), **Bank of Ireland** (☎21079), and **Ulster Bank** (☎21064). All have 24hr. **ATMs.** All open M 10am-5pm, Tu-F 10am-4pm.

Laundry: Masterclean, Tyrconnell St. (☎22155), just off the Diamond. Wash and dry 5-10 lb. €6.50, 11-15 lb. €9.50, 16-20 lb. €11. Open M-Sa 9am-6pm.

Police *(Garda):* ☎21021.

Internet Access: The Blueberry Tea Room (p. 807) has a cyber cafe upstairs. €6 per hr. Open M-Sa 9am-7pm.

Post Office: Tyrconnell St. (☎21007), past Donegal Castle and over the bridge. Open M-Sa 9am-5:30pm.

⌂ ACCOMMODATIONS

Donegal Town has some of the most welcoming hostels in the country. The tourist office provides a list of B&B options for travelers hooked on the full fry. During the high season, beds are in demand, so plan and call ahead.

▨ **Donegal Town Independent Hostel (IHH/IHO),** Killybegs Rd. (☎20749), a 10min. walk from town. Linda and her daughters greet guests with smiles and muralled walls frame unbroken views of the Donegal outdoors. Call ahead, especially for possible pickup. Open June-Aug. Dorms €12; doubles €28. **Camping** €7 per person. ❶

▨ **Ball Hill Youth Hostel (An Óige/HI),** Ball Hill (☎21174), 3 mi. from town. Go 1½ mi. from town on the Killybegs Rd., turn left at the sign, and continue toward the sea. Kevin and Áine keep guests well entertained—past activities include horseback riding, boating, and a shipwreck. Dorms €14.50, under 18 €13; low season €12.50/11.50. ❶

Atlantic Guest House, Main St. (☎21187). Central location, plush carpets, TVs, and phones. All rooms ensuite. Singles €30-35; doubles €45-60. ❸

🍴 FOOD

A good selection of cafes and takeaways occupies the Diamond and nearby streets. For **groceries,** head to **SuperValu,** minutes from the Diamond down the Ballyshannon Rd. (☎22977. Open M-W and Sa 9am-7pm, Th-F 9am-9pm, Su 10am-6pm.) **Simple Simon's,** the Diamond, sells fresh baked goods, local cheeses, and homeopathic remedies. (☎22687. Open M-Sa 9:30am-6pm.)

▨ **The Blueberry Tea Room,** Castle St. (☎22933), on the corner of the Diamond toward the Killybegs Rd. Popular homemade sandwiches, daily specials, and all-day breakfasts. Cyber cafe upstairs. Entrees around €6.50. Open M-Sa 9am-7pm. ❷

▨ **The Harbour,** Quay St., opposite the tourist office. Great new restaurant, lauded for its delicious and affordable evening meals. Open M-F 4-10:30pm, Sa-Su noon-10:30pm.

Dom Breslin's Restaurant and Bar, Quay St. (☎22719), next to the tourist office. Takes the mariner theme to new levels—customers can eat below in the "Galley," in the "Captain's Office" on the mezzanine, or at the "Crow's Nest" above. Steak and seafood specialties €15-20. Open daily in summer 12:30-4pm and 5-10pm, in winter 12:30-9:30pm. Trad nightly July-Aug.; Sept.-June F-Sa. Nightclub open July-Aug. W and Sa. ❹

 PUBS

Donegal's pubs are well-equipped to accommodate thirsty visitors. Weekends in the summer are busy and full of music, particularly in early July during the Summer Festival, when many pubs host touring acts.

The Coach House, Upper Main St. (☎22855). Spontaneous sing-alongs are standard at this wood-beamed local. Downstairs **Cellar Bar** opens nightly in July and Aug. at 9:15pm for trad and ballads; musicians and singers are encouraged to join. Cover €2.

The Schooner Bar and B&B, Upper Main St. (☎21671). Great mix of hostelers and locals gather in this lantern-lit James Joyce Award-winning pub. Best trad and contemporary sessions in town on weekends from June-Aug. Sa nights summon trendy DJs.

The Scotsman, Bridge St. (☎25838). The best trad in town. There is not much mingling, but the nightly sessions are unforgettable.

O'Donnell's, the Diamond (☎21049). The biggest bar in town packs in well-mannered locals and tourists for blues and ballads on weekends. Food served M-F noon-4pm.

The Reveller, the Diamond (☎21201). Caters to a younger crowd that likes loud music and late drinks. Rock music on weekends, pop through speakers during the week.

The Olde Castle Bar and Restaurant, Castle St. (☎21062). Stone walls and corbel windows for that medieval feel. Low-key place for soulful conversation with a lovely lad or lass. Food served noon-3pm. Open June-Aug. M-Th until 11:30pm, F-Su until 12:30am; Sept.-May until 11pm.

 SIGHTS

Donegal was torn apart by Irish-English conflict in the 17th century. Evidence of this turmoil remains at **Donegal Castle,** Castle St., the former residence of the O'Donnell clan and various English nobles. (☎22405. Open daily Mar.-Oct. 10am-5:15pm; Nov.-Feb. Sa-Su 10am-5:15pm. Guided tours on the hr. €3.50, seniors €2.50, students and children €1.25, families €8.25.) A new addition to Donegal Town's tourism machine, the **Waterbus** shuttle provides aquatic tours of Donegal Bay. Among the highlights are a colony of seals, a shoreside castle, and an oyster farm. Ferries leave from the quay next to the tourist office, depending on tides; call ahead. (☎23666. €10; concessions €5.)

Six craftspeople open their workshops to the public in ☒**Donegal's craft village,** about 1 mi. south of town on the Ballyshannon Rd. The innovative works of a potter, a jeweler, a painter, an ironsmith, and two sculptors make great gift alternatives to the legions of mass-produced leprechauns sold elsewhere. (☎22225. Open July-Aug. M-Sa 10am-6pm, Su noon-6pm; Sept.-June call ahead.) A few miles outside of town at **Lough Eske** ("fish lake"), an idyllic pond set among a fringe of trees and the crumbling but majestic grounds of **Lough Eske Castle,** built in 1861, provide a gorgeous site for picnics and afternoon rambles. Follow the path around front to find a **Celtic high cross,** surrounded by breathtaking gardens that contain the burial site of the castle's former master. The hike to the lough and back takes about 2hr. Follow signs for "Harvey's Point," marked from the Killybegs Rd. About 3 mi. down the path is a stone pillar; turn right and follow the path.

SLIEVE LEAGUE PENINSULA

Just west of Donegal Town, the Slieve League Peninsula's rocky cliffs jut imposingly into the Atlantic. The cliffs and mountains of this sparsely populated area harbor coastal hamlets, untouched beaches, and some of Ireland's most dramatic scenery. R263 extends along the peninsula's southern coast, linking each charming village to the next. Backpackers and cyclists navigating the hilly terrain are advised to work their way westward, then northward, toward Glencolmcille. **Ardara** and **Glenties** make pleasant stops along the inland return and fine points of departure for a deeper trek into northern Donegal. Though most easily covered by **car**, the peninsula is spectacular for **cycling** (with bike walking on frequent, serious hills). Despite recent improvements in service, **buses** remain infrequent.

THE SLIEVE LEAGUE WAY

🚶**Slieve League Mountain** lays claim to the hotly contested title of the highest sea cliffs in Europe. The face of its sheer 2000 ft. drop is spectacular—on a clear day, a hike over the cliffs overlooks the infinite expanse of the Atlantic and the compact hamlets along the inland portion of the peninsula. To reach the mountain, turn left halfway down Carrick's Main St. and follow the signs for Teelin. A right turn at the Cúl A' Dúin pub will put you on the inland route to Slieve League. The more popular path involves hanging a left at the pub and following the coastal route to **Bunglass** (a 1½hr. walk from Carrick). From a car park, the trail heads north and then west along the coast. One hour along, the mountaintop path narrows to 2 ft., becoming the infamous **One Man's Pass**. On one side, the cliffs drop 1800 ft. to the ocean below. No worries, though—the rocky floor on the other side is only 1000 ft. down. There are no railings here, and those prone to vertigo generally opt to lower their centers of gravity by slithering across the 33 yd. platform. The path continues along the cliffs all the way to **Rossarrell Point**, 6 mi. southeast of Glencolmcille. The entire hike from the Teelin carpark to Rossarrell Point takes about 4-6hr. **Never go to Slieve League in poor weather;** ask a local expert for advice and tell someone when you expect to return. The *Ordnance Survey Discovery Map #10* helps to navigate the trek.

GLENCOLMCILLE (GLEANN CHOLM CILLE) ☎074 97

Wedged between sea-cliffs at the northwestern tip of the Slieve League peninsula, 🚶**Glencolmcille** (Gleann Cholm Cille; glen-kaul-um-KEEL) is actually a parish—a collection of several tiny, Irish-speaking villages that have come to be regarded as a single entity. This sometime-pilgrimage site centers around the street-long village of **Cashel,** which lies just off R236 along the aptly-named Cashel St. Though few venture to the desolate, wind-battered cliffs that lie beyond civilization, buses often roll in to Glencolmcille to see the **Folk Village Museum and Heritage Centre,** the town's attraction for non-hiking, non-Irish-speaking tourists. The museum is housed in thatch-roofed stone cottages that date from 1700, 1850, and 1900; guided tours describe the furniture and tools from each of these eras in Irish history. (☎30017. Open Easter-Sept. M-Sa 10am-6pm, Su noon-6pm. Tours July-Aug. every 30min.; Apr.-June and Sept. every hr. Tours €2.50.) Today, the town is renowned for its handmade products, particularly sweaters, which are on sale at numerous "jumper shops" on the surrounding roads. The **Foras Cultúir Uladh** (FOR-us KULT-er UH-lah; "The Ulster Cultural Institute") runs the **Oideas Gael institute** for the preservation of the Irish language and culture, and offers language classes. (☎30248. Open daily June-Aug. 9am-6pm; Sept.-May M-F 9am-5pm.)

Fine beaches and cliffs make for excellent hiking in all directions. Close by Malinbeg, the **Silver Strand** rewards with stunning views of the gorgeous beach and surrounding rocky cliffs. An hour's walk north of town through land dotted with prehistoric ruins (including St. Columcille's stations of the cross, his well, and his church), **Glen**

Head is easily identified by the Martello tower at its peak. Another 3hr. walk from town begins at the Protestant church and climbs over a hill to the ruins of the ghostly "Famine villages" of **Port** and **Glenloch** in the valley on the other side. Port has been empty since its last, hunger-stricken inhabitants emigrated. The road east from Glencolmcille to Ardara proceeds through the stunning **Glengesh Pass,** 900 ft. above sea level.

Bus Éireann (☎21101; www.buseireann.ie) leaves from the village corner to Donegal Town (July-Sept. M-Sa 3 per day, Su 1 per day; Oct.-June M-Sa 1 per day). **McGeehan's** buses leave from Biddy's Bar for **Carrick, Kilcar, Killybegs, Ardara, Glenties, Fintown,** and **Letterkenny.** (☎074 95 46150, July-Sept. 2 per day; Oct.-June M-Th 1 per day, F-Su 2 per day.) The **tourist office** is on Cashel St. (☎30116. Open July-Aug. M-Sa 10am-7:30pm, Su 11am-6pm; Apr.-June and Sept. to mid-Nov. M-Sa 10am-6pm, Su 11am-1:30pm.) The nearest **banks** are in Killybegs and Ardara; the nearest **ATM** is in Carraig. A **bureau de change** is in the Folk Village. The **post office** is east of the village center. (☎30001. Open M-F 9am-1pm and 2-5:30pm, Sa 9am-1pm.)

A trip to Donegal wouldn't be complete without a visit to Mary at ◼**Dooey Hostel (IHO)** ❶. To get there, turn left at the end of the village and follow the signs uphill for almost a mile. The hostel is built into the hillside overlooking the sea, and a garden's worth of flowers sprouts from the rocky face that is the hostel's corridor. (☎30130. Dorms €11.50; doubles €25. **Camping** €7 per person.) **Byrne and Sons Food Store,** Cashel St., sells **groceries.** (☎30018. Open M-Sa 9am-10pm, Su 9am-1pm and 6-9pm.) **An Chistin** ❸ (AHN KEESHT-ahn; "the Kitchen"), at the Foras Cultúir Uladh, is affordable and tasty for lunch. (☎30213. Entrees €10-15. Open daily May-Sept. 9am-9pm; Apr. and Oct. noon-9pm.) The most famous of the bunch is 120-year-old **Biddy's,** at the mouth of Carrick Rd. The town's three pubs have a dark 1950s Ireland feel: imagine spare rooms with plastic covering and, for once, a minimal amount of wood paneling. A favorite of the older crowd, this is the place to meet Irish speakers. (☎30016. Trad most nights in summer.)

THE NORTHWEST GAELTACHT

The four parishes in Co. Donegal's northwest corner comprise the largest *gaeltacht* in the Republic. Though the Rosses, Gweedore, Gartan, and Cloghaneely all maintain distinct identities, they are united by their intensely traditional culture, which has flourished unperturbed in geographic isolation. There are few visitors to the area, and locals often feign incredulity about its appeal. Do not let them fool you—there will always be plenty to discover in the isolated north.

DUNLEWY, ERRIGAL MOUNTAIN, AND GLENVEAGH ☎074

R251 runs east through the village of **Dunlewy** *(Dún Lúiche)*, past the conical **Errigal Mountain,** and on to **Glenveagh National Park.** Dunlewy, which straddles the border of Gweedore and Cloghaneely parishes, makes a great base for exploring the **Derryveagh Mountains.** Its hostels offer proximity to a pub and store and their own set of scenic trails, including the ascent to Errigal Mountain, a ramble through the **Poison Glen,** and the paths in the national park. The **Errigal Youth Hostel (An Óige/HI)** ❶, only 1 mi. from the foot of Errigal, is clean but basic—perfect for backpackers with their minds on the trail. (☎953 1180. Lockout 10am-5pm. Curfew 1am. June-Sept. dorms €13; bunked private rooms €15. Oct.-May €12/€14.)

A few minutes up the road is a turnoff to **Dunlewy Lake** and the **Poison Glen.** Within the glen is the former **manor** of an English aristocrat and his **abandoned church.** Continuing along the paved road around a few curves leads to an unmarked car park that signals the beginning of the trail up the side of **Errigal Mountain** (at 2466 ft., Ireland's second-highest peak). The scramble through loose scree and over a narrow ridge takes 3hr. round-trip. Be sure to keep an eye on the clouds—descending the mountain in poor visibility is dangerous.

IRELAND

Glenveagh National Park's 37 mi.² of forest glens, bogs, and mountains stretch east of Dunlewy on R251. The park is often fairly deserted, so don't lose your map. Rangers lead guided nature walks and more strenuous hill walks. The Visitors Center has information about these and self-guided routes, as well as a cafeteria-style restaurant. (☎913 7090. Open daily Mar.-Nov. 10am-6pm; car park gates don't close until 8pm. Call ahead for info or to schedule a walk.)

BUNBEG, DERRYBEG, AND THE BLOODY FORELAND ☎074

Bunbeg Harbour, the smallest enclosed harbor in Ireland, lies on the R257 in a region great for cycling. Relics of British occupation line the harbor. Boats (☎953 1320 or 953 1340) sail from Bunbeg *(An Bun Beag)* to Tory Island *(Oileán Thoraigh)* and Gola Island, a nearer, but not larger, land mass that has deserted beaches and beautiful views. The mile of R257 between Bunbeg and Derrybeg (Doirí Beaga) has not escaped the hand of tourism; those who have grown tired of remote wilderness are sure to find relief in Derrybeg's suburban splendor. North of Derrybeg on R257, the Bloody Foreland, a short length of rough scarlet rock, juts out into the sea. At sunset on clear evenings, the sea reflects the deep red hue of the rocks and sea, composing one of Ireland's most famous views. Farther west, the headland at Meenlaragh (Magheraroarty) offers miles of unspoiled beaches.

To reach Derrybeg by bus, try Swilly (☎912 2863), whose Donegal-Derry service stops in town (2-3 per day). Derrybeg's streets have several banks, but only the AIB has both a bureau de change and an ATM. The local post office (☎953 1165) is open M-F 9am-1pm and 2-5:30pm. There are no budget accommodations in Bunbeg or Derrybeg; the best places to seek beds are Crolly, Dunlewey, and, for the truly adventurous, Tory Island. The waterfront Bunbeg House ❸ greets guests with serene rooms. (☎953 1305; www.bunbeghouse.com. €35 per person.) At the west end of Derrybeg is Teach Niocáin, which is not only a grocery with a fantastic hot bar and sandwich shop, but also a launderette. (☎953 1065. Wash €3.80, dry €1.90. Open daily 8am-10pm.) The irresistible ⬛Hudi Beag's pub, at the west end of town, grounds Derrybeg's musical tradition. (☎953 1016. M trad.)

LETTERKENNY (LEITER CEANAINN) ☎074

Letterkenny is the commercial center of Donegal and the region's primary transportation hub. Though its heavy traffic may be a civil engineer's nightmare, the town is a cosmopolitan breeze through otherwise rustic Donegal—the large student population supports hipster cafes and pubs all about the town center.

⌷ TRANSPORTATION. The almighty Bus Depot is on the eastern side of the roundabout at the junction of Port (Derry) Rd. and Pearse Rd., in front of the shopping center. Bus Éireann (☎912 1309) runs a "Hills of Donegal" tour, going to Dungloe, Glenveagh National Park, and Gweedore (July-Aug. Tu-Sa 11:05am; €20, children €15) and has regular service to: Derry (30min.; M-Sa 9 per day, Su 3 per day; €6.70, students €5.20, children €4.40); Dublin (4½hr.; M-Sa 6 per day, Su 4 per day; €15/€13.50/€10); Galway (4¾hr., 4 per day, €27.50/€22/€17.50) via Donegal Town (50min.; M-Sa 6 per day, Su 5 per day; €7.50/€6.20/€4.80); Sligo (2hr.; M-Sa 5 per day, Su 4 per day; €12/€11/€8). Doherty's Travel (☎952 1105) sends buses to Dungloe and Burtonport, departing from Dunnes Stores daily at 3:30pm. Feda O'Donnell Coaches (☎954 8114 or 091 761 656) go to Galway (2-3 per day) via Donegal Town (€6.50). Lough Swilly Buses (☎22863) head to: Derry (M-Sa 12 per day, €6); Dungloe (M and W-Sa 4 per day, Tu 3 per day; €10.50); Fanad Peninsula (M-F 3 per day, Sa 4 per day; €9.20); Inishowen Peninsula (M-Th 2 per day, F 3 per day) via Buncrana (€6). McGeehan's (☎954 6150) sends 2 buses per day to Glencolmcille (€11.50) and Killybegs (€8.90); McGinley Coaches (☎973 5201) sends 2 buses per day to Dublin (€14) and to Gweedore via Dunfanaghy. Northwest Busways (☎938 2619) buses cruise Inishowen (M-F 4 per day, Sa 2 per day), making stops in Buncrana (€6.50), Carndonagh (€7), and Moville (€8).

🛈 PRACTICAL INFORMATION. The **tourist office** is off the second rotary at the intersection of Port (Derry) Rd. and Blaney Rd. (☎912 1160; www.irelandnorthwest.ie. Open July-Aug. M-F 9am-6pm, Sa 11am-5pm, Su noon-3pm; Sept.-June M-F 9am-5pm.) The **Chamber of Commerce Visitors Information Centre,** 40 Port Rd., is closer but has less information. (☎912 4866. Open M-F 9am-5pm.) **AIB** (☎912 2877), **Bank of Ireland** (☎912 2122), and **Ulster Bank** (☎912 4016) are all on Main St. (All open Tu-F 10am-4pm, M until 5pm. AIB and Bank of Ireland have 24hr. **ATMs.**) **Internet access** at the **Letterkenny Central Library,** Main St. (☎912 4950. Open M, W, F 10:30am-5:30pm; Tu and Th 10:30am-8pm; Su 10:30am-1pm. Book ahead.) The **post office** is halfway down Main St. (☎912 2287. Open M-F 9am-5:30pm, Sa 9am-1pm.)

🛏 ACCOMMODATIONS. In a sheltered glade up the hill from the An Grianán Theatre, **⬛The Port Hostel (IHO) ❶,** Orchard Crest, has easy access to the city center. Safe in the care of their hostess Karen, who also works as a nurse in the hospital, residents can enjoy organized pub-crawls, barbecues, and roadtrips. (☎912 5315. Laundry €5. Dorms €15; private rooms €18-20.) **Pearse Road Guesthouse ❸** is a 7min. walk down Pearse Rd. from the bus depot. Cool green, ensuite rooms sweep guests away from the traffic outside. You may rub shoulders with Ireland's *artistes,* as many performers in the Earigal Arta Festival reside here in the summer. (☎912 3002. Singles €35; doubles €60.) **Covehill House B&B ❷,** on a turnoff just before An Grianán Theatre, offers all the amenities one could need. (☎912 1038. Singles €25; doubles €50, ensuite €56.)

🍴🍺 FOOD AND PUBS. Letterkenny is a culinary haven for budget travelers, with several quirky options for cheap meals with fresh ingredients. **Tesco,** in the shopping center behind the bus station, has it all, including an **ATM.** (Open M-Tu and Sa 8:30am-7pm, W 8:30am-8pm, Th-F 8:30am-9pm, Su noon-6pm.) At **The Brewery ❹,** Market Sq., enjoy the town's best pub grub on barrel tables, or take a table for the à la carte dinner (€12-20) upstairs. (☎912 7330. Carvery lunch €7.50. Bar food M-F noon-10pm, Sa-Su noon-8pm.) **Yellow Pepper ❷,** 36 Lower Main St., serves savory, sophisticated dishes in a bright interior. Lunch specials (€8) change daily, but guarantee at least one vegetarian option. (☎912 4133. Open daily noon-10pm.)

    McGinley's, 25 Main St., has a hugely popular student bar in its chapel-like upstairs, while an older-but-still-hip crowd gathers on the Victorian ground floor. (☎912 1106. W trad at 10:30pm, F-Sa rock and blues.) **The Old Orchard Inn,** High Rd., features occasional trad and other live music (Th-F and Su) downstairs, a hip scene upstairs, and a disco on the top floor. (☎912 1615. Disco W-Su until 2am. Cover €8-10. Bar food served daily 12:30-10pm.)

🎭🎟 SIGHTS AND ENTERTAINMENT. **St. Eunan's Cathedral,** perched high above town on Church Ln., looks like the heavenly kingdom when it's lit at night. (Church Ln. is on the right up Main St. away from the bus station.) Proposed as a "resurrection of the fallen shrines of Donegal," its construction took 11 years—all years of economic hardship and depression. (☎912 1021. Open daily 8am-5pm, except during Su masses 8-11:15am and 12:30pm. Free.) In the old town Workhouse, the **Donegal County Museum,** High Rd., displays exhibits on all things Donegal. (☎912 4613. Open M-F 10am-12:30pm and 1-4:30pm, Sa 1-4:30pm. Free.)

    Anglers hook salmon in a number of nearby lakes. Call **Letterkenny Anglers** for more details (☎912 1160). Golfers of all ages perfect their short game at the 18-hole **Letterkenny Pitch & Putt** (☎912 5688 or 912 6000). Those looking to hit the long ball try **Letterkenny Golf Club** (☎912 1150). **Black Horse Stables** (☎915 1327) and **Ashtree Riding Stables** (☎915 3312) have treks and lessons for all experience levels. If horses don't meet your need for speed, rev up at **Letterkenny Indoor/Outdoor Karting Centre.** (☎912 9077. Open M-Sa 1-11pm.) Off-road fun abounds at **Letterkenny ATV Co. Ltd.** (☎912 4604). After it all, relax in the sauna, swimming pool, and whirlpool at **Letterkenny Leisure Centre** (☎912 5251), on High Rd.

APPENDIX

CLIMATE

Avg Temp (lo/hi), Precipitation	January			April			July			October		
	°C	°F	mm	°C	°F	mm	°C	°F	mm	°C	°F	mm
London	2/6	36/43	77	6/13	43/55	56	14/22	57/72	59	8/14	46/57	70
Cardiff	2/7	36/45	91	5/13	41/55	56	12/20	54/68	74	8/14	46/57	97
Edinburgh	1/6	34/43	57	4/11	39/52	39	11/18	52/64	56	7/12	45/54	65
Dublin	1/8	34/46	67	4/13	39/55	51	11/20	52/68	51	6/14	43/57	70

2005 BANK HOLIDAYS

Government agencies, post offices, and banks are closed on the following days (hence the term "Bank Holiday"). Businesses, if not closed, may have shorter hours. Transportation in rural areas grinds to a halt, while congestion in urban areas can reach ridiculous levels. Sights are more likely to be open at these times.

DATE	HOLIDAY	AREAS
Jan 3	New Year's Day	UK and Republic of Ireland
Jan 4	New Year's Day	Scotland
Mar 17	St. Patrick's Day	Republic of Ireland and Northern Ireland
Mar 25	Good Friday	UK and Republic of Ireland
Mar 28	Easter Monday	UK and Republic of Ireland except Scotland
May 2	May Day Bank Holiday	UK and Republic of Ireland
May 30	Spring Bank Holiday	UK
June 6	First Monday in June	Republic of Ireland
July 12	Battle of the Boyne (Orangemen's Day)	Republic of Ireland and Northern Ireland
Aug 1	Summer Bank Holiday	Scotland and Republic of Ireland
Aug 29	Summer Bank Holiday	UK except Scotland
Oct 31	Halloween Weekend (last monday in October)	Republic of Ireland
Dec 25	Christmas Day	UK and Republic of Ireland
Dec 26	Boxing Day/St. Stephen's Day	UK and Republic of Ireland
Dec 27	In lieu of Dec 25th	UK and Republic of Ireland

MEASUREMENTS

Britain and Ireland use the metric system, though Britain's conversion is still in progress; road signs indicate distances in miles. Gallons in the US and those across the Atlantic are not identical: one US gallon equals 0.83 Imperial gallons.

Pub aficionados will note that an Imperial pint (20 oz.) is larger than its US counterpart (16 ounces). Below is a list of Imperial units and their metric equivalents.

MEASUREMENT CONVERSIONS	MEASUREMENT CONVERSIONS
1 inch (in.) = 25.4mm	1 millimeter (mm) = 0.039 in.
1 foot (ft.) = 0.30m	1 meter (m) = 3.28 ft. = 1.09 yd.
1 yard (yd.) = 0.914m	1 kilometer (km) = 0.62 mi.
1 mile (mi.) = 1.61km	1 gram (g) = 0.035 oz.
1 ounce (oz.) = 28.35g	1 kilogram (kg) = 2.202 lb.
1 pound (lb.) = 0.454kg	1 milliliter (ml) = 0.034 fl. oz.
1 fluid ounce (fl. oz.) = 29.57ml	1 liter (L) = 0.264 gal.
1 UK gallon (gal.) = 4.546L	1 square mile (sq. mi.) = 2.59km^2
1 acre (ac.) = 0.405ha	1 square kilometer (km^2) = 0.386 sq. mi.

LANGUAGE

The worldwide use of a single language has given rise to countless variations. Below is a list of British words that travelers are most likely to encounter.

BRITISH ENGLISH	AMERICAN ENGLISH	BRITISH ENGLISH	AMERICAN ENGLISH
aubergine	eggplant	fag	cigarette
bap	a soft bun	fanny	vagina
barmy	insane, erratic	first floor	second floor
bed-sit, or bed sitter	studio apartment	fortnight	two weeks
beer mat	coaster	full stop	period (punctuation)
biro	ballpoint pen	geezer	adult male
biscuit	a cookie or cracker	grotty	grungy
bobby	police officer	give a bollocking to	shout at
bonnet	car hood	high street	main street
boot	car trunk	hire	rental, to rent
braces	suspenders	holiday	vacation
brilliant	awesome, cool	hoover	vacuum cleaner
caravan	trailer, mobile home	ice-lolly	popsicle
car park	parking lot	interval	intermission
cheeky	mischievous	"in" a street	"on" a street
cheers, cheerio	thank you, goodbye	jam	jelly
chemist/chemist's	pharmacist/pharmacy	jelly	Jell-O
chips	french fries	jumper	sweater
chuffed	pleased	kip	sleep
coach	intercity bus	kit	sports team uniform
concession	discount on admission	knackered	tired, worn out
courgette	zucchini	lavatory, "lav"	restroom
crisps	potato chips	lay-by	roadside turnout
dear	expensive	legless	intoxicated
dicey, dodgy	sketchy	lemonade	lemon soda
the dog's bollocks	the best	lift	elevator
dual carriageway	divided highway	loo	restroom
dustbin	trash can	lorry	truck
ensuite	with attached bathroom	mate	pal

BRITISH ENGLISH	AMERICAN ENGLISH	BRITISH ENGLISH	AMERICAN ENGLISH
motorway	highway	single carriageway	non-divided highway
naff	cheap, in poor taste	sod it	forget it
pants	underwear	snogging	making out
petrol	gasoline	sweet(s)	candy
pissed	drunk	swish	swanky
plaster	Band-Aid	take the piss	to make fun of
prat	stupid person	toilet	restroom
pudding	dessert	to let	to rent
pull	to seduce	torch	flashlight
public school	private school	tosser	term of abuse; see prat
punter	average person	trainers	sneakers
queue up, queue	to line up	trousers	pants
quid	pound (in money)	trunk call	long-distance call
roundabout	rotary road intersection	vest	undershirt
rubber	eraser	waistcoat (weskit)	men's vest
self-catering	with kitchen facilities	wanker	masturbator; see prat
self-drive	car rental	way out	exit
serviette	napkin	W.C. (water closet)	toilet, restroom
a shag, to shag	sex, to have sex	"zed"	the letter Z

BRITISH PRONUNCIATION

Berkeley	BARK-lee	Magdalen	MAUD-lin
Berkshire	BARK-sher	Norwich	NOR-ich
Birmingham	BIRM-ing-um	Salisbury	SAULS-bree
Derby	DAR-bee	Shrewsbury	SHROWS-bree
Dulwich	DULL-idge	Southwark	SUTH-uk
Edinburgh	ED-in-bur-ra	Thames	TEMS
Gloucester	GLOS-ter	Woolwich	WOOL-ich
Greenwich	GREN-ich	Worcester	WOO-ster
Hertfordshire	HART-ford-sher	gaol	JAIL
Grosvenor	GROV-nor	quay	KEY
Leicester	LES-ter	scones	SKONS

WELSH WORDS AND PHRASES

Consult **Language,** p. 451, for the basic rules of Welsh pronunciation. Listed below are a number of words and phrases you may encounter on the road.

WORD/PHRASE	PRONUNCIATION	MEANING
allan	ahl-LAN	exit
ar agor	ahr AG-or	open
ar gau	ahr GUY	closed
bore da	boh-RA DAH	good morning, hello
croeso	CROY-so	welcome
diolch	dee-OLCH	thank you
dydd da	DEETH dah	good day
dynion	dihnion	men
Ga i peint o cwrw?	gah-EE "pint" oh coo-roo?	Can I have a pint of beer?
hwyl	huh-will	cheers

APPENDIX

WORD/PHRASE	PRONUNCIATION	MEANING
ia	eeah	yes (sort of—it's tricky)
iawn	eeown	well, fine
llwybr cyhoeddus	hlooee-BIR cuh-HOY-this	public footpath
merched	mehrch-ED	women
na, nage	nah, nahgah	no (sort of—it's tricky)
nos da	nos dah	good night
noswaith dda	nos-WAYTHE tha	good evening
os gwelwch yn dda	ohs gwell–OOCH uhn tha	please
perygl	pehr-UHGL	danger
preifat	"private"	private
safle'r bws	savlehr boos	bus stop
stryd Fawr	strihd vahor	high street
dwn i ddim	dun ee thim	I don't know

IRISH WORDS AND PHRASES

The following words or phrases are either used often in Irish English or are common in Irish place names. Spelling conventions almost never match English pronunciations: for example, "mh" sounds like "v," and "dh" sounds like "g." See **History of the Irish Language**, p. 729, for more on the Irish Language.

WORD/PHRASE	PRONUNCIATION	MEANING
an Lár	on lahr	city center
Baile Átha Cliath	BAL-yah AW-hah CLE-ah	Dublin
bodhrán	BOUR-ohn	traditional drum
Bord Fáilte	bored FAHL-tshuh	Irish Tourist Board
Conas tá tú?	CUNN-us thaw too?	How are you?
céilí	KAY-lee	Irish dance
craic	krak	good cheer, good pub conversation
Dáil	DOY-il	House of Representatives
Dia dhuit	JEE-a dich	Good day, hello
dia's Muire dhuit	JEE-as MWUR-a dich	reply to "good day"
dún	doon	fort
Éire	AIR-uh	Ireland; official name of the Republic of Ireland
fáilte	FAWLT-cha	welcome
fir	fear	men
fleadh	flah	a musical festival
gaeltacht	GAYL-tokt	a district where Irish is the everyday language
garda, Garda Síochána	GAR-da SHE-och-ANA	police
go raibh maith agat	guh roh moh UG-ut	thank you
inch, innis, ennis	inch, innis, ennis	island, river meadow
kil	kill	church, cell
knock	nok	hill
lei thras	LEH-hrass	toilets
lough	lohk	lake
mná	min-AW	women
ní hea	nee hah	no (lit. "it is not")
oíche mhaith dhuit	EE-ha woh ditch	good night
Oifig an Phoist	UFF-ig un fwisht	Post Office
rath	rath or rah	earthen fort

WORD/PHRASE	PRONUNCIATION	MEANING
sea	shah	yes (sort of—it's tricky)
Seanad	SHAN-ud	Senate
sláinte	SLAWN-che	cheers, to your health
slán agat	slawn UG-ut	goodbye
sraid	shrawd	street
Taoiseach	TEE-shukh	Prime Minister
trá	thraw	beach

SCOTTISH GAELIC WORDS AND PHRASES

Consult **Language**, p. 541, for information on Scottish Gaelic. Listed below are a number of words and phrases you may encounter on the road.

WORD/PHRASE	PRONUNCIATION	MEANING
allt	ALT	stream
baile	BAL-eh	town
beinn	BEN	mountain
Ciamar a tha sibh?	KI-mer a HA shiv?	How are you?
De an t-ainm a th'oirbh?	JAY an TEN-im a HO-riv?	What's your name?
Failte gu...	FAL-chuh goo	Welcome to...
gleann	GLAY-ahn	valley
Gle mhath	GLAY va	very well
Gabh mo leisgeul	GAV mo LESH-kul	excuse me
Is mise...	ISH MISH-uh	My name is...
Latha ma	LA-huh MA	good day
ionad	EE-nud	place, visitor center
Madainn mhath	MA-ting VA	good morning
Oidhche mhath	a-HOY-chuh VA	good night
rathad	RAH-hud	road
Seo	SHAW	This is... (to introduce someone)
Slainte mhath	SLAN-che VA	cheers, good health
sraid	SRAHJ	street
Tapadh leibh	TA-pa LEEV	Thank you
Tha gu math	HA gu MA	I'm fine

SCOTS WORDS AND PHRASES

Consult **Language**, p. 541, for more info on Scots, a distinct dialect of English. Listed below are a few of the many Scots words and phrases used in standard Scottish English and their pronunciation if applicable:

WORD/PHRASE	MEANING	WORD/PHRASE	MEANING
aye	yes	eejit	idiot
ben	mountain	nae	no (NAY)
blether, or guid blether	talk idly, chat (good BLA-ther)	sassenach	Lowlander (SAS-uh-nach)
bonnie	beautiful	strath	broad valley
brae	hill near water (BRAY)	tatty	potato
braw	bright, strong, great	teuchter	Northerner (TYOOCH-ter)
burn	stream	tipple	a drink
cannae	cannot	weegie	Glaswegian (WEE-gee)

INDEX

INDEX

Edinburgh 63, 551, 562
Eton 263
Galway 64
Glasgow 63, 586, 589
Glasgow School of Art 590
Leeds 63
London School of Economics 64
National Univ. of Ireland 64
Oxford 64, 263
Queen's Univ. Belfast 64, 705
Sabhal Mor Ostaig 657
St. Andrews 598, 64
Stirling 608
Strathclyde 586
Trinity, Dublin 64, 727, 744
Ulster 64
Univ. College Cork 64, 774
Univ. College Dublin 64, 746
Univ. College London 64, 114
Westminster 64
Colsterworth 315
Coniston 373, 379
Connemara 798–806
Connolly, James 749
Conrad, Joseph 81, 146
Conwy 522–524
Cook, Captain James 230, 233, 422
Cooper, Susan 498
Corbridge 436
Corgis (Welsh) 448
Cork 770–775
Cornwall 234–254
Costelloe 798
Cotswolds, the 287–293
Coventry 297
Cowes 176
Cragside 441
craic 731
Craighouse 620
Craignure 621
Craig-y-nos 473
Crail, Fife 598
Craven Arms 306
Cregneash 392
Criccieth 505
cricket 88
Crickhowell 476
Cromer 330, 336
Cromwell, Oliver 73, 182, 328, 420, 537, 630, 636, 726
Crowden-in-Longdendale 366
Cúchulainn 657, 729
Cuillin Hills 657
Culloden 643
Cumbria 372–376
currency exchange 16
Cushendall 714
Cushendun 713
customs 16

cycling
Beara Way 778
Borderloop 566
Dartmoor 227
Four Abbeys 566
Great Glen Cycle Route 644, 649
Inis Mór Way 791
Isle of Man 387
Lake District 376
North York Moors 419
Peak District 367
Swansea Bikepath 479
Tarka Trail 222
tours 39
Tweed Cycleway 566
Wight Cycling 178
Yorkshire Dales 407

D

Dahl, Roald 452
Dáil 744
Danby 417, 424
Darwin, Charles 111, 306, 323
D-Day Invasion 75
de Valera, Éamon 747
Deal 152
Dean Village 558
Dentdale 405
Derry 713, 716–720
Derrybeg 811
Derryveagh Mountains 810
Devil's Bridge 496
devolution 75
Devon 216–234
Diana, Princess of Wales 77, 117
Dickens, Charles 80, 115, 175, 193, 429
dietary concerns 56
Dingle Peninsula 783–788
Dingle Town 784
disabled concerns 55
diseases 24
distilleries 543
Ardberg 618
Arran 580
Ben Nevis 648
Blair Athol 601, 606
Bowmore 619
Bruichladdich 619
Bunnahabhainn 619
Bushmills 716
Caol Ila 619
Edradour 606
Glenfiddich 638
Glenlivet 638
Highland Park 682
Jura 619, 620

Lagavulin 618
Laphroaig 619
Oban 615
Old Jameson 748
Plymouth Gin 233
Speyside Cooperage 638
Strathisla 638
Talisker 659
Tobermory 622
Dolgellau 499
Domesday Book 72, 179
Donegal 806–808
Dooagh 802
Doolin 788
Dorchester 212–215
Dornie 673
Dorset Coast, the 210–215
double-decker buses 95
Douglas 389
Dover 148–152
Down 710
Dowth 761
Doyle, Arthur Conan 118, 542
Drake, Sir Francis 72, 230, 232, 324
driving permits 37
Drumnadrochit 644
Dublin 732–757
Temple Bar 746
Dublin Suburbs 753–757
Dufton 397
Dumfries 572
Dumfries and Galloway 571–576
Dún Laoghaire 754
Dunkeld 602
Dunlewy 810
Dunmanway 776
Dunquin 784
Dunster 223
Durham 425–429
Durness 678
Dursey Island 778

E

Earby 397
East Anglia 316–338
Eastbourne 157
Easter Rising 728
Eastern Ireland 757–761
Eastwood 311
Edale 369
Eday 687
Eden Project 245
Edinburgh 546–564
Eigg, Isle of 653
Eildon Hills 567
Elgar, Edward 84, 280, 282
Elgin 636

Fortingall 604
Foula 694
Franz Ferdinand 543
fried Mars bar 543

G

Gaelic (Irish) 729, 816
Gaelic (Scottish) 541, 817
gaeltacht 729
Gairloch 675
Galashiels 566
Galway 793–797
Ganlochhead 616
Garenin 662
genealogy 749
Giant's Causeway 716
Glasgow 581–592
Glastonbury 208–210
GLBT concerns 55
  Cork 773
  Dublin 737
  Edinburgh 547
  Glasgow 584
  London 98
Glen Affric 645
Glen Cannich 645
Glen Coe 649–650
Glenariff 713
Glenbrittle 658
Glencolmcille 809
Glendalough 758
Glenfinnan 538, 651
Glengarriff 778
Glenmore 633
Glenridding 373, 384
Glens of Antrim 713
Glorious Revolution 73
Glyndŵr, Owain 448, 477
Goathland 417, 422
golf 593, 596
Golspie 643
Good Friday Agreement 695, 699, 729
Goodwood House 170
Gower Peninsula 479–480
grail. See Holy Grail.
Grampian Coast 630, 637
Grantchester 325
Grantham 315
Grasmere 373, 374, 381
Grassholm Island 487
Grassington 404, 408
Great Ayton 417
Great Bernera 665
Great Famine, the 727
Great Glen, the 638–652
Great Langdale Valley 379
Great Malvern 282

Great Yarmouth 336
Greenhead 436
Greenwich 125
Greyfriars Bobby 557
Grinton 405
Grosmont 422
Guernsey 256
guesthouses 49
Guinness 731, 747
Guinness
  the perfect pint 742
Guisborough 418

H

Haddon Hall 371
Hadrian 384, 536
Hadrian's Wall 71, 384, 436–437
haggis 543
HAGGiS tours 35, 534
Haltwhistle 436
Hamlet 630
Hampshire 170–183
Hampton Court 126
Handel, George 84, 122
Hardy, Thomas 80, 212
Harlech 501
Harris, Isle of 666–667
Hartington 366
Harvard, John 279, 324
Harwich 316
Hastings 154
Hatfield House 261
Hathaway, Anne 279
Hathersage 366, 368
Haverfordwest 484, 485
Hawes 404, 409
Hawkshead 374, 380
Haworth 399
Haydon Bridge 436
Hay-on-Wye 465
Haytor Vale 224
health 24
Healy Pass 778
Heaney, Seamus 730
Heart of England 258–294
Hebden Bridge 399
Hebrides. See Road to the Isles.
Helmsdale 643
Helmsley 417, 420
Helvellyn 384
Henson, Jim 279
Hepstonstall 399
Hereford 293
Herm 256, 257
Hexham 437
Highland Clearances 538
Highlands and Islands 624–694

hiking equipment 52
Hill of Tara 761
hitchhiking 39
Hobbes, Thomas 73
Holkham Hall 331
Holmes, Sherlock 185, 223, 227
Holst, Gustav 84, 285
Holwick 398
Holy Grail 4, 185, 208, 565
Holy Island 444
Holyhead 520
Holyroodhouse 556
home exchange 50
Home Office 66
Hopkins, Gerard Manley 81, 271, 746
Horning 336
Horringer 337
horseracing 89
Horton in Ribblesdale 408
hostels 46, 47
Houghton Hall 330
House of Lancaster 72
House of Tudor 72
Hoveton 336
Howmore 662
Howth 753
Hoy 686
Hundred Years' War 72
Hunstanton 330
hurling 731
Hyde Park 117

I

Iarnród Éireann. See Irish Rail
Ickworth House 337
identification 14
Industrial Revolution 74
Ingleton 408
Ingram 439
Inishbofin 799
Inisheer 792
Inishmaan 792
Inishmore 791
Inner Hebrides 652–661
insurance 23, 36
International Driving Permit (IDP) 37
International Youth Discount Travel Card 14
Internet 46
Inveraray 613
Inverie 652
Inverness 638–642
Iona, Isle of 623
IRELAND, Republic of 722–812

Coriusk 658
Etive 616
Fyne 613
Insh 633
Katrine 610
Leven 649
Linnhe 616, 646
Lomond 611
Long 673
Morar 651
Morlich 633
Na Dal 657
Ness 644
Rannoch 607
Shiel 651
Sligachan 658
Tarbet 619
Tay 604
Tommel 607
Torridon 674
Locke, John 73
Lockton 418
London 90–140
　accommodations 99
　food and pubs 102
　museums 127
　nightlife 134
　practical information 98
　shopping 132
　sights 108
　theater 137
　transportation 90
　Underground (Tube) 94
London Eye 106, 119
Long Melford 337
Looe 234
Lossiemouth 637
Lough Leane 780
Luss 613
Lyndhurst 183
Lynmouth 222
Lynton 221, 222
Lyveden New Bield 10

M

Maamturk Mountains 798
Mabinogion, the 451
MacBackpackers 35, 534, 655
Macbeth 602
MacDonald, Flora 660, 670
Macgillycuddy's Reeks 780
MacGregor, Rob Roy 568, 610
Machynlleth 497–499
Mackintosh, Charles Rennie 542, 581, 587, 589
Macpherson, James 542
Mad Cow Disease. See diseases.
Magna Carta 72, 190
Maidstone 148

mail 40
Malhamdale 404
Mallaig 652
Man, Isle of 386–392
Manchester 74, 354–360
Mankinholes 397
Manorbier 485
Marloes Sands 485
Marlowe, Christopher 80, 119, 324
Marx, Karl 117, 121
MasterCard 17
Matlock 364
May, Isle of 599
Mead 444
Medic Alert 25
medical assistance 24
Meenlaragh 811
Melford 337
Mellerstain House 570
Melrose 567
Merlin 4, 237, 451
Merthyr Tydfil 469
metric system 814
Midlands, the 295–315
Milford Haven 485
Milton, John 80, 323
Minehead 222
Minginish Peninsula 659
Mingulay 672
minority concerns 56
Mizen Head 776
Model Mugging 22
money 16
Monmouth 462
Monty Python 4, 87, 324, 325, 610, 616
Mordred 4, 185
More, Sir Thomas 114, 115, 147
Moreton-in-Marsh 291
Mourne Mtns. 710
Mousa 693
Muck, Isle of 653
Mull, Isle of 620–622
Mumbles 479

N

Napoleonic Wars 73
National Gallery (London) 127
National Gallery (Scotland) 559
National Health Service (NHS) 25
National Parks
　Brecon Beacons 471–476
　Cairngorm Mtns. 632–636
　Connemara 800
　Dartmoor 223–227
　Derrynane 782
　Exmoor 219–223
　Glenveagh 810

Killarney 780
Lake District 372
North York Moors 415–419
Northumberland 438–440
Peak District 363–372
Pembrokeshire Coast 484–487
Snowdonia 510–516
South Downs 154–159
Trossachs and Loch Lomond 610–613
Yorkshire Dales 404–407
Nelson, (Admiral Lord) Horatio 112, 174
Nether Wasdale 376
New Forest 183
New Lanark 592
Newcastle (N. Ireland) 710
Newcastle-upon-Tyne 429–435
Newgrange 760
Newport (Isle of Wight) 176
Newport (Wales) 485
Newquay 239
News 352
Newton Dale 422
Newton, Sir Isaac 73, 111, 315, 322
NHS. See National Health Service.
Norfolk 328–336
North Ronaldsay 688
North Wales 492–532
Northeast England 393–444
NORTHERN IRELAND 695–720
　history 696–700
　money 695
　politics 696
　safety 695
　trains 32
Northern Ireland Peace Agreement. See Good Friday Agreement
Northern Norfolk Coast 330
Northumberland 438–444
Northwest England 339–392
Northwest Gaeltacht 810–811
Northwest Highlands 672–679
Northwest Ireland 806–810
Norwich 331–335
Noss 692
Nottingham 308–311

O

Oban 614–616
O'Connell, Daniel 727
Okehampton 225
Old Course, St. Andrews 596
Old Sarum 192, 193
Old Sessions House 117
Orange Day 695, 727

Orkney Islands 680–688
Orwell, George 81, 263, 619
Osborne House 178
Osmotherley 418
Ostaig 657
Out Skerries 694
Outer Hebrides 661–672
Oxford 263–274

P

Padstow 238
Papa Stour 694
Papa Westray 687
Parliament
    Cardiff 450
    Dublin 744
    Early English 72
    Edinburgh 539, 556, 557
    Isle of Man 386
    London 76, 109
Parracombe 222
passports 13
pasty (Cornish) 245
Patterdale 384
Pearse, Padraig 747
Peebles 568
Peel 391
Pembroke 487
Pennard 480
Pennine Way 396–398
Penrith 384
pensions 49
Penwith Peninsula 252–254
Pen-y-Fan 474
Penzance 246–249
Perth 600–601
Petworth House 167
Pevensey 153
phone cards 41
phones 41
    GSM 44
    pay-as-you-go 44
Pickering 417, 420
Picts 536
Pitlochry 605–607
Plas Newydd 531
Plockton 673
PLUS 18
Plymouth 230–233
Pollagh 802
polo 89
Polperro 234
Pontsticill 474
Pooley Bridge 373
Porlock 222
Port Charlotte 619
Port Ellen 617
Port Village 810

Porthcurno 250
Porthmadog 504
Porthor 507
Portmagee 781
Portmeirion 504
Portnalong 659
Portree 659
Portsmouth 170–175
post 40
Postbridge 224, 225
poste restante 41
Potter, Beatrix 378, 380, 603
Powerscourt 756
Prime Ministers
    Blair, Tony 75
    Chamberlain, Neville 74
    Churchill, Winston 75, 111,
        123, 152, 274, 685
    George, David Lloyd 449, 506,
        728
    Thatcher, Margaret 75, 271,
        315
    Walpole, Robert 73, 330
Princetown 224, 225
priories. See abbeys.
pubs 78
Pwll Deri 485
Pwllheli 506
Pyecombe 158

Q

queens
    Anne 193
    Boudicca 71, 334
    Elizabeth I 72, 111, 167, 261,
        271, 307, 385
    Elizabeth II 76, 109, 169, 448
    Isabella, She-Wolf of France 330
    Lady Jane Grey 113
    Mary II 73, 117, 126
    Mary, Queen of Scots 73, 111,
        261, 370, 384, 385, 537,
        569, 596, 598, 599, 609,
        642
    Victoria 74, 262, 443

R

Radiohead 85
railways
    narrow-gauge 445, 474, 496,
        504, 511
    North Yorkshire Moors 417,
        418, 422
    Volk's 163
    West Highland 646, 648, 651
Raleigh, Sir Walter 233

Ramsey Island 487, 489
Ranworth 336
rarebit. See Welsh rabbit.
Rathlin Island 715
Ravenstor 367
real ale. See beer.
Red Cross 24
Reeth 405
Regent's Park 118
renting a car 35, 36
Rhenigidale 662
Ring of Kerry 779
Ringaskiddy 770
Road to the Isles 651–652
Robert the Bruce. See kings.
Robin Hood 311
Robin Hood's Bay 417, 424
Robinson, Mary 728
Rock of Cashel 765
Rodel 667
Rodmell 158
Roman Empire 71, 447
Roslin 565
Rossetti, Christina 81
Rosslare Harbour 487, 767
Rosslyn. See Roslin.
Rosthwaite 383
Rothbury 441
Rousay 686
Rowardennan 612
Rowen 529
Royal Deeside 630–632
Royal Shakespeare Company
    279, 435
rugby 88, 543
Rum, Isle of 653
Ruskin, John 115, 270, 379, 395
Russell, Mary 158
RVs 53
Ryde 175
Rye 152

S

Saffron Walden 326
St. Albans 71, 258
St. Andrews 593–598
St. David's 489
St. Helier 255
St. Ives 250–252
St. Just 253
St. Mawes 244
St. Ninian's Isle 693
St. Patrick 712, 726
St. Paul's Cathedral 111
St. Peter Port 257
Salisbury 186–191
Sanday 687
Sandown 176

INDEX

go the distance with

HOSTELLING INTERNATIONAL

An HI membership card gives you access to friendly and affordable accommodations at over 4,000 hostels in 60 countries, including all across Britain and Ireland.

HI Members also recieve:
 FREE Travel Insurance
 FREE stay vouchers*
 Global reward points*
 Long distance calling card bonus
 *at participating hostels

Join millions of members worldwide who save money and have more fun every time they travel.

**Get your card online today!
HIUSA.ORG**

MAP INDEX

MAP LEGEND

Hospital	Airport	Hotel/Hostel	Stone Monument
Police	Bus Station	Camping	Cave
Post Office	Train Station	Food & Drink	Waterfall
Tourist Information Centre	London Tube Station	Nightlife/Clubs	Park Ranger Station
National Park Information Centre	Subway Station	Pubs	Mountain Peak
Bank	Ferry Terminal	Theatre	Mountains
Pharmacy	Taxi Stand	Museum	Countour Lines
Service	Beach	Mountain Pass	Tunnel
Site or Point of Interest	Church/Cathedral	Observatory	Ferry Route
Embassy or Consulate	Parking	Castle	Pedestrian Zone
Library	Gate or Entrance	Lighthouse	Stairs
Internet Café	Ship/Submarine	Surfing	Footpaths/Trails
	Wildlife Reserve		Railroads